SOCIAL SCIENCE AND THE CULTS

SECTS AND CULTS IN AMERICA
BIBLIOGRAPHICAL GUIDES
(General Editor: J. Gordon Melton)
(VOL. 17)

GARLAND REFERENCE LIBRARY
OF SOCIAL SCIENCE
(VOL. 564)

SECTS AND CULTS IN AMERICA
BIBLIOGRAPHICAL GUIDES
(General Editor: J. Gordon Melton)

1. *Magic, Witchcraft, and Paganism in America: A Bibliography*
   by J. Gordon Melton
2. *The Anti-Cult Movement in America: A Bibliography and Historical Survey*
   by Anson D. Shupe, Jr., David G. Bromley, and Donna L. Oliver
3. *The Old Catholic Sourcebook*
   by Karl Pruter and J. Gordon Melton
4. *Jehovah's Witnesses and Kindred Groups: A Historical Compendium and Bibliography*
   by Jerry Bergman
5. *The Children of God/Family of Love: An Annotated Bibliography*
   by W. Douglas Pritchett
6. *The Baha'i Faith: A Historical Bibliography*
   by Joel Bjorling
7. *Jewish Christians in the United States: A Bibliography*
   by Karl Pruter
8. *The Churches of God, Seventh Day: A Bibliography*
   by Joel Bjorling
9. *The Unification Church in America: A Bibliography and Research Guide*
   by Michael L. Mickler
10. *Psychiatry and the Cults: An Annotated Bibliography*
    by John A. Saliba
11. *The Latter Day Saint Churches: An Annotated Bibliography*
    by Steven L. Shields
12. *American Communes to 1860: A Bibliography*
    by Philip N. Dare
13. *American Communes, 1860–1960: A Bibliography*
    by Timothy Miller
14. *The Radhasoami Tradition: An Annotated Bibliography*
    by David Lane
15. *Mediumship and Channeling: A Bibliography*
    by Joel Bjorling
16. *The Church of Scientology: A Bibliography*
    by June D. Littler
17. *Social Science and the Cults: An Annotated Bibliography*
    by John A. Saliba

SOCIAL SCIENCE AND THE CULTS
An Annotated Bibliography

John A. Saliba

GARLAND PUBLISHING, INC. • NEW YORK & LONDON
1990

Library of Congress Cataloging-in-Publication Data

Saliba, John A.
    Social science and the cults: an annotated bibliography / John A.
Saliba.
        p.   cm. — (Sects and Cults in America: Bibliographical Guides, vol. 17)
(Garland reference library of social science; vol. 564)
    ISBN 0–8240–3719–7 (alk. paper)
    1. Cults—Periodicals—Indexes. 2. Sects—Periodicals—Indexes.
3. Religion and sociology—Periodicals—Indexes. 4. Cults—
Bibliography. 5. Sects—Bibliography. 6. Religion and sociology—
Bibliography. I. Title. II. Series: Sects and Cults in America.
Bibliographical guides; v. 17. III. Series: Garland reference
library of social science; v. 564.
Z7835.C86S34   1990
[BP603]
016.3066'91—dc20   90–32106
                                                                                                  CIP

Printed on acid-free, 250-year-life paper
Manufactured in the United States of America

CONTENTS

ACKNOWLEDGMENTS

The compilation of this bibliography would have been impossible without the help of many people. Sue and John Ditsky proofread the first draft of the manuscript and Janise A. Grey made invaluable suggestions and corrections in its final stages. The reference librarians of the University of Detroit dedicated their skills and energies to help in the location of a large percentage of the items listed in the following pages. Many scholars have contributed to make this volume as complete as possible. To the following, I am especially grateful: Drs. Angela Aidala, Hans Baer, Robert Balch, Eileen Barker, James A. Beckford, David G. Bromley, Peter B. Clark, Mary Ann Groves, Jeffrey K. Hadden, John R. Hall, Charles L. Harper, Paul Heelas, Irving L. Horowitz, J. Gordon Melton, James T. Richardon, Anthony Robbins, Larry D. Shinn, Anson Shupe, Rodney Stark, Roy Wallis, Bryan Wilson, and Stuart Wright.

THE NATURE, SCOPE, AND LIMITATIONS OF THIS BIBLIOGRAPHY

The study of contemporary cults, sects, new religious movements, or alternative religions has been conducted in an atmosphere of controversy. Debates about the nature of cults and of the behavior of both their leaders and members have not always been restricted to popular magazines and newspaper reports, nor have they always been conducted with professional courtesy and propriety. The acrimonious quality of the exchanges between "experts" in the field has left a mark not only on the content and quality of the research carried out on the new movements, but, sometimes, also on the characters of those who have dedicated their time and energies to observe and offer explanations of the current religious scene.

Studying new religious or spiritual movements has practically ceased to be simply an academic pursuit. It has become a matter of taking sides, or at least of being accused of doing so. The terms "procult" and "anticult" have become emotional labels that designate the theoretical approach to, and attitude towards, the cults one chooses to study. This dichotomy is frequently conceived of in absolute fashion as a matter of black or white, right or wrong. Any critic of the cults is automatically dubbed an irrational, biased cult-basher, while a scholar who does not state clearly in public talks and printed word that the cults are evil institutions whose activities should at least be curtailed ends up on the black list of the Anti-Cult Movement or, worse still, finds himself or herself accused of being a cult sympathizer or suspected of being a secret member of one of the cults themselves! Many scholars have been explicitly excluded from participation in conferences on cults because they are conceived of as being pro- or anticult in their respective orientations.

Procultists or cult defenders, we are told, consist chiefly of college teachers in departments of sociology and religion, of those involved with civil liberties' issues, and of clergy and laymen representing religious organizations and institutions. These scholars and ministers of religion assume that the cults are 1) genuine, even if mistaken and misguided, religious endeavors similar to other religious revivals in different historical eras, and 2) alternative spiritual options that provide solutions to the problems of many young people in times of social unrest and religious turmoil. The rise of new movements can be examined as one expression of the religious pluralism and tolerance that have become major cultural features in the Western world, particularly in North America.

Anticultists or cult critics, on the other hand, take quite a different stand. Consisting mainly of ex-cult members and families of cult

members who are supported by some psychologists, psychiatrists, lawyers,
and clerics, anticultists view the new movements not as representations
of authentic religiosity or spirituality, but rather as evil pseudoreli-
gious organizations. Instead of helping those who join them to alleviate
or solve their problems, cults tend to aggravate them or create new ones,
sometimes inflicting serious physical, mental, and psychological harm.
And rather than being concrete signs of religious liberty, they violate
this very freedom by inducing young people to join them with subtle psychological techniques and with false or insufficient information about the
total and demanding commitment they are being asked to make. Cult membership is not brought about by conversion, that is, an honest change of
heart, but by deceptive manipulation. Those who remain members are so
heavily indoctrinated or brainwashed that they are likely to become virtual prisoners in the group they so enthusiastically and unwittingly
joined.

The debate outlined above has reached an impasse with no solution in
sight. It has also cast a dark shadow on the very nature of social
science, particularly sociology, which has provided, by and large, the
best and fullest descriptions of cult beliefs and lifestyles and articulated sophisticated theories about their origin, development, and import
in the twentieth century. Skepticism and distrust of social-scientific
studies on the new movements require, in our opinion, some reflection and
reevaluation. We think that one way of doing so is to make a comprehensive examination of what social science, especially sociology, has contributed to our understanding of the cultic phenomenon of our time. One of
the main aims of this bibliography is, therefore, to make available for
ready reference a broad and comprehensive listing of social-scientific
materials in the field of the cults, sects, and new religious groups. By
annotating the many books and articles cited in the following pages, this
volume intends to give an overall picture of what social scientists are
really saying about the new movements, of any agreements they may have
reached about cult beliefs, practices, and membership, of the many disagreements among them about the nature and significance of the cultic
phenomenon, and of the implicit and explicit criticisms of cults that one
comes across in their writings.

Assumptions of This Study

There are several assumptions that have guided the selection of the
materials in this volume. The first concerns the meaning of the word
"cult." We have opted for a broad, inclusive, and neutral definition of
a cult as a minor, alternative religious system that is outside the mainstream of traditional religion and is usually judged negatively by society
at large. Cults, sects, and other small religious organizations are,
therefore, included.

Several reasons have led us to ascribe to this extended meaning of the
word "cult." First of all, it would be difficult, if not altogether impossible, to draw up a precise narrow definition of a cult that would be
universally accepted by those currently studying the cultic phenomenon.
Secondly, because new religious groups are in constant flux, the labels of
cult and/or sect might cease to be applicable to some groups as they develop over time. Thirdly, the words "cult" and "sect" have been used to

designate the same movement. Thus, to quote one flagrant example, SOCIO-
LOGICAL ABSTRACTS (December 1987) lists in the Subject Index one essay
(item 1658) on the Rajneesh Movement under "cults" and another essay (item
1818) on the same group under "sects." And, finally, in current debate,
the new cults, several established sects, and some fundamentalist Christian churches are repeatedly lumped together as destructive organizations
that are harmful both to the individual's and society's well-being. The
accusation, for instance, that children are abused or mistreated has been
leveled against some independent fundamentalist Christian Churches, Christian Science, and the Hare Krishna Movement.

The definitional problem is further aggravated by the fact that social-
scientific writings have frequently considered sects and cults to be a
species of social movements, communal lifestyles, and millenarian or utopian societies and have even compared them to religious orders and monasteries that appear to have some cultic or sectarian features. Besides,
the labels "cult," "sect," "denomination," and "church" are discussed and
defined in relation to one another. Social science does not divide religious organizations in two neat categories of cults and noncults, but
rather sees the cults as part of a continuum of a variety of evolving
religious movements and institutions that do not always conform to ideal
typologies. Comparison between traditional sects and new cults is deemed
necessary not only because it might generate more plausible theories about
their emergence and development, but also because it might lead to the
clarification of the very concepts of sect and cult.

Instead of starting with a narrow, value-laden definition of a cult, we
have, therefore, opted for an admittedly vague description. By so doing,
we believe that we are representing the situation in the social sciences
more accurately. We are also allowing the reader to draw his or her own
definition of a cult after having sampled the abundant material on the
subject. This value-free, definitional approach appears to be more compatible with a bibliographic collection that is not a treatise on cultism,
but a research guide.

Another basic assumption deals with the religious or spiritual nature
of the new religious movements. While social-scientific studies seem to
take it for granted that cults are religious phenomena, there is a growing
popular, theological, and psychological literature that rejects the cultic
claim of genuine religiosity or spirituality.

We have decided once again to take an impartial stand in the sense that
this volume does not aspire to settle the issues of the nature of religion
and of whether the cults can be included in the definition of religion
and, therefore, present viable spiritual options to those who join them.
Because the majority of social scientists regard the new cults to be religious manifestations, the cited literature heavily favors the opinion
that, generally speaking, the so-called cults are religious in nature.
Many of the new cults are seen in the context of the major Eastern or
Western tradition out of which they emerged or in comparison with other
religious or spiritual revivals in the history of religion. The inclusion
of the new cults under the species of religion follows the social-scientific approach that opts for a broad, inclusive definition of religion and
avoids discussions on the truth or falsehood of belief systems.

This position does not imply that cults cannot and/or should not be evaluated from religious, theological, or moral points of view. It merely adopts the social-scientific perspective that is not concerned with formulating such evaluations and judgments. Because cults make statements about spiritual reality, they can be recognized as religious, irrespective of whether the beliefs they espouse are false and irrational and whether their religious leaders are motivated by religious values or by more mundane goals. People can be mobilized by political, economic, and religious reasons at the same time. Material success and wealth, for instance, have often been seen as signs of acceptance by God, in which case the pursuit of wealth becomes a religious endeavor. In like manner, leaders of religious movements may pursue a luxurious lifestyle that contrasts sharply with the austere living conditions of their followers, but cults can be still considered religious. Religion has been known to inspire people to perform both good and bad actions. And not all the effects of religion can be guaranteed to be beneficial. In fact, social scientists talk about both the (positive) functions and (negative) dysfunctions of religion. False religions and religious aberrations are still, to some degree at least, "religious."

Thirdly, we have assumed throughout that the social-scientific study of the cults is not an isolated area of research, but rather part of the total endeavor of the social sciences. The modes of inquiry, research methods, and theoretical formulations that one comes across in the writings on the cults are those commonly used in other areas of investigation. As one reads the literature on the new movements, one becomes aware that cults cannot be studied, much less understood, as isolated forms of human behavior, since they are an integral part of the culture and society in which they thrive and with which they clash. Thus, to give but one example, some cults follow a communitarian lifestyle, which can only be understood in the framework of various forms of communitarian living that have developed throughout history.

Since the social-scientific study of cults could include a large number of academic disciplines, we have found it necessary to restrict, to some degree, our use of the reference to "social science" to those disciplines that take a social or cultural approach, that is, one that examines the cults in relation to society or culture or to some aspect thereof.

Finally, this bibliography stands on the assumption that social science has made, and can still advance, important contributions for an understanding of the new religious movements, an understanding that is required before arriving at a religious, social, and ethical evaluation that promotes a constructive response to their presence in our midst. Several sociologists (for example, Van Driel and Richardson, item 2213) have complained that the media have ignored the abundant research on cults by social scientists in the last two decades. The same criticism can be leveled against many of those who have embarked on an anticult campaign. Our stance in this respect is quite patent. We cannot even begin to grasp the phenomenon of cultism without delving into the copious social-scientific literature on the subject. In our opinion, it is a truism to state that an in-depth knowledge of the cults should precede a theological evaluation, a psychiatric assessment, and, finally, any social action taken in response to their presence and activities in our midst.

Works Selected for Inclusion in Bibliography

The social-scientific literature on the cults is extensive. Scholars with different academic backgrounds have contributed to our knowledge of the new movements in the context of Western society and culture, where they may have already acquired a secure foothold. To include all related material would be a task of encyclopedic proportions. Several guidelines have, therefore, been adopted to keep this collection within manageable proportions.

First, we have tried to be comprehensive in our coverage of materials that directly address themselves to the new religious movements. We have made special efforts to trace publications that overview the presence of the cults in Western culture, propose both general and specific theories to explain their presence, discuss selected features of cultism, and explore individual groups in depth. Because the new religions are routinely seen as alternative, utopian, millenarian, and/or communitarian societies, no coverage of the literature would be complete without reference to the many studies of these societies. We have, therefore, included that literature on alternative and other groups that we found quoted by scholars doing research on the new religious movements.

In like manner, students of the new religions tend to compare them with those that came into being in different periods of history, particularly those that flourished in nineteenth-century America. Instead of making an effort to cover all the literature on nineteenth-century communes, sects, and cults, we have quoted those that figure more prominently in the references cited in books and articles on the new religions.

The effects the presence of new movements has had on the study of religion in the social sciences became apparent by the early 1970's. Our coverage of the literature encompasses an 18-year span, from 1970 to 1988. We have included earlier material in the historical section. We have also added some books and articles published in early 1989 as they became available for our perusal. All the books and articles listed in this bibliography have been read or consulted. The availability of the materials quoted in this research guide was also an important criterion in selecting the literature. Besides making use of the resources of the libraries in the greater Detroit area (namely those of the University of Detroit, Wayne State University, Eastern Michigan University, Michigan State University, The University of Michigan, and the University of Windsor in Canada), we have also spent some time at the Institute for the Study of American Religion in Santa Barbara, California, where many resource materials on various aspects of cultism are located. Moreover, we have, relied heavily on the OCLC Online System for borrowing books and getting photocopies of articles in professional journals.

Works Omitted

Several areas of cultic studies have not been incorporated in this collection. We have left out those works that examine the new movements from the perspective of the psychological disciplines. Our previous volume, PSYCHIATRY AND THE CULTS: AN ANNOTATED BIBLIOGRAPHY (New York:

Garland, 1987) amply covered this material and could be used as a companion to this bibliography. With few exceptions, we have consciously
avoided repeating material cited in our earlier work.

Also omitted is the legal literature on the cults. Besides articles
published in many law reviews and journals, there are many court documents
that add a unique dimension to the relationship between the cults and the
society in which they flourish. This literature deserves separate treatment. In this volume we have made mention of several seminal works that
deal with both the social and legal issues that the cults have raised.
Readers interested in this aspect of cultism can consult the ample bibliographies that these works contain and such publications as 1) the JOURNAL
OF LAW AND RELIGION that, though not dedicated to the study of cultism,
contains discussions of problems that are also applicable to the cults,
2) the RELIGIOUS FREEDOM REPORTER, which covers pending and decided court
cases involving religious groups and lists references to legislation and
to scholarly articles, and 3) INDEX TO LEGAL PERIODICALS (Bronx, NY: H. W.
Wilson Co.), which incorporates articles on cults published in law journals
and reviews.

This bibliography is further limited to books and articles published in
the English language. Fortunately, there are some publications in English
that survey the cult problem in other parts of the Western world and that
make some comparisons between the presence of the new cults in North America and in Europe. We have not included studies on the many new religious
and prophetic movements in Africa, Asia, and other Third World countries.
Moreover, we have restricted coverage to papers published in professional
journals and magazines. We recognize that popular magazine articles and
newspaper reports, often referred to in the essays cited in the following
pages, are important data and primary source material that are necessary
for a complete assessment of the public image of, and reaction to, the new
movements, but they do not pertain to the social-scientific study of the
cults, technically speaking.

Divisions of the Bibliography

The works and articles cited in this volume are divided into four chapters. Chapter 1 lists the sources for the Social Scientific Study of the
Cults, that is, the volumes and periodicals where most of the materials on
the new movements can be located.

Chapter 2 covers the historical background, including: 1) theoretical
essays on, and general surveys of, sects, cults, and other religious groups
that were in print before the current intensive study of the new movements
got under way; and 2) representative studies on particular cults and sects
during the same period. This historical section is important for two
major reasons. It furnishes the conventional sociological framework under
which many of the current studies of the new movements are conducted and
it brings to light the issues discussed in the social sciences before the
current debate on the cults emerged.

Chapter 3 includes general, theoretical, and methodological studies on
cults, sects, and new religious movements. We have further subdivided the
material for more convenient reference into four sections. The first

deals with background materials to the study of new religious movements.
This consists of: 1) general studies on social movements, communal groups,
millenarian movements, utopian societies, and religious revivals; 2) some
basic studies on countercultures and alternative lifestyles; and 3) main
works on various theories (e.g., resource mobilization, secularization,
labeling theory, and charismatic leadership) that have been applied to the
new movements. The second section includes edited works on, and surveys
of, new religious movements. Included are: 1) volumes that combine theoretical essays with studies of particular movements and deal with a variety of cults from different academic perspectives; 2) surveys that map the
presence of the new movements in particular countries or geographic areas;
3) studies that assess the literature on, and theories about, the new
religious movements; and 4) thematic essays that consider specific ideals,
practices, or shared features of the new movements as a whole. The third
section lists theoretical studies on the new religious movements as a
whole. Under this section are included: 1) discussions on the meaning of
cult and its alleged "newness," on the "consciousness" reformation, and on
the typology of church, denomination, sect, and cult; 2) theories of cult
formation that refer to the secularization process and to the counterculture; 3) general topics, like conversion to, defection from, and charismatic leadership in the new movements; and 4) applications of specific
interpretations (e.g., resource mobilization theory) to the cultic phenomenon. The last section in Chapter 3 consists of methodological essays
that deal with the problems involved in the actual investigation of the
cults.

Chapter 4 is dedicated to contemporary studies on specific cults,
sects, and new religious movements, and is divided into three parts, the
first dealing with those works on the so-called established sects or religious movements, the second with studies of cults that have arisen since
the mid-1960's. We have purposely refrained from subdividing the two parts
into clusters of sects and cults in order to avoid adopting or constructing
a typology. To locate books and articles on individual sects and cults,
we have compiled a special Index of Religious Groups, where the main works
on individual movements can be traced. Other references to these movements can be found in the General Subject Index. Part Three is dedicated
to studies on the societal response, including the accusation of brainwashing, to the new movements.

These divisions are intended to give some order to a large collection
of essays and to indicate the variety of studies that deal with, or are
related to, the new cults. They are, to some degree, arbitrary, since the
material sometimes overlaps. Many sociological essays, for instance,
follow a common pattern by starting with a short discussion on theory with
reference to traditional sociological materials, then giving the method
pursued in the research project, describing some of the main features of
the cult under investigation, and lastly showing the applicability of a
specific hypothesis that is being tested.

Type of Annotations

The annotations in this bibliography are mainly descriptive. They are
intended to summarize some of the major contents of the works cited, particularly in relation to the issues discussed in the introduction. It

should be emphasized that the annotations are not a substitute for reading the original books and articles. A short paragraph cannot possibly contain all the factual data, the theoretical contributions, the methodological procedures, and the detailed argumentation regularly found in social-scientific writings on the cults.

The descriptive nature of the annotations should not be interpreted to mean that the works are beyond critique or that the present author subscribes to the theories referred to. Many of the authors listed in the following pages disagree about the nature of the cultic phenomenon and its interpretation. They further criticize one another, both with respect to research methods and about factual statements relating to the beliefs and practices of individual cults. To give one example, Wallis (item 2054) takes Davis and Richardson (item 1680) to task for describing the way the Children of God operate in a manner that was already out of date by the time their paper was published in 1976, and further accuses them of thoroughly misconceiving changes in Berg's role as leader.

Social-scientific literature proves beyond any doubt that a healthy debate has been going on about the presence, functioning, and meaning of the cults in Western culture. We have endeavored to portray this controversy in our annotations.

INTRODUCTION

SOCIAL SCIENCE AND THE CULTS: AN OVERVIEW AND EVALUATION

The decade of the 1960's was one of great social and religious turmoil. Social discontent, religious change, and disregard of traditional authority in civil, moral, and religious matters seemed to prevail, especially among young adults. This was the age when religion appeared to be in decline, when secularization, the process through which religion becomes less of a factor in sociopolitical matters and in the public domain in general, was deemed irreversible, and when religious beliefs looked as if they were crumbling under the advance of modern science. In retrospect, the appearance of the "Death of God Theology" by the mid-1960's was not a surprising development.

The late 1960's, however, did not witness the death of God nor the disappearance of religion. On the contrary, there are some indications that it experienced a resurgence of religious enthusiasm. This revival expressed itself in several distinct forms. On the one hand, Christianity witnessed an internal dynamic to growth and relevance. On the other, the influx of Eastern traditions to the West, particularly to the United States, attracted disillusioned and dissatisfied youngsters and gave impetus to an alternative religious tradition that has been part of Western culture for some time. Further, the growth of interest in occult matters rekindled religious beliefs and practices that had never quite died down in Western society. Added to these explicitly religious manifestations, the flowering of many human growth movements, though often secular in orientation, manifested itself in ideals, language, and rituals reminiscent of traditional spiritual paths. As the decade of the 1970's rolled in, it was already becoming increasingly clear that what was taking place in the West was no passing fad.

The Social Scientific Study of Religion

The resurgence of religion and the advent of new religious movements have revitalized the study of religion in the social sciences (Robbins, item 919). Scholars interested in the field of religion have been given the opportunity to observe firsthand how new religions might come into being, how they interact with their sociocultural environment, and how they die out or else develop, adapt, and become gradually institutionalized. Insights gleaned from these direct personal observations have been used to reexamine other movements in different periods of history. And

comparative analyses have been employed to determine to what degree the
new movements of the second half of the twentieth century can be considered a unified phenomenon, sharing similar features among themselves and
with other alternative groups that came before them.

The Scope of the Social Scientific Study of Cults

The social-scientific study of new religious movements is concerned
with the existence of these groups as marginal subcultures and with the
interrelationships between them and society and/or culture at large. It
examines 1) the way religious institutions and organizations are formed
and maintained, 2) the internal dynamics that make them viable social
entities, 3) the economic, social, and political features that characterize them as deviant, 4) the type of charismatic leadership that often
provides divine legitimation for the movements' beliefs and practices, and
5) the level of commitment they demand of their devotees. It explores the
social correlates that go with membership and the cultural factors that
influence recruitment policies. And it follows the development of particular movements and their efforts to seek respectable niches in society.
Since new religions must start by being marginal movements, social scientists are also interested in the conflicts that exist between new groups
and the mainline religious traditions and the effects such conflicts might
have on both. New religious movements are expressions of human diversity
and, as such, they contribute to our understanding of the nature of religion and its place in the fabric of human life.

Social scientists do not usually dwell on religious beliefs and values
as systems of thought, but rather as modes of influencing group behavior.
Neither are they concerned with the evaluation of the new beliefs and
practices from moral and theological points of view. What is important to
them is the exploration of those processes whereby new values and lifestyles create new symbolic expressions, experimental communities, and
subcultures that, while existing in various levels of friction with their
surroundings, may express or contribute to the process of religious and
social change.

While social science has itself often existed in some form of tension
with its cultural environment, it has achieved a high degree of recognition and respectability and has affected social, educational, and political decisions in the West. In the area of the cults, however, social
scientists have not been very successful in influencing people's attitudes
about, understanding of, and responses to, the cults and have often supported, in vain, the cults' point of view in legal suits.

Conflicts between social scientists in general and other observers of
the cultic scene dominate the literature on new religious movements. The
various issues that have arisen in the study of cults have to be addressed,
if for no other reason because social scientists have become embroiled in
the acrimonious debates about modern cultism. We have identified six
major issues around which the debate about the cults has revolved. The
first deals with the definition of a cult. The second questions the reasons for studying the cults and the methods that should be used to examine
them. The third concerns the variety of cults and hinges on whether we
can make any generalizations about them. The fourth centers around their
distinguishing characteristics. The fifth focuses on the models that are

devised to understand the reasons why they come into being and their significance for, and possible impact on, modern Western culture. The sixth
discusses the societal response that is appropriate to their persistent
presence, a response that is determined by the answers that are given to
the first five issues.

The Definition of Cult

The first major area of debate lies in the very definition of a cult.
Two basic rules of the social-scientific approach are impartiality and
objectivity. By training, social scientists are inclined to be dispassionate and open-minded and, hence, to adopt a neutral position. The
underlying issue at stake, however, is whether a nonpartisan definition
of a cult is at all possible.

It should be observed from the start that, though an impartial approach
is highly commendable, it is certainly fraught with difficulties, particularly when it relates to religious and ideological matters. Social-scientific attempts to give a nonjudgmental, factual definition of a cult may
not be as value-free as they might appear. All scholars are faced with
the initial task of identifying and defining the various kinds of religious groups they are studying. In so doing, it is practically impossible
to avoid making an implicit evaluative statement on the movement under
study. Neutral definitions of a cult or a sect may not incorporate a
religious appraisal of its orthodoxy, but they state something about the
cult and may influence both our opinion of their importance and worth and
the kind of response we make to their challenging presence. A definition
of a cult, for instance, may steer away from the question as to whether
its claim to be a genuine Christian or Judaic tradition is a legitimate
one. But it can hardly avoid making a statement on its nature and/or
functions and selecting certain constitutive features that determine its
makeup. That empirical and objective observation should play the key role
in the making of a definition is taken for granted. One question, however, remains unanswered: to what degree do the scholars' own religious
background or lack of it, their academic training, and their own attitudes
towards religion influence the definition?

Social scientists have been active participants in the debate on cultism for the simple reason that they view a cult as just one type of socio-
religious group and organization. Consequently, they frequently write
about a particular cult as if it were just another religious entity and
option, sharing some features with other religious organizations and tra-
ditions--a position that contrasts sharply with the conviction that a cult
is a pseudoreligion and, therefore, should in no way be compared and confused with the major Western religions and their main branches. Social
scientists also contend that contemporary cults share at least some characteristics with religious movements in other periods of Western history--
a point of view not usually shared by those who maintain that the new
cults are destructive entities and are essentially different from religious groups that sprung up in the eighteenth and nineteenth centuries.

Four major concepts or types of religious organizations are discussed
in sociological literature, namely "church," "denomination," "sect," and
"cult." These concepts were designed both to explain differences between

existing religious groups in the largely Christian West and to account for
religious change and pluralism. The initial work in this area was spearheaded by Weber (items 139-40), Troeltsch (item 134), and Niebuhr (item
119), who dwelt particularly on the features that distinguished a church
from a sect. Their writings still lie at the roots of contemporary speculations on the subject. Fundamental to the original distinction between
church and sect is the relationship that these two religious entities have
with society at large. Briefly stated, the church and the denomination
are organizations that have achieved some level of accommodation with
society and culture, whereas a sect tends to maintain a degree of tension
with its environment. In this respect the cult (which did not figure
explicitly in the speculations of these early sociologists) is similar to
the sect. Sociologists disagree on exactly how cults differ from sects.
One common explanation sees sects are groups that have split off from a
major Christian church, while cults as composed of people recruited by a
charismatic leader to a relatively new and syncretistic system of religious beliefs and practices (see, for example, Stark and Bainbridge, item
966, pp. 11-12). Sects and cults are then subdivided into a variety of
types based on their ideology, goals, and/or position in, and relationship
to, the larger society.

The debate in the social sciences on the various kinds of religious
organizations has not led to a commonly accepted definition of terms nor
to a universal typology. Critical evaluations of both the original terms
and of the many existing typologies, as well as attempts to amend the
theoretical formulations of early sociologists, tend to support the view
that this area of the sociology of religion is likely to continue to be
the subject of debate for a long time to come.

Several major conclusions, however, can be drawn from the voluminous
literature on the subject: 1) the different kinds of religious groups
represent ideal types and are more accurately placed on a continuum with
the church and the cult situated at the ends; 2) religious organizations
must be examined, not as static, but as dynamic entities that change over
time; 3) all religious groups must be defined and understood in the context of their relationship with the society or culture in which they
thrive; and 4) cults, like sects, are to be considered as marginal or
fringe religions and/or subcultures. This viewpoint of cults contrasts
sharply with the position that defines them as destructive, pseudoreli-
gious organizations that have deviant (and often criminal) tendencies.

It follows that, from a social-scientific perspective, the emergence of
new religious movements, be they labeled sects or cults, and their confrontation with society are considered almost a natural process that will
occur, given the correct sociocultural conditions. From this general picture it is easy to conclude that the rise of new religious movements is an
interesting but unremarkable event in a society that is changing rapidly
under the influence of technology. While this does not logically lead to
the view that sectarian and cultic developments are necessarily good in
themselves or beneficial to the individual and society, it certainly leans
toward the position that cults and sects should not be the subject of overwhelming concern, much less fear. Consequently, most social scientists do
not exhibit the same level of anxiety, apprehension, and panic that one
finds among psychiatrists and psychologists, parents of cult and ex-cult
members, self-styled deprogrammers, and news media reporters.

Why and How Does One Study the Cults?

A second major issue regards both the reasons why and the manner in which cults should be studied (see, especially, items 1050 ff.). In general, the social scientists' interest in the cults is part of their academic concerns. The cults are a specific form of human behavior. They reveal some aspects of humanity and are an expression of religious, social, and cultural dynamism. Social scientists, ideally at least, are not dedicated to the investigation of the new movements for personal reasons. Their research is not an aspect of their involvement in, or reaction to, a new religion, nor is it directly related to their own personal quest for religious meaning and experience, even though there might be some exceptional cases. How and to what extent or degree this initial attitude influences one's research is a debatable point. Because of this rather dispassionate motivation for studying cults, social scientists could easily appear to be cult sympathizers or even cult promoters.

The above approach contrasts sharply with the view of those whose study of the cults is motivated by the desire to combat them and to curtail their activities. Here the study of the new movements is not an end in itself, an academic activity pursued for the quest of human knowledge. Cults are studied because they threaten Christianity and/or Judaism and one cannot refute their doctrines and criticize their practices without first knowing what these are. Or else, cults are judged to be a menace to the social order, to family traditions, and to the established cultural values and must be scrutinized carefully in order that appropriate ways might be found to keep them at bay and to defeat their efforts to overrun Western civilization. While social scientists can at least make an effort at impartiality, students who are engaged in exposing the cults have already taken a negative stand on the nature of cultism and its effects on individuals and society. They become religious crusaders, champions of traditional moral values and family unity, and defenders of social norms. That such a zealous attitude could negatively influence the study of the new movements does not require much verification. Because of this highly charged, emotional stand, those people who denounced the cults as evil institutions can be readily perceived as "cult opponents" with little to offer to the academic study of cultism.

The two opposing views of the cults and of the reasons for studying them are buttressed by similar arguments. Social scientists insist that their firsthand investigation of these movements has led them to a non-pejorative opinion of a cult. Those who attack the cults are also convinced that their studies on the effects cults have on people support the strong, negative stand on the matter they have embraced.

Methods of Studying the Cults

Examining the methods used to investigate the cults is necessary because the validity of the information about the cults and its consequent interpretation ultimately depends on how researchers go about studying them. What are the procedures one should adopt for finding out exactly what cult members believe, what their goals and practices are, what effects they have on those who join them, and what demands do gurus make of

their devotees? How does one reach conclusions about the way cults operate as distinct subcultures that are at variance or in conflict with the
mainline religions and culture? Are there suitable methods that can help
the researcher not only record the facts faithfully, but also understand
their significance?

The methods employed by social scientists to investigate the new religious movements are essentially those that have been applied to the study
of traditional religion and religions across cultures and to social processes in general. These methods are: the use of historical materials,
comparisons between similar phenomena in the same society and across cultures, controlled experimentation where possible, sample surveys, content
analysis, and participant observation. Many of these approaches emphasize
the need for an investigation that entails direct contact and interaction
with the people under study. The underlying assumptions are that 1) the
social scientist can achieve some degree of objectivity and impartiality,
and 2) those being studied are reliable informants.

The method of participant observation is at the heart of the current
debate on how new religious movements should be studied. It should be
borne in mind that such an approach is not new in the social sciences
(cf., for instance, Bryun, item 73). Developed initially by Western anthropologists for the study of non-Western peoples, this method, which has
been standard in anthropological circles for almost half a century, has
been analyzed and discussed for decades and been adopted by most social
scientists. The heart of this approach, to understand people who have
different worldviews and who follow diverse lifestyles, lies in its insistence that the observers should not apply an interpretation or judgment
based solely on their own cultural assumptions and points of view. Rather,
they should attempt to understand people's behavior from the perspective
of the latter's own cultural norms and values. Thus, scholars are encouraged to beware of their own ethnocentrism, to be nonjudgmental, and to
adopt a posture of cultural relativism. Some participation, be it overt
or covert, in the activities of the subjects being studied is, therefore,
considered necessary.

Several reasons have been advanced to show that participant observation
has distinct advantages over most other methods (see, e.g., Bernard, item
1056). First of all, it allows the observer to see things from inside.
Reports of what cult members do are based on direct eyewitnessing rather
than on hearsay or on what is publicly acknowledged by cult and ex-cult
members.

Secondly, the observer can notice discrepancies between what people say
and what they actually do. Religions tend to advertise the ideal that is
often not realized at all. Thus, for instance, the utopian goals of religious communes hardly ever materialize. Some statements that cult members
make can be seriously questioned. The devotees of some cults have at
times assured their audiences that joining their organizations does not
imply that one has to abandon one's own religious heritage. Contact with
the group may show, however, that the nature of the beliefs, practices,
and commitment of a cult are incompatible with other religious systems and
that most members actually abandon the religion of their upbringing as
they become socialized in their new ideology and lifestyle.

Thirdly, it is only observational studies that can answer some of the disputed questions about cults. Thus, for instance, whether the leader of the group lives a luxurious lifestyle while his devotees follow the path of poverty and self-denial is not always easily noticed from the outside; and whether the leader's lifestyle is given a meaningful interpretation by those who are involved in the movement can only be fully answered by close and trusting contact with cult members. Similarly, the actual training that the initiated go through can only be fully evaluated if seen from the perspective of believers. The kind of hardships that a communal lifestyle demands cannot simply be determined by a comparison with the difficulties and advantages of a traditional religious or secular style of living. To argue, for instance, that fundraising is a demeaning and exhausting exercise may be an imposition of the outsider's perspective rather than an understanding of the meaningfulness of such activity to those who accept the ideology that supports it.

Fourth, participant observation enables those scholars interested in symbolic interaction to examine human behavior at close quarters. It would be difficult to describe the type of family and peer relationships that characterize a religious group or the political system that prevails within the organization without some prolonged face-to-face contact with those who are personally involved and committed.

One way of explaining this approach is to state that students of an alien culture or religion use empathy in their efforts to understand another person's beliefs, values, and practices (Saliba, item 1088). Empathy, a method applied in the context of psychological counseling, is also applicable in the study of those individuals who have joined a new religious movement. It aims at relating with cult members on their own level in order to see the world from their own perspective and to elicit understanding of how events are interpreted by those who are involved.

Participant observation, however, is not to be equated with surveillance, a sort of advantaged position that gives access to information that cannot be retrieved in any other way. Some genuine participation that is both intellectual and emotional is called for. Anthropologists, in their studies of non-Western cultures, have insisted that the researcher should not only learn the language of those under study, but also adopt at least some aspects of their culture. This partial assimilation facilitates the flow of information from the subjects to the scholars investigating them and helps researchers assess and interpret that information.

The issue at stake is to what extent does one "go native;" in other words, how does one determine the parameters of a mode of participation that is not just an outward conformity to some aspects of the behavior of the members of a new religion under study (see Geertz, item 1067). Because religion deals with matters of ultimate truth and moral worth, it is hardly possible to accept the ideology and lifestyle of a new religion on a temporary and uncommitted basis. Social scientists do not endorse conversion to the cult one is studying, but they do insist that one must see cult life from the "inside out" rather than from the "outside in." This implies that scholars must find some common ground between what they are studying and some of their own religious and/or cultural beliefs, values, practices, and experiences. In so doing, social scientists might be

indirectly criticizing some aspects of modern culture and traditional
religion. Incidentally, this approach is not restricted to social scientists. Those religious writers--including those who draft representative
statements on the new movements--who maintain that the cults are being
successful in precisely those areas where the mainline churches have
failed, are indirectly following a similar method.

The use of the method of participant observation highlights the tension
that exists between most social scientists and those scholars who have
opted for an anticult stand. The former have often pointed out that the
alleged facts (such as brainwashing and violence) have not been verified
by researchers who have examined the cults at close quarters. The latter,
on the other hand, have accused social scientists of having accepted some
of the beliefs and values of the new movements and to have sided with
their members in the family conflicts that membership has given rise to or
aggravated. Anticultists have responded with their own method which, by
and large, consists of studying cult life through the eyes of those who
have defected, willingly or by force, from the movements. Cult literature
and activities are interpreted not in the total context of the members'
lifestyle and commitment, but from the cultural presuppositions of those
who have embarked on an anti-cult crusade. The fact that most social
scientists consider this methodological approach highly inadequate, if not
completely misleading, has intensified the conflict.

The criticism that the method of participant observation is indicative
of an approach that favors cultic involvement is, however, a misunderstanding of the whole anthropological and sociological enterprise. First
of all, social scientists are aware that this method is not immune to
difficulties that have been openly recognized and debated in social-scientific literature for decades (consult Becker, item 73, as a typical example). Thus, to mention just one problem, to what extent can scholars
actually assume a worldview and lifestyle that are foreign to their upbringing and convictions is not easy to determine. The many monographs on
non-Western societies that Western scholars have produced testify, however, that participant observation is, within limitations, a possible
venture. Its application has advantages that far outweigh its weaknesses
and its contributions cannot be replicated by other methods. Hence, it is
more than likely that it will continue to be a major tool for exploring
the new religions.

Moreover, except in a few cases, there is little evidence that social
scientists look favorably on the beliefs and practices of the new movements. Not many scholars in their face-to-face approach to the cults have
been converted to the worldview and lifestyle of the new movements. Some
social scientists have, in fact, been very critical. Thus, to cite but a
couple of examples, both Wallis (item 2062) and Bainbridge and Stark have
expressed serious reservations about Scientology (item 1089). When responding to negative studies on cults, critical reviewers have directed
their questions to scholarly issues and not to the truth or falsehood of
cultic beliefs. Angela Burr's anthropological analysis of the Hare
Krishna Movement (item 1654), that does not depict a favorable view of the
movement's lifestyle, has been criticized for its use of biased rhetoric,
inattention to detail, and misapplication of anthropological insights (see
the lengthy review of her book by Charles R. Brooks in ISKCON REVIEW, vol.
2, 1986, pp. 148-64).

The Variety of Cults

The phenomena that fall under such labels as "cults," "new religious movements," "alternative religions," and "marginal or fringe religions" number at least several hundred. When one reflects on the many new religious groups that have sprouted over the course of history, one is faced with several thousands of religious entities. Whether they can all be included under the one label of "cult" becomes an important issue. Social scientists insist that cults differ among themselves in their belief systems, their ritual practices, their ethical rules, their political, social, and economic structures, and their relationships with society. Too much generalization about cults might distort our understanding of their nature, structure, and import.

Two areas of research result from this preoccupation with the variety of cults and the quest for the generic denominators that unify them all into one phenomenon, namely attempts to draw up typologies and to list those features that cults share in common. Here one can identify, respectively, the third and fourth major issues that have divided those studying the cults into two distinctive groups, that is, how does one classify the new religions, and what are the distinctive features of cults that separate them from the established religious traditions?

Ideological Cult Typologies

In social-scientific literature one comes across two types of cult classifications, one historical and ideological in emphasis, the other sociological. Probably the most elaborate of the former is Melton's classification of all religions into 17 family groups, each with its distinct heritage, theology, and lifestyle (item 47). Contemporary cults fall into six of these clusters, namely the 1) Pentecostal, 2) Communal, 3) Metaphysical, 4) Psychic and New Age, 5) "Magick," and 6) Eastern and Middle Eastern families. This classification is largely descriptive and aims at situating the individual groups within one of the major philosophical and/or religious traditions. In so doing, Melton's typology stresses the continuity that contemporary cults have with other alternative religions in the history of the Christianity and other major religions and provides an intellectual framework for understanding cultic beliefs and practices.

A similar, though somewhat eclectic approach has been adopted by Ellwood and Partin (item 598) who restrict their classification largely to those cults that are based on Eastern religious and philosophical traditions. Basically, these two historians of religion propose five main divisions: 1) Theosophical and Rosicrucian traditions; 2) Spiritualism and UFO groups; 3) Initiatory groups; 4) Neo-Paganism; and 5) Oriental traditions. They see the so-called new cults not as complete novelties, but rather as developments of traditions that have existed concomitantly with the mainline Christian Churches. Cults, in the approach of Melton and Ellwood and Partin, are ideologically and ritually different groups. They often follow quite different lifestyles. Consequently, they cannot be evaluated morally, theologically, or socially as one homogeneous phenomenon.

The appeal of this approach seems to have had some impact on traditional sociological literature. In a recent article, Eileen Barker adopts a simplified typology based on ideological and theological differences (item 546). She constructs five major models that might distinguish contemporary cults, namely: 1) those that derive from the Christian tradition; 2) those that are based on Eastern religions and philosophies; 3) those that are parareligious (such as the Human Potential Movement); 4) the esoteric tradition; and 5) occult movements (including Witchcraft, neo-Paganism, and Satanism).

The difficulty of constructing a perfect typology is admitted by all the scholars mentioned above. Melton adds a category of "New Unaffiliated Religious Groups." Ellwood and Partin omit Jewish and Christian cults because they are not alternative religious groups in the sense adopted by the authors. And Barker recognizes that many of the movements do not fit easily in any one of the categories she mentions, that some would fit comfortably in more than one, and that several have altered sufficiently enough to merit being placed in a category different from the one they belonged to when they first came into being. The problems of classification are highlighted when one considers the fact, for example, that the Unification Church is listed by Melton with the unaffiliated groups or with Christian cults, by Ellwood as an Oriental movement, and by Barker with Christian groups.

Sociological Cult Typologies

Strictly sociological classifications of cults have tended to focus on the divergent conflicting relationships that cults might have with society at large. Wallis (item 906), for instance, proposes a much-used classification of cults in three different categories, that is: 1) the world-rejecting; 2) the world-affirming; and 3) the world-accommodating. This typology would be applicable to both sects and cults. Its main stress is not on the content of belief, but rather on the way each group defines itself vis-a-vis society. Implicit in such a classification is the principle that new religious movements cannot be understood simply as religious revivals or resurgences. They are rather envisaged as ways of reacting to society or to some particular sociocultural condition.

Another more elaborate proposal has been put forward by Bryan Wilson (item 1023) to account for the variety of sects, which he considers to be "deviant responses to the world." Seven types of such responses are then distinguished: 1) conversionist; 2) revolutionist (or transformative); 3) introversionist; 4) manipulationist; 5) thaumaturgical; and 6) reformist; and 7) utopian. Though developed primarily to account for the divisions within Christianity, several of the characteristics that are associated with each of this typology have been used to classify some of the new cults.

A typology tailored specifically for the new cults has been proposed by Stark and Bainbridge (item 966) who take the degree of organization, or lack of it, as the principal criterion for their distinction between the various new religious groups. These two sociologists classify cults into three types, namely audience cults, client cults, and cult movements. The first type (audience cults) is characterized by having virtually no organization; its members remain largely on the consumer level; they do not, as a rule, meet as a group; and they adopt cult beliefs and practices through printed materials, the radio, and television. This kind of cult provides a mythology for its participants. The second type (client cults) is made up of individuals who develop a relationship with their leaders similar to that of patients with their therapists. These cults never become organizations or communities; they have clients, not members, who may retain their formal association with an established church. They make serious magical practices available to those interested. The final type (cult movements) consists of organized religious entities which attempt to satisfy all the needs of their adherents. Though the levels of organizational development, the intensity of commitment, and the demands made on the membership may vary, all cult movements look for converts who will break off their attachment to other religious organizations. Cult movements are genuinely religious and they alone provoke great hostility from their sociocultural surroundings.

It may be argued that these sociological typologies neglect both the ideological differences between the new religious and cultic groups as well as the experiential dimensions that most of them claim. It may be further objected that none of them would encompass all the cults. Moreover, they all seem to have been originally constructed to account for the divisions within Christianity, making their application to a broader religious base somewhat strained. Whatever the weaknesses of these sociological classifications, they certainly direct our attention to some crucial questions that must be answered if we are to understand the cults at some depth. When is the sociocultural environment conducive to the emergence and success of cults? What types of relationships with society do cults promote? To what extent is knowledge of the cult's organizational structure necessary for an understanding of the cult itself? What factors will lead a cult to grow or fail or to cultivate a lower or higher tension with society?

Popular Cult Typologies

It is not difficult to see why these historical and sociological discussions on the varieties of cults challenge the more popular classifications. Two cult typologies dominate popular religious or theological literature (see McDowell and Stewart, item 2162, and Enroth and others, item 600). One adopts a theological position and distinguishes between genuine Christianity and unorthodox and/or aberrant groups. The other takes a sociopsychological stance and divides cults into destructive and benign groups. From a social-scientific perspective, these typologies look rather naive. They fail to address themselves to the real diversity that exists among the cults themselves and end up by placing side by side religious groups that require more careful differentiation. Moreover, they concentrate on one theme, orthodoxy or psychological deviancy, with the result that many, and possibly more important, aspects of cults are neglected or ignored.

The first typology (orthodox Christianity/unorthodox cults) leaves unsolved the main area of contention, namely what orthodox Christianity is. Though it concentrates on an important trait, namely the cult's ideological content, its weakness lies precisely in that fact that it

leaves fundamental theological differences unaddressed and unsolved. To
place as, for example, McDowell and Stewart have done, such groups as
Mormonism, Jehovah's Witnesses, Christian Science, the Worldwide Church of
God, the Way International, the Unification Church, Theosophy, EST, Transcendental Meditation, and the Hare Krishna Movement in the same category
of unorthodox groups that are a perversion and distortion of Biblical
Christianity, fails to draw attention to the great theological, sociological, and practical differences that exist between them. This typology
fails to realize that, since some new religious movements stem from Eastern religions, they have, first, to be evaluated in the context of the
traditions from which they have emerged. Further, it has no sense of the
historical roots of many cults and ignores religious pluralism, which has
been part of the Christian tradition and world religions in general. It
also tends to lose all objectivity, since the interpretation of a cult's
Christian orthodoxy or unorthodoxy depends on the denominational background of the individual assessing the cult's theology. It also treats
religious and theological factors as independent entities unrelated to
other social aspects of life. To state that the Hare Krishna Movement is
an Eastern religious group that espouses beliefs and practices that oppose
and contradict fundamental Christianity may be quite accurate, but it
doesn't throw much light on those who become members of the movement, on
the motives, factors, and influences that might lead a person to abandon
one's faith to join it, on why it should enjoy a measure of success in the
West, and on the reasons why society reacts with such great hostility to
its presence.

     The second popular typology (destructive/benign cults), which is pro-
moted by the Anti-Cult Movement, is based on the premise that certain
cultic beliefs and practices are harmful both to the individual and to
society (see Levine, item 858). But it is precisely the nature of this
harm and its applicability to specific religious groups that have to be
determined. While in extreme cases, Jonestown being a case in point, it
is evident that cultic life has led to suicide and murder, it is certainly
less obvious how most of the so-called cults could even remotely be placed
in the same category as the People's Temple (Richardson, item 1947). The
tendency of those who oppose the new marginal religions is to place them
all indiscriminately under the label of "destructive cults," with Jonestown as the all-encompassing paradigm. This method, instead of illuminating the tragic events at Jonestown, maligns all cultic groups. It would
seem more reasonable to see the Jonestown phenomenon as one species of the
various kinds of religious violence that has been recorded in different
religions and cultures and in diverse historical periods.

     The simplicity and clarity of popular typologies are probably their
major appealing features. They neatly divide the varieties of religious
expressions into absolute categories that leave little room for doubts or
errors. Careful consideration and examination of the many types of cults,
however, show that different cults make different demands on their adherents with, consequently, quite different physical, mental, social, and
psychological repercussions. Further, the effects of cults on those who
join them vary, if for no other reason than because people differ. Reading the literature on "destructive cultism," one wonders whether underlying
this typology lurks the assumption that complete commitment, passionate
devotion, and total dedication in a religious or semireligious context
are impossible without serious physical, psychological, and mental harm to

the individual. It is not surprising that some religionists and social
scientists have interpreted anticult literature as an attack against
religion in general. Social-scientific studies of cults do not support
sweeping statements on the harmful effects of cult involvement and find
that the application of the medical model lacks sufficiently objective
criteria to make it a viable one (Robbins, item 2186).

Major Cultic Features

The fifth major area of debate centers around the main characteristics
of cults that mark them off as unique religious manifestations distinct
from more traditional expressions. Since there seems to be a general
agreement that the cults or new religious movements in contemporary Western society, however much they differ, form a discernible phenomenon dis-
tinguishable from the mainline churches and denominations, the question of
what theological, moral, social, psychological, ritual, and practical
dimensions set them apart as a distinct group must be answered.

Two elaborate attempts to specify the major features of cultism will
suffice to illustrate the issues involved in studying, understanding, and
responding to the new movements. Ellwood and Partin (item 598), who rely
heavily on social-scientific literature, list the following five major
identifying marks of the new cults: 1) they represent a distinct alternative to mainline traditions from which they differ in size and in theoretical, practical, or sociological expressions; 2) they have strong authoritative and charismatic leadership; 3) they are oriented to bringing about
deep subjective experiences and fulfilling personal needs; 4) they are
separatist in that they make a clear distinction between their respective
members and outsiders; and 5) they tend to see themselves as representa-
tives of a long tradition of wisdom and practice.

In contrast to this list of relatively neutral elements, those who
vigorously oppose the cults (like McDowell and Stewart, item 2162, and
Levine, item 858) have brought together all the objections that have been
raised against the new religions. Anticult organizations list many negative features of cults that are generalized and applied to all groups,
even though little attempts are made to demonstrate that these features
are applicable in each individual case. One can summarize these traits as
follows: 1) total allegiance to an all-powerful leader; 2) discouragement
or forbidding of rational thought; 3) deceptive recruitment techniques;
4) psychological weakening of the members who end up believing that all
the problems can be solved within the group; 5) manipulation of guilt;
6) isolation from the outside world; 7) assumption of all life decisions
by the leader or cult; 8) vain promise to improve society; 9) full-time
work for the respective cult; 10) an antiwoman, antichild, and antifamily
orientation; 11) belief that the world is coming to an end; 12) a philosophy that the "end justifies the means;" 13) an atmosphere of mystery and
secrecy; 14) an aura of violence or potential violence (see, for example,
PRISON OR PARADISE?, by James and Marcia Rudin, Philadelphia: Fortress
Press, 1980, pp. 20 ff.).

These two contrasting and irreconcilable descriptions of cultic features
are symptomatic of two separate assumptions about, approaches to, and
understandings of the cultic phenomenon. They show exactly why the two

views of the cults are irreconcilable and why the debate has been carried
out at a level of intensity not common in the social sciences. And they
explain why, in court cases involving the cults, expert witnesses on both
sides of the litigating parties have been identified as procultists and
anticultists.

From a social-scientific point of view, generalizations about cults
suffer from several major flaws. Any list of cultic features would be
practically inapplicable to more than a handful of cults. Thus, for
example, the above-mentioned list of fourteen cultic features, which are
often highlighted at conferences run by anticult organizations, seems to
be a combination of negative elements taken from diverse cults and lumped
together to create an impressive, negative image of cults in general.
Many of the features listed--for instance, deceptive recruitment techniques and an aura of violence--cannot be applied to more than one or two
groups. Several cultic traits, such as obedience to a leader and full-
time work for the cult, are applicable to many traditional sects and religious and monastic institutions. Others, like the psychological weakening of the members, are somewhat difficult to substantiate. The same list
assumes that all the mentioned attributes, such as authoritarianism and
charismatic leadership, are always negative and harmful. It also fails to
take into account the changing nature of many of the cults. And finally,
the method employed is misdirected and misleading. It starts with several
absolute generalizations, finds a few (sometimes questionable) examples in
different cults, and then uses these instances to buttress the generalizations themselves.

The anticult depiction of the new movements has captured the imagination of the general public. Why is it, one might ask, that the list of
negative features of cultism has become part of the folklore on cults?
One reason, we may surmise, is that the alternative descriptions of cult
features listed by social scientists and religionists are not without
their flaws. The portrait of a cult outlined by Ellwood and Partin has
several qualities that are, to the person who has been personally affected
by cultic behavior, both problematic and unappealing.

To begin with what is probably the heart of the matter, these two
authors assume an aura of impartiality in dealing with the thorny problem
of religious pluralism, an approach that might seem both confusing and
threatening to the average believer. Unless theological and cultural ways
of handling religious pluralism are made available to the average person,
any impartial attempt to study, describe, and understand the cults is
bound to evoke hostile reactions. Second, the two scholars seem to suggest that, in spite of the differences between the mainline traditions and
the new religions, both groups are equally valid. Third, they assign only
positive functions to the cults. Fourth, they consequently appear to be
critical of the main religions that are indirectly judged to be unable to
satisfy the spiritual needs of some of their adherents, a position that
several of the cults have explicitly advanced. Fifth, they fail to take
into account that cultic behavior has, in some cases at least, created
serious problems. The fact that some cults and sects (and several Christian fundamentalist churches) have refused medical treatment to their
children cannot be neglected, no matter how isolated and untypical the
instances might be. And lastly, they do not address themselves to the
real difficulties that parents of cult members have to face.

The reason why the anticult view of a cult has had such an impact on the public is because it offers parents some psychological reassurance and a definite program for reacting to the cults. Ellwood and Partin's view of a cult, though objectively more accurate than that promulgated by anticult networks (like the American Family Foundation and the Cult Awareness Network), seems to have little to offer to those people who have been negatively affected by the presence of the cults.

A more sociological approach, advanced by Bryan Wilson (item 1023), avoids some of the failings of the above descriptions. Wilson's catalog of ideal sect characteristics, most of which are applicable to the cults, might be a good example of an attempt to avoid giving either a good or a bad image of a cult. He enumerates the following eight features of sectarianism: 1) voluntariness; 2) exclusivity; 3) merit (such as the claim of a specific experience) for admission; 4) self-identification with clear boundaries; 5) elite status; 6) expulsion; 7) self-consciousness and conscientious commitment; and 8) legitimation by claiming sacred authority. These characteristics do not, by themselves, imply any positive or negative functions of sectarianism or cultism. Some of them, like authoritarianism and exclusivity, can conceivably have both good and/or bad effects, depending on the social circumstances and the state of mind of the individuals who join the cults.

Theories Explaining the Rise of New Religious Movements

The fifth major debate about the cults concerns their significance. Their apparently sudden emergence requires an explanation. Why is it that this particular period in the history of Western culture should witness the rise of so many cults? What factors must be taken into account to understand the dynamics of new movements? Most social-scientific literature takes it for granted that the roots of cultism lie in contemporary culture. Quite a few theories have been proposed to show how the Western world in the second half of the twentieth century has become a fertile ground for the successful presence of new religions.

The Functional Approach

Probably the most common interpretation of cult formation has been the functional one. Cults are seen as religious revivals that come into being to satisfy practical human needs that are not being met, to help people cope with new problems that cannot be addressed in other ways, and to act as catalysts for religious change. This view is usually labeled the deprivation theory of cult formation because it starts with the observation that disgruntled, alienated, and dissatisfied individuals look outside the religion of their upbringing to satisfy their normal human needs.

The functional approach is hardly new in the social sciences, especially in sociology and anthropology, where exploring the functions of religion has been a common undertaking. The following five major functions or needs which religion in general and, by extension, cults serve have dominated social-scientific literature, particularly anthropological studies on nonliterate cultures.

1) Explanatory functions. Religion is said to offer explanations, interpretations, and rationalizations of the many facets of human existence. It satisfies cognitive and intellectual needs by providing sure and definite answers. Inexplicable problems, which cannot be resolved by any other means, are unraveled by recourse to theological and religious arguments. The new religions have come into being at a time when the mainline churches appear to have retreated in part from their dogmatic stance and when scientific progress has brought to the fore new moral and religious questions for which there are no definite answers. Cults are known for providing intellectual security. They counteract contemporary moral ambiguity, providing definite and religiously legitimated answers about human behavior.

2) Emotional functions. The most common sociopsychological functions assigned to religion are emotional. Religion--by giving the person identity, security, and courage--reduces, relieves, and allays anxiety, fear, tension, and stress. It helps the individual cope with life and face human problems with comfort and confidence. It contributes to emotional integration both on an individual and social level. The argument, found repeatedly in social-scientific literature, is that when traditional religions cease to fulfill these needs, new religious movements come into being. This view considers the rise of the cults as a response to human psychological needs, which the major religious traditions are are not fully satisfying. Thus, more precisely, the cults could be offering a holistic self-conception in an culture where the diffusion of personal identity has left many people lost, confused, and afraid.

3) Social functions. Following Durkheim, many social scientists concur that religious beliefs and practices are instrumental in maintaining, if not creating, social solidarity. Religion is judged to be a force of integration, a unifying bond contributing to social stability and social control and to the preservation of knowledge. Recent developments in the West leave doubt as to whether the established religions are fulfilling this important function. To what degree cults can take the place of these traditionally assigned social functions is not clear. From one point of view, they stress community living in an age when both religious, social, and kinship ties have become rather tenuous and diffuse. They offer a shared lifestyle in a society where dislocation of communal patterns has become the norm. They further propound, and at times eagerly await, an ideal future situation when the relationship between religion and society will be more harmonious. Yet, from another perspective, cults create conflict with society and between family members and can be judged to be dysfunctional.

4) Validating functions. Another function of religion, closely allied with the social ones, is that of validating cultural values. Religious beliefs and practices support, at times with moral and spiritual sanctions, the basic institutions, values, and aspirations of a society. Religion inculcates social and ethical norms; it justifies, enforces, and implements a people's ideological assumptions and the way of life of a group. Again, the applicability of these functions to the cults is not obvious. Joining a new religious movement indicates a break with traditional religious and cultural values. The cults, rather than stamp with approval their member's previous lifestyles, pass a condemnatory judgment

on them. Yet, at the same time, they give the new ideology and ritual behavior the endorsement of charismatic and revelatory authority and validate the members' abandonment of their previous religion.

5) Adaptive functions. Several anthropologists have emphasized the adaptive functions of religious beliefs and rituals. Observing that there is a definite relationship between religion and the environment, they argue that through the use of religion, human beings have been able to adjust and utilize the environment to cater to their own needs. Religion, in this view, is seen as a tool for survival and can be better understood in terms of recurrent adaptive processes. This approach has been applied to show how many of the rituals (like divination and totemism) of primitive and prehistoric religions may originally have had ecologically relevant results. Marc Galanter's (item 799) application of the theory of sociobiology to cults like the Unification Church is an example of how adaptive functions can be attributed to new religious movements.

While it would be difficult to outline any direct relationship between the new cults and ecology, it is possible to build a case for their adaptive function. Many of the new movements, particularly those that align themselves with the New Age Movement, are very ecologically minded. In a time in history when the human race is overusing, polluting, and destroying the natural environment, it is possible that theological and moral views that bestow a divine quality to nature or see it as an expression of divine creativity that must be preserved may have a survival value.

Further, since membership in the new movements is largely transient, they may be indirectly acting as stages in an individual's psychological development and/or reentry into the larger society. It can also be maintained that some cults or cultic activities play the role of mental health care and counseling agencies. Astrology, a form of divination, is clearly a process of self-reflection leading to a decision under the guidance of experts whose role is similar to that of counseling psychologists. Alternative forms of marriage, like the prearranged mass marriages carried out in the Unification Church, are a contrasting substitute for the current precarious married state embodied, for example, in the custom of "serial monogamy" that has become common in Western culture. There are different ways through which a person learns to cope with the stress of sexual gratification and regulation and one of them is to adopt a novel family life in a religious cult.

Current Theories of Cultism

The tendency among social scientists, particularly anthropologists and sociologists, to highlight the positive functions of religion is also reflected in their writings on the cults. If the new religious movements gratify some of the needs of those individuals who join them, then it is easy to conclude that they are beneficial institutions. And if the new cults offer genuine alternatives in an age of social turmoil, then one can readily be led to the view that cults perform a necessary and useful service for humanity. It is not surprising, therefore, that cult opponents have seen social scientists as supporters of or sympathizers with the cults. The functional viewpoint is in direct conflict with the anticult conception of a cult as a spurious religious organization that can be better likened to a cancerous growth in an otherwise healthy organism.

It is necessary to bear in mind, however, that the functional explanation of religion and of cults has come under serious attack by several social scientists, even though it has not completely lost its appeal (see, for example, Fowler, item 798, and Glock, item 804). Besides the admission that religious beliefs and practices may not always have positive results, there are some who are questioning the whole approach that treats the cults as remedies for deprivation (see, for instance, Beckford, item 752, Heelas and Heelas, item 829, and Bibby and Brinkerhoff, item 297). Because this approach neglects the religious functions that cults might fulfill, it could easily be perceived as reductionistic, ignoring the fact that the human religious quest might be responsible for the success of the cults that may function, in part, as vehicles for mystical experiences. Several explanatory theories, some of which overlap, have been devised either to bypass the question of deprivation or else to reformulate it more cogently.

1) One approach considers the new cults as genuine religious and spiritual revivals (see Stark and Bainbridge, item 962). Observing that religious revivals or awakenings have been common in the history of the West, particularly the United States, it can be argued that such revivals appear in cycles and/or take place whenever traditional religions appear to have lost some of their original vitality. The advent of the new cults in the last few decades has coincided with a period in history when the mainline churches have so accommodated themselves to society that their ability to satisfy the religious needs of their adherents has diminished. In sociological terms, when religion becomes too secularized one can expect new religious groups to come into being. Secularization and cult formation go hand in hand. Most of those cults that survive will, in time, be swept away by the secularization process, thus recreating the conditions that give rise to new cults.

2) A second approach that contradicts the above considers the presence of the new religions as a confirmation of the secularization hypothesis (Wilson, item 1020). The new cults are a trivialization of religion and not a genuine religious resurgence. They may be considered to be the final gasp of religion, a last but futile attempt to restore the importance that religion used to have in daily life. In this view, secularization is an inevitable process because contemporary social developments leave no room for religion and spirituality. The cults could be considered a reaction to the process of secularization, but a reaction that will have little impact on that process.

3) A third hypothesis interprets the cults as a form of experimental religion (Wuthnow, 1141). Contemporary society is marked by a system of communication and mobility that increases one's knowledge of different religious options and makes available several spiritual opportunities. In a society that values individual experience and stresses freedom of choice, young adults, who form the bulk of people cults attract, become prone to experiment even with religious forms. This experimental outlook may also be a result, in part at least, of the loosening of family ties. Unlike members of tribal societies, people in contemporary Western culture may be less attached to their cultural, family, and religious roots and more likely to embark on their own personal quest than to accept unquestionably the religion of their parents. More psychologically inclined scholars would stress the prevailing narcissism in our culture and maintain that the new movements are an expression of this growing trend.

4) Another theory focuses on the current political scene and argues that the new cults have sprung from political disenchantment (cf. Richardson, item 910, and Wuthnow and Glock, item 1046). The late 1960's saw for the first time widespread antagonism towards, and rebellion against, the economic and sociopolitical system in the West. Material success has become an all-embracing value that neglects or denies the spiritual dimension of life. It may also have created more problems (such as rivalry and intense competition) than it has solved. Joining a new religious movement is a way of opting out of the system, a form of escapism. One can expand this theory to include rebellion against Western culture as a whole and against one's parental authority. The values and lifestyles that have been passed on by the family and society are rejected as inadequate and unsatisfying.

5) Related to the aforementioned theory is the view that contemporary change has been too rapid and has, consequently, uprooted people from their parental and cultural moorings. The Western world is in a state of culture crisis (Bellah, item 756, Anthony and Robbins, item 735, and Eister, item 788). People feel lost and insecure in a world that questions all absolute values and norms and has become highly impersonal and utilitarian. Cults provide encouragement and certainty to people who are beset by moral and religious confusion and who are in a state of anomie. They fulfill needs that traditional religions have ceased to take care of. This is one form of the deprivation theory of religion tailored to suit the emergence of the new cults.

6) Another hypothesis, which has some similarities to the second theory mentioned above, speculates that the new cults are indicators of the emergence of new humanism (See Wuthnow, items 1035 and 1038). It starts with the assumption that religion is an evolving phenomenon and attempts to pinpoint the universal religious trends for the future. It implies that that religion as we know it is on the decline and that a new worldview is coming into being, a worldview that has been influenced by Eastern traditions and stresses the immanent, rather than the transcendent, nature of the divine. This new humanism is thisworldly-oriented. Though such a perspective has been present in the West for centuries, it now shows signs of becoming the dominant feature in contemporary spiritual life. This theory does not necessarily maintain that the traditional religious worldview will be replaced by a new one. But it does suggest that traditional religion might be undergoing some radical changes and might not remain the only dominant force in human spirituality.

7) The rise of the cults has also been related to the breakdown of the "American Civil Religion" (Robbins et al., item 1961, and Hammond, item 817). In many societies throughout history, there has been a religious or quasi-religious regard for civic values and traditions. The complexity of special festivals, rituals, creeds, and dogmas that flow from this nationalist attitude has been given the label of "Civil Religion." The United States is a vivid example of such a religion, which began with the divine mission ascribed to America by the Puritan settlers in New England. The cultural developments and turbulence of the 1960's are related to the incipient breakdown of Civil Religion in the United States. The cults may be considered as attempts to fill the void left by the decline of Civil Religion. Some cults, like the Mormon Church in the nineteenth century and the Unification Church in the twentieth century, that exalt the place

of America in the divine plan, may in fact be offering a substitute Civil
Religion that permeates cultural values and filters into every aspect of
life.

8) A final explanation of cult formation that has captured the popular
imagination is the brainwashing theory, which has been proposed mainly by
social psychologists and psychiatrists (see my PSYCHIATRY AND THE CULTS:
AN ANNOTATED BIBLIOGRAPHY, New York: Garland, 1987). This theory insists
that those who join the cults do not do so voluntarily. Rather, they are
recruited by skillful, dishonest, and manipulative techniques and then
heavily indoctrinated by mechanisms similar to those employed by communist
countries to change the political allegiances of their prisoners-of-war.
Psychological conditions might render an individual susceptible or vulnerable to cult recruitment. The cults, led by charismatic individuals whose
principal goals are to achieve personal wealth and power, have mounted an
attack against the established sociocultural institutions. Cults attract
young adults, who are often in need of therapy or counseling, with the
vain promise of a better and happier life. Instead, they have the effect
of creating new problems or aggravating already existing ones.

Social-Scientific Critique of the Brainwashing Theory

The brainwashing theory or coercive persuasion contrasts sharply with
the majority of explanations that social scientists have advanced to
account for the rise and success of the cults. These researchers share
one thing in common: they see the emergence of the new movements as a
complex sociocultural phenomenon that cannot be explained simply in terms
of individual psychology or as a result of the recruitment practices of
the cults themselves.

The brainwashing theory is judged deficient precisely because it fails
to take the sociocultural conditions of Western society seriously and,
therefore, ignores some of the main issues that must play a central role
in any explanation of the phenomenon of cultism. Thus, to uphold the view
that cults attract people who are mentally ill or psychologically weak
does not answer the question of why cults have arisen in a certain period
of history and why it is that so many young adults join them. To claim
that power-seeking cult leaders use their charismatic powers to entice, by
some kind of hypnotic power, naive youngsters into their folds, reveals
nothing about the reasons why such leaders actually emerge and little
about the causes of the alleged vulnerability of those attracted to them.
And to explain the success of the cults by stating that they use carefully
planned, deceptive and brainwashing techniques to gain members reduces
young adults to virtual prisoners of cult activity. Most of those individuals who join cults, however, have already embarked on a spiritual or
religious quest before they ever came in contact with a cult and are,
therefore, not just passive bystanders who have been unwittingly lured
into a new religious movement. In like manner, to insist that continuous
heavy socialization or indoctrination into cult beliefs and values practically destroys the free wills and minds of cult members contradicts the
evidence that many members disengage themselves from the new movements on
their own initiative and that a few cult members are actually critical of
some of the activities of the cult to which they belong.

Moreover, to conceive of the emergence of the cults as the result of some kind of attack on Western culture from outside sources is, to say the least, unrealistic. Many of the ideals, values, and lifestyles adhered to by modern cults are hardly novel; their roots are well established in marginal groups that have been part of the Western cultural tradition for some time. Cults are not an external problem, a kind of invasion from outside that can be stopped. Rather they are an internal problem and, hence, direct attacks against them will not succeed in exterminating them. The evidence suggests that Western culture is not being overrun by Eastern traditions; rather Eastern traditions are adapting themselves to Western utilitarian values and being influenced to some degree by Western secularization processes. While there is every reason for some concern, both for those individuals who have joined new religious movements hastily and without careful reflection on the profound implications of their actions and for the parents of cult members who have been affected by the the presence of the cults, social-scientific studies do not condone hysterical fear of the cults, nor do they warrant a panicky reaction to them.

It is certainly not difficult to see why social-scientific views on the new religions have not been very popular. Those who hold that membership in cults implies pathology have at their disposal a simple, professional answer to involvement in a cult, namely optional or forced therapy. On the other hand, those who maintain that the cults are responsible for enticing and brainwashing young adults against their wills propound the equally straightforward solution that cult members should be deprogrammed and the cults suppressed. Both groups of people seem to find no great flaws in contemporary society and put the blame elsewhere--the former having recourse to mental illness, the latter to malicious people who found cults for their own profit. Social scientists think that these solutions do not fit the facts and offer superficial and simplistic explanations that neglect consideration of the many problems caused by modern industrialized society and by evolutionary forces that may not be easily controlled by human endeavors.

The social-scientific theories of cult formation alert us to the sociocultural matrix that makes cults possible. They direct our attention to the problems of Western society in a period of rapid social change and argue that it is precisely these problems that explain the reason why cults succeed and that, consequently, must be addressed. They make us reflect not only on the possible inevitability of the cults, but also on their manifold functions. Though social-scientific studies could lead to the conclusion that the problems that the cults have brought in their wake may not be easily solved, they also provide the information and reflection for ways of coping with them.

Responses to the Cults

The sixth and final issue in contemporary cultism has to do with the response that society should make to the cults. Two opposing viewpoints have gradually emerged and solidified since the early 1970's. The first and more common one has been identified largely with the activity of the Anti-Cult Movement and has attracted the support of many psychiatrists, lawyers, ministers of religion, and the general public. Its main concerns

are the effects of cultism on family members, on the well-being of the
individuals who become cult members, and on what are perceived to be negative results on society and/or religion as a whole. Its methods are
mostly confrontational. Besides the dissemination of literature that
discredits the cults and the foundation of counseling centers that assist
parents in their efforts to remove their offspring from the cultic milieu,
those who adhere to this approach have had recourse to the courts to
counteract cultic practices and to achieve their goals.

A second response, to which many social scientists subscribe, is aimed
more towards diagnosing the activities of the Anti-Cult Movement itself
and analyzing the various reactions to cultism than dealing directly with
the personal problems brought into being by the presence and influence of
the new religions (cf. Shupe et al., item 62). Instead of concentrating
largely on the psychological and personal aspects of cultic involvement,
many social scientists have drawn attention to the serious social implications that might follow a legally sanctioned anti-cult stand (Kelley, item
2149). They have stressed the importance of religious pluralism and freedom, particularly in American culture, and have contended that any legal
curtailment of the cults threatens both. Their defense of religious freedom has regrettably been seen as a procult stance. Some scholars have
also drawn attention to the common sociological view that the persecution
of cults has the effect of strengthening them, by making martyrs of their
leaders and members, by enhancing their ideological goals, and by contributing to a stronger sense of unity and purpose among cult members.

The issues about cultism are expressive of a deep division between two
approaches to, and interpretations of, the new religious movements. The
debates have assumed a crusading spirit that has intensified the split
between so-called opponents and defenders of cults. Because of the antagonism that exists between these two camps, it would be unrealistic at this
stage to hope for a quick and easy resolution to the problems discussed in
this introduction.

Some Observations on the Social Scientific Study of the Cults

Because social science has taken a leading role in the study of the
cults, it is legitimate to ask how it can contribute to the resolution of
the social problems that the cults have inevitably brought with them. The
approach to the new movements adopted by the majority of social scientists
has much to recommend it; it has definitely broadened our understanding of
cultic phenomena, thus laying the foundation for a solid response to their
presence. However, it still suffers from a number of flaws that need to
be corrected if any impact is to be made on public opinion and policy.

Several deficiencies become apparent to anyone who surveys the abundant
literature on the new movements. The first thing one observes is that,
given the number of cults and of scholars who have spent some time studying them, the ethnographic monographs on individual cults are relatively
few. Without denying the role of theory in studying the new movements and
without neglecting the fact that there is some excellent descriptive material on some of the more prominent new movements (like the Unification

Church, the Hare Krishna Movement, the Charismatic Movement, and the
Children of God Movement in its early phases), more comprehensive ethnographic studies of individual cults are needed.

A second observation, related to the first, is that too many of the
studies on the cults are overshadowed by the debate about brainwashing.
Barker's excellent study on the Unification Church (item 1698) is a case
in point; the author subtitles her book "Brainwashing or Choice." Two
recent studies on the Hare Krishna Movement (Rochford, item 1964, and
Shinn, item 1983) have been written with the precise intention of disprov-
ing and discrediting the brainwashing hypothesis. Just as anticultists
have studied cults with the intention of proving their basic assumption,
namely that the cults are destructive organizations that brainwash or
indoctrinate their members, so also have social scientists often begun
their investigation of a cult with the aim of demonstrating that this
assumption is false. Works like those of Chidester on Jonestown (item
1664) and Norquist on Ananda Cooperative Village (item 1892) are like a
breath of fresh air. Instead of exerting their efforts to prove or dis-
prove the claim that members of these new religious groups are intentionally brainwashed, the authors pursue a different line of investigation to
give a meaningful interpretation of the Jonestown phenomenon in the context of religious history and of Ananda Village in the context of a long
tradition of communal lifestyles. The results may not be emotionally
arousing, but they certainly open up new perspectives and opportunities
for making some sense out of the violence of Jonestown and out of the
relatively restrictive environment of life in a commune.

A third observation deals with the rather lopsided volume of studies on
the new cults. While certain new religious movements, like the Unification Church, the Hare Krishna Movement, and, more recently, the People's
Temple, have been the object of numerous and intense research projects by
different scholars, there are many cults about which there are few, if
any, exhaustive studies. Scientology can be taken as a case in point.
There are many popular books that describe and/or criticize some aspects
of this new religious movement, but this writer could trace only two major
works in the English language, i.e., Wallis's sociological monograph
(item 2062) and Whitehead's anthropological study (item 2089).

Several reasons can be adduced to explain this state of affairs. While
a handful of cults have actually encouraged researchers, many cults seem
weary of inquisitive scholars and reporters. Developments in some cults
have made them less accessible for study. The Children of God/Family of
Love and the Divine Light Mission, about which there are several excellent
publications, have been in some form of self-imposed hibernation since the
early 1980's. Others do not seem to encourage researchers. Some groups
may have not attracted scholars to explore them. Or, in some cases, not
enough funds could be generated to make the research feasible. Ideally,
the student of cultism should have at his or her disposal several monographs on each cult written by different researchers. Recent publications
on, for instance, the People's Temple, provide the needed factual information and historical background on this religious movement plus a variety
of approaches and interpretations of its tragic demise. While admittedly
there are a number of intensive studies on many cults, more are required
for a better understanding of the individual movements and of the cults as
a whole.

A fourth observation deals with the response to the new religious movements. That their presence has raised religious, moral, social, and legal
issues can hardly be questioned. That some of these issues are urgent and
relate to personal problems that the families of cult members have to face
is equally obvious. Unless social science is alert and responsive to
these issues, its efforts to understand the cults are likely to be ignored
or repulsed. While it is difficult to endorse or condone the neglect of
social-scientific studies on the new cults, one must concede that social
scientists have to share the blame for their inability to influence the
public and the news media.

The success of cult-counseling and information agencies that take a
negative attitude to the cults has been due to two major facts: they have
addressed themselves to the personal problems of those who have been negatively affected by cults' presence and activities; and they have proposed
simple and direct answers to the challenge--real or apparent--of cultism.
Those individuals who consult these agencies are likely to have their
social and religious values reinforced and to have their hopes of getting
people out of cults bolstered.

Scholars who have used social-scientific data and theory to address the
same problems have run into serious difficulties. They have discovered
that it is irrelevant to quote the statistics on cult defection to the
parents of a cult member, no matter how correct these statistics are. And
it is quite unappealing and impractical to offer them, say, the theory of
resource mobilization to help them come to terms with what they experience
as a traumatic event in their lives. While it is relatively easy to support in principle the need to safeguard religious pluralism and freedom,
it is quite another matter to try and convince religiously minded parents
of these values when their offspring have abandoned the religious and
cultural traditions of their upbringing. Although the attitude of cultural relativism is certainly a necessary scholarly requirement for a fair
study, understanding, and evaluation of exotic movements, it cannot be
easily incorporated in a popular societal response to the cults. On the
contrary, it appears to be incompatible with most mentalities that are
still very ethnocentric when religious and cultural values appear threatened by outside forces.

What is needed is some kind of applied sociology and/or anthropology
of the cults whereby social-scientific data, analyses, and theories are
translated into intellectual tools and practical means to help people cope
socially, psychologically, and religiously with the new movements. Though
there are both academic and ethical problems in any applied social-scientific method, we are convinced that the risks are well worth it. Otherwise, the social-scientific study of the cults might remain an academic
discipline with very limited impact on the social, moral, religious, and
legal responses to the new religious movements that have acquired a
permanent footing in contemporary Western society.

Social Science and the Cults

CHAPTER I

SOURCES FOR THE SOCIAL-SCIENTIFIC STUDY OF CULTS, SECTS, AND NEW RELIGIOUS MOVEMENTS

The social-scientific literature on the new religious movements is voluminous. There is no single book or bibliography available that could possibly contain all the materials that have been published in the last two decades or that deal with the historical antecedents to, or contemporary aspects of, the current investigation of cults. The cult researcher has to explore many avenues to locate the publications on the phenomena under study. In this chapter, we include those materials that we found helpful in tracing a large proportion of the works listed in the following pages and that can be utilized for locating many of the primary and secondary sources necessary for the social-scientific study of the new movements.

Three types of literature referred to in this chapter can be distinguished. The first consists of bibliographic surveys, encyclopedias, and commentaries that deal specifically and exclusively with sects and cults and of abstracts of sociological, anthropological, and religious essays among which literature on new religious movements can be found. Though some of the surveys are dated, they are essential for understanding the history of the study of cultism, the development of social-scientific theory, and the changes that have occurred among the cults themselves.

A second type of literature pertains not directly to the cults but to the background information necessary to understand the social-scientific discussions on cultism. Thus, to give but a few examples, cults are often called deviant. Deviance, however, may be assigned several meanings: it may refer to unorthodoxy (or religious deviancy), to mental illness (or psychological deviancy), or to criminal behavior (one form of sociological deviancy). Whether and to what extent these three types of aberrant and/or atypical behaviors are related is a debatable issue. The cults, as one form of socially deviant phenomena, must be understood in the context of the sociology of deviancy, which will enable the student to determine if, and in what sense, the label "deviant" can be used to describe the cults.

Similarly, many writers on the new movements, irrespective of their academic orientation, have seen some relationship between the rise of the cults and alienation among modern youth, particularly since the late 1960's. In order to determine the role played by alienation in the emergence of the cults, one has to explore at some depth the concept itself and the ways it has been used in the social sciences. If one stresses

social alienation, then one will be led to consider involvement in cults
not merely as an expression of individual psychology and/or of carefully
orchestrated recruitment practices, but mainly as a symptom of broader
sociocultural conditions.

And as a final example, one can take the theory of resource mobilization
that has been recently applied to the new religions. Those students who
endeavor to explore the significance of the mobilization theory and its
potential for interpreting and shedding light on the cult phenomenon must
begin with the literature that gives the background to this sociological
approach and to its application to social movements in general, of which
religious movements are but a species.

As one reads the social-scientific literature on the cults, one becomes
increasingly aware that the approach social scientists take, the methods
they employ, and the hypotheses they adopt must be seen in the context of
their disciplinary backgrounds. In other words, one cannot fully understand, much less appreciate, the social-scientific study of cults unless
one is familiar with social science in general. Several areas of social
science, particularly sociology and anthropology, need to be explored if
one wishes to follow their debates on cults. Thus, the anthropological
study of cults has emphasized the need to explore their symbolic systems
and to interpret their functions in terms of rites of passage, while the
sociological study of the reactions to the new movements has found, for
instance, the labeling theory a useful tool to decipher the interactions
between the cults and society at large. Throughout this volume we have
referred to bibliographies that help situate the social-scientific study
of cults within this wider framework.

The third type of literature mentioned in this chapter consists of
annuals and professional journals that publish materials on cults and
sects. Most social-scientific and religious periodicals regularly
include refereed articles, and quite a few have occasionally dedicated a
whole issue to the phenomenon. Three journals, namely the JOURNAL FOR
THE SCIENTIFIC STUDY OF RELIGION, SOCIOLOGICAL ANALYSIS, and the REVIEW
OF RELIGIOUS RESEARCH, stand out in their many theoretical and descriptive
articles on cults. A substantial bibliography can be amassed by listing
the relevant essays that have appeared in these journals over the last
two decades and their many references to cultic studies. These journals
have taken a somewhat neutral approach to the new movements, in the sense
that they have not passed judgment on their "religious orthodoxy." Moreover they have tended to underscore the religious, sociological, and psychological functions that many cults fulfill, to focus their attention on
the sociological variables associated with cultism, and to devise sociological theories that explain their presence and persistence. Though
there is a definite trend in these journals to pay attention to the positive functions of cults and to look on them as expressions of genuine
religiousness, nevertheless conflicting opinions on the origins of cults,
the kind of members they attract, their relations to, and effects, on
society and other religious organizations, and their possible outcomes are
frequently expressed.

Two of the journals cataloged below, namely UPDATE: A QUARTERLY
JOURNAL OF NEW RELIGIOUS RELIGIOUS MOVEMENTS and CULTIC STUDIES JOURNAL,
are dedicated exclusively to the study of the new cults. The former, now

defunct, was published from 1977 to 1986 from the Dialog Center in Aarhus, Denmark; the latter, a relatively recent addition to the scene, has been issued semiannually since 1984 by the American Family Foundation of Weston, Massachusetts. Both have taken a largely anticult stand, the former from religious point of view, the latter from a social-psychological and legal perspective. In spite of this negative theoretical stance, both have provided informative and reflective essays on many of the new movements. CULTIC STUDIES JOURNAL publishes regular, exhaustive bibliographies that often contain materials not easily traced elsewhere.

A. BIBLIOGRAPHIES, ENCYCLOPEDIAS, AND MANUALS

1. Ahlstrom, Sydney. A RELIGIOUS HISTORY OF THE AMERICAN PEOPLE. New Haven, CT: Yale University Press, 1972. xvi, 1158 pp.

   Presents a history of religion in the United States that gives constant attention to the radical and colorful diversity of religious movements and revivals. The rise of sects and cults, particularly those that came into being in the eighteenth and nineteenth centuries, is fully recorded. One chapter deals with the influence of non-Western religions in America, while another examines the turbulent 1960's that were characterized by a steady escalation of "religious antitraditionalism." There are many bibliographic footnotes. This book is a basic and practically indispensable reference for the study of the history of American religious movements in the sociocultural setting.

2. American Theological Library Association. RELIGION INDEX TWO: MULTI-AUTHOR WORKS. Chicago: American Theological Library Association, 1960-1988.

   Provides comprehensive coverage of articles published in collective works, Festschriften, and conference proceedings. Materials covering the years 1960-1969 were published in one volume, while those between 1970 and 1975 appeared in two volumes, one being an author-editor index, the other a subject index. Since 1976, RELIGION INDEX TWO has come out on a yearly basis. It has been edited by different scholars throughout the years. Relevant materials can be located under the headings of "cult," "sect," "new religious movements," and "sociological study of religion," and/or under the names of the religious groups under investigation. These volumes are an indispensable source for the study of new religions since they list many essays not easily traceable elsewhere. A companion publication is dedicated to periodical literature (see item 18).

3. Baer, Hans A. "Bibliography of Social Science Literature on Afro-American Religions in the United States." REVIEW OF RELIGIOUS RESEARCH 39 (1988): 413-30.

   Lists social-scientific studies on Afro-American churches and religious groups including the following: the Holiness and Pentecostal sects; the Spiritual and Spiritualistic sects; the Moorish

Science Temple; the Black Jews; the Black Muslims; the African
Orthodox Church; and the Father Divine Peace Mission Movement.
The author observes that the "separatism of Black religion has
been the single most important vehicle by which Blacks have been
able to assert their social identity as well as to protest the
racism of the larger society" (p. 413). The bibliographic materials are divided into the following five sections: 1) overviews
of Black religion; 2) community studies with extensive discussions
of Black religion; 3) studies of Black churches in specific locales;
4) White churches, Racism, and Black Americans; and 5) the occult
among Black Americans: Voodoo, Hoodoo, and magic.

4.   Barker, Eileen. "Religious Movements: Cult and Anti-Cult Since
       Jonestown." ANNUAL REVIEW OF SOCIOLOGY 12 (1986): 329-46.

       Overviews theoretical and empirical studies by sociologists of
       religion on the new religious movements and the Anti-Cult Movement
       since 1978. The aftereffects of Jonestown, the different theories
       advanced to explain why people join cults, and the social roles of
       witnesses in court cases and participant observers at conferences
       organized by the cults themselves are the main areas covered. The
       author observes that the differences between the various religious
       movements are considerably greater than is often recognized.

5.   Beckford, James A. "Religious Organization: A Survey of Recent
       Publications." ARCHIVES DE SCIENCES SOCIALES DES RELIGIONS 57
       (1984): 83-102.

       Surveys the major English publications on religious organization
       since 1975. The materials are divided into four general headings:
       1) changing problematics (where the current trend not to deal with
       questions of organization is discussed); 2) cults and networks
       (where the emphasis is on how members of the new religious move-
       ments are united by a series of social networks); 3) mobilization
       and management (where the strategies for generating, directing,
       and monitoring resources are studied); and 4) power and leadership
       (where various notions of power in a religious context are inves-
       tigated). This is a useful bibliography that amply covers some
       major publications. Though by no means exhaustive, it gives the
       reader a good idea of where sociological interest in the new
       religious movements lies.

6.   Beckford, James A., and James T. Richardson. "A Bibliography of
       Social Scientific Studies of New Religious Movements." SOCIAL
       COMPASS 30 (1983): 111-35.

       Lists sociological books and articles on new religious movements
       published between the 1970's and early 1980's. Though most of the
       items listed are in the English language, several significant works
       in French, Italian, German, and Dutch are cited. This collection
       of materials does not include anticult literature and theological
       evaluations. This is a useful introductory bibliography that
       covers most of the major issues discussed in contemporary
       sociology.

7.   Bergman, Jerry. JEHOVAH'S WITNESSES AND KINDRED GROUPS: A HISTOR-
        ICAL COMPENDIUM AND BIBLIOGRAPHY. New York: Garland, 1984.
        xxix, 370 pp.

        Presents a comprehensive list of books, articles, theses, and
        book reviews on Jehovah's Witnesses and their offshoots. The
        material is divided into five parts: 1) official church documents;
        2) materials associated with the Russel Movement; 3) publications
        about the Jehovah's Witnesses; 4) offshoots of the Watchtower Bible
        and Tract Society; and 5) non-American Bible study groups. One
        short section (pp. 200-208) lists magazine articles that approach
        Jehovah's Witnesses from a psychological or sociological point of
        view. Though the publications listed are largely in English,
        there are several references to books and articles in different
        languages. A short introduction to each section is provided, but
        there are no annotations.

8.   Blood, Linda Osborne. COMPREHENSIVE BIBLIOGRAPHY ON THE NEW CULT
        PHENOMENON. Weston, MA: American Family Foundation, n.d. 111 pp.

        Compiles an exhaustive bibliography of materials dealing with
        the new cults. The works cited, which are catalogued by author,
        are divided into two sections: 1) books and scholarly literature
        and 2) popular literature, the latter section comprising about
        one-fourth of the volume. There are well over 2000 references to
        psychological, psychiatric, sociological, and legal studies on
        cults, to book reviews, and to reactions to the cult's presence.
        Since the materials are not annotated or arranged in any sub-
        divisions to facilitate reference, and since there is no subject
        index to help locate specific materials, this book is by no means
        an easy guide to the new religious movements. The citations cover
        publications up to the early 1980's.

9.   Brunkow, Robert de V., editor. RELIGION AND SOCIETY IN NORTH
        AMERICA: AN ANNOTATED BIBLIOGRAPHY. Santa Barbara, CA: American
        Bibliographic Society--Clio Press, 1983. xi, 515 pp.

        Amasses a bibliography that "reflects the subtle but still
        drastic shifts on writings about religion in America." Relevant
        chapters on communal movements and utopian thought, the occult,
        revivals, and many small religious groups in the nineteenth and
        twentieth centuries provide a variety of annotated literature
        particularly rich in historical studies. Most of the titles are
        in English.

10.   Burgess, Stanley M., and Gary B. McGee, editors. DICTIONARY OF
        PENTECOSTAL AND CHARISMATIC MOVEMENTS. Grand Rapids, MI:
        Zondervan Publishing House, 1988. xiii, 914 pp.

        Presents a comprehensive treatment of twentieth-century Pente-
        costalism in Europe and North America and covers both classical
        Pentecostalism and the more recent Charismatic Movement in encyclo-
        pedic form. An introduction by the editors traces the historical
        roots of Pentecostalism and outlines the differences and tensions

between the earlier and newer forms of revivals. Besides entries
on individual movements, the dictionary includes the founders and
leaders of the movements and various topics such as the role of
women, global statistics, and publications. There also are general
essays on glossolalia, Black-Holiness Pentecostalism, the Catholic
Charismatic Renewal, and on the psychology and sociology of Pentecostalism. Bibliographies are attached to each entry. Though
largely theological in orientation, this volume brings together
plenty of information on many Pentecostal movements.

Contains item 689.

11.   Chall, Leo P., editor. SOCIOLOGICAL ABSTRACTS. San Diego, CA:
       Sociological Abstracts, 1953-1988.

       Summarizes the contents of periodical literature in sociology
       and related disciplines. Materials on cults and new religious
       movements are included under the section "Sociology of Religion."
       Some references can also be found under "Social Movements," a sub-
       section of "Mass Phenomena." This is an indispensable source for
       periodical articles on cults, sects, and new religious movements.
       It also contains sections giving summaries of papers read at
       sociological conferences.

12.   Choquette, Diane, compiler. NEW RELIGIOUS MOVEMENTS IN THE UNITED
       STATES AND CANADA: A CRITICAL ASSESSMENT AND ANNOTATED BIBLIOG-
       RAPHY. Westport, CT: Greenwood Press, 1985. xi, 235 pp.

       Covers scholarly materials on new religious movements and orders
       them by their respective disciplines, namely history, sociology
       and anthropology, psychology and psychiatry, theology and religion,
       and law. Other sections include reference works, the cultural
       background, and interdisciplinary studies. Most of the 738 items
       cited are annotated. The last three sections of the bibliography
       include personal accounts, popular studies, and the spiritualiza-
       tion of knowledge. The author holds that these last-mentioned
       sections complement the scholarly studies and provide some evalu-
       ation of the material that is available to the general public. An
       introduction by Robert Ellwood proposes several areas of future
       research. This is a good bibliographical introduction to the new
       religious movements.

13.   Claire, Thomas C. OCCULT/PARANORMAL BIBLIOGRAPHY: AN ANNOTATED
       LIST OF BOOKS PUBLISHED IN ENGLISH, 1976 THROUGH 1981. Metuchen,
       NJ: Scarecrow Press, 1984. xviii, 561 pp.

       Continues the author's previous research (item 13) on occult
       phenomena. A total of 1714 books (including some dissertations)
       are included, starting with item number 2001 (even though his
       early book had listed only 1856 books). As in his earlier bibli-
       ography, this selection is strong on primary sources and on the
       heated debate on the validity of occult beliefs in a scientific
       age, though somewhat weak on social-scientific studies. Witch-
       craft, astrology, prophecy, supernatural phenomena, and para-
       psychology are among the many topics covered. Author, book title,
       and subject indices are appended.

14.   Claire, Thomas C. OCCULT BIBLIOGRAPHY: AN ANNOTATED LIST OF BOOKS
        PUBLISHED IN ENGLISH, 1971 THROUGH 1975. Metuchen, NJ: Scare-
        crow Press, 1978. xxvii, 454 pp.

        Attempts a comprehensive, mostly annotated, list of occult books
        and a few dissertations in English aimed to fill in the vast gaps
        in the field of occult research. Those publications that fail to
        live up to the criteria of excellence the author outlines in his
        introduction are omitted. The 1856 items included are listed in
        alphabetical order by author. Works by proponents of occult
        beliefs and practices as well as critical and interpretative
        studies are included. There are many invaluable primary sources
        in this collection. However, one has to wade through the book to
        locate the relatively few social and psychological studies. At
        the beginning of the bibliography, a useful survey of important
        events in the occult world and a list of the most important books
        between 1971-1975 are provided. Author, book title, and subject
        indices are added.

15.   Delaney, Oliver J. "The Occult: Diabolica to Alchemists." R Q
        (REFERENCE QUARTERLY) 11 (1971): 7-14.

        Defines the occult as a science "that investigates the doctrines,
        practices, and rites of things mysterious and hidden" (p. 7).
        Students of the occult work with the intention of helping human
        beings understand the universe in order to achieve protection from
        evil, to foretell the future, and to gain personal power. Topics
        like alchemy, astrology, demonology, Satanism, witchcraft, and
        parapsychology are included. With his definition in mind, the
        author presents a select annotated bibliography, largely of books
        and articles in English. The materials are divided into several
        sections including reference works, bibliographies, dictionaries,
        encyclopedias, handbooks, histories, and yearbooks. Though obvi-
        ously dated, this volume contains some excellent historical sources
        going back to the middle of the nineteenth century.

16.   Demerath, Nicholas J., and Wade C. Roof. "Religion--Recent Strands
        in Research." ANNUAL REVIEW OF SOCIOLOGY 2 (1976): 19-33.

        Overviews recent sociological literature on religion under three
        major headings: 1) the sources of religious sentiment; 2) the con-
        sequences of religious commitment; and 3) recent research on old
        and new forms of religious organizations. In the last-mentioned
        section, the authors discuss church organizations and clerical
        roles, sectarianism, youth movements and protests, and civil
        religion. It is observed that the following trends are prominent
        in contemporary studies of religion: the use of new methodological
        techniques and approaches, the importation of theoretical insights
        from other disciplines, and the extension of sociological inquiry
        beyond the conventional subject matter. A short bibliography (pp.
        31-33) is attached.

17.   Dickenson, G. Fay, et al. RELIGION INDEX ONE: A SUBJECT INDEX TO
        PERIODICAL LITERATURE INCLUDING AN AUTHOR INDEX AND SCRIPTURE
        INDEX. Chicago: American Library Association, vols. 10-20
        (1969-1988).

Contains references to articles published in over 400 regular indexed titles and selected essays from other journals. Both the subject and author-editor indices are comprehensive. Most of the materials on new religious movements can be located under the name of the particular religious group and/or under several subject listings, including sects, cults, religious movements, and sociology of religion. These volumes (which are published quarterly) are indispensable for the study of the new religious movements from various academic perspectives.

18.   Eliade, Mircea, editor in chief. THE ENCYCLOPEDIA OF RELIGION. New York: Macmillan, 1987. 16 vols.

Brings together several general essays on the new religious movements and individual entries on the major groups. Most of these essays have been written by social scientists, especially sociologists, and contain basic bibliographies. There are also essays dealing with topics that are related to the cults, such as astrology, conversion, glossolalia, messianism, millenarianism, and utopianism. This encyclopedia is also rich in materials on Eastern religious traditions.

Contains items 547, 553, 682, 1606, 1647, 1972.

19.   Evans, Hilary, and John Spencer, compilers and editors.   UFOS, 1947-1987: THE 40-YEAR SEARCH FOR AN EXPLANATION. London: Fortean Tomes, 1987. 383 pp.

Presents a compendium of articles on UFOs and on the various attempts to explain them. The appearance of unidentified flying phenomena in history and in different countries since 1947 is covered in some detail. The problem of assessing the evidence is discussed. There are several essays offering psychological and/or sociological explanations of the phenomenon of flying saucers. Societal reactions to the UFOs include those of governments, skeptics, pranksters, and true believers. The underlying premise of this collection is that UFOs have left a permanent impact on society and have become part of contemporary mythology. There are bibliographical references appended to almost every essay, though, unfortunately, there is no subject index nor a cumulative bibliography. A directory of current UFO research organizations in 17 countries and a list of books about UFOs are added. This volume is a major reference work on the UFO phenomenon.

Contains items 1708, 1844, 1861, 2004, 2218.

20.   Galbreath, Robert. "Occult and the Supernatural." HANDBOOK OF AMERICAN POPULAR CULTURE. Edited by M. Thomas Inge. Westport, CT: Greenwood Press, 1980, vol. 2, pp. 213-36.

Argues that since the increased interest in occult matters is often related to periods of social tension and rapid change, the study of popular occultism "may contribute to understanding the persistence and displacement of beliefs and the processes of social change" (p. 213). The areas included in the occult are PSI phenomena, transpersonal experiences, occult sciences, arts, and

technologies, occult religions, and metaphysics. The author
reviews books and articles on the occult under the following four
headings: 1) reference works; 2) research collections; 3) historical outline and criticism; and 4) anthologies and reprints. He
limits his reflections on materials pertinent to American culture
and focuses his attention particularly on the history of the
occult and the supernatural. A bibliography of over 140 books and
articles is appended.

21.   Galbreath, Robert. "The History of Modern Occultism: A Biblio-
          graphical Survey." JOURNAL OF POPULAR CULTURE 5 (1971): 725-54.

Offers an introductory guide to selected scholarly and popular
publications in the history of Western occultism in the nineteenth
and twentieth centuries. The material is divided into five
headings: 1) bibliographies; 2) reference works; 3) general histories of magic and occultism; 4) occult sciences and themes (such
as magic, alchemy, and astrology); 5) occultism from Romanticism
to the present day. The rise of occult literature in the late
1960's is cited as evidence for the occult revival. The author
maintains that the formation of the Theosophical Society in New
York in 1875 marks the rebirth of occult interest in the West,
while Krishnamurti and Gurdjieff are "two new stars in the occult
firmament" (p. 748). Nearly 300 items are cited, mostly in the
English language, but with several publications in French and
German. Some of the early works on the new religions, including
Scientology, are quoted. The author, writing almost two decades
ago, complains that scholarly works are still very few and makes a
plea for more interdisciplinary studies.

22.   Gibbs, Jack P., and Maynard L. Erickson. "Major Developments in
          the Sociological Studies of Deviance." ANNUAL REVIEW OF
          SOCIOLOGY 1 (1975): 21-42.

Concentrates on surveying literature on the new conception of
deviance that has emerged in sociology. The various societal
reactions to deviance are discussed. This article restricts itself
to criminology and indirectly raises the question whether, and in
what sense the concept of deviance can be applied to the new religious movements. In the literature cited (pp. 40-42) there is
reference to only one study of religious deviance, namely Erickson's
WAYWARD PURITANS (item 181).

23.   Gollin, G. Lindt. "Religious Communitarianism in America: A
          Review of Recent Research." ARCHIVES INTERNATIONALES DE SOCIO-
          LOGIE DE LA COOPERATION ET DU DEVELOPMENT 28 (1970): 125-40.

Surveys early studies on those organizations in America that
have stressed the value of collectivism, particularism, and exclu-
sivism in a religious communitarian setting. The principal religious features of the following groups are summarized: the colonial
communities (such as the Ephrata Brethren), the Amish, the Oneida
Community, the Harmony Society, the Mennonites, the Hutterites, and
the Doukhobors. The author observes that there is "a striking
growth in the number of multi-institutional, sociologically-oriented

studies" (p. 133) which focus on the structures and functions of
these groups and ignore their dynamics. He discusses the origin
and development of religiously oriented communitarian societies,
their persistence, and their social implications. An annotated
bibliography is appended.

24.   Hexham, Irving. "A Bibliographical Guide to Cults, Sects, and New
        Religious Movements (2)." UPDATE: A QUARTERLY JOURNAL ON NEW
        RELIGIOUS MOVEMENTS 8.1 (1984): 36-48.

        Continues the author's introductory bibliography on new reli-
        gious movements by listing major works on the following groups: the
        Baha'i Faith, the Children of God, the Divine Light Mission, Meher
        Baba, the Occult, Rajneesh Foundation, Scientology, Krishnamurti,
        Holistic Health, Theosophy, Transcendental Meditation, and the
        Unification Church. Most of the references, which are partly
        annotated, are to publications in English, though there are some
        encyclopedic texts in a number of other languages. Besides several
        social-scientific studies, this bibliography contains primary
        sources, Christian responses, and anticult materials.

25.   Hexham, Irving. "A Bibliographical Guide to Cults, Sects, and New
        Religious Movements (1)." UPDATE: A QUARTERLY JOURNAL OF NEW
        RELIGIOUS MOVEMENTS 7.4 (1983): 40-46.

        Introduces the reader to a bibliography of materials in English
        on new religious movements. The author thinks that the references
        cited will help readers understand the appeal of the new cults.
        The books and articles quoted are annotated and divided into seven
        sections: 1) sources of information on world religions (including
        some basic books on world religions); 2) introductory works on
        comparative religion; 3) religious and social background to the
        rise of the new religions; 4) psychological studies on religion;
        5) deprogramming and the anticult controversy; 6) the new reli-
        gions and the drug subculture; and 7) the rise of new religions.
        This is a useful, though limited, introductory bibliography that
        places many of the new religions in the context of world religions
        and that contains some basic materials on most of the cultic issues
        discussed in both sociological and psychological literature on the
        new movements.

26.   Hinnells, John R., editor. THE PENGUIN DICTIONARY OF RELIGIONS.
        Harmondsworth, England: Penguin Books, 1984. 550 pp.

        Contains about 30 entries dealing directly and indirectly with
        new religious movements. The articles on the new cults, written
        by Eileen Barker, cover such groups as the Unification Church,
        the Hare Krishna Movement, the Children of God, and the People's
        Temple. Several short items, written by Roger Beck, deal with
        astrological topics, while others, authored by Grevel Lindop,
        survey the occult, including such areas as magic, Anthroposophy,
        witchcraft, Satanism, and Voodoo. There ia a section on tradi-
        tional sects. Introductory bibliographies on each subject are
        appended.

27.   Homan, Roger, compiler. THE SOCIOLOGY OF RELIGION: A BIBLIOGRAPH-
       ICAL SURVEY. New York: Greenwood Press, 1986. x, 309 pp.

       Annotates over 1000 books and articles dealing with the sociology
       of religion. The author provides lists of general works, classical
       sociological studies, and commentaries. The following sections are
       especially useful for the study of cults and sects: 1) typologies
       of religious organizations; 2) sect development, sects, cults, and
       new religious movements; and 3) membership, recruitment, and social-
       ization. Most of the works cited are in English, though some works
       in other European languages, particularly French, are included.
       The annotations are largely descriptive in nature. An introductory
       essay overviews the field of the sociology of religion. Author,
       subject, and title indices are appended.

28.   HUMANITIES INDEX. New York: H. W. Wilson Co., vols. 1-15 (1974-
       1988).

       Presents a quarterly cumulative index, by author and subject, of
       nearly 300 English-language periodicals. History, religious
       studies, and theology are among the disciplines represented. A
       separate listing of book reviews is included. Most of the rele-
       vant material on new religious movements can be located under such
       headings as "cults," "sects," and/or the name of the individual
       religious group under investigation. A companion volume in the
       social sciences is also published by the same company.

29.   International Committee for Social Science Information and Docu-
       mentation. INTERNATIONAL BIBLIOGRAPHY OF SOCIOLOGY. New York:
       Tavistock Publications. Vols. 1-38 (1951-1988).

       Presents a comprehensive, multilingual bibliography of socio-
       logical studies on many aspects of human society. One major sec-
       tion is given over to books and articles on magic, mythology, and
       religion. Materials relevant to new religions can also be located
       in the subject index under such headings as religious movements and
       revivals, sects, and cults (the last also being used to designate
       rituals). These volumes are an indispensable source, especially
       for researchers comparing the new religions in various parts of the
       Western world.

30.   International Committee for Social Science Information and Docu-
       mentation. INTERNATIONAL BIBLIOGRAPHY OF SOCIAL AND CULTURAL
       ANTHROPOLOGY. New York: Tavistock Publications. Vols. 1-34
       (1955-1988).

       Offers, like its companion volume, a broad and thorough listing
       of books and articles in the field of social and cultural anthro-
       pology. One section is dedicated to materials on religion, magic,
       and witchcraft. Largely concerned with the traditional anthropo-
       logical area of tribal and folk religious beliefs, practices, and
       movements, these multilingual volumes are a necessary tool for
       cross-cultural comparisons.

31.   Jenkins, J. Craig. "Resource Mobilization Theory and the Study of
       Social Movements." ANNUAL REVIEW OF SOCIOLOGY 9 (1983): 527-53.

Discusses the emergence of resource mobilization theory as a new
alternative explanatory model of the rise of social movements.
The literature on the formation of such movements, on the manner
they activate those resources necessary for collective action, and
on their organizational structures and political systems is surveyed. Though restricting itself largely to social and political
movements, this essay presents the necessary sociological background for understanding the resource mobilization theory and its
application to the new religious movements. Over 150 books and
articles are cited (pp. 550-53).

32.   Jones, Charles Edwin. BLACK HOLINESS: A GUIDE TO THE STUDY OF
        BLACK PARTICIPATION IN WESLEYAN PERFECTIONIST AND GLOSSOLALIC
        PENTECOSTAL MOVEMENTS. Metuchen, NJ: American Theological
        Library Association and Scarecrow Press, 1987. xxxi, 388 pp.

        Presents a compilation of books, articles, and other publications,
        mainly in the English language, on Black Holiness Churches in var-
        ious countries. This author divides the material into six parts,
        each with a short introduction: 1) Black Holiness (in which general
        works on Wesleyan and Pentecostal Movements are listed); 2) Wesleyan-
        Armenian Orientation (Holiness Perfectionist and Pentecostal groups);
        3) Finished Work of Calvary Orientation (Baptist Trinitarian and Bap-
        tism Oneness Churches); 4) Leader-Centered Orientation; 5) Schools;
        and 6) Biography. In each of the first four chapters, the churches
        and movements are listed in alphabetical order; under each church
        various subheadings, such as doctrinal and controversial works,
        history, statistics, pastoral theology, and the geographic location
        (where necessary), are used. There are no annotations. This vol-
        ume is particularly useful for historical and theological materials
        and for primary sources. There is a good index, but tracing the
        relatively few social-scientific studies is far from easy.

33.   Jones, Charles Edwin. A GUIDE TO THE STUDY OF THE PENTECOSTAL
        MOVEMENT. Metuchen, NJ: Scarecrow Press and the American Theo-
        logical Library Association, 1983. 2 vols., lxv, 1199 pp.

        Compiles a monumental bibliography of books, articles published
        in magazines and scholarly journals, theses, leaflets, and sermons
        (mainly in English) on the Pentecostal Movement in many countries
        throughout the world. The bibliography is divided into four major
        sections, namely: 1) Pentecostal Movements; 2) Doctrinal Tradi-
        tions (which cover the Wesleyan-Armenian Churches and the Finished
        Work of Calvary or Baptist Traditions; 3) Schools; and 4) Biogra-
        phies. There are short introductions to each section and to the
        listed churches, but no annotations except an occasional one-liner.
        This volume is useful particularly for the many primary sources it
        contains. There is a substantial index, though it is difficult to
        locate the relatively few social-scientific studies included.

34.   Jorstad, Erling. "A Review Essay of Sources and Interpretations
        of the Jesus Movement." LUTHERAN QUARTERLY 25 (1973): 295-303.

        Reviews 14 books on the Jesus Movement published between 1970
        and 1972. Besides several personal biographical accounts, a
        number of general surveys and critical works are listed. Though

the author does not refer to any social-scientific study of this
movement, he does include some primary sources and several early
reactions to the Jesus Movement.

35.   Keel, John A. "The Flying Saucer Subculture." JOURNAL OF POPULAR
       CULTURE 8 (1975): 871-95.

       Surveys UFO literature which is divided into three periods, each
       occurring a couple of years after a wave of sightings: 1) publica-
       tions in 1950, after the wave of sightings in 1947; 2) those
       between 1955-1956, after the 1952 wave; and 3) those between 1966-
       1969, after and during the sightings between 1964 and 1967. The
       author discusses various interpretations of the UFO myth and draws
       attention to the fact that flying saucers have also been linked
       with religious manifestations. The author divides the literature
       into four categories: 1) descriptions of sightings; 2) studies on
       the official conspiracy of silence and attacks against the United
       States Air Force; 3) theories and speculations about the origins
       and purpose of UFOs; and 4) contactee stories. It is maintained
       that the ranks of the hard-core flying saucer cultists are rapidly
       growing. Over 100 items are quoted and a short (now dated) list of
       UFO organizations and publications is given.

36.   Keeney, Steven H. "Witchcraft in Colonial Connecticut and Massa-
       chusetts: An Annotated Bibliography." BULLETIN OF BIBLIOGRAPHY
       AND MAGAZINE NOTES 33.2 (1976): 61-72.

       Provides an exhaustive listing of scholarly literature on witch
       scares in New England during the Colonial period. Several bibli-
       ographies, some published in the nineteenth century, are included.
       This partly annotated collection is rich in historical and primary
       sources with a few references to sociological studies.

37.   Kies, Cosette N. THE OCCULT IN THE WESTERN WORLD: AN ANNOTATED
       BIBLIOGRAPHY. Hamden, CT: Shoe String Press, 1986. xii, 223 pp.

       Presents a beginner's sourcebook to the study of the occult,
       stressing "the occult as it is viewed today." Nearly 900 items
       are listed and briefly annotated. Besides an introduction on
       general works on the occult, there are sections on traditional and
       modern witchcraft and Satanism, the magic arts, secret societies,
       astrology, UFOs, etc. This volume contains many primary sources
       and critical works on the various occult beliefs and practices.
       Name and title indices are provided. Several social-scientific
       works are included, but they are difficult to locate.

38.   La Barre, Weston. "Materials For a History of Studies of Crisis
       Cults: A Bibliographic Essay." CURRENT ANTHROPOLOGY 12 (1971):
       3-44.

       Overviews studies on new religious movements that are caused by
       culture shock and by the strains of acculturation. The materials
       listed deal with new movements in different cultural settings and
       are divided into four major sections, namely: 1) general works on

crisis cults; 2) empirical studies; 3) synoptic surveys; and 4)
theories of causality (political, military, economic, messianic,
acculturation, psychological stress, and the "Great Man" theory).
Included are crisis cults in the United States. Though obviously
dated, this much-quoted essay provides a summary of some of the
major theories of cult origin and development that have also been
applied to the new movements of the 1970's and 1980's. Its cross-
cultural perspective places the rise of new religious movements in
the West in a balanced perspective. Comments by various scholars
and a reply by the author are included. A useful bibliography is
attached.

39.   Lippy, Charles H. BIBLIOGRAPHY OF RELIGION IN THE SOUTH. Macon,
        GA: Mercer University Press, 1985. xvi, 898 pp.

        Contains a comprehensive listing of books, articles, and disser-
        tations on religion in the southern regions of the United States.
        Besides a chapter on the sources for such a study, there are chap-
        ters on Native American religions (including Indian Sectarianism),
        Black religions and sects, and various other religious groups, like
        the Mormons, the Holiness Pentecostal Churches, the Quakers, the
        Shakers, the Campbellites, and the Unitarian-Universalists. There
        are no annotations and indices, though each chapter is introduced
        by a survey of the field. There is an obvious stress on the his-
        tory of the churches and movements surveyed.

40.   Lippy, Charles H., and Peter W. Williams, editors. ENCYCLOPEDIA
        OF THE AMERICAN RELIGIOUS EXPERIENCE: STUDIES OF TRADITIONS AND
        MOVEMENTS. New York: Charles Scribner's Sons, 1988. 3 vols.,
        1872 pp.

        Includes a series of essays that address the total scope of reli-
        gious activity and its impact on American life. The first part
        outlines some of the approaches to religion in America and includes
        the perspectives of history, sociology, psychology, geography,
        folklore, and theology. Two sections are particularly useful: one
        deals with religion outside the Jewish and Christian traditions and
        includes many different cults, Eastern religions, and the occult;
        the other studies movements in American religion and examines re-
        vivals, great awakenings, and millenarian, Adventist, and communal
        groups. Though largely historical and descriptive in character,
        these essays contain many other references to studies and interpre-
        tations of new religious movements.

        Contains items 593, 681.

41.   Lo, Clarence Y. H. "Countermovements and Conservative Movements in
        the Contemporary United States." ANNUAL REVIEW OF SOCIOLOGY 8
        (1982): 107-34.

        Covers literature on conservative movements since 1970 and the
        countermovements which have arisen to oppose them. The following
        areas are examined: 1) theories of status preservation, status
        symbolism, and status discrepancy; 2) constituencies of conser-
        vative movements; 3) countermovements linkages; 4) conservative

Protestantism (including fundamentalism and revitalization movements); and 5) the new right as a general social movement. Though not directly related to the new cults or religious movements, these studies offer the necessary background for understanding their emergence in broader sociocultural and religious contexts. Further, countercultural and conservative movements are often related, as are cults, to alienation, frustration, and anomie. Directions for further research are given. There are 130 references cited.

42. Mauss, Armand L. "Sociological Perspectives on the Mormon Subculture." ANNUAL REVIEW OF SOCIOLOGY 10 (1984): 437-60.

Reviews about 250 books and articles (published in English in the United States) in the twentieth century. The author distinguishes between early Mormon studies, which focus on economic, family and fertility, and community life, and the new generation of Mormon scholarship, which, over the last two or three decades, has produced sociological and historical studies which are broader in scope. Among new areas being pursued by contemporary Mormon scholars are: 1) modernization, secularization, and accommodation; 2) Mormon politics; 3) social and ethnic relationships and sex roles; and 4) the expansion of Mormonism. It is argued that the sociology of Mormon religion has become a respectable research area. "Both Mormon and non-Mormon scholars in religious studies now understand that religious experiences, myths, and commitments should be taken seriously as data, rather than explained away as pathological" (p. 441). This is an indispensable article for those exploring the sociology of Mormonism.

43. Mauss, Armand L., and Jeffrey R. Franks. "Comprehensive Bibliography of Social Science Literature on the Mormons." REVIEW OF RELIGIOUS RESEARCH 26 (1984): 73-115.

Comprises a lengthy list of about 500 books and articles in 50 topical categories and subcategories on the Church of Jesus Christ of Latter Day Saints. Included in the journals cited are Mormon publications, such as DIALOGUE: A JOURNAL OF MORMON THOUGHT, SUN-STONE, and BRIGHAM YOUNG UNIVERSITY STUDIES, which the authors insist are professional journals in their own right. Among the categories included are general histories and descriptions of Mormon culture, social and psychological sources of Mormon origins, Mormon religiosity, and various aspects of Mormon subculture, like education, health, community living, economics, politics, and family life. This collection is an indispensable source for the study of Mormonism.

44. Melton, J. Gordon. ENCYCLOPEDIC HANDBOOK OF CULTS IN AMERICA. New York: Garland Publishing Inc., 1986. vi, 272 pp.

Contains short, descriptive essays on many established sects (such as Christian Science, Mormonism, the "I AM" Movement, Theosophy, Satanism, and the Father Divine Movement) and new religious groups (such as Scientology, the Church Universal and Triumphant, Eckankar, the Divine Light Mission, and modern Witchcraft). There

is a section on countercult groups, Evangelical Christianity and
the Anti-Cult Movement, and two essays, one on the New Age Movement, the other on violence and the cults. Bibliographies are
appended throughout. In an introductory essay the author discusses
the definition of a cult and the lifestyle of its members and makes
an assessment of the emergence of cults in the twentieth century.

Contains item 1863.

45.   Melton, J. Gordon. BIOGRAPHICAL DICTIONARY OF AMERICAN CULT AND
        SECT LEADERS. New York: Garland Publishing Inc., 1986. xiii,
        354 pp.

        Provides short biographies of the founders and leaders of cults
        and sects in the United States. Inclusion in the volume is limited
        to those founders and/or prominent leaders of these minority and
        alternative religious groups who died before January 1, 1983. Each
        of the 200 or so entries is accompanied by a short bibliography.

46.   Melton, J. Gordon. MAGIC, WITCHCRAFT, AND PAGANISM IN AMERICA: A
        BIBLIOGRAPHY. New York: Garland Publishing Co., 1982. xi, 231 pp.

        Gives a comprehensive survey of literature written by and about
        the American magical community. The material is divided into 11
        major sections (including one on neo-Paganism), each preceded by a
        short introduction. A general introduction provides a brief his-
        tory of Paganism in the United States, an overview of its revival
        since the 1960's, and a description of magic beliefs and practices.
        The inclusion of material published by the Pagan community makes
        this bibliography an indispensable reference for primary sources,
        while the references to newspaper reports and popular magazine
        essays indicate the extent of interest in magic and witchcraft in
        contemporary Western society.

47.   Melton, J. Gordon. THE ENCYCLOPEDIA OF AMERICAN RELIGION. Wil-
        mington, NC: McGrath Publishing Co., 1978. 2 vols., xxxvi, 608
        and 593 pp.

        Explores the variety of American religions, describing 1200 or
        so churches and religious organizations. Using a classification
        that groups churches, sects, and cults into families, the author
        concentrates on describing and understanding their heritage, world-
        view, ideology, and lifestyle. Volume Two includes those religious
        groups that are often classified as cults or sects in social-scien-
        tific literature. Though primarily historical in orientation, this
        encyclopedia has become a source of many sociological studies on
        new religious movements. Besides its broad and thorough coverage
        of religious organizations, it contains references to many primary
        sources. A second edition in one volume (Gale Research, 1987, xv,
        899 pp.) has also been published. A third edition is in print.

48.   Mickler, Michael L. THE UNIFICATION CHURCH IN AMERICA: A BIBLIOG-
        RAPHIC RESEARCH GUIDE. New York: Garland Publishing Co., 1987.
        xi, 227 pp.

Presents a comprehensive bibliography of materials on the Unification Church in America. Books, articles published in professional journals, dissertations, and popular publications are all included. Besides many references to primary sources, there are sections on the psychological study of the Unification Church and its members, on theological investigations of its doctrines, and on the controversy that the movement has aroused. One section is dedicated to sociological analyses of the movement. The author observes that most of these studies have not been solicited by, or published under the auspices of, the church. Rather, sociologists of religion "have sought out the UC and have been able to publish their findings in both commercial and academic presses" (p. 177).

49.   Midelfort, H. C. Erik. "Recent Witch Hunting Research, or Where Do We Go From Here?" PAPERS OF THE BIBLIOGRAPHICAL SOCIETY OF AMERICA 62 (1968): 373-420.

Describes and evaluates the various approaches to the study of witchcraft and witch-hunting, including more recent anthropological interpretations. The author draws attention to several sociological, intellectual, scientific, and theological problems inherent in the study of witchcraft. A lengthy bibliography lists materials, mostly in English with several titles in a number of continental European languages, under the following four divisions: 1) literature before 1940; 2) European witchcraft, 1940-1967; 3) republications of primary sources since 1940; and 4) witchcraft in art and literature since 1940. One section includes about 50 medical, psychological, and anthropological studies. Though dated, this bibliography provides a useful historical background to the study of European witchcraft and contains some materials relevant to the revival of the occult in the twentieth century.

50.   Mills, Watson E. GLOSSOLALIA: A BIBLIOGRAPHY. New York: Edwin Mellen Press, 1985. ix, 129 pp.

Lists over 1100 items, mainly books and essays, but also some dissertations and unpublished papers, on the phenomenon of glossolalia. In the introduction the author divides the materials into several categories. Though social-scientific studies on the phenomenon of speaking in tongues are not included separately, there is a section on psychological studies and one on cross-cultural studies. Several sociological items can be easily located through the subject index.

51.   Mills, Watson E. CHARISMATIC RELIGION IN MODERN RESEARCH: A BIBLIOGRAPHY. Macon, GA: Mercer University Press, 1985. xii, 178 pp.

Gives a sampling of over 2000 books, published and unpublished articles, and dissertations, mostly in the English language, on classical Pentecostalism and on the neo-Charismatic Renewal. Though leaning heavily towards theological evaluations of charismatic religion, this bibliography contains several social and/or psychological studies on the Catholic Charismatic Movement, glossolalia, and the Jesus Movement. Author and subject indices are included.

52.   Nugent, Donald. "Witchcraft Studies, 1959-71: A Bibliographical
        Survey." JOURNAL OF POPULAR CULTURE 5 (1971): 711-25.

        Supplies a general survey on witchcraft studies, centering on
        historical investigations with some concern for anthropological,
        psychological, psychiatric, and theological analyses. The survey
        is not done in the form of an index, but is annotated and provides
        critical comments and clarifications of the materials cited. It
        includes mainly English works on Western witchcraft from antiquity
        to modern times. Three main historical periods are distinguished:
        1) antiquity; 2) Renaissance (1350-1650); and 3) contemporary. The
        author thinks that older studies on witchcraft too readily equated
        it with mental illness and suggests that witchcraft should be
        approached on its own terms.

53.   Pingree, Elizabeth, editor. SOCIAL SCIENCE AND HUMANITIES INDEX.
        New York: H. W. Wilson Co., vols. 1-27 (1928-1974).

        Contains an author and subject index to English periodicals
        covering various academic disciplines including anthropology,
        religious studies, and sociology. Materials on new religious
        movements can be located under the headings of "cult," "sect,"
        and/or the name of the religious group under study. Till 1965
        these volumes were issued under the title of INTERNATIONAL INDEX.
        In 1974 they were superseded by two publications, namely SOCIAL
        SCIENCES INDEX and HUMANITIES INDEX. They are particularly useful
        in tracing early writings on cults.

54.   Ralston, Helen. "Strands of Research of Religious Movements in
        Canada." STUDIES IN RELIGION 17 (1988): 257-77.

        Overviews research on three types of religious movements in
        Canada, namely: 1) "old" religious movements; 2) new cults; and
        3) contemporary conservative revivals. Major references to books
        and articles in English and French are included in the copious
        footnotes.

55.   Rambo, Lewis R. "Current Research on Religious Conversion."
        RELIGIOUS STUDIES REVIEW 8 (1982): 146-59.

        Incorporates in a survey essay a series of bibliographies, each
        with an introductory comment, surveying the literature on conver-
        sion in anthropology, sociology, history, psychology, psychoanal-
        ysis, and theology, and stressing the different disciplinary foci,
        methodologies, and interpretations. The author points out that
        anthropological studies on conversion tend to bring to light the
        cultural factors and dynamics in the process of conversion. He
        finds little consensus among sociologists but believes that in
        sociology "the groundwork is being laid for a formulation of a
        theory (or theories) of conversion which would account for the
        diversity and complexity of the phenomenon" (p. 149).

56.   Ramsell, Jean E. "A Bibliography of Superstition." R Q (REFER-
        ENCE QUARTERLY) 10 (1970): 45-48.

Gives a list of several basic sources (encyclopedias, dictio-
naries, and books) on "superstition," which is defined as the
acceptance of belief or practice that has no empirical foundation
and that contradicts the knowledge of the community one belongs
to. Astrology is judged to be one of these superstitions that are
probably encouraged by political, social, economic, and religious
tensions and that provide security and comfort. In the author's
view superstition is connected with folklore, primitive religion,
mythology, occultism, and spiritism. Though dated, this bibliography contains several useful sources.

57.   Robbins, Thomas. "New Religious Movements, Brainwashing, and
       Deprogramming--The View From the Law Journals: A Review Essay
       and Survey." RELIGIOUS STUDIES REVIEW 11 (1985): 361-70.

       Maintains that, although practical, legal questions regarding
       taxes and finances may determine the very survival of the new
       religious movements, "issues involving conversion and deconversion
       processes are particularly important both from the standpoint
       of civil liberties and the study and appreciation of religion"
       (p. 362). Legal and philosophical arguments that address the issue
       of conversion and deconversion are reviewed under three headings:
       1) introduction and reviews; 2) legal defense of deprogramming; and
       3) the state as deprogrammer. The contrasting approaches, repre-
       sented by Richard Delgado and Robert Shapiro, are examined. The
       relatively short bibliography provides an introductory sampling of
       the literature pertaining to the current legal debates that have
       followed in the wake of the cults. For other bibliographical refer-
       ences on the cults and the law, see items 684 and 2194.

58.   Robbins, Thomas. "Sociological Studies of New Religious Movements:
       A Selective Review." RELIGIOUS STUDIES REVIEW 9 (1983): 233-39.

       Surveys literature on new religious movements or cults, focusing
       primarily on monographs, collections of papers, and special issues
       of various journals. The material is divided into four general
       areas, namely: 1) collections and anthologies; 2) volumes on
       specific groups; 3) works explaining the emergence of the move-
       ments; and 4) conversion dynamics. About 70 items are cited.
       This is a useful introduction to the sociology of the cults; it
       covers the major theoretical issues being discussed in contempo-
       rary sociology of religion.

59.   Robbins, Thomas, and Dick Anthony. "The Sociology of Contemporary
       Religious Movements." ANNUAL REVIEW OF SOCIOLOGY 5 (1979): 75-89.

       Surveys the literature on new religious movements under four
       divisions: 1) the historical significance and sociocultural
       sources of the present ferment. In this section several theo-
       retical formulations are briefly summed up: the relationship
       between the new religions and secularization; the crises of values
       and community that are thought by many scholars to be among the
       causal factors in the rise of the movements; and the new individu-
       alism that lies behind many of their teachings. 2) The social
       consequences of the new movements. Here the authors examine the

"integrative hypothesis" that maintains that by joining a new
religious group, the individual is eventually rehabilitated into
mainstream culture. 3) The classification of the new movements.
In this context the meanings assigned to the word "cult" in
contemporary literature are discussed. 4) The conversion and
indoctrination process. Special emphasis is given to the brain-
washing/deprogramming controversy that has raged in both psychological and sociological literature. The authors hold that the
new religions have raised theological and epistemological issues
that involve several disciplines, particularly anthropology. About
140 references are cited.

60.   Robbins, Thomas, Dick Anthony, and James Richardson. "Theory and
         Research on Today's 'New Religions.'" SOCIOLOGICAL ANALYSIS 39
         (1978): 95-112.

         Surveys the theoretical formulations and typological divisions
         that have been made by scholars studying the new religious move-
         ments. Several sources of contemporary religious innovations,
         such as secularization, the crisis of community, value crisis, and
         the need for a holistic self-definition, are assessed. A reli-
         gious typology, which divides the movements into dualistic and
         monistic, is described. In simplified form, dualistic groups are
         those that react against the relativistic and pessimistic trends
         of modern Western culture. They can be divided into two sub-
         groups: 1) those which are fundamentalist, stressing Biblical
         literalism and the imminence of the apocalypse (like the Jesus
         People); and 2) those who are revisionist and syncretistic and
         whose aim is to establish a religious theocracy (like the Moonies).
         Monistic groups are those Eastern sects in the West that stress a
         mystical unity and promote the expansion of human consciousness.
         These are also subdivided into two main groups: 1) the technical
         ones, which use ritual methods for achieving a gradual spiritual
         development (like the Hare Krishna Movement and the Integral Yoga
         Institute); and 2) the charismatic ones, which focus on spiritual
         masters (like the Divine Light Mission and the Meher Baba Movement).
         A common feature of all groups is their "emotional and experiential
         thrust." The church-sect theory and the process of conversion and
         commitment are also discussed. Over 250 references are given.

61.   Seeman, Melvin. "Alienation Studies." ANNUAL REVIEW OF SOCIOLOGY
         1 (1975): 91-123.

         Overviews sociological studies of alienation. Several varieties
         of alienation, such as powerlessness, meaninglessness, normless-
         ness, self-estrangement, social isolation, and cultural estrange-
         ment, are discussed. Since many of those studying the new reli-
         gious movements maintain that the majority of those who join them
         are alienated youth, this survey provides excellent background for
         understanding the roots and expressions of alienation. A bibliog-
         raphy of about 300 items is included (pp. 116-23).

62.   Shupe, Anson D., David G. Bromley, and Donna L. Oliver. THE ANTI-
         CULT MOVEMENT IN AMERICA: A BIBLIOGRAPHY AND HISTORICAL SURVEY.
         New York: Garland Publishing, 1984. xiii, 169 pp.

Examines in some detail the contemporary reaction to the new
religious movements or cults. Three separate but interrelated
components of the Anti-Cult Movement are distinguished: 1) local
and regional groups of family members of converts and ex-cult
members; 2) a loose network of deprogrammers; and 3) a network of
religious groups. The materials cited are divided into the following sections, each preceded by an introductory essay: 1) the
history of the Anti-Cult Movement; 2) family-based associations
and deprogrammers; 3) the reaction of the churches; 4) the Anti-
Cult Movement and social science; 5) the Anti-Cult Movement and
the law; 6) opposition to the Anti-Cult Movement. About 1000
items are listed, none of which are annotated. An author index is
included. This volume is a necessary tool for the study of the
social, religious, and legal reactions to the new religious movements.

63.   Skarsten, Trygve R. "Marginal Religious Movements: A Bibliograph-
      ic Essay." TRINITY SEMINARY REVIEW 3.1 (1981): 22-27.

      Gives a select, annotated bibliography on cults intended for
      religious ministers and lay people who are interested in a Chris-
      tian response to their presence. The material is divided into four
      sections: 1) general works; 2) studies on specific cults; 3) films
      and filmstrips; and 4) resource centers. Several major references
      to social-scientific material are included. Most of the well-known
      new religious movements are covered.

64.   Smith, Linda, J., managing editor. ABSTRACTS IN ANTHROPOLOGY.
      Farmington, NY: Baywood Publishing Co., vols. 1-15 (1970-1988).

      Contains a comprehensive list of anthropological materials pub-
      lished in a variety of anthropological, sociological, ethnological,
      and other journals. Relevant materials on new religious movements
      are grouped under a section entitled "Symbol System: Religion,
      Ritual, and World View," and can also be located in the subject
      index under such headings as "cults" and "religion." Most of the
      items cited deal with the traditional anthropological areas of
      tribal and folk societies. These volumes provide invaluable mate-
      rials for cross-cultural comparisons. Earlier volumes have been
      edited by different scholars.

65.   Snow, David A., and Richard Machalek. "The Sociology of Conver-
      sion." ANNUAL REVIEW OF SOCIOLOGY 10 (1984): 167-90.

      Critically reviews recent works on religious conversion, partic-
      ularly to new religious movements or cults. The authors first
      discuss the conceptualization and nature of conversion. They point
      out that conversion can be seen as a radical personal change or as
      an alteration in "one's universe of discourse." Several indicators
      of conversion are considered: membership status, demonstration
      events, and rhetorical indicators (the latter including biographi-
      cal reconstruction, suspension of analytical thinking, and embrace-
      ment of the convert role). Next, they dwell on analytic status of
      the accounts of converts, showing how accounts have a socially

structured, retrospective character. Finally, they explore the
causes of conversion, which include psychophysiological response to
coercion and induced stress, predisposing personality types and
cognitive orientations, situations that induce stress, and social
influences. Several research questions are proposed. Studies on
the maintenance of conversion and of apostasy or defection are
encouraged. There are over 130 references. This essay provides a
useful survey that touches on a much debated issue in the study of
new religions.

66.   SOCIAL SCIENCES INDEX: A QUARTERLY AUTHOR AND SUBJECT INDEX TO
       PUBLICATIONS IN THE FIELDS OF ANTHROPOLOGY, ETC. New York: H.
       W. Wilson Co., vols. 1-15 (1974-1988).

       Cumulatively indexes articles from hundreds of periodicals in
       the English language. Sociology and anthropology are among the
       disciplines represented. Materials relating to new religious
       movements can be located under one or more of the following head-
       ings: cults, sects, conversion, social movements, Christian and
       Hindu sects, or the name of the religious group or organization
       under study. This publication is a must for research on new reli-
       gions. A companion publication indexes papers published in the
       humanities.

67.   Story, Ronald D., editor. THE ENCYCLOPEDIA OF UFOS. New York:
       Doubleday and Co., 1980. 440 pp.

       Seeks "to reflect a reasonably accurate picture of the past and
       present state of UFOlogy" (vii). Besides being a useful collec-
       tion of information and primary source materials on UFOs, this
       volume has brief essays on religion and UFOS, on the sociological,
       psychological, and psychiatric aspects of the flying saucer
       phenomenon, and on scientific approaches to UFO research. Several
       appendices include a chronology of important events in UFO history
       from 1947 to 1978, a list of UFO-related periodicals, and a direc-
       tory of organizations involved in the study of UFOs. A bibliog-
       raphy (pp. 426-440) is added.

       Contains items 1701, 1977.

68.   Truzzi, Marcello, compiler. "Scientific Studies of Classical
       Astrology." ZETETIC SCHOLAR 1 (1978): 79-87.

       Gives a list of strictly scientific and science-relevant mate-
       rials on classical astrology. The citations, which are not anno-
       tated, are divided into five headings: 1) studies favoring astrol-
       ogy; 2) studies denying astrology; 3) psychological, sociological,
       and science-related studies on astrology and astrologers; 4) the
       current debate; and 5) public opinion polls on astrology. The
       articles cited in this bibliography are taken both from profes-
       sional journals and popular magazines. A few sociological studies
       are included.

69.   Wagner, Jon. "Sexuality and Gender Roles in Utopian Communities:
       A Critical Survey of Scholarly Work." COMMUNAL SOCIETIES 6
       (1986): 172-88.

Stresses the need to study sexuality and gender roles in utopian communities because they raise issues related to contemporary social change and to experiments in social structure and dynamics. The literature survey is divided into four areas: 1) the early literature prior to 1970; 2) perennial issues; 3) trends in the history of sexuality; and 4) recent works. The author concludes that the study of sexuality in these societies is "leaving its infancy behind," reformulating the issues, and breaking down old categories of thought.

70.   Wallis, Roy. "What's New on the New Religions?: A Review of Recent Books." ZETETIC SCHOLAR 6 (1980): 155-69.

Divides the approaches used by authors in their studies of new religious movements into two categories, externalist and internalist; the first is based on observations of these groups from outside, the latter seeks an understanding through the movement's own worldview and by close association with the daily lives of their members. Each approach can be hostile or not. About 13 books, published between 1977 and 1979, are classified under the categories drawn up. The author concludes by stating that new religious movements "must be carefully understood before they are explained" (p. 168), and that close firsthand observation is a necessary step towards understanding.

71.   Wilcox, Laird M. ASTROLOGY, MYSTICISM, AND THE OCCULT: A CRITICAL BIBLIOGRAPHY. Kansas City, MO: Editorial Research Service, 1980. (29) pp.

Lists over 400 books and articles that "tend to represent critical analysis and opinion regarding the claims made by advocates and practitioners of the occult and paranormal." Among the subjects included in this selection are astrology, UFOs, mediums, witchcraft and magic, Yoga, and such groups as Scientology and the Unification Church. There are no annotations and no indices, making it hard to locate specific materials. The author, who admits that he "sees evil in all mystical beliefs," thinks that many of the groups who practice the occult arts are a danger to a rational and free society because occult practices are destructive of human intelligence and reasoning powers. An expanded 1988 edition is available.

B. LIST OF PERIODICALS CITED

ACTA SOCIOLOGICA
ADMINISTRATIVE SCIENCE QUARTERLY
ADVANCEMENT OF SCIENCE
ALCOHOL HEALTH AND RESEARCH WORLD
ALTERNATIVE FUTURES: THE JOURNAL OF UTOPIAN STUDIES
ALTERNATIVE LIFESTYLES
ALTERNATIVES: THE JOURNAL OF MARRIAGE, FAMILY, AND CHANGING LIFESTYLES
AMERICAN ANTHROPOLOGIST

AMERICAN BEHAVIORAL SCIENTIST
AMERICAN HISTORICAL REVIEW
AMERICAN JOURNAL OF ACUPUNCTURE
AMERICAN JOURNAL OF CHINESE MEDICINE
AMERICAN JOURNAL OF PSYCHIATRY
AMERICAN JOURNAL OF SOCIOLOGY
AMERICAN JOURNAL OF THEOLOGY AND PHILOSOPHY
AMERICAN QUARTERLY
AMERICAN REVIEW OF SOCIOLOGY
AMERICAN SCHOLAR
AMERICAN SCIENTIST
AMERICAN SOCIOLOGICAL REVIEW
AMERICAN SOCIOLOGICAL SOCIETY PAPERS AND PROCEEDINGS
AMERICAN SOCIOLOGIST
AMERICAN STUDIES
ANGLISTIK UND ENGLISCHUNTERRICHT
ANNALI DI SOCIOLOGIA
ANNALS OF THE AMERICAN ACADEMY OF POLITICAL AND SOCIAL SCIENCE
ANNALS OF THE AMERICAN ASSOCIATION OF GEOGRAPHERS
ANNALS OF SCIENCE
ANNUAL REVIEW OF STUDIES OF DEVIANCE
ANNUAL REVIEW OF SOCIOLOGY
ANTHROPOLOGICA
ANTHROPOLOGICAL JOURNAL OF CANADA
ANTHROPOLOGICAL LINGUISTICS
ANTHROPOLOGICAL QUARTERLY
ANTONIANUM
ARCHIVES DE SCIENCES SOCIALES DES RELIGIONS
ARCHIVES DE SOCIOLOGIE DES RELIGIONS
ARCHIVES EUROPÉENNES DE SOCIOLOGIE
ARCHIVES INTERNATIONALES DE SOCIOLOGIE DE LA COOPERATION AND DU
        DÉVELOPMENT
AUSTRALIAN AND NEW ZEALAND JOURNAL OF SOCIOLOGY
AUSTRALIAN JOURNAL OF SOCIAL ISSUES
BERKELEY JOURNAL OF SOCIOLOGY
BRITISH JOURNAL OF SOCIOLOGY
BULLETIN OF BIBLIOGRAPHY AND MAGAZINE NOTES
BULLETIN OF THE JOHN RYLANDS UNIVERSITY LIBRARY OF MANCHESTER
BULLETIN: THE COUNCIL ON THE STUDY OF RELIGION
CALIFORNIA SOCIOLOGIST
CANADIAN ETHNIC STUDIES
CANADIAN JOURNAL OF SOCIOLOGY
CANADIAN REVIEW OF SOCIOLOGY AND ANTHROPOLOGY
CENTENNIAL REVIEW
CENTER MAGAZINE
CENTRAL ISSUES IN ANTHROPOLOGY
CHURCH HISTORY
CHURCHMAN
CIVIL LIBERTIES REVIEW
CLERGY REVIEW
COMMENTARY
COMMUNAL SOCIETIES
COMMUNAL STUDIES NEWSLETTER
COMMUNITIES
COMPARATIVE STUDIES IN SOCIETY AND HISTORY

CONCILIUM
CONTEMPORARY SOCIETY: A JOURNAL OF REVIEWS
CULTIC STUDIES JOURNAL
CURRENT ANTHROPOLOGY
CURRENT PERSPECTIVES IN SOCIAL THEORY
CURRENT SOCIOLOGY
CURRENTS IN THEOLOGY AND MISSION
DAEDALUS
DEVIANT BEHAVIOR: AN INTERDISCIPLINARY JOURNAL
DIALOGUE: A JOURNAL OF MORMON THOUGHT
DIOGENES
DISSENT
EASTERN ANTHROPOLOGIST
ENCOUNTER
ETHNICITY
ETHNOLOGY
ETHOS
EUROPEAN JOURNAL OF SOCIOLOGY
FABULA
FAMILY COORDINATOR
FLYING SAUCERS REVIEW
FREE INQUIRY IN CREATIVE SOCIOLOGY
FUTURIST
GEORGIA REVIEW
GRADUATE JOURNAL
HIBBERT JOURNAL
HISTORY OF RELIGIONS
HORIZONS
HUMAN CONTEXT
HUMAN MOSAIC
HUMAN ORGANIZATION
HUMAN RELATIONS
HUMAN STUDIES
HUMANIST
HUMANITY AND SOCIETY
ILIFF REVIEW
INTELLECT: THE MAGAZINE OF EDUCATIONAL AND SOCIAL AFFAIRS
INTERNATIONAL JOURNAL OF COMPARATIVE SOCIOLOGY
INTERNATIONAL JOURNAL OF HEALTH SERVICES
INTERNATIONAL JOURNAL OF MASS EMERGENCIES AND DISASTERS
INTERNATIONAL JOURNAL OF MORAL AND SOCIAL STUDIES
INTERNATIONAL JOURNAL OF SOCIAL PSYCHIATRY
INTERNATIONAL JOURNAL OF SOCIOLOGY AND SOCIAL POLICY
INTERNATIONAL JOURNAL OF WOMEN STUDIES
INTERNATIONAL REVIEW OF MISSION
INTERNATIONAL REVIEW OF MODERN SOCIOLOGY
INTERNATIONAL YEARBOOK FOR THE SOCIOLOGY OF RELIGION
ISKCON REVIEW
JAPANESE JOURNAL OF RELIGIOUS STUDIES
JEWISH JOURNAL OF SOCIOLOGY
JOURNAL FOR THE SCIENTIFIC STUDY OF RELIGION
JOURNAL OF AMERICAN CULTURE
JOURNAL OF AMERICAN FOLKLORE
JOURNAL OF AMERICAN HISTORY
JOURNAL OF AMERICAN STUDIES

JOURNAL OF ASIAN STUDIES
JOURNAL OF COMMUNICATION
JOURNAL OF COMPARATIVE FAMILY STUDIES
JOURNAL OF COMMUNITY PSYCHOLOGY
JOURNAL OF CROSS-CULTURAL PSYCHOLOGY
JOURNAL OF CURRENT SOCIAL ISSUES
JOURNAL OF DHARMA
JOURNAL OF HUMANISTIC PSYCHOLOGY
JOURNAL OF INTEGRATIVE AND ECLECTIC PSYCHOTHERAPY
JOURNAL OF INTERDISCIPLINARY HISTORY
JOURNAL OF MARRIAGE AND THE FAMILY
JOURNAL OF MEDICINE AND PHILOSOPHY
JOURNAL OF MODERN HISTORY
JOURNAL OF OCCULT STUDIES
JOURNAL OF OPERATIONAL PSYCHIATRY
JOURNAL OF PARAPSYCHOLOGY
JOURNAL OF POPULAR CULTURE
JOURNAL OF PSYCHOLOGICAL ANTHROPOLOGY
JOURNAL OF RELIGION AND HEALTH
JOURNAL OF RELIGIOUS HISTORY
JOURNAL OF RELIGIOUS THOUGHT
JOURNAL OF SOCIAL HISTORY
JOURNAL OF SOCIAL ISSUES
JOURNAL OF SOCIAL PSYCHOLOGY
JOURNAL OF SOCIAL RESEARCH
JOURNAL OF SOCIOLOGY
JOURNAL OF SOCIOLOGY AND SOCIAL WELFARE
JOURNAL OF STUDIES ON ALCOHOL
JOURNAL OF THE AMERICAN ACADEMY OF RELIGION
JOURNAL OF THE AMERICAN DIETIC ASSOCIATION
JOURNAL OF THE AMERICAN SCIENTIFIC AFFILIATION
JOURNAL OF THE EARLY REPUBLIC
JOURNAL OF THE FOLKLORE INSTITUTE
JOURNAL OF THE ILLINOIS STATE HISTORICAL SOCIETY
JOURNAL OF THE INTERDENOMINATIONAL CENTER
JOURNAL OF THE STEWART ANTHROPOLOGICAL SOCIETY
JOURNAL OF THE THEORY OF SOCIAL BEHAVIOR
JOURNAL OF VOLUNTARY ACTION RESEARCH
JUDAISM
KENTUCKY FOLKLORE RECORD
KEYSTONE FOLKLORE QUARTERLY
LEXINGTON THEOLOGICAL QUARTERLY
LABOR HISTORY
LISTENING: JOURNAL OF RELIGION AND CULTURE
LOUISIANA REVIEW
LSI QUARTERLY
LUTHERAN QUARTERLY
MARRIAGE AND FAMILY REVIEW
MEDICAL ANTHROPOLOGY
MEDICAL JOURNAL OF AUSTRALIA
MENNONITE QUARTERLY REVIEW
MID-AMERICAN FOLKLORE
MID-AMERICAN REVIEW OF SOCIOLOGY
MISSISSIPPI VALLEY HISTORICAL REVIEW
MODERN ASIAN STUDIES

MODERN UTOPIAN
NEBRASKA HUMANIST
NEW COMMUNITY
NEW ENGLAND JOURNAL OF MEDICINE
NEW ENGLAND QUARTERLY
NEW JERSEY HISTORY
NEW PHYSICIAN
NEW SOCIETY
NEW YORK FOLKLORE
NEW ZEALAND JOURNAL OF SOCIOLOGY
PACIFIC SOCIOLOGICAL REVIEW
PACIFIC HISTORICAL REVIEW
PAPERS OF THE AMERICAN BIBLIOGRAPHIC SOCIETY
PAST AND PRESENT
PEASANT STUDIES
PERKINS JOURNAL
PERSPECTIVES IN RELIGIOUS STUDIES
PHYLON
PLAINS ANTHROPOLOGIST
PLATTE VALLEY REVIEW
POLICY REVIEW
POLITICAL PSYCHOLOGY
PRAIRIE FORUM
PROCEEDINGS OF THE CENTRAL STATES ANTHROPOLOGICAL SOCIETY
PSYCHIATRY
PSYCHOLOGY TODAY
QUAKER HISTORY
QUALITATIVE SOCIOLOGY
QUARTERLY JOURNAL OF SPEECH
QUARTERLY JOURNAL OF IDEOLOGY
QUARTERLY REVIEW: A SCHOLARLY JOURNAL FOR REFLECTION ON MINISTRY
RACE AND CLASS
RADICAL HISTORY REVIEW
RADICAL RELIGION
R Q (REFERENCE QUARTERLY)
RELIGION
RELIGION IN COMMUNIST LANDS
RELIGION IN LIFE
RELIGION TODAY
RELIGIOUS EDUCATION
RELIGIOUS STUDIES
RELIGIOUS STUDIES REVIEW
RESEARCH IN SOCIAL MOVEMENTS, CONFLICT, AND CHANGE
REVIEW OF RELIGIOUS RESEARCH
REVUE FRANCAISE D'ETUDE AMERICAINES
RURAL SOCIOLOGY
SCHOOL REVIEW
SCIENCE
SCOTTISH JOURNAL OF RELIGIOUS STUDIES
SCOTTISH JOURNAL OF SOCIOLOGY
SEMIOTICA
SIGNS: JOURNAL OF WOMEN IN CULTURE AND SOCIETY
SKEPTICAL INQUIRER
SOCIAL ANALYSIS
SOCIAL AND ECONOMIC STUDIES

SOCIAL COMPASS
SOCIAL FORCES
SOCIAL HISTORY
SOCIAL PROBLEMS
SOCIAL RESEARCH
SOCIAL SCIENCE AND MEDICINE
SOCIAL SCIENCE INFORMATION
SOCIAL STUDIES OF SCIENCE
SOCIAL STUDIES REVIEW
SOCIAL STUDIES: IRISH JOURNAL OF SOCIOLOGY
SOCIALIST REVIEW
SOCIETY
SOCIOLOGIA NEERLANDICA
SOCIOLOGICAL ANALYSIS
SOCIOLOGICAL FOCUS
SOCIOLOGICAL INQUIRY
SOCIOLOGICAL PERSPECTIVES
SOCIOLOGICAL QUARTERLY
SOCIOLOGICAL REVIEW
SOCIOLOGICAL SPECTRUM
SOCIOLOGICAL SYMPOSIUM
SOCIOLOGICAL YEARBOOK OF RELIGION IN BRITAIN
SOCIOLOGY: JOURNAL OF THE BRITISH SOCIOLOGICAL ASSOCIATION
SOCIOLOGY AND SOCIAL RESEARCH
SOCIOMETRY
SOUNDINGS: AN INTERDISCIPLINARY JOURNAL
SOUTH AFRICAN JOURNAL OF PSYCHOLOGY
SOUTHERN QUARTERLY
SOUTHERN SPEECH COMMUNICATIONS JOURNAL
SOUTHWESTERN SOCIAL SCIENCE QUARTERLY
SPECTRUM: A QUARTERLY JOURNAL OF THE ASSOCIATION OF ADVENTISTS FORUMS
STUDIES IN COMPARATIVE RELIGION
STUDIES IN RELIGION
SUICIDE AND LIFE THREATENING BEHAVIOR
SWEDISH PIONEER HISTORICAL QUARTERLY
SYMBOLIC INTERACTION
TECHNOLOGICAL FORECASTING AND SOCIAL CHANGE
TEILHARD REVIEW
TELOS
TEMENOS: STUDIES IN COMPARATIVE RELIGION
THEOLOGY TODAY
THEORY AND SOCIETY
THOUGHT: A REVIEW OF CULTURE AND IDEA
TRANS-ACTION
TRANSACTIONAL ANALYSIS JOURNAL
TRANSACTIONS OF THE NEW YORK ACADEMY OF SCIENCES
TRINITY SEMINARY REVIEW
ULTIMATE REALITY AND MEANING
UNION THEOLOGICAL SEMINARY QUARTERLY
UPDATE: A QUARTERLY JOURNAL ON NEW RELIGIOUS MOVEMENTS
URBAN ANTHROPOLOGY
URBAN LIFE: A JOURNAL OF ETHNOGRAPHIC RESEARCH
URBAN LIFE AND CULTURE
UTAH HISTORICAL QUARTERLY
VIRGINIA QUARTERLY REVIEW

WESTERN HUMANITIES REVIEW
WESTMINSTER THEOLOGICAL JOURNAL
WILLIAM AND MARY QUARTERLY
WISCONSIN MEDICAL JOURNAL
WISCONSIN SOCIOLOGIST
YOUTH AND SOCIETY
ZETETIC
ZETETIC SCHOLAR

CHAPTER II

THE HISTORICAL BACKGROUND

The advantages of looking at the historical background to the current debate about the cults are several. The pre-1970 social-scientific literature on sects and cults is devoid of the emotionally charged debates that characterize more recent studies. Therefore, one can assume a more detached approach in studying them, thus increasing one's chances of understanding them more deeply and evaluating them more accurately. Many of the religious groups cited in this earlier literature have, to a large degree, become part of the contemporary religious and social environment, in some cases adapting their beliefs and practices to more conventional norms. In an atmosphere that is not focused on just one problem that cults might bring with them, scholars are likely to find it easier to direct their attention to several important factors and issues brought to the fore by the presence of sects and cults.

The first underlying issue in the discussions on churches, sects, and cults deals with the meaning of religion. Two motifs appear to dominate the social-scientific studies of this period. Religion, in the view of those studying the emergence of new religious movements, is a dynamic entity and thus constantly changing. Sects and cults are, therefore, expressions of religious change. Though social scientists are not interested in determining the level of orthodoxy of new religious groups, their writings indirectly support the views that religious diversity is the norm and that the emergence of new religious groups is a natural phenomenon. The second motif deals with the relationship between religion and society. Though not all social scientists would accept the position of Durkheim that religion is largely, if not completely, the reflection of society, there is a tendency, particularly in sociological and anthropological literature, to see the proliferation of new religious groups as largely a sociocultural phenomenon. In other words, these new religious groups cannot be understood simply by listing their ideological and ritual differences and by evaluating them from some universal criterion of orthodoxy. The meaning of the rise of religious bodies, whether they are splinter bodies from larger churches or denominations, new entities imported from other cultures, or syncretistic belief systems devised by prophetic leaders, must be sought in social and cultural conditions. These two assumptions are still evident in contemporary social-scientific writings on new religious movements. They probably account for one major reason why the influence of social scientists on the public attitude toward the cults has been minimal.

The second issue is a definitional one. This early literature concentrated heavily on the distinction between church and sect, the latter being often used synonymously with the word "cult." Though the initial works of Weber, Troeltsch, and Niebuhr have made a lasting contribution to the study of different religious groups and organizations, by the late 1960's social scientists had begun to raise serious questions about the accuracy and usefulness of a simple church-sect typology. Some scholars, like Eister (item 90) and Goode (items 98 and 99), seem to suggest that this typology should be abandoned; others, like Gustafson (item 101) and Demerath (items 85, 86 and 87), defend it strongly; and still others, like Nelson (item 118) and Johnston (items 105 and 106) have attempted to refine it and make it more suited to the religious scene of the 1960's.

A third issue is concerned with the main features of cults and sects. Probably the most common characteristic assigned to both religious groups is the marginality that separates them from mainstream culture with which they exist in varying levels of tension and/or conflict. Many of the sectarian traits ascribed to both cults and sects are negative. Werner Stark, for instance, lists six types of cults, including the antinomian, rigoristic, and violent ones (item 130). Cults may also be deficient in social responsibility (Binder, item 77). The most extreme view of cults and sects is probably that of Coser, who describes them as "greedy institutions" (see items 83 and 84). Sects (and cults) are exclusive and totalistic. They demand total commitment and devotion of those who become members. Coser views them "with pain and sympathy and terror." His position, however, is hardly typical. Bryan Wilson, for example, a British sociologist of religion who has made a lasting contribution to the study of sects and cults, appears to be much more neutral and balanced in his opinion of what a cult is. His typology (item 144) tends to stress the main thrust of the cult, such as its conversionist, utopian, or communal goals, none of which connote obviously derogatory traits that should be the cause for alarm or concern.

A fourth issue centers around the reasons why cults and sects come into being. Here social scientists seem to agree that their origins must be traced to the sociocultural conditions, particularly those that are related to class distinctions and to social mobility. Cults may reflect social problems (Mann, item 113) or political and cultural disintegration (Niebuhr, item 119). They arise in times of social stress (Parucci, item 122), when meaninglessness (Klapp, item 109), disillusionment (Wallace, item 136), alienation (Catton, item 80), and threat of personal disintegration in a period of social change (Smith, item 129) lead people to search for some relief and security. New religious movements may also play the role of socializing agents (Johnston, item 106); or they may function as a mechanism for dealing with "culture shock" brought about by change (Yinger, item 151). This deprivation theory of sect and cult formation, which has been most cogently articulated by Charles Glock (item 94), still occupies a central place in contemporary sociological and anthropological explanations of cults. In spite of the somewhat negative connotation that the words "sect" and "cult" carry with them, social science has assigned more positive than negative functions to them. The deprivation theory is, in fact, based on the assumption that sects and cults fulfill valid human needs that are not met by traditional religious and social institutions.

Finally, social scientists tend to relate the presence of sects and cults to the lower socioeconomic classes. In other words, those who join new religious movements are considered less educated and less financially well-off than the average member of society. It is precisely because of the lack of opportunities that besets the lower classes of society that

sects and cults succeed in attracting followers. Therefore one can con-
sider new movements as forms of protest against the established order
(Redecop, item 125 and Wach, item 135) and/or as agents of social change
(Weber, item 139).

One of the main observations that can be made, even by a casual reading
of the studies of individual sects and cults, is that the above issues are
debated in the context of a large variety of religious groups. Besides
the more well known Christian sects and denominations, the following groups
are incorporated in the social-scientific debates on new religious movements: one particular Catholic sect (O'Dea, item 228), food cultists (New
and Priest, item 227), Hasidic communities (Poll, item 233 and Rubin, item
239), and Hebrew Christians (Sobel, item 244).

One could possibly divide most of the religious groups that are the
focus of individual studies and that are frequently quoted in social-
scientific literature into six general categories, some of which may overlap: 1) traditional groups which originated in Europe during the first few
centuries after the Protestant Reformation (such as the Amish, the Mennonites, the Hutterites, the Methodists, and the Quakers); 2) nineteenth-
century religious movements which would encompass the Mormons, Christian
Scientists, the Seventh-Day Adventists, the Baha'i Faith, and other established sects; 3) various Pentecostal and Holiness churches; 4) occult
traditions that include Theosophy, New Thought, astrology, UFOs, and
Anthroposophy; 5) Black religious movements and practices, including the
Black Muslims, the Rastafarians, and storefront churches; and 6) new religious movements that appeared on the scene by the mid-1960's and began to
attract the attention of scholars by the late 1960's.

Several dominant themes turn up repeatedly in descriptions of sectarian
beliefs and lifestyles. First of all, these groups are marginal, that
is, they are on the fringes of culture, mainline religion, or church;
this implies that their adherents are relatively small in number and that
their impact on society as a whole is minimal. Secondly, these groups are
deviant in the sense that they consciously break away from traditional
religion and social norms. Thirdly, they exist in various levels of conflict with religion and society. The tension exists because traditional
religious beliefs and social norms are attacked either directly by word of
mouth or by a variety of publications and/or indirectly by the adoption of
customs (such as polygamy by the Mormons) or ideologies (such as millenarianism or utopianism) that are at variance with what is conceived to be
the norm. Fourthly, the new religions have a tendency to form smaller,
tighter, more closely knit and extended-family relationships. They adopt
controlled, often communal, lifestyles and belief systems that make them
stand apart from the rest of society. Fifthly, many of these sects and
cults are concerned with the problems of the individual. They preach and
promise spiritual and material well-being to those who join them. Spiritualism (Nelson, item 224), food cults (New and Priest, item 227), healing
cults (Reed, item 235, Romano, item 238), and alternative medical systems
(Wardwell, item 256) promise the improvement of the mental and/or physical
condition of those who join them. Many of these themes can be found also
in new cults.

The social scientists who have studied new religious movements are more
interested in describing their lifestyles than in evaluating them; they
concentrate on giving accounts of how the authority system works rather

than on making judgments on its legitimacy and rigidity. The underlying
assumption seems to be that people join sects or cults under the pressure
of sociopsychological needs, but still of their own free will. There is
no discussion before the 1970's on whether those who become sect or cult
members are coerced to do so.

The few contemporary religious movements that were explored by social
scientists during the late 1960's are treated in the same way as other
older sects. The studies on such new religions as Meher Baba (Robbins,
item 236), Synanon (see Garrett, item 186 and Yablonski, item 269), and
the Unification Church (Lofland, item 215) assign positive functions to
them. Membership in Meher Baba and Synanon leads to the resocialization
of drug addicts, while joining the Unification Church may contribute to
reduction of tension in one's life.

The reader of social-scientific studies on new religious movements is
likely to conclude that, for those who have certain needs, there are
definite benefits linked to membership. Not all writings on these new
religions, however, depict such a positive image. Robert Graves, writing
on the revival of Witchcraft in Britain in the early 1960's, thinks that it
is hysterical and perverted people that end up within the ranks of the
witches, though he does not say whether their condition improves or dete-
riorates by doing so. And George Hillery, in a study of convent life
(item 195), raises the question of whether convents can be compared to
total institutions like prisons, mental asylums, or military barracks. He
prefers to classify them as folk villages. His discussions provide, in
part, a hint of the main debate about sects and cults that would emerge
in the 1970's, namely whether they are totalistic institutions that
restrict human freedom.

A. THEORETICAL ESSAYS AND GENERAL SURVEYS

72.   Armytage, W. H. G. HEAVENS BELOW: UTOPIAN COMMUNITIES IN ENGLAND,
        1560-1960. Toronto: University of Toronto Press, 1961. vii,
        458 pp.

        Provides a descriptive account of Utopian communities in England
        over four centuries. Among those groups included are the Quakers,
        the Philadelphians, the Camisards, the Owenites, and various eso-
        teric, anarchist, and socialistic communities that abounded during
        the period. The author thinks that these experimental lifestyles
        are a universal way in which societies maintain their vitality.

73.   Becker, Howard E. "Problems of Inference and Proof in Participant
        Observation." AMERICAN SOCIOLOGICAL REVIEW 23 (1958): 652-59.

        Explains, with reference to specific instances, the participant-
        observation method of collecting data and then pinpoints "the basic
        analytic operations" carried out by the researcher in the field.
        Four stages of analysis are distinguished: 1) the selection and
        definition of the problem, concepts, and indices; 2) the check on
        the frequency and distribution of the phenomena; 3) the incorpora-

tion of the individual findings into a descriptive model that best
explains the data; and 4) the presentation of the evidence. The
credibility of the informants, the kind of statements elicited from
them, and the role of the researcher are among the issues discussed.

74. Berger, Peter L. "Sectarianism and Religious Sociation." AMERICAN
     JOURNAL OF SOCIOLOGY 64 (1958): 41-44.

     Discusses the classical typology of church-sect developed by
     Weber (item 140) and Troeltsch (item 134) and points out that re-
     cent studies favor a continuum, rather than a dichotomy, between
     the two religious groups. Sectarian characteristics can be found
     in Protestant churches in Germany, while Pietist sects may exhibit
     church-like behavior. Sectarianism, it is argued, can be regarded
     as a form of religious community or group whose social structure is
     similar or identical to that of an established church.

75. Berger, Peter L. "The Sociological Study of Sectarianism." SOCIAL
     RESEARCH 21 (1954): 467-85.

     Discusses in the context of sociological theory the contribution
     of Weber and Troeltsch to the definition of sect as a social entity
     distinct from the church. The church is distinguished from a sect
     in that its members are born into it. Sect members, on the other
     hand, join as adults. They conceive of the Holy Spirit as being
     immediately present, whereas church members think of the Spirit as
     somewhat remote. Monastic institutions in the Catholic Church and
     revival movements in Protestant denominations are cited as examples
     of sectarian phenomena within the churches. A general typology of
     sects in three major divisions is proposed: 1) Enthusiastic sects,
     where experience is stressed (like the Billy Graham Crusade and the
     Salvation Army); 2) Prophetic sects, where a new message is pro-
     claimed (as in Jehovah's Witnesses); and 3) Gnostic sects, where
     secret knowledge and revelation are claimed (as among the Rosicru-
     cians).

76. Bestor, Arthur Eugene. BACKWOOD UTOPIAS: THE SECTARIAN AND OWENITE
     PHASES OF COMMUNITARIAN SOCIALISM IN AMERICA: 1663-1829. Phila-
     delphia: University of Pennsylvania Press, 1950. xi, 288 pp.

     Presents a historical study of North American communes from the
     mid-seventeenth to the early nineteenth centuries. The Owenite
     communities and New Harmony are given special attention. The
     author chronologically traces the development of sectarian communi-
     ties and looks at ways in which religious bodies were transformed
     into colonies. An appendix (pp. 235-42) includes a list of commu-
     nitarian experiments divided into three periods: 1) communes prior
     to 1825; 2) those between 1825 and 1939; and 3) those between 1940
     and 1960. There is also a useful bibliographical essay (pp. 245-
     68).

77. Binder, Louis Richard. MODERN RELIGIOUS CULTS AND SOCIETY: A
     SOCIOLOGICAL INTERPRETATION OF A MODERN RELIGIOUS PHENOMENON.
     New York: AMS Press, 1970. viii, 213 pp. (First published in
     1933.)

Presents a study of many sects and cults (including Christian
Science, Spiritualism, Mormonism, the Holy Rollers, the Mennonites,
New Thought, and the Shakers). The author gives the backgrounds
of these religious groups and discusses the social factors sustain-
ing them. Though the author thinks that cults and sects are related both to social adjustment and social progress, his view of
these fringe religions is negative--they actually contribute to
maladjustment and are deficient in social responsibility.

78.   Bourque, Linda Brookover. "Social Correlates of Transcendental
       Experiences." SOCIOLOGICAL ANALYSIS 30 (1968): 151-63.

       Explores the mystical dimensions of religion and records two
       major conclusions, namely 1) that such experiences are widespread
       and can be easily identified, and 2) that the events that seem to
       trigger such experiences are many and not limited to traditional
       religious disciplines. The author investigates the contexts in
       which these experiences occur and the specific differences between
       religious and esthetic experiences both of which, he thinks, have
       an ecstatic quality. She concludes that the esthetic experience is
       acceptable among middle-class, well-educated, white suburbanites,
       while the religious one is more common among marginal, poorly
       educated, rural, Black populations.

79.   Bruyn, Severyn. "The Methodology of Participant Observation."
       HUMAN ORGANIZATION 22 (1963): 224-35.

       Discusses the research technique of participant observation that
       originated in anthropology and has now been adopted by the social
       sciences in general. The author considers the main epistemological
       issues it raises and the challenges it puts to the traditions of
       science. After exploring the epistemology of knowledge as explored
       by the philosophical traditions of naturalism and idealism, he
       analyzes the basic types of symbols used in culture, namely signs,
       denotive symbols, abstract symbols, emotive symbols, ideological
       symbols, and substantive symbols. Two major perspectives, an inner
       and an outer, that dominate the researcher's approach, as well as
       the scientific standards of objectivity, reliability, and validity,
       are also discussed.

80.   Catton, William R. "What Kind of People Does a Religious Cult
       Attract?" AMERICAN SOCIOLOGICAL REVIEW 22 (1957): 561-66.

       Asks whether it is possible to predict what classes of people may
       be attracted to join new religious cults. The author postulates
       that in a large population there are always some people whose
       intense spiritual needs are not adequately met by existing reli-
       gious institutions and that the objective characteristics of these
       individuals can be determined. He tests his hypothesis in the
       context of a new religious cult in Seattle, Washington. Members of
       this cult believed that their leader was Christ who was referred to
       as "Krishna Venta." A description of the six meetings that the
       author attended and of the kind of audience that was attracted are
       given. The people present are divided into two types, the seekers
       and the observers. The former were more inclined than the latter

to accept the leader's claims to be Christ. These people are said
to be cult-prone, that is, "institutionally alienated but religiously intense."

81.   Clark, S. D. CHURCH AND SECT IN CANADA. Toronto: University of
        Toronto Press, 1948. viii, 459 pp.

        Presents a historical outline of church development in Canada,
        stressing the sociological significance of a number of general
        religious revivals. The Great Awakening in Nova Scotia (1760-
        1783), the great revival in the Maritime Provinces (1787-1832), and
        the great revival in Canada (1783-1832) are among the main topics
        covered. The author discusses the rise of various sects, their
        conflicts with the mainline traditions, and their break with Ameri-
        can sectarianism. Besides the many Methodist and Baptist revivals,
        various movements, like the Millerites, Holiness and Pentecostal
        groups, the Salvation Army, and the Mormons, are included in the
        author's discussions.

82.   Coleman, John A. "Church-Sect Typology and Organizational Precari-
        ousness." SOCIOLOGICAL ANALYSIS 29 (1968): 55-66.

        Reviews the history and usage of the church-sect typology in the
        social sciences. Weber's original theory, the first critical reac-
        tions to it, and various sociological attempts to reformulate it
        are outlined. It is argued that the distinction between church and
        sect becomes confusing if it is detached from the original intent
        of its framers. The typology is useful "in the context of an anal-
        ysis of organizational precariousness in non-institutionalized or
        already institutionalized religion" (p. 66). Organizational pre-
        cariousness is measured by the status of membership, the stability
        of leadership, the tangibility of organizational goals, and the
        degree of militant commitment.

83.   Coser, Lewis A. "Greedy Organizations." EUROPEAN JOURNAL OF SOCI-
        OLOGY 8 (1967): 196-215.

        Focuses on one main aspect of totalistic or greedy institutions:
        the attempts that are sometimes made to destroy all family attach-
        ment of some or all its members and to direct sexual energy into
        channels that do not interfere with the organization's main goal.
        Two instances of such institutions that demand total allegiance,
        sacerdotal celibacy in the Catholic Church and the peculiar sexual
        patterns of nineteenth-century American Utopian communities, are
        explored. The author speculates that the custom of having a celi-
        bate clergy survived because the Catholic Church was a legitimate,
        professional community, while the practices of Utopian communities
        failed because they were regarded as "deviant."

84.   Coser, Lewis A. "Sects and Sectarians." DISSENT 1 (1954): 360-69.

        Discusses several characteristic patterns of behavior that flow
        from the exclusive structure of both religious and political sects.
        The sect creates a morality in opposition to that of the society at
        large. It does not strive for large membership and discourages any

attachment, occupation, or behavior that tends to minimize or limit the devotion and commitment of its members. Sects encompass one's total personality and inculcate uniformity and homogeneity through de-individualization. They are intolerant of pluralism both from outside and inside the group and insist that they have a special monopoly on the truth. The author views the sect "with pain and sympathy and terror" (p. 369).

85.   Demerath, Nicholas J. "Son of Sow's Ear." JOURNAL FOR THE SCIEN-
        TIFIC STUDY OF RELIGION 6 (1967): 275-77.

        Continues the debate with Goode (item 99) on the use of the con-
        cepts of church and sect in connection with social class. Goode's
        major points are rebutted, though it is admitted that his arguments
        raise important questions about the "causal dynamic" that underlies
        the traditional sociological distinction between church and sect.

86.   Demerath, Nicholas J. "In a Sow's Ear: A Reply to Goode." JOURNAL
        FOR THE SCIENTIFIC STUDY OF RELIGION 6 (1967): 77-84.

        Takes up some of the issues raised by Goode (item 98) in his
        critique of the traditional church-sect typology. The author dis-
        cusses whether the typology is now out-of-date. While agreeing
        with some of the critical reflections on the sociological distinc-
        tion between church and sect and with the need for revising the
        social correlates of these two religious organizations, he insists
        that the concepts are still valuable and useful for understanding
        religious groups in the contemporary world.

87.   Demerath, Nicholas J. "Social Stratification and Church Involve-
        ment: The Church-Sect Distinction Applied to Individual Partici-
        pation." REVIEW OF RELIGIOUS RESEARCH 2 (1961): 146-54.

        Questions the "implications of a person's 'social status' for his
        religious behavior" (p. 146). After reviewing the somewhat contra-
        dictory literature on the subject, the author endorses the view
        that a church-like mode of religious expression (that is, formal
        participation in church activities) is characteristic of high-
        status groups, while the sect-like mode (that requires greater
        emotional involvement and concern with purity of doctrine) is typi-
        cal of low-status groups. Sect members appear to be more rewarded
        by their intense religious involvement in the community than church
        members. Data from the National Lutheran Council is used to test
        the author's hypothesis.

88.   Dynes, Russell R. "The Consequences of Sectarianism For Social
        Participation." SOCIAL FORCES 35 (1957): 331-34.

        Theorizes that members of sectarian religious groups center their
        social participation within their congregation and that friendship
        and religious grouping within sects tend to coincide. A scale
        designed to measure these sectarian tendencies was tested on a
        random sample of the adult population in the metropolitan area of
        Columbus, Ohio. It was discovered that sectarians attended church
        more frequently and belonged to fewer organizations outside their

religious congregation than regular church members. Sects are linked to a type of loyalty, satisfaction, and religious intensity not found in complex religious organizations.

89.   Dynes, Russell R. "Church-Sect Typology and Socio-Economic Status." AMERICAN SOCIOLOGICAL REVIEW 20 (1955): 555-60.

Points out that, while the classic church-sect typology has been useful in historical and theological analyses, few attempts have been made to apply it to contemporary religious phenomena. The author focuses on Liston Pope's distinction between church and sect in his book MILLHANDS AND PREACHERS (New Haven, CT: Yale University Press, 1942). He draws up an attitudinal scale to test the church and sectarian qualities of a large Protestant church in Columbus, Ohio. He concludes that church-type organizations are related to higher socio-economic status of their members, while sect-type groups attract members of lower socioeconomic levels.

90.   Eister, Alan W. "Toward a Rational Critique of Church-Sect Typology: Comment of 'Some Critical Observations on the Church-Sect Dimension.'" JOURNAL FOR THE SCIENTIFIC STUDY OF RELIGION 6 (1967): 85-90.

Reflects critically on Goode's essay (item 99) on the traditional church-sect typology and goes further in questioning not just the unreliability of the construct, but also the possibility that it hinders sociological development in the field. Theory and research on new religious movements have moved beyond the limitations of the concepts of church and sect with the introduction of such labels as messianic movements, nativistic and Cargo Cults, separatist churches, etc.

91.   Festinger, Leon, Henry W. Riecher, and Stanley Schachter. WHEN PROPHECY FAILS. Minneapolis: University of Minnesota, 1956. vi, 256 pp.

Presents a study on millenarian and messianic movements, focusing on how believers react when prophetic utterances do not come to pass. The main part of the book deals with a UFO cult founded by a Mrs. Keech and her prophecies of impending catastrophes. The authors give an account of the movement's ideology, the members' personal histories and involvements in the cult, and their preparations for the coming flood. The various reactions to the failure of the prophecy are recorded at some length. The authors think that members of such groups do not lose their faith when prophecies fail, but rather emerge stronger and with greater fervor and enthusiasm to spread the goals and ideology of the cult they belong to.

92.   Francis, E. K. "Toward a Typology of Religious Orders." AMERICAN JOURNAL OF SOCIOLOGY 55 (1950): 437-49.

Discusses the different forms of religious life that are possible within the Catholic Church. The author first distinguished between the community of "religiosi" who are not organized as religious orders and the religious and monastic institutions themselves. Religious orders, which are complex and abstract forms of social organization, are distinguished in four types: 1) monasticism (a implication of a total way of life); 2) common regular and military orders (a combination of religious life with the status of priest or knight in the world); 3) the friars (purposeful organizations in the service of the Church); and 4) the Jesuits (devoted to objective institutions that stress reason, individualization, and depersonalization of intragroup relationships). The common social denominators of these orders are among the topics investigated.

93.   Gillin, John L. "A Contribution to the Sociology of Sects." AMERICAN JOURNAL OF SOCIOLOGY 16 (1910): 236-52.

Points out that sects are social movements because they express social ideals and values and result from social conflicts and conditions. The economic, political, and intellectual impact upon the origins of sects are considered. Intellectual unrest and sociopolitical change must be taken into account in any explanation of the rise of sects. "More fundamentally, sects are the result of forces stimulated to activity by a heterogeneity of the population of any social group" (p. 240). Class consciousness brought about by conquest or immigration is at the root of sectarianism, a position the author tries to show with reference to early Christianity and to the Protestant Reformation. Various other factors, such as the presence of an unusual person who assumes leadership, are also accounted for.

94.   Glock, Charles Y. "The Role of Deprivation in the Origin and Evolution of Religious Groups." RELIGION AND SOCIAL CONFLICT. Edited by Robert Lee and Martin E. Marty. New York: Oxford University Press, 1964, 24-36.

Reviews sociological theories about the conditions that give rise to new religious groups, proposes a theory of deprivation to explain their origin, and suggests a broad theoretical framework to explain the evolution of new religions. The church-sect typology as proposed by Weber (item 139) and Troeltsch (item 134) and revised by Niebuhr (item 119) is described and its weakness, when applied to such groups as the I Am Movement and Theosophy is, specified. A theory of deprivation explains not only the rise of new religions but also their development and potentiality for survival. Five kinds of deprivation are distinguished: economic, social, organismic, ethical, and psychic.

95.   Glock, Charles Y. "On the Study of Religious Commitment." RELIGIOUS EDUCATION 52.4 (Supplement, 1962): 98-110.

Attempts to construct a theoretical framework for the study of different types of religious commitments. Five dimensions of religiosity--experiential, ideological, ritualistic, intellectual, and consequential--are described. Several areas for further research, such as the effects of religiosity, are indicated.

96.   Glock, Charles Y. "The Religious Revival in America." RELIGION AND THE FACE OF AMERICA. Edited by Jane C. Zane. Berkeley: University Extension, University of California, 1958, pp. 25-42.

Reflects on the various opinions that have been expressed on the state of religiosity in America. The author examines the religious indicators and evidence and concludes that there has been some post-war growth in religious affiliation and observance, but that there are no clear signs of a great religious revival. He further states that the scientific studies carried out to assess the state of religion in American are deficient.

97.   Glock, Charles Y., and Rodney Stark. RELIGION AND SOCIETY IN TEN-
      SION. Chicago: Rand McNally and Co., 1965. 316 pp.

      Presents a synthesis of the early work of two sociologists who have made a substantial contribution to the study of religion and of the contemporary religious scene in the United States. Some of the materials included had already been published in academic journals. Four major areas are covered: 1) religion as a social phenomenon; 2) religion in contemporary America; 3) religion and social change; and 4) religion and humanistic perspectives. The authors outline a taxonomy of religious experience, explore its social contexts, discuss the religious revival of the 1960's, and probe into the emergence of new religious groups.

98.   Goode, Erich. "Further Reflections on the Church-Sect Typology."
      JOURNAL FOR THE SCIENTIFIC STUDY OF RELIGION 6 (1967): 270-75.

      Replies to the criticism of Demerath (item 86) and Eister (item 90) of the author's earlier observations on the church-sect typol-ogy. Four specific points are elaborated: 1) the question of class and church-sect differences in church attendance; 2) meaningful alternatives to these distinctions; 3) functional alternatives to the common sociological typology; and 4) friendship patterns. The author restates his position that the church-sect typology "has outlived its usefulness" (p. 274) and is a hindrance to further theoretical developments.

99.   Goode, Erich. "Some Critical Observations on the Church-Sect Divi-
      sion." JOURNAL FOR THE SCIENTIFIC STUDY OF RELIGION 6 (1967):
      69-77.

      Discusses the distinction between church and sect as first devel-oped by Weber (item 140), substantially elaborated by Troeltsch (item 134), and later refined by many sociologists, including Niebuhr (item 119). Several questions about the classification, especially its definition and correlation with social class, are raised. Attendance at formal religious services, the felt sense of importance of these services, and friendship patterns within the church do not seem to fit into the traditional church-sect pattern.

100. Gusfield, Joseph R. "Functional Areas of Leadership in Social
      Movements." SOCIOLOGICAL QUARTERLY 7 (1966): 136-56.

      Examines the conflicting types of demands made upon persons in leadership positions in social movements. The leader in these movements is both the head of a hierarchical authority system and an operative in an environment of clients, enemies, adherents, and

recruits. Basing his reflections on an examination of the Women's
Christian Temperance Society at the turn of the twentieth century
and in the mid-1950's, the author reflects on role differentiation
and leadership types. The problem of dual environments in social
movements and the mobilization and articulation of leadership in
the Women's Christian Temperance Society are among the main areas
covered. The function of leadership and the various mechanisms for
lessening role-set conflict are discussed.

101.   Gustafson, Paul M. "UO-US-PS-PO: A Restatement of Troeltsch's
       Church-Sect Typology." JOURNAL FOR THE SCIENTIFIC STUDY OF RELI-
       GION 6 (1967): 64-68.

       Reexamines the Troeltsch's typology (item 134) of religious
       organizations as they are applicable to the American scene. The
       author points out that Troeltsch uncovered two central dimensions
       upon which he built his typology: 1) the objective-subjective mean-
       ing of grace and 2) the universalistic-particularistic concept of
       membership. Four particular ideological categories of sect members
       within Christianity can be found. It is insisted that Troeltsch's
       typology is still a useful tool for analyzing religious groups.

102.   Hazelrigg, Lawrence E. "A Re-Examination of Simmel's 'The Sociol-
       ogy of Secrecy and Secret Societies': Nine Propositions." SOCIAL
       FORCES 47 (1969): 323-30.

       Examines George Simmel's seminal article on secret societies,
       published in the AMERICAN JOURNAL OF SOCIOLOGY 11 (1906): 441-98.
       Some of their central features are analyzed and reviewed. Simmel's
       suggestions are discussed in the context of Hawthorne's more recent
       case study of the Doubhobors (item 194), a religious community that
       settled in British Columbia, Canada. The author maintains that
       Simmel's approach is useful for generating explanations of how
       secret societies come into being and develop.

103.   Jackson, John, and Ray Jobling. "Towards an Analysis of Contempo-
       rary Cults." SOCIOLOGICAL YEARBOOK OF RELIGION IN BRITAIN 1
       (1968): 94-105.

       Discusses various sociological and anthropological definitions of
       cult and concludes that, in spite of their ambivalence and ambi-
       guity both in conceptualization and application, some general con-
       clusions can be reached on the nature of cultism. Two types of
       cults are distinguished: 1) the mystic-religious cult where esoteric
       practices are employed to increase the individual's experience; and
       2) the non-religious, world-affirming cult where esoteric and
       quasi-religious practices are used to enhance the members' success,
       prestige, and power. Cults may develop into sects (as is the case
       with Christian Science and Scientology) and sects into cults (as in
       Quakerism). The author argues against a rigid distinction between
       a sect and a cult. Cults, in his view, remain on the fringe of
       institutionalized religion.

104.   Jarvie, I. C. "The Problems of Ethical Integrity in Participant
       Observation." CURRENT ANTHROPOLOGY 10 (1969): 505-8.

Points out that the method of participant observation precipi-
tates role clashes since the researcher must decide when to be a
participant and when to assume the stance of an observer. The
author believes that the role of observer should be chosen to preserve the researcher's integrity. He decries the "relativist"
position often selected by scholars and insists that honesty and
truthfulness should be the guiding principles.

105.   Johnson, Benton. "On Church and Sect." AMERICAN SOCIOLOGICAL
       REVIEW 28 (1963): 539-49.

Discusses Troeltsch's church-sect typology (item 134) and the
many attempts by sociologists to revise it in order to make it more
serviceable in sociological research. The author reformulates
Weber's definitions (item 140) and adopts the following distinction
between church and sect: "A church is a religious group that accepts the social environment in which it exists. A sect is a religious group that rejects the social environment in which it exists"
(p. 542). He then applies this distinction to the religious scene
in the United States and finds that the majority of American religious bodies actually support the dominant values in Western culture. Extreme forms of liberalism and conservatism are indicators
of great dissatisfaction with traditional values.

106.   Johnson, Benton. "A Critical Appraisal of the Church-Sect Typol-
       ogy." AMERICAN SOCIOLOGICAL REVIEW 22 (1957): 88-92.

Critically examines the definitions of church and sect with the
aim of improving the traditional sociological typology. After
reviewing the contributions of Niebuhr (item 119) and Troeltsch
(item 134), the author directs his attention towards those "regularly undertaken set of behaviors which out of all other permissible
behaviors enjoy a primacy with affirmation of religious status"
(p. 90). The process and kind of justifications that religions use
become the basis of a typology and of a theory of sect development.
This approach is tested with reference to the Holiness Churches.
It is concluded that, contrary to Holt's analysis (item 198), which
saw the rise of these churches as a way of helping people cope with
the disruption of traditional rural life patterns, the Holiness
groups were powerful agents in socializing lower-class people into
the values of middle-class society.

107.   Kanter, Elizabeth Moss. "Commitment and Social Organization: A
       Study of Commitment Mechanisms in Utopian Societies." AMERICAN
       SOCIOLOGICAL REVIEW 33 (1968): 499-517.

Defines commitment as "the process through which individual
interests become attached to the carrying out of socially organized
patterns of behavior which are seen as fulfilling those interests,
as expressing the nature and needs of the person" (p. 500). Three
major elements in commitment—social control, social cohesiveness,
and continuation of the system—are identified and discussed.
Cognitive, cathetic (affective), and evaluative orientations form
the personality system axis of commitment. Examples from several
nineteenth-century American communities—some successful ones, like

Amana, Oneida, and Harmony, and several unsuccessful ones, like
Brook Farm and the Jasper community--are provided. A number of
continuance mechanisms (e.g., sacrifice and investment), cohesion
tools (e.g., renunciation and communion), and methods of control
(e.g., mortification and surrender) are explored in detail.
Commitment is a process binding participants to the social system.

108.   King, Morton. "Measuring the Religious Variable: Nine Proposed
       Dimensions." JOURNAL FOR THE SCIENTIFIC STUDY OF RELIGION 6
       (1967): 173-90.

       Tests the hypothesis that religion is one-dimensional on a local
       sample of Methodists and concludes that 1) the "unidimensionality"
       of religion must be rejected; 2) nine dimensions can be identified;
       and 3) some of the nine dimensions are similar to those proposed in
       sociological literature. Among the nine dimensions of religion
       expounded are personal commitment and religious experience, partic-
       ipation in congregational activities, and dogmaticism.

109.   Klapp, Orrin E. COLLECTIVE SEARCH FOR IDENTITY. New York: Holt,
       Rinehart, and Winston, 1969. xiii, 383 pp.

       Argues that identity-seeking movements, including religious
       cults, crusades, and cults of celebrities, come into being because
       some modern social systems leave people with a sense of alienation
       and meaninglessness. The author discusses the sources of identity
       problems and the various responses to them. He states that "the
       cultic response is an effort of man to rescue himself from banality
       and meaninglessness by creating new symbols capable of carrying
       mystiques" (p. 148). The centering functions of cults, such as the
       Self-Realization Fellowship, Jehovah's Witnesses, the Shakers, and
       Father Divine's Movement, their rituals, instructions and communal
       spirit, conversion to the cults, and the monastic path are among
       the topics discussed.

110.   Kloss, Peter. "Role Conflicts in Social Fieldwork." CURRENT
       ANTHROPOLOGY 10 (1969): 509-23.

       Reflects on the different roles that the fieldworker has to
       assume towards the group being studied, his or her own society, and
       the scientific community. It is argued that in some situations,
       the researcher, no matter what choices are made, cannot avoid being
       criticized. Some examples of such choice situations are presented.
       Greater sensitivity to the problem of role conflicts in fieldwork
       is urged. The responses of several scholars and the author's reply
       are added. This debate tackles the issue of participant observa-
       tion without reference to the study of the new cults, and indi-
       rectly clarifies some of the questions that scholars, who apply
       this method to the new movements, have had to face.

111.   Lipset, Seymour. "Religion in America: What Religious Revival?"
       REVIEW OF RELIGIOUS RESEARCH (Summer 1959): 17-24.

       Questions the claims that contemporary religion (that is, in the
       late 1950's) is undergoing a revival because 1) there has been a
       gradual growth in religious affiliation and 2) there has occurred a

change in the quantitative character of religion from transcendental belief to secularized churchgoing. Citing statistics that
demonstrated that the ratio of clergy to the total population has
not altered over the last 100 years, the author states that institutionalized religion has remained pretty much the same. Secularization may have led to the increase of evangelical sects, but it
may also have been a characteristic feature of American life in the
past. Basic continuity rather than renewal is the striking aspect
of religion in America.

112.   Mann, William E. SECT, CULT, AND CHURCH IN ALBERTA. Toronto:
       University of Toronto Press, 1955. xi, 166 pp.

       Studies the way in which sects and cults come into being at the
       expense of the more established churches. The author concentrates
       on the religious scene in the Canadian Province of Alberta where
       evangelical groups, older sects from Europe, and esoteric cults
       flourished. He distinguishes between sects and cults by stating
       that the former emphasize the revival of primitive, first-century
       Christian doctrines, while the latter blend alien religious or
       psychological notions with Christian doctrine with the aim of
       creating a more adequate or modern faith. The history of sects and
       cults in Alberta, their nature and composition, their programs and
       organizational forms, the role of leadership, and their techniques
       of evangelization are among the topics discussed. The author's
       view is that sects assist people from rural backgrounds to adjust
       to an urban environment, defend the interests of marginal groups
       among the rural and urban lower classes, contribute to social inte-
       gration, and meet the social needs of dislocated groups. Cults,
       however, had little influence on the social life of the Province.
       Their success reflected the social problems of the period. Besides
       some well-known sects like Christian Science, the Church of Divine
       Science, Seventh-Day Adventism, the author incorporates in his
       discussion several cultic groups like the I Am Movement, New
       Thought, and Theosophy.

113.   Martin, David. "The Denomination." BRITISH JOURNAL OF SOCIOLOGY
       13 (1962): 1-14.

       Suggests that the religious denomination should be considered an
       independent sociological type of religious organization on the same
       level as church and sect. The distinguishing features of the de-
       nomination are discussed. Primarily, the denomination rejects the
       classical principle "extra ecclesiam nulla salus" (that is, "out-
       side the church there is no salvation"), which is commonly accepted
       by church and sect. It differs from the church in its approach to
       the sacraments and from the sect, which rejects the sacramental
       idea completely. Unlike the sect, the denomination has a genuine
       stake in the present social order and stresses individualism,
       liberalism, and pragmatism. It "flourishes in conditions and
       countries where social change proceeds at a steady pace according
       to agreed criteria" (p. 13).

114.   Marty, Martin E. "Sects and Cults." ANNALS OF THE AMERICAN ACAD-
       EMY OF POLITICAL AND SOCIAL SCIENCE 332 (1960): 125-34.

Considers sects and cults to be a third force (after Protestantism and Catholicism) in Christianity in America. Cults and sects
are noted particularly for their lack of conformity to the mainstream religion and culture. The author discusses their growth in
contemporary society. He distinguishes between negatively and
positively oriented sects, the former characterized by their
efforts to isolate people from competing value systems, the latter
by providing "surrogates for interpersonal relations or attachment
to significant persons in an apparently depersonalizing society"
(p. 129). He lists the Adventist Church, the Churches of God,
Jehovah's Witnesses, the Pentecostals, and the Assemblies of God
among the negatively oriented sects, and Father Divine's Peace
Mission Movement, the I Am Movement, Theosophy, the Unity School
of Christianity, and New Thought with the more positively oriented
ones. Cults differ from sects in that the former attempt to establish a spatial and psychic context of isolation. The appeal of
sects is compared to that of monasticism. Both sects and cults are
"uneroded, unexposed, intransigent, and withdrawn" (p.125).

115.   Mauss, Armand L. "Dimensions of Religious Defection." REVIEW OF
       RELIGIOUS RESEARCH 10 (1969): 128-35.

       Examines "the causes and types of religious defection that can
       lead to effective programs of prevention and reactivation" (p.
       128). Three dimensions of religious defection, namely intellec-
       tual, social, and emotional, are explained. An eightfold typology
       deriving from these dimensions is developed. Disaffiliation can be
       1) total, 2) psychological, 3) alienated, 4) emotional, 5) cultural,
       6) intellectual, 7) social, and 8) circumstantial. Empirical sup-
       port for this typology is found in a pilot study of a small group
       of Mormons in the San Francisco Bay Area of California.

116.   McCall, George J., and J. L. Simmons, editors. ISSUES IN PARTICI-
       PANT OBSERVATION: A TEXT AND READER. Reading, MA: Addison-Wesley,
       1969. 359 pp.

       Discusses at length one of the most commonly used methods in both
       sociology and anthropology, namely participant observation. Eight
       major areas are explored: 1) the nature of this method; 2) field
       relations; 3) data collection, recording, and retrieval; 4) quality
       of the data; 5) general hypotheses; 6) evaluation of hypotheses; 7)
       publication of results; 8) comparison of methods. This book pre-
       sents an objective survey of the method's merits and problems and
       should provide some insights in the controversy which has arisen
       regarding the use of participant observation in the study of reli-
       gious movements. Of particular interest is one essay (pp. 105 ff.)
       that discusses the reliability of inside informers.

117.   Moberg, David O. "Potential use of the Church-Sect Typology in
       Comparative Religious Research." INTERNATIONAL JOURNAL OF COM-
       PARATIVE SOCIOLOGY 2 (1961): 47-58.

       Suggests that Troeltsch's classification of religious groups into
       churches and sects (item 134) can, with some modifications, be
       applied also to other religions besides Christianity. The author

gives a description of Troeltsch's typology and accepts the common
view that in Christianity there is a definite tendency for a sect
to develop into a church. Criticisms of Troeltsch's position are
then discussed and refuted. Moberg's position is that Troeltsch's
typology has the advantage of helping us understand the natural
history of religious institutions, the conflicts within and between
religious groups, the relationships between religious organizations
and society, and the impact of religion on social change and individual behavior.

118.   Nelson, Geoffrey K. "The Concept of Cult." SOCIOLOGICAL REVIEW 16
        (1968): 351-62.

        Points out how the church-sect dichotomy of Weber (item 140) and
        Troeltsch (134) was expanded by Niebuhr (item 119) to include the
        "denomination" and to explain how religious bodies that began as
        sects for the socially deprived and underprivileged developed into
        middle-class religious entities. Various elaborations of these
        categories by different sociologists to include a new religious
        group labeled "cults" are noted. The author remarks that mysti-
        cism, Troeltsch's third type of religion has been usually ignored
        even though it is very similar to the concept of "cult." He sug-
        gests that the category of "mystical religion" could be refined to
        include groups from different religions. Criteria for distinguish-
        ing cults from sects, denominations, and churches are outlined.
        Two types of cults, charismatic and spontaneous, may come into
        being, dependent on their mode of origin. All successful charis-
        matic cults that include the early stages of all founded religions
        can develop into new religions.

119.   Niebuhr, H. Richard. THE SOCIAL SOURCES OF DENOMINATIONALISM.
        Hamden, CT: Shoe String Press, 1954. viii, 304 pp. (First pub-
        lished in 1929.)

        Presents a classic study of the origin of theological and reli-
        gious differences from social sources. The author elaborates on
        the works of Weber (item 140) and Troeltsch (item 134) on the dif-
        ferences between church and sect and the social correlates of these
        two religious organizations. He discusses at length the churches
        of the "disinherited," that is, the poor and the middle class. The
        way national, racial, ethnic, and immigrant churches are formed is
        also taken into consideration. The rise of sectarianism and denom-
        inationalism in American culture is seen in the context of the
        social, cultural, and historical backgrounds. This book is a land-
        mark in the study of sects and was among the first to examine
        sectarianism in terms of political and cultural disintegration.

120.   O'Dea, Thomas E. "Sects and Cults." INTERNATIONAL ENCYCLOPEDIA OF
        THE SOCIAL SCIENCES. Edited by David L. Shils. New York: Mac-
        millan and Free Press, 1968, vol. 14, pp. 130-36.

        Summarizes the common sociological theory that is connected with
        the terms "sect" and "cult." The distinction between church and
        sect is outlined, and various themes, such as the accommodation of
        sects to society and sectarian ideology, are described. The social

base of sectarianism, the functions usually ascribed to these marginal religious groups, and their politics are among the topics
covered. Sects, it is pointed out, are one form of religious protest. Monasticism, a non-secessionist type of protest, exhibits
several sectarian characteristics. The concept of cult, which,
when this essay was written, was still relatively unencumbered by
the issues that now permeate sociological literature, is discussed
in relation to Troeltsch's "mysticism" (item 134). A basic bibliography of materials published before 1962 is included.

121.   Orlans, Harold. "Ethical Problems in the Relations of Research
        Sponsors and Investigators." ETHICS, POLITICS, AND SOCIAL RE-
        SEARCH. Edited by Gideon Sjoberg. Cambridge, MA: Schenkman
        Publishing C., 1967, pp. 3-24.

        Reviews some of the ethical issues that affect the relationship
        between scholars and those who sponsor their research. The strings
        that are sometimes attached to research grants, the difficulties
        that the researcher faces in his or her choice of research topic
        and of the methods to be used, and the conflicts of interest are
        among the topics discussed. The author thinks that most of the
        ethical problems arise during the research itself and center
        around the scholar's relationships with her or his informants. The
        sponsoring of a research project implies that a bargain has been
        made between the sponsor and the researcher, a bargain that should
        deal with most of the issues involved.

122.   Parucci, Dennis J. "Religious Conversion: A Theory of Deviant
        Behavior." SOCIOLOGICAL ANALYSIS 29 (1968): 144-54.

        Proposes a typology of religious conversion that takes into
        account not only the sensational varieties linked with sects and
        cults, but also those that occur within the more conventional reli-
        gious bodies. A sixteen-fold typology is constructed, based on the
        degree and direction of change both with regard to the structure
        and within the content of the belief system. Conversion is seen as
        a deviant form of behavior in the sense that it departs from the
        normative rules of the convert's society. A stress-inducing socio-
        cultural environment is a major precondition to conversion.

123.   Pfautz, Harold W. "The Sociology of Secularization: Religious
        Groups." AMERICAN JOURNAL OF SOCIOLOGY 61 (1955): 121-28.

        Argues that five types of religious groups--cults, sects, insti-
        tutionalized sects, churches, and denominations--represent increas-
        ing degrees of secularization. A religious movement starts as a
        cult, the most elementary form of religious organization, then
        develops into a sect, later developing into an established sect, a
        church, or a denomination. Five social perspectives are used as
        frames of reference for constructing the different types of reli-
        gious organizations: demographic, ecological, associational, struc-
        tural, and social-psychological. Christian Science is taken as an
        example of a healing (cultic) movement that first became a sect and
        later adopted the characteristics of an institutionalized sect.

124.   Poblete, R. "Sociological Approach to the Cults." SOCIAL COMPASS
        7 (1960): 383-406.

        Gives 1) a typology of sect, church, and denomination; 2) an
        outline of the main theories that explain the origin of sects;
        3) an analysis of the problem of anomie and of the search for com-
        munity; and 4) an interpretation of the motivation at work in the
        functions of Pentecostal sects. The author accepts Durkheim's view
        that anomie, which results from the absence of guiding principles
        and the weakening of the moral forces that regulate human relation-
        ships, and the search for community that follows, are the major
        reasons for the proliferation of sects among working-class people.
        This view is corroborated by the author's study of Pentecostal
        sects among the Puerto Ricans of New York City.

125.   Redekop, Calvin. "The Sect From a New Perspective." MENNONITE
        QUARTERLY REVIEW 39 (1965): 304-17.

        Advances an operational definition of a sect in the context of a
        case study of the Old Colony Mennonites who emigrated from Russia
        to Canada and then to Mexico. Sects, in the author's view, come
        into being as a protest to the cultural goals that cannot be recon-
        ciled to religion, or as a protest against a religious group that
        is becoming too accommodated to cultural (and secular) values. The
        Mennonites experienced the second kind of protest. Sects, there-
        fore, come into being when the realms of the sacred and the profane
        are confused, when a shift in these realms has taken place, or
        when the boundaries between the two worlds have been relaxed. From
        a sociopsychological perspective, sects emerge when personality
        integration is threatened by outside forces and when sanctions that
        govern relationships between people are eased. Sects are concerned
        with the reaffirmation of belief, especially that regarding a basic
        dualistic understanding of life in times of social upheaval and
        change.

126.   Roucek, Joseph S. "The Changing Concept of Charismatic Leadership."
        INTERNATIONAL YEARBOOK FOR THE SOCIOLOGY OF RELIGION 3 (1967):
        87-100.

        Discusses the concept of charismatic leadership and its develop-
        ment in sociological literature since Weber. The author describes
        Weber's view (item 139) that three forms of authority--rational,
        traditional, and charismatic--can be used to make people's obedi-
        ence look respectable or legitimate. Some problems with the appli-
        cation of these concepts are briefly examined. The author main-
        tains that charismatic leaders can only be understood in their
        sociocultural contexts and that their influence is related to the
        needs and tendencies of those attracted to their authority.

127.   Scanzoni, John. "Innovation and Constancy in the Church-Sect
        Typology." AMERICAN JOURNAL OF SOCIOLOGY 71 (1965): 320-27.

        Examines the various efforts that have been made to rethink the
        church-sect typology in the context of social change and constancy.
        After surveying the data relative to the distinction between the

two religious organizations, the author raises some questions
regarding 1) the sect group that is dissatisfied and agitates for
social change in a society where the religious system is not in
control, 2) the developmental change from sect to church, and
3) the structural conditions under which innovation emerges.

128.   Smelser, Neil J. THEORY OF COLLECTIVE BEHAVIOR. New York: Free
        Press of Glencoe, 1963. xi, 436 pp.

        Presents an outline of a theory of collective behavior that is
        applicable to both social and religious movements. Two chapters
        deal respectively with norm-oriented and value-oriented movements,
        a distinction that has been applied to sects and cults that tend
        to be value-oriented. Value-oriented movements "possess a distinc-
        tive generalized belief and proceed through a definite value-added
        process" (p. 28). They have a potential for violence because of
        the hostile component of their belief system. The author reflects
        on the kind of structural arrangements that favor the rise of the
        value-oriented movements and concludes that they are likely to
        emerge under the conditions of strain.

129.   Smith, Timothy L. "Historic Waves of Religious Interest in Amer-
        ica." ANNALS OF THE AMERICAN ACADEMY OF POLITICAL AND SOCIAL
        SCIENCE 332 (November 1960): 9-19.

        Overviews four periods of religious uprising in U. S. history: 1)
        the First Great Awakening of the Colonial era; 2) the Second Great
        Awakening of the early 1800's; 3) the Third Great Awakening of the
        late nineteenth and early twentieth centuries; and 4) the most
        recent one of the late 1950's. The author concentrates on those
        periods that seem to have occurred independent of great charismatic
        leaders. Various problems of interpretation are discussed. The
        use of revivals as an opiate for the masses or as a way of fulfill-
        ing psychic needs is considered. During all four periods Chris-
        tianity made major adjustments in thought and practice to cope with
        new social conditions. Attempts to generalize on these social
        conditions or on cyclical occurrences of religious revivals are
        questioned. The author concludes that "the main factors common to
        recurrent cycles of religious interest which this essay describes
        have been tension resulting from rapid social change, the determi-
        nation of large numbers of religious leaders to do something about
        them, and the persistence among the mass of ordinary men of the
        simple ideas of evangelical religion" (pp. 18-19).

130.   Stark, Werner. THE SOCIOLOGY OF RELIGION: A STUDY OF CHRISTENDOM.
        Vol. 2: Sectarian religion. New York: Fordham University Press,
        1967. viii, 357 pp.

        Discusses the traditional sociological definition of a sect as an
        organization that is born of a negative attitude to the established
        social, economic, and political system. Three major areas of sec-
        tarian religion are investigated: 1) its origin; 2) its nature and
        variety; and 3) its decay. Various examples, including Christian
        Science and the Christadelphians, are adduced to illustrate that
        sects are basically groups that reject the social environment. Six

types of sects are distinguished: 1) retrogressive; 2) progressive; 3) rigoristic; 4) antinomian; 5) violent; and 6) nonviolent. The development of sects is also discussed in terms of their conflict with society which can result in their annihilation, withdrawal, or adjustment.

131. Talmon, Yonina. "Millenarian Movements." ARCHIVES EUROPÉENNES DE SOCIOLOGIE 7 (1966): 159-200.

Traces the historical roots of millennial movements to Persian Zoroastrianism and Judaism, from which it was transmitted to Christianity and Islam and later passed on to non-literate societies who came into contact with Western culture. Defining millenarian or chiliastic movements as those "religious movements that expect imminent, total, ultimate, this-worldly, collective salvation" (p. 159), the author goes on to describe in detail their major traits. Several dimensions of religious and social differentiation are also discussed. Multiple and cumulative deprivations, social isolation, and periods of transition are believed to be the main conditions for the emergence of millennial movements. The author speculates on the consequences of millenarianism, which has often been thought of as a kind of "dangerous collective madness" and "paranoid fantasy." She thinks that it is rather an integrative movement that brings hope and not despair and stresses its positive social and psychological functions.

132. Talmon, Yonina. "Pursuit of the Millennium: The Relation Between Religion and Social Change." EUROPEAN JOURNAL OF SOCIOLOGY 2 (1962): 125-48.

Overviews sociological and anthropological studies of millenarian movements and observes that they reflect a common concern with the relationship between these movements and social change. The main features of millenarian movements, such as their view of salvation as a collective enterprise and their forward-looking orientation, are outlined. The author thinks that deprivation alone does not explain the rise of these movements. Rather, the "uneven relation between expectations and the means of their satisfaction" (p. 137) is singled out as the predisposing factor. Besides being a much-needed response to severe deprivation, frustration, and social isolation, millennial movements can be seen as a prepolitical phenomenon or as a prototype of modern revolutionary movements.

133. Thomas, Keith. "Women and the Civil War Sects." CRISIS IN EUROPE: 1560-1660. Edited by Trevor Aston. Garden City, NY: Doubleday and Co., 1967, pp. 332-57.

Discusses the impact of the patriarchal family in general and of women in particular on the U. S. Civil War sects in the seventeenth century. These sects (like the Baptists, the Millenarians, and the Quakers) were largely "separatist," i.e., stressing the need for members to separate themselves from society. They laid great stress upon the spirituality of both sexes and recruited more women than men to their ranks. Women's high involvement in sects throughout the ages is briefly traced from the Montanist Movement through the Waldenses and Cathars of the Middle Ages and up to contemporary times. The growth of sectarianism created family conflicts. Sects were always accused of reducing household piety, alienating family members, and disrupting the bonds of obedience that held the family members together. The sectarian insistence on spiritual equality between the sexes, however, had little importance on the historical development of female emancipation.

134.   Troeltsch, Ernst. THE SOCIAL TEACHINGS OF THE CHRISTIAN CHURCH.
       Translated by Oliver Wyon. London: Allen and Unwin, 1931.
       2 vols., 1017 pp.

       Presents a seminal and influential study of the sociology of religion and discusses in some depth the church-sect typology which has influenced sociological reflections on the subject for over half a century. Chapter three contains a section that outlines the differences between sect-type organizations and mysticism (spiritual religion) in Protestantism.

135.   Wach, Joachim. SOCIOLOGY OF RELIGION. Chicago: University of
       Chicago Press, 1944. xii, 418 pp.

       Presents a sociological approach to religion that stresses the relationship between religion and society and the various functions of religion. The author's analysis is carried out in the context of the world's great religions. Several forms of natural religious groupings are considered. Sects are said to be modes of radical protest leading to secession, while monastic institutions are forms of protest within the mainline institutions. Types of religious authority are also discussed.

136.   Wallace, Anthony F. C. "Revitalization Movements." AMERICAN
       ANTHROPOLOGIST 58 (1956): 264-81.

       Presents a much-quoted article in the anthropological and sociological circles that explains the rise of new religious movements, particularly in third world countries. Revitalization is defined as "a deliberate, organized, conscious effort by members of a society to construct a more satisfying culture" (p. 265). The author argues that all organized religions are relics of old revitalization movements. The structure of the revitalization process is described in five overlapping stages: 1) steady state; 2) period of individual stress; 3) period of cultural distortion; 4) period of revitalization; and 5) new steady state. These movements are often religious in nature and perform the following six major tasks: mazeway reformulation, communication, organization, adaptation, cultural transformation, and routinization. High stress for individual members of a society and disillusionment with a distorted cultural worldview are the main conditions for the emergence of new religious movements.

137.   Wallace, Anthony F. C. "Mazeway Synthesis: A Biocultural Theory of
       Religious Inspiration." TRANSACTIONS OF THE NEW YORK ACADEMY OF
       SCIENCE 18 (1956): 626-38.

Maintains that the study of religious inspiration in prophets is "of central importance in the analysis both of processes of socio-cultural change and of individual therapeutic reorganization" (p. 626). The main features of religious inspiration are examined. The variety of perceptions or cognitive levels of perception is referred to as the "mazeway" that has the basic function of giving meaning to messages. It also restores an internal biopsychic equilibrium. Basing his reflections on anthropological data from a Seneca Tribe Indian named Handsome Lake, the author thinks that his theory has wider applicability.

138. Wallis, Wilson D. MESSIAHS: THEIR ROLE IN CIVILIZATION. Washington, DC: American Council on Public Affairs, 1943. 217 pp.

Reviews the concepts of messiah in various cultures and religious traditions, including nonliterate societies, and major religions, such as Judaism, Christianity, and Islam. The following three major common views about messiahs are considered: 1) the messiah represents the return of a god or a leader; 2) the messiah is a culture hero; and 3) the messiah represents the millennial Christ. The author discusses the supernatural, political, and cultural aspects of messianism. A bibliography, useful for its historical sources, is added.

139. Weber, Max. ON CHARISMA AND INSTITUTION BUILDING: SELECTED PAPERS. Edited with an introduction by S. N. Eisendstadt. Chicago: University of Chicago Press, 1968. lvi, 313 pp.

Contains 23 essays dealing with charismatic authority in various spheres of human life. The final section deals with charisma in religion and culture and includes discussions on the sociological aspects of prophets, various paths to salvation, mysticism, and asceticism, and caste and class in relation to religion. In the introduction the editor presents an analysis of Weber's concerns and contributions and reflects on the implications of his theories of contemporary societies. The select bibliography lists the works of Weber that have appeared in English translation and major books and articles on his theoretical formulations. This volume contains the work of one of the most influential contributors to the sociology of religion and is indispensable for the sociological study of charismatic authority.

140. Weber, Max. THE SOCIOLOGY OF RELIGION. Translated by Ephraim Frischoff. Boston: Beacon Press, 1963. (First published in 1922.) lxvii, 304 pp.

Presents a classical and influential study of the sociology of religion. Among the topics dealt with are religion and the problem of social evolution, the main components of a religious system, prophecy and charisma, and religion and social status. Of special interest to those scholars studying new religious movements is Weber's analysis of the prophet as an agent of social change and his distinction between world-rejecting asceticism and mysticism, the former being a path of mastery, the latter a way of resignation and adjustment.

141.   Weiss, Robert F. "Defection From Social Movements and Subsequent
        Recruitment to New Movements." SOCIOMETRY 26 (1963): 1-20.

        Proposes a theory of recruitment to social movements of people
        who have defected from other movements. Four processes underlying
        defection and new recruitment are distinguished and described: 1)
        simple stimulus generalization; 2) extinction; 3) displacement; and
        4) counterconditioning. The author further names four causes that
        lead to defection: 1) the movement becomes unavailable to the
        member; 2) the strength of belief and participation is decreased
        because of lack of rewards; 3) the same strength wanes because of
        punitive punishments; and 4) attachment to an alternative movement
        develops and eventually leads to the breaking of ties with the
        original group. The author applies a social-institutional and
        learning-theory approach to understand these processes and gives
        examples of various movements, such as Cargo Cults.

142.   Westhues, Kenneth. THE RELIGIOUS COMMUNITY AND THE SECULAR STATE.
        New York: J. B. Lippincott Co., 1968. 127 pp.

        Speculates on the reasons why religious communities are founded,
        on their development, and on their future. After discussing the
        definition of a religious community in the context of the Catholic
        religion and monastic institutions, the author analyzes the primi-
        tive type of religious community, its growth in the Middle Ages,
        and its status in the twentieth century. The rejection of this
        world by religious communities, their problem of adaptation, and
        their functions are among the topics discussed. A small community
        of men, called the Brothers of Joseph, founded in Oklahoma City in
        the late 1950's and often referred to as an example of "secular
        monasticism," is described.

143.   Wilner, Ann Ruth, and Dorothy Wilner. "The Rise and Role of Charis-
        matic Leaders." ANNALS OF THE AMERICA ACADEMY OF POLITICAL AND
        SOCIAL SCIENCE 358 (November 1965): 77-88.

        Analyzes the charismatic quality of certain leaders, stressing
        that what is really decisive for the validity of their charisma is
        its acceptance by their followers. The conditions that are condu-
        cive to charismatic leadership, the process by which leaders emerge
        and gain recognition, and the functions and significance of leader-
        ship are discussed. The authors restrict their observations to
        political leaders that emerged in those countries that were under
        colonial rule, though their reflections are, to some extent,
        applicable also to religious leaders.

144.   Wilson, Bryan R. "A Typology of Sects." SOCIOLOGY OF RELIGION:
        SELECTED READINGS. Edited by Roland Robertson. Baltimore: Pen-
        guin, 1969, pp. 361-83.

        Criticizes theological or doctrinal classifications of sects and
        proposes a more universal social typology that is also applicable
        to religious movements on the fringes of Christianity. A seven-
        fold classification is then proposed and described. Sects can be,
        according to the author, 1) conversionist (e.g., the Salvation Army

and Pentecostal Movements); 2) revolutionary (e.g., Jehovah's Witnesses and the Christadelphians); 3) introversionist (e.g., the European Pietist Movement in the eighteenth century); 4) manipulationist (e.g., Christian Science, Scientology, and the Rosicrucians); 5) thaumaturgical (e.g., the Spiritualist Churches); 6) reformist (e.g., the Quakers); and 7) utopian (e.g., the Oneida Community and the Bruderhof). To what extent this typology is suitable for "mission territories" is examined.

145. Wilson, Bryan R. "Establishment, Sectarianism, and Partnership." SOCIOLOGICAL REVIEW 15 (1967): 213-20.

Reviews Werner Stark's SOCIOLOGY OF RELIGION (item 130) and criticizes some of his major generalizations on sects, particularly his view that sects are rebellious or revolutionary movements that arise out of frustrated, lower middle-class people who suffer from inferiority complexes. Stark's opinion that all sects decay into denominations is also questioned.

146. Wilson, Bryan R. "Sectarianism and Schooling." SCHOOL REVIEW 72.1 (1964): 1-21.

Identifies various types of sectarian responses to the social order, responses that are related to social attitudes and consequently towards education. The type of education to which sects are usually opposed is discussed in the context of such groups as the Puritans, Quakers, and adventist groups like the Seventh-Day Adventists, the Christadelphians, and the Jehovah's Witnesses. The areas where sects and schools clash are identified with special reference to the pietistic (introversionist), fundamentalist evangelical (conversionist), and gnostic (manipulationist) groups. The author concludes that the sects have become less antagonistic to schools because the material taught has been increasingly neutral from a religious point of view and, therefore, less challenging to the sects' theological stance.

147. Wilson, Bryan R. "Millennialism in Comparative Perspective." COMPARATIVE STUDIES IN SOCIETY AND HISTORY 6 (1963): 93-114.

Surveys the increasing number of studies on millennial movements that are categorized in four main groups, namely: 1) collectivist, other-worldly (traditional religion); 2) collectivist, this-worldly (millennial movements); 3) individualistic, other-worldly (Evangelical Christian sects); and 4) individualistic, this-worldly (gnostic sects). Millennial movements aim to awaken and prepare people for a transformation that is expected to be sudden and soon. Four types of action within millennial movements are distinguished: 1) activity that is limited to calling people to make themselves ready for the coming millennium (Jehovah's Witnesses and the Seventh-Day Adventists); 2) specific activities, like taboos and ordeals, that are deemed necessary if one is to be ready for the coming millennium (Christadelphians and Seventh-Day Adventists); 3) collective activities that are not directly related to the new dispensation, but are thought to be of symbolic significance (the Ghost Dance of the American Indians); and 4) activities that are directly aimed at bringing about the millennium and which will bring the movement into conflict with the authorities. Charismatic leadership, the role of cultural diffusion, and the causal interpretation of millenarianism are among the topics discussed.

148.   Wilson, Bryan R. "An Analysis of Sect Development." AMERICAN SOCIOLOGICAL REVIEW 24 (1959): 3-15.

Considers the following elements in the development of religious sects: the conditions under which they emerged, their internal structure, the degree of separateness from the external world, the coherence of their values, the groups' commitment, and the social relationships characteristic of sect involvement. The sect is clearly distinguished from the denomination. Four subtypes of sects are described: conversionist, adventist, introversionist (pietistic), and gnostic. The way in which a sect comes into being, the specific factors that stimulate its growth, and the external prevailing conditions are analyzed. Several features that facilitate a sect's development into a denomination are identified.

149.   Wilson, Bryan R., editor. PATTERNS OF SECTARIANISM: ORGANIZATION AND IDEOLOGY IN SOCIAL AND RELIGIOUS MOVEMENTS. London: Heinemann, 1967. vii, 416 pp.

Contains 11 papers (four of which had been previously published) dealing with the organizational development and the interrelationship of ideology and structure of several established sects. In an introduction the editor outlines some of the minimum requirements for sect organization and several ways in which sects can come into being. The essays are grouped under three types: 1) conversionist, like the Salvation Army, the British Holiness Movement, and Pentecostal groups; 2) introversionist, like the Quakers, the Society of Friends, the Plymouth Brethren, and the Churches of God; and 3) non-sectarian movements, like British Israelism and Humanist societies.

Contains items 205, 255, 260, 265, 268, 1250.

150.   Wolpe, Harold. "A Critical Analysis of Some Aspects of Charisma." SOCIOLOGICAL REVIEW 16 (1968): 305-18.

Examines the concept of charisma in the context of Weber's theory (item 139) and concludes that it is not "analytically useful" because of several obscure and contradictory elements. The author maintains that charisma cannot explain authority relationships and that structural factors (such as economics and other support given to the leaders) must be taken into account when interpreting charismatic leadership.

151.   Yinger, J. Milton. "Religion and Social Change: Functions and Dysfunctions of Sects and Cults Among the Disprivileged." REVIEW OF RELIGIOUS RESEARCH 4 (1963): 65-84.

Outlines the possible types of relationships between religious and social change. The main function of sects and cults is, in the author's view, to help people deal with the conditions of "culture

shock" that is brought about by change. New religious movements
thus "serve a bridging function." Several examples, including the
Cargo Cults of Melanesia, the Ghost Dance of the American Indians,
the Black Muslims, and the Rastafari cult, are considered. The
conditions under which the new groups achieve a stable condition
within the larger society (that is, when they move from sect to
church) are discussed. The depth of social alienation may affect
the course of a new movement's development. Various Black movements, which are said to be responses of a disprivileged minority,
are also taken into consideration.

152.   Yinger, J. Milton. "Contraculture and Subculture." AMERICAN
        SOCIOLOGICAL REVIEW 25 (1960): 625-35.

        Identifies three usages of the concept of "subculture" in socio-
        logical and anthropological sources: 1) certain unique universal
        tendencies that seem to be present in all societies; 2) normative
        systems of social and frequently ethnic groups that are found in a
        society; and 3) norms that arise in a frustrating situation or from
        a conflict between a small group and the larger society. The
        author prefers to call the last-mentioned definition "subculture."

153.   Zald, Mayer N., and Roberta Ash. "Social Movement Organizations:
        Growth, Decay, and Change." SOCIAL FORCES 44 (1966): 327-41.

        Elaborates the common sociological view that new movements often
        develop a bureaucratic structure and a general accommodation to
        society once the charismatic leadership is replaced or changed and
        its economic and social bases stabilized. Three types of change
        usually occur, namely a goal transformation, a shift in organi-
        zational maintenance, and "oligarchization." Some of the major
        factors influencing the direction of change in political and social
        movements are discussed. Seventeen propositions are outlined,
        specifying the internal and external processes that lead to the
        growth, development, and decline of movement organizations.

154.   Zenner, Walter P. "The Case of the Apostate Messiah: A Reconsid-
        eration of the 'Failure of Prophecy.'" ARCHIVES DE SOCIOLOGIE
        DES RELIGIONS 21 (1966): 111-18.

        Reflects on various reasons why unfulfilled prophecies do not
        usually cause messianic movements to disintegrate. Festinger et
        al.'s work (item 91) on the failure of prophecy is criticized for
        not taking into account the available cultural explanations of such
        failure. The popular Jewish seventeenth-century movement founded
        by Sabbatai Sevi is described and the explanations that his own
        followers gave to justify continued belief in him, even after he
        had actually apostatized, examined. While the failure of this
        movement generally confirms Festinger's analysis it also points to
        the need to modify it.

155.   Zetterberg, Hans L. "The Religious Conversion as a Change in
        Social Roles." SOCIOLOGY AND SOCIAL RESEARCH 36 (1952): 159-66.

        Studies a club affiliated with the Swedish Mission Covenant
        Youth, a revivalist church in Sweden. The author questions the

view that religious conversions are sudden and that they are always
accompanied by a change in beliefs and habits. Conversion can mean
a more conscious acceptance of a person's traditional religious
beliefs and practices. Conversions linked with a sudden change in
role are more common in rural districts, among less-educated
people, and more frequently among men than women.

B.   STUDIES ON PARTICULAR SECTS AND CULTS

156.   Arrington, Leonard J. "Early Mormon Communitarianism: The Law of
       Conservation and Stewardship." WESTERN HUMANITIES REVIEW 7
       (1953): 341-69.

       Examines the first of many Mormon experiments in community
       living, namely the law of conservation and stewardship, that was
       made up of the following four elements: "economic equality, social-
       ization of surplus incomes, freedom of enterprise, and group eco-
       nomic self-sufficiency" (p. 342). This regulation, the practical
       operation of which was suspended, was a novel combination of indi-
       vidualism and collectivism and throws light on the social unity and
       cohesiveness of the Mormons. The implications of this law, which
       was held to be divinely inspired, on the daily lives of the Mormons
       and some of its weaknesses are examined. The reasons why the law
       was unsuccessful during its short term of operation are spelled
       out.

157.   Babbie, Earl T. "The Third Civilization: An Examination of Soka-
       gakkai." REVIEW OF RELIGIOUS RESEARCH 7 (1966)): 101-21.

       Studies several factors that account for the rise of Soka Gakkai,
       a new Japanese religion, which has a branch in the U.S.A. known as
       Nichiren Shoshu. The origin and history of the movement are traced
       and some of its doctrines outlined. The sociological literature on
       the movement is reviewed and a theoretical model to explain this
       "world-proselytizing religion" is proposed. The principal elements
       of this model, namely the field in which the religion came into
       being, the condition of cultural change and state of deprivation,
       the message, the initial group, and the expansion phase, are de-
       scribed and then applied to Sokagakkai. The manner in which Soka
       Gakkai has adapted to the modern scene is explained. The author
       thinks that the main mantra of this religion, Nam-myoko-renge-kyo
       (Hail to the Mystery of the Lotus Sutra), is a magical formula.

158.   Bayer, A. E. "The Man Who Died: A Narrative Account of the Dutch
       Fisherman Lou, and His Group." REVIEW OF RELIGIOUS RESEARCH 10
       (1969): 81-88.

       Describes the emergence of a Dutch fisherman who in the late
       1960's began to preach about the imminent end of the world and new
       reality and consciousness, claiming that he himself had already
       reached a state beyond getting ill and dying. A short biographical
       sketch of Lou is given and his main doctrines briefly examined.

His followers never developed a clear organizational structure but kept the features of a primary group where all members lived in almost daily contact with one another. The breakup of this group started when Lou became ill and could not solve the conflicts among his followers. At his death his followers split into two factions. One group lost faith in Lou and abandoned the movement, the other (about one-third of the original members) remained and rationalized the death of their founder by stating that their sinful condition actually brought it about.

159.   Benyon, Erdmann Doane. "The Voodoo Cult Among Negro Immigrants in Detroit." AMERICAN JOURNAL OF SOCIOLOGY 43 (1938): 894-907.

Identifies the Black sect known to its members as the "Nation of Islam" or the "Muslims" and to the police as the "Voodoo Cult." The author thinks that the significance of the cult lies in its synthesis of diverse cultural elements and in its function of expressing race consciousness. The origin of the cult in Detroit, Michigan, is traced to the prophet Wali Farrad (or Fard), whose teachings are summarized. This cult, which gradually became organized, at first attracted unemployed, maladjusted migrant Blacks. Persecutions and schisms tended to increase the cultural isolation of the its members. This cult, however, slowly adjusted itself to an urban economy, and can be seen as an effort of migrant Blacks to secure a better socioeconomic status for themselves and their families.

160.   Blumstock, Robert E. "Fundamentalism, Prejudice, and Mission to the Jews." CANADIAN REVIEW OF SOCIOLOGY AND ANTHROPOLOGY 5 (1968): 27-35.

Examines the effects of the efforts of Christian fundamentalists to convert Jews, focusing on the work of the American Board of Mission to the Jews, Inc. It is argued that the works of this board have indirectly attacked the basic doctrinal position that fosters anti-Semitism. Consequently, the attempts to evangelize may contribute to the encouragement of religious toleration, thereby easing intergroup tensions and strengthening the social system. The author propounds a much more positive view of missionary efforts in Western culture than is normally admitted.

161.   Brewer, Earl D. C. "Sect and Church in Methodism." SOCIAL FORCES 30 (1952): 400-8.

Outlines the sociological view of the division of religious institutions into two main types, sect and church. This typology is seen as a continuum between two extreme types of religious organizations. The sect and church are considered in their conceptual and ideological differences, in their various associational and organizational patterns, in their usages, rituals, and other behavioral prototypes, and in their material and instrumental aspects. The author indicates to what extent Methodism was a sect-type organization between 1780-1790 and a church-type in the 1930's. The institutional characteristics of Methodism point to a development from a sect-type toward a church-type religious organization.

162.   Brown, Ira V. "Watchers of the Second Coming: The Millenarian
       Tradition in America." MISSISSIPPI VALLEY HISTORICAL REVIEW 39
       (1952): 441-58.

       Traces millenarian thought in American history to its Judeo-
       Christian origins and states that, as the main churches abandoned
       or neglected belief in the second coming, new sects came into being,
       basing their appeal on the conviction that the millennium is at
       hand. The Shakers, the Oneida Community, Harmony Society, early
       Mormonism, the Millerites, and Jehovah's Witnesses are the main
       groups cited. Millenarianism has stressed two opposing pictures of
       the world: a pessimistic one that sees the world as coming to an
       end soon and human efforts to reform as useless, and a more opti-
       mistic perspective that envisages the establishment of a heaven on
       earth in the near future.

163.   Buckner, H. Taylor. "The Flying Saucerians: An Open Door Cult."
       SOCIOLOGY IN EVERYDAY LIFE. Edited by Marcello Truzzi. Engle-
       wood Cliffs, NJ: Prentice-Hall, 1961, pp. 223-30.

       Examines an organization that investigates UFO phenomena and
       which itself has taken the form of a new religious cult. The his-
       tory of this cult is reviewed in two main phases, those of popular
       excitement and occult colonization. The first phase is further
       subdivided into three main periods: sensitization (1947-1950,
       during which time records of UFO sightings were made), hysteria
       (1952, a period when personal contacts with UFOs were reported),
       and secondary hysteria (which began in 1957 following the first
       Russian satellite launched into space). The author describes
       briefly the occult worldview and points out that the flying saucer
       movement began as another occult philosophy and then changed into
       an Open Door Cult. The main features of this cult are described
       and the personal characteristics of its members outlined. Several
       organizational difficulties of flying saucer clubs are discussed.

164.   Carden, Maren Lockwood. ONEIDA: UTOPIAN COMMUNITY TO MODERN COR-
       PORATION. Baltimore: Johns Hopkins University Press, 1969. xx,
       228 pp.

       Presents a historical account of the Oneida Community in two
       idealistic periods, the first being that of a Perfectionist
       society, the second that of an organized community. The author
       concentrates on how in both phases the ideals and values of the
       group were kept alive and suggests some conditions that contribute
       to the success or failure of utopias. The origin of Oneida, the
       beliefs and lifestyle of its members, and the breaking up of the
       community and its consequent development into a corporation and
       decline of its ideals are among the topics discussed.

165.   Carden, Maren Lockwood. "Experimental Utopia In America."
       DAEDALUS 94 (1965): 403-18.

       Discusses nineteenth-century utopianism, focusing on the Oneida
       Community, which produced several innovative practices including a
       complex marriage system in which childbearing was carefully con-

trolled. The development and gradual demise of the community are
outlined. The author thinks that utopian ideals have shifted from
the level of community to that of society or the nation as a whole.

166. Chamberlayne, John H. "From Sect to Cult in British Methodism."
      BRITISH JOURNAL OF SOCIOLOGY 15 (1964): 139-49.

      Distinguishes between sect-type and church-type religious organi-
      zations and shows how Methodism passed from the first to the second
      type from 1740-1750 (the decade of organization) to 1930-1940 (the
      decade of unification within British Methodism). The author shows
      how Methodism seems to have originated as a conversionist sect with
      an ideology, rituals, and material aspects stressing its separation
      from society or the world. It retained some church-type features
      from the beginning, but it was more revolutionary and anticlerical
      in nature and its process toward self-awareness was slow. Psycho-
      logical, economic, sociological, and theological factors led to its
      growth in numbers and to a complete self-awareness leading to its
      development to a church-type organization.

167. Clark, Elmer T. THE SMALL SECTS IN AMERICA. New York: Abingdon-
      Cokesbury Press. Second edition, 1949. 256 pp.

      Presents a descriptive account of various religious sects, giving
      brief historical sketches of each. In the introduction the author
      discusses the main features of sects and suggests that "a narrow
      dogmatism is perhaps the most nearly universal characteristic of
      the typical sectarian spirit" (p. 21). The economic influence on
      the emergence and success of sects is stressed. The following
      typology of sects based on their ideological emphasis is proposed:
      1) pessimistic or adventist; 2) perfectionist or subjectivist; 3)
      charismatic or Pentecostal; 4) communistic; 5) legalistic or objec-
      tivistic; 6) egocentric or New Thought; and 7) esoteric or mystic.
      Two appendices give a list of sects included under the last two
      mentioned types. A bibliography of now-dated materials (pp. 236-
      40) is useful for historical studies.

168. Cohn, Norman. THE PURSUIT OF THE MILLENNIUM. London: Secker and
      Warburg, 1957. xvi, 476 pp.

      Deals with the various European messianic and millennial move-
      ments of the Middle Ages. The author's view is that apocalyptic or
      eschatological visions can function as dynamic social myths giving
      "direction and concentration" to social discontents. Medieval
      sects, such as the Flagellants, can thus be interpreted as collec-
      tive experiments in adaptation and as efforts to cope with strain
      and conflict. Besides this sociocultural explanation, the author
      also considers millennial fantasies as examples of individual para-
      noia that bind people together and stimulate them to collective
      action. Besides a lengthy appendix (pp. 315-72) on the Ranters in
      seventeenth-century England, there are copious notes and two bib-
      liographies, one on the original sources and one on various studies
      of millennial movements.

169. Cohn, Werner. "Jehovah's Witnesses as a Proletarian Movement."
      AMERICAN SCHOLAR 24 (1955): 281-98.

Attempts to show that Jehovah's Witnesses "are actually separated by an almost airtight spiritual barrier from the rest of American society" (p. 281). The author maintains that this religious group can be labeled as "proletarian" and listed with radical religious sects and fanatical movements (like the German Youth Movement and some Zionist groups). These movements are characterized by social estrangement and by their stress on a cataclysmic end of the world and a future millennium. The author thinks that proletarian movements are an escape from the conflicts and ambiguities of reality and their millennial dreams are fantasy fulfillments of their desire to abolish all the difficulties of life. The similarities in organizational structure and in charismatic leadership that these movements share are explored. Both adolescent fixation and anomie are causal conditions that give rise to proletarian movements, whose strength is "a good barometer of the cohesion and permissiveness" of the society in which they prosper.

170. Cole, Alan. "The Quakers and the English Revolution." CRISIS IN EUROPE, 1560-1660. Edited by Trevor Aston. New York: Doubleday and Co., 1967, pp. 358-76.

Discusses the quietism and pacifism of the Quakers and their relationship to the political struggles of the seventeenth century. The political circumstances in which Quakerism developed is first outlined, stressing the fact that the Quakers "were by no means consistent pacifists" (p. 361). The reason why Quakers found it hard to remain in the army was not their pacifism, but rather their refusal to recognize the social division within the army's ranks. Because of their insistence on human equality, Quakers challenged both the ecclesiastical and political systems. Their involvement in political matters during the British monarchical struggles is explored.

171. Cross, Whitney B. THE BURNED-OVER DISTRICT: THE SOCIAL AND INTELLECTUAL HISTORY OF ENTHUSIASTIC RELIGION IN WESTERN NEW YORK, 1800-1850. Ithaca, NY: Cornell University Press, 1950. xiii, 383 pp.

Describes the religious turmoil in Western New York during the first half of the nineteenth century and shows how it must be taken into account for any thorough understanding of social phenomena, like the Civil War. The author outlines the social and environmental backgrounds of the area and traces the developments of the many revival and utopian movements of the period. He suggests that both internal and external causes led to the revival's decline in the middle of the century.

172. Dator, James Allen. SOKA GAKKAI, BUILDERS OF THE THIRD CIVILIZATION: AMERICAN AND JAPANESE MEMBERS. Seattle: University of Washington Press, 1969. xiii, 171 pp.

Examines the social functions of Sokagakkai, the lay organization of the Nichiren Shoshu Buddhist sect, the kind of people who join the movement, the reasons why they do so, and its political and social principles, goals, and aims. The author gives a brief history of Soka Gakkai, which was founded by T. Makiguchi (1871-1944), and outlines its organizational features and overseas expansion. Japanese members are compared with their American counterparts in their demographic characteristics, their marital status, attitudes toward work, and other personal characteristics. The relative deprivation theory is used to explain the movement's success.

173. Davis, David Brion. "Some Themes of Counter-Subversion: An Analysis of Anti-Masonic, Anti-Catholic, and Anti-Mormon Literature." MISSISSIPPI VALLEY HISTORICAL REVIEW 47 (1960): 205-24.

Examines the nineteenth-century literature that accused Masons, Catholics, and Mormons of subverting American ideals and way of life. This literature reflects the fears, prejudices, hopes, and unconscious motives of the participants in the movement against these three religious groups. Certain similarities between the campaigns against them are noted. In each case there was the belief that an un-American conspiracy was being plotted and that treason and criminal behavior were being perpetrated. Accusations that members of the minority religious groups committed heinous crimes were common. The author points out that the exposure of subversion promoted unity, clarified national values, gave individuals a sense of high moral righteousness, and legitimized American institutions. Conversion to the countersubversion movement followed the pattern of religious conversions.

174. Davis, J. Kenneth. "The Accommodation of Mormonism and Politico-Economic Reality." DIALOGUE: A JOURNAL OF MORMON THOUGHT 3 (1968): 42-54.

Discusses the problem of the relationship between Mormonism and society at large and suggests that when Mormonism could not integrate the prevailing institutions with its principles, these were adapted to worldly realities. The process of mutual adaptation is traced throughout Mormon history. Mormonism had to renounce both political power and economic isolation and change its very concept of Zion. The accommodation, however, was particularly difficult for manual workers, especially since Mormonism did not favor trade unions. In fact, Mormonism has adapted to the reality of the business world but not yet to unionism.

175. Davis, J. Kenneth. "The Mormon Church: Its Middle Class Propensities." REVIEW OF RELIGIOUS RESEARCH 4 (1963): 84-95.

Argues that the Mormon Church has participated in the movement of the United States from a rural-agrarian socioeconomic structure to an urban-industrial one. Four main characteristics of Mormonism--education, political leanings, occupational structure, and union activity--are examined and it is concluded that there is a close correlation between Mormon activity and all of them except unionism. There is evidence that the attitudes of the working class are becoming less favorable and that the Church leaders and active members have become more disposed towards the middle-class worldview, a trend encouraged by Mormon organization and theology.

176.   De Pillis, Mario S. "The Social Sources of Mormonism." CHURCH
        HISTORY 37 (1968): 50-79.

        Critically examines Cross's view of the origin of Mormonism (see
        item 171) and concludes, among other things, that the evidence does
        not support the "anti-frontier" hypothesis. The author argues that
        the birth of Mormonism "was related to the disorientation of values
        associated with migration to and within the backwood areas of the
        United States" (p. 79). The population lived in newly settled,
        rural locales (frontiers) and was evangelical and sectarian in
        religious outlook. The organization, personnel, and doctrines of
        this new religion must be understood not in the context of the
        Burned-Over District of New York nor in the long-settled areas of
        eastern New England. Rather, Mormon origins must be sought in the
        complex, ethnic, institutional, and denominational conditions of
        Mormon culture of Eastern Ohio, Western Missouri, and Western
        Illinois.

177.   Eddy, G. Norman. "Store-Front Religion." RELIGION IN LIFE 28
        (1959): 68-85.

        Examines Store-Front Religion, that is, those religious groups
        "found in socially disorganized areas of large urban communities
        and generally housed in small secular buildings" (p. 69). These
        churches deviate from the established religious bodies, particularly
        in that their clergy are much less educated and their members are
        drawn from the lower economic classes. Independence from, or loose
        association with, other groups is also a main feature of Store-Front
        Churches. Three basic varieties of such churches are identified:
        1) the transitory local group (e.g., the Pentecostal Church of
        Hope); 2) the charismatic group (e.g., the House of Prayer); and
        3) the group that unifies people around a myth that gives them a
        distinctive ritual and belief system (e.g., the Church of God and
        Saints of Christ).

178.   Eister, Alan W. "The Oxford Movement: A Typological Analysis."
        SOCIOLOGY AND SOCIAL RESEARCH 34 (1949): 116-24.

        Discusses the problem of classifying religious movements in the
        context of the Oxford Group Movement, which came into being in the
        1920's and was known under several names, including the First Cen-
        tury Christian Fellowship, Moral Rearmament, and Buchananism. The
        origin and structure of the movement as well as its internal disci-
        pline and governance are explored. The author thinks that the
        Oxford Group was "neither closed or selective nor entirely assess-
        able, but that it approached nearer the latter type than the former"
        (p. 122). The uncritical, nonintellectual attitudes of the Group
        towards religious experience are among the issues raised.

179.   England, R. W. "Some Aspects of Christian Science." AMERICAN
        JOURNAL OF SOCIOLOGY 59 (1954): 448-53.

        Endeavors, through an analysis of a sample of 500 published
        letters of testimony by Christian Scientists, to determine some
        of the personal features of those who find the Church of Christ,

Scientist, appealing. The largest group of adherents are drawn
from urban, middle-class, married females who suffer from several
bodily disorders that are either physically or emotionally caused.
Financial difficulties, the use of alcohol, tobacco, tea, and coffee, and various conditions of unhappiness (like family discord and
bereavement) have also led people to join this Christian sect. The
alleged power of the Church to cure bodily diseases has been the
largest factor that sustains interest and membership in the church.
The author thinks that Christian Science has a function similar to
that of professional psychotherapy with its practitioners playing
the role of psychotherapists.

180.   Ericksen, Ephraim Edward. THE PSYCHOLOGICAL AND ETHICAL ASPECTS
       OF MORMON GROUP LIFE. Salt Lake City: University of Utah Press,
       1975. xix, 101 pp. (First published in 1922.)

       Presents a sociopsychological approach to Mormonism, focusing on
       group sentiment and on the genetic development of Mormon group
       consciousness. The author deals with three "maladjustments" in
       Mormon life: 1) between Mormons and gentiles in Mormonism's first
       stage of history; 2) between Mormons and nature in the second
       stage; and 3) between new thought and old institution in the third
       stage. The relationship of the prophet Joseph Smith to those who
       joined his church, Mormon colonization, and various Mormon institu-
       tions (such as marriage) are among the topics dealt with. It is
       argued that the moral concepts of Mormonism developed out of ini-
       tial group experience.

181.   Erikson, Kai T. WAYWARD PURITANS: A STUDY IN THE SOCIOLOGY OF
       DEVIANCE. New York: John Wiley and Sons, 1966. xiii, 228 pp.

       Uses the Puritan community as a background for an analysis of
       deviant behavior. After discussing the sociology of deviance, the
       author examines the Puritan community and the various crises that
       occurred during the first century of its settlement in New England.
       The Puritan attitude that encouraged relentless punishment for
       those who deviated from the norm is seen in the context of their
       theological doctrine of predestination. The author argues that
       "deviant persons often supply an important service to society by
       patrolling the outer edge of group space and by providing a con-
       trast which gives the rest of the community some sense of their
       territorial identity" (p. 196).

182.   Fauset, Arthur Huff. BLACK GODS OF THE METROPOLIS: NEGRO RELIGIOUS
       CULTS IN THE URBAN NORTH. Philadelphia: University of Pennsyl-
       vania Press, 1971. xi, 128 pp. (First published in 1944).

       Attempts to unravel the story of Afro-American religious history
       by exploring Afro-American culture in its main forms and functions.
       The following five cults representing the variety of Black reli-
       gions in America are the focus of this study: 1) Mount Sinai Holy
       Church of America; 2) United House of Prayer for All People; 3)
       Church of God (Black Jews); 4) Moorish Science Temple of America;
       and 5) Father Divine's Peace Mission Movement. The origins,
       organization, finance, beliefs, rituals, and practices of each

group are described. These cults are compared with the established
and traditional churches. Among the attractive features of these
Black cults are the personality of their leaders, the relief from
physical and mental illness that they promise, and their efforts to
combat race prejudice.

183.   Fishman, Aryei, compiler and editor. THE RELIGIOUS KIBBUTZ MOVE-
        MENT: THE REVIVAL OF THE JEWISH RELIGIOUS COMMUNITY. Jerusalem:
        Zionist Organization, 1957. 159 pp.

        Brings together a collection of essays that discuss the religious
        kibbutz and its implications for Israeli society. In the introduc-
        tion, the editor traces the history of the movement and outlines
        its features. The materials are divided in three sections. The
        first deals with the religious pioneering community; the second
        with the various aspects of community life; and the third with
        several individual settlements.

184.   Galbreath, Robert. "Traditional and Modern Elements in the Occult-
        ism of Rudolf Steiner." JOURNAL OF POPULAR CULTURE 3 (1969):
        451-67.

        Traces the rise of contemporary interest in occult matters to the
        late nineteenth and early twentieth centuries. The life and ideas
        of Rudolph Steiner (1861-1925), who dominated the occultism of the
        1920's, are overviewed "with particular attention to the interwork-
        ing of traditional and modern elements in his conception of occult-
        ism as a spiritual science which could be used to combat the mate-
        rialism of contemporary civilization" (p. 452). Anthroposophy,
        Steiner's system of occultism, is a mixture of ideas derived from
        Christianity, Theosophy, the thought of Goethe, nineteenth-century
        occultism, and Steiner's own personal experience. Steiner's
        efforts to harmonize traditional beliefs with modern scientific
        principles is stressed. The author thinks that Steiner's system
        need not be a form of escapism; it has the potential for bringing
        about social change and promoting spiritual health.

185.   Garabedian, John H., and Orde Coombs. EASTERN RELIGIONS IN THE
        ELECTRIC AGE. New York: Grosset and Dunlap, 1969. 160 pp.

        Accounts "for the serious conflicts in the United States and in
        the Western world that produce a search for the serenity of the
        East" (p. 8). After describing the 1960's mood of disenchantment
        among young Americans, the author gives brief sketches of the var-
        ious Eastern religions. He then describes the encounter between
        East and West in Zen, Esalen, and Transcendental Meditation.

186.   Garrett, Dan L. "Synanon: the Communiversity." HUMANIST 25.5
        (1965): 185-89.

        Describes and discusses Synanon's view of education. The author
        explains how Synanon looks on personality disorder, of which the
        addiction to drugs is one manifestation, as an educational problem.
        He maintains that Synanon is not to be understood as a therapeutic
        or educational community, but rather a "communiversity," that is,

a living arrangement in which the reciprocal relationship between the teacher and the student is translated into action. The following four devices in the Synanon's educational system are outlined: 1) the "Synanon Game"; 2) "dissipation"; 3) "cerebration"; and 4) the "wizard concept."

187. Gerlach, Luther P., and Virginia H. Hine. "Five Factors Crucial to the Growth of a Modern Religious Movement." JOURNAL FOR THE SCIENTIFIC STUDY OF RELIGION 7 (1968): 23-40.

Examines the newer pentecostal groups of the 1960's and proposes a set of five internal factors that account for their spread. These factors are: 1) a reticulate, acephalous structure, with an infrastructure that includes several personal ties; 2) a fervent and convincing recruitment program, carried out mainly through face-to-face contacts; 3) a commitment act or experience; 4) a change-oriented and action-motivating ideology; and 5) a perception of real or imaginary opposition. The author also provides a description of the movement where glossolalia is one of its most important manifestations. It is argued that, though the condition of relative deprivation, social disorganization, and psychological maladjustment may explain the genesis of the movement, its development into a dynamic social structure should be sought in the dynamics of the movement itself.

188. Glick, Ira O. "The Hebrew Christians: A Marginal Religious Group." THE JEWS: SOCIAL PATTERNS OF AN AMERICAN GROUP. Edited by Marshall Sklare. Glencoe, IL: Free Press, 1958, pp. 415-31.

Describes a Hebrew Christian Church that was organized in 1934 and whose roots lie in the early twentieth century when Herman Kaufman, a young Romanian Jew, emigrated to the United States. The author seeks to discover the reasons why some Jewish converts to Christianity insist on maintaining the dual identification of both Jewish and Christian. The status dilemma of the Hebrew Christian is solved by the group's ideology, which is best understood with reference to the realities it reflects. Hebrew Christianity "is a protest against the position which Jewish converts to Christianity must occupy in our society" (p. 427). The author thinks that, because of the inherent contradiction and problems of Hebrew Christianity, the Hebrew Christian Church is not likely to survive.

189. Graves, Robert. "Witches in 1964." VIRGINIA QUARTERLY REVIEW 40 (1964): 550-59.

Reflects on the "sudden spread of organized witch groups in modern Britain" (p. 550). The works of Margaret Murray are said to be at the basis of such a revival that was spearheaded by Gerald Gardner. The author describes some of the general activities of witches and outlines briefly the origins of the Two-Horned cult that entered Great Britain as early as the thirteenth century. He thinks that witchcraft attracts largely "hysterical or perverted characters." In his opinion, schisms that followed the death of Gardner present some serious problems for the future of Witchcraft.

190.   Griswold, Alfred Whitney. "New Thought: A Cult of Success." AMER-
        ICAN JOURNAL OF SOCIOLOGY 40 (1934): 309-18.

        Traces the origin of New Thought to the Mesmerism of Phineas
        Quimby and the Transcendentalism of Ralph Waldo Emerson and the
        Concord group. Some of the main features of New Thought are out-
        lined. It is stated that the movement was not a church and that
        its members, who were mainly city-dwellers, were motivated primar-
        ily by profit and not by its theology and metaphysics. Those who
        joined the movement believed that success in business was acquired
        by magical magnetism. The movement's appeal and popularity were in
        its nature of a "get-rich-quick-religion" (p. 31). A select list
        of early authorities and writings is appended.

191.   Hackett, Herbert. "The Flying Saucer: A Manufactured Concept."
        SOCIOLOGY AND SOCIAL RESEARCH 32 (1948): 869-73.

        Shows how the concept of the "flying saucer" was developed and
        how it became accepted through the authority of the press and of
        experts. The belief in flying saucers is related to the "public
        tensions of the moment."

192.   Hand, Wayland D. "Folk Medical Magical and Symbolism in the West."
        FORMS UPON THE FRONTIER. Edited by Austin Fife, Alfa Fife, and
        Henry H. Glassie. Salt Lake City: Utah State University Mono-
        graph Series xvi, no. 2, 1969, pp. 103-118.

        Gives several examples of folk medical magical beliefs and sym-
        bols found in the United States. Both sympathetic and contagious
        magic, involving the use of animals and plants, are used widely to
        cure various kinds of illnesses. Though largely descriptive in
        content, this essay shows convincingly that magical beliefs and
        practices are common in modern industrialized societies in the
        West.

193.   Harrison, Ira E. "The Storefront Church as a Revitalization Move-
        ment." REVIEW OF RELIGIOUS RESEARCH 7 (1966): 160-63.

        Views the phenomenon of storefront churches as a conscious, orga-
        nized effort to create a more satisfying culture and religion.
        Basing his reflections on a study of such churches in Syracuse, New
        York, the author concludes that they have the function of relieving
        "stress and disillusionment through their organizational structure,
        leadership, membership, and ritual" (p. 161). Like all revitali-
        zation movements, the storefront church has 1) a code (the Bible);
        2) a system of communication (the Word of God from the Pastor); 3)
        an organization (the storefront); 4) adaptation (to the urban con-
        text); 5) a routinization process (in the order of their services);
        and 6) a goal of cultural transformation (of Black rural cultural
        heritage). The author thinks that some storefront churches develop
        into organized churches.

194.   Hawthorn, H. B. "A Test of Simmel on the Secret Society: The
        Doukhobors of British Columbia." AMERICAN JOURNAL OF SOCIOLOGY
        62 (1956): 1-7.

Discusses Simmel's view of secret societies in the context of the
Sons of Freedom sect of the Doukhobors of British Columbia, Canada.
This sect had several features that are usually assigned to secret
societies. The Doukhobors are chosen as an extreme example of a
persecuted religious group that adopted secrecy as a means of survival. The Sons of Freedom refused to make any compromise with the
Canadian government and thus found themselves even more threatened.
Simmel's views as to how secret societies operate and their culture
transmitted from one generation to the next are extended. The
author suggests, among other things, that when power and authority
in a secret society acquire mystic overtones, the opportunities for
exploiting both members and outsiders increase.

195.   Hillery, George, A. The Convent: Community, Prison, or Task
       Force?" JOURNAL FOR THE SCIENTIFIC STUDY OF RELIGION 9 (1969):
       140-51.

Attempts to clarify the sociological nature of the convent that
has been at times compared to a prison, mental asylum, and military
barracks. Two types of convents are examined: 1) the cloistered,
monastic one and 2) the apostolic one. Several types of social
groups are clustered together in two broad categories: 1) prisons,
i.e., custodial institutions, which can be called total institutions; and 2) "vills," i.e., communities or social organizations
like folk villages. The author maintains that convents are not
total institutions nor vills. Monastic convents are communal
organizations similar to vills and apostolic convents are formal
organizations stressing specific goals.

196.   Hine, Robert V. CALIFORNIA'S UTOPIAN COLONIES. New Haven: Yale
       University Press, 1966. xi, 209 pp. (First published in 1953.)

Describes 17 utopian colonies in California that were founded
between 1850 and 1950. Two Theosophical colonies and a Mormon
settlement are included in the author's investigation. The author
attempts to make some generalizations on communal life, to identify
those features these communes shared with society at large, and to
explain why they so often failed. Though religious colonies tend
to survive twice as long as secular ones, the author thinks that
religious faith does not account for longevity. Political, economic, social factors, as well as internal dissensions and conflicts
with society, are the main reasons why communes do not last long.

197.   Hine, Virginia H. "Pentecostal Glossolalia: Toward a Functional
       Interpretation." JOURNAL FOR THE SCIENTIFIC STUDY OF RELIGION 9
       (1969): 211-26.

Rejects attempts to explain glossolalia as a sign of psychopathology, hypnosis, or suggestibility, or as an indication of
social deprivation or disintegration. The author maintains that a
functional interpretation that considers speaking in tongues a
factor in the movement's dynamics provides a better understanding
of the phenomenon. The personality changes (like conversion, the
acceptance of a fundamentalist ideology, and the adoption of new
personal attitudes and moral behavior) that are associated with

Pentecostal glossolalia are described. Glossolalia plays a functional role in the process of personal change. It is one of the components that generates religious commitment.

198.   Holt, John B. "Holiness Religion: Cultural Shock and Social Reorganization." AMERICAN SOCIOLOGICAL REVIEW 5 (1940): 740-47.

Reflects on the phenomenological growth of the Holiness and Pentecostal sects in the southeastern parts of the United States. The members of these sects are often labeled the "holy rollers," even though the highly emotional character of their worship has been largely eliminated. Four hypotheses that explain the growth of these religious groups are discussed: 1) the movement is largely a product of social disorganization and culture conflict due to rapid urban migration; 2) it is mainly social in its character and is aimed at reestablishing a lost sense of security; 3) it is a reactionary and reformist movement; and 4) it is simply a regional and southern phenomenon. The author maintains that religious experience tends to develop out of conditions of economic stress, personal isolation, and insecurity due to migration, and social discrimination. He thinks, however, that not enough information has been gathered to fully support any one particular thesis.

199.   Hostetler, John A. "Folk and Scientific Medicine in Amish Society." HUMAN ORGANIZATION 22 (1963/1964): 269-75.

Investigates the medical knowledge of the Amish and suggests that both folk and scientific concepts are present in attempts to explain and treat illnesses. The author attempts to explain how the two apparently incompatible forms of medicine, namely the folk and the scientific, exist side by side. Among the Amish, scientific healing is applied in cases of chronic, non-incapacitating sickness, while folk medicine is used in instances of chronic, incapacitating illnesses. The physician-patient relationship among the Amish is outlined. It is suggested that "the practice of folk medicine persists in a culture that places a premium on isolation" (p. 275). Folk medical concepts and treatments are consistent with Amish culture as a whole.

200.   Hostetler, John A. "Religious Mobility in a Sect Group: The Mennonite Church." RURAL SOCIOLOGY 19 (1954): 244-55.

Studies the factors that attract outsiders to, or repel people from, the Mennonite Churches in the United States and Canada. The proportion of converts from outside the group, their previous religious affiliation, and the membership losses by denominational choice are recorded. The sex, age, education, income, and occupation of converts and ex-members are analyzed. The author discovers that in the Mennonite Church "the turnover in membership is higher in urban churches than in churches located in rural places" (p. 255). It is further gaining more new members from the low-income classes and losing more from the upper-income ones.

201.   Huelett, J. E. "The Kenny Healing Cult: Preliminary Analysis of Leadership and Patterns of Interaction." AMERICAN SOCIOLOGICAL REVIEW 10 (1945): 364-72.

Traces the process of a cult that centered round a method of
healing infantile paralysis, a method invented by an Australian
nurse, Elizabeth Kenny. The author traces the history of the cult
to the early twentieth century and examines the leadership patterns
within it as well as the resulting conflicts between those who
accepted Kenny's healing techniques and those who dismissed them as
unscientific. Kenny is described as a typical charismatic leader
who accepted the role of "hypotheist" of the cult. The public
anxiety regarding the disease created a social condition conducive
to the emergence of the cult and elevated Nurse Kenny to the status
of a public heroine.

202.   Hurston, Zora Neale. "Hoodoo in America." JOURNAL OF AMERICAN
        FOLKLORE 44 (1931): 320-417.

Provides an extensive ethnography of the practice of Hoodoo in
America. After a brief historical introduction in which the main
influences on Hoodoo (namely the Catholic Church and Spiritualism)
are mentioned and a description of Bahamian "Obeah" (conjure) is
given, the author focuses on the practice of Hoodoo in the Southern
states and transcribes many magical texts used by the practitioners
of this cult.

203.   Inglis, Brian. FRINGE MEDICINE. London: Faber and Faber, 1964.
        288 pp.

Distinguishes between orthodox and fringe medicine, the former
pertaining to a professional organization. Fringe medicine is
divided into three types, based on whether it emphasizes the body
(like herbalism and acupuncture), the mind (as in Yoga), or the
spirit (as in Christian Science and spiritual healing). It is
an alternative medical system that assumes that healing forces are
actually within the individual. Some areas of conflict between
orthodox and fringe medicine are discussed.

204.   Isichei, Elizabeth A. "From Sect to Denomination in English
        Quakerism, with Special Reference to the Nineteenth Century."
        BRITISH JOURNAL OF SOCIOLOGY 15 (1964): 207-22.

Presents the common sociological distinction between sect and
denomination with reference to their relationship with the society
in which they thrive. Religious movements, in this view, tend to
start as sectarian ones that, unlike denominations, stress separatism and totalitarianism, demand great fervor and dedication from
the membership, and claim exclusive possession of truth. The
author questions the view that sects develop into denominations,
citing the English Quakers as an example to show that this process
is not necessarily the norm. It is suggested that sectarian and
denominational outlooks may exist side by side in the same movement. Further, while prosperity and denominational membership are
certainly linked, socioeconomic criteria do not sufficiently explain the divergences between sects and denominations. In the case
of Quakerism, sectarian impulses, though weakening, may have been
revived by the introduction of historical studies that led to the
abolition of the customs of recording ministers and birthright
membership.

205.   Isichei, Elizabeth A. "Organization and Power in the Society of
        Friends." PATTERNS OF SECTARIANISM (item 149), pp. 182-212.

        Discusses the government of the Society of Friends (Quakers).
        The author analyzes a Quaker business meeting's deliberation and
        decisions in the 1880's in order to find out how their highly indi-
        vidualistic system worked in practice. The conflicts at the time
        are interpreted as a clash between conservative and reformist ten-
        dencies. The Quaker theory of authority, as it was enunciated by
        George Fox, and its development throughout history are explained.
        Among the areas examined are the way in which proposals were for-
        mulated, the kind of information that led to decisions, the way
        influential groups that swayed opinion were formed, and various
        interest groups among the decisions makers.

206.   Jennings, George J. "An Ethnological Study of Glossolalia." JOUR-
        NAL OF THE AMERICAN SCIENTIFIC AFFILIATION 20.8 (March 1968): 5-
        16.

        Gives an ethnographic description of glossolalia and identifies
        six forms of glossolalic utterances: 1) the language of spirits;
        2) sacerdotal language; 3) the language of animas; 4) nonsense
        syllables; 5) xenoglossia (speaking in foreign tongues); and
        6) ermeneglossia (interpretation of tongues). The glossolalic
        features of the contemporary Charismatic Renewal are compared with
        similar phenomena in non-Christian cultures. The author adopts the
        deprivation theory to explain glossolalia. He writes that "there
        is a positive correlation between the disappearance of traditional
        supports sustaining man's self-confidence and the emergence of
        charismatic revivalism with its glossolalic phenomena" (p. 14).
        A useful bibliography of pre-1968 materials is included.

207.   Johnson, Benton. "Do Holiness Sects Socialize in Dominant Values?"
        SOCIAL FORCES 39 (1961): 309-16.

        Argues that enough evidence can be mustered to support the theory
        that the Holiness Movement in American Protestantism has the impor-
        tant function of socializing marginal, lower-class groups into the
        values commonly found among the middle class, that is, the dominant
        value of institutionalized society. Stress on conversion suggests
        that Holiness groups attempt to reorient their values and motiva-
        tions into channels that are not as opposed to secular values as
        they might appear at first sight. The Holiness churches try to win
        respect and acceptance of outsiders and, in so doing, adopt some of
        the dominant values and attitudes. Holiness churches are not
        alienated from secular society; they are rather positively oriented
        to it "in terms of an ethic of inner-worldly asceticism" (p. 314).

208.   Judah, J. Stillson. THE HISTORY AND PHILOSOPHY OF THE METAPHYSICAL
        MOVEMENTS IN AMERICA. Philadelphia: Westminster Press, 1967.
        317 pp.

        Describes the origin and ideology of the Metaphysical Movement in
        nineteenth-century America. Included in the groups examined are
        Spiritualism, Theosophy (especially the Arcane School and the

Astara Foundation), New Thought, Divine Science Church, Church of
Religious Science, Unity School of Christianity, and Christian
Science. The author holds that since these movements "contributed
to and fitted into American culture, their strength and growth are
partly due to their becoming a mirror of the hope, thoughts, and
aspirations of a large part of the the American population" (p.
12). He discovers that the reasons for the origin of these movements lies within American cultural history. Some of the main
themes expounded by these movements, namely religious freedom, new
revelation, idealism, a utilitarian deity, religious experience,
mysticism, and monism, are considered to be an integral part of
American culture. The Metaphysical Movement, in the author's view,
represents a shift towards meeting the mental and bodily needs of
individuals.

209.   Keene, James J. "Baha'i World Faith: Redefinition of Religion."
       JOURNAL FOR THE SCIENTIFIC STUDY OF RELIGION 1 (1967): 221-235.

       Compares members of the Baha'i faith with Jews, Catholics, and
       Protestants in the structure of their religious behavior and in
       some personality traits. Baha'is were found to differ from the
       rest. The cognitive, experiential, self-defining, administrative,
       and meditative aspects of their religious life were then analyzed
       and it was concluded that only the Baha'i group exhibited total,
       balanced religious activity. The findings are then defined in
       terms of the concept of community.

210.   Kitzinger, Sheila. "Protest and Mysticism: The Rastafari Cult of
       Jamaica." JOURNAL FOR THE SCIENTIFIC STUDY OF RELIGION 8 (1969):
       240-62.

       Takes an anthropological approach to the Rastafari Movement that
       originated in Jamaica in the 1930's and has since spread to other
       countries. The history of the movement is summarized and its roots
       traced to the Garvey Movement and the condition of slavery. The
       author explains how a person becomes a "rasta," elaborates on the
       idea of God within the movement, accounts for its various taboos
       and religious services, and analyzes its main doctrines and socio-
       religious attitudes. The repressed psychological drives, namely
       male dominance and maternal rejection, form the basis of faith and
       action for the Rastafarians. A process of mother-rejection and
       father-identification dominates the movement. The cult "canalizes
       aggression and permits the expression of hostility in symbolic and
       ritualized forms," and "it takes paranoid fantasies and institu-
       tionalizes them, and at the same time it virtually rids them of
       much of their social danger" (p. 261). In spite of its positive
       function of reducing hopelessness, the author maintains that the
       Rastafari Movement fails to reconcile its members to the world.

211.   Lang, Kurt, and Gladys Engel Lang. "Decisions For Christ: Billy
       Graham in New York City." IDENTITY AND ANXIETY: SURVIVAL OF THE
       PERSON IN MASS SOCIETY. Edited by Maurice R. Stein, Arthur J.
       Vidich, and David Manning White. Glencoe, IL: Free Press, 1960,
       pp. 415-27.

Discusses a Billy Graham crusade held in Madison Square Garden,
New York, in 1957. The authors distinguish between inquirers and
converts, the former indicating a kind of revivalism in the modern
urban crusade, the latter referring to the more old-fashioned personal form of revivalism. In their view, the modern revival is a
mass performance that is carefully planned and relies heavily on
gimmickry. Unlike older revivals, the new crusades do not entail a
public confession of one's conversion. The kind of people drawn to
Billy Graham and to the techniques used to solicit them to attend
the meetings are the main focus of this essay. The rally, from its
conception up to the time when people step forward to make their
decision for Christ, is described. Most of the people who respond
to Graham's invitation are not "converts." The crusades leave no
lasting impact on their behavior and mentality, nor do they elicit
their permanent commitment. The modern revival tends to be "an
organized drive to re-establish the importance of religion by
dramatizing its urgency" (p. 426).

212.   Laue, James H. "A Contemporary Revitalization Movement in American
        Race Relations: The 'Black Muslims.'" SOCIAL FORCES 42 (1964):
        315-23.

        Uses Wallace's theory of revitalization movements (that proposes
        that such movements are a "deliberate, organized, conscious effort
        by members of a society to construct a more satisfying culture")
        to develop a social theory and research program for understanding the
        Black Muslims. A brief history of the development of this Black
        nationalist group and a description of its values and artistic
        expression are provided. Wallace's five-stage theory of how reli-
        gious movements develop is applied to the Black Muslims. Several
        doctrinal modifications, which seem to indicate that the movement
        is changing from a sect into a church, are listed. Some lines for
        further research are suggested.

213.   Lawton, George. THE DRAMA OF LIFE AFTER DEATH: A STUDY OF THE
        SPIRITUALIST RELIGION. London: Constable and Co., 1933. xxvii,
        688 pp.

        Presents an extensive study of Spiritualism, describing its
        beliefs and practices and showing how people arrive at such beliefs
        and derive psychic benefit from them. The Spiritualist theory on
        the nature of the human being and what life is like in the spirit
        world are depicted in some detail. The faith as practiced in the
        believer's daily life is then outlined. Spiritualism as a church
        organization, its membership requirements, its general services,
        the prayer life of its adherents, and mediumship are dealt with.
        Methods of evangelization and defense of the belief system are also
        summarized. The author endorses the view that Spiritualism satis-
        fies the needs for sociability and for belonging to a secret con-
        fraternity. It often enables a person to adjust to the problems of
        life, compensates for frustrations, releases tensions, and makes up
        for many human deprivations.

214.   Lincoln, C. Eric. "The Black Muslims as a Protest Movement."
        ASSURING FREEDOM TO THE FREE. Edited by Arnold Rose. Detroit:
        Wayne State University Press, 1964, pp. 220-40.

Presents an analysis of the Black Muslims in America as "a symbol and a product of social conflict." The rise of this movement, which has parallels in other parts of the world, expresses the anxiety and discontent of a group that is reacting against a discrepancy of power. The history of the movement is traced and its main features described. The author thinks that the Black Muslims reflect the failure of a society to meet the needs of those who want to participate in the social values that are taken for granted by the majority of the population.

215.   Lofland, John, and Rodney Stark. "Becoming a World-Saver: A Theory of Conversion to a Deviant Perspective." AMERICAN SOCIOLOGICAL REVIEW 30 (1965): 862-74.

Outlines a model of the conversion process in the context of a small millennial, religious cult in the San Francisco Bay Area (a cult later identified as the Unification Church in its earliest stage in the United States). A brief historical background is given and the predisposing conditions and situation contingencies that led to its success are discussed. Among the major predisposing conditions of its members are listed: 1) tension in one's life; 2) a religious problem-solving perspective; and 3) the spirit of religious seekership. The following are identified as the main situation contingencies: 1) encountering the cult at a turning point in life; 2) the creation of cult affective bonds; 3) diminution of extra-cult attachments; and 4) intense interaction leading to conversion.

216.   MacKensie, Norman, editor. SECRET SOCIETIES. London: Aldus Books, 1967. 350 pp.

Edits 11 essays on various secret societies including, the Rosicrucians and Free Masons. In an introductory essay the editors stress the importance of studying these societies particularly in order to understand human relationships. The initiation ritual, the ordeal, the myth that supports the secrecy, and the segregation of the sexes are said to be among the principal features of these societies.

217.   Maiolo, John R., William V. D'Antonio, and William T. Liu. "Sources and Management of Stress in a Social Movement: Some Preliminary Considerations." SOCIOLOGICAL ANALYSIS 29 (1968): 67-78.

Discusses the emergence of the Christian Family Movement, pointing out the need that all social movements experience for managing tension. The origins of this movement, which reflects and identifies the shared discontent of American Catholics in a transitional society, are traced to its social and religious roots. The authors suggest that structural strain in the movement is caused by the control of the internal erosive tendencies. Among the problem-solving features are selective recruitment, transitory membership, guided action programs aimed at socialization, and decentralized decision-making processes. The study of such movements helps us understand the way they eventually become complex organizations.

218.   Maitre, Jacques. "The Consumption of Astrology in Contemporary
        Society." DIOGENES 53 (Spring 166): 82-98.

        Seeks to understand why the gains made by science and communica-
        tion seem to favor the spread of ideas (including astrology and the
        occult) that run counter to science. The author's main thesis is
        that "the limitations of specific knowledge, whether theoretical,
        practical, or pedagogical, demand an asceticism often experienced
        as frustration in terms of the felt needs of individuals and groups"
        (p. 83). Astrology is examined as a form of divinatory procedure.
        Its scope, its features that appeal to the consumer public, and its
        social functions are examined. The exorcising of change, the
        unbridling of fate, and popularization of psychology are among the
        functions assigned to the practice of astrology.

219.   McCall, George J. "Symbiosis: The Case of Hoodoo and the Numbers
        Racket." SOCIAL PROBLEMS 10 (1963): 361-71.

        Compares the practice of Hoodoo with gambling and argues that
        they are closely related. Basing his reflections on his observa-
        tions of Hoodoo belief and practice in Harlem, New York, the author
        gives a brief description of this imported religion, which is a
        blend of Christian and African religious traditions. He describes
        the artifacts used in Hoodoo to secure good luck in gambling. His
        theory is that the Hoodoo belief system "bolsters the profits of
        the numbers racket" in that it increases "the volume of business"
        and "the already overwhelming odds in favor of the 'bank'" (p. 367).
        At the same time Hoodoo goods and services are in greater demand
        because of the widespread interest in gambling.

220.   McLaughlin, Wayman B. "Symbolism and Mysticism in the Spirituals."
        PHYLON 24 (1963): 69-77.

        Attempts a comparative analysis of the symbolic and mystical
        thinking among Black Spirituals. The experience of cosmic exile
        from the world and from God, the search for unity, and the denial
        of temporal time are among the more common themes that appear in
        spiritualist hymnology. It is argued that the exploration of these
        motifs are necessary for understanding this religion.

221.   McLoughlin, William G. "Pietism and the American Character."
        AMERICAN QUARTERLY 17 (1965): 163-86.

        Proposes the view that religious pietism is central to the Ameri-
        can character. It is the author's opinion that the "dynamic, sec-
        tarian form of Pietistic-perfectionism" (p. 164) is at the basis of
        American civilization. Two types of pietism are distinguished: 1)
        Puritan and separatist; 2) conservative and antinomian. The author
        traces the history and development of both through the various
        revivals that have taken place in the history of America. He
        further discusses pietism in the context of the claim that America
        is a materialistic and secular culture--a view which he rejects.

222.   Monaghan, Robert R. "Three Facets of the True Believer: Motivation
        for Attending a Fundamentalist Church." JOURNAL FOR THE SCIEN-
        TIFIC STUDY OF RELIGION 1 (1967): 237-45.

Explores the motivations, aspirations, and gratifications that
are typical of members of a fundamentalist church (which is defined
as one where adherence to an anthropomorphic concept of God and to
a literal interpretation of the Bible is central). The characteristics and structure of the church under study, located in Georgia,
are described. Three types of members are distinguished: 1) the
comfort-seeker (who fears illness, death, and the possibility of
hell); 2) the social participator (who looks for social interaction); and 3) the authority seeker (who needs definite doctrinal
and moral guidelines).

223.   Moore, LeRoy. "Another Look at Fundamentalism: A Response to
        Ernest R. Sandeen." CHURCH HISTORY 37.2 (1968): 195-202.

Contends that Sandeen's view that the theological roots of fundamentalism lie in dispensationalism and biblical literalism fails to
account for developments that have occurred since the early 1920's.
The author suggests that a distinction between "doctrinaire fundamentalism" and "fundamentalism as a party movement" might more
accurately account for the historical situation and explain the
unique features of Fundamentalism of the 1920's.

224.   Nelson, Geoffrey K. SPIRITUALISM AND SOCIETY. New York: Schocken
        Books, 1969. xi, 307 pp.

Presents a historical and sociological study of Spiritualism. In
the first part the author traces the social and religious factors
in the rise of Spiritualism in America and its development as an
organization. In the second part he concentrates on describing
Spiritualism in Great Britain. The final section is dedicated to
an analysis of Spiritualism in terms of the sociological theory of
church, sect, and cult. Spiritualism, like occult and flying-
saucer movements, is "a cult movement containing within it centralized cults and a large number of independent local cults" (p. 234).
The following cultic features are stressed: 1) the quest for religious experience; 2) the break with religious traditions and with
societal values; and 3) the preoccupation with the problems of the
individual. The sources of Spiritualism are traced "to the conditions of anomie brought about by the change in life conditions and
expectations among people whose pattern of life had been disrupted
by the effects of migration" (p. 256).

225.   Nelson, Geoffrey K. "The Spiritualist Movement and the Need for a
        Redefinition of Cult." JOURNAL FOR THE SCIENTIFIC STUDY OF RELI-
        GION 8 (1969): 152-60.

Examines the spiritualist movement with its two main beliefs,
namely the survival of human personality after death and the possibility of communicating with the spirits of the dead. The main
difficulties in fitting Spiritualism into the church-sect typology
are discussed. The concept of cult, implicit in Troeltsch's works,
where he regards "mysticism" together with church and sect as
another type of religious group, provides a better avenue for classifying Spiritualism and similar organizations. A definition of a

cult is proposed and the origin and its success or dissolution are
discussed. Cults could develop into new religions, survive in
competition with dominant religion, or become secret societies.

226.   Nelson, Geoffrey K. "The Analysis of a Cult: Spiritualism."
        SOCIAL COMPASS 15 (1968): 469-81.

Traces the development of the concept of cult and applies it to
spiritualism. Three traits peculiar to cults are noted: 1) the
stress on the need for a religious experience (psychic, mystical,
or ecstatic); 2) the fundamental break from traditional religion;
and 3) the concern with the problems of the individual rather than
with those of the group. Cults are classified into 1) cult movements (diffused collectivities, such as the spiritualist movement,
Witchcraft, and the occult); 2) local cults (that come into being
to satisfy the religious needs of people, like Theosophy and
charismatic groups); and 3) centralized cults (that are made up of
several local groups linked together). Spiritualism is a cult
movement that has two main centralized divisions (the Spiritualist
National Federation and the Spiritualists' National Union Limited)
and many local cults.

227.   New, Peter Kong-Ming, and Rhea Pendergrass Priest. "Food and
        Thought: A Sociological Study of Food Cultists." JOURNAL OF
        THE AMERICAN DIETIC ASSOCIATION 51.1 (1967): 13-18.

Discusses the interest in health food that often contradicts
orthodox medical practices. Two groups of health food users are
distinguished: 1) the general users who claim that a variety of
foods contribute to human health; and 2) the unitary users who
insist on one particular type of health food diet. The second type
of health food users form a more cohesive entity and may have some
cultic features. The author holds that "the use of health food is
but one manifestation of a feeling of unrest and dissatisfaction
among the users" (p. 14) and may have some countercultural elements,
including a negative attitude towards physicians. Health food is
symbolic of both life and the quest for peace of mind.

228.   O'Dea, Thomas F. "Catholic Sectarianism: A Sociological Analysis
        of the So-Called Boston Heresy Case." REVIEW OF RELIGIOUS RE-
        SEARCH 3 (1961): 49-63.

Presents a study of a Catholic sectarian group that originated in
1940 as a Catholic student organization in St. Benedict Center in
Cambridge, Massachusetts. After some reflections on the strains
inherent in the pre-Vatican II Catholic Church, the author describes three overriding themes of this movement: 1) its opposition
to secular education and to Catholic students attending secular
colleges and universities; 2) its complaints about the secular
emphasis within the Catholic Church; and 3) its attempt to draw a
very sharp distinction between Catholics and non-Catholics. Separation, austerity, and conviction of persecution were among the
sectarian tendencies that St. Benedict Center had developed by the
late 1940's. The crisis with church authorities, which led the
group to become a "dissenting sect," are chronicled.

229.   O'Dea, Thomas F. THE MORMONS. Chicago: University of Chicago
        Press, 1957. xiii, 289 pp.

        Presents a classical sociological study of Mormonism. Besides an
        attempt to view the origin of the Mormons in the sociocultural
        context of the nineteenth century, this book analyzes the values of
        Mormonism, its social institutions, and its sources of strain and
        conflict. Because Mormonism has, to a large degree, been reinte-
        grated into its parent culture and has made accommodations to, and
        compromises with, American society, the issue of its relevance is
        discussed. While the author thinks that stress and discord are
        inherent to Mormonism, he still believes it is a vital institution
        that will survive.

230.   O'Dea, Thomas F. "Mormonism and the Avoidance of Sectarian Stagna-
        tion: A Study of Church, Sect, and Incipient Nationality." AMER-
        ICAN JOURNAL OF SOCIOLOGY 60 (1954): 285-93.

        Dwells on two major questions regarding Mormonism: 1) how did the
        Church avoid becoming a sect?; and 2) can it be considered an
        ecclesiastical body or a church in the way the term has been used
        in sociological literature? The criteria for distinguishing church
        and sect commonly found among sociologists are then applied to
        Mormonism. The author sketches the origin of the Mormon Church and
        discovers ideological, historical, social, and structural factors
        that hindered its development into a typical sect. He thinks that
        Mormonism is neither a church (or denomination) nor a sect, though
        it has adopted characteristics from both. It developed from being
        a "near-sect" to a "near-nation," a development similar to the
        emergence of ancient nations and empires from religious groups.

231.   Peven, Dorothy E. "The Use of Religious Revival Techniques to
        Indoctrinate Personnel: The Home-Party Sales Organizations."
        SOCIOLOGICAL QUARTERLY 9 (1968): 97-106.

        Compares ways in which home-party companies (like Tupperware)
        maintain an effective sales program by using methods similar to
        those employed by evangelical crusaders like Billy Graham to lead
        people to religious conversion and commitment. Loyalty-building,
        recognition, rewards, weekly sales assemblies, local rallies, and
        national meetings are buttressed by a kind of religious philosophy.
        The following religious elements are observed in the home-party
        sales organizations: a belief system, faith, the promise of future
        rewards, a sense of communion, a sense of belonging to an esoteric
        group, the idea of salvation, and a missionary spirit.

232.   Pfautz, Harold W. "Christian Science: A Case Study of the Social
        Psychological Aspect of Secularization." SOCIAL FORCES 34
        (1956): 246-51.

        Theorizes that religious groups change from emotional to rational
        associations when they grow in size, variety, age, and power.
        Christian Science is taken as an example to illustrate this
        hypothesis. About 3,000 testimonies from Christian Scientists in

the United States published in official periodicals between 1890
and 1950 are analyzed. The author concludes that Christian Science
has been subjected to the process of secularization, a process
demonstrated by the fact that purposeful rational motives and
secular, sociopsychological explanations have increased.

233.   Poll, Solomon. THE HASIDIC COMMUNITY OF WILLIAMSBURG: A STUDY IN
       THE SOCIOLOGY OF RELIGION. New York: Schocken Books, 1969. x,
       308 pp.

       Presents a sociological study of a closely-knit Hasidic Jewish
       community in Brooklyn, New York. The author describes the
       characteristics of these Jews, their origin, the way they maintain
       their isolation from the rest of society including other Jews, and
       the norms that shape their community. A major part of this book is
       dedicated to the study of their economic activities. The impor-
       tance of religious performances that bestow status on members is
       underscored. In an appendix the author discusses several problems
       that the researcher encounters in the study of Hasidic communities.

234.   Redekop, Calvin. "Decision Making in a Sect." REVIEW OF RELIGIOUS
       RESEARCH 2 (1960): 79-86.

       Reports on how decisions are made in the Old Colony Mennonite
       Church. Pointing out that sect ideology has a cognitive orienta-
       tion based on a dichotomy of the world in clear categories of black
       and white, the author discusses four major principles of sectarian
       decisions: 1) shock insulation; 2) efficiency; 3) pressure from
       uncontrollable sources; and 4) perpetuation. The desire to keep
       out any secular encroachment into sect life is behind many
       decisions that regulate sects.

235.   Reed, Louis S. THE HEALING CULTS. A STUDY OF SECTARIAN MEDICAL
       PRACTICE: ITS EXTENT, CAUSES, AND CONTROL. Chicago: University
       of Chicago Press, 1932. 134 pp.

       Presents a study of healing beliefs and practices that are out-
       side the limits of scientific medicine. Five major areas or types
       of cultic and sectarian healing practices are discussed: 1) osteo-
       pathy; 2) chiropractic; 3) naturopathy and other drugless healing
       methods; 4) Christian Science and various forms of New Thought
       healing; and 5) other types of healings, such as spiritual and
       religious healing in the mainline churches and magical practices.
       The author thinks that, while several of the above-mentioned heal-
       ing groups, like osteopathy, chiropractic, and naturopathy, can
       gradually be absorbed by the regular medical system, cults like
       Christian Science, which deny the very existence of disease, can
       hardly follow the same evolutionary course. Medical sects, in the
       author's opinion, "exist in part because they provide a short cut
       for those who lack time, money, or mental capacity to attain the
       qualifications demanded of the medical profession" (p. 110). It is
       admitted that the deficiencies in the scientific method are also
       one of the causes that propel people to medical cults. The ques-
       tion of whether and to what extent should these cults be socially
       and legally controlled is finally discussed.

236. Robbins, Thomas. "Eastern Mysticism and the Resocialization of
        Drug Users: The Meher Baba Cult." JOURNAL FOR THE SCIENTIFIC
        STUDY OF RELIGION 9 (1969): 308-17.

        Observes that Eastern mystical movements in the United States
        of America draw their membership partly from young adults who had
        previously experienced psychedelic drugs. The view is advanced
        that religious sects or cults can function as resocialization
        agents in that they "a) provide continuity with the initial values
        of the clientele thus avoiding sharp breaks, and b) allow their
        clients to express their resentment against dominant mores while
        simultaneously c) socializing these persons into aspects of these
        mores" (p.309). The resocialization process is illustrated by a
        study of the Meher Baba cult. According to the author, those who
        join it make a shift "from mysticism to inner worldly asceticism"
        and from a hippie lifestyle to a more acceptable one. Commitment
        to Meher Baba provides a rationale for giving up the deviant
        behavior that is linked with alienation.

237. Robertson, Roland. "The Salvation Army: The Persistence of Sec-
        tarianism." PATTERN OF SECTARIANISM (item 149), pp. 49-105.

        Explores the reasons why the Salvation Army maintains some sepa-
        ration from society at large in spite of some accommodations that
        have taken place throughout its history. Three areas of investi-
        gation are pursued: 1) the Salvation Army's doctrine, worship, and
        social teachings (including its eschatological beliefs and faith
        healing practices); 2) its organization; and 3) its social constit-
        uency. Its membership is divided into those who want to maintain
        the original communal features of the movement, those who prefer to
        keep up the basic elements but are willing to allow some changes,
        and, finally, those who see the need to revitalize the Army and
        adapt it to modern, social conditions. The author suggests that
        the Salvation Army is an established sect and a religious order
        within Anglicanism.

238. Romano, Octavio Ignacio. "Charismatic Medicine, Folk-Healing, and
        Folk-Sainthood." AMERICAN ANTHROPOLOGIST 67 (1965): 1151-73.

        Studies the popular beliefs about medicine men among Mexican-
        Americas in South Texas. The author first gives an outline of
        traditional behavioral patterns that govern the daily lives of the
        Mexican-American community and defines the role of the healer.
        Then he shows how there is a healing hierarchy among practitioners
        that depends on success in healing. Finally, the specific case of
        a healer is considered and his rise from obscurity to sainthood
        after his death is discussed. The nature of charisma and its
        effects on the peasants under study are considered. The faith
        healer in this instance was an example of a "charismatic-renovator,"
        who is likely to meet institutional resistance.

239. Rubin, Israel. "Chassidic Community Behavior." ANTHROPOLOGICAL
        QUARTERLY 37 (1964): 138-48.

        Presents a field study of the Satmarer Hasidic Jews of Brooklyn.
        The circumstances that gave rise to the movement are summarized and

several behavior patterns of the group analyzed. Hasidism is described as a revitalization movement that came into being in "an
atmosphere of extreme stress," coupled with disorganization, ignorance, and despair. Hasidic Jews have differed from Orthodox Jews
in two main respects: they belong to a particular type of closely
knit community under a charismatic leader; and they stress the
expressive element in their behavior. Hasidic Judaism is a type of
community that may lead to reduced stress in the urban society of
the twentieth century, which explains its success and tenacity.

240.   Sargent, Leslie N. "Occupational Status in a Religious Group."
       REVIEW OF RELIGIOUS RESEARCH 4 (1963): 149-55.

       Suggests that the Seventh-Day Adventist Church, which recruits
       its members largely from farmers and other low middle-class occu-
       pational groups, has not maintained its low-class membership in
       spite of its unique religious practices, like the observance of the
       Sabbath and the rigid prohibition of alcohol and tobacco. Church
       members are pressured to improve their social standing and, conse-
       quently, their occupational status has improved. This upward
       mobility, according to the author, does not seem to have brought
       with it a substantial risk to their church allegiance.

241.   Schniederman, Leo. "Ramakrishna: Personality and Social Factors in
       the Growth of a Religious Movement." JOURNAL FOR THE SCIENTIFIC
       STUDY OF RELIGION 8 (1969): 60-71.

       Describes the main features of the Ramakrishna Movement that
       originated in India in the late nineteenth century. Two develop-
       ments are considered in this study: 1) the movement as a permanent,
       organized network of agencies with barely no traces of the charis-
       matic leadership that brought it into being; and 2) a service-
       oriented organization that contrasts sharply with the founder's
       mystical, other-worldly view of religion. The author contends that
       Ramakrishna's personality was the vehicle through which the psycho-
       logical needs of his disciples were expressed and satisfied, that
       his personality and teachings provided the meaningful basis for
       reforms within Hinduism, and that his own detachment from organiza-
       tional roles permitted his followers to develop the movement along
       other lines that it had taken at its birth.

242.   Sharot, Stephen. "A Jewish Christian Adventist Movement." JEWISH
       JOURNAL OF SOCIOLOGY 10 (1968): 35-45.

       Examines a small Jewish-Christian community that resulted from
       the persecution of the Jews by the Germans during World War II and
       that emphasized messianism. It was founded by Abram Poljak, a
       Russian-born Jew who opened the first "Christian Synagogue" or
       "Jewish Church" in London in 1944. The history of the group is
       traced and its strong leadership under Poljak (who died in 1963)
       underscored. Though the belief system of the group was a response
       to the conditions in Europe at a specific time in history, the
       followers of Poljak maintained an identity by interpreting their
       initial experience and world events in terms of their basic belief
       system. The Arabs have now replaced the Germans as the tools of

Satan. This religious sect had tended to unite Jewish and Christian religious practices, celebrating, for example, both the Jewish
Pesach and the Christian Easter. Jewish practices have declined
since the group has attracted more gentiles than Jews into its
fold.

243.   Simmons, J. L. "On Maintaining Deviant Belief Systems: A Case
        Study." SOCIAL PROBLEMS 11 (1964): 250-57.

        Explains the means by which the beliefs of a small group of
        mystics (called the "Espers" by the author), who live in a rather
        isolated mountainous area in the State of Georgia, are maintained
        in the face of a disbelieving larger society. Their main occult
        beliefs, including reincarnation, are described. Five mechanisms
        that make belief in a deviant religious perspective easier are
        identified: 1) attention is kept on those perceptions that are in
        harmony with one's beliefs; 2) social situations are structured to
        support one's belief system; 3) ambiguous evidence is interpreted
        as a confirmation of one's beliefs; 4) association with people who
        share the same beliefs is encouraged; and 5) an ambivalent attitude
        of larger culture toward deviant belief systems tends to strengthen
        the believer's involvement. Religious beliefs cannot be tested and
        are, therefore, safe from the challenge of empirical events.

244.   Sobel, B. Z. "The Tools of Legitimization--Zionism and the Hebrew
        Christian Movement." JEWISH JOURNAL OF SOCIOLOGY 10 (1968):
        241-50.

        Explains how the Hebrew Christian Movement, which had its roots
        in the missionary failures of the nineteenth century, adopted the
        view that conversion to Christianity did not entail the loss of
        Jewish ethnicity. The history of the Hebrew Christian Movement,
        from its birth in London in 1813 as a group calling itself "Sons of
        Abraham," is traced. The basic beliefs of the movement are out-
        lined. The author examines "the devices utilized by Hebrew Chris-
        tians to underscore the traditional acceptability and legal basis
        for the avowal of Christianity as the 'bona fide' religious
        expression of the Jews" (p. 245). One such device to legitimize
        Hebrew Christianity was Zionism.

245.   Sprague, Theodore W. "Some Notable Features in the Authority
        Structure of a Sect." SOCIAL FORCES 21 (1943): 344-50.

        Studies the authority structure of the Jehovah's Witnesses. Four
        principal agencies that exercise authority within this sect are
        distinguished: Jehovah, the Bible, The Watchtower Bible and Tract
        Society, and the president of the corporation. The personal and
        impersonal relationships that church members have with the above-
        mentioned agencies are examined.

246.   Stahlman, William D. "Astrology in Colonial America: An Extended
        Query." WILLIAM AND MARY QUARTERLY 13 (1956): 551-63.

        Suggests various lines of inquiry that could determine the extent
        and seriousness of the use of astrology in Colonial America. In
        spite of the fact that astrology is often relegated to the history

of human error, no one seems to doubt "its social role in the formation of the present-day world, nor its influence on many human
activities" (p. 551). After giving a brief historical background,
several areas of research are suggested.

247.   Steinberg, Stephen. "Reform Judaism: The Origin and Evolution of
        a 'Church Movement.'" JOURNAL FOR THE SCIENTIFIC STUDY OF RELI-
        GION 5 (1965): 117-29.

        Discusses whether Reform Judaism is a church or a sect. After
        summarizing Benton Johnson's refinement of the church-sect typol-
        ogy, the author attempts to show that the Jewish Reform Movement is
        an anomaly in that it aims "to modify institutional norms and
        values that were discrepant with those of the larger society" (p.
        120). Reform Judaism is said to be a "church movement" that, in
        opposition to Orthodox Judaism from which it sprang, attempted to
        conform more closely to secular society. The various stages of the
        movement are analyzed. Reform Judaism created a new form of
        Judaism for those Jews who wished to maintain their marginality and
        yet achieve some adaptation to society.

248.   Trevor-Roper, H. R. "Witches and Witchcraft: An Historical Essay
        (II)." ENCOUNTER 28.6 (June 1967): 13-34.

        Continues the examination of the European witch-craze of the
        sixteenth and seventeenth centuries. Differences between Catholic
        and Protestant reactions to witches are discussed and various en-
        cyclopedias and manuals of witchcraft produced during the period
        analyzed. So entrenched was the intellectual basis of the witch-
        craze that "every crucial state in the ideological struggle of the
        Reformation was a stage also in the revival and perpetuation of the
        witch-craze" (p. 22). The mythology surrounding witchcraft was, in
        the author's view, more than mere fantasy; it was also a stereotype
        of fear. Witchcraft was created out of a social situation, namely,
        the conflict between the feudal society of the time and social
        groups that could not be assimilated into it. The decline and
        collapse of the witch-craze are documented.

249.   Trevor-Roper, H. R. "Witches and Witchcraft: An Historical Essay
        (I)." ENCOUNTER 28.5 (May 1967): 3-25.

        Discusses the European witch-craze of the sixteenth and seven-
        teenth centuries and states that its origins in the Alps is well
        established. "The mountains, then are the home not only of sorcery
        and witchcraft but also of primitive religious forms and resistance
        to new orthodoxies" (p. 11). The persecutions, to which both Jews
        and witches were subjected, share several features and can be
        more readily interpreted as forms of "social intolerances" rather
        than of intellectual differences. Both Jews and witches symbolized
        social nonconformity. The genesis of the sixteenth-century witch-
        craze is explained in two stages, the first being the tension be-
        tween orthodox believers and social nonconformists that generated
        the systematic mythology of witchcraft, the second the interpre-
        tation of unorthodox and antisocial behavior in terms of that myth-
        ology.

250.   Vann, Richard T. THE SOCIAL DEVELOPMENT OF ENGLISH QUAKERISM,
         1665-1755. Cambridge: Harvard University Press, 1969. xiv,
         260 pp.

         Examines various aspects of the development of English Quakerism
         during its first century in existence. Conversion to this sect is
         discussed in the terms used by Quakers themselves. The main social
         and religious features of Quakerism, its changing place within the
         social order, the dynamics of its organization, and the response of
         its members to persecution are dealt with. The author discusses
         the transition of Quakerism from a movement into a sect. A lengthy
         bibliography (pp. 216-50) includes a comprehensive list of primary
         sources.

251.   Vann, Richard T. "Quakerism and the Social Structure in the Inter-
         regnum." PAST AND PRESENT, No. 43 (May 1969): 71-91.

         Suggests that the early Quakers came from the middle and upper-
         middle classes (yeomen and traders) and examines the historical
         records in some parts of England (including Norfolk and Norwich) to
         support his view. This article contains many references to the
         debate among social historians on the social composition of early
         Quakerism.

252.   Vogt, Evon Z., and Peggy Golde. "Some Aspects of the Folklore of
         Water Witching in the United States." JOURNAL OF AMERICAN FOLK-
         LORE 71 (1958): 519-31.

         Provides a brief historical background of water witching in
         Europe and then describes its practice and folklore in the United
         States. The authors dismiss the view that water witching is just a
         superstitious custom that persists among uneducated people as in-
         adequate. They insist that magical divination, of which water
         witching is an example, persists in Western culture "because there
         are potent psychological and social reasons for its continued
         practice" (p. 528). Their research led them to conclude that there
         is a definite relationship between the degree of uncertainty and
         risk and the flourishing of water-witching beliefs and practices.
         Water witching is a response to anxiety that has been created or
         aggravated by modern science. Its practice can be interpreted as a
         denial that science is able to provide answers to all human ills
         and problems. This essay contains references to other works of the
         authors on the subject of water witching.

253.   Vogt, Evon Z., and Ray Hyman. WATER WITCHING: U.S.A. Chicago:
         University of Chicago Press, 1959. ix, 248 pp.

         Presents a study of water witching or divining in the United
         States. The history of its practice from ancient to current times
         is traced and the technique and folklore surrounding it described.
         Case histories and field tests are analyzed in order to determine
         whether water divining really works. The movement of the rod in
         the divining process is discussed in the context of other psychic
         phenomena. The authors draw a portrait of American diviners with
         reference to their training, sex, age, education, and ethnic back-

ground. They focus largely on the social role of water diviners. Water witching is a form of magical divination and persists in those areas where lack of adequate water supply causes anxiety and uncertainty. It is, therefore, a way of coping with these psychological problems and functions, as magic does in nonliterate societies, to reduce stress.

254.   Warburton, T. Rennie. "Holiness Religion: An Anomaly of Sectarian Typologies." JOURNAL FOR THE SCIENTIFIC STUDY OF RELIGION 9 (1969): 130-39.

Argues that Holiness and Pentecostal religion should not be classified in the same religious type since they stress different kinds of religious experiences. A brief examination of the origin, development, and essential features of Holiness religion is made. Both Holiness and Pentecostal religion are conversionist, sect-type organizations; both enjoin social proscriptions on their members; and both encourage ideological separateness from other religions. They differ, however, in their doctrines, their organizations, their inspirational meetings, and in the social background of the individuals they recruit. The factors that prevented Holiness religion from becoming as widespread and varied as Pentecostalism are scrutinized. Holiness religion, with its stress on moral purity and subjective experience, was never really distinct from Orthodox Protestantism and its evangelical environment.

255.   Warburton, T. Rennie. "Organization and Change in a British Holiness Movement." PATTERNS OF SECTARIANISM (item 149), pp. 106-37.

Traces the origin of the Holiness Movement to Methodist revivals in the early nineteenth century. The author contends that early Holiness groups were essentially interdenominational, though they acquired a more distinct denominational character by the end of the century. He focuses on one particular Holiness group, the Emmanuel Holiness Church founded by J. D. Drysdale in 1916 in Edinburgh, Scotland. The history of the church, its distinctive, sectarian traits, and its major goals are summarized. It is held that the Emmanuel Church is more "an independent Mission than a distinctive independent sect" (p. 120), even though it possesses a number of sect-like attributes (like the injunction that members abstain from smoking and dancing). The movement has since experienced a process of bureaucratization that has led to a modification of its structure, becoming less charismatic and acquiring a professional ministry. The author's view is that the church has become more like a "missionary agency."

256.   Wardwell, Walter I. "A Marginal Professional Role: The Chiropractor." SOCIAL FORCES 30 (1952): 339-48.

Discusses the role of the chiropractor whose profession lacks social prestige and status and is marginal in comparison to the well-institutionalized position of the medical doctor. The functions of the chiropractor as they relate to the practitioners themselves, their patients, and society as a whole are investigated. The chiropractic profession provides "a channel for therapeutic

innovation alternate to that of the medical profession" (p. 346).
The chiropractor performs the function of legitimizing the sick
status of individuals who are found to be healthy by medical
doctors. The author thinks that the two professions might eventually merge. This type of marginality of role is common in modern
society because of the frequent and rapid changes that take place
in role-definitions.

257.   Whitam, Frederick J. "Revivalism as Institutionalized Behavior: An
        Analysis of the Social Base of a Billy Graham Crusade." SOUTH-
        WESTERN SOCIAL SCIENCE QUARTERLY 49 (1968): 115-27.

        Argues that revivalism is not a form of unstructured, irrational,
        and emotional behavior; rather, it is institutionalized and predic-
        table. The occupations, ethnicity, and the religious backgrounds
        of the converts of the 1957 Billy Graham Crusades in New York are
        carefully recorded. The conclusions indicate that those people who
        made religious decisions at these crusades came "from the ranks of
        White, middle class, 'old' Americans who were already identified
        with major Protestant denominations" (p. 117). The social base of
        Billy Graham's Crusades is not, as it is so commonly assumed to be,
        the disgruntled minority, the deprived members of the lower class,
        or the unchurched members of society. The author insists that
        social or normative, rather than psychological or psychopathologi-
        cal, theories of religious behavior are more likely to explain the
        success of these crusades.

258.   Whitley, Oliver Read. "The Sect-to-Denomination Process in an
        American Religious Movement: The Disciples of Christ." SOUTHWEST
        SOCIAL SCIENCE QUARTERLY 36 (1955): 275-81.

        Discusses whether historical data support the conclusion that a
        religious movement has a "natural history," and whether the sect/
        denomination typology can be used to describe the development of
        the Disciples of Christ. The author's view is that this religious
        group has some sectarian features and is in the process of becoming
        a denomination. Both its own political system and the American
        political milieu act as major hindrances to its becoming a church.
        It is suggested that, in the case of the Disciples of Christ, the
        movement from sect to denomination is associated with their shift
        from a largely rural group to an increasingly urban one.

259.   Whitten, Norman E. "Contemporary Patterns of Malign Occultism
        Among Negroes in North Carolina." JOURNAL OF AMERICAN FOLKLORE
        75 (1962): 311-25.

        Examines occult beliefs and practices (called "maleficia") among
        Blacks in North Carolina, emphasizing those that attribute misfor-
        tunes to evil activities. The role of the professional diviner or
        curer is one of the topics dealt with. The author traces the ori-
        gins of Black occultism to European practices of the seventeen and
        eighteenth centuries and maintains that it has survived because of
        "cultural lag," that is, because of the lower educational and
        social positions of Blacks in the United States. Occult practices
        are said to have the function of relieving tension and diminishing
        anxiety.

260.   Willis, Gordon, and Bryan Wilson. "The Churches of God: Patterns
        and Practice." PATTERNS OF SECTARIANISM (item 149), pp. 244-86.

        Studies the Church of God, a sect of some 3000 members that split
        from one branch of the Plymouth Brethren. The context of belief
        and practice among the Open Brethren and the history of previous
        divisions within that body are first reviewed. The Church of God's
        different view of its own origins is explained. The authority
        system within the Churches of God, their social teachings, and
        their social composition are outlined and compared with those of
        the Open Brethren. These churches, according to the authors,
        experience tension in retaining their members, a tension common to
        similar separatist movements.

261.   Wilson, Bryan R. "The Migrating Sects." BRITISH JOURNAL OF
        SOCIOLOGY 18 (1967): 303-314.

        Reviews several books on the Hutterite Society, Mormonism, and
        George Rapp's Harmony Society. The author labels all these groups
        "migrating sects" because they were forced to move from their place
        of origin, a movement that became the most important factor influ-
        encing their development. They share the following features: the
        establishment of colonies for the faithful, the adaptation to col-
        lectivist and communitarian lifestyles, and the maintenance of a
        different language that strengthened their separate identity.

262.   Wilson, Bryan R. SECTS AND SOCIETY: A SOCIOLOGICAL STUDY OF THE
        ELIM TABERNACLE, CHRISTIAN SCIENCE, AND CHRISTADELPHIANS. Berke-
        ley: University of California Press, 1961. x, 397 pp.

        Presents a study of three sects or small religious groups "in
        which membership is voluntary and conditional upon some marks of
        merit--understanding the groups' teachings or experience of some
        personal religious ecstasy--upon the basis of which association can
        arise" (p. 3). These sects are identified as a Pentecostal church
        (Elim Tabernacle), a gnostic cult (Christian Science), and a pre-
        millenarian adventist group (Christadelphians). The organization
        of each is examined in terms of its main teachings, history, social
        structure, and social composition. The way each group interprets
        itself, specifies its relations to outsiders, and conducts its
        recruitment of new members is also covered. The role of the leader
        in each group and the internal schisms are described. The author
        maintains that all three are "established sects" because of the
        denominational tendency to compromise with the outside world.

263.   Wilson, Bryan R. "The Origins of Christian Science." HIBBERT
        JOURNAL 225 (1959): 161-70.

        Points out that Christian Science reflected the prevailing ethos
        of its time, particularly with respect to "the optimism, progres-
        sivism, utopianism, feminism, and pragmatism of that era" (p. 162).
        Some of the early influences on Christian Science are traced and
        the author thinks that there is clear evidence of plagiarism on the
        part of its founder, Mrs. Eddy. Her idea of "malicious animal
        magnetism," which is similar to the primitive notion of sympathetic
        magic, is probably the one original element in her revelations.

264.   Wilson, Bryan R. "The Pentecostal Minister: Role Conflicts and the
        Contradictions of Status." AMERICAN JOURNAL OF SOCIOLOGY 64
        (1959): 494-504.

        Explores the part played by the minister in Pentecostal groups in
        England, where their gradual development from sects to denominations
        can be clearly seen. The acceptance of a permanent, paid minister
        is one feature of such a transformation. Pentecostal ministers
        have become guardians of sectarianism in a denominational setting
        in which revivalism is the main form of recruitment. Their role
        tends to be ambivalent because sects generally stress the priest-
        hood of believers and spontaneous leadership, yet their leaders'
        status has become uniquely different from that of the rest of the
        congregation and their selection depends on conventionality and
        training rather than on charismatic qualities. The main focus of
        attention in this essay is the Foursquare Gospel Alliance.

265.   Wilson, Bryan R. "The Exclusive Brethren: A Case Study in the
        Evolution of a Sectarian Ideology." PATTERNS OF SECTARIANISM
        (item 149), pp. 287-342.

        Discusses schisms within the Plymouth Brethren and the rise of
        one of its splinter groups, the Exclusive Brethren, who adopted
        doctrinal and organizational differences. The author holds that
        the history of these Brethren denotes a progressive development of
        distinctive beliefs and an intensification of sectarian tendencies.
        The debates that took place within the Exclusive Brethren and the
        schisms that came into being are discussed. The Exclusive Brethren
        are an example of a sect that does not evolve into a denomination
        in the course of two generations.

266.   Wilson, John. "British Israelism." SOCIOLOGICAL REVIEW 16 (1969):
        41-57.

        Gives an account of the origin and growth of British Israelism, a
        nineteenth-century movement founded on the belief that the Anglo-
        Saxons are descended from the lost 10 tribes of Israel and are
        destined to inherit their blessings in the last days. The member-
        ship and social composition of several British Israelite groups in
        England are described. It is observed that gradual changes have
        been taking place in the ideology and social base of the movement.
        Its appeal today is to the lower-middle class, whereas originally
        it attracted members from the aristocracy, the military, and the
        colonial middle class. Contemporary British Israelism has a pes-
        simistic view of history and joining it has become a denial of
        social change.

267.   Wilson, John. "The Relation Between Ideology and Organization in a
        Small Religious Group: The British Israelites." REVIEW OF RELI-
        GIOUS RESEARCH 10 (1968): 51-60.

        Examines a religious group that cannot be classified either with
        sects or cults. The author argues that this ambiguous position
        influences the organization, authority, structure, membership, and
        ecclesiology of the group. A brief description of the British

Israelism belief system is given and its features as a religious movement outlined. Unlike many new movements, British Israelism does not have an exclusive membership, makes no claim of having a monopoly on the saving theological truth, and does not require its members to abandon their previous beliefs. British Israelism can thus be regarded as a reformist or restorative, denominational movement that believes in preserving the social order. It is an intellectual persuasion with no promise of a religious experience and no demand of total commitment from its members. British Israelism is compared with the Moral Rearmament Movement.

268.   Wilson, John. "British Israelism: The Ideological Restraints on Sect Organization." PATTERNS OF SECTARIANISM (item 149), pp. 345-76.

Investigates the features of British Israelism which, in spite of its distinctiveness, does not constitute a sect or religious order within British Protestantism. Some of the major beliefs of the group, particularly its central tenet that the British are the literal descendants of the Lost Tribes of Israel, and its historical origins are discussed. The major contributions of some of its leading members, like Richard Brothers, Ralph Wedgewood, and Edward Hine, are dealt with at some length. The author's view is that British Israelism did not become a sect because its teachings did not contradict the main Protestant belief system nor did they offer a protest against society. Those who joined British Israelism kept their church alliances, national obligations, and public service to the community.

269.   Yablonski, Lewis. SYNANON: THE TUNNEL BACK. New York: Macmillan, 1965. vii, 403 pp.

Presents an account of Synanon in its early days. The origins of this alcohol and drug rehabilitation organization and its development from 1958 to 1964 are described in some detail. The social structure of Synanon, with its political and administrative system, its training or indoctrination methods, and its religious observances are accounted for. The evaluations of the group made by the State of California and by the Federal government, as well as some of the early objections to its activities, are recorded. The author sees Synanon, which was founded by Chuck Dietrich, as a new social phenomenon. He maintains that "it is a new kind of group therapy; an effective approach to social integration; a human solution to some facets of bureaucratic organization; a different way of being religious..." (xi). Synanon, he insists, is not a deviant group but the "tunnel back to the human race," offering the newcomer a new direction in life.

270.   Young, Frank W. "Adaptation and Pattern Integration of a California Sect." REVIEW OF RELIGIOUS RESEARCH 1 (1960): 137-150.

Studies a Pentecostal Church in an urban setting in California and discusses several variables of the sect activities, including the intensity of expression during the meetings. The value orientations that mark the relationship between the members and out-

siders are specified. A transition from sect to church seems to
have taken place. The author thinks that his study of this church
supports "the general hypothesis that anomic social conditions are
associated with sect activity and, additionally, that the adaptive
and pattern integrative aspects of sect activity are inversely
related under differing conditions of anomie" (p. 150).

271.   Young, Kimball. ISN'T ONE WIFE ENOUGH? New York: Henry Holt and
        Co., 1954. xii, 476 pp.

        Presents the history of the Mormon custom of polygamy, focusing
on, among other things, how individuals "learn to accept radical
changes in their habits and values" (xi). Three views of polygamy
are described: 1) the antagonistic view, which decried the practice;
2) the official Mormon doctrine; and 3) the position of the average
person who lived a polygamous life. Several chapters are dedicated
to a psychological analysis of the spouses and their children in a
polygamous family. The place of women in Mormon society, the roles
and statuses of the wives in a single household, and the relationship between sex, polygamy, and religion are discussed. The public
controversy over the practice is summarized. The author finally
offers some speculations on the wider implications of plural
marriages in modern society.

272.   Zald, Mayer N., and Patricia Denton. "From Evangelism to General
        Services: The Transformation of the YMCA." ADMINISTRATIVE
        SCIENCE QUARTERLY 8 (1963): 214-34.

        Deals with the transformation of the Young Men's Christian Asso-
ciation (YMCA) from an evangelistic social movement into a general
service organization. The authors trace the history and expansion
of this movement that originally stressed religious proselytization
among single young men who, at the time of the movement's foundation in London in 1844, were migrating in large numbers to the
city. The movement has successfully adapted itself to a changing
society and to the consequent demands made by its clientele. Its
current organizational structure and operation as well as its
organizational dilemmas and role problems are discussed. Several
principles of religious organizational change that might be
applicable to other groups are outlined.

CHAPTER III

GENERAL, THEORETICAL, AND METHODOLOGICAL STUDIES ON

SECTS, CULTS, AND NEW RELIGIOUS MOVEMENTS

The presence of new religious movements or cults in Western society is a widespread phenomenon that has attracted the interests of scholars with different academic backgrounds. It would be difficult to find a social-scientific issue that has received as much attention in the public litera-ture and in mass media than that surrounding the cults.

In this chapter we list general materials on the cults under four inter-related topics, namely: 1) the background to the cults; 2) the extent of their presence in the West and of the scholarly interest in them; 3) the theoretical speculations that have been advanced to explain their emer-gence and persistence; and 4) the debate about the methods that should be employed to study them.

The Background to the Cults

It seems to be an assumed maxim in the social sciences that the rise of new religious movements should not be studied in isolation from their historical antecedents and apart from the sociocultural conditions in which they occur. Cults cannot be interpreted simply by an examination of the motives of their founders or by listing the various psychological needs that membership might satisfy.

Several major factors must be taken into account in the study of con-temporary cults. The first is the nature of religion and the general religious situation of our times. Religious movements are an aspect of religious change and development that can be grasped only if one starts with a dynamic view of religion. One question that has been raised re-gards the "newness" of the the new religious groups. Scholars debate whether they are part of an awakening cycle or a recurrent pattern of religious revivalism in American history (see Barkum, item 284; Gordon-McCutchan, item 353; McLoughlin, items 418-20; and Smith, item 476). Some writers favor an explanation of the cultic phenomenon in the context of other religious developments, such as the success of televangelism (Hadden and Shupe, item 357 and Hadden and Swan, item 359), the growth of conser-vative churches (see Kelley, items 389 and 390; Bibby, item 295; and Bibby and Brinkerhoff, item 298), and the increased strength of fundamentalism in different parts of the world (see, for instance, Marsden, item 412 and Sandeen, item 1450). Members of these movements manifest features, like authoritarianism and antagonism to society, that are often linked with cultism and sectarianism.

An added reason why cults must be studied in relation to broader religious phenomena is because they share several major religious dimensions with the so-called mainline traditions. Conversion (Ferris, item 337 and Heirich, item 366), religious involvement (Roberts and Davis, item 456 and Roof, item 461), religious commitment (Hall, item 360; Kanter 383; and Stark and Bainbridge, item 478), and disaffiliation (Hunsberger, items 373-375) are related features shared by all religious groups. They cannot be studied as detached, unrelated phenomena since, to mention one example, disaffiliation from one's traditional religious upbringing and conversion to a new cult may be two sides of the same coin.

The second factor that social science takes for granted is that religious movements are a species of social movement (see Freeman, item 343; and Ash, item 277; and Banks, item 282). Communes, utopias, and millennial groups must be included since new religious movements are often communal, utopian, and/or millenarian. Nonreligious movements cannot be ignored since they share some elements and features with religious groups. Wilson (item 507), for instance, includes the Charismatic Movement and Soka Gakkai in his study of social movements. Both religious and secular movements can be seen as revitalization movements. Studies of communes (see, for instance, Rigby, items 454 and 455), utopias (Berger, items 292 and 293; Cohen, item 331; and Fairfield, item 334), and millenarian societies (Barkum, item 283) provide a broader perspective in which the new cults can be placed. Topics like charismatic leadership and sex roles, both of which are heavily criticized in the context of the new cults, have been studied in depth in noncultic groups (see Barnes, item 288; Camic, item 308; Downton, item 325; Lauer and Lauer, item 402; Lewis, item 505; and Muncy, items 429 and 431).

The third factor, almost universally accepted by social scientists, is the relationship between contemporary religious and social movements to similar phenomena in the past. New and old communes (Kephart, item 391; Gardner, items 347 and 348; and Oved, item 438) and utopias (Moment and Kraushaar, item 425) are often studied together in the belief that their comparison will contribute to a deeper understanding of both past and present communitarian lifestyles. The nineteenth-century religious ferment (see Gaustad, item 350) manifests both many of the characteristics of contemporary cults and the societal reactions to their presence. Examples of how historical data can help towards understanding are plentiful. The current interest in Holistic Health acquires a new meaning when seen in the framework of traditional folk medicine (Jackson, item 376, and Jarvis, item 378). The emergence of Black religious movements with their frequent reliance on African beliefs and practices is deeply rooted in history (Simpson, item 474). Even recent arrivals, such as Buddhism and Hinduism, can be traced to the end of the nineteenth century. The apparent increase in witchcraft and magical beliefs and practices should not come as a surprise to those acquainted with the history of magic (see Douglas, item 324; Ehrenreich and English, item 328; O'Keefe, item 436; and Winkelman, 510; and Thomas, item 487). The new cults have their roots not only in foreign lands, but also in American culture.

The main feature of social-scientific studies of social and religious movements is the relationship between social factors and participation in these movements (see, for example, Bland and Wallis, item 300). It is a generally accepted view among social scientists that the rise of the new

religious movements must be traced to the counterculture of the 1960's
(Bellah, item 290; Carroll, item 309; Flacks, item 339; and Shepherd, item
470). Many would hold that it would be next to impossible to understand
the emergence of the cults without reference to the secularization process
(Martin, item 413; Dobbelaere, items 321-23; and Duke and Johnson, item
326). More specifically, one can refer to Lasch's attempt (item 399) to
characterize Western culture as being essentially narcissistic, a condition that has been interpreted as conducive to the formation and success
of cults and to the studies of Zurcher and Kirkpatrick (items 525-29) who
have related the rise of moral crusades to status inconsistency and defense (see also Wilson and Zurcher, items 408 and 409, and Wallis's critique, item 496).

The Extent of the Cultic Presence

The many surveys and assessments of new religious movements over the
last 15 years lead to the conclusion that the cults have spread to all
Western countries. Even Northern European countries, such as Sweden
(see items 635, 670, 721, and 722), where secularization has reached an
advanced state, have not been spared from the surge of new religions since
the late 1960's. Though the United States is often assumed to lead in the
proliferation of cults, some scholars have raised doubts whether this is
really the case (see Stark, item 959).

While there is evidence that membership in the cults was never as high
as the cults themselves advertised or as the public and some commentators
on the cultic scene believed, the activities of some cults and the public
campaigns against them made it seem that the new religious movements were
just about to supplant the Judeo-Christian tradition. The "Great Cult
Scare" (see Bromley and Shupe, item 581) was based on an exaggeration of
cultic membership and influence. This assessment is confirmed by the fact
that most cults peaked by the 1980's and that some of them have experienced
a decline.

It would be incorrect, however, to assume that most of the new cults
will die out in the near future. The new religious movements are here to
stay, even though by far the large majority of them comprise, at most,
only a few thousand members. To what extent the cults will influence
traditional religious beliefs and practices is still unclear. The fact
that churches have responded to the cults is already indicative of some
impact (Brockway and Rajashekar, item 577). Any response to the cults
implies not only critique of their belief systems and activities, but also
self reflection. Therefore, cults might indirectly influence the established churches to stress certain aspects of their doctrines and to make
specific practical recommendations to their members. It will not be surprising if some cultic behavior will be adopted and reinterpreted. Christian theologians and spiritual directors were talking of "Christian Yoga"
and "Christian Zen" before the cultic presence was felt as a social menace
and a religious threat. It will certainly not come as a surprise if the
emphasis on an inner religious experience, which is central to most cults,
will eventually find its way into the mainline churches.

This state of affairs suggests that the new movements in the West are
a unified phenomenon that cannot be fully explained by simple deprivation
theory or by some kind of medical model of individual psychopathology.

Religion toward the end of the twentieth century may be undergoing changes
that are too complex to analyze or to predict. What makes the social-
scientific study of new religious movements interesting and challenging
is precisely the possibility that many theories can be adduced to explain
them. As one reads the scholarly attempts to grasp the significance of
the cults in a secularized world, one is led to the inevitable conclusion
that their presence is somewhat enigmatic.

Theoretical Speculations

The major theories of cult formation and success have been briefly
outlined in the introduction. At the root of many of these theories lies
the presupposition that cults fulfill genuine religious, social, and psychological needs not met by the established churches. While such theories
are attractive, it is becoming increasingly clear that they cannot provide
a completely satisfactory explanation (cf. Heelas and Haglund-Heelas, item
829). One has to bear in mind that many individuals who abandon the faith
of their upbringing do not join a cult. Cults may not be the only way in
which certain types of human needs are met. Why only a relatively small
number of people join a deviant cult, rather than find meaning and fulfillment in their respective tradition or just become agnostics or
atheists, is not an easy question to answer.

It is also possible that several theories are needed to account for
the presence of the cults. Social, religious, and psychological factors
may have to be combined to provide an interpretation of the emergence of
new religions. An analysis of the general cultural conditions in the West
could throw some light on the reasons why people might be looking into
other religious options. Western culture stresses the individual and his
or her freedom to chose, for example, one's career and, consequently,
offers people many options in various spheres of life. The development of
this Western trait may have reached a stage where religion, too, has become
an option. In other words, just as young adults may choose a career and
political allegiance that differ radically from those of their parents,
now they have the opportunity to select their own religion, which may not
be that of their parents. One can surmise that the proliferation of cults
makes sense in a market economy in which religion in different forms has
become a marketable item. Cults arise and succeed because they are in
demand, a demand that depends not necessarily on one's needs but on the
fact that people are socialized into a culture in which one has to make
important choices affecting one's ideology and lifestyle. The selection
of a particular cult might depend on one's individual experiences, education, and contacts.

Studying the Cults

The controversy about the methods of studying the cults discussed in
the introduction has repercussions on the kind of explanatory theories
that scholars devise and on the manner in which research is conducted.
Two issues in this respect have been disputed in scholarly literature.

The first debate concerns itself with conferences sponsored by the new
religious movements. Three major groups, namely the Unification Church,
the Hare Krishna Movement, and Scientology, have led the way in planning
and funding the meetings of scholars from various academic fields to

discuss religious issues, especially those pertaining to their presence in the West. The focus of the debate has been whether the cult's influence on the scholars in such conferences minimizes their objectivity to such a degree that they become tools in the cult's own propaganda machine. Although the majority of social scientists maintain that their scholarly research has not been marred by their participation in and contribution to these meetings, several writers have accused the cults of using scholars to enhance their position in society and scholars themselves of aiding the cults by indirectly promoting their goals (see, for instance, O'Toole, item 1079).

There is little doubt that the effort and money invested by some cults in scholarly gatherings has been well worth it. These meetings have certainly boosted the morale of members. They have further fostered the cults' claim to legitimacy and respectability in the eyes of their own members. Whether they have had the same effect on the public and on the scholars themselves is not so obvious. Social scientists who regularly participate in the Unification Church's conferences know exactly what the church is trying to achieve. To suggest that such participation automatically means acceptance of the cult's beliefs and/or endorsement of its practices and claims borders on the ridiculous.

The relationship between many scholars and the cults, especially the three mentioned above, has been symbiotic. The movements have come up with the funds and opportunity for research and travel. Scholars, by conducting their studies in a neutral, nonjudgmental fashion, have contributed to the individual movement's self-image of a church or religion on an equal par with other religious traditions. This relationship is, in some respects, similar to that between the new religions and the Anti-Cult Movement. To accuse scholars of intentionally or unintentionally aiding the cults in their evangelization and proselytizing efforts is, to say the least, unrealistic. Much of the debate that has been conducted on the topic of participation in cult-organized conferences has been initiated by those whose negative views of new religions have been seriously questioned by eminent and highly respected social scientists. If social-scientific descriptions of cultic beliefs and behavior and theoretical speculations on their impact and significance cannot be refuted, then the only option left is to reject the methodological approaches used to gather information and the theoretical frameworks adopted to explain their presence and success.

Another issue, less discussed than the foregoing one, centers round the participation of cult members in academic conferences. The argument can be stated as follows: cult members who are allowed to read papers at meetings organized by the cults themselves or by a professional society (like the American Academy of Religion, the Society for the Scientific Study of Religion, and the Association for the Sociology of Religion) are basically taking advantage of the opportunity to advertise their faith commitment. Underlying the assumption is the contention that a cult member cannot write a research paper or reflect critically on his or her newly acquired belief system.

The social-scientific response to this line of reasoning is that there is no reason why Moonies and Scientologists could not be trained as sociologists, psychologists, historians, or theologians and apply their training to study their new faiths and that of others. There are Catholic, Lutheran, and Mormon sociologists and historians who have conducted sociological and historical research both on their respective faiths and on other religions and who enjoy the respect of their peers for the integrity of their work and the insight of their theories. There is no way one can evaluate the papers read by members of cults at scholarly conferences except on their own merit. There is evidence that some cult members can reflect critically and perceptively on their own faith commitment and on the beliefs and activities of their movement (see, for instance, Gelberg, items 1725-28, and Mickler, items, 1870-72) and are able to respond intelligently to the anti-cult propaganda (Biermans, item 2122). The same reflections are applicable to those who have left a fringe religious movement and questioned its beliefs and values. It is not difficult to distinguish between evangelical Christians who conduct anticult tirades (such as those of McDowell and Stewart, item 2162) and ex-members who offer intelligent criticism (see Swan, item 2208). It would be disastrous if scholarship were to be judged solely by taking into consideration the religious conviction of the scholars themselves.

A. BACKGROUND MATERIAL FOR THE STUDY OF NEW RELIGIOUS MOVEMENTS

273.   Ald, Roy. THE YOUTH COMMUNES. New York: Tower Publications, 1970. 170 pp.

Provides a journalistic, inside view of of communes that are classified in four types, namely collective settlements, communes, expanded or extended families, and tribal groups. The hippie who lives in a commune is either 1) the high priest, guru, or enlightened teacher; or 2) the disciple or apostle; or 3) the true and committed believer. The author describes the commune scene and dwells on the problems encountered by its members. A now dated guidebook for the new communitarianism (including shelters available and basic foodstuffs), it lists communes in the United States and Canada and various underground newspapers.

274.   Alexander, Daniel. "Is Fundamentalism an Integrism?" SOCIAL COMPASS 32 (1985): 373-92.

Discusses the question whether integrism--first used to refer to the antimodern Catholic current at the turn of the century--is similar to the modern wave of "reactionary ideological-political movements" that are sweeping parts of the world, Iran in particular. The roots of integrism, i.e. the Roman Catholic reaction to secularization and liberalism best exemplified in the Pius X Institute led by Archbishop Lefebvre, are examined. The widespread rise of fundamentalism and the problem of secularization in the United States are described and related to the overall picture of integrism. The author holds that integrism is fundamentally a form of millenarianism.

275.   Alexander, Peter, and Roger Gill, editors. UTOPIAS. London: Duckworth, 1984. xx, 218 pp.

Presents a collection of 17 essays dealing with different aspects
of utopian and millenarian beliefs and practices. The material is
divided in three sections: 1) essays discussing the concept of
utopia and its definitions; 2) essays exploring the features and
impact of utopian thought; and 3) papers questioning the uses and
necessity of utopian thought. The main thrust of these studies is
to examine the values of utopian thinking in making plans for the
future. Several social aspects of utopianism are brought to the
fore. Each essay contains many references to some of the major
writings on utopianism.

Contains item 444.

276. Allain, Mathé, editor. FRANCE AND NORTH AMERICA: UTOPIAS AND
      UTOPIANS: PROCEEDINGS OF THE THIRD SYMPOSIUM OF FRENCH AMERICAN
      STUDIES, March 4-8, 1974. Lafayette: University of Southwest
      Louisiana Press, 1978. xii, 195 pp.

      Presents a collection of essays in which the study of utopianism
      is approached from different historical perspectives. A common
      assumption throughout this volume is that the rise of utopias is
      rooted in the social problems of the various historical periods.
      Among the groups studied are Icaria and Fourierism.

      Contains item 430.

277. Arens, W., and Susan P. Montague, editors. THE AMERICAN DIMENSION:
      CULTURAL MYTHS AND SOCIAL REALITY. Port Washington, NY: Alfred
      Publishing Co., 1977. xvii, 221 pp.

      Presents a collection of essays that examine American culture
      from an anthropological perspective. The material is divided into
      two sections, one dealing with the symbolic analysis of cultural
      phenomena, the other with ways "people adapt and use information to
      formulate real behavior in varieties of social contexts" (ix). The
      essays deal with symbols and rituals as portrayed in sports, in
      popular movies, like STAR TREK and THE EXORCIST, and in TV soap
      operas. Several mythical and ideological themes can be deduced
      from a study of mainstream American culture that manifests, among
      other tendencies, a growing interest in astrology.

      Contains item 2074.

278. Atkinson, Paul. "From Honey to Vinegar: Lévi-Strauss in Vermont."
      CULTURE AND CURING: ANTHROPOLOGICAL PERSPECTIVES ON TRADITIONAL
      BELIEFS AND PRACTICES. Edited by Robert Morley and Roy Wallis.
      Pittsburgh: University of Pittsburgh Press, 1979, pp. 168-88.

      Discusses folk medicine in Vermont from the point of view of the
      sociology of medicine. The types of legitimacy which are claimed
      in the system are briefly outlined. Folk medicine is believed to
      be natural, hallowed by age, simple, efficacious, and scientific.
      The authors analyze the data in terms of Lévi-Strauss's view of the
      antimony between, and integration of, nature and culture. The mix-
      ture and use of honey and vinegar, commonly used in folk medicine,
      are accepted as conducive to happiness and health. It offers "a

logical and a symbolic solution to a number of puzzles posed by the belief system itself--puzzles concerning Man and Nature, health, illness, and curing" (p. 176). Honey and vinegar are ambiguous in nature, combining opposite qualities. United, they bring together once again urban (and cultural) human nature with the innocent, natural grace and health enjoyed in rural Vermont. Given the rise of interest in new diets and views about their effects on human health, this essay offers an anthropological perspective for understanding their popularity.

279.   Bainbridge, William Sims. "The Religious Sociology of Deviance." AMERICAN SOCIOLOGICAL REVIEW 54 (1989): 288-95.

Tests the common sociological view that religion deters individual deviance by encouraging the observance of the norms and values of society. The author uses data on suicide, crime, homosexuality, and cultism. Statistics of church membership and rates of deviance are tabulated. Among the cults are included Christian Science, occult science, the New Age Movement, Transcendental Meditation, and Scientology. It is concluded that religion does deter crime and cultism.

280.   Bainbridge, William Sims. "Utopian Communities: Some Theoretical Issues." THE SACRED AND THE SECULAR: TOWARD REVISION IN THE SCIENTIFIC STUDY OF RELIGION (item 623), pp. 21-35.

Discusses and rejects, in the contexts of utopian communities and religious millenarian movements, the common sociological view that society at large is becoming progressively more secular. The major theoretical and methodological issues in studying these groups are considered. Nineteenth-century communes (like the Shakers and Oneida Community) and more recent ones (like the Lama Foundation and Ananda Cooperative Village) are among the groups studied. The works of Kanter (see items 380-85) and Zablocki (items 514 and 1552) are assessed. The author suggests that it is possible to develop "reliable, valid measures of utopianism itself." He concludes by asserting that "the role of religion in promoting the perfect society remains open" (p. 32).

281.   Baker, Jean Harvey. "Women in Utopia: The Nineteenth-Century Experience." UTOPIAS: THE AMERICAN EXPERIENCE (item 425), pp. 56-71.

Examines the position of women in three nineteenth-century utopian groups, namely the Shakers, the Oneida Community, and the Mormons. The author holds that, although the variety of sexual arrangements makes any generalization on women's place in these societies impossible, it is safe to state that women who joined these groups changed their positions and roles dramatically. Women Shakers and Oneidans moved towards sharing equal rights with men, while Mormon women became more subservient in their traditional female status. The sexual arrangements adopted by the three groups became clear identifying features: the Shakers opted for celibacy; the Oneidans for a complex marriage system; and the Mormons for polygamy. All three groups maintained that, in a perfect society, the traditional role of women has to be drastically altered.

282.   Banks, J. A. THE SOCIOLOGY OF SOCIAL MOVEMENTS. New York: Mac-
       millan, 1972. 62 pp.

       Criticizes the structural-functional approach to the study of
       social movements because one of its main flaws is that it fails to
       explain social change. Instead, the author adopts a method which
       regards social movements as "social technologies" or "invention
       mechanisms." These movements are seen not as the product of social
       change, but rather as the creators of change. The conditions, that
       are historically determined by the social organization and that
       contribute to successful social innovation, are among the topics
       discussed. The author finds similarities between the spread of
       social innovation and technological diffusion. Religious movements
       are not directly included in the author's speculations, but several
       of his theoretical formulations can be applied to them.

283.   Barkum, Michael. CRUCIBLE OF THE MILLENNIUM: THE BURNED-OVER DIS-
       TRICT OF NEW YORK IN THE 1840s. Syracuse, NY: Syracuse Univer-
       sity Press, 1986. xi, 194 pp.

       Examines the causes, forms, and significance of the religious
       ferment in New York State in the middle of the nineteenth century.
       It is argued that Millerism and the utopian communities of the
       period arose from common causes, that is, the rural nature of the
       district and the New England origins of most of the people. The
       differences between Millerism (an urban phenomenon) and utopian
       communities (a rural phenomenon) are explained by their respective
       environments. The relationship between natural and socioeconomic
       disasters and millenarianism are discussed at some length. Miller-
       ism is seen as stressing natural catastrophes, while utopian commu-
       nities focus on social and economic breakdowns. The author finally
       discusses the "millenarian process" which he sees as a recurring
       "social coping mechanism for the management of collective stress"
       (p. 143). He reflects on the current apocalyptic mood of the last
       three decades (from the 1950's to the 1980's), drawing parallels
       between them and the movements of the nineteenth century. A bibli-
       ography of primary and secondary sources (pp. 177-88) is included.

284.   Barkum, Michael. "The Awakening-Cycle Controversy." SOCIOLOGICAL
       ANALYSIS 46 (1985): 425-43.

       Contributes to the discussion on recurrent religious awakenings,
       a discussion that has tended to obscure the issue by equating
       awakenings with peaks in religious activity. The author comments
       on those theorists, who favor the awakening-cycle, and on their
       critics. He favors this theory, but believes it can be modified
       especially by stressing the outbursts of millenarianism. Various
       cyclical models that link revivals with economic depressions, poli-
       tical despair, or revitalization are examined. Areas for further
       study are identified.

285.   Barkum, Michael. "Communal Societies as Cyclical Phenomena."
       COMMUNAL SOCIETIES 4 (1984): 35-48.

       Briefly outlines four intense communal periods that occurred in
       the United States of America in 1) the early nineteenth century; 2)
       the end of last century; 3) the years of the great depression; and

4) the 1960's. These periods are linked with utopian and millennial
ideals and goals. The author maintains that these waves do not
arise "in spontaneous or accidental fashion." He speculates on the
factors, mostly the weakening economic conditions, that influence
their timing. The 1960 wave differed somewhat from the preceding
ones. It is argued that "millenarianism in general and utopianism
in particular are responses to perceived disturbances in the moral
order" (p. 47).

286. Barkum, Michael. DISASTERS AND THE MILLENNIUM. New Haven, CT:
      Yale University Press, 1974. x, 243 pp.

      Explores the relationship between disasters that connote death
and destruction and the millennium that promises salvation and
fulfillment. Four representative millennial movements, namely the
Vailala Madness in Melanesia, the Taiping Rebellion in China, the
Ghost Dance among the Sioux Indians, and the Taborites of late
Medieval Europe, are described. A critical review of theories of
millenarianism is provided and it is concluded that social change
by itself does not sufficiently explain the rise of these movements.
The author maintains that many factors are needed to account for
outbursts of millenarianism, past and present. He discusses the
conversion process to these groups, the nature of the ecstatic
behavior of those who join them, and the social and educational
background of their membership. He thinks that millenarianism has
moved out of its former rural confines into modern, urban, industrialized society.

287. Barkum, Michael. "Movements of Total Transformation." AMERICAN
      BEHAVIORAL SCIENTIST 16 (1972): 145-51.

      Introduces a special issue of the AMERICAN BEHAVIORAL SCIENTIST
in which millenarian movements are comparatively discussed in terms
of their causes, effects, and internal dynamics. The author points
out that these movements have to be understood in terms of their
leaders, that millennialism has now entered the mainstream of contemporary life, and that judgments about the rationality or
irrationality of a movement cannot be easily made. Two types of
transformation are sought by these renewals: 1) a change in the
world as a whole, including its political, social, and religious
fabrics; and 2) an alteration of the values, attitudes, and behavior of individuals. "The tendency to regard these as fringe movements, interestingly exotic but largely irrelevant" (p. 14), is
clearly diminishing. Various aspects that need to be explored are
mentioned. Though millenarianism appears to be the product of
agrarian societies, they have definitely entered the life of
modern, industrial, urban cultures.

288. Barnes, Douglas F. "Charisma and Religious Leadership: An Histor-
      ical Analysis." JOURNAL FOR THE SCIENTIFIC STUDY OF RELIGION 17
      (1978): 1-18.

      Proposes a theory of charismatic leadership and institutionalized
religion that takes into account the sociohistorical conditions
under which charisma emerges. For data, the author relies not on

case studies but rather on the biography of the following 15 religious founders and their secondary leaders: Mahavira, Bal Shem Tov,
Guru Nanak, Baha'ullah, Muhammad, Buddha, Nichiren, Calvin, Luther,
Joseph Smith and Brigham Young, George Fox, Confucius, Gandhi,
Jesus and Peter, and Martin Luther King. Charisma is defined as
"that authority relationship which arises when a leader, through
the dynamics of a set of teachings, a unique personality, or both,
elicits responses of awe, deference, and devotion from a group of
people" (p. 2). The conditions necessary for charisma to exist are
explained. Religious founders were "de-alienated," i.e., had "the
conscious realization that the social world is humanely constructed
and therefore unstable" (p. 3). They lived through periods of
radical social change, reacted against traditional religion, and
proposed innovative teachings.

289.   Bartelt, Pearl W. "Sex Roles in American Communes." COMMUNAL LIFE
        (item 354), pp. 559-84.

        Suggests that a study of sex role differentiation can provide
        insight into the beliefs, occupations, family arrangements, and
        authority systems of a commune. From information gathered on 24
        historic communes and 46 modern ones, it is concluded that sex dif-
        ferentiation is common in all communes. A better understanding of
        sex roles can be achieved if communes are seen in the context of
        the larger society, rather than from preconceived notions of egali-
        tarianism and/or perfectionism.

290.   Bellah, Robert N., et al. "Symposium on Shepherd: 'Religion and
        the Counter Culture--A New Religiosity." SOCIOLOGICAL INQUIRY 42
        (1972): 155-72.

        Contains three responses to Shepherd's view (item 470) that the
        counterculture can be viewed as a new religiosity in harmony with
        rock music. A reply by Shepherd is included.

291.   Bennett, John W. "Communes and Communitarianism." THEORY AND
        SOCIETY 2 (1975): 63-94.

        Examines the "communitarian tradition" as an expression of the
        search for cultural integrity and personal identity. Communes are
        a "recurrent pattern of ideals and social arrangements" (p. 64)
        which take the form of millenarian revitalization or utopian move-
        ments. A brief historical overview is presented, starting with the
        Galilean Essenes down to the twentieth-century groups like the
        Hutterites and the kibbutzim. Some of the main themes of modern,
        nonmonastic movements are outlined. These groups have rejected
        the majority culture and formed voluntary communitarian lifestyles.
        The author thinks that communes are an escape from society and
        present a challenge to both culture and the family.

292.   Berger, Bennett M. "Utopia and Its Environment." SOCIETY 25.2
        (1988): 37-41.

        Explores the efforts to realize a communal ideal by examining the
        mutual adaptation of a rural counterculture commune with its Paci-
        fic Northwest environment. The author finds it extremely difficult

to distinguish between communards and noncommunards. Several contextual features of the local scene help commune members become
integrated into the life of the larger community. The stress on
survival skills is common to both commune members and to rural
people whose economic existence is interdependent. It is observed
that the educational endeavors of the communards has had beneficial
repercussions on the community at large.

293.   Berger, Bennett M. "Utopia and Its Environment." COMMUNAL LIFE
        (item 354), pp. 419-30.

        Studies a counterculture commune on the Pacific Northwest Coast
        of Canada and mentions some of the values that led to its estab-
        lishment, the equality of the sexes, views about childbearing, a
        high prestige for manual and practical survival skills, and the
        desire for open, personal relationships. Several contextual
        features of the local environment, in spite of persisting conflicts
        and tensions, helped the communards become integrated with the
        larger community. The author points out that the "strong religious
        component in the counterculture tradition, radical though it was,
        contains spiritual resources that can not only alienate its
        partisans from the community but also integrate with it" (p. 427).

294.   Berger, Bennett M., Bruce Hackett, and R. Mervyn Millar. "The
        Communal Family." FAMILY COORDINATOR 21 (1972): 419-27.

        Reports on anthropological investigations of communes along the
        West Coast of the United States, focusing on the specific nature
        of the interaction between children, and between children and their
        parents in a communal life setting. A basic distinction between
        urban and rural communes is made, the former being easier to start,
        more fluid in their membership, and less demanding of total commit-
        ment. Rural communes require a more radical change in lifestyle
        and a greater demand on their members. They are, further, a purer
        form of a New Age Movement. Communes can also be creedal or non-
        creedal, the former being organized around a systematic statement
        of counterculture beliefs or doctrines to which all members must
        adhere. Recruitment and childrearing practices are described and
        some of the problems that commune dwellers have to face are
        discussed.

295.   Bibby, Reginald W. "Why Conservative Churches Really Are Growing:
        Kelley Revisited." JOURNAL FOR THE SCIENTIFIC STUDY OF RELIGION 17
        (1978): 129-37.

        Examines the reason why conservative churches--among which are
        included the Salvation Army, the Seventh Day Adventists, Jehovah's
        Witnesses, and the Mormon Church--have registered an increase in
        their membership. Kelley's theory (see item 390) to explain this
        phenomenon, namely that conservative churches are providing people
        with answers to ultimate questions and encouraging members to make
        serious commitments, is examined. The author uses the demographic
        approach to compare conservative and mainline groups in Canada and
        relates the increase of the former to the following factors: birth
        and religious socialization; switching of denominations; and higher

level of participation. These factors explain the growth in membership. Kelley's view, though correct in its implication that conservative churches are more successful in retaining people in their commitment, does not prove that these churches have a greater impact on unchurched individuals. Conservative churches are compared to sectarian religious groups that "appear to perform a number of spiritual, social, and psychological functions which ring a responsive chord with many people" (p. 137).

296.   Bibby, Reginald W., and Merlin B. Brinkerhoff. "When Proselytization Fails: An Organizational Analysis." SOCIOLOGICAL ANALYSIS 35 (1974): 189-200.

Argues that a comprehensive study of proselytization should include not only those who are proselytized, but also the religious groups and organizations that carry out the missionary activity aimed at converting people. Conservative churches who seek out converts must develop mechanisms for reaching out to individuals (contact), making them members (bridging), and maintaining their commitment (assimilation). The authors examine the mechanisms used by 20 conversion-oriented churches (including several Pentecostal groups, the Salvation Army, and a Plymouth Brethren Congregation) in a Western Canadian city. They found out that conversions to these churches were largely limited to relatives of their members. The programs aimed at converting outsiders have some success, but they have also the latent functions of entertaining people and of perpetuating the evangelical subculture.

297.   Bibby, Reginald W., and Merlin B. Brinkerhoff. "Sources of Religious Involvement: Issues For Future Empirical Investigation." REVIEW OF RELIGIOUS RESEARCH 15 (1974): 71-79.

Questions the adequacy of intellectual, psychic, or social deprivation as an explanation of religious involvement. Four points regarding theories of deprivation are raised: 1) their a priori proofs often exclude other possible explanations; 2) control group comparisons are seldom used; 3) deprivation indicators tend to be subjective rather than objective; and 4) little attention is paid to questions about the sources and continuation of religious involvement. The authors explore other alternatives, such as socialization, accommodation, and cognition, and find that they account for the majority of involvement in the following groups in Western Canada's "Bible Belt:" Baptist, Pentecostal, Nazarene, Salvation Army, Christian and Missionary Alliance, and Plymouth Brethren. The variations observed by the authors might explain why people not only get involved in a religious group, but also keep up their involvement throughout their lives. Certain types of deprivation might still be dominant in various religious groups, influencing recruitment, culture, and organization.

298.   Bibby, Reginald W., and Merlin B. Brinkerhoff. "The Circulation of Saints: A Study of People Who Join Conservative Churches." JOURNAL FOR THE SCIENTIFIC STUDY OF RELIGION 12 (1973): 273-83.

Explores the reasons why and how conservative churches are growing. Three types of church memberships are discussed: 1) by affiliation; 2) by birth; and 3) by proselytism. In the 20 evangelical congregations studied by the authors it was found that 70% of new-comers had been members of other evangelical churches, that nearly 70% were children of members, and that less than 10% were converts from other, more liberal churches. Converts to evangelical groups tend to be switchers. The growth of conservative churches is a retention of those families with evangelical culture and not a gain of new members from other denominations.

299.   Bird, Frederick. "Max Weber's Perspectives on Religious Evolution." STUDIES IN RELIGION 13 (1984): 215-25.

Argues that Max Weber made use of an evolutionary, developmental perspective in his analysis of world religions. Three major areas of religious evolution are discussed, namely those of religious symbols, cults, and norms of conduct. The author points out that, for Weber, cultic practices start by being magical acts performed with the intention of producing concrete worldly results and then develop into organized rituals in the hands of priests who ascribe to them transcendent goals.

300.   Bland, Richard, and Roy Wallis. "Comment of Wilson and Zurcher's 'Status Inconsistency and Participation in Social Movements.'" SOCIOLOGICAL QUARTERLY 18 (1977): 426-29.

Responds to Wilson and Zurcher's study (item 509) on the anti-pornography movement on three levels: numerical aspects of their analysis, inferences drawn, and theoretical assumptions. Fault is found with these two authors' efforts to relate involvement in the antipornography crusade and various elements of the social struc-ture. Bland and Wallis insist that "pornography crusades are a matter of cultural defense, not status defense" (p. 429).

301.   Bouvard, Marguerite. THE INTENTIONAL COMMUNITY MOVEMENT: BUILDING A NEW MORAL WORLD. Port Washington, NY: National University Publi-cations, 1975. 207 pp.

Presents a study of new alternative communal lifestyles that constitute a special form of social dissent. Self-sufficiency, ecological concerns, and detachment from political involvement are among the shared features in these groups. The reasons underlying the search for community are explored and it is maintained that they "constitute a response to needs experienced in a vast, highly modernized, Western political society" (p. 21). One chapter is dedicated to religious communities, such as the Society of Brothers (Bruderhof), the Koinonia Partners, and the Brotherhood of the Spirit, while another describes several utopian communities, includ-ing Walden Two and Twin Oaks. The author endorses the view that these experimental communities, which embody dreams of perfection, are laboratories for social change.

302.   Braumgart, Richard G. "Historical Generations and Youth Movements." RESEARCH IN SOCIAL MOVEMENTS, CONFLICT, AND CHANGE 6 (1984): 95-141.

Explores how historical-generational forces interact to produce youth movements and endeavors to construct an adequate theory of generations. Two main historical approaches to the study of youth

movements, namely the social discontinuity or breakdown approach
and the resource mobilization theory, are first discussed. The
author then surveys the generational approach to the study of these
movements, an approach that sees the difference in age as a source
of conflict and change. He finally combines the historical and
generational perspectives and presents a typology of the sources
for youth movements. Though largely concerned with political and
cultural movements, this essay discusses sociological theories that
have been applied to the new religious movements.

303.   Brinkerhoff, Merlin B., and Kathryn L. Burke. "Disaffiliation:
        Some Notes on 'Falling From the Faith.'" SOCIOLOGICAL ANALYSIS
        41 (1980): 41-54.

        Proposes a typology, based on "loss of religiosity" and "abandon-
        ment of communal identity," to understand the process of apostasy.
        Instead of employing demographic factors and secularization themes
        to explain why people leave their faith, the author adopts the
        symbolic interactionist approach that uses labeling to illustrate
        the process of apostasy in a fundamentalist sect. Disaffiliation
        is thus seen as a gradual, social process in which "official typing"
        and consequent stigmatization can act as a catalyst that accelerates
        the journey to apostasy.

304.   Brinkerhoff, Merlin B., and Marlene M. Mackie. "The Applicability
        of Social Distance for Religious Research: An Exploration."
        REVIEW OF RELIGIOUS RESEARCH 28 (1986): 151-67.

        Attempts to measure the lack of tolerance of religious groups
        among university students in the Western United States and Canada.
        New religions (like the Unification Church), followed by proselyti-
        zing and conservative Christian groups (like the Mormons), were the
        least accepted and tolerated. Mainline Protestants and Catholics
        were the most favored. Several suggestions for measuring social
        distance between groups are made.

305.   Bromley, David G. "Religious Disaffiliation: A Neglected Social
        Process." FALLING FROM THE FAITH (item 578), pp. 9-25.

        Introduces a series of essays discussing the social process of
        religious disaffiliation. It is the author's contention that
        research in this area will contribute to the understanding of mem-
        bership in religious groups in processual terms. Several issues in
        the study of disaffiliation are identified: 1) the problems of ter-
        minology, where the following words have all been used to denote
        the action of leaving a religious organization: exiting, defection,
        apostasy, disaffiliation, and disengagement; 2) the need to inte-
        grate research on disaffiliation from both the mainline churches
        and the new movements; 3) the lack of research done on examining
        the effects of disaffiliation; 4) the need to look at entering a
        religious organization as a process rather than a sudden event; and
        5) inherent problems in interpreting both affiliation and disaffil-
        iation since the accounts of both may be colored by socialization.

306.   Bruce, Steve, and Roy Wallis. "Homage to Ozymandias: A Rejoinder
        to Bainbridge and Stark." SOCIOLOGICAL ANALYSIS 46 (1985): 73-75.

Continues the debate on Bainbridge and Stark's theory of religion, particularly on the concepts of "rewards" and "compensators" that are central to religion and religious change. Bruce and Wallis reassert their previous position that this theory of religion is inadequate, incoherent, and ultimately reductionistic.

307.   Butler, Jon. "Enthusiasm Described and Decried: The Great Awakening as Interpretative Fiction." JOURNAL OF AMERICAN HISTORY 69 (1982): 305-325.

Gives an account of the commonly accepted historical appraisal of the First Great Awakening as a great religious revival and suggests that this interpretation "distorts the character of eighteenth-century American life and misunderstands its relationship to pre-revolutionary American society and politics" (p. 322). A four-fold model of eighteenth-century Colonial revivals is proposed with the following main features: 1) the revivals were mainly Calvinistic-inspired regional events that took place in the "colonial backwaters;" 2) they were part of a long-term pattern of erratic movements for spiritual renewal; 3) they had modest effects on Colonial religion; and 4) they had practically no link with the American revolution.

308.   Camic, Charles. "Charisma: Its Varieties, Preconditions, and Consequences." SOCIOLOGICAL INQUIRY 50 (1980): 5-23.

Maintains that progress in the sociological study of charisma has been limited because sociologists have assumed with Weber that charisma is homogeneous. A brief outline of the sociology of charisma is given. The findings of psychoanalysis are then applied to charisma. The following topics related to charisma are then discussed: 1) its preconditions, namely the various human needs like dependency and the superego; 2) its various modes, that is, omnipresence, excellence, sacredness, and the uncanny; and 3) its consequences, including the formation of relationships, a sense of awe, devotion, and obedience to need-gratifying persons.

309.   Carroll, Jackson W. "Transcendence and Mystery in the Counter-Culture." RELIGION IN LIFE 42 (1973): 361-75.

Makes some generalizations regarding the common features of the counterculture, particularly those about the type of people involved and the emerging social relationships. "The styles and symbols of the counter-culture are the cultural expressions of persons who find themselves alienated from the establishment and who are seeking alternative social relationships based on cooperation and community" (p. 365). The author suggests a typology of orientations towards the transcendent based on its goals (individual or social) and on its basis (within or beyond history). The counterculture is credited with a recovery of the sense of mystery. A way of evaluating the counterculture is suggested.

310.   Cavan, Ruth Shonle. "Roles of the Old in Personal and Impersonal Societies." FAMILY COORDINATOR 27 (1978): 315-19.

Compares and contrasts the role of old people in three types of societies: 1) religious communities like the Old Order Amish and the Hutterites; 2) contemporary communes; and 3) urban society. The family unit and its stability, the status the old have in their respective communities, their geographic stability, their place of residence, and their economic support are the factors considered.

311. Cavan, Ruth Shonle. "Introduction to Historical and Contemporary Communes." INTERNATIONAL REVIEW OF MODERN SOCIOLOGY 6.1 (1976): 1-11.

Suggests a more precise terminology for describing communes and proposes a threefold classification into 1) religious, closed sub-societies, 2) socialist, closed sub-societies, and 3) escapist, closed groups. Voluntary self-segregation is deemed to be the most important feature for survival. Adaptability, value systems, decline of opposition, boundary maintenance, economic adaptation, and organized governance are the main topics that have to be considered in any discussion of these sub-societies.

312. Cavan, Ruth Shonle, and Man Singh Das, editors. COMMUNES: HISTORICAL AND CONTEMPORARY. New Delhi, India: Vikas Publishing House, 1979. xiv, 359 pp.

Presents 25 studies that were published, in one form or another, in the INTERNATIONAL REVIEW OF MODERN SOCIETY (vol. 6, Spring, 1976). The papers deal with a variety of communes, past and present, and cover a wide variety of subjects, religions, and communes. The editors, in a short essay at the end of the book, point out some of the important features of commune movements, which they classify under five types: 1) old and well-established; 2) extinct; 3) newly emerging; 4) escapist; and 5) contemporary communes in the United States of America. An index is included.

Contains items 485, 1204, 1374.

313. Cohen, Jean L., editor. "Social Movements." SOCIAL RESEARCH 6 (1985): 663-690.

Presents six essays discussing various aspects of new social movements. Different types of, and theories about, these movements are distinguished and discussed, and their challenges considered. Though none of the articles deals explicitly with new religious movements, this collection as a whole supplies the background for understanding some of the general theories (like resource mobilization) that explain social and political movements and that have been applied to the new cults.

314. Connor, John W. "Misperception, Folk Belief, and the Occult: A Cognitive Guide to Understanding." SKEPTICAL INQUIRER 8.4 (1984): 344-54.

Applies cognitive theory and research to understanding folk beliefs, particularly those related to the occult. It is argued that "humans will interpret and reinterpret information to make it

compatible with what is already known" (p. 348). The author insists that people perceive reality in terms of the ideal models
that culture gives them.

315.   Conover, Patrick W. "An Analysis of Communes and Intentional Com-
        munities With Particular Attention to Sexual and Genderal Rela-
        tions." FAMILY COORDINATOR 24 (1975): 453-64.

        Describes the contemporary development of communes and intention-
        al communities that are seen as an institutionalizing response to
        the emergence of an alternate culture. A historical perspective is
        provided and the sources of such a culture explored. The author
        holds that "an alternate culture is seen as flowing from distinctly
        cultural sources rather than as an adjustment to social changes
        such as class conflict and technological change" (p. 457). Prob-
        lems of order, commitment, and economical management provide the
        basis for diverse social arrangements in communes. The male/
        female relationship is examined with Twin Oaks Community as an
        example. It is maintained that the alternate culture "can become
        institutionalized in the meeting of the domestic functional neces-
        sities without giving up distinctive values" (p. 462).

316.   Conover, Patrick W. "The Alternate Society: Its Sources and Its
        Future." TECHNOLOGICAL FORECASTING AND SOCIAL CHANGE 5 (1973):
        295-304.

        Gives an account of the counterculture of the late 1960's and
        early 1970's and explores its religious and secular themes. The
        rise of the new religious movements is seen as an expression of
        alternative religious ventures. It is suggested that the sources
        of the alternative culture are "the broadly disseminated secondary
        themes in American culture that have been raised, often in
        resymbolized forms, to primary significance" (p. 299). These
        themes are specified as women's culture, modernistic Christianity,
        the American cultural ideals, and existentialism. The movement
        toward an alternate society should not, in the author's view, be
        considered transitory and marginal. It functions as a way of meet-
        ing the needs of many of those who become part of it, even though
        it has some disintegrative forces. The author speculates that, if
        the alternate culture solves its problem of disorganization, it may
        survive and have an impact on American society as a whole.

317.   Coser, Lewis A. GREEDY INSTITUTIONS: PATTERNS OF UNDIVIDED COMMIT-
        MENT. New York: Free Press, 1974. ix, 166 pp.

        Discusses those organizations that the author labels "greedy
        institutions" because they "seek exclusive and undivided loyalty
        and they attempt to reduce the claims of competing roles and status
        positions on those they wish to encompass within their boundaries"
        (p. 4). Such institutions, be they religious or political, do not
        externally coerce individuals; rather, they put various pressures on
        them to weaken or sever their ties with people and groups who make
        conflicting demands. The author examines the structural conditions
        that favor recruitment. Three goals of greedy institutions are
        distinguished, namely those of serving the rules, the family, and

the collective. Sects and sectarians, who play major roles on the stage of history, are discussed in the context of "collectives," among which are included such groups as the Jesuits and Jansenists, both of which were militaristic organizations. The sexual require- ments of utopias and the functions of sacerdotal celibacy are also discussed.

318.   Curtis, Russell L., and Louis A. Zurcher. "Social Movements: An Analytical Exploration of Organizational Forms." SOCIAL PROBLEMS 21 (1974): 356-70.

Reviews some of the literature on social movements and finds that there are two key organizational variables: 1) the nature of the goals (instrumental, specific, or expressive-diffuse); and 2) the nature of membership requirements (exclusive or inclusive). Other conceptual components are listed: the kind of membership incentives (solidarity or purposiveness); the degree of detachment from commu- nity; the leadership styles; etc. Nine types of social movements are divided into two main categories: the congruent ones--those with expressive goal orientations and exclusive membership condi- tions; and the noncongruent ones--those with instrumental goal orientations and inclusive membership conditions. The author holds that one can distinguish between those social movements which en- courage social innovation and those which resist it. Judging from the bibliographic references, several cults and sect (like Voodoo and the Snake-Handling Pentecostals of W. Virginia) are treated as social movement organizations.

319.   Davidson, James D. "Glock's Model of Religious Commitment: Assess- ing Different Approaches and Results." REVIEW OF RELIGIOUS RESEARCH 16 (1975): 83-93.

Discusses some of the conflicts that have followed the applica- tion of Glock's five dimensions of religious commitment (see item 95). The author derives ten components of religious commitment by combining a liberal/conservative distinction with Glock's dimen- sions and testing the resultant model on Baptist and Methodist church members. He concludes that Glock's model is generally sup- ported by his own conclusions. Implications for future research are outlined.

320.   Davidson, James D., and Dean D. Knudsen. "A New Approach to Reli- gious Commitment." SOCIOLOGICAL FOCUS 10 (1977): 151-73.

Proposes a new model for studying religious commitment, stressing the theoretical aspect but also presenting dates from six Christian churches (i.e., United Methodist, Presbyterian Church, United Church of Christ, Friends, Christian Disciples, and Church of the Brethren). Religious commitment, according to the authors, refers to the extent of the individual's involvement in various aspects of life and includes subjective (psychological) and behavioral (parti- cipatory) components that are closely interrelated. People's reli- gious commitment can both shape, and be shaped by, some components of their religious orientations. The determinants and consequences of commitment are finally considered.

321.   Dobbelaere, Karel. "Secularization Theories and Sociological Para-
       digms: A Reformulation of the Private Public Dichotomy and the
       Problem of Social Integration." SOCIOLOGICAL ANALYSIS 46 (1985):
       377-87.

       Examines various sociological paradigms used to explain the secu-
       larization process and religious change. Three distinct levels of
       secularization are distinguished, namely the societal, the organi-
       zational, and the individual. The author thinks that different
       paradigms can be employed to elucidate various questions and diffi-
       culties.

322.   Dobbelaere, Karel. "Secularization Theories and Sociological Para-
       digms: Convergences and Divergences." SOCIAL COMPASS 31 (1984):
       199-219.

       Discusses several major sociological theories of secularization
       and attempts to find the relationships between various levels of
       sociological interpretation. The different paradigms and processes
       of secularization with the ensuing religious changes are schemati-
       cally outlined. The author stresses the need to look on seculari-
       zation as a process that unfolds in a cultural context.

323.   Dobbelaere, Karel. "Secularization: A Multi-Dimensional Concept."
       CURRENT SOCIOLOGY 29.2 (1981): 1-216.

       Deals comprehensively with the secularization theory which has
       held the center stage in discussions between sociologists of reli-
       gion over the last few decades. After explaining the concept of
       secularization as one containing a number of dimensions, the author
       accounts, in some detail, for three major theories that conceive of
       secularization as a process of laicization, or of religious change,
       or of church involvement. It is insisted that the cultural context
       in which secularization takes place is a major factor that must be
       taken into consideration. A comprehensive bibliography (pp. 161-
       213), mainly in English with several citations in German, French,
       and Dutch, is included.

324.   Douglas, Mary, editor. WITCHCRAFT CONFESSIONS AND ACCUSATIONS.
       New York: Tavistock Publications, 1970. xxxviii, 387 pp.

       Presents a collection of essays, derived from the Annual Confer-
       ence of the Association of Social Anthropologists of the Common-
       wealth, that discuss witchcraft mainly in the traditional anthropo-
       logical area of research, that is, nonliterate societies. The
       articles are grouped in four parts: 1) the context of witchcraft
       in Europe; 2) confessions of witches; 3) idioms of power; 4) alter-
       native interpretations of misfortunes. The editor outlines the
       main two patterns of witch beliefs that consider witchcraft as the
       activity of internal or external inimical forces. Though largely
       concerned with non-European witchcraft, many of the essays assume
       that the anthropological analysis of witch beliefs and accusations
       can be applied universally.

       Contains item 1506.

325. Downton, James V. REBEL LEADERSHIP: COMMITMENT AND CHARISMA IN
      THE REVOLUTIONARY PROCESS. New York: Free Press, 1973. x, 306 pp.

      Studies the nature and functions of rebel leaders in the context
      of the sociological and psychological theories that explain the
      relationship between leaders and their followers, the nature of
      commitment, and the process of revolutionary change. Two types of
      functions of leadership are distinguished, the instrumental (that
      is, goal-setting, communication, and mobilization) and the expres-
      sive (such as ego-support). The determinants of commitment and the
      inter-transactional relationships between the leaders and their
      followers are discussed at length. The concept of charisma is
      analyzed in terms of Weber's seminal study.

326. Duke, James T., and Barry L. Johnson. "The Stages of Religious
      Transformation: A Study of 200 Nations." REVIEW OF RELIGIOUS
      RESEARCH 30 (1989): 209-24.

      Refutes each of the four major assumptions of the secularization
      theory, namely that the process is 1) linear, 2) inevitable, 3) a
      recent phenomenon caused by modernization, and 4) largely a Western
      event. The authors examine extensive data on religious changes
      between 1900 and 1980, assess the usefulness of the secularization
      theory to explain these changes, and formulate a set of hypotheses
      that account for the changes. They propose a cyclical view of
      religious change in four stages: 1) decline (that is, the loss of
      influence of traditional religions and the emergence of new ones);
      2) dominance (that is, the growth of a new minority religion into a
      majority faith); 3) sustained growth (that refers to consolidation
      and increase of influence of newly established traditions); and 4)
      transition (that is, the dominant religions reach a peak and then
      begin to decline). Religious transformation is cyclical and is not
      restricted to Western culture.

327. Dupertius, Lucy G. "American Adaptation to Hinduism." RELIGION
      AND BELIEF SYSTEMS (item 701), pp. 101-11.

      Examines the impact of Western culture on Hindu religious tradi-
      tions that have been in America since last century. The ways in
      which Americans have adapted 1) Hindu beliefs and symbols (like
      reincarnation), 2) Hindu practices (such as Hatha Yoga and medita-
      tion), and 3) Hindu social forms (as nonviolent protest) are con-
      sidered. It is argued that, in some instances, genuine Hindu reli-
      gious ideas are misunderstood and Hindu practices altered to fit
      Western materialistic goals.

328. Ehrenreich, Barbara, and Deirdre English. WITCHES, MIDWIVES, AND
      NURSES: A HISTORY OF WOMEN HEALERS. Old Westbury, NY: Feminist
      Press, second edition, 1973. 45 pp.

      Gives a brief overview of the part played by women in the healing
      profession in Western Europe. The churches saw witches, who func-
      tioned as folk healers, as a serious threat to the established
      socioreligious order. The unrelenting persecution of witches is
      linked with an anti-empiricist, anti-feminist, and anti-sexual

obsession. The witch was, in fact, an agent of change. This book
is largely written from a contemporary feminist perspective that
criticizes the attitudes commonly associated with witches, midwives, and nurses, and suggests areas of reform.

329. Eichler, Margarit. "Leadership in Social Movements." SOCIOLOGICAL
      INQUIRY 47.2 (1977): 97-107.

Maintains that social movements are one of the major vehicles for
social change and explores the role of leadership in four different
movements, namely the Nazis of Germany, the Manson Family, the
Millerites, and the Women's Liberation Movement. The concept of
charismatic leadership is rejected because it has been used too
indiscriminately. Instead, the author suggests that the legitimacy
of the leader's authority and the source and nature of this legitimacy are central features of social movements. Various types of
leadership are distinguished and their consequent control over
decisions and membership commitment assessed in each of the four
types of movement. The Nazi Movement and the Manson Family are said
to be closed-access movements, while the Millerites and the Women's
Liberation Movement are open-access ones.

330. Eichler, Margarit. "Some Comments Concerning Murvar's 'Messianism
      in Religion: Religion and Revolutionary.'" JOURNAL FOR THE
      SCIENTIFIC STUDY OF RELIGION 11 (1972): 187-91.

Responds to Murvar's long essay (item 432) in which he develops a
dichotomy between religious and revolutionary (political) messianism. The author criticizes this distinction because it fails to
realize that religious movements can contain political elements and
that, vice versa, political movements are often imbued with religious fervor and ideology. She prefers the old distinction between
religious and secular movements, both of which can be revolutionary
or nonrevolutionary.

331. Erasmus, Charles J. IN SEARCH OF THE COMMON GOOD: UTOPIAN EXPERI-
      MENTS PAST AND FUTURE. New York: Free Press, 1977. xiii, 424 pp.

Presents a comprehensive study of utopian communities from a
political-economic point of view. Among the groups surveyed are
19 communities and modern Israeli communes (kibbutzim). The monastery is seen as a typical institution stressing the common lifestyle in an idealistic setting. Amana, the Hutterites, Oneida, and
the Shakers are among the religiously motivated communes included.
The author holds that these communities agree that the common good
should prevail over individual interests. He thinks that the
development of capitalism has altered the situation and has led to
the formation of different kinds of utopian quests.

332. Evans, Robert P., editor. SOCIAL MOVEMENTS: A READER AND SOURCE
      BOOK. Chicago: Rand McNally, 1973. xvi, 605 pp.

Offers a collection of previously published articles and selections from books on the rise and development of various social and
religious movements. The essays are intended to provide some basic

and introductory orientation to the study of these movements. The
first part of this volume is dedicated to discussion on theoretical
and methodological issues. The rest covers individual movements as
they relate to 1) ethics and moral questions, 2) the conflicts they
bring about, 3) their impact on individuals, and 4) their changing
views on war and women. Several essays deal specifically with
religious movements. There are bibliographies attached to each
essay.

Contains item 394.

333.   Fairfield, Richard. COMMUNES USA: A PERSONAL TOUR. Baltimore:
        Penguin Books, 1972. x, 400 pp.

Describes the rapid growth of communes in the late 1960's when
over 2000 were in operation. After a brief historical survey of
utopian communities, the author divides the communes he visited
into seven different types: 1) Marxist/anarchist ideological communes; 2) scientific ones; 3) modern religious communities (including the Lama Foundation, Ananda Cooperative Village, and the
Himalayan Academy); 4) Hippie communes of rural America; 5) group
marriage communes; 6) service communities; and 7) youth communes.
Five major ideals held by most of these utopian communes are identified: 1) getting back to essentials; 2) getting back to the land;
3) concern for people; 4) searching for the self; and 5) social
change by example.

334.   Fairfield, Richard, editor. UTOPIA USA. San Francisco: Alterna-
        tives Foundation, 1972. 231 pp.

Presents a collection of largely descriptive essays on communes
in America. Most of the essays had been previously published in
various magazines and newspapers and contain photographic illustrations. They cover a large variety of communal lifestyles including
religious-oriented ones, like the Amish, the Hutterites, and the
Jesus People. An extensive typology of communes is attempted. The
author thinks that joining a commune is a way of opting out of the
system. The reasons why so many of them fail and the problems of
communal living are among the topics discussed.

335.   Fallding, Harold. THE SOCIOLOGY OF RELIGION: AN EXPLANATION OF
        UNITY AND DIVERSITY IN RELIGION. Toronto: McGraw-Hill Ryerson,
        1974. xii, 240 pp.

Presents a social-scientific study of religion in two parts, the
first dealing with the unity found in religion, the second with the
diversity. Several classical theories of religion and the basic
modes of religious expression, namely doctrine, ritual, ethics,
fellowship, and experience, are among the topics discussed. The
rise of religious diversity is attributed to the sectarian protest
of the alienated. Geographic separation and social change are the
two distinct bases of religious differences. A typology of religious organizations based on their stages of development is given.
Sects are divided into "militant" and "withdrawing" types. Cultism

is used to refer to the tendency of "ascribing sacred status to anything in the profane, actualized world" (p. 29). Humanism, the Nazi Movement, Communism, and Hippieism are among the new modern religions of natural need-fulfillment.

336.   Ferree, Myra Marx, and Frederick D. Miller. "Mobilization and Meaning: Toward an Integration of Social Psychological Research Perspective on Social Movements." SOCIOLOGICAL INQUIRY 55 (1985): 38-61.

Discusses the resource mobilization theory of social movements, a theory that stresses that these groups are organized activities that form part of social and political life rather than a symptom of social disorganization and decay. The resource mobilization approach brings into focus the political processes that the movements use to gain control and distribute resources rather than the psychological processes that drive individual members to join the movement. The authors find this approach inadequate, because it neglects the individual participant. They propose a view that combines the resource mobilization theory and the role that ideology and perception have in the recruitment of members.

337.   Ferris, William R. "The Negro Conversion." KEYSTONE FOLKLORE QUARTERLY 15 (1970): 35-51.

Examines the conversion experience of Black Americans in terms of its source, nature, and function and then analyzes specific Black experiences. The imprint of White culture is taken for granted and interpreted functionally within the context of a society where racial inequality prevails. Conversion, in the author's opinion, gives Blacks dignity and self-respect, enabling them to endure social injustices.

338.   Fishman, Aryei. "Is Religion Always Functional For Communal Life?: An Evolutionary Perspective." COMMUNAL LIFE (item 354), pp. 440-46.

Proposes the view that, in order to have functional values for communal life, religion must possess two unified, evolutionary modes, namely mystical otherworldliness and rational thisworldly orientation. The author illustrates his view with reference to the kibbutz, the Hasidic Jews, and Christian communal experiments in the nineteenth century, like those of the Hutterites and Shakers.

339.   Flacks, Richard. YOUTH AND SOCIAL CHANGE. Chicago: Rand McNally, 1971. xi, 147 pp.

Argues that the youth counterculture movement of the 1960's was an unparalleled development in American society and an expression of a fundamental sociocultural crisis. More specifically, it was a youth identity crisis, that is, "an inability to define the meaning of one's life and to accept the meanings and models of adulthood offered by parents and other elders" (p. 6). The author attempts to outline the type of young person who was attracted to the counterculture and some possible future trends.

340.   Fogarty, Robert S. DICTIONARY OF AMERICAN COMMUNAL AND UTOPIAN
        HISTORY. Westport, CT: Greenwood Press, 1980. xxvi, 271 pp.

        Presents a rich source of information on 270 American communes or
        utopian settlements established between 1787 and 1919. The data
        is divided into two main sections: 1) biographies of all communal
        founders, leaders, and other noteworthy figures; and 2) descrip-
        tions of the various communities. An annotated list of communal
        and utopian societies (compiled by Otohiko Okugawa) and a biblio-
        graphic essay on communal history in America are provided. A short
        annotated bibliography is added (pp. 246-53).

341.   Fogarty, Robert S. "American Communes, 1865-1914." AMERICAN
        STUDIES 9 (1975): 145-62.

        Groups American communes that came into being in the second half
        of last century into the following three general categories, based
        on their leaders and interests of their members: 1) "Cooperative
        Colonizers;" 2) "Charismatic Perfectionists;" and 3) "Political
        Pragmatists." The main features of each group are described and
        illustrated by specific examples. The author holds that this his-
        torical period testifies to numerous collective settlements engaged
        in community building. A strong social purpose and an attempt to
        respond to emerging social conditions of the time were also charac-
        teristic of communes, many of which were religious in nature.

342.   Fogarty, Robert S. AMERICAN UTOPIANISM. Itasca, IL: Peacock Pub-
        lishers, 1972. xi, 175 pp.

        Attempts to present American utopian communities in the words of
        the participants themselves. Concentrating largely on communes
        from the eighteenth to the early twentieth centuries, the author
        gives very brief sketches of such groups as the Shakers, New
        Harmony, and Koinonia Community, and then provides selections from
        materials published by the respective groups to explain their life-
        styles and goals.

343.   Freeman, Jo, editor. SOCIAL MOVEMENTS OF THE SIXTIES AND SEVEN-
        TIES. New York: Longman, 1983. xvii, 382 pp.

        Presents a collection of 21 previously published essays that
        study the various aspects of social movements. The materials are
        divided into five topical sections dealing respectively with the
        origins, mobilization, organization, strategy, and decline of these
        movements. Though only one essay concentrates exclusively on reli-
        gious movements, these essays embody sociological theories that have
        been applied to the new religious movements.

        Contains item 2131.

344.   Furman, D. RELIGION AND SOCIAL CONFLICTS IN THE U.S.A. Moscow:
        Progress Publishers, 1981. 254 pp.

        Examines how specific features of religion affect the ideology
        and politics of social conflicts in the United States. The author
        discusses the role of religion and of secularization in a bourgeois

society. One chapter deals with sects in American society. The author sees a connection between the acceptability of sectarian ideology and dissatisfaction with society and one's place in it. He maintains that the sect fulfills a major psychological role: "it reverses his (that is, the member's) social status in his mind, thus freeing him from his agonizing social and personal inferiority hang ups" (p. 98). The reasons for the spread of the sects, their significance, and manifold functions are explored.

345.   Gabernnesch, Howard. "Authoritarianism as World View." AMERICAN JOURNAL OF SOCIOLOGY 77 (1972): 857-75.

Examines the view of several sociologists that authoritarianism can be the result of a lack of "broad social perspective" and need not be explained in psychological terms. After evaluating some of the literature on the subject, the author suggests that by exploring the worldview that authoritarianism encourages, one might be able to specify the relationship between broad perspectives and authoritarian attitudes. He maintains that the authoritarian worldview is a "reified" one, that is, it sees the social reality "as it if were fixed rather than a process, absolute instead of relative, natural rather than conventional and, in general, as a product of forces which are more than human" (p. 863). The reified worldview is self-justifying, morally and ontologically superior to men and women and demands that people adjust themselves to it.

346.   Gallup, George, and David Poling. THE SEARCH FOR AMERICA'S FAITH. Nashville: Abingdon, 1980. 153 pp.

Examines, through various national and local polls, the present state of organized religion and finds hopeful trends pointing to its revival and strength. The yearning of young people and the rediscovery of the family are among the topics discussed. The rise of the new cults (particularly that of the Unification Church) and the problem they pose for the established churches are dealt with and suggestions for responses to them are recommended. One chapter is dedicated to the study of the "unchurched Christians," concentrating on their attitudes, values, and beliefs and on the forces that alienate them from becoming members of one particular church. The roles of women, of youth, and of television in shaping the future church are also explored. Several statistical tables are provided.

347.   Gardner, Hugh. THE CHILDREN OF PROSPERITY: THIRTEEN AMERICAN COM-MUNES. New York: St. Martin's Press, 1978. xi, 281 pp.

Attempts to 1) compile a history of a representative sample of rural communal groups established between 1965 and 1970; 2) describe their social and organizational structure in a uniform pattern; and 3) report on later development to assess the groups' success or failure. Several (pseudonymously named) rural communes in Colorado, New Mexico, Oregon, and New England are chosen as the basis of the study. They are described in the words of their members and then analyzed in terms of Kanter's six types of commitment (sacrifice, investment, renunciation, communion, mortification, and

transcendence). The changes which took place in the communes in
the early 1970's are assessed. There are many references to new
religiously oriented communes such as a Yogi Bhajan Ashram, Ananda
Cooperative Village, the Lama Foundation, and the Ram Das Ashram.

348. Garner, Roberta Ash. SOCIAL MOVEMENTS IN AMERICA. Chicago: Rand
     McNally, second edition, 1977. xii, 233 pp.

Presents a comprehensive historical study of various social and
religious movements in America. Two introductory chapters attempt
to give analytic and descriptive overviews respectively: the first
defines and classifies social movements and explores their determinants and effects; the second looks at the particular sociocultural
setting in which they flourish. Most of this volume is dedicated
to an account of social movements in the United States from the
Colonial period to the 1960's and early 1970's. One chapter investigates the rise of religious movements in the seventeenth and eighteenth centuries and includes such groups as the Puritans and the
Quakers. Several conclusions based on historical materials are
outlined. The rise of new religious movements is not included in
the author's survey of recent movements in the United States.

349. Garrett, William R. "Religion and the Legitimation of Violence."
     PROPHETIC RELIGIONS AND POLITICS: RELIGION AND THE POLITICAL
     ORDER (item 358), pp. 103-22.

Discusses the recent resurgence of radical religious violence.
Three types of radical religion are first described, namely: 1)
totalitarian rigid; 2) liberal, democratic centrist; and 3) totalitarian, democratic right. Several propositions about the nature
of radical religion are then outlined. The author cautions that
religion is not always benign and that "it holds the potential for
unleashing the most demonic of social forces" (p. 120).

350. Gaustad, Edwin, editor. THE RISE OF ADVENTISM: RELIGION AND
     SOCIETY IN MID-NINETEENTH CENTURY AMERICA. New York: Harper and
     Row, 1974. xx, 329 pp.

Presents a collection of historically oriented essays that examine the religious ferment in America in the nineteenth century.
Besides discussions on the health reform movement and the conflict
between science and religion, there are studies on communitarianism,
spiritualism, millennialism, and modernism. A lengthy bibliography
(pp. 207-307) contains many primary sources.

Contains item 420.

351. Gerlach, Luther P. "Movements of Revolutionary Change: Some Struc-
     tural Characteristics." AMERICAN BEHAVIORAL SCIENTIST 14 (1971):
     812-36.

Discusses various movements, including the Students for a Democratic Society, the Black Panthers, and the sixteenth-century Protestant Reformation, which bring about or endeavor to create social
upheaval. Several theories explaining the rise of these new move-

ments are evaluated. The author's previous work (item 187) outlining five factors operative in the these groups is assumed. This
essay focuses on a movement organization which is described as 1)
segmentary, i.e., composed of different groups which grow, proli-
ferate, or simply dissipate; 2) polycephalous, i.e., with no central common or decision-making structure, having, instead of one
leader, several rival ones; and 3) reticulate, i.e., organized into
a network or structure with overlapping connections between the
members. Several adaptive functions of these movements are examined. They are said to: 1) prevent suppression by the opposition;
2) penetrate a number of social niches; 3) maximize adaptive variations at a time of marked environmental change; 4) contribute to
system reliability by the duplicating and overlapping of functions
by different groups; and 5) escalate effort and dynamism. Among
the many examples given is the rivalry between Pentecostal groups
and Voodoo, which seek to outdo each other. These movements are
said to encourage innovation and problem solving.

352.   Glock, Charles Y., editor. RELIGION IN SOCIOLOGICAL PERSPECTIVE:
        ESSAYS IN THE EMPIRICAL STUDY OF RELIGION. Belmont, CA: Wads-
        worth, 1973. ix, 315 pp.

        Presents a collection of, and some abstracts from, previously
        published essays arranged under five topics: 1) on being and becom-
        ing religious; 2) on the effects of religion; 3) on conformity and
        rebellion among the religious professionals; 4) on the origins and
        evolution of religious groups; and 5) on the future of religion.

        Contains items 157, 215, 804, 1929, and excerpts from items 95, 115.

453.   Gordon-McCutchan, R. C. "Great Awakenings?" SOCIOLOGICAL ANALYSIS
        44 (1983): 83-95.

        Discusses whether the great religious awakenings come in cycles,
        whether they can be traced to social sources and stress, and
        whether they have a profound impact on culture. Various theories
        about the relationship between revivals and social stress and about
        their periodic recurrence are examined. The author accepts the
        view that "social stress leads to a renewal cycle--a revival cycle
        leads to radical reform" (p. 94).

354.   Gorni, Yosef, Yaacov Oved, and Idit Paz, editors. COMMUNAL LIFE:
        AN INTERNATIONAL PERSPECTIVE. New Brunswick, NJ: Transaction
        Books, 1987. 758 pp.

        Presents 78 essays covering the various perspectives of communal
        lifestyle. The articles are divided into the following six sec-
        tions: 1) ideological aspects, including the religious, spiritual,
        and utopian dimensions; 2) historical and comparative approaches
        (where there are essays on the Essenes and on medieval and Renais-
        sance communities); 3) the educational experience and social tech-
        niques used by different groups; 4) sociological perspectives; 5)
        family and sex roles; and 6) economic issues. There are many
        essays that deal with the kibbutzim in Israel.

        Contains items 289, 293, 338, 429, 445, 2168.

355.   Gotz, Ignacio L. "The Commune as Symbol." ALTERNATIVE FUTURES:
        THE JOURNAL OF UTOPIAN STUDIES 2.1 (1979): 76-96.

        Discusses the meaning of communes that, in spite of their anti-
        institutionalism, express a desire for the improvement of the human
        condition. Communal living, in the author's view, is "not merely a
        matter of dynamics, of fraternal spirit, or of economic expediency"
        (p. 82). Among the factors that contribute to the emergence of
        communes is the dissatisfaction with materialistic conditions.
        Communes "symbolize the dreams of human solidarity, and awaken in
        us the consciousness of its possibility" (p. 92).

356.   Greeley, Andrew M., and William C. McCready. "Some Notes on the
        Sociological Study of Mysticism." ON THE MARGINS OF THE VISIBLE
        (item 799), pp. 303-22.

        Presents an outline of a sociological study of religious mysti-
        cism (that excludes occult phenomena and trance experiences).
        Various descriptions of mysticism are examined and the four main
        elements of the mystical experience, namely ineffability, noetic
        quality, transiency, and passivity, described. The authors contend
        that the ecstatic person, no matter how deviant he or she might be,
        should be taken seriously. The social, cultural, and structural
        contexts in which the mystical experiences occur should also be
        carefully and thoroughly investigated. Examples of the kind of
        questions the authors asked are given in an appendix.

357.   Hadden, Jeffrey K., and Anson Shupe D. TELEVANGELISM: POWER AND
        POLITICS ON GOD'S FRONTIER. New York: Henry Holt and Co., 1988.
        viii, 325 pp.

        Examines the efforts of contemporary television evangelists and
        their followers to bring about a cultural revival in America.
        Focusing on the key figures in the emergence of the New Christian
        Right, such as Pat Robertson and Jerry Falwell, the authors see
        conservative Christianity as a powerful force in American politics.
        They show how modern communication technology in the hands of these
        evangelists is transforming American religion. The main themes,
        namely religion, society, and politics, of the Televangelical
        Movement are described. The resource mobilization theory is used
        to understand the success of the New Christian Right. Several
        reasons are advanced to explain why, in the authors' view, this
        movement will continue unabated for some time.

358.   Hadden, Jeffrey K., and Anson Shupe D., editors. PROPHETIC RELI-
        GIONS AND POLITICS: RELIGION AND THE POLITICAL ORDER, VOLUME 1.
        New York: Paragon House, 1986. xxix, 458 pp.

        Presents the papers read at an interdenominational conference
        organized by the New Ecumenical Research Association (a Unification
        Church affiliate) to discuss the relationship between prophetic
        religions and politics. The material is divided into five clusters
        of papers, namely: 1) a theoretical assessment of Weber's theory;
        2) prophetic religions at the grass roots level; 3) prophetic reli-
        gions as nation builders; 4) prophetic religions and accommodation;

and 5) conflict and institutionalization. The subject matter dealt
with in these essays covers Christian and Islamic fundamentalism,
various prophetic leaders (including Marcus Garvey, Sun Myung Moon,
and Ram Mohan Roy), and several specific movements like Soka
Gakkai, the Rastafari Movement, and Pentecostalism.

Contains items 349, 867, 1871, 1929.

359.   Hadden, Jeffrey K., and Charles Swan. PRIME TIME PREACHERS: THE
        RISING POWER OF TELEVANGELISM. Reading, MA: Addison-Wesley
        Publishing Co., 1981. xxi, 217 pp.

        Investigates the activities and roles of evangelical preachers on
        American television who represent a socioreligious movement. The
        authors define who these preachers are, how they became important,
        their television followers, and the effect they might have on the
        country as a whole. Television preachers are classified into seven
        types: 1) supersavers (Billy Graham, Oral Roberts, Rex Humbard, and
        Jerry Falwell); 2) mainliners (Robert Schuller); 3) talkies (Jim
        Bakker, Pat Robertson, and Paul Crouch); 4) entertainers (Jimmy
        Swaggart and Ross Bagley); 5) teachers (Richard De Haar and Paul
        Van Gorder); 6) rising stars (James Robison, Kenneth Copeland, and
        Jack Van Impe); and 7) unconventional (Ernest Angley). Their
        audiences are transformed into communicants who "are able to tran-
        scend their sense of loneliness and little worth" (p. 67) in the
        privacy of their living rooms. The main themes of television ser-
        mons, the financial operations, the political involvement of the
        evangelists, and the reaction to the Moral Majority are among the
        topics discussed.

360.   Hall, John R. "Social Organization and Pathways of Commitment:
        Types of Communal Groups, Rational Choice Theory, and the Kanter
        Thesis." AMERICAN SOCIOLOGICAL REVIEW 53 (1988): 679-92.

        Discusses, in the context of Kanter's theory (item 383), ways in
        which commitment in communes is achieved. The author reexamined
        Kanter's data on nineteenth-century communes and suggests an ideal
        typology of five groups, namely communes, intentional organiza-
        tions, ecstatic associations, communities, and otherworldly sects.
        He discovers "distinctive causal pathways to commitment at work at
        the two successful types of communal groups--the community and the
        other-worldly sect" (p. 688), both of which tend to last longer
        than other communes. Commitment in these two types is achieved by
        different means: communities stress the need for social cohesion
        through authority, while otherworldly sects emphasize social con-
        trol through spiritual hierarchy.

361.   Hall, John R. THE WAYS OUT: UTOPIAN COMMUNAL GROUPS IN AN AGE OF
        BABYLON. London: Routledge and Kegan Paul, 1978. x, 269.

        Presents a comparative study of alternative communal groups which
        the author observed from 1970 to 1976. The formation of such
        groups, the conditions that attract people to seek them, and the
        creation of a group myth are traced. The author describes the
        number of ways time is constituted in communes, examines the

communal life with its various forms of government, and considers
the needs that such a life caters to. There are two appendices
that deal with research methods.

362.   Hammond, John L. "The Reality of Revivals." SOCIOLOGICAL ANALYSIS
        44 (1983): 111-16.

        Admits that religious revivals not only fall outside the natural
        course of events, but also have striking effects. Four areas of
        debate are outlined: 1) the reasons why revivals take place; 2) the
        number of people who take part in them; 3) the nature of the belief
        systems; and 4) the effects on society at large. The author holds
        that revivals do not occur because of anomie or discontent, but
        rather because of the internal dynamics of the churches themselves.
        Past revivals did not contribute to social consensus or harmony,
        and led to disruption rather than social cohesion. He agrees with
        those scholars who maintain that religious revivals are genuine
        religious awakenings that occur intermittently and that sometimes
        introduce new patterns of belief and behavior that have an impact
        on social life in general.

363.   Harrell, David Edwin. WHITE SECTS AND BLACK MEN IN THE RECENT
        SOUTH. Nashville: Vanderbilt University Press, 1971. xix,
        166 pp.

        Presents a study of the types of religious expression in the
        southern United States and argues that "the racial views of south-
        ern religious spokesmen are primarily related to class values
        rather than theological presuppositions" (xvi). The author draws
        attention to the diverse and large White sects and cults in the
        South and to their middle-class and lower-class positions in soci-
        ety. The more radical sects and cults are said to be atypical in
        their racial attitudes and patterns of behavior. A lengthy biblio-
        graphical essay that also covers sociological literature is
        included (pp. 135-52).

364.   Hayden, Brian. "Alliances and Ritual Ecstasy: Human Response to
        Resource Stress." JOURNAL FOR THE SCIENTIFIC STUDY OF RELIGION
        26 (1987): 81-89.

        Applies archaeological models and theories to explain the dis-
        tinctly human behavior called "religion" and more specifically the
        tendency and susceptibility to ecstatic experiences. It is main-
        tained that religious behavior and emotional bonds have "clear-cut
        and major selective advantages;" in other words, they are critical
        in maintaining alliances that were essential for survival. Ritual
        ecstasy among primitive societies was a means to deal with long-
        term, periodic resource shortages and daily problems of survival.
        Though not applied to the new religious movements, this essay
        offers an anthropological theory of the origin of ecstatic
        experiences.

365.   Hayden, Dolores. SEVEN AMERICAN UTOPIAS: THE ARCHITECTURE OF
        COMMUNITARIAN SOCIALISM, 1790-1975. Cambridge: MIT Press,
        1976. ix, 401 pp.

Investigates "the relationship between social organization and the building process in particular community groups" (p. 4) and tries to explain how these groups define their own lifestyles. The author theorizes that communal groups use the design process to explore the transition from sociological theory to practice. The following seven communities, four of which are religious, are chosen for intensive study: the Shakers, the Fourierites, the Mormons, the Perfectionists, the Inspirationists, the Union Colonists, and the Llano Colonists. The book's material is organized around three major themes: seeking utopia, building utopia, and learning from utopia. Illustrations by photographs and drawings of the buildings of the groups studied are given .

366.   Heirich, Max. "Change of Heart: A Test of Some Widely Held Theories About Religious Conversion." AMERICAN JOURNAL OF SOCIOLOGY 83 (1977): 653-80.

Reviews critically three major trends in social science to explain the nature and course of religious conversion, namely: 1) conversion is a fantasy solution to social and/or psychological stress; 2) conversion is brought about by previous conditioning or socialization processes; and 3) conversion is explained by looking at the patterns of interactions between people. The author puts these theories to the test by applying them to the Charismatic Renewal and finds them all unsatisfactory. He suggests that the questions about conversion need to be reformulated in such a way that conversion is not treated as an odd experience and that its content is taken seriously.

367.   Hepworth, Mike, and Bryan S. Turner. CONFESSION: STUDIES IN DEVIANCE AND RELIGION. London: Routledge and Kegan Paul, 1982. viii, 200 pp.

Discusses the relationship between criminal and religious confessions in the context of law and religion as mechanisms of social control. After explaining the meaning of confession, the authors examine various confessions as "rituals of social closure." One chapter is dedicated to the study of Christian confession, the functions of which are outlined and critically examined and its relationship to social stratification is explored.

368.   Hillery, George A. "Freedom and Social Organization: A Reconceptualization: A Comparative Analysis." AMERICAN SOCIOLOGICAL REVIEW 36 (1971) 51-65.

Provides a general taxonomy of human groups into two broad divisions, that is, the formal and the communal. Among the latter are listed intentional communities (like the Hutterites) and limited communities (like the Shakers and the Trappists). The author maintains that the antagonism of members increases proportionately to the deprivation of freedom and that "only if a group is not primarily oriented to the attainment of a specific goal will it maximize the freedom of its members" (p. 62). Though this essay was written before the cults had become an issue, it deals with one of the major topics about cult life, namely the degree to which members are deprived of individual freedom.

369.   Hillery, George A. "Families, Communes, and Communities." PER-
        SPECTIVES ON THE AMERICAN COMMUNITY (item 498), pp. 511-26.

        Considers in some detail the principal components of communes,
        namely: 1) spatial integration and the family; 2) cooperation and
        space; and 3) cooperation and the family. The importance of the
        ideology and common goals of the communal life are stressed. Among
        groups from which data is collected are the following: the Roman
        Catholic Trappist monks, various Protestant communes, the
        kibbutzim, Oneida Community, the Hutterites, and the Shakers.

370.   Himmelfarb, Harold S. "Measuring Religious Involvement." SOCIAL
        FORCES 53 (1975): 606-18.

        Critically reviews some of the more prominent typologies of reli-
        gious involvement and argues that they all suffer from problems of
        definition and classification. Besides a lack of clear focus on
        the meaning of religious involvement, many typologies are deficient
        in one or more of the following ways: "a) the lack of mutual exclu-
        siveness and exhaustiveness between categories; b) the mixture of
        temporally unrelated phenomena; and c) the inclusion of phenomena
        that are at different levels of abstraction" (p. 607). A synthesis
        of religious involvement typologies is attempted. The author dis-
        tinguishes between 1) four objects of orientation, that is, super-
        natural, communal, cultural, and interpersonal, 2) two types of
        orientation, namely behavioral and ideational, and 3) three speci-
        fically religious (supernatural) dimensions, namely devotional,
        doctrinal, and experiential.

371.   Hostetler, John A. COMMUNITARIAN SOCIETIES. New York: Holt, Rine-
        hart, and Winston, 1974. vii, 65 pp.

        Presents an anthropological study of societal groups commonly
        described as "communities, brotherhood, communal experiments, and
        utopian movements" which are growing rapidly in the modern world.
        The author describes their basic lifestyles and attempts to under-
        stand them in their social and cultural contexts. Among the groups
        included are the Essenes, the Cathars in France, the Labadists in
        Holland, the Lollards in England, the Waldenses in Italy, the Ana-
        baptists in various parts of Europe, various religious orders, and
        more recently formed communities in the U.S.A. The author focuses
        on three major groups: 1) "The Family," a modern experiment in
        group marriage; 2) the Oneida Community in the nineteenth century;
        and 3) the Hutterites in the sixteenth century. In each case the
        origins, ideology, structure, social patterns, and policy are
        sketched. It is maintained that interest in communes cannot be
        dismissed as a passing fad. Communes are seen as a reaction to
        alienation and to fractured human relationships and as a means for
        self-discovery and exposure to a broader range of human potential.

372.   Howard, John R. THE CUTTING EDGE: SOCIAL MOVEMENTS AND SOCIAL
        CHANGE IN AMERICA. Philadelphia: J. B. Lippincott Co., 1974.
        ix, 276 pp.

Examines the social movements that flourished in the 1960's and 1970's. The author takes a socio-historical approach. He identifies the social base of the support of each movement and for personal involvement, describes their ideologies and analyzes their functions. One section deals with the youth movement (which includes the Hippie Movement of the 1960's) and the flowering of communes and new religions, which are alternative and more viable expressions of the same impulses that gave rise to the counter-culture. The main new religions dealt with are the Hare Krishna Movement, the Jesus Movement, and the Jews for Jesus.

373.   Hunsberger, Bruce E. "Apostasy: A Social Learning Process." REVIEW OF RELIGIOUS RESEARCH 25 (1983): 21-38.

Examines the process of apostasy, that is, the abandonment of one's religious upbringing, and attempts to understand it as a product of socialization. The author maintains that, to some extent, apostates report less religious influences in their early education than nonapostates. The parents of apostates are less religious. Consequently, response to parental teaching and the stress placed on religion at home are likely to influence apostasy. Poorer relationships with parents might be due to apostasy rather than the cause of it.

374.   Hunsberger, Bruce E. "A Re-Examination of the Antecedents of Apostasy." REVIEW OF RELIGIOUS RESEARCH 21 (1980): 158-70.

Explores the conditions that might lead individuals to abandon the religion of their upbringing. Apostates are usually less religious people even before they abandon their faith. They report more doubts about their religious beliefs, react more negatively against their religious practices, and find themselves disagreeing more strongly with what they were taught. The relationship between those who keep the faith and their parents, especially the father, tends to be better. Though the author's research does not include the new religious movements, his results offer materials for comparative studies between apostates from mainline religions and from the new cults. The bibliography included in this essay refers to further studies on apostasy, particularly among college students.

375.   Hunsberger, Bruce E., and L. B. Brown. "Religious Socialization, Apostasy, and the Impact of Family Background." JOURNAL FOR THE SCIENTIFIC STUDY OF RELIGION 23 (1984): 239-51.

Compares apostasy rates from mainline churches in Australia with those in Canada, taking into account the religious socialization apostates received in their youth and their family backgrounds. Apostates were found to report poorer relationships with parents (contrary to Hunsberger's previous study). The importance of home environment and of early religious socialization in influencing later religious orientations is underscored.

376.   Jackson, Bruce. "The Other Kind of Doctor: Conjure and Magic in Black American Folk Medicine." AMERICAN FOLK MEDICINE: A SYMPOSIUM. Edited by Wayland D. Hand. Berkeley: University of California Press, 1973, pp. 59-72.

Discusses the uses of folk magical beliefs and practices among Black Americans. The author thinks that medical treatments by magic are declining because of the change of social status that is taking place among Blacks. The movement to urban centers is one of the main causes of the decline of folk medicine.

377.   Janzen, Donald E. "The Intentional Community--National Community Interface: An Approach to the Study of Communal Societies." COMMUNAL SOCIETIES 1 (1981): 37-42.

Argues that the study of communes as closed units is deficient and that the comparison between past and present communes may not help us understand the nature of communal societies. It is suggested that intentional communities should be compared to other communities in the same historical period. The daily schedules and the nature of religious life within intentional communities should be compared with those of national communities. This paper focuses on the overlap between these two communities. The social organizations, political structures, economic patterns, and belief systems are compatible and constantly interact with each other. Modern communes, like the larger society, must deal with social security, workers' compensation, and medicine.

378.   Jarvis, Peter. "Towards a Sociological Understanding of Superstition." SOCIAL COMPASS 27 (1980): 285-95.

Draws attention to a neglected area in sociology, namely folk religion and superstition. After discussing the definitional problem and referring to research being done on superstition, the author proposes a definition and a typology of superstition. For him superstition is firmly rooted in folk religion, that is, it lies outside the institutionalized belief systems of a society. Three main types of superstition--omen, taboo, and spell--are distinguished, each type having its own clearly defined objectives. Beliefs in taboos and spells are magical in nature. Though the basic structure of superstition remains constant, its contents appear to be susceptible to change.

379.   Jerome, Judson. FAMILIES OF EDEN: COMMUNES AND THE NEW ANARCHISM. New York: Seabury, 1974. xiii, 271 pp.

Presents an autobiographical approach to the study of communes. The author argues that visits to communes and other standard means of sociological inquiry are unsatisfactory approaches to understanding communal living. Instead, he combines the impressions and observations of many reporters, who were themselves members of communes, with the many underground publications by different communes. The information is topically arranged under such headings as economics, communication, political structure, interpersonal and sexual relationships, education, religion, and changing consciousness. The study is limited to communes founded after 1965. A typical commune is "one which is urban, internally oriented, pluralistic, noncredal, private, poor, closed, organic, omnivorous, unincorporated, without industry or business, in a rented house, with partial economic sharing, both sexes, non-monogamous, non-

academic, composed of six to eight peers with one or two children
under six" (p. 13). Sketchy accounts of 14 communes are given.
Communes, the author thinks, are an effort to regain the state of
the Garden of Eden. They represent an escape from reality and are
the antithesis of the centralized system of communism. This book
contains no index or bibliography.

380.   Kanter, Elizabeth Ross. "Communes in Cities." CO-OPS, COMMUNES,
        AND COLLECTIVES: EXPERIMENTS IN SOCIAL CHANGE IN THE 1960S AND
        1970S. Edited by John Case and Rosemary C. R. Taylor. New York:
        Pantheon Books, 1979, pp. 112-35.

        Examines the many urban communes in the United States that were
        in existence in the 1960's and 1970's. The author describes the
        various communal lifestyles, the way children grew up in communes,
        and the tensions and conflicts that beset most of them. She thinks
        that urban communes are "too temporary, transient, and conflict-
        ridden" to replace the traditional family structure. "But they do
        signify shifts in family process, and they are laboratories for new
        kinds of family relationships" (p. 113).

381.   Kanter, Elizabeth Ross. "The Romance of Community: Intentional
        Communities as Intensive Group Experiences." THE INTENSIVE GROUP
        EXPERIENCE (item 464), pp. 146-85.

        Considers the kinds of group experiences that people who join
        communes (among which is included the Hare Krishna settlement near
        Moundsville, West Virginia) are seeking. Three communal images--
        the spiritual, the familial, and the pastoral--dominate the life-
        styles of communes. The author traces the historical background of
        intentional communities in monasticism, millennialism, and utopian-
        ism. She holds that people who join a community (or "communitas")
        are looking for "the immediate ecstatic experience of oneness with
        other people," and that such a quest is a "recurrent human longing"
        (p. 159). The community-building process, which the author has
        outlined in several of her other works (see, for instance, item
        383) are described and the benefits and conflicts of communal liv-
        ing discussed.

382.   Kanter, Elizabeth Ross. "Utopian Communities." SOCIOLOGICAL
        INQUIRY 43 (1973): 263-90.

        Studies alternative communities that came into being to make up
        for the "loss of community" that characterizes advanced industrial
        societies and that aim to create a more perfect and cooperative
        human society. The origins of these groups from value-based social
        movements, their early stages of organization, the problems they
        face, and their political and economic arrangements are discussed.
        In spite of their idealism, most utopian communities do not last
        more than a few years. Those that survive change drastically over
        the years, just as Oneida became a business, Amana turned into a
        church and a business, and Zoar developed into a township.

383.   Kanter, Elizabeth Ross. COMMITMENT AND COMMUNITY: COMMUNES AND
        UTOPIAS IN SOCIOLOGICAL PERSPECTIVE. Cambridge: Harvard Univer-
        sity Press, 1972. x, 303 pp.

Considers the ideas and values underlying utopian communities, presents the results of research done on such groups which flourished in the nineteenth century, and outlines some of the major problems that these experimental lifestyles faced. The links between these communes and the more recent ones are explored and two contemporary communes (Synanon, a drug rehabilitation community, and Cumbres, a personal growth community in New Hampshire) are described in detail. Some of the moral and social issues raised by these groups are discussed. The focus throughout is on how a commune is built and maintained. Six commitment-building processes are described: 1) sacrifice; 2) investment; 3) renunciation; 4) communion; 5) mortification; 6) and transcendence. Alternate styles of communal living are major social experiments on, or living laboratories of, human behavior, motivation, and interpersonal relationships. The relevance of communes for social life in general is explored. There is an appendix that includes a sample of nineteenth-century communes and the method of studying them (pp. 241-69). A bibliography is also attached (pp. 270-86).

384.   Kanter, Elizabeth Ross. "Commitment and the Internal Organization of Millennial Movements." AMERICAN BEHAVIORAL SCIENTIST 16 (1972): 219-43.

Argues that, in many cases, millennial movements are attempts to build a radical moral community. The author focuses on the social nature and internal characteristics of these movements rather than on their origins and goals, and sees their millennial ideas as secondary to the social act of mobilization and the formation of a new community. The various commitment-building processes (see her book above) are described. Examples from different societies and historical periods are provided. Millennial movements have several functions: they create a place where believers can gather; they offer the excitement and chance of doing the forbidden; they provide an outlet for frustration; and enable a person to reach a new identity.

385.   Kanter, Elizabeth Ross. "Communes." PSYCHOLOGY TODAY 4 (July 1970): 56-61, and 78.

Discusses the contemporary communal movement and compares it to nineteenth-century utopian communes. The family arrangement, group support, and property ownership are among the main areas covered. Two of the more common forms of communes operating today are anarchistic groups and growth centers like Esalen. A comparison of some successful and many unsuccessful communes is made, focusing on the following areas: communal farming, structure, ritual, mutual criticism, communal sharing, and labor. Growth communes are more likely to succeed that anarchistic ones. The former create a place for enduring commitment with their roots well established in communal life.

386.   Kanter, Elizabeth Ross, editor. COMMUNES: CREATING AND MANAGING THE COLLECTIVE LIFE. New York: Harper and Row, 1973. xiv, 544 pp.

Presents a collection of 45 essays dealing with various types of religious and social communes. The material is organized under four headings: 1) how communes come into being; 2) the arrangements within a commune (leadership, organization, work, and property); 3) the relationships between the members (family, children, and interpersonal issues); and 4) the crises of communes (the reason why so many of them dissolve and the problems which confront those that survive). Three types of communes--religious, political, and psychological--are distinguished. The Bruderhof, Hutterites, Shakers, Oneida, and a typical kibbutz are among the groups studied. The author, in an overview chapter, discusses communal living from Plato's REPUBLIC to the counterculture of the 1960's. Underlying theme throughout all utopias is the desire for wholeness and integration.

387.   Kaplan, Robert E. "Maintaining Relationships Openly: Case Study of Total Openness in a Communal Organization." HUMAN RELATIONS 31 (1978): 375-93.

Studies "expressive maintenance" in the Farm, a utopian organization where instrumental, affective, and moral commitments are clearly manifested. In these communal organizations, face-to-face relationships are encouraged to promote constructive social ties and to enable members to cope with conflict and hostility. Integration, regulation, and education are three main functions of expressive maintenance.

388.   Katz, Jack. "Deviance, Charisma, and Rule-Defined Behavior." SOCIAL PROBLEMS 20 (1972): 186-202.

Discusses the concept of deviance as rule breaking and the labeling of people as deviants in the context of five cases of witchcraft. The author maintains that deviance cannot be applied to witches. He thinks that both deviance and charisma imply an orientation to behavior as defined by rules.

389.   Kelley, Dean M. "Why Conservative Churches are Growing." JOURNAL FOR THE SCIENTIFIC STUDY OF RELIGION 17 (1978): 165-72.

Reflects on the continued growth of conservative churches like the Southern Baptist Convention, the Church of Jesus Christ of Latter-Day Saints, Jehovah's Witnesses, the Seventh-Day Adventists, and the Salvation Army. The author responds to the criticism leveled at his book (item 390) and reconfirms his view that these churches are successfully recruiting new members because they do a better job "of making life meaningful in ultimate terms" (p. 166). He admits that the reasons why this growth has happened in our times are not clear. He suggests that conservative churches are more effectively preaching the Gospel and winning others for Christ. It is the seriousness, costliness, and strictness with which this is done (and not the content) that makes one system of ultimate meaning more convincing than another.

390.   Kelley, Dean M. WHY CONSERVATIVE CHURCHES ARE GROWING: A STUDY IN SOCIOLOGY OF RELIGION. New York: Harper and Row, 1972. xiii, 184 pp.

Reflects on the statistical evidence that, while the mainline churches seem to be declining, sectarian and conservative religious groups are making amazing gains. After discussing the meaning and function of religion, the author develops a scale for measuring success and failure. Four religious movements, namely Anabaptist, Wesleyan, Mormon, and Jehovah's Witnesses, are examined in order to determine the traits of a "strong" religion. An elaborate chart is drawn to show how and in what respect strong groups differ from weak ones. Sectarian traits are said to be linked with strong groups, while ecumenically minded churches are the weakest.

391. Kephart, William M. EXTRAORDINARY GROUPS: THE SOCIOLOGY OF UNCON-
       VENTIONAL LIFE-STYLES. New York: St. Martin's Press, 1976. vii,
       311 pp.

Selects for examination the seven following American institutions and lifestyles: the Old Order Amish, the Oneida Community, the Father Divine Movement, the Shakers, the Mormons, the Hutterites, and modern communes. Assimilation and culture conflict are among the main themes that all these groups manifest in their origin and development. The appeal of modern communes is explored and reasons for their success or failure discussed. The background, origins, membership, family system, and major beliefs of each group are presented. The author thinks that, though communes have provided people with genuinely alternative lifestyles, most of them will probably not survive because they cannot compete with society at large, nor can they satisfy the basic human needs as well as, or better than, the larger society. Good introductory bibliographies are attached to each chapter.

392. Kephart, William M. "Why They Fail: A Socio-Historical Analysis of
       Religious and Secular Communes." JOURNAL OF COMPARATIVE FAMILY
       STUDIES 5.2 (1974): 130-40.

Questions the reasons why internal dissensions have so often been the cause of the failure of communes. Several factors, such as economics, aberrant membership, leadership, social organization and commitment, primary group needs, and children, are considered. Most communes in America, with the notable exceptions of groups like the Hutterites, Bruderhof, and Synanon, have been so charac-terized by lack of success that they do not pose any discernible threat to the American family system. Several problems that face communes, such as outside pressures, home influences, legal diffi-culties, drugs, jealousies, and quarrels dealing with sex, are discussed. Both religious and secular communes face the same endemic problems.

393. Kilbourne, Brock, and James T. Richardson. "A Social Psychological
       Analysis of Healing." JOURNAL OF INTEGRATIVE AND ECLECTIC PSY-
       CHOTHERAPY 7 (1988): 20-34.

Attempts to identify the common structure underlying psychother-apy and other healing practices by offering a model of healing in diverse social and cultural contexts. The authors examine the universal roles and attributes of healers and of those healed and discover several similarities between traditional psychotherapy and religious and spiritual healers and shamans and between the clients of both groups. The common factors of psychotherapy and religious conversion are discussed.

394. Killian, Lewis M. "Social Movements: A Review of the Field."
      SOCIAL MOVEMENTS: A READER AND SOURCE BOOK (item 332), pp. 9-53.

      Surveys the field of sociological studies of social movements in the early 1970's. The features, norms, and structures of these movements and their membership are described. Other areas of interest to sociologists, like interaction within an individual movement, the effects movements have on society, and their relationship to social change, are among the major topics covered. A short bibliography is added.

395. Klandermans, Bert. "New Social Movements and Resource Mobilization: The European and American Approach." INTERNATIONAL JOURNAL OF MASS EMERGENCIES AND DISASTERS 4 (1986): 13-37.

      Examines student, environmental, women's, and peace movements in Europe and North America and observes that, in spite of their similar developments, diverse theoretical approaches have been applied to study them. In the United States, resource mobilization theory has shifted attention away from deprivation and has attempted to explore cycles of protest as reactions to the availability to resources. In Europe, attention has centered on a new social movement approach that looks for the role of postindustrial society in generating the movements that are considered to be innovative or creative reactions to Western culture. The author thinks that the two approaches are complementary. Though this essay does not deal directly with the new religious movements, it clearly outlines two theoretical approaches that have been used to explain them.

396. Klandermans, Bert. "Mobilization and Participation: Social-Psychological Expansion of Resource Mobilization Theory." AMERICAN SOCIOLOGICAL REVIEW 49 (1984): 583-600.

      Contrasts social-psychological theories of social movements with the resource mobilization approach, the latter stressing the importance of structural factors, such as the availability of resources and social networks, the former seeing participation as a consequence of predisposing psychological traits. The author attempts to combine the two approaches and, using data from a Dutch workers' union, concentrates on participation and the way it changes through mobilization efforts. He maintains that those who join new movements do not do so simply to relieve some deprivation or strain; they have to perceive their goals as instrumental to the elimination of these feelings. Such perception is brought about by a "consensus mobilization." A bibliography of some basic works on resource mobilization theory is given.

397. Krippner, Stanley, and Don Ferish. "Mystic Communes." MODERN UTOPIAN 4 (Spring 1970): 1-9.

Gives a brief account of 18 communes that practiced some form of mysticism. Three types of organizations are identified: 1) secular communes with little formal administration; 2) secular communes that have some administrative network; and 3) religious communes that are highly structured and organized. A list of communes with their inhabitants, religious orientations, sexual practices, and drug usage is provided.

398.   Larkin, Ralph W. SUBURBAN YOUTH IN CULTURAL CRISIS. New York: Oxford University Press, 1979. xi, 259 pp.

Provides a picture of the cultural crisis in America by an analysis of an American middle-class suburb and its high school. The development of youth in "post-scarcity America" is traced from the 1950's to the 1970's. The author thinks that pleasure (sex and drugs) has become routinized and that beneath its regular consumption lies both a malaise and a lack of meaning in life. He finds contradictions between the material wealth of the surroundings and the inner poverty of the people he studied. He suggests that technological society has been unable to provide young adults with a bold vision.

399.   Lasch, Christopher. THE CULTURE OF NARCISSISM: AMERICAN LIFE IN AN AGE OF DIMINISHING EXPECTATIONS. New York: W. W. Norton and Co., 1978. xviii, 268 pp.

Advances the view that the culture of competitive individualism is dying out in Western society and that the result of this decay has been an extreme pursuit of happiness, which is indicative of a narcissistic preoccupation with the self. The author discusses the awareness movement of modern times and thinks that it points to a climate that is therapeutic and not religious. Though the author does not link the emergence of cults with the narcissistic trend, other scholars have done so, stressing that narcissism is one of those conditions that contributes to the success of the religious movements.

400.   Lauer, Robert H. "Social Movements: An Interactionist Analysis." SOCIOLOGICAL QUARTERLY 13 (1972): 315-28.

Applies the interactionist perspective to explore the dynamics of the social movement to legitimize the use of the drug popularly known as LSD. The history of the movement, led by Timothy Leary, Richard Alpert, and others, is traced and its objectives and values specified. It is hypothesized that "the genesis of a social movement involves an interactional process between an interest group and its social environment" (p. 320). The development of the movement's ideology and program is identified in three areas: 1) the symbol system to express the ideology; 2) the idea of the "messiah game" that included the feeling of superiority that came with the experience of drugs and the homage paid to Leary and his followers; and 3) the idea of social withdrawal which led to the belief in a utopia based on the drug's allegedly therapeutic and creative powers. The motivational factors in the recruitment of people to join the movements are discussed.

401.   Lauer, Robert H., editor. SOCIAL MOVEMENTS AND SOCIAL CHANGE.
       Carbondale: Southern Illinois University Press, 1976. xxviii,
       292 pp.

       Presents a collection of essays, most of which had been published
       in professional journals, on the various dimensions of social inno-
       vation. The contributions are thematically divided in four major
       areas, each preceded by a short introduction: 1) the impact of
       change upon movements; 2) the movements' strategies for change; 3)
       the effects of movements on change; and 4) the consequences of
       social movements. In his introduction, the editor sketches the
       interrelationships between social movements and social change and
       in his summary conclusion suggests directives for the future. Some
       of the contributors to this volume include millenarian movements in
       their speculations. A useful bibliography is appended.

402.   Lauer, Robert H., and Jeanette C. Lauer. THE SPIRIT AND THE
       FLESH: SEX IN UTOPIAN SOCIETIES. Metuchen, NJ: Scarecrow Press,
       1983. viii, 244 pp.

       Studies sexual relations in the utopian societies of nineteenth-
       and twentieth-century America. The authors investigate the various
       arrangements that different groups considered ideal, the ideology
       and mechanisms of social control used to maintain the sexual prac-
       tices, the experiences of people in different communes, and the
       nature of sexuality. They examine the following methods employed
       to insure conformity to the preferred sexual patterns: 1) spatio-
       temporary structuring, such the separation from the outside world;
       2) interaction patterns and experiences, like rituals, confessions,
       and the pressure of collective opinion; 3) cognitive input, such as
       the use of music, educational programs, and the promulgation of
       explicit rules to legitimate the sexual customs; and 4) coercive
       measures, such as surveillance and punishment. Examples are given
       from many religious movements, including Oneida Community; the
       Shakers, and the Bruderhof, and more recent groups like Ananda
       Cooperative Village, Twin Oaks, and Brook Farm.

403.   Lebra, Takie Sugiyama. "Millenarian Movements and Resocialization."
       AMERICAN BEHAVIORAL SCIENTIST 16 (1972): 195-217.

       Discusses those aspects of millenarian movements that are related
       to the socialization of adults. It is claimed that these movements
       can change a person's behavior through enlightenment, integration,
       and commitment, leading to a better adaptation to the larger, secu-
       lar society. The author distinguished between institutionalized
       and millenarian socialization, the latter being more intense and
       voluntary, demanding the individual's involvement. He presents
       a somewhat detailed analysis of enlightenment, integration, and
       commitment that are seen as specific mechanisms of socialization.
       The adaptation of the individual can be examined both as a change
       in the individual's behavioral system and as a change in his or her
       social environment.

404.   Leger, Daniele. "Charisma, Utopia, and Communal Life: The Case of
       Neorural Apocalyptic Communes in France." SOCIAL COMPASS 29
       (1982): 41-58.

Examines the notion of charisma in those neo-rural communes in France that came into being since the early 1970's. Several difficulties regarding the notion of charisma as it applies to these communes are discussed. The author thinks that charismatic activity transcends the contradictions on which apocalyptic and utopian communes are built and functions on three levels, namely those of knowledge, work, and enjoyment. It is argued that the charismatic relationship is a complex social one that cannot be reduced to the psychological attraction that the charismatic leader engenders.

405. Lewis, I. M. RELIGION IN CONTEXT: CULTS AND CHARISMA. Cambridge: Cambridge University Press, 1986. x, 139 pp.

Contains several of the author's lectures and previously published papers on the relationship between cults and charisma or mystical power. Anthropological theories of witchcraft, the various types of witchcraft and sorcery, the relationship between cannibalism and witchcraft, and the shaman's charismatic role are among the topics discussed. One chapter is dedicated to local cults in African Islam. Though largely concerned with nonliterate cultures, this book is a good illustration of the anthropological approach to the study of marginal and new religious movements. A useful bibliography is added (pp. 118-32).

406. Lewis, I. M. ECSTATIC RELIGION: AN ANTHROPOLOGICAL STUDY OF SPIRIT POSSESSION AND SHAMANISM. Harmondsworth, England: Penguin Books, 1971. 221 pp.

Emphasizes the need to treat religious enthusiasm as a social phenomenon. Some of the most striking common elements found in diverse ecstatic religions and the social contexts in which they occur are examined. Because possession cults are so often limited to women, the author argues that they are "thinly disguised protest movements against the dominant sex" (p. 31). Possession cults function as agents of political and social control.

407. Lipp, Wolfgang. "Charisma--Social Deviation, Leadership, and Cultural Change: A Sociology of Deviance Approach." ANNUAL REVIEW OF THE SOCIAL SCIENCES OF RELIGION 1 (1977): 59-77.

Adopts an interactionist-dialectic approach to the study of charisma and suggests that charismatic behavior should be treated as a phenomenon of deviance. Elaborating on Weber's views on the subject, the author attempts to show how charisma affects society and changes its values.

408. Lofland, John, and Michael Jamison. "Social Movement Locals: Model Member Structure." SOCIOLOGICAL ANALYSIS 45 (1984): 115-29.

Discusses movement organization as a type of formal organization whose members are consciously arranged into a unified but differentiated pattern of actions for the pursuit of their goals. Six structures of movement locals are distinguished, one of which, namely an association that is sustained by volunteers, is examined in detail. The sect is identified as one level of such an associa-

tion. Three sectarian features are listed: 1) exclusiveness of
membership; 2) totalitarianism of organization and outlook; and 3)
hostility towards, or separation, from society. Some areas for
further research are indicated.

409.   Lynch, Frederick R. "Sociology and Parapsychology." JOURNAL OF
       PARAPSYCHOLOGY 39 (1975): 297-305.

       Compares the disciplines of sociology and parapsychology from the
       perspective of the sociology of science. The author observes that
       these two disciplines are engaged in similar struggles with pre-
       viously established academic subjects and perceived as threatening
       by other scholars. Several suggestions for interdisciplinary
       research are made. It is the author's view that sociology and
       parapsychology "can learn a great deal from one another" (p. 304).

410.   Mandelker, Ira L. RELIGION, SOCIETY, AND UTOPIA IN NINETEENTH-
       CENTURY AMERICA. Amherst: University of Massachusetts Press,
       1984. 181 pp.

       Studies utopian communities, exploring particularly their sacred
       histories, values, and prophecies that often accompany their forma-
       tion. Three areas are investigated: 1) the relationship between
       secular values and worldviews and the sacred ones adopted by uto-
       pian religious communities; 2) the extent to which this relation-
       ship affects the social structure of utopias; and 3) the outcome of
       the same relationship on the growth, stability, success, or failure
       of utopian groups. The author's investigation is carried out
       mainly in the context of the mid-nineteenth-century Perfectionist
       Community of Oneida. The tensions between the various components
       of communal life, such as religion, economics, sex, marriage, and
       the family, and science are discussed. The Oneida Community is
       seen as an attempt to resolve and transcend these tensions.

411.   Mandic, Oleg. "A Marxist Perspective on Contemporary Religious
       Revivals." SOCIAL RESEARCH 37 (1970): 237-58.

       Maintains that religion is one of those forces that influences
       the direction of social evolution and distinguishes some general
       features of the process of religious revival. The activities of
       the Roman Catholic Church in Yugoslavia are quoted as an example of
       a religious revival in a state where religion does not exist offi-
       cially. The following general conditions determine the revival of
       religious thought and practice: 1) the conflict between the rapid
       advance of technology and the consciousness of the average person;
       2) the conflicts deriving from the processes of social change; 3)
       the conflict between the young and the old; 4) the loneliness of
       the urban individual in a large society; 5) the conflict between
       spirituality and pragmatism; 6) changes in the aims of institution-
       alized religion. The absence of administrative compulsion in reli-
       gious matters and the reduction of militant atheism also contribute
       to religious revival.

412.   Marsden, George M. FUNDAMENTALISM AND AMERICAN CULTURE: THE SHAP-
       ING OF TWENTIETH-CENTURY EVANGELICALISM, 1870-1925. New York:
       Oxford University Press, 1980. xiv, 306 pp.

Traces the origin and growth of American Fundamentalism, which is
seen "as a distinct version of evangelical Christianity uniquely
shaped by the circumstances of America in the early twentieth century" (p. 3). The influence of social, intellectual, and religious
crises on the movement are traced. After looking at the emergence
of Fundamentalism through the accounts of its prominent leaders
(like D. L. Moody), the author discusses the movement's distinctive
features, namely dispensational pre-millennialism, its stress on
holiness, its efforts to defend the faith, and its views on the
relationship between Christianity and culture. One final chapter
looks at four main interpretations of Fundamentalism, that is as
a social, political, intellectual, or American phenomenon.

413.   Martin, David. A GENERAL THEORY OF SECULARIZATION. New York:
        Harper and Row, 1978. ix, 353 pp.

Outlines the four basic patterns of a theory of secularization,
namely: 1) the European pattern; 2) the mixed pattern; 3) the pattern of secular monopoly (mainly in Eastern Europe); and 4) the
pattern of "reactive organicism" (with Spain cited as a typical
example). The following factors indicative of the process of religious change in different countries are discussed: 1) religious
pluralism; 2) anti-clericalism; 3) clerical status; 4) the political situation; 5) civil religion; 6) the relationship between the
church and the state; and 7) the presence of religious parties. A
substantial bibliography of materials published up to the mid-1970's
is provided (pp. 309-41).

414.   Marx, John H., and David L. Ellison. "Sensitivity Training and
        Communes: Contemporary Quests for Community." PACIFIC SOCIOLOGI-
        CAL REVIEW 18 (1975): 442-62.

Discusses the quest for community that, from a sociological point
of view, satisfies the need for greater individual power, commitment, and participation, and, from a psychological viewpoint caters
to the basic personal longing for meaningful social relationships.
The authors interpret this quest as a sectarian reaction. Two
areas are covered: 1) sensitivity training and communal movements
in America; and 2) intensive groups which form part-time communities that have quasi-religious characteristics. It is suggested
that independent movements have a common source in the search for
community, collective meaning, and identity. Intensive groups and
communes share similar features, such as, cohesiveness, solidarity,
support, intimacy, de-bureaucratization, antistructuralism, and
utopianism--features which are symptomatic of disenchantment with
society. Sensitivity training and communes "provide permissive,
sheltered, collective contexts for adult resocialization which
invent and manufacture alternative life styles and identities"
(p. 460).

415.   Mauss, Armand L. SOCIAL PROBLEMS AS SOCIAL MOVEMENTS. Philadel-
        phia: J. B. Lippincott, 1975. xviii, 718 pp.

Presents a case "for considering social problems as simply a
special kind of social movement." The first two chapters of this
book provide a theoretical background that, though not directly

related to the cults by the author, has provided the sociological
framework for social-scientific studies on new religious movements.
Theories that rely on functionalism, strain and control, social
learning, social interactionism, and social change are summarized.
The genesis and types of social movements and their organization,
mobility, and natural history are also considered.

416. McCarthy, John D., and Mayer N. Zald. "Resource Mobilization and
      Social Movements: A Partial Theory." AMERICAN JOURNAL OF SOCIOL-
      OGY 82 (1977): 1212-39.

      Approaches the study of social movements from the theoretical
      viewpoint of resource mobilization, that is, an approach that deals
      with the dynamics and tactics of social-movement growth, change,
      and decline. The manner in which this theory deals with the
      support base of new movements, their strategies and recruitment
      techniques, and their relationship with the larger society in which
      they thrive is contrasted with the traditional method that stresses
      the connection between frustrations and the growth and decline of
      the movements. The theoretical elements of the resource mobiliza-
      tion theory are explained in detail. A basic bibliography is added
      (pp. 1238-39).

417. McCready, William C. "A Survey of Mystical Experiences: A Research
      Note." LISTENING: JOURNAL OF RELIGION AND CULTURE 9.3 (1974):
      55-70.

      Points out that current research shows that mystical experiences
      are common among a large proportion of the population and should
      not be considered bizarre phenomena. The author summarizes the
      results of a study carried out at the National Opinion Research
      Center, a study that explored the relationship between mystical and
      psychic experiences, demographic variables, and family experiences.
      The various kinds of stimuli that triggered mystical experiences,
      their duration, and the way people describe them are also recorded.
      Those who have mystical experiences "do not appear to be those
      people who inhabit the fringes and recesses of our society, rather
      they appear to be ordinary people with, perhaps, extraordinary
      sensitivities to forces outside themselves" (p. 67). They differ
      from those who have had ESP experiences and are generally happier.

418. McLoughlin, William G. "Timepieces and Butterflies: A Note on the
      Great-Awakening Construct and Its Critics." SOCIOLOGICAL ANALY-
      SIS 44 (1983): 103-10.

      Refutes the major opponents of the theory that religious revivals
      occur periodically. The following four major views are examined
      and found inadequate: 1) revivals are not normal and much less
      constant (the minimalist approach); 2) revivals occur within the
      framework of grandiose theories of social change (the microcosmic
      approach); 3) American revivals have taken place in such a diverse
      and pluralistic environment that no large-scale theory of social
      change is applicable (the precisionist-pluralistic approach); and
      4) revivals emerge out of the inner dynamics of Christian theology
      and faith (the neo-orthodox view).

419.   McLoughlin, William G. REVIVALS, AWAKENINGS, AND REFORM: AN ESSAY
        ON RELIGION AND SOCIAL CHANGE IN AMERICA, 1607-1977. Chicago:
        University of Chicago Press, 1978. xv, 239 pp.

        Seeks to explain America's five great awakenings or periods of
        "ideological transformation." The author relies on anthropological
        ideas and interprets these religious revivals as a revitalization of
        culture that alters the nation's worldview. After a discussion of
        the Puritan revitalization of early seventeenth-century England, he
        states that social, political, and economic changes in America led
        to the disruption of the Puritan system and prepared the group for
        revival. Besides the Puritan Awakening, four other revivals, Pro-
        testant rituals at first spontaneous but since 1830 routinized, are
        described: 1) the First Great Awakening (1730-1760); 2) the Second
        Great Awakening (1800-1830); 3) the Third Great Awakening (1880-
        1920); and 4) the Fourth Great Awakening (1960-1990?).

420.   McLoughlin, William G. "Revivalism." THE RISE OF ADVENTISM (item
        350), pp. 119-53.

        Examines and evaluates four functions served by religious reviv-
        als in America, that is, the spiritual, ecclesiastical, social, and
        historical. The author observes that religion has often been seen
        either as a means of maintaining social control and conformity or
        as a way of encouraging experimentation and social change. Reviv-
        als can have the radical social functions of reforming social and
        ecclesiastical systems and of bringing about political and social
        reform. Contemporary revivalism is, in the author's view, premil-
        lennial and apocalyptic.

421.   Melucci, Alberto. "The New Social Movements: A Theoretical
        Approach." SOCIAL SCIENCE INFORMATION 19 (1980): 199-226.

        Suggests that a social theory of collective action is necessary
        to combine various factors that are at the roots of the rise of new
        social movements. Several characteristics of these movements, like
        direct participation and solidarity, are described. Regressive
        utopia with a strong religious component plays a key role in some
        contemporary movements.

422.   Melville, Keith. COMMUNES IN THE COUNTER CULTURE: ORIGINS, THEO-
        RIES, STYLES OF LIFE. New York: William Morrow, 1972. 256 pp.

        Studies the growing communal movement in America, a movement
        that, while not yet able to provide a truly alternative culture,
        may throw some light on the problems of contemporary society.
        After examining the uses of utopia and its proliferation in the
        nineteenth century, the author dwells on the counterculture of the
        1960's and attempts to understand it as a social-class phenomenon
        rather than as a generational revolt. Communes typify the rejec-
        tion of middle-class culture. They introduce those who join them
        into the counterculture and act as agents for social change.

423.   Mills, Richard. YOUNG OUTSIDERS: A STUDY OF ALTERNATIVE COMMUNI-
        TIES. New York: Pantheon Books, 1973. xi, 208 pp.

Presents a study of the 1960 Hippie Movement based on research done in England. The author describes the life of a typical London Hippie, the process of transformation whereby one actually becomes a Hippie, and the sacraments of renewal (music, drugs, and festivals). The decay of the Hippie culture is traced in part to its own values (that couldn't reasonably be lived by) and its goals (that had little chance of being fulfilled). Finally, the relationship between the Hippie pattern of thought and behavior to changes taking place in Western society are discussed and the response of society assessed. The author thinks that the labeling process helped create the hippies and that legislation against them can never be completely successful. He suggests that society is faced with two options: 1) "either to leave subcultures free to work;" or 2) "to cripple them by legislating against core practices, and consequently to create for society as a whole generally insoluble problems" (p. 193).

424.   Miyahara, Kojro. "Charisma: From Weber to Contemporary Sociology." SOCIOLOGICAL INQUIRY 53 (1983): 368-87.

Critically examines the study of charisma, starting with Weber's concept and covering the many sociological efforts to use it in the explanation of social movements, collective behavior, social change, etc. Three concepts of charisma used in contemporary sociology, namely prophetic, routinized, and magical, are discussed. The author thinks that there is "conceptual anarchy surrounding charisma" and suggests that charismatic phenomena "are essentially the expressions of the pure process of alienation" (p. 383). The important elements within the idea of charisma are outlined.

425.   Moment, Gairdner B., and Otto F. Kraushaar, editors. UTOPIAS: THE AMERICAN EXPERIENCE. Metuchen, NJ: Scarecrow Press, 1980. vii, 251 pp.

Contains 14 essays on various utopian communities in the United States, written from the perspectives of different academic disciplines. An introductory essay discusses the meaning of utopia and the impulses that lead to the foundation of utopian societies. Besides articles discussing issues like economics and women in several utopian societies, there are a number of articles dedicated to the study of individual utopias (such as Harmony Society, Jonestown, the Quakers, Stephen Gaskin's Farm, and Koinonia Community).

Contains items 281, 1878.

426.   Mouly, Ruth, and Roland Robertson. "Zionism in American Premillenarian Fundamentalism." AMERICAN JOURNAL OF THEOLOGY AND PHILOSOPHY 4.3 (1983): 96-109.

Reflects on the support that pre-millenarian fundamentalist Christians have given to the modern State of Israel, particularly on the high visibility of this support since the rise of the Moral Majority and other right-wing evangelical groups. The authors give an account of the birth of pre-millenarian Zionism in the second half of the nineteenth century and on its development in recent

years. The authors endeavor to show how "the future of a religious
movement can be affected by political and instrumental factors,
leading possibly in the long-run to reshaping of theological empha-
ses on one or both sides of the 'alliance'" (p. 108).

427.   Mowri, Jeni. "Systematic Requisites of Communal Groups." ALTERNA-
       TIVE LIFESTYLES 1 (1978): 235-61.

       Discusses various communal groups in America that share the feel-
       ings of powerlessness, occupational alienation, and personal loss
       of human significance. The author examines the economic needs,
       social organization, and goal attainment of these communes and
       offers two hypotheses: 1) there is a direct relationship between
       the financial situation and the duration of a commune; and 2) there
       is also a direct link between the type and degree of social organi-
       zation and the commune's duration. Communes, it is argued, repre-
       sent "a viable alternative to the traditional nuclear family" (p.
       252), even though most of them fail to endure for any great length
       of time. A catalog of nearly 100 nineteenth- and twentieth-century
       communal groups, with their duration, type of social organization,
       and financial situation, is provided (pp. 255-61).

428.   Muncy, Raymond Lee. "Sex and Marriage in Utopia." SOCIETY 25.2
       (1988): 46-48.

       Summarizes some of his previous studies on sex and marriage in
       American utopias of the nineteenth century (see items 429, 430, and
       431).

429.   Muncy, Raymond Lee. "Sex and Marriage in Nineteenth-Century Uto-
       pian Communities in America." COMMUNAL LIFE (item 354), pp.
       585-90.

       Points out that the utopian communities of the nineteenth century
       removed the monogamous nuclear family from its central position in
       Western society. The Icarians, the Shakers, the Mormons, and the
       Perfectionists (like Oneida) all tried different kinds of sexual
       arrangements and marital life. It is argued that one of the main
       reasons why these experiments failed is "the inability of the mem-
       bers to subordinate their own selfish interests to the interests of
       the community at large" (p. 587). Those communities that abolished
       private property and the nuclear family survived longer than those
       that maintained these two institutions. Similarly, those groups
       that adopted pure communism and strict celibacy, which required a
       strong religious commitment, tended to last longer.

430.   Muncy, Raymond Lee. "Women in Utopia." FRANCE AND NORTH AMERICA:
       UTOPIA AND UTOPIANS (item 276), pp. 57-69.

       Reasserts his previous division of utopian communities into three
       distinct types (see item 431). The position of the sexes in each
       type is described. The author thinks that, though communal experi-
       ments of the nineteenth century made concessions to women, incen-
       tives such as relief from housework and the care of children
       attracted relatively few women.

431.   Muncy, Raymond Lee. SEX AND MARRIAGE IN UTOPIAN COMMUNITIES: NINE-
        TEENTH-CENTURY AMERICA. Bloomington: Indiana University Press,
        1973. 275 pp.

        Distinguishes between three types of utopian communities formed
        in nineteenth-century America: 1) sectarian religious groups that
        peaked in the first half of last century; 2) reform, perfectionist
        groups that were popular during the three decades preceding the
        Civil War; and 3) purely economic cooperatives that were alterna-
        tives to capitalism and that blossomed in the last quarter of the
        century. The author focuses his research on those communities,
        like the Owenites, Fourierists, Shakers, Mormons, Amana, and Brook
        Farm, that appeared to be original and unique in the way they han-
        dled sex and marriage. One chapter is dedicated to a discussion of
        women's rights in utopias. Several factors that led to the down-
        fall of these communities, such as the loss of leadership, economic
        failure, outside opposition, and the inability of members to put
        the interests of the community before their own individual desires,
        are identified. Those communes that adopted celibacy seem to have
        survived the longest.

432.   Murvar, Vatra. "Messianism in Russia: Religious and Revolutionary."
        JOURNAL FOR THE SCIENTIFIC STUDY OF RELIGION 10 (1971): 277-338.

        Examines two kinds of messianic movements in Russia, namely
        religious and revolutionary, and explores their similar features
        and their intense contribution to the dominant cultural values of
        the Soviet Union today. The background of two messianic movements
        and a theoretical scheme of their common doctrines and practices
        are given. Religious messianism is seen as being very pervasive in
        prerevolutionary Russia. Unrelated to Protestantism, it was a
        response to the threats of westernization and was deeply rooted in
        monasticism. Millennialism, a dual cosmology, and a spiritual,
        political, and economic monism and/or collectivism are said to be
        the main elements in both kinds of messianism. The development of
        many revolutionary messianisms is described. Among its many reli-
        gious features, the following are listed: eschatological expecta-
        tions, dogmaticism, exclusivism, intolerance, totalism, asceticism,
        guilt and expiation, and an apocalyptic vision.

433.   Musgrove, Frank. ECSTASY AND HOLINESS: COUNTERCULTURE AND THE OPEN
        SOCIETY. London: Methuen, 1974. vi, 236 pp.

        Examines the attitudes of the counterculture of the 1960's and
        suggests that it is linked not with alienation, but with anomie,
        that is, a sense of loneliness, social dislocation, and uprooted-
        ness. The author believes that "the politics of the counter cul-
        ture ties it to mainstream society" (p. 16) in a dialectical manner
        of confrontation, interaction, exchange, and transformation. Var-
        ious aspects of the counterculture are sketched and the relation-
        ship between ecstasy and the economic order discussed. Examples
        are provided from diverse cultures in different historical periods.
        Countercultures, it is argued, arise in rich societies that are
        characterized by steep population growth and intensive migrations
        brought about by great economic changes.

434. Najman, J. M., G. M. Williams, J. P. Deeping, J. Morrison, and M.
      J. Anderson. "Religious Values, Practices, and Pregnancy Out-
      comes: A Comparison of the Impact of Sect and Mainstream Religi-
      ous Affiliation." SOCIAL SCIENCE AND MEDICINE 26.4 (1988):
      401-407.

      Raises the issue of the relationship between sect lifestyles and
      health and specifically considers the connection between religious
      affiliation and pregnancy outcomes. Three groups of women, who
      were members of religious sects (such as Jehovah's Witnesses, the
      Mormons, and Ananda Marga) who attended a mainstream church regu-
      larly and who identified themselves with a major denomination but
      did not go to church regularly, took part in research carried out
      in Brisbane, Australia. The sociodemographic characteristics of
      each group are outlined. It is concluded that the data indicates
      that sect mothers who are committed to their religious lifestyle
      have better pregnancy outcomes than those whose religious affili-
      ation is weak.

435. Nunn, Clyde Z. "The Rising Credibility of the Devil in America."
      LISTENING: JOURNAL OF RELIGION AND CULTURE 9.3 (1974): 84-100.

      States that recent surveys point to a decline in the belief in
      God and an increase in the presence of the devil and that this
      suggests that "Satanism is making dramatic gains in America" (p.
      86). The author sees some relationship between belief in the devil
      and the contemporary sociocultural conditions that are often per-
      ceived as threatening and as being under some evil force. The rise
      of the belief in Satan has been greater among the less-educated and
      less-religious people.

436. O'Keefe, Daniel L. STOLEN LIGHTENING: THE SOCIAL THEORY OF MAGIC.
      New York: Continuum Publishing Co., 1982. xxii, 581 pp.

      Attempts to construct a general theory of magic based on data
      from several academic fields, but organized from a sociological
      point of view. After an introductory discussion on the meaning of
      magic, the author presents his material in three parts. The first
      deals with the symbolism in magic and is largely phenomenological
      in its approach. The second discusses the relationship between
      magic and religion. The third considers the functions of magic.
      The occult sciences (such as astrology), the paranormal (like ESP
      and flying saucers), millennial and magical cults and sects, and
      communes where small-group interaction is aimed at renewing the
      magical experience, are all included in the author's exhaustive
      coverage of magical beliefs and practices. A postscript gives an
      overview of the history of magic from the ancient times to the
      occult upsurge in the twentieth century.

437. Okugawa, Otohiko. "Intercommunal Relationships Among Nineteenth-
      Century Communal Societies in America." COMMUNAL SOCIETIES 3
      (1983): 68-82.

      Examines the nature and extent of intercommunal relationships
      between 270 communes that existed between 1787 and 1919. Five
      types of such relationships are identified: 1) branch or offshoot

communes; 2) ideological confederates; 3) schismatic communities;
4) sequential communes, such as those that relocated their residents; and 5) parent communes. Various diagrams are drawn to
illustrate the major interrelationships and the complex migration
patterns. It is concluded that when a group did not survive, its
members often went to live in another, usually related, commune.

438. Oved, Yaacov. TWO HUNDRED YEARS OF AMERICAN COMMUNES. New Bruns-
     wick, NJ: Transaction Books, 1988. xvi, 500 pp.

     Presents an extensive study of American communes from 1663 to the
     present time. The author attempts to understand the establishment
     of communes in the context of American history and to discover the
     common typical trends. He divides his work in two main parts. The
     first part gives a descriptive account of the various communes,
     drawing the reader's attention to their various types and features.
     The second part analyzes the communes as religious, social, and
     ideological movements. Among the topics treated are the social
     activities and management of the communes, their financial and
     educational systems, their ritual practices, their family arrange-
     ments and the status of women within the commune, their relation-
     ships with the outside world, and their viability. A comprehensive
     list of American communes between 1663 and 1984 is given in an
     appendix. The copious footnotes to each chapter provide an exten-
     sive historical bibliography.

439. Parrinder, Patrick. "The Prophets of Doom." NEW SOCIETY 69 (Sep-
     tember 1984): 354-55.

     Examines the accounts of contemporary visions of a catastrophic
     end that have often been foretold in terms of nuclear and environ-
     mental disasters. The subliminal effects of these forebodings
     uttered by fortune-tellers and other oracles can be seen by means
     of an analogy with the process of being ill. The author maintains
     that fascination with future disasters, including the Christian
     notion of Armageddon, is a sign that society does not satisfy all
     our needs.

440. Perinbanayagam, R. S. "The Dialectics of Charisma." SOCIOLOGICAL
     QUARTERLY 12 (1971): 387-402.

     Expands on Wilner and Wilner's view that charismatic leadership
     "involves a process of interaction between a leader and his follow-
     ers where the leader transmits and the followers accept his presen-
     tation of himself as their predestined leader, his definitions of
     their world as it is and as it ought to be, and his convictions of
     his mission and their duty to reshape it" (p. 388). Two cases of
     charismatic leadership, namely those of Mahatma Gandhi and Adolph
     Hitler, are contrasted. The author considers charisma to be a
     result of social processes that involve selective and purposeful
     activities. Charisma can elicit a variety of responses that create
     and sustain conflicting structures. The case of Gandhi shows that
     charismatic leadership need not develop to the "illusions of
     grandeur" that are manifested in the leadership of Hitler.

441.   Photiadis, John, and William Schweiker. "Attitudes Toward Joining
        Authoritarian Organizations and Sectarian Churches." JOURNAL FOR
        THE SCIENTIFIC STUDY OF RELIGION 9 (1970): 227-43.

        Contends that attempts to adapt to a rapidly changing society
        create alienation and could lead people to authoritarian institu-
        tions (like the John Birch Society) or sectarian churches. Four
        indicators of alienation, namely powerlessness, bewilderment, need
        to avoid social contact and exposure, and anomie, are taken into
        consideration together with the drift to conservatism and authori-
        tarianism. Among the several correlations found is that between
        powerlessness and the attraction to sectarian churches.

442.   Piazza, Thomas. "Jewish Identity and the Counterculture." THE NEW
        RELIGIOUS CONSCIOUSNESS (item 614), pp. 245-64.

        Discusses Jewish participation in the counterculture of the late
        1960's and the effects of such involvement on a Jewish sense of
        identity. Conducting his research at the University of California
        at Berkeley, the author investigates the nature of Jewish identity
        before the college experience. He concludes that, while the number
        of young Jews active in the counterculture was relatively high,
        there are no reasons to believe that their Jewish background led
        them to such activity. He further suggests that the counterculture
        did not seem to be a hindrance to this identity.

443.   Pitts, Jesse R. "On Communes." CONTEMPORARY SOCIETY: A JOURNAL OF
        REVIEWS 2 (1973): 351-354.

        Reviews critically five books on communes published in the early
        1950's. The reviewer points out that the authors are essentially
        "pro-commune" in their orientation, even though some of them
        attempt a sociological analysis of the communal movement.

444.   Pitzer, Donald E. "Collectivism, Community, and Commitment: Amer-
        ica's Religious Communal Utopians From Shakers to Jonestown."
        UTOPIAS (item 275), pp. 119-35.

        Examines the utopian nature of communitarianism and the utopian
        roots of American religious communes that have abounded since the
        nineteenth century. The various lessons that can be learned from
        these experiments are discussed. Jonestown is cited as receiving
        one of the most justified denunciations ever made of a commune.
        The author's view is that intentional communities were seen by
        young people in the 1960's as "a means of security, sanctuary, and
        a 'raison d'etre,' that is, an alternative environment in which to
        humanize an otherwise depersonalized society" (p. 132-33).

445.   Poldervaard, Saskia. "The Position of Women in Commune-Movements
        Especially in Dutch Live-In Groups." COMMUNAL LIFE (item 354),
        pp. 606-13.

        Examines the position women have held in communes throughout
        history and accounts for their present status in contemporary com-
        munes in Holland. It is stated that women held high positions

among groups like the Essenes, Cathari, Waldenses, Anabaptists, and
Shakers. In the communes of the 1960's, however, women played a
secondary role because women's emancipation in the West was thought
to have been complete and hence male/female relationships were no
longer regarded as a problem. In contemporary Dutch live-in groups,
members are more involved in politics outside the communes and thus
have a better chance of furthering the equality of the sexes.

446.   Prebish, Charles. "Reflection on the Transmission of Buddhism
       to America." UNDERSTANDING THE NEW RELIGIONS (item 667), pp.
       141-52.

       Explores the transplanting of Buddhism in America from the second
       half of the nineteenth century to the present time. The initial
       activity of the two Buddhist sects (Joho Shinshu and Zen), the
       influx of new form of Buddhism (such as Soto Zen and Tibetan Bud-
       dhism) by the mid-1950's, and the expressions of Buddhism in the
       1960's and 1970's are described. Buddhism is related to the recent
       religious turmoil in American and to the drug culture. Some of the
       problems with which Buddhist communities are faced are discussed.
       Two distinct developments in Buddhism are noted: 1) the stress on
       sound, basic doctrine and practice shared by all Buddhists; and 2)
       the trend towards a novel element, which is often centered on a
       charismatic leader.

447.   Pritchard, Linda K. "Religious Change in Nineteenth-Century Amer-
       ica." THE NEW RELIGIOUS CONSCIOUSNESS (item 614), pp. 297-330.

       Examines the religious upheaval that took place during the Second
       Great Awakening in America between 1820 and 1860, a period of rapid
       social and economic shifts in American society. The religious
       transformation that occurred at this time in divided into four
       stages: 1) the crisis of the established churches; 2) the emergence
       of new theological perspective and religious practices; 3) the
       development of many new sects; and 4) the condition of the estab-
       lished religion. The sects themselves are classified in four main
       types: 1) regenerative (that stayed within the established tradi-
       tions); 2) schismatic (that formed new modes of Christianity); 3)
       cultic (that include non-Christian groups, like the Mormons, Spiri-
       tualism, Swedenborgianism, Mesmerism, and Astrology); and 4) quasi-
       religious (that were largely secular sects, like New Harmony,
       Fourierism, and the Oneida Community).

448.   Ramey, James W. "Emerging Patterns of Innovative Behavior in
       Marriage." FAMILY COORDINATOR 21 (1972): 435-56.

       Discusses various forms of alternative marriage arrangements
       found in communes or intentional communities that are classified in
       four principal types: 1) religious; 2) utopian; 3) revolutionary;
       and 4) student. The fourth type is said to be somewhat unique
       because it is temporary. Religious communes have several distin-
       guishing characteristics, including a rigid structure, an authori-
       tarian leader, a work ethic, withdrawal from society, and a family
       orientation. The author considers the different marriage systems
       as alternative, rather than deviant, arrangements.

449.   Ramirez, Francisco O. "Comparative Social Movements." INTERNA-
        TIONAL JOURNAL OF COMPARATIVE SOCIOLOGY 22.1-2 (1981): 2-21.

        Compares and contrasts two perspectives on social movements,
        namely the social-integration approach and the more recently
        developed resource-mobilization paradigm. After identifying the
        key concepts and assumptions of both theories, the author focuses
        on the resource-mobilization approach. Criticisms of both views
        are briefly outlined. Finally, the world-system perspective, that
        considers social movements as part of a broader collective social
        reality, is described and its application to new movements noted.

450.   Redecop, Calvin. "Religious Intentional Communities." INDIANA
        SOCIAL STUDIES JOURNAL 29.1 (1976): 52-65.

        Specifies four major traits that distinguish religious inten-
        tional communities from other alternative ones, namely: 1) their
        religious ideology; 2) their commitment to this ideology; 3) their
        desire to save the world by attracting people to their respective
        community; and 4) their longevity. American freedom, mobility, and
        change are said to be the main conditions that have given rise to
        communal societies. Statistics of the number of communal groups
        and the number of adherents from 1790 to 1970 are provided.
        Several features of Christian religious communities are described
        and their impact on American culture assessed.

451.   Redlinger, Lawrence J., and Philip K. Armour. "Changing Worlds:
        Observations on the Process of Resocialization and the Transfor-
        mation of Subjective Social Reality." VIOLENCE AND THE CULTS
        (item 653), pp. 88-102.

        Presents an analytic framework for understanding the resocializa-
        tion that takes place in radical conversions. Five elements in
        this process are identified and discussed: 1) the necessity of a
        plausible structure; 2) the replication of childhood dependencies
        with new significant others; 3) new embodied models of the world;
        4) isolation and segregation from the past in a community that
        stresses the present; and 5) reinterpretation of, alienation from,
        and fabrication of the past in order to legitimize the newly
        adopted lifestyles. The authors think that this process can be
        applied to a further understanding not only of cults and sects, but
        also of business corporations, the military, and traditional reli-
        gious orders.

452.   Richardson, James T. "A Data Frame for Commune Research." COMMU-
        NAL STUDIES NEWSLETTER 4 (March 1977): 1-13.

        Develops a program for conducting research on communes, including
        such religious groups as the Jesus Movement. Three major areas of
        investigation are outlined in schematic form: 1) general character-
        istics; 2) economic organization; and 3) belief and value systems.
        The organizational arrangements on individual, local (or communal),
        and national (or federal) levels should also be taken into account.

453.   Richter, Peyton E., editor. UTOPIAS: SOCIAL IDEALS AND COMMUNAL
        EXPERIMENTS. Boston: Holbrook Press, 1971. xi, 323 pp.

Presents 24 essays on utopianism, focusing on utopian speculation
and planning. The material is divided into four parts. The first
reflects on the many reasons why utopias are sought. The second
describes several utopian communities, including the Shakers, New
Harmony, Icaria, and Oneida. The third and fourth parts deal with
the arguments for utopia and their rebuttals respectively. In the
introduction the editor describes the various approaches to the
study of utopianism and discusses the relationship between utopian
thinking and social goals, various kinds of utopias, utopian views
of human nature, and utopia and the problem of freedom.

454. Rigby, Andrew. COMMUNES IN BRITAIN. London: Routledge and Kegan
     Paul, 1974. 157 pp.

Classifies communes in Great Britain in six different types,
namely: 1) self-actualizing; 2) mutual-support; 3) activist; 4)
practical; 5) therapeutic; and 6) religious. Several examples are
given and in each case the author outlines the commune's origin and
recruitment practices, its internal organization, its financial
structure, its relationship with the outside world, and its problems and future prospects. Communes, in the author's view, can
provide answers "to the isolation and loneliness of the nuclear
family life, the meaninglessness of the rat-race, the futility of
consumerism, the boredom of nine to five work, and so on" (p. 148).

455. Rigby, Andrew. ALTERNATIVE REALITIES: A STUDY OF COMMUNES AND
     THEIR MEMBERS. London: Routledge and Kegan Paul, 1974. ix, 341.

Gives an insider's overview of the commune scene in Great Britain
in the late 1960's. After an introduction to the communitarian
tradition, the author discusses the youth culture of the period as
a movement of people seeking self-realization. The communes in
Britain are divided in five types: 1) self-actualizing communes; 2)
communes for mutual support; 3) activist communes; 4) practical
communes; and 5) therapeutic communes. Religious communes are said
to be of two kinds, the mystic (like Findhorn Community) and the
ascetic (like Kingsway Community and the Grail Community). Those
who join communes are freedom seekers, or security-seekers, or
activists. The worldview of communitarianism, the problems encountered in communal settings, and the relationship between communes
and social change are dealt with. A basic bibliography that
includes material up to the early 1970's is added.

456. Roberts, Michael K., and James D. Davidson. "The Nature and
     Sources of Religious Involvement." REVIEW OF RELIGIOUS RESEARCH
     25 (1984): 334-50.

Briefly outlines two major theories about the nature of religious
involvement, namely Weber's approach that stresses the meaning
religion has for the individual and Durkheim's functional view
that highlights the importance of the group. Four major sources
of religious involvement are assessed: 1) sociodemographic influences; 2) the individual's meaning system; 3) the individual's
social relationships with church members; and 4) religious belief.
The authors observe that for church members, the meaning and belong-

ing components of religious involvement are positively correlated;
that that sociodemographic variables affect this involvement
indirectly; that one's meaning system determines the level of
involvement; that social relationships have the strongest effect
on one's involvement; and that religious beliefs are the least
important factor.

457.   Roberts, Ron E. THE NEW COMMUNES: COMING TOGETHER IN AMERICA.
        Englewood Cliffs, NJ: Prentice-Hall, 1971. x, 144 pp.

        Describes some of the utopian and communitarian movements that
        were extant around 1970. After dwelling on young people's attempts
        to create an alternative society, the author lists several major
        characteristics of communal groups, namely: 1) rejection of social
        classes; 2) rejection of the large-scale organization of modern
        societies; and 3) the adoption of a nonbureaucratic type of gover-
        nance. One chapter deals with nineteenth-century communes and
        included the Shakers, New Harmony (Owenism), Fourierism, Oneida,
        and German colonies like Amana and the Mennonites. Religious com-
        munes, such as the Lama Foundation, Quaker colonies, and Koinonia
        Farm, are also described. The author thinks that the success of
        these communities should be judged by their stability and endurance
        and by the effects they have on the individual lives of their
        members.

458.   Rogers, Joseph W., and M. D. Buffalo. "Fighting Back: New Modes
        of Adaptation to a Deviant Label." SOCIAL PROBLEMS 22 (1974):
        101-18.

        Discusses the reaction of people who are labeled deviant. The
        author develops a typology of adaptation to counteract this nega-
        tive characterization. Reactions to deviancy may be: 1) acquies-
        cence; 2) repudiation; 3) flight; 4) channeling; 5) modification; 6)
        evasion; 7) reinterpretation; 8) redefinition; and 9) alteration.
        Although the authors do not discuss the issue of labeling in con-
        nection with the cults, they provide the background for understand-
        ing the labeling theory that has been applied to cult members.

459.   Rohrlich, Ruby, and Elaine Hoffman Baruch, editors. WOMEN IN
        SEARCH OF UTOPIA: MAVERICKS AND MYTHMAKERS. New York: Schocken
        Books, 1984. xxvii, 325 pp.

        Presents a collection of essays, some previously published, dis-
        cussing women's search for, and place in, utopias in different his-
        torical periods. The material is grouped in four parts dealing
        with, respectively, utopias in the distant past (such as among the
        early Celts and Cretans), those in the recent past (for example,
        the nineteenth-century Oneida Community), contemporary groups (such
        as the Twin Oaks community, Findhorn, and the Children of God), and
        utopian visions. The role and status of women in these utopias is
        considered and the differences between groups that admitted both
        women and men or women only are outlined.

        Contains items 1441, 2070.

460.   Roof, Wade Clark. "The Study of Social Change in Religion." THE
        SACRED AND THE SECULAR: TOWARD REVISION IN THE SCIENTIFIC STUDY
        OF RELIGION (item 623), pp. 75-89.

        Outlines briefly three strands of current research in the area of
        religious change: 1) the tracing of historical patterns of general
        religious change; 2) the examination of secular context of reli-
        gious belief, which studies the place of traditional faith in a
        secularized society; and 3) the analysis of the varieties of mean-
        ing systems in modern society, covering the plurality of alterna-
        tive meaning systems (new religious movements or cults). The
        author thinks that significant developments are taking place in the
        field of religion. The current situation is one that encourages
        inquiry into a rich and exciting field of study.

461.   Roof, Wade Clark. "Social Correlates of Religious Involvement:
        Review of Recent Survey Research in the United States." ANNUAL
        REVIEW OF THE SOCIAL SCIENCES OF RELIGION 2 (1978): 53-70.

        Gives an overview of the research being carried out in three
        areas: 1) current patterns of age, sex, and social class in reli-
        gious involvement; 2) theories of religious involvement, especially
        the deprivation-compensation theory; and 3) new directions in re-
        search and theory. One section covers Wuthnow's study (item 1043)
        of value changes and commitments among young people.

462.   Roozen, David A. "Church Drop-Outs: Changing Patterns of Disen-
        gagement and Re-Entry." REVIEW OF RELIGIOUS RESEARCH 21 (1980):
        427-50.

        Examines the patterns and rates of religious dropouts who even-
        tually return to the religious tradition of their upbringing.
        Historical trends, age variations, reasons for abandoning the prac-
        tice of one's faith, and return statistics are discussed. The part
        played by maturation, personal life crises, intrachurch discord,
        and church experiences that might lead to disengagement are also
        considered. The author concludes that religious disengagement
        decreases with age. Once a person goes beyond the teens, disrup-
        tion of one's life routines and crises are the predominant reasons
        for leaving one's church. Though this study is limited to those
        who leave the mainline churches, it may provide materials for
        understanding why people join cults and for making comparisons with
        dropouts from the new religious movements. A useful bibliography
        is added (pp. 429-50).

463.   Rosen, George. "Social Change and Psychopathology in the Emotional
        Climate of Millennial Movements." AMERICAN BEHAVIORAL SCIENTIST
        16 (1972): 153-67.

        Reviews many different millennial movements that have arisen
        throughout history and maintains that messiahs appear during
        periods of social conflict in order to instill new life among con-
        quered or suppressed peoples. The strange phenomena, like group
        dances, glossolalia, and trances, that frequently accompany these
        movements, are not evidence of psychopathology, but are rather

occurrences that take place when "there is a contradiction between
cultural goals and the institutional means to attain them" (p. 164).
These movements are reactions to stressful conditions; they are
critical of the present state of affairs and endeavor to bring
about beneficial changes in the human condition.

464.   Rosenbaum, Max, and Alvin Snadowsky, editors. THE INTENSIVE GROUP
        EXPERIENCE. New York: Free Press, 1976. xiv, 210 pp.

        Presents a collection of essays discussing participation in in-
        tensive group experiences from different academic perspectives.
        The authors maintain that such participation may be helpful, but
        should not be equated with religious experience. Besides describ-
        ing communal lifestyles and extended family relationships, these
        papers attempt an evaluation. The rise of the encounter group is
        related to the contemporary cultural crisis, particularly the
        breakdown of the ethical system.

        Contains item 381.

465.   Rossel, Robert D. "The Great Awakening: An Historical Analysis."
        AMERICAN JOURNAL OF SOCIOLOGY 75 (1970): 907-25.

        Examines the religious revival in Puritan New England that took
        place between 1730 and 1745 as a "mechanism for social change."
        The author outlines his argument in detail by describing the his-
        torical context of the revival, the Puritan social organization at
        the time, the deterioration of public morals, the cultural strains,
        and the political and religious situation in which the so-called
        "Great Awakening" emerged. He maintains that the clash between the
        institutional order and its material substructure led to tensions
        and change within the social system and that the Great Awakening
        led to a religious order more compatible with individualism, volun-
        tarism, and democracy.

466.   Samarin, William J. "Glossolalia." PSYCHOLOGY TODAY 6 (August
        1972): 48-50, 78-79.

        Maintains that glossolalia is "linguistic nonsense" comparable to
        child's play and that, in spite of the insistence by Pentecostals
        that it is a God-given gift, is simply not a supernatural phenome-
        non. Glossolalia, in the author's view, should be considered as
        one type of religious language. It functions symbolically by mark-
        ing the discontinuity between the sacred and the profane and by
        arousing and expressing religious feelings.

467.   Selengut, Charles. "Eschatology and the Construction of Alterna-
        tive Realities: Toward a Social Conflict Perspective of Millen-
        nialism." THE RETURN OF THE MILLENNIUM. Edited by Joseph Bettis
        and S. K. Johannesen. Barrytown, NY: New Era Books, 1984, pp.
        167-79.

        Suggests that millenarian movements can be studied as "cognitive
        minorities," that is, groups that violate the normative and theo-
        logical concerns of the dominant society and thus challenge its

political and economic interests. Millennial societies create
strong communal structures to counteract society's opposition.
They propose an alternative reality and are, consequently, placed
in an inferior social and political status. Some of the social and
religious consequences of "majority labeling and stigmatizing" are
considered. Millennial groups are marginal and they encourage
social and psychic separation from outsiders through their rituals,
proselytization efforts, and truth claims.

468.   Sheils, Dean, and Philip Berg. "A Research Note on Sociological
       Variables Related to Belief in Psychic Phenomena." WISCONSIN
       SOCIOLOGIST 14 (1977): 24-31.

       Remarks that sociological research on psychic phenomena has
       lagged behind studies on new religious movements and explores the
       sociological variables among those who believe in such phenomena.
       Social status, sex, church attendance, and political preference
       were found to be unrelated to psychic beliefs, though believers in
       psychic phenomena ascribed also to other unconventional cultural
       convictions. Religious orthodoxy was significantly and negatively
       related to psychic beliefs which are usually accompanied by knowl-
       edge of psychic concepts and the claim of psychic experiences.

469.   Shenker, Barry. INTENTIONAL COMMUNITIES: IDEOLOGY AND ALIENATION
       IN COMMUNAL SOCIETIES. London: Routledge and Kegan Paul, 1986.
       280 pp.

       Presents a study of intentional communities that are defined as
       relatively small groups of people "who have created a whole way of
       life for the attainment of a certain set of goals" (p. 10). These
       small societies share certain features with sects and social move-
       ments. Two central elements in their existence are alienation and
       ideology. Three well-established intentional communities, the
       Hutterites, the kibbutzim, and therapeutic communities, are exam-
       ined in some detail. In each case, the origin, development, social
       structure, ideology, socialization techniques, the individual's
       place in the group, deviance and conformity within the group it-
       self, and the exclusive relationship with outsiders are examined.
       Among the many conclusions that are summarized in a final chapter
       (pp. 239-58) is the statement that intentional communities "emerged
       at a time of great social change, a time of social and moral un-
       certainty" (p. 240). A useful select bibliography is included
       (pp. 268-75).

470.   Shepherd, William C. "Religion and the Counterculture--A New Reli-
       giosity." SOCIOLOGICAL INQUIRY 42.1 (1972): 3-9.

       Attempts to clarify the difference between the religious aspects
       of the youth counterculture movement and traditional religion. The
       author first dwells on the concepts of "being religious" and "being
       musical." Then he stresses the importance of truth claims in the
       Western tradition, where religious experience is subordinated to
       the acceptance of religious truth. Finally, he argues that drugs
       and rock music are a form of symbolic ritual that creates and main-
       tains the sense of social solidarity among members of the counter-

culture. The author thinks that the counterculture represents "the birth of a new religious lifestyle in which religious experience is precisely analogous to the aesthetic experience of music" (p. 6).

471.   Shey, Thomas H. "Why Communes Fail: A Comparative Analysis of the Viability of Danish and American Communes." JOURNAL OF MARRIAGE AND THE FAMILY 39 (1977): 605-13.

Compares Danish and American communes and finds out that while the former fail largely for economic or practical reasons, the latter do so for personal motives. The high drop-out rate from both groups is due to internal conflicts, the stress on individualism, the general lack of organization, and the diversity among the members. Fairfield's typology of American communes (see item 333) is taken as an accurate description of the American scene. Though religious communes are not considered, some of the author's reflections may be applicable to those religious groups that promote a communal lifestyle.

472.   Shupe, Anson D., and Jeffrey K. Hadden, editors. THE POLITICS OF RELIGION AND SOCIAL CHANGE: RELIGION AND THE POLITICAL ORDER, VOLUME 2. New York: Paragon House, 1988. xx, 284 pp.

Presents a second volume (see item 358) aimed at exploring the role of religion in the transformation of the political order. The essays are grouped under four thematic headings: 1) the politics of world-transforming movements; 2) the varieties of liberation theologies; 3) religious minorities and integration, especially in India and in the Soviet Union; and 4) Israel as an example of precarious pluralism.

Contains item 544.

473.   Simmons, Herbert W. "Requirements, Problems, and Strategies: A Theory of Persuasion For Social Movements." QUARTERLY JOURNAL OF SPEECH 56 (1970): 1-11.

Provides a framework for analyzing how people are persuaded to join social movements, particularly the reformist and revolutionary ones. The rhetorical arguments of the leaders, the difficulties they encounter, and the strategies they adopt are examined. It is the author's opinion that the leaders of these movements face rhetorical dilemmas in the methods they use to attract potential followers. Successful leaders are able to combine conflicting strategies and to justify them with appeals to higher principles.

474.   Simpson, George Eaton. BLACK RELIGIONS IN THE NEW WORLD. New York: Columbia University Press, 1978. ix, 415 pp.

Brings together several of the author's previously published studies of Black religions that have their roots in Africa and have migrated to America. One chapter covers the role of Blacks in the traditional churches in the United States and Canada, while another discusses Black sects and cults in North America and Great Britain. Among the Black sects and cults in the United States, the following

are included: 1) Father Divine's Peace Mission Movement; 2) the
Black Jews; 3) the Moorish American Temple and Islamic cults;
4) the Black storefront church; and 5) West Indian Pentecostal
churches in England. The author states that for many of their
members, the cults compensate for their lowly social positions and
offer emotional support and healing for those who distrust or cannot afford modern physicians.

475.   Smith, Ralph R., and Russel R. Windes. "The Rhetoric of Mobiliza-
        tion: Implications for the Study of Movements." SOUTHERN SPEECH
        COMMUNICATION JOURNAL 42 (1976): 1-19.

        Discusses rhetorical movements that are defined as "the set of
        acts which include mobilization appeals" (p. 1). This study con-
        centrates on the speakers in movements who respond to mobilization
        exigencies. After some methodological considerations, the authors
        illustrate the importance of their approach by considering Anglo-
        American revivals in the eighteenth and nineteenth centuries. The
        emergence of organization and the need to develop a rhetoric suit-
        able to arouse people to collaborate on resources are examined.
        Evangelical revivals, according to the authors, favor a rhetoric of
        identification rather than one of agitation or coercion.

476.   Smith, Timothy. "My Rejection of a Cyclical View of 'Great Awaken-
        ings.'" SOCIOLOGICAL ANALYSIS 44 (1983): 97-102.

        Overviews the attempts by historians to interpret the rise of
        evangelicalism in the United States in terms of revival cycles and
        maintains that none of the themes "that overlapped one another at
        the end of the nineteenth century yields readily to a cyclical or
        psycho-social interpretation" (p. 99). It is argued that the roots
        of evangelicalism lie deep in American history and, therefore, must
        be explained by recourse to some inner dynamic forces. The current
        evangelical surge must be understood as part of American history
        and not as a revival triggered by "psychic insecurities, economic
        dislocations, or crass motivations of new rich television evangeli-
        cals" (p. 101). A short bibliography of the author's works on
        revivalism is included.

477.   Smith, William L. "The Uses of Structural Arrangements and Orga-
        nizational Strategies by Urban Communes." COMMUNAL STUDIES 6
        (1986): 118-37.

        Points out that communitarian developments in the 1970's and
        1980's have been largely in urban areas and that religious ideology
        has been the primary motivating force that brought them into exis-
        tence. The author adopts Kanter's theoretical position to investi-
        gate the following seven modern urban communes in the Chicago area:
        1) Austin Community Fellowship; 2) Mennonite Volunteer Services,
        North of Howard Unity; 3) Gospel Outreach; 4) The Olive Branch; 5)
        the Emissaries of Divine Light; 6) Jesus People USA; and 7) the
        Institute of Cultural Affairs. These communes are described and
        compared and their commitment measured with reference to Kanter's
        commitment-building mechanisms (item 383).

478.   Stark, Rodney, and William Sims Bainbridge. "Towards a Theory of
        Religion: Religious Commitment." JOURNAL FOR THE SCIENTIFIC
        STUDY OF RELIGION 19 (1980): 114-28.

        Constructs a theory to explain why religions exist, how they
        originate, and how religious movements are transformed. Several
        axioms, definitions, and theoretical statements are schematically
        listed. The authors observe that the anthropological and sociolog-
        ical theory of deprivation, commonly ascribed to explain religious
        beliefs and practices, is very incomplete. After defining religion
        as a system of general compensators (rewards) based on supernatural
        assumptions, they show how in sects "the power of the individual or
        group will be negatively associated with accepting religious com-
        pensators, when desired rewards exist" (p. 126).

479.   Stephan, Karen H., and G. Edward Stephan. "Religion and the Sur-
        vival of Utopian Communities." JOURNAL FOR THE SCIENTIFIC STUDY
        OF RELIGION 12 (1973): 89-100.

        Examines the records of utopian communities in the continental
        United States between 1776 and 1900 in order to determine those
        factors that affect their chances for survival. The authors con-
        tend that religion makes a significant contribution to the stabil-
        ity of communes by helping them overcome difficulties that would
        otherwise lead to their demise. A list of communes included in
        this study is given in an appendix.

480.   Strauss, Roger. "Religious Conversion as a Personal and Collective
        Accomplishment." SOCIOLOGICAL ANALYSIS 40 (1979): 158-65.

        Criticizes the conventional approach to conversion, which treats
        it as an occurrence in one's personal life. The author thinks that
        this view is a rather passive model that relies on the mechanistic
        worldview of classical science. He proposes, instead, an activist
        paradigm. Collective organization, the use of ritual, and other
        institutions are conceived as having direct impact on the partici-
        pants' endeavors to improve and transform their lives.

481.   Swanson, Guy E. "Trance and Possession: Studies on Charismatic
        Influence." REVIEW OF RELIGIOUS RESEARCH 19 (1978): 253-78.

        Studies charismatic encounters that occur both outside and within
        the established frameworks of traditional rite and worship. The
        author focuses on trance and possession experiences which, though
        often considered exotic, are common to, and central in, human lives.
        Two forms of trance, namely hypnosis in Western society and posses-
        sion states in primitive societies, are distinguished. The social
        condition associated with each is then specified. The author sees
        both as related to social experiences or collective purposes.

482.   Synan, Vinson. THE HOLINESS-PENTECOSTAL MOVEMENT IN THE UNITED
        STATES. Grand Rapids, MI: Eerdmans, 1971. 248 pp.

        Attempts to place the major Holiness and Pentecostal groups in
        America "in their proper setting as part of the total social and
        intellectual history of the United States" (p. 8). The origins of

Pentecostalism are traced and nineteenth- and twentieth-century churches and sects (such as the Churches of God and Black Pentecostalism) are included in the author's reflections. The Pentecostal rejection of society and the resulting social conflicts are discussed. The author's view is that Pentecostalism is an heir of the frontier, enthusiastic type of religion that is indigenous to American religious life.

483.   Tarrow, Sidney. "Comparing Social Movement Participation in Western Europe and the United States: Problems, Uses, and a Proposal for Synthesis." INTERNATIONAL JOURNAL OF MASS EMERGENCIES AND DISASTERS 4 (1986): 145-70.

Argues in favor of comparing social movements from different countries in order to clarify the problems scholars encounter in analyzing and interpreting their origin and development. The following areas that are in need of further study are specified: 1) the formation and activation of recruitment networks; 2) networks that occur within the movements themselves; 3) already existing social networks; new cultural contexts; and 4) individual norms and values. The author proposes a synthesis between two current approaches, namely the American model of resource mobilization and the European paradigm of new social movements.

484.   Taylor, Brian. "Recollection and Membership: Converts' Talk and the Ratiocination of Commonality." SOCIOLOGY: JOURNAL OF THE BRITISH SOCIOLOGICAL ASSOCIATION 12 (1978): 316-24.

Examines religious conversion not just as a form of patterned behavior, but rather as a "transition on a cognitive and ontological plane from non-religious to religious folk-epistemologies" (p. 316). The common grounds on which converts base and express their religious experiences are the focus of the author's reflections. He examines the way converts talk about their conversion experiences. It is stated that accounting for conversion is a mode of remembering the past. The conversion experience itself and the accounts of it given by converts are in a relationship of "reciprocal origination."

485.   Terjesen, Nancy Conn. "Longevity Factors in Past and Present Communal Societies." COMMUNES: HISTORICAL AND CONTEMPORARY (item 312), pp. 272-81.

Discusses those social factors that appear to contribute to the survival of communal societies. Using data from religious and secular groups in the United States (such as the Brotherhood of the Spirit, Twin Oaks, Gould Farm, and the Bruderhof), the author explores the following five factors that are related to the longevity: community, leadership, boundary maintenance, religion or its functional alternative, and commitment mechanisms (cf. Kanter, item 383). Noting that most of the successful historic communes have been religiously oriented, the author insists that religion (or a strong political ideology) unifies the group and helps develop an "esprit de corps."

486.   Thomas, George M. "Rational Exchange and Individualism: Revival
       Religion in the U.S., 1870-1890." THE RELIGIOUS DIMENSION: NEW
       DIRECTIONS IN QUANTITATIVE RESEARCH. Edited by Robert Wuthnow.
       New York: Academic Press, 1979, pp. 351-72.

       Suggests that "changes in organizational and cultural context or
       in patterns of institutionalized exchange are sufficient for
       effecting the rise of revivalism or for conversion from one reality
       to another" (p. 353). The author attempts to illustrate this posi-
       tion with reference to data from nineteenth-century revivalism in
       the United States. He describes the relationship between rational
       exchange (in which individuals become their own agents) and the
       myth of individualism, shows how a culture centered on the individ-
       ual was created by the expansion of rational exchange, and suggests
       that revivalism was linked to the mythology of the individual.
       Quantitative data from several states are used to buttress the
       author's theory. He concludes that nineteenth-century revivalism
       was an attempt to bring a new moral and political order, in which
       individualism was emphasized and that its emergence is linked with
       similar developments in nineteenth-century culture as a whole.

487.   Thomas, Keith. RELIGION AND THE DECLINE OF MAGIC. New York:
       Charles Scribner's Sons, 1971. xviii, 716 pp.

       Attempts to explain why beliefs in astrology, witchcraft, magical
       healing, divination, and ancient prophets were popular in England
       during the sixteenth and seventeenth centuries. The author shows
       how all these beliefs are indicative of a preoccupation with human
       misfortune and reflect the intensely insecure environment of the
       period. The decline of magic is linked with the growth of urban
       living, the rise of science, and the ideology of self-help.

488.   Travisano, Richard V. "Alternation and Conversion as Qualitatively
       Different Transformations." SOCIAL PSYCHOLOGY THROUGH SYMBOLIC
       INTERACTION. Edited by Gregory P. Stone and Harvey D. Faberman.
       Waltham, MA: Ginn-Blaisdell, 1970, pp. 594-606.

       Discusses two different kinds of personal transformations, largely
       in the context of Hebrew Christians and Jewish Unitarians. Jews
       who become fundamental Christians are converts who have broken from
       their past without abandoning their previous identity. The Jew who
       joins a Unitarian Church, on the other hand, does not have to break
       the past, but simply extends one's activities in one of the many
       permissible directions. The former Jew undergoes a change of heart,
       a conversion, that is not permitted within Judaism; the latter
       makes a change of identity, an alternation, that is allowed or
       tolerated within certain limits.

489.   Treece, James William. "Theories on Religious Communal Develop-
       ment." SOCIAL COMPASS 18 (1971): 85-100.

       Considers various theories of religious communal formation and
       development, particularly in their application to the rise of sects
       and cults. Five religious groups are examined: Bethany Fellowship

(a Christian missionary endeavor), Koinonia Farm (a Christian commune), the Hutterites, St. Julian's (a Christian community in England that restricts membership to women), and Mayeem Kareem (an
Israeli kibbutz). The stability of each group, its charismatic
leadership, and its future prospects are among the topics examined.

490. Turner, Ralph H. "Determinants of Social Movement Strategies."
      HUMAN NATURE AND COLLECTIVE BEHAVIOR: PAPERS IN HONOR OF HERBERT
      BLUMER. Edited by Tamotsu Shibutani. Englewood Cliffs, NJ:
      Prentice-Hall, 1970, pp. 145-64.

      Attempts to specify some of the variables that lead a movement to
      select specific strategies for exercising power. The following
      broad types of strategies are examined: 1) persuasion, which uses
      strictly symbolic manipulation; 2) bargaining, which stresses the
      exchange of valuable goods; and 3) coercion, which employs punish-
      ment to further the movement's actions. Several limiting factors
      that affect the use of strategies are discussed. Nonviolence as
      a strategy in social movements is discussed at some length.

491. Verbit, Mervin F. "The Components and Dimensions of Religious Be-
      havior: Towards a Reconceptualization of Religiosity." AMERICAN
      MOSAIC. Edited by Phillip Hammond and Benton Johnson. New York:
      Random House, 1970, pp. 24-39.

      Identifies six components of religion, namely ritual, doctrine,
      emotion, knowledge, ethics, and community. The content, frequency,
      intensity, and centrality of each dimension are then discussed. An
      elaborate scale to measure religiosity is then constructed.

492. Veysey, Laurence. THE COMMUNAL EXPERIENCE: ANARCHIST AND MYSTICAL
      COUNTER-CULTURES IN AMERICA. New York: Harper and Row, 1973.
      xi, 495 pp.

      Explores the "distinctive tradition of cultural radicalism in
      America" (p. 3). Two types of intentional communes, the anarchist
      and the mystical, which were the two most striking intellectual
      tendencies of the counterculture of the 1960's, are distinguished.
      The mystical communes are labeled "communities of discipline."
      Several Vedanta Societies and a New Age Social Order in Mexico are
      examined in some detail. In a final chapter the author attempts to
      trace some of the features of American cultural radicalism.

*   Wagner, Jon. "Sexuality and Gender Roles in Utopian Communities:
      A Critical Survey of Scholarly Work." Cited above as item 69.

493. Wagner, Jon. "Success in Intentional Societies: The Problem of
      Evaluation." COMMUNAL SOCIETIES 5 (1985): 89-100.

      Lists and discusses seven criteria for an evaluation of whether
      intentional communities are successful or not. For such a commu-
      nity to succeed: 1) it has to fulfill its goals; 2) it must come
      close to achieving its goal of social perfection; 3) it must exist
      for some length of time; 4) it must develop in proportion to its

size; 5) it must maintain social cohesion; 6) its influence on society should be judged to be important; and 7) it must provide for the personal growth of its members.

494.   Wagner, Jon. "Utopian Societies and the Charismatic Individual." ESSAY IN HUMANISTIC ANTHROPOLOGY. Edited by Bruce T. Grindal and Dennis M. Warren. Washington, DC: University Press of America, 1978, pp. 167-85.

Discusses two recurring themes of American utopias: 1) the reliance on the teachings of one individual; and 2) the organization of those teachings into ideologies that form the basis of a new social system. The charismatic person is described as both a revolutionary and reactionary individual who demands both intellectual assent and active participation in a plan of action of which he or she is the sole source of inspiration. The author illustrates these themes with examples of Western communes that were operative in the early 1970's. Visionary utopias are deemed to be important cultural developments since they have left an imprint on American consciousness and provided successful models of alternative social arrangements. The rise of charismatic movements is linked to the cultural crisis in the West and the need to solve the problems that followed in its wake.

495.   Wallace, Anthony F. C. "Nativism and Revivalism." INTERNATIONAL ENCYCLOPEDIA OF THE SOCIAL SCIENCES. Edited by David L. Shils. New York: Crowell Collier and Macmillan, 1972, vol. 11, pp. 75-80.

Examines two forms of social movements, namely nativism and revivalism, the former referring either to an attitude that rejects foreign persons or cultures or to a kind of utopian thought, the latter to an attitude that seeks to return to a previous golden age. The author traces the history of the concept of nativism, which often includes revivalist elements, and describes the stages through which nativistic movements go through. The following four theories that have been advanced to explain these movements are discussed: 1) absolute deprivation; 2) acculturation; 3) social evolution; and 4) relative deprivation. The current status of research is assessed and two examples from nonliterate societies, namely the Ghost Dance of the Plains Indians of North America and the Paliau Movement of the Admiralty Islands after World War II, are given.

496.   Wallis, Roy. "A Critique of the Theory of Moral Crusades as Status Defense." SCOTTISH JOURNAL OF SOCIOLOGY 1 (1977): 195-203.

Discusses the theory of symbolic crusades developed by Gusfield (see item 1286) in the context of the American Temperance Movement and criticizes Zurcher and Kirkpatrick for using the theory to interpret antipornography crusades (item 526). After an outline of both studies, Wallis summarizes the problems they share. He finds fault particularly with the "debunking drift" of both studies. In his opinion, both fail to adduce "any clear evidence that desire for status improvement motivated the crusading activity" (p. 201).

497.   Warner, R. Stephen. "Theoretical Barriers to the Understanding of
        Evangelical Christianity." SOCIOLOGICAL ANALYSIS 40 (1979): 1-9.

        Maintains that sociologists have made little contribution to the
        understanding of Evangelical Christianity, which is an "important
        contemporary phenomenon." Class, liberal, and evolutionary bias
        are responsible for this failure. Scholars are often repelled by
        the conservatism, supernaturalism, and emotionalism so often dis-
        played by these Christians. They tend to label evangelism a lower-
        middle class, politically conservative, and historically retrogres-
        sive phenomenon. The author suggests that these scholars should
        abandon their evaluative approach and return to the stand of cul-
        tural relativism. He insists that the current Evangelical revival
        meets emotional, moral, and cognitive needs and contains a value
        system that merits study on its own.

498.   Warren, Richard L., editor. PERSPECTIVES ON THE AMERICAN COMMU-
        NITY. Chicago: Rand McNally, 1973. ix, 542 pp.

        Reprints selections from books and previously published papers on
        various aspects of contemporary communal lifestyles. One section
        is dedicated to alternative communities and communes. Their func-
        tions, structures, diverse forms, lifestyles, and the nature of the
        commitment required of their respective members are among the
        topics discussed.

        Contains item 369.

499.   Webster, Colin, "Communes." RESISTANCE TO RITUALS: YOUTH SUB-
        CULTURES IN POST-WAR BRITAIN. Edited by Stewart Hall and Tony
        Jefferson. London: Hutchinson and Co., 1976, pp. 127-34.

        Examines the commune movement among some disenchanted youth in
        Britain between 1965 and 1975. A thematic typology is constructed.
        Communes can be 1) rural, 2) utopian, 3) monogamous, 4) childbear-
        ing, 5) religious, 6) urban-activist, 7) infrastructural, and 8)
        therapeutic. Attention is drawn to the contradictions that are
        part of the communal movement.

500.   Wegner, Eldon L. "The Concept of Alienation: A Critique and Some
        Suggestions for a Context Specific Approach." PACIFIC SOCIOLOG-
        ICAL REVIEW 18 (1975): 171-93.

        Discusses sociological approaches to the study of alienation.
        Four issues that are essential to any definition of alienation are
        examined: 1) the nature of the human being; 2) the question whether
        alienation is a general orientation toward the social order or a
        set of context-specific attitudes; 3) the debate about whether
        there are specific causes of alienation; and 4) the discussion
        about the one-dimensional or multidimensional nature of alienation.
        The author maintains that alienation is to be related to acquired
        personality characteristics, rather than to human nature as such,
        that it is a response towards a specific social context, and that
        its measurement and study should take place in the situations in
        which it occurs. Alienation is defined as a set of "negative feel-

ings and cynical beliefs toward a particular social context, where
disenchantment is based on the incompatibility between the individual's personal characteristics and the social role he is
performing" (p. 189).

501.   Weisbrod, Carol. THE BOUNDARIES OF UTOPIA. New York: Pantheon
        Books, 1880. xxii, 297 pp.

        Offers a legal perspective on nineteenth-century utopias in the
        United States, focusing on the controversies between ex-members of
        utopian communities and the societies themselves. Four major
        groups, namely the Shakers, Harmony Society, Zoar, and Oneida, are
        discussed. One chapter is dedicated to utopian contracts that
        involve "the volitional assumption of obligation." The process of
        leaving a community and the settlement reached in the disengagement
        process are explored. The author points out that suppression by
        the State through its legal system was never the reason why utopian
        communities either failed or were dissolved and that the law always
        recognized the rights that these communities held in relation to
        their members.

502.   Westhues, Kenneth. SOCIETY'S SHADOW: STUDIES IN THE SOCIOLOGY
        OF COUNTERCULTURES. Toronto: McGraw-Hill Ryerson, 1972. vi,
        223 pp.

        Presents a collection of essays that assess the Hippie movement
        of the 1960's. Several introductory articles focus on the sociology
        of countercultures that are said to be alternative realities.
        Three major areas of concern are investigated: 1) the Hippie Move-
        ment as an alternative culture; 2) the social origins of Hippiedom;
        and 3) patterns in Hippiedom's history. The rise of countercul-
        tures and charismatic leaders occurs under two conditions, namely
        the contradiction or insufficiency of society's ideology and the
        insoluble discrepancies between this ideology and lived experience.
        There are plenty of references to major early writings on the
        counterculture.

503.   Westhues, Kenneth. "Hippiedom 1970: Some Tentative Hypotheses."
        SOCIOLOGICAL QUARTERLY 13 (1972): 81-89.

        Argues that a counterculture movement, which is distinctive for
        its radical opposition to its parent society, tends not towards
        revolutionary social change, but rather to the sectarian alterna-
        tive of building an intentional island within that society. The
        author outlines the social origins of Hippie communes whose values
        are narrowed down to the following six: 1) close personal relation-
        ships; 2) total honesty with other people; 3) doing things with
        others; 4) a sense of community; 5) greater sensitivity to others;
        and 6) opportunity to be creative. It is maintained that the
        Hippie Movement, though pleasure-seeking, is not antinomian.

504.   Whitworth, John M. "Communitarian Groups and the World." SECTAR-
        IANISM: ANALYSES OF RELIGIOUS AND NON-RELIGIOUS SECTS (item 713),
        pp. 117-37.

Theorizes that "the life-changes of communitarian groups in Western industrialized society are extremely slim" (p. 117). The author first presents a twofold typology of communitarian groups into introversionist and utopian communities. Then, he illustrates his position by describing the Shakers and analyzing their decline. Finally, he discusses those geographic, political, and socio-cultural aspects of Western society, such as urbanization and bureaucracy, that minimize the chances of success these groups might have.

505. Wilder, D. Lawrence, and Don H. Zimmerman. "Becoming a Freak: Pathways into the Counter-Culture." YOUTH AND SOCIETY 7 (1976): 311-44.

Examines the personal and societal changes that take place when a person becomes a "freak," that is, one who has rejected most of the values and aspirations of one's parents. This process of personal and cultural change is deemed to be "a self-initiated and socially supported therapeutic strategy which is in some sense comparable to undertaking a course of psychotherapy" (p. 312). The transformation of the individual is described and the accompanying disengagement and desocialization discussed. The attire and mannerisms of freaks, once adopted, act as identification marks for freaks and nonfreaks alike.

506. Williams, Peter W. POPULAR RELIGION IN AMERICA: SYMBOLIC CHANGE AND THE MODERNIZATION PROCESS IN HISTORICAL PERSPECTIVE. Engle-wood Cliffs, NJ: Prentice-Hall, 1980. xiv, 258 pp.

Applies sociological and anthropological insights to the study of popular (extraecclesiastical) religion in America and tries to correlate its symbolic expressions with social experiences. The author uses the phrase "popular religion" to refer to those movements that exist in tension with the established churches, whose beliefs and values are transmitted through different channels (such as direct revelation or popular literature), and who look for signs of the divine in daily experiences. He considers in turn: 1) traditional religion and the clash of cultures with reference to American Indian and Black religious movements; 2) American folk religions and their transformations, including several sects like the Amish, the Hutterites, and the Mormons; 3) popular religion in the modern world in the context of Pentecostalism, faith-healing movements, fundamentalism, evangelicalism, and attacks on witchcraft; and 4) religion in mass society, during which period new religious movements that look for the attainment of religious experience or a transformation of consciousness come into being.

507. Wilson, John. INTRODUCTION TO SOCIAL MOVEMENTS. New York: Basic Books, 1973. vi, 369 pp.

Provides a general introduction to the study of social and religious movements that are defined as "a conscious, collective, organized attempt to bring about or resist change in the social order by noninstitutionalized means" (p. 8). Three kind of typologies of these movements are discussed: 1) value-oriented, power-oriented, and participant-oriented movements; 2) transformative, reformative,

redemptive, and alternative movements; and 3) value-oriented and
norm-oriented movements. The author considers the structures of
social movements, the problems they face, the tactics they use for
recruiting members, and the level of commitment they demand. There
are references throughout the book to traditional groups like Pentecostal sects, snake-handling cults, the Mormons, the Salvation
Army, the Millerites, the Hutterites, and the Disciples of Christ,
and to new movements, such as the Black Muslims, the Charismatic
Movement, and Soka Gakkai. Bibliographies are attached to every
chapter, making this book a useful resource manual for literature
published before 1973.

508.   Wilson, Kenneth L., and Louis A. Zurcher. "Status Inconsistency
       and Participation in Social Movements: A Rejoinder to Bland and
       Wallis' Comments." SOCIOLOGICAL QUARTERLY 18 (1977): 430-50.

       Responds to the criticism of the authors' original essay that
       attempts to account for those who take part in anti-pornography
       campaigns. The authors state that Bland and Wallis (item 300)
       misunderstand and misinterpret the main thrust of their theory and
       strongly reassert their own statistical results. They admit, how-
       ever, that "status inconsistency is only one factor that accounts
       for pornoactivity" (p. 432).

509.   Wilson, Kenneth L., and Louis A. Zurcher. "Status Inconsistency
       and Participation in Social Movements: An Application of Goodman's
       Hierarchical Model." SOCIOLOGICAL QUARTERLY 17 (1976): 520-33.

       Examines the status inconsistency levels of active participants
       in an antipornography movement and of those who actively opposed
       them. After reviewing the literature on the theory of status in-
       consistency, the author adopts a new statistical model to find out
       whether the status theory explains an individual's involvement in a
       social movement. He considers the income, occupation, and educa-
       tion of those who take part in crusades and concludes that status
       inconsistency appears to improve the odds that persons become par-
       ticipants in social movements.

510.   Winkleman, Michael. "Magic: A Theoretical Reassessment." CURRENT
       ANTHROPOLOGY 23 (1982): 37-66.

       Examines the possibility that magic has a psi-related aspect,
       that is, that "some magical practices facilitate or produce empiri-
       cally verifiable effects outside the currently understood cause-
       and-effect processes of nature" (p. 38). The parallels between
       magic and parapsychology are listed. In both cases, several condi-
       tions, such as an altered state of consciousness, visualization,
       and belief, are necessary. Theoretical similarities between magic
       and parapsychology are observed in three distinct areas, namely
       mana and psi, magic and psychokinesis, and divination and psi-
       mediated information gathering. A distinction is also made between
       psi-related and nonpsi-related magic. Though the discussion is
       carried largely in the context of nonliterate societies, it raises
       several issues regarding the contemporary Western interest in many
       occult matters that include both magic and psi-related practices.
       Comments by several reviewers of the article and the author's res-
       ponse, as well as a lengthy bibliography, are included.

511.   Wuthnow, Robert. "The Growth of Religious Reform Movements."
       ANNALS OF THE AMERICAN ACADEMY OF POLITICAL AND SOCIAL SCIENCE
       480 (July 1985): 106-11.

       Discusses the role in Western culture of such movements as the
       Moral Majority, the Charismatic Renewal, the Anti-Nuclear Coali-
       tion, and religious feminist groups. These groups, according to
       the author, have deep roots in American history and can shape the
       course of religious organization. Moreover, they function as revi-
       talization movements.

512.   Wuthnow, Robert. "Peak Experiences: Some Empirical Tests." JOUR-
       NAL OF HUMANISTIC PSYCHOLOGY 18.3 (1978): 59-75.

       Reports, from a random sample survey of San Francisco Bay Area
       residents, on the differences between those people who have had
       intense religious experiences and those who have never had such
       experiences. The incidents of peak experiences and the effects
       these have on one's life, such as a lowering of one's concern for
       material possessions, a decrease in one's status consciousness, and
       an increase in social concern, are discussed. The author insists
       that, while the psychological benefits of peak experiences should
       not be neglected, their potential for relieving such problems as
       social disintegration, prejudice, and poverty should be stressed.

513.   Yinger, J. Milton. "Countercultures and Social Change." AMERICAN
       SOCIOLOGICAL REVIEW 42 (1977): 833-53.

       Discusses the definition of "counterculture" and its various
       forms, including religious sectarianism. The following three over-
       riding elements are found in all countercultures: 1) a belief that
       truth is attained by empirical insight rather than by scientific
       research; 2) an insistence on an ethical code which contradicts the
       values of the dominant society; and 3) a view that culture is fully
       defined not only by its system of knowledge and morality, but also
       by its aesthetic standards. The author also deals with rituals of
       opposition as constitutive elements of subcultures found in all
       societies. Three interpretations of countercultures as avenues of
       social change, symbols of change, or as faddish expressions are
       explored. Countercultures, in the author's opinion, reveal some-
       thing about the human condition and take a position regarding what
       can be done in a period when civilization is undergoing a major
       transformation.

514.   Zablocki, Benjamin. ALIENATION AND CHARISMA: A STUDY OF CONTEM-
       PORARY AMERICAN COMMUNES. New York: Free Press, 1980. xxii,
       453 pp.

       Presents a study of communes, stressing the process of collective
       decision making and the conflicts between ideology and structure
       that make this process difficult. After an introductory chapter in
       which the meaning and significance of communes are discussed, the
       author overviews the distribution of communitarian movements from
       the early Roman Empire up to the turn of the twentieth century.
       One chapter is dedicated to American communitarianism as a social

movement. The people who join communes, the methods through which
one becomes a member, the effects of communal living, and the reasons for leaving a commune are all dealt with. One chapter, co-
authored with Angela Aidala, describes the varieties of communal
ideologies (see item 516).

515.   Zablocki, Benjamin. "Communes, Encounter Groups, and the Search
        for Community." IN SEARCH FOR COMMUNITY: ENCOUNTER GROUPS AND
        SOCIAL CHANGE. Edited by Kurt Back. Boulder, CO: Westview
        Press, 1978, pp. 97-142.

        Contends that 1) communes and encounter groups are part of one
        monolithic social movement, even though there are historical and
        cultural differences in their origin and development, and 2) they
        are an expression of cultural and demographic changes that took
        place in the late 1960's and early 1970's. Yoga, group and individ-
        ual psychotherapy, consciousness-raising groups, and sensitivity
        training are included in encounter groups. Both communes and en-
        counter groups are a response to the waning of "spontaneous commu-
        nity" in Western society. Three mechanisms of commitment-- sacri-
        fice, renunciation, and mortification--are discussed. Meditation,
        prayer, yoga, mantras, and speaking in tongues are cited as types
        of commitment-inducement rituals in communal life.

516.   Zablocki, Benjamin, and Angela Aidala. "The Varieties of Commu-
        nitarian Ideology." ALIENATION AND CHARISMA (item 514), pp.
        189-246.

        Provides a general picture of the many different ideologies that
        can be found within the communal movement. The communes are divid-
        ed into eight distinct types, namely: 1) Eastern religions; 2)
        Christian; 3) psychological; 4) rehabilitational; 5) cooperative;
        6) alternative-family; 7) countercultural; and 8) political. Short
        descriptions of several representative types are given. The orga-
        nizational background of each type is one of the topics discussed.
        According to the authors, communal movements "occur in times of
        sudden increase in complexity of social differentiation, when con-
        sensus underlying existing social arrangements begins to show large
        cracks" (p. 245).

517.   Zald, Mayer N. "Theological Crucibles: Social Movements in and of
        Religion." REVIEW OF RELIGIOUS RESEARCH 23 (1982): 317-36.

        Discusses the interplay between religious movements and socio-
        political change and examines the forces that "create social move-
        ments and political conflict within religious organizations" (p.
        319). The relationship between global order or disorder, religious
        movement, and resource mobilization is discussed in the context of
        Wuthnow's view that a discrete group of religious phenomena can be
        understood in its connection with global (political and economic)
        processes. The major tenets of the resource mobilization approach
        are outlined. The author's opinion is that the internal structure
        of new movements conditions their potentiality. Religious organi-
        zations provide an infrastructure for the activities of these
        movements and may affect their readiness to participate in politi-

cal life. An organizational model for understanding conflict in
religious movements is developed. The implication of this approach
and areas of further research are explored.

518.   Zald, Mayer N. "Issues in the Theory of Social Movements." CUR-
        RENT PERSPECTIVES IN SOCIAL THEORY 1 (1980): 61-72.

        Critically reflects on three main areas of research on social
        movements, namely: 1) the relationship between movement and
        countermovement (including resource mobilization processes and
        relations to authority); 2) the structure of industries and the way
        they are managed, especially the ways in which a movement organiza-
        tion can dominate an industry through charisma, coercion, and the
        survival of the fittest; and 3) the shape, size, and orientation of
        the aggregate of all social movement industries working for social
        change.

519.   Zald, Mayer N., and Michael A. Berger. "Social Movements in Orga-
           nizations: Coup d'Etat, Insurgency, and Mass Movements." AMERI-
        CAN JOURNAL OF SOCIOLOGY 83 (1978): 823-61.

        Examines the impact on organizational change that social move-
        ments might have. It is argued that much conflict in organizations
        occurs outside normal channels and that conflict and unconventional
        opposition are subject to social movement analysis. Three types of
        social-movement phenomena are distinguished: organizational coup,
        bureaucratic insurgency, and mass movement; and three areas of
        stress in these situations are listed: 1) the distribution and
        intensity of grievances and deprivation; 2) the role ideology; and
        3) the processes of resource mobilization and social control.
        Several hypotheses are drawn up in support of the resource mobili-
        zation perspective. Though this essay does not directly deal with
        sects and cults, it provides the theoretical background of a social
        approach that has been applied to the new religious movements.

520.   Zald, Mayer N., and John D. McCarthy. "Religious Groups as Cruci-
           bles of Social Movements." SOCIAL MOVEMENTS IN AN ORGANIZATIONAL
        SOCIETY (item 521), pp. 67-95.

        Gives a revised and expanded version of a previously published
        article by one of the authors (see item 517).

521.   Zald, Mayer N., and John D. McCarthy, editors. SOCIAL MOVEMENTS
        IN AN ORGANIZATIONAL SOCIETY: COLLECTED ESSAYS. New Brunswick,
        NJ: Transaction Books, 1987. x, 435 pp.

        Presents 13 previously published essays, most of which were co-
        authored by the two editors. After a general essay on the resource
        mobilization theory, the material is grouped under the following
        five sections, each of which is prefaced by an introduction: 1) the
        infrastructure of movements; 2) processes of organizational change;
        3) movements within organizations; 4) movements and countermove-
        ments; and 5) social movements and the future. A bibliography is
        appended (pp. 393-419).

        Contains items 153, 272, 416, 519, 520.

522.   Zald, Mayer N., and John D. McCarthy, editors. THE DYNAMICS OF
        SOCIAL MOVEMENTS: RESOURCE MOBILIZATION, SOCIAL CONTROL, AND
        TACTICS. Cambridge, MA: Winthrop Publishers, 1979. viii, 264 pp.

        Contains the revised versions of papers delivered at the Fifth
        Frontiers of Sociology Symposium held at Vanderbilt University in
        1977. Nine papers in this collection analyze new social movements
        by applying the resource mobilization approach which "de-emphasizes
        grievances and focuses upon societal supports and constraints on
        movements, tactical dilemma, social control, media message, and the
        interplay of external supports and elites" (vii). The essays are
        grouped under three general headings: 1) collective action and
        response of authorities; 2) mobilization tactics in contemporary
        movements; and 3) the course and outcome of social movements. This
        volume contains one essay (item 1831) that applies this theory to a
        group called "Divine precepts" (which is usually identified with
        the Unification Church). A basic bibliography (pp. 247-58) is
        included.

        Contains item 1831.

523.   Zicklin, Gilbert. COUNTERCULTURE COMMUNES: A SOCIOLOGICAL PER-
        SPECTIVE. Westport, CT: Greenwood Press, 1983. xv, 198 pp.

        Provides an overview of contemporary experiments in communal
        living in the framework of the counterculture. The author first
        describes the principal themes of the counterculture: 1) natural-
        ism; 2) spiritual quest; 3) an expressive mode of thought and be-
        havior; and 4) a movement for a new America. Then, he shows how
        these themes are translated into the lifestyles of the new communes.
        His reflections are based on the study of about twenty communes
        that include Christian, Jewish, and Hindu movements. The growth of
        the counterculture is said to be a response to tensions in advanced
        capitalistic countries. A short, useful bibliography is added (pp.
        185-91).

524.   Zurcher, Louis A., and Russell L. Curtis. "A Comparative Analysis
        of Propositions Describing Social Movement Organizations." SO-
        CIOLOGICAL QUARTERLY 14 (1973): 175-88.

        Assesses the theory of Zald and Ash (item 153) concerning the
        structure and dynamics of social-movement organizations. Four
        major organizational variables, namely exclusiveness of membership
        requirements, leadership characteristics, origin of organization,
        and organizational goals, are examined; and it is concluded that
        the data in general supports Zald and Ash's theory. In particular,
        exclusiveness of membership requirements is associated with resis-
        tance to pressures for organizational requirements, stability of
        organizational goals, task-oriented leadership style, and avoidance
        of coalitions and mergers. The routinization of charisma is linked
        with conservative tendencies and the emergence of radical splinter
        groups.

525.   Zurcher, Louis A., and R. George Kirkpatrick. "Status Discontent
        and Anti-Pornography Crusades: A Rejoinder to Roy Wallis'
        Critique." SCOTTISH JOURNAL OF SOCIOLOGY 2 (1977): 105-113.

Responds to the critique of their interpretation of antipornography crusades (item 496). The authors argue that these crusades
can be seen as status defense "only in the context of other social
and psychological factors" (p. 105). They contend that they have
seriously taken into consideration the accounts of those involved
in the movements, even though they favor a structuralist interpretation.

526.   Zurcher, Louis A., and R. George Kirkpatrick. CITIZENS FOR DEMOC-
        RACY: ANTIPORNOGRAPHY CRUSADES AS STATUS DEFENSE. Austin: Uni-
        versity of Texas Press, 1976. xv, 412 pp.

        Tests the hypothesis that antipornography crusades are symbolic
        activities of people who are "status discontents," that is, who
        believe that the prestige and attendant power of their lifestyles
        is threatened. After elaborating on the theoretical aspects of
        these moral crusades, the author compares and discusses two case
        histories in the United States. He describes their origins and
        characteristics, their important attitudes and perceptions, and the
        experiences of both their participants and opponents. These cru-
        sades are also examined as social-movement organizations that
        attempt to influence social legislation. A useful bibliography is
        added (pp. 374-96).

527.   Zurcher, Louis A., R. George Kirkpatrick, Robert G. Cushing, and
        Charles K. Bowman. "Ad Hoc Anti-Pornography Organizations and
        Their Active Members: A Research Summary." JOURNAL OF SOCIAL
        ISSUES 29.3 (1973): 69-94.

        Presents a study of two antipornography organizations that was
        made for the Commission on Obscenity and Pornography. The cam-
        paigns conducted by these organizations and the characteristics of
        their leaders and active participants are analyzed. Those involved
        in these movements were generally older, and female members were
        more numerous. Their backgrounds were largely rural. They were
        more alienated and less educated than the average population.
        Antipornography crusades are norm-oriented movements that occur
        when there is some structural strain which is indicative of some
        disequilibrium, inconsistency, or conflict. Antipornography cam-
        paigners are "status discontents" who formed associations to defend
        basic values.

528.   Zurcher, Louis A., R. George Kirkpatrick, Robert G. Cushing, and
        Charles K. Bowman. "The Anti-Pornography Debate: A Symbolic
        Crusade." SOCIAL PROBLEMS 19 (1971): 217-38.

        Examines two antipornography crusades and concludes that their
        participants are "status discontents." Their activities tend to
        enhance the lifestyles to which they were previously committed.
        Antipornography crusades are symbolic, norm-oriented rather than
        utilitarian, social movements, that is, they demonstrate belief in
        and support of a particular lifestyle or basic value system.

529.   Zurcher, Louis A., and Kenneth Monts. "Political Efficacy, Politi-
        cal Trust, and Anti-Pornography Crusading: A Research
        Note." SOCIOLOGY AND SOCIAL RESEARCH 56 (1972): 211-20.

Tests, with reference to antipornography crusades, the sociological view that a higher degree of political efficacy and a low degree of political trust are the best conditions for mobilizing citizens' political action. It is suggested that two case studies of such crusades support the theory that an imbalance of political efficacy and trust can be related to the success of such political-religious movements.

530.   Zygmunt, Joseph F. "When Prophecies Fail: A Theoretical Perspective on the Comparative Evidence." AMERICAN BEHAVIORAL SCIENTISTS 16 (1972): 245-67.

Uses the method of comparative analysis to formulate a theory that explains what happens when the drastic transformations forcasted by millennial movements do not materialize. The collective dimension of these movements is thought to be a major contributing factor in their survival in the face of crises. Millennial collectivities are classified in four types, based on their functional characteristics: expressive, agitational, preparatory, and interventional. People in these movements suffer cognitive and motivational distress when the expected prophecy does not come about or when organizational strains ensue, leading to the loss of marginal or potential supporters and rendering recruitment ineffective. When prophecy fails, millennial movements may disintegrate, become institutionalized, or adapt to the new situation.

B.   EDITED WORKS ON, AND GENERAL SURVEYS OF, THE NEW RELIGIOUS MOVEMENTS

531.   Aagaard, Johannes. "The World-view/Cosmology of the New Religious Movements." NEW RELIGIOUS MOVEMENTS AND THE CHURCHES (item 577), pp. 39-59.

Describes, analyzes, and interprets the common cosmological assumptions of many of the new religious movements, a cosmology that, the author maintains, is based on yogic ideology with its chakras that are believed to influence human thinking and psychic powers. Two movements, namely Theosophy and Anthroposophy, are taken as examples of organizations that transmit this yogic worldview, which has its roots in the occult tradition. The author compares this worldview with that of Christianity and concludes that the symbolic language of the Christian tradition differs from that of the new religious movements.

532.   Aagaard, Johannes. "Modern Syncretist Movements--A General View." UPDATE: A QUARTERLY JOURNAL OF NEW RELIGIOUS MOVEMENTS 5.2 (1981): 29-36.

Divides modern movements that combine diverse religious elements into two mainstreams: 1) the Western occult tradition that includes such established groups as Theosophy, Rosicrucianism, and diverse occult groups; and 2) the oriental movements. Recent movements like Scientology, Eckankar, Arica, Esalen, Synanon, EST, and the

Church Universal and Triumphant would fall under the first group; movements like those led by Muktananda, Sathya Sai Baba, Bhagwan Shree Rajneesh, and Maharaj Ji are examples of Eastern movements in the West. The author concludes by grouping the new movements in three principal geographical areas: 1) Mediterranean (Hellenistic groups); 2) Atlantic (apocalyptic and fundamentalist movements); and 3) Pacific (groups that combine Eastern and Western features).

533.   Aagaard, Johannes, and Linda W. Duddy. "Denmark Vis-a-Vis New Religious Movements." UPDATE: A QUARTERLY JOURNAL OF NEW RELIGIOUS MOVEMENTS 8.2 (1984): 37-42.

Argues that in Scandinavia, particularly in Denmark, the success of a movement is largely determined by its "religious conformity to general social, rather than Judeo-Christian, norms" (p. 37). New groups like Scientology, Transcendental Meditation, and other schools of meditation have been more successful than the Hare Krishna Movement, Ananda Marga, and the Children of God. A brief survey of these movements is given.

534.   Ahern, Geoffrey. "Esoteric 'New Religious Movements' and the Western Esoteric Tradition." OF GODS AND MEN (item 550), pp. 165-76.

Examines the social growth of esoteric new religious movements in the West in the context of the Western esoteric tradition and argues that the movements depend on the "relative plausibility of esoteric cosmology." After briefly discussing the meaning of esotericism, the author outlines esoteric beliefs and practices in the Middle Ages and in the Renaissance period. Then he traces their modern revival to the Rosicrucians in England in 1865 and later to Madame Blavatsky's Theosophy. Modern esotericism is linked with the rise of scientific materialism. The author speculates that developments in depth psychology will be related to any further increase in esoteric cosmology and consequently to esoteric movements.

535.   Aidala, Angela A. "Social Change, Gender Roles, and New Religious Movements." SOCIOLOGICAL ANALYSIS 46 (1985): 287-314.

Studies religious and nonreligious communes to explore the relationship between gender role ambiguities and the new movements. The author holds that to understand the cultural crisis of our present age (a crisis often used to explain the rise of the cults), one must take into account both the age and the sex of those who become members. Rapid social change and cultural fragmentation are expressed in gender role confusion and uncertainty. Religious movements are successful also because they offer certainties in areas dealing with sex and gender roles.

536.   Allison, Paul D. "Experimental Parapsychology as a Rejected Science." ON THE MARGINS OF SCIENCE (item 712), pp. 27-91.

Traces the beginnings of academic interest in parapsychology to the second half of the nineteenth century and the rise of psychical research on a scientific basis due to the effort of Dr. Rhine in the

1930's. The quest for legitimizing the study of parapsychology and
the resistance to it by the scientific world are discussed and the
failure of parapsychology to acquire equal footing with orthodox
science explained. It is observed that parapsychology stresses its
difference with mainstream science "to maintain internal esprit de
corps in the face of an opposition that would resist them in any
case" (p. 283). The connection between parapsychology and the
occult tends to increase the opposition of the scientific world.

537.   Anker, Roy M. "Popular Religion and Theories of Self-Help." HAND-
       BOOK OF AMERICAN POPULAR CULTURE. Edited by M. Thomas Inge.
       Westport, CT: Greenwood Press, 1980, vol. 2, pp. 287-316.

       Gives a historical outline of the efforts towards self-help in
       healing, a trend that originated in the Puritan culture and reached
       its peak in the Mind Cure Movement of the nineteenth century and
       has experienced a revival in charismatic and faith-healing prac-
       tices of the twentieth century. The tradition of self-healing that
       stresses the "instrumental utility of religious belief" has been an
       influential alternate to medicine. Included in this essay is a
       review of studies on the self-help movement and a short bibliog-
       raphy (pp. 314-16).

538.   Appel, Willa. CULTS IN AMERICA: PROGRAMMED FOR PARADISE. New
       York: Holt, Rinehart, and Winston, 1983. 204 pp.

       Presents an overview of the cult phenomenon and tackles some of
       the main issues it has raised: 1) the reason why cults are prolif-
       erating; 3) the kind of people they attract; 2) the socialization
       processes they employ; and 4) different ways people get involved in
       them. The author, an anthropologist by training, compares the
       ideologies of messianic and millenarian movements to children's
       fairy tales and holds that cult members actually abandon adulthood.
       She adheres to the brainwashing theory of cult recruitment and
       indoctrination and to the consequent view that makes exit from the
       cults "a difficult and protracted process." She maintains that the
       new cults are dangerous institutions. They are an outgrowth of the
       counterculture movement of the 1960's and their ultimate role may
       be to revitalize the established churches.

539.   Back, Kurt W. BEYOND WORDS: THE STORY OF SENSITIVITY TRAINING AND
       THE ENCOUNTER MOVEMENT. New York: Russell Sage Foundation, 1972.
       xii, 266 pp.

       Offers an overall picture of the intensive group process, sensi-
       tivity training, and encounter group experience as a social move-
       ment. The social setting and scientific base of this movement are
       described. The historical, ideological, and conceptual contexts in
       which intensive group experience was sought for and assimilated are
       discussed. Many of the practices used in these encounters, like
       Zen, Yoga, and other forms of Eastern mysticism, are recorded. The
       author concludes that sensitivity training springs out of a need to
       come to grips with the implications of modern science. A lengthy
       bibliography, now somewhat dated, is provided (pp. 239-45) and a
       list of reports that evaluate sensitivity training (1945-1970) is
       given (pp. 247-255).

540.   Back, Kurt W., editor. IN SEARCH OF: ENCOUNTER GROUPS AND SOCIAL
        CHANGE. Boulder, CO: Westview Press, 1978. xiii, 175 pp.

        Consists of papers presented at two symposia of the American
        Association for the Advancement of Science held in 1971 and 1977,
        respectively. Encounter groups are examined from several disci-
        plinary perspectives. They are discussed as rites of passage and
        as one expression of humanistic psychology. Encounter groups often
        function as self-realization cults, promote communal living, and
        use meditation, yoga, the chanting of mantras, and other practices
        that are associated with the new religions. The author argues that
        encounter groups and self-realization methods are new devices in a
        time of rapid social change designed to exalt communal practices in
        terms of interpersonal relationships.

        Contains item 515.

541.   Bainbridge, William Sims. "In Search of Delusion: Television
        Pseudo Documentaries." SKEPTICAL INQUIRER 4.1 (1979): 33-39.

        Argues that television programs that claim to be documentaries on
        occult and similar topics have become a "serious social issue."
        Two such programs ("In Search of" and "Project UFO") are examined.
        The effects of these programs were measured by examination ques-
        tions given to nearly 400 people attending the 1978 World Science
        Fiction Convention in Phoenix, Arizona. The two programs are
        saturated with occult and folk science and are typical examples of
        "fantasy wish-fulfillment." Though they retain their character as
        fiction, they encourage belief in extrasensory perception and other
        occult beliefs.

542.   Bainbridge, William Sims, and Rodney Stark. "Superstitions: Old
        and New." SKEPTICAL INQUIRER 4.4 (1980): 18-31.

        Contends that the contemporary age is replete with superstitious
        beliefs and practices, a view supported by the magic of the new
        cults and the widely held beliefs in the occult. The authors try
        to evaluate the effects of traditional religion on attitudes to-
        wards supernatural and paranormal ideas. They conclude, through
        the analysis of several surveys and publications, that 1) conserva-
        tive and fundamentalist groups tend to reject Darwin's theory of
        evolution; 2) born-again Christians condemn occult beliefs and
        practices; and 3) cult and occult activity exist, where traditional
        churches are the weakest.

543.   Baker, George, et al., editors. NEW RELIGIOUS MOVEMENTS IN AMER-
        ICA. New York: Rockefeller Foundation, 1979. xiii, 78 pp.

        Transcribes in abridged form the discussions held at a conference
        on new religious movements in Berkeley, California in 1977. The
        exchange between the scholars who participated in the meeting
        covers the following areas: 1) new religious movements and American
        society; 2) elitism and populism in American religious criticism;
        3) new religions and mental health; 4) adult religion; and 5) the
        building of new religious institutions. Several methodological
        issues are also discussed.

544.   Barker, Eileen. "Kingdom of Heaven on Earth: New Religious Move-
        ments and Political Orders." THE POLITICS OF RELIGION AND SOCIAL
        CHANGE (item 472), pp. 17-39.

        Examines various ways in which new religious movements conceive
        of the political order. The material is grouped around four basic
        questions the new religions have attempted to answer: 1) what is
        wrong with the present political system?; 2) why is it that the
        present evil conditions exist?; 3) what should a future, improved
        order look like?; and 4) how should we go about establishing the
        new order? The author finds that Wallis's distinction (item 991)
        into world-accommodating, world-affirming, and world-negating types
        of movements does not account for the diversity that exists within
        each type. She differentiates four types of "kingdom builders"
        among Unification Church members to illustrate the variety within
        just one movement. And she suggests that the new religions, by
        promising more than conventional political institutions, actually
        achieve less in their efforts to establish God's kingdom on earth.

545.   Barker, Eileen. "Bringing Them In: Some Observations on Method of
        Recruitment Employed by New Religious Movements." NEW RELIGIOUS
        MOVEMENTS AND THE CHURCHES (item 577), pp. 69-83.

        Describes briefly the types of social environments in which the
        new religions freely recruit members and the different methods that
        are used to attract young adults. The author refutes the brain-
        washing theory, though she admits that some nonphysical coercive
        measures and deceptive techniques are found in several of the new
        cults. Basing most of her reflections on her studies of the Unifi-
        cation Church, she argues that what makes potential recruits become
        actual members is something they "brought with them." People join
        freely because they feel themselves "at home" in the new groups.
        She suggests ways in which the recruitment methods of the cults can
        be approached from the traditional churches' point of view.

546.   Barker, Eileen. "New Religious Movements in Modern Western
        Society." THE ENCYCLOPEDIA OF WORLD FAITHS. Edited by Peter
        Bishop and Michael Darton. London: Macdonald Orbis, 1987, pp.
        294-306.

        Gives a general overview of the new religious movements in the
        West and divides them into four broad categories: 1) those that
        derive from the Christian tradition; 2) those that stem from East-
        ern traditions; 3) parareligious groups of the Human Potential
        Movement; and 4) esoteric traditions (including Witchcraft, Satan-
        ism, Paganism, and the Occult). The author deals with the history
        and distribution of these various movements, their leaders, and
        some of their rituals. Various explanations of the rise of new
        religions are summarized. The societal reaction to them is briefly
        discussed. The author thinks that these movements will appear less
        exotic and threatening with the passage of time.

547.   Barker, Eileen. "New Religions and Cults in Europe." ENCYCLOPEDIA
        OF RELIGION (item 18), vol. 10, pp. 405-410.

Examines the immediate historical setting, the origins, and the
spread of new religious movements in Europe where secularization
seems to have been widespread and where, consequently, the new
movements have been more readily received. The author suggests a
simple classification based on the geographical origins of the
movements. Other classifications, she admits, are also possible
and useful. The hostility toward the new religions is outlined and
their long-term (slightly exaggerated) significance discussed.

548.   Barker, Eileen. "New Religious Movements in Britain: The Context
       and the Membership." SOCIAL COMPASS 30 (1983): 33-48.

       Describes the historical and cultural contexts of the new reli-
       gious movements in Britain, drawing attention to the religious
       situation and to patterns of social dissension among young people.
       The author attempts some generalizations about those movements
       that are religious or quasi-religious in orientation, which demand
       that converts make a radical change, and which are considered a
       threat by the general public. The age, sex, class, educational
       background, and commitments of those who join are briefly sketched.
       Two general needs, that is, to express freely and explore a reli-
       gious aspect of life and to desire to be of use, are being met by
       the new religions.

549.   Barker, Eileen. "Free to Choose: Some Thoughts on the Unification
       Church and Other Religious Movements, II." CLERGY REVIEW 65
       (1980): 365-68.

       Surveys the new religious movements scene in Great Britain and
       reflects on some of the questions they have raised. The membership
       patterns and recruitment techniques of these movements are briefly
       discussed. Though admitting that the issues of free will and
       determinism are not easy to solve, the author maintains that one
       must seriously take into consideration that freedom to choose might
       play an important part in a person's decision to join a cult. (See
       item 1612 for part one of this essay.)

550.   Barker, Eileen, editor. OF GODS AND MEN: NEW RELIGIOUS MOVEMENTS
       IN THE WEST. Macon, GA: Mercer University Press, 1983. xii,
       347 pp.

       Edits the Proceedings of the Religion Study Group of the 1981
       Annual Conference of the British Sociological Association. The
       18 papers included in this volume cover a variety of theoretical
       themes and individual religious groups, such as the Charismatic
       Renewal, the Unification Church, the Hare Krishna Movement, the
       Divine Light Mission, and the Human Potential Movement. There are
       bibliographies attached to each essay, making this collection a
       good reference source-book.

       Contains items 534, 763, 865, 950, 1341, 1653, 1688, 1978, 2027,
       2047, 2111, 2205.

551.   Barker, Eileen, editor. NEW RELIGIOUS MOVEMENTS: A PERSPECTIVE FOR
       UNDERSTANDING SOCIETY. New York: Edwin Mellen Press, 1982. xxv,
       398 pp.

Aims to bring together the ideas of those scholars who have professional knowledge of the new religious movements and who also propose broader hypotheses to interpret their rise and significance. The contributors of this volume seek to find out how the study of these movements might contribute to our self-understanding as social animals, to our knowledge of social processes, and to our analysis of those societies within which the movements emerge. The material is divided into five sections: 1) the wider comparative perspective; 2) the individual and society; 3) accommodation, rejection innovation, assimilation, and disinterest; 4) social resources, indicators, or reflections; and 5) revelation and control. A list of characteristics that are shared by the new religious movements and by similar groups in different historical periods and societies is included (pp. 325-29). Besides a glossary of new religions mentioned in the text (pp. 331-58), a good bibliography on these movements is added.

Contains items 670, 733, 749, 771, 828, 861, 992, 1007, 1014, 1039, 1535, 1641, 1752, 2117.

552.   Barkum, Michael. "The Language of Apocalypse: Premillennialists and the Nuclear War." THE GOD PUMPERS (item 604), pp. 159-73.

Comments on the modern millenarian wave that has been brought into the mainstream of American cultural awareness by means of modern mass communications. Contemporary chiliastic thought has adopted the view of dispensational premillennialism which maintains that the course of human history will proceed along the following lines: there will be first a period of tribulation, which will be followed by the Second Coming of Christ and the Rapture, after which a new millennium under the reign of Christ will begin. The author describes the premillennial position on nuclear war as portrayed in such popular writings as those of Hal Lindsey and Jerry Falwell. He speculates on the influence they might have on the political scene.

553.   Beckford, James A. "New Religions." ENCYCLOPEDIA OF RELIGION (item 18), vol. 10, pp. 390-94.

Discusses the concepts of new religions, religious movements, and cults and the various theories that have been proposed to interpret them. Religious innovation has been linked with periods of rapid social change and disruptions of social structure. Unlike many new religious movements in nonliterate societies and contemporary movements in Christian Africa and elsewhere, the cults in the West "have shown little interest in history" (p. 392). Experimentation in new religious forms has been fueled by a "fragmented, rationalized, and mobile society." The new cults have stimulated interest among social scientists whose contributions to their study is not always recognized. The author stresses the importance of the cults even though they may be individually insignificant and short-lived.

554.   Beckford, James A. "Religious Organizations." THE SACRED IN A SECULAR AGE (item 623), pp. 125-38.

Outlines some of the sociological studies on religious organizations, with special reference to the works of Weber, Durkheim,
Troeltsch, and Niebuhr. Since the 1960's, the research on these
systems represents a reversal of classical priorities. Religious
institutions are, first of all, being studied in terms of their
inner structure and dynamics, with less stress on their relationships with the sociocultural environment. Secondly, the implicit
equation between the Christian religion and organized churches
has been challenged. A new concept of religious organization is
deemed necessary because of the diversity of religious and social
structures. Studies of religious systems since the 1970's have
been dominated by considerations of new alternative religious movements and have tended to stress the power of organization to sustain recruitment, socialization, and mobilization. An agenda of
future research is proposed. This includes comparative questions
about religion; the study of semireligious and nonreligious estab-
lishments with reference to their environment; and the voluntary
nature of religious associations.

555.   Beckford, James A. "Holistic Images and Ethics in New Religions
       and Healing Movements." SOCIAL COMPASS 31 (1984): 259-72.

       Proposes the view that some new religions and healing movements
       in the United States and Western Europe are making a distinction
       between ethics, spirituality, and healing by using holistic world-
       images and that this might be one of the novelties of the new move-
       ments. The holistic imagery is applicable to the individual self,
       to the healing theme, and to the cosmic context in which healing is
       believed to occur. The author maintains that, though these move-
       ments generate a lot of interest and activity within a restricted
       sphere, the milieu in which they operate is rather narrow and
       small. He pinpoints some of the sociocultural conditions that re-
       inforce the holistic worldview, namely the high value placed on
       training and adaptability among the educated middle class in the
       West.

556.   Beckford, James A. "Young People and New Religious Movements."
       SOCIAL COMPASS 30 (1983): 3-15.

       Introduces a special issue of SOCIAL COMPASS on new religious
       movements. The essays focus attention on those features of the
       cults in Europe that distinguish them from their counterparts in
       the United States. The editor observes that social investigations
       of the cults in Europe are uneven. While there are many social
       studies on them in the United States, little work has been done in
       France. Eastern Europe has been virtually unaffected by the rise
       of the new movements.

557.   Beckford, James A. "Religious Organization: A Trend Report and
       Bibliography." CURRENT SOCIOLOGY 21.2 (1973): 1-170.

       Presents a general view of the major contributions to the sociol-
       ogy of religious organizations since 1960. The following areas are
       covered: 1) the history of the concept of religious organization;
       2) the reasons for studying such organizations and the factors

that make them distinct; 3) a description of the open-systems
approach; 4) the effects of the social environment; 5) the use of
environmental resources for the continuing operation of religious
associations; 6) the processes that transform people's outlooks;
and 7) the structured dimensions of organizations, namely speciali-
zation, formalization, centralization, and distribution of authority. The author proposes a moratorium on the use of the terms
"church," "sect," "denomination," "cult," and "eccelsia." Various
attempts to redefine the church-sect typology are outlined.

558.   Beckford, James A., editor. NEW RELIGIOUS MOVEMENTS AND RAPID
        SOCIAL CHANGE. London: Sage, 1986. xv, 245 pp.

        Presents a collection of essays, the result of a close coopera-
        tion between UNESCO and the International Sociological Association.
        The aim of the papers is to throw light on social factors influenc-
        ing the ride and expansion of religious movements without, however,
        minimizing the place of individual belief and action. The underly-
        ing assumption is that institutional influences, financial support,
        and conflicts between ethnic groups can play a preponderant role in
        the formation of new religious movements. Religious movements are,
        in the editor's view, indicative of the fact that broad shifts in
        people's ideas and sensibilities may occur independently of orga-
        nized religion.

        Contains items 559, 1037.

559.   Beckford, James A., and Martine Levasseur. "New Religious Move-
        ments in Western Europe." NEW RELIGIOUS MOVEMENTS AND RAPID
        SOCIAL CHANGE (item 558), pp. 29-54.

        Demonstrates how some young adults have responded to the rapidly
        changing Western world by joining one of the new cults which are
        compared to similar movements in the late nineteenth and early
        twentieth centuries. It is one of the authors' main contentions
        that "a host of demographic, social, and cultural changes," parti-
        cularly in the means of communication, have provided a specific
        audience for the new religious movements. The American contribu-
        tion to the rise and spread of the new religions and their impor-
        tation to Europe as well as their composition are considered.
        Three types of interpretations, namely the cults as 1) refuges
        from society, 2) attempts to improve or reform sociocultural
        conditions, 3) providers of a service to clients, are described.
        The public response to the new religious movements in France is
        described.

560.   Bednarowski, Mary Farrell. "Women in Occult America." THE OCCULT
        IN AMERICA: NEW HISTORICAL PERSPECTIVES (item 849), pp. 177-95.

        Compares three movements, namely Spiritualism, Theosophy, and
        Feminist Witchcraft, with the aim of showing that 1) the concern
        for women's rights has figured prominently in some occult movements
        in America and 2) the expressions of the occult have taken various
        forms (including spirit messages in Spiritualism, Eastern esoteri-
        cism in Theosophy, and psychological-oriented occultism in feminist

witchcraft). The three movements provided avenues through which women have addressed the issues of gender and sexuality, the female relationship with the holy, and woman's subjection to male authority. They have also been instrumental in arousing protest against the prevailing structures and in exploring ways in which women can affirm their sexuality and spirituality.

561.   Belil, J. M. "The Religious Climate in Spain." UPDATE: A QUAR-
        TERLY JOURNAL OF NEW RELIGIOUS MOVEMENTS 8.2 (1984): 59-61.

Relates the continuing growth of new religious movements in Spain to the political, social, and economic crises of the country. Scientology, the Hare Krishna Movement, Transcendental Meditation, the Unification Church, Ananda Marga, and the Rajneesh Foundation are among the more important groups mentioned. The Temple of Light of the New Age Universal Christianity Without Religion, with its headquarters in the Canary Islands, is also very active. Some cults have been officially recognized as cultural or religious associations.

562.   Bell, Daniel. "Religion in the Sixties." SOCIAL RESEARCH 38
        (1971): 447-97.

Presents a lengthy overview of the religious situation of the 1960's and examines some of the consequences that followed the "transvaluation of religion" during that decade. Four basic themes are judged to be at the root of this change: 1) a turning away from theology to anthropology; 2) a revival of Protestant liberalism that attempts to harmonize Christian thought with progressive cultural thinking and to adapt to modern concerns; 3) a stress on personal ethics rather than on law; and 4) a return to Pelagianism that saw evil embedded in social institutions. Several elements that contribute to cults are mentioned: a belief and interest in the Oriental world; a flight from the self; a spread and acceptance of syncretism; and the drug culture.

563.   Benassi, Victor A., Barry Singer, and Craig B. Reynolds. "Occult
        Belief: Seeing is Believing." JOURNAL FOR THE SCIENTIFIC STUDY
        OF RELIGION 19 (1980): 337-49.

Reports on experiments conducted to show how psychic powers can be wrongly attributed to people who are involved in ordinary and amateur magic routines. Two plausible hypotheses--that belief in psychic powers is either a sign of reasoning deficiency or a confirmation of strong prior beliefs--are considered. The current preoccupation with the occult in Western society is explained by 10 the high prior availability of occult beliefs; 2) the intransigence of these beliefs to disconfirmation; 3) the tendency to trust intuitive experience rather than rational knowledge; and 4) the failure to look at alleged psychic experiences and manifestations abstractly and critically.

564.   Benor, Daniel J. "Psychic Healing." ALTERNATIVE MEDICINES (item
        687), pp. 165-90.

Points out that, in spite of the suspicion with which orthodox medicine looks on psychic healing, this latter phenomenon demands "a re-evaluation of the basic understanding and assumptions of nature and of one's place in the universe" (p. 166). The author briefly outlines the principles of psychic healing, gives a historical overview of its practice, spells out the distinction between psychic healing and modern medicine, and suggests some possible explanations for the success of the former. He reviews the different situations in Britain and the United States and observes that in the former country, healers are well organized and officially licensed. The potential impact of psychic healing on society is stressed.

565.   Biezais, Haralds, editor. NEW RELIGIONS. Stockholm, Sweden: Almquist and Wiksell International, 1975. 223 pp.

Contains sixteen essays based on the papers read at the Symposium on New Religions held in Abo, Sweden, in September 1974. Most of the essays are in English and mainly cover new religious movements in the West.

Contains items 655, 1156, 1278, 1364, 1496, 1699, 1813, 1918.

566.   Bird, Frederick B. "Theories of Justice in New Religious and Parareligious Movements." STUDIES IN RELIGION 15 (1986): 17-28.

Complains that the new religious movements, while expressing concern for the development of the integrity of the individual and the peaceful relationship between people, exhibit a general indifference to issues of justice. Three major points are underscored: 1) many of the movements speak authoritatively on moral standards, but rarely address themselves to the moral value of justice; 2) the forceful encouragement of the virtue of selfless virtue, common in many movements, is not linked with social reform and justice; and 3) the virtue of tolerance that appears in Hindu- and Buddhist-inspired groups is not related to the principles of justice. On the contrary, justice in the new religions is overshadowed by the tolerant, detached acceptance of the world as it is and the stress on the hierarchical system within the groups themselves. The author thinks that the ahistorical, fatalistic, apolitical, and frequently nontheistic worldview is responsible for the lack of interest in social justice.

567.   Bird, Frederick B. "The Nature and Function of Ritual Forms: A Sociological Discussion." STUDIES IN RELIGION 9 (1980): 387-402.

Formulates a theory about the nature and function of ritual forms and distinguishes between the manifest objective of rituals and their latent social function. Six major types of rituals with their corresponding manifest and latent functions are identified: 1) taboos; 2) purification rites (cleansing, exorcisms, and confessions); 3) spiritual exercises (ascetic or mystical); 4) rites of passage (life cycle, initiation, and season rituals); 5) worship; and 6) shamanistic rituals. The author distinguishes four major developments in the ritual customs in North America: 1) rituals performed by evangelical Christian and non-Christian groups (like the Charismatics, the Jesus People, the Divine Light Mission, and Nichiren Shoshu); 2) rituals of cultic groups (including various Buddhist associations, Silva Mind Control, Transcendental Meditation, Gurdjieff, astrology, and palmistry); 3) the decline of consensus on rituals in American society at large (with special reference to puberty, etiquette, and the presence of new secular rituals); and 4) an ever-increasing pluralism in ritual practice.

568.   Bird, Frederick B. "The Contemporary Religious Milieu." RITUAL AND CEREMONIES IN POPULAR CULTURE. Edited by Ray B. Browne. Bowling Green, OH: Bowling Green University Popular Press, 1980, pp. 19-35.

Sets forth a general theory about the nature and function of ritual forms that are considered to be "culturally transmitted symbolic codes that are stylized, regularly respected, dramatically structured, authoritatively designated, and intrinsically valued" (p. 19). An elaborate chart of various ritual forms according to their main ritual objectives and latent social functions is drawn. The various types of rituals are discussed in the context of the new religious movements.

569.   Bird, Frederick B. "Initiations and the Pursuit of Innocence: A Comparative Analysis of Initiation Rites of New Religious Movements and Their Influence on Feelings of Moral Accountability." RITUAL SYMBOLISM AND CEREMONIALISM IN THE AMERICAS. Edited by N. Ross Crumrine. Greeley, CO: Museum of Anthropology, University of Northern Colorado, 1979, part 2, pp. 250-77.

Examines the new religious movements in the Montreal area of Canada, and proposes the view that they are providing the ritual means through which their adherents assume moral accountability and accept certain patterns of moral authority. The author discusses the "modern dilemma of moral accountability" caused in part by the increasing relativity of moral standards in the West. The following main features of initiation rites in religious and parareligious movements are described: 1) imparting of power and knowledge; 2) submission to authority; 3) giving of some sort of license to the person who is initiated; 4) the assumption of moral accountability; and 5) a change of status. The author maintains that initiation rites are means by which the initiate's sense of moral responsibility is reduced and sense of innocence augmented, both processes being highly sought in a pluralistic society where the demand for personal, moral accountability is on the rise.

570.   Bird, Frederick B. "Charismatic Cults: An Examination of the Ritual Practices of Various New Religious Movements." RITUAL SYMBOLISM AND CEREMONIALISM IN THE AMERICAS. Edited by N. Ross Crumrine. Greeley, CO: Museum of Anthropology, University of Northern Colorado, 1979, part 2, pp. 214-49.

Argues that new religious movements stress ritual patterns rather than ideology. The rituals function not as a means of establishing ordered social relationships but as ways of strengthening the sense

of self necessary to sort out confusing interpersonal relationships and to solve problems dealing with careers, success, and
happiness. An analytic typology for identifying major differences
among new religious movements is proposed: 1) rites of initiation;
2) rites of meditation; and 3) therapeutic rites for healing and
purification. The author maintains that the new cults are not
compensatory movements and cannot be explained by a theory of
deprivation.

571.   Bird, Frederick B. "The Pursuit of Innocence: New Religious Move-
        ments and Moral Accountability." SOCIOLOGICAL ANALYSIS 40 (1979):
        335-46.

Explores the impact that most of the new religious movements have
on the feelings of moral accountability, that is, "the individual
awareness that a person is expected to act in keeping with moral
expectations" (p. 335). Three types of new movements are distinguished, based on the relationship between the leaders and their
followers or between religious seekers and sacred power: devotee,
disciple, and apprentice relationships. The way people relate to
the holy, the type of authority structure, and the morality of each
group are described. The author argues that the contemporary cultural situation encourages or multiplies relativistic and comparatively permissive moral expectations. This results in moral
confusion. He thinks that the new religious movements remedy this
problem by fostering reduced feelings of moral accountability and
enhance feelings of innocence.

572.   Bird, Frederick B. "Charisma and Ritual in New Religious Move-
        ments." UNDERSTANDING THE NEW RELIGIONS (item 667), pp. 173-89.

Points out that ritual practice is one of the important features
present in new religious movements. It is argued that rituals are
important because they foster certain authenticating experiences
for those who practice them. Three types of ritual found in new
movements are distinguished: 1) therapeutic rituals for healing or
purification (as in Silva Mind Control, Self-Realization Fellowship, and Yoga groups); 2) meditation rites (as in Zen monasteries,
Divine Light Mission, Hare Krishna Movement, Transcendental Meditation, and Nichiren Shoshu of America); and 3) rituals of initiation
(as in Transcendental Meditation, Scientology, Divine Light Mission,
and Integral Yoga Institute). The adherents of new religions are
classified into devotees, disciples, and apprentices. People are
drawn to these movements not because they are deprived of some
material or social benefits but rather because they desire to
achieve a personal well-being by faithfully following authoritative
ritualized forms that bestow secret knowledge and charisma on the
practitioners themselves.

573.   Bird, Frederick B. "A Comparative Analysis of the Rituals Used by
        Some Contemporary 'New' Religious and Para-Religious Movements."
        RELIGION AND CULTURE IN CANADA. Edited by Peter Slater. Water-
        loo, Ontario: Canadian Corporation For Studies in Religion, 1977,
        pp. 448-69.

Explores the common features of new religious movements by an analysis of their rituals. The meaning and function of ritual are first discussed. The following seven ritual traits of the new religions are mentioned: 1) rituals usually led by lay persons; 2) intense involvement of core members in the rites; 3) the presence of an initiation rite; 4) pietism in ritual, during which devotion is paid to the leader or the testimony of converts is heard; 5) some common linguistic features, like mantras, chants, and body language; 6) ritual used as a means to step outside secular time and space; and 7) a communal aspect. A list of rituals practiced by several groups is provided.

574.   Bird, Frederick B., and Frances Westley. "The Economic Strategies of New Religious Movements." SOCIOLOGICAL ANALYSIS 46 (1985): 157-70.

Suggests that the best way to understand the economic strategies of the new movements is to compare them with those of more traditional ones. The latter have recruited members by socializing the young, by political and cultural conquest, by direct proselytizing, and by offering various services. Four different categories of followers are distinguished: affiliates, clients, members, and adepts. The economic strategies of the new movements are examined in detail and the various services offered by different groups are schematically outlined in three distinct types, namely: 1) the devotee type; 2) the apprenticeship type and 3) the mixed type.

575.   Bjornstad, James. "Cults And Christian Conversion: Is There a Difference?" UPDATE: A QUARTERLY JOURNAL ON NEW RELIGIOUS MOVEMENTS 6.1 (1982): 50-59.

Summarizes some major social scientific views of conversion that stress the common elements, but fail to distinguish between conversion to Christianity and to other religions, including the cults. The author contests that the study of conversion should be carried out in the context of the worldview in which it occurs and in the sociological setting and psychological character of the individuals. A short bibliography (pp. 60-64) on conversion is added.

576.   Bourguignon, Erika. "Cross-Cultural Perspectives on the Religious Uses of of Altered States of Consciousness." RELIGIOUS MOVEMENTS IN CONTEMPORARY AMERICA (item 727), pp. 228-43.

Reports on a major cross-cultural study of institutionalized forms of altered states of consciousness and discusses their implications on the study of minority religions in the United States. The distribution of trance and possession types throughout the world are recorded. It is maintained that those people in the United States who experience altered states of consciousness are the most alienated ones in society. Such states have functional values in the sense that "they can be cathartic and give a sense of conviction and righteousness not present before" (p. 224).

577.   Brockway, Allan P., and J. Paul Rajashekar, editors. NEW RELIGIOUS MOVEMENTS AND THE CHURCHES. Geneva, Switzerland: WCC Publications, 1987. xix, 201 pp.

Contains the reports to, and papers read at, a consultation sponsored by the Lutheran World Federation and the World Council of
Churches held in Amsterdam in September 1986. The material is
divided into the following three aspects of the new religious movements: 1) understanding their emergence; 2) different perspectives
and interpretations; and 3) responses to their presence and activities. Besides a general essay that considers the cults as a global
phenomenon, there are articles on their worldviews and religiosity,
on their recruitment methods, on some of the legal issues involved,
and on the churches' responses to new movements in the past and in
the present. Most presentations are accompanied by replies by the
conference participants. Two documents, namely the summary and
recommendations of the Lutheran World Federation and the World
Council of Churches and the Vatican's lengthy response, are
included.

Contains items 531, 545, 638, 880, 984, 2140, 2149, 2155.

578.   Bromley, David G., editor. FALLING FROM THE FAITH: CAUSES AND
        CONSEQUENCES OF RELIGIOUS APOSTASY. Beverly Hills, CA: Sage
        Publications, 1988. 260 pp.

Presents a collection of original essays dealing with the social
processes of religious disaffiliation. One section groups together
several essays discussing apostasy from the mainline churches (such
as conservative denominations, the Catholic Church, and Mormonism),
while another considers defections from alternative religions (such
as the Unification Church and the People's Temple). A bibliography
is added (pp. 251-62).

Contains items 305, 932, 1030, 1603, 1744, 2124.

579.   Bromley, David G., and Phillip E. Hammond, editors. THE FUTURE OF
        NEW RELIGIOUS MOVEMENTS. Macon, GA: Mercer University Press,
        1987. 278 pp.

Contains 17 papers originally presented at a three-day conference
on the new religions held in Berkeley, California in 1983 and
sponsored by the New Ecumenical Research Association (which is
affiliated with the Unification Church). The papers are grouped
under four headings: 1) historical and comparative perspectives;
2) structural elements of the new religious movements; 3) implications of social research on the new religious groups; and 4) speculations on their future and lasting impact.

Contains items 594, 816, 839, 883, 956, 1013, 1057, 1102, 1584,
1601, 1727, 1830, 1837, 1960, 1985, 2001, 2050, 2129.

580.   Bromley, David G., and Larry D. Shinn, editors. KRISHNA CONSCIOUS-
        NESS IN THE WEST. Lewisburg, PA: Bucknell University Press,
        1989. 295 pp.

Edits a selection of papers, most of which were presented at
an interdisciplinary conference held in 1985 at the Hare Krishna
settlement in New Vrindaban, near Moundsville, West Virginia. The

material, which represents both outsiders' and insiders' points of
view, is divided into five main sections: 1) the emergence of
ISKCON; 2) ISKCON in American culture; 3) conversion to the Krishna
Consciousness Movement; 4) Hare Krishna communities; and 5) the
social responses to the movement. In the introduction, the editors
assess the presence of ISKCON in the West and the areas of conflict that have plagued the movement in the 1980's, namely the
question of guru authority, economic troubles, and legal setbacks.

Contains items 1645, 1681, 1700, 1725, 1781, 1869, 1983, 2123,
2163, 2191.

581.   Bromley, David G., and Anson D. Shupe. STRANGE GODS: THE GREAT
        AMERICAN CULT SCARE. Boston: Beacon Press, 1981. xvii, 249 pp.

        Represents a popularized sociological approach to the study of
        the new religious movements. The authors deal with most of the
        problems that have arisen in the wake of the cults. The origins,
        beliefs, and organizations of six of the most controversial groups,
        namely the Children of God, the Unification Church, the Divine
        Light Mission, the Church of Scientology, the Hare Krishna Move-
        ment, and the People's Temple, are described. Among the issues
        discussed are whether those who join these movements are converted
        or brainwashed, whether their leaders are gurus or madmen, and
        whether the fundraising methods are charities or rip-offs. A short
        bibliography (pp. 238-44) is given covering 1) scientific studies,
        2) religious studies, and 3) popular criticisms.

582.   Campbell, Colin, and Shirley McIver. "Cultural Sources of Support
        For Contemporary Occultism." SOCIAL COMPASS 34 (1987): 41-60.

        Considers those facets in Western culture that encourage interest
        in occult matters, pointing out several interconnections between
        culture and the occult. The authors argue that the labeling of the
        occult as "rejected," "anomalous," or "esoteric" knowledge has
        contributed to its mystification and has led sociologists to link
        its adherents to marginality and mobility. They hold that people
        might become interested in the occult because superstitions, folk
        religion, and popular culture are deeply embedded in the West and
        because mass media, with its regular astrology column, have also
        provided a supportive environment for occultism.

583.   Clarke, Peter B. "Religions Traditional and New in THE ENCYCLOPE-
        DIA OF RELIGION." RELIGIOUS STUDIES 24 (1988): 19-27.

        Evaluates the many articles on traditional and new religions
        published in THE ENCYCLOPEDIA OF RELIGION (item 18). Despite some
        omissions, such as the treatment of the demise of new religious
        movements, most articles are judged to be of good quality.

584.   Clarke, Peter B. "New Religions in Britain and Western Europe: In
        Decline?" THE NEW EVANGELISTS (item 587), pp. 5-15.

        Examines the membership statistics of participants in new reli-
        gious movements in Britain and other European countries to deter-
        mine whether they have actually peaked and are now in decline. The

author offers some reflections on the methods of evangelization,
noting that the transmission of vibrations during meditation and
personal contact are frequently used techniques that have received
little attention. Stressing the difficulties researchers encounter
in their efforts to get reliable estimates on cult membership, he
concludes that most groups are undergoing "a slower but more steady
growth rate" (p. 15).

585.   Clarke, Peter B. "Trends in New Religions in Contemporary Britain."
       UPDATE: A QUARTERLY JOURNAL OF NEW RELIGIOUS MOVEMENTS 8.2 (1984):
       17-25.

       Surveys the religious scene in Great Britain where over 400 new
       religions have emerged since 1945 and concentrates on the types of
       movements that have been successful and the questions they pose to
       society at large. Millenarianism, charismatic leadership, and the
       stress on the control of one's mind are among the main features
       mentioned. The author observes that the spread of the new reli-
       gions is slow when compared to the adventist-oriented House Church
       Movement, though some Hindu groups are registering a steady growth.
       The self-religions, namely those that stress psycho-religious
       means to self-improvement, and some African movements are concerned
       with the question of self-identity. The new movements have raised
       questions that deal with education and the effectiveness of the
       traditional churches.

586.   Clarke, Peter B., editor. "New Religious Movements." THE WORLD'S
       RELIGIONS. Edited by Stewart Sutherland, et al. London: Rout-
       ledge, 1988, pp. 905-66.

       Introduces a selection of essays that assess the presence of new
       religious movements in different parts of the world, especially
       North America, Europe, Japan, and Africa. Besides a short intro-
       duction to the essays as a whole, there is a final paper that dis-
       cusses secularization. The novelty in this collection is that it
       is included as a major and separate section in a book on world
       religions and that it treats new religions on a par with other
       well-established religious traditions.

       Contains items 629, 706, 1012.

587.   Clarke, Peter B., editor. THE NEW EVANGELISTS: RECRUITMENT METHODS
       AND AIMS OF NEW RELIGIOUS MOVEMENTS. London: Ethnographica,
       1987. 160 pp.

       Presents a collection of essays that describe and discuss the
       various procedures movements like the Unification Church, the
       Nichiren Shoshu of America, EST, and the Sathya Sai Baba followers
       use to recruit members. These essays are restricted to the activi-
       ties of the new movements in Great Britain.

       Contains items 584, 1604, 1665, 1669, 1764, 1882, 2023, 2100.

588.   Clecak, Peter. AMERICA'S QUEST FOR THE IDEAL SELF: DISSENT AND
       FULFILLMENT IN THE 1960S AND 1970S. New York: Oxford University
       Press, 1983. ix, 395 pp.

Takes an approach to the cultural changes of the 1960's and 1970's
that stresses thematic and ideological continuities. Characteriz-
ing these two decades as "a quest for personal fulfillment within a
small community (or several communities) of significant others" (p.
9), the author shows how this quest was explored in the various
religious and social movements that flourished during this period.

589.   Coleman, John, and Gregory Baum, editors. NEW RELIGIOUS MOVEMENTS.
        (CONCILIUM: RELIGION IN THE EIGHTIES, vol. 161, no. 1). New
        York: Seabury Press, 1983. x, 83 pp.

        Presents a collection of essays dealing with the rise of new
        religious movements in different parts of the world, particularly
        in Western culture. Two essays give an overview of the presence of
        Asian religions in Europe and North America, respectively. There
        is an emphasis throughout on the religious significance and impact
        of these movements on traditionally Christian countries, though
        several sociological factors are taken into consideration by most
        of the contributors.

        Contains items 595, 639, 736, 1900.

590.   Cooper, John Charles. RELIGION IN THE AGE OF AQUARIUS. Philadel-
        phia: Westminster Press, 1971. 175 pp.

        Discusses the rise of interest in occult beliefs and practices in
        the 1960's. In the occult the author finds both a healthy desire to
        find a religious framework for one's life and a dark, psychotic
        side full of superstition. Astrology, mediumship, witchcraft, and
        Satanism are among the topics discussed. The author relates the
        rise of the occult to the "emotional sterility of our industrial-
        ized, technologized world" (p. 35). Occult practices like witch-
        craft flourish when human needs are not being met. A general
        feeling of anxiety and insecurity are among the reasons why people
        get involved in occult matters. Some speculations on future
        developments and on the impact of the occult on religion are made.

591.   Dyson, Anthony, and Eileen Barker, editors. "Sects and New Reli-
        gious Movements." BULLETIN OF THE JOHN RYLANDS UNIVERSITY
        LIBRARY OF MANCHESTER 70.3 (1988): 3-240.

        Edits 17 studies of sects and cults from diverse academic per-
        spectives and different historical periods mainly in the Western
        world. Besides essays on early Christian sects, sects during the
        French Revolution, the Quakers and the Plymouth Brethren, there are
        articles on several nineteenth-century sects, like the Mormons and
        the Jehovah's Witnesses and on the new cults, like the Hare Krishna
        Movement. In a short introduction the editors outline their cri-
        teria for selecting the variety of essays in this collection.

        Contains items 1096, 1590, 1726, 1966.

592.   Edge, Hoyt L. "Sociocultural Aspects of Psi." FOUNDATIONS OF
        PARAPSYCHOLOGY: EXPLORING THE BOUNDARIES OF HUMAN CAPABILITY. By
        Hoyt L. Edge, Robert L. Morris, Joseph H. Rush, and John Palmer.
        Boston: Routledge and Kegan Paul, 1986, pp. 361-78.

Presents an anthropological perspective of parapsychology. The
author reports on the attitude of anthropologists towards psi
research and on various empirical studies of psychic phenomena. He
observes that there is a connection between parapsychology and non-
Western cultures, a connection that can also be found in psychic
archaeology "in which paranormal abilities are used as an aid in
examining the past" (p. 68). The implications that would follow
if parapsychology became part of the Western educational system are
briefly assessed.

593. Ellwood, Robert S. "Occult Movements in America." ENCYCLOPEDIA OF
      THE AMERICAN RELIGIOUS EXPERIENCE (item 40), vol. 2, pp. 711-22.

      Presents a general overview of the occult movement in American
      history and explores reasons for its periodic resurgence. The main
      argument advanced in this essay is that the radical pluralism of
      contemporary society leads some people to occultism, which fits
      well with the current stress on individualism and with the variety
      of religious forms that pervade Western culture. The success of
      the occult is due, in part at least, to its ability to give those
      involved in it a sense of significance, power, and harmony with the
      universe. The following movements are included in the occult:
      Witchcraft and ceremonial magic, Masonry, Swedenborgianism, Mesmer-
      ism, Spiritualism, UFO groups, Theosophy, Anthroposophy, Satanism,
      and Rosicrucianism.

594. Ellwood, Robert S. "A Historian Looks at the Future of New Reli-
      gious Movements." THE FUTURE OF NEW RELIGIOUS MOVEMENTS (item
      579), pp. 235-50.

      Relates the debate on the future of the new cults to the wider
      discussion of the process of secularization. The new religions
      could articulate a reaction against this process, or provide a
      spiritual interpretation of secular values, or could themselves
      succumb to secularization. The author adopts Robert Redfield's
      concept of the "Great and Little Traditions" and suggests that
      while the little traditions continue to exist, the great ones are
      losing their vitality under the influence of modern secular trends.
      He thinks that Little Traditions, like neo-Paganism, are more
      likely to grow numerically.

595. Ellwood, Robert S. "Asian Religions in North America." NEW RELI-
      GIOUS MOVEMENTS (item 589), pp. 17 -22.

      Divides Asian religions in North America into two categories,
      namely those imported by immigrants and those oriented primarily
      to Westerners seeking an alternative spirituality and religious
      experience. Several stages, which Western interest in oriental
      philosophy and theology have gone through since last century, are
      described. A brief survey of the main Eastern religious groups in
      the West is given. The author concludes that "the spiritual East
      in North America, then, while more visible in some times and places
      than others, is a deeply-rooted and inseparable part of American
      culture" (p. 21).

596.   Ellwood, Robert S. ALTERNATIVE ALTERS: UNCONVENTIONAL AND EASTERN
        SPIRITUALITY IN AMERICA. Chicago: University of Chicago Press,
        1979. xiii, 192 pp.

        Investigates "religious life in this country outside the Judeo-
        Christian mainstream and its significance for American spiritual
        culture" (xi). The author focuses on theoretical models for under-
        standing the presence of Eastern religions and philosophies in the
        West and employs various models to grasp the difference between
        established traditions (the "Temple") and new religions (the "Cave")
        and to understand how they coexist in the same society. New reli-
        gions are seen as an "excursus" away from the familiar and toward
        strange forms that appear to offer "a new kind of self-discovery."
        One chapter is dedicated to the psychology of "excursus religion."
        The history of Spiritualism, Theosophy, and Zen are used to illus-
        trate the author's views on alternative religions in the West.

597.   Ellwood, Robert S. "Notes on a Neopagan Religious Group in Amer-
        ica." HISTORY OF RELIGIONS 2 (1971): 125-39.

        Makes some general remarks on the history and typology of new
        religious movements using Wach's three categories of verbal, prac-
        tical, and social religious expressions (see item 135). The cults,
        according to the author, do not simply share a negative reaction to
        the Judeo-Christian tradition, but also focus on a different kind
        of experience of the holy. The following stages in the recent
        history of new religious movements are identified: 1) from the
        nineteenth century to World War I (with groups like Spiritualism,
        Theosophy, New Thought, and various magical religions); 2) between
        the two World Wars, 1918-1939, (with groups like the I Am Move-
        ment, Self-Realization Fellowship, and Krishnamurti); 3) from the
        end of World War II up to the late 1960's (including the wave of
        Oriental imports such as Zen, the Hare Krishna Movement, and Scien-
        tology; and 4) a new phase which began in 1971 and which stresses
        not peak experiences, but rather a desire to create sacred space
        and time in the world at large. One neopagan group, Feraferia,
        located in Pasadena, California, is described particularly with
        reference to the main features of modern paganism.

598.   Ellwood, Robert S., and Harry B. Partin. RELIGIOUS AND SPIRITUAL
        GROUPS IN MODERN AMERICA. Englewood Cliffs, NJ: Prentice-Hall,
        second edition, 1988. vii, 328 pp.

        Gives an introductory survey of alternative religions in America
        with particular attention to Eastern and Occult groups. After
        discussing the several meanings of the word "cult" and describing
        its main features, the authors trace the history of alternative
        religions in the West from the Hellenistic period to the present
        times. Short descriptive summaries of many groups, including The-
        osophy, Rosicrucianism, UFO cults, Gurdjieff, Scientology, Witch-
        craft and Paganism, and Hindu and Buddhist movements are provided.
        Bibliographies are added to every chapter.

599.   Enroth, Ronald, and Neil T. Duddy. "Legitimation Processes in Some
        New Religions." UPDATE: A QUARTERLY JOURNAL ON NEW RELIGIOUS
        MOVEMENTS 7.3 (1983): 22-37.

Examines the ways by which new religions gain public respectability. The authors first look at the way the Mormon Church
achieved legitimation by changing some of its major policies and
stressing public relations to forge a better image of itself. Then
they explore how Scientology and the Unification Church have conducted their campaigns to alter the public view of them as "deviant
cults." The Moonies-sponsored conferences have been the most powerful tactic used to acquire professional legitimation. Another
strategy is that of "co-opting luminaries," that is, the use of
public figures, like governors and mayors, to bestow on the Rev.
Moon honorary titles and official good wishes for his religious
work. The authors think that, of these two groups, the Unification
Church is more likely to achieve legitimation.

600. Enroth, Ronald, and Others. A GUIDE TO CULTS AND NEW RELIGIONS.
      Downers Grove, IL: InterVarsity Press, 1983. 215 pp.

      Provides descriptions and Christian evaluations of the ten main
      new religions and cults, namely: the Baha'i Faith; the Rajneesh
      Foundation; Eckankar; EST; the Hare Krishna Movement; Jehovah's
      Witnesses; the Mormons; Transcendental Meditation; the Unification
      Church; and the Way International. In the introduction, Ronald
      Enroth deals with the definition of a cult and its main features.
      He maintains that a social definition must include "the authoritar-
      ian, manipulative, totalistic, and sometimes communal features of
      cults" (p. 12). He classifies cults and new religions into five
      groups, namely: 1) Eastern mystical; 2) aberrational Christian; 3)
      psychospiritual or self-improvement; 4) eclectic-syncretistic; and
      5) psychic-occult-astral.

601. Eve, Raymond A., and Francis B. Harrold. "Creationism, Cult
      Archaeology, and Other Pseudoscientific Beliefs." YOUTH AND
      SOCIETY 17 (1986): 396-421.

      Reports on the prevalence of unscientific beliefs among college
      students at a public university, focusing on two commonly held
      beliefs, namely: 1) creationism, that refers to the literal inter-
      pretation of the Bible's account of creations; and 2) pseudo-
      archaeology, that implies the acceptance of accounts of the human
      past, exemplified in such popular works as Eric Von Daniken's book,
      CHARIOTS OF THE GODS? (New York: Putnam's Sons, 1969). The authors
      observe that "creationism and pseudo-archaeology, although both
      pseudo-scientific, are differentially influenced by social back-
      ground and personality factors" (p. 400).

602. Fenton, John Y. TRANSPLANTING RELIGIOUS TRADITIONS: ASIAN RELI-
      GIONS IN AMERICA. New York: Praeger, 1988. xiii, 270 pp.

      Overviews the settlement and adaptation of Asian Indians in the
      United States, focusing on the successful transportation of their
      religious traditions. Based on the author's research in Atlanta
      Georgia between 1979 and 1988, this book covers such groups as the
      Vedanta Society, the Radha Soami Satsang, the Hare Krishna Move-
      ment, the Sathya Sai Baba Movement, and the Healthy, Happy, Holy
      Organization (3HO) as well as traditional Hindu Temples and Muslim
      Mosques.

603.   Fichter, Joseph H., editor. ALTERNATIVES TO AMERICAN MAINLINE
        CHURCHES. New York: Rose of Sharon Press, 1983. xxi, 199 pp.

        Presents a collection of essays that examine "fringe religious
        groups" that are outside the conventional religious traditions in
        America. The papers were originally read and discussed at a con-
        ference sponsored by the New Ecumenical Research Organization
        (New ERA), which is sponsored by the Unification Church. They are
        grouped under two main categories, one dealing with metaphysical
        alternatives (including Spiritual Frontiers Fellowship, Thelemic
        Magick, and Scientology), the other with groups like the Hare
        Krishna Movement and the Catholic Traditionalist Movement. In the
        introduction the editor reflects on a major theme common to all the
        essays, namely that Americans are being faced with the possible
        choice of other religious commitments besides the churches in which
        they were raised.

        Contains items 873, 966, 1689, 1715, 1865, 1988, 2043.

604.   Fishwick, Marshall, and Ray B. Browne, editors. THE GOD PUMPERS:
        RELIGION IN THE ELECTRONIC AGE. Bowling Green, OH: Bowling Green
        State University Press, 1987. 196 pp.

        Presents a series of essays that discusses television evangelists
        like Oral Roberts, Pat Robertson, Jimmy and Tammy Bakker, Jerry
        Falwell, and Jimmy Swaggart. The editors see the growth of tele-
        vision ministry as part of the resurgence of fundamentalism that is
        also present on college and university campuses in such groups as
        CAUSA (Confederation of the Associations for the Unity of the
        Sciences in the Americas) and CARP (Collegiate Association for the
        Research of Principle), both of which have ties with the Unifica-
        tion Church. Besides bibliographies at the end of most essays
        there is a short select bibliography (pp. 191-96).

        Contains items 552, 1290, 1761.

605.   Flinn, Frank, editor. HERMENEUTICS AND HORIZONS: THE SHAPE OF THE
        FUTURE. New York: Rose of Sharon Press, 1982. xvii, 445 pp.

        Presents the proceedings of a seminar on hermeneutics sponsored
        by the Unification Church in 1980. About 20 essays discuss the
        methodological principles of interpretation as used in scripture,
        theology, history, and other disciplines. Several papers discuss
        different aspects of the Unification Church from sociological per-
        spectives. The exchange between scholars that followed the presen-
        tation of the papers is also reproduced.

606.   Fornaro, Robert J. "Neo-Hindu Acculturation: An Alternative to
        'Instant Chemical Religion.'" THE REALM OF THE EXTRA-HUMAN.
        Edited by Agehananada Bharati. The Hague: Mouton, 1976, pp.
        17-30.

        Discusses neo-Hinduism in America as an alternative form of per-
        sonal religious experience that many young Americans who had exper-
        imented with drugs have adopted. The presence of neo-Hinduism in

America is linked with the secularization process. Both neo-
Hinduism and drugs provide for a "spiritual lifestyle" that is
frowned upon by current sociocultural trends in the West. Those
who joined the neo-Hindu groups in the late 1960's and early 1970's
abandoned the drug culture and turned to Yoga and other spiritual
exercises. Neo-Hindu religious groups, like the Hare Krishna Movement, Sivananda Yoga centers, and the Integral Yoga Institute, can
act as a drug rehabilitation program for those who voluntarily seek
help and have become viable agents of acculturation.

607.   Fornaro, Robert J. "Neo-Hinduism in America." JOURNAL OF SOCIAL
       RESEARCH 16 (1973): 1-15.

       Explores the presence of new forms of Hinduism which are a prod-
       uct of the Hindu Renaissance and the process of desanskritization
       and which are spreading their ideas in the West. Three basic ques-
       tions are asked: 1) when did this resurgence begin?; 2) who is
       responsible for it?; and 3) what institutional profile does it have
       in the United States of America? Relying on data drawn from neo-
       Hindu religious groups in New York City, the author traces the
       structural development of the beliefs and devotions of some of the
       many gurus and swamis operating in the West. He sees the rise of
       interest in neo-Hindu groups as a response to secularization and as
       an attempt to discontinue the use of drugs common among devotees
       before their conversion.

608.   Fracchia, Charles A. LIVING TOGETHER ALONE: THE NEW AMERICAN
       MONASTICISM. New York: Harper and Row, 1979. vi, 186 pp.

       Examines the new vitality or revival of monastic institutions in
       the United States of America. The kind of people who join them and
       their motivations are explored and the significance of the movement
       assessed. The author maintains that the new monasticism, which is
       genuine religious revival, will be a catalyst for change. Among
       the Christian and non-Christian groups studied are 1) the New Trap-
       pists at St. Joseph's Abbey (in Spencer, Massachusetts); 2) the
       Benedictine Monastery of Christ in the Desert (near Albuquerque,
       New Mexico); 3) Our Lady of Guadalupe Monastery (in Pecos, New
       Mexico); 4) Swami Muktananda's ashram in Oakland, California; 5)
       The House of the Holy Order of MANS (with its main center in San
       Francisco); and 6) Vajradhatu (a Tibetan Buddhist center located in
       Boulder, Colorado).

609.   Fuchs, Stephen. "The Cultural and Religious Dimensions of Neo-
       Hinduism." UPDATE: A QUARTERLY JOURNAL OF NEW RELIGIOUS MOVE-
       MENTS 8.1 (1984): 9-15.

       Describes the revival of Hinduism through contact with Western
       civilization and explains why many Westerners are responding posi-
       tively to the Hindu claims of spiritual superiority. The fact that
       Hinduism does not make hard demands on its followers and the claim
       that individuals can attain superhuman levels of being are said to
       be attractive to the West where the social, economic, and political
       situation has tended to dehumanize people and leave them spiritu-
       ally unfulfilled.

610.   Gaines, M. Josephine, et al. "The Effects of Cult Membership on
        the Health Status of Adults and Children." UPDATE: A QUARTERLY
        JOURNAL ON NEW RELIGIOUS MOVEMENTS 8.3-4 (1984): 9-17.

        Studies reports that health-related abuses are frequently report-
        ed, particularly with reference to the Unification Church, the
        Divine Light Mission, and the Way International. Basing their
        analysis only on the reports by, and comments of, ex-cult members
        (since not a single questionnaire sent to cult members was re-
        turned), the authors outline the treatment of children in cults.
        It is concluded that the dietary regimen of cults was in most cases
        the reason for health problems. The implications of these findings
        for public health are discussed.

611.   Galanter, Marc, editor. CULTS AND NEW RELIGIOUS MOVEMENTS: A RE-
        PORT OF THE AMERICAN PSYCHIATRIC ASSOCIATION. Washington, DC:
        American Psychiatric Association, 1989. xv, 346 pp.

        Presents a report by the Committee on Psychiatry and Religion of
        the American Psychiatric Association on the controversial issues
        that surround the new religious movements in the West. Conflicting
        perspectives are represented in the 16 essays included in this
        volume. After a couple of overviews of the cult issues, the essays
        are grouped into five sections: 1) perspectives on cults and new
        religions; 2) the impact of membership; 3) group functions and
        social control; 4) entry in, and departure from, the cults; and
        5) legal and social implications. Though largely psychological and
        psychiatric in orientation, this volume includes several sociolog-
        ical analyses of the new cults. Each essay includes many refer-
        ences, making this book an important sourcebook, especially on
        psychiatric implications of the cults.

        Contains items 654, 899, 1006, 2128.

612.   Galbreath, Robert, editor. "In-Depth: The Occult." JOURNAL OF
        POPULAR CULTURE 5 (1971): 628-754.

        Presents a collection of essays dealing with occult topics, such
        as metaphysical themes, parapsychological experiences, and witch-
        craft. Several bibliographical essays are included.

        Contains items 21, 2025.

613.   Garde, Michael. "New Religious Movements' Inroads into Ireland."
        UPDATE: A JOURNAL OF NEW RELIGIOUS MOVEMENTS 8.2 (1984): 25-31.

        Remarks that in Ireland the public's tolerance of new religious
        movements has increased in proportion to the waning of traditional
        religious values. The presence and activities of the following
        groups that have been popular in Ireland is briefly accounted for:
        the Hare Krishna Movement, Theosophy, and Anthroposophy.

614.   Glock, Charles Y., and Robert N. Bellah, editors. THE NEW RELI-
        GIOUS CONSCIOUSNESS. Berkeley: University of California Press,
        1976. xvii, 391 pp.

Presents the results of research carried out by advanced graduate
students of the University of California and of the Graduate Theological Union, both located in Berkeley. Two scholarly research
methods—cultural-historical and the quantitative-empirical—are
combined in the study of several new religious movements in the
Eastern and Western traditions. The editors, in two concluding
chapters, question the abiding meaning and significance of the
changing consciousness among young people. Bellah discusses three
interpretations of reality in America that have provided meaning
and generated loyalty, namely Biblical religion, utilitarian individualism, and, more recently, Asian spirituality. Glock argues
that the counterculture of the 1960's did not initiate or bring
about any significant change in American society but rather
expressed and accelerated fundamental changes that were already
under way.

Contains items 442, 447, 756, 803, 1044, 1066, 1548, 1771, 1788,
1815, 1868, 1903, 2012, 2029.

615.   Glock, Charles Y., and Robert Wuthnow. "Departures From Conven-
       tional Religion: The Nominally Religious, the Non-Religious, and
       the Alternatively Religious." THE RELIGIOUS DIMENSION: NEW
       DIRECTIONS IN QUANTITATIVE RESEARCH. Edited by Robert Wuthnow.
       New York: Academic Press, 1979, pp. 47-68.

       Presents a portrait of religion in the San Francisco Bay Area of
       California, covering the adherents of both traditional faiths and
       new religious movements. The survey conducted by the authors
       showed that, in spite of the decline of the influence of tradi-
       tional religion, people, especially young adults, were interested
       in both alternative and conventional religious forms. It is con-
       cluded that the prospects for the growth of new religions seem
       promising, but it is doubtful whether they will ever become dominant
       or greatly influence religious lifestyles.

616.   Gordon, James S. "Holistic Health Centers in the United States."
       ALTERNATIVE MEDICINES (item 687), pp. 229-51.

       Discusses the concepts of "holism" and "holistic health" and
       traces the historical origins of the growing number of holistic
       health centers in the United States. The characteristics of these
       centers are described in some detail, and some speculations about
       their future are made. A list of resources for holistic health is
       appended.

617.   Greeley, Andrew M. THE SOCIOLOGY OF THE PARANORMAL: A RECONNAIS-
       SANCE. Berverly Hills, CA: Sage Publications, 1975. 88 pp.

       Presents a sociological study of extraordinary experiences, in-
       cluding psychic events (like clairvoyance and déjà vu), contact
       with the dead, mysticism, and ecstasy. Two themes run throughout
       this little monograph: 1) the paranormal is normal; and 2) those
       who have paranormal experiences are not deviants, social misfits,
       drug addicts, or mentally sick people. The author states that
       people who are psychics are not "narrow, rigid, punitive, authori-
       tarian personalities" (p. 15).

618.   Greeley, Andrew M. "Implications For the Sociology of Religion of
        Occult Behavior in the Youth Culture." ON THE MARGIN OF THE
        VISIBLE (item 700), pp. 295-302.

        Maintains that there are several major strains in the deviant
        behavior of the upper-middle classes and that occult beliefs and
        practices are linked with such behavior. The interest in the "neo-
        sacral" takes three principal forms: 1) divination (as in the use
        of astrological charts, the I Ching, and Tarot cards); 2) mysticism
        (such as oriental meditation groups); and 3) bizarre cultic groups
        (such as Witchcraft covens). Like religion, occult beliefs and
        behaviors can have a number of functions: they provide people with
        meaning and with norms to live by and help them make contact with
        the transcendent and identify themselves with a community of
        believers.

619.   Guizzardi, Gustavo. "New Religious Phenomena in Italy: Towards a
        Post-Catholic Era?" ARCHIVES DE SCIENCES SOCIALES DES RELIGIONS
        42 (1976): 97-116.

        Surveys the presence of new religious movements in Italy and
        discusses their significance in a country where the Catholic Church
        enjoys a special status and where religion and politics are often
        confused. An outline of the historical development of the new
        movements is given and several trends identified. The author's
        view is that the new movements are a response to two distinct
        strains, namely the youth protest and the ecclesiastical protest,
        both of which arose in the context of social change and class con-
        flict. A dynamic, explanatory model that takes into account the
        religious situation in Italy is proposed.

620.   Hadden, Jeffrey K., editor. "Review Symposium: "The New Religious
        Consciousness." JOURNAL FOR THE SCIENTIFIC STUDY OF RELIGION 16
        (1977): 305-24.

        Introduces four major reviews of the book THE NEW RELIGIOUS CON-
        SCIOUSNESS (item 614). The editor's view is that, in spite of its
        shortcomings, this book is a contribution to what it symbolizes,
        rather than to what is accomplishes. He thinks that the variety
        of the backgrounds of the collaborators provides evidence for a
        new way of doing sociology.

621.   Hadden, Jeffrey K., and Theodore E. Long, editors. RELIGION AND
        RELIGIOSITY IN AMERICA: STUDIES IN HONOR OF JOSEPH H. FICHTER.
        New York: Crossroads, 1983. 167 pp.

        Explores the new relevance of religion in American life by exam-
        ining new religions, new politics, and new therapeutic systems.
        Besides the editors' introduction that seeks to identify the rela-
        tionship between religion and various social problems, there are
        many essays that cover the main trends in contemporary religious
        development. Three previously published essays on the cults are
        included.

        Contains items 571, 740, 2203.

622.   Haines, Richard F., editor. UFO PHENOMENA AND THE BEHAVIORAL
          SCIENTIST. Metuchen, NJ: Scarecrow Press, 1979. xiv, 450 pp.

          Contains thirteen essays that explore the social and cultural
          dimensions of beliefs regarding UFOs. The authors concentrate on
          the various reports of UFO phenomena and they critically examine
          the human and social factors that influence the reliability of
          these reports. They group the essays in four main areas of study:
          1) cultural factors; 2) eyewitness factors; 3) eyewitness reporting
          factors; and 4) selected UFO research data and theory.

          Contains items 1719, 1990.

623.   Hammond, Phillip E., editor. THE SACRED IN A SECULAR AGE: TOWARD
          REVISION IN THE SCIENTIFIC STUDY OF RELIGION. Berkeley: Univer-
          sity of California Press, 1985. 379 pp.

          Assumes that secularization is an established thesis in social
          science and explores its adequacy to explain the current shift in
          religious consciousness. The following areas are dealt with: con-
          ceptual and methodological issues; the sacred in traditional form;
          culture and the sacred; religion and psychology; and the sacred
          and the exercise of power. The editor admits that the findings
          presented in these essays may seem scattered and the theories
          fragmented, yet they direct us toward revision in the scientific
          study of religion.

          Contains items 280, 460, 554, 747, 910, 957, 1015, 2197.

624.   Hardesty, Nancy, Lucille Sider Dayton, and Donald W. Dayton.
          "Women in the Holiness Movement: Feminism in the Evangelical
          Tradition." WOMEN OF SPIRIT: FEMALE LEADERSHIP IN JEWISH AND
          CHRISTIAN TRADITIONS. Edited by Rosemary Reuther and Eleanor
          McLaughlin. New York: Simon and Schuster, 1979, pp. 225-54.

          Examines the part played by women in the evangelical tradition,
          beginning with the Wesleyan revival. The participation of women in
          public prayer, in giving testimony, and in preaching is documented.
          Six factors contributing to the Holiness Movement's consistent
          feminist thrust are listed, namely: 1) a theology centered on ex-
          perience; 2) its basis in the doctrine of holiness in Scripture;
          3) a stress on the work of the Holy Spirit; 4) freedom to experiment;
          5) an implicit critique of the status quo; and 6) sectarian ten-
          dencies. The nineteenth-century feminist vision in the Holiness
          sects waned and as they evolved into churches, the number of
          ordained women decreased.

625.   Harman, Willis W. "The Social Implications of Psychic Research."
          PSYCHIC EXPLORATIONS: A CHALLENGE FOR SCIENCE. Edited by John
          White. New York: G. P. Putnam, 1974, pp. 640-69.

          Suggests that, because psychic research affects human thinking
          and perception, it has repercussions on social institutions and
          culture. The author examines the challenge that psychic discov-
          eries present to the dominant scientific and social paradigms of

knowledge. He advocates the use of a new, more humanistic and spiritual paradigm that he calls the New Transcendentalism, or Perennial Philosophy, or the New Freemasonry, and in which he includes psychic phenomena.

626. Hartman, Patricia A. "Social Dimensions of Occult Participation: The Gnostica Study." BRITISH JOURNAL OF SOCIOLOGY 27 (1976): 169-83.

Investigates the reasons for the rise of interest in occult phenomena and for its apparent neglect in social science research. The author relies on a national survey that included astrologers, spiritualists, Rosicrucians, Cabalists, and neo-Pagans. She concludes that the current trend in occult revival is not in the direction of an occult establishment, but rather of new religious forms composed of young adults and those involved in the counter-culture. The interest in the occult points to a new religious commitment that is especially clear in neo-Paganism.

627. Hauth, Rudiger. "The New Religious Scene in West Germany." UPDATE: QUARTERLY JOURNAL OF NEW RELIGIOUS MOVEMENTS 8.2 (1984): 42-45.

Distinguishes three categories of new religious movements in West Germany, namely: 1) pseudo-Christian groups (like the Unification Church, the Children of God, and the Way International); 2) Hindu meditation and guru movements (such as the Divine Light Mission, the Hare Krishna Movement, Ananda Marga Yoga Society, and Transcendental Meditation); and 3) "psycho-cults" (like Scientology, EST, Eckankar, and the Rajneesh Foundation). The author believes that the "psycho-cults" will dominate the 1980's. "The inarticulated yearning for self-realization and religious experience of many contemporaries will provide a propitious and fertile soil" (p. 45).

628. Haywood, Carol Lois. "The Authority and Empowerment of Women Among Spiritualist Groups." JOURNAL FOR THE SCIENTIFIC STUDY OF RELIGION 22 (1983): 157-66.

Explores the position of women in spiritualist groups in the United States where female leaders (mediums, pastors, and healers) predominate. The author provides a short description of spiritualist worship services, which are characterized by a utilitarian orientation and intensity of participation. The role and authority of spiritualist leaders is discussed and compared with those of the mainline churches. It is held that spiritualism modifies female identity by its active concept of self, its notion of divine power, and its stress on altered states of consciousness and meditation. Though the lifestyle of spiritualists is not radically different from the social norm, spiritualist groups have significant impact on women and on institutional authority.

629. Heelas, Paul. "Western Europe: Self Religions." NEW RELIGIOUS MOVEMENTS (item 586), pp. 925-31.

Gives an overview of the new religions that offer people an experience of the self, that is, of the divine within them. The author suggests that these religions are new in the sense that they

fuse together the religious and psychological domains. Most of the
self-religions in Europe spring from developments in the United
States, and the establishment of the Institute for the Harmonious
Development of Man (by Gurdjieff) in 1922 is seen as the one central event that opened the way for new religions to establish themselves in Europe. Groups like Scientology, EST, and Church for the
Movement of Inner Spiritual Awareness are among those mentioned as
examples. These movements are not expanding in Europe as fast as
they are in the United States.

630.   Heelas, Paul. "Self Religions in Britain." RELIGION TODAY 1.1
        (1984): 4-5.

        Points out that "self-religions" like Scientology, Silva Mind
        Control, Lifespring, and Exegesis offer a different religious path
        from that pursued by more traditional new religions like the Unifi-
        cation Church and the Hare Krishna Movement. Self-religions are
        grounded in the self; they tend to be immanent rather than trans-
        cendental; and they require no worldly rejection. The author con-
        siders self-religions as an extension of the Human Potential Move-
        ment and thinks that they appeal to those individuals who are
        already acquainted with popular psychotherapies and who desire to
        fulfill their potentials.

631.   Heenan, Edward F., editor. MYSTERY, MAGIC, AND MIRACLE: RELIGION
        IN A POST-AQUARIAN AGE. Englewood Cliffs, NJ: Prentice-Hall,
        1973. vii, 179 pp.

        Contains several articles, some original, and selections from
        various books dealing with the current religious revival in the
        youth culture. The editor, in an introduction, dwells on what
        he considers to be the three integral parts of religion, namely
        mystery, magic, and miracle. The emerging forms of religious
        beliefs and practices are understood in the context of the larger
        cultural background, the change in American Civil Religion, and the
        relationship of youth culture to religion. The place of drugs in
        mystical experience, the occult, and the Jesus Movement are the
        main areas covered.

        Contains item 1765.

632.   Heino, Harri. "New Religious Communities in Finland." UPDATE: A
        QUARTERLY JOURNAL OF NEW RELIGIOUS MOVEMENTS 8.2 (1984): 27-31.

        Gives a picture of the changing religious and social situation in
        Finland in order to account for the inroads of new religious move-
        ments whose progress has been hampered by language barriers and
        geographical location. Spiritualism, parapsychology, Yoga, Anthro-
        posophy, Theosophy, and various Christian groups (like the Mormons
        and the Jehovah's Witnesses) are the main groups mentioned. The
        late 1970's saw the influx of new movements like Scientology, the
        Hare Krishna Movement, and the Summit Lighthouse, an influx which
        could have been caused in part by the critical stand of public
        opinion against them. The influence of these new religions on
        Finnish society is said to be relatively small.

633.   Hexham, Irving, Raymond F. Currie, and Joan B. Townsend. "New
        Religious Movements." NEW CANADIAN ENCYCLOPEDIA. Edmonton,
        Alberta: Hurtig, 1985, vol. 2, pp. 1479-82.

        Defines new religious movements as "unorthodox, splinter reli-
        gions that are usually outgrowths of ancient religious traditions"
        (p. 1479). The authors discuss the conflicting evidence on the
        number of people who have joined these movements, the reasons why
        young adults join, and the methods used to attract them. They
        maintain that the deprogramming of cult members is "unnecessary"
        and that considerable evidence supports the view that most people
        join a cult voluntarily. One section of this article is dedicated
        to new religions of Canadian origin, such as the Latter Rain Move-
        ment, the Children of God (who moved to Canada in 1971) the Aquarian
        Foundation, Kabalarian Philosophy, and the Emissaries of Divine
        Light. Appended to this essay is a short article on Spiritualism
        by Joan Townsend.

634.   Hexham, Irving, and Karla Poewe. UNDERSTANDING CULTS AND NEW RELI-
        GIONS. Grand Rapids, MI: Eerdmans, 1986. xi, 170 pp.

        Aims at developing an understanding of the new religious move-
        ments using an interdisciplinary perspective. The authors reject
        both the idea of brainwashing and the claims of deprogrammers and
        suggest that the conversion process of cult members should be seen
        in the broader framework of Evangelical conversion. New religious
        movements are said to propound a new mythology that is a return to
        magic and that is reinforced by primal experiences of the para-
        normal. The authors divide the religions of the world into two
        major contrasting traditions, the Yogic and the Abramic. The for-
        mer is described as a religion that denies individual choice and
        replaces trust in God with magical notions. The psychological
        aspects of conversion and the social dimensions of cultic involve-
        ment are also dealt with.

635.   Holm, Nils G. "Revivals and Society in Nordic Countries." RELI-
        GION AND THE PUBLIC DOMAIN: ACTS OF THE SEVENTEENTH INTERNATIONAL
        CONFERENCE FOR THE SOCIOLOGY OF RELIGION. Paris: C.I.S.R., 1983,
        pp. 243-51.

        Briefly surveys religious revivals in Denmark, Sweden, Norway,
        and Finland from the seventeenth to the nineteenth centuries and
        raises the question whether these renewals promoted social change.
        One religious movement, namely Laestadianism, that is found in all
        the aforementioned countries, is taken as an example to show how
        the conservative and segregationist tendencies of sects are counter-
        balanced by the demands for uniformity imposed by central authori-
        ties. The author suggests that, in their early stages, revivals
        enabled people to adopt new social and cultural innovations by
        acting as regulating and legitimizing instruments. As new move-
        ments develop, they tend to become conservative social forces. The
        correspondence between revivals and economic boons is explained
        with reference to the concept of anomie.

636.   Holroyd, Stuart. PSI AND THE CONSCIOUSNESS EXPLOSION. London:
        Bodley Head, 1977. 345 pp.

Attempts to show "the points at which the interests of contemporary parapsychology and the counterculture converge to consolidate
attitudes and concepts which may constitute a valuable 'new gnosis'"
(p. 19). These points are: altered states of consciousness, the
positive attitude towards the unconscious, the openness to exotic
cultural influence (such as that of Zen and Tantra), body and sen-
sory awareness, and theory about psychic phenomena. The author
discusses the move from spiritualism to paraphysics and elaborates
on the differences and similarities between the study of psychic
events and orthodox science.

637.   Hultberg, Thomas. "Political Implications of Neo-Buddhism." UP-
        DATE: A QUARTERLY JOURNAL OF NEW RELIGIOUS MOVEMENTS 2.1 (1978):
        14-20.

        Reflects on the presence of Buddhism in the West and on its
        potential of influencing Western culture. Although the number of
        adherents to Buddhism is small, Buddhist ideas and values are
        becoming widespread. Among the neo-Buddhist groups are included
        the Theosophical Society and various Buddhist missions to the West.
        The political implications of Buddhist influence are assessed.

638.   Hummel, Reinhart. "Contemporary New Religions in the West." NEW
        RELIGIOUS MOVEMENTS AND THE CHURCHES (item 577), pp. 16-29.

        Argues that the new religious movements in the West, unlike those
        elsewhere, are not indigenous reactions against outside influence,
        but are rather foreign importations. A simple typology grouping
        these religions into three clusters is adopted: 1) those originat-
        ing from within Christianity; 2) those that stress Eastern reli-
        gious thought; and 3) those based on Western psychology and thera-
        peutic subcultures. The author discusses the tensions between the
        new religions and society and analyzes different types of conflicts
        in terms of organizational structure and degree of commitment. The
        attitudes of the members of the new religions to Christianity and
        to religious pluralism in general are examined.

639.   Hummel, Reinhart, with Bert Hardin. "Asiatic Religions in Europe."
        UPDATE: A QUARTERLY JOURNAL OF NEW RELIGIOUS MOVEMENTS 7.2
        (1983): 3-13.

        Discusses the presence of Eastern religions in the West, focusing
        on the movement founded by Bhagwan Shree Rajneesh. The birth and
        development of this movement is briefly traced. The authors offer
        some reflections on this new group, which they think can be con-
        sidered as 1) a psychoreligious movement, or 2) a syncretistic
        'guru-cult' or 3) an esoteric school of the mysteries.

640.   Huotari, Voitto. "Finnish Revivalism as an Expression of Popular
        Piety." SOCIAL COMPASS 29 (1982): 113-23.

        Discusses five revival movements that are currently active within
        the Finnish Lutheran Church, namely Supplicationism, Pietism,
        Laestadianism, Evangelical groups, and the Evangelizing movements.
        The functions these revivals fulfill both in the church and on

society are explored and the nature of popular piety they represent analyzed. Three types of movements, namely lay, protest, and traditional, are distinguished in terms of their functions within the church. From society's point of view, revivals can function as a means of status compensation, as forms of political protest, or as a source of continuity in times of upheavals.

641.   Hurst, Jane, and Joseph Murphy. "New and Transplanted Religions." MOVEMENTS AND ISSUES IN WORLD RELIGIONS--A SOURCE AND ANALYSIS OF DEVELOPMENTS SINCE 1945: RELIGION, IDEOLOGY, AND POLITICS. Edited by Charles Wei-hsun Fu and Gerhard F. Spiegler. New York: Greenwood Press, 1987, pp. 215-41.

Studies the influx of new religious movements in the West with the aim of identifying the reasons for their presence and growth. A threefold typology is adopted and several representative movements described: 1) Afro-American movements; 2) movements of Eastern origin; and 3) New Age religious movements. These movements, in the authors' view, are a "response to religious gaps within a culture" (p. 216) and "creative responses to the changes and stresses of the postwar world" (p. 237). They are not merely novel compensators for social frustrations and satisfactions for various forms of deprivation, but rather creative opportunities for new religious experiences.

642.   Isser, Natalie, and Lita Linzer Schwartz. THE HISTORY OF CONVERSION AND CONTEMPORARY CULTS. New York: Peter Lang, 1988. ix, 230 pp.

Takes a historical and psychological approach to understanding conversion to the cults, though it is acknowledged that they "came in the tumultuous decade, 1965-75, when many changes occurred in American society" (p. 2). After analyzing some major case histories of conversion, the authors briefly examine a handful of the new movements (the Unification Church, Scientology, the Way International, the Divine Light Mission, and the Children of God) out of an estimated 1000 to 3000 cults. The authors subscribe to the theory of brainwashing or thought reform and outline the largely negative effects of conversion on both cult members and their families. A final chapter is dedicated to community responses to counteract the proselytization efforts of the cults.

643.   Jones, R. Kenneth, editor. SICKNESS AND SECTARIANISM: EXPLORATORY STUDIES IN MEDICAL AND RELIGIOUS SECTARIANISM. Brookfield, VT: Gower Publishing Company, 1985. ix, 158 pp.

Presents a series of essays that "attempt to bring together marginal medicine and religious sectarianism and to see in what ways they bare some similarities to each other" (vii). Besides several general articles dealing with the development of medical sects and the relationship between mental health and sect members, there are studies on specific groups like Transcendental Meditation and the Human Potential Movement.

Contains items 1326, 1933, 2053.

644.   Kaslow, Florence, and Marvin B. Sussman, editors. CULTS AND THE
           FAMILY. New York: Haworth Press, 1982. 192 pp.

           Reprints a special issue of the MARRIAGE AND FAMILY REVIEW (vol.
           4, nos. 3/4, 1982) that was dedicated to the study of the dynamics
           of the interrelationships between the family and contemporary cults.
           Several sociologists, psychologists, and ex-cult members contribute
           to the ongoing debate on the effects of cult membership on family
           life. Among the areas covered are a typology of family responses
           to the new movements, involvement in cultism, and the negative
           effects of this involvement on the family.

           Contains items 920, 936, 1644, 2116, 2153, 2161.

645.   Kilbourne, Brock K., editor. SCIENTIFIC RESEARCH AND NEW RELI-
           GIONS: DIVERGENT PERSPECTIVES. San Francisco: American Associa-
           tion for the Advancement of Science, Pacific Division, 1985.
           180 pp.

           Presents the papers read at the symposium "Science and the New
           Religions" held as part of the annual meeting of American Associa-
           tion for the Advancement of Science, Pacific Division. The essays
           cover a variety of hotly debated issues, such as the methods used
           to study the new movements, the relationship between them and
           psychopathology, and the question of brainwashing or conversion.
           The editor lists and discusses the major points of conflict that
           emerged out of the meeting: 1) definitions of terms; 2) levels of
           analysis; 3) research methodologies; 4) assumptions and value
           orientations; 5) hypothetical processes; 6) research bias; and
           7) similarities between the new religions and psychotherapy.

           Contains items 730, 858, 871, 1048, 1050, 1081, 2180.

646.   Kowalewski, David, and Arthur L. Greil. "Religious Sectarianism
           and the Soviet State: The Dynamics of Believer Protest and Regime
           Response." REVIEW OF RELIGIOUS RESEARCH 24 (1983): 245-60.

           Attempts to apply the church-sect typology to the U.S.S.R. where
           several sectarian and nonsectarian demonstrations occurred between
           1965 and 1977. The social features of both kinds of protests in
           this hostile political environment are compared. The authors state
           that "little systematic analysis has been conducted to validate the
           claim that sectarians do indeed more often suffer discriminating
           treatment at the hands of Soviet authorities" (p. 252). They
           conclude that members of sects, such as Baptists, Pentecostals,
           Seventh-Day Adventists, and Jehovah's Witnesses, seem to be treated
           more harshly than nonsectarians because of the different forms of
           protest they indulge in.

647.   Lane, Christel O. "The New Religious Life of the Soviet Union: How
           and Why Does It Differ?" INTERNATIONAL JOURNAL OF SOCIOLOGY AND
           SOCIAL POLICY 2.1 (1982): 44-57.

           Outlines the significant new developments in religious matters
           that have recently taken place in Russia and shows how they differ
           from similar movements elsewhere. Renewal among Evangelical Bap-

tists and Orthodox believers has been the major sign of religious
change. The former's success is seen as resulting from a reaction
to the characteristics of the Soviet Union, the latter's as a response to developments that have led educated young people to find
meaning in the old religion. The author states that the Soviet
Union has "remained completely untouched by the new religious movements prominent in the U.S.A." (p. 49) and then explores the why
this is the case and concludes that the conditions favoring the
spread of cults in the West are not found in the U.S.S.R.

648.   Lauer, Roger M. "Urban Shamans: The Influence of Folk-Healers
       on Medical Care in Our Cities." NEW PHYSICIAN (August 1973):
       486-89.

       Reflects on the common practice among educated, middle-class
       people to consult shamans to seek help through a variety of psychic
       phenomena, like telepathy, clairvoyance, and premonition. The
       activities of two main folk healers--psychic readers and religious
       healers--are discussed. Scientology, the Association for Research
       and Enlightenment (Edgar Cayce), and Spiritualist churches are
       among the contemporary "psychic religions" that are attracting many
       people looking for relief from their physical and/or psychological
       problems. The author thinks that these urban shamans are likely to
       remain popular. "Their niche is secure since they give a service
       that physicians never could duplicate" (p. 489).

649.   Lawren, Bill. "Apocalypse Now?" PSYCHOLOGY TODAY 23.5 (May 1989):
       38-44.

       Reflects on the current interest in, and concern about, the end of
       the world at the approaching end of the second millennium. The
       views of various prophets of doom, like Hal Lindsey, Jerry Falwell,
       and Ruth Montgomery, are described. Millenarian consciousness is
       viewed by some as a potential for danger, such as a surge in world
       terrorism, panic, or anxiety. The possible reasons for this "ap-
       petite for apocalypse" are briefly discussed.

650.   Lee, John A. "Social Change and Marginal Therapeutic Systems."
       MARGINAL MEDICINE (item 715), pp. 23 -41.

       Discusses fringe medical systems, including therapeutic sugges-
       tion, New Thought, mind cure, Spiritualist healing, and the Unity
       Church of Truth. Current attempts to advance unorthodox healing
       techniques, like those offered by Scientology, are also considered.
       The author outlines three fundamental doctrinal differences between
       faith healing and mind cure. The latter, unlike the former, starts
       with an abstract form of the divine that is always within the reach
       of the human mind, endorses a belief in a monistic worldview, and
       employs the power of suggestion. The author's view is that "mind
       cure may be understood as a response to certain social and techni-
       cal conditions in the field of health care, but it has also had an
       impact, in turn, on the development of medicine" (p. 37).

651.   Lee, John A. SECTARIAN HEALERS AND HYPNOTHERAPY. Toronto: Queen's
       Press, 1970. x, 173 pp.

Presents a study made for the Committee on the Healing Arts on
those forms of therapy in Toronto that are regarded to rely primarily on the use of occult healing methods, suggestion, and hypnosis
and that attribute the power of healing to the Divine Mind, the
Thetan, the Life Force, Spirits, and similar conceptions of supernatural power. A historical overview of these alternative forms of
healing is provided. The history, organization, beliefs, and
practices of the following groups are dealt with: Dianetics and
Scientology, Christian Science, Electropsychometry, Concept-Therapy,
Spiritualist Healing, faith healing (Oral Roberts), Unity, and
Ontology. Legislation on occult healing in Canada and the United
States is summarized.

652.   Lehman, Arthur C., and James E. Myers. MAGIC, WITCHCRAFT AND RELI-
       GION: AN ANTHROPOLOGICAL STUDY OF THE SUPERNATURAL. Mountain
       View, CA: Mayfield Publishing Company, second edition, 1988. xi,
       482 pp.

       Reproduces a collection of essay that approach religious phenom-
       ena from an anthropological point of view. Besides several selec-
       tions dealing with the ways in which anthropologists define and
       approach religion, and with religious beliefs, rituals, and activi-
       ties of both nonliterate and modern Western societies, there are
       several papers on the new religious movements in the West. The
       many bibliographic references make this volume a major source for
       the anthropological study of these movements.

       Contains items 192, 495, 1228, 1647, 1695, 1720, 1746, 1860, 1880,
       1886, 1945, 1972, 1995, 2006, 2033, and selections from item 1821.

653.   Levi, Ken, editor. VIOLENCE AND RELIGIOUS COMMITMENT: IMPLICATIONS
       OF JIM JONES'S PEOPLE'S TEMPLE MOVEMENT. University Park: Penn-
       sylvania State University Press, 1982. xv, 207 pp.

       Presents a collection of papers discussing the events at Jones-
       stown and their aftermath. After a brief chronology of this cult,
       the material is divided into four parts. The first examines the
       People's Temple in comparative perspective, seeing it as one aspect
       of violence often found in connection with religious experience
       and relating it to the activities of other contemporary religious
       groups. Part Two proposes ways of understanding the People's
       Temple Movement. Part Three attempts to analyze the reactions to
       Jonestown from sociological, philosophical, and theological
       viewpoints. The final part contains one personal report by a
       former member of the People's Temple.

       Contains items 451, 1049, 1821, 1875, 2188, 2199.

654.   Levine, Saul V. "Life in the Cults." CULTS AND NEW RELIGIOUS
       MOVEMENTS (item 611), pp. 95-107.

       Examines some common features of cults, such as belief systems,
       leadership, rules and regulations, and membership, using as exam-
       ples four major groups, namely the Hare Krishna Movement, the
       Unification Church, the Children of God, and the Divine Light Mis-
       sion. The daily routines and rituals of each cult are sketched.

655. Ljungdhal, Axel. "What Can We Learn From Non-Biblical Prophetic
      Movements." NEW RELIGIONS (item 565), pp. 84-91.

      Examines about 50 different prophetic movements from different
      historical periods and parts of the world and attempts a brief
      account of the fundamental patterns they reveal. Three main ques-
      tions are asked: 1) what are the causes leading to the appearance
      of a prophet?; 2) what are the significance and function of his
      message?; and 3) why do only some movements have prophets? The
      author thinks that all prophetic movements promise better living
      conditions to their followers and provide outlets for aggression
      and self-assertion. Both external and internal hardships contrib-
      ute to the rise of prophetic movements. Several flying-saucer
      cults are among the groups considered.

656. Lofland, John. PROTEST: STUDIES OF COLLECTIVE BEHAVIOR AND SOCIAL
      MOVEMENTS. New Brunswick, NJ: Transaction Books, 1985. xii,
      349 pp.

      Presents a collection of the author's previously published mate-
      rials. One section is dedicated to his main contributions to the
      study of conversions to the cults.

      Contains item 1365.

657. Macioti, Maria. "New Religious Movements in Italy." UPDATE: A
      QUARTERLY JOURNAL OF NEW RELIGIOUS MOVEMENTS 8.2 (1984): 54-58.

      Surveys new religious movements in Italy, focusing mainly on
      Transcendental Meditation, the Hare Krishna Movement, the Unifica-
      tion Church, the Divine Light Mission, the Rajneesh Foundation, and
      the Catholic Charismatic Renewal. The problems of accepting and
      legitimizing most of these new movements in a Catholic context are
      briefly mentioned. Some groups, like the Children of God, have
      barely survived, while others, like the Hare Krishna Movement, are
      prospering. Transcendental Meditation and the Rajneesh Foundation
      claim several thousand members. The author thinks that the new
      movements have profited by the weaknesses of the Catholic Church
      and by the legislation that no longer recognizes it as the sole
      state religion.

658. Marty, Martin E. A NATION OF BEHAVERS. Chicago: University of
      Chicago Press, 1976. xi, 239 pp.

      Stresses the need to study social behavior in order to understand
      religious activity. The author explores the various religious
      aspects of America life, including the mainline traditions, the
      evangelical and pentecostal churches, and the new religions. He
      investigates the reasons for the growth and appeal of the cults,
      such as boredom or discontent with the existing churches and the
      search for identity. According to the author, the most interesting
      feature in relation to these movements is not the counterculture
      "but the cultural (and subcultural) context of the enduring occult
      and metaphysical trends" (p. 135). Various types of new religions
      or revitalization movements are briefly examined.

659.   Mitchison, Amanda. "The Witch Guide to Turin." NEW SOCIETY 77
        (September 12, 1986): 13-15.

        Surveys the rise of witchcraft (Satanism) and parapsychology in
        Turin, Italy. Occult practices, like card and hand fortune-telling,
        numerology, mediumship, and telepathy, are said to originate in
        traditional folk practices common throughout the Mediterranean.
        Several well-known occultists and their practices are described.
        Most of these occult beliefs and rituals are found among estranged
        middle-class people working mostly in the service industries.
        Turin, according to the author, is an unfriendly city with various
        philosophical and religious traditions and seems an ideal place for
        the occult.

660.   Moberg, David O., editor. SPIRITUAL WELL-BEING: SOCIOLOGICAL PER-
        SPECTIVES. Washington, DC: University Press of America. x, 358
        pp.

        Presents a pioneering study on the sociology of spiritual well-
        being, which refers to the health of the total person including
        one's ultimate concerns, central philosophy, and meaning system
        that influence individual and social behavior. The 24 essays
        included in this volume represent several different methodological
        and theoretical perspectives. After an introductory chapter in
        which the editor discusses the nature of social indicators of
        spiritual well-being and gives an overview of the research done so
        far, the material is divided in the following four major sections:
        1) conceptual studies of spiritual well-being; 2) spiritual well-
        being and social theory; 3) qualitative research on spiritual well-
        being; and 4) quantitative research on spiritual well-being. A
        concluding chapter by the editor reflects on the future of research
        in the field and deals with some basic research problems.

        Contains items 761, 784, 1613.

661.   Mol, Hans. FAITH AND FRAGILITY: RELIGION AND IDENTITY IN CANADA.
        Burlington, Ontario: Trinity Press, 1985. 354 pp.

        Gives an overview the religious situation in Canada, examining in
        the process traditional Indian religions, various ethnic groups,
        the major denominations, and the new religious movements. Among
        the groups are included the Mennonites, the Hutterites, and the
        Doukhokors. Jehovah's Witnesses, the Salvation Army, and the Pen-
        tecostal churches are cited as examples of sects. One section
        deals with new religious movements with special emphasis on Scien-
        tology (pp. 162-70), which promises calmness and confidence. There
        is a short discussion on the deprogramming issue (pp. 160-62).

662.   Moore, Robert Lawrence. IN SEARCH OF WHITE CROWS: SPIRITUALISM,
        PARAPSYCHOLOGY, AND AMERICAN CULTURE. New York: Oxford Univer-
        sity Press, 1977. xvii, 310 pp.

        Presents a historical overview of beliefs about Spiritualism
        (that is, communication with spirits through human mediums) and of
        psychical research (that is, investigation of alleged mental powers

that are apparently inexplicable by known science). The first part of the author's treatment covers the rise of the Spiritualist Movement in the 1850's, its development from 1850 to 1875, and its decline in the last quarter of the nineteenth century. The second part concentrates on the activities of those involved in psychical research, like the American Society for Psychical research and the work initiated by Dr. Rhine at Duke University. The author finally discusses the relationship between Spiritualism, parapsychology, and the occult (including Theosophy). Though Spiritualism and parapsychology are not necessarily linked with the occult, both reflect some of the concerns that motivate modern occult movements.

663. Mosatche, Harriet S. SEARCHING: PRACTICES AND BELIEFS OF THE RELI-
      GIOUS CULTS AND HUMAN POTENTIAL GROUPS. New York: Stravon Educa-
      tional Press, 1983. 437 pp.

      Presents a social-psychological study of the following nine new
      religious movements: 1) the Unification Church; 2) EST; 3) Scien-
      tology; 4) the Association for Research and Enlightenment; 5) the
      Himalayan International Institute; 6) the Institute for Psychic
      Integrity; 7) the Divine Light Mission; 8) Wainwright House; and
      9) the Hare Krishna Movement. The organization, belief system,
      recruitment procedures, and possible future developments of each
      group are among the topics covered. Several significant issues,
      such as the reason why the new movements came into being, their
      relationship with the mainline religious traditions, the conversion
      or brainwashing of members, and the family reactions are discussed.

664. Musgrove, Frank, with Roger Middleton and Pat Hawes. MARGINS OF
      THE MIND. London: Methuen and Company, 1977. vi, 247 pp.

      Presents several case studies about the "transformation of con-
      sciousness." Attention is focused on several aspects of conscious-
      ness and some important changes (like joining a commune of mystics)
      are examined. Changes in personal identity are most apparent in
      members of the Sufi groups and the Hare Krishna Movement. Recent
      studies of adult change are surveyed. The author maintains that
      the importance of "liminality" as a prelude to transformation has
      not been sufficiently recognized.

      Contains item 1873, 1885.

665. Nanninga, Rob, and Arjaan Wit. "Contemporary Religious Movements
      in the Netherlands." UPDATE: A QUARTERLY JOURNAL OF NEW RELI-
      GIOUS MOVEMENTS 8.2 (1984): 46-50.

      Points out that the influence of the traditional churches in
      Holland has declined and that about one third of the Dutch popula-
      tion is religiously inclined but unattached to any particular de-
      nomination and, therefore, open to other religious alternatives.
      Most of the new movements, with the exception of Transcendental
      Meditation, the Rajneesh Foundation, and the Young Christian Evan-
      gelical Movement, have attracted very few followers. Studies are
      quoted to suggest that conversion to the new cults is related to
      identity and authority problems which were in existence before the

individuals joined a cult. The authors think that the negative public reaction to the new movements has led to an exaggeration of the effects they have on their membership.

666. Needleman, Jacob. THE NEW RELIGIONS. New York: Crossroad, second edition, 1984. xxxv, 243 pp. (First published in 1973.)

Provides reflective descriptions of several Eastern religious groups, such as Zen and Tibetan Buddhism, Meher Baba, Subud, and Transcendental Meditation, that have become part of the new religious scene over the last two decades. There are chapters dedicated to Krishnamurti, the Occult, and Gurdjieff. In the introduction the author gives brief outlines of the philosophical systems of the major Eastern traditions. How and to what extent the new religions will influence Western culture are some of the questions that preoccupy the author. New religions are seen as a means of satisfying desires and allaying fears, even though people may be actually looking for something more fundamental than self-gratification.

667. Needleman, Jacob, and George Baker, editors. UNDERSTANDING THE NEW RELIGIONS. New York: Seabury Press, 1978. xxi, 314 pp.

Presents revised versions of essays given at the national Conference on the Study on New Religious Movements held in Berkeley, California, in June 1977. The papers are grouped under three headings: 1) new religions in American history; 2) the nature and meaning of the new religions; and 3) the phenomenon of the new cults. Besides general articles explaining the reasons why these movements should appear in the second half of the twentieth century, there are several studies of particular groups, including the Unification Church, the Radha Soami Movement, and the Jesus People. Underlying most of these studies is the assumption that the new religious movements are indicative of a profound cultural change in American society.

Contains items, 446, 572, 792, 823, 1042, 1082, 1092, 1573, 1673, 1798, 2138.

668. Nelsen, Hart M., Raytha L. Yokley, and Anne K. Nelsen, editors. THE BLACK CHURCH IN AMERICA. New York: Basic Books, 1971. 375 pp.

Brings together 33 previously published articles or selections from books on various aspects of Black religion in the United States. The material is divided into four main sections dealing with 1) historical perspectives, 2) differentiation in the Black Church, 3) sects and cults within Black religion, and 4) Black ministers and Black power.

Contains items 193, 212, 1173, and selections from item 182.

669. Noonan, Eddie. "A Random Sampling: A Brief Survey of 20 New Age Groups From the Festival of Mind, Body, and Spirit." UPDATE: A QUARTERLY JOURNAL OF NEW RELIGIOUS MOVEMENTS 5.2 (1981): 6–21.

Contains summaries of 20 religious movements, some of relatively
recent origin. A brief historical statement and some basic beliefs
about most of the groups included are given. Among the newer
groups, the following are mentioned: the Atlanteans, the Church
Universal and Triumphant (Summit Lighthouse), Claregate College (a
metaphysical school in England), Da Free John and the Crazy Wisdom
Fellowship (now known as the Laughing Man Institute), Findhorn,
Silva Mind Control, and the Sufi Order in the West.

670.   Nordquist, Ted A. "New Religious Movements in Sweden." NEW RELI-
       GIOUS MOVEMENTS: A PERSPECTIVE FOR UNDERSTANDING SOCIETY (item
       551), pp. 173-87.

Focuses on about 30 Swedish religious movements in order to gain
an understanding of the general social process of Swedish society.
Several features (including number, age of membership, and sex) of
six of these groups, namely the Divine Light Mission, Sri Chinmoy
Center, the Hare Krishna Movement, Ananda Marga, the Unification
Church, and Siddha Yoga Dham, are described. The author seeks to
offer an explanation of why new cults in Sweden have been relatively unsuccessful, even though the country is one of the world's
most secularized, a condition which is supposed to be conducive to
cult origin and development. It is argued that Sweden does not
contain within itself "a latent symbology for the expression of
discontent in alternative religious form" (p. 181). Further, the
Swedish legal system does not favor new religions. Since the organizational structure of Sweden is very centralized, it allows for
little innovation and slow acceptance of new religious expressions.

671.   O'Toole, Roger, editor. "Symposium on Religious Awakening."
       SOCIOLOGICAL ANALYSIS 44 (1983): 81-122.

Contains the proceedings of a session on "Historical Perspectives
in Religious Awakenings" held at the 1982 joint meeting of the
Association for the Sociology of Religion, the Religious Research
Association, and the Society for the Scientific Study of Religion.
The discussions raise several theoretical and methodological issues
both to historians and sociologists.

Contains items 353, 362, 418, 476.

672.   Palmer, Susan. "AIDS as Metaphor." SOCIETY 26.2 (1989): 44-50.

Examines how the presence of the disease AIDS has become a powerful symbol in the following religious groups: Jimmy Swaggart's
Ministry; the Jehovah's Witnesses; Seventh-Day Adventism; Christian
Science; the Unification Church; and the Rajneesh Movement. After
describing the religious response to AIDS in the groups mentioned
above, the author observes that their literature refers to the
disease in the context of four major themes, namely: 1) millenarian
beliefs; 2) sexual mores; 3) magical approaches to illness; and 4)
the definition and strengthening of the boundaries that separate
them from society.

673.   Palmer, Susan. "Performance Practices in Meditation Rituals Among
       the New Religions." STUDIES IN RELIGION 9 (1980): 403-13.

Argues that meditation rituals can be, and often are, used for
outer-directed social ends. Basing her analysis on several new
religious groups, like the Sivananda Yoga Society, the American
Sufi Order, Dharmadatu, and Tai Chi Chuan, where meditation is the
central mystical practice believed to lead one to a higher consciousness, the author demonstrates how the ritual is employed for
social communication. Timing, voice inflection, facial expression,
body posture and gesture, touching, clothing, and space are means
by which meditators express ritual ecstasy, membership, courtship,
and disaffiliation from, or devotion to, the group and its teaching.
Formal meditation rituals are distinguished from informal ones.
The former express the cosmology of the group and also enable the
practitioners to experience and realize that cosmology; the latter
reflects the social organization and the relationships and power
struggles within it.

674.   Partin, Harry B. "Modern American Religious Cults: An Overview."
        ENCOUNTER 47 (1986): 291-307.

Gives an overview of contemporary cults, that is, religious
groups that differ from, and are an alternative to, the dominant
religion of American society. The author holds that the presence
of the cults is important because they are an expression of American pluralism. Six types of cults are distinguished: 1) those that
stress ancient wisdom (like the Theosophical Society, the I Am
Movement, Eckankar, and Anthroposophy); 2) those that are based on
belief in visitors from outer space (Spiritualism and UFO cults);
3) those that strive for an initiatory experience (Gurdjieff and
Scientology); 4) neopagan groups (nature religion, Witchcraft, and
Satanism); 5) those that stem from Hindu traditions (the Hare
Krishna Movement and the Self-Realization Fellowship); and 6) other
Eastern and Middle-Eastern groups (Zen, Nichiren Shoshu of America,
Subud, the Unification Church, and the Baha'i Faith). The author
points out that the People's Temple does not fit into his classification because it emerged out of a mainline denomination (the Dis-
ciples of Christ). He maintains that the cults will remain a part
of the American religious scene.

675.   Peters, Ted. "Post-Modern Religion." UPDATE: A QUARTERLY JOURNAL
        OF NEW RELIGIOUS MOVEMENTS 8.1 (1984): 16-30.

Points out that the current religious consciousness has a gnostic
orientation that has become part of diverse movements and philosophies, including Transcendental Meditation, the Hare Krishna Movement, EST, Lifespring, Holistic Health, the Occult, Astrology,
Teilhardianism, UFO cults, and Freemasonry. The following eight
major features of "perennial gnosticism" are described: 1) cosmic
unity; 2) the higher self; 3) the divine spark; 4) human potential;
5) reincarnation; 6) evolution and transformation; 7) gnosis; and
8) Jesus. Though basically a theological essay that aims at
evaluating the New Age Movement, this article provides a solid
philosophical reason for looking at the new religions as a whole
and for making a connection between modern and ancient cults.

676.   Richardson, James T. "New Religious Movements in the United
        States: A Review." SOCIAL COMPASS 30 (1983): 85-110.

Concentrates on reviewing quantitative works that focus on individual members of new religious movements. The efforts of a number
of institutions and groups involved in researching new religions
are assessed. The Institute for the Study of American Religion
(under the direction of J. Gordon Melton at the University of California at Santa Barbara) and the now-defunct Center for the Study
of New Religious Movements (founded by Jacob Needleman at the Graduate Theological Union in Berkeley, California) are mentioned.
Some groups studying the new religions are included under the head-
ing of "anti-cult movement," and are made up of such groups as the
Spiritual Counterfeits Project, and FREECOG (Free Our Children From
the Children of God). Others, such as APRL (Association for the
Preservation of Religious Liberty) and New ERA (Ecumenical Research
Organization) are seen as opponents of the anticult movement. The
media's treatment of new religions and the actions taken by public
officials and organizations are briefly summarized. A relatively
short, select bibliography is included (pp. 107-10).

677. Richardson, James T. "Financing the New Religions: A Broader View."
     OF GODS AND MEN (item 550), pp. 65-88.

     Presents a slightly revised version of his previously published
     essay (item 678) that discusses the methods that the new cults,
     especially the Unification Church and the Hare Krishna Movement,
     use to raise money. A "data frame" for gathering information on
     the economic policies of the new religions is given in an appendix.

678. Richardson, James T. "Financing the New Religions: Comparative
     and Theoretical Considerations." JOURNAL FOR THE SCIENTIFIC
     STUDY OF RELIGION 21 (1982): 255-68.

     Examines fundraising methods used by several of the new religious
     movements, methods which have become a major issue in our society.
     Three types of techniques for soliciting funds are investigated: 1)
     fundraising procedures of evangelical groups like the Hare Krishna
     and the Unification Church; 2) ways of raising money by groups that
     do not use public solicitation, like the Divine Light Mission and
     Ananda Cooperative Village; and 3) fundraising in some noncommunal
     groups and movements, such as Transcendental Meditation and Scien-
     tology. The author maintains that the one-sided stress on public
     solicitation is too narrow in scope. Most of the new religions go
     through an experimental period, using several methods and finally
     selecting the most successful and acceptable to their ideology.

679. Richardson, James T., editor. CONVERSION CAREERS: IN AND OUT OF
     THE NEW RELIGIONS. Beverly Hills, CA: Sage Publications, 1978.
     160 pp.

     Contains nine articles previously published in the AMERICAN
     BEHAVIORAL SCIENTIST (vol. 20, no. 6, 1977). Besides an introduc-
     tory essay by the editor, this volume includes several studies
     on the Jesus People, the Unification Church, the occult, and the
     Catholic Charismatics. There is also one essay discussing the
     deprogramming issue.

     Contains items 870, 1575, 1598, 1833, 1950, 1992, 2082, 2207.

680.   Robbins, Thomas.   "Old Wine in Exotic New Bottles."   JOURNAL FOR
       THE SCIENTIFIC STUDY OF RELIGION 16 (1977): 310-13.

       Reviews Glock and Bellah's NEW RELIGIOUS CONSCIOUSNESS (item 614)
       and suggests that some of the "ugly and facile" new religions are
       driving out the attractive and subtle ones. The two fastest grow-
       ing movements, namely EST and the Unification Church, are quoted as
       examples of the former kind of movements, in that EST embodies a
       nondualistic ideology that goes against the traditional utilitar-
       ian individualism and Western culture, while the Unification Church
       seems to promote totalitarian religious attitudes.

681.   Robbins, Thomas, and Dick Anthony.   "'Cults' in the Late Twentieth
       Century."   ENCYCLOPEDIA OF THE AMERICAN RELIGIOUS EXPERIENCE
       (item 40), vol. 2, pp. 741-54.

       Presents an overview of the new religious movements and the
       issues they have raised. After debating the problem of defining a
       cult, the authors discuss the significance of the contemporary
       resurgence of cults. Theories that offer explanations of their
       presence are grouped under four headings: 1) cults and secularity;
       2) cults and the material world; 3) cults and the breakdown of
       community; and 4) cults and cultural confusion. Various attempts
       to classify the new religions are outlined and brief summaries of
       the Unification Church, the Way International, Scientology, and
       EST are provided. The controversies surrounding cults, particu-
       larly the attempt to "medicalize" them and deprogram their members,
       are mentioned and the sources of conflict identified.

682.   Robbins, Thomas, and Dick Anthony.   "New Religious Movements in
       the United States."   ENCYCLOPEDIA OF RELIGION (item 18), vol.
       10, pp, 394-405.

       Presents a summary of the current cultic scene in the United
       States. The following areas are considered: 1) the sources and
       significance of the contemporary religious ferment; 2) the type of
       groups that have emerged; and 3) the general hostility towards the
       new cults. The emergence of the new religions can be interpreted
       as a revival of magic that aims for wealth and power, as an attempt
       to stem the progress of secularization, as a reaction to moral
       ambiguity, as an outcome of dislocation in communal patterns, or as
       an attempt to counteract the diffusion of personal identity in
       Western culture. The authors propose a typology based on meaning
       systems, monistic and dualistic systems of belief, and univocal and
       multivocal cognitive styles. The conflicts that cults have brought
       with them are outlined and the issue of brainwashing discussed.
       The authors hold that, though some manipulation and intense indoc-
       trination is present in many new religious movements, members are
       not unwillingly brainwashed and forced to give their allegiances to
       cults.

683.   Robbins, Thomas, and Dick Anthony, editors.   IN GODS WE TRUST: NEW
       PATTERNS OF RELIGIOUS PLURALISM IN AMERICA.   New Brunswick, NJ:
       Transaction Books, 1981.   338 pp.

Presents a collection of 18 essays, many of which were originally
published in SOCIETY (15.4, 1978). Apart from the introductory
essay by the editors, the material is divided into five sections:
1) religious ferment and cultural transformation; 2) disenchantment
and renewal in mainline traditions; 3) civil religious groups,
oriental mysticism, and therapy groups; 4) the brainwashing theory;
and 5) new religions and the decline of community. A short bibliography of basic materials (pp. 327-35) is included.

Contains items 735, 783, 840, 1040, 1746, 1782, 1930, 1960, 2003,
2010, 2190.

684.   Robbins, Thomas, William C. Shepherd, and James McBride, editors.
        CULTS, CULTURE, AND THE LAW: PERSPECTIVES ON NEW RELIGIOUS MOVE-
        MENTS. Chico, CA: Scholars Press, 1985. 238 pp.

Presents the papers read at a seminar held at the Center for the
Study of New Religious Movements at the Graduate Theological Union
in Berkeley, California in 1982. Four major themes are dealt with
in these essays: 1) the global and sociological dimensions of the
new movements; 2) the issue of brainwashing; 3) legal intervention;
and 4) the state regulation of new movements. In an introductory
essay, Thomas Robbins maintains that "controversies surrounding
cults are closely related to an emerging general crisis on church
and state relations as well as to significant currents of social
transformations in the United States" (p. 7).

Contains items 909, 923, 1038.

685.   Romarheim, Arild. "New Religious Movements in Norway." UPDATE: A
        QUARTERLY JOURNAL OF NEW RELIGIOUS MOVEMENTS 2.2 (1978): 39-46.

Outlines the conditions that have contributed to the spread of
new religious movements in Norway and surveys their distribution.
Secularization, though proceeding at a slower rate in Norway than
in other European countries, is said to be weakening the established religions and opening up opportunities for religious minorities whose message fits into a situation that creates a crisis of
identity. Those movements that have established themselves in
Norway are classified in five types according to their respective
background: 1) Hindu (such as Transcendental Meditation, Ananda
Marga Yoga Society, and the Divine Light Mission); 2) Buddhist
(like Kargyudpa Buddhism); 3) Islamic (for example, the Baha'i
Faith, Subud, and the Ahmedia Movement); 4) Christian (such as the
Worldwide Church of God, the Children of God, and the Unification
Church); and 5) occult (Theosophy, Anthroposophy, Astrology,
Eckankar, and the Rosicrucian Order).

686.   Sachs, Viola. "The Occult, Magic, and Witchcraft in American Cul-
        ture." SOCIAL SCIENCE INFORMATION 22 (1983): 941-45.

Comments on the conference, held in Paris in 1982, on the uses
of the occult in American culture. The author maintains that the
presence and vitality of occult beliefs and practices can be traced

to the Puritan heritage, to certain elements in American history,
and to certain social conditions, "particularly the pressure of
uniformization upon the self and the desire it breeds for secrecy"
(p. 941).

687.   Salmon, J. Warren, editor. ALTERNATIVE MEDICINES: POPULAR AND
        POLICY PERSPECTIVES. New York: Tavistock Publications, 1984. x,
        302 pp.

        Contains nine essays that explore the differences between alter-
        native medical systems that have recently experienced a resurgence
        and the implications they might have on society. The editor, in
        the introduction, overviews the field of alternative medicines. He
        thinks that two social developments have facilitated the rise of
        interest in, and use of, alternative medical treatment: 1) the
        increased quest for health in Western societies, and 2) the organi-
        zational and financial problems of contemporary scientific medicine.
        Homeopathy, chiropractic, acupuncture, psychic healing, and the
        encounter between alternative and orthodox medicines are among the
        topics covered. Useful bibliographies are appended to every essay.

        Contains items, 564, 616, 2024.

688.   Schiller, Johannes A. "The Sociology of Charismatic Movements."
        GIFTS OF THE SPIRIT AND THE BODY OF CHRIST" PERSPECTIVES ON THE
        CHARISMATIC MOVEMENT." Edited by J. Elmo Agrimson. Minneapolis,
        MN: Augsburg Publishing House, 1974, pp. 57-69.

        Speculates on the way cultural and social systems influence the
        development and nature of charismatic movements. The contemporary
        social environment is said to be normless, massive, pluralistic,
        bureaucratic, and technological. The problems created by such a
        condition are usually alleviated by religion. When traditional
        religion fails to perform this function of satisfying human needs,
        people look for other avenues to find meaning in life, develop
        their personal identity, and create systems of support and secu-
        rity. Charismatic movements offer one alternative for helping
        people cope with their problems.

689.   Shepherd, Jerry W. "Sociology of Pentecostalism." DICTIONARY OF
        PENTECOSTAL AND CHARISMATIC MOVEMENTS (item 10), pp. 794-99.

        Examines Pentecostalism as "a specific movement engaged in by
        persons attempting to make sense of, and thus bring cognitive order
        to, what is seen as a complex and, at times, alien world structure"
        (p. 794). After outlining the background to the sociological
        approach to the Pentecostal Movement, the author argues in favor of
        understanding it as a "value-oriented," rather than "norm-oriented"
        society. A basic bibliography is attached.

690.   Sihvo, Jouko. "Expanding Revival Movements and Their Circumstances
        in Finland." THE CONTEMPORARY METAMORPHOSIS OF RELIGION: ACTS OF
        THE 12th INTERNATIONAL CONGRESS ON SOCIOLOGY OF RELIGION, The
        Hague, Netherlands, 1973. Lille, France: C.I.S.R., 1973, pp.
        257-69.

Analyzes the nature of the more successful religious movements
in Finland and investigates their social structure and the circumstances that facilitated their emergence. The religious situation
in Finland is described and the features of the new movements outlined. The main groups studied are the evangelical movements, the
pietists, the People's Bible Society, the People's Mission, the
Pentecostals, the Jehovah's Witnesses, and the Laestadian Movement.
The universal priesthood of all believers is a prominent characteristic shared by all of these groups. The rise and spread of religious movements is related to population growth, agrarian lifestyle, and church attendance. The current revival is considered
a response to the needs of people who are alienated and socially
isolated.

691.   Sobal, Jeff, and Charles F. Emmons. "Patterns of Belief in Reli-
        gious, Psychic, and Other Paranormal Phenomena." ZETETIC SCHOLAR
        9 (1982): 7-17.

        Analyzes various beliefs about the following 12 unexplained phe-
        nomena: angels, devils, life after death, the Loch Ness monster,
        Sasquatch (Bigfoot), witches, ghosts, astrology, ESP, precognition,
        déjà vu, and clairvoyance. Three underlying dimensions in the
        attitudes towards these phenomena are distinguished: religious
        beliefs, belief in psychic powers, and belief in the existence of
        other, not quite human beings. Paranormal phenomena, like ancient
        astronauts, need not be religious in content. The authors think
        that unexplained phenomena are "related to myth and paradigm in our
        culture" (p. 13) and should be interpreted in their sociocultural
        contexts.

692.   Stark, Rodney, editor. RELIGIOUS MOVEMENTS: GENESIS, EXODUS, AND
        NUMBERS. New York: Paragon House, 1985. 354 pp.

        Presents papers held at a convention in Washington State and
        sponsored by the New ERA, an organization associated with the Uni-
        fication Church. The editor discusses the nature of such sponsor-
        ship and stresses the fact that all participants are well-known
        and respected scholars, mostly sociologists. Contrary to the fears
        from some quarters, no restrictions were made to their academic
        freedom, a fact corroborated by the papers themselves. This volume
        represents the state of the art in the field of the sociology of
        new religious movements. The bibliographies attached to each essay
        give an indication of the voluminous research being done by sociol-
        ogists in this relatively new area.

        Contains items 739, 959, 1594, 1608, 1864, 1986, 2052.

693.   Stark, Rodney, and William Sims Bainbridge. "American-Born Sects:
        Initial Findings." JOURNAL FOR THE SCIENTIFIC STUDY OF RELIGION
        20 (1981): 130-49.

        Presents and discusses "the distribution of certain primary fea-
        tures of American-Born sect movements" (p. 131) based largely on
        Melton's ENCYCLOPEDIA OF AMERICAN RELIGION (item 47). Sects are
        defined as high tension, schismatic religious movements that remain

within an established religious tradition while cults are considered to be deviant groups because they depart from one of the conventional religions. The authors examine 417 different sects,
their racial and ethnic backgrounds, their expansion, location, and
distribution, and their usually high level of tension with society.
They observe that the larger a sect is in membership, the lesser is
the tension. Over half of the sects originated from a Pentecostal,
Holiness, or Baptist tradition.

694. Stark, Rodney, William Sims Bainbridge, and Daniel Doyle. "Cults
in America: A Reconnaissance in Space and Time." SOCIOLOGICAL
ANALYSIS 40 (1979): 347-59.

Examines the geographic distribution of American cults based on
over 500 independent groups listed in Melton's ENCYCLOPEDIA OF
AMERICAN RELIGIONS (item 47). Their location, number, variety, and
names adopted are among the areas investigated. Nevada is found to
be the cult capital in terms of number of cults per million inhabitants. The authors think that the study of contemporary cults
help us understand how religions began and why some survive while
others die out.

695. Stark, Rodney, and Lynne Roberts. "The Arithmetic of Social Movements: Theoretical Implications." SOCIOLOGICAL ANALYSIS 43
(1982): 53-68.

Examines the implications of the growth of the new religions "for
the structure and fate of social movements per se" (p. 53). Several questions are raised specifically in relation to the Unification
Church: 1) what rate of growth is needed for a movement to succeed?;
2) what factors govern the rates of growth?; and 3) what effect has
the rate of growth on the founder's morale and on the movement's
ideology? New religions, it is stated, must grow rapidly or fail.
One main reason why most of them do not grow large enough to survive is the fact that they exist in the midst of large societies.
Cults, it is concluded, grow more rapidly through preexisting
social networks, and growing cults tend to maintain their doctrinal
intensity.

696. Stupple, David, editor. "The Occult." JOURNAL OF POPULAR CULTURE
8 (1975): 859-911.

Presents a series of papers dealing with a variety of occult
topics and organizations, like astrology, UFOs, and the I Am
Society. The nature of the occult experience and the reasons why
interest in the occult has risen so dramatically are among the
questions explored.

Contains items 35, 2017, 2030, 2085.

697. Sundback, Susan. "New Religious Movements in Finland." TEMENOS 16
(1980): 132-39.

Recapitulates the work of a conference held in 1979 by the Finnish Society for the Study of Comparative Religion, a conference
that was convoked with the aim of describing the variety of new

religious movements in Finland and of analyzing their relationship
with the mainstream culture. The influx of new religions in Finland is said to have taken place in two waves, the first of which
took place at the turn of this century and was represented by such
groups as Theosophy and Anthroposophy; the second began in the late
1960's and includes groups like the Baha'i Faith, Transcendental
Meditation, the Divine Light Mission, the Friends of the Buddhist
Order, and the Charismatic Renewal. Whether or not the presence of
the recent surge of cults can be related to the counterculture is
debated.

698.   Thung, Mady A. "From Pillarization to New Religious Pluralism: A
       Social Science Congress on Religion and Politics, Amsterdam,
       1983." SOCIAL COMPASS 30 (1983): 503-24.

       Reflects on the papers read at a meeting of Dutch and Flemish
       social scientists who discussed the topic of religion and politics.
       Though the congress was not directly concerned with the new reli-
       gious movements, one paper describes the new religiotherapeutic
       cult led by a Dutch woman who claimed heavenly powers. The clash
       of this cult with the government points to a large area of conflict
       between new religions and the state and between the mainline reli-
       gions and the state. Cases of this type of new religion have been
       marginal in the religious life of Holland.

699.   Thung, Mady A., reporter. EXPLORING THE NEW RELIGIOUS CONSCIOUS-
       NESS: AN INVESTIGATION OF RELIGIOUS CHANGE BY A DUTCH WORKING
       GROUP. Amsterdam, The Netherlands: Free University Press, 1985.
       xi, 246 pp.

       Studies contemporary religious change in the Netherlands, a
       change that is affecting traditional religion and expressing itself
       in such groups as the Charismatic Renewal, the Hare Krishna Move-
       ment, and Transcendental Meditation. A sketch of the Dutch reli-
       gious scene is provided and various worldviews described.

700.   Tiryakian, Edward A., editor. ON THE MARGIN OF THE VISIBLE: SOCI-
       OLOGY, THE ESOTERIC, AND THE OCCULT. New York: Wiley, 1974. xv,
       364 pp.

       Presents a collection of previously published articles and selec-
       tions from books on occult belief and practices. The material is
       divided into three sections. The first gives examples of esoteric
       doctrines and expressions from such classic occult writers as P. D.
       Ouspensky, H. P. Blavatsky, and Rudolph Steiner. The second repro-
       duces some studies on medieval and modern witchcraft, stressing the
       social setting of the occult. The third reprints essays on social
       theory and research on esoteric and occult phenomena. The purpose
       of this volume is to explore the sociological significance of the
       esoteric teachings that are propagated in various associations. A
       short topical bibliography, mainly of pre-1970's materials, is
       provided.

       Contains items 356, 618, 1714, 1880, 2028, 2034, and selections
       from item 2033.

701. Tomasson, Richard F., editor. RELIGION AND BELIEF SYSTEMS. COM-
      PARATIVE SOCIAL RESEARCH, volume 10. Greenwich, CT: JAI Press,
      1987. ix, 251 pp.

      Contributes a collection of genuinely comparative papers on dif-
      ferent religious belief systems. Besides, there are several essays
      that discuss theoretical and methodological issues in the process
      of comparison. A number of essays deal specifically with the be-
      lief systems of new religious movements and one essay discusses the
      definitions of sect and cults. There are substantial bibliogra-
      phies attached to each essay.

      Contains items 327, 848, 1227, 1388.

702. Valentin, Friederike. "New Religions in Austria." UPDATE: A
      QUARTERLY JOURNAL OF NEW RELIGIOUS MOVEMENTS 8.2 (1984): 50-54.

      Outlines the activities of the more successful new religious
      movements in Austria, namely the Unification Church, Scientology,
      the Children of God, the Hare Krishna Movement, the Rajneesh Foun-
      dation, and Transcendental Meditation. Few of the new cults have
      attracted a large following. The churches have responded by
      disseminating information and offering counseling programs.

703. Van de Castle, Robert L. "Anthropology and Psychic Research."
      PSYCHIC EXPLORATIONS: A CHALLENGE FOR SCIENCE. Edited by John
      White. New York: G. P. Putnam, 1974, pp. 269-87.

      Argues that anthropology has contributed little to psychic
      research, even though anthropologists have studied magical beliefs
      and practices mainly in nonliterate societies. The author reviews
      ethnographic and experimental literature that supports the exis-
      tence of psychic phenomena. He suggests that non-Western peoples
      exhibit greater incidences of psychic experiences because of their
      strong beliefs in magic and of cultural pressures to participate in
      altered states of consciousness. Several suggestions for further
      research are advanced. The implications for anthropology are
      briefly assessed.

704. Van der Lans, Jan. "Meditation: A Comparative and Theoretical
      Analysis." ANNUAL REVIEW OF THE SOCIAL SCIENCES OF RELIGION 6
      (1982): 133-65.

      Maintains that current models of meditation that rely on hypnosis,
      psychoanalysis, or psychotherapy are inadequate explanations of why
      people get involved in meditation programs. The author thinks that
      most scholars tend to examine the technique aspect of meditation
      and neglect both its functions and the characteristics of the set-
      ting in which it is practiced. The following structural elements
      of meditation are described: 1) body relaxation and motionless
      posture; 2) reduction of sensory stimulation and the increase of
      cognitive faculties; and 3) the activation of "a specific religious
      meaning programme." The author prefers a research model that
      stresses the symbolic meanings that are associated with body pos-
      ture, respiration rhythm, and the object of concentration.

705.   Wagner, Jon, editor. SEX ROLES IN CONTEMPORARY AMERICAN COMMUNES.
        Bloomington: Indiana University Press, 1982. ix, 242 pp.

        Presents a collection of essays exploring one issue concerning
        utopian communities in America, namely the extent to which they
        seek to change the traditional roles (statuses, rights, obligations,
        and character) ascribed to the sexes. The editor provides an over-
        view of the nineteenth- and twentieth-century data and the theoret-
        ical framework that has guided sex relationships in communes with
        reference to the following groups: 1) the New Age Brotherhood (a
        pseudonym of a group led by a disciple of Paramahansa Yogananda);
        2) the Levites of Utah (a Mormon schismatic group); 3) the Shiloh
        Farm Community; 4) Haran (a pseudonym for a Christian fundamental-
        ist commune); and 5) the Black Hebrew Israelite community.

        Contains items 1119, 1841, 1997.

706.   Wallis, Roy. "New Religious Movements: North America." NEW RELI-
        GIOUS MOVEMENTS (item 586), pp. 912-24.

        Outlines the new religious scene in North America where the free
        market economy is applicable also to religious commodities. The
        author gives a broad picture of the various new movements that have
        emerged since World War II. The roots of these movements are
        traced to indigenous traditions, imported traditions, or psycholog-
        ical religions. Their orientations are either world-rejecting,
        world-affirming, or world-accommodating. The types of members
        that are attracted to these are also examined. The author suggests
        that the demise of the counterculture has removed the recruitment
        base of the world-rejecting movements like the Unification Church.

707.   Wallis, Roy. "Sex, Violence, and Religion: Antinomianinsm and
        Charisma." SOCIOLOGICAL THEORY, RELIGION, AND COLLECTIVE ACTION
        (item 714), pp. 115-27.

        Discusses sex and violence in such groups as Charles Manson's
        Family, Jim Jones's People's Temple, Chuck Dederich's Synanon, and
        Moses David Berg's Children of God. It is a main theme of this
        essay that sex and violence are not isolated features in these
        movements, but rather represent "the extremity of unconventional
        behaviors which characterizes them much more generally" (p. 117).
        These movements also display a volatile and erratic nature coupled
        with unpredictability, change, and innovation. The arbitrary and
        unpredictable changes that occur in these movements form a pattern
        in itself. The sharp rejection of society provokes hostility with
        the consequent creation of fear, anxiety, and paranoia that in-
        crease the possibility of sex and violence. The author rejects as
        unsatisfactory those theories that explain the apparent lack of
        pattern in these groups by claiming that their leaders were insane
        and their members brainwashed. Through constant changes, charis-
        matic leaders maintain their influence on their followers and pre-
        vent the emergence of institutional structures.

708.   Wallis, Roy. "Sex, Violence, and Religion." UPDATE: A QUARTERLY
        JOURNAL OF NEW RELIGIOUS MOVEMENTS 7.4 (1983): 3-11.

Discusses the prevalence of unusual sexual behavior among the leaders of several new movements (see item 707). These movements have histories that "are curiously violent and erratic in terms of the diversity of their innovations and the abruptness and unpredictability with which these innovations are introduced" (p. 4). The author holds that these activities cannot be satisfactorily explained by appeals to the madness of their leaders and/or to the brainwashing techniques they use. He suggests instead that the charismatic leaders of these world-rejecting cults change the rules and demands of their organizations whenever their authority is threatened; in so doing, they eliminate restrictions on the leaders themselves. Rejection of the world results in a reciprocal hostility that leads to anxiety and fear, thus increasing the possibility of sex and violence.

709.   Wallis, Roy. SALVATION AND PROTEST: STUDIES OF SOCIAL AND RELIGIOUS MOVEMENTS. New York: St. Martin's Press, 1979. vii, 231 pp.

Presents a collection of the author's essays on several religious and social movements. Part One looks at the various aspects and characteristics of movements like the Children of God, Scientology, and Christian Science. Part Two examines moral crusades, including two recent British ones, namely the Nationwide Festival of Light and the National Viewers' and Listeners' Association. Part Three discusses theory and method.

Contains items 994, 1094, 2058-59, 2064.

710.   Wallis, Roy. "Varieties of Psychosalvation." NEW SOCIETY 50 (December 20-27, 1979): 649-61.

Considers several contemporary religious groups, such as Scientology, Transcendental Meditation, Synanon, and EST, that offer instant, labor-saving ways to salvation or resolutions of personal problems. These movements share the view that human beings can be made perfect and, hence, focus their attention on the transformation of the individual and not on society. Although they tend to be psychologically oriented, they differ from psychoanalysis in several important aspects. Individual achievement, accommodation, liberation from social inhibitions, and intimacy or instant community are central to these groups. It is argued that "psychosalvationism has its roots in the central characteristics of an advanced capitalist society" (p. 651).

711.   Wallis, Roy, editor. MILLENNIALISM AND CHARISMA. Belfast, Northern Ireland: Queen's University, 1982. viii, 318 pp.

Presents a collection of six essays that deal with the connection between the social phenomena of millennialism and charismatic manifestations. Millennialism is a movement "which anticipates a total and supernatural transformation of the physical world, with the elimination of its present evils, its indignities, and, characteristically, the elevation of believers to the status of an elite" (p. 1). The essays explore the founding of these movements, the

recruitment of new followers, the influence of the charismatic
leaders, and the development of the movements through time. Most
of the essays deal with movements that have either originated in
the U.S.A. (like a UFO cult) or have established a foothold in the
West (like the Children of God, the Unification Church, and the
Baha'i faith).

Contains items 1486, 1595, 2009, 2021, 2055.

712.   Wallis, Roy, editor. ON THE MARGINS OF SCIENCE: THE SOCIAL CON-
        STRUCTION OF REJECTED KNOWLEDGE. Keele, England: University of
        Keele, 1979. 337 pp.

        Contains a series of essays that discuss the sociology of knowl-
        edge that is not part of currently accepted scientific information.
        The materials include studies on astrology, UFOs, paranormal occur-
        rences, acupuncture, the creation/evolution debate, and nineteenth-
        century topics like phrenology, mesmerism, and spiritualism.

        Contains items 536, 1417, 1523, 1550, 1626, 2083, 2137, 2166.

713.   Wallis, Roy, editor. SECTARIANISM: ANALYSES OF RELIGIOUS AND NON-
        RELIGIOUS SECTS. London: Peter Owen, 1975. 212 pp.

        Presents a collection of the editor's largely original essays
        dealing with various sects and cults in Western culture. The
        material is arranged under three headings: 1) cults and their
        development; 2) structure and process in sectarian movements; and
        3) nonreligious sects. The Aetherius Society, the Hare Krishna
        Movement, and Scientology are the three main new religious groups
        covered.

        Contains items 504, 997, 1144, 1327, 1486, 1675, 2019, 2216.

714.   Wallis, Roy, and Steve Bruce. SOCIOLOGICAL THEORY, RELIGION, AND
        COLLECTIVE ACTION. Belfast, Northern Ireland: Queen's Univer-
        sity, 1986. xi, 259 pp.

        Contains 12 previously published essays that are divided into four
        parts dealing with the following topics respectively: 1) sociolog-
        ical theory; 2) studies on charisma; 3) new movements; and 4) com-
        parative Protestant politics. Of particular interest are Wallis's
        essays on the Human Potential Movement and the Rajneesh Movement.

        Contains items 707, 989, 2051.

715.   Wallis, Roy, and Peter Morley, editors. MARGINAL MEDICINES. New
        York: Free Press, 1976. 173 pp.

        Contains seven essays that explore various aspects of the nature,
        development, and clientele of marginal medicines in Western socie-
        ties. The relationship between medical and social change and the
        belief systems of a couple of fringe medical groups are discussed.
        In their introduction, the editors reflect on the link between the

emergence of an orthodox consensus in medicine and the rise of
marginal medical alternatives. Besides bibliographical references
to each essay, there is a short bibliography at the end of the book.

Contains items 650, 716, 1104, 1405, 2063.

716.   Wardwell, Walter I. "Orthodox and Unorthodox Practitioners: Changing Relationships and the Future Status of Chiropractors." MAR-
GINAL MEDICINES (item 715), pp. 61-73.

Classifies nonorthodox medical practitioners in the West into
four basic types, namely: 1) ancillary practitioners; 2) limited
medical practitioners; 3) marginal or parallel practitioners
(including chiropractors); and 4) quasi-practitioners (such as
faith healers, Christian Science practitioners, shamans, and folk
healers). The accommodation between marginal and orthodox medicines is discussed. Chiropractors are contrasted with Christian
Science practitioners and the fundamental difference is pinned down
to the latter's denial of the reality of matter, the body, sickness, and death. Unlike Christian Science, chiropractic (which,
like homeopathy and osteopathy, is a healing sect) shares a common
ground with orthodox medicine and, again unlike Christian Science,
it has the possibility of developing into an orthodox medical
system.

717.   Weldon, John. "A Sampling of the New Religions." INTERNATIONAL
REVIEW OF MISSION 67 (1978): 407-26.

Describes four new religious movements, namely the Unification
Church, the Children of God, Scientology, and Transcendental Meditation. The authors maintain that many factors, including the
failure of optimistic humanism, cultural alienation, and a number
of global crises, are responsible for their success in the West.

718.   Westley, Francis R. "Purification and Healing Rituals in New Religious Groups." RITUAL SYMBOLISM AND CEREMONIALISM IN THE AMERI-
CAS: STUDIES IN SYMBOLIC ANTHROPOLOGY, PART II. Edited by N.
Ross Crumrine. Greeley, CO: Museum of Anthropology, University
of Northern Colorado, 1979, pp. 195-213.

Applies the anthropological theory of ritual process proposed by
Mary Douglas to explain the rites of purification and healing in
new religious movements. The author argues that the many cultic
rites are actually body rituals aimed at restoring or maintaining
the psychic selves of the members. Two kinds of rituals are distinguished: 1) purification rituals (such as Kriya Yoga, pranayana,
and dietary regulations aimed at self-healing) that are practiced
in counterculture groups, usually of Eastern origin and that have
no sense of sin or guilt connected with them; and 2) healing
rituals (such as those practiced by Spiritualists, Charismatics,
Christian Scientists, and members of Silva Mind Control) where the
sense of sin and guilt play a key role and where outside help is
needed for healing. The author suggests that ritual symbolizes and
reflects concern for social issues but does not resolve them.

719.   Westley, Francis R. "Purification and Healing Rituals in New Reli-
        gious Movements." RITUAL AND CEREMONIES IN POPULAR CULTURE.
        Edited by Ray B. Browne. Bowling Green, OH: Popular Press, 1980,
        pp. 36-47.

        Presents a slightly different version of her previous essay. A
        typology of healing and purificatory rituals in the Montreal area
        is included.

720.   Whitt, Hugh, and John Turner. "Other Realities: New Religions and
        Revitalization Movements." HUMANIST 8.2 (1985): 9-16.

        Introduces a selection of essays presented at a Conference on New
        Religions held at the University of Nebraska (Lincoln) in 1985.
        The authors maintain that cults are revitalization movements that
        provide alternatives to the dominant religious traditions that have
        become secularized and highly bureaucratic. (For other papers read
        at this conference, see items 819, 876, 2164).

721.   Wikström, Lester. "Strategies on the '80s of New Religions in
        Sweden." UPDATE: A QUARTERLY JOURNAL OF NEW RELIGIOUS MOVEMENTS
        8.2 (1984): 31-36.

        Suggests that the positive thinking encouraged by such groups as
        Scientology and the Rajneesh Foundation is attractive, particularly
        in a society plagued by a high rate of unemployment and beset by
        pessimism about the future. The rising interest in astrology and
        horoscopes is also related to economic depression and uncertainty.
        Diverse new religious movements (such as the Church Universal and
        Triumphant, Transcendental Meditation, and Satanism) that stress
        self-realization, self-transformation, and the acquisition of power
        and those (like the Rajneesh Foundation) that combine religion with
        psychotherapy are gaining momentum in Sweden.

722.   Wikström, Lester. "The Present Situation in Sweden and Recent
        Developments in the New Religious Scene." UPDATE: A QUARTERLY
        JOURNAL OF NEW RELIGIOUS MOVEMENTS 2.2 (1978): 47-52.

        Describes the presence of Transcendental Meditation in Sweden and
        the various experiments that have been conducted to test the effec-
        tiveness of this movement's techniques. The author also reviews a
        book on Scientology that, in his view, should not be persecuted.

723.   Wilson, Bryan R. "American Religious Sects in Europe." SUPER
        CULTURE: AMERICAN POPULAR CULTURE AND EUROPE. Edited by C. W. E.
        Bigsby. London: Paul Elek, 1976, pp. 107-22.

        Examines the influence of several American sects, especially the
        Jehovah's Witnesses, Seventh-Day Adventism, Christian Science,
        Mormonism, New Thought, and Scientology. According to the author,
        all these sects are, or have been to some extent, protest movements
        against the moral and social conditions of their times. They
        appeal to different social classes and all offer those who join
        them hope in an uncertain world and meaning in a confused state of
        affairs.

724.   Wilson, Bryan R. "American Religion: Its Impact on Britain."
       CONTAGIOUS CONFLICT: THE IMPACT OF AMERICAN DISSENT ON EUROPEAN
       LIFE. Edited by A. N. J. Den Hollander. Leiden, The Nether-
       lands: E. J. Brill, 1973, pp. 233-63.

       Discusses the effects of developments in religion in America on
       European life. Revivalism, Pentecostalism, Mormonism, Adventist
       Movements, Jehovah's Witnesses, and Christian Science are the main
       religious sects and denominations considered. Some more recent
       groups, like the Jesus Movement and the Charismatic Movement, are
       also mentioned. The author states that "the advantage enjoyed by
       American cultural exports was their freshness and their direct-
       ness," that "cut through the rigid, and sometimes fossilized stra-
       tification of British society in a way not possible for native men
       or movements" (p. 261). Egalitarianism and voluntarism are among
       the features that American religions have contributed to the Brit-
       ish scene.

725.   Wilson, Bryan R., editor. THE SOCIAL IMPACT OF NEW RELIGIOUS MOVE-
       MENTS. New York: Rose of Sharon Press, 1981. xix, 234 pp.

       Presents the papers read at a symposium sponsored by the Unifica-
       tion Church and held at this church's seminary in Barrytown, New
       York. In a somewhat lengthy foreword, the editor discusses the
       issue of sponsorship of sociological conferences by new religious
       movements. The material in this volume covers four major areas,
       namely: 1) the general social context in which the new movements
       come into being; 2) case studies of the Unification Church, the
       Children of God, and Transcendental Meditation; 3) theories that
       explain why new movements emerge; and 4) the societal response to
       the movements.

       Contains items 794, 835, 874, 960, 1017, 1587, 1611, 2057, 2198.

726.   Woods, Richard, editor. HETERODOXY: MYSTICAL EXPERIENCE, RELIGIOUS
       DISSENT, AND THE OCCULT. River Forest, IL: Listening Press,
       1975. 153 pp.

       Publishes, in book form, a collection of essays from LISTENING: A
       JOURNAL OF RELIGION AND CULTURE. The Jesus Movement, witchcraft
       and magic, and religious experience are the main topics covered.

       Contains items 417, 435, 1845, 1866, 1949.

727.   Zaretzky, Irving I., and Mark P. Leone. RELIGIOUS MOVEMENTS IN
       CONTEMPORARY AMERICA. Princeton, NJ: Princeton University Press,
       1974. xxxvi, 837 pp.

       Presents a large and comprehensive volume covering various dimen-
       sions of the new religious movement in the United States. In the
       introduction, the editors identify those common features shared by
       contemporary religious groups and speculate on the sociocultural
       factors that generated their emergence in the second half of the
       twentieth century. Among their conclusions is the observation that
       religious innovations are not a sign of mental weakness, pathology,

or even radical change. Rather, new religious movements tend to
introduce modern changes and to protest against the established
order. The 27 essays included in this volume are divided into
seven sections, each preceded by a short introduction. Some speculations on future research are made and a rather lengthy bibliography (pp. 771-813), now somewhat dated but still useful, is added.

Contains items 576, 788, 834, 901, 1027, 1217, 1236, 1270, 1359,
    1553, 1574, 1733, 1797, 1879, 2031, 2090.

728.   Zikmund, Barbara Brown. "The Feminine Thrust of Sectarian Chris-
        tianity." WOMEN OF SPIRIT: FEMALE LEADERSHIP IN THE JEWISH AND
        CHRISTIAN TRADITIONS. Edited by Rosemary Reuther and Eleanor
        McLaughlin. New York: Simon and Schuster, 1979, pp. 205-24.

        Points out that the masculine bias in traditional Christianity
        has been modified repeatedly by sectarian groups (like the Shakers,
        the Quakers, the Adventists, Christian Scientists, the Mormons, and
        Pentecostals). The author explores the correlation between femi-
        nism and sectarianism, particularly in the first half of the nine-
        teenth century. She examines the sectarian concepts of God, life-
        styles, church reform, and female leadership, and she concludes that
        many women were won over to the new sects by the theological idea
        of an "androgynous or married deity," by the vision of an easier
        way of life, and by the hope of attaining leadership positions.

                C.   THEORETICAL STUDIES ON SECTS AND CULTS

729.   Aidala, Angela A. "World Views, Ideologies, and Social Experimen-
        tation: Clarification and Replication of the Consciousness Refor-
        mation." JOURNAL FOR THE SCIENTIFIC STUDY OF RELIGION 23 (1984):
        44-59.

        Examines a number of conceptual and methodological ambiguities in
        Wuthnow's study, THE CONSCIOUSNESS REFORMATION (item 1043), and
        tries to resolve these ambiguities and to replicate his findings
        regarding different worldviews and social experimentation. The
        author distinguishes eight major types of communes: 1) political;
        2) hippie; 3) Christian; 4) Eastern; 5) personal growth; 6) alter-
        native family; 7) cooperative household; and 8) rehabilitation.
        She relates these types to five major worldviews, namely theistic,
        social-scientific, mystical, countercultural, and spiritual. She
        concludes by confirming Wuthnow's views regarding the current shift
        from traditional meaning systems and the propensity for social
        experimentation.

730.   Anderson, Susan M. "Identifying Coercion and Deception in Social
        Systems." SCIENTIFIC RESEARCH AND NEW RELIGIONS (item 645), pp.
        12-23.

        Discusses criteria for identifying some major features of cults
        and questions whether deviancy, religiosity, and ethical behavior
        are useful and realistic qualities that can be ascribed to all

cults. The author suggests that "the most relevant criterion should concern the presence of high degrees of coercion over individual freedoms because such control can easily be misused" (p. 14). She outlines sixteen techniques of psychological coercion and deception and argues that if at least half of them are present within an organization, then it can be labeled a cult.

731. Anthony, Dick, and Bruce Ecker. "The Anthony Typology: A Framework for Assessing Spiritual and Consciousness Groups." SPIRITUAL CHOICES (item 732), pp. 35-105.

Summarizes the major research being done by social scientists on the new religious movements and develops a basic typology that categorizes these movements in monistic and dualistic groups. Both groups are then subdivided into multilevel and unilevel dimensions, which in turn can be either charismatic or technical. The eight types that flow from this typology are described in some depth. The authors also discuss the cultural and historical contexts in which spiritual groups thrive.

732. Anthony, Dick, Bruce Ecker, and Ken Wilbur, editors. SPIRITUAL CHOICES: THE PROBLEM OF RECOGNIZING AUTHENTIC PATHS TO INNER TRANSFORMATIONS. New York: Paragon House, 1987. xi, 374 pp.

Considers the insights of transpersonal psychology and the scientific study of religion in order to develop criteria for evaluating religious groups and spiritual paths. The first part of this volume contains a long essay that develops an elaborate typology as a framework for assessing these movements. The second part transcribes interviews with several individuals who are involved with such movements as EST and Meher Baba. The third part contains several essays that discuss the transpersonal perspectives of the new religions and their gurus. Finally, in a transcribed conversation with Jacob Needleman, the editors reflect on the transformative power of religion.

Contains item 731.

733. Anthony, Dick, and Thomas Robbins. "Contemporary Religious Ferment and Moral Ambiguity." NEW RELIGIOUS MOVEMENTS: A PERSPECTIVE FOR UNDERSTANDING SOCIETY (item 551), pp. 243-63.

Contends that both Eastern and Christian new religious groups are a response to a cultural situation in which moral meanings have become pluralistic and somewhat problematic. Eastern movements have tended to adopt a monistic, relativistic view of morality, while Christian-oriented groups, like fundamentalists and evangelicals, have reacted to this interpretation with a return to a traditional, dualistic worldview and to a reemphasis on moral absolutes. The authors schematically compare the position of the Jesus Freaks and Meher Baba Lovers on five major religious themes: 1) salvation; 2) exclusivity; 3) possibility of judgment in terms of moral categories; 4) orientation to the American success ethics of competitive individuals; and 5) apocalyptic worldview.

734.   Anthony, Dick, and Thomas Robbins. "Spiritual Innovation and the
            Crisis of American Civil Religion." DAEDALUS 111 (1982): 215-34.

            Upholds the view that the contemporary religious ferment in Amer-
            ica must be understood in the context of American Civil Religion,
            which is "a complex of symbolic meanings that many Americans share
            and that unite them in a moral community" (p. 215). Seculariza-
            tion is at the root of the rise of the new religious movements.
            Civil religion sects (like the Unification Church and the People's
            Temple) are contrasted with monistic movements (like the Meher Baba
            Movement, Yoga and Meditation groups, and the Human Potential Move-
            ment). The former propose a new form of civil religion, uniting
            political and religious themes, while the latter stress the need to
            develop a higher spiritual consciousness. Moral ambiguity and the
            consequent polarization of dualistic and monistic worldviews are
            related to the breakdown of the American civil religion.

735.   Anthony, Dick, and Thomas Robbins. "Culture Crisis and Contempo-
            rary Religion." IN GODS WE TRUST (item 683), pp. 9-31.

            Summarizes contemporary religious developments in the context of
            the major problems in Western culture. The religious ferment of the
            1960's and 1970's is related to the decline of the American Civil
            Religion, a decline that has caused the individual personality to
            "become increasingly differentiated from the social system in which
            it participates" (p. 12). Mainline traditions have been unable to
            effectively deal with the problem. New movements have, therefore,
            come into being to deal with the frustration that the breakdown of
            civil religion has caused. These movements are divided into three
            groups: 1) civil religious sects (like the Unification Church, the
            People's Temple, and Synanon); 2) oriental mysticism (like Zen
            Buddhism and Meher Baba); and 3) psychotherapy groups (like EST and
            Scientology). The reaction against the new cults, especially the
            accusation of brainwashing, is briefly discussed. The new reli-
            gions are a response to the hunger for community, the erosion of
            the Protestant ethical assumptions about free will, and the dis-
            solution of moral consensus and national identity.

736.   Anthony, Dick, Thomas Robbins, and Paul Schwartz. "Contemporary
            Religious Movements and the Secularization Premise." NEW RELI-
            GIOUS MOVEMENTS (item 589), pp. 1-8.

            Pinpoints the key elements in the current religious revival and
            the major issues that have arisen in their wake. The main view
            presented in this essay is that theoretical "issues embroiled in
            controversies over 'narcissism,' religious authoritarianism, and
            brainwashing are in part derivative from the broader issues of
            secularization and the compatibility of religion with modernity"
            (p. 1). Because new religious movements share the common emphasis
            on inner spiritual experience, they seem to disprove the secular-
            ization theory that religion will inevitably lose influence in
            modern societies.

737.   Attwoood, D. James, and Ronald B. Flowers. "Early Christianity as
            a Cult Movement." ENCOUNTER 44 (1983): 245-61.

Argues that, from a sociological point of view, cults are not inherently evil and that this can be shown by looking at early Christianity as a cult. The author attempts to show how Christianity in the first two centuries fits into the concept of a cult-movement that utilized the various cult mechanisms (see Kanter, item 383) to enhance cohesion among, and control of, its members. From the Jewish standpoint, Christianity was a deviation from standard Jewish theology and from the Roman point of view it was a dangerous "importation cult." The tensions between Roman society and early Christianity are reminiscent of the contemporary conflict between modern society and the new cults.

738.   Austin, Roy L. "Empirical Adequacy of Lofland's Conversion Model." REVIEW OF RELIGIOUS RESEARCH 18 (1977): 282-87.

Investigates Lofland's model of conversion in the context of a group of young "born-again" Christians who are usually considered deviant. Most of Lofland's seven determinants of conversion, i.e., tension, religious problem-solving experience, religious seekership, turning point in one's life, cult-affective bonds, extra-cult affective bonds, and intensive interaction, "can be rejected as necessary determinants of conversion" (p. 283). The only condition necessary for total conversion appears to be the last mentioned above. A revised, broader form of Lofland's model is presented.

739.   Bainbridge, William Sims. "Cultural Genetics." RELIGIOUS MOVEMENTS: GENESIS, EXODUS, AND NUMBERS (item 692), pp. 157-94.

Argues that since "cult is culture writ small," sociologists can more easily develop a theory of cultural genetics from studying cults, which are small, relatively simple phenomena. The entrepreneur mode, which clearly points the way toward cultural genetics, is briefly outlined and applied to the cults. The author delves into the "genes" of culture and the way they mutate. Though there are definite differences between cultural and biological genes, he maintains that the former possesses enough stability and coherence to permit a science of cultural genetics that begins with a systematic research on cults.

740.   Bainbridge, William Sims, and Rodney Stark. "Cult Formation: Three Compatible Models." SOCIOLOGICAL ANALYSIS 40 (1979): 283-95.

Outlines in some detail three fundamental models of cult innovation. The first sees the rise of cults as the result of individual psychopathology. The second looks on cult formation as a process by which individuals "consciously develop anew compensator-systems in order to exchange them for great rewards" (p. 287). Within this model three levels of cults are possible: 1) audience cults that provide a mythology; 2) client cults that add magic; and 3) cult movements that eventually become religions. The final model suggests that cults are the result of "group interaction processes" that indicate radical cultural developments. The author holds that these models can be combined to explain why cults come into being.

741.   Bainbridge, William Sims, and Rodney Stark. "Formal Explanations of Religion: A Progress Report." SOCIOLOGICAL ANALYSIS 45 (1984): 145-58.

Replies to the critical essay of Wallis and Bruce (item 999) who found serious flaws in the authors' general scientific theory of religion that incorporates the rise and development of sects and cults and who expressed doubt as to whether a scientific theory of religion is at all possible. Bainbridge and Stark strongly defend their theory and refer to their major works that outline it at some length and to the voluminous empirical evidence from traditional and new religions that supports their main contentions.

742.   Bainbridge, William Sims, and Rodney Stark. "Church and Sect in Canada." CANADIAN JOURNAL OF SOCIOLOGY 7 (1982): 351-66.

Adduces evidence from Canada to buttress the view that secularization among the major religious traditions does not herald the demise of religion; rather, it creates opportunities for the rise of new religious movements that are based on supernatural assumptions that provide the only plausible answer to certain human desires. The authors give an overview of the main religious affiliations in Canada and survey those religious cults that differ from sects and churches in their novel or exotic beliefs and practices.

743.   Bainbridge, William Sims, and Rodney Stark. "The 'Consciousness Reformation' Revisited." JOURNAL FOR THE SCIENTIFIC STUDY OF RELIGION 20 (1981): 1-16.

Reports on a study designed and conducted "to explore the network basis of competing meaning systems" which Robert Wuthnow had uncovered in his book THE CONSCIOUSNESS REFORMATION (item 1043). The four meaning systems explored are: theism, individualism, social science, and mysticism. The ways these systems are employed as explanations of lifestyles are briefly described. The authors conclude that of the four systems, only theism emerges as a true religious meaning system, namely a traditional religion which is based on supernatural beliefs and promulgated by a formal church organization and which prevents experimentation with radical lifestyles and occult practices.

744.   Bainbridge, William Sims, and Rodney Stark. "Client and Audience Cult in America." SOCIOLOGICAL ANALYSIS 41 (1980): 199-214.

Distinguishes three types of cults: 1) cult movements that are full-fledged religions living in high tension with their sociocultural environment; 2) client cults that provide magical services; and 3) audience cults in which people participate through the mass media. Client cult directories that furnish the most comprehensive sources of geographical data about the cults are assessed. FATE magazine is said to be the prime audience cult medium. Transcendental Meditation and astrology are said to be examples of client and audience cults respectively.

745.   Bainbridge, William Sims, and Rodney Stark. "Sectarian Tension." REVIEW OF RELIGIOUS RESEARCH 22 (1980): 105-24.

Discusses the possibility of measuring tension in the context of religious cults. These groups live in a state of conflict with their sociocultural environment, a state "equivalent to subcultural deviance, marked by difference, antagonism, and separation" (p. 108). Six major topics to measure tension as sectarian rejection of society are explored: 1) deviant norms; 2) deviant beliefs; 3) deviant behavior; 4) particularism; 5) conversion and defense; and 6) social encapsulation. Tension as rejection of sects is also investigated by measuring the social distance members of the major religious groups feel towards cult members.

746. Bankston, William B., Craig J. Forsyth, and H. Hugh Floyd. "Toward a General Model of the Process of Radical Conversion: An Inter-actionist Perspective in the Transformation of Identity." QUALI-TATIVE SOCIOLOGY 4 (1981): 279-97.

Maintains that radical conversions differ from other kinds of self-change both in time and degree; they are relatively sudden and involve a dramatic change in one's status. The author thinks that radical conversion can be explained as a moral career and takes place in six stages: 1) tension; 2) failure to find an acceptable identity; 3) seekership; 4) a turning point; 5) relatively small stakes in maintaining current identity; and 6) intensive inter-action. The model is tested and confirmed.

747. Barker, Eileen. "New Religious Movements: Yet Another Religious Awakening?" THE SACRED IN A SECULAR AGE (item 623), pp. 36-57.

Raises the issue whether the new religious movements are the "final flurry" of religiosity in an increasingly rational and secu-lar world, a symptom of the vulgar and superstitious in a demysti-fied age, or the dawn of a new religious consciousness. The novelty and the religious expressions of these movements, their diversity, and their demographic distribution are briefly dealt with. The author believes that they "represent simply a highly publicized collection of options selected from the enormous variety already available in modern societies, which celebrate neither belief nor ideology under any single category" (p. 47).

748. Barker, Eileen. "'And So To Bed:' Protest and Malaise Among Youth in Great Britain." YOUTH WITHOUT A FUTURE? (CONCILIUM: RELIGION IN THE EIGHTIES). Edited by John Coleman and Gregory Baum. Edinburgh: T. & T. Clark, 1985, pp. 74-80.

Discusses unrest among young people in Britain and suggests that some of them have joined charismatic groups or new religious move-ments as a reaction to the permissiveness and/or secularity of Western culture. Many have abandoned the traditional churches because they seem to be hypocritical, apathetic, or irrelevant.

749. Barker, Eileen. "From Sect to Society: A Methodological Programme." NEW RELIGIOUS MOVEMENTS: A PERSPECTIVE FOR UNDERSTANDING SOCIETY (item 551), pp. 3-15.

Points out some areas where the study of new religious movements might further the understanding of society by examining three main social processes, namely: 1) the new movements as means of satisfy-ing major human needs; 2) their strange beliefs and practices as

reflections of some aspects of society; and 3) the socialization of
new members as manipulative methods designed to control their beliefs and actions. The author stresses the need to make comparative studies. She points out that in the case of the Unification
Church, the objections to this movement's activities differed from
country to country, thus possibly telling more about societal reactions to the Moonies than about the Moonies themselves. Studies
of conversion and apostasy "could illumine important dimensions in
our understanding of the human conditions at the level of societal
interaction and symbolic meaning" (p. 12).

750.   Barkum, Michael. "Millenarianism in the Modern World." THEORY AND
        SOCIETY 1 (1974): 117-46.

        Points out that since millenarian movements tend to flourish in
        relatively isolated rural areas, the question arises as to whether
        similar movements in our times are "mere sputterings, the last
        volatile by-products of an irreversible process of change" (p. 117).
        Various modern urban movements, like Rastafarianism, Garveyism, and
        the Black Muslims, are considered. The author thinks these move-
        ments occur "when incomplete urbanization leaves some groups rela-
        tively more vulnerable than others, cut off in homogenous enclaves
        from both external stresses and supports" (p. 125).

751.   Battan, Jesse F. "The 'New Narcissism' in 20th-Century America:
        The Shadow and Substance of Social Change." JOURNAL OF SOCIAL
        HISTORY (Winter 1983): 199-220.

        Discusses Lasch's book on the new narcissism (item 399) and con-
        cludes that his main theme, namely that there is a relationship
        between the large-scale reorientation in American culture and indi-
        vidual psychopathology (narcissism), is questionable. While deny-
        ing the prevalence of pathological narcissism in America, the
        author admits that important changes have taken place in patterns
        of behavior. Citing the work of Clecak (item 588), he states that
        America's recent concern with personal growth reflects a culture
        that is changing rapidly in the rights, responsibilities, and obli-
        gations of individuals and in the growing pursuit of personal
        dignity and social justice.

752.   Beckford, James A. "Functionalism and Ethics in Sociology: The
        Relationship Between 'Ought' and 'Function.'" ANNUAL REVIEW OF
        THE SOCIAL SCIENCES OF RELIGION 5 (1981): 101-31.

        Analyzes the ethical implications of attempts to promote tolerant
        attitudes or encourage hostility towards the new religious move-
        ments in the West. The author first gives an account of the cult
        controversy, then examines the theory of functionalism in soci-
        ology, and lastly speculates on how social interpretations are
        related to ethical considerations. Functional analyses of new
        religious movements tend to be conservative, condescending, and
        reductionistic. They further "distract attention from the content
        of their teachings, beliefs, practices, etc." (p. 119). The author
        thinks that an evaluation of the cults' highly divergent teachings
        and values is necessary before one can make any judgment on the
        usefulness of their presence.

753.   Beckford, James A. "Cults and Cures." JAPANESE JOURNAL OF RELI-
          GIOUS STUDIES 5 (1978): 225-57.

          Expounds on the interpretation of new religious movements as
          organizations that might "help members to overcome a wide range of
          personal problems and eventually reintegrate them into mainstream
          ways of thinking, feeling, and associating with others" (p. 226).
          The author discusses some of the alleged adaptive effects on mem-
          bership in the context of the Unification Church. The experience
          of a monastic lifestyle within the movement may create many prob-
          lems for ex-members as they try to readapt to life outside the
          movement. The author concludes that this church cannot be consid-
          ered an adaptive religious movement that helps people achieve per-
          sonal integration and reentry into mainstream culture.

754.   Beckford, James A. "Explaining Religious Movements." INTERNATION-
          AL SOCIAL SCIENCE JOURNAL 29 (1977): 235-49.

          Reviews conventional practice and current trends in the sociolog-
          ical explanations of new religious movements. The author suggests
          that these movements, because they are interpreted as struggles
          against traditional structures, are not given equal status with
          more established groups and are further seen as somewhat abnormal
          manifestations of deviant social conditions. This abnormality is
          often explained in terms of experiences of deprivation or frustra-
          tion that people go through prior to their involvement. The move-
          ments are consequently studied as mere surface phenomena. The
          author favors current attempts to explain the new religions in
          terms of social networks and organizational fields and of their
          role as social indicators. The new movements can also be explored
          as alternative symbolic articulations of the experiences of their
          adherents.

755.   Bell, Daniel. "The Return of the Sacred?: The Argument on the
          Future of Religion." BRITISH JOURNAL OF SOCIOLOGY 28 (1977):
          419-49.

          Discusses whether there is a future for religion in modern cul-
          ture and the forms it might take. The author finds flaws with the
          views that hold that religion will not die out because it has the
          important functions of social control and integration or because it
          is constitutive of human nature. He thinks that the permanence of
          religion lies more on existential grounds, namely the awareness of
          finitude and limitation of power. He links the rise of cults with
          the breaking up of the institutional framework of traditional reli-
          gions. Cults provide direct experience and esoteric knowledge.
          Three kinds of future religious forms--moralizing, redemptive, and
          mythic--are possible.

756.   Bellah, Robert N. "New Religious Consciousness and the Crisis
          in Modernity." THE NEW RELIGIOUS CONSCIOUSNESS (item 614), pp.
          333-52.

          Traces the rise of the new religious movements in the social
          developments of the 1960's, a decade characterized by the erosion of
          the legitimacy of established institutions. Biblical religion and

utilitarian individualism, the most successful systems for providing meaning and generating loyalty, are briefly discussed. The
author thinks that Asian spirituality provides a great contrast to
Western values. Oriental religions stress the belief in the unity
of all beings, a view that is directly opposed to individual liberalism. Some speculations on the possible outcome of the current
crisis are offered.

757.   Bibby, Reginald W. "Religion and Modernity: The Canadian Case."
        JOURNAL FOR THE SCIENTIFIC STUDY OF RELIGION 18 (1979): 1-17.

        Examines the effects of industrialization on personal religiosity
        in Canada. The origins of the universe, the purpose of life, the
        means to attain happiness, the reasons for suffering, and belief in
        life after death were the topics investigated in a survey intended
        to explore religious meaning. The data, according to the author,
        suggest that the new movements may function as alternatives to
        traditional Christianity. It is concluded that religion in Canada
        has been adversely influenced by industrialization and that the
        secularization process is likely to continue.

758.   Bibby, Reginald W., and Harold R. Weaver. "Cult Consumption in
        Canada: A Further Critique of Stark and Bainbridge." SOCIOLOGI-
        CAL ANALYSIS 46 (1985): 445-60.

        Discusses Stark and Bainbridge's theory of the emergence of new
        religious movements in the West in the second half of the twentieth
        century (see item 961). Three assumptions are singled out as
        being debatable: 1) human beings need supernaturally based answers
        to the questions about life; 2) these answers must be provided by
        religion; and 3) cults flourish where religions are weak. The
        authors state that scientific answers are usually supplemented by
        "a-scientific" ones and that the presence of supernatural explana-
        tions in new movements is hardly original. In Canada, for instance,
        secularization has not been followed by the expected weakening of
        conventional religions and the rise of new ones to replace them.
        Canadians have retained their old affiliations with traditional
        religions, but have tended to address questions of ultimate meaning
        by drawing both from Christianity and other religious forms.

759.   Bird, Frederick, and Bill Reimer. "Participation Rates in New
        Religious and Para-Religious Movements." JOURNAL FOR THE SCIEN-
        TIFIC STUDY OF RELIGION 21 (1982): 1-14.

        Explores the rate of participation in new religious movements in
        order to discern their significance. Four questions are raised: 1)
        what percentage of the adult population has ever participated in
        these movements?; 2) what is the typical form this participation
        takes?; 3) do the participants exhibit any significant character-
        istics?; and 4) are there any major differences between the parti-
        cipants in different religious groups? Basing their reflections
        on research conducted in Montreal, Canada in 1975 and 1980, the
        authors conclude that while participation rates are high, the per-
        centage of members who remain affiliated with these movements is
        rather low. They see in the rise of the new movements a return
        to magic and a concomitant decrease of confidence in science.

760.   Bird, Frederick, and Bill Reimer. "New Religious and Para-Reli-
        gious Movements in Montreal." RELIGION IN CANADIAN SOCIETY.
        Edited by Stewart Crysdale and Les Wheatcroft. Toronto: Macmil-
        lan, 1976, pp. 307-20.

        Focuses on the religious activities of the participants in new
        religious movements and compares them with traditional Western
        practices. The authors discuss the religiousness or nonreligious-
        ness of these groups as well as their "newness" in the West. Var-
        ious aspects of religion are identified and several criteria are
        constructed to distinguish two kinds of movements, namely the
        "cultic-mystical" and the "ascetic-sectarian." The principal fea-
        tures of the new religious movements are reviewed, including their
        optimistic worldview, their concern for the therapeutic, and their
        attempts to explore the subconscious dimension of the human mind.

761.   Blaikie, Norman W. H., and G. Paul Kelsen. "Locating Self and
        Giving Meaning to Existence: A Typology of Paths to Spiritual
        Well-Being Based on New Religious Movements in Australia."
        SPIRITUAL WELL-BEING: SOCIOLOGICAL PERSPECTIVES (item 660), pp.
        132-51.

        Attempts to construct a typology of new religious movements on
        the notion of spiritual well-being as it relates to the process of
        joining and maintaining membership in these movements in Melbourne,
        Australia. Two theoretical backgrounds to the rise of the cults,
        namely the problem of preserving a satisfactory self-identity in a
        pluralistic society and the sociopolitical turmoil of the 1960's,
        are discussed. The major source of information for the authors'
        speculations came from the Divine Light Mission and two main
        branches of Buddhism. Three paths to spiritual well-being are
        distinguished: 1) ritualistic; 2) charismatic; and 3) mystical;
        these are in turn related to Troeltsch's typology of church, sect,
        and mysticism (item 134).

762.   Bodemann, Y. Michael. "Mystical, Satanic, and Chiliastic Forces in
        Counter Culture Movements: Changing the World--or Reconciling
        It?" YOUTH AND SOCIETY 5 (1974): 433-47.

        Examines some of the causes of the counterculture of the 1960's
        and uncovers three major themes: 1) "a preoccupation with the ex-
        isting symbolic locus in American society" (p. 435); 2) a concern
        with the boundaries of group-identity feeling; and 3) a very clear
        bipolarity in mainstream culture. Several trends in the counter-
        culture are described. The author observes, among other things, a
        process of desocialization accompanied by an interest in mysticism.
        Satanism is interpreted as another attack against the dominant
        value system, while millenarian groups provide an escape from the
        threat of chronic anomie.

763.   Bourg, Carroll J. "The Politics of Religious Movements." OF GODS
        AND MEN (item 550), pp. 45-64.

        Discusses the ways in which contemporary religious cults are new
        movements in modern society. These cults are first compared with
        youth movements of the twentieth century (like the German Youth

Movement) which were historical and critical. The religious movements of the 1970's and 1980's are analyzed according to themes
summarized by McGuire (item 882), namely: 1) religious experience;
2) access to power; 3) a sense of order; 4) moral norms; and 5)
unity through communalism or a new type of family. The author
demonstrates how the cults have continued to express the stresses
that had emerged in the Civil Rights Movement and in the Ecumenical
Movement of the 1960's. The following three approaches to the new
movements, all of which are recommended by the author, are then
discussed: the deprivation theory, the mobilization theory, and
the view that sees the movements as a reflection of society that
demands the researcher's intervention.

764.   Bourg, Carroll J. "Contemporary Religious Consciousness Among Some
        Young Adults." HUMAN CONTEXT 6 (1974): 632-41.

        Suggests that understanding human beings as pluralistic in nature
        is the best approach to contemporary religious diversity. Some of
        the major attributes of those participating in various religious
        movements in the 1960's are outlined. Pluralism is seen as a mode
        "of being religious today which provides a challenge and at most a
        threat to existing religious institutions." (p. 640).

765.   Braden, William. THE AGE OF AQUARIUS: TECHNOLOGY AND THE CULTURAL
        REVOLUTION. Chicago: Quadrangle Books, 1970. 306 pp.

        Maintains that contemporary society is comprised of two conflict-
        ing cultures, one technological, the other humanistic. The former
        is based on scientific advances that lead to the manipulation of
        the environment and the domination of the universe, the latter on
        the more romantic view that the dignity, values, and welfare of
        individual human beings should be the main concern. Various move-
        ments in contemporary Western society, such as Hindu and Zen Bud-
        dhist groups, the faddish enthusiasm for astrology, witchcraft, and
        sensitivity training, are a result of this conflict. It is the
        author's opinion that the rise of the new religious movements is
        related to the contemporary crisis of identity.

766.   Bromley, David G., and Anson D. Shupe. "Affiliation and Disaffilia-
        tion: A Role-Theory Interpretation of Joining and Leaving New
        Religious Movements." THOUGHT: A REVIEW OF CULTURE AND IDEA 61
        (1986): 197-211.

        Applies a role-theory model to explain how people leave communal
        organizations and new religious groups. The authors first examine
        how affiliation and disaffiliation are understood by the religious
        movements themselves and by the anticult movement and observes
        that they both make the same assumption, namely that the individ-
        ual is autonomous and self-contained. The role-theory approach
        sees affiliation, membership, and disaffiliation not as emanating
        from one's personality structure, but rather as coming from the
        social structure, that is, as socially structured events arising
        out of social relationships. In this view all participants play
        influential roles. Deprogramming is said to be a special form of
        disaffiliation.

767.   Bromley, David G., and Anson D. Shupe. "Financing the New Reli-
           gions: A Resource Mobilization Approach." JOURNAL FOR THE SCIEN-
           TIFIC STUDY OF RELIGION 19 (1980): 227-39.

        Examines the financial structure of new religious movements from
        a sociological perspective, which sees and understands them "as
        organizations facing certain perennial developmental problems" (p.
        227) including the accumulation of necessary economic resources.
        Using the Unification Church and the Hare Krishna Movement as exam-
        ples, the authors analyze the dynamics of economic resource mobili-
        zation in world-transforming new religions. It is maintained that
        this mobilization is a function of resource availability, congru-
        ence of organization requisites, individual role requirement and
        motives, and the management of exchanges between movement and
        society. Such an approach resolves the issue of how the two move-
        ments, with relatively few members and in a short period of time,
        achieved financial success in spite of the intense hostility from
        society at large. Their success has been due to their use of pub-
        lic solicitation strategy, which is a characteristic solution of
        these kinds of movements.

768.   Bucher, Glenn B. "Words of Total Meaning: An Interpretation of
           Cult Religion." SOUNDINGS: AN INTERDISCIPLINARY JOURNAL 63
           (1980): 274-85.

        Rejects those interpretations of the cultic phenomenon that
        attribute their emergence to social permissiveness or to the hunger
        for transcendence as reductionistic or pejorative. The author
        advances a theory based on historical, sociological, and anthropo-
        logical perspectives. "In the cult story," he states, "there is a
        chapter about social and religious life in late twentieth-century
        Western, mechanical, desacralized, atomistic society" (p. 274).
        From a sociological viewpoint cult religion answers the question
        about cultural universals; it offers affirmation, meaning, and
        hope. From an anthropological point of view, cults represent rites
        of passage in which liminality, "communitas," and the struggle for
        meaning are expressed.

769.   Caird, Dale, and Henry G. Law. "Non-Conventional Beliefs: Their
           Structure and Measurement." JOURNAL FOR THE SCIENTIFIC STUDY OF
           RELIGION 21 (1982): 152-63.

        Presents arguments in favor of studying nonconventional beliefs
        and then examines the nature of such beliefs and the ways they can
        be studied. Subjects from Christian denominations, from non-Chris-
        tian religions, from non-conventional groups, and from nonreligious
        people participated in an intensive questionnaire. The authors
        discovered that many people involved in non-conventional religions
        tend to have multiple group memberships.

770.   Campbell, Bruce. "A Typology of Cults." SOCIOLOGICAL ANALYSIS 39
           (1978): 228-40.

        Attempts to clarify the differences between religious groups
        by introducing a new concept of cult based on the sacred/profane
        distinction. Cults are founded on the belief that the sacred is

located within the individual and can be defined as "non-traditional religious groups based on belief in a divine element in
the individual" (p. 239). The various definitions of cult and
Troeltsch's use of mysticism as a basis for the cult (item 134) are
examined and a new typology presented. Three kinds of cults are
distinguished: the illumination cult, the instrumental cult, and
the sense-oriented cult. Three illumination cults, namely Theosophy, Wisdom of the Soul, and Spiritualism, and three instrumental
ones, namely New Thought, Scientology, and Transcendental Meditation, are briefly described.

771.   Campbell, Colin. "Some Comments on the New Religious Movements:
        The New Spirituality and the Post-Industrial Society." THE NEW
        RELIGIOUS MOVEMENTS: A PERSPECTIVE FOR UNDERSTANDING SOCIETY
        (item 551), pp. 232-42.

        Maintains that the common functionalist interpretation of the new
        religious movements is deficient in that it directs our attention
        away from the cultural context and trends in which the movements
        rise and grow. The new movements are not, according to the author,
        "functional alternatives to the churches." The new spirituality
        supports the view that the major shift in the last couple of de-
        cades has not been from belief to unbelief, but rather from "belief
        to seekership," a position supported by Wuthnow's research (item
        1041). The author subscribes to the view that the conflict between
        the secular and the spiritual-mystical worldviews gives rise to new
        religious movements.

772.   Campbell, Colin. "Accounting For the Counter-Culture." SCOTTISH
        JOURNAL OF SOCIOLOGY 4 (1980): 38-51.

        Rejects three attempts to explain the emergence of the counter-
        culture movement of the 1960's. The first sees this movement not as
        new or novel, but rather as a recurring phenomenon in Western cul-
        ture; the second considers it new but not novel, in the sense that
        it has one or more precedents; the third maintains that it is both
        new and novel and that, consequently, it can only be explained with
        reference to features present in contemporary society. The author
        insists that the origin of the beliefs and values underlying the
        counterculture must first be explored.

773.   Campbell, Colin. "The Secret Religion of the Educated Masses."
        SOCIOLOGICAL ANALYSIS 39 (1978): 146-56.

        Maintains that religious changes in contemporary society can be
        best understood as a transition from "Church religion" to "spiri-
        tual and mystical religion" (see Troeltsch, item 134), and that
        these changes are related to the process of secularization.
        Troeltsch's typology of religion in three major forms, namely
        church, sect, and mysticism, is explained. The author thinks that
        Troeltsch's view of mysticism can help "relate the two apparently
        irreconcilable trends of secularization and the rise of the new
        religiosity" (p. 149). He thinks that spiritual and mystical
        religion is more acceptable to modern educated people who live in
        an industrialized, scientifically minded world and is, therefore,
        well adapted to survive in the modern sociocultural conditions.

774. Campbell, Colin. "Clarifying the Cult." BRITISH JOURNAL OF SOCI-
OLOGY 28 (1977): 375-88.

Argues in favor of a more adequate concept of "cult" in the light
of the cultic phenomena of the late 1960's and early 1970's. The
problems linked with the concept are identified, and it is proposed
that there is a need to distinguish between "the empirical construct of a cult and the ideal type concept of mystic collectivity"
(p. 375). The structural features of a cult, the criteria of cultic belief, the religion of mysticism, and the mystic collectivity
are among the types discussed. The author prefers the use of the
phrase "mystic collectivity." Religious cults are seen as an
ephemeral organization that will dissolve into collectivity.

775. Campbell, Colin. "The Cult, the Cultic Milieu, and Secularization."
SOCIOLOGICAL YEARBOOK OF RELIGION IN BRITAIN 5 (1972): 119-35.

Traces the concept of cult to Troeltsch's tripartite division of
religious groups into church, sect, and mysticism (item 134). The
author points out that, because of the trend to de-emphasize the
link between cult and mysticism, two contrasting concepts of cults
are now in existence. The first follows Troeltsch's view of asso-
ciating cults with mystical aspiration; the second stresses the
deviant or heterodox dimensions of cults. A distinction is made
between the cultic milieu, a constant feature of society, and the
cults, that are transitory phenomena. The sociological focus
should be the cultic milieu, which is a combination of mysticism
and the personal services and practices of healing and divination.
The author thinks that this cultic milieu might have the function
of cultural diffusion and innovation.

776. Casanova, José V. "The Politics of Religious Revival." TELOS No.
59 (Spring 1984): 3-33.

Discusses the contemporary religious revival in the context of
sociological theories on secularization. Four different phenomena
are examined: 1) the new religious movements; 2) new forms of religiosity and private, secular quests for salvation (as in the Human
Potential Movement); 3) the Christian fundamentalist revival; and
4) renewal within the established churches. The new religions, in
the author's view, are "both symptom of and contributive factor to
not only the legitimation crisis of advanced capitalism but the
general crisis of modernity" (p. 16). The Human Potential Movement
(including encounter groups) is interpreted as a typical expression
of the modern quest for salvation which is secular rather than
religious in its orientation and can be called a religion of narcissism. Astrology, Spiritism, Occultism, Satanism, and UFO cults
are regressions to primitive religious forms.

777. Champlin, Carole. "Neo-Oriental Religious Sects in America: Opiate
of Impoverished Middle-Class Youth." SOCIAL SCIENCE FORUM: AN
INTERDISCIPLINARY JOURNAL 2.1 (1978): 27-35.

Seeks to discover why religious sects that traditionally have
been the product of the economically depressed are now making head-
way among the middle-class youth in the the United States. The

author thinks that what leads young adults to join a new religious movement is not their social status or class, but rather their anomalous social locations, that is, the discrepancy between their cultural expectations and the social situations in which they live. It is the strains that result from anomalies that lead youngsters to alternative religions. The author shows how the Unification Church and the Hare Krishna Movement alleviate some of the strains and dissonance of modern youth.

778.   Cohen, Eric, and Nachman Ben-Yehuda. "Counter-Cultural Movements and Totalitarian Democracy." SOCIOLOGICAL INQUIRY 57 (1987): 372-93.

Identifies the following four types of movements and examines their potential for "totalitarian democracy": 1) those that stress self-fulfillment; 2) cults of self-realization; 3) radical protest movements; and 4) revolutionary movements. The inner or outer direction of liberation they propose and the degree of their absoluteness are explored. Cults that focus on self-realization, like Scientology, are monopolistic and inner-directed.

779.   Crippen, Timothy. "Old and New Gods in the Modern World: Towards a Theory of Religious Transformation." SOCIAL FORCES 67 (1988): 316-36.

Challenges the secularization thesis that is based on the assumption that religion is on the decline. Though traditional religions are losing their hold over their adherents, religious consciousness, in the author's opinion, remains powerful and is manifesting itself in a variety of new beliefs and rituals that are more in tune with modern culture. The transformation of religion is outlined with reference "to the relation between the evolution of sacred symbols and the market and political dimensions of sovereign organization in the modern world" (p. 316). The emergence of liberation theory in Latin America, the vitality of Islamic fundamentalism, and the strength of the New Christian Right in the United States are the main examples cited.

780.   Cushman, Philip. "The Self-Besieged: Recruitment-Indoctrination Processes in Restrictive Groups." JOURNAL OF THE THEORY OF SOCIAL BEHAVIOR 16.1 (1986): 1-32.

Distinguishes two types of authoritarian cults, the religious and psychological. The author endeavors to explain, by analyzing the methods of cult recruitment and indoctrination, two contradictory points of view, namely the apparent happiness of cult members and the negative psychiatric reports on the effects of cult life on its members. He understands conversion or personality change by using the theory of self-image management, development, and maintenance of a cohesive self. Thought reform techniques plus the vulnerability of young adults, who suffer from "a chronic low-level narcissistic wound," are said to explain why people join cults. Restrictive groups first attack the self of the recruit, causing an identity fragmentation, during which critical thought and democratic processes are suspended, and then offer a cure by imposing a substitute identity.

781. Dent, Owen. "Church/Sect Typologies in the Description of Religious Groups." AUSTRALIAN AND NEW ZEALAND JOURNAL OF SOCIOLOGY 6.1 (1970): 10-27.

   Reviews some of the substantive and methodological issues in the sociological typologies of religious organizations and suggests areas of research in the field. After discussing the various ways in which typologies are built, the author gives a short history of the church-sect distinction and the main features of the literature on the subject. Five states in the development of the typology are noted: those of innovation, of elaboration, of consolidation, of reconsideration, and of rejection.

782. Dittes, James E. "Typing the Typologies: Some Parallels in the Career of Church-Sect and Extrinsic-Intrinsic." JOURNAL FOR THE SCIENTIFIC STUDY OF RELIGION 10 (1971): 375-83.

   Points out that the sociological typology of church and sect and the psychological distinction between extrinsic and intrinsic type of religious behavior have similar origins and characteristics. Both are loaded with value judgments and are carelessly formulated. It is argued that those who proposed the typologies were mainly concerned with the purity of religion and animated by a prophetic ardor. These classifications are culture-bound and applicable only to Western Christianity.

783. Doress, Irving, and Jack Nusan Porter. "Kids in Cults." SOCIETY 15.4 (1978): 69-71.

   Proposes several reasons why young people join cults, why they remain members, and why they leave. The authors believe that people are drawn to new religious groups to find a family, to search for spiritual answers to questions about life, and to achieve security. Adolescent rebellion, adventure, and unemployment are also factors to be taken into account. Cults provide loving personal relationships and a better physical and moral environment. Cult members are afraid of leaving for moral and religious reasons and not because they are physically restrained from doing so. Disillusionment, completion of one's stage of development, and kidnaping and deprogramming are the main reasons why they leave. Cults will persist because they satisfy human needs, which are not otherwise met.

784. Dowdy, Edwin. "The Dialectic of Spiritual Experience and Social Structure." SPIRITUAL WELL-BEING: SOCIOLOGICAL PERSPECTIVES (item 660), pp. 113-18.

   Defines religious experience as a search for self-transcendence and then explores the relationship between this experience and social structure. An attempt is made to locate the parameters of the relationships between the individual and society, the church and society, and the individual and the church or sect. The question is raised whether church and society tend to facilitate or hinder spiritual experiences, thereby either preventing or encouraging new sects or cults.

785.   Drane, James. THE NEW AMERICAN REFORMATION: A STUDY OF YOUTH CUL-
       TURE AND RELIGION. New York: Philosophical Library, 1973. 166 pp.

       Makes an effort to understand the youth culture of the 1960's and
       interprets it as a "threat to social stability and cultural conti-
       nuity." Young adults of the period are described as alienated from
       the establishment's goals and practices. The rise of youth culture
       is related to the decline of religion in the West and to the inter-
       est in communal living, meditation, and other religious activities.
       One chapter is given to a discussion on the Jesus Freaks and the
       new Charismatic Movement.

786.   Duddy, Neil T. "Conversion--Under the Microscope and Under the
       Guru." UPDATE: A QUARTERLY JOURNAL OF NEW RELIGIOUS MOVEMENTS
       6.1 (1982): 1-10.

       Discusses the issue of conversion to new religious movements with
       reference to the debate in the social sciences. The author insists
       that the work of social scientists, though invaluable, should not
       be a substitute for theological reflection and evaluation.

787.   Ebaugh, Helen Ross Fuchs, and Sharon Lee Vaughn. "Ideology and
       Recruitment in Religious Groups." REVIEW OF RELIGIOUS RESEARCH
       26 (1984): 148-57.

       Stresses the importance of structural variables in the study of
       conversion to new religious groups. The very nature of the group
       influences both the way individuals are first contacted and the
       process of incorporation into the new community. Cultic affective
       bonds and intensive interaction within the group are major factors
       in recruitment and conversion. The authors focus on the different
       types of social ties and on how these are related to ideological
       differences in three religious groups, namely the Catholic Charis-
       matics (who form a conversionist, fundamentalist, and evangelical
       sect), Christian Scientists, and the Baha'is (the latter two being
       gnostic sects that emphasize esoteric teachings in order to achieve
       this-worldly goals). It is concluded, contrary to what Snow and
       Phillips (item 952) hold, that "the more isolated of our three
       groups tended to recruit through casual, acquaintance-like friend-
       ship ties, while the two less isolated groups drew members by means
       of more intimate, primary-type relationships" (p. 155).

788.   Eister, Allan W. "Culture Crises and New Religious Movements: A
       Paradigmatic Statement of a Theory of Cults." RELIGIOUS MOVE-
       MENTS IN CONTEMPORARY AMERICA (item 727), pp. 612-27.

       Relates the emergence of cult organizations in the West to the
       "culture crises" of "dislocations in the communicational and orien-
       tational institutions of advanced societies" (p. 612). Religious
       movements that arise in periods of disruption to satisfy the human
       need for giving meaning to life have four critical functions, those
       of: 1) ordering and identifying signs and symbols used in communi-
       cation; 2) clarifying the rules of discourse; 3) specifying the
       rules for reasoning; and 4) defining the conditions of human exis-
       tence. Various responses to the culture crises are also discussed.

789.   Eister, Allan W. "Quasi-Groups and New Religious Movements: Some
        Theoretical Considerations and Some Empirical Findings." THE
        CONTEMPORARY METAMORPHOSIS OF RELIGION: ACTS OF THE 12TH INTER-
        NATIONAL CONFERENCE ON SOCIOLOGY OF RELIGION, The Hague, The
        Netherlands, 1973. Lille, France: C.I.S.R., 1973, pp. 435-49.

        Raises the question whether cults are quasi-groups "in the sense
        of their being regarded as 'loose configurations' which crystallize
        into associations under specific conditions" (p. 438), as opposed
        to sects which are highly structured. The discussion is carried on
        in the context of several of the new religious movements, including
        the Jesus People and the Hare Krishnas. The author thinks that
        these groups are new in the sense that they are free, independent
        inventions of young people. He maintains that the cults contain
        some organized structure since they often offer a communal setting
        in which stated religious goals can be attained. What attracts
        young adults to these cults is also considered.

790.   Eister, Allan W. "An Outline of a Structural Theory of Cults."
        JOURNAL FOR THE SCIENTIFIC STUDY OF RELIGION 11 (1972): 319-33.

        Discusses the emergence and some features of cult movements that
        are a result of "cultural crises." The author hypothesizes that
        such crises are "dislocations in the communicational and orienta-
        tional institutions of advanced societies--dislocations which open
        the way for cults to flourish" (p. 320). The conditions for the
        rise of cults are explored in some detail and the various cultic
        responses to culture crises outlined. The orientations offered
        by cults are diverse and unconventional and may be syncretistic,
        eclectic, or esoteric. Several questions that might be asked about
        individual cults are listed.

791.   Ellwood, Robert S. "The Several Meanings of Cult." THOUGHT: A
        REVIEW OF CULTURE AND IDEA 61 (1986): 212-24.

        Discusses the different definitions that have been given to the
        word "cult." Several common features assigned to the concept are
        noted: isolation from the larger community; conformity with the
        group; dependence on a powerful leader; and tension with society at
        large. The author then cautiously suggests his own definition of
        a cult, a definition that displays several features that need not
        apply to all cults. A cult is "a group offering an alternative to
        the dominant spiritual tradition, a group which is small, has
        strong authoritative and charismatic leadership, offers powerful
        subjective experiences to meet personal needs, is separatist, and
        claims a relation to a legitimizing tradition" (p. 223).

792.   Ellwood, Robert S. "Emergent Religion in America: An Historical
        Perspective." UNDERSTANDING THE NEW RELIGIONS (item 567), pp.
        267-84.

        Explores various metaphors used in understanding new religious
        movements, particularly the diachronic and synchronic models. The
        latter, which stress short histories of the cults and their contem-
        porary social contexts, are divided into contact and disequilibrium

theories, the first stressing contact with more advanced cultures, the second concentrating on revitalization or deprivation. Diachronic models tend to see cults in historical perspective. Both approaches share the view that new movements are a crisis-response that has to be understood in its particular historical period. The author thinks the phrase "emergent religions" accurately expresses the latent religious values that most alternative religions in the United States stress. The strengths and weaknesses of the historical model are discussed.

793.   Fabian, Johannes. "The Anthropology of Religious Movements: From Explanation to Interpretation." SOCIAL RESEARCH 46 (1979): 4-35.

Provides an overview of the areas covered by anthropologists when they approach new religious movements, the study of which is divided into three categories: 1) causal explanations (such as political or socioeconomic oppression); 2) typologies and taxonomies; and 3) interpretations based on the interests of Western society. Future trends are discussed. The author thinks that research on religious movements is an investigation into religious processes. Though largely concerned with the study of new religions in nonliterate societies, several of the author's observations are applicable to the study of cults in the Western world.

794.   Fichter, Joseph H. "Youth in Search of the Sacred." THE SOCIAL IMPACT OF NEW RELIGIOUS MOVEMENTS (item 725), pp. 21-41.

Examines new religious movements as a search for truth, transcendence, and the sacred. The modern trends to industrialization, urbanization, and secularization are judged to be the causes of the current religious revival. The author's view is that a "large number of people have been programmed into the routine of consumerism, materialism, and secularism" (p. 25) and that conversion to the new movements is a kind of deprogramming from utopian materialism to transcendental religion. Dismissing the functional approach as inadequate, he thinks that people join cults freely because they are convinced that by so doing they gain an experience of the holy.

795.   Flowers, Ronald B. RELIGION IN STRANGE TIMES: THE 1960S AND 1970S. Macon, GA: Mercer University Press, 1984. xiv, 242 pp.

Presents a study of religious changes and trends over the last two decades. One chapter is dedicated to the understanding of the Charismatic Movement, while another examines the various cults, particularly the Unification Church. Classical and contemporary Pentecostalism are compared and the social characteristics of the former are described. Three major types of religious groups are distinguished, namely the church, sect, and cult, the last mentioned being further categorized into "innovation" and "important" cults. Cult movements, which can be individual-transforming (like Scientology) or world-transforming (like the Unification Church) are the most organized of all cultic groups. The author insists that the words "sect" and "cult" are sociological terms and should not contain value judgment. He does admit, however, that the Children of God is the most visible and alarming of cults.

796. Foss, Daniel A., and Ralph W. Larkin. "The Roar of the Lemming: Youth, Post-Movement Groups, and the Life Construction Crisis." SOCIOLOGICAL INQUIRY 49 (1979): 264-85.

Discusses various possible explanations of why the new religious movements came into being and attracted people involved in the counterculture movement of the 1960's. The structure of these movements is sketched and the nature of their appeal analyzed. Several characteristics of these movements are identified: 1) an authoritarian structure; 2) a vision of peace and love among young people in the 1960's; 3) nonconflict stance with society; 4) denigration of sexual indulgence; 5) minute regulation of the lives of their members; 6) maintenance of a fierce exclusivity; and 7) claims to solution to the problem of the meaninglessness of life. The authors think that the emergence of the cults can be better explained by a "life construction" rather than an "identity" crisis.

797. Foss, Daniel A., and Ralph W. Larkin. "From 'Gates of Eden' to 'Day of the Locust:' An Analysis of the Dissident Youth Movement of the 1960s and Its Heirs of the Early 1970s--the Post-Movement Groups." THEORY AND SOCIETY 3 (1976): 45-64.

Redefines a social movement in terms of its dissident nature. Three mutually reinforcing lines of development are said to be central to a social movement: 1) the intensification of social conflict by the introduction of new lifestyles for the purpose of struggle; 2) the reinterpretation of social reality, including the repudiation of dominant values and the construction of models for future society; and 3) the reevaluation of the self and its capacities, leading to what amounts to mass therapy. New movements like the Divine Light Mission, the Alamo Foundation, Scientology, and the Hare Krishna Movement aim at transforming the social order and have broken sharply with some of the values of the movements of the 1960's by advocating self-discipline, hard work, the renunciation of the pleasures of the flesh, exclusivity, and new remedies for coping with meaninglessness.

798. Fowler, Newton B. "Religion Beyond the Churches: The Appeal of Sect and Non-Traditional Religions." LEXINGTON THEOLOGICAL QUARTERLY 16 (April 1981): 78-84.

Interprets the reason why people join sects and cults in terms of relative deprivations. The variety of new religious movements, we are told, "reflect the range of human needs" (p. 83), whether these are physical, social, or psychological.

799. Galanter, Marc. CULTS: FAITH, HEALING, AND COERCION. New York: Oxford University Press, 1989. viii, 230 pp.

Applies the systems theory to analyze the structure and functioning of charismatic groups, an approach that does not start with the investigation of the motives in individual members, but rather with the way the group's needs are met. The author concentrates on one aspect of the systems theory, namely the role of feedback among the system components. He examines the forces in the charismatic

group and constructs a model that sees cults as social systems.
Four functions characteristic of systems, namely transformation,
monitoring, feedback, and boundary control, are discussed. Jonestown, the Unification Church, and Alcoholics Anonymous are the
major case histories used to illustrate the author's theory.
Cults, according to the author, emerge when society does not
adequately address major social issues and provide intellectual
answers and relief from anxiety and distress.

800.   Gallup, George. "U. S. in Early State of Religious Revival."
        JOURNAL OF CURRENT SOCIAL ISSUES 14 (1977): 50-55.

        Adduces evidence to show that a profound religious revival is
        taking place in the United States and cites five main factors that
        confirm the results of polls and surveys: 1) "a turning inward to
        seek refuge from the pressures of everyday existence" (p. 50); 2) a
        quest for nonmaterial values; 3) President Carter's open discus-
        sion of his own religious experience; 4) an increase in religious
        interest and activity; and 5) efforts to adapt religion to the
        younger generation. Results of the Gallup Poll are included. The
        following figures of those involved in "experimental religions" are
        given: Transcendental Meditation, 6% (six million); Yoga, 3% (five
        million); Charismatic Renewal, 2% (three million); mysticism, 2%
        (three million); and Eastern religions, 1% (2 million).

801.   Garrett, William R. "Maligned Mysticism: The Maledicted Career
        of Troeltsch's Third Type." SOCIOLOGICAL ANALYSIS 36 (1975):
        205-223.

        Traces the development of Troeltsch's third type of religion and
        reevaluates its possible use in social research (see item 134).
        The early discussions on Troeltsch's and Weber's church-sect-mysti-
        cism typology (see items 134 and 140, respectively) are summarized.
        It is pointed out that Niebuhr (item 119) was responsible for elim-
        inating mysticism from the typology. Two main traits of Troeltsch's
        mysticism are noted: 1) the individuality and inwardness of reli-
        gious experience; and 2) the lack of an internal pressure to devel-
        op an enduring social organization. The author's opinion is that
        mysticism, as used by Troeltsch, is still a relevant and practical
        concept for understanding different types of religiosity.

802.   Gartrell, C. David, and Zane K. Shannon. "Contacts, Cognitions,
        and Conversion: A Rational Choice Approach." REVIEW OF RELIGIOUS
        RESEARCH 27 (1985): 32-48.

        Starts with Lofland and Skonovd's distinction (item 866) between
        various conversion motifs and attempts to develop a theory of con-
        version that links together the many variables that make up the
        experience of conversion. The authors stress that "conversion
        hinges on actors' perceptions of the expected rewards of conversion
        relative to not converting" (p. 32). The features of the recruits'
        social networks, cognitive structures, and conversions are derived
        from the principle of rational choice. Relying particularly on
        studies on the Divine Light Mission, the authors specify the condi-
        tions that lead potential recruits to evaluate a new religious
        movement and then to decide whether or not to become members.

803.   Glock, Charles Y.   "Consciousness Among Contemporary Youth: An
        Interpretation." THE NEW RELIGIOUS CONSCIOUSNESS (item 614), pp.
        353-66.

        Proposes the view that the youth countercultural movement of the
        1960's did not initiate a significant change in American society,
        but was rather an indication of changes already under way. The
        author discusses the causes that set the counterculture in motion,
        the reasons why it lost its momentum, the meaning of the crisis of
        consciousness that followed in its wake, and possible future devel-
        opments. New movements may be a sign that the search for an alter-
        native reality that began with the counterculture is still going on.

804.   Glock, Charles Y.   "On The Origin and Evolution of Religious
        Groups." RELIGION IN SOCIOLOGICAL PERSPECTIVE (item 352), pp.
        207-220.

        Reproduces a slightly different version of an earlier essay. The
        types of deprivation and the corresponding forms and success expec-
        tations of religious groups are clarified as follows: 1) economic
        deprivation that leads to the formation of sects that either die
        out or are radically transformed; 2) social deprivation that is
        associated with churches that retain their original form; 3) organ-
        ismic deprivation, which gives rise to healing movements that be-
        come cult-like or die out when medical discoveries become commonly
        accepted healing procedures; 4) ethical deprivation, which leads to
        reform movements that can expect early extinction due to success,
        opposition, or irrelevancy; and 5) psychic deprivation that creates
        cults that either succeed and thus become extinct through transfor-
        mation or fail, due to extreme outside opposition.

805.   Greeley, Andrew M.   "Superstition, Ecstasy, and Tribal Conscious-
        ness." SOCIAL RESEARCH 37 (1970): 203-11.

        Argues that recent, bizarre manifestations of religion are not
        indicative of a return to the sacred, since society has not in fact
        been desacralized. Contemporary society is witnessing new forms of
        the sacred becoming available in the marketplace because of the
        increased demand for contact with the holy. Several sociocultural
        crises and the alienation of the younger generation are responsible
        for this demand. The author discusses three "new gods," or reli-
        gions, namely superstition, ecstasy, and groupism, all of which
        are nonrational, Pelagian in their orientation to human nature,
        salvationist, millennial, charismatic, and liturgical.

806.   Greeley, Andrew M., and Gregory Baum, editors. THE PERSISTENCE OF
        RELIGION. (CONCILIUM: RELIGION IN THE SEVENTIES, vol. 1, no. 9).
        New York: Herder and Herder, 1973.   160 pp.

        Presents a collection of sociologically-oriented essays devoted
        to the question of the persistence of religion in an age when the
        process of secularization seems to be at its peak. The revival of
        the sacred, the emergence of small religious communities, and the
        interest in mystical experiences are among the topics covered.

        Contains item 1943.

807.   Greil, Arthur L. "Previous Dispositions and Conversion to Per-
           spectives of Social and Religious Movements." SOCIOLOGICAL ANAL-
           YSIS 38 (1977): 115-25.

        Investigates the individual conversion process, particularly the
        dispositions that eventually lead a person to conversion. The
        major areas examined are the social nature of the individual's
        perspectives and what the author labels the "conversion and re-
        ference others" (p. 117). A number of factors that are likely to
        increase or decrease a person's acceptance of a new perspective are
        listed. The author concludes that, among other things, a person's
        "perspective is more likely to be discredited in periods of rapid
        social change" (p. 120). He holds that individuals who convert
        have a certain degree of choice and some contact and affinity with
        the members of the group they join. It is argued, however, that
        many converts do not change their perspectives at all, or else
        experience only a partial change.

808.   Greil, Arthur L., and David R. Rudy. "Social Cocoons: Encapsula-
           tion and Identity Transforming Organizations." SOCIOLOGICAL
           INQUIRY 54 (1984): 260-78.

        Discusses those religious or nonreligious movements (such as the
        new cults, Alcoholics Anonymous, and Weight Watchers) that aim to
        transform a person's identity. Basing their analysis largely on
        research carried out among Alcoholics Anonymous, the authors de-
        scribe an essential feature of these organizations, namely "encap-
        sulation," which is the mechanism used to restrict communication
        and interaction between members and outsiders. Three modes of
        encapsulation--physical, social, and ideological--are distinguished
        and reasons why different groups stress different ways of limiting
        their members' contact with the outside world are suggested. Psy-
        chical encapsulation, for example, is practiced by groups that,
        like the Unification Church and Scientology, recruit young adults
        who do not have strong family ties.

809.   Greil, Arthur L., and David R. Rudy. "Have We Learned From Process
           Models of Conversion?: An Examination of Ten Case Studies."
           SOCIOLOGICAL FOCUS 17 (1984): 305-23.

        Examines conversion to new religious movements in the context of
        Lofland and Stark's model (item 215). The authors take into con-
        sideration the conversions to several groups representing the
        1) Eastern religions 2) Christianity, and 3) the occult tradition.
        Four major questions are asked: 1) does the group advocate a mini-
        mal lifestyle?; 2) does membership involve a radical discontinuity
        in social roles?; 3) are members regarded as "deviant" by the gen-
        eral public?; and 4) do members see themselves as having adopted a
        new ideology? Various models of conversion are examined and the
        authors propose an organizational model that considers conversion
        as one form of socialization.

810.   Groves, Mary Ann. "Marginal Religious Movements as Precursors of a
           Sociocultural Revolution." THOUGHT: A REVIEW OF CULTURE AND IDEA
           61 (1986): 267-76.

Maintains that cult participants are reacting against the consequences of the modern world with which most Americans are now
satisfied. Three major causes for the dissatisfaction of cult
members are then analyzed, namely: 1) the growth of bureaucratization in all spheres of life; 2) social disorganization due to the
breakdown of family and social ties; and 3) secularization which
stimulates people to seek transcendental experiences. The factors
that influence commitment to new religious movements are listed.
The author maintains that those who join cults are the forerunners
of a sociocultural evolution now taking place in America.

811.   Groves, Mary Ann. "A Sociological Discussion of Contemporary Reli-
         gious Movements." RELIGION AND CULTURE: EXPLORING THE INTERFACE.
         New York: Manhattan College, 1979, pp. 73-90.

Explores three questions that the rise of new religions has
brought to the fore: 1) what social conditions are necessary for
such movements to emerge?; 2) what are the social characteristics
of the people who join them?; and 3) what social organization factors affect the maintenance or disappearance of the new groups?
The author dwells on four themes that predominate the sociological
literature that seeks to explain the emergence of marginal religious movements. These themes are 1) social disorganization,
2) economic, political, or social deprivation, 3) secularization,
and 4) the stress on individuals. It is suggested that the study
of the relationship between social context, social organization,
and human behavior can add to our understanding of the popularity
of the new religious movements.

812.   Gurney, Joan Neff, and Kathleen J. Tierney. "Relative Deprivation
         and Social Movements: A Critical Look at Twenty Years of Theory
         and Research." SOCIOLOGICAL QUARTERLY 23 (1982): 33-47.

Attempts to analyze and evaluate the theory of religious deprivation that has been widely used to explain the origin of social (and
religious) movements. The concept of relative deprivation and its
theoretical basis are criticized and its empirical adequacy questioned. The author surveys the literature that employs this model
and concludes that it is not useful as a tool for understanding
these movements. Several reasons that might account for the
model's popularity are advanced. A bibliography that includes
basic writings on religious deprivation is included.

813.   Gussner, R. E., and S. D. Berkowitz. "Scholars, Sects, and Sanghas,
         1: Recruitment to Asian-Based Meditation Groups in America."
         SOCIOLOGICAL ANALYSIS 49 (1988): 136-70.

Criticizes the dominant explanation of the rise of the new religious movements, namely what the authors label the "disruption-
neediness-belongingness thesis." After an overview of the research
on the cults that support this hypothesis, the authors describe the
sampling method they used to collect data from the following 10
major Asian-based groups that are usually neglected by social
scientists: 1) The Ramakrishna Vedanta Society; 2) Zen Centers; 3)
Tibetan Buddhist Kagu Lineage; 4) Sri Chinmoy Meditation Society;

5) the Healthy, Happy, and Holy Organization (3HO); 6) the Divine
Light Mission; 7) Rajneesh Foundation International; 8) Siddha Yoga
Dham of America; 9) the Himalayan Institute; and 10) small Hindu
societies like the Lama Foundation and Arunchala. It is contended
that deprivation needs played a minor role in attracting people to
the aforementioned new movements.

814. Haack, Friedrich. "New Youth Religions, Psychomutation, and Tech-
      nological Civilization." INTERNATIONAL REVIEW OF MISSION 67
      (1978): 436-47.

      Outlines three major features shared by the new religious move-
      ments, namely: 1) they attract mainly young people; 2) they have
      founders who exercise authority and bring salvation; and 3) they
      form a cohesive family. Western technology, according to the
      author, has brought with it a loss of meaning and security, thereby
      creating a crisis. New religious movements have capitalized on
      this weakness of the Western world and have employed techniques
      that change the personality of their members.

815. Hadden, Jeffrey K. "Towards Desacralizing Secularization Theory."
      SOCIAL FORCES 65 (1987): 587-611.

      Offers a critical examination of the secularization theory that
      has been also used to explain the rise of new religious movements.
      The author first attempts to understand how the theory itself be-
      came "sacralized." He then outlines several recent challenges to
      the theory. Four critical approaches to secularization are sum-
      marized: 1) the theory is a medley of ideas rather than a syste-
      matic hypothesis; 2) the general data do not support it; 3) the
      rise of new religious movements suggests that religion is still a
      powerful force in human life; and 4) the increasing involvement of
      religion in politics, revolution, and reform.

816. Hammond, Phillip E. "Cultural Consequences of Cults." THE FUTURE
      OF NEW RELIGIOUS MOVEMENTS (item 579), pp, 261-73.

      Discusses the possible effects of the new religious movements on
      American society as a whole. The author suggests that these move-
      ments offer individuals not only a wider religious choice, but also
      a broader selection of values. This results in the continued weak-
      ening of the link between religion and the family and of the power
      of the established churches. New religions tend to increase insti-
      tutionalized individualism which in turn contributes to the secu-
      larization process.

817. Hammond, Phillip E. "Civility and Civil Religion: The Emergence of
      Cults." VARIETIES OF CIVIL RELIGION. Edited by Robert E. Bellah
      and Phillip E. Hammond. New York: Harper and Row, 1980, pp.
      188-99.

      Expounds on the view that "the trivialization or corruption of
      American Civil Religion has been an important factor in the explo-
      sion of cults" (p. 193). The author thinks that various forms of
      superficiality in the American way of life in the 1950's and 1960's,

the absurdity of the Vietnam War, the use of the tenets, symbols,
and rituals of Civil Religion by those in power to maintain the
status quo, and the publicity of the Watergate Scandal all contributed to the decline of Civil Religion. The cults offer an opportunity which Civil Religion has failed to do, that is,, "to commit
oneself and to do so in ways that were neither middle class nor
even particularly American" (p. 197). The great negative reaction
to the cults indicates that they are perceived as a threat to
traditional values.

818.   Hammond, Phillip E., and R. C. Gordon-McCutchan. "Cults and the
       Civil Religion: A Tale of Two Centuries." REVUE FRANCAISE
       D'ETUDES AMERICANES 21 (1981): 173-85.

       Discusses the theory that the rise of the new cults is a direct
response to the breakdown of American Civil Religion. The authors
examine this religion in the first part of the nineteenth century
and the activities of cults at the same period and observe that at
that time the cults seemed to have arisen as a response to a vi-
brant Civil Religion. One common feature of the American Civil
Religion of both the nineteenth and twentieth centuries is said to
be the self-consciousness of people as American citizens, an identity that is religious and political. In both periods people had
grounds for questioning their nation's behavior and, consequently,
their own behavior. Civil rebels tend to express rebellion in
religious forms, that is, in cultic activity, whether their dissent
occurs in an age of national expansion and enthusiasm (as in the
early nineteenth century) or in a period of national folly and
despair (as in the mid-twentieth century).

819.   Hargrove, Barbara. "New Religions and the Search for a Public
       Morality." NEBRASKA HUMANIST 8.2 (1985): 61-70.

       Examines the social sources that lie behind the rise of new reli-
gious movements. Unlike movements in the past, the new cults are
recruiting people, not from the marginal or disinherited, but from
relatively privileged and affluent classes. The author points out
that contemporary political and economic structures "have also
undermined the traditional voluntaristic patterns of work and soci-
ality that have been the basis of our cultural self-understanding"
(p. 63). In her opinion, new religions attempt to give legitimacy
and purpose at a time when Western culture has become an efficient
machine without a definite goal and has stressed utilitarian individualism with the consequent neglect of public morality.

820.   Hargrove, Barbara. "New Religious Movements and the End of the
       Age." ILIFF REVIEW 34 (Spring 1982): 41-52.

       Explores a common feature shared by many new religious movements,
namely the belief that our present historical era is coming to an
end and/or a new one is about to emerge. Several major views of
this new beginning are described. The author thinks that the great
changes taking place in contemporary society are bound to lead to
speculations about the end of the world. Apocalyptic visions offer
an explanation of what is already happening and assist people in
the transition period.

821.   Hargrove, Barbara. RELIGION FOR A DISLOCATED GENERATION: WHERE
        WILL THOSE WHO GREW UP IN THE SIXTIES FIND FAITH? Valley Forge,
        PA: Judson Press, 1980. 141 pp.

        Reflects on the rise of new religious movements in the 1970's and
        attempts to understand its antecedents. The author's aim is to
        find out whether the new religions stand for a major cultural break
        and what kind of effects they might have on society. Major social
        changes since World War II are examined, with particular reference
        to the dislocation of the population and the migrations from the
        cities to suburbia. Educational changes since the war are also
        examined. The disillusionment with traditional religion is seen as
        a direct cause of the rise of the new movements that attempt to
        meet unanswered religious needs. The effects of the counterculture
        on mainstream society and some possible responses from the churches
        are also discussed.

822.   Hargrove, Barbara. "Religion For a Dislocated Generation." ILIFF
        REVIEW 97.2 (1980): 3-23.

        Looks into the condition of those young adults who were part of
        the post-World War II baby boom and who were caught up in the great
        sociocultural changes that have taken place over the last few
        decades. The sources and consequences of their rebellion and dis-
        location are discussed. It is stated that their quest for mystery
        often led them to occult practices or to nature religions, Eastern
        traditions, or fundamentalist or charismatic Christian groups. The
        impact on the mainline churches is assessed.

823.   Hargrove, Barbara. "Integrative and Transformative Religion."
        UNDERSTANDING THE NEW RELIGIONS (item 567), pp. 257-66.

        Discusses whether, and in what sense, contemporary religious
        movements can be called "new" and "religious" and whether they form
        a single phenomenon. It is maintained that "deviant" religions are
        new: 1) if they are based on religions imported from other cultures;
        2) if they indicate a radical shift in social traditions; and 3) if
        they unite uniquely various familiar elements. The distinction
        between integrative and transforming religion is offered as a
        typology, the former indicating a more organized religious form,
        the latter a more open-ended one in its ritual and myth.

824.   Hargrove, Barbara. "Dilemmas of the New Spirituality." RELIGIOUS
        EDUCATION 75 (1978): 259-65.

        Maintains on the need to recognize that new religious movements
        always come into being to fulfill vacuums in people's lives and
        that sufficient people are getting involved in them that a common
        need is present. The new spirituality is, according to the author,
        characterized by experience, community, and commitment. The impli-
        cations for religious education are discussed.

825.   Hargrove, Barbara. "The Rise of the New Polytheism." RELIGIOUS
        EDUCATION 72 (1977): 459-72.

Examines the current religious situation in the United States
where several religions and/or centers of values are accepted as
legitimate and where people can switch their allegiance from one
group to another. The author shows how the study of new movements
indicates that religion is becoming a quest for personal improvement and ecstatic experience and that people are faced with a wider
choice. She distinguishes between genuine pluralism and destructive polytheism and suggests that the task of the churches and
synagogues is to meet the needs that the new religious groups are
addressing.

826.   Harrison, Michael I. "Dimensions of Involvement in Social Move-
        ments." SOCIOLOGICAL FOCUS 10 (1977): 353-66.

Argues on the basis of the author's research on the Catholic
Charismatic Renewal in Michigan that there are several ways in
which an individual can become involved in a new religious movement. After a brief introduction to the Charismatic Renewal, five
distinct modes of involvement, each with its specialized activities, are identified: 1) regular, organized activities; 2) spiritual gifts; 3) communal involvement; 4) individual forms of
involvement; and 5) elite activities. A typology is constructed
based on a distinction between popular and elite involvement, both
of which can be either instrumental or expressive.

827.   Heelas, Paul. "New Religious Movements in Perspective." RELIGION
        15 (1985): 81-97.

Gives a lengthy, reflective review of Wallis's book, THE ELEMEN-
TARY FORMS OF NEW RELIGIOUS LIFE (item 991). Two major questions
about his typology of new religious movements into world-affirming
and world-rejecting are raised: 1) does it portray coherence and
distinctiveness?; and 2) are the ideal types applicable to individual cases? While the author reluctantly concedes that Wallis's
approach might be useful, he still thinks that the typology does
not function well at all when applied to specific movements.

828.   Heelas, Paul. "California Self-Religions and Socializing the Sub-
        jective." NEW RELIGIOUS MOVEMENTS (item 551), pp. 69-85.

Maintains that some new movements, like the Farm, Primal Therapy,
and EST, are concerned both with psychology and meaning and can be
labeled "self-religions" because they aim at the individual's perfection. The author argues "that the self-religions shed light on
a distinctive social response which is open to mankind" (p. 69), a
response that aims at socializing inner experiential states. Self-
religions function to provide a middle way between traditional
public institutions and the private subjectivity of anomie. The
author illustrates how this is done with reference to Kerista, a
self-religion in San Francisco.

829.   Heelas, Paul, and Anna Marie Haglund-Heelas. "The Inadequacy of
        'Deprivation' as a Theory of Conversion." VERNACULAR CHRIS-
        TIANITY: ESSAYS IN THE SOCIAL ANTHROPOLOGY OF RELIGION PRESENTED
        TO GODFREY LIENHARDT. Oxford: JASO, 1988, pp. 112-19.

Argues that criticisms of the deprivation theory of religious
conversion are justified because experiences of deprivation "cannot
lend themselves to scientific scrutiny." This common theory fails
to take into account the complexity of conversion and its varieties.
The authors hold that, though the deprivation theory does not offer
a complete explanation of conversion, it should be taken into
consideration in any examination of the conversion process. Though
written largely in the context of conversions to Christianity, the
authors' comments are also applicable to conversions to the new
religions.

830.   Hervieu-Léger, Daniele. "Signs of a Contemporary Religious Reviv-
        al?" SPIRITUAL REVIVALS. (CONCILIUM: RELIGION IN THE SEVENTIES,
        Vol. 9, no. 9). Edited by Christian Duquoc and Casiano Floristan.
        New York: Herder and Herder, 1973, pp. 11-25.

        Reflects on the contemporary revival within Christianity, focus-
        ing on the Jesus Movement. The author detects ambivalent features
        in most new movements, features that are augmented by ambiguities
        in the social and cultural environment of the West.

831.   Hill, Michael. "The Cult of Humanity and the Secret Religion of
        the Educated Masses." NEW ZEALAND SOCIOLOGY 2 (1987): 112-27.

        Examines the sociological interest in minority and fringe reli-
        gions and therapies with special reference to those that can be
        found in New Zealand, where the relative weakness of mainline,
        institutional religion opened up market opportunities for the new
        movements. Two sociological frameworks that throw light on these
        groups, namely Durkheim's idea of "the cult of humanity," and
        Troeltsch's "secret religion of the educated masses," (item 134)
        are discussed. Religions of modern, complex societies are said to
        be individualistic, tolerant, monistic, and syncretistic; they
        further stress an idealized human personality and the process by
        which human beings are remade morally. These features are examined
        in relation to the complimentary (fringe) therapies in New Zealand.
        It was found that a monistic/holistic conception of therapy was
        common among practitioners and their clients. Two groups, Trans-
        cendental Meditation and Centerpoint (which has its origins in
        Esalen) are examined in some detail.

832.   Hill, Michael. "Do Sects Thrive Where the Churches Languish?"
        RELIGION IN NEW ZEALAND SOCIETY. Edited by Brian Colless and
        Peter Donovan. Edinburgh: T. & T. Clark, 1980, pp. 115-32.

        Discusses briefly the sociological approach to religion and then
        observes that while the churches stress continuity, the sects lead
        towards spontaneity. Wilson's typology of sects (item 1023) is
        outlined and related to the New Zealand material. Besides tradi-
        tional or established sects, newer religious groups, particularly
        those that stem from Hinduism and Buddhism, are taken into consid-
        eration. The author maintains that sectarianism is a "thriving
        condition in contemporary society" (p. 126). The personal relation-
        ship encouraged by sects is an appealing feature especially in the
        context of the anonymity of the large, institutionalized churches.

Sectarian groups are in harmony with several aspects of modern society. Joining a sect may be a solution to economic or cultural deprivation or an alternative route to success.

833.   Hiller, Harry H. "Continentalism and the Third Force in Religion." CANADIAN JOURNAL OF SOCIOLOGY 3 (1978): 183-207.

Contends that significant differences exist in both the nature and extent of the activities of traditional and newer sectarian groups in the United States and Canada. Those groups that include such religious movements as the Mormons, the Salvation Army, Christian Science, Scientology, Spiritualism, and New Thought are called a "third force." The author thinks that they engage in greater activity in the United States. In Canada, these movements tend to stress religious conservatism, congregational ecumenism, and cooperation; in the United States, they emphasize religious fundamentalism, congregational independence, and individualism. Various theories explaining the differences between these sects in the two countries are discussed.

834.   Hine, Virginia H. "The Deprivation and Disorganization Theories of Social Movements." RELIGIOUS MOVEMENTS IN CONTEMPORARY AMERICA (item 727), pp. 628-45.

Reviews literature that supports either of two sociological and anthropological theories that are adduced to explain social and religious movements, namely the theories of disorganization and deprivation. While admitting that the intimacy and emotional support in charismatic groups are a help to those individuals experiencing social dislocation or family disruption, the author states that her data do not support the application of these reasons to explain the success of contemporary Pentecostalism. Similarly, she concludes that an economic and social deprivation theory is useful only "in pinpointing a particular type of status, or power" (pp. 659-60). The author prefers a relative deprivation theory to explain certain aspects of the Pentecostal Movement.

835.   Hunter, James Davison. "The New Religions: Demodernization and the Protest Against Modernity." THE SOCIAL IMPACT ON THE NEW RELIGIOUS MOVEMENTS (item 725), pp. 1-19.

Explores several reasons brought forth to explain the rise of new religious movements. Modern society is characterized by a high degree of deinstitutionalization in some major areas of human life, a condition that leads to a crisis of meaning and identity. The sources of the new religious consciousness lie in "the anthropological protest against modernity," more specifically in the protest against "the anomic situation intrinsic to modernity" (p. 7). New religions' attempts to neutralize these anomic effects and present utopian ideals that are radically antimodern. The main features, namely absolutism and expressiveness, of the new religious movements are directly opposite to contemporary trends of institutional ambiguity and utilitarianism, respectively. The author states that his approach incorporates the view that sees the new movements as a response to the breakdown of norms and the lack of agreement on values.

836.   Iannaccone, Laurence R. "A Formal Model of Church and Sect."
        AMERICAN JOURNAL OF SOCIOLOGY 94 (Supplement, 1988): S241-68.

        Criticizes the sociological typology of church and sect as inade-
        quate and attempts to show "why the characteristics commonly asso-
        ciated with church and sect tend to correlate and how they derive
        from more fundamental considerations" (p. 244). An economic model,
        outlined in mathematical form, is proposed. The individual is seen
        as allocating resources or commodities as a means of maximizing his
        or her overall satisfaction. Out of this model a distinction be-
        tween church and sect emerges based on one variable, namely the
        extent to which a religious organization accepts the sociocultural
        environment in which it exists. The author claims to have laid the
        foundation for a theory, rather than a typology, of church and
        sect.

837.   Jacobs, Janet. "Deconversion From Religious Movements: An Analysis
        of Charismatic Bonding and Spiritual Commitment." JOURNAL FOR
        THE SCIENTIFIC STUDY OF RELIGION 26 (1987): 294-308.

        Examines the process of disengagement from new religious move-
        ments "as a gradual voluntary phenomenon that reflects disillusion-
        ment with both the social and emotional dimensions of religious
        commitment" (p. 294). In some instances deconversion is expressed
        in the severing of the bonds that unite the cult member with the
        religious leader. Forty religious devotees from four clusters of
        movements (including Charismatic Christianity, Hindu traditions,
        Buddhist movements, and other less-easy-to-specify groups) were
        interviewed. The author points out that the devotee who abandons
        his or her commitment slowly ceases to allocate power to the guru,
        who is now conceived as unworthy of the homage demanded from his
        or her followers, and becomes more autonomous and less emotionally
        dependent. Deconversion is more likely to take place as the
        devotee becomes aware of other religious systems.

838.   Jacobs, Janet. "The Economy of Love in Religious Commitment: The
        Deconversion of Women from Nontraditional Religious Movements."
        JOURNAL FOR THE SCIENTIFIC STUDY OF RELIGION 23 (1984): 155-71.

        Examines the features of female religious commitment by focusing
        on conversion to, and disaffection from, nontraditional religious
        groups, including Charismatic Christianity, Eastern mysticism, the
        Baha'i Faith, the Divine Light Mission, the Hare Krishna Movement,
        the Unification Church, and Tibetan Buddhism. The male authority
        structure and the sex roles in these movements are briefly out-
        lined. It is maintained that religious commitment emphasizes an
        economy of love where affection, approval, and intimacy play a
        major part. A male hierarchy controls the emotional rewards of
        these religious communities, thus influencing the lives of the
        female converts. Sexual exploitation, abuse, and discrimination
        are often the result. The women who leave religious movements have
        often been disenchanted by the romantic idealism of the group.
        Through rejection the devotee begins to perceive the imbalance in
        the emotional exchange relationship common in the new religions.

839.   Johnson, Benton. "A Sociologist of Religion Looks at the Future of
        the New Religious Movements." THE FUTURE OF NEW RELIGIOUS MOVE-
        MENTS (item 579), pp. 251-60.

        Criticizes Stark's model (see item 956) for explaining why new
        religious movements succeed and makes several suggestions regarding
        the power of religious ideology, which is ignored in Stark's theory.
        Several speculations on the future of Scientology, the Hare Krishna
        Movement, and the Unification Church are offered. The author does
        not think that the new religions will make great strides in Western
        society unless the general public image of them changes.

840.   Johnson, Benton. "A Sociological Perspective on the New Religions."
        IN GODS WE TRUST (item 683), pp. 51-56.

        Maintains that new religious movements share one important fea-
        ture with most of their predecessors, namely "a focus on the
        therapeutic transformation of the self" (p. 51). New movements
        respond to structural and cultural sources of distress that are
        defined in psychological and spiritual terms. The author contends
        that the current preoccupation with the self derives from modern
        work conditions. New religions might improve the quality of life
        by providing an experience of transcendence, a common purpose and
        motivation, and a support group bound by a moral code.

841.   Johnson, Benton. "Church and Sect Revisited." JOURNAL FOR THE
        SCIENTIFIC STUDY OF RELIGION 10 (1971): 124-37.

        Discusses the conceptual and methodological issues regarding the
        common sociological distinction between church and sect and specu-
        lates on the theoretical possibilities of revising such a distinc-
        tion. Troeltsch's typology (see item 134) is criticized and more
        recent attempts by sociologists to refine his views examined.
        Theories about sect development are also discussed. The author
        rejects elaborate formal typologies of church and sect and opts for
        a simple distinction that is conceptually independent of historical
        cases.

842.   Johnson, Joan. THE CULT MOVEMENT. New York: Franklin Watts, 1984.
        106 pp.

        Adopts the view that cults differ from religions in that the
        former have a living leader who leads a luxurious lifestyle, exerts
        pressure on his or her followers, aims primarily to amass wealth,
        prevents members from thinking critically, and encourages depen-
        dence. A description of the life, ideas, and goals of the leaders
        of the most well-known cults is given. Jim Jones is taken as an
        example of "the cult leader, the messianic personality, gone hay-
        wire" (p. 26). The author briefly relates the emergence of the
        cults to the cultural conditions of the 1960's and 1970's and sug-
        gests that young people are attracted to the cults because they
        function as substitute parents.

843.   Johnstone, Ronald L. RELIGION AND SOCIETY: A SOCIOLOGY OF RELI-
        GION. Englewood Cliffs, NJ: Prentice-Hall, second edition, 1983.
        viii, 312 pp.

Presents a standard introduction to the sociology of religion
that discusses, among many other topics, religion as a social organization and the relationship between religion and other aspects of
culture. The traditional typology of church, denomination, and
sect and the recent refinements of these concepts are outlined.
The impact of deprivation on sect formation and development is also
covered. The stress on a new revelation is said to be the distinguishing feature of cults that are, in the author's opinion, transitory religious groups. The People's Temple of Jonestown is
examined as a "representational cult."

844.   Judah, J. Stillson. "From Political Activism to Religious Partici-
       pation." UPDATE: A QUARTERLY JOURNAL OF NEW RELIGIOUS MOVEMENTS
       6.1 (1982): 11-20.

       Defines cults as "a new religion that is not one of the estab-
       lishment of a given culture" (p. 12) and states that cults arise in
       periods of rapid cultural change and are generally persecuted by
       the mainline traditions. Conversion to the cults is a response to
       sociocultural needs and, hence, often transitory. The author
       insists that the brainwashing model is not necessary to account for
       conversions to the new religious movements. The common backgrounds
       and features that contributed to the conversion process of young
       adults are examined in the context of the Hare Krishna Movement.

845.   Judah, J. Stillson. "Belief and Behavior Amid Cultural Change:
       Some Thoughts on the Dynamics of New Religious Movements Like the
       Unification Church and Others." LIFESTYLES: CONVERSATIONS WITH
       MEMBERS OF THE UNIFICATION CHURCH. Edited by Richard Quebedeaux.
       New York: Rose of Sharon Press, 1982, pp. 185-96.

       Views the new religious movements in the context of the history
       of religions. The origin of new cults is attributed to cultural
       upheaval caused by immigration, invasion, oppression, and rapid
       social change. These cults come into being by 1) forming a new
       synthesis of ideas, or 2) rejecting changes made by the established
       religions and returning to the original values, or 3) discovering a
       new rationale for one's faith. The author traces the history of
       new religious movements in nineteenth-century America and relates
       their growth to sociocultural roots. In the twentieth century the
       Unification Church has proposed a new synthesis to meet contempo-
       rary needs. The author states that new religious movements play a
       role in eliminating violence and crime and in encouraging construc-
       tive means for creating a better world.

846.   Keiser, Thomas W., and Jacqueline Keiser. THE ANATOMY OF ILLUSION:
       RELIGIOUS CULTS AND DESTRUCTIVE PERSUASION. Springfield, IL:
       Charles C. Thomas, 1987. xv, 144 pp.

       Discusses one of the main issues regarding the new cults, namely
       whether their members are converts who have freely chosen a new
       lifestyle and worldview or whether they have been coerced into
       their new belief system. The authors do not accept the view that
       "coercive techniques like those used by the communists in the
       fifties are responsible for the success of modern cults and sects"
       (p. 30). They distinguish between coercion and persuasion and

argue that no mysterious forces are necessary to account for either
conversion or deprogramming and that ordinary processes are employed by destructive cults to change people's attitudes. Several
strategies of destructive persuasion, such as the manipulation of
needs and the control of information, and several principles of
indoctrination are outlined. A final chapter discusses the legal
issues involved.

847. Kent, Stephen A. "Slogan Changers to Mantra Chanters: A Mertonian
      Deviance Analysis of Conversion to Religiously Ideological Orga-
      nizations in the Early 1970s." SOCIOLOGICAL ANALYSIS 49 (1988):
      104-118.

      Explores various reasons why people participating in the social
      protests of the 1960's became involved in new religious movements.
      Questioning the commonly held interpretation that the crisis of
      moral meaning was the major cause of the upheaval, the author sug-
      gests instead that the causal factor was "a crisis of meaning with-
      in the political counterculture" (p. 107). In his view, the parti-
      cipants in the new religions are adopting the same means to achieve
      the same goal they had pursued in the counterculture movement by
      changing the focus of discontent from the social to the individual.
      The resource mobilization theory is used to explain the cults as
      deviant social movements.

848. Kent, Stephen A. "Puritan Radicalism and the New Religious Move-
      ments: Seventeenth-Century England and Contemporary America."
      RELIGION AND BELIEF SYSTEMS (item 701), pp. 3-46.

      Identifies the many comparisons scholars have made between seven-
      teenth-century Puritan cults and the new religions of the last two
      decades, and then applies an expanded version of the relative depri-
      vation theory to explain the phenomena. The author first describes
      the emergence of such groups as the Quakers and Ranters in England
      and maintains that "a collectively held sense of frustration in
      relation to unfulfilled societal reforms can generate millenarian
      movements" (p. 18). Then he examines the rise of the new cults
      with special reference to the Hare Krishna Movement, the Divine
      Light Mission, and Transcendental Meditation, and concludes that
      the members of these groups had lost hope in the efforts of the
      1960's to implement fundamental social and political changes. The
      reaction to the rise of new movements was similar in both histori-
      cal periods and can also be explained by the deprivation theory.

849. Kerr, Howard, and Charles C. Crow, editors. THE OCCULT IN AMERICA:
      NEW HISTORICAL PERSPECTIVES. Urbana: University of Illinois
      Press, 1983. 246 pp.

      Presents a collection of essays on the occult that is explored
      from a variety of historical and methodological perspectives.
      These studies cover a wide range of occult theory and practice,
      including the Salem witchcraft trials, Spiritualism, Theosophy,
      and UFOs.

      Contains items 560, 1392, 1722.

850.   Kilbourne, Brock K., and James T. Richardson. "Paradigm Conflict,
       Types of Conversion, and Conversion Theories." SOCIOLOGICAL
       ANALYSIS 50 (1988): 1-21.

       Examines two perspectives that dominate research on conversion
       to new religious movements, namely: 1) the active vs. the passive
       (where the convert is seen either as an agent in one's own reli-
       gious change or as merely an individual influenced by outside
       forces); and 2) the the intraindividual and interindividual (where
       the factors that influence conversion are conceived as coming from
       within the individual or from contacts with outsiders). The
       authors construct a typology of conversion and propose a theory
       that would "always involve some choice of perspective by both the
       convert and the observer" (p. 15). A basic bibliography is added
       (pp. 18-21).

851.   Kilbourne, Brock K., and James T. Richardson. "Social Experimenta-
       tion: Self Process or Social Role." INTERNATIONAL JOURNAL OF
       SOCIAL PSYCHIATRY 31 (1985): 13-22.

       Proposes an alternative social-psychological view of Robert Lif-
       ton's self-process notion of "protean man" to describe the social
       experimentation that takes place when people join new religious,
       cultic, and self-growth movements in America. A role-theory per-
       spective is judged to be a better model for understanding these
       movements. The authors defining the social role of the experi-
       menter, describe some of its main features, and examine the socio-
       cultural system that supports it. The role of the person who joins
       a new cult fits into a contemporary society that has moved from
       product consumption to experience consumption, a novel situation
       where experiences are available in the open marketplace.

852.   King, Winston L. "Eastern Religions: A New Interest and Influ-
       ence." ANNALS OF THE AMERICAN ACADEMY OF POLITICAL AND SOCIAL
       SCIENCE 387 (1970): 66-76.

       Describes the new climate of interest in, and openness to, Asian
       religions and proposes the following three steps to understanding
       this phenomenon and its implications: 1) a study of American reli-
       gion and its cultural situation; 2) an exploration of contemporary
       American needs that the religions of the East might satisfy; and 3)
       an estimation of the nature and depth of Eastern religious influ-
       ence in America. Uncertainty about classical Christian theology
       and secular utopianism, coupled with a distrust of intellectualism
       and an alienation from nature, make the West amenable to Eastern
       influences. The stress on experience, intuition, and relationship
       with nature are the Eastern elements that attract people in Western
       countries. Though Eastern religiosity has become a possible option,
       the author thinks that it is still too alien to survive intact in a
       largely Judeo-Christian environment.

853.   Knudsen, Dean D., John R. Earl, and Donald W. Shriver. "The Con-
       ception of Sectarian Religion: An Effort at Clarification."
       REVIEW OF RELIGIOUS RESEARCH 20 (1978): 44-60.

Endeavors to clarify the essential features of sectarianism by an investigation of four religious groups in Gastonia, North Carolina, namely the Renewal Center, The Chapel of Faith, St. Mark House of God, and the Holy Spirit Church. Each group is briefly described and the differences in organizational and leadership patterns identified. To what degree the various sociological features of sectarianism are applicable to these groups is discussed. The author proposes a definition of a sect that has exclusive membership based on religious experience and a total ideology of life and ethics.

854. Kvideland, Karin. "New Religions and Old Definitions." TEMENOS 16 (1980): 62-67.

Contributes to the debate about the religiousness of the cults. The author holds that the new movements conform to the anthropological definition of religion as a culturally based and transmitted system of beliefs, values, and actions that revolve around the idea of a supernatural being. New religions cannot be adequately analyzed by traditional models of religion. Some theoretical suggestions for studying the new movements are offered.

855. Langone, Michael D. "Cultism and American Culture." CULTIC STUDIES JOURNAL 3 (1986): 157-72.

Contends that the cults are in direct conflict with the very basis of American culture. The following six fundamental values that cults oppose are outlined: 1) life, liberty, and the pursuit of happiness ; 2) freedom; 3) connectedness; 4) common sense; 5) tolerance; and 6) fair play. The author makes several suggestions for coping with the cultic challenge.

856. Lanternari, Vittorio. "Nativistic and Socio-Religious Movements: A Reconsideration." COMPARATIVE STUDIES IN SOCIETY AND HISTORY 16 (1974): 483-503.

Distinguishes between movements that have come into being in tribal, colonial, and oppressed societies and those that arose in medieval and modern Western societies. The former, which the author calls "exogenous" and "acculturative," arose as a response to specific social factors, like slavery, colonization, political, social, and economic exploitation and dominion, and racial segregation. The latter, called "endogenous" and "non-acculturative," are a reaction to the process of intense sociocultural change and internal conflict. The author lists over 30 labels which have been used to designate and identify these various movements and assesses the theories and classificatory schemes that have been proposed by scholars. Though written largely in the context of religious movements in nonliterate societies, this essay includes reflections on medieval and modern European sects and provides basic materials for comparisons with more recent movements. A short bibliography of major writings is included (pp. 599-503)

857. Leininger, C. Earl. "The Dynamics of Conversion: Toward a Working Model." PERSPECTIVES IN RELIGIOUS STUDIES 2 (1975): 192-202.

Distinguishes four types of religious conversions, namely psycho-social, restrictive, limited, and comprehensive. The author holds that the comprehensive conversion represents real conversion, which means personality integration. Such a conversion must also be holistic and progressive and include a variety of experiences.

858.   Levine, Edward M. "Religious Cults: A Social-Psychiatric Analysis." SCIENTIFIC RESEARCH AND NEW RELIGIONS: DIVERGENT PERSPECTIVES (item 645), pp. 114-22.

Contends that cult members do not become converts through a reasoned understanding of cult ideology and that cult leaders are not genuine religious personages. Most sociological studies on the cults are dismissed as being pro-cultist in orientation since they ignore the evidence that shows that cults misuse reason and manipu-late and abuse their members. The author admits that the cults are "symptoms of the deterioration of basic values and of the weakness of the middle-class family" (p. 121). In contemporary society young adults too often fail to achieve a sound sense of identity and develop a sense of anomie, thus becoming vulnerable to cults.

859.   Levine, Edward M. "The Motives Behind Cult Converts and Cult Lead-ers." UPDATE: A QUARTERLY JOURNAL OF NEW RELIGIOUS MOVEMENTS 9.4 (1985): 11-23.

Argues that an examination of the motives of cult leaders is necessary for understanding the nature of the new cults. Several incentives used to attract prospective members are reviewed. The author thinks that those who are drawn to the cults fall under three categories, namely: 1) those who have "unresolved dependency needs" that originated in their childhood; 2) those who are ideal-istic and deeply concerned with modern social problems; and 3) those who are intellectually searching for a new identity. Cult leaders, in the author's view, are authoritarian personalities who want to dominate others and gain material wealth. The medical model is necessary for understanding the real issue in cultism.

860.   Lewis, James R. "Reconstructing the 'Cult' Experience: Post-Involvement Attitudes as a Function of Mode of Exit and Post-Involvement Socialization." SOCIOLOGICAL ANALYSIS 47 (1986): 151-59.

Reports on a survey of 154 ex-members of controversial religious movements, mainly the Unification Church, the Hare Krishna Move-ment, and the Healthy, Happy, and Holy Organization (3HO), who left the cult either without exit counseling or with some form of volun-tary or involuntary counseling. The age at the time of involvement, the duration of membership, and the time lapse between their exit and the completion of the questionnaire are among the data recorded. Cult stereotypes about deception, brainwashing, and leadership style, as well as the attitude of ex-members towards their previous commitment to the cults, are explored. The author concludes that ex-members who hold negative, stereotypical attitudes towards the cult they belonged to left through forced counseling and have been exposed to the socializing influences of the Anti-Cult Movement.

861.   Lewis, Warren. "Coming-Again: How Society Functions Through Its
        Religious Movements." NEW RELIGIOUS MOVEMENTS: A PERSPECTIVE FOR
        UNDERSTANDING SOCIETY (item 551), pp. 191-215.

        Argues that new religious movements are an expression of "society
        seeking the resolution of its own cultural needs" (p. 207). The
        author sees a pattern in which new religions come into being, then
        experience rejection by society, and finally adapt themselves to
        the culture from which they sprang. In the U.S.A., the nineteenth
        century saw the rise of millenarianism and social reformism in the
        context of the war between the states. The twentieth century is
        experiencing a wave of new religions under the threat of an expand-
        ing communism. The Unification Church is cited as an example of an
        anti-Communist organization that sees itself embarking on a defen-
        sive war of righteousness.

862.   Liebman, Charles S. "Extremism as a Religious Norm." JOURNAL FOR
        THE SCIENTIFIC STUDY OF RELIGION 22 (1983): 75-86.

        Maintains that religious extremism, rather than moderation, is
        the norm that requires explanation. Within the context of Judaism
        in Israel, three dimensions of religious extremism are proposed:
        1) the expansion of religious laws; 2) social isolation; and 3)
        cultural rejection. Religious extremism is entirely consistent
        with basic religious tenets and authentic religious orientations.
        The rise of modern Jewish extremists is discussed and the decline
        of religious moderation accounted for. Total commitment reflects
        and supports an extreme orientation. Because religion claims
        absolute truth about ultimate reality, it rejects other views and
        leads to fanaticism.

863.   Lofland, John. "Crowd Joys." URBAN LIFE 10 (1982): 355-81.

        Draws attention to crowd behavior that is characterized by either
        sacred or profane joy. Sacred joys are those to which a sacred
        meaning is ascribed and are subdivided, in declining order of
        arousal, into ecstatic upheavals, conventions and congregations,
        euphoric moods, and revivalist behavior. Profane crowd joys can be
        revelous, exciting, adoring, ersatz, revivalist, and comic. The
        ritual services at the Zion Tabernacle Church and at a snake-handl-
        ing Pentecostal group are examples of ecstatic joy, the Bruderhof's
        decision-making process an example of euphoric mood, and a Billy
        Graham   crusade an example of a revivalist congregation. The
        Unification Church combines elements of an ecstatic congregation,
        the euphoric mood, and the revival meeting. The author suggests
        that the rarity of crowds joys and our inability to understand them
        might explain the appeal of "brainwashing," "programming," and
        "snapping" notions of affiliation with new religions.

864.   Lofland, John, and James T. Richardson. "Religious Movement Orga-
        nizations: Elemental Forms and Dynamics." RESEARCH IN SOCIAL
        MOVEMENTS, CONFLICTS, AND CHANGE 7 (1984): 29-51.

        Endeavors to outline the most fundamental and generic forms of
        religious organizations in order to clarify some of the issues that
        have arisen in the wake of a recent surge of new religious move-

ments. The authors suggest that the basic units are to be found in
the "corporateness" of each movement whose members share income,
residence, food provision, support, and faith sharing. The five
basic forms, in order of increasing corporateness, are identified
as follows: clinic; congregation; collective; corps; and colony.
The authors discuss the dynamics of religious movement organization
and maintain that the concepts of ·"cult" and "sect" are too general and imprecise.

865. Lofland, John, and Norman Skonovd. "Patterns of Conversion." OF
      GODS AND MEN (item 550), pp. 1-24.

      Develops in some depth the authors' views presented in a
      previously published paper (see item 866).

866. Lofland, John, and Norman Skonovd. "Conversion Motifs." JOURNAL
      FOR THE SCIENTIFIC STUDY OF RELIGION 20 (1981): 373-85.

      Distinguishes, in the context of new religious movements, six
      conversion motifs: 1) intellectual; 2) mystical; 3) experimental;
      4) affectional; 5) revivalist; and 6) coercive. These in turn are
      related to five major variations: 1) degree of social pressure; 2)
      temporal duration; 3) level of affective arousal; 4) affective
      content; and 5) belief-participation sequence. Coercive conversion
      "entails an extremely high degree of external pressure over a rela-
      tively long period of time, during which there is intense arousal
      of fear and uncertainty, culminating in empathetic identification
      and even love" (p. 383). Several sociopsychological and socio-
      historical implications of conversion are discussed.

867. Long, Theodore E. "Prophecy, Charisma, and Politics: Reinterpret-
      ing the Weberian Thesis." PROPHETIC RELIGIONS AND POLITICS (item
      358), pp. 3-17.

      Sums up the common sociological interpretation of Weber's view
      on prophecy and politics (see items 139-40) in the statement that
      "prophecy is conceived as a special form of leadership which gains
      significance as an agent of social change" (p. 4). The author con-
      tends that such an interpretation is both misleading and incomplete.
      Three main areas of inquiry are pursued: 1) the meaning of prophecy
      and charisma; 2) the social location of prophecy (where the sources,
      conditions, and institutional locus of prophecy are examined); and
      3) the social and political relevance of prophecy (where the revo-
      lutionary force and consequences of prophecy and the ways it gains
      relevance are discussed). The development of prophecy depends on
      historical and situational factors as well as on its emergence
      trajectory and the response given to it.

868. Long, Theodore E., and Jeffrey K. Hadden. "Religious Conversion
      and the Concept of Socialization: Integrating the Brainwashing
      and Drift Models." JOURNAL FOR THE SCIENTIFIC STUDY OF RELIGION
      22 (1983): 1-14.

      Argues that both conversion models of brainwashing and gradual
      drift are partially correct, but they rely on a faulty paradigm of
      socialization as internalization and social learning. The authors

redefine socialization to include the following three central components: 1) the nature and requirements of membership; 2) the participants in the socialization process; and 3) the creating and
incorporating activities. They attempt to show, by outlining the
process of socialization in the Unification Church, that the brainwashing and drift models are both employed. Unification Church
methods create a stumbling block to long-term affiliation, but
have been successful in fostering strong, initial commitment. A
strategy for studying conversion is outlined.

869. Long, Theodore E., and Jeffrey K. Hadden, editors. "Sects, Cults,
      and Religious Movements." SOCIOLOGICAL ANALYSIS 40 (1979): 280-82.

      Introduces a special issue of this journal dedicated to the study
      of past and present religious movements. Besides several essays
      discussing theoretical issues of cult formation and significance,
      two recent movements, namely the Unification Church, and the
      People's Temple, receive special attention.

      Contains items 571, 694, 740, 924, 1172, 1787, 2203.

870. Lynch, Frederick R. "Toward a Theory of Conversion and Commitment
      to the Occult." AMERICAN BEHAVIORAL SCIENTIST 20 (1977): 887-908.

      Constructs "a descriptive framework for studying conversion and
      commitment to the occult" (p. 888). The methodological procedures
      and theoretical framework the author used to study the Church of
      the Sun, a pseudonym for an occult organization, are briefly out-
      lined. A short account of the history and organization of the
      church and the social characteristics of its members and ex-members
      is provided. The complex conversion and commitment process takes
      place in four stages over a period of several years. These stages
      are identified as follows: intellectual curiosity, emotional con-
      viction, contact with charismatic occultists or attendance at an
      occult session, and joining the occult community. The author
      maintains that the contemporary "occult explosion" facilitates
      conversion and commitment to occult organizations.

871. Machalek, Richard, and David A. Snow. "Neglected Issues in the
      Study of Conversion." SCIENTIFIC RESEARCH AND NEW RELIGIONS:
      DIVERGENT PERSPECTIVES (item 645), pp. 123-29.

      Discusses the possibility of constructing general process models
      of conversion and analyzing it from a macrosociological point of
      view. The authors suggest that, because conversion (like divorce)
      can be studied not only as an occurrence that happens to individ-
      uals, but also as a form of collective behavior, its rates can be
      understood as a function of the social structure. They maintain
      that specifying the causes of conversion does not by itself help us
      understand the phenomenon. The meaning of conversion, the accounts
      given by converts, and the social aspects of conversion must all be
      taken into consideration.

872. Maron, Neil, and Joel Braverman. "Family Environment as a Factor
      of Vulnerability to Cult Involvement." CULTIC STUDIES JOURNAL 5
      (1988): 23-43.

Investigates the role of the family as a predisposing factor in
cult involvement. The authors assess the family environments "as
retrospectively perceived by the parents, prior to their offspring's
cult membership" (p. 25). The main cults included in this study
are the Unification Church, the Children of God, Scientology, the
Divine Light Mission, the Hare Krishna Movement, and the Way International. Cult involvement, the authors conclude is not related to
family factors. The typical recruit is a person who has experienced a stressful event within the last 12 months.

873.   Martin, David. "A Definition of Cult: Terms and Approaches."
        ALTERNATIVES TO AMERICAN MAINLINE CHURCHES (item 603), pp. 27-42.

Offers a "critical but sympathetic commentary" on Stark and Bainbridge's theory of cults (see item 966), concentrating on the meanings assigned to the terms "church' and "cult." The author argues
that the state of being in tension with the environment, a quality
so often assigned to cults, is an important attribute that requires
some clarification and specification. The view that holds that
cults are novel and foreign is also questioned. It is maintained
that individualism is the fundamental criterion that distinguishes
cults from other religious groups. Cults differ from sects because
they (the cults) are more congruent with modern individualism and
not group-oriented.

874.   Martin, David. "Disorientations to Mainstream Religion: The Con-
        text of Reorientations in New Religious Movements." THE SOCIAL
        IMPACT OF THE NEW RELIGIOUS MOVEMENTS (item 725), pp. 43-58.

Relates the rise of new religious movements to the declining
social influence and increasing organizational uncertainty of, and
disorientation within, the mainline traditions, coupled with an
increase of doctrinal diversity. These trends are organized around
three major themes: 1) bureaucracy and charisma; 2) ecumenicity and
fragmentation; and 3) liturgical change and politicization. Quot-
ing examples from Great Britain, the author shows how the new religious movements, like the Charismatic Renewal and the Unification
Church, provide reorientation for those who find that the religion
of their upbringing was unable to meet their expectations, to provide hope for their disillusionment, and to offer a comprehensive
explanation of life.

875.   Martin, David. "Revived Dogma and Cult." DAEDALUS 111.1 (1982):
        53-71.

Examines the evangelical revival within the Protestant churches
in the context of the liberalized Christian tradition, which is
experiencing a decline in Northern Europe. This revival is also
seen in the background of the cultural upheavals of the 1960's.
Some reflections are offered about the rise of the Moral Majority,
the Catholic Charismatic Renewal, the House Church Movement, and on
the new cults like the Unification Church, the Children of God, the
Hare Krishna Movement, and Transcendental Meditation. The new
movements draw "the young in comprehensive, total loyalties" and
have the "capacity to attract idealists who seek a purpose to life,
and even to history" (p. 67).

876.   Marty, Martin E. "Old New Religions and New Old Religions." NE-
       BRASKA HUMANIST 8.2 (1985): 9-16.

       Distinguishes between "old new religions," (those imported ones
       that are new to America), and "new old religions," (those Christian
       evangelical revivals that have occurred several times in the his-
       tory of the West). The author seeks an understanding of both
       groups in the disarray of secular society, in people's quest for
       spiritual meaning and solace, and in cultural revolution that
       favors those religions that exploit spiritual resources.

877.   Marty, Martin E. "Transpositions: American Religion in the 1980s."
       ANNALS OF THE AMERICAN ACADEMY OF POLITICAL AND SOCIAL SCIENCE
       480 (July 1985): 11-23.

       Points out that the major religious event of the last decade has
       been the change in both religious and secular forces and movements,
       a change typified by the disarray of secularists, the aggressive-
       ness of Protestant evangelical moralism, and the entry of extraor-
       dinary religion into the mainstream of American life. The author
       argues that the injection of new religions creates an opportunity
       for appraisal.

878.   Marx, John H., and Burkart Holzner. "The Social Construction of
       Strain and Ideological Models of Grievance in Contemporary Reli-
       gious Movements." PACIFIC SOCIOLOGICAL REVIEW 20 (1977): 411-38.

       Endeavors to formulate a paradigm of stress or strain that has
       been popular in the explanation of socioreligious movements. The
       main point of the authors is that "both individual psychological
       stress and collective social strain are socially constructed, sub-
       jectively experienced, interpretative (meaning) systems that sym-
       bolically define problematic or dissatisfying experiences and con-
       ditions as structurally determined injustices" (p. 412). The
       strain model is criticized as inadequate. In the authors' view,
       those who join a new religious movement participated in a socially
       constructed personal strain leading to a personal and collectively
       shared anger.

879.   Marx, John H., and Burkart Holzner. "Ideological Primary Groups in
       Contemporary Cultural Movements." SOCIOLOGICAL FOCUS 8 (1975):
       311-29.

       Examines the unique features of contemporary ideological move-
       ments from a "social construction of reality" perspective. Among
       these new movements are included the Jesus Movement, the Women's
       Liberation Movement, and the Sensitivity Training-Encounter Move-
       ments. These new groups "reflect a synthesis of previously incom-
       patible attributes associated with 'ideological groups,' 'primary
       groups,' and intensive (Sensitivity-Training Encounter) groups"
       (pp. 313-14). The main characteristics of ideological primary
       groups are described and their latent functions and significance
       explored. Such groups are seen as "legitimate contexts for
       intentional adult resocialization or identity transformation and
       reconstruction among 'normals'" (p. 325).

880.   Mayer, Jean-François. "The Emergence of a New Religiosity in the
        Western World." NEW RELIGIOUS MOVEMENTS AND THE CHURCHES (item
        577), pp. 60-68.

        Suggests that the new religious movements indicate a "mutation of
        the sacred" rather than a return to the sacred, because "religious
        feelings are now being expressed--albeit with some skepticism and
        in a diluted form--in areas where they had not been customary in
        the West" (p. 61). The author thinks that the new movements ex-
        press some common, universal, and synthesizing themes and attempt
        to go beyond traditional religions rather than oppose them. The
        stress on experience, a central theme in most new religions, is
        said to be behind the shift from the religious to the therapeutic.

881.   Mayrl, William W. "Marx's Theory of Social Movements and the
        Church-Sect Typology." SOCIOLOGICAL ANALYSIS 37 (1976): 19-31.

        Shows that Marxism shares some organizational and doctrinal fea-
        tures with some utopian religious movements and proposes that Mar-
        xist theory itself can explain this similarity. The Marxist theory
        of praxis and the traditional church-sect theory with some recent
        developments are briefly described. The author thinks that the
        works of Weber (item 140), Troeltsch (item 134), and Niebuhr (item
        119) provide a useful model for understanding Marxism. While Marx-
        ist theory gives a general view of social reality, the church-sect
        typology accounts for common tendencies in all movements of social
        change.

882.   McGuire, Meredith B. RELIGION: THE SOCIAL CONTEXT. Belmont, CA:
        Wadsworth Publishing Co., 1981. xii, 297.

        Presents a standard textbook on the sociology of religion, dis-
        cussing such topics as: 1) religion, social cohesion, and conflict;
        2) the impact of religion on social change; 3) secularization;
        4) official and unofficial religion; and 5) the dynamics of reli-
        gious organizations and groups. New religious movements are
        included in the last-mentioned topic. The typology of religious
        groups into churches, denominations, sects, and cults is discussed.
        Three social factors--deprivation, social dislocation, and socio-
        economic change--are said to be important in the formation of sects
        and cults. The processes through which a religious group or cult
        is transformed into another type of organization are outlined, with
        particular reference to the theory of movement organization. Var-
        ious religious movements, especially the Catholic Charismatic re-
        newal and Silva Mind Control, are quoted as examples.

883.   Melton, J. Gordon. "How New Is New?: The Flowering of the 'New'
        Religious Consciousness since 1965." THE FUTURE OF NEW RELIGIOUS
        MOVEMENTS (item 579), pp. 46-56.

        Outlines briefly the alternative religious tradition in America
        and the increased presence of Eastern religions since the Oriental
        Exclusion Act, which forbade Asians from immigrating to the U.S.A.,
        was repealed by President Johnson in 1965. Three developments in
        the scientific community have contributed to the growth of new
        religions in the last two decades: 1) the growth of parapsychology;

2) the discovery of LSD and its mind-altering effects; and 3) contemporary developments in psychiatry and psychology (e.g., psychosynthesis) that led to an openness to alternative religions. The author's view is that the new religions have been part of the American scene for over 150 years and that the so-called new religious movements represent nothing else but the growing presence of alternative religions in Western culture.

884. Melton, J. Gordon. "Spiritualization and Re-affirmation: What Really Happens When Prophecy Fails." AMERICAN STUDIES 26.2 (1985): 17-29.

Discusses the problems that millennial groups face when predicted events fail to transpire and argues that the way devotees or adherents cope with these problems reveal basic religious dynamics. The author discusses the issues in the context of Festinger's book WHEN PROPHECY FAILS (item 91). The theory that the adherents of such groups try to reduce their dissonance by intensifying their proselytization efforts is evaluated by an examination of the cultural and societal responses. The author concludes that Festinger's theory has not been confirmed by later studies (for example, on the Millerites). It is pointed out that what appears to be failure to outsiders may not be the case with members of millennial groups such as Jehovah's Witnesses, the Worldwide Church of God, and the Children of God. These groups tend to spiritualize the prophecy and to reaffirm their faith and lifestyle.

885. Melton, J. Gordon, and Robert L. Moore. THE CULT EXPERIENCE: RESPONDING TO THE NEW RELIGIOUS PLURALISM. New York: Pilgrim Press, 1982. x, 180 pp.

Discusses some of the major issues, such as conversion and deprogramming, in connection with the new cults and presents an overall theory for understanding their emergence in contemporary Western culture. The authors borrow the anthropological theory on rites of passage and interpret the new movements as a transformation process in three stages: the psychosocial state prior to transition, the transition stage (liminality), and the psychosocial state after transition. An appendix gives brief summary descriptions of the major cults.

886. Moellering, Ralph. "Ancient and Modern Gnosticism." CURRENTS IN THEOLOGY AND MISSION 10 (1983): 221-32.

Interprets the rise of the new religious movements as a resurgence of Gnosticism. The author outlines the origins and main features of ancient Gnosticism and then shows how modern cults, among which he includes Theosophy, Rosicrucianism, the Unification Church, the Hare Krishna Movement, Scientology, and Satanism, express gnostic beliefs. Though largely theological in scope, this essay indirectly points out that the new religions may not be very new.

887. Mol, J. J. "Secularization and Cohesion." REVIEW OF RELIGIOUS RESEARCH 11 (1970): 183-91.

Distinguishes between cultural and institutional secularization, the former concept used in research that focuses on religion as an independent variable, the latter in research which considers religion as a dependent variable. The phenomena and findings that support this distinction are examined. Pentecostal sects in Latin America, Charismatics in the U.S.A., and other denominations in Australia and New Zealand are among the groups considered. Major counterforces (like church attendance and religious education) to the secularization of religious institutions are discussed. The author questions whether the secularization process is irreversible.

888.   Moore, R. Lawrence. RELIGIOUS OUTSIDERS AND THE MAKING OF AMERICA. New York; Oxford University Press, 1986. xv, 263 pp.

Discusses the religious pluralistic scene in American history, focusing on the significance and nature of the many sects that have appeared since the nineteenth century. In the first part of his book, the author pays attention to the relationship between ethnicity, outsider religion, and American identity in the context of three religious groups, namely the Mormons, the Catholics, and the Jews. In the second part he analyzes what he calls the "religions of the average American," among which he includes Christian Science, millennial sects, and Black churches. The author maintains that these religions are not deviations, but rather normal ways in which Americans have invested their lives with meaning. Civil Religion is briefly discussed in a postscript. Though largely historical in orientation, this book treats the rise of new religions as part of American culture.

889.   Morrison, Denton E. "Some Notes Toward Theory on Relative Deprivation, Social Movements, and Social Change." AMERICAN BEHAVIORAL SCIENTIST 14 (1971): 675-90.

Argues that much of the evidence linking the rise of social movements to relative deprivation is indirect. The proponents of the theory of religious deprivation have little to say on absolute deprivation and on the structural conditions that gives rise to it. The author attempts to elaborate the theory by stating that the desires of those who are deprived "must become 1) legitimate expectations that are 2) perceived as blocked" (p. 677). Religious deprivations involve a type of cognitive dissonance. They result in involvement in new religious movements when different options to resolve the dissonance are rejected and the individuals feel hampered by the larger society to attain their wishes. The structural conditions necessary for the emergence of social movements are outlined and the problems of recruitment of members and effective growth discussed. Social movements bring about social change, but social change itself creates relative deprivation, which is the reason why social movements come into being.

890.   Murvar, Vatro. "Towards a Sociological Theory of Religious Movements." JOURNAL FOR THE SCIENTIFIC STUDY OF RELIGION 14 (1975): 229-56.

Shows how one can compare the revolutionary function of various religious movements in different countries and historical eras within the Christian cultural context. The basic distinction,

namely the ecclesia versus the sect (or monasticism versus sectarianism), is discussed. Early Christianity, the Donatist religious
movement, third-century monasticism, Western monasticism, and four-
teenth-century movements of apostolic poverty, and many other religious uprisings in Europe before and during the Reformation, are
all interpreted as protest movements challenging religious and
social structures. The features of these new religious groups are
identified. The author holds that his research supports Weber's
qualified, tentative, and neutral position (items 139-40) rather
than Durkheim's dogmatic, value-loaded statements.

891. Murvar, Vatro. "Nontheistic Systems of Belief: An Urgently Needed
      Conceptual Tool." AMERICAN BEHAVIORAL SCIENTIST 16 (1972):
      169-94.

      Points out that messianism is a great force in the present world
      and attempts to account, mainly in terms of Marxist theory, for
      political, but "religion-like" messianic belief systems that come
      into being as responses to the need for social change. Three major
      types of nontheistic systems of belief are outlined: 1) nationalism;
      2) revolutionary messianism; and 3) contemporary messianic move-
      ments in America. The following characteristics of revolutionary
      messianism are described: 1) the search for purpose, meaning, and
      destiny in life; 2) dogmatism, exclusiveness, and intolerance;
      3) elitism; 4) totalism; 5) asceticism and martyrdom; 6) guilt and
      expiation; and 7) apocalyptic vision.

892. Nelsen, Hart A. "Sectarianism, World View, and Anomie." SOCIAL
      FORCES 51 (1972): 226-33.

      Starts with the assumption that "religion is related to social
      classes and additional variables involved in the formation of one's
      world view" (p. 226). The author's position is that sectarianism
      is not a direct result of economic deprivation or the state of
      anomie, but rather a reflection of the worldview of simplistic
      people from the lower classes and from rural areas. This theory is
      tested in the context of Presbyterians in Southern Appalachia. It
      is concluded that sectarianism is inversely related to social class,
      level of literacy, and place of residence.

893. Nelson, Geoffrey K. CULTS, NEW RELIGIONS, AND RELIGIOUS CREATIVITY.
      London: Routledge and Kegan Paul, 1987. vii, 245 pp.

      Endeavors to develop a theoretical synthesis of the studies on
      new religious movements since World War II and to arrive at an
      understanding of the causes and consequences of this unparalleled
      period in religious activity. The following issues are discussed:
      1) why did these movements emerge at this particular time?; 2) what
      are the common factors leading to their emergence?; 3) what are
      their functions?; and 4) how do they grow, decline, and cease to
      exist? One chapter discusses the traditional sociological typology
      of sect and cult and modern attempts to correct its weaknesses,
      while another chapter deals with parapsychology and the sociology
      of religion. The author stresses human creativity, which tradi-
      tional religions tend to suppress. A substantial bibliography (pp.
      213-40) is appended.

894.   Nelson, Geoffrey K. "Cults and New Religions: Towards a Sociology
            of Religious Creativity." SOCIOLOGY AND SOCIAL RESEARCH 68
            (1984): 301-25.

        Critically reviews recent studies of new religious movements in
        the West. The following five problematic areas of investigation
        are distinguished: 1) the factors that gave rise to these move-
        ments; 2) the social conditions that lead to the current wave of
        religious creativity; 3) the manner in which new members are re-
        cruited; 4) the reason for the success of some of these movements;
        and 5) the organization adopted to achieve their goals. The author
        states that "the emergence of new religious movements is a final
        stage of the process of emergence of a non-materialistic economic
        ethic that is a necessary precondition for the successful estab-
        lishment of a stable post-industrial society" (p. 313).

895.   Nock, David A. "Cult, Sect, and Church in Canada: A Re-Examination
            of Stark and Bainbridge." CANADIAN REVIEW OF SOCIOLOGY AND
            ANTHROPOLOGY 24 (1987): 514-24.

        Evaluates the contribution of Stark and Bainbridge to the socio-
        logical theory of cult and sect (see item 961) and attempts to
        replicate their research by a careful examination of the Canadian
        scene. According to the author, the evidence sustains the view
        that, also in Canada, the "development of cults is directly corre-
        lated with the growth of irreligion" (p. 519). Spiritualism,
        Theosophy, Baha'ism, New Thought, Mormonism, and Paganism are the
        main cults considered.

896.   O'Toole, Roger. "'Underground' Traditions in the Study of Sectari-
            anism: Non-Religious Uses of the Concept 'Sect.'" JOURNAL FOR
            THE SCIENTIFIC STUDY OF RELIGION 15 (1976): 145-56.

        Examines the usage of the word "sect" in a non-religious context
        by two sociological traditions, namely Marxist sociology and the
        Chicago school of collective behavior. It is held that comparison
        between religious and nonreligious sects is necessary for under-
        standing sectarianism, which can be located in many areas of human
        life, including politics, art, literature, and science.

897.   O'Toole, Roger. "Some Social-Psychological Aspects of Sectarian
            Social Movements." INTERNATIONAL YEARBOOK FOR THE SOCIOLOGY OF
            RELIGION 9 (1975): 162-99.

        Explores the social-psychological features of political sects,
        claiming that their study has important consequences on the study
        of all new movements. Some sectarian characteristics can be found
        in both religious and nonreligious contexts. The author focuses
        on two late-1960's political sects (namely the Internationalists
        and the Socialist Workers Party) in Toronto, Canada. He covers
        such areas as the process of conversion, the maintenance of commit-
        ment, the satisfaction of membership, and the aftermath of the
        failure of prophecy.

898.   Pace, Enzo. "New Paradigms of Popular Religion." ARCHIVES DE
            SCIENCES SOCIALES DES RELIGIONS 64.1 (1987): 7-14.

Maintains that changes in society demand different approaches to
new religions. Three characteristics are said to distinguish modern Western culture: 1) a loss of unifying center; 2) the fluidity
of the divisions between social strata; and 3) the emergence of new
forms of social discrimination. One way of solving the conflicts
that arise in a highly complex society is the formation of religious groups that conform to the type Troeltsch called "mysticism"
(item 134). The author thinks that participation in mysticism
creates fellowship for those struggling with an identity crisis.

899.   Pattison, E. Mansell, and Robert C. Ness. "New Religious Movements
       in Historical Perspective." CULTS AND NEW RELIGIOUS MOVEMENTS
       (item 611), pp. 43-83.

       Relies on insights from history, sociology, political science,
       and anthropology to develop a sociological and historical perspec-
       tive on new religious movements. The following areas are pursued
       in the authors' lengthy analysis: 1) the nature of fundamental
       social relationships; 2) the increasing complexity of society and
       the consequent repercussions on religious forms; 3) the relation-
       ship between religion, politics, and social organization and the
       influence of this relationship on the formation of cults and sects;
       4) the way in which religious forms in contemporary America reflect
       social and political organizations; and 5) the question of distin-
       guishing between fact and value (or professional and ideological)
       assessment of religious movements. Included in the authors' study
       are nineteenth-century sects and many contemporary movements, such
       as Eastern religious groups, UFO cults, Satanism, Witchcraft, and
       the Charismatic Renewal. A brief outline of the geographic distri-
       bution of sects and cults is given.

900.   Payne, Barbara P., and Kirk W. Elifson. "Commitment: A Comment on
       Uses of the Concept." REVIEW OF RELIGIOUS RESEARCH 17 (1976):
       209-215.

       Reflects on the use of the concept of commitment by sociologists
       of religion and social scientists in general. The major works in
       the field are reviewed and contrasted. Nonreligious commitment
       usually refers to a consistent and/or focused line of action or to
       a new way of life. It may also be described in terms of penalties
       and costs and may contain an element of conformity and control.
       Students of religious commitment have often relied on Glock's five
       dimensions of religiosity (see item 95). The authors think that
       the relationship between belief and commitment, the consequences of
       commitment, and the possibility of conflicting commitments are
       areas that require further investigation.

901.   Prince, Raymond H. "Cocoon Work: An Interpretation of the Concern
       of Contemporary Youth With the Mystical." RELIGIOUS MOVEMENTS IN
       CONTEMPORARY AMERICA (item 727), pp. 255-71.

       Discusses the development of the movement towards mysticism and
       interprets it as a self-imposed rite of passage. The author de-
       scribes the mystical experience and traces the modern mystical move-
       ment from the nineteenth-century Transcendentalists to the late

1960's. Modern youth's interest in the mystical is related to the
rejecting of materialistic values, to developing of interpersonal
relationships, and to communal lifestyles. Because of the increasing separation of the phases of childhood and adulthood in American
society and the lack of religious rites of initiation, neo-Trans-
cendentalism can be seen as a rite of passage that brings about a
psychological change. Various anthropological explanations of the
current quest for the mystical are briefly discussed.

902.   Prus, Robert C. "Religious Recruitment and the Management of Dis-
        sonance: A Sociological Perspective." SOCIOLOGICAL INQUIRY 46
        (1976): 127-34.

        Relates the new religious movements' concern with acquiring new
        members, maintaining their beliefs, inspiring commitment, and de-
        terring defections to their ability of managing dissonance. The
        author points out that, although cognitive dissonance is a personal
        experience, it is socially and culturally "negotiable." The pro-
        cess of resolving any inconsistencies in one's religious commitment
        is influenced by the methods the group adopts to counteract the
        members' doubts.

903.   Quarantelli, Enrico L. "Emergent Accommodation Groups: Beyond
        Current Collective Behavior Typologies." HUMAN NATURE AND COL-
        LECTIVE BEHAVIOR: PAPERS IN HONOR OF HERBERT BLUMER. Edited by
        Tamotsu Shibutani. Englewood Cliffs, NJ: Prentice-Hall, 1970,
        pp. 111-23.

        Develops a typology of new social groups and gives the details of
        the specific conditions for their emergence, development, and es-
        tablishment. Two general situational contexts, namely a consensus
        and a dissensus crisis, are said to be the reason why these new
        groups come into being. In the former crisis, there is agreement
        about the goals and the course of action that needs be taken; in
        the latter, basic differences lead participants to form contending
        factions. Each situational crisis can lead to a conflict or accom-
        modation group, which, in turn, could result in a change or an
        adjustment of the social structure. Various basic types of emer-
        gent accommodation groups are described.

904.   Raschke, Carl A. THE INTERPRETATION OF ETERNITY: MODERN GNOSTICISM
        AND THE ORIGINS OF THE NEW RELIGIOUS CONSCIOUSNESS. Chicago:
        Nelson-Hall, 1980. xi, 271 pp.

        Advances the theory that the new religious movements are mainly
        "the cresting waves" of forces in Western culture that can be
        traced back to several hundred years. The new movements are gnos-
        tic not only because they include underground religious commitments,
        but also because they propose certain attitudes towards the world
        and society. They are best considered as a reaction to material
        progress in the contemporary Western culture. They further seek
        salvation in a plane outside time. The forms and variations of
        gnosticism in its rebellion against time are examined and the
        flowering of the occult and the Mind Cure Movement in America since
        the turn of this century are described. The author maintains that

though the quest for the eternal is inherent in human nature, it
runs the risk of becoming an obsession and thus becomes destructive
of humanity itself.

905.   Redekop, Calvin. "A New Look at Sect Development." JOURNAL FOR
THE SCIENTIFIC STUDY OF RELIGION 13 (1974): 345-52.

Discusses the process of sect development which, in the author's
opinion, involves a dialectical process between the sect and the
host society. Three variables are taken into account, namely: 1)
the degree to which the sect rebels against the central values of
society; 2) the ability of different societies to tolerate or integrate radical protest; and 3) the strategies that the sects adopt
to confront opposition. The Old Colony Mennonites and the Mormons
are chosen as examples to illustrate the author's position.

906.   Restivo, Sal. "Parallels and Paradoxes in Modern Physics and Eastern Metaphysics: II--A Sociological Perspective on Parallelism."
SOCIAL STUDIES OF SCIENCE 12 (1982): 37-71.

Continues his previous study on the common elements between
physics and Eastern mysticism and discusses this parallelism as "a
strategy in intellectual conflict." The sociological view of mysticism is contrasted with that proposed by those who favor the view
that psychics and mysticism have similar characteristics. The
author suggests that contemporary parallelism is a reaction and an
alternative to the counterculture criticism of science and to anti-
mystical movements. The social context in which parallelism emerges
is described. Parallelism is an attempt to come to terms with new
modes of thought and behavior in developing human communities. A
bibliographic essay (pp. 60-71) includes a section on the sociology
of mysticism.

907.   Restivo, Sal. "Parallels and Paradoxes in Modern Physics and Eastern Metaphysics: I--A Critical Reconnaissance." SOCIAL STUDIES
OF SCIENCE 8 (1978): 143-81.

Presents the background for an elaborate study on the social
origins and functions of the theory that there is a parallelism
between modern physics and eastern mysticism. It is the author's
view that those favoring such a parallelism have tended to be its
advocates rather than critical analysts. The theory of parallelism
is outlined in some detail and the pitfalls associated with making
connections between science and religion or physics and mysticism
are discussed at length.

908.   Richardson, James T. "Proselytizing Processes of the New Religions." PUSHING THE FAITH: PROSELYTISM AND CIVILITY IN A PLURAL-
ISTIC WORLD. Edited by Martin E. Marty and Frederick E. Greenspahn. New York: Crossroad, 1988, pp. 143-54.

Examines the recruiting practices of three new religious movements, namely the Unification Church, the Hare Krishna Movement,
and the Jesus People, and constructs a typical "nonmysterious pattern" of proselytization. At first, each group tended to spend

more time and resources on public witnessing. As they became somewhat established, they relied more on friendship and kinship networks to gain new converts. Once they developed into organizations, their lifestyle and recruitment methods became more congregational than communal in style. These groups experimented with different techniques on a trial-and-error basis because they encountered difficulties both in attracting and maintaining members.

909.   Richardson, James T. "The 'Deformation' of New Religions: Impacts of Societal and Organizational Factors." CULTS, CULTURE, AND THE LAW: PERSPECTIVES ON NEW RELIGIOUS MOVEMENTS (item 684), pp. 163-75.

Dismisses the mythology that has surrounded some explanatory models of cult formation and argues that more "normal" explanations of how and why people join and leave the new movements are available. The social-historical context in which the cults arose is briefly described. The author thinks that the new religions have developed in a negative climate that has dictated the forms they have taken. Internal pressures have also partly determined the growth of these movements, many of which have already been domesticated and bureaucratized. The beliefs of many cults have changed because of organizational factors and material considerations. A dynamic feedback model of development is proposed.

910.   Richardson, James T. "Studies of Conversion: Secularization or Re-Enchantment." THE SACRED IN A SECULAR AGE (item 623), pp. 104-121.

Points out that the secularization theory is being reexamined by some scholars in the light of the rise of interest in the new religious movements in the West. The author rejects the deterministic paradigm for conversion and describes the shift to a new model that is more humanistic and activist in orientation. Converts to new religions are seen as active human beings seeking meaning and appropriate lifestyles, and their conversion is more of a social event that takes place more than once in the lifetime. After examining alternative paradigms, the author concludes that there seem to be signs of a possible "re-enchantment" of the world and sees some positive and significant results emerging from the new movements.

911.   Richardson, James T. "The Active vs. Passive Convert: Paradigm Conflict in Conversion/Recruitment Research." JOURNAL FOR THE SCIENTIFIC STUDY OF RELIGION 24 (1985): 163-79.

Argues that the old mechanistic and deterministic model of conversion assumed that a passive subject was led to conversion by external forces beyond one's control. A more active paradigm that stresses human freedom is preferred. Taking a more humanistic approach, some sociologists studying converts to the new religious movements see them as active individuals seeking self-development. The author maintains that the shift to the participant-observation method to understand conversion phenomena is largely responsible for the emergence of the activist paradigm and for the rejection of the brainwashing theory by social scientists.

912.   Richardson, James T. "Psychological and Psychiatric Studies of New
       Religions." ADVANCES IN THE PSYCHOLOGY OF RELIGION. Edited by
       L. B. Brown. New York: Pergamon Press, 1985, pp. 209-23.

       Presents a standard sociological assessment of psychological and
       psychiatric interpretations of the new cults. The author points
       out that the focus of psychiatric literature has centered around
       three main themes: 1) the evaluation of the mental health of cult
       members before and after joining a new religion; 2) the assessment
       of their personality features and syndromes; and 3) the examination
       of the effects cultic life has on its members. Psychological works
       on the Jesus People, the Ananda Marga Yoga Society, the Unification
       Church, and the Divine Light Mission are among those surveyed. The
       author emphasizes the "social location" of the recruits to the new
       religious movements and maintains that, in spite of the very nega-
       tive view of cults held by a few psychiatrists, "the personality
       assessment of these group members reveal that life in the new reli-
       gions is often therapeutic rather than harmful" (p. 221).

913.   Richardson, James T. "Conversion Careers." SOCIETY 17.3 (1980):
       47-50.

       Attempts an understanding of conversion through the interactionist
       theory, which sees the convert as an active participant in the con-
       version process. The author criticizes social and psychological
       studies that assume that the convert is a passive individual influ-
       enced by outside sources, and discusses the brainwashing theory, the
       most extreme form of such an approach. Studies on the Jesus People
       are utilized to explore the active role a convert plays and to
       avoid the usual distinction of conversions into two types, namely
       the sudden and the gradual. The author prefers the phrase "conver-
       sion careers" to highlight the "sequential trying out of new beliefs
       and identities in an effort to solve felt difficulties" (p. 49).
       The ways in which conversion careers can be differentiated are
       briefly outlined.

914.   Richardson, James T. "An Oppositional and General Conception of
       Cult." ANNUAL REVIEW OF THE SOCIAL SCIENCES OF RELIGION 2 (1978):
       29-52.

       Provides a critique of the concept of "cult" and attempts to
       extend it by applying it to the early phase of the Jesus Movement.
       Cults, which are transitory entities, are known for their "loosely
       defined ideologies and behavioral boundaries." Cults can be de-
       fined with reference to three major contrasts: 1) individualist/
       collectivistic; 2) rational/mystical; and 3) dominant culture/
       counterculture.

915.   Richardson, James T. "Comment on Austin's Article 'Empirical Model
       of Lofland's Conversion Model.'" REVIEW OF RELIGIOUS RESEARCH 19
       (1978): 320-32.

       Finds some problems with Austin's critique (item 738) of Lofland's
       conversion model (see items 215 and 866) and specifies those areas
       where this critique is not valid. Among the difficulties mentioned
       are Austin's apparent passive model of human beings.

916.   Richardson, James T.   "Critique of Bibby and Brinkerhoff's 'Sources
        of Religious Involvement.'" REVIEW OF RELIGIOUS RESEARCH 17
        (1976): 158-60.

        Criticizes Bibby and Brinkerhoff's paper (item 297) for two
        conceptual reasons. First, it doesn't carefully define conversion
        and, secondly, it fails to distinguish between "cognition" and
        "psychic deprivation." The four types of explanations usually
        brought forward to explain religion and religious involvement,
        namely socialization, cognition, accommodation, and deprivation,
        are applicable to a wider variety of subjects than Bibby and
        Brinkerhoff maintain. A short reply to Richardson is included.

917.   Richardson, James T., Jan Van der Lans, and Frans Derks. "Leaving
        and Labeling: Voluntary and Coerced Disaffiliation From Religious
        Social Movements." RESEARCH IN SOCIAL MOVEMENTS, CONFLICTS, AND
        CHANGE 9 (1986): 97-127.

        Explores two types of disaffiliation from new religious move-
        ments, namely voluntary exiting or forced extraction carried out by
        outsiders. The work of Brinkerhoff and Burke (item 303) that con-
        centrates on expulsions is evaluated. Some relationships between
        communal groups (sects or cults) and the types of disaffiliation
        are suggested. The ways ex-cult members are labeled are also exam-
        ined. The process of labeling in various disaffiliation contexts
        and the main types of disaffiliations are summarized (pp. 112-13).

918.   Robbins, Thomas. CULTS, CONVERTS, AND CHARISMA: THE SOCIOLOGY OF
        NEW RELIGIOUS MOVEMENTS. Beverly Hills, CA: Sage, 1988. vi,
        252 pp.

        Provides a comprehensive overview of the sociology of contempo-
        rary religious movements in the West. The following major topics
        are discussed: 1) theories about, and explanations of, the rise and
        presence of the new cults; 2) the processes of conversion, commit-
        ment, and disaffiliation; 3) their organization and development;
        and 4) typologies and evaluations. One final chapter discusses the
        impact of the new movements on the sociology of religion. Included
        is a substantial bibliography that covers most of the areas of
        research (pp. 208-48). Chapter One includes a brief survey (pp.
        17-23) by James A. Beckford of the literature on new religious
        movements in the West outside the U.S.A. and Great Britain.

919.   Robbins, Thomas. "The Transformative Impact of the Study of New
        Religions on the Sociology of Religion." JOURNAL FOR THE SCIEN-
        TIFIC STUDY OF RELIGION 27 (1988): 12-31.

        Contends that the study of new religious movements is important
        because of the impact it has had on the sociology of religion in
        general. The presence of the cults has opened up areas for compar-
        ative and interdisciplinary research, encouraged the use of anthro-
        pological methods like participant-observation and linguistic anal-
        ysis, and led to a reconsideration of the secularization thesis and
        the church-sect theory. Further, the role of the sociologist of
        religion has been questioned in terms of the issues of objectivity

and partnership. The author maintains that the study of new religious movements is revitalizing the discipline of the sociology of
religion.

920.   Robbins, Thomas, and Dick Anthony. "Cults, Culture, and Community."
        CULTS AND THE FAMILY (744), pp. 3-30.

Overviews the sociological and historical sources that led to the
resurgence of new religious movements and the various social processes and structures within them. Three major features, namely
authoritarianism, loose organization, and deviancy, that are frequently assigned to cults are discussed. Cults are related to the
secularization trends in the West and to the culture crisis of the
twentieth century. Contemporary society, in the authors' view,
lacks mediating structures that stand between the individual's
private life and the large social institutions. The increasing
isolation of the nuclear family further contributes to the need for
mediating structures. Cults fulfill the roles of face-to-face
organizations or institutions. The authors hold that involvement
in cults can lead to either integration or disintegration.

921.   Robbins, Thomas, and Dick Anthony. "New Religious Movements and
        the Social System: Integration, Disintegration, or Transforma-
        tion." ANNUAL REVIEW OF THE SOCIAL SCIENCES OF RELIGION 2
        (1978): 1-28.

Examines the effects the new religious movements might have on
the stability, tensions, and changes in the social system. Three
main theses are discussed: 1) the new movements contribute to the
individual's integration through social adjustment in traditional
norms, through a synthesis of counterculture and traditional
values, through renewing commitment to conventional routines, or
through redirecting protest in less destructive channels; 2) they
lead to social integration by managing or redirecting tension in
the social system; and 3) they are a means of sociocultural transformation in that they are linked with constructive cultural innovation.

922.   Robbins, Thomas, Dick Anthony, and Thomas Curtis. "Youth Culture
        Religious Movements: Evaluating the Integrative Hypothesis."
        SOCIOLOGICAL QUARTERLY 16 (1975): 48-64.

Examines the possibility that new religious movements may succeed
in reintegrating individuals into the social system, that is, they
may rehabilitate drug users, assimilate young people into conventional educational and vocational careers, mitigate feelings of
alienation, and rechannel protest away from sociopolitical institutions. Four ways of integration, namely adjustive socialization,
combination, compensation, and redirection, are discussed and their
strengths and weaknesses evaluated. The authors point out, however, that the new religious movements "appear on the surface to
have only very limited integrative consequences" (p. 55). Two
kinds of movements are distinguished and described: 1) adaptive
movements, those that reassimilate converts into traditional social
roles, and 2) marginal movements, those that draw converts away
from the mainstream

culture and lock them into a fringe subculture. It is contended
that interpretations of new movements in terms of latent, integrative functions often make unwarranted, logically untenable, and
reductionistic assumptions.

923.   Robertson, Roland. "The Relativization of Societies, Modern Reli-
            gion, and Globalization." CULTS, CULTURE, AND THE LAW (item
            684), pp. 31-42.

        Maintains that the study of new religious movements has a broader
        frame of empirical reference and relevance and should include the
        contemporary surge in evangelicalism and fundamentalism. The new
        cults are just one expression of an evolutionary shift at a global
        sociocultural level. A suitable approach to account for modern
        religious trends in terms of "world order" is outlined. The issues
        of the quality of life, the ends of human existence, and the nature
        of humanity are being addressed throughout the world. Society is
        being relativized because, with globalization, the individual be-
        comes more involved in world problems and seeks solutions on a
        global scale rather than on a national or societal level.

924.   Robertson, Roland. "Religious Movements and Modern Societies:
            Towards a Progressive Problemshift." SOCIOLOGICAL ANALYSIS 40
            (1979): 297-314.

        Examines the classical sociological church-sect theory and its
        historical limitations. The author reviews the attempts to study
        new religious movements as marginal groups. He argues that the
        most important aspect of this study is not to find out whether the
        movements are new and what the causes are that brings them into
        being. The main task is to find out "their general significance
        with regard to the changing conceptions of the relationships be-
        tween the individual and society, and between extra-societal
        agencies and society itself" (p. 306). The study of new religious
        movements is given a different focus by a discussion on the chang-
        ing societal distinction between religion and the secular.

925.   Robertson, Roland. "Church-Sect and Rationality: Reply to Swatos."
            JOURNAL FOR THE SCIENTIFIC STUDY OF RELIGION 16 (1977): 197-200.

        Responds to the article of William Swatos (item 979), which crit-
        icizes the author for being tied down to Troeltsch's analysis of
        church and sect (item 134) and to the Judeo-Christian tradition and
        for neglecting the interaction between religious collectivity and
        the environment. Both charges are strongly refuted. The author
        holds that the continuing use of the church-sect typology will
        certainly not resolve the problems that beset the efforts at
        drafting a typology of religious movements.

926.   Robertson, Roland. "On the Analysis of Mysticism: Pre-Weberian,
            Weberian, and Post-Weberian Perspectives." SOCIOLOGICAL ANALYSIS
            36 (1975): 241-66.

        Highlights Weber's interest in mysticism by sketching and reflec-
        ting on the mystical tendencies in modern Western society. Mysti-
        cism is distinguished from asceticism, the former seeking inner-

worldliness, the latter other-worldliness. Weber's (item 140) and Troeltsch's (item 134) views of mysticism are explained and the need to revise them is stressed. Modern sociology of religion tends to equate mysticism with the "cultic."

927.   Robertson, Roland, and JoAnn Chirico. "Humanity, Globalization, and Worldwide Religious Resurgence: A Theoretical Exploration." SOCIOLOGICAL ANALYSIS 46 (1985): 219-42.

Proposes a global theory to explain the emergence of religious phenomena, including fundamentalism, new cults, and increase of church-state tensions. The following basic components of such a theory are discussed: 1) individual national societies; 2) a system of national societies; 3) the individual selves; and 4) the category to which individuals belong (humankind). In the authors' view we are witnessing the globalization of religion, which means the release from the security of life-in-society leading to questions dealing with the legitimacy of the world order and the meaning of human life on a broader scale.

928.   Roof, Wade Clark. "Alienation and Apostasy." SOCIETY 15.4 (1978): 41-45.

Maintains that the presence of new religious movements raises important questions for society at large. The author examines data from the General Social Survey of the National Opinion Research Center to estimate the extent of religious defection and to determine its social correlates (like sex, region, education, income, occupation, and marital status). Cultural alienation and the new morality are linked with the rise of the new religious movements.

929.   Ross, Joan. "Adolescents and Cults." UPDATE: A QUARTERLY JOURNAL OF NEW RELIGIOUS MOVEMENTS 8.3-4 (1984): 20-29.

Discusses the resources, tasks, and vulnerability that are usually linked with adolescence and explains why both cult ideology and lifestyle are attractive to young people. Though largely psychologically oriented, this essay raises many issues regarding the adolescents' position within the family power structure. The author maintains that the cults offer answers to young people's confusion about their role models and peer relationships. She views the cults as destructive, robbing their members of their continuity with the past and restricting their freedom.

930.   Rossel, Robert D. "Religious Movements and the Youth Culture." HUMAN CONTEXT 6 (1974): 621-31.

Speculates on the similarities and differences between the Great Awakening (1730-1750) and the counterculture movement of the late 1960's and thinks that both have occurred in periods characterized by a crisis in meaning. The author singles three areas out for investigation: 1) the nature of the worldview of the new movements; 2) the common themes they share with past revivals; and 3) the way in which new belief systems become institutionalized. He attempts

a study of religious awakenings similar to Lévi-Strauss's "verti-
cal" (i.e. structural) analysis of myths and hopes to unveil the
implicit forms that are present in all human quests for self-
transcendence.

931.   Roth, Guenther. "Social-Historical Model and Developmental Theory:
        Charismatic Community, Charisma of Reason, and the Counter-Cul-
        ture." AMERICAN SOCIOLOGICAL REVIEW 40 (1975): 148-57.

        Starts with Weber's contribution to the study of charisma and
        discusses the differences between sociohistorical and developmen-
        tal theories of charismatic authority. Weber's "charismatic commu-
        nity of ideological virtuosi" is contrasted with the charisma of
        reason. The author reflects on charisma in the context of the
        counterculture. The members of two kinds of counterculture groups
        are distinguished, namely the renunciates or pacifist virtuosi and
        the radicals or militant charismatics.

932.   Rothbaum, Susan. "Between Worlds: Issues of Separation and Iden-
        tity After Leaving a Religious Community." FALLING FROM THE
        FAITH (item 578), pp. 205-28.

        Reflects on the period of transition in which those who leave
        cults find themselves. Basing her analysis on research carried out
        at "Sorting It Out," a transition counseling center in Berkeley,
        California, that caters to those who leave groups that do not
        practice aggressive and deceptive recruitment techniques, the
        author explores the ways ex-members handle and come to terms with
        their leave-taking transitions. She thinks that those who leave
        alternative communities separate themselves from group identity and
        rediscover themselves as unique individuals. They further experi-
        ence their exits as both liberating and challenging and evaluate
        their cult involvement, keeping those elements they judge to be
        useful.

933.   Roucek, Joseph S. "The Changing Role of Sects in American Life."
        ANNALI DI SOCIOLOGIA 8 (1971): 32-49.

        Discusses the phenomenon of sects and cults in America and the
        problems of classifying them from a sociological point of view.
        Among sects are included the Mennonites, Quakers, Mormons, and
        Holiness and Pentecostal groups, while among cults are listed
        Jehovah's Witnesses, Christian Science, Spiritualism, New Thought,
        Faith Healing, the Oxford Group, and Moral Rearmament. Brief notes
        on many of these movements are given. The author holds that many
        sects have not evolved into denominations, a change that would
        indicate their new role in American religious life.

934.   Sandeen, Ernest R. "The 'Little Tradition' and the Forms of Modern
        Millenarianism." ANNUAL REVIEW OF THE SOCIAL SCIENCES OF RELI-
        GION 4 (1980): 165-81.

        Suggests that Robert Redfield's concept of the "Little Tradition"
        be applied to millenarian movements which reflect local issues and
        gain power by opposing the larger society, or the "Great Tradition."

The author theorizes that British and American nineteenth- and twentieth-century millenarian movements "developed a different configuration from preindustrial millenarian movements because they are symbiotically related to a much different, modernizing culture" (p. 166). Four religious movements--the Seventh-Day Adventists, Jehovah's Witnesses, the Bible and Prophecy Conference Movement, and Jim Jones' People's Temple--are taken as examples to illustrate the author's model. The People's Temple was originally a modernizing millenarian movement; in Guyana, however, it became more like a millenarian group in a primitive society. Jonestown's holocaust was "an archetypal millenarian disaster."

935.   Schwartz, Lita Linzer. "Leaving the Cults." UPDATE: A QUARTERLY JOURNAL OF NEW RELIGIOUS MOVEMENTS 9.4 (1985): 3-10.

Examines cases when both cult leaders and members defect or disengage themselves from their respective organizations. Three cases of "absent leadership" are examined, namely those of Bhagwan Shree Rajneesh, Ron Hubbard (of Scientology) and the Reverend Moon (of the Unification Church). Voluntary or forced defection of members raises a number of questions relevant to counseling. The literature on defection is briefly surveyed.

936.   Schwartz, Lita Linzer, and Florence K. Kaslow. "The Cult Phenomenon: Historical, Sociological, and Familial Factors Contributing to Their Development and Appeal." CULTS AND THE FAMILY (item 644), pp. 3-30.

Contends that the search for identity, rendered acute in modern societies, has made young adults vulnerable to the attraction of cults that promise security and freedom from responsibility. After looking briefly at the historical background of the new religious movements, the authors discuss the development of cults, compare their major features with those of the mainline traditions and sects, explore the causes of young adult vulnerability, and analyze conversion techniques used by the cults. The reaction of the parents to the news that their son or daughter has joined a cult is described. Various ways of extracting people from cults are summarized.

937.   Seggar, John, and Phillip Kunz. "Conversion: Evaluation of a Step-Like Process for Problem-Solving." REVIEW OF RELIGIOUS RESEARCH 43 (1972): 178-84.

Describes conversion as a problem-solving process in five stages: 1) the occurrence of events which raises problematic issues; 2) the resulting tensions in one's life; 3) the definition of these issues in sacred or secular terms; 4) the encountering of an organization that offers solutions to one's problems in the context of a community; and 5) the formation of affective bonds with members of the new community, with the consequent diminution of attachment to outsiders. Converts to the Church of Jesus Christ of Latter-Day Saints supply the data for testing the authors' theory. They conclude that the data do not fully support the theory. Converts to Mormonism are not always in a life-crisis situation and are usually sought out by missionaries.

938.   Shearmur, J. F. G. "The Religious Sect as a Cognitive System."
        ANNUAL REVIEW OF THE SOCIAL SCIENCES OF RELIGION 4 (1980): 149-63.

        Argues in favor of the need to study sects as "a cognitive system"
        and develops a theory that clarifies the relationship between social
        institutions and such systems. Sects that stress their own unique
        views about the world (such as the Unification Church and Jehovah's
        Witnesses) are taken as examples to support the author's position
        that these sects exhibit "patterns of dogmatism." The author con-
        siders his approach to complement the theory of cognitive dissonance.

939.   Shepherd, William C. "The New Religions and the Religion of the
        Republic." JOURNAL OF THE AMERICAN ACADEMY OF RELIGION 46 (Sup-
        plement 1978): 575.

        Summarizes the author's view of the new religious and cultic
        movements that are seen in the context of civil religious develop-
        ment. The new religions are an expression of extremely high reli-
        gious involvement that has characterized America. They flourish
        because religion is still considered to be socially valuable.

940.   Shupe, Anson D. SIX PERSPECTIVES ON NEW RELIGIONS: A CASE STUDY
        APPROACH. Lewiston, NY: Edwin Mellen Press, 1981. x, 235 pp.

        Provides six different interpretations currently used by scholars
        in their studies on new religious movements. In an introduction,
        the author discusses the definitions of "sect" and "cult" and opts
        for the phrase "fringe religions" to include all kinds of alterna-
        tive religious groups. Six scholarly perspectives, namely: 1)
        criminological; 2) philosophical; 3) anthropological; 4) social
        psychological; 5) social structural; and 6) historical, are distin-
        guished and illustrated with reference to case studies.

941.   Shupe, Anson D. "New Developments in Church-Sect Theory: The Cult
        to Sect Transformation." PROCEEDINGS OF THE ASSOCIATION FOR THE
        SCIENTIFIC STUDY OF RELIGION: SOUTHWEST REGION, 1981. 10 pp.

        Examines the common sociological definition of "cult," "sect,"
        "church," and "denomination" and criticizes the view that some
        modern religious movements are moving from cults to sects. The
        author states that when cults survive, they either remain "tran-
        sient cults" or else develop into churches, that is, they become
        established. The consequences of organizational changes in a given
        religious tradition are also reviewed.

942.   Shupe, Anson D. "Toward a Structural Perspective of Modern Reli-
        gious Movements." SOCIOLOGICAL FOCUS 6.3 (1973): 83-99.

        Identifies two areas of analysis in the study of new religious
        movements, namely their origin and their persistence or demise.
        Two general theories to account for the fate of these movements are
        advanced: 1) the "con-game" hypothesis that assumes a criminologi-
        cal approach in which such factors as fraudulence, profit-motives,
        shady financial deals, and sexual exploitation are central in the

understanding of the development of cults; and 2) the "cargo cult" hypothesis, an anthropological-sociological view that sees the new religions as revitalization movements that transform culture, provide security in times of social instability, and satisfy human needs. The author offers some criticisms of both approaches and suggests a structural view that sees the new movements as social organizations interacting with the larger social milieu. It is precisely this interaction that determines whether a particular movement will survive or die out. The discussion is carried out largely in the context of new Japanese religions.

943.   Sirkin, Mark I., and Bruce A. Grellong. "Cult vs. Non-Cult Jewish Families: Factors Influencing Conversion." CULTIC STUDIES JOURNAL 5 (1988): 20-22.

Attempts to discover whether the family background influences conversion to new religious movements. By comparing Jewish families who have children in one of the cults with those who do not, the authors reach three main conclusions: 1) cult members have a history of psychological problems and problems in living; 2) their families were less emotionally expressive and more critical than the families whose children had not joined a cult; and 3) cult members are inclined to look for religious solutions to life's difficulties. The authors conclude that vulnerable adolescents are more likely to respond positively to the psychological techniques of recruitment used by the cults.

944.   Skonovd, Norman. "Leaving the 'Cultic' Milieu." THE BRAINWASHING/ DEPROGRAMMING CONTROVERSY (item 2127), pp. 91-105.

Examines how cult members decide to leave the religious groups they had committed themselves to and the strategies that are used in the actual defection. Ex-members from the Unification Church, Scientology, the People's Temple, various Eastern religious groups, and extreme fundamentalist Christian churches were interviewed at length about their defections. The process that leads a person to question one's allegiance is considered and it is argued that a deterioration of one's social bonds is the critical factor underlying religious disaffiliation. The decision to leave can be intellectual, that is, when one loses one's faith, or instrumental, that is, when one realizes that the rigid practices are detrimental to one's health. Various problems linked with defection and ways in which a defector announces his or her departure are discussed.

945.   Slotten, Ralph. "Exoteric and Esoteric Modes of Apprehension." SOCIOLOGICAL ANALYSIS 38 (1977): 185-208.

Examines esoteric and exoteric religious traditions as ways of knowledge. Several case studies, including Kabbalah, Sufism, Tantrism, and Yoga, are presented. The author offers several rather complex models with their respective features. One model includes "ascetic control," "priestly function," and "Appollonian" within the exoteric mode, while "mystical surrender," "prophetic," and "Dionysian" are within the esoteric mode.

946.   Smith, Archie. "Black Reflections on the Study of the New Reli-
        gious Consciousness." RADICAL RELIGION 4.1 (1978): 31-36.

        Maintains that the so-called new religious consciousness is a
        phenomenon found almost exclusively among the White population and
        that scholars who study the new religious movements have failed to
        pay attention to the racism that is prevalent in America. Reflect-
        ing on a conference held at the Graduate Theological Union in
        Berkeley, California, the author observes that at this meeting
        there were no discussions on Black religion's "impact upon social
        reality in the United States and its implications for their own
        life and work" (p. 34). Several reasons why Blacks are not embrac-
        ing the same new forms of religion as Whites are advanced. The
        author questions the authenticity and universality of a new reli-
        gious consciousness that ignores "personal and systemic sources of
        racism, sexism, and class oppression" (p. 36).

947.   Snelling, Clarence H., and Oliver R. Whitley. "Problem-Solving
        Behavior in Religious and Para-Religious Groups: An Initial Re-
        port." CHANGING PERSPECTIVES IN THE SCIENTIFIC STUDY OF RELI-
        GION. Edited by Allan W. Eister. New York: John Wiley and Sons,
        1974, pp. 315-34.

        Reports on a preliminary study of those religious groups that are
        outside the mainstream American religious traditions. The follow-
        ing groups, all of which share the same problem-solving motive, are
        explored: 1) small Alcoholics Anonymous groups; 2) Cenikor House, a
        Denver live-in center for drug addicts and people convicted of
        various crimes; 3) a group connected with the Denver temple of the
        Hare Krishna Movement; and 4) a Denver astrology group. The
        authors observe that all these groups tend to reduce or narrow the
        size of the world to make it more manageable and to accept the
        Protestant ethic.

948.   Snook, John B. "An Alternative to Church-Sect." JOURNAL FOR THE
        SCIENTIFIC STUDY OF RELIGION 13 (1974): 191-204.

        Favors a multidimensional, rather than a typological, model to
        analyze religious groups. It is argued that the church-sect dis-
        tinction does not facilitate a comparison between these groups in
        so far as they are religious. Four dimensions of religious author-
        ity are described: symbolism, organization (structure), intensity,
        and pervasiveness. Each dimension is divided into three ranges
        (high, moderate, and low) and its characteristics and indicators
        are listed. Two cases are provided to illustrate the author's
        analysis: 1) the controversy between the gnostics and orthodox
        Christians in the early Christian era; and 2) the changes in the
        Catholic Church after Vatican Council II. The implications of this
        multidimensional approach for the church-sect theory are assessed.

949.   Snow, David A., and Richard Machalek. "The Convert as a Social
        Type." SOCIOLOGICAL THEORY. Edited by Randall Collins. San
        Francisco: Jossey-Bass Publishers, 1983, pp. 259-89.

Treats religious converts as a social type with identifiable
properties or characteristics that are manifested in various interactions. The features are deduced by the way converts talk and
reason. Basing their comments on a study of the Nichiren Shoshu of
America, the authors first evaluate the existing conceptions of
conversion. They suggest that it is "the universe of discourse"
that changes when a person is converted. The following properties
of conversion are analyzed: biographical reconstruction, adoption
of a master attribution scheme, suspension of analogical reasoning
(which compares one's beliefs to those of others), and the acceptance of a master role.

950. Snow, David A., and Richard Machalek. "Second Thoughts on the
      Presumed Fragility of Unconventional Beliefs." OF GODS AND MEN
      (item 550), pp. 25-44.

      Expands a previously published paper (item 951), where the
      authors challenge the common view that unconventional belief sys-
      tems are inherently fragile.

951. Snow, David A., and Richard Machalek. "On the Presumed Fragility
      of Unconventional Belief." JOURNAL FOR THE SCIENTIFIC STUDY OF
      RELIGION 21 (1982): 15-25.

      Challenges the view that unconventional beliefs, like those found
      in religious cults, are necessarily fragile and persist primarily
      because of the power of plausibility structures (such as cognitive
      dissonance). The common view that many cultic beliefs are highly
      incredible, vulnerable to everyday experience, or plain nonsense
      actually impedes our understanding of new religious movements.
      The authors critically examine the relationship between plausibil-
      ity structures and unconventional beliefs, assess the self-validat-
      ing nature of such beliefs, and question the theory of cognitive
      dissonance.

952. Snow, David A., and Cynthia L. Phillips. "The Lofland-Stark Con-
      version Model: A Critical Assessment." SOCIAL PROBLEMS 27 (1980):
      430-47.

      Examines Lofland and Stark's conversion model (item 215) in the
      context of data from the study of the Nichiren Shoshu of America.
      The following elements of the model are explored: 1) predisposing
      conditions (such as tension, problem-solving perspective, and reli-
      gious seekership); and 2) situational factors (including turning
      points in one's life, cult affective bonds, and intensive inter-
      action with cult members). The authors maintain that their data do
      not support the model in its entirety. They question whether per-
      sonal tension, ideological congruence, and religious seekership are
      necessary preconditions for conversion. They refute the assumption
      that explanations by converts of their conversions (that include a
      reconstruction of their pasts) are necessarily those that actually
      motivated them to join a cult. Further, in the case of the Nichi-
      ren Shoshu of America, recruitment and commitment are contingent on
      the maintenance of extracult affective ties. It is the authors'
      view that the "interactive process holds the key to understanding
      conversion" (p. 44).

953.   Snow, David A., Louis A. Zurcher, and Sheldon Ekland-Olson. "Social
        Networks and Social Movements: A Microstructural Approach to
        Differential Recruitment." AMERICAN SOCIOLOGICAL REVIEW 45
        (1980): 787-801.

        Explores the reasons why some people join one movement rather
        than another and why some movements attract a larger following and
        grow at a more rapid rate than others. Relying on data from sev-
        eral movements, including Soka Gakkai and the Hare Krishna Movement,
        the authors stress the importance of social networks in accounting
        for differential availability. Recruitment is, in their view,
        strongly influenced by structural mobility, availability, and
        affective interaction with movement members.

954.   Spae, Joseph J. "Eastern Cults in Western Culture." INTERNATIONAL
        REVIEW OF MISSION 67 (1978): 426-35.

        Examines the kind of people who join Eastern religious movements
        and discovers four definite patterns. Members of these groups are
        in search of 1) simple human friendship, 2) a direct experience of
        God, 3) some authority in their lives, and 4) something more natu-
        ral than the West has provided them with. The rise of these move-
        ments is "one symptom of a serious malaise" in Western civilization
        and religion.

955.   Staples, Clifford, and Armand L. Mauss. "Conversion or Commitment:
        A Reassessment of the Snow and Machalek Approach to the Study of
        Conversion." JOURNAL FOR THE SCIENTIFIC STUDY OF RELIGION 26
        (1987): 133-47.

        Examines the factors that Snow and Machalek suggest are indica-
        tors of conversion (see items 949-51). While agreeing with the
        approach that considers the language and rhetoric of converts a
        promising tool for understanding conversion, the authors think that
        the wrong implications of convert rhetoric are stressed. They
        suggest, instead, that attention should be focused on the role of
        language in the conversion process, thereby stressing the essen-
        tially subjective nature of conversion. Basing their reflections
        on a study of Christian evangelicals, the authors conclude that
        language and rhetoric are not a reflection of some underlying
        changes in consciousness, but rather tools individuals use to
        achieve a self-transformation.

956.   Stark, Rodney. "How New Religions Succeed: A Theoretical Model."
        THE FUTURE OF NEW RELIGIOUS MOVEMENTS (item 579), pp. 11-29.

        Draws on materials from Christian Science and Mormonism and from
        historical data from Pauline Christianity and Islam to propose a
        theory explaining why new religions succeed, that is, achieve a
        measure of dominance over one or more cultures. Eight conditions
        necessary for a new religious movement to develop into an estab-
        lished religious tradition are analyzed. These conditions are: 1)
        cultural continuity; 2) medium level of tension; 3) effective mobi-
        lization; 4) normal age and sex structure; 5) favorable ecology;
        6) dense internal network relationships; 7) resistance of secular-
        ization; and 8) adequate socialization. Several areas requiring
        further research are listed.

957.   Stark, Rodney. "Church and Sect." THE SACRED IN A SECULAR AGE:
        (item 623), pp. 139-49.

        Criticizes Niebuhr's social distinction between church and sect
        (item 119) because it has been "fashioned into a host of idiosyn-
        cratic typologies that defeated the possibility of theorizing about
        anything" (p. 139). The major developments since the 1960's are
        sketched. The author develops Benton Johnson's major contributions
        (items 105 and 106) and describes cults and sects as high tension
        religious movements, the former occurring within a deviant reli-
        gious tradition, the latter within a conventional one. Client and
        audience cults practice deviant magical activities but have not yet
        developed into deviant religions. The growth of new religious
        movements is related to religious economies that cater to special
        interest groups. The author thinks that secularization will not
        bring in a "postreligious era," but rather set into motion the
        revival of otherworldly, religious organizations.

958.   Stark, Rodney. SOCIOLOGY. Belmont, CA: Wadsworth Publishing Co.,
        1985. xxiv, 563 pp.

        Presents a general introduction to sociology with one chapter on
        religion in which cults are treated (pp. 318-29). A cult is de-
        fined as "a religious movement that represents a faith that is new
        and unconventional in society" (p. 319), as opposed to a sect, that
        is an organization aimed at reviving traditional religion. The
        author maintains that all religions started as cult movements which
        prospered because of the weaknesses of the old faiths. The dynamic
        character of religious economics and the processes by which sects
        and cults are formed are briefly explained. The geography of cult
        movements and the characteristics of those who join them are among
        the topics dealt with. It is argued that the majority of cult
        members are brought up in irreligious homes. The author restates
        his view that secularization contributes to cult formation.

959.   Stark, Rodney. "Europe's Sensitivity to Religious Movements."
        RELIGIOUS MOVEMENTS: GENESIS, EXODUS, AND NUMBERS (item 692), pp.
        301-343.

        Puts forward the theory that sects are a reaction to the secular-
        ization process that occurs in all religious organizations and
        that secularization itself actually stimulates revival and reli-
        gious innovation. Cult movements are distinguishable from sect
        movements in that the former are religious organizations in a
        deviant religious tradition, while the latter are deviant as orga-
        nizations, but remain within a conventional religious tradition.
        The author examines many sects and cults in Europe and concludes
        that "religious cults do abound in the more secularized parts of
        Europe" (p. 334), while sect activity is more notably present where
        conventional churches remain strongest. State repression, estab-
        lished state-supported churches, and left-wing political movements
        are among the other factors that influence the rise and growth of
        new religious movements.

960.   Stark, Rodney. "Must All Religions Be Supernatural?" THE SOCIAL
        IMPACT OF NEW RELIGIOUS MOVEMENTS (item 725), pp. 159-77.

Argues that the supernatural component is the distinctive and unique feature of any religion, which provides "compensators" when highly desired rewards seem unavailable. When the supernatural element of traditional religious institutions wanes, new faiths arise offering a stronger version of the supernatural. The Process Church of the Final Judgment (called, pseudonymously, The Power), Synanon, and Scientology are given as examples. In these groups, one can observe supernatural ideologies replacing secular psychotherapies that had ceased to satisfy the desires of those who joined these movements.

961.   Stark, Rodney, and William Sims Bainbridge. A THEORY OF RELIGION. New York: Peter Lang, 1987. 386 pp.

Presents a comprehensive sociological theory of religion and its development. It is argued that religious commitment is the core of religion and that religion appeals mostly to the weak and is thus a way of compensating human deprivations. The concepts of "sects" and "cults" are used to explain the evolution of religion. Two chapters are dedicated to the study of the emergence of sects (schismatic religious movements) and cults (innovative religious movements), respectively. The process of sect and cult affiliation is analyzed and the influences that propel these movements to grow or stagnate, to become more conventional, or to remain deviant are discussed. The conditions under which religions lose their power and new ones emerge are explored. A lengthy bibliography (pp. 351-74) is included.

962.   Stark, Rodney, and William Sims Bainbridge. THE FUTURE OF RELIGION: SECULARIZATION, REVIVAL, AND CULT FORMATION. Berkeley: University of California Press, 1985. vii, 571 pp.

Presents a collection of essays by two of the foremost sociologists of religion. These articles, most of which had been previously published between 1979 and 1984, are divided into five main areas, namely: 1) the religious economy; 2) sect movements; 3) cults; 4) recruitment methods; and 5) sources of religious movements. A lengthy bibliography (pp. 531-57) is appended.

Contains items 659, 693-94, 742-44, 959, 963-65, 969-70, 1494, 1587-89.

963.   Stark, Rodney, and William Sims Bainbridge. "Sect Transformation and Upward Mobility: The Missing Mechanisms." THE FUTURE OF RELIGION (item 962), pp. 149-67.

Clarifies and expands the church-sect theory. It is maintained that sects tend to become churches because 1) their members are inclined to move with the passage of time to a higher social class, and 2) such a move reduces the tension between sect and society. The offspring of converts to sect movements become socialized in their parents' religion and experience less tension with society than the original converts. Data from the following churches is adduced to support the authors' views: Church of God, Church of Christ Nazarene, Assemblies of God, Seventh-Day Adventists, Gospel Lighthouse, and the Church of the Foursquare Gospel.

964.   Stark, Rodney, and William Sims Bainbridge. "Who Joins Cult Move-
        ments?" THE FUTURE OF RELIGION (item 962), pp. 394-424.

        Discusses some individual characteristics that influence recruit-
        ment to cult movements. The main thesis defended in this essay is
        that "under present sociocultural conditions, cults have great
        success recruiting persons who are fully normal in terms of almost
        any characteristic one wants to measure" (p. 395). Cults attract
        those who are "most adrift from conventional faith." The social
        origins of cult members, their educational level, and their pre-
        vious participation in the psychedelic movement are considered.
        While nineteenth-century cults appear to have attracted more women
        than men to their ranks, contemporary cults have a more balanced
        proportion of the sexes. It is argued that the theory of brain-
        washing is largely a product of Freudian psychotherapy, which is
        itself a client cult.

965.   Stark, Rodney, and William Sims Bainbridge. "The External Exodus:
        Causes of Religious Dissent and Schism." THE FUTURE OF RELIGION
        (item 962), pp. 149-67.

        Describes how religious sects come into being from established
        religious bodies. The basis of schism, the sources of conflict,
        and the roles of sect leaders are discussed. External forces, such
        are the attitude towards religious diversity, also influence sect
        formation. The authors maintain that the presence of sect move-
        ments within Christianity has been a constant factor in the history
        of the Church and that religious orders (like monastic institutions)
        function as official sects. The continuous demand for magic and
        the Church's attempt to suppress religious dissent by its attacks
        on witchcraft practices are also dealt with. It is the authors'
        view that religious schism is inevitable because of the presence of
        relatively deprived people who abandon the Church to form less-
        worldly faiths.

966.   Stark, Rodney, and William Sims Bainbridge. "Concepts for a Theory
        of Religious Movements." ALTERNATIVES TO AMERICAN MAINLINE
        CHURCHES (item 603), pp. 3-25.

        Starts by defining religion and then examines the church-sect
        typology developed by Weber (item 140), Troeltsch (item 134), and
        Niebuhr (item 119), a typology that is judged to be inadequate.
        The authors praise the work of Benton Johnson (items 105 and 106)
        who reexamined the concepts and attempted to draw up a typology
        including the concept of cult. Elaborating on Johnson's efforts,
        Stark and Bainbridge distinguish between three types of cults:
        audience cults, client cults, and cult movements. The levels of
        organization and commitment in each group are explored. Only cult
        movements are judged to be true religions because they offer their
        members an ultimate worldview, which includes a system of "general
        compensators" (i.e. postulations of rewards based on faith and
        hope) and depends on supernatural assumptions. (This essay is
        basically a revision of a previously published essay, item 970.)

967.   Stark, Rodney, and William Sims Bainbridge. "Secularization and
        Cult Formation in the Jazz Age." JOURNAL FOR THE SCIENTIFIC
        STUDY OF RELIGION 20 (1981): 360-73.

Tests the authors' hypothesis that secularization leads to the
formation of new religious groups rather than to the removal of
religious beliefs and values as a significant factor in modern
society. Assuming the common sociological and anthropological
position that supernaturalism is at the core of religion, Stark and
Bainbridge maintain that "supernatural assumptions are the only
plausible source of many rewards that humans seem to desire intensely" (p. 361). Several indicators that supernaturalism is
bound to remain dominant in Western culture are listed. According
to the authors, cult movements are strongest when conventional
religions are weakest--a view confirmed by a study of Christian
Science, Theosophy, the Liberal Catholic Church, Divine Science,
the Baha'i, and those groups that deal primarily with magic and
the occult. It is argued that the rise of cults in the last two
decades is not new.

968.   Stark, Rodney, and William Sims Bainbridge. "Secularization, Re-
       vival, and Cult Formation." ANNUAL REVIEW OF THE SOCIAL SCIENCES
       OF RELIGION 4 (1980): 85-119.

Argues that contemporary society exhibits both a trend towards
secularization (that is, the erosion of belief in the supernatural)
and a trend towards religious revival and suggests that secularization is the primary cause of the current religious ferment. Revival leads to new sects which are responses to the early stages of
weakness in established religions; innovation leads to cults, that
are responses to latter stages of such weakness. To demonstrate
these theories, the authors start by formulating a general theory
of religion and then sketch the forces of secularization in modern
society. The responses to secularization are finally analyzed.

969.   Stark, Rodney, and William Sims Bainbridge. "Networks of Faith:
       Interpersonal Bonds and Recruitment to Cults and Sects." AMERI-
       CAN JOURNAL OF SOCIOLOGY 85 (1980): 1376-95.

Discusses two theories of recruitment to cults and sects, one
stressing that they provide an ideological appeal and a fulfillment
of deprived needs, the other that centers on the part social networks play in attracting new members. The authors hold that both
approaches can be combined to form a more thorough explanation of
how individuals join marginal religious groups. Three religious
groups--a Christian church that preaches the coming of an atomic
Armageddon, Ananda Cooperative Village, and the Mormons--are
adduced to illustrate the author's position. It is argued that
all faiths rely on network influences for evangelization.

970.   Stark, Rodney, and William Sims Bainbridge. "Of Churches, Sects,
       and Cults: Preliminary Concepts for a Theory of Religious Move-
       ments." JOURNAL FOR THE SCIENTIFIC STUDY OF RELIGION 18 (1979):
       117-31.

An earlier version of a more recently published essay (item 966).

971.   Staude, John Raphael. "Alienated Youth and the Cult of the Occult."
       SOCIOLOGY FOR THE SEVENTIES: A CONTEMPORARY PERSPECTIVE. Edited
       by M. L Medley and J. E. Congers. New York: Wiley, 1971, pp. 86-95

Reflects on the evidence that young middle-class Americans are exhibiting a growing interest in, and acceptance of, occult and mystical ideals and practices. The use of the I Ching, the Tarot, astrology, palmistry, and Scientology are all based on the rejection of rational planning and on the reliance on some kind of supernatural force. The author maintains that Western culture is experiencing a spiritual, religious, and cultural renaissance. The interest in occult matters is symptomatic of a deepening spiritual crisis and a disillusionment with science, of alienation from contemporary society, and of identity-confusion. Young people are experiencing a metaphysical anxiety and are turning to mysticism and the occult to find meaning in a world dominated by progressive and liberal worldviews and totalistic ideologies.

972. Steeman, Theodore M. "Troeltsch and Modern American Religion." ARCHIVES DE SCIENCES SOCIALES DES RELIGIONS 58.1 (1984): 85-116.

Adopts Troeltsch's sociological typology of religion (item 134) into church, sect, and mysticism as a tool for understanding the contemporary religious scene. The author first provides a brief description of Troeltsch's perspective in which his concerns for the church type of organization, the free church, and ascetic Protestantism are underscored. He then suggests that "the rise and decline of ascetic Protestantism as a culturally formative embodiment of Christianity" (p. 93) would be a major focus of Troeltsch's analysis of contemporary American religion.

973. Steeman, Theodore M. "Church, Sect, Mysticism, Denomination: Periodological Aspects of Troeltsch's Types." SOCIOLOGICAL ANALYSIS 36 (1978): 181-204.

Examines Troeltsch's typology of religious groups (item 134) to determine to what extent they can be applied to contemporary American religion. It is pointed out that these concepts are historically dated and applicable largely to Christianity. For Troeltsch, sects and mysticism are two forms of protest that come into being because of the Church's neglect of religious experience. Church, sect, and mysticism occur in different periods of Church history.

974. Stone, Donald. "New Religious Consciousness and Personal Religious Experience." SOCIOLOGICAL ANALYSIS 39 (1978): 123-34.

Makes some generalizations about the features of contemporary religious movements based on research carried out in the San Francisco Bay Area. Pluralism, pragmatism, organizational openness, holism, and divine immanence are among the major attractive cultic characteristics. The author suggests that "the significance of current religious groups may be less as social movements than as part of a cultural drift toward an 'inner-worldly mysticism' that is compatible with (non-reductionistic) scientific orientations" (p. 131).

975. Strauss, Roger. "Changing Oneself: Seekers and the Creative Transformation of Life Experience." DOING SOCIAL LIFE: THE QUANTITATIVE STUDY OF HUMAN INTERACTION IN NATURAL SETTINGS. Edited by John Lofland. New York: Wiley and Sons, 1976, pp. 252-73.

Rejects the common view that the person who undergoes an identity change is essentially passive and explores the opposite assumption that such people are active seekers. Restricting himself to the study of religious seekers, the author identifies the sequence of events that lead to the discovery and use of transformative means. The first step, called "creative bumbling," is one in which the seeker gradually moves from a covert to an open quest and looks for and recognizes some tactics for changing oneself. The second step, called "strategies of creative exploration," includes the checking out of the discovery, experimentation, and realization of a life change.

976.   Swanson, Guy E. "Travels Through Inner Space: Family Structures and Openness to Absorbing Experiences." AMERICAN JOURNAL OF SOCIOLOGY 83 (1978): 890-919.

Relates family structure to absorbing experiences, which are said to have three types of tendencies, namely: 1) to become immersed in nature, past events, etc.; 2) to treat imagined objects as real; and 3) to become dissociated from reality. Absorbing experiences which, like mysticism, alter one's consciousness are related to hypnosis. They bring out changes in the relationships of individuals to themselves and to others. The author tested college students who reported such experiences and concluded that these experiences bear a close relationship to the respective family situations. The various indicators of absorbing experiences and several social factors dealing with personal data, like family size and relationships within the family, are outlined.

977.   Swatos, William H. "Church, Sect, and Cult: Bringing Mysticism Back In." SOCIOLOGICAL ANALYSIS 42 (1981): 117-26.

Discusses sociological attempts to relate the concept of "cult" to the classical church-sect distinction and maintains that such efforts misunderstand both the function of the church-sect typology and the significance of the new religious movements. The author suggests that the best approach to these movements is in the application of Weber's typological distinction between asceticism and mysticism (item 139-40), a distinction that was adopted and confused by Troeltsch (item 134). He compares the cults to religious orders and thinks that the rise of cultism is related to the corresponding decline of religious orders.

978.   Swatos, William H. "Quo Vadis: Reply to Robertson." JOURNAL FOR THE SCIENTIFIC STUDY OF RELIGION 16 (1977): 201-204.

Continues the debate with Roland Robertson on Weber's church-sect typology (see item 925).

979.   Swatos, William H. "Weber or Troeltsch?: Methodology, Syndrome, and the Development of the Church-Sect Theory." JOURNAL FOR THE SCIENTIFIC STUDY OF RELIGION 15 (1976): 129-44.

Analyzes the historical development of the church-sect theory and examines Weber's (item 140) and Troeltsch's (item 134) approaches to the variety of religious groups. Weber's theory is endorsed for

not being a "generalized abstraction nor an evaluative stereotype
nor a quantitative average" (p. 133), and also for being a useful
tool for analytic comparisons. Troeltsch's hypothesis, however, is
an attempt to use a sociological theory to solve a theological
problem and hence departs radically from Weber's original intention
of formulating the typology. Current developments in the field in
the last twenty-five years up are assessed. The author recommends
scholars to return to Weber's approach which applies church-sect
theory as a means for studying certain aspects of religion.

980.   Tipton, Steven M. GETTING SAVED FROM THE SIXTIES: MORAL MEANING
       IN CONVERSION AND CULTURAL CHANGE. Berkeley: University of
       California Press, 1982. xviii, 364 pp.

       Theorizes that people join new, alternative religious movements
       in order "to make moral sense of their lives." After a discussion
       on the countercultural scene of the 1960's, the author describes the
       change in moral meaning of the young adults who joined 1) the Liv-
       ing Word Fellowship (a millenarian Pentecostal sect), 2) the Pacif-
       ic Zen Center (a Buddhist meditation organization), and 3) Erhard
       Seminary Training (a human potential institution). In each case
       the history of the movement is traced and its social organization
       and composition of its members outlined. The formal ethic of each
       group as it is presented to newcomers is expounded. Several appen-
       dices provide a typology of ethical evaluation, a schematic presen-
       tation of the three movements, an account of the methods used by
       the author, and a demographic analysis of EST.

981.   Tipton, Steven M. "The Moral Logic of Alternative Religions."
       DAEDALUS 111.1 (1982): 185-213.

       Contends that people join new religious movements to make sense
       of their moral lives. Therefore, conversion is not just a per-
       sonal transformation, but also an intellectual change that provides
       life with a new moral meaning. Because moral problems are embedded
       in the social situation, the styles of American moral culture need
       to be investigated. The author illustrates the change in moral
       attitudes through an examination of a Human Potential Movement,
       namely EST (Erhard Seminary Training, now called "The Forum"). EST
       teaches a consequential theory of right and an expressive theory of
       good where rules play an instrumental role. It presents an engag-
       ing, yet detached therapeutic ideal that responds adaptively to
       the social conditions prevailing in urban bureaucratic life. Con-
       version is described as an "ethical recombination" of expressive
       hip culture and utilitarian individualism without reference to the
       authoritarianism of a revealed religion.

982.   Tipton, Steven M. "New Religious Movements and the Problem of
       Modern Ethic." SOCIOLOGICAL INQUIRY 49.1-2 (1979): 286-311.

       Argues that one reason why young people have joined alternative
       religions is to "make moral sense of their lives" (p. 286). Bibli-
       cal religion and utilitarian individualism, the two conceptions of
       reality in contemporary America, had been rejected in the counter-
       culture of the 1960's. The author concentrates on showing how

changes in ethical outlook are rejected and how Zen provides an
alternative. The ethics of Zen Buddhism, with its moral and social
accountability, are examined and the part played by Jerry Brown
(former Governor of California) in the acceptance of neo-Oriental
ethos is traced. The new religious movements, unlike those of the
1960's, are not iconoclastic. They draw their ethic both from Biblical religion (which repudiates rationalism and utilitarianism)
and from non-Western religions. They can revitalize tradition as
well as change it.

983.   Townsend, Joan B. "Anthropological Perspectives on the New Reli-
        gious Movements." THE RETURN OF THE MILLENNIUM. Edited by
        Joseph Bettis and S. K. Johannesen. Barrytown, NY: New Era
        Books, 1984, pp. 137-51.

        Summarizes the most commonly accepted anthropological views on
        the rise of new religious movements in Western culture. Various
        types of movements are distinguished: 1) revitalistic or nativistic
        (that signal a return to an original culture); 2) millenarian or
        utopian (that announce the coming of a golden age through divine
        intervention); 3) messianic (that focus around the presence of a
        prophetic leader); 4) assimilative or syncretistic (that come into
        being from contacts between different cultures); and 5) expropriate
        (that are offshoots of imperialism in colonized countries). Var-
        ious explanations, particularly those of social disintegration and
        relative deprivation, are briefly described. Several conditions in
        Western culture (including scientific materialism and rapid social
        change) are said to lead to feelings of helplessness, powerless-
        ness, and deprivation, all of which can be considered to be the
        causes of the emergence of new movements.

984.   Turner, Harold. "A Global Phenomenon." NEW RELIGIOUS MOVEMENTS
        AND THE CHURCHES (item 577), pp. 3-15.

        Sees the rise of the new religious movements in a wider histori-
        cal and geographic context and divides them into two broad types:
        1) those that arose from "within one of the universal traditions"
        (sects); and 2) those that resulted from the "interaction between
        two or more universal faiths" (cults). The Jesus People, the
        Children of God, and the Way International are cited as examples of
        sects, while the Divine Light Mission and the Hare Krishna Move-
        ment are typical of cults. The author further distinguishes be-
        tween movements related to primal religions ("Prinerms") and those
        arising amid the universal religions ("Nerms"). He then examines
        the response of the established churches and concludes that the
        twentieth century is "the great age of religious persecution."

985.   Veysey, Laurence. "Ideological Sources of American Movements."
        SOCIETY .25.2 (1988): 58-60.

        Suggests that one approach to understanding the significance of
        religious and secular movements in the United States is to look for
        the role of an alternate ideology in creating and maintaining them.
        Two fairly distinct movements, the pietistic and the apocalyptic,
        are distinguished. The question whether the communal movements of

the 1960's and 1970's represent a historical continuity with earlier ones is discussed. The author thinks that "American society has never been a very receptive environment for communal experiments" (p. 61). The ideology of commune requires self-sacrifice which is not in harmony with American acquisitiveness and individualism. The part played by idealism in the rise of new movements has, in the author's opinion, been vastly overrated.

986. Wallace, Dewey D. "Sects, Cults, and Mainstream Religion: A Cultural Interpretation of New Religious Movements in America." AMERICAN STUDIES 26.2 (1985): 5-15.

Defines sects and cults as "small religious groups that are generally perceived as being outside the mainstream of the religious life of a community and that hold views which the large society finds unusual" (p. 5). The author attempts to analyze some of the teachings of these groups in relation to the American mainstream and wonders whether the differences are substantial. It is suggested that the new religions hold views that are variations of central themes in American religious life. These themes, namely restoration, millennial age, spiritual age, and perfect community, are traced to the long-standing Protestant mainstream since the sixteenth century, to the Biblical and Christian traditions, and to the way Americans see themselves as a people and as a nation (Civil Religion). Mormons and Christian Scientists are an illustration of these themes in the nineteenth century. Modern groups, like the Children of God, the Divine Life Mission, the Unification Church, and Scientology are contemporary expressions of these trends, which are deeply entrenched in the American ethos.

987. Wallis, Roy. "New Religious Movements and the Potential For Worldly Re-Enchantment: Religion as a Way of Life, Preference, and Commodity." SECULARIZATION AND RELIGION: THE PERSISTING TENSION. ACTS OF THE XIXth INTERNATIONAL CONFERENCE ON THE SOCIOLOGY OF RELIGION. Lausanne, Switzerland: C.I.S.R., 1987, pp. 87-98.

Maintains that new religious movements are unlikely to bring about a radical transformation of Western society and that no single movement is strong enough to replace the Judeo-Christian tradition. Because religion has become a consumer item, it tends to cease being an all-pervasive way of life and becomes, instead, a matter of preference among consumers and "finally a commodity."

988. Wallis, Roy. "Figuring Out Cult Receptivity." JOURNAL FOR THE SCIENTIFIC STUDY OF RELIGION 25 (1986): 494-503.

Rejects Stark and Bainbridge's theory (see item 961) that schismatic religious groups come into being where traditional religion is strong and that new forms of religion appear where it is weak. He further argues against their conclusion that Europe is particularly receptive to culturally innovative forms of religion. Based on the author's own research on Scientology and the Children of God, it is concluded that cult activity 1) increases with declining church attendance and 2) is also particularly high in

Anglo-Saxon Protestant-dominated, immigrant based societies, despite continuing high rates of church attendance. New religious movements should not be related only to secularization, as in Stark and Bainbridge, but also to cultural pluralism and to lessened demands of traditional religions.

989.   Wallis, Roy. "The Social Construction of Charisma." SOCIOLOGICAL THEORY, RELIGION AND COLLECTIVE ACTION (item 714), pp. 129-54.

Argues that charisma is "essentially a relationship born out of interaction between the leader and his followers" (p. 130) and explores the emergence, recognition, and maintenance of charisma as an interactional process. A particular example of charismatic leadership, namely that of Moses Berg who founded the Children of God, is taken to illustrate the social dimension of charisma. The biography of Berg before his prophetic calling is outlined and his transformation into a prophet of God described. Berg developed "an antinomian theology with a variety of exotic features" (p. 141). The dispersal of charismatic recognition and the management of charisma are explained in terms of the relationships between himself and his followers.

990.   Wallis, Roy. "The Sociology of the New Religions." SOCIAL STUDIES REVIEW 1.1 (1985): 3-7.

Describes the variety of new religions in the West and points out that they differ from traditional religions not only in their beliefs and practices, but also in their organizational structures which often resemble those of multinational business corporations. The author's typology (elaborated in several of his writings) of new religions into world-rejecting, world-accommodating, and world-affirming groups is outlined. The rationalization tendencies in the West are said to be at the basis of the rise of the cults which are preoccupied with a search for a remedy to cope with the modern world, among other things.

991.   Wallis, Roy. THE ELEMENTARY FORMS OF THE NEW RELIGIOUS LIFE. London: Routledge and Kegan Paul, 1982. x, 156 pp.

Offers a framework for understanding new religious movements that have emerged in the last quarter of the twentieth century. Three analytical types of movements, based on their orientation to the world, are distinguished: 1) world-rejecting new religions (like the Hare Krishna Movement, the People's Temple and the Children of God); 2) world-affirming new religions (such as Transcendental Meditation, EST, and Scientology; and 3) world-accommodating movements (such as neo-Pentecostalism and Subud). The characters, recruitment bases, social sources, and developmental patterns of each group are described. Among the topics discussed are the issues of social change and secularization as they relate to the new religions. Various theories on the development of new religions are analyzed in the context of the precariousness of the market and of charisma. An appendix on substance and method in the study of new religious movements is added (pp. 132-44).

992.   Wallis, Roy. "The New Religious Movements as Social Indicators."
       NEW RELIGIOUS MOVEMENTS: A PERSPECTIVE FOR UNDERSTANDING SOCIETY
       (item 551), pp. 216-31.

       Explains that new religious movements provide insight into the
       nature of society because they either reject or celebrate major
       social features and because their emergence can be traced to those
       social factors that lead to their development. Two types of move-
       ments are examined: 1) the world-rejecting ones; 2) the world-
       affirming ones (see item 991). The author agrees with Weber's
       theory (item 140) that rationalization and secularization bring a
       sense of loss of the mysterious and of the sacred and provides the
       underlying causes for the emergence of the new religions. The
       first type (world-rejecting) offers an alternative to anonymity and
       impersonalization, the second type (world-affirming) offers salva-
       tion in the context of society and its problems.

993.   Wallis, Roy. "The Elementary Forms of Religious Life." ANNUAL
       REVIEW OF THE SOCIAL SCIENCES OF RELIGION 3 (1979): 191-211.

       Provides a theoretical framework for understanding the new reli-
       gious movements in the West by identifying their social sources and
       by relating these to their forms, beliefs, and development. Three
       types of new movements are distinguished (see item 991). The char-
       acteristics of each of these groups are listed, and the sources of
       support for the world-affirming and world-denying groups traced.
       The author states that "the new religions have developed in re-
       sponse to, and as attempts to grapple with the consequences of,
       rationalization" (p. 198).

994.   Wallis, Roy. "Reflections on 'When Prophecy Fails.'" SALVATION
       AND PROTEST (item 709), pp. 44-50.

       Utilizes Festinger's work (item 91) to support the author's views
       on the features of cults. The view advanced is that sectarianiza-
       tion is "a solution to the problem of the institutional frailty
       of the cult" (p. 45). A brief account of the cult dealt with in
       Festinger's book is given and its founder, Mrs. Keech, is compared
       to George King, the founder of the Aetherius Society. The differ-
       ence between the two explains why Mrs. Keech's group remained a
       cult, while King's organization developed a sectarian character.

995.   Wallis, Roy. THE REBIRTH OF THE GOD?: REFLECTIONS ON THE NEW RELI-
       GIONS IN THE WEST. Belfast, Northern Ireland: The Queen's Uni-
       versity, 1978. 30 pp.

       Admits that in advanced industrialized societies, religion becomes
       less prominent in human affairs, but observes that the predicted
       demise of religion has not come about, as the rise of new religious
       movements since the late 1960's amply demonstrates. These movements
       are ranged along a continuum between two basic types, namely world-
       rejecting and world-affirming, both of which have to be seen in the
       context of the failure and disintegration of the counterculture.
       The world-rejecting movements "offer an alternative to the anony-
       mity, individualism, segmentalization of modern life" (p. 17); the

world-affirming religions, on the other hand, offer salvation to those attached to modern industrial society and are not searching for an alternative lifestyle. Several movements (like the Healthy, Happy, and Holy Organization and the Divine Light Mission) combine elements from conventional religion and the counterculture. The author thinks that world-affirming movements have a better chance of survival.

996. Wallis, Roy. "Relative Deprivation and Social Movements: A Cautionary Note." BRITISH JOURNAL OF SOCIOLOGY 26 (1975): 360-63.

Comments briefly on the use and misuse of the concept of relative deprivation to explain the origin of religious and social movements. The author observes that not all people who are deprived join a new religious movement and that it is difficult to specify the types of people who join specific religious groups. The author finds fault with the deprivation theory, because it fails to take into account the social environment and circumstances that contribute to a person's decision to become a member of a new religion. The unmet needs of individuals can only be determined by interviewing those who actually joined new movements. Motivations for doing so fall into a limited number of typical patterns.

997. Wallis, Roy. "The Cult and Its Transformation." SECTARIANISM: ANALYSIS OF RELIGIOUS AND NON-RELIGIOUS SECTS (item 713), pp. 35-49.

Examines the concepts of cult and sect and their development as outlined by Glock and Stark (item 97) and Nelson (item 118) and criticizes these authors for failing "to capture the organizational factors that distinguish these forms of religious organization" (p. 40). Wallis's view is that while a sect, like a church, is a uniquely legitimate means to truth and salvation, a cult is more pluralistic and allows for a variety of paths to reach the same goals. Some religious movements emerge as cults, of which several may develop into sects. This happens when the movement's ideology changes and is conceived as the way to salvation.

998. Wallis, Roy. "Ideology, Authority, and the Development of Cultic Movements." SOCIAL RESEARCH 41 (1974): 299-327.

Discusses the differences between sects and cults and contends that cults usually emerge as fragile institutions that face the problems of doctrinal precariousness and authority. The ways through which this fragility is overcome, leading the cult to develop into a sect, are discussed in the context of Dianetics, Christian Science, the Aetherius Society, and the Unity School of Christianity. The author considers the sect and the cult as parts of a continuum, with the "centralized cult" as an intermediate concept and stage through which those cults that become sects pass.

999. Wallis, Roy, and Steve Bruce. "The Stark-Bainbridge Theory of Religion: A Critical Analysis and Counterproposal." SOCIOLOGICAL ANALYSIS 45 (1984): 11-27.

Examines the theory of religion proposed by Stark and Bainbridge
(item 478) and concludes that it has major internal difficulties
and unwarranted assumptions and fails to understand the motivations
leading to religious commitment. The authors maintain that their
view is based on two invalid procedures used by Bainbridge and
Stark, namely "ontological atheism and explanatory dualism." Basing their reflections on studies of several new religious movements
(including Transcendental Meditation, Rajneeshism, and Scientology),
Wallis and Bruce argue that people join new movements not because
the religion of their upbringing fails to provide them with "compensators" and hence leave them dissatisfied, but rather because
they have been raised in a precarious condition caused by the diffuse belief system itself.

1000.   Wallis, Roy, and Steve Bruce. "Network and Clockwork." SOCIOLOGY
        16 (1982): 102-07.

        Examines the arguments of Snow et al. (item 953) that explain why
        people join new social movements and why some of these movements
        are more successful than others. Wallis and Bruce think that the
        influence of networks in the recruitment of new members has been
        overstressed. Evidence is adduced to show that interpersonal ties
        and social networks are not necessary for a movement's success.

1001.   Warren, Carrol A. B. "Destigmatization of Identity: From Deviant
        to Charismatic." QUALITATIVE SOCIOLOGY 3.1 (1980): 59-72.

        Develops a systematic theory of "destigmatization," that is an
        entrance into normality from deviance. The structural elements
        that promote destigmatization, its aims, and degrees of success are
        discussed. The process of changing one's status from that of devi-
        ant to charismatic can take place in three modes: 1) individual
        purification; 2) individual transcendence; and 3) "aristocratiza-
        tion," that is, a self-definition as better than normal. The trans-
        formation from deviant to charismatic can occur when a person joins
        a self-help group of alcoholics or a church of reborn Christians.

1002.   Weiman, Gabriel. "'New Religions:' From Fear to Faith." CANADIAN
        JOURNAL OF SOCIOLOGY 12 (1987): 216-29.

        Thinks that the emergence and growth of cults in the last two
        decades is due to the anxiety needs of those individuals who join
        them and proceeds to relate the various elements that make up
        anxiety to cult types. The author finds that a high level of exis-
        tential anxiety and general interest in cults go together, while
        the choice of cult is mediated by the "locus of control," that is,
        the perceived source of control over one's behavior. Astrology,
        Transcendental Meditation, and Scientology are among the examples
        cited to illustrate the author's position. People whose locus of
        control is internal, that is, those who tend to take responsibility
        for their own actions, choose Transcendental Meditation or Scien-
        tology; those whose locus of control is external, that is,
        who see control residing in outside forces, prefer astrology.

1003. Weiser, Neil. "The Effects of Prophetic Disconfirmation on the
          Committed." REVIEW OF RELIGIOUS RESEARCH 16 (1974): 19-30.

          Discusses the repercussions on a cult when the prophetic state-
          ments of its leader fail to materialize. In several recorded
          instances, like those of the Anabaptist Movement in 1534 and the
          Millerites in 1843, prophetic failure gave new life to the reli-
          gious group. The author thinks that millennial beliefs remain
          intact for a while after they have been disconfirmed by the unfold-
          ing events. Believers rationalize the situation by "1) an eventual
          displacement of the goal with marginal goal modification; 2) the
          welcoming of imitator prophets; and 3) increase proselytizing
          activity in order to ascertain social support" (p. 20). The author
          goes beyond the theory of cognitive dissonance (see Festinger, item
          91) and introduces the concept of rationalization, which assuages
          present and future suffering and permits the adherents to alter or
          revise their messianic hopes. A search for social advocacy fre-
          quently follows prophetic failure.

1004. Welch, Michael R. "Quantitative Approaches to Sect Classification
          and the Study of Sect Development." THE RELIGIOUS DIMENSION: NEW
          DIRECTIONS IN QUANTITATIVE RESEARCH. Edited by Robert Wuthnow.
          New York: Academic Press, 1979, pp. 93-109.

          Gives an overview of the many sociological studies on the concept
          of "sect," explores a mathematical, multidimensional approach to
          sect classification, and finally advances some proposals for the
          study of religious organizational change. The author stresses the
          need to examine the empirical relationships between sectarian
          attributes. He suggests that the organization and ideational fea-
          tures of American sects should be related to Wilson's sect typology
          (1969). The study of a sect's organization and doctrine at differ-
          ent periods in its history is one of the requirements for plotting
          its transformation.

1005. Welch, Michael R. "Analyzing Religious Sects: An Empirical Exami-
          nation of Wilson's Sect Typology." JOURNAL FOR THE SCIENTIFIC
          STUDY OF RELIGION 16 (1977): 125-41.

          Attempts to find out the correspondence between Wilson's sect
          typology (see, for example, items 144 and 1023) and the various
          sects; to identify the dimensions underlying sect structures and
          purposes; and to discover the actual characteristics that differen-
          tiate sects from one another. Wilson's seven-fold sect typology is
          briefly described. Tables that outline the dimensions of sectarian
          responses to the world, sect classes, and distinctive sect features
          are drawn. The author claims that his multidimensional scaling
          facilitates the analysis of religious organizations. The value of
          empirical approaches to sect analysis is finally discussed. A
          listing of organizational and doctrinal indicators used in this
          study and of sect's responses to the world are added in an
          appendix.

1006. Wenegrat, Brant. "Cult Membership: A Sociobiologic Model." CULTS
          AND NEW RELIGIOUS MOVEMENTS (item 611), pp. 193-208.

Applies the theory of sociobiology to understand the presence of cults in contemporary Western society. In essence, this approach argues that people join cults to seek in-group experiences "that are more or less central to human nature" (p. 199) and to satisfy needs that are left unaddressed by culture. The author relies on the pioneering work of Galanter in this field (see item 799 and other citations to his writings in my PSYCHIATRY AND THE CULTS: AN ANNOTATED BIBLIOGRAPHY).

1007. Werblowsky, R. J. Zwi. "Religions New and Not So New: Fragments of an Agenda." NEW RELIGIOUS MOVEMENTS: A PERSPECTIVE FOR UNDER-STANDING SOCIETY (item 551), pp. 32-46.

Questions the newness of the so-called "new religious movements" because history gives evidence of the presence of such movements in different eras and cultures. Several points of interest to both sociologists and historians are discussed. The people who join new religions, the social role of the new sects, the relation they have to science, their claims to healing power, the political tendencies of some of them, and the sociology of hostility towards them are among the general areas covered.

1008. Westley, Frances. THE COMPLEX FORMS OF RELIGIONS LIFE: A DURK-HEIMIAN VIEW OF NEW RELIGIOUS MOVEMENTS. Chico, CA: Scholars Press, 1983. ix, 199 pp.

Applies Durkheim's causal, representational, and functional theory to the new religious movements. Several commonly accepted, alternative theories are examined and rejected because they assume that religions perform a compensatory function in human life. The author organizes his data, collected from the Montreal area over a five-year period, under Durkheim's concept of the "cult of man." Two main areas are investigated: the relationship between beliefs and social organization (in groups like the Catholic Charismatic Renewal), and the movements' rituals of purification, manipulation, and transformation that are centered on the cult of the person. These cults that hold that the human person is a sacred being have pollution fears that reflect the personal and social flux that individuals experience. The rituals themselves are expressive of the sensitivity and potential to change in a diverse and complex culture.

1009. Westley, Frances. "'The Cult of Man:' Durkheim's Predictions and New Religious Movements." SOCIOLOGICAL ANALYSIS 39 (1978): 135-45.

Maintains that Durkheim's theory about the future of religion sheds light on the theoretical issues that contemporary religious movements have raised. Durkheim postulated a structural correspon-dence between social organization and religious beliefs and rituals, the latter being derived from the former. He further held that religion functions to order life, both on individual and social levels, and made some predictions about rituals in his work on "the cult of man." The author attempts to apply these views to explain some of the characteristics of the new movements, namely the middle-

class origins of their adherents, their system of ethics, and their
relation to contemporary rational-scientific thought. Two contemporary groups, Silva Mind Control and the Catholic Charismatics,
are specifically considered.

1010. Willis, Gary. "What Religious Revival?" PSYCHOLOGY TODAY 11.4
       (April 1978): 74-81.

       Questions the common view that America is experiencing a new
       religious revival or another great awakening. The evidence,
       according to the author, indicates that there is a "long-term
       stability of religious experiences and practices" (p. 77). Polls
       measuring people's religious beliefs have not changed since the
       1940's. Revival meetings and evangelistic uprisings do not point
       to new trends, but are rather typical of the way American religion
       expresses itself.

1011. Wilson, Bryan R. "The Functions of Religion: A Reappraisal."
       RELIGION 18 (1988): 199-216.

       Discusses the social functions of religion and the effect that
       secularization has had on them. It is pointed out that secular-
       ization has turned religion from a matter of public obligation to
       one of private choice. Traditional religions have been unable to
       accommodate themselves to the new pattern of social organization
       where religion and society are two distinct realities. The rise of
       new religious movements is judged to be a creative and innovative
       attempt to deal with this new situation. The controversies that
       have come in the wake of the cults are assessed and some method-
       ological remarks about the way sociologists might focus their
       studies are made.

1012. Wilson, Bryan R. "'Secularization:' Religion in the Modern
       World." NEW RELIGIOUS MOVEMENTS (item 586), pp. 953-66.

       Defines secularization as "the process through which religious
       thinking, practice, and institutions lose social significance, and
       become marginal to the operation of the social system" (p. 954).
       The way in which religious groups, like the Catholic Church in
       Belgium, the Mormons, the Shi'ites in Iran, and the Catholic Char-
       ismatic Renewal in America, tried to resist or limit the process of
       secularization are described. Religious movements serve as mediat-
       ing structures between the individual and the increasingly powerful
       state. They can be considered as recurring phenomena that come
       into being in the face of the persisting and irreversible secular-
       ization of the social order.

1013. Wilson, Bryan R. "Factors in the Failure of the New Religious
       Movements." THE FUTURE OF NEW RELIGIOUS MOVEMENTS (item 579),
       pp. 30-45.

       Examines the social criteria that lead to the failure of new
       religious movements to achieve their own goals. Five endogenous
       factors, namely ideology, leadership, organization, constituency,
       and institutionalization, are reviewed. The author suggests, among

other things, that the failure of ideological promise may not lead
a religious movement to decline or cease to exist. Charismatic
leaders, however, may be discredited both in the eyes of the public
and among their own followers, thus causing the movement to fail.
Several exogenous elements, such as the hostile reaction of the
media, the public, and civil and religious authorities, the competition among the various movements, and the decline in stable relationships in modern society, play an important role in a new movement's success or failure.

1014. Wilson, Bryan R. "The New Religions: Some Preliminary Considera-
       tions." NEW RELIGIOUS MOVEMENTS: A PERSPECTIVE FOR UNDERSTANDING
       SOCIETY (item 551), pp. 16-31.

       Discusses the problems of understanding the new religious move-
       ments which are "a phenomenon that taxes our existing conceptual
       apparatus" (p. 17). One major feature of these movements, namely
       their promise to offer a more proximate salvation and a wider
       access to it, is described. The author thinks that their implicit
       assault on spiritual elitism, their availability to a wider public,
       the accessibility of their techniques, their therapeutic claims,
       and the spiritual mobility they facilitate are all life-enhancing.
       Functional explanations fail to discriminate sufficiently between
       the different kinds of movements. Urbanization, the new tech-
       nology, and impersonal social contexts are among the general cir-
       cumstances in which new religions arise. Though they can achieve
       much for individuals and might even create a new subculture, they
       are unlikely to transform the structure of society.

1015. Wilson, Bryan R. "Secularization: The Inherited Model." THE
       SACRED IN A SECULAR AGE (item 623), pp. 9-20.

       Reflects on the social model of secularization, which stresses
       the following shifts: 1) from supernatural to empirical specula-
       tions; 2) from transcendent to natural entities; 3) from revealed
       knowledge to practical concerns; 4) from belief systems to testable
       hypotheses; and 5) from charismatic manifestations of the divine to
       structured, planned management of human affairs. The theory that
       secularization is a means by which religion is purified (or revi-
       talize) is discussed and rejected. The view is advanced that per-
       iodic reform and revivalism (as in the case of the Reformation, the
       rise of Methodism, and the revival of Pentecostalism), though often
       interpreted as a reversal of the secularization process, are them-
       selves evidence that religion is slowly but surely accommodating
       itself to the pressing needs of mundane matters.

1016. Wilson, Bryan R. RELIGION IN SOCIOLOGICAL PERSPECTIVE. Oxford:
       Oxford University Press, 1982. vii, 185 pp.

       Presents a general introduction to the sociology of religion.
       Two chapters deal with the sociology of sects and new religious
       movements, respectively. The main features of the traditional
       sects--exclusivism, radicalism, conservatism, and total commit-
       ment--are discussed. The author also covers such topics as the
       applicability of the concept of sect outside its Western Christian

context, the social consequences of sectarianism, the relative
deprivation theory, and the conditions for conversion and commitment. The rise of the new cults is related to the inability of
traditional religions "to cope with human needs in the contemporary
social context" (p. 125). The author holds that the new religious
movements throughout the world, in spite of some common features
and functions, are too different, both in style and in the role
they play in their respective cultures, to warrant a unified theory
to explain their emergence and continuance in the contemporary
world.

1017. Wilson, Bryan R. "Time, Generation, and Sectarianism." THE SOCIAL
       IMPACT OF THE NEW RELIGIOUS MOVEMENTS (item 725), pp. 217-34.

       Discusses the presence of the new religious movements, which have
       a disproportionate appeal to the young generation. It is shown how
       the sense of time promoted by these movements differs radically
       from that of traditional religions. "Whereas the church has
       offered timeless truths, the sects have always canvassed timely
       truths" (p. 225). The second generation of believers will signal a
       shift in time-orientations as well as in the nature of ideological
       commitment. The author thinks that changes in recruitment and
       socialization are likely to occur and that these changes will indi-
       cate that the impact of contemporary society on the new movements
       will be greater than that of the new movements on society.

1018. Wilson, Bryan R. "The Return of the Sacred." JOURNAL FOR THE
       SCIENTIFIC STUDY OF RELIGION 18 (1979): 268-80.

       Discusses the question of whether the contemporary religious
       ferment indicates a religious revival that goes counter to the
       secularization tendencies of the last few decades. Noticing that
       several scholars, David Martin, for example (see item 413), who
       have written on the secularization process seem to have changed
       their position on the matter, the author refutes their application
       to the new movement of Durkheim's theory that religion is an agency
       of social cohesion. Criticism is leveled against Bell's position
       (item 755) that the new religious movements are a "return of the
       sacred" and, hence, a re-sacralization of society and culture.

1019. Wilson, Bryan R. "Becoming a Sectarian: Motivation and Commitment."
       RELIGIOUS MOTIVATION: BIOGRAPHICAL AND SOCIOLOGICAL PROBLEMS FOR
       THE CHURCH HISTORIAN. Edited by Derek Baker. Oxford: Blackwell,
       1978, pp. 481-506.

       Explores the reasons people give for joining sects. Responses
       from members of Jehovah's Witnesses in the south of England reveal
       that the motives of these converts were conscious, point to the
       circumstances in which decisions were knowingly made, and hint at
       some unconscious predispositions. Several functions of believing,
       such as that of bestowing a sense of intellectual certainty and
       purpose and of providing mutual help in a segregated group, are
       admitted by the Witnesses themselves. The author rejects the
       theory that sects arise in social conditions that create anomie.
       He discusses the relative deprivation theory, particularly as

refined by Glock (item 94). He finally observes that "individuals
are socialized into conversion, and subsequently they learn how to
express, in appropriate language, just what has happened" (p. 506).

1020. Wilson, Bryan R. CONTEMPORARY TRANSFORMATIONS OF RELIGION. London:
      Oxford University Press, 1976. ix, 116 pp.

      Reflects on the cultural implications of contemporary seculariza-
      tion and on the widely diverse religious movements of our time.
      This volume consists of three lectures in which the author discus-
      ses the current changes taking place in the traditional churches,
      the apparent revival of religion, and the social meaning and impli-
      cations of religious change. The author expounds his theory that
      the new cults do not represent a religious revival but, rather,
      reconfirmation of the process of secularization.

1021. Wilson, Bryan R. THE NOBLE SAVAGES: THE PRIMITIVE ORIGINS OF
      CHARISMA AND ITS CONTEMPORARY SURVIVAL. Berkeley: University
      of California Press, 1975. xi, 131 pp.

      Examines charismatic leadership in primitive societies. The
      author first discusses the concept of charisma and its social con-
      texts. He then explores charismatic leadership in less-developed
      societies, giving examples from American Indian culture, the Ivory
      Coast, and the Congo. Charisma, even though the faith in healing
      and miracles it elicits is never confirmed, is "the occasion for
      social transformation." The author holds that charisma is a primi-
      tive trait and its presence in the modern world shows how slowly
      simple wish-dreams die out.

1022. Wilson, Bryan R. "The Debate Over Secularization: Religion,
      Society, and Faith." ENCOUNTER 45.4 (1975): 77-83.

      Scrutinizes the arguments for and against the theory that society
      is becoming more secularized, even though the process of secular-
      ization takes place on different patterns in diverse countries.
      The author refutes the view that insists that the proliferation of
      new cults questions the secularization hypothesis. He thinks that
      these cults "thrive precisely because culture is secularized."

1023. Wilson, Bryan R. RELIGIOUS SECTS: A SOCIOLOGICAL STUDY. New York:
      World University Library, 1970. 256 pp.

      Discusses the problems of defining "sects" and lists their main
      features, namely voluntariness, exclusivity, merit, self-identifi-
      cation, elite status, expulsion, conscience, and legitimation.
      Seven types of sectarian responses to the world--conversionist,
      revolutionist, introversionist, manipulationist, thaumaturgical,
      reformist, and utopian--are distinguished and described at length.
      Some exceptional cases, like the Mormons, the Shakers, and the
      Catholic Apostolic Church, are briefly analyzed. A final chapter
      deals with the origins, functions, and development of sects.

1024. Wilson, Bryan R., and Daisaku Ikeda. HUMAN VALUES IN A CHANGING
      WORLD: A DIALOGUE ON THE SOCIAL ROLE OF RELIGION. Secaucus, NJ:
      Lyle Stuart, 1987. xv, 364 pp.

Presents an exchange of views between Ikeda, the Japanese leader
of the world's largest Buddhist organization, and Wilson, a noted
British sociologist who has written extensively on sects and cults.
The nature of religious feeling, human reason and responsibility,
and ethical issues are among the topics discussed. Wilson confirms
his position on the rise of new religious movements, namely that
they are a response to contemporary malaise, a spiritual and social
uncertainty that has come into being in response to cultural change
and various deprivations. He regards these movements as ephemeral
and strongly denies that they are an indication of a permanent
religious renewal that will affect culture as a whole or leave any
substantive impact on world order.

1025.   Wilson, John. RELIGION IN AMERICAN LIFE: THE EFFECTIVE PRESENCE.
        Englewood Cliffs, NJ: Prentice-Hall, 1978. xv, 492 pp.

        Provides a comprehensive coverage of recent literature in the
        sociology of religion. The author discusses the concepts of
        "church," "denomination," "sect," and "cult" and concludes that a
        "cult is not a different type of religious group but merely one
        form in which new religious movements appear" (p. 93). Seven types
        of sects are distinguished: conversionist, introversionist, revolu-
        tionist, utopian, manipulationist, thaumaturgical, and reformist.
        Various theories that have been proposed to explain why people join
        new religious movements are critically examined. These movements
        arise out of a changing social order that creates or intensifies
        discontent, anxiety, or isolation. Faith-healing, magic, witch-
        craft, and astrology are seen as part of a "common religion."
        There are references throughout the book to traditional sects and
        new cults. A lengthy bibliography is appended (pp. 454-86).

1026.   Wilson, John. "Making Inferences About Religious Movements." RELI-
        GION: 7 (1977): 149-66.

        Refutes a common anthropological and sociological approach to new
        religious movements that treats them as examples of distorted ra-
        tionality or as ways through which their members overcome their
        distress. Instead, the author stresses the "active and imaginative
        process by which the actors involved in religious movements exter-
        nalize and apprehend their world" (p. 150). The need to study the
        symbolic dimensions of these new cults is underscored. The con-
        tribution of anthropology in this area is sketched with reference
        to some major works on ritual, myth, and symbol.

1027.   Wilson, John. "The Historical Study of Marginal Religious Move-
        ments." RELIGIOUS MOVEMENTS IN CONTEMPORARY AMERICA (item 727),
        pp. 596-627.

        Discusses the interpretations of marginal religious groups that
        have been put forward by historians of American religions, comments
        upon the influence of the social study of sectarianism on the study
        of religious history, and suggests various ways in which historical
        studies of these movements can be pursued. The author thinks that
        American historians of religion have exhibited a declining interest
        in marginal religious movements that were often judged to be on

the fringes of society and, therefore, insignificant. He maintains
that the anthropological study of these movements will directly
benefit historical research. A morphology of marginal movements in
three broad families is outlined: 1) occult groups (such as Spiritualism, Satanism, Scientology); 2) mystical or transcendental
movements (like the Hare Krishna Movement); and 3) Ecstatic or
enthusiastic movements (like Pentecostalism and Seventh-Day Adventism), which are a response to emotional deprivation.

1028.   Wilson, John. "The Sociology of Schism." A SOCIOLOGICAL YEARBOOK
        OF RELIGION IN BRITAIN 4 (1971): 1-20.

        Applies a model of social movements to analyze schism where one
        can observe not only the creation and intensification of conflict,
        but also a qualitative transformation into an open break. This
        model of change and separation is applied to the Plymouth Brethren,
        the Hicksite Quakers, and the Methodists, all of which experienced
        schisms in the late 1920's. The impact of the force of social con-
        trol on the process of schism is discussed. The author suggests
        that "schism can be described in terms of a natural sequence of
        stages, each of which is dependent on the occurrence of the preced-
        ing stage" (p. 19). The progressive components of schism are
        structural conduciveness, structural strain, precipitating factors,
        modifying agents, and forces of social control.

1029.   Wright, Stuart A. LEAVING THE CULTS: THE DYNAMICS OF DEFECTION.
        Washington, DC: Society For the Scientific Study of Religion,
        1987. x, 124 pp.

        Focuses on the process of defection from the new religious move-
        ments. The author first discusses whether cult members are brain-
        washed or whether they are voluntary participants in the movements
        they join. He then outlines some causes and patterns of defection,
        noting the precipitating factors leading to defection and to the
        "tactical modes of exit" (such as covert, overt, and declarative
        departure). And finally, he considers 1) the post-involvement
        attitudes of voluntary defectors over 65% of which claim they were
        wiser for the cult experience, and 2) the problems ex-cult members
        have in reentering society. He discovers that about 50% of these
        ex-cult members become active in conservative, fundamentalist, or
        evangelical denominations or charismatic groups. This book con-
        tains a chapter on method in which the issue of cult sponsorship
        and the presumed legitimation by some sociologists are discussed.
        The author concludes that brainwashing or coercive persuasion is a
        result of popular misconception of the cult involvement process.

1030.   Wright, Stuart A. "Leaving New Religious Movements: Issues,
        Theories, and Research." FALLING FROM THE FAITH (item 578),
        pp. 143-65.

        Examines the recent sociological shift to the study of disengage-
        ment, exiting, and apostasy from new religious movements. These
        studies are arranged in three major areas: 1) the concept of disaf-
        filiation; 2) substantive issues in disaffiliation; and 3) the
        implications of research findings. Departure from the cults is

discussed in terms of three sociological analytical frameworks, namely role theory, causal process model, and organizational model. The most debated areas relating to disaffiliation, namely the activist or passivist model of cult members and the sudden or gradual nature of the conversion process, are outlined. The author offers some speculations on the future of new religious movements which, he thinks, will continue the trend of accommodating themselves to mainstream culture.

1031. Wright, Stuart A. "Dyadic Intimacy and Social Control in Three Cult Movements." SOCIOLOGICAL ANALYSIS 47 (1986): 137-50.

Studies the prohibition against exclusive dyadic relationships in three new religious movements (the Unification Church, the Hare Krishna Movement, and the Children of God), all of which regulate such relationships by arranged marriage, celibacy, and group marriage, respectively. Distinguishing between romantic love (eros) and spiritual love (agape), the author investigates the former to find out to what extent it preserves commitment and deters withdrawal from the cult. He concludes, from interviews with voluntary defectors from each of these movements, that the low incidence of defections that result from dyadic relationships indicates that they have been successfully controlled and that dyadic relationships, when they occur, increase the probability of defection.

1032. Wright, Stuart A. "Post Involvement Attitudes of Voluntary Defectors From Controversial New Religious Movements." JOURNAL FOR THE SCIENTIFIC STUDY OF RELIGION 23 (1984): 172-82.

Studies 45 members of three religious movements (the Unification Church, the Hare Krishna, and the Children of God) who had left without the aid of deprogramming or other counseling. Two-thirds of the defectors could look back on their involvement with some degree of social and emotional distance and express the view that they felt "wiser for the experience." The tendency of these defectors, who admitted joining the group voluntarily, was to be more tolerant and less critical of the movements they once belonged to. The process of disengagement, sometimes lasting for months, is similar in some respects to what occurs in any major transition in life (from marriage to divorce, from one career to another, etc.). Several organizational or sociopsychological factors that are operative in the process of deconversion from a new religious movement are discussed. The author claims that his research finds no support whatsoever for the brainwashing hypothesis. The impact of cult environment cannot be equated with mind control or with the destruction of free will.

1033. Wright, Stuart A. "Defection From New Religious Movements: A Test of Some Theoretical Propositions." THE BRAINWASHING/DEPROGRAMMING CONTROVERSY (item 2126), pp. 106-21.

Examines the more common voluntary defections from the new cults. The nature of voluntary commitment to "world transforming movements" like the Children of God, the Hare Krishna Movement, and the Unification Church is discussed. Four major factors that might play a

role in defection--social isolation, interpersonal dependency, the
imminence of transformation, and the cult's leadership--are considered. The author thinks that defection is likely to take place if
social isolation isn't great, if the regulation of two-person intimacy is less effective, if the regulation of time, lifestyle,
labor, and sexual conduct is perceived to be less strict, and if
the leadership is not seen as exemplary.

1034. Wright, Stuart A., and Elizabeth S. Piper. "Families and Cults:
      Familial Factors Related to Youth Leaving or Remaining in Deviant
      Religious Groups." JOURNAL OF MARRIAGE AND THE FAMILY 48 (1986):
      15-25.

      Interviews 90 former and current members of three highly contro-
      versial cults (the Unification Church, the Hare Krishna Movement,
      and the Children of God) to determine the families' role in their
      leaving or staying in the group. The common deprivation theory,
      which states that young persons join new movements "to compensate
      for unfulfilled needs resulting from family dissatisfaction," is
      questioned. The author discusses the relationships between 1) the
      emergence of cults and the declining family and 2) youth culture,
      life cycle factors, and cult affiliation. Family closeness, paren-
      tal attitudes, and adolescent experience are all necessary to ex-
      plain both defection from, and continued membership in, a cult.
      Whether a cult member remains committed is "to some degree influ-
      enced by the person's parents and the quality of family life in the
      years preceding conversion" (p. 22).

1035. Wuthnow, Robert. THE RESTRUCTURING OF AMERICAN RELIGION: SOCIETY
      AND FAITH SINCE WORLD WAR II. Princeton, NJ: Princeton Univer-
      sity Press, 1988. xiv, 374 pp.

      Surveys the developments in American religion over the last four
      decades, drawing attention to the growing polarization between
      religious liberals and conservatives. The author maintains that
      this split is accompanied by a declining denominationalism and by
      the growth of "special purpose groups," among which he includes
      sects and cults. He considers these groups an American tradition
      and offers some reflections on their rise, character, numbers,
      memberships, social sources, and implications on the mainline
      churches. The growth of these special purpose groups, which are
      one way in which faith is revitalized, "constitutes a significant
      form of social restructuring in American religion" (p. 101).

1036. Wuthnow, Robert. "Indices of Religious Resurgence in the United
      States." RELIGIOUS RESURGENCE: CONTEMPORARY CASES IN ISLAM,
      CHRISTIANITY, AND JUDAISM. Edited by Richard T. Antoun and Mary
      Elaine Hegland. Syracuse, NY: Syracuse University Press, 1987,
      pp. 15-34.

      Examines the contemporary revival in the United States where
      secularization has been the prevailing trend. The author warns
      that the pluralistic nature of American religion and the debate on
      the conditions that give rise to religious revivals make the task
      of assessing the current religious scene difficult. He observes

that there is an overwhelming lack of evidence to suggest 1) that
the strength of the established religions is increasing, and 2) that
the resurgence is not taking place among young people. There is,
however, a growth in membership, resources, and organizational
structures of evangelical denominations. The impact of society and
politics on evangelical activity is assessed. Though not directly
assessing the state of new religious movements, this essay draws a
general picture of the religious scene in the United States in
which these new movements do not seem to be playing a very significant role.

1037. Wuthnow, Robert. "Religious Movements and Counter-Movements in
        North America." NEW RELIGIOUS MOVEMENTS AND RAPID SOCIAL CHANGE
        (item 558), pp. 1-25.

        Attempts to chart the main trends in religious developments over
        the last 30 years and to relate them to the broader cultural and
        social changes that gave rise to them. The religious movements of
        the 1950's (which include the growth of the Seventh-Day Adventists
        and the Mormons) can be understood as efforts to accommodate new
        opportunities or as sectarian reactions against social change. The
        decade of the 1960's is considered to be one of great religious
        turbulence that accounts for the rise of new cults and of the Anti-
        Cult Movement. Developments in society are having an effect on
        religious communities and on the presence and success of the new
        movements.

1038. Wuthnow, Robert. "The Cultural Context of Contemporary Religious
        Movements." CULTS, CULTURE, AND THE LAW (item 684), pp. 43-56.

        Argues that, though the new religious movements have reached
        their peak, many of them have a solid financial and organizational
        base and still claim many followers. The issues that they have
        raised, namely whether their presence signals the decline of secu-
        lar humanism, reflects a deeper shift in the focus of American
        faith, or indicates that our cultural values to need be reexamined,
        are still very much alive. The author holds that the new movements
        are "a product of broader, more pervasive tendencies in American
        culture" (p. 46). The legitimation of religious protest, its vari-
        eties, and its tactics are considered. The new religions do not,
        in the author's opinion, challenge the theoretical basis of the
        modern scientific worldview, but they criticize the problems
        resulting from technology and offer social experiments to overcome
        these difficulties.

1039. Wuthnow, Robert. "World Order and Religious Movements." NEW RELI-
        GIOUS MOVEMENTS: A PERSPECTIVE FOR UNDERSTANDING SOCIETY (item
        551), pp. 47-65.

        Argues that religious movements have emerged from the central
        social processes of the modern world itself and that the study of
        their historical antecedents is a necessary prelude to understand-
        ing them. Sociological efforts to seek their cause in some form of
        rapid social change are judged to be deficient because they do not
        stand up to the test of historical reality. The author proposes

the view that modern new religious movements can better be related
to world order, i.e., "the presence of transnational division of
labor in which societies and members of societies participate,
necessitating recurrent, patterned exchange (economic, political,
and cultural) across national boundaries" (p. 49). He examines
several types of new religious movements, namely revitalization,
reformation, religious militancy, counterreforms, religious accommodation, and sectarianism, and explores the relation between them
and world affairs.

1040. Wuthnow, Robert. "Political Aspects of the Quietist Revival." IN
      GODS WE TRUST (item 683), pp. 229-43.

      Discusses the political attitudes and commitments of the members
      of new religious movements, explores ideological links between
      mysticism and political action, and tests the view that political
      activists have become absorbed in new religions. Basing his re-
      flections on the data gathered during a study of the new religious
      consciousness in the San Francisco Bay Area, the author concludes
      that, though mysticism and political action are not incompatible,
      there is some evidence that mysticism may be redirecting the energy
      of political activists into quietist directions. Mysticism is
      described as "a shortcut to modernity" and as a "ritual release,"
      providing a much-needed rest from daily routines. It is an anti-
      dote to, rather than an expression of, narcissism.

1041. Wuthnow, Robert. EXPERIMENTATION IN AMERICAN RELIGION: THE NEW
      MYSTICISMS AND THEIR IMPLICATIONS FOR THE CHURCHES. Berkeley:
      University of California Press, 1978. x, 221 pp.

      Presents some empirical data relevant to the understanding of
      religious experimentation outside the Judeo-Christian tradition.
      The attractive features of new religious movements, the new values
      and experiences they offer, and the reasons why people defect from
      the church of their upbringing are among the topics discussed.
      Part One of this volume covers religious experimentation and in-
      cludes materials already published elsewhere. Part Two examines
      several developments within the religious mainstream and considers
      the extent of its decline under the influence of the counterculture.
      The author thinks that the recent quest for religious experience is
      a social phenomenon that has been nourished by the rising role of
      popular education, by mass media coverage, by the West's high stan-
      dard of living, and by cultural pluralism. He maintains that this
      quest is also indicative of a "re-enchantment" of the natural and
      social worlds, a reinfusion of divine immanence in worldly affairs.

1042. Wuthnow, Robert. "Religious Movements and the Transition in World
      Order." UNDERSTANDING THE NEW RELIGIONS (item 667), pp. 63-79.

      Argues that the social and cultural conditions of the twentieth
      century are not sufficient to explain the present religious turmoil,
      and the roots of new religious movements must be sought in the
      fabric of social experience itself. In the contemporary situation
      of change, the validation of our "construction of reality" (includ-
      ing supernatural reality) is also being transformed. The author

maintains that there is a world crisis and compares contemporary
responses to it to those that occurred in the late seventeenth and
early nineteenth centuries. He insists that the new religious
movements must be understood in a global perspective.

1043. Wuthnow, Robert. THE CONSCIOUSNESS REFORMATION. Berkeley: Univer-
       sity of California Press, 1976. x, 309 pp.

       Records the results of one of the earliest research projects on
       the new religious scene in the early 1970's, a project that was
       carried out by several scholars in the San Francisco Bay Area. The
       author stresses "the role of long-range cultural shifts which have
       created a 'new consciousness' in which experimentation with social
       alternatives tends to be regarded as more meaningful and legitimate
       than it has in the past" (p. 1). Four systems of meaning, namely
       theism, individualism, social science, and mysticism, are the focus
       of this study. Many tables and statistics, as well as the lengthy
       interview schedule used by the researchers (pp. 269-302), are in-
       cluded in this volume.

1044. Wuthnow, Robert. "The New Religions in Social Context." THE NEW
       RELIGIOUS CONSCIOUSNESS (item 614), pp. 267-93.

       Discusses the significance of the new religious movements in the
       context of research conducted in the San Francisco Bay Area. Three
       questions are raised: 1) how many people are involved in these
       movements?; 2) are these movements promoting changes in the value
       system of American society?; and 3) what kind of people are drawn
       to them? The author distinguishes between countercultural groups
       (that is, offshoots of non-Western or non-Christian traditions,
       like Zen Buddhism, Transcendental Meditation, and the Hare Krishna
       Movement), personal growth groups (like EST, Synanon, and Scien-
       tology), and new Christian groups (that is, Western groups that are
       essentially neutral to Christianity, such as the Children of God,
       the Jews for Jesus, Campus Crusade for Christ, and the Charismat-
       ics). The author thinks that though the membership in these groups
       is not very large, they might continue to provide some people with
       a meaningful alternative to their religious quest.

1045. Wuthnow, Robert. "Recent Patterns of Secularization: A Problem of
       Generations." AMERICAN SOCIOLOGICAL REVIEW 41 (1976): 850-67.

       Suggests that the counterculture generation contributed to the
       shift in religious trends since the 1960's and that the seculariza-
       tion process in the 1950's was more pronounced among the younger
       generation. Basing his argument on Gallup Polls and other surveys,
       the author stresses the importance of age differences in under-
       standing discontinuities in the secularization process.

1046. Wuthnow, Robert, and Charles G. Glock. "Religious Loyalty, Defec-
       tion, and Experimentation Among College Youth." JOURNAL FOR THE
       SCIENTIFIC STUDY OF RELIGION 12 (1973): 157-80.

       Reports on a survey of students at the University of California
       at Berkeley that points to a trend away from conventional religion
       and a movement towards new forms of religious beliefs and practices.

The nature and sources of religious loyalty, defection, and experimentation with new religious movements are examined. Religious
defection from the mainline churches is interpreted as one of the
signs of general disenchantment with the familiar. Those who join
an alternative religion are breaking away from their traditional
upbringing rather than with religion itself. They are suffering,
according to the author, from "psychic stress."

1047. Yinger, Milton J. COUNTERCULTURE: THE PROMISE AND THE PERIL OF
A WORLD TURNED UPSIDE DOWN. New York: Free Press, 1982. xi,
371 pp.

Defines counterculture as "all those situationally created designs for living formed in contexts of high anomie and intra-
societal conflict; the designs being inversions of, in sharp opposition to, the historically created designs" (pp. 39-40). Countercultures can be measured through four sets of observations: perceived (by outsiders), experienced (by participants), measured
(by observers through records and comparisons), and interpreted
(through informal judgments of observers). The various sources of
countercultures (such as economic and demographic factors and
relative deprivations) are discussed. Some of the new religious
groups, like Satanism, gnostic sects, and chiliastic groups, "turn
the spiritual world upside down." Others, though still deviant,
remain closer to the established traditions. Three perspectives on
the new religions are possible, namely those of the participants,
of the anticultists, and of those who take a neutral stand and
explore the implications of the controversy for religious freedom
and civil liberties. It is pointed out that "frontal attack also
promotes deviance amplification rather than a removal of the
desired behavior" (p. 245). Countercultures are not mere fads;
they symbolize fundamental dilemmas and deeply influence the course
of human life.

1048. Zerin, Marjorie Fisher. "The Pied Piper Phenomenon: Family Systems
and Vulnerability to Cults." SCIENTIFIC RESEARCH AND NEW RELI-
GIONS (item 645), pp. 160-73.

Focuses on the preliminary recruitment phase of cult involvement
before the individual has made his or her full commitment. Both
personal and familial factors can contribute to variation in a
person's vulnerability to cult recruitment. The author maintains
that the family factors are related to the larger social system.
Some proposals for future research are made.

1049. Zurcher, Louis A. "A Self-Concept for Religious Violence." VIO-
LENCE AND THE CULTS (item 653), pp. 57-87.

Argues that contemporary social and technological changes have
eroded familiar self-concepts and that some people resolve the
ensuing discomfort by joining a highly cohesive religious cult.
Social change can lead to problematic personal adaptation to escape
the anxiety associated with dislocation. Four types of self-con-
ception--physical, social, reflective, and oceanic--can become
exaggerated or exclusive and lead to violence.

D. METHODOLOGICAL STUDIES

1050.   Balch, Robert W. "What's Wrong with the Study of New Religions and
        What We Can Do About It." SCIENTIFIC RESEARCH AND NEW RELIGIONS:
        DIVERGENT PERSPECTIVES (item 645), pp. 24-39.

        Reviews some of the problems inherent in current research on new
        religious movements and proposes several solutions. Bias, confu-
        sion over terms, overgeneralizations, causal analogies, and data
        collection are discussed and it is concluded that "the study of
        new religions suffers from serious methodological deficiencies"
        (p. 34). The use of a variety of data sources whenever possible,
        the standardization of data collection techniques, and the creation
        of more outlets for ethnographic studies are strongly recommended.
        An outline of a comprehensive guide for ethnographers is provided.
        The author thinks that there is a need for a new journal dedicated
        to the ethnography of new religious movements and for a monographic
        series on new religions.

1051.   Barker, Eileen. "Brahmins Don't Eat Mushrooms: Participant Obser-
        vation and the New Religions." LSE QUARTERLY (June 1987): 127-52.

        Discusses the problems of the method known as participant ob-
        servation, a method that the author has used consistently in her
        studies on new religious movements, particularly the Unification
        Church. The tensions involved in such research are illustrated
        with examples from the author's experience. Three vertical levels
        or visions of social reality are distinguished, namely the indi-
        vidual (personal), the social (interpersonal), and the sociological
        (impersonal). These levels should be understood by the respective
        application of the tools of interviews, participant observation,
        and questionnaires. The advantages and disadvantages of studying a
        religious movement as an outsider or as an insider are debated. It
        is argued that "too much detachment or too much attachment becomes
        counterproductive" (p. 51).

1052.   Barker, Eileen. "Supping With the Devil: How Long a Spoon Does the
        Sociologist Need?" SOCIOLOGICAL ANALYSIS 44 (1983): 197-206.

        Discusses the issue of doing research on the Unification Church
        in the context of the author's extensive studies on this church in
        Britain. She questions Horowitz's (item 1072) two assumptions that
        social scientists cannot conduct conscientious research on a church
        that sponsors their work and that a religious organization cannot
        possibly sanction, much less approve of, proper sociological anal-
        ysis of itself. She strongly insists that the researcher's results
        must be judged on their own merits and maintains that "any system-
        atic observation of the movement which did not include attendance
        at Unification conferences would, to say the least, be methodolog-
        ically deficient" (p. 199). The social-scientific method of par-
        ticipant observation requires that researchers take part in the
        conferences sponsored by the organization. It is only through such
        participation than much invaluable data can be collected.

1053. Barker, Eileen. "Sun Myung Moon and the Scientists." TEILHARD
       REVIEW 14 (1979): 35-37.

       Discusses the science conferences organized and sponsored by the
       Unification Church. In spite of the objections that have been
       raised against them, it is argued that they are useful in making
       the participants aware of the complexity of knowledge and the vari-
       ety of human opinions. Besides confronting science with values,
       the conferences provide good publicity for the Unification Church
       and function as morale boosters among its members. The author
       favors such conferences if for no other reason than because they
       provide a forum for the exchange of views between scholars from
       various disciplines.

1054. Barker, Eileen. "Confessions of a Methodological Schizophrenic:
       Problems Encountered in a Study of Reverend Sun Myung Moon's
       Unification Church (1)." RESEARCH BULLETIN--INSTITUTE FOR THE
       STUDY OF WORSHIP AND RELIGIOUS ARCHITECTURE, University of Bir-
       mingham, England, (1978): 70-89.

       Discusses the various methodological issues that the author en-
       countered in her study of the Unification Church. Among the prob-
       lems she investigated were the reasons why young adults join this
       new religion and the freedom of choice they had in so doing. Three
       different lines of approach, namely participant in-depth interviews,
       participant observation, and the use of questionnaires, are outlined.
       The author further describes her role as stranger. She admits that
       "realizing that making statements about value-judgments was both
       necessary and impossible" (p. 84). She concludes that, while she
       rejects the lifestyle and ideology of the church, she learned a lot
       from its members.

*   Becker, Howard E. "Problems of Inference and Proof in Participant
       Observation." Cited above as item 73.

1055. Beckford, James A. "Some Questions About the Relationship Between
       Scholars and the New Religious Movements." SOCIOLOGICAL ANALYSIS
       44 (1983): 189-96.

       Reflects on the ethical issues raised by the sponsorship of aca-
       demic scholarship by the New Ecumenical Research Association (NEW
       ERA) of the Unification Church. The author distinguishes between
       different kinds of sponsorship, participation, and accusations
       brought against this church. Four different types of meetings that
       are organized by the Unification Church are briefly described. The
       author reflects seriously on the following three major accusations
       against the church's sponsorship and organization of meetings of
       scholars: 1) the meetings are a cover-up of its authoritarian and
       anti-intellectual ideology; 2) they are a means for gaining legiti-
       macy and respectability; and 3) they are also a way of finding out
       which scholars are on its side. Whether "social scientists attend-
       ing meetings sponsored by the Unification Church can be considered
       as consultants" (p. 193) is one of the questions raised by the
       author. It is claimed that the intentions of the church are to
       counteract the hostile propaganda of the Anti-Cult Movement and its

leaders have on a number of occasions interfered with research
results and procedures. The ease with which it can publish conference material also raises questions about the quality of the papers
published.

1056. Bernard, H. Russell. RESEARCH METHODS IN CULTURAL ANTHROPOLOGY.
       Beverly Hills, CA: Sage Publications, 1988. 259 pp.

       Gives an overview of the research methods used by anthropologists
       in field research. Three major areas are discussed, namely prepa-
       rations for field research, collecting information, and analyzing
       data. Participant observation is one of the topics treated at
       length. Because this book does not enter into the question of how
       to study new religious movements, it provides a clear and neutral
       picture of this anthropological research procedure. A basic bib-
       liography (pp. 486-503) is added.

1057. Bromley, David G., Jeffrey K. Hadden, and Phillip E. Hammond.
       "Reflections on the Scholarly Study of New Religious Movements."
       THE FUTURE OF NEW RELIGIOUS MOVEMENTS (item 579), pp. 210-217.

       Discusses two major obstacles in the scholarly studies of new
       religious movements: 1) the opposition of anticultists to such
       efforts; and 2) the ambivalent relationships of cult members. It
       is argued that self-consciousness results from studying new reli-
       gions and that this self-consciousness has had an impact on the
       study itself. The issue of the close contact that social scien-
       tists adopt to study the cults is also brought up. Because some
       scholars have gained inside knowledge of new religions, they have
       ended up defending them against anticult accusations. The authors
       maintain that in the debate about the study of the cults there has
       emerged a "major disagreement regarding the proper interpretation
       of human behavior" (p. 214).

1058. Bromley, David G., and Anson Shupe. "Evolving Foci in Participant
       Observation: Research as an Emergent Process." FIELDWORK EXPERI-
       ENCE: QUALITATIVE APPROACHES TO SOCIAL RESEARCH. Edited by
       William B. Shaffir, Robert A. Stebbins, and Allan Turowetz. New
       York: Saint Martin's Press, 1980, pp. 191-203.

       Describes how the authors shifted their research focus as they
       applied the method of participant observation in their studies of
       two conflicting groups, namely the Unification Church and the
       National Ad Hoc Committee Engaged in Freeing Minds (CEFM). The
       first contacts with the groups and the subsequent involvement in
       their activities led the researchers to adopt "a much more complex
       and relativistic view of both groups" (p. 196). The authors found
       that participant observation helped them understand and sympathize
       with both positions. They discovered, however, that the popular
       view of the Unification Church did not conform with their observa-
       tions and was rather a social construction. Their sympathies thus
       tended to swing in favor of the church. They describe their ef-
       forts to maintain some relationship with both groups and advance
       some practical suggestions for researchers.

*   Bruyn, Severyn. "The Methodology of Participant Observation."
        Cited above as item 79.

1059.   Bulmer, Martin. "When is Disguise Justified?: Alternatives to
        Covert Participant Observation." QUALITATIVE SOCIOLOGY 5 (1982):
        251-64.

        Debates the ethical and practical merits of the method of covert
        participant observation, that is, when the researcher's identity
        and intentions are not revealed to those being studied. The author
        outlines the various research roles that may be adopted, pointing
        out that a variety of these roles exist even though they are not
        often recognized. Besides the overt and covert methods, the author
        lists other possible approaches that can be taken, such as those of
        1) the overt native as stranger, 2) the covert native as stranger,
        3) the overt stranger, and 4) the covert stranger. Though not
        particularly concerned with the study of new religious movements,
        this essay deals with several issues that have played an important
        part in the debate on how to study the cults.

1060.   Bulmer, Martin. "Comments on the 'Ethics of Covert Methods.'"
        BRITISH JOURNAL OF SOCIOLOGY 31 (1980): 59-65.

        Takes issue with Homan's position (item 1070) that covert methods
        of research do not have an impact on the people under study. The
        author holds that covert participation may be a gross invasion of
        personal privacy and must be used only in highly exceptional cases.

1061.   Cole, John P. "Anthropology Beyond the Fringe." SKEPTICAL INQUIR-
        ER 2.2 (1978): 62-71.

        Discusses the anthropological approach of cultural relativism
        when it is applied to the study of strange beliefs and practices
        that include extrasensory perception (ESP), magic, the Atlantis
        and Lemuric myths, and the history of ancient astronauts. It is
        argued that the nonjudgmental, relativistic viewpoint need not
        abstain from evaluating claims of objective reality. The author
        focuses on two main theories: 1) that native American Indian cul-
        tures stem from old, pre-Columbian sources; and 2) that the peoples
        of America are so ancient that the beginnings of the human race are
        to be traced to America rather than to Africa. According to the
        author, anthropologists do nothing else but further misunderstand-
        ing when they refrain from debunking popular misconceptions.

1062.   Davis, Fred. "The Martian and the Convert: Ontological Polarities
        in Social Research." URBAN LIFE AND CULTURE 2 (1973): 333-43.

        Discusses the problem of knowledge when scholars are studying
        their fellow human beings. The metaphors of "martian" and "con-
        vert" are used to designate two different approaches to the object
        of study. The "martian" drastically distances himself or herself
        from the immediate concern and involvement with those being studied.
        The convert, on the other hand, immerses himself or herself in the
        ideological framework and lifestyle of those under investigation in
        order to gain greater insight and understanding. The author thinks
        that neither way suffices by itself.

1063. Dole, Arthur A., and Steve K. Dubrow Eickel. "Moon Over Academe."
      JOURNAL OF RELIGION AND HEALTH 20 (1981): 35-40.

      Analyzes the reasons scholars give for attending the Annual In-
      ternational Conference of the Unity of Sciences sponsored by the
      Unification Church. The authors conclude that these scholars are
      being manipulated into supporting this new religious movement.
      Their attitudes "represent a case history in manipulation, in the
      calculated misapplication of the principles of open oppression,
      religious freedom, and the search for values" (p. 35).

1064. Duster, Tony, David Matza, and David Wellman. "Fieldwork and the
      Protection of Human Subjects." AMERICAN SOCIOLOGIST 14 (1979):
      136-42.

      Reflects on the issues brought about by the use of participant
      observation employed by the U. S. Department of Housing and Urban
      Development and suggests that laws should be introduced to protect
      the rights of those under study. The legal problems involved are
      also applicable to the EST program, which is part of the psycho-
      logical services industry that requires evaluation.

1065. Ellwood, Robert S. "The Study of New Religious Movements in Amer-
      ica." BULLETIN OF THE COUNCIL FOR THE STUDY OF RELIGION 10.3
      (July 1979): 69-72.

      Explains that the study of new religions should avoid the nega-
      tive connotations of words like "cult" and "sect," be aware of the
      variety that exists among these various groups, and examine care-
      fully the historical perspective. The author reviews some models
      that have been used in the study of new religions and favors the
      systems approach that sees American spirituality as "an interlock-
      ing whole in which all subsystems are interaction with all others"
      (p. 71). He maintains that alternative religions are not periph-
      eral to American religion but rather a part of it.

1066. Filstead, William J., editor. QUALITATIVE METHODOLOGY: FIRSTHAND
      INVOLVEMENT WITH THE SOCIAL WORLD. Chicago: Markham Publishing
      Co., 1970. xi, 352 pp.

      Contains a collection of essays describing and discussing socio-
      logical approaches to fieldwork. The roles scholars adopt in field-
      work, the collection and analysis of data, the problems of validity
      and reliability of the information collection, and the ethical
      issues that arise in the field are among the topics covered. Many
      of the essays deal specifically with the method of participant
      observation as applied to different social contexts.

1067. Geertz, Clifford. "From the Native's Point of View: On the Nature
      Anthropological Understanding." INTERPRETATIVE SOCIAL SCIENCE: A
      READER. Edited by Paul Rabinow and William M. Sullivan. Berke-
      ley: University of California Press, 1979, pp. 225-41.

      Reflects, in the context of the author's fieldwork in Africa and
      Southeast Asia, on the problems of seeing and understanding matters
      from the point of view of those who are being studied, without

letting one's own biases and assumptions dictate the conclusions of
one's research. The issue, according to the author, is whether and
how the researcher can actually describe perceptions, sentiments,
outlooks, and experiences. Understanding "the natives' inner lives
is more like grasping a proverb, catching an allusion, seeing a
joke...than it is like achieving communion" (p. 241).

1068.   Gutwirth, Jacques. "Fieldwork Method and the Sociology of Jews:
        Case Studies of Hassidic Communities." JEWISH JOURNAL OF SOCIOL-
        OGY 20 (1978): 49-58.

        Argues that the anthropological methods of participant observa-
        tion and open-ended interviews are best suited for the study of
        Hasidic communities. The author describes his own studies of var-
        ious Hasidic groups, particularly those in Boston. He describes his
        work as "urban ethnology" since most Hasidic communities are
        located in large cities. Differences between the various Hasidic
        groups can only be brought to light by anthropological methods.

1069.   Hillery, George A. "Triangulation in Religious Research: A Socio-
        logical Approach to the Study of Monasteries." REVIEW OF RELI-
        GIOUS RESEARCH 23 (1981): 22-38.

        Focuses on the basic research tools, namely questionnaires,
        participant observation, interviews, and documents, used in the
        study of monks. The author holds that a combination of these
        methods, which he calls "triangulation," is a distinctive approach
        that yields new and unique information and that can help in the
        formulation and testing of hypotheses.

1070.   Homan, Roger. "The Ethics of Covert Methods." BRITISH JOURNAL OF
        SOCIOLOGY 31 (1980): 46-59.

        Reflects critically on the author's own study (item 1309) of
        the members of a sect known as the "Old Time Pentecostals." After
        a brief description of the main features of the group and a state-
        ment on the use of clandestine and dishonest methods sometimes used
        in sociological and anthropological research, the author raises two
        types of ethical problems, namely those of individual morality and
        professional ethics. It is pointed out that casual and purposeful
        observation is not always distinguishable and that researchers may
        find themselves observing human behavior without informing the
        subjects of the nature of their inquiry and intentions. The author
        thinks that covert methods do not significantly affect the people
        under study.

1071.   Horowitz, Irving Louis. "A Reply to Critics and Crusaders." SO-
        CIOLOGICAL ANALYSIS 44 (1983): 221-26.

        Replies to his many critics of his view that sponsorship of con-
        ferences by the Unification Church is in conflict with the main
        principles of scientific research. The author argues that "the
        romance of intimate and intense participation in the lives of sects
        and cults is not without its dangers" and that the limits of an
        "empiricist ethnography or symbolic interactivism" must be care-
        fully drawn.

1072. Horowitz, Irving Louis. "Universal Standards, Not Uniform Beliefs:
       Further Reflections on Scientific Method and Religious Sponsors."
       SOCIOLOGICAL ANALYSIS 44 (1983): 179-82.

       Discusses the thorny question of whether scientific research
       projects conducted under religious or government sponsorship raise
       the same issues. The author thinks that there is the danger that
       scholars may become representatives, spokepersons, or even apolo-
       gists for governmental and theological special interests. Three
       major points of contention that have emerged in the study of the
       Unification Church are listed: 1) the distinction between church
       and state which is denied or downplayed in Reverend Moon's theol-
       ogy; 2) the stress in American religion on individual conscience
       and judgment that seems to have been replaced by the collectivism
       of the Unification Church; and 3) the insistence in the Unification
       Church on the absolute character of its goals. The author main-
       tains that faith-oriented institutions and scientific research are
       distinct and in tension and that new religious movements tend to
       resist sociological analysis and investigation.

1073. Horowitz, Irving Louis. "Sin, Science, and Scholarship." SIN,
       SCIENCE, AND SCHOLARSHIP (item 1783), pp. 261-81.

       Discusses the proceedings of the Fifth International Conference
       on the Unity of the Sciences. The author states that this confer-
       ence, organized and sponsored by the Unification Church, was "based
       on a powerful a priori belief that only the wall of the absolute
       could stem the tide of totalitarian pragmatism" (p. 263). Despite
       the various academic disciplines that were represented, all the
       scholars present appeared to share an animosity towards the Commu-
       nist menace. The author is particularly concerned with the rules
       for participation in these meetings. He points out that, because
       participation contributes to the overt legitimization goal of the
       Unification Church, it is necessary for those who agree to take
       part in the conferences to be fully aware of what they are doing.
       He thinks that the role of the Reverend Moon in such meetings is
       carefully screened and muted and that those scholars who attend
       them are indirectly supporting the Unification Church's ideology
       and activities.

1074. Lewis, James R. "The Scholarship of 'Cults' and the 'Cult' of
       Scholarship." JOURNAL OF DHARMA 12 (1987): 96-107.

       Insists that, as a member of a new religious movement (namely
       Yogi Bhajan's Healthy, Happy, Holy Organization), the author finds
       contemporary scholarly studies on cults deficient in understanding
       and one-sided in their assumptions. Modern scholarship has taken
       for granted that rationality and secularity are the best paths to
       knowledge. Two major suggestions are made for humanizing the
       approach to the new movements: 1) the "life world" of the members
       of new religious movements should be more adequately described;
       and 2) the models used in the study of these groups should be re-
       examined and judgmental aspects eliminated. Thus, rather than
       viewing people who join a cult as ethically deprived individuals,
       one can see them as seeking a context in which they can engage in

moral self-affirmation. It is the author's view that adjustment to contemporary secular culture should not be taken as an absolute standard of health, maturity, and rationality.

1075. Lynch, Frederick R. "Field Research and Future History: Problems Posed for Ethnographic Sociologists by the 'Doomsday Cult' Making Good." AMERICAN SOCIOLOGIST 12 (1977): 80-87.

Examines the difficulties brought to the fore by Lofland's study (item 1832) of a cult (namely "Divine Precept") which, in spite of his attempts to keep it anonymous, is now recognized to have been the Unification Church in its early stages in the United States. Knowing that the group Lofland studied was in fact this church is important for researchers who must take into account the history and development of the church. Among the questions raised is "how should an ethnographic sociologist respond to attempts of government authorities to gain access to research data in order to check upon the possible genesis of illegal activities by a group or movement which has emerged as a potential threat to the well-being of society?" (p. 85).

1076. Mackie, Marlene, and Merlin B. Brinkerhoff. "Moonie Conferences: Dialog or Duplicity?" UPDATE: A QUARTERLY JOURNAL ON NEW RELIGIOUS MOVEMENTS 7.3 (1983): 22-37.

Evaluates the scholarly conferences sponsored and funded by the Unification Church as "one of the cleverest tactics ever devised by a social movement" (p. 22). Three main motives, namely consultation, instruction, and proselytization, that are clearly behind these conferences are discussed. The current debate on the ethics of scholarly participation in these meetings is summarized. The authors think that further discussion on scholarly involvement in these conferences is necessary. They conclude by stating that, for the Moonies, the conferences are a "legitimation seeking strategy."

1077. Merton, Robert K. "Insiders and Outsiders: A Chapter in the Sociology of Knowledge." AMERICAN JOURNAL OF SOCIOLOGY 78 (1972): 9-47.

Reflects on current social change that is being initiated by, and funneled through, diverse social movements, all of which aim at achieving a new collective consciousness, solidarity, and total allegiance to a new ideology. New movements usually propound an "insider doctrine" that is sharply contrasted to the knowledge of outsiders. The author discusses the social basis of the insider's knowledge and contrasts the social structure of the movement with that of the mainline culture. He explores the perspectives of both insiders and outsiders from the point of view of the sociology of knowledge. He thinks that the claims made by both parties are a hindrance to understanding. For example, the insider's insistence that you have to belong to the group to understand it is an instance of sheer ethnocentrism.

1078. Naroll, Raoul, and Ronald Cohen, editors. A HANDBOOK OF METHOD IN CULTURAL ANTHROPOLOGY. New York: Columbia University Press, 1970. xxi, 1017.

Presents comprehensive coverage of anthropological approaches
to the study of cultures. Besides a general introductory section,
the following areas are the subject of the discussions: 1) general
problems in anthropological method; 2) the fieldwork process;
3) the various methods of ethnographic analysis; 4) comparative
approaches; 5) problems of categorization; and 6) special problems
of the comparative method. Though somewhat dated and largely
limited to the study of nonliterate societies, this volume is
useful because it examines methods that have been applied to the
new religious movements before the current issues surrounding the
study of the cults had surfaced.

*   Orlans, Harold. "Ethical Problems in the Relations of Research
         Sponsors and Investigators." Cited above as item 121.

1079.   O'Toole, Roger, editor. SYMPOSIUM ON SCHOLARSHIP AND SPONSORSHIP.
         SOCIOLOGICAL ANALYSIS 44 (1983): 177-223.

         Presents the discussions on the methodological and ethical issues
         that began at a joint session of three professional societies,
         namely the Society for the Scientific Study of Religion, the Amer-
         ican Sociological Association, and the Religious Research Associa-
         tion. The debate centered on whether the funding of research on
         new religious movements by some of the new movements themselves
         (notably the Unification Church) has a deleterious effect on the
         research results.

1080.   Pilarzyk, Thomas, and Lakshmi Bharadwaj. "What is Real?: The Fail-
         ure of the Phenomenological Approach in a Field Study of the
         Divine Light Mission." HUMANITY AND SOCIETY 2.4 (1978): 16-34.

         Examines the nature, utility, and limitations of the phenomeno-
         logical method for obtaining objective accounts of cult beliefs and
         practices. The criteria of validity in this type of research are
         discussed and an overview of the various types of such research
         given. The method is then tested in relation to the Divine Light
         Mission. The authors point out that in order to understand the
         members of this cult on its own terms, they had to get involved in
         the daily lives of the devotees or "premies," and thus abandon
         their stance as observers. The problems involved in such partici-
         pation are discussed. Because of the competing and irreconcilable
         ontological assumptions in the sociologists' and devotees' world-
         views, the phenomenological method posits problems that cannot be
         resolved.

1081.   Richardson, James T. "Methodological Considerations in the Study
         of New Religions." DIVERGENT PERSPECTIVES ON THE NEW RELIGIONS
         (item 645), pp. 130-37.

         Considers the disagreement between two groups of scholars who are
         studying the new religions and who have often been labeled "pro-
         cultists" or "anti-cultists" in their respective approaches. The
         author thinks that the level and strength of the debate on the
         matter deserve serious consideration. Three reasons are advanced
         to explain why scholars disagree so strongly on the cults: 1) the

divergent perspectives and social locations of researchers; 2) the differences in what is actually studied; 3) the tendencies to overgeneralize; and 4) the different methodologies used in the research project itself.

1082. Richardson, James T., Mary M. Stewart, and Robert B. Simmonds. "Researching a Fundamentalist Commune." UNDERSTANDING THE NEW RELIGIONS (item 667), pp. 235-51.

Describes the authors' approach to the study of a large, communal, evangelical Christian group that is part of the Jesus Movement, and compares their research experiences with those of other scholars. Various problems encountered during the research, such as the intense proselytizing efforts of the Jesus People, are discussed. The authors state that they were open about their objectives in studying the group because they believe that to deceive the members would have been "unnecessary, impractical, and unethical." It is argued that certain group practices and the authoritarian belief system actually made positive contributions to the research project, since they rendered the members passive in the face of a concerted effort to study them. The success of the authors' approach is attributed to two main factors: 1) the major data was gathered by a team of researchers; and 2) those participating in the project allowed a more open discussion of their own beliefs with some of the commune members.

1083. Robbins, Thomas. "Nuts, Sluts, and Converts--Studying Religious Groups as Social Problems: A Comment." SOCIOLOGICAL ANALYSIS 46 (1985): 171-78.

Discusses the proposal by Horowitz (item 1071) that new religious movements should be studied as social problems. The issues of funding research on these movements and of exploring them in an objective, nonjudgmental manner are raised. The author approaches these problems within the broad framework of the sociology of religion which, he thinks, has become too "clerical" in orientation. He thinks that sociology faces a "credibility gap" because of the controversial nature of the cults. The strictly value-neutral, scientific study of religion and the "detente" between religion and the social sciences may suffer in the long run.

1084. Robbins, Thomas. "The Beach Is Washing Away: Controversial Religion and the Sociology of Religion." SOCIOLOGICAL ANALYSIS 44 (1983): 207-14.

Reflects on the criticism of some scholars, especially Irving Horowitz (see item 1071), that social scientists are favoring the cults. One accusation in particular, namely "whether a cultist whose group practices mind control can be trusted to analyze groups objectively" (p. 210), is discussed at some length. The study of contemporary religious movements is compared to the traditional anthropological studies of "exotic" cultures. The author thinks that just as anthropologists felt protective towards these cultures, so too contemporary students of new religions might assume a protective attitude towards their adherents. He states that if the

Catholic Church can sponsor research, and if a Jesuit can be both
a sociologist of religion and an expert in his faith, then there
seems to be no reason why the Unification Church cannot sponsor
research and a Moonie be engaged in scientifically oriented studies.

1085. Robbins, Thomas, Dick Anthony, and Thomas E. Curtis. "The Limits
      of Symbolic Realism: Problems of Empathetic Field Observation in
      a Sectarian Context." JOURNAL FOR THE SCIENTIFIC STUDY OF RELI-
      GION 12 (1973): 259-71.

      Argues that an approach to the study of religion that combines
      neutral scientific objectivity with a generic sympathy for reli-
      gious beliefs runs into difficulties when applied to rigid sects
      that do not accept the legitimacy of other religious institutions.
      The authors discuss the problem in relation to their study of the
      Jesus Freaks in California and point out that such researchers may
      come under heavy proselytization pressures by the subjects they're
      studying. Tension between researchers and their subjects may ham-
      per the research itself. The pressures exerted by the subjects
      under study may create intellectual and practical drawbacks.

1086. Robertson, Roland. "Scholarship, Partnership, and Sponsorship
      and the 'Moonie Problem': A Comment." SOCIOLOGICAL ANALYSIS 46
      (1978): 179-84.

      Comments on the Symposium on Scholarship and Sponsorship (item
      1079) that debated the influence of the new religious movements on
      social-scientific research. It is argued that both the integrity
      of individual scholars and the effects on scholarship itself must
      be taken into consideration. While favoring some involvement in
      conferences sponsored by the Unification Church, Robertson warns
      that this involvement complicates the vocational and research as-
      pects of sociological inquiry. He contrasts the functional with
      the critical analysis of new religious movements. In his view some
      rethinking concerning the study of the cults is needed.

1087. Ryan, Joseph M. "Ethnoscience and Problems of Method in the Social
      Scientific Study of Religion." SOCIOLOGICAL ANALYSIS 39 (1978):
      241-49.

      Discusses the methodological issue of how one can study religion
      scientifically without falling into reductionism and suggests that
      developments in anthropology (mainly cognitive anthropology and
      ethnoscience) offer valuable insights for theoretical development
      and methodological procedures. The advantages of the scientific
      approach are outlined. Ethnoscientists shift the focus of the
      questions asked in their research: they ask how people are reli-
      gious, rather than how religious people are. This procedure allows
      researchers to discover "how people become religious, how a given
      socio-religious identity is achieved and validated, how religious
      meaning is created, and other related problems" (p. 244). A short
      bibliography of the ethnoscientific method is included.

1088. Saliba, John A. "The New Ethnography and the Study of Religion."
      JOURNAL FOR THE SCIENTIFIC STUDY OF RELIGION 13 (1974): 145-59.

Describes one anthropological method of research, namely the new ethnography or ethnoscience, and explores its applicability to the study of religion. The author explains how this approach, which stresses participant observation, is suitable for describing religious beliefs, experiences, and behavior from the perspective of the believers themselves. Because it encourages empathy on the part of the student, this method helps towards greater objectivity and accuracy and increases one's understanding of other people's religious lives. Though not concerned specifically with the study of the cults, this essay hints that ethnoscience can be profitably applied to the study of all kinds of religious phenomena.

1089. Shaffir, William. "Some Reflections on Approaches to Fieldwork in Hassidic Communities." JEWISH JOURNAL OF SOCIOLOGY 27 (1985): 115-34.

Reflects on the author's own experience in studying various Hasidic communities and focuses on some of the ethical issues that arise in the fieldwork approach. The way the author presented himself to the people he was studying and the attitudes and emotions he assumed are described. The author states that "fieldwork often involves carefully constructed and managed self-presentations" (p. 124). Participant observation is, in his opinion, inherently deceptive. He relates in some detail his own covert research among the Tasher Hasidic community. The problems of establishing contact and creating a trusting relationship with the people chosen to be studied are treated. It is maintained that these problems are not solved through a fixed and rigid methodology.

1090. Shupe, Anson, and David G. Bromley. "Walking a Tightrope: Dilemma of Participant Observation of Groups in Conflict." QUALITATIVE SOCIOLOGY 2 (1980): 3-21.

Discusses some of the difficulties the authors encountered in their application of the participant observation method to two opposing groups, namely the Unification Church and the Anti-Cult Movement. Five major methodological issues are raised: 1) the researcher's role definition and justification; 2) the pressures to go native; 3) public pressure to take a stand; 4) evolving commitments; and 5) gaining comparable information and insights. The authors explain their involvement with both groups and the serious obstacles they had to overcome to maintain a working relationship with both.

1091. Snow, David A. "The Disengagement Process: A Neglected Problem in Participant Observation Research." QUALITATIVE SOCIOLOGY 3 (1980): 100-22.

Discusses the process by which field researchers disengage themselves from their participant-observation roles. Three questions are raised: 1) when does the researcher decide that the research has come to an end?; 2) what outside factors can hasten one's disengagement?; and 3) what obstacles impede the researcher from leaving the field? The author attempts to answer these questions in the context of his field studies of the Nichiren Shoshu of America.

1092. Stone, Donald. "On Knowing How We Know About the New Religions."
       UNDERSTANDING THE NEW RELIGIONS (item 667), pp. 141-52.

       Discusses the issues involved in researching the new religious
       cults, especially those of objectivity and fair-mindedness. Var-
       ious research methods, especially that of participant observation,
       are dealt with. The author finds some flaws in the methods of
       personal involvement (or experiential participation) and in the
       attitude of cognitive openness (which takes the new movements
       seriously), even though they have the advantage of preventing re-
       ductionism, that is, explaining the new movements simply as ways of
       fulfilling one's needs. Some complementary approaches, such as the
       viewpoints of both apostates and practicing members, are also de-
       sirable.

1093. Wallis, Roy. "Religion, Reason, and Responsibility: A Reply to
       Professor Horowitz." SOCIOLOGICAL ANALYSIS 44 (1983): 215-20.

       Responds to Horowitz's view (see items 1071-73) that research
       sponsored by the new religious movements themselves should be
       avoided. Wallis outlines his own participation in various academic
       meetings organized and funded by the Unification Church and con-
       cludes that the hostility shown to the church on this account is
       unwarranted and the accusation that it is actually opposed to crit-
       ical inquiry is unsubstantiated. He insists that attendance at
       gatherings sponsored by the church does not imply acceptance of its
       ideology and/or approval of the lifestyle of its members. It is
       argued that it should not be surprising that the Moonies use the
       presence of scholars at conference to redress the balance of nega-
       tive publicity that has been directed against them.

1094. Wallis, Roy. "The Moral Career of a Research Project." DOING
       SOCIAL RESEARCH. Edited by Colin Bell and Howard Newby. New
       York: Free Press, 1977, pp. 149-69.

       Reflects, in the context of the author's study on Scientology
       (see item 2062), on the moral and political issues that research on
       human subjects necessarily brings to the fore. A brief description
       of Scientology is given and the method used to investigate this new
       religious movement outlined. The author considers the relation-
       ships he established with members and ex-members alike and the
       discussions about his research project with the movement's leaders.
       The negative reaction to his earlier publication on Scientology
       and the campaign of harassment that Scientology apparently con-
       ducted against him are sketched. A reply by David Gaiman of the
       Church of Scientology is appended.

1095. Whyte, William F. "On Making the Most of Participant Observation."
       AMERICAN SOCIOLOGIST 14 (1979): 56-66.

       Discusses a common sociological and anthropological method of
       studying human subjects, namely participant observation. Three
       major questions are the focus of the author's reflections: 1) what
       role does the participant observer have in developing relationships
       with the people and institutions under study?; 2) what should those
       being studied get out of the research project?; and 3) can the

scholar combine some involvement without jeopardizing his or her
study? The author distinguishes between overt and covert participant observation and explores the advantages and disadvantages of
each. It is maintained that the people being studied should be
viewed as active collaborators in the research process.

1096. Wilson, Bryan R. "Methodological Considerations in the Study of
        Religious Minorities." BULLETIN OF THE JOHN RYLANDS UNIVERSITY
        LIBRARY OF MANCHESTER 70.3 (1988): 225-40.

        Explains how the term "sect" in sociological literature is a
        neutral concept "without evaluative or emotional connotations" and
        how the "reputation of the sociological study of sects stands in
        sharp contrast to the esteem in which historical studies of sects
        are held" (p. 228). The goals of the sociological study of sects
        and the problems inherent in the method of participant observation
        are outlined. The use of members of, and apostates from, minority
        religious groups as informants is assessed.

1097. Wilson, Bryan R. "Sympathetic Detachment and Disinterested Involve-
        ment: A Note on Academic Integrity." SOCIOLOGICAL ANALYSIS 44
        (1983): 183-88.

        Replies to the accusation by Horowitz (item 1071) that sponsor-
        ship of research by new religious movements does not conform to
        academic procedures. The author points out that to explain the
        social and psychological needs of religious groups is in no way a
        justification of their beliefs and practices; and that, while empa-
        thy is required for understanding people involved in religious
        movements, empathetic understanding does not necessarily lead to
        advocacy. Evidence that the new cults are generally opposed to
        sociological study is lacking. Wilson's view is that religious
        sponsorship does not hinder sociological research, nor does it
        jeopardize the integrity of the researcher, and does not turn him
        or her into a apologist for the church under study. He has no
        difficulty attending academic conferences sponsored by the Unifica-
        tion Church (or any other religious organization) provided the
        conditions for such participation safeguard academic freedom. (For
        Wilson's own specific conditions for taking part in conferences of
        this kind, one may consult his introduction to the volume THE SOCIAL
        IMPACT OF THE NEW RELIGIOUS MOVEMENTS, item 725, v-xvi.)

1098. Yinger, Milton. "Salvation and Witches in a 'Secular' Age." CON-
        TEMPORARY SOCIOLOGY 9 (1980): 472-77.

        Reviews several books on the new religious movements and shows
        how they answer the sociological questions that their presence
        raises. The author criticizes in particular the methods by which
        information is gathered. He states that "those who prefer more
        hard-nosed methods of research will find little to satisfy them
        here" (p. 476). He further questions the ethical nature of some
        of the methods used. The need for reliable methods is underscored
        because of the importance of the study of the new religious move-
        ments, a study that might lead to a better understanding of society
        and of the human condition.

CHAPTER IV

CONTEMPORARY STUDIES ON SPECIFIC SECTS, CULTS,

AND NEW RELIGIOUS MOVEMENTS

An examination of contemporary social-scientific literature on the new cults leads to the conclusion that one cannot ignore similar movements in the past. If one considers the recent religious upheavals, not in isolation but in relation to similar occurrences in the history of Western culture, several relevant questions must be taken into account: 1) how new are the new religious movements?; 2) how and in what manner can the new cults be compared to those of earlier centuries?; and 3) what is the difference between the study of the new cults and the old ones?

The Novelty of the New Cults

There is a tendency in popular literature on the cults and in some scholarly explanations of their presence in the second half of the twentieth century to consider them as a unique phenomenon, unparalleled in the history of Western culture. The argument advanced is that even though religious movements have emerged in the past, modern cults cannot be compared to them. The new movements that have appeared in the last twenty years differ from older ones in their nature, goals, methods of recruitment, and effects they have on individuals. Unlike previous ones, modern cults are so prevalent, numerous, and successful that they are threatening the very fabric of Western culture and religion. They are destructive because of the negative repercussions on those who join them, on family life, and on society in general.

The social-scientific study of the cults simply does not support this view of cultism. Many of the ideas and practices common among the Eastern religious groups that have flourished in the West since the late 1960's have roots in earlier centuries. Ellwood and Partin (item 598), for instance, have traced the history of alternative religion and shown convincingly that even though each generation of new cults in America has had a distinctive character, there is a common thread which unites them throughout history. Many of the New Thought ideas that are rampant in the New Age Movement are hardly new as even a cursory history of the nineteenth-century New Thought Movement shows (see, e.g., Judah, item 208). More specifically, anyone who examines the current interest in, for example, karma and reincarnation will conclude that these beliefs are not foreign to Western thought and can be traced to early gnostic movements and have appeared repeatedly in the religious history of the West.

It is not surprising, then, that social scientists question the very newness of contemporary cults (Willis, item 1010). The past roots of many current new movements are obvious. The revival of Witchcraft as a religion may be a novel and startling revelation to the average person, but its link with similar phenomena in the past is an attested historical fact (see Russell, item 1447). Not only are modern cults similar to those that preceded them in earlier centuries, but some of the reasons why people join them are the same (confer Jackson, item 1321)--even some of the reactions to them have been similar (see Bromley and Shupe, item 1172). Levack (item 1361), for instance, who has studied the witch hunt in early modern Europe, has concluded that contemporary attempts to investigate new religious movements bear striking resemblances to those used to persecute alleged witches in the past.

The view that the current cults do not represent a completely new phenomenon in the religious history of the West is corroborated by the common social-scientific approach that considers cultism the initial stage in the development of new religions. Major religions, including Christianity, initially, had sectarian or cultic features (Scroggs, item 1457). Rodney Stark (item 1493) observes that when Jesus began his public ministry he behaved like a leader of a Jewish sect, which was transformed into a cult after his death and resurrection. It was only later, especially when it became the official religion of the Roman Empire, that Christianity acquired the full stature of an established religion and shed many of its cultic characteristics.

Moreover, several of these features, such as the practice of celibacy and the common pooling of financial resources, are also found in traditional Buddhist and Christian monastic institutions. Thomas Gannon (item 1268), writing on Catholic religious orders, mentions several characteristics, such as the separation of members from the outside world and the demand of total commitment, that have figured prominently in the debate on the cults. Those who attack the cults for their counterculture mentality and for the restrictions they place on human freedom must realize that these accusations can easily be applied to monastic institutions (see Capps, item 1195 and Dudley, item 1237). In many respects monasteries can be studied as communes (Hillery, item 1305). Even the mechanisms of control used in monasteries and cultic communes have a lot in common (Ebaugh, item 1243). Though there are serious differences between cults and religious orders (the traditional legitimation of the latter being an excellent case in point), the student of cultism who takes into consideration all the data at one's disposal is bound to reach the conclusion that the newness of the cults has been greatly exaggerated.

Comparison Between New and Old Cults

Social scientists have found it both informative and useful to draw comparisons between several of the new religious movements and those of the nineteenth century. The Unification Church, for example, has been compared with the Hutterites (Miller, item 1386), with Mormonism (Hampshire and Beckford, item 1293), with Hasidism (Berger, item 1154), and with Jehovah's Witnesses (Beckford, item 1144). In the first study, the author observes that among both Unificationists and Hutterites, the sexual and emotional relationships between married couples are subordinate to the

perceived spiritual brotherhood of the group. In the second study, the
authors compare the hostility that the activities of the Moonies and the
Mormons have elicited and discuss its effects on the deviance of each
group. In the third study, the writer compares two charismatic religions.
Though he has a very negative opinion of the Unification Church, he admits
that there are some glaring similarities between this religious movement
and Hasidism, such as the indoctrination techniques and the stress on
commitment to the community. In the final study, James Beckford traces
the different organizational structures of the two religious groups in
question, namely Jehovah's Witnesses and the Unification Church, and
states that in spite of their contrasting modes of political involvement
and lifestyle, they share similar objectives.

A good example of how the comparative approach might contribute to our
understanding of extreme cults is the comparison Thomas Robbins makes
between the People's Temple and the Russian Old Believers (item 1439).
The popular and scholarly reflections that followed the tragic events at
Jonestown illustrate how difficult it is to account for this catastrophic
demise of a new movement without having recourse to the argument that the
behavior of the leaders and members of the People's Temple are instances
of severe pathology. After carefully comparing the violent ends of the
two religious groups, Robbins suggests that, among other things, apocalyptic pessimism and a conviction that evil had triumphed on earth provided
adequate reasons for the suicidal frenzy that led both groups to self-
destruction.

While it has to be admitted that such comparative attempts have been
relatively few, the results have questioned not only the newness of the
current religious ferment, but also the appropriateness of giving a negative connotation to the term cult and of applying it almost indiscriminately to most, if not all, contemporary fringe religions.

The Study of New and Old Cults

One of the major differences between current social-scientific studies
of new movements and those that came into being in the past, particularly
in the nineteenth century, is that the former are very often discussed in
the framework of the brainwashing debate. Studies of earlier movements,
on the other hand, are more neutral, more objective, and less involved in
the emotional issues that the new cults have brought to the fore.

The comparative study of new and old cults has corroborated the view
that clear-cut distinctions between religious movements are not always
possible. It has also drawn attention to the fact that even religious
groups cannot always be distinguished from social or political ones. The
Mormons, Black Muslims and the Unification Church are typical examples of
groups that unite both religious and nonreligious themes in a common
goal. Other groups, like Alcoholics Anonymous and Synanon, seem at first
sight to be nothing more than alcohol and drug rehabilitation programs.
Sociologists, however, have observed that the former has developed several
sectarian features while the latter has changed radically since its foundation and become a tight cultic organization. Both emphasize a worldview
that has religious overtones.

Among the many contemporary religious revivals, Witchcraft and Paganism have attracted more followers than those notorious cults which have been targeted by the Anti-Cult Movement. Adler's book (item 1563) provides evidence of how widespread the movement towards a religion of nature is. Witchcraft as a religion has links with the feminist movement and has attracted many women who feel that traditional Christianity is largely a male-dominated religion. The quest for a female spirituality and for an equal place for women in religion has its recent roots in a number of nineteenth-century religious movements in which women played leadership roles.

A closer look at the religious upheavals of the past shows that many of the questions raised about the new cults are also applicable to older movements. Some of the strange behavior of contemporary cults is far from new. One has only to call to mind the unusual marital relationships in the Oneida Community (see, for instance, items 1262-63) and the wild behavior of the Ranters (items 1214, 1247, and 1395) to realize that bygone cults were subject to the same kind of reaction that their newer counterparts have met.

Criticism of the Study of the New Movements

One of the main criticisms of the study of the new movements has been that it has been largely restricted to those groups that have attracted White middle-class youth (Smith, item 946). Religious movements among minorities, particularly Blacks, have not often figured prominently in scholarly assessment of the contemporary religious scene and in reflections on future religious trends.

While there is no doubt that this weakness in the study of the new religions needs to be remedied, the current emphasis on the study of cults that have attracted middle- and upper-middle class White Americans should not be readily dismissed as an expression of racial prejudice or as a negative judgment on the importance of minority (Black) religious revivals. Rather, it is indicative of a social condition or trend. For example, the success that Indian gurus have had among members of the mainline churches points to the social, economical, and educational differences between Blacks and Whites in the United States.

Several reasons can be adduced to explain why different movements have appealed to different social groups. The new religious movements that are based on Eastern religions and philosophies or on a revival of New Thought have attracted people who are rebelling against their own cultural heritage. They can rightly be labeled countercultural movements. Members of these groups are protesting against the affluence of modern secularized society that has left little place for the sacred in public life and which has relegated religion to ritual practices that are performed out of tradition rather than genuine commitment. The return to communal life, for instance, challenges the current stress on individual competition and accumulation of wealth. Movements like the Unification Church, the Hare Krishna, Scientology, and Transcendental Meditation attract people who are tired of and dissatisfied with many aspects of Western industrialized culture, in which members of these new groups were raised.

Black movements of the twentieth century, on the other hand, have been concerned not with a countercultural philosophy but with an ideology that questions and rejects the inferior socioeconomic conditions of Blacks in America. The Black minority does not need salvation from the evils of affluence, but rather from oppression and prejudice. Black religious revivals, like Garveyism, the Father Divine Movement, the Black Muslims, and the Rastafari Movement, have been concerned not just with the spiritual development or improvement of the individual (as so many of the new cults are). They have been involved in working for social and economic changes that will improve the status of Blacks. Members of most of the new cults are rebelling against their own culture; members of black sects and cults against a foreign one. While those new religious movements that attract middle-class Whites can afford to ignore or transcend the political scene, Black spiritual revivals could not survive without attempts to transform or influence the political process and to achieve for their members an equal status with the rest of the population. Black religious movements are expressions of social rebellion, and the political, economic, and spiritual reforms they advocate cannot always be easily distinguished. White religious movements have tended to be more spiritual in nature, stressing classic themes like quiet contemplation, mystical union with nature, and, at times, celibacy. Members of these cults have often chosen to opt out of society in a symbolic fashion.

The study of new religious movements, past and present, is somewhat uneven. A number of groups dominate the social-scientific scene of emergent religions. Among the long-established groups, the Amish and the Hutterites figure prominently in both historical and social studies. The Mormons, Jehovah's Witnesses, Seventh-Day Adventists, and the Pentecostal Movement, together with communal-living groups, like Oneida, are still the focus of great attention. The Unification Church and the Hare Krishna must be listed among the most intensely studied new religions. The study of the Charismatic Movement, Black religions, and, more recently, the New Age Movement, has not been neglected but, in our opinion, lags somewhat behind. There are many small movements, like the Aetherius Society, about which little has been written (see Wallis, item 2067, for one exception). The materials on cults, sects, and new religions annotated in this chapter not only record what has been accomplished by social scientists, but also indirectly point to the many areas of research that must be pursued for a more comprehensive description of individual cults and for a better understanding of the significance of the new religious movements in the West.

A. STUDIES ON ESTABLISHED SECTS

1099.   Agogino, George. "An Overview of the Yeti-Sasquatch Investigations and Some Thoughts on Their Outcome." ANTHROPOLOGICAL JOURNAL OF CANADA 16.2 (1978): 11-13.

Examines the evidence brought in support of the existence of the popularly called "abominable snowman" and leans in favor of the Indian folklore theory as an explanation of the sighting and beliefs surrounding this strange creature. By implication, many contemporary views on occult topics, such as the belief in Atlantis, would be subject to folkloristic interpretations.

1100. Ahern, Geoffrey. SUN AT MIDNIGHT: THE RUDOLPH STEINER MOVEMENT AND
       THE WESTERN ESOTERIC TRADITION. Wellingborough, England: Aquar-
       ian Press, 1984. 256 pp.

       Attempts an interpretation of Anthroposophy, founded by Rudolph
       Steiner, in the context of Western esoteric tradition, which in-
       cludes gnosticism, Rosicrucianism, and modern occultism. The
       author provides in turn: 1) a short account of 18 converts to the
       movement and the reasons for their conversion; 2) a description of
       the different communities, social institutions, and groups with the
       movement; 3) a statement on the place of meditation in the life of
       an anthroposophist; 4) a biographical account of Steiner, including
       the establishment of his movement; and 5) a description of the
       movement's philosophy. The author maintains that anthroposophy
       "has much to tell us about the age that shapes us" (p. 211). Bib-
       liographies on Anthroposophy and esotericism are included.

1101. Albrecht, Stan L., and Howard M. Bahr. "Patterns of Religious
       Disaffiliation: A Study of Lifelong Mormons, Mormon Converts, and
       Former Mormons." JOURNAL FOR THE SCIENTIFIC STUDY OF RELIGION 22
       (1983): 366-79.

       Explores patterns of religious disaffiliation (or apostasy) from
       the Mormon Church and attitudes of current members and compares
       them with those of other major religious groups, including Greek
       Orthodox, Catholic, Lutheran, Episcopal, Unitarian, and Pente-
       costal. Defection, preambles to conversion, and dropping out are
       considered. It is concluded that: 1) churches from which Mormon
       converts are drawn differ from those to which Mormons usually turn
       to when they leave their church; 2) converts to Mormonism have the
       highest religiosity scores; and 3) former Mormons are more likely
       than dropouts of other denominations to claim that they have no
       religion. The author stresses the need to study the actual experi-
       ence of religious disaffiliation.

1102. Albrecht, Stan L., Marie Cornwall, and Perry H. Cunningham. "Reli-
       gious Leave-Taking: Disengagement or Disaffiliation Among Mormons.
       FALLING FROM THE FAITH (item 579), pp. 62-80.

       Focuses on the processes by which Mormons abandon their faith,
       either through decreased participation (disengagement) or by the
       loss or change of organizational identification (disaffiliation).
       Disengagement and return rates are examined and the part played by
       age and parental socialization assessed. Various reasons, such as
       problems with the church, for nonattendance at Mormon functions
       are examined. Those who become disaffiliated had always been mar-
       ginal in the church, had not been raised in a religious home, or
       had married outside their faith. The disaffiliation process is
       related to the conversion process to another church, although the
       doctrinal issues are not central to the process.

1103. Allan, Graham. "A Theory of Millennialism: The Irvingite Movement
       as an Illustration." BRITISH JOURNAL OF SOCIOLOGY 25 (1974):
       295-311.

Discusses the conditions under which millennial movements come into being in the context of an early nineteenth-century Scottish revival under the direction of a Presbyterian minister, Edward Irving. It is maintained that the Irvingite Movement had an "internal logic" and that its development is understandable in the context of the cultural conditions of the period and the character of its followers. Unlike similar phenomena, the Irvingite Movement did not emerge at a time of disaster and those who joined it were middle-class and well-educated people. The author maintains that "millennial movements are attempts to interpret and order situations in which a group of individuals feel that their total worth is being denied" (p. 309). This movement cannot be explained simply with reference to its leader's charisma. It was a reaction, expressed in absolute, dogmatic, and authoritarian terms, against the doubt and relativism of early nineteenth-century Britain.

1104.   Allen, Gillian, and Roy Wallis. "Pentecostals as a Medical Minority." MARGINAL MEDICINE (item 715), pp. 100-37.

Studies the Assemblies of God, a Pentecostal Church in a Scottish city, with the aim of determining its members' knowledge and attitude towards illness and its cure. Besides natural theories of causation, Assembly members accept supernatural explanations that ascribe illness to demonic, theistic, and metaphysical causes and that stress future compensations in this world at the imminent Second Coming of Christ. The influence of these beliefs on the illness behavior of church members and the mechanisms that reinforce nonmedical systems of knowledge are examined. The authors conclude that these Pentecostals accepted at the same time the scientific and religious beliefs about the origin and treatment of illness without experiencing any conflict or contradiction.

1105.   Alston, Jon P., and B. E. Aguirre. "Congregational Size and the Decline of Sectarian Commitment: The Case of the Jehovah's Witnesses in South and North America." SOCIOLOGICAL ANALYSIS 40 (1979): 63-70.

Tests three hypotheses concerning the effects of the growth of membership among Jehovah's Witnesses: 1) the average size of the local congregation increases; 2) the members become less active; and 3) few members are highly committed. The authors found that as the sect grows in membership, it acquired church-life characteristics with fewer members getting involved in the group's organized religious activities. It is concluded that the classic church-sect model needs to be modified, for it unveils little about the internal dynamics of a religious group.

1106.   Altheide, David L., and John M. Johnson. "Counting Souls: A Study of Evangelical Crusades." PACIFIC SOCIOLOGICAL REVIEW 20 (1977): 323-48.

Examines the work of religious counselors at a Billy Graham Evangelical crusade to discover how they define and direct converts who accept Christ in their lives during an evangelical meeting. The role played by the organization in the success of the crusade is

stressed. The author describes the way counselors were instructed
and prepared and the tasks they performed at one crusade held in
Phoenix, Arizona. The reasons why counting the number of converts
is so important are spelled out in detail.

1107. Andelson, Jonathan C. "The Gift to Be Single: Celibacy and Reli-
       gious Enthusiasm in the Community of True Inspiration." COMMUNAL
       SOCIETIES 5 (1985): 1-31.

       Maintains that the rate of celibacy among the Community of True
       Inspiration (Amana Society) reflected the intensity of religious
       enthusiasm among individual communities. The scriptural foundation
       of Inspirationist celibacy and the relationship between German
       radical pietism and the Inspirationist Movement are outlined. The
       author sketches the demographics of Inspirationist celibacy in
       Europe and in the United States. He concludes that between 1800
       and 1840 Inspirationist men and women adopted a celibate life more
       often than members of any other group. This high incidence of
       celibacy is explained by a rise in religious enthusiasm. The de-
       cline in celibacy was influenced by some internal factors and by
       the general decline of enthusiasm.

1108. Andelson, Jonathan C. "The Double Bind and Social Change in Commu-
       nal Amana." HUMAN RELATIONS 34 (1981): 111-25.

       Discusses the processes that led to the break-up of the Amana
       community. After a short historical introduction and description
       of the Amana organization, the author expounds on the double-bind
       theory and its application to Amana. The double bind in Amana
       "resulted from the conflicting demands of the sect's plan for sal-
       vation, which required self-denial and isolation, and the groups'
       economic dependence on external markets" (p. 124). The death of
       the sect's charismatic leader intensified the double bind, which in
       turn lead to many defections, thereby creating a second double bind
       of preserving the community and upholding its roots. Both binds
       were resolved through a reinterpretation of communal organization.

1109. Anderson, Alan, and Raymond Gordon. "The Uniqueness of English
       Witchcraft: A Matter of Numbers?" BRITISH JOURNAL OF SOCIOLOGY
       30 (1979): 359-61.

       Continues the debate on the differences between British and Euro-
       pean witchcraft and the possible social causes that underlie them
       (see item 1110). The authors argue that their critics (Swales and
       McLachlan, item 1498) actually corroborate their main thesis that
       the lower status of women in continental Europe accounts for the
       harsh treatment witches received in comparison to their British
       counterparts.

1110. Anderson, Alan, and Raymond Gordon. "Witchcraft and the Status of
       Women--The Case of England." BRITISH JOURNAL OF SOCIOLOGY 29
       (1978): 171-84.

       Briefly examines various theories of witchcraft and suggests that
       one might profitably start with reflecting on the fact that the
       majority of accusations were against women. Several distinctive

features of British witchcraft in the sixteenth and seventeenth
centuries are outlined. Witch hunts were relatively few and mild;
they also differed qualitatively from those carried out in most
other societies at the time; the sentences meted out were usually
lenient; and they were, as a rule, not linked with devilry. The
authors explore the distinctive social traits of England, especially the improved status of women in economic, religious, and
political matters. They conclude that, because England did not see
women as inferior or inherently evil, witches were treated much
better.

1111.   Anderson, Robert Mapes. VISION OF THE DISINHERITED: THE MAKING
        OF AMERICAN PENTECOSTALISM. New York: Oxford University Press,
        1979. 334 pp.

        Presents a study of the formative stage of the Pentecostal Move-
        ment from the late nineteenth century to the early 1930's. The
        types of people who become Pentecostals and the circumstances under
        which they joined the movement are explored. The author stresses
        the historical and social contexts in which Pentecostalism took
        shape. The charismatic tradition, the holiness background, and the
        Apostolic Faith Movement are described. In a final chapter the
        sources and functions of Pentecostalism are explored. A theory of
        deprivation is adopted to explain the movement as originating in
        social discontent. Pentecostalism was a rebellion against moder-
        nity, a rebellion that was nurtured by the social turmoils at the
        turn of the twentieth century. Some comparisons are made between
        traditional Pentecostalism and the Neo-Pentecostal (Charismatic)
        Movement; those individuals who join the latter do not suffer from
        material deprivation. Besides copious notes, there is an appendix
        listing 45 Pentecostal leaders and somewhat lengthy selective bib-
        liographies.

1112.   Apel, William D. "The Lost World of Billy Graham." REVIEW OF
        RELIGIOUS RESEARCH 20 (1979): 138-49.

        Examines the theology of Billy Graham, focusing on his modified
        premillennial views which, together with the preaching of Dwight
        Moody, modern existentialism, and the American Dream, contributed
        to his cosmology. The author criticizes social scientific studies
        of Billy Graham's revivalism for not paying enough attention to his
        theology.

1113.   Archer, Anthony. "Remaining in the State in Which God Has Called
        You: An Evangelical Revival." ARCHIVES DE SCIENCES SOCIALES DES
        RELIGIONS 40 (1975): 67-78.

        Studies an Evangelical, Methodist revival movement that was
        formed in New England in the late 1960's. The author explores the
        ways in which young people came to join the movement, their world-
        view, and the circumstances that influenced their decision to be-
        come members. The proselytizing methods that were concentrated in
        "the evangelistic coffee bar" are described. The repetitive and
        stereotyped messages given at meetings are seen as a ritual leading
        to conversion, which led to further evangelization. This revival

movement, according to the author, differed little from the traditional pattern of Methodist revivalism. The group's religious
world "provided legitimation for a particular way of life" (p. 77)
and contributed to the group's assimilation of society's dominant
attitudes and values.

1114. Baer, Hans A. RECREATING UTOPIA IN THE DESERT: A SECTARIAN CHAL-
       LENGE TO MODERN MORMONISM. New York: State University of New
       York Press, 1988. xxii, 225 pp.

       Presents a study of a Mormon sect, the Aaronic Order (also known
       as the "Levites of Utah"), a small millenarian and communal group
       that came into being in the 1930's under the leadership of Maurice
       L. Glendenning. It is argued that the social transformation of
       Mormonism into an institutionalized religion that has reached some
       degree of accommodation with society at large has led to several
       Mormon splinter groups. After an analysis of Mormonism, the author
       describes the origin of the Aaronic Order as a revitalization move-
       ment, the conversion experience of its members, the religious world-
       view that guided its communitarian goals, the social system of the
       Eskdale commune which embodies these goals, and the development of
       the Aaronic Order as a distinct Mormon sect. The author maintains
       that the theory of deprivation does not sufficiently explain the
       emergence of the Aaronic Order, which is "the product of a complex
       interaction of several variables at several levels of analysis" (p.
       192). A bibliography is included (pp. 207-220).

1115. Baer, Hans A. "The Metropolitan Spiritual Churches of Christ: The
       Socio-Religious Evolution of the Largest Black Spiritual Associa-
       tions." REVIEW OF RELIGIOUS RESEARCH 30 (1988): 140-50.

       Examines the origin and development of the Spiritual Church of
       Christ, which is interpreted as a Black response to racial and
       social stratification. Three stages in the development of this
       church are listed: 1) the early years, since its beginning in 1925
       in Kansas, Missouri; 2) the long tenure of its leader, the Reverend
       Clarence Cobb; and 3) the schism that followed Cobb's death in
       1974. The expansion and institutionalization of this church moved
       in step with the massive migration of Blacks from the rural South
       to the industrial centers around the country. Attempts at revital-
       ization within the church have led to certain aspects of Voodoo and
       Catholicism to be rejected and elements of New Thought and Mind
       Science to be incorporated into its system.

1116. Baer, Hans A. "Nineteenth-Century Mormonism as a Partial 'Asiatic'
       Social formation." PERSPECTIVES IN U. S. MARXIST ANTHROPOLOGY.
       Edited by David Hakkim and Hanna Lessinger. Boulder, CO: West-
       view Press, 1987, pp. 102-22.

       Applies, to Mormonism, Marx's concept of the Asiatic mode of
       production, which consists essentially of kinship-based, primitive
       communities that owned land communally and operated under the power
       of the state. The development of Mormonism is traced in five
       stages: 1) the quasi-communal; 2) the incipient Asiatic; 3) the
       mature Asiatic; 4) the declining Asiatic; and 5) the corporate

church. According to the author, Mormonism changed "from a relatively independent theocratic state into a respectable religious
denomination which today exhibits many of the characteristics of a
modern transnational corporation" (p. 104). Mormonism's Asiatic
stage was only a transitional one, because it could not sever its
ties with the capitalistic economy of its parent society.

1117. Baer, Hans A. THE BLACK SPIRITUAL MOVEMENT: A RELIGIOUS RESPONSE
       TO RACISM. Knoxville: University of Tennessee Press, 1984.
       viii, 221 pp.

       Attempts to understand a specific religious movement in the Black
       community that includes a variety of "spiritual" churches. A his-
       torical outline of the movement is given and its main features
       described. The author locates the movement in the larger context
       of Black Religion and American society. Arguing that the develop-
       ment of Black religion has been largely neglected and/or misunder-
       stood, he rejects some of the stereotypes of the alleged uniformity
       of Black religion. One chapter is dedicated to a description of a
       Black sect founded in 1923 by Father George E. Hurley, a contempo-
       rary of Father Divine, who also declared himself to be God; another
       chapter deals with the syncretism of the spiritual movement that
       combines elements from Black Protestantism, Spiritualism, Roman
       Catholicism, and Voodoo. The author interprets the Spiritual Move-
       ment as "one of several possible Black religious responses to the
       racist and class structure of American society " (p. 6). The Spi-
       ritual Movement has compensatory, integrative, manipulative, and
       psychotherapeutic dimensions.

1118. Baer, Hans A. "Toward a Systematic Typology of Black Folk Healers."
       PHYLON 43 (1982): 327-43.

       Discusses the diversity of ethnomedicine among Black Americans,
       focusing on the folk healers associated with it. After outlining
       early typologies of Black folk healers, the author proposes his own
       fourfold classification that takes into consideration their insti-
       tutional context and their particular practices. The following
       four principal types are described in some detail: 1) independent
       generalists (e.g., conjurers, root workers, and spiritualists);
       2) independent specialists (e.g., neighborhood prophets and magic
       vendors); 3) cultic generalists (e.g., Voodoo priests or priest-
       esses and spiritual prophets); and 4) cultic specialists (e.g.,
       evangelistic faith healers and spiritual divine healers).

1119. Baer, Hans A. "Sex Roles in a Mormon Schismatic Group." SEX ROLES
       IN CONTEMPORARY AMERICAN COMMUNES (item 705), pp. 111-54.

       Describes and analyzes sex roles among the Levites of Utah, a
       Mormon schismatic group also known as the Aaronic Order founded by
       Maurice L. Glendenning in the 1930's. After a historical overview
       of the Levite community, the author examines the group as a revi-
       talization movement. The composition of the Order and its symbols
       of male domination and female submission are explored. The author
       thinks that its complex system of offices and councils acts to
       legitimize male dominance. He outlines the Levite view of sex

roles as expressed in the family and marriage systems, in the sexual division of labor, and in the educational system. The Levite
community is an example of the common custom of combining communal
living with a male-supremacist perspective.

1120. Baer, Hans A. "Black Spiritual Churches: A Neglected Socio-Reli-
        gious Institution." PHYLON 42 (1981): 207-23.

        Explores the pluralism and religious syncretism of one variety of
        Black religion, namely the spiritual or spiritualist churches. A
        history of their rather obscure development is attempted and their
        origin is traced to Mother Anderson, a Black Spiritualist medium
        in New Orleans in the early twentieth century. Several religious
        services at different Spiritualist churches in the Southern and
        Midwestern parts of the United States are described, highlighting
        their pluralistic nature and syncretistic elements. The author
        thinks that the spiritualist religion appeals to certain socially,
        upwardly mobile Blacks and validates their achievements by its
        positive-thinking ideology.

1121. Baer, Hans A. "An Anthropological View of Black Spiritual Churches
        in Nashville, Tennessee." CENTRAL ISSUES IN ANTHROPOLOGY 2.2
        (1980): 53-68.

        Examines the religious beliefs and practices of Black Spiritual
        churches and provides the historical background necessary to under-
        stand their origin and development. Focusing on 11 churches in
        Nashville, Tennessee, the author studies the role of those churches
        that conduct their religious services in a nonresidential building
        (a regular or storefront church). These churches are syncretistic
        and have been heavily influenced by Voodoo. Their greatest appeal
        lies in their use of magicoreligious rituals. It is argued that
        these religions "meet the sociocultural and psychocultural needs of
        lower-class Blacks, who continue to be the victims of a racist and
        stratified social order" (p. 62).

1122. Baer, Hans A. "The Aaronic Order: The Development of a Modern
        Mormon Sect." DIALOGUE: A JOURNAL OF MORMON THOUGHT 12 (1979):
        57-71.

        Describes a Mormon sect founded by Maurice L. Glendenning in the
        early 1930's. An outline of its history and its main beliefs is
        provided. The Order is made up of two congregations, a cooperative
        community, and a commune called Eskdale. Two significant factors
        in the development of the Aaronic Order, namely the dynamic and
        charismatic leadership of Glendenning and the group's contact with
        fundamentalist Protestant congregations, are discussed. The author
        notices that there has been a shift towards fundamental Protestant-
        ism in the younger members of the Order, a shift that has led to
        internal conflict leading to the expulsion of those conceived of as
        departing from Mormon norms. Similarities between the Aaronic
        Order and the Mormon Church are noted. The author thinks that the
        Order will not likely grow in size, but may still attract certain
        alienated individuals from the mainstream Mormon tradition.

1123. Baer, Hans A. "A Psychocultural View of a Modern-Day Prophet Among
       the Mormons." JOURNAL OF PSYCHOLOGICAL ANTHROPOLOGY 2 (1979):
       177-95.

       Focuses on the founder of the Aaronic Order, an offshoot of Mor-
       monism in the 1930's. A brief biographical sketch of Maurice L.
       Glendenning, the found of the sect, is given. The development of
       the Order and the role of its founder in its origin and growth are
       outlined. The author's view is that the Aaronic Order serves as a
       defense mechanism for psychologically troubled individuals and as a
       framework for revitalization among some disaffiliated and deprived
       Mormons.

1124. Baer, Hans A. "A Field Perspective of Religious Conversion: The
       Levites of Utah." REVIEW OF RELIGIOUS RESEARCH 19 (1978): 279-94.

       Presents a study of religious experiences of members of the Aaro-
       nic Order, a Mormon schismatic group. A short description of the
       sect is given. Several questions asked of converts to determine
       the factors involved in their conversion experience are listed.
       The background of the converts (particularly their sex and economic
       status) and the types of conversions are recorded. Five types of
       deprivation are discussed: ethical, economic, social, psychic, and
       organismic. Various other factors, like previous religious affil-
       iation and intensive interaction with members of the Aaronic Order,
       that predisposed or led people to join this order are considered.

1125. Baer, Hans A. "The Levites of Utah: A Twentieth-Century Attempt to
       Revitalize Mormonism." PROCEEDINGS OF THE CENTRAL STATES ANTHRO-
       POLOGICAL SOCIETY 19 (1977): 9-16.

       Espouses the view that the Levites of Utah, a Mormon sect known
       also as the Aaronic Order or the Order of Aaron, came into being as
       an attempt to revitalize the community spirit and worldview of
       nineteenth-century Mormonism before it developed into an elaborate
       bureaucratic institution. An account of the early development of
       the Order is given. The charismatic personality of, and the new
       code promulgated by, the founder Maurice L. Glendenning were the
       main factors contributing to the movement's success. Several
       features of the social structure and ideology of the Levites, such
       as their desire to reestablish cooperative and egalitarian ideals
       and practices, their stress on eschatological beliefs, and their
       return to polygamy, are a clear indication that the movement
       emerged as an attempt to revitalize Mormonism.

1126. Baer, Hans A. "The Effect of Technological Innovation on Hutterite
       Culture." PLAINS ANTHROPOLOGIST 21 (1976): 187-97.

       Attempts to show that technological changes open the door for
       other changes in Hutterite culture. A brief description of the
       Hutterites--their beliefs, social organization, and division of
       labor--is provided. Modern technology leads the Hutterites to
       greater contact with the outside world and to the consequent adop-
       tion of customs and views that are foreign to Hutterite culture and

shunned by most Hutterites. Several control mechanisms, such as
a strong superego and social disapproval, have come into play to
enable the Hutterites to deal with deviations and innovations. The
possibility that the Hutterites might be assimilated into mainstream culture is discussed.

1127. Baer, Hans A. "The Hutterites and the External World." PLATTE
        VALLEY REVIEW 1 (1973): 33-43.

        Studies six Hutterite colonies in South Dakota, focusing on their
        views of, and relationships with, the outside world. After a brief
        historical introduction, the author outlines the Hutterite atti-
        tudes towards worldly pleasures, education, technology, and mili-
        tary involvement. The reasons why some members defect from the
        Hutterite colonies are discussed. In spite of the common opinion
        that the Hutterites will eventually be assimilated into mainstream
        American culture, the colonies examined by the author are stable,
        cohesive, and vital. Several factors stabilizing their lifestyle
        and new problems which will eventually threaten it are noted.

1128. Baer, Hans A., and Merrill Singer. "Toward a Typology of Black
        Sectarianism as a Response to Racial Stratification." ANTHROPO-
        LOGICAL QUARTERLY 54 (1981): 1-14.

        Constructs a fourfold typology of Black religious groups in the
        United States: 1) established sects (e.g., the African Methodist
        Episcopal Church and the National Baptist Convention); 2) messianic
        nationalist sects (e.g., Noble Drew Ali's Moorish Science Temple
        and the Nation of Islam); 3) conversionist sects (e.g., Holiness
        and Pentecostal congregations); and 4) thaumaturgical/manipulation-
        ist sects (e.g., Spiritual Churches and the United Church and
        Science of Living Institute). This diversity is traced to the
        influences of African cultures, Euro-American cultures, and reli-
        gious responses to cope with the Blacks' minority status in Western
        society. The movement of Father Divine is seen as an example of a
        mixed type, combining elements from the first two groups listed
        above. The authors hold that the rise of Black sects and cults is
        basically a response to the sense of powerlessness that is inherent
        in the social position Blacks have in the United States.

1129. Bahr, Howard M. "Religious Contrasts in Family Role Definition and
        Performance: Utah Mormons, Catholics, Protestants, and Others."
        JOURNAL FOR THE SCIENTIFIC STUDY OF RELIGION 21 (1982): 100-17.

        Attempts to find how Latter-Day Saints differ from the rest of
        the population of Utah in their role definition and enactment of
        family life. The central position of the family, the preferred
        division of labor, and tolerance of nontraditional roles are the
        main areas explored. It is concluded that Mormons differ from non-
        Mormons more in attitudes about the family than in actual family
        behavior. They are certainly more family-centered and less toler-
        ant of modern female roles and activities. No differences were
        observed in family decision-making processes and conflicts.
        Several reasons for these findings are offered.

1130. Bahr, Howard M. "Religious Intermarriage and Divorce in Utah and
       the Mountain States." JOURNAL FOR THE SCIENTIFIC STUDY OF RELI-
       GION 20 (1981): 251-61.

       Compares marriage and divorce rates between Catholics, Protes-
       tants, and Mormons with the aim of finding out the relationship
       between religion and divorce. Several statistical tables are pre-
       sented for both Utah and other Mountain States. Three major con-
       clusions are reached: 1) Same-faith marriages are much more stable
       than interfaith ones; 2) Catholic and Mormon same-faith marriages
       are slightly more stable than the rest; and 3) interfaith marriages
       between Mormons and the other two groups are less stable than those
       between Catholics and Protestants.

1131. Bahr, Howard M., and Stan L. Albrecht. "Strangers Once More: Pat-
       terns of Disaffiliation from Mormonism." JOURNAL FOR THE SCIEN-
       TIFIC STUDY OF RELIGION 28 (1989): 180-200.

       Explores the processes of disaffiliation from Mormonism by ana-
       lyzing in-depth interviews with 30 ex-Mormons from the State of
       Utah. The various types of defection and disaffiliation are out-
       lined with reference to some basic studies like those of Roozen
       (item 426) and Brinkerhoff and Burke (item 1171). The authors
       describe the characteristics of ex-Mormons (their marital status,
       age, religious preference, and Mormon membership status), review
       the usefulness of the various typologies of disaffiliation, and
       give some individual examples of the disengagement process at work.
       They maintain that disaffiliation from Mormonism is "a matter of
       multiple causation."

1132. Bainbridge, William Sims. "The Decline of the Shakers: Evidence
       From the Unites States Census." COMMUNAL SOCIETIES 4 (1984):
       19-34.

       Uses the U.S. census data from 1850 t0 1970 to chart the begin-
       ning of the Shaker decline in numbers, to further an understanding
       of Shaker demographics and to determine the social processes that
       led to the Shaker fate. The author records in some detail the
       decline in membership during the said period, the defection and
       death of members, and the number of new recruits. He discovers
       that the losses through defection and death by far outnumbered new
       members. Shaker colonies became refuges for members of broken
       families and for people experiencing social problems; they func-
       tioned more like religious asylums than utopian communities.

1133. Bainbridge, William Sims. "Shaker Demographics, 1840-1900: An
       Example of the Use of the U.S. Census Enumeration Schedules."
       JOURNAL FOR THE SCIENTIFIC STUDY OF RELIGION 21 (1982): 352-65.

       Studies the changing demographic structure of Shaker communities
       with the aim of evaluating theories about the fates of utopian
       experiments. The author makes an analysis of the U.S. census mate-
       rials, focusing on the structure of the Shaker colonies. Several
       plausible explanations for increasing sex balance among the members
       are rejected. It is suggested that the census reports support the

view that the sex imbalance "was a more or less conscious choice of
the sect" (p. 361). It is concluded that the U.S. Census contains
enough information for many research projects.

1134. Balch, Robert W., Gwen Farnsworth, and Sue Wilkins. "When the
       Bombs Drop: Reaction to Disconfirmed Prophecy in a Millennial
       Sect." SOCIOLOGICAL PERSPECTIVES 26 (1983): 137-58.

       Studies a small Baha'i sect that predicted a nuclear disaster to
       occur in 1980 and a consequent twenty years of turmoil followed by
       the establishment of God's kingdom on earth. A description of the
       sect, known as "Baha'is Under the Provision of the Covenant" and led
       by Dr. Leland Jensen, is given. Festinger et al.'s theory (item
       91) that prophetic failure results in increased conviction and
       greater proselytization is tested and found wanting. Internal
       conflict, demoralization, and widespread defection followed the
       realization that the prophecy did not materialize. Public ridicule
       and the uncertainty of the believers probably account for the fact
       that proselytization did not resume after the failure of the proph-
       ecy. The demoralization and ambiguity of the remaining faithful
       are explained by the fact that the small groups of believers had no
       plans of staying in contact with each other and by the failure of
       their leader to act decisively. "The reactions to disconfirmed
       prophecy," the authors suggest, "depend on the nature of the social
       situation in which prophetic failure occurs" (p. 156).

1135. Barclay, Harold B. "The Religious Society of Friends." ULTIMATE
       REALITY AND MEANING 2 (1979): 135-42.

       Discusses the history and teachings of the Quakers whose organi-
       zation has been more influential than its membership would indicate.
       Quakerism is, in the author's view, a unique blending of mysticism,
       empiricism, and pragmaticism. Instead of stressing an individual
       and solitary form of mysticism, as in oriental religions and Chris-
       tian monasticism, Quakerism considers mysticism as directed both
       towards God and the group. This approach has social significance
       because it introduces a mechanism of social control in Quaker life.

1136. Barthell, Diane L. AMANA: FROM PIETIST SECT TO AMERICAN COMMUNITY.
       Lincoln: University of Nebraska Press, 1984. xv, 210 pp.

       Presents a historical study of the Amana Community, integrating
       the sociological concerns about sect function and adaptation, cha-
       rismatic leadership, and societal development. Amana, existing on
       the margin of American society, is seen as responsive to, and to
       some degree reflective of, larger historical developments, particu-
       larly the movement to greater individual choices. Amana's trans-
       formation from a religious sect to a tourist attraction has led,
       according to the author, to the creation of myths about social and
       utopian groups. A bibliographical essay (pp. 195-203) is included.

1137. Baxter, John. "The Great Yorkshire Revival 1792-6: A Study of Mass
       Revival Among the Methodists." SOCIOLOGICAL YEARBOOK OF RELIGION
       IN BRITAIN 7 (1974): 46-76.

Describes one of the most dramatic outbursts of mass revival in the history of Methodism that took place in Yorkshire, England in the late eighteenth century. It is suggested that such revivals are a characteristic form of Methodist expansion and occurred every 18 years as a natural, "generational" pattern of renewal and growth. The author further attempts to relate this particular revival to the wider social context of "soaring statistics of unemployment, prices, and poor law expenditure" (p. 61). Five major apocalyptic signs, namely war, pestilence, famine, flooding, and earthquake, were witnessed by individual communities at West Riding where the revival began. Revivals offered not only the temporary emotional release provided by cathartic conversion, but also a new birth that comes with a new identity and confidence.

1138. Beckford, James A. "Accounting for Conversion." BRITISH JOURNAL OF SOCIOLOGY 29 (1978): 249-62.

Starts with the sociological assumption that accounts of religious conversion cannot be understood as objective reports of experience, but must be seen in the light of the conditions under which they are retold. The author's study of Jehovah's Witnesses led him to examine three topics, namely: 1) the Witness's rules for speaking about conversion; 2) the way these rules are related to other aspects of the movement; and 3) the historical changes in the rules. The contextual features of talking about conversion are examined and the logic relating conversion accounts to the social context is outlined. Several guidelines for expressing one's conversion experience are summarized. The author thinks that the convert's motives, needs, and attractions are less important than the organizational framework in which the stories of conversion are related.

1139. Beckford, James A. "Sociological Stereotypes of the Religious Sect." SOCIOLOGICAL REVIEW 26 (1978): 109-23.

Argues that sociologists are prejudiced in the type of questions they ask about sects and in their common assumption that members of the lower social classes join sects because in them they find compensation for their various deprivations. The author attempts to illustrate his point with reference to the Jehovah's Witnesses in Britain. He outlines the social stratification of this sect in which he finds that occupational status is evenly distributed. He holds that this sect challenges traditional sociological wisdom that the sect attracts people "from the lowest socio-economic groups, suffering multiple deprivations and dis-privileges" (p. 118). He thinks that the appeal of the Witnesses lies not in the revolutionary character of their beliefs, but rather in the certainty, coherence, practicality, and imagery of their teachings.

1140. Beckford, James A. "Jehovah's Witnesses Worldwide." SOCIAL COMPASS 24 (1977): 5-31.

Introduces a special issue of the international journal, SOCIAL COMPASS, that is dedicated to the study of Jehovah's Witnesses in various parts of the world. The author gives a brief description

of the Watch Tower Movement. He observes that recent developments
have caused structural strain within this movement, a strain
brought about by the increasing disaffection among the membership.
The current problems of commitment and activism that the church is
experiencing and the persecution it has provoked are discussed.

1141. Beckford, James A. "Structural Dependence in Religious Organiza-
        tions: From 'Skid-Road' to Watch Tower." JOURNAL FOR THE SCIEN-
        TIFIC STUDY OF RELIGION 15 (1976): 169-175.

        Examines the "skid-road" rescue mission in Seattle, Washington,
        and explores the ways in which a study of this mission can contrib-
        ute to the understanding of the organizational dynamics of the
        Watch Tower Movement. The theme of structural dependence in both
        groups is discussed and it is argued that the level of dependence
        can influence the discrepancy between the personal and formal goals
        of those who participate in the two groups. The difference between
        the local leaders of the skid-road mission and of the Jehovah's
        Witnesses congregations are partly explained in terms of organiza-
        tional structure.

1142. Beckford James A. "New Wine in New Bottles: A Departure from
        Church-Sect Conceptual Tradition." SOCIAL COMPASS 23.1 (1976):
        71-85.

        Examines the problems of classifying religious organizations
        with reference to the Jehovah's Witnesses in Great Britain. The
        author gives an overview of the "conceptual confusion" that domi-
        nates scholarly literature on church-sect theory and examines the
        contribution of several typologies for clarifying the issues at
        stake. He finds fault with church-sect theories for not answering
        the important question of why people join one particular sect
        rather than another. It is suggested that the question should be
        approached by studying in some detail the modes of affiliation to
        religious sects. Several hypotheses concerning affiliation to
        marginal religious groups are constructed and then tested on
        Jehovah's Witnesses.

1143. Beckford, James A. THE TRUMPET OF PROPHECY: A SOCIOLOGICAL ANALY-
        SIS OF JEHOVAH'S WITNESSES. Oxford: Blackwell, 1975. xii, 244 pp.

        Examines the Watch Tower Movement in Great Britain with special
        focus on the sociological factors that have influenced its growth
        and development since its inception in the 1870's. Its organiza-
        tion, doctrines, social composition of its members, and methods of
        recruiting and training of new recruits are described. The social,
        moral, and religious conditions that draw people to the Jehovah's
        Witnesses are considered. Five predispositions to conversion are
        listed: 1) Christian upbringing; 2) marginal occupation; 3) lack of
        intermediary associations and communal ties; 4) young family with
        nominal Christian values and standards; and 5) other family members
        in the movement. The ideology of the movement is considered under
        the headings of "historicism," "absolutism," "activism," "rational-
        ism," "authoritarianism," and "extremism." Several problems in the
        sociological study of the Witnesses are discussed.

1144. Beckford, James A. "Two Contrasting Types of Sectarian Organiza-
       tion." SECTARIANISM: ANALYSIS OF RELIGIOUS AND NON-RELIGIOUS
       SECTS (item 713), pp. 70-85.

       Examines the organizational aspects that are accompanying reli-
       gious change in the Western world, concentrating on two religious
       bodies, namely the Jehovah's Witnesses, an established sect, and
       the Unification Church, a new religious movement. A brief descrip-
       tion of both groups is given and some of the organizational prob-
       lems they respectively face are brought up. It is argued that the
       structures of sects vary in relation to their basic teachings and
       ideologies and that their evangelistic or proselytizing methods and
       type of political involvement depend on the organization. The two
       groups have similar objectives but have adopted different kinds of
       solutions to the problem of "enrollment economy," the Jehovah's
       Witnesses utilizing mass-movement strategies, the Unification
       Church fostering an intensive form of communal living.

1145. Beckford, James A. "Organization, Ideology, and Recruitment: The
       Structure of the Watch Tower Movement." SOCIOLOGICAL REVIEW 23
       (1975): 893-909.

       Examines the recruitment procedures of the Watch Tower Movement
       in the context of its unusual organizational structure. The foun-
       dation of the movement is briefly sketched and its structure is
       said to differ from that of the majority of religious organizations
       in three respects: 1) it denies any sort of charisma to its non-
       elite officials; 2) it refuses to apply any form of regional or
       representative democracy; and 3) it claims direct control of all
       congregations. The "political economy" of its recruitment system
       is then discussed. The author maintains that the Watch Tower Move-
       ment, seen as a movement organization, does not conform to common
       sociological models of sect formation. However, its recruitment
       process depends, as in many other sects, on preexisting social
       relationships between members and nonmembers. It also relies
       heavily on carefully rehearsed "door-step" evangelism. This sect
       continues to recruit members largely through a systematic and un-
       relenting proselytization, a process that fits well with its cen-
       tralized structure.

1146. Beckford, James A. "The Embryonic Stage of a Religious Sect's
       Development: The Jehovah's Witnesses." SOCIOLOGICAL YEARBOOK OF
       RELIGION IN BRITAIN 5 (1972): 11-32.

       Discusses the origin and development of the evangelistic agency,
       Zion's Watch Tower Tract Society, that was founded by Charles Taze
       Russell, and argues that it does not fit into the pattern outlined
       by Wilson (item 149). The factors that kept the movement from
       developing like other sects are discussed. Although Russell's
       publishing venture fitted well into the millenarian spirit of his
       times, it had a novel feature, namely it began as a commercially
       sophisticated publishing enterprise and only later became a full-
       fledged sect. The reason why the Jehovah's Witnesses differ
       from apparently similar sects in organization and activities is
       explained by their rather unique origin and development.

1147. Bednarowski, Mary Farrell. "Outside the Mainstream: Women's Reli-
       gion and Women's Religious Leaders in Nineteenth-Century America."
       JOURNAL OF THE AMERICAN ACADEMY OF RELIGION 48 (1980): 207-231.

       Analyzes the status of women in the marginal religious movements
       of the nineteenth century with reference to four main beliefs and
       practices of these religious groups: 1) the character of the holy;
       2) the essence of human nature; 3) the function of the clergy; and
       4) the nature of marriage. The author attempts to demonstrate,
       with reference to Shakerism, Spiritualism, Christian Science, and
       Theosophy, that certain religious movements have given women leader-
       ship roles. The aforementioned groups are characterized by a view
       of God that is less masculine, a modification or denial of the
       Genesis doctrine of the Fall of Adam and Eve, a departure from the
       traditional male clergy, and a view of marriage that allows a wider
       variety of roles for women. Consequently, they attracted women
       because, unlike the mainline traditions, they gave them a wider say
       and greater choice of roles.

1148. Bednarski, Joyce. "The Salem Witch-Scare Viewed Sociologically."
       WITCHCRAFT AND SORCERY: SELECTED READINGS. Edited by Max Mar-
       wick. Harmondsworth, England: Penguin Books, 1970, pp. 151-63.

       Analyzes from a sociological point of view the major events of
       the seventeenth-century witch trials at Salem, Massachusetts. The
       author looks on these events as an indication that the society at
       the time had gone mad and became "blind to reason, driven by fear
       and distrust" (p. 156). Two major conditions that caused the
       witch scare, namely the political and religious crises of the time
       and the deterioration of the strong sense of community within the
       colony, are explored. Other factors, like the prevailing Puritan
       ethic, are also believed to have contributed to the problem. The
       witch scare served as a valve by which the community let off steam.
       The most apparent effects of the Salem trials were the hastening of
       the Puritan era and the ushering in of the Age of Reason.

1149. Bennett, John W. "Social Theory and the Social Order of the Hut-
       terite Community." MENNONITE QUARTERLY REVIEW 51 (1977): 292-307.

       Discusses the methods employed by the Hutterites "to maintain
       internal discipline in the face of the powerful external and inter-
       nal inducements to deviate from the chartered rules and tradition"
       (p. 292). It is suggested that their continuous reviewing of the
       social order acts as a kind of adaptive mechanism. The social
       structure creates conformity while leaving room for adjustment and
       change. The author maintains that the basis for social order among
       the Hutterites is belief and not commitment.

1150. Bennett, John W. "The Hutterites: A Communal Sect." RELIGION IN
       CANADIAN SOCIETY. Edited by Stewart Crysdale and Les Wheatcroft.
       Toronto: Macmillan, 1976, pp. 256-77.

       Studies the only Anabaptist sect that has rigorously preserved a
       communal lifestyle requiring the sharing of all major property and
       the raising of children mainly in collective institutions. The

author briefly sketches the movement of the sect from the U.S.A. to Canada and concentrates on the community in Jasper, Alberta. Its major beliefs, family and marriage practices, colony organization, and relationship with the community at large are outlined. Because the Hutterites do not mingle with outsiders and do not participate in political and social matters, they are looked upon with suspicion. Cultural changes might, in the future, have important repercussions on their lifestyle and could eventually modify their belief system to fit more comfortably into a secular society.

1151. Bennett, John W. "Frames of Reference For the Study of Hutterite Society." INTERNATIONAL REVIEW OF MODERN SOCIOLOGY 6.1 (1976): 23-39.

Proposes a discussion of Hutterite society from the following points of reference: 1) as a nuclear agricultural village; 2) as a system of conflict avoidance and resolution; 3) as a mode of inter-colony relationships for cooperative exchange; 4) as an agricultural conservationist system; and 5) as a homeostatic system that sees the community fluctuate in regular cycles.

1152. Ben-Yehuda, Nachman. "The European Witch Craze of the 14th to the 17th Centuries: A Sociologist's Perspective." AMERICAN JOURNAL OF SOCIOLOGY 86 (1980): 1-31.

Examines the rise and treatment of European witches and explores the reasons for the widespread craze, for the sudden increased attention to witchcraft, and for singling out women as the main victims. Several conditions are responsible for these developments: 1) the vested interest of the control organization within the established church (particularly that of the Dominicans and the Inquisition); 2) the dissolution of the medieval worldview; and 3) economic, demographic, and familial changes, particularly those affecting the role of women who became symbols of witchcraft. A basic bibliography is added (pp. 26-31).

1153. Ben-Yehuda, Nachman. "The European Witch Craze: Still a Sociologist's Perspective." AMERICAN JOURNAL OF SOCIOLOGY 88 (1983): 1275-79.

Replies to Hoak's critique (item 1307) that a sociological interpretation of the European witch craze is deficient. The author argues that historical explanations do not account for the fact that women were the main victims. They also fail to show how the religious conflicts of the Reformation ended up in a witch craze rather than in some other kind of religious persecution.

1154. Berger, Alan L. "Hasidism and Moonism: Charisma in the Counter Culture." SOCIOLOGICAL ANALYSIS 41 (1980): 357-90.

Examines two kinds of charismatic religion as presented by Hasidism and the Unification Church. Both groups share a response to world disenchantment, a stress on experience, a demand for commitment and community, elaborate indoctrination techniques, similar recruitment patterns, and a clearly defined social organization

based on charismatic leadership. The Unification Church differs in
that its founder is still alive. The authority in the Unification
Church differs from that in Hasidism in that in the former, ultimate
authority rests with the Reverend Moon. The author maintains that
there are crucial differences between the two religious groups in
the areas "of humility and mystery." He thinks that the charisma
of Reverend Moon has the "trappings of infantilization" (p. 390).

1155.   Birkelbach, Ronald A., and Louis A. Zurcher. "Some Socio-Political
        Characteristics of Anti-Pornography Campaigns." SOCIOLOGICAL
        SYMPOSIUM No. 4 (Spring 1970): 13-21.

        Outlines some of the features of those who actively campaigned in
        antipornography organizations and tests the hypothesis that par-
        ticipants in such movements are highly resistant to social and
        political change. Participants in antipornography movements are
        usually middle-class people reared in small communities. They have
        less formal education, are more religiously dogmatic, tend to be
        more authoritarian, and are less politically tolerant.

1156.   Björkstrand, Gustav. "Formative Factors of Maria Akerblom Move-
        ment." NEW RELIGIONS (item 565), pp. 133-40.

        Traces the history of a Finnish movement founded by Ida Maria
        Akerblom, who claimed to be the prophet of the Lord. The author
        holds that her movement must be seen against the background of her
        youth and of the charismatic qualities she manifested particularly
        in reading thoughts and faith healing. Her movement passed through
        four main phases: 1) origins (1917-1920); 2) consolidation (1920-
        1923); 3) struggle (1923-1927); and 4) dissolution (1927). Its
        emergence was due to Akerblom's complicated personality, the reli-
        gious situation of the time, and the social unrest and insecurity
        of the period.

1157.   Blauvelt, Martha Tomhave. "Women and Revivalism." WOMEN AND RELI-
        GION IN AMERICA. VOL. I: THE NINETEENTH CENTURY. Edited by
        Rosemary Radford Reuther and Rosemary Skinner Keller. San Fran-
        cisco: Harper and Row, 1981, pp. 1-45.

        Investigates the prominent role women played both as subjects and
        promoters of American revival movements in the nineteenth century.
        Two major areas are explored: 1) whether women were more suscepti-
        ble than men to evangelical revivals, and 2) what methods women
        used to foster religious interest in others. The periodic awaken-
        ings, according to the author, "revived not only religion but a
        spirit of sisterhood and high purpose among women" (p. 9). Several
        documents that exhibit women as members and promoters of revivals
        are reproduced.

1158.   Blauvelt, Martha Tomhave, and Rosemary Skinner Keller. "Women and
        Revivalism: The Puritan and Wesleyan Traditions." WOMEN AND
        RELIGION IN AMERICA. VOL. II: THE COLONIAL AND REVOLUTIONARY
        PERIOD. Edited by Rosemary Radford Reuther and Rosemary Skinner
        Keller. San Francisco: Harper and Row, 1983, pp. 316-67.

Maintains that Colonial Revivalism was significant not only because it brought preachers and theologians to prominence, but also because it expanded the activities of women. The work of several Puritan women, such as Sarah Goodhue, Deborah Prince, and Sarah Osborne, in spreading the evangelical message is explored. Puritan and Wesleyan revivals during this period are briefly described with special emphasis on the part played by women. The Wesleyan revival "proved to be the most liberating religious tradition for women in all areas of religious expression" (p. 237). Twelve Puritan and Wesleyan documents are given to illustrate women's participatory role in these religious revivals.

1159. Boldt, Edward D. "The Death of Hutterite Culture: An Alternative Interpretation." PHYLON 41 (1980): 390-95.

Maintains that external harassment is no longer a major threat in the decline of the Hutterites as a distinctive, separatist group. A brief description of Hutterite culture is given. It is argued that the erosion of values and traditions has increased. Changes in the dress code, violations of traditional taboos, and the adoption of less austere house furnishings are among the obvious signs of this decline. The defensive posture adopted by the Hutterites because of persecution has now been relaxed, with the consequence that the acceptance or assimilation of the ideology and values of the larger cultural context has become common. The danger that Hutterite culture now faces is the loosening of their own social structure.

1160. Boldt, Edward D. "Structural Tightness, Autonomy, and Observability: An Analysis of Hutterite Conformity and Orderliness." CANADIAN JOURNAL OF SOCIOLOGY 3 (1978): 349-63.

Challenges the common view that Hutterite conventionality is due to socialization practices that create deeply internalized norms and values, thus making the individual subservient to the group. Instead, it is argued that simplicity and structural tightness in Hutterite culture, coupled with the conditions of high observability, reduce individual autonomy and, therefore, increase conventional conduct.

1161. Boldt, Edward D. "Acquiescence and Conventionality in a Communal Society." JOURNAL OF CROSS-CULTURAL PSYCHOLOGY 7 (1976): 21-36.

Discusses, in the context of the Hutterites of North America, whether the tendency to social compliance is the cause of conventional behavior or conformity. A brief account of a Hutterite colony and a description of the tests conducted on 100 Hutterite children from 12 colonies in Alberta, Canada are given. The author concludes that the length of exposure to socialization has little influence on the relative vulnerability to group pressure. Various ways, such as selective recruitment, isolation, and expulsion, that a group can select to reduce individual autonomy are briefly explored.

1162. Bosk, Charles L. "The Routinization of Charisma: The Case of the Zaddik." SOCIOLOGICAL INQUIRY 49.1-2 (1979): 150-67.

Examines the role of the Hasidic leader, the zaddik, and its
cultural legitimation. The zaddik is said to have the personal
charismatic authority of an "exemplary prophet," an authority that
is usually propagated by his powers of curing and performing miracles and by the magical qualities he sometimes exhibits. Three
personality types are distinguished: the rational scholar, the
questioning peasant, and the messianic mystic. The ways in which
the charisma of the zaddik is legitimized and factional differences
dealt with are explored. A common cultural source, namely the
Kabbala and its representation of creation in mythical form, is
examined. The creation myth, according to the author, stabilizes
and legitimizes the office of the zaddik by basing his authority on
his personal contact with the feminine element of God. It also
gives order to the diverse Hasidic teachings.

1163.   Bosk, Charles L. "Cybernetic Hasidism: An Essay on Social and
        Religious Change." SOCIOLOGICAL INQUIRY 44.2 (1974): 131-44.

Employs a cybernetic model (or a religious symbol system) to
explain competition among Rabbinists, Messianists, and the Hasidim
in the Jewish communities of nineteenth-century Poland. Jewish
history is interpreted as a struggle between two religious viewpoints, namely ascetical rationalism and worldly mysticism. The
author explores why and on what grounds Hasidism and messianism
competed with Rabbinism and what elements gave Hasidism the capacity to adapt for survival. The historical background and theological differences in theodicy, soteriology, and cosmology between
the three mentioned Jewish groups are described and contrasted.
The author's view is that this model explains the various ways the
Jews used to adapt to their environment in Eastern Europe between
1750-1850.

1164.   Botting, Heather, and Gary Botting. THE ORWELLIAN WORLD OF JEHO-
        VAH'S WITNESSES. Toronto: University of Toronto Press, 1984.
        xxxiv, 213 pp.

Presents an examination of the Jehovah's Witnesses by two church
members who adopt a "more objective perspective in order to come to
understand the dynamics of attraction to, as well as defection from,
the Witnesses' world" (xxvii). The authors provide an account of
the worldview and historical development of the Witnesses. They
further discuss the following topics: 1) the Witnesses' interpretation of prophecy; 2) their conversion and indoctrination processes;
3) the role of the Watch Tower Bible and Tract Society in keeping
the symbols alive for the membership; and 4) the internal crises.
The socialization of children is described as a disciplinary regu-
lating of youth. The authors see a similarity between George
Orwell's 1984 and the structure of Jehovah's Witnesses in that
both propound an "totalitarian, oligarchical collectivism."

1165.   Boyer, Paul, and Stephen Nissenbaum. SALEM POSSESSED: THE SOCIAL
        ORIGINS OF WITCHCRAFT. Cambridge: Harvard University Press,
        1974. xxi, 231 pp.

Examines the seventeenth-century witch trials at Salem, Massachusetts in a broader social framework and discovers that the witch
hunters' offensive against witches is a fleeting one in the midst

of a general retreat. Some new perspectives, such as the patterns of accusation, are explored. An attempt is made to depict the dynamics of village factionalism and the problems that confronted Salem village during the period in question. Witchcraft accusations "moved in channels that were determined by years of factional strife" (p. 181). The authors show how the struggles between various parties in Salem were intimately related to the outburst of witch hunting.

1166.   Brady, Margaret K. "Transformations of Power: Mormon Women's Visionary Narratives." JOURNAL OF AMERICAN FOLKLORE 100 (1987): 461-68.

Explores how in the Mormon patriarchal system women "come to terms with the varied personal, feminine, and ecclesiastical goals of reproduction and mothering" (p. 461). Folk traditions express how women themselves conceive of their own power within a male-oriented society. This essay attempts to demonstrate how this is done through a description of personal experiences of Mormon women concerning visionary predictions during pregnancy. Women in contemporary Mormon society, unlike their counterparts in the nineteenth century, are debarred from healing the sick, speaking in tongues, casting out devils, and prophesying; they are permitted to have only personal visions that give them access to spiritual power in their church.

1167.   Braude, Ann D. "Spirits Defend the Rights of Women: Spiritualism and Changing Sex Roles in Nineteenth-Century America." WOMEN, RELIGION, AND SOCIAL CHANGE. Edited by Yvonne Yazbeck Haddad and Ellison Banks Findly. New York: State University of New York Press, 1985, pp. 419-31.

Surveys the relationship between the religious content of Spiritualism and the changes in sex roles advocated by Spiritualists and those involved in the Women's Rights Movement. In the nineteenth century, Spiritualism, which has been conspicuous for the number and celebrity of its female leaders, adhered to the principle of the equality of the sexes and presented women with the opportunity to resolve the contradictions of the mainline religious traditions. The Spiritualists "created a model of female power which made sense to many women's rights advocates" (p. 429).

1168.   Brewer, Priscilla J. "'Numbers Are Not the Thing For Us To Glory In:' Demographic Perspectives on the Decline of the Shakers." COMMUNAL SOCIETIES 7 (1987): 25-35.

Examines the reasons for, and timing of, the decline of the United Society of Believers in Christ's Second Appearing through Shaker records and U. S. census records. The relatively large decline in numbers, which began in 1840, was not caused by external factors, like urbanization and industrialization, but rather by internal conflicts (such as the debate about vegetarianism) and by the sect's inability to maintain converts permanently. By the mid-nineteenth century, the Shakers suffered from a weakened leadership combined with the declining proportion of young and middle-aged adults.

1169. Brewer, Priscilla J. SHAKER COMMUNITIES, SHAKER LIVES. Hanover,
       NH: University Press of New England, 1986. xviii, 273 pp.

       Investigates the Shakers from within the boundaries of their own
       society and attempts to draw a picture of Shaker life as it was
       experienced by the members of the community. After tracing the
       socioreligious background that fostered the growth of Shakerism in
       the last quarter of the eighteenth century, the organization's
       growth under its various leaders is chronologically outlined. The
       serious internal and external difficulties that plagued the sect
       and the adjustments it made are discussed in some depth. The suc-
       cess of the Shakers is attributed to their ability "to combine
       tradition and innovation in ideology, economics, social structures"
       (p. 203). Internal dissension and external social forces are re-
       sponsible for their decline. Several demographic characteristics
       are included in the appendices. A bibliography of primary and
       secondary sources is added (pp. 259-68).

1170. Brewer, Priscilla J. "The Demographic Features of the Shaker
       Decline, 1787-1900." JOURNAL OF INTERDISCIPLINARY HISTORY 15
       (1984): 31-52.

       Maintains that there are some misconceptions about both the qual-
       ity and quantity of Shaker membership. The decline of the Shakers
       cannot be attributed solely to industrialization, to dislocation
       due to the Civil War, or to the lessening appeal of celibacy. Nor
       was the sect always more popular with women. Five stages of the
       demographic and social history of the New Lebanon Church Family
       (the name of the Shaker central community and residence of its
       governing body) between 1787-1900 are distinguished and described.
       During this period the United Society of Believers of Christ's
       Second Appearing (the full title of the sect) underwent significant
       modification, but its early decline was not fundamentally numerical.
       The Shaker community "was characterized by considerable instability
       throughout its history" (p. 52). This essay contains the major
       references to demographic studies on Shakerism.

1171. Brink, T. L. "The Rise of Mormonism: A Case Study in the Symbology
       of Frontier America." INTERNATIONAL JOURNAL OF SYMBOLOGY 6
       (1975): 31-38.

       Discusses the "innovative and intricate symbology" that Joseph
       Smith introduced when he founded Mormonism. After outlining the
       importance of symbolism, with particular reference to the work of
       Jung, three major symbols are described: 1) the return to original
       purity; 2) the Indians as ancient Hebrews; and 3) the American
       destiny under God. The American frontier symbolism undercut "the
       cult of consciousness found in Calvinism and deism, and also the
       uncontrollable irruptions found in frontier revivalism" (p. 37).

1172. Bromley, David G., and Anson D. Shupe. "The Tnevnoc Cult." SOCIO-
       LOGICAL ANALYSIS 40 (1979): 361-66.

       Examines a hypothetical nineteenth-century religious movement
       that, like other cults today, was embroiled in a controversy re-
       garding its recruitment and socialization practices. A brief

ethnography of "Tnevnoc" ("convent" spelled backwards) is provided.
The authors find many similarities between the "desocialization"
and "resocialization" techniques of the Tnevnoc cult and the new
religions. Some of the reactions to all these movements have been
the same. It is maintained that what shapes public reactions and
definitions of a religious group is the legitimacy accorded it
rather than its practices. The authors suggest that several societal responses to the new religious movements might impede them
from following the same course of accommodation that nineteenth-
century cults pursued.

1173.   Brotz, Howard M. "Negro 'Jews' in the United States." PHYLON 13
        (1952): 324-37.

        Describes a Black Jewish cult in Harlem, New York, namely The
        Commandment Keepers Congregation of the Living God (also known by
        the name of the respective lodge, such as the Royal Order of
        Aethiopian Hebrews). The emergence of this group under "Rabbi"
        Wentworth Arthur Matthew, who came from the West Indies in 1913,
        and its beliefs and rituals are outlined. The social structure of
        this cult or sect, led by a typically charismatic individual, is
        examined. The author observes that at the roots of this cult lies
        an explicit self-differentiation from the Black lower class. The
        religious practices of this group have a important magical compo-
        nent that is related to the concerns of Blacks, namely mental and
        physical health and affection. There is reference to another eight
        cults that originated in the New York area between 1919 and 1931
        and disintegrated with the deaths of their founders.

1174.   Bruce, Steve. "The Moral Majority: The Politics of Fundamentalism
        in a Secular Society." STUDIES IN RELIGIOUS FUNDAMENTALISM.
        Edited by Lionel Chapman. London: Macmillan Press, 1987, pp.
        177-94.

        Gives an account of the New Christian Right in America and iden-
        tifies some of the problems it faces in its efforts to reintroduce
        religion into a largely secular society. The author disputes the
        theories of status defense and status inconsistency to account for
        the origin of the movement. He maintains that the New Christian
        Right is a movement of culture defense that was triggered by in-
        creased encroachment by the cultural and political center and by
        the heightened permissiveness of that center. The rise, impact,
        and goals of the Moral Majority are outlined and their failure to
        achieve political success discussed in the context of motivational
        problems that the movement faces.

1175.   Bruce, Steve. "Born Again: Conversion, Crusades, and Brainwash-
           ing." SCOTTISH JOURNAL OF RELIGIOUS STUDIES 3.2 (1982): 107-23.

        Critically examines the adequacy of the brainwashing model to
        explain conversion to new religious movements. An account of a
        typical Christian crusade meeting is given and the nature of cru-
        sades discussed. Crusades have become highly routinized with lit-
        tle enthusiasm. They are frequently interdenominational, aimed at
        regular churchgoers and at sustaining the morale of Christians.

Conversion during a crusade does not involve a major shift in one's faith, but rather a pledge to a more serious commitment. The modern crusade is not something to be explained by crowd psychology. The conversion at crusades is a product of gradual socialization rather than a dramatic, immediate transformation.

1176. Bruce, Steve. "The Student Christian Movement: A Nineteenth-Century Movement and Its Vicissitudes." INTERNATIONAL JOURNAL OF SOCIOLOGY AND SOCIAL POLICY 21 (1982): 67-82.

Studies the rise and demise of the Student Christian Movement in Great Britain. The various types of bonding that form the network of relationships and communications within the movement and that are necessary for the movement's success are described. The importance of legitimated leadership is stressed. The demise of this British movement is traced mainly to its diffuse and precarious belief system, though other factors, such as competition from other evangelical groups, could also have contributed to its disintegration.

1177. Brutz, Judith L., and Craig M. Allen. "Religious Commitment, Peace Activism, and Marital Violence in Quaker Families." JOURNAL OF MARRIAGE AND THE FAMILY 48 (1986): 491-502.

Explores the relationship between religious commitment and marital violence in nearly 300 Quaker spouses to determine whether religious commitment has a positive outcome on the way married couples relate to each other. After a short description of the Quaker orientation towards peace, the authors test their hypothesis that those Quakers who are committed to peace react less violently when faced with marital problems. It is concluded that the Quaker religion has an important impact on the rates of marital violence. The various factors that contribute to the relationship between religious beliefs and family violence are discussed.

1178. Brutz, Judith L., and Bron B. Ingoldsby. "Conflict Resolution in Quaker Families." JOURNAL OF MARRIAGE AND THE FAMILY 46 (1984): 21-26.

Investigates the degree to which nonviolence actually characterizes Quaker family life. The beliefs of Quakers (who live in the Lake Erie region) about violence are summarized and the way they resolve family disputes recorded. The authors' findings are apparently contradictory in that, while the rates of violence are the same or higher than the national averages, there are clear signs that Quaker families experience less violence than other families. The possible interpretation of these findings are discussed and several research questions posed.

1179. Buchanan, Frederick S., and Larry W. Scott. "The Eskdale Commune: Desert Alternative to Secular Schools." INTELLECT 102 (1974): 226-30.

Describes a Mormon sect, the Order of Aaron, founded by Maurice L. Glendenning in 1943. The educational system of Eskdale, the central commune of the Order, is outlined. The Montessori method

is used for children under six, and the county and state authorities
approve and support the remaining grades. The authors observe that
the "holistic approach to education and the close integration of
the schools with the community" (p. 230) make the Eskdale school
system unique.

1180. Buck, Roy C. "Boundary Maintenance Revisited: Tourist Experience
       in an Old Order Amish Community." RURAL SOCIOLOGY 42 (1978):
       221-34.

       Assesses the presence of tourism in the Old Order Amish settle-
       ment in Lancaster County, Pennsylvania and attempts to convey "the
       essential character and meaning of tourist experience" among these
       Amish. Tourist literature advertises the Amish as a separate,
       peculiar, and religious people. It uses a boundary maintenance
       mechanism as a strategy to attract people to visit the Amish.
       While reinforcing the visitor's helplessness in a strange land,
       tourism offers well-orchestrated stage productions and other ser-
       vices that are not really part of Amish life and that actually keep
       tourists from direct contact with the Amish. While the Amish feel
       the presence of tourism, they do not seem to be bothered by it.
       Rather than erode their culture or cause personal distress, the
       presence of tourists strengthens the Amish in their self-perception
       of a community separate from the rest of society.

1181. Buckle, Robert. "Mormonism in Britain: A Survey." SOCIOLOGICAL
       YEARBOOK OF RELIGION IN BRITAIN 4 (1971): 160-79.

       Reports on a survey of Mormonism in Britain aimed at finding out
       what attracted people to join the Mormon church and comparing the
       Mormon attitudes on social and religious matters with those of
       other churches. Among the attractive features of Mormonism, the
       following are included: influence of missionaries; approval of the
       way of life Mormonism offered; enthusiasm for the way the church is
       run; friendliness of church members; the ability of the Mormon
       church to fulfill the needs of individuals; reading the Book of
       Mormon; and youth activities. Mormon attitudes are compared with
       those of members of the Church of England, of the Catholic Church,
       and the general population.

1182. Bull, Malcolm. "The Seventh-Day Adventists: Heretics of American
       Civil Religion." SOCIOLOGICAL ANALYSIS 50 (1989): 177-87.

       Discusses the relationship between the Seventh-Day Adventists and
       American culture, stressing the importance of this religious orga-
       nization and its uniqueness in that "it is cult-like in its origins
       but sect-like in its ideology and social practice" (p. 178). The
       author maintains that the Adventists, who define themselves in
       opposition to the state, developed their ideology in the image of
       contemporary Civil Religion; thus, Seventh-Day Adventism can be
       considered a heretical form of the American Civil Religion.

1183. Bull, Malcolm. "Eschatology and Manners in Seventh-Day Adventism."
       ARCHIVES DE SCIENCES SOCIALES DES RELIGIONS 65.1 (1988): 145-59.

Complains that scholars have neglected to ask some of the following questions on the Seventh-Day Adventists: 1) what is the significance of their preoccupation with the Second Coming?; 2) how does
one accurately describe the sect's social orientation?; and 3) what
interpretation best explains the origins of the movement? The
author seeks to answer these questions by looking into the early
history of the sect and the teachings of its prophet, Ellen White.
He holds that by analyzing the relationship between her eschatology
and ethics, one can identify the characteristics of Adventism. The
movement's eschatology "was postmillennialist rather than premil-
lennialist, reactionary rather than revolutionary" and its call for
restraint "is better understood as a social ethic than as a work
ethic" (p. 157).

1184. Bunker, Gary L., Harry Coffey, and Martin A. Johnson. "Mormons and
       Social Distance: A Multidimensional Analysis." ETHNICITY 40
       (1977): 352-69.

Investigates the attitudes of Mormons towards outsiders concentrating on two major questions: 1) are Mormon ethical attitudes in
conflict with those of the larger culture? and 2) do Mormons gener-
alize from their ecclesiastical norms (which hold that they have a
common Semitic origin and cooperative destiny with Jews, American
Indians, etc.) to secular tolerance or intolerance? The authors
explore the following factors: formal social distance; marital
acceptance; friendship; and subordination. They conclude that with
the exception of marital acceptance, the Mormons responded favorably
to other ethnic and religious groups. For Mormons, race was the
strongest determinant of social distance.

1185. Bunker, Gary L., and Martin A. Johnson. "Ethnicity and Resistance
       to Compensatory Education: A Comparison of Mormon and Non-Mormon
       Ethnic Attitudes." REVIEW OF RELIGIOUS RESEARCH 16 (1975): 74-82.

Attempts to determine whether Mormon teachings advocate tolerance
towards ethnic minorities in the United States. The basic theological position of the Church of Latter-Day Saints on racial differences is briefly outlined. A method of measuring group prejudice
is developed and used to contrast Mormon and non-Mormon views towards American Blacks, American Indians, and Mexican-Americans. It
was concluded that Mormons are not significantly more resistant
than non-Mormons to compensatory education for ethnic minorities.
Mormons do not differ much from the average population in their
secular, racial attitudes.

1186. Burfield, Diana. "Theosophy and Feminism: Some Explorations in
       Nineteenth-Century Biography." WOMEN'S RELIGIOUS EXPERIENCE:
       CROSS CULTURAL PERSPECTIVES. Edited by Pat Holden. Totowa, NJ:
       Barnes and Noble, 1983, pp. 27-56.

Sketches the historical background of the Theosophical Society
and sees it in the context of the social movements of the nineteenth century (like the British National Association of Spiritualists and the Fabian Society). Some of the Theosophical feminists
are examined individually and three ideal types of women theoso-
phists are proposed, namely the leaders, loners, and disciples.

The Theosophical Society's appeal to ancient wisdom and occult traditions and its future-oriented programs are compatible with socialist and feminist goals.

1187. Burkett, Randall K. GARVEYISM AS A RELIGIOUS MOVEMENT: THE INSTITUTIONALIZATION OF A BLACK CIVIL RELIGION. Metuchen, NJ: Scarecrow Press, 1978. xxvi, 216 pp.

Gives an account of the rise of the Universal Negro Improvement Association and African Communities League led by Marcus Garvey in the early part of the twentieth century. The religious ethos of this organization and its rituals are described and the theology of Garvey is outlined. The author's view is that Garvey was attempting to create a Black civil religion based on traditional Christian themes but with the belief that Blacks were the Chosen People and Africa the Promised Land. The reaction of the Black clergy to Garvey is dealt with at some length. Garveyism was deliberately nonsectarian and was broad enough to attract Christian and non-Christian Blacks alike.

1188. Burnham, Kenneth E. GOD COMES TO AMERICA: FATHER DIVINE AND THE PEACE MISSION MOVEMENT. Boston: Lambeth Press, 1979. ix, 167 pp.

Studies the rise of a religious movement in the depression years of the 1930's. The place of Father Divine as God in the movement is explained and his mission of economic, social, political and educational reforms examined. The structure and organization of the Peace Mission (with its strict moral code) from its initial, family-type, charismatic setting to a larger, more complex, formal organization are outlined. The movement, according to the author, is one large religious order that divides its members into various groups. The problem of succession to Father Divine is discussed. The social conditions, namely political and economic stresses, in which charismatic leadership emerges and flourishes are considered. Father Divine provided an avenue for rebellion against anomie and for the adoption of new norms.

1189. Burns, Thomas A., and J. Stephen Smith. "The Symbolism of Becoming in the Sunday Service of an Urban Black Holiness Church." ANTHROPOLOGICAL QUARTERLY 57 (1978): 185-204.

Focuses on the symbolic actions and belief statements in the Sunday morning ritual of an urban Black Holiness church. It is the author's contention that these symbols "function first to locate the members of the congregation in terms of their current position in the sect and second to symbolically promote the members' commitment to more advanced status within the sect" (p. 185-86). The symbolism of the Sunday ritual is analyzed in terms of several factors, such as the types of speech used and the signs of spirit manifestation. An overall pattern of the service is provided and interpreted as a service concerned with "becoming" that refers to levels of contact with the Spirit, and not with identity confirmation or transformation. The service thus reveals the social hierarchy of the church and confirms its social structure.

1190. Butler, Jon. "Magic, Astrology, and the Early American Religious
       Heritage, 1600-1760." AMERICAN HISTORICAL REVIEW 84 (1979):
       317-46.

       Discusses occult beliefs and practices in early American history
       in the context of the publications of the seventeenth and eigh-
       teenth centuries. The author thinks that the English occult tradi-
       tion survived to some extent in early America in spite of the rise
       of science and skepticism. He endeavors to explain the decline of
       occult religious practices with reference to the change of the
       literary taste of England's educated elite, to the personal discord
       and intellectual vacillation in occult literature, and to the
       attacks on occult religion by traditional Christian churches and
       colonial governments.

1191. Campbell, Bruce, and Eugene E. Campbell. "The Mormon Family."
       ETHNIC FAMILIES IN AMERICA. Edited by Charles H. Mindel and
       Robert W. Haberstein. New York: Elsivier, 1976, pp. 379-412.

       Presents a picture of the family system that Joseph Smith, the
       founder of Mormonism, promoted and then examines the development of
       Mormon family life. The main Mormon ideology surrounding the fam-
       ily is described in terms of four concepts, namely the eternal
       family, the extended family by adoption, the patriarchal family,
       and the polygamous family. The contemporary Mormon family, with
       its divorce rate, husband-wife relationship, extended family kin-
       ship system, and socialization process, is analyzed. The impor-
       tance of the family in maintaining Mormonism as a distinct and
       vital religious group is underscored.

1192. Campbell, D'Ann. "Women's Life in Utopia: The Shaker Experiment in
       Equality Reappraised." NEW ENGLAND QUARTERLY 51 (1978): 23-38.

       Studies the Shaker literature to determine 1) whether Shaker
       society reflected their view of sexual equality, 2) the economic
       background of Shaker women, and 3) the reasons that attracted women
       to join and remain in the movement. The author thinks that the
       extended family network that the Shaker communities provided for
       members of broken families was especially appealing to women and
       their children. Women became members to satisfy their needs for
       stability and security. In Shaker society they functioned as the
       political, economic, and social equals of men.

1193. Campbell, Mary Ann. "Labeling and Oppression: Witchcraft in Medi-
       eval Europe." MID-AMERICAN REVIEW OF SOCIOLOGY 3.2 (1978):
       55-82.

       Discusses the underlying social conditions and processes through
       which witches in medieval Europe were labeled, hunted, and perse-
       cuted. The author's view is that the witch image was created by
       the Christian Church as a means of entrenching its power, which was
       maintained by the Inquisition. She further holds that the mythol-
       ogy of witches was based on distortions of the real beliefs and
       practices of pagan religions. The author thinks that both witch-
       craft and the Inquisition have a contemporary significance.

1194. Capp, Bernard. ENGLISH ALMANACS, 1500-1800: ASTROLOGY AND THE
       POPULAR PRESS. London: Faber and Faber, 1979. 452 pp.

       Presents a history of the English almanac from 1500 to 1800,
       noting its astrological calculations and its effects on politics,
       society, religion, and medicine. The author maintains that the
       almanac played an invaluable role "in its ability to span the in-
       tellectual and social horizons" (p. 292). Besides copious biblio-
       graphical notes on compilers and publishers of almanacs, there is
       an appendix on the bibliography of English almanacs up to 1970.

1195. Capps, Walter. THE MONASTIC IMPULSE. New York: Crossroads, 1983,
       163 pp.

       Explores the basis for the current interest in, and revival of,
       monastic lifestyles. Various monastic institutions in the West are
       described. The author relates the development in monastic life to
       a number of significant sociocultural changes, namely the loss of
       confidence in social progress, the impatience with bureaucracy, and
       cultural malaise. He discusses the problems monasticism must over-
       come to avoid becoming a narcissistic escape. He suggests that
       "monasticism may be functioning as one of the primary vehicles
       through which the aspirations of the counterculture are being car-
       ried out" (p. 7).

1196. Cardwell, Jerry D. "On Keeping the Sabbath Day Holy: Perceived
       Powerlessness and Church Attendance of Mormon Males and Females."
       THE SOCIAL CONTEXT OF RELIGIOSITY. By Jerry D. Cardwell. Wash-
       ington, DC: University Press of America, 1980, pp. 145-56.

       Discusses the theory that traditional church attendance declines
       as the perceived powerlessness of church members increases. The
       research was conducted in a state university and all the respon-
       dents were Mormons. Several features of powerlessness are listed.
       The author holds that the students' response supported his assump-
       tion, namely that the sense of power, or lack of it, a church-goer
       feels has important implications on his or her attendance at church
       functions. Neither Mormon men nor women, however, responded in an
       an alienated manner to the absence of power to influence social and
       religious issues within their church.

1197. Carroll, Robert P. WHEN PROPHECY FAILED: REACTIONS AND RESPONSES
       TO FAILURE IN OLD TESTAMENT PROPHETIC TRADITION. London: SCM
       Press, 1979. 250 pp.

       Takes a cross-disciplinary approach to understand how people
       reacted to Old Testament prophecies that failed to materialize. The
       author first outlines a general interpretation of the prophetic
       tradition. Then he summarizes the theory of cognitive dissonance
       and applies it to the Biblical prophets. He shows how 1) reinter-
       pretation, 2) adaptive predictions, and 3) the stress on the need
       to exercise faith in response to prophetic visions were among the
       methods used in the Bible to account for, or explain, prophetic
       failures--in other words, to resolve or reduce the level of cogni-
       tive dissonance.

1198. Carwardine, Richard. "The Religious Revival of 1857-8 in the Unit-
       ed States." RELIGIOUS MOTIVATION: BIOGRAPHICAL AND SOCIOLOGICAL
       PROBLEMS FOR THE CHURCH HISTORIAN. Edited by Derek Baker. Ox-
       ford: Blackwell, 1978, pp. 393-406.

       Explores the motivations and reasons of the many Americans who
       participated in the religious revival in the mid-nineteenth cen-
       tury. Economic regression is seen as one of the main forces that
       triggered the revival. The feeling of guilt in the business commu-
       nity and the need for people to find strength and consolation are
       among the underlying motives that made the revival a success. Two
       objectives were among the main motives of the evangelical leaders:
       1) to begin a new era in church/state relations; and 2) to create a
       perfect Protestant republic freed from Catholicism, socialism, and
       infidelity. Some saw the revivals as a means of soothing tensions
       in society at large, of harmonizing various sectional differences,
       of spreading conservative Christian influence, or of achieving a
       better society.

1199. Carwardine, Richard. "The Second Great Awakening in the Urban
       Areas: An Examination of Methodism and the 'New Measures.'"
       JOURNAL OF AMERICAN HISTORY 59 (1972): 327-40.

       Questions the view that Charles Grandison Finney was responsible
       for the mid-nineteenth-century revival in the cities and examines
       more closely the situation in the urban centers before and during
       the revival. Various types of restrained and cautious Calvinistic
       revivals were taking place at the time without the more emotional
       or enthusiastic forms of religious behavior that Methodist preach-
       ers introduced. Among the "new measures" of revivalism was the
       introduction of the "anxious seat" or "mourners' bench," the pew
       "set aside at the front of the congregation to which those in a
       state of concern over their souls could go to be exhorted and
       prayed for at the close of the sermon" (p. 333). Itinerant evange-
       lism, mixed assemblies, direct and colloquial preaching, and sus-
       tained sessions of private and public prayer were methods used by
       Finney. These methods, though new to other Protestant churches,
       were not novel to Methodism. Finney was not innovative, though he
       did give the new measures a wider popular base.

1200. Casanova, José V. "The First Secular Institute: The Opus Dei as
       a Religious Movement-Organization." ANNUAL REVIEW OF THE SOCIAL
       SCIENCES OF RELIGION 6 (1982): 243-85.

       Presents a sociological study of the Catholic Organization Opus
       Dei. After tracing the origins of the movement in the late 1920's
       and describing the work of its founder, José Maria Escriva, the
       author suggests that it could be seen as a resolution to the Catho-
       lic dilemma in the modern world. The process of conversion to Opus
       Dei, its inner tensions with the Catholic Church, and its internal
       contradictions are dealt with. The author's view is that Opus Dei
       is a compromise between inner-worldly asceticism and Catholic tra-
       ditionalism. He identifies its sectarian traits, including its
       demand of total commitment, and considers it a modern Catholic
       order characterized "by a high degree of stratification, special-
       ization of functions, and a rigid notion of community" (p. 259).

1201. Caudrey, Adriana. "Keepers of the Faith." NEW SOCIETY 75 (January 24, 1986): 137-39.

Describes briefly some of the practices of various Hasidic groups in Stanford Hill, London, England. The sanctity of the family is said to be one of the major strengths of the movement. Missionary attempts by the Lubavitcher are surveyed.

1202. Cavan, Ruth Shonle. "Analysis of Health Practices Among the Amish With Reference to Boundary Maintenance." COMMUNAL SOCIETIES 4 (1984): 59-73.

Investigates the health hazards and care among the Amish. Three areas are explored: 1) how are health hazards, especially accidents, related to Amish farm life?; 2) to what extent do these hazards integrate the community and hence function to maintain the village boundary?; and 3) to what degree is outside medical care sought? The author sees a contradiction between the Amish rejection of science and technology and their acceptance of Western medicine, though she thinks that the Amish still "preserve a delicate balance between the community and the world, between traditional methods and outside medical care" (p. 73).

1203. Cavan, Ruth Shonle. "The Contrasting Roles of Women at Oneida Community, the Mid-Western Frontier, and the Urban East in the Mid-Nineteenth Century." COMMUNAL SOCIETIES 1 (1981): 67-79.

Contrasts the conditions of women in three nineteenth-century situations: seclusive communes, the American Western frontier, and industrialized cities. The social structure, the role of women in the family, and the advantages and disadvantages of Oneida women as compared to other women are the topics discussed. Women at Oneida lived in a more controlled and economically secure condition, but they were denied the roles of wives and mothers and played an inferior role in commune life. In the East, these roles were still dominant, but women were already taking an active part in other areas of life. On the frontier, women, though still subservient to men, were expected to be resourceful, knowledgeable in household skills, and strong enough to withstand the hardships of the isolated lifestyle. The author concludes that Oneida women had an easier, more comfortable, and more secure life, but lacked the opportunities for individual achievements.

1204. Cavan, Ruth Shonle. "The Future of a Historic Commune: Amana." COMMUNES: HISTORIC AND CONTEMPORARY (item 312), pp. 257-71.

Explores the Amana Community, otherwise known as the Religion of True Inspiration, under six aspects: 1) the historical background; 2) the crises of the Amana communities in the United States; 3) the great change that took place in 1932; 4) some positive features and threats to survival; 5) adjustment to society at large; and 6) some speculations about the future. Material security, religious life, strong family ties, and the continued use of the German language all contributed to the survival of the community. The lack of charismatic leadership, loss of members, lack of colonization,

economic problems, and tourism have tended to weaken Amana as a
distinct entity. The author thinks that in spite of Amana's efforts to adapt to modern times, its traditional way of life will
continue to diminish.

1205. Chevannes, Barry. "The Literature of Rastafari." SOCIAL AND ECO-
NOMIC STUDIES 26 (1977): 239-62.

Reviews those studies on the Rastafari Movement that are based on
original research and traces some major themes, like racial identity, that run throughout this literature. The author maintains
that the movement is becoming more religious in outlook and in its
activities, even though some members are playing an increasingly
active role in politics. A short bibliography of 40 items is added.

1206. Christensen, Harold T. "Stress Points in Mormon Family Culture."
DIALOGUE: A JOURNAL OF MORMON THOUGHT 4.4 (1972): 20-24.

Examines the "structural weakness" of the Mormon family. The
divorce rate, dating habits, youthful marriage, sexual guilt,
underplanned marriages, and the authoritarian family relationships
are among the major topics discussed.

1207. Christie-Murray, David. VOICES FROM THE GODS: SPEAKING IN TONGUES.
London: Routledge and Kegan Paul, 1978. xiii, 280 pp.

Surveys the phenomenon of glossolalia and the main debates about
its significance and function. After a chapter on the speaking in
tongues in non-Christian religions, the author focuses on the history of glossolalia in Christianity from the first century up to
contemporary times. There are chapters on twentieth-century Spiritualism and on the Charismatic Movement. The psychological effects
of speaking in tongues are also discussed.

1208. Clark, Peter. "Leadership and Succession Among the Hutterites."
CANADIAN REVIEW OF SOCIOLOGY AND ANTHROPOLOGY 14 (1977): 294-
302.

Studies 42 Hutterite colonies in order to find out "the degree to
which succession to leadership positions departs from a model of
complete equality of opportunity" (p. 294). The author examines
social mobility among the Hutterites paying special attention to
the "intergenerational political mobility." After a short introductory assessment of Hutterite population, the political hierarchy
is described. Political mobility tends to offer equality of opportunity more readily in those colonies that break up into distinct
groups more rapidly. The type of inequality observed was familial
nepotism.

1209. Clarke, Garrett. SPIRIT POSSESSION AND POPULAR RELIGION: FROM THE
CAMISARDS TO THE SHAKERS. Baltimore: Johns Hopkins University
Press, 1987. viii, 294 pp.

Deals mainly with the origin of the Shakers, though several chapters are dedicated to the eighteenth-century Camisards, the Methodist Awakening, and the Great Awakening in America. The author, who

combines anthropological and historical approaches to the study of religion, attempts to see how several eighteenth-century religious revivals touched the lives of the average individual. The focus of this book is on the phenomena of spirit possessions, which are seen as various kinds of "sacred theatres." The Shakers are compared to ecstatic cults in other cultures.

1210. Clasen, Claus-Peter. ANABAPTISM: A SOCIAL HISTORY, 1525-1618: SWITZERLAND, AUSTRIA, MORAVIA, SOUTH AND CENTRAL GERMANY. Ithaca, NY: Cornell University Press, 1972. xviii, 523 pp.

Traces the evolution of the Anabaptism movement from its beginnings in 1525 to the outbreak of the Thirty Years' War in 1618, concentrating on its effects on society at large, its numerical strength, and the internal conflicts that led to its breakup into many different groups. The organization of this sect, its appeal largely to craftsmen and peasants, its rejection of the official church, its spiritual life, and its relationship to society are the main topics discussed. Among the reasons for its success are said to be the religious conditions of the time and government persecutions.

1211. Clear, Val. "The Church of God: A Study in Social Adaptation." REVIEW OF RELIGIOUS RESEARCH 2 (1961): 129-33.

Speculates on the reasons why the Church of God, which grew out of the Holiness Movement, has experienced rapid and extreme change since its inception in 1880. Three influential forces are identified: 1) the variety of the religious backgrounds of the church's early members; 2) its movement from a rural to an urban setting; and 3) the consequent adoption of bourgeois attitudes. Eight overlapping stages of development, starting with social unrest and including institutionalization and sophistication, are outlined.

1212. Clelland, Donald A., and Thomas C. Hood. "In the Company of the Converted: Characteristics of a Billy Graham Crusade Audience." SOCIOLOGICAL ANALYSIS 35 (1974): 45-56.

Examines the social features of a Billy Graham Crusade audience in Knoxville, Tennessee. Various questionnaires given to those attending the crusade plus a survey of area residents are used to collect information that supports the view that the respectable middle-class form the bulk of Billy Graham's followers. Crusade attenders are more educated and of higher income and occupational prestige than the average area residents. They are further disproportionately young, female, active in an organized church, and orthodox in their beliefs. They tend to attract those who feel that their lifestyle is threatened and tend to reaffirm their traditional worldview.

1213. Cohen, David Steven. "The 'Angel Dancers:' The Folklore of Religious Communitarianism." NEW JERSEY HISTORY 95.1 (1977): 5-20.

Proposes a folkloristic approach to the study of religious sects that stress communal living and focuses on a late nineteenth-century group called the "Angel Dancers," a small religious commune in

Woodcliff, New Jersey. The author gives a vivid description of the various popular accounts of the sect's activities. He thinks that the case of the "Angel Dancers" demonstrates the process of rumor formation, a process which can also be detected in other cults, such as the Ephrata Community, the Shakers, and more recently the Unification Church and the Children of God. Because many of the rumors had no foundation in reality, the author thinks that the allegation that communitarianism is incompatible with American society is untenable.

1214.   Cohn, Norman. "The Ranters." ENCOUNTER 34.4 (April 1970): 15-26.

Discusses a mid-seventeenth-century English sect of mystical anarchists known as "the high attainers," or, more popularly, "the Ranters," whose behavior attracted the attention of the British parliament. The Ranters were believed to be an antinomian community that practiced free love. The author maintains that, even though the Ranters did not survive as a group for a long period of time, they are important because they serve as a link between a long series of mystical or quasi-mystical anarchists extending from the thirteenth century to the present day. A hippie commune in California in the late 1960's is cited as an example of modern mystical anarchists with ideological ties to the Ranters.

1215.   Coleman, Linda. "The Language of 'Born Again' Christianity." PROCEEDINGS OF THE SIXTH ANNUAL MEETING OF THE BERKELEY LINGUIS- TICS SOCIETY. Edited by Bruce M. Caron, et al. Berkeley, CA: Berkeley Linguistic Society, 1980, pp. 133-42.

Examines the language of evangelical Christians who are described as holding strong, orthodox protestant beliefs based on a conversion experience in which they accept Jesus Christ as their personal savior. The author examines how the evangelical worldview affects syntax, points to various ways in which both worldview and practical realities have an impact on semantics, and gives some examples to illustrate her findings. Evangelical language not only helps create and sustain a religious event, but it may also be used to transform a secular situation into a religious one.

1216.   Connor, John W. "The Social and Psychological Reality of European Witchcraft Beliefs." PSYCHIATRY 38 (1975): 366-80.

Contends that European belief in witchcraft was not irrational or delusory, but rather made sense in the context of the culture and belief system of late medieval post-Reformation Europe. The author holds that the Black Death of the fourteenth century helped spread the belief in witchcraft and encouraged the search for scapegoats. The process of identifying witches and the pattern of witchcraft accusations are examined. The decline of witchcraft in the sixteenth and seventeenth centuries is related to the increase in natural wealth and to political and religious stability. The current wave of interest in occult matters indicates that many people are alienated from society and feel they have little control over their own lives.

1217.	Cooper, Lee R. "'Publish' or Perish: Negro Jehovah's Witness Adaptation in the Ghetto." RELIGIOUS MOVEMENTS IN CONTEMPORARY AMERICA (item 727), pp. 700–21.

Examines the reasons why Jehovah's Witnesses have been successful in recruiting American Blacks by their house-to-house visits known as the "publishing" method of evangelizing. The author explores the ways the Witnesses conduct their work, the obligations and rewards which go with their activities, and the training they undergo in doctrine and evangelization techniques. It is maintained that their lifestyle "has positive adaptive functions for certain segments of America's Black ghetto population" (p. 715), because it offers an alternative lifestyle that minimizes the hardships of low-income people and provides them with a strategy for coping with racial prejudice.

1218.	Cooper, Matthew. "Relations of Modes of Production in Nineteenth-Century America: The Shakers and Oneida." ETHNOLOGY 26 (1978): 1–16.

Compares the Shakers and Oneida Community in their modes of production and in the economic relationships they developed with the larger society. The author first gives a short history of each group and then outlines their belief systems, particularly as they relate to their economic goals. He finally discusses how the economic systems of both groups developed in such a way that external economic relationships became necessary. Though both communities were critical of the capitalistic system of Western culture, capitalism "determined the conditions that allowed them to reproduce their own modes of production" (p. 14). Oneida, in particular, became a capitalistic system through a series of steps which eventually undermined the Biblical communism on which the community was founded.

1219.	Crapo, Richley H. "Grass-Roots Deviance from Official Doctrine: A Study of Latter-Day Saint (Mormon) Folk-Beliefs." JOURNAL FOR THE SCIENTIFIC STUDY OF RELIGION 26 (1987): 465–85.

Explains the existence within the Mormon Church of two levels of beliefs, namely the official doctrine promulgated by ecclesiastical authorities, who claim an ongoing divine revelation, and various credal systems at the grass-roots level. The official position on several main issues, like the age of the earth and the creation of Eve, is examined. The author suggests that the "de-emphasis on the existence of diversity in the beliefs of members makes possible the perpetuation of folk-beliefs that are contrary to official doctrinal position..." (p. 474). In areas not central to Mormon doctrine, diversity exists. The church has carefully avoided confrontations and conflicts, stressing at the same time the divine authority of its leaders and tolerance of deviance among members.

1220.	Crider, Charles C., and Robert C. Kistler. THE SEVENTH-DAY ADVENTIST FAMILY: AN EMPIRICAL STUDY. Berrien Springs, MI: Andrews University Press, 1979. xii, 284 pp.

Presents an in-depth study of the Seventh-Day Adventist Church. After a brief look at the impact and change on the family in America, the authors examine the family in the Seventh-Day Adventist tradition and find that it conforms to the pattern of other family groups in America. In spite of similarities in art forms, recreational activities, and attitudes towards material possessions, Seventh-Day Adventists differ significantly in their dating and mating patterns, in their views regarding sex, marriage and divorce, and in their family organization and religiosity. Some speculations on the possible impact of modern changes in family life on this religious group are made.

1221. Crowley, William K. "Old Order Amish Settlement: Diffusion and Growth." ANNALS OF THE ASSOCIATION OF AMERICAN GEOGRAPHERS 68 (1978): 249-64.

Maps the historical development and diffusion of the Old Order Amish, an Anabaptist sect that originated in Europe in the seventeenth century. A pattern of contemporary Amish settlements is provided. The author thinks that the Amish illustrate that acculturation and assimilation are not the unavoidable results of living in a modern, industrialized society. Their order has been one of the fastest-growing religious denominations in the United States. Greater daily contacts with the non-Amish population and the pressure to limit the size of the family are seen as possible threats to its survival.

1222. Cunningham, Raymond J. "From Holiness to Healing: The Faith Cure in America, 1872-1892." CHURCH HISTORY 43 (1974): 499-513.

Traces the rise and development of faith healing in America and attempts to understand its popularity. The author maintains that "the subsidence of the faith cure movement and the controversy surrounding it by the mid-1980s is an important indication of the transition of perfectionism from denominational to sectarian status" (p. 500). The connection between perfectionism or holiness teachings and faith-cure movements is demonstrated with reference to the establishment of faith-cure homes and hospitals. The author sees the emergence of faith healing as a counteraction to the rise of Biblical criticism and natural science.

1223. Curtis, Russell L., and Louis A. Zurcher. "Stable Resources of Protest Movements: The Multi-Organizational Field." SOCIAL FORCES 52 (1973): 53-61.

Studies the histories and membership characteristics of two anti-pornographic organizations in the 1960's, that often functioned as crusades. The interests, goals, and audiences shared by the two protest movements are outlined. The characteristics of the active members--their age, income, and education--are compared. Among the authors' conclusion is the assertion that "the findings disclose multiple affiliation career paths for voluntary association members" (p. 60). Though not directly related to the new cults, this study offers possible areas of research of those religious groups that function as voluntary associations whose members can belong to different religious organizations.

1224. Damrell, Joseph. SEEKING SPIRITUAL MEANING: THE WORLD OF VEDANTA.
       Beverly Hills, CA: Sage Publications, 1977. 249 pp.

       Provides an ethnographic account of the lifestyle of the Vedanta
       Society, which was founded by Sri Ramakrishna in the second half of
       the nineteenth century and imported to the United States at the
       turn of the century. The author, a sociologist who, in order to
       explore this society, joined an unidentified Vedanta Temple for six
       years, accounts for the movement's history, cultural and philosoph-
       ical contexts, contemporary social location, and its temple's daily
       activities. He then spends some time discussing his methodological
       and theoretical perspectives in the context of his own participa-
       tion and the movement's spirituality.

1225. Daniel, Vattel Elbert. "Ritual and Stratification in Chicago Negro
       Churches." SOCIOLOGICAL OBSERVATION: A STRATEGY FOR NEW SOCIAL
       KNOWLEDGE. Edited by Matilda White Riley and Edward E. Nelson.
       New York: Basic Books, 1974, pp. 243-48.

       Classifies Black churches in Chicago in four groups: 1) ecstatic
       sects or cults; 2) semi-demonstrative groups; 3) deliberative
       churches; and 4) liturgical denominations. The author suggests
       that religious ritual has different functions depending on the
       economic status of the people participating in it. One common
       function of ritual is social adjustment, which refers to the degree
       of adaptation to the social pressures that led people to join a
       particular church with middle- or upper-middle class features.
       Various elements of worship in nine ecstatic cults are outlined.

1226. Dann, Norman K. "Special Diffusion of a Religious Movement."
       JOURNAL FOR THE SCIENTIFIC STUDY OF RELIGION 15 (1976): 351-60.

       Attempts to explore the the ways and reasons why religious move-
       ments spread over space and time. Several descriptive and explana-
       tory models are examined. The author's research focuses on the
       Holiness Movement, a brief history of which is given and its diffu-
       sion patterns in the United States traced. He suggests that the
       "directional sector" model of diffusion, which sees the movement
       expanding away from the center in well-defined directions, best
       explains how "the movement consistently spread West from its area
       of origin, avoiding the Southern States until after 1890" (p. 359).
       Immigration, national crises, and the presence of Methodism account
       for the reasons why the Holiness Movement spread in specific areas
       of the country.

1227. Danzer, M. Herbert. "Toward a Redefinition of 'Sect' and 'Cult':
       Orthodox Judaism in the United States and Israel." RELIGION AND
       BELIEF SYSTEMS (item 701), pp. 113-25.

       Reflects on the resurgence of Orthodox Judaism in the United
       States and Israel and maintains that, though this branch of Judaism
       is neither a sect nor a cult, it may be better understood if com-
       pared to these two religious organizations. After a brief descrip-
       tion of the movement towards Orthodox Judaism and of its seminaries
       (yeshivot), the author discusses the sociological concepts of church,

denomination, sect, and cult. He points out that Orthodox Jewish
groups like the Hasidic, which in the United States are at times
listed with, and compared to, cults like the Hare Krishna and the
Unification Church, are considered as major expressions of Judaism
in Israel. He suggests that the term "cult" should be used to
apply to those groups who are believed to recruit people by
illegitimate means and some coercive measures.

1228. Daugherty, Mary Lee. "Serpent Handling as Sacrament." THEOLOGY
TODAY 33 (1976): 232-43.

Describes the religious practice of serpent-handling in some
Holiness churches in West Virginia and argues that it reflects the
geographic and economic harshness of the environment. The main
theme of the author is that the handling of snakes during religious
services is not simply an example of how some Christians interpret
the Bible literally; it is rather a forceful sacramental ritual in
the sense that it is believed to be a divinely bestowed way in
which "physical signs communicate spiritual reality." The rich
symbolism of the practice is explored.

1229. Davis, Douglas J. "Aspects of Latter Day Saint Eschatology."
SOCIOLOGICAL YEARBOOK OF RELIGION IN BRITAIN 6 (1973): 122-35.

Examines the Mormon attitude toward the world with specific reference to the sectarian eschatology that it so clearly expresses.
The development of Mormon eschatology is outlined in three periods:
1) initiated eschatology (1830-1900) that is characterized by the
early expectation of the Second Coming of Christ and the building
of a holy society; 2) transition eschatology (1900-1950) that is
based on the fact that the Second Coming did not materialize and
Mormon groups were scattered in various parts of the world; and
3) reinterpretation eschatology (1950 onwards) that justified the
proselytizing activity and the establishment of a worldwide Mormon
community.

1230. Dearman, Marion. "Christ and Conformity: A Study of Pentecostal
Values." JOURNAL FOR THE SCIENTIFIC STUDY OF RELIGION 13 (1974):
437-53.

Discusses Johnston's hypothesis (item 207) that converts to Pentecostal Churches adopt an "inner-worldly asceticism" after their
conversion, an asceticism which, rather than the charismatic gifts,
is the core of their religious life. The author focuses on the
the United Pentecostal Church (in Oregon). A short history of the
church is given and the following church values described: activity
and work; achievement and success; moral orientation; humanitarian-
ism; efficiency and practicality; science and secular rationality;
nationalism and patriotism; individual personality; racism; and
superiority of selected groups. The author agrees with Johnston's
theory that Pentecostals socialize their members in the dominant
values of American culture.

1231. Della Fave, L. Richard, and George A. Hillery. "Status Inequality
in a Religious Community: The Case of a Trappist Monastery."
SOCIAL FORCES 59 (1980): 62-84.

Remarks that in recent studies of intentional communities (communes and utopian colonies), monasteries have been, to a large degree, neglected. The authors apply the stratification theory to the study of monastic institutions, concentrating their efforts on a Trappist monastery. They examine the following criteria of respect: love and friendliness; basic monastic values; spirituality; integrity; sacrifice; self-control, and instrumental values. They find evidence for a clear-cut status of inequality, based on the observance of monastic norms. The implications for monasticism in general and for other intentional communities are discussed.

1232.   Demos, John Putnam. ENTERTAINING SATAN: WITCHCRAFT AND THE CULTURE OF EARLY NEW ENGLAND. New York: Oxford University Press, 1982. xiv, 543 pp.

Presents a comprehensive and multidimensional study of witchcraft in early seventeenth-century New England. The author first gives a sampling and summary of witchcraft biography and then presents a couple of life histories in detail. He draws a group portrait of witches in an attempt to find out who became witches and why. He deals at length with the psychological, sociological, and historical aspects of witchcraft, which is seen as related to the structure of group life at the time. Witchcraft accusations express recurrent tensions in society and perform the functions of sharpening its boundaries, reinforcing its values, and deepening the loyalty of its members. Over 130 cases of witchcraft are listed. There are copious bibliographical notes, but no separate bibliography.

1233.   Demos, John Putnam. "Underlying Themes in the Witchcraft of Seventeenth-Century New England." AMERICAN HISTORICAL REVIEW 75 (1970): 1311-26.

Explores the social and psychological characteristics of the principal actors in the witchcraft accusations in Salem, Massachusetts. The complex relationships between witches and their victims, witnesses, and accusers are discussed. Most witches came from the lower economic class and were usually irascible and contentious in their personal relationships and expressed their hostile feelings freely. All had "some kind of personal eccentricity, some deviant or even criminal behavior that had long since marked them out as suspect" (p. 98). The author suggests that witchcraft in seventeenth-century New England reveals a lot about the culture of the time.

1234.   De Wert, Elly. "Folk Healers as Part of Local Health Care Systems: A Case Study in Northern Norway." TEMENOS 20 (1984): 101-21.

Examines how people on a small island in the Helgeland district of Norway look upon, and make use of, various folk healers. The author aims at discovering the sociocultural processes that determine the choice of healers. The folk beliefs about health in the context of the total health care system are first examined. The diagnosis of disease, its etiology, the role-behavior of patients,

their choice of treatment, and its evaluation are explored. A
brief taxonomy of healers is given and various cases of patients
who sought their help recorded. People who consider themselves ill
and who have found professional medical treatment insufficient are
likely to have recourse to folk healers.

1235. Dobbelaere, Karel, and Bryan R. Wilson. "Jehovah's Witnesses in
       a Catholic Country: A Survey of Nine Belgian Congregations."
       ARCHIVES DE SCIENCES SOCIALES DES RELIGIONS 50 (1980): 89-110.

       Examines the presence of Jehovah's Witnesses in Belgium. A short
       history of their missionary activities, particularly with Polish
       immigrant workers in the 1930's and with Italian and other immi-
       grants in recent times, is provided. Various statistical data,
       such as the social class of those who become Witnesses, are given
       and the reasons they proffer for leaving the Catholic Church and
       joining Jehovah's Witnesses are recorded. Jehovah's Witnesses in
       Belgium are generally not integrated into the wider society.

1236. Dolgin, Janet L. "Latter-Day Sense and Substance." RELIGIOUS
       MOVEMENTS IN CONTEMPORARY AMERICA (item 727), pp. 519-46.

       Attempts to show that the Church of Jesus Christ of Latter-Day
       Saints is a modern religious movement in the sense that it exhibits
       "a radical attenuation of the role of traditional churches and a
       flexible, individualistic system of thought" (p. 519). Focusing
       attention on the relationship between the individual members of the
       church and its organizational framework, the author demonstrates
       how 1) the authoritarian Mormon Church sustains and fosters credal
       independence, and 2) church members perceive themselves as belong-
       ing to one Church in spite of the diversity that exists among them.
       The Mormon Temple ritual indicates how Mormons use their cultural
       symbols to order and define their world and to promote both unity
       and tolerance in the Church.

1237. Dudley, Charles J., and George A. Hillery. "Freedom and Monastic
       Life." JOURNAL FOR THE SCIENTIFIC STUDY OF RELIGION 18 (1979):
       18-28.

       Examines the nature of freedom in Cistercian monastic institu-
       tions which, because of their stress on the ascetical life, are
       likely to leave an impact on the concept and practice of human
       freedom. A short description of the rather stern monastic life is
       given. It is concluded that "perceived disciplined freedom is a
       central ingredient in the social life of a monastery" (p. 26).
       Several positive consequences of disciplined freedom are noted.
       Monks registered lower scores of alienation and deprivation of
       feeling than members of other organizations. The concept of free-
       dom is discussed and the authors suggest that religious freedom
       itself must be defined in terms of discipline.

1238. Dudley, Roger L. "Alienation From Religion in Adolescents From
       Fundamentalist Religious Homes." JOURNAL FOR THE SCIENTIFIC
       STUDY OF RELIGION 17 (1978): 389-98.

Discusses the reasons why young people sometimes reject the faith of their parents in the context of Seventh-Day Adventism. Three general hypotheses are formulated: 1) authoritarianism and harshness are positively related to alienation; 2) inconsistency between profession of faith and its practice observed by young people in their parents and leaders is also positively related with alienation from religion; and 3) the common view which young people have of religion as a set of rules is also one factor which leads to alienation. Several scales are drawn up to measure alienation from religion as an independent variable. Only the first hypothesis was amply supported by the research results. It is suggested that the reduction or prevention of alienation can be achieved by the improvement in the quality of the relationship between adolescents and their parents and teachers.

1239. Dudley, Roger L., and Des Cummings. "A Study of Factors Relating to Church Growth in the North American Division of Seventh-Day Adventists." REVIEW OF RELIGIOUS RESEARCH 24 (1983): 322-33.

Presents a study which the North American Division of the Seventh-Day Adventist Church commissioned the Institute of Church Ministry at Andrews University to conduct, with the aim of identifying the factors leading to church growth. The research concluded that a growing church is probably one that 1) stresses growth, 2) believes that growth is possible, and 3) is providing spiritual nourishment to its members. The authors conclude by making several theoretical and programmatic implications.

1240. Dudley, Roger L., Patricia B. Mutch, and Robert J. Cruise. "Religious Factors and Drug Usages Among Seventh-Day Adventist Youth in North America." JOURNAL FOR THE SCIENTIFIC STUDY OF RELIGION 26 (1987): 218-33.

Examines those factors that contribute to the lower frequency of drug abuse among Seventh-Day Adventists. Alcohol, tobacco, and marijuana are less common among young Adventists than they are among young adults in North America. This is explained by the fact that Seventh-Day Adventists are more influenced by religious reasoning, participate more often in religious devotions, and are protected by other attitudes and social behaviors (such as the acceptance of their church's recreational standards). The results highlight "the importance of religious commitment in preventing or limiting drug abuse" (p. 231).

1241. Dunford, Franklyn W., and Phillip R. Kunz. "The Neutralization of Religious Dissonance." REVIEW OF RELIGIOUS RESEARCH 15 (1973): 2-9.

Discusses, in the context of the theory of cognitive dissonance, the problem of religious deviance and the control of members in a Church of Jesus Christ of Latter-Day Saints (Mormons). Focusing in particular on Church's Sunday observance, which encourages members to attend long worship services and to refrain from shopping, the authors conclude that active church members who shopped on Sunday experienced dissonance. The following techniques of neutralization were explored: denial of responsibility; denial of inquiry; denial of victim; condemnation of the condemners; and appeal to higher authorities. Mormons used, to varying degrees, one or several of these methods--particularly the denial of responsibility and the appeal to higher authorities--to justify their behavior. It is concluded that 1) the neutralization techniques are "analytically" useful; 2) religious organization and values do not always serve as powerful controlling forces; and 3) the techniques themselves provide a basis for action.

1242.   Ebaugh, Helen Rose Fuchs. "Leaving the Convent: The Experience of Role Exit and Self-Transformation." THE EXISTENTIAL SELF IN SOCIETY. Edited by Joseph A. Kotarba and Andrea Fontana. Chicago: University of Chicago Press, 1984, pp. 156-76.

Describes the process by which a nun decides to leave the convent and begins to create a new identity and role. Basing her conclusions on both her own personal experience and on a sociological study of ex-nuns, the author outlines six stages in the leaving process: 1) first doubts; 2) the freedom to decide; 3) trying out options; 4) the vacuum; 5) the turning point; and 6) creating the ex-role. Throughout these stages there is a continual interaction between the issues of self-identity and relevance to others. The author thinks that her model is applicable to a wider range of ex-roles emerging in American life.

1243.   Ebaugh, Helen Rose Fuchs. OUT OF THE CLOISTER: A STUDY OF ORGANIZATIONAL DILEMMAS. Austin: University of Texas Press, 1974. xxii, 155 pp.

Discusses, from historical, sociological, and social-psychological perspectives, the movement of Catholic nuns from a cloistered way of life towards a more open and socially involved existence. After describing religious orders before and after Vatican Council II, the author explores several social aspects of religious life, such as utopianism, boundary maintenance and ideology, totalism, the costs and rewards of membership, and organizational problems. She points out that the mechanisms to obtain and keep commitment and solidarity are similar to those used by other groups like the Bruderhof and Oneida Community.

1244.   Ebaugh, Helen Rose Fuchs, Kathe Richman, and Janet Saltzman Chafetz. "Life Crises Among the Religiously Committed: Do Sectarian Differences Matter?" JOURNAL FOR THE SCIENTIFIC STUDY OF RELIGION 23 (1984): 19-31.

Analyzes the perceptions of, and responses to, life crises among members of three different sectarian groups, namely Christian Scientists, Catholic Charismatics, and Baha'is. Three hypotheses are examined: 1) Christian Scientists experience fewer crises than either of the other groups; 2) Catholic Charismatics experience more self-crises than either of the other two sects, while Christian Scientists experience more health problems and Baha'is have greater life-structure/life-goals crises than Catholic Charismatics and Christian Scientists; and 3) Catholic Charismatics and Baha'is

are more likely to react to a crisis by turning toward group membership for help and support, while Christian Scientists will rely
more on the self to solve their problems. The first hypothesis was
not supported by the data which showed no statistically significant
differences between the three groups. The second and third hypotheses were confirmed.

1245. Eglin, Trent. "Introduction to a Hermeneutics of the Occult: Alchemy." ON THE MARGINS OF THE VISIBLE (item 700), pp. 323-50.

Presents an ethnomethodological study of the occult sciences,
focusing on alchemy. The author finds fault with social-scientific
studies of the occult in that they fail to acknowledge the fact
that occult sciences form "a unitary body of thought in no wise
deficient in empirical referent, in consistency, cogency, reproduc-
tibility, and, specifically, in no wise lacking in sheer efficacy"
(p. 324). A distinction between exoteric (or popular) and esoteric (or exclusive) occult teachings is made. Occult sciences have
the transformation of the very structures of human awareness as
their main objective. A brief history of alchemy is given and
several theories that attempt to explain it discussed. It is insisted that alchemy is a subject that deserves to be studied on its
own terms.

1246. Eliav-Feldon, Miriam. "'If You Will, It Is No Fairy Tale': The
First Jewish Utopias." JEWISH JOURNAL OF SOCIOLOGY 25 (1983):
85-103.

Examines those Jewish utopias that came into being in the late
nineteenth century and maintains that Herzl's Zionist group was "a
distinct case in the history of utopian literature" (p. 91). The
ideology of this utopia is outlined and interpreted as the last
chapter in Western utopianism. In spite of its Jewish character,
it was well within the stream of utopists and social reformers of
the period.

1247. Ellens, G. F. S. "The Ranters Ranting: Reflections on a Ranting
Counter Culture." CHURCH HISTORY 40 (1971): 91-107.

Describes briefly the sect called "Ranters" which, together with
other counterculture religious groups, flourished in Puritan England in the seventeenth century. The author thinks that the presence of these sects was indicative of the instability of the age,
an instability aggravated by "the violence of the politico-reli-
gious turmoil, the insecurity of the state, and the contentions of
the religions" (p. 96). The Ranters were drawn largely from the
lower socioeconomic classes. Some similarities between them and
the Hippies of the 1960's are noted, even though the latter were
middle class in background. Both belonged to a counterculture
characterized by skepticism, subjectivism, and introversion.

1248. Elliot, P. Currie. "Crimes Without Criminals: Witchcraft and its
Control in Renaissance Europe." THE COLLECTIVE DEFINITION OF
DEVIANCE. Edited by F. James Davis and Richard Stivens. New
York: Free Press, 1975, pp. 296-316.

Proposes the view that the differences between witchcraft in
England and Continental Europe are the result of the differences in
the legal systems. While witchcraft on the Continent was usually
conceived of, and prosecuted as, a form of heresy, in England it
assumed the form of a mental felony, namely the practice of magic.
The response to witchcraft in Continental Europe was repressive
control, while in England it was restrained control. The former
control, coupled with powerful economic motives, led to "the mass
stigmatization of witches and the confiscation of their property"
(p. 307). The author strongly maintains that witchcraft is a
social construct.

1249. Elmen, Paul. WHEAT FLOUR MESSIAH: ERIC JANSSON OF BISHOP HILL.
      Carbondale: Southern Illinois University Press, 1976. xv,
      222 pp.

Relates the story of Eric Jansson (1808-1850) and of the colony
he founded. Jansson, a wheat-flour salesman, is described as a
"copybook example" of Weber's idea of a charismatic leader of a
sect in the classical definition of the term. His followers were a
small group of people who strove for perfection and personal fellowship. Their clash with both the Lutheran Church and the Swedish
State led to their migration to the United States at a time when
America began to emerge as a utopian dream in the consciousness of
Europe. Their migration to the United States, where they settled
in Illinois at a place they called Bishop Hill, led to their gradual loss of self-identity and final disintegration. A bibliography
of Swedish and English publications is added.

1250. Embley, Peter L. "The Early Development of the Plymouth Brethren."
      PATTERNS OF SECTARIANISM (item 149), pp. 213-43.

Presents a historical account of the beginnings and early development of the Plymouth Brethren who acquired a reputation for proselytizing rather than evangelizing and who maintained the complete
rejection of a formally appointed ministry and the practice of
charismatic worship, especially at the Lord's Supper. The part
played by the leaders of the movement in spreading the ideology of
the Brethren is discussed. The stages through which the movement
developed in the first 20 years of its existence are described, and
the early internal disputes that led to the schism of 1848 are
chronicled.

1251. Ericksen, Julia, and Gary Klein. "Women's Roles and Family Produc-
      tion Among the Old Order Amish." RURAL SOCIOLOGY 46 (1981): 282-
      96.

Examines ways in which women help maintain the Old Order Amish of
Lancaster County, Pennsylvania and concludes that they do so in
two ways, namely they engage in subsistence production and in the
bearing of children. The relationships between women's productiv-
ity and family life and networks and between fertility and farming
are among the areas explored. One of the factors that lessens
women's powers is that they are not involved in the larger distribution networks. The authors think that the position of women is

ambiguous since there is "an incompatibility between the patriarchal ideology and the egalitarian patterns of decision making
necessitated by the contingencies of survival" (p. 295).

1252. Estes, Leland L. "The Medieval Origins of the European Witch Craze:
       A Hypothesis." JOURNAL OF SOCIAL HISTORY (Winter 1983): 271-84.

       Discusses the ways people use witchcraft accusations to attack
       certain social groups and suggests that the late Renaissance period
       actually produced the intellectual basis for belief in witches and
       for the witch hunting craze. Reflecting on the medical aspects of
       the witch craze and the role of the physician in witchcraft cases,
       the author concludes that the medical revolution did not bring an
       end to witch hunting, but rather gave it an intellectual basis and
       an emotional impetus. This article contains many references to
       studies on the relationship between witchcraft and psychiatry.

1253. Fields, Karen E. "Charismatic Religion as Popular Protest: The
       Ordinary and the Extraordinary in Social Movements." THEORY AND
       SOCIETY 11 (1982): 321-61.

       Espouses the view that speaking in tongues among Pentecostals can
       be a tactic of revolution. The author attempts to demonstrate her
       hypothesis by a historical analysis of a religious revival (namely
       the Jehovah's Witnesses) in Zambia. In a postscript she suggests
       that her view might be applicable to contemporary religious move-
       ments in the West.

1254. Fine, Howard D. "The Koreshan Unity: The Chicago Years of a Uto-
       pian Community." JOURNAL OF THE ILLINOIS STATE HISTORICAL ASSO-
       CIATION 68 (1975): 213-27.

       Gives an account of a celibate millennial community founded in
       New York State in 1880. The author describes the activities of its
       founder, Cyrus Read Teed, during his stay in Chicago from 1886 to
       1903. The various levels of membership of the Koreshan Unity, its
       cosmology, and its goals to form a federation of celibate societies
       (such as the Shakers and Harmony Society) are outlined. The author
       also discusses the legal conflicts in which Teed was involved
       because of attracting married women to his commune. The Koreshan
       Unity lost its momentum with the death of its founder in 1908 and
       eventually ceased to exist, its property becoming a recreational,
       historical, and educational site.

1255. Fishman, Aryei. "The Religious Kibbutz: Religion, Nationalism, and
       Socialism in a Communal Framework." THE SOCIOLOGY OF THE KIBBUTZ:
       STUDIES OF ISRAEL SOCIETY. Edited by Ernest Krauz and David Glanz.
       New Brunswick, NJ: Transaction Books, 1983, vol. 2, pp. 115-23.

       Studies the Religious Kibbutz Federation ("Hakibbutz Hadati") as
       a Zionist movement of religious renewal within Orthodox Judaism.
       The author shows how the Federation, through its religious ideol-
       ogy, changed a secular, socialist institution into a community
       governed by the Torah, thus becoming a religious community that was
       made up of three components: a national collectivity, a socialist
       commune, and a "halakhic" order.

1256.   Flanagan, Thomas. "Social Credit in Alberta: A Canadian 'Cargo
        Cult'?" ARCHIVES DE SOCIOLOGIE DES RELIGIONS 34 (1974): 39-48.

        Examines an economic movement in Canada founded by Major Clifford
        Hugh Douglas in the 1920's and later led by a charismatic fundamen-
        talist preacher named William Aberhart. The author attempts to
        show that this movement contains millenarian aspects common to
        religious movements. The millenarian features of this movement are
        described under the following headings: 1) ideology; 2) generative
        conditions; 3) leadership; 4) social basis; 5) magic and irratio-
        nality; and 6) syncretism with Christian premillennialism. It is
        stressed that "severe strain and the resulting disorientation can
        produce phenomena resembling the millenarian movements of more
        primitive peoples" (p. 47).

1257.   Flora, Cornelia Butler. "Social Dislocation and Pentecostalism: A
        Multivariate Analysis." SOCIOLOGICAL ANALYSIS 34 (1973): 296-304.

        Hypothesizes that those people who experience great social dis-
        location are the most likely to become Pentecostals. The following
        socioeconomic preconditions to joining a Pentecostal church are
        explored: 1) migration because of violence; 2) migration unrelated
        to family ties; 3) change in type of employment; and 4) unemploy-
        ment. Pentecostalism provides new meaning to those whose self-
        conception has become ambiguous and vague. When Pentecostal groups
        "provide a total ideology, an environment is created where, to use
        religious phraseology, the self can be 'reborn'" (p. 297).

1258.   Fogarty, Robert S. THE RIGHTEOUS REMNANT: THE HOUSE OF DAVID.
        Kent, OH: Kent State University Press, 1981. xiii, 195 pp.

        Provides a historical sketch of a millennial and adventist sect,
        the Israelite House of David, founded by Benjamin Purnell in the
        early twentieth century at Benton Harbor, Michigan. The author
        considers this movement as part of the prophetic tradition that
        took root in the United States. The conflicts with civil authori-
        ties that beset this sect and its efforts to avoid the criminal and
        civil prosecution of its prophet are described. The focus of this
        study are the community survival and the dynamics of the relation-
        ship between the prophet and his disciples. There are several
        appendices that give biographical information on Purnell's follow-
        ers, the Colony's membership list, and the 60 propositions that
        outline the sect's theology. A bibliography provides references to
        the Colony's literature and other major sources.

1259.   Fogarty, Robert S. "Oneida: A Utopian Search for Security." LABOR
        HISTORY 14 (1973): 202-27.

        Discusses the initial success of the Oneida Community, whose first
        recruits came from the background of "frantic religious and social
        upheaval." In Oneida, labor was made part of a larger commitment
        that united family affection, business, reeducation, and religion.
        Religious dedication and socialist spontaneity "created an atmo-
        sphere of great relaxation" (p. 218) and "security from sin" (p.
        227).

1260.   Foster, Lawrence. "The Rise and Fall of Utopia: The Oneida Commu-
            nity Crises of 1852 and 1879." COMMUNAL STUDIES 8 (1988): 1-17.

        Reflects on the two occasions in the history of the Oneida Commu-
        nity when its members announced that, while not giving up their
        ideological position on sexuality and marriage, they were discon-
        tinuing their practices because of public sentiment against them.
        The author attempts to analyze these developments from the Oneida
        Community's point of view. The religious and social beliefs of
        John Humphrey Noyes, the founder of Oneida, are examined and their
        relationship to his introduction of a complex marriage system ex-
        plained. The personal and communal problems experienced by Noyes
        and their effects on the suspension of the new regulations are
        outlined. The factors leading to the end of the complex marriage
        system in 1879 and to the breakup of the community in 1881 are also
        discussed. The author suggests that the crises of 1852 and 1879
        can be viewed as "a triumph of the human spirit rather than a
        failure" (p. 17).

1261.   Foster, Lawrence. "Shaker Spiritualism and Salem Witchcraft:
            Social Perspectives on Trance and Possession Phenomena." COMMU-
            NAL STUDIES 5 (1985): 176-93.

        Describes and contrasts the behavior of the Salem witches (in
        1692) and of the first Shakers (in 1837) and finds some striking
        similarities. These phenomena were, however, interpreted differ-
        ently by the affected individuals and the communities in which they
        lived. The author attempts to explain why the behavior of the
        witches was seen as diabolical and threatening, while that of the
        Shakers as a sign of divine blessing. Relying on anthropological
        theory, he finally asks broader questions about the social signifi-
        cance of trance and possession, which usually occur among people
        (women, lower-class men, and teenagers) who are outside the normal
        power channels of society. "Trance phenomena," he concludes,
        "illustrate how fine is the line which divides mental and social
        disruption from ecstasy and the highest visionary activity" (p.
        193).

1262.   Foster, Lawrence. RELIGION AND SEXUALITY: THREE AMERICAN COMMUNAL
            EXPERIMENTS OF THE NINETEENTH CENTURY. New York: Oxford Univer-
            sity Press, 1981. xi, 363 pp.

        Presents an anthropological study of three nineteenth-century
        American religious groups--the Shakers, the Mormons, and Oneida
        Community--which developed three different types of marriage alter-
        natives, namely celibacy, group marriage, and a form of polygamy,
        respectively. In each case the author explores the formative reli-
        gious experience of the leaders, examines how their communities
        came into being and how they attracted people to join them, and
        shows how each group dealt with the issues of marriage and the
        family. The author maintains that millennial and ecstatic sects
        are efforts to create an intellectual and social synthesis for a
        new society during a period of extensive cultural interaction and
        perceived social crisis. Rejecting the psychopathological model,
        he has recourse to anthropological views on the rites of passage to

understand the transition periods or processes of moral regeneration that members of these movements went through. There are
voluminous footnotes (pp. 257-339) and a short essay on sources
(pp. 341-52).

1263. Foster, Lawrence. "Free Love and Feminism: John Humphrey Noyes and
       the Oneida Community." JOURNAL OF THE EARLY REPUBLIC 1 (1981):
       165-83.

       Comments on the widely divergent interpretations of Noyes's views
       regarding the role of women. The author stresses the "systematic
       and institutionally radical character of Noyes's innovations" re-
       garding sexual practices and relationships between sexual partners.
       He points out that although Noyes believed in the superiority of
       men to women, he was sympathetic to women's issues, if not to the
       solutions that were being proposed in the nineteenth century.
       Further, Noyes's views about the feminist movement must be seen in
       the context of his wider concern for social order and the changes
       he envisaged for social institutions.

1264. Foster, Thomas W. "Amish Society: A Relic of the Past Could Become
       a Model for the Future." THE FUTURIST 15.6 (1981): 33-40.

       Reflects on the lifestyle of the Old Order Amish (known also as
       the Pennsylvania Dutch) and sees it as an ecologically balanced
       society that could set a model for human society as a whole. Amish
       society is an example of a "frugal community" that combines self-
       government, self-sufficiency, escape from fossil-fuel dependency,
       freedom from structural employment, population decentralization, a
       people-centered technology, and a profound sense of spirituality.

1265. Fox, Margaret. "Protest in Piety: Christian Science Revisited."
       INTERNATIONAL JOURNAL OF WOMEN STUDIES 1 (1978): 401-16.

       Interprets Christian Science, an American therapeutic religion,
       as a nineteenth-century women's protest movement, its latent func-
       tion being to rebel against women's social limitations at the time
       the movement was founded. The author examines the social stereo-
       types for women in the nineteenth century and holds that the role
       conflicts and discontinuities that women felt led many of them,
       including Mary Baker Eddy, to express and draw attention to them-
       selves by hysterical behavior. Mrs. Eddy attracted people who,
       like herself, wanted to be cured and to assume dominant social
       roles by becoming healers. Christian Science not only cured the
       symptoms of hysteria, but also attacked its social causes.

1266. Fretz, J. Winfield. "Newly Emerging Communes in Mennonite Communi-
       ties." INTERNATIONAL REVIEW OF MODERN SOCIOLOGY 6 (1976): 103-112.

       Reports on a social phenomenon among the Mennonites, namely the
       growing numbers of small intentional communes that are seeking a
       more disciplined lifestyle, demanding greater personal commitment,
       and requiring stricter church laws. Twenty-four of these new enti-
       ties founded in America since 1970 are examined and their social
       characteristics determined. It is suggested that the new groups

are the by-product of the college influence on the Mennonite Church and a reaction to the increasing influence of the secular worldview and value system and materialistic lifestyle of the larger society. Several needs that these communes cater to are listed. The impact that communes might have on the economy, education, the family, and the established churches is assessed.

1267. Frideres, James S. "The Death of Hutterite Culture." PHYLON 33 (1972): 260-65.

Discusses how Canadian legislation contributes to the demise of Hutterite culture. The values and social structure of the Hutterites are briefly outlined. The author thinks that these structures are related to the social control mechanisms that have been imposed on the Hutterites and which have led to the decay of their culture. Legislation prohibits them to move freely and decisions to allow them to split colonies are being delayed, thus creating internal problems. One main element of their value structure, namely life as transient, is changing faster than the others. Some Canadian provinces are further destroying the controlled acculturation techniques traditionally used by the Hutterites. The author holds that the Hutterite religious beliefs will persist and they will become a quasi-religious group.

1268. Gannon, Thomas P. "Catholic Religious Order in Sociological Perspective." AMERICAN DENOMINATIONAL STRUCTURE: A SOCIOLOGICAL VIEW. Edited by Ross P. Scherer. Pasedena, CA: William Carey Library, 1980, pp. 159-93.

Examines the organizational structure of Catholic religious orders as a major instrument for carrying out the mission of the Church. After a brief historical survey of their origin and development up to recent times, a summary of the empirical research of their members' changing attitudes and beliefs is given. Several features (often found mentioned in the context of sects and cults) of these orders are outlined: 1) their separation from the world; 2) their founding by charismatic leaders in times of crisis; 3) the routinization of charisma; and 4) their demand of total voluntary commitment. What distinguishes religious orders from sects is the former's traditional legitimation. Unlike sects, religious orders do not reject the church's compromises with the world and neither do they encourage hostility to society.

1269. Garrett, Clarke. "Women and Witches: Patterns of Analysis." SIGNS: JOURNAL OF WOMEN IN CULTURE AND SOCIETY 3 (1977): 461-70.

Argues in favor of combining historical with anthropological approaches to witchcraft and focuses on several patterns of analysis to throw light on European witchcraft in a global context. A number of studies that relate witchcraft to social conditions, particularly to social tensions, are reviewed. The relationship between witchcraft and women, who were often marginal and powerless, has to be explored in the context of both sociological and psychological reflections.

1270. Gerlach, Luther P. "Pentecostalism: Revolution or Counter-Revolu-
       tion?" RELIGIOUS MOVEMENTS IN CONTEMPORARY AMERICA (item 727),
       pp. 669-99.

       Maintains that Pentecostalism in the United States, even though
       it might appear like a therapeutic and system-maintaining form of
       spirit possession, "functions to generate personal transformation
       and social change" (p. 673). A lengthy description of the Pente-
       costal Movement in the United States is given and the various types
       of Pentecostal churches with their organization, recruitment proce-
       dures, ideology, social opposition, and commitment processes out-
       lined. The author perceives Pentecostalism not as some form of
       sect activity or as an opiate for the deprived, but rather as a
       widespread movement of social and possible revolutionary change.
       The nature of Voodoo and Pentecostalism in Haiti is also explored.

1271. Gerlach, Luther P., and Virginia H. Hine. PEOPLE, POWER, CHANGE:
       MOVEMENTS OF SOCIAL TRANSFORMATION. New York: Bobbs-Merrill Co.,
       1970. xxii, 257 pp.

       Studies, from an anthropological perspective, the dynamics of
       change in social, political, or religious institutions. Five
       significant key factors that bring people together to form a move-
       ment are identified and discussed separately at some length: 1) a
       segmented, usually acephalous, organization; 2) face-to-face re-
       cruitment; 3) personal commitment; 4) an ideology; and 5) real or
       perceived opposition from society at large. Two movements, namely
       the Pentecostal Movement and the Black Power Movement, are explored.
       In both, the authors found the same generic features, the same
       basic type of organization, similar ideology, the stress on per-
       sonal transformation, and religious and revolutionary ideas. The
       authors reject the theories of deprivation and psychological mal-
       adjustment as unsatisfactory. Several steps in the commitment
       process to these movements are identified (pp. 110 ff.). The
       methods of data collection are specified in an appendix (pp. 219-
       29). A useful, though somewhat dated, bibliography is provided
       (pp. 229-50).

1272. Gianakos, Perry E. "The Black Muslims: An American Millennialistic
       Response to Racism and Cultural Deracination." CENTENNIAL REVIEW
       23 (1979): 430-51.

       Suggests that the eschatology and social myth of the Black Mus-
       lims (the Nation of Islam) is one variety of the American paradigm
       of the millennium, a paradigm that can be found in most American
       radical, salvationist movements. Both nationalistic and religious
       elements have contributed to the formation of the Black Muslim
       mythology. The author attempts to trace the social myth to its
       millennial sources. He tries to show that basic Black Muslim be-
       liefs are a variation of the fundamental American concepts of
       "manifest destiny" and "redeemer nation." They are a response to
       racism and industrialization.

1273. Gildrie, Richard P. "Visions of Evil: Popular Culture, Puritanism,
       and the Massachusetts Crisis of 1692." JOURNAL OF AMERICAN CUL-
       TURE 8.4 (1985): 17-33.

Points out that witchcraft is not merely a symptom of social conflict, but also an "embodiment of rich traditions about the nature of evil" (p. 17). The symbolic complexity of witchcraft is examined in the context of the seventeenth-century witchcraft crisis. The author points out that beliefs in magic and witchcraft were part of the culture and religious tradition of the period. He maintains that the "Salem crisis erupted when the carefully forged clerical interpretation of witchlore failed to account adequately for what was happening in Salem village and the crisis ended when the magistrates and populace concluded that they had no intelligible substitute" (p. 30).

1274. Glanz, David, and Michael I. Harrison. "Varieties of Identity Transformation: The Case of Newly Orthodox Jews." JEWISH JOURNAL OF SOCIOLOGY 20 (1978): 129-42.

Discusses four types of identity transformation in the context of Jews who embrace Orthodox Judaism and thus assume "an identity which is little known in contemporary Jewish life and which deviates substantially from more popular alternative life styles" (p. 129). These types of identity changes are: 1) alternation sequence, which entails a series of gradual changes; 2) direct consolidation, which is a reaffirmation of one's identity; 3) indirect consolidation, which is a process of return after a stage of disjunction from the home environment; and 4) conversion, a radical shift and a break with the past. Newly Orthodox Jews experience a less disjunctive process of identity transformation than that which takes place in conversion.

1275. Glick, Deborah C. "Symbolic, Ritual, and Social Dynamics of Spiritual Healing." SOCIAL SCIENCE AND MEDICINE 27 (1988): 1197-1206.

Explores the characteristics of spiritual healing groups in the Baltimore area. Two types of groups are investigated: 1) Christian, Pentecostal, and Charismatic; and 2) New Age and metaphysical. The similarities and differences between them in the following areas are outlined: 1) the social features and illnesses of the participants; 2) the leadership patterns; 3) the ideological systems; and 4) the ritual processes. The author shows how social roles, myths, rituals, and symbols are essential in the therapeutic effect of spiritual healing. A bibliography of 69 items is included.

1276. Goldenberg, Sheldon, and Gerda R. Wekerle. "From Utopia to Total Institution in a Single Generation: The Kibbutz and the Bruderhof." INTERNATIONAL REVIEW OF MODERN SOCIOLOGY 2 (1972): 224-32.

Discusses two institutions, a religious (the Bruderhof) and a secular one (the Kibbutz), that have been forced to deal with two highly priced though inconsistent values, namely personal freedom of choice and the maintenance of their social system. The author attempts to show how both groups have created utopias that deny freedom to those born in them. The socialization system of each group is examined and the way it restricts the freedom of its members specified. The second generation defines its community not as a utopia, but rather as a total institution.

1277. Goldsmith, Peter. "Revivalism and the Advent of Cash Economy on the
      Georgia Coast." REVIEW OF RELIGIOUS RESEARCH 29 (1988): 385-97.

      Discusses the emergence of a Pentecostal revival movement among
      American Blacks on the island of St. Simon, Georgia in 1928. The
      author examines the view that this revival can be linked to the
      sudden and disturbing change in the group's socioeconomic condition.
      He argues that the implicit ideology of religious movements can
      challenge the dominant view of the social order and insists that
      the relationship between these movements and political ideologies
      cannot be taken for granted.

1278. Gooden, Rosemary D. "A Preliminary Examination of the Shaker Atti-
      tude Toward Work." COMMUNAL SOCIETIES 3 (1983): 1-16.

      Examines the Shakers and their work "within the broader social
      and cultural contexts of nineteenth-century America during the
      growth of early industrial capitalism" (p. 3). The author attempts
      to outline the meaning of work for the Shakers in this period of
      socioeconomic change. She finds that Shaker values with respect
      to work were basically the same as those of mainline society, even
      though the Shakers were not profit-oriented capitalists. The
      Shakers' tenet of the "separation, but equality of the sexes" is
      clearly expressed in their work patterns.

1279. Gothóni, René, and Kirsti Suolinna. "The Religious Message in
      Action--A Case Study." NEW RELIGIONS (item 565), pp. 189-201.

      Analyzes and clarifies the structure of the religious message of
      the Laestadian movement, which arose in Finland and populated the
      northern regions of Sweden by the 1840's. The way the message
      operates, the response of the members, and the functions the move-
      ment fulfills are considered. A brief history of the movement and
      a description of the context of its message that is recorded in
      sermons are provided. The author proposes a combined structural
      and interactional analysis of the movement. The members are so-
      cialized into the movement's lifestyle through the interactional
      situations at meetings. Close personal relationships are kept
      even when individuals move to settle in other locations. The move-
      ment acts as a channel for those people who move into urban areas.

1280. Gottlieb, Robert, and Peter Wiley. AMERICA'S SAINTS: THE RISE OF
      MORMON POWER. San Diego: Harcourt Brace Jovanovich, 1984. 278 pp.

      Chronicles the rapid rise of the Mormon Church since World War
      II. The spiritual appeal of Mormonism, its complex and well-run
      bureaucratic system, its political influence, and its religious
      hierarchy are among the topics covered. The authors show how the
      Mormon belief system penetrates and controls the daily lives of
      church members. The extensive Mormon economic empire, which has
      both national and international dimensions, is assessed. Some of
      the Mormon attitudes towards sexuality, authority, and racism are
      also described. The tensions within Mormonism and between Mormon-
      ism and mainstream society are examined. A section on sources
      lists some major works on Mormonism.

1281. Graybill, Ronald. "Millenarians and Money: Adventist Wealth and
       Adventist Beliefs." SPECTRUM: A QUARTERLY JOURNAL OF THE ASSOCI-
       ATION OF ADVENTIST FORUMS 10.2 (1979): 31-41.

       Tests the common view of the social sources of millenarian move-
       ments by examining the economic state of the Seventh-Day Adventists
       in 1860. The author discovers that those who joined the movement
       came not from economic, social, and politically distressed life-
       styles, but rather from those characterized by upward social and
       economic mobility. Early Adventists were prosperous and overwhelm-
       ingly rural in background. They experienced "relative status de-
       privation" after their conversion. They were "neither pessimistic,
       passive, or fatalistic, but perfectly consistent with a striving
       for human betterment in both spiritual and economic matters" (p.
       36). Millennialism in its adventist form appealed to both those
       who were economically comfortable and to those economically de-
       prived and "may have actually functioned to inspire the accumula-
       tion of wealth" (p. 37).

1282. Green, Ernest J. "The Labadists of Colonial Maryland (1683-1722)."
       COMMUNAL SOCIETIES 8 (1988): 104-21.

       Examines a seventeenth-century European religious sect, called
       the Labadists after its founder Jean de Labadie, which "aroused the
       same passions and provokes the same antipathy characteristic of
       many other dynamic post-Reformation religious movements (p. 105).
       After a brief outline of the sect's origin in France and its set-
       tlement in Maryland, the author describes its social organization
       that was based on asceticism and communalism. The author considers
       this sect important because it is "the original link in the trun-
       cated chain of America's colonial utopian experiments" (p. 121).

1283. Green, Henry A. "Religion in Valentinian Gnosticism: A Sociologi-
       cal Interpretation." JOURNAL OF RELIGIOUS HISTORY 12 (1982):
       109-24.

       Probes the institutionalization of Valentinian Gnosticism and
       shows how ritual expresses the standard behavioral patterns of
       organizational structure. The influence of Valentinian (circa 135-
       160 A. D.) is sketched and his theories are said to have influenced
       many religious movements of his time. Sectarian tendencies within
       Gnosticism are exposed. Ritual, in the author's opinion, played a
       key role in the socialization of new and old members of Valentinian
       Gnosticism.

1284. Greil, Arthur L., and David R. Rudy. "Conversion to the World View
       of Alcoholics Anonymous: A Refinement of Conversion Theory."
       QUALITATIVE SOCIOLOGY 6 (1983): 5-28.

       Maintains that, like converts to cults and sects, those who join
       Alcoholics Anonymous acquire a worldview with which they reinter-
       pret their past experiences. The authors describe the worldview of
       Alcoholics Anonymous and the process whereby an individual becomes
       a member, a process that is expressed in such phrases as "hitting
       bottom," "first stepping," "accepting your problems," and "telling

your story." Becoming a member is similar in some respects to
religious conversion, even though it does not fit into the widely
accepted model of Lofland and Stark (item 215). It is suggested
that instead of focusing narrowly on conversion to fringe religions, scholars should study the process of conversion in a variety
of settings.

1285. Gruneir, R. "The Hebrew-Christian Mission in Toronto." CANADIAN
       ETHNIC STUDIES 9.1 (1977): 18-28.

       Reflects on the efforts of various churches to convert Jews who
       migrated to Toronto in large numbers at the turn of the century.
       The foundation of the first Christian Synagogue and the emergence
       of Hebrew Christianity with the consequent Jewish reaction are
       described. The author points out that eventually the Protestant
       Church of Canada came "to see the intrusion of large numbers of
       Jews into Canada's Christian cities not as a problem of proselytiz-
       ing and assimilating, but one of neighborliness and social adjust-
       ment."

1286. Guarneri, Carl. "Who Were the Utopian Socialists?: Patterns of
       Membership in American Fourierist Communities." COMMUNAL
       SOCIETIES 5 (1985): 65-81.

       Presents a preliminary analysis of membership data of the Fouri-
       erist or Associationist Movement of the nineteenth century. Three
       geographically representative and successful communities or "pha-
       lanxes" are analyzed: Brook Farm (1844-1947), the North American
       Phalanx of New Jersey (1843-55), and the Wisconsin Phalanx (1844-
       1855). The following topics are discussed: 1) ethnic unity and
       religious diversity; 2) class cooperation; 3) the occupational
       spectrum; and 4) the stable families and transient individuals.
       Complex motives were at play in the formation of these utopian
       groups whose members produced a pioneering social movement. Demo-
       graphic factors helped shape the life of these communities and also
       hasten their demise.

1287. Gusfield, Joseph R. SYMBOLIC CRUSADE: STATUS POLITICS AND THE
       AMERICAN TEMPERANCE MOVEMENT. Urbana: University of Illinois
       Press, 1980. viii, 226 pp.

       Describes "the relationship between Temperance attitudes, the
       organized Temperance Movement, and the conflicts between divergent
       subcultures in American society" (p. 3). The author first dis-
       cusses the relationship between social status and the temperance
       ethic. He argues that the nineteenth-century Temperance Movement
       is not to be attributed to the effects of Puritanism, but should
       rather be understood in the context of sociocultural changes of the
       pre-Civil War period. The Temperance Movement is one of social
       status, reflecting clashes between rival social systems, cultures,
       and status groups. Temperance is "both a protest against a chang-
       ing status system and a mechanism for influencing the distribution
       of prestige" (p. 12).

1288. Gutwirth, Jacques. "The Structure of a Hassidic Community in
       Montreal." JEWISH JOURNAL OF SOCIOLOGY 14 (1972): 43-62.

Outlines the structure of a Belzer Hasidic community in Montreal
and compares it with its sister community in Antwerp. The history
of the Montreal community since its inception in 1952 and the various splinter groups are traced. The author finds that the religious, social, and economic organizations of both groups are very
similar. "The Hassidic cult of the rebbe and the belief in his
wonder-working powers are very much alive in the community" (p. 51)
of Montreal. The occupation and social status of the Hasidic members are outlined and it is concluded that both Hasidic and Orthodox Judaism have a typical economic structure and a middle-class
ideology.

1289. Hadden, Jeffrey K. "Indemnity Lost, Indulgences Found: Theological
Convergence in American Televangelism." RESTORING THE KINGDOM.
Edited by Deane William Ferm. New York: Paragon House, 1984, pp.
211-23.

Examines the concept of "indemnity" in both the Unification
Church and in traditional Christianity in order to understand the
teachings of modern evangelists. The author summarizes the theological message of televangelists and their role. He thinks that
their success is due to the fact that mass communications enable
them to reinforce "the positive image of self-worth." Further,
their teaching permits the "privatization of evangelical faith."
The audiences of the televangelists, who are loyal participants in
the electronic church, pay indemnity in the form of sacrificial
giving; in other words, they take part in the church by "buying
indulgences."

1290. Hadden, Jeffrey K., Anson D. Shupe, James Hawdon, and Kenneth
Martin. "Why Jerry Falwell Killed the Moral Majority." THE GOD
PUMPERS (item 604), pp. 101-15.

Argues that the success of the Moral Majority was the reason
behind Jerry Falwell's move to form a new organization (Liberty
Federation) that would incorporate the interest of the Moral Majority in a broader agenda. The authors assess the strength of the
Moral Majority and survey its activities and participants. They
conclude that it did not have a significant grass-roots organizational structure. Once the movement had served the purpose of the
New Christian Right, it had run its course as a social movement and
was ready to be replaced.

1291. Halford, Larry J., and C. LeRoy Anderson. "When Prophecy Fails
Again: The Morrisites." FREE INQUIRY IN CREATIVE SOCIOLOGY 9.1
(1981): 5-10.

Describes one Mormon schismatic group, known as the Morrisites.
Several variables--social-structural, demographic, interactional,
and environmental--are investigated. The Morrisite belief in the
imminent Second Coming of Christ was disconfirmed. The believers'
reaction was a public reaffirmation that acted as an "important
mechanism through which support for the belief system may be maintained, even in the face of repeated non-confirmation" (p. 10).
The Morrisites used testimony sharing and public ceremonies to
maintain their solidarity and to reduce doubt and skepticism.

1292. Hammond, Phillip E. "An Approach to the Political Meaning of Evan-
          gelicalism in Present-Day America." ANNUAL REVIEW OF THE SOCIAL
          SCIENCES OF RELIGION 5 (1981): 187-202.

          Reflects on one aspect of the contemporary religious revival,
          namely the Evangelical Movement within Protestantism. The author
          advances the view that "rather than being the religious channel by
          which people are atomized, Evangelicalism is the religious channel
          by which they participate in society" (p. 189). He uses Alexis de
          Tocqueville's notion of voluntary association and self-interest
          rightly understood to gauge the political meaning of the evangeli-
          cal revival of the 1970's and 1980's. Individual, structural, and
          cultural influences are examined to determine whether contemporary
          evangelicalism will have the same political effects as other re-
          vivals in the past.

1293. Hampshire, Annette, and James A. Beckford. "Religious Sects and
          the Concept of Deviance: The Mormons and the Moonies." BRITISH
          JOURNAL OF SOCIOLOGY 34 (1983): 208-29.

          Examines the internal dynamics that engender hostility between
          sects and the society in which they emerge in the context of the
          Mormons in the mid-nineteenth century and the Moonies in the 1970's.
          A brief introduction to each of the two religious groups, focusing
          on the antagonism they aroused, is given. The concept of deviance
          and the assumptions underlying it are examined. It is the authors'
          view that deviance is not the result of behavior, but rather "a
          product of the social process of definition" (p. 211). Deviance is
          a form of social labeling that can accentuate or encourage untypi-
          cal conduct (deviance amplification theory). A comparison between
          the Mormons and the Moonies shows that in neither case did the
          social reaction increase the deviant behavior of the two religious
          groups.

1294. Hansen, Klaus J. MORMONISM AND THE AMERICAN EXPERIENCE. Chicago:
          University of Chicago Press, 1981. xvii, 257 pp.

          Investigates the transformation of Mormonism from a separatist
          cult to a more tolerated, and finally highly respected, religious
          organization. The author traces the origins of Mormonism and then
          discusses its relationship with American culture, especially to the
          social and intellectual condition of New England. Four major areas
          of change in Mormon thought and practice are covered: 1) the Mormon
          "rationalization of death;" 2) the politics and economics of the
          kingdom of God; 3) sexuality and marriage; and 4) attitudes and
          practices regarding race. The author maintains that the Mormon
          transformation represents a radical change in content.

1295. Hardy, B. Carmon. "The Schoolboy God: A Mormon-American Model."
          JOURNAL OF RELIGIOUS HISTORY 9 (1976): 173-88.

          Discusses the Mormon emphasis on education with reference to
          their theological tenet that human beings have an "inherited and
          divine potential." According to the author, Mormon theism has
          succeeded in elevating human intellectual work to a godly level.

The author contends that there is a continuity between Mormon and American values expressed in the educational experience. In other words, Mormonism followed, and at times anticipated, the general drift of American educational thought.

1296. Heeren, John, Donald B. Lindsey, and Marylee Mason. "The Mormon Concept of Mother in Heaven: A Sociological Account of Its Origin and Development." JOURNAL FOR THE SCIENTIFIC STUDY OF RELIGION 23 (1984): 396-411.

Focuses on the Mormon belief in a Heavenly Mother (female deity). Its historical expressions are considered and some explanatory models used to account for its origin assessed. The belief in a Mother in Heaven provides divine justification not for equality between sexes, but rather for the patriarchal, plural marriage system that the Mormons introduced. Patriarchal authority among the Mormons provides for an extreme separation or division of labor between men and women. This sharp separation is the basis for the appearance of the concept of the Heavenly Mother, which is associated with conservative politics and has functioned to sustain institutional ends rather than feminist concerns.

1297. Heilman, Samuel C. "Inner and Outer Identities: Sociological Ambivalence Among Orthodox Jews." JEWISH JOURNAL OF SOCIAL STUDIES 39 (1977): 227-40.

Distinguishes between traditional Orthodox Jews who eschew the contemporary world and the modern Orthodox Jews who embrace it. The former stress Jewish identity as opposed to the outside world; the latter maintain another inner identity that is linked with modern society. Modern Orthodox Jews suffer from a sociological ambivalence because they have feelings of support and hostility towards more traditional Jews. The various types of sociological ambivalence are sketched and their sources discussed.

1298. Heinerman, John, and Anson Shupe. THE MORMON CORPORATE EMPIRE. Boston: Beacon Press, 1985. xiv, 293 pp.

Examines the Mormon Church's financial and political involvement in the larger society. The authors claim that Mormonism constitutes a formidable economic force and political power. Since Mormons reject the values of religious pluralism, they present a danger to society that cannot be matched by new religious movements like the Unification Church and the Hare Krishna Movement. This view is corroborated by an exploration of the Church's investments in mass communication, its extensive corporate empire, and its military/political dimensions. The commonly held view that Mormons are involved in large social-welfare efforts is challenged. The authors argue that the Mormon Church "has engaged in a good deal of authoritarian control of its own members, stifling dissent and criticism in a manner inconsistent with democratic ideals" (p. 179). Court cases are a clear indication that Mormons are, in fact, a social problem. Many of the criticisms leveled at the Mormon Church are similar to the popular attacks against some of the new religious movements.

1299. Heinz, Donald. "Clashing Symbols: The New Christian Right as
       Countermythology." ARCHIVES DE SCIENCES SOCIALES DES RELIGIONS
       59.1 (1985): 153-73.

       Examines several sociological interpretations of the rise of the
       New Christian Right in the United States as a significant social
       movement. The argument advanced is that this movement is creating
       a countermythology that opposes that of secular humanism, liberal
       Christianity, and the rival mythology within the Christian Right
       Movement itself. Important symbols that convey systems of meaning
       (like television, public education, and the family) have become the
       target of the Christian Right. The author rejects the view that
       this movement is 1) a response to widespread anomie in relation to
       the sociopolitical scene; 2) a maladaptive or outmoded response
       to modernity; or 3) a naive repressive reaction to current socio-
       political developments. He suggests, rather, that it is "an emerg-
       ing coalition of social movements engaged in a contest over the
       meaning of America's story" (pp. 169-70).

1300. Hill, Clifford. "Immigrant Sect Development in Britain: A Case of
       Status Deprivation?" SOCIAL COMPASS 18 (1972): 231-36.

       Discusses various conservative Christian sects in Britain that
       are exclusively made up of West Indian and African immigrants. One
       particular church, The New Testament Church of God, which is the
       oldest of these immigrant sects dating to 1953, is examined. The
       author contends that the experience of social deprivation due to
       ethnic prejudice is responsible for the growth of these sects.
       "Deprivation has the effect of driving together in social solidar-
       ity members of a pariah group" (p. 233). He thinks that the dete-
       rioration of race relations in Britain will contribute to the
       increase of sect membership.

1301. Hill, Clifford. "From Church to Sect: West Indian Religious Sect
       Development in Britain." JOURNAL FOR THE SCIENTIFIC STUDY OF
       RELIGION 10 (1971): 114-23.

       Studies the growth of The New Testament Church of God, a West
       Indian sect whose members first migrated to Britain in 1953. Their
       rejection by the English churches in explained in sociocultural
       terms. Several features of the sect, like worship, preaching style,
       pentecostal doctrine, and authoritarian lifestyle, are described.
       Withdrawal is seen as a response to social deprivation and func-
       tions as a means of providing members with a social network. Reli-
       gious status becomes a substitute for social status that is denied
       to the members by the larger society. Originally an offshoot of the
       Church of God, the New Testament Church of God has moved from a
       church to a sect, indicating its rejection of the middle-class
       cultural heritage of the established English church.

1302. Hill, Marvin S., and James B. Allen, editors. MORMONISM AND AMERI-
       CAN CULTURE. New York: Harper and Row, 1972. 189 pp.

       Maintains that "the central theme of Mormon history has been the
       search for community, and that this has also been the ultimate
       American concern" (p. 3), and presents a collection of previously

published essays dealing with that theme. The essays are divided
into three sections. The first deals with the origins of the
Mormon community; the second considers the early Mormon struggles
to create a community that both reflected and at the same time
conflicted with American cultural goals; and the third looks at the
challenges that the Mormon community faces in the twentieth century.
A short select bibliography is added (pp. 185-89).

1303. Hill, Michael. "Methodism as a Religious Order." SOCIOLOGICAL
       YEARBOOK OF RELIGION IN BRITAIN 6 (1973): 91-99.

       Discusses the sect-church typology and its application to Method-
       ism. The author points out that eighteenth- and nineteenth-century
       observers note a resemblance between Methodist and religious orders.
       Methodists were sometimes compared to Jesuits and Wesleyans with
       Franciscans. Several parallels between Methodism and religious
       orders are listed. Early Methodism had the character of a reli-
       gious order within the Church of England.

1304. Hiller, Harry H. "A Reconceptualization of the Dynamics of Social
       Movement Development." PACIFIC SOCIOLOGICAL REVIEW 18 (1975):
       342-60.

       Examines the stages of social movement development using as exam-
       ples the social credit movement in England and the religious funda-
       mentalist movement in the Canadian Province of Alberta. Three
       phases of their development, namely interest, protest, and perspec-
       tive, are described. The author demonstrates how in each phase the
       participants were forced to reorganize their commitment to the
       movement. The author's analysis shifts the focus of study from the
       routinization and organization of social movements to the dynamics
       of social participation.

1305. Hillery, George A., and Paula C. Morrow. "The Monastery as a Com-
       mune." INTERNATIONAL REVIEW OF MODERN SOCIOLOGY 6 (1976): 139-54.

       Analyzes data from two Trappist monasteries, three communes, five
       semicommunes, and seven student populations. The following three
       hypotheses are tested: 1) monasteries are similar to communes (like
       yoga ashrams); 2) monasteries differ from semicommunes (such as
       cooperatives); and 3) monasteries differ from student groups (like
       sororities and fraternities). The authors conclude that the
       results support their claims that monasteries and communes are
       homogeneous and that communards can learn from monks about how
       communal life should be conducted.

1306. Hine, Virginia H. "Bridge Burners: Commitment and Participation
       in a Religious Movement." SOCIOLOGICAL ANALYSIS 31 (1970): 61-77.

       Studies involvement in the Pentecostal movement at the earliest
       stage of its development and relates it to "an identity-altering
       experience and a bridge-burning act" (p. 65). Four features of
       committed individuals are listed: 1) assurance or deep conviction;
       2) willingness to sacrifice various social ties; 3) charisma (the
       capacity to influence others and to inspire a devoted following);

and 4) attitudinal and behavioral change. A subjective experience
and a severance of former ties, both of which are expressed in
glossolalia, are interpreted as commitment-generating mechanisms.
A topology of involvement and an operational definition of commitment are proposed.

1307. Hoak, Dale. "The Great European Witch Hunt." AMERICAN JOURNAL OF
       SOCIOLOGY 88 (1983): 1270-74.

       Criticizes Ben-Yehuda's sociological interpretation of European
       witch hunts (item 1153) as too imprecise "to reveal the changing
       patterns of witch-hunts in Europe" (p. 1270). The author proposes
       instead a historically based explanation that holds that witch
       hunting was more common in those areas where the Reformation had
       precipitated religious violence. The Reformation intensified the
       awareness of Satan in those areas already possessing a rich tradi-
       tion of folklore about Satan. Various crises (like inflation,
       disease, and war) were blamed on the devil, whose agents were iden-
       tified as witches. The collision of two cultures, the village
       culture and the reformation culture, explain the witch craze.
       Witch hunting was "a socially destructive by-product of the Euro-
       pean transition to modernity" (p. 1274).

1308. Holm, Nils G. "Ritualistic Patterns and Sound Structure of Glosso-
       lalia in Material Collected in the Swedish-Speaking Parts of
       Finland." TEMENOS 11 (1975): 143-60.

       Attempts to determine the position of glossolalia and the glosso-
       lalist in the ritual of speaking in tongues and to find whether
       glossolalic utterances by different people are similar or not.
       Conducting his research among Swedish-speaking Pentecostals in
       Finland, the author analyzes the ritual patterns of glossolalia and
       compares two types of glossolalia, namely the prophetic type and
       the prayer type. He concludes that certain glossolalic utterances
       are similar to those existing in other languages. Glossolalia is a
       common "pseudolangauge" that everyone has the ability to produce.

1309. Homan, Roger. "Interpersonal Communication in Pentecostal Meetings."
       SOCIOLOGICAL REVIEW 26 (1978): 499-518.

       Explores modes of communication in Pentecostal assemblies, focus-
       ing on indirect speech and taboos relating to the expression of
       sympathy and appreciation. The way words like "family," "fellow-
       ship," "assembly," "brother," and "sister" are used is described.
       Reports about the illness of a member are made to elicit prayer
       rather than to invoke sympathy. Pentecostals, especially those in
       Europe, do not like applause since it may ascribe the role of "star"
       to the performer. They tend to express appreciation in terms of
       praise to God rather than in terms of congratulations to the per-
       former or the pastor. A sequence of learning Pentecostal behavior
       and language is proposed. The theocentric element in interaction
       and the conscientious denial of personal merit are said to be the
       reasons for the taboo of expressing the sentiments of sympathy and
       appreciation.

1310. Horsley, Richard A. "Further Reflections on Witchcraft and Euro-
        pean Folk Religion." HISTORY OF RELIGIONS 19 (1979): 71-95.

        Explores the relationship between European folk religion and
        witchcraft belief in order to understand why witch hunts were
        carried out. The author thinks that the study of popular religion
        might also throw light on the socioeconomic conditions of the six-
        teenth and seventeenth centuries and on the manner in which beliefs
        about witches were used to suppress popular religion. The basic
        practices of folk religion, which included mostly beneficial magical
        rituals performed by wise women and sorcerers, are outlined. The
        author's view is that religious and civil authorities used witch
        beliefs to divide and control the peasantry during a period of
        social and economic transition.

1311. Horsley, Richard A. "Who Were the Witches?: The Social Roles of
        the Accused in the European Witch Trials." JOURNAL OF INTERDIS-
        CIPLINARY HISTORY 9 (1978): 689-715.

        Examines the social status, role, and relationships of the vic-
        tims of the great witch hunt. After discussing the popular versus
        the official concepts of witchcraft, the author maintains that the
        evidence supports the position that a few of the victims of the
        witch hunts were indeed sorcerers, but many of them folk healers
        and diviners who were perceived as quarrelsome or eccentric. The
        increase in the accusations of witchcraft must be understood in the
        context of the pressures that broad historical developments brought
        on village life.

1312. Hostetler, John A. AMISH SOCIETY. Baltimore: Johns Hopkins Uni-
        versity Press. 3rd edition, 1980. xv, 414 pp.

        Presents a comprehensive picture of Amish society from its birth
        to the challenges it faces in contemporary Western culture. After
        tracing its historical roots and migrations to America, the author
        dwells on the main features that stabilize it, namely its communal
        living, subsistent agriculture, the family, child nurture and edu-
        cation, life ceremonies, and communal rituals. The patterns of
        change in Amish society caused by its controversy with the govern-
        ment about education, by internal diversities and tensions, and by
        its contact with modern medicine are discussed. The author finally
        offers some reflections on whether the Amish can survive in the
        modern world. A select bibliography (pp. 385-401) is included.

1313. Hostetler, John A. HUTTERITE SOCIETY. Baltimore: Johns Hopkins
        University Press, 1974. xvi, 403 pp.

        Presents an ethnographic account of Hutterite culture. The mate-
        rial is divided in three major sections: 1) historical development;
        2) contemporary social and cultural organization; and 3) the prob-
        lems and techniques of survival. The author holds that the Hutter-
        ites have had more than sufficient resources to overcome their
        difficulties and have demonstrated a remarkable ability to adapt to
        natural, geographic, and agrarian environments. A selected bibli-
        ography is given (pp. 373-92).

1314. Hostetler, John A. "Folk Medicine and Sympathy Healing Among the
      Amish." AMERICAN FOLK MEDICINE: A SYMPOSIUM. Edited by Wayland
      D. Hand. Berkeley: University of California Press, 1973, pp.
      349-58.

      Maintains that to understand folk medicine in Amish society, one
      "must observe the totality of Amish medical practices and observe
      how folk and scientific knowledge function in a cultural system"
      (p. 251). The author describes the Amish attitudes towards sick-
      ness and their folk treatments. The Amish have a practice of
      changing doctors as "a means of achieving social integration by
      acquiring all available means of healing" (p. 254). The author
      thinks that the Amish have health problems that are linked with
      sociocultural changes. The persistence of folk medicine is under-
      standable in the context of their society.

1315. Hostetler, John A., and Gertrude Enders Huntington. "Children in
      Amish Society: Socialization and Community Education." New York:
      Holt, Rinehart, and Winston, 1971. xiv, 119 pp.

      Describes the educational system of the Old Order Amish, which
      presents a challenge to the fundamental assumptions and goals of
      the larger American society. The authors provide a brief descrip-
      tion of Amish culture and education and then in turn treat the
      Amish socialization patterns, school system and the training of
      teachers, and vocational schools. In spite of the conflicts be-
      tween the government and the Amish, the latter have resisted the
      influence of the public school system with its secular values.

1316. Huber, Elaine C. WOMEN AND THE AUTHORITY OF INSPIRATION: A REEXAM-
      INATION OF TWO PROPHETIC MOVEMENTS FROM A CONTEMPORARY FEMINIST
      PERSPECTIVE. Lanham, MD: University Press of America, 1985.
      vii, 252 pp.

      Studies two religious movements, namely the Montanist Movement
      in the early Church and the Antinomian Movement in the sixteenth-
      century Massachusetts Bay Colony. The author locates both move-
      ments in their respective historical backgrounds, analyzes the
      position of women in each, and examines the way in which the move-
      ments have been commonly presented. The authority of prophesy, the
      actual prophetic utterances, and the conditions under which women
      have exercised leadership are discussed. The author finally offers
      some reflections on the significance of the current resurgence of
      the authority of inspiration in the Christian feminist movement.

1317. Huber, Elaine C. "'A Woman Must Not Speak': Quaker Women in the
      English Left Wing." WOMEN OF SPIRIT: FEMALE LEADERSHIP IN THE
      JEWISH AND CHRISTIAN TRADITIONS. Edited by Rosemary Reuther and
      Eleanor Mclaughlin. New York: Simon and Schuster, 1979, pp. 153-
      81.

      Describes the rise of women to positions of leadership in the
      Society of Friends, which provided a setting "where women were en-
      couraged to share full responsibility" (p. 155). The following
      features of Quakerism that were attractive to women are singled

out: 1) simplicity; 2) "empowerment in the present moment" (which followed from the Quaker belief that all human beings have a divine spark within them); 3) a sense of adventure; and 4) opportunity for full participation. By the middle of the seventeenth century, however, the trend to treat women on an equal basis had begun to wane. The author thinks that there is a need to understand the social conditions that enabled women to break through traditional boundaries in early Quakerism.

1318. Huntington, Gertrude Enders. "The Amish Family." ETHNIC FAMILIES IN AMERICA. Edited by Charles H. Mindel and Robert W. Haberstein. New York: Elsivier, 1976, pp. 295-322.

Shows how the family institution helps maintain the Amish culture and society. After providing the historical background of the Amish in the United States, the author concentrates on the family system among the Old Order Amish. Its demographic characteristics, social structure, kinship relationships, family order, social class, and lifestyles are described. The socialization of the Amish is outlined in six stages of life, namely those of infancy, preschool children, school children, young people, adulthood, and old people. Various threats to their community structure and family organization, such as social security, state education, and the draft, are discussed. The author thinks that, in spite of change and adaptation, the Amish have maintained their unique worldview and social and cultural lifestyle.

1319. Hurwick, Judith Jones. "The Social Origins of the Early Quakers." PAST AND PRESENT, No. 48 (1970): 156-64.

Questions Richard Vann's view (item 251) that by the middle of the eighteenth-century, Quakerism was becoming a movement largely of urban middle-class people. Evidence is adduced to show that Vann's picture of the Quakers cannot be generalized. A rejoinder by Vann is added (pp. 162-63).

1320. Itzkin, Elissa S. "The Halevy Thesis--A Working Hypothesis? English Revivalism: Antidote for Revolution and Radicalism, 1789-1815." CHURCH HISTORY 44 (1975): 47-56.

Examines the theory that religious beliefs and sanctions are the roots of England's social solidarity and political stability and that, in particular, the Methodist revival influenced British society at large and spared the country from a sociopolitical upheaval. The view that under the conservative influence of the Wesleyan revival (1792-1815) the revolutionary spirit declined is positively evaluated.

1321. Jackson, Carl T. "The New Thought Movement and the Nineteenth-Century Discovery of Oriental Philosophy." JOURNAL OF POPULAR CULTURE 9 (1975): 523-48.

Explores the historical roots of the current interest in Asian thought and traces them back to the early nineteenth century, particularly to the Transcendentalist Movement led by Emerson. The

author concentrates on one single manifestation of the interest in
oriental ideas, namely the New Thought Movement or Mind Cure. The
main features of New Thought, a significant social and religious
movement of the period, are outlined. The Indian doctrines of
Karma and reincarnation and the practice of Yoga are said to be
among the movement's more attractive characteristics. The writings
and activities of some of the major personalities in New Thought
are described. The author thinks that those contemporary Americans
who are exploring Eastern religious thought are doing it for the
same reasons that their nineteenth-century forerunners did.

1322. Jioultsis, Basil. "Religious Brotherhoods: A Sociological View."
        SOCIAL COMPASS 22 (1975): 67-83.

        Examines religious brotherhoods within the Greek Orthodox Church.
        Their history and social conditions under the Ottoman occupation
        and their development in the eighteenth century are outlined. Four
        major brotherhoods (Life, Savior, Cross, and Comforter) that follow
        the monastic rule of poverty, chastity, and obedience are described.
        The author attempts a "microsociology" of these associations, whose
        work lies primarily in preaching and religious education. He con-
        siders in turn: 1) their internal organization and coordination;
        2) their administration and functioning; and 3) their inner life
        and unity in conjunction with the social activities of the monks.
        The brotherhood's critical attitude toward ecclesiastical authority
        and the way it differs from traditional monastic institutions and
        other religious associations leads the author to categorize it as
        an "autonomous" (self-governed) religious group.

1323. Johnson, Norris R., David A. Choate, and William Bunis. "Atten-
        dance at a Billy Graham Crusade." SOCIOLOGICAL ANALYSIS 45
        (1984): 383-92.

        Applies the resource mobilization theory of social movements to
        explain the attendance at an evangelical crusade led by the Rever-
        end Billy Graham. The authors explore the ways in which the local
        church organizations brought together their resources to promote
        the crusade. It is argued that the greater the mobilization
        efforts made by the local churches, the more likely were regular
        church members enticed to go to the meeting. Those churches that
        believed Billy Graham was either too liberal or too conservative
        did not participate in the mobilization efforts with the result
        that fewer of their members participated in the crusade.

1324. Johnson, Weldon T. "The Religious Crusade: Revival or Ritual?"
        AMERICAN JOURNAL OF SOCIOLOGY 76 (1971): 873-90.

        Discusses, in the context of of Lang and Lang's study of Billy
        Graham's crusades (item 211), whether revivalism is a condition of
        religious change. The author thinks that such crusades do not lead
        to radical conversions, but rather to an increase of religious com-
        mitment. He views revivalist meetings as a "subcultural tradition
        whose norms define and prescribe ritualistic religious 'conver-
        sions,' without changing either verbal or non-verbal religious
        behavior" (p. 888).

1325. Jolicoeur, Pamela M., and Louis L. Knowles. "Fraternal Associ-
          ations and Civil Religion: Scottish Rite Freemasonry." REVIEW OF
          RELIGIOUS RESEARCH 20 (19780: 3-22.

       Maintains that Freemasonry, "the oldest, largest, and most pres-
       tigious of American fraternal associations, is an organization
       dedicated to the maintenance and propagation of civil religion" (p.
       4). A brief description of the Scottish rite, the most prominent
       system of Masonic higher degrees, is provided. The author reviews
       the literature on Civil Religion and analyzes the content of The
       New Age, a major national Masonic magazine that contains key civil-
       religious concepts. The Masonic Rite is to a large extent an ex-
       pression of American Civil Religion, though the interpretation of
       this religion in Masonic literature differs from that usually given
       in sociological literature.

1326. Jones, R. Kenneth. "The Development of Medical Sects." SICKNESS
          AND SECTARIANISM (item 643), pp. 1-21.

       Compares the origin and development of medical sects and reli-
       gious sects and finds that both groups have a similar organization
       and structure. A brief overview of cultic quackery (which includes
       Christian Science), phrenology, mesmerism, chiropractic, and oste-
       opathy is provided. The cultic element in medicoreligious sects is
       characterized by membership in associations "whose adherents claim
       access to gnosis of a special and ephemeral kind" (p. 14), and by
       the presence of a charismatic founder. The author thinks that these
       medical sects fall into Wilson's category of "manipulationist" sects
       (see item 1023).

1327. Jones, R. Kenneth. "Some Sectarian Characteristics of Therapeutic
          Groups With Special Reference to Recovery, Inc., and Neurotics
          Nomine." SECTARIANISM: ANALYSIS OF RELIGIOUS AND NON-RELIGIOUS
          SECTS (item 713), pp. 190-210.

       Maintains that therapeutic groups share some similarities with
       religious sects both in their belief structure and organization.
       Two groups, Recovery, Inc. and Neurotics Nomine, are analyzed with
       respect to their origins, goals, literature, language, and develop-
       ment. Though only the former used the confessional technique, both
       employed conversion and resocialization procedures.

1328. Jones, R. Kenneth. "The Swedenborgians: An Interactionist Analy-
          sis." SOCIOLOGICAL YEARBOOK OF RELIGION IN BRITAIN 7 (1974):
          132-53.

       Gives an account of the origins and development of Swedenborgian-
       ism, an eighteenth-century sect. Focusing on one major schismatic
       group founded in Britain in 1910 and known in England as the Sweden-
       borgian Society and in America as the Swedenborgian Foundation, the
       author describes the nature of the church's revelation and its
       doctrines regarding the Bible, the Second Coming, the Trinity,
       Heaven and Hell, and the world of spirits. The group is said to be
       a transcendental and value-oriented one. Its meaning is ascribed
       to an interactive social and intellectual milieu that maintains the

esoteric aspect of its doctrines. Swedenborgianism is at variance with the prevailing culture, but seeks an accommodation with society to which it offers no serious threat.

1329. Jones, R. Kenneth. "The Catholic Apostolic Church: A Study of Diffused Commitment." SOCIOLOGICAL YEARBOOK OF RELIGION IN BRITAIN 5 (1972): 127-60.

Provides an account of the origins of the Catholic Apostolic Church in the early nineteenth century and of the part played by its two main advocates, namely Edward Irving and Henry Drummond. The charismatic period of the movement, during which speaking in tongues was common, and its belief system and organizational structure are described. The Catholic Apostolic Church has, in the author's opinion, several sectarian features, such as a fundamentalist interpretation of the Bible, the acceptance of, and stress on, prophecy, an intolerance of dissenters, and an interpretation of political events as "signs of the times." Its emergence is attributed to the powerlessness of the middle classes who were unable to have any impact on society at a time of rapid social change and consequent strain. A couple of appendices give a list of churches in England and their geographic location that shows a substantial decline in the twentieth century.

1330. Jones, R. Kenneth. "Alcoholics Anonymous: A New Revivalism." NEW SOCIETY (July 16, 1970): 102.

Presents a short and slightly different version of the author's essay in SOCIOLOGY. Alcoholics Anonymous is clearly portrayed not just as a therapeutic fellowship, but also as a religious sect.

1331. Jones, R. Kenneth. "Sectarian Characteristics of Alcoholics Anonymous." SOCIOLOGY 4 (1970): 181-95.

Argues that Alcoholics Anonymous is similar to sects both in its organization and belief system. After a brief account of its origin, the author describes its organizational structure in various units, each of which is assigned a distinctive purpose. Like a sect, Alcoholics Anonymous is a voluntary association requiring a high level of commitment and utilizing social controls like rituals, prestige symbols, resocialization, and leadership. Though largely secular in theory, Alcoholics Anonymous has a formal belief system that is transcendental in character.

1232. Juster, Susan. "'In a Different Voice:' Male and Female Narratives of Religious Conversions in Post-Revolutionary America." AMERICAN QUARTERLY 41 (1989): 34-62.

Examines over 200 detailed accounts of religious conversions published in several evangelical magazines between 1800 and 1830 and compares the male and female narratives that "reveal a rich portrait of men and women caught in a moment of intense self-scrutiny and self-assessment" (p. 37). Various common motifs, such as the metaphor of rebirth, are outlined. Two models of authority are found in these accounts, a male view that sees authority as an

abstract system of rules and principles and a female view that
experiences authority as a personal power. The author points out
that these two views closely coincide with contemporary research on
psychology and moral development. She finds that the conversions
of both men and women suggest "an androgynous model of the conversion experience," a model which has far-reaching implications.

1333. Katelansky, Sandra. "The Lubavitch Hasidim: The Relationship Be-
      tween Attraction, Socialization, and Social Control in a Reli-
      gious Movement." PROCEEDINGS: ASSOCIATION FOR THE SCIENTIFIC
      STUDY OF RELIGION: SOUTHWEST, 1981. 6 pp.

Suggests that the same elements that attract recruits to the
Lubavitch Hasidic Movement are also used in the socialization and
control of its new members. The following reasons given by the new
members for joining the movement are outlined and discussed: 1) the
well-defined guidelines for social and religious behavior of Hasidism; 2) the Lubavitcher education programs; 3) its initial acceptance of recruits regardless of their knowledge and practice of
orthodox Judaism and Hasidism; and 4) the sociability of the members of the movement. The Lubavitcher Movement, according to the
author, serves the function of molding a distinctive Jewish identity.

1334. Kauffman, J. Howard. "Social Correlates of Spiritual Maturity
      Among North American Mennonites." SOCIOLOGICAL ANALYSIS 40
      (1979): 27-42.

Reports on the development and use of "religious life scales" to
measure spiritual maturity, examines the relationship between such
maturity and several social factors, and then checks whether Mennonites differ significantly from other religious groups. Nine religious dimensions are considered: belief, practices, experience,
knowledge, consequences, particularism, ethicalism, friendship, and
communal involvement. The author finds that, though spiritual
maturity is strongly related to age and weakly, but significantly,
related to socioeconomic status, rural residence, and sex, it is
not significantly related to educational achievement. The most
religious Mennonite "would be an elderly female with a professional
education, residing in a rural non-farm area, and having a low to
moderate income" (p. 39).

1335. Kauffman, J. Howard, and Leland Harder. ANABAPTISTS FOUR CENTURIES
      LATER: A PROFILE OF FIVE MENNONITE AND BRETHREN IN CHRIST DENOMI-
      NATIONS. Scottsdale, PA: Herald Press, 1975. 399 pp.

Presents a sociological profile of two Mennonite Churches in the
United States. After a historical introduction, the characteristics of church members, namely their residence, age, sex, educational attainment, occupation, and income, are outlined. The
authors, who are Mennonite college teachers, overview the patterns
of faith, life, and work of the church, and the sources and consequences of church membership. Several unresolved tensions, such
as sectarian versus ecumenical tendencies, the attitudes towards
political participation, and the fear of assimilation, are discussed. Some implications for the churches are drawn up.

1336.   Kent, Stephen A. "The Quaker Ethic and the Fixed Price Policy: Max
        Weber and Beyond." SOCIOLOGICAL INQUIRY 53 (1983): 16-31.

        Starts with an examination of Max Weber's research on the Quakers
        and their fixed price policy in order to understand the part played
        by Protestant sects in the rise of capitalism. The author finds
        Weber's analysis deficient in historical perspective. He inter-
        prets the Quaker economic customs against the background of the
        English Civil War rather than in the context of their religious
        ideology. The Quaker economic reforms are, thus, seen as arising
        after a period of conflict and high expectations. He concludes
        that in Quakerism there is a clear relationship between religious
        doctrines and social frustrations.

1337.   Kent, Stephen A. "Relative Deprivation and Resource Mobilization:
        A Study of Early Quakerism." BRITISH JOURNAL OF SOCIOLOGY 33
        (1982): 529-44.

        Contends that models of resource mobilization that have been used
        extensively in recent analyses of sectarian movements should be
        seen as complimentary to theories of relative deprivation. The
        author attempts to illustrate how both theories can be applied at
        the same time with reference to the origin and development of
        Quakerism, particularly its protest against the payment of tithes.
        Many people at the close of the Civil War in England felt "aspira-
        tional deprivation" since their hopes for the abolition of tithes
        were not fulfilled. Quakerism came into being as a social movement
        among people who opposed the tithe-supported ministry. While the
        resource mobilization theory explains how people muster their re-
        sources to achieve their goals, the deprivation theory explains the
        motivation that initiates the formation of a sect.

1338.   Kern, Louis J. AN ORDERED LOVE: SEX ROLES AND SEXUALITY IN VICTO-
        RIAN UTOPIANS--THE SHAKERS, THE MORMONS, AND THE ONEIDA COMMUNITY.
        Chapel Hill: University of North Carolina Press, 1981. xiii,
        430 pp.

        Examines three nineteenth-century communities that offered dif-
        ferent alternatives to monogamous marriage. After discussing nine-
        teenth-century attitudes towards the self and sexuality, the author
        describes, in turn, the sexual ideology and practices of the Shakers
        (who opted for celibacy), the Mormons (who chose polygamy), and the
        Oneida Community (which favored a rather complex form of plural
        marriage called "pantagamous"). The maternal-familial paradigm of
        utopian societies is described and related to broader cultural
        patterns. The author thinks that the three groups were a utopian
        rejection of the Victorian romantic-love ideology and sexual
        practices. Each community provided a structural environment with
        a different vision of male/female relationships and, in so doing,
        promised stability and order in sexual life and some degree of
        freedom from anxiety about sexual problems. The bibliography (pp.
        395-419) includes both primary and secondary sources.

1339.   Kern, Louis J. "Ideology and Reality: Sexuality and Women's Status
        in the Oneida Community." RADICAL HISTORY REVIEW 20 (1979): 180-
        204.

Discusses the aggressive attack on the material spirit carried out by the Oneida Community to change traditional sexual and family practices. Women's work patterns, female fashions, and the community's reaction to the women's movement are examined. It is noted that the women in Oneida Community did not like the sexual and social arrangements, particularly the introduction of a selective reproduction plan and the development of a spirit of "masculine independence" for all. While women in Oneida made some real gains in achieving equality with men, diametrically opposed views of women's status and function in society led to the break-up of the commune in 1889.

1340. Khoshkish, A. "Decision-Making Within a Communal Setting: A Case Study of Hutterite Colonies." INTERNATIONAL REVIEW OF MODERN SOCIOLOGY 6.1 (1976): 41-55.

Points out that the Hutterites offer three major solutions to the problems of power complexes: adult baptism, pacifism, and communal living and property. While recognizing both the spiritual and functional attributes of the individual, the Hutterites ascribe a sense of the holy to personal freedom and to decision making. The author speculates on how decision making fits into an egalitarian communal lifestyle and outlines the nature and level of the process of making decisions within the authority system of the Hutterites. Just as in primitive tribes, the whole church or commune takes up the responsibility of enforcing the law.

1341. King, Christine E. "Strategies For Survival: Sectarian Experiences in the Third Reich." OF GODS AND MEN (item 550), pp. 239-53.

Studies the religious situation in Germany in the 1930's when the majority of sects were banned by the government. The responses to new situation of five sects, namely Jehovah's Witnesses, the Mormonism, Christian Science, Seventh-Day Adventism, and the New Apostolic Church, are compared. Of the five groups, only the Jehovah's Witnesses resisted the regime and refused to give allegiance to the new state on theological grounds. Christian Science and Mormonism used whatever international influence they had to safeguard their position. Seventh-Day Adventism and the New Apostolic Church stressed the nationalistic and conservative leanings of their members. The author explores the theologies of these sects to find explanations for their varied responses.

1342. King, Robert R., and Kay Atkinson King. "The Effect of Mormon Organization on Group Cohesion." DIALOGUE: A JOURNAL OF MORMON THOUGHT 17.1 (1984): 61-75.

Focuses on the organizational aspect of Mormonism in order to throw light on some facets of its history. The author is particularly interested in how the nature of its organization, its internal cohesion, and its relationship to the environment determined the way social boundaries are formed and maintained. Six elements that play a significant role in maintaining Mormons' sense of boundary, namely ritual, unique beliefs and doctrines, a strong sense of community, conflicts with other groups, polygamy, and

dietary restrictions, are examined. The effects firm boundaries
and a high level of social cohesion have on the Mormon Church are
outlined.

1343. Kohn, Rachael L. E. "Dual-Membership and Sectarian Status: The
       Case of a Hebrew Christian Group." STUDIES IN RELIGION 12.2
       (1983): 157-66.

       Studies a Hebrew Christian group, the "Friends of Israel," that
       was founded in 1892 in a middle-sized Canadian city as a mission
       devoted to Jewish evangelism. Some of its attitudes, beliefs, and
       activities are described. Although not exclusive in its member-
       ship, the Friends of Israel has sect-like features, such as a
       unique teaching, a special status conferred on its members, and a
       demand of strict loyalty. Formal links with several Protestant
       churches are maintained for several reasons that include the oppor-
       tunity to make converts and the need for financial backing that is
       necessary for survival. The view that religious groups that prac-
       tice dual membership are not sects is questioned. It is argued,
       instead, that the Friends of Israel actually enhance its distinc-
       tiveness by allowing its members to belong also to a regular Chris-
       tian church.

1344. Kohn, Rachael L. E. "Praising the Lord and Penetrating the Commu-
       nity: Transition and Dual Leadership in a Contemporary Hebrew
       Christian Group." SOCIOLOGICAL ANALYSIS 45 (1984): 29-39.

       Presents a study of a Hebrew Christian group, the Hamilton
       Friends of Israel, that generated a Messianic Jewish sub-group in
       October 1980. A short history of the main group (founded in 1892)
       is given and its organizational structure described. The author
       then dwells on the emergence of the new sub-group whose leader also
       heads the Friends of Israel. She applies the theories of Zald and
       Ash (1966) and Gusfield (1966) to explain how the symbolic values
       of the leader's role as Jewish pastor function to maintain dual
       leadership.

1345. Kolmerten, Carol A. "Unconscious Sexual Stereotyping in Utopia: A
       Sample From the New Harmony Gazette, 1825-1827." UTOPIAS: THE
       AMERICAN EXPERIENCE (item 425), pp. 72-86.

       Argues that, despite the reforms introduced by the nineteenth-
       century New Harmony commune, "real sexual equality was impossible,
       because in New Harmony, as in the mainstream culture, women were
       regarded as more pure, more moral, and more delicate than their
       male counterparts" (p. 73). Citing the many articles in the offi-
       cial voice of the community, NEW HARMONY GAZETTE, the author shows
       that while adopting new assumptions about education, marriage, and
       divorce, the leader of the new commune believed that women were not
       quite equal to men. The editors of the gazette constantly advised,
       lectured to, and admonished women. And the leaders of the commu-
       nity held that women's "female character" dictated that they took
       up different roles and more servile occupations than men.

1346. Kring, Hilda Adam. THE HARMONISTS: A FOLK-CULTURAL APPROACH.
       Metuchen, NJ: Scarecrow Press, 1973. xv, 260 pp.

Presents a study of the Harmony celibate community founded by
George Repp in 1805. The author takes a holistic approach and
attempts to show how religion was an integral part of the members'
daily living, which created tension with society at large. Their
creed, social organization, rites of passage, place of worship,
feasts, and community relationships are among the topics treated.
A bibliography and a list of manuscripts are appended.

1347. Kroll-Smith, J. Stephen. "The Testimony as Performance: The Relationship of an Expressive Event to the Belief System in a Holiness Sect." JOURNAL FOR THE SCIENTIFIC STUDY OF RELIGION 19
(1980): 16-25.

Discusses the belief system of a Pentecostal-Holiness church,
stressing the peculiar structural conditions underlying the system.
The practice of giving testimony is seen "as a form of identity
work, as a ritual means for addressing the tension between present
status or identity, and aspired status or potential identity" (p.
18). Further, testimony is a performance that specifies one's
social status in the group and signals one's commitment to a more
advanced and prestigious rank. Several typical testimonies are
examined, with special emphasis on their style and content. The
author maintains that testimony is a ritual of affirmation rather
than one of transformation.

1348. Kurtz, Ernest. "Why A.A. Works: The Intellectual Significance of
Alcoholics Anonymous." JOURNAL OF STUDIES ON ALCOHOL 43 (1982):
38-80.

Argues that Alcoholics Anonymous has an intellectual place in the
larger social history of ideas. The author offers an analysis of
Alcoholics Anonymous' origins and sources, of the parallels between
it and existential philosophy, and of the readiness with which it
has influenced other social phenomena. He describes the organization's worldview and maintains that Alcoholics Anonymous is "a
therapy for shame." Many references that discuss the therapeutic
qualities of Alcoholics Anonymous are included.

1349. Lane, Christel O. "Socio-Political Accommodation and Religious
Decline: The Case of the Molokan Sect in Soviet Society." COM-
PARATIVE STUDIES IN SOCIETY AND HISTORY 17 (1975): 221-37.

Presents a historical and sociological analysis of the Molokan
sect that emerged as a reaction to the ritualistic, liturgically
oriented, and hierarchical Russian Orthodox Church in the second
half of the eighteenth century. The belief system of this sect is
outlined and an account of its relationship to the state between
1871 and 1959 given. The social and demographic structures of the
Molokan groups are discussed. The author attributes the decline of
the sect to the fact that it has adjusted itself to Soviet reality
and its utopia has become realized by political means.

1350. Larner, Christina. WITCHCRAFT AND RELIGION: THE POLITICS OF POPU-
LAR BELIEF. Edited with an introduction by Alan McFarlane.
Oxford: Basil Blackwell, 1984. xi, 172 pp.

Presents a collection of essays dealing primarily with witchcraft in sixteenth- and seventeenth-century Europe, especially Scotland. The author shows where witchcraft persecutions occurred, who the accused people were, how the accusations proceeded, and what legal means were employed to bring the alleged witches to trial. Several preconditions, such as the peasant economy, the belief in witches among the peasants, and the common belief in the Devil, that led to the witch hunts are examined. The timing of the witch hunts is explained by the judicial revolution at the time, the rapid development of printing, the Christian stress on the need of personal salvation, and the rise of the Christian nation state.

1351. LaRuffa, Anthony L. "Pentecostalism and Assimilation: Puerto Rico and New York City." JOURNAL OF THE STEWARD ANTHROPOLOGICAL SOCIETY 1 (1970): 113-19.

Examines the effects of Pentecostalism on the structural and cultural assimilation among Puerto Ricans in their native country and in New York City. The main features of Pentecostalism and some statistical data on Pentecostal churches and membership are given. The main thesis advanced in this essay it that Pentecostalism "as practiced by Puerto Ricans in the New York area helps to maintain ethnicity, in both a cultural and structural sense, thereby retarding the process of assimilation" (p. 117).

1352. Lawless, Elaine J. "Piety and Motherhood: Reproductive Images and Maternal Strategies of the Woman Preacher." JOURNAL OF AMERICAN FOLKLORE 100 (1987): 469-78.

Studies the methods Pentecostal women use to become preachers and pastors of congregations whose conservative theology would favor their exclusion from important roles in church services and government. It is maintained that women who succeed in becoming religious leaders use maternal and reproductive images to remove the most threatening aspects of the religious roles they assume. Women often represent the denial of the secular, noninvolvement in the public arena, and the ideal family-based community--all of which appeal to conservative Pentecostals. Women pastors who "mother" a congregation are more easily accepted. While women pastors and preachers are not freed from sexual discrimination common in conservative, fundamentalist churches, they are liberated from the typical mold of cloistered wife and mother.

1353. Lawless, Elaine J. "'I Know If I Don't Bear My Testimony, I'll Lose It:' Why Mormon Women Bother to Speak at All." KENTUCKY FOLKLORE RECORD 30 (1984): 79-86.

Seeks to discover whether there is a traditional expressive forum for Mormon women. Though both men and women find a common platform in the religious services of the Mormon Church, the testimonies of women, unlike those in Pentecostal churches, do not contribute any power to women and seem to function as a means of maintaining the status quo. The Mormon attitudes regarding the role of women as centered around the home are indirectly expressed in the testimonies where grief is frequently expressed. Unlike those of men,

women's testimonies "suggest a significant discomfort with her role
and a distress about her plight, although her distress and anger
cannot be articulated" (p. 91). Women testify because they fear
they will lose what little they have in their church. Their testimonies are a public affirmation of humility in that they acknowledge
the power of the priesthood denied to them.

1354. Lawless, Elaine J. "Shouting for the Lord: The Power of Women's
      Speech in the Pentecostal Religious Service." JOURNAL OF AMERI-
      CAN FOLKLORE 96 (1983): 434-59.

      Presents a study of women's speech in Pentecostal meetings in
      Southern Indiana, a study which supports the anthropological theory
      of Lewis (item 406) that such services attract those who are polit-
      ically powerless and provides them with a means of expressing their
      group identity. In Pentecostal services, women and their audiences
      are freed from the domination of the male members of their reli-
      gious communities. The role women play in Pentecostal meetings is
      described. Their testimonies, which are a blend of standardized
      formulae and creative materials, are linguistically analyzed.

1355. Lee, Carleton L. "Toward a Sociology of Black Religious Experience."
      JOURNAL OF RELIGIOUS THOUGHT 29 (1972): 5-18.

      Explores religious experiences of Black Americans, pointing out
      that the sociological study of Black religion has focused on its
      protest character and on its tendency to assume sectarian and cul-
      tic features. After reviewing some of the literature on the sub-
      ject, the author mentions two organizations that express and en-
      courage Black religious experience, namely the Olivet Baptist
      Church in Chicago and Black Christian Nationalism (the Shrine of
      the Black Madonna) in Detroit. The stereotyping of Black religious
      experience is criticized and suggestions are made for exploring the
      "qualitative, regenerative, and survival character of the Black
      religious experience" (p. 17).

1356. Lee, Shu-Ching. "Group Cohesion and the Hutterite Colony." HUMAN
      NATURE AND COLLECTIVE BEHAVIOR: PAPERS IN HONOR OF HERBERT BLUMER.
      Edited by T. Shubitani. Englewood Cliffs, NJ: Prentice-Hall,
      1970, pp. 165-78.

      Tries to specify the properties of group cohesion by an analysis
      of Hutterite colonies. A brief historical sketch of the Hutterite
      Brotherhood, an Anabaptist sect founded by Jacob Hutter in Central
      Europe in the early sixteenth century, is provided. Four elements
      of group cohesion are discussed: 1) shared consensus; 2) organized
      attitudes; 3) structural integration; and 4) sense of group identi-
      fication. All of these factors, which are necessary for a group to
      be socially cohesive, are found in Hutterite colonies.

1357. Leonard, Bill J. "Independent Baptists: From Sectarian Minority to
      'Moral Majority.'" CHURCH HISTORY 56 (1987): 504-17.

      Attempts to identify independent, fundamentalist Baptists from
      historical and theological perspectives and then questions their
      relationship to American culture. The author questions, among

other things, the implications of their transition from a small
sectarian group to a leadership role in the Moral Majority? The
author summarizes these independent Baptists' approach to politics
and morality and concludes that they have become an important
phenomenon in American life.

1358. Leone, Mark P. ROOTS OF MODERN MODERNISM. Cambridge: Harvard
        University Press, 1979. ix, 250 pp.

        Examines from sociological and anthropological perspectives the
        origin, development, and adaptation of a religious minority. Among
        the areas investigated are the Mormon Church's history, its church
        structure, its tithing policy, its adjustment to the desert condi-
        tions, and its institution of ecclesiastical courts. The change
        that took place when Mormonism abandoned its theocratic goals are
        discussed. The author holds that Mormonism provides a way of
        thinking for those who are powerless in society.

1359. Leone, Mark P. "The Economic Base For the Evolution of Mormon
        Religion." RELIGIOUS MOVEMENTS IN CONTEMPORARY AMERICA (item
        727), pp. 722-66.

        Attempts to show how the economic transformations that took place
        between the nineteenth and twentieth centuries have been accompa-
        nied by religious changes in Mormonism. Rapid economic shifts and
        undifferentiated revolving tasks "are accompanied by decentralized
        formation of creeds and an increase in means for personal defini-
        tion of paradigms for belief and behavior" (p. 765). The author
        investigates, among other things, the connection between Mormon
        ritual and the organization of the irrigation system that the
        early Mormons constructed and some of the modifications that took
        place when the economic conditions changed.

1360. Leone, Mark P. "The Evolution of Mormon Culture in Eastern Arizona."
        UTAH HISTORICAL QUARTERLY 40 (1972): 122-41.

        Discusses the Mormon goal to create a utopian community that was
        an independent, self-sustaining entity, separated from mainline
        culture. The author, focusing on Mormon settlements on the Little
        Colorado River in Arizona, "attempts to show Mormonism's changing
        relationship to the economic and social circumstances of its popu-
        lation from 1880-1965" (p. 127). He examines several unifying
        features of Mormon society and concludes that it stressed indepen-
        dence and self-sufficiency through cooperation. In the twentieth
        century, Mormonism has faced the problem of a changing American
        culture by emphasizing the roles rather than the tasks members have
        and by moving towards ideological decentralization. Economic adap-
        tability and ideological independence have become the tools of
        Mormon success in the twentieth century.

1361. Levack, Brian P. THE WITCH-HUNT IN EARLY MODERN EUROPE. London:
        Longman, 1987. xii, 267 pp.

        Endeavors to explain why the great European witch hunt took place
        by "adopting a multi-causal approach which sees the emergence of
        new ideas about witches and a series of fundamental changes in the

criminal law as the necessary preconditions of the witch hunt, and
both religious changes and social tension as its more immediate
causes" (p. 3). The intellectual and legal foundations of witchcraft are explored and the impact of the Reformation assessed. The
author describes the social context of the witch hunt, which played
a role in relieving anxiety and widespread feelings of guilt. He
suggests that contemporary efforts to investigate the new religious
movements bear striking similarities to witch hunts. Several bibliographies are added (pp. 239-56).

1362. Lewis, Russell E. "Controlled Acculturation Revisited: An Examina-
      tion of Differential Acculturation and Assimilation Between the
      Hutterite Brethren and the Old Amish Order." INTERNATIONAL RE-
      VIEW OF MODERN SOCIOLOGY 6.1 (1976): 75-85.

      Compares the different rates of acculturation and assimilation
      for the Hutterites and the Amish. Various criteria for controlled
      acculturation, such as institutionalized mechanisms, community,
      racial, and spatial integration, socialization, and economic self-
      sufficiency, are considered. The author maintains that the Hutter-
      ites have been more successful than the Amish in controlled accul-
      turation and hence the former's chances of survival are greater.

1363. Lincoln, C. Eric, and Lawrence H. Mamiya. "Daddy Jones and Father
      Divine: The Cult as Political Religion." RELIGION IN LIFE 49
      (1980): 6-23.

      Discusses, in the context of Jim Jones and Father Divine, the
      characteristics of those cults that attract Black people. The cult
      leader's role and the social and physical isolation he or she en-
      couraged are examined. Cult members live in a private cosmos and
      have their sense of identity and reality partially determined by
      their leader. They are recruited from those who have lost hope and
      need relief or fulfillment. The political dimensions of a cult are
      brought into focus by a comparison between the movements founded by
      Father Divine and Jim Jones, both of whom had their greatest impact
      in times of social upheaval. There is some evidence that a "doc-
      trine of suicide" existed within the ideological framework of
      Father Divine's Movement. The author attempts to understand the
      mass suicides at Jonestown by seeing the cult as a "political
      religion."

1364. Lindén, Ingemar. "Millerism—An Historical Enigma?" NEW RELIGIONS
      (item 565), pp. 123-33.

      Looks into some of the major works on Millerism and deals briefly
      with its main characteristics and phases. It is the author's view
      that Millerism is frequently misunderstood. Three main historical
      periods are distinguished and it is shown how by the second period.
      Millerism had changed from a tolerant, ecumenical group to a sec-
      tarian movement that specified the exact date of Christ's Second
      Coming. Contrary to the many accounts of this religious group, the
      Millerites were not recruited from the ranks of the poor. Miller-
      ism cannot be classified as a typical cult for the economically
      disinherited because none of its principal leaders had a "definite

left-wing ideology." The social structure of Millerism and British millenarianism had many conspicuous similarities. Millerism, at first, was a typical American revival movement within the American Protestant tradition.

1365. Lofland, John. "Mankind United." PROTEST: STUDIES OF COLLECTIVE BEHAVIOR AND SOCIAL MOVEMENTS (item 665), pp. 249-54.

Examines a social movement founded in the 1930's by Arthur L. Bell, an American businessman. The origin of the movement is traced and its organization described. In its seventeen years of history, four stages of development can be detected: 1) popularization; 2) commitment; 3) collectivization; and 4) decline.

1366. Lovett, Leonard. "Perspective on the Black Origins of the Contemporary Pentecostal Movement." JOURNAL OF THE INTERDENOMINATIONAL CENTER 1 (Fall 1973): 36-49.

Discusses the origins of the Holiness-Pentecostal Movement that has its foundation in the religious experience of Black Americans. The nineteenth-century American Holiness Movement is seen as a direct precursor of twentieth-century Pentecostalism. The view that the origins of the Pentecostal Movement are interracial is refuted.

1367. Lundmark, Lennart. "Prophecy and Protest: The Korpela Millenarians of Northern Sweden in the 1930s." ETHOS 10 (1985): 231-47.

Applies Norman Cohn's view (item 168) that millenarian movements envision salvation as collective, earthly, imminent, total, and miraculous to the Swedish Korpela Sect. The religious and social background of this sect are described with particular attention given to Laestadianism, the conservative religion dominant at the time. The rise of the prophetic figure, Toivo Korpela, who began his career in Finland during a period of cultural oppression and economic crisis, and his message are outlined. The author suggests that one of the central features of such movements, a feature labeled "social temporalization," is the connection participants make between their interpretation of the past and their understanding of the present and hopes for the future.

1368. Mack, Phyllis. "Feminine Symbolism and Feminine Behavior in Radical Religious Movements: Franciscans, Quakers, and the Followers of Gandhi." DISCIPLES OF FAITH: STUDIES IN RELIGION, POLITICS, AND PATRIARCHY. Edited by Jim Obelkevitch, Lyndal Roper, and Raphael Samuel. London: Routledge and Kegan Paul, 1987, pp. 115-30.

Outlines the feminine symbolic behavior found in movements led by St. Francis of Assisi, George Fox, and Mahatma Gandhi. The symbol of outward and inward nakedness used in the three movements is associated with their stress on community and their image of salvation as a return to childhood. The three founders "buttressed their support of women by a faith in their own ability to transcend desire and by the belief that women, by their humility and chastity,

would help them do it" (p. 120). The place of women in these
movements is discussed in the context of Victor Turner's idea of
"communitas." An earlier version of this essay was published in
SIGNS: JOURNAL OF WOMEN IN CULTURE AND SOCIETY 11 (1986): 457-77.

1369. Mackie, Marlene. "Defection From Hutterite Colonies." SOCIALIZA-
TION AND VALUES IN CANADIAN SOCIETY. Edited by Robert M. Pike
and Elia Zureik. Toronto: McClelland and Stewart, 1975, vol. 2,
pp. 291-316.

Inquires into the experience of those few Hutterites (less than
one half of one percent of their total population) who leave their
closely knit colonies and endeavors to determine the role of culture in the process of defection. Two major areas are covered,
namely: 1) the conditions under which defection occurs and 2) the
adjustment of defectors to modern, urban society. Competition for
prestige roles within their community and the conflict between
traditional and modern values have significant consequences on
defection. Disorganization among the Hutterites has led to factions within the communities and the consequent weakening of
authority. Deviant behavior, like alcoholism, illegitimacy, and
petty thievery, has resulted. The adjustment of defectors to the
main culture, an adjustment that includes the problems of finding
work and maintaining contact with their Hutterite friends, is
discussed.

1370. Madsen, William. "Alcoholics Anonymous as a Crisis Cult." ALCOHOL
HEALTH AND RESEARCH WORLD (Experimental Issue, Spring 1974):
27-30.

Places Alcoholics Anonymous within the history of movements that
attract deprived members of society who want to improve their lot
and seek justice. Alcoholics Anonymous, like so many other crisis
cults, has acquired a spiritual or supernatural dimension. A brief
account of its origins is given and the process of joining the
organization is described, stressing the social bonding that is
appealing to its members. The change from uncontrolled alcoholism
to total abstinence is drastic and can be compared to the experiences of religious converts. Indoctrination into the movement's
principles keeps the members from returning to their drinking
habits. Alcoholics Anonymous provides an integrated value system
and the personalized caring relationships that are found in folk
societies.

1371. Mamiya, Lawrence H. "From Black Muslim to Bilalian: The Evolution
of a Movement." JOURNAL FOR THE SCIENTIFIC STUDY OF RELIGION 21
(1982): 138-52.

Analyzes the evolution of Black Muslim Movement in America into
Sunni Orthodoxy ("Bilial" being the official replacement of such
terms as "Afro-American" and "Black"). The author examines the
name "Bilial," the name of an Ethiopian Muslim slave, and the theme
of Ethiopianism in Black religion. Bilial is seen as a symbolic
representation of the movement towards orthodox Islam. The roles
of Louis Farrakhan, Malcolm X, and Wallace Muhammad in the movement

are compared and the religious messages and programs of the latter
two are scrutinized. It is maintained that the "internal socioeconomic conditions of the Nation have also contributed to the
shift in ideology now affecting both groups" (p. 145). The Nation
of Islam, which began as a lower-class movement, is becoming increasingly middle-class. Some speculations on the future of the
movement are made.

1372. Mappen, Marc, editor. WITCHES AND HISTORIANS: INTERPRETATIONS OF
      SALEM. Malabar, FL: Robert E. Krieger, 1980. 120 pp.

      Presents 15 essays that examine the trail and execution of the
      so-called witches in Salem, Massachusetts from different academic
      perspectives. The editor points out that "social research has
      revolutionized our understanding of this seventeenth-century trag-
      edy." Several sociological and anthropological viewpoints are
      included.

1373. Marcoux, Marcene. CURSILLO: ANATOMY OF A MOVEMENT. THE EXPERIENCE
      OF SPIRITUAL RENEWAL. New York: Lambeth Press, 1982. viii,
      290 pp.

      Studies, from an anthropological perspective, the Cursillo Move-
      ment, which emerged in Spain in the late 1940's and which strives
      at renewing traditional Catholicism. After a description of the
      movement's origins, the preparation and training for initiation,
      and the conversion experience, the author discusses two interpreta-
      tions of the Cursillo—one that sees it as a club-like association,
      the other that considers it a religious movement. The elements in
      the Catholic Church that Cursillo opposes and the language it
      espouses are explored. The author maintains that this movement is
      not just a short course on Catholicism, but a renewal movement with
      its own distinct way of life. There is an appendix on the research
      method used by the author. A list of the major documents (pp. 257-
      62) and a bibliography (pp. 274-84) are included.

1374. Mariampolski, Hyman. "Religion and the Survival of Utopian Commu-
             nities: The Case of New Harmony, Indiana (1824-1827)." COMMUNES:
             HISTORICAL AND CONTEMPORARY (item 312), pp. 215-34.

      Presents a sociological analysis of the utopian community founded
      by Robert Owen at New Harmony, Indiana in 1824. Since this com-
      mune, which lasted only three years, was founded on secular rather
      than religious principles, it provides a testing ground for eval-
      uating the role of religion in the success or failure of communes.
      The author maintains that the absence of a consistent religious
      ideology meant that the New Harmony commune could not elicit the
      commitment of its members and thus failed to survive. Other
      issues, such as the religious differences among its members, the
      lack of awareness of the founder's own religious orientation, reli-
      gious schisms, the absence of a transcendent ideology, and antago-
      nism from outsiders, also contributed to the commune's demise.

1375. Marini, Stephen A. RADICAL SECTS OF REVOLUTIONARY NEW ENGLAND.
      Cambridge: Harvard University Press, 1982. 213 pp.

Discusses and compares the origins and development of three major
sects, namely the Shakers, the Universalists, and the Free Will
Baptists, all of which came into being in rural New England during
the American Revolution--a period of religious, political, social,
and economic unrest. The author defines a sect as "a new form of
religious culture that emerges from and in opposition to an ante-
cedent tradition" (p. 1). He holds that successful sects bring
into being distinctive social organizations, ideologies, and liturgical symbols. Sectarianism, in his opinion, accounts to a large
degree for American religious pluralism and creates alternative
cultures intent on finding ultimate meaning in the midst of rapid
and violent change.

1376. Marinich, Vladimir G. "Revitalization Movements in Kievan Russia."
       JOURNAL FOR THE SCIENTIFIC STUDY OF RELIGION 15 (1976): 61-68.

Examines, from an anthropological perspective, the rise of new
movements in tenth-century Russia when Christianity was accepted by
the ruling classes. The pagan reactions to Russia's official conversion and the pagan revivals, which have shamanistic features,
are described. These occasional uprisings, led by shamans who had
social and religious power before the advent of Christianity, are
interpreted as struggles for survival and reactions to persecution.

1377. Martin, Bernice. "The Spiritualist Meeting." SOCIOLOGICAL YEAR-
       BOOK OF RELIGION IN BRITAIN 3 (1970): 146-61.

Describes the main features of the Spiritualist religious service
and suggests that its main analogues are to be found in shamanism,
spirit possession, and divination. The author outlines in sequence
the setting in which a Spiritualist meeting takes place and the
main components of the service (hymns and prayers, the medium's
address, and the demonstration of clairvoyance). The labeling of
Spiritualism as a cult or gnostic sect is inadequate, because
Spiritualism is more similar to the religions of some of the small-
scale, nonliterate societies than to the Judeo-Christian tradition.
The differences and similarities between priests, prophets, shamans,
and spiritualist mediums are outlined. Various issues, such as the
nature of the kin and community structures in Spiritualist churches,
are raised.

1378. Matalene, Carolyn. "Women as Witches." INTERNATIONAL JOURNAL OF
       WOMEN STUDIES 1 (1978): 573-87.

Examines the period in European history when witches were persecuted. Relying particularly on data from England, the author
observes that most people accused of witchcraft were women. The
definition of witchcraft was made by the persecutors themselves and
the evidence for the practice of witchcraft came from the persecutors, the witches, and the witnesses called to testify against
them. The social contexts of the persecutions are outlined with
special emphasis on the relationship between witchcraft accusations
and social change. The author thinks that women provided scapegoats for the community of believers. These women, she suggests,
were social outcasts by virtue of their age, that is, they had

outlived the social definition of women as "a biological female
functioning as a wife and mother within the institution of the
family" (p. 584).

1379. Mauss, Armand L. "Moderation in All Things: Political and Social
       Outlooks of Modern Urban Mormons." DIALOGUE: A JOURNAL OF MORMON
       THOUGHT 7.1 (1972): 57-69.

       Contends that the political and social attitudes of most Mormons
       are "moderate" and "mainstream." Political preference, religious
       libertarianism, racism, and anti-Semitism are among the themes
       explored.

1380. Mayers, Marvin K. "The Behavior of Tongues." SPEAKING IN TONGUES:
       LET'S TALK ABOUT IT. Edited by Watson E. Mills. Waco, TX: Word
       Books, 1973, pp. 112-27.

       Studies, from anthropological and linguistic viewpoints, the
       behavior associated with speaking in tongues. Glossolalia, which
       is classified as a distorted pattern of speech, is examined as
       learned behavior and as a system of reciprocating statements and
       responses. The sociocultural background, particularly conflict,
       is related to the use of glossolalia. The underlying values that
       are at its root are discussed.

1381. McIntosh, Christopher. THE ROSY CROSS UNVEILED: THE HISTORY,
       MYTHOLOGY, AND RITUAL OF AN OCCULT ORDER. Wellingborough, En-
       gland: Aquarian Press, 1980. 160 pp.

       Provides a basic history and description of the Rosicrucian Order.
       One chapter is dedicated to the Hermetic Order of the Golden Dawn,
       a magical society that came into being in England in the 1880's and
       still exists today. The modern Rosicrucian Order, particularly in
       America, is described. The author states that this order is not a
       cult nor a philosophical system; rather, it is a solid, coherent
       movement with a recognizable doctrine, code, and set of practices.
       Its members did not give up their allegiance to Christianity. A
       short select bibliography is appended (pp. 156-58).

1382. McLachlan, Hugh V. "Witchcraft and Anti-Feminism." SCOTTISH JOUR-
       NAL OF SOCIOLOGY 4 (1980): 141-58.

       Considers why and to what extent the accusations of witchcraft
       were mainly directed at women and questions whether these accusa-
       tions were simply an expression of an antifeminine mentality.
       Scottish and other European data on witchcraft are compared. The
       following theories are discussed: 1) witchcraft was an attempt by
       women to compensate for their relative lack of social power; 2) the
       persecutions of witches were attacks on women by legal authorities;
       3) witches were essentially folk healers who, though largely female,
       were persecuted for their medical practices; and 4) the persecution
       of witches was a form of scapegoating.

1383. Michaelsen, Robert S. "Enigmas in Interpreting Mormonism." SOCIO-
       LOGICAL ANALYSIS 38 (1977): 145-73.

Discusses, in the context of O'Dea's study on Mormonism (item 229), the sociological problems in classifying and assessing this American religion in the twentieth century. The author detects in Mormonism "an extraordinary combination of this- and other-worldliness, or religious ideology and of practicality" (p. 148). The vitality of Mormonism is seen to rest, in part, in the polarities of human experiences, namely the sacred versus the secular, tradition versus change, and the individual versus community.

1384. Midelfort, H. C. Erik. WITCH HUNTING IN SOUTHWESTERN GERMANY: THE SOCIAL AND INTELLECTUAL FOUNDATIONS. Stanford, CA: Stanford University Press, 1972. viii, 306 pp.

Presents a study of witchcraft in one area of Germany during the sixteenth and seventeenth centuries and, following anthropological research, stresses the fundamental social mechanisms at work and the social patterns of those involved in witch hunts. Two factors that point to the social realities that affected the course of the witchcraft panic, namely the material interests of the witch hunters and the social position of the witches, are examined in detail. Some witch trials may have served the function "of delineating the social threshold of eccentricity tolerable to society, and registering fear of a socially indigestible group, unmarried women" (p. 195). Witch trials, however, tend to increase, rather than decrease, social tensions. The appendix contains a list of trials between 1300-1800. A lengthy bibliography (pp. 261-300) is added.

1385. Miller, Robert L'H. "The Religious Value System of Unitarian Universalists." REVIEW OF RELIGIOUS RESEARCH 17 (1976): 189-208.

Studies the value system of Unitarian Universalists, focusing on their distinctive elements. The author finds that frequency of church attendance, perceived importance of religion, and economic class have little influence on their value patterns. The following values were ranked higher by Unitarian Universalists than by members of other religious and nonreligious groups: 1) terminal values--self-respect, wisdom, inner harmony, mature love, a world of beauty, and exciting love; and 2) instrumental values or qualities in people--love, independence, intellectual activity, imagination, and logic.

1386. Miller, Timothy. "Families Within a Family: Spiritual Values of Hutterites and Unificationists." THE FAMILY AND THE UNIFICATION CHURCH (item 1785), pp. 53-63.

Compares the dual family structure of two communal movements, the Moonies and the Hutterites, the latter also known as the Bruderhof or The Farm. In both groups the sexual and emotional relationships of the married couple are subordinate to, and based on, the spiritual brotherhood of the group as a whole. There are major differences between the two religious groups. The Moonies, unlike the Hutterites, are not an Anabaptist Church, do not live in permanent colonies, and do not till the soil. In spite of these differences, however, the two religious communities look on the nuclear family

as part of a larger family. The author maintains that alienation
from one's biological family is a common problem in contemporary
society. This alienation is intensified when a young adult decides
to join another group that stresses different kinds of family ties
and obligations.

1387. Mitchell, Douglas, and Leonard Plotnicov. "The Lubavitch Movement:
       A Study in Contexts." URBAN ANTHROPOLOGY 4 (1975): 303-15.

       Maintains that the attraction of young American Jews to the mys-
       ticism and enthusiasm of the Lubavitcher Hasidic missionaries is
       motivated by the same forces that draw many young adults to orien-
       tal philosophies and religions, to the establishment of Christian
       communes, and to the rise of fundamentalism. The cultural context
       is held to be essential for an understanding of all these movements.
       The authors trace the local activity, the ethnic context, the his-
       torical background, the international political situation, and the
       religious and cultural situation of the Lubavitcher Jews in Pitts-
       burgh, Pennsylvania in order to expose the unique features of these
       Hasidic Jews.

1388. Moberg, David O. "The Paradox of Modern Evangelical Christianity:
       The United States and Sweden." RELIGION AND BELIEF SYSTEMS (item
       701), pp. 47-99.

       Starts with the observation that the rise of evangelical Chris-
       tianity has been somewhat enigmatic in that it runs counter to the
       secularization trend in Western culture. The author maintains that
       social scientists have slighted and misinterpreted this movement
       and attempts a more sympathetic interpretation. He first describes
       the movement in the United States, noticing its historical context,
       the different kinds of evangelicalism, its social concern, and the
       significant role it plays in American life. Then he describes the
       religious situation in Sweden and compares it to that in the United
       States. The evangelical attitude towards ecumenism is discussed.
       Evangelicalism is said to be a global, and not just a national,
       movement and its presence calls for a reevaluation of the secular-
       ization thesis.

1389. Moberg, David O. "Fundamentals and Evangelicals in Society." THE
       EVANGELICALS: WHAT THEY BELIEVE, WHO THEY ARE, WHERE ARE THEY
       CHANGING. Edited by David F. Wells and John D. Woodridge. Nash-
       ville: Abingdon Press, 1975, pp. 143-69.

       Examines, from a sociological viewpoint, the meaning of evangeli-
       calism through an analysis of those people who join an evangelical
       church, the social relationships within the evangelical movement,
       and its rising strength in contemporary society. The theory of
       deprivation is critically applied to those who join this conserva-
       tive movement. The author states that the social, theological,
       cultural, and ethnic backgrounds of evangelicals are so varied that
       "stereotyped images of evangelicals as low middle-class people are
       unwarranted" (p. 149). The resurgence of evangelicalism is linked
       to secularization and to the human need for commitment.

1390. Monter, E. William. "The Historiography of European Witchcraft:
       Progress and Prospects." JOURNAL OF INTERDISCIPLINARY HISTORY 2
       (1972): 435-51.

       Maintains that the two approaches applied to European witchcraft,
       namely those of intellectual history and social development, are
       complementary. Some main contributions to witchcraft studies are
       discussed. Three ways of studying witchcraft are distinguished:
       1) the rationalist method, in which it is seen as a form of mass
       hysteria; 2) the romantic method, in which it is considered a
       socially oppressed, pre-Christian religion; and 3) the social-
       scientific method, in which it is seen as a result of internal,
       social pressures. Some suggestions for future research are made.

1391. Monter, E. William. "Patterns of Witchcraft in the Jura." JOURNAL
       OF SOCIAL HISTORY 5 (1971): 1-25.

       Investigates the history of witchcraft in the Jura mountains of
       Western Europe (France and Switzerland). The witch trials that
       took place in this region are examined and the author observes that
       not all the accused were women and not all were poor, powerless, or
       deviant. Jura witches were stereotypes found all over Europe. The
       conditions that prevailed during witch trials and the type of accu-
       sations leveled at witches are discussed.

1392. Moore, R. Lawrence. "The Occult Connection?: Mormonism, Christian
       Science, and Spiritualism." THE OCCULT IN AMERICA: NEW HISTORI-
       CAL PERSPECTIVES (item 849), pp. 135-61.

       Speculates on the appeal of the Occult in nineteenth-century
       America by examining the presence of magical and esoteric ideas in
       three religions that came into being during this period. Though
       Mormonism, Christian Science, and Spiritualism are not typical
       representatives of occultism, traces of the occult tradition can be
       found in all of them. Joseph Smith claimed Mormonism was founded
       on ancient wisdom which he recovered in an obscure manner. Mary
       Baker Eddy maintained an inner circle of trusted friends who often
       met in secret. Her early followers were attracted mainly to her
       esoteric culture. Spiritualism, with its attempts to contact the
       spirits of the dead, was associated from the start with the occult
       tradition. The author thinks that Occultism permeated American
       culture in the nineteenth century and that the Occult Movement
       should be understood as a part of a "dominant popular outlook."

1393. Moore, Willard B. "Communal Experiments as Resolutions of Sectar-
       ian Identity Crises." INTERNATIONAL REVIEW OF MODERN SOCIOLOGY
       6.1 (1976): 85-102.

       Discusses a group of Russian Spiritual Christians calling them-
       selves "Molokans," who emigrated to America in 1904. After a his-
       torical sketch of this religious sect that was formed as a splinter
       group from the Doukhobors, the author looks into two Molokan experi-
       ments in communal settlement, one in Canada, the other in the
       United States. Several factors that undermined these experiments
       are examined.

1394. Moran, Gerald F. "Conditions of Religious Conversion in the First
       Society of Norwich, Connecticut, 1718-1744." JOURNAL OF SOCIAL
       HISTORY 5 (1972): 331-43.

       Discusses conversions to Puritanism and seeks to add a new per-
       spective to Puritan religious behavior by examining the sociocul-
       tural conditions of the eighteenth century. Age, sex, marital
       status, familial relationships, and the economic and social status
       of converts are taken into consideration. The author thinks that
       new converts "were trying to solve more complex demands arising
       from conditions of crisis similar to those faced by Elizabethan
       Puritans--deteriorating social institutions, growing divergence
       between 'operational and ideal values,' breakdown in parental
       control, and increasing population and mobility" (p. 339).

1395. Morton, A. L. THE WORLD OF THE RANTERS: RELIGIOUS RADICALISM IN THE
       ENGLISH REVOLUTION. London: Lawrence and Wishart, 1970. 224 pp.

       Contains several of the author's essays, some of which had been
       previously published. The main topic discussed throughout is the
       relationship between religion and politics in seventeenth-century
       Britain. The author attempts to show why certain kinds of reli-
       gious and political behavior go together. One essay is dedicated
       to a discussion on the Ranters, an extreme, unorganized group that
       flourished during the English Revolution. The author demonstrates
       how their political views were the outcome of their antinomian,
       pantheistic mysticism.

1396. Moses, Wilson Jeremiah. BLACK MESSIAHS AND UNCLE TOMS: SOCIAL AND
       LITERARY MANIFESTATIONS OF A RELIGIOUS MYTH. University Park:
       Pennsylvania State University Press, 1982. xii, 278 pp.

       Explores the social and literary expressions of Black messianism
       that is considered to be a powerful myth that has permeated the
       thinking of both Blacks and Whites. The myth, in the author's
       view, serves the function of motivating Black advancement. Among
       the Black religious movements discussed are: 1) that initiated by
       Marcus Garvey; 2) the Black Muslims; and 3) the Black Jews. There
       are also references to the Father Divine Movement and to other mes-
       sianic figures, including that of Jim Jones. Black messianism is
       essentially a Christian movement that is related to American destiny.

1397. Mullett, Michael. "From Sect to Denomination?: Social Developments
       in Eighteenth-Century Quakerism." JOURNAL OF RELIGIOUS HISTORY
       13 (1984): 168-91.

       Examines the "appropriateness of the model of sect and denomina-
       tion to the life of the early Quakers" (p. 170). The following
       features that usually represent the sect-denomination dichotomy are
       discussed: isolation-cultural integration; relationships with other
       churches; group behavioral rules; the practice of endogamy or exog-
       amy; the use of excommunication; attitudes toward education and
       scholarship; and the emergence of a formal ministry. The author
       thinks that the Quakers cannot be easily classified into a sect or
       a denomination.

1398. Munters, Q. J. "Recruitment as a Vocation: The Case of Jehovah's
       Witnesses." SOCIOLOGIA NEERLANDICA 2 (1971): 88-100.

       Attempts a sociological interpretation of the missionary activi-
       ties of the Jehovah's Witnesses. The goals and motives of their
       missionary work are analyzed in the context of the author's first-
       hand investigation of this religious group in Utrecht. The origins,
       growth, and recruitment policies of the Witnesses are outlined.
       The focus in on what the author calls "external recruitment", that
       is, the readiness to accept outsiders as members and the tendency
       to reject cultural elements that are deemed incompatible with the
       movement. It is argued that the attraction to Jehovah's Witnesses
       "cannot be explained solely on the grounds of a certain dissatis-
       faction with the situation of the outsider" (p. 95). Various
       deprivations that must also be taken into account to explain the
       conversion process are discussed.

1399. Neff, H. Richard. "The Cultural Basis for Glossolalia in the Twen-
       tieth Century." SPEAKING IN TONGUES: LET'S TALK ABOUT IT. Ed-
       ited by Watson E. Mills. Waco, TX: Word Books, 1973, pp. 26-35.

       Assumes that glossolalia is "just one experience among the many
       ecstatic experiences that are associated with religious revivals"
       (p. 27), which have usually occurred when people experienced dislo-
       cation. Religious revivals are related to cultural changes that
       take place when mobility increases. The emergence of glossolalia
       in the twentieth century is traced to Los Angeles in 1906 when many
       people began to move to urban areas. The growth of the movement in
       the 1920's and 1930's is also related to heavy migrations from rural
       farming areas to the cities. Various needs that glossolalia satis-
       fies are enumerated. The author thinks that glossolalia is a rite
       of passage that gives people a sense of security by membership in an
       elite group. Pentecostalism and speaking in tongues are also part
       of the counterculture movement within the Christian churches.

1400. Nelson, Charles H. "The Eric Janssonist Movement of Pre-Industrial
       Sweden." SOCIOLOGICAL ANALYSIS 38 (1977): 209-25.

       Studies a nineteenth-century religious sect in Sweden as a social
       movement and explores its structural implications. The processes
       of sectarian development, which led to its origin and spread, are
       seen not as an exclusively intrachurch controversy, but rather as
       part of a wide range of social encounters. The author attempts to
       show how three typical modes of consciousness common to the period,
       namely the conservative, traditional pietist, and liberal humani-
       tarian, throw light on sectarian action and reaction, which led to
       the formation of the sect as a distinct entity. Various charis-
       matic signs and theological symbols are used to assess the movement,
       both from the members' point of view and that of its detractors.
       Sectarian movements, according to the author, emerge out of con-
       flict and change.

1401. Nelson, Charles H. "Toward a More Accurate Approximation of the
       Class Composition of the Erik Janssonists." SWEDISH PIONEER
       HISTORICAL QUARTERLY 26.1 (1975): 3-15.

Examines the wave of immigrants of the members of the Erik Janssonist sect and evaluates the previous estimates of their social-
class background. It is concluded that these immigrants were
neither largely lower-class workers nor prosperous farmers. Those
with the least economic potential in their country of origin,
Sweden, comprised only one third of the group's membership.

1402. Nelson, Geoffrey K. "The Membership of a Cult: The Spiritualists
        National Union." REVIEW OF RELIGIOUS RESEARCH 13 (1972): 170-77.

        Defines a cult as "a religious movement which makes a fundamental
        break with religious tradition of a culture and which is a) com-
        posed of individuals who have or seek mystical, psychic, or
        ecstatic experiences, and b) is concerned with the problems of
        individuals" (p. 171). Cults tend to prosper during periods of
        rapid social change. The author examines the Spiritualist National
        Union in Great Britain to determine the characteristics of its
        members. It is theorized that people join cults either 1) because
        they have become disillusioned by the churches, or 2) after they
        have had a mystical experience, or 3) because they have embarked on
        a positive search for meaning. The social composition of member-
        ship of the Spiritualist National Union is mainly middle-class and
        occupationally mobile. Among the determining factors leading to
        cult membership is the influence of parents, relatives, and friends
        and the healing and comfort that cults offer in time of grief.

1403. Ness, Robert C. "The Impact of Indigenous Healing Activity: An
        Empirical Study of Two Fundamentalist Churches." SOCIAL SCIENCE
        AND MEDICINE 14B (1980): 167-80.

        Studies two fundamentalist Christian churches in Newfoundland
        focusing on religious healing rituals that are their primary re-
        sponse to illness and misfortune. The author explores the rela-
        tionship between physical and psychological complaints of ill
        health and participation in religious rituals and finds that people
        who take part in such rituals are likely to report fewer symptoms
        of psychological distress. He also observes that "participation in
        specific religious activities in Northwest Harbor (a pseudonym) is
        largely structured in terms of social roles" (p. 174). A useful
        bibliography of 82 items (pp. 178-80) is added.

1404. Nickless, Karen K., and Pamela J. Nickless. "Trustees, Deacons,
        and Deaconesses: The Temporal Role of the Shaker Sisters, 1820-
        1890." COMMUNAL STUDIES 7 (1987): 16-24.

        Points out that the part played by women in Shaker communities
        became gradually more active and that the men resisted the women's
        acquisition of equal privileges and responsibilities. The roles of
        trustees, deacons, and deaconesses are examined with special atten-
        tion given to the financial relationship between the sexes. It is
        concluded that Shaker sisters were not viewed as equal partners
        till the late nineteenth century. The increasing involvement of
        women in finances and industries may have been the result of their
        larger number in Shaker colonies. The authors suggest that the
        sisters may have been trying to change the church into a feminist
        institution.

1405. Nudelman, Arthur E. "The Maintenance of Christian Science in
       Scientific Society." MARGINAL MEDICINE (item 715), pp. 42-60.

       Speculates on how Christian Science has survived in modern secu-
       lar societies. Three major factors that are relevant to the main-
       tenance of Christian Science faith are discussed: 1) the beneficial
       effects on physical and emotional health; 2) several institutional
       concessions to reality that have kept some confrontations with
       society at bay; and 3) individual behavior and belief, such as sug-
       gestion and unintentional, health-promoting customs like abstinence
       from tobacco and alcohol. The author holds that certain beliefs
       and practices of Christian Science (and of other healing cults)
       "enhance the viability" of the group.

1406. Nudelman, Arthur E. "Christian Science and Secular Science: Adap-
       tation on the College Scene." JOURNAL FOR THE SCIENTIFIC STUDY
       OF RELIGION 11 (1972): 271-76.

       Examines the attitudes towards, and involvement in, the secular
       sciences of Christian Science college students. The author found
       that while Christian Scientists were less likely than other stu-
       dents to major in the behavioral and life sciences, they were no
       less likely to major in the physical sciences and more likely to
       major in engineering. Devoted Christian Scientists were more apt
       to choose science than nondevoted members. The author speculates
       that they enter the field of physical science for two reasons:
       1) scientists are often confronted with evidence to change their
       view about the inanimate world and 2) Christian Science stresses
       success in worldly endeavors.

1407. Nudelman, Arthur E. "Dimensions of Religiosity: A Factor-Analytic
       View of Protestants, Catholics, and Christian Scientists." RE-
       VIEW OF RELIGIOUS RESEARCH 13 (1971): 42-56.

       Compares the religiosity of Christian Scientists with members of
       other churches. The following nine variables are examined: devo-
       tionalism, orthodoxy, experience, ritualism, communal involvement,
       knowledge, particularism, ethicalism, and friendship. These themes
       are then related to four major components of religiosity, namely
       belief, experience, knowledge, and lesson-sermon. Specific Chris-
       tian Science practices, such as membership in the Mother Church,
       weekly church attendance, testimonies, and the role of the practi-
       tioner, are also considered. Devotion and ritual participation
       stand out as distinctive features of Christian Science.

1408. Nudelman, Arthur E., and Barbara E. Nudelman. "Health and Illness
       Behavior of Christian Scientists." SOCIAL SCIENCE AND MEDICINE
       6 (1972): 253-62.

       Describes the Christian Science view of sin, sickness, and death,
       stressing that Christian Scientists do not believe in faith healing
       and that sometimes they do offer recourse to physicians for "mech-
       anical problems" (including bone fractures and dental and visual
       problems). The sick-role behavior of members of Christian Science
       is compared to that of nonmembers and a typology of the former is
       constructed.

1409.   Olim, Spencer C. "The Oneida Community and the Instability of
        Charismatic Authority." JOURNAL OF AMERICAN HISTORY 67 (1980):
        285-300.

        Speculates on the reasons why the nineteenth-century Oneida Com-
        munity failed to survive after several decades of successful exis-
        tence. John Humphrey Noyes's charismatic leadership is described
        and the problem of charismatic succession and the challenge to
        his authority by a rival group led by James Towner discussed. The
        breakup of Oneida is interpreted as the result of a classic Weber-
        ian conflict over legitimate domination, which led to the failure
        of charisma to become routinized and for charismatic authority to
        become transformed into legal authority.

1410.   Olshan, Marc A. "Modernity, Folk Society, and the Old Order Amish:
        An Alternative Explanation." RURAL SOCIOLOGY 46 (1981): 297-309.

        Rejects the position of those who depict the Amish as an "unre-
        flective, unselfconscious, folk society" that is largely anachro-
        nistic, representing an early stage of cultural development. The
        author discovers that Amish society differs more from the typical
        folk society than from modern culture. He insists that the Amish
        are modern in the sense that they control their self-development
        and consciously maintain their level of technology and their form
        of social organization.

1411.   O'Sullivan, Ralph G. "Structure, Function, and Cognitive Develop-
        ment in Cursillo: An Interactionist Analysis." SOCIOLOGICAL
        SPECTRUM 8 (1988): 257-75.

        Discusses the Cursillo Movement, which aims at revitalizing or
        converting people through short courses in Christian education and
        socialization. A brief history of this Catholic movement, which
        originated in Spain in the 1930's, is given. Three stages of so-
        ciolinguistic integration of Cursillo members are distinguished:
        the preparatory stage, the interactional stage, and the participa-
        tory stage. The themes and activities of each stage (or day) are
        described. Religious conversion and revival in Cursillo are dis-
        cussed and some criticisms of the movement are raised. The author
        thinks that the Cursillo programs "provide their participants with
        direct contact with primary relationships with whom they interact
        on a regular basis" (p. 273).

1412.   Owen, Alex. "Women and Nineteenth-Century Spiritualism: Strategies
        in the Subversion of Femininity." DISCIPLES OF FAITH: STUDIES IN
        RELIGION, POLITICS, AND PATRIARCHY. Edited by Jim Obelkevitch,
        Lyndal Roper, and Raphael Samuel. London: Routledge and Kegan
        Paul, 1987, pp. 130-53.

        Argues that Spiritualism allowed women the kind of freedom of
        language and behavior they would not have enjoyed outside the cir-
        cle of believers. Spiritualists were concerned with women's issues
        and discussed them openly. They regarded women as good trance
        mediums because they were able to surrender to the Spirit. The
        author examines the condition of trance and suggests that during

trance, unconscious desires and impulses were expressed, thus making women aware of themselves as powerful individuals. Women Spiritualists were able to reformulate the passive and subservient image of women.

1413. Owens, Joseph. DREAD: THE RASTAFARIANS OF JAMAICA. London: Heinemann, 1976. xix, 282 pp.

Presents a study of the Rastafarian Movement, which the author considers to be a symbolical "dialectical representation of a society and indeed of an entire epoch of history" (p. 2). It is the main theme of this book that Rastafarian theology revolves around the experience of "dread," that is, the "fearful confrontation of a people with a primordial but historically denied racial selfhood" (p. 3). The Rastafarian worldview is described in the words of those who are part of the movement. The origin and development of Rastafarianism, its location, and its membership are briefly sketched. The main theological and ideological views the Rastafarians have about their identity, their oppressors, their conversion, their special knowledge, and their apocalyptic vision are outlined in the context of their major experience of "dread."

1414. Paris, Arthur E. BLACK PENTECOSTALISM: SOUTHERN RELIGION IN AN URBAN WORLD. Amherst: University of Massachusetts Press, 1982. vii, 180 pp.

Offers a study of three Boston congregations of the Mount Calvary Holy Church of America, Incorporated, an offshoot of the Black Holiness-Pentecostal churches that developed in the post-Civil War period and expressed a racial rupture within the movement. The author gives a short history of this Church and then focuses on the social and historical backgrounds of the Boston congregations. The life of the church is discussed in terms of its ritual, which exemplifies the way people give meaning to the world around them. The church's organization, social life, and relationship to the outside world are considered. The author thinks that these churches are not exotic and peculiar cults, but rather "a viable development, rooted in a particular moment of Southern religious history" (p. 139).

1415. Parker, Gordon, and Hilary Tapling. "The Chiropractic Patient: Psychosocial Aspects." MEDICAL JOURNAL OF AUSTRALIA 2 (1976): 373-76.

Examines 84 patients who went for the first time to an Australian-trained chiropractor in order to determine some of the psychosocial aspects influencing their accounts and responses to the new treatment. The healing effects of the treatment and the characteristics of chiropractors are among the topics briefly discussed. It is concluded that these patients do not differ from the general population. They are "normal" people "whose condition has not been catered to by medical techniques" (p. 375) and who turn to a chiropractor as a last resort for the relief of their ailments.

1416. Parkin, Christine. "The Salvation Army and Social Questions of the Day." SOCIOLOGICAL YEARBOOK OF RELIGION IN BRITAIN 5 (1972): 103-118.

Examines the Salvation Army's approach to the problem of poverty
between 1865-1890. The ideology of the movement is traced to Wesleyan theological thought. General Booth, the Salvation Army's
founder, was convinced that his message of salvation was not one of
resignation and submission to poverty, but rather a religious call
to combat poverty by making rich people aware of their obligations.
Booth's scheme to relieve the poverty of the underprivileged is
outlined. The Army's survival as one of the leading voluntary
agencies in the West testifies to the movement's success.

1417.   Parssinen, Terry A. "Professional Deviants and the History of
        Medicine: Medical Mesmerists in Victorian Britain." ON THE MAR-
        GINS OF SCIENCE (item 712), pp. 113-20.

        Suggests that Mesmerism was shunned by the medical profession in
        Britain in the mid-nineteenth century because 1) its practitioners
        required no special training or formal education, 2) it presented
        an economic challenge to orthodox medicine, and 3) it had features
        similar to the practices of magicoreligious healers. Mesmerists
        not only challenged medical theory and practice, but also threatened
        the social and political goals of the reformers. They were branded
        as "deviants." The author thinks that an exploration of the role
        of mesmerists is needed for an understanding of the history of
        medicine.

1418.   Penton, M. James. APOCALYPSE DELAYED: THE STORY OF JEHOVAH'S WIT-
        NESSES. Toronto: University of Toronto Press, 1985. xviii,
        400 pp.

        Presents a study of a particular community of Jehovah's Witnesses
        which, contrary to prediction, has not become an institutionalized
        and accommodated sect (denomination), but has maintained its hos-
        tility to society. The history, major doctrines, and organization
        of the group are described. Millennialism has been the Witnesses'
        main basis for growth and success, but also their greatest weakness.
        The author's view is that Jehovah's Witnesses will eventually have
        to come to terms with the world. Besides copious footnotes, this
        volume includes an annotated bibliography of the major scholarly
        works on Jehovah's Witnesses, a list of scholarly articles on the
        movement, and a list of its own publications.

1419.   Peter, Karl A. THE DYNAMICS OF HUTTERITE SOCIETY: AN ANALYTICAL
        APPROACH. Edmonton: University of Alberta Press, 1987. xxiii,
        232 pp.

        Contains 13 previously published essays authored or coauthored
        by Karl Peter. The material is divided into five main sections:
        1) religion and history; 2) religion and the social structure;
        3) demography; 4) contemporary social changes; and 5) ethnic rela-
        tions. The author sees the Hutterite phenomenon "as an ongoing
        sociocultural entity constantly adapting to environmental, politi-
        cal, and social circumstances" (xiii).

1420.   Peter, Karl A. "The Certainty of Salvation: Ritualization of Reli-
        gion and Economic Rationality Among Hutterites." COMPARATIVE
        STUDIES IN SOCIETY AND HISTORY 25 (1983): 222-40.

Proposes that the contradiction between the traditional and rational aspects of Hutterite society be approached in the context of Weber's theory regarding the Protestant ethic. The rational dimension of Hutterite economics is seen as an adaptive response for survival in a host culture. The ideal religious interests of the Hutterites became ritualized while the material concerns remained under the control of reason.

1421.   Peter, Karl A. "The Decline of Hutterite Population Growth." CANADIAN ETHNIC STUDIES 12.3 (1980): 97-110.

Attempts to explain the reversal of the growth of the Hutterite population since the 1960's, a reversal caused by the impact with modern technological society. The author sees a definite correlation between fertility, structural stability, opportunities for expansion, and a value system favorable to high fertility. The adoption of technology by the Hutterites has had serious repercussions on their division of labor and has led to the postponement of marriage. A critical response and the author's reply are included (pp. 111-123).

1422.   Peter, Karl A. "The Death of Hutterite Culture: A Rejoinder." PHYLON 14 (1979): 189-94.

Responds to article of Frideres (item 1267) who holds that the Canadian provincial governments are contributing to the demise of the Hutterite culture. Peter contends that these conclusions are artificial; they have not been derived from empirical observations nor tested in an appropriate setting. He concludes that "there is no danger whatsoever of Hutterite culture dying at the hand of Western Canadian Governments" (p. 194). The Hutterites, he thinks, will successfully adapt to modern changes.

1423.   Peter, Karl A., Edward D. Boldt, Ian Whitaker, and Lance W. Roberts. "The Dynamics of Religious Defection Among the Hutterites." JOURNAL FOR THE SCIENTIFIC STUDY OF RELIGION 21 (1982): 327-37.

Reflects on significant transformations in contemporary Hutterite values and practices and examines the accompanying serious increase in permanent defections from this Anabaptist sect in North America. The researchers focus on the evangelical appeal to the Hutterites and how conversion eases the process of defection. The origin of Hutterite belief, particularly that regarding salvation, and their application to contemporary times are discussed. Individualism is making its appearance in Hutterite life, thus intensifying their susceptibility and accessibility to evangelical overtures. Proselytizing agents are recording greater success in their missions because the Hutterite community is not as closed as it might appear to be. The Hutterites' own attempts to win converts often result in the loss of their members. The trend toward individual autonomy and decision making is one of the reasons why Hutterite lifestyle faces the serious problem of survival in contemporary society.

1424.   Peter, Karl A., and Ian Whitaker. "The Acquisition of Personal Property Among Hutterites and Its Social Dimension." ANTHROPO-LOGICA 23.2 (1982): 145-55.

Documents the growing practice among the Hutterites of setting apart specific articles and products as private property, which is a departure from the traditional ideal of communal living and sharing of goods. The social consequences of this new practice are stressed. Redefinition of community goods has been a continuing process in the history of the Hutterites who, thus, avert major discontinuities and make changes without directly challenging traditional norms. The study of the Hutterite ideology of private property shows the role of informal social control in the process of cultural change.

1425. Peter, Karl A., and Ian Whitaker. "The Changing Role of Hutterite Women." PRAIRIE FORUM 7 (1982): 267-77.

Discusses the role of Hutterite women, a role that, together with other aspects of their culture, is undergoing many changes. The religiously supported male authority that legitimized male/female difference is now under pressure. The Hutterite stress on individual salvation has an egalitarian component attractive to women and conducive to changes in self-perception and in their level of dependence on men. The same theology can have an impact on courtship and marriage customs, on education, and on the lifestyle of the community as a whole. Material changes have also brought about not only modernization in equipment, but also changes of roles and work assignments. Though formal authority and power structures have remained the same, the authors observe that the current trend will lead to further changes among the Hutterites.

1426. Peters, Victor. "The Process of Colony Division Among the Hutterites: A Case Study." INTERNATIONAL REVIEW OF MODERN SOCIOLOGY 6.1 (1976): 57-64.

Explains the system of Hutterite colony division when the population reaches around 150 members. The author examines the Minnesota Big Stone colony division and thinks that such splits lead to an increase in agriculture production and industrial diversity that might eventually bring about changes in the social structure.

1427. Petrunik, Michael A. "Seeing the Light: A Study of Conversion to Alcoholics Anonymous." JOURNAL OF VOLUNTARY ACTION RESEARCH 1 (1972): 30-38.

Maintains that Alcoholics Anonymous "has many features of religious sects or cults, perhaps most notably a model of resocialization as conversion or redemption" (p. 30). The author examines the imputation of moral meaning to drunkenness and the ways in which members of this alcohol-rehabilitation organization reconstruct the phase of their moral career before they joined Alcoholic Anonymous. Conversion is then explored in some detail. It is pointed out that conversion to Alcoholic Anonymous requires the acceptance of a radically new meaning system amounting to a moral rebirth. The "Twelve Steps" of the new ideology are a religious statement about the need and means of regeneration. Among the mechanisms of coping with failure and guilt are laughter and joking, self-forgiveness, confession to a sympathetic audience, elevation ceremonies, and social integration.

1428. Pickering, W. S. F. "Hutterites and Problems of Persistence and
       Social Control in Religious Communities." ARCHIVES DE SCIENCES
       SOCIALES DES RELIGIONS 44 (1977): 75-92.

       Prefers to understand the Hutterites in the United States and
       Canada not as a sect, but rather as a religious community or order,
       that is "a group of people who are closely associated with one
       another for the purpose of leading a distinctly religious way of
       life" (p. 75). The origin of the Hutterites and their history in
       the United States and Canada are briefly traced. Because the Hut-
       terites maintain their numbers not by conversions, but by internal
       growth, social control is a major necessary mechanism for keeping
       their membership from declining. The Hutterites maintain their
       geographic and ideological distance from the larger society and use
       disciplinary measures to maintain their isolation. Whether and to
       what extent these mechanisms can survive in the modern world is
       debated.

1429. Procter-Smith, Marjorie. WOMEN IN SHAKER COMMUNITY AND WORSHIP: A
       FEMINIST ANALYSIS OF THE USES OF RELIGIOUS SYMBOLISM. Lewistown,
       NY: Edwin Mellen Press, 1985. xvii, 253 pp.

       Attempts to clarify our understanding of historic Shakerism and
       its relevance to current feminist theological concerns, especially
       the maleness of God and Christ. The origin of the Shakers as a
       charismatic community and its development into an institutionalized
       form of communal living are traced. The role of women in worship
       services is described and the portrait of a woman that emerges from
       Shaker spirituality, hymns, and songs is outlined. The author
       thinks that the Shaker criticism of male-centered theology still
       has relevance today for it anticipates some of the religious con-
       cerns expressed in current feminist theology. Liturgical changes
       that the Shakers initiated took place in a social context similar
       to that of the twentieth century, namely one that restricts and
       degrades women.

1430. Rausch, Paul A. MESSIANIC JUDAISM: ITS HISTORY, THEOLOGY, AND
       POLITY. New York: Edwin Mellen Press, 1982. xviii, 283 pp.

       Presents a history of Hebrew Christianity covering its renais-
       sance in the beginning of the nineteenth century and its more
       recent revival in the last two decades. The distinctive messianic
       character of a Hebrew-Christian congregation is outlined and its
       theology explained. There is a chapter dedicated to each of the
       following congregations: the Messianic Jewish Congregation of Min-
       neapolis, the Ben Yeshua Congregation of Philadelphia, and Beth
       Messiah in the Washington, D.C. area. Information on the Union of
       Messianic Jewish Congregations is provided and the conflict between
       Jews and Messianic Jews in Toronto described. A final chapter
       deals with the general Christian and Jewish responses to Messianic
       Jews. A useful bibliography is added (pp. 263-75).

1431. Reay, Barry. "Quakerism and Society." RADICAL RELIGION IN THE
       ENGLISH REVOLUTION. Edited by J. F. McGregor and Barry Reay.
       New York: Oxford University Press, 1984, pp. 141-64.

Explores the religious and political backgrounds of those who
joined the Quaker Movement in the seventeenth century and the sect's
socioeconomic composition. Some of the radical views of the Quakers
are described. Dissatisfaction with the central government was one
reason why Quakerism flourished. The impact of the movement on
society and the latter's reaction to its presence are assessed.
The governing class reacted negatively to Quakerism because Quakers
were believed to promote social anarchy. Hostility to the Quakers
was one of the factors that contributed to the restoration of the
Stuarts in 1660. The author thinks that the main political impact
of Quakerism was to stimulate political conservatism.

1432. Reay, Barry. "The Social Origins of Early Quakerism." JOURNAL OF
       INTERDISCIPLINARY HISTORY 11.1 (1980): 55-72.

       Outlines and reviews the scholarly debate on the social origins
       of the Quakers and summarizes the author's research on the subject.
       The view endorsed by the author is that the social structure of
       early Quakerism differed from that of the population as a whole.
       Quakerism attracted members mainly from the well-to-do rural areas.

1433. Reay, Barry. "The Muggletonians: A Study of Seventeenth-century
       English Sectarianism." JOURNAL OF RELIGIOUS HISTORY 9 (1976):
       32-49.

       Deals with the sectarian features of the Muggletonians, one of
       the sects that emerged during the English Revolution. Its leader-
       ship, organization, social composition, and distribution are sum-
       marized. The Muggletonians are presented as an excellent example
       of a sect in conflict with society.

1434. Redekop, Calvin. "The Social Ecology of Communal Socialization."
       INTERNATIONAL REVIEW OF MODERN SOCIOLOGY 6.1 (1976): 113-25.

       Analyzes the socialization practices of contemporary communes
       with special reference to two Mennonite communities. The con-
       stituents of formal socialization, namely technical and religious
       education and social training, and of informal socialization,
       namely the learning of religious rules, social roles, values, and
       beliefs, are outlined and comparisons made between the two groups.
       The author's view is that the relationship between the Mennonite
       communities and the cultural and social environment of the larger
       society directly influences the forms of socialization.

1435. Rettig, Richard P. "Mormonism as a System of Deviant Behavior in
       American Society." PROCEEDINGS OF THE ANNUAL MEETING OF THE
       ASSOCIATION FOR THE SCIENTIFIC STUDY OF RELIGION, SOUTHWEST,
       1980. 9 pp.

       Illustrates, largely from historical data, how Mormonism deviates
       significantly from mainline culture and religion in social customs,
       processes, and organization. Two common American social customs,
       namely the celebration of July Fourth as the biggest national
       holiday and drinking coffee at breakfast, are discussed in the
       context of Mormon values and practices. Dietary habits and tithing

set Mormons apart. Their educational system is cohesive and ethnocentric and its welfare system and economic goals are unique. Some
Mormon religious customs, such as relief programs for the poor and
the required two-year missionary service for all young adults,
stress the distinctive nature of the Mormon subculture as a whole.

1436. Reuther, Rosemary Radford. "Women in Utopian Movements." WOMEN
      AND RELIGION IN AMERICA, VOL. 1: THE NINETEENTH CENTURY. Edited
      by Rosemary Radford Reuther and Rosemary Skinner Keller. San
      Francisco: Harper and Row, 1981, pp. 46-100.

      Reflects on four aspects of utopian communities that flourished
      in the second half of the nineteenth century in America: 1) the
      androgynous God and the new communities; 2) the issue of marriage;
      3) patterns of female leadership; and 4) utopianism and feminism.
      These movements are interpreted as "a protest of the preindustrial,
      agrarian, handicraft economy against the alienation of the new
      industrialized world" (p. 53). They also stimulated radical specu-
      lation about women's social roles. Seventeen documents from various
      sources, including Shakerism, Christian Science, and Mormonism, are
      reproduced.

1437. Reuther, Rosemary Radford, and Catherine M. Prelinger. "Women in
      Sectarian and Utopian Groups." WOMEN AND RELIGION IN AMERICA,
      VOL. 2: THE COLONIAL AND REVOLUTIONARY PERIODS. Edited by Rose-
      mary Radford Reuther and Rosemary Skinner Keller. San Francisco:
      Harper and Row, 1983, pp. 260-315.

      Examines briefly the role women played among the seventeenth-
      century Quakers, the Ephrato Cloister (in Lancaster County, Penn-
      sylvania), and the Moravian Brethren. The lives and works of two
      female messiahs of the revolutionary war era, namely Mother Ann
      Lee (1736-84) and Jemima Wilkinson (1752-1819), are briefly de-
      scribed. The authors point out that the advocacy of women's
      spiritual and administrative powers was strong, especially at the
      beginning of the nineteenth century. Fourteen documents dealing
      with these religious groups are given.

1438. Richardson, James T. "New Forms of Deviancy in a Fundamentalist
      Church: A Case Study." REVIEW OF RELIGIOUS RESEARCH 16 (1975):
      134-40.

      Discusses the events leading to the dismissal of a loyal, doc-
      trinally sound member of a fundamentalist church for disagreeing
      with the financial handling of church funds. The political nature
      of the deviancy is discussed in the context of social theory, that
      is, in terms of boundary maintenance, moral entrepreneurship, and
      degradation ceremonies. The author thinks that the incident might
      lead to a devaluation of doctrinal matters and to the admission
      that some churches are seen as businesses rather than religious
      institutions.

1439. Robbins, Thomas. "Religious Mass Suicide Before Jonestown: The
      Russian Old Believers." SOCIOLOGICAL ANALYSIS 47 (1986): 1-20.

Focuses on a comparative analysis between the suicides of tens of thousands of "old Believers" in seventeenth- and eighteenth-century Russia and those of Jonestown. A description of the Russian case, where members of the schismatic Old Believers Movement committed mass suicide at a monastery or peasant commune, is provided and the reasons that led to the apocalyptic despair and suicidal frenzy examined. Both groups were beset by apocalyptic pessimism and a sense that evil had triumphed on earth; both failed to resolve the strident confrontation with the perceived demonic powers and authorities.

1440. Roemer, Kenneth M. "Sex Roles, Utopia, and Change: The Family in Late Nineteenth-Century Utopian Literature." AMERICAN STUDIES 13.2 (1982): 33-47.

Distinguishes three types of ideal families that utopian communities strove for: 1) the conventional Victorian family; 2) the feminist-oriented family that freed women from economic dependence on men; and 3) the ideal family that eliminated both the economic and social differences between the sexes. The utopian literature that advances reform in family structure not only offers various examples of attitudes towards sex roles that were seen as problematic, but also helps us understand the mixture of old and new values, which reformers and utopians tried to incorporate in communal societies.

1441. Rohrlich, Ruby. "The Shakers: Gender Equality in Hierarchy." WOMEN IN SEARCH OF UTOPIA: MAVERICKS AND MYTHMAKERS (item 459), pp. 54-61.

Gives a brief account of the origins of the Shakers and of some of the basic features of their community. The Shakers are depicted as liberal gnostic Christians and sexual egalitarians whose view of God is expressed in both male and female images. Men and women in Shaker communities participated equally in religious matters, governance, and politics.

1442. Rowe, David L. "A New Perspective on the Burned-Over District: The Millerites in Upstate New York." CHURCH HISTORY 47 (1978): 408-20.

Examines critically Cross's theory of the early nineteenth-century religious revivals in Western New York State (see item 171) and suggests that the mistrust of the mainline churches coupled with the belief that truth can be attained without theological training help account for the rise of sects during this period. The emergence of Millerism is taken as an example of the author's position. The Millerites' hostility against the worldliness of the mainline churches and their clergy is described.

1443. Rudy, David R., and Arthur L. Greil. "Is Alcoholics Anonymous a Religious Organization?: Meditations on Marginality." SOCIOLOGICAL ANALYSIS 50 (1988): 41-51.

Questions whether Alcoholics Anonymous can be considered a religious organization and maintains that "both the religious features of A.A. and the denial of A.A.'s religious nature are integral to

the structure and functioning of the organization" (p. 44). The
authors trace the roots of Alcoholics Anonymous to the Moral Rearmament Movement (the Oxford Group) and explore whether it can be
called a religion. They think that the ideology of Alcoholics
Anonymous is quasi-religious in character and that the tension
between the sacred and the secular is an essential part of its
program.

1444. Rudy, David R., and Arthur L. Greil. "Taking the Pledge: The Commitment Process of Alcoholics Anonymous." SOCIOLOGICAL FOCUS 20
(1987): 45-59.

Develops a four-stage model of the commitment process and then
applies it to an Alcoholics Anonymous group in a Midwestern city.
The following four stages are described: 1) managing tension;
2) escalating commitment and encapsulation; 3) solidification of
ideological commitment and the commitment act; and 4) demonstrating
and reaffirming commitment.

1445. Ruff, Ivan. "Baha'i--The Invisible Community." NEW SOCIETY 29
(September 12, 1974): 665-68.

Describes the main features of the Baha'i Faith, a religion without a church, that embraces a program of social change with a
policy of quietism and conformism and that has a strong sense of
social cohesion and family unity. The author explores the reasons
why this sect has persisted and grown since its origin in the
nineteenth century. He theorizes that its success may partly stem
from its worldview "of general enlightened liberalism unrelated to
specific problems, with a belief in a benevolent destiny" (p. 668).
Further, Baha'ism lives in relative harmony with society and builds
strong social networks among its members. The average Baha'i member is communally oriented, peaceful, and free from strife, exploitation, and alienation.

1446. Rushby, William F., and John C. Thrush. "Mennonites and Social
Compassion: The Rokeach Hypothesis Considered." REVIEW OF RELI-
GIOUS RESEARCH 15 (1973): 16-28.

Criticizes Milton Rokeach's view that orthodox Christianity fosters "uncompassionate social attitudes." The relationship between
religious orthodoxy and compassionate values is examined through a
sample of Mennonite students attending Goshen Mennonite College.
These students were measured on the Rokeach Terminal Value Scale
and were found to be highly orthodox and socially compassionate.

1447. Russell, Jeffrey B. A HISTORY OF WITCHCRAFT: SORCERERS, HERETICS,
AND PAGANS. New York: Thomas and Hudson, 1980. 192 pp.

Provides a historical overview of witchcraft in various cultures.
European witchcraft since the Middle Ages is treated at some length
and the relationship between witchcraft and society is carefully
examined. The author maintains that the history of witchcraft is
"also an attempt to understand the social conditions and interactions that encouraged the development of the concept" (p. 109).

European witchcraft had important social functions, such as that of
defining the boundaries of the Christian community. One section
of this volume deals with modern witchcraft under which is incorporated Satanism (including LaVey's Church of Satan and the practices
of Charles Manson) and the religion of Witchcraft (including the
Church of Wicca and the practices of Sybil Leek, Gerald Gardner,
and Alex Sanders).

1448. Sadler, Patricia O. "The 'Crisis Cult' as a Voluntary Organiza-
       tion: An Interactional Approach to Alcoholics Anonymous." HUMAN
       ORGANIZATION 36 (1977): 207-10.

       Disagrees with Madsen's view (item 1370) that Alcoholics Anony-
       mous is a "crisis cult." The limitations of approaching this drug-
       rehabilitation program as a cult are outlined and a broader anthro-
       pological perspective is proposed. The author applies the theory
       of interactional analysis to Alcoholics Anonymous, hoping to under-
       stand it as voluntary association. People who join Alcoholics
       Anonymous "seek a relationship with the supernatural in order to
       cease managing their own lives," while members of crisis cults
       look for ways "to remedy uncontrollable situations" (p. 208). The
       differences between religious converts and those who join Alcohol-
       ics Anonymous are discussed.

1449. Sandeen, Ernest R. THE ROOTS OF FUNDAMENTALISM: BRITISH AND AMERI-
       CAN MILLENARIANISM, 1800-1930. Chicago: University of Chicago
       Press, 1970. xix, 328 pp.

       Provides "historical evidence for the argument that Fundamental-
       ism existed as a religious movement before, during, and after the
       controversies of the twenties" (xiii). Traditional interpretations
       of fundamentalism are refuted. The author maintains that millenar-
       ianism gave life and shape to the Fundamentalist Movement. He
       traces the origin and development of the millenarian tradition and
       shows its impact on fundamentalism.

1450. Sandeen, Ernest R. "Fundamentalism and American Identity." ANNALS
       OF THE AMERICAN ACADEMY OF POLITICAL AND SOCIAL SCIENCE 389 (Jan-
       uary 1970): 56-65.

       Rejects the explanation that relates the rise of Fundamentalism
       in the 1920's to socioeconomic factors and traces its roots to the
       nineteenth-century movement that stressed the Second Coming of
       Christ (millennialism) and to the literal interpretation of the
       Bible. The author holds that Fundamentalism lives in "a symbiotic
       relationship" with its rivals, the National Council of Churches and
       the liberal establishment. Fundamentalism is an authentic conser-
       vative tradition that defines the American character.

1451. Sawatsky, Rodney J. "Domesticated Sectarianism: Mennonites in the
       U.S. and Canada in Comparative Perspective." CANADIAN JOURNAL OF
       SOCIOLOGY 3 (1978): 233-44.

       Examines the differences between the Mennonites in the United
       States and Canada and argues that their acculturation has proceeded
       along different routes. The sectarian identity of the two national

groups is, consequently, different. The denominational process of this religious sect moved more slowly in the United States than in Canada--a result of diverse immigration policies and constitutional assumptions. The demographic differences--ethnic origins, population size, regional distribution, and relative urbanization--that exist between U.S. and Canadian Mennonites are outlined. Canadian Mennonites have a stronger sense of ethnic identification and have experienced less sectarian-type tension with their nation than have their counterparts in the United States.

1452. Scanzoni, Lethe Dawson, and Susan Setta. "Women in Evangelical, Holiness, and Pentecostal Traditions." WOMEN AND RELIGION IN AMERICA: VOL. 3, 1900-1968. Edited by Rosemary Radford Reuther and Rosemary Skinner Keller. San Francisco: Harper and Row, 1986, pp. 223-66.

Examines the active role of women in revival churches in the late nineteenth and early twentieth centuries. The authors observe that there are many inconsistencies in the way women were regarded and treated and that restrictive attitudes towards women in these traditions were actually on the rise. Though these traditions often stressed the equality of the sexes in principle, the position of women was always qualified and restricted. Besides the changing political, economic, and social roles of women were seen as detrimental to the family and to society. Conservative churches tended to tighten the restrictions against women, even in religious matters. Fourteen documents that illustrate the active role played by some women in the revivalist movements of the period are included.

1453. Schoeneman, Thomas J. "The Witch Hunt as a Cultural Change Phenomenon." ETHOS 3 (1975): 529-54.

Argues that new theories must be constructed in order to combine effective historical and anthropological approaches to the study of Western witchcraft. The author first discusses Wallace's revitalization theory (item 136) and its possible application to understanding the role of the witch hunt in culture change. He suggests a processual model in which the orderly progression of events that surround the witch hunt are taken into account. He theorizes that witch hunts are "at once reflective of and an agent of sociocultural change" (p. 531), and that, like revitalization movements, they come into being "from mazeway changes caused by situations of chronic cultural distortion and disorganization" (p. 552).

1454. Schwartz, Gary. SECT IDEOLOGIES AND SOCIAL STATUS. Chicago: University of Chicago Press, 1970. x, 260 pp.

Examines, from an anthropological perspective, the religious ideology of two sectarian groups, namely the Pentecostals and the Seventh-Day Adventists, and explores the "social roots of sect affiliation and the impact this commitment has upon the believer's everyday existence" (p. 1). After discussing the problem of sect affiliation with reference to the church-sect typology and to the relationship between status deprivation and sect membership, the author gives an outline of the belief system of each group. He

also explains how the Pentecostals and the Seventh-Day Adventists
view their "status trajectory," that is, their conception of their
previous, current, and future position in the occupational system.
The differences between the two groups are outlined. Seventh-Day
Adventists are said to be classical examples of a transformative
movement, while Pentecostals are a redemptive type of movement.
There is a short discussion on the research method of participant
observation (pp. 27-31) and two appendices on various other methods
and the interview schedule, respectively (pp. 323-49).

1455. Schwieder, Elmer, and Dorothy Schwieder. "The Paradox of Change in
       the Life-Style of Iowa's Old Order Amish." INTERNATIONAL REVIEW
       OF MODERN SOCIOLOGY 6.1 (1976): 65-74.

       Discusses the variety of lifestyles within the Amish Order and
       the manner in which the Amish population accommodates individual
       differences while maintaining their beliefs and traditions. After
       a brief outline of the early history of the Amish and their basic
       beliefs and practices, the authors dwell on the high degree of
       communication and interaction between the Amish and on the creation
       and significance of new communities. Those Amish who question
       relatively minor Amish traditions are accommodated through the
       process of continual mobility.

1456. Schwieder, Elmer, and Dorothy Schwieder. A PECULIAR PEOPLE: IOWA'S
       OLD ORDER AMISH. Ames: Iowa State University Press, 1975. ix,
       188 pp.

       Presents a description of the Old Order Amish who live in several
       settlements in Iowa. After a historical introduction, which traces
       their birth from the Swiss Anabaptist Movement in the sixteenth
       century till their migration to America, the author describes their
       religious practices, economic organization, and family life. The
       author thinks that Amish mobility is "a safety valve for their
       discontent." The controversy with state officials over education
       and its solution are discussed. One chapter is dedicated to the
       "Beach Amish," a distinct group that, unlike the Old Order, wor-
       ships in churches.

1457. Scroggs, Robin. "The Earliest Christian Communities as Sectarian
       Movements." CHRISTIAN, JUDAISM, AND OTHER GRECO-ROMAN CULTS.
       Part 2: EARLY CHRISTIANITY. Edited by Jacob Neusner. Leiden: E.
       J. Brill, 1975, pp. 1-23.

       Argues that the community that Jesus gathered around him had the
       essential features of a religious sect. The following major sec-
       tarian traits are first described and then applied to this early
       Christian community: 1) protest; 2) rejection of the reality taken
       for granted by the established religion; 3) egalitarianism; 4) the
       creation of a community of love and acceptance; 5) voluntary asso-
       ciation; 6) total commitment; and 7) an adventist mentality. The
       early Christian community provoked hostility both because it led to
       the breakup of families and because it engaged in widespread mis-
       sionary activities. The author thinks that by looking at early
       Christianity as a sect, new insights about its emergence as a world
       religion can be gained.

1458. Sebald, Hans. "Justice by Magic: Witchcraft as Social Control
         Among the Franconian Peasants." DEVIANT BEHAVIOR: AN INTERDIS-
         CIPLINARY JOURNAL 7 (1986): 269-87.

         Examines how witchcraft among the Franconian peasants in the Jura
         mountains of Central Germany still functions as a personal and egal-
         itarian judicial system and as an alternative to the official legal
         procedures. In spite of its decline, witchcraft in this region has
         survived because of the geographic seclusion of the area, which has
         not been fully incorporated into modern technological society. The
         ways in which witchcraft and magic worked in this community are
         explained. The author maintains that witchcraft has strengthened
         family cohesion and helped subordinate personal wishes to the goals
         of the family. It has further provided respect for ownership and
         checked criminal acts. Some negative functions of witchcraft are
         discussed. Several cases of witchcraft are described.

1459. Sebald, Hans. "Franconian Witchcraft: A Discussion of Functional-
         ism." DEVIANT BEHAVIOR: AN INTERDISCIPLINARY JOURNAL 2 (1981):
         349-70.

         Gives an account of the "last phase of a long tradition of folk
         magic among the peasants in a secluded area of Central Germany
         called Franconian Switzerland" (p. 350). The meaning and functions
         of the belief in witchcraft are explored. Witchcraft serves as a
         personal explanation for misfortune in a society that inhabits a
         harsh environment and was plagued by poverty, poor sanitation, and
         malnutrition. The author thinks that witchcraft functioned as a
         sanction system that erased all differences between social class,
         sex, and age, and that was more effective than the sanctions of
         the Catholic Church. Witchcraft also acted as a form of boundary
         maintenance; it separated from the rest of the community those who
         have certain personality characteristics as a way of overcoming
         one's sense of powerlessness and as a less harmful way of express-
         ing one's feelings of aggression. Witchcraft explains events in a
         prescientific age and will eventually lose some of the functions
         it performs in Franconian society.

1460. Sebald, Hans. WITCHCRAFT: THE HERITAGE OF HERESY. New York:
         Elsivier, 1978. x, 262 pp.

         Presents a study of contemporary beliefs in the power of witch-
         craft of the peasants who live in that part of Bavaria called Fran-
         conian Switzerland. The author's analysis is divided into three
         sections: 1) the setting of witchcraft, in which the the history of
         the area is outlined and its occult traditions described; 2) the
         workings of witchcraft, where the main beliefs and practices and
         the healing activities of witches are described; and 3) the meaning
         of witchcraft, which is functionally explained as a natural phenom-
         enon, as a system of social sanctions and boundary maintenance, as
         a quest for individual power, and as a channel for aggression.

1461. Seggar, John F., and Reed H. Blake. "Post-Joining Participation:
         An Exploratory Study of Convert Inactivity." REVIEW OF RELIGIOUS
         RESEARCH 11 (1970): 204-209.

Discusses the factors that lead to the disengagement of individuals who had converted to the Mormon Church. The following four major factors that affect affiliation are explored: 1) latent perceptual discrepancies (i.e., negative perceptions of the church); 2) latent reservations (such as disagreement with the dietary laws and the payment of tithes); 3) ideologies that conflict with the position of the church; and 4) crises experienced since conversion. Recent converts to Mormonism are more likely to leave the church if 1) the church's doctrine, services, and other activities have ceased to be attractive, 2) the church's regulations have become difficult to follow, and 3) they have experienced economic problems since their conversion.

1462. Shaffir, William. "Separation From the Mainstream in Canada: The Hassidic Community of Tash." JEWISH JOURNAL OF SOCIOLOGY 29 (1987): 19-35.

Studies the flourishing Hasidic institutional life in the Montreal area, focusing on the Tasher Movement (that derives its name from a Hungarian town called "Tash," from which the present rebbe's ancestors originated). The author outlines the history of the community and examines the reasons why these Hasidic Jews stress the need for geographical isolation. He also looks into their efforts at self-regulation and self-sufficiency and at the way they organize their secular studies. The high birthrate and negligible number of defections are a sign of the group's success, but at the same time they might signal a future problem, namely the need for expansion that threatens their self-imposed isolation.

1463. Shaffir, William. "Hassidic Jews and Quebec Politics." JEWISH JOURNAL OF SOCIOLOGY 25 (1983): 105-18.

Examines the reaction of the Lubavitcher and Tasher Hasidic Jews to the changing political scene in the Province of Quebec, Canada. The conditions of these Hasidic Jews are compared and contrasted with the Jewish population in Montreal. The Hasidic Jews in Quebec have tended to rely on their rebbe for guidance and to ignore as much as possible the political debates in the province, even though they did react rather strongly to the language legislation that had a direct impact on their schools. Hasidic Jews, unlike other Jews, rather than being afraid of alienation from the larger society, have always sought cultural insulation and the preservation of their unique identity under the guidance of their religious leaders.

1464. Shaffir, William. "Witnessing as Identity Consolidating: The Case of the Lubavitcher Chassidim." IDENTITY AND RELIGION. Edited by Hans Mol. Beverly Hills, CA: Sage Publications, 1978, pp. 39-57.

Argues that witnessing and proselytizing tend to intensify one's identity, rather than threaten it. The Lubavitcher Hasidic Jews illustrate how their activities sharply defined and strengthened their religious identity. A short description of the community and their missionary ideology is provided. Contact with other Jews, particularly through the observance of religious precepts, is one of their common proselytizing techniques. The Telfillin campaign,

for instance, stressed the need of all adult male Jews to wear
phylacteries (i.e. two small leather cubes, each containing a piece
of parchment inscribed with Bible verses and worn during morning
services other than the Sabbath and holy days; one is strapped to
the left arm, while the other is bound around one's forehead).
This campaign made the Hasidic Jews more aware of, and secure in,
their identity.

1465. Shaffir, William. "The Organization of Secular Education in a
      Chassidic Jewish Community." CANADIAN ETHNIC STUDIES 8.1 (1976):
      38-51.

      Examines the methods used by the Lubavitcher Jews in Montreal to
      minimize their children's exposure to secular schooling. Their
      rebbe's negative view of secular education, which exposes the indi-
      vidual to secular ideas and distracts him or her from the study of
      the Torah, is outlined. The curriculum of the Lubavitcher schools
      and the methods their teachers use are described. The author holds
      that the Lubavitcher use "identity shaping mechanisms" to maintain
      their distinctiveness.

1466. Shaffir, William. LIFE IN A RELIGIOUS COMMUNITY: THE LUBAVITCHER
      CHASSIDIM IN MONTREAL. Toronto: Holt, Rinehart, and Winston,
      1974. xi, 244 pp.

      Presents a study of one Hasidic community, a Jewish religious
      group that aims at maintaining the integrity of Orthodox Judaism.
      The author shows how these Hasidic Jews manage to survive in an
      urban setting. A short history of the movement as a whole and of
      Chabad (Lubavitcher) Hasidism is given and its presence in Montreal
      is traced back to 1941. The distinctive identity of the group,
      with the very-present influence of its leader, the "Rebbe," the
      maintenance of its lifestyle, its educational system, its relation-
      ship with outsiders, and its missionary work are the main topics
      dealt with. It is argued that the Lubavitcher differs from other
      Hasidic groups in that it actively seeks contact with the larger
      Jewish community. Its proselytizing efforts actually reinforce and
      strengthen the community's distinctive identity. The symbolic-
      interactionst perspective, which holds that the life of the group
      is controlled by the everyday activities of the people as they
      respond to problematic situations of life, is used to explain why
      the Lubavitcher community persists.

1467. Shaffir, William, and Robert Rockaway. "Leaving the Ultra-Conser-
      vative Fold: Haredi Jews Who Defected." JEWISH JOURNAL OF SOCI-
      OLOGY 29 (1987): 97-114.

      Deals with the process of disengagement of ultra-Orthodox Jews
      from Haredi society, a disengagement that the authors see in the
      context of contemporary cults. Three areas of investigation are
      pursued: 1) the motivation for leaving; 2) the process of depar-
      ture; and 3) the problems encountered in secular society. Those
      who defected apparently "believed that it was easier to cope with
      the stresses and shortcomings of secular society than to conform
      again obediently but without faith to the rigorous standard of
      ultra-Orthodox Judaism" (p. 111).

438   SOCIAL SCIENCE AND THE CULTS

1468.   Sharot, Stephen. MESSIANISM, MYSTICISM, AND MAGIC: A SOCIOLOGICAL
        ANALYSIS OF JEWISH RELIGIOUS MOVEMENTS. Chapel Hill: University
        of North Carolina Press, 1982. viii, 306 pp.

        Presents a study of popular religious traditions and movements
        that have emerged out of the Jewish community, focusing on the
        relationships between them and the social conditions in which they
        arose. The author overviews the practice of religion and magic in
        the tradition of Judaism and in various Jewish millenarian move-
        ments, such as Sabbatism and Hasidism. He distinguishes between
        several types of movements and discusses the following theories
        brought forth to explain them: 1) the remedy-compensation view
        (which interprets the rise of religious movements to oppression,
        disaster, relative deprivation, social disorganization, or anomie);
        2) the social-congruency theory (that explains religious changes
        by parallel changes in the social structure); 3) the theory that
        stresses the relative autonomy of religion and explains the rise of
        new movements by internal factors; and 4) the processual perspec-
        tive (which looks on religion as a system that develops without
        necessarily having any relationship to sociocultural conditions).

1469.   Sharot, Stephen. "Jewish Millenarianism: A Comparison of Medieval
        Communities." COMPARATIVE STUDIES IN SOCIETY AND HISTORY 22
        (1980): 394-415.

        Examines several outbreaks of millenarianism among European Jews
        in the Middle Ages. Four possible causes of such outcomes are
        discussed: 1) millenarianism as a response to economic and politi-
        cal oppression; 2) millenarianism as a reaction to disaster, anomie,
        social disorganization, and relative deprivation; 3) millenarianism
        as a spontaneous outgrowth of already existing beliefs about the
        end of the world; and 4) millenarianism as a response to the appeal
        of a prophet. The author concludes that no single theory or combi-
        nation of theories can account for all the cases of Jewish move-
        ments, about which few generalizations can be made and little per-
        vading patterns can be detected.

1470.   Sharot, Stephen. "Hasidism and the Routinization of Charisma."
        JOURNAL FOR THE SCIENTIFIC STUDY OF RELIGION 19 (1980): 325-36.

        Traces the origins of the Hasidic movement in the Western Ukraine
        in the middle of the eighteenth century, and relates its features
        to the social structure of Eastern Europe at the time. The charac-
        teristics of Hasidism are discussed in the framework of Weber's
        "routinization of charisma." Focusing on one aspect of this rou-
        tinization, i.e., its charismatic succession, the author argues
        that the forms of succession developed in Hasidism explain its
        phenomenal success in Eastern Europe. Several types of succession
        that appeared in the history of Hasidism are described. These led
        to the segmentation and decentralization of the movement and to a
        wide variety of religious forms. Charisma in Hasidism and Pente-
        costalism are then contrasted.

1471.   Shepherd, Gary, and Gordon Shepherd. "Modes of Leader Rhetoric in
        the Institutional Development of Mormonism." SOCIOLOGICAL ANAL-
        YSIS 47 (1986): 125-36.

Concerns itself with an elaboration of different modes of expression in the conference rhetoric of Mormon authorities over time. Two main types of rhetoric are distinguished: that of exposition (in which meaning is articulated and policies and teachings are clarified) and that of admonition (in which moral exhortation and counseling is given). Exposition rhetoric is divided into four kinds, namely explanation, justification, repudiation, and narration, while admonition rhetoric is divided into prescription, proscription, and chastisement. Mormon leaders have always favored the expository style, with the defense and definition of God's Kingdom receiving the paramount concern. Narration was the second most frequently used method. Recent changes indicate an increase of explanatory discourse that the authors attribute to the growth of mass communications. There has also been some increase in repudiation rhetoric that is related to the leadership's concern that secular social trends might be weakening traditional values.

1472. Shepherd, Gary, and Gordon Shepherd. "Mormon Commitment Rhetoric." JOURNAL FOR THE SCIENTIFIC STUDY OF RELIGION 23 (1984): 129-39.

Studies the way in which the Mormon Church has urged commitment from its members during its 150-year history, using Kanter's classification of commitment mechanisms (see item 383). The authors maintain that commitment rhetoric is influenced by environmental and historical circumstances. The identification with a greater collective good plus the sense of transcendence are means for encouraging submission and sacrifice to group interests. While commitment rhetoric is not to be equated with the actual level of commitment, the authors think that it can reflect organizational preoccupation with different levels of commitment. Commitment rhetoric is linked with the dynamics of adaptation.

1473. Shepherd, Gordon, and Gary Shepherd. A KINGDOM TRANSFORMED: THEMES IN THE DEVELOPMENT OF MORMONISM. Salt Lake City: University of Utah Press, 1984. 307 pp.

Presents a study of Mormonism's adaptation as a religious movement, a social organization, and a cultural system, to both internal and external pressures since its emergence up to the present time. The authors attempt to show how Mormonism has fundamentally changed and suggest reasons why changes occurred. Social themes, such as group identity, social solidarity, organizational commitment, sectarianism, and secularization, that appear in the main addresses given at Mormon General Conferences are explored. The tension between Mormonism and society has declined considerably over the last few generations, even though Mormonism has not become a "thoroughly accommodated modern religion."

1474. Shepherd, Gordon, and Gary Shepherd. "Mormonism in Secular Society: Changing Patterns in Official Ecclesiastical Rhetoric." REVIEW OF RELIGIOUS RESEARCH 26 (1984): 28-42.

Records the changes that have taken place in the official statements of Mormon leaders over the last 150 years through a study of a sample of the addresses given at Mormon general conferences.

Themes such as utopianism, the supernatural, eschatology, personal
morality, family life, and doctrinal distinctiveness are explored.
The effects of secular society on Mormonism are examined, and it is
concluded that the stress of all traditional rhetoric themes, with
the exception of personal morality and family life, has declined.
Mormonism has made significant accommodations to secular society,
yet has succeeded in maintaining its sectarian spirit. Its attractiveness remains in its authoritarian, centralized leadership, its
moral certitude, its strong sense of community, and its transcendental goals.

1475. Shor, Francis. "The Utopian Project in a Communal Experiment in
       the 1930's: The Sunrise Colony in Historical and Comparative
       Perspective." COMMUNAL SOCIETIES 7 (1987): 82-94.

       Presents a study of a mostly Jewish commune that flourished near
       Saginaw, Michigan during the economic depression in the United
       States. The author first analyzes the basic elements of the commu-
       nal experiment, its leadership under Joseph J. Cohen, group cohe-
       sion, division of labor, and educational system. Then he compares
       it from different perspectives to the Kibbutz movement in Israel.
       Several internal divisions within Sunrise Colony are described.

1476. Sill, John Stewart. "The Spirit Brings Life: The Process of Change
       in Houston's Church of the Redeemer." PROCEEDINGS OF THE ANNUAL
       MEETING OF THE ASSOCIATION FOR THE SCIENTIFIC STUDY OF RELIGION,
       SOUTHWEST, 1981. 10 pp.

       Discusses the transformation of a traditional Episcopal congre-
       gation, the Church of the Redeemer in Houston, Texas, into a char-
       ismatic community. A brief description of the church is given and
       the initial change traced to the arrival of a new pastor who began
       to experiment with neighborhood ministry. The birth of a neo-Pen-
       tecostal group, with the pastor as its head, and the eventual evo-
       lution of a mainline church into a charismatic group are described.
       Several factors that brought about the transformation are discussed.

1477. Simpson, George Eaton. "Black Pentecostals in the United States."
       PHYLON 35 (1974): 203-11.

       Traces the origins of the Pentecostal Movement to a revival among
       Black Americans led by W. J. Seymour, a Black Holiness prophet.
       It is shown that the emergence and growth of this movement was
       partly due to the neglect of lower classes by the major Christian
       denominations in America. The main features of Pentecostalism are
       outlined and a typology of Black Pentecostalism given. The author
       finally discusses the social and political aspects of Black Pente-
       costalism in the United States.

1478. Singelenberg, Richard. "'It Separated the Wheat From the Chaff':
       The '1975' Prophecy and Its Impact Among Dutch Jehovah's Wit-
       nesses." SOCIOLOGICAL ANALYSIS 50 (1989): 23-40.

       Discusses the prophecy of the Watchtower Bible and Tract Society
       that the year 1975 would see the Apocalypse. While this prophecy
       had the effect of increasing the missionary efforts of Jehovah's

Witnesses before the fated date, there was a corresponding decline
in their zeal after the date when the prophecy was not fulfilled.
He concludes that the theory of Festinger et al. (item 91) is not
applicable to this case because the prophecy contained an "uncertainty" clause that became more pronounced as the foretold date
approached. Several phases of the Witnesses' proselytizing activities are distinguished. Dutch reaction to the 1975 prophecy was
"one of initial hope, expectancy, and tension" (p. 33). After
1975, these activities decreased, recruitment dropped, and many
left the church.

1479. Singer, Merrill. "The Use of Folklore in Religious Conversion: The
      Chassidic Case." REVIEW OF RELIGIOUS RESEARCH 22 (1980): 170-85.

      Discusses the use of folklore as a proselytizing tool among the
      Lubavitcher Hasidic Jews. Several phases of the conversion process
      are examined. Folklore plays an important role both in attracting
      new members and in furthering their commitment and affiliation.
      Folklore is seen as an "influence mechanism in interpersonal inter-
      action" (p. 172), because it symbolically transmits messages and a
      worldview; it also helps in the process of resocialization by fos-
      tering an attitude of fellowship. A description of Lubavitcher
      Hasidic folklore is given and the four phases of conversion are
      applied to the Hasidic context. The Lubavitcher consciously apply
      folklore as an effective conversion technique. The author believes
      that folklore can be viewed as a mechanism of social change and as
      one way of supporting the spread of a new religious movement.

1480. Singer, Merrill. "Chassidic Recruitment and the Local Context."
      URBAN ANTHROPOLOGY 7 (1978): 373-83.

      Presents an account of the founding (in 1967) and the current
      status of the Lubavitcher in Los Angeles and shows the importance
      of the local context in analyzing their proselytizing efforts.
      Geographic location, city size, history, special distribution of
      ethnic groups, regional values, and the origins of the local popu-
      lation are the variables taken into account. The historical con-
      text and the local urban situation are briefly described and a
      comparison is made between the Lubavitcher of Pittsburgh (see
      Mitchell and Plotnicov, item 1387) and those of Los Angeles. It is
      suggested that the variation between these two groups may account
      for the differences in the proselytizing efforts and community
      responses. The Los Angeles Lubavitcher have attracted many Jewish
      youth who have been disenchanted with drugs and are still alienated
      from mainstream American culture and life. Their proselytizing
      efforts reflect a generally lower level of adherents to Jewish
      religious tradition as well as a sense of being removed from the
      Chassidic centers of New York.

1481. Skultans, Vieda. "Mediums, Controls, and Eminent Men." WOMEN'S
      RELIGIOUS EXPERIENCE; CROSS-CULTURAL PERSPECTIVES. Edited by Pat
      Holden. Totowa, NJ: Barnes and Noble, 1983, pp. 15-26.

      Offers some reflections on the origins of nineteenth-century
      Spiritualism that grew out of family and domestic preoccupations
      and that, from its very beginnings, accorded women a special place.

Spiritualist mediumship has been primarily a female vocation. The
author elaborates on those traditional female characteristics that
are particularly suited to the task of mediumship and thinks that
Spiritualism provided women with ideal career opportunities. The
alliance between Spiritualism and the Society of Psychical Research
is described, the latter being a predominantly male organization.
The relationship between Spiritualism and this society mirrored
several aspects of the male-female relationship, according to the
author

1482. Skultans, Vieda. "Empathy and Healing: Aspects of Spiritualist
      Ritual." SOCIAL ANTHROPOLOGY AND MEDICINE. Edited by J. B.
      Loudon. London: Academic Press, 1976, pp. 190-222.

Deals with Spiritualism in South Wales, focusing on the ways in
which Spiritualists respond to pain and sickness. Three Spiritualist churches in Swansea are described. The author lists several
types of health problems that these churches take care of and compares their treatments with those of orthodox medicine. The importance of the spirit world, which mirrors the varieties of human
distress, is underscored. The author shows how Spiritualists
manage illness and indicates the precise topography and content of
Spiritualist pain experiences, which are related to group activities
by a consideration of key rituals. The author holds that Spiritualism is a ritual of reconciliation, functioning as a supportive and
therapeutic system.

1483. Skultans, Vieda. INTIMACY AND RITUAL: A STUDY OF SPIRITUALISM,
      MEDIUMS, AND GROUPS. Boston: Routledge and Kegan Paul, 1974.
      vii, 106 pp.

Presents an anthropological study of Spiritualism in South Wales.
Two churches, whose 400 members are three-fourths female, are the
focus of the author's research. The part played by illness in
Spiritualist belief and practice and the competition that takes
place between individual mediums and groups (that is, circles and
churches) are carefully examined. Spiritualism is judged to be a
coping device that enables women to accept their often frustrating
female roles. The weekly healing rituals and mediumistic activities and messages from the spirits are rituals of acceptance of a
situation that cannot be altered. Spiritualist meetings have,
therefore, a strong therapeutic element. The deprivation theory is
used to account for the presence of Spiritualism in Western culture.

1484. Slagle, A. Logan, and Joan Weibel-Orlando. "The Indian Shaker
      Church and Alcoholics Anonymous: Revivalist Curing Cults." HUMAN
      ORGANIZATION 45 (1986): 310-19.

Describes how the Indian Shaker Church, an intertribal religious
movement started by John and Mary Slocum about 100 years ago, functions as a culture-based alcohol rehabilitation center. The origins of the church, in the ecstatic experiences of their charismatic
founders who were exemplary cult figures, are outlined. The institutionalization of the church along the lines of Alcoholics Anonymous is examined. The similarities and differences between the

two organizations are discussed. Their success is attributed
partly to their function as substitutes for alcohol consumption and
its social-behavioral contexts.

1485. Smidt, Corwin. "'Praise the Lord' Politics: A Comparative Analysis
of the Social Characteristics and Political Views of American
Evangelicals and Charismatic Christians." SOCIOLOGICAL ANALYSIS
50 (1988): 53-72.

Compares and contrasts the social base and political viewpoints
of evangelicals and charismatics. After a brief historical overview, the author points out the religious differences between the
two groups and observes that, while evangelicals have played a
significant role in American politics, charismatics have tended to
be apolitical. Statistics are provided on 1) the distribution of
evangelicals and charismatics in American society, 2) their social
composition, 3) their religious practices, and 4) their stands on
issues of personal morality, social justice, and church-state relationships. It is concluded that the charismatic experience tends
to heighten social and political conservatism and that charismatics
are less likely than evangelicals to be mobilized into political
action.

1486. Smith, Peter. "Millenarianism in the Babi and Baha'i Religions."
MILLENNIALISM AND CHARISMA (item 713), pp. 231-83.

Examines the origins and history of the Baha'i religion in the
light of social-scientific studies of millenarian movements. The
Babi, a Shi'ite messianic movement in the nineteenth century represents a typical example of such movements with the following features: charismatic leadership, goals to establish a new state,
conflict with society, and antagonism with the existing clerical
order. The emergence of Baha'u'llah and the transformation of
Babism into the Baha'i religion is traced and an account of the
modern Baha'i Faith with its millennial aspirations is provided.

1487. Smith, Peter. "Motif Research: Peter Berger and the Baha'i Faith."
RELIGION 8 (1978): 210-34.

Examines the way Peter Berger has applied motif research to the
study of the Baha'i Faith and his conclusions that this religion
developed from a sect into a church when the messianic motif grew
weaker. Several other motifs derived from Islamic esotericism are
discussed. The author thinks that, while charisma in the Baha'i
has been routinized, the transition from sect to church has not
been completed.

1488. Smith, Peter, and Moojan Momen.   "The Baha'i Faith, 1952-1988: A
Survey of Contemporary Developments." RELIGION 9 (1989): 63-91.

Outlines the developments in the Baha'i Faith over the last three
decades under the following headings: 1) leadership and organization; 2) quantitative growth; 3) expansion and development plans;
4) central issues (including authoritative and charismatic leadership, development of a religious law, millenarianism, universalism,

social reformism, and liberalism). Some of the problems and prospects of the religion are also discussed. The authors think that the Baha'i Faith will experience growth in the Third World but will remain weak in Western Europe and in the Middle East.

1489. Smucker, Joseph. "Religious Community and Individualism: Conceptual Adaptation by One Group of Mennonites." JOURNAL FOR THE SCIENTIFIC STUDY OF RELIGION 25 (1986): 273-91.

Studies the experience of Mennonites who move from rural communities to urban areas. The author finds that Mennonites who abandon rural communities are influenced by the values of individualism that are dominant in large cities. The tensions of practicing their religion in the new setting are strongly felt and partly resolved through a revision of the concepts of "community" and "service." A high degree of involvement in philanthropic projects leads to participation in the urban environment and at the same time reinforces their religious identity. A new language of psychological support and assurance has been developed to provide urban Mennonites with "an escape without dealing with the problem of what it means to be a Mennonite" (p. 289).

1490. Sobel, B. Z. HEBREW CHRISTIANITY: THE THIRTEENTH TRIBE. New York: Wiley and Sons, 1974. xx, 413 pp.

Presents a comprehensive study of Hebrew Christianity. The author presents several cases of Jewish converts, describes their worldview and religious practices, outlines a history of the messianic tradition in Judaism, and finally attempts a sociological evaluation of the movement. He holds that these conversions are a necessary act of freedom in a society that has failed to provide for "crucial human needs." By converting to Christianity, some Jews find a constructive resolution to their problems and a meaning that society didn't succeed in providing them. Hebrew Christianity is a "reluctant sect," with little chance of survival in any form, save that of a fringe phenomenon. A useful bibliography is included.

1491. Sorenson, John. "Mormon World View and American Culture." DIALOGUE: A JOURNAL OF MORMON THOUGHT 8.2 (1973): 17-29.

Reviews the relationship of Mormon lifestyle and the mainline American culture. It is pointed out that behavioral sociologists tend to view Mormon culture as thoroughly compatible with American life, while anthropologists, who draw attention to the symbol system of a society, are inclined to see a greater dichotomy between Mormon and American cultures. The author discusses the concept of a Mormon culture and concludes that 1) such a culture exists in the sense that Mormonism has a worldview characterized by a unique ideology and value system, but 2) there is also a Mormon American culture since Mormonism has adopted the features of the larger society in which it thrives.

1492. Stark, Rodney. "The Class Basis of Early Christianity: Inferences From a Sociological Model." SOCIOLOGICAL ANALYSIS 47 (1986): 216-25.

Attempts to show, by a comparison with the new religious movements in the West, that early Christianity was a new religious
movement or cult that recruited members largely from the more
privileged classes. The author suggests that, during his ministry,
Jesus behaved like a leader of a sect within Judaism, a sect which
was transformed into a cult after his death and resurrection.

1493.   Stark, Rodney. "The Rise of a New World Faith." REVIEW OF RELI-
        GIOUS RESEARCH 26 (1984): 18-27.

Attempts to show that Mormonism "will soon achieve a worldwide
following comparable to that of Islam, Buddhism, Christianity,
Hinduism, and other dominant world faiths" (p. 18). The author
explains why the Mormon Church has been successful and stresses the
impact of its recruitment strategies that are based on gaining
access to new social networks. He suggests that, while Mormon
fertility offsets mortality and defection, conversions account for
the rapid growth of church membership. The rates of growth of the
church in the United States and overseas and a projection of membership up to the year 2080 are given.

1494.   Stark, Rodney, William Sims Bainbridge, and Lori Kent. "Cult Mem-
        bership in the Roaring Twenties: Assessing Local Receptivity."
        SOCIOLOGICAL ANALYSIS 42 (1981): 137-62.

Presents a historical dimension to the study of cults, which are
defined as "religious movements within a deviant religious tradition" (p. 137). Relying on the survey of religious bodies by the
U. S. Bureau of Census in the early part of the twentieth century
(1906-1936), the authors locate 15 cult groups. The following ones
are examined in some detail: the Theosophical Society; the Church
of Christ, Scientist; the Reorganized Church of Latter-Day Saints;
the Liberal Catholic Church; the Divine Science Church; and Swedenborgianism. Client cults, which deal primarily with magic, and
their memberships are recorded. It is concluded that there is a
"remarkable stability in the location of cult activity between the
roaring twenties and the 1970s" (p. 160).

1495.   Stewart, Gordon. "Charisma and Integration: An Eighteenth-Century
        North American Case." COMPARATIVE STUDIES IN SOCIETY AND HISTORY
        16 (1974): 138-49.

Examines the relationship between charisma and social integration
through a study of Henry Alline, a popular religious leader in Nova
Scotia during the American Revolution. The author gives an account
of the economic, social, and political conditions in Nova Scotia
between 1776 and 1783. He then analyzes the message of Alline,
whose success depended more on the message he proclaimed than on
his messianic style of preaching. His movement increased "Yankee
self-awareness and created a new-found solidarity" and began the
process of "creating a coherent sense of identity of Yankee Nova
Scotia" (p. 145). But since Alline's leadership also brought division, his charisma did not promote harmony in the settlements where
he preached. The relationship between charisma and social integration does not always apply whenever there is a religious revival.

1496. Ström, Ake. "Jehovah's Witnesses' Three Periods." NEW RELIGIONS
       (item 565), pp. 141-53.

       Analyzes the three periods in the history of the Jehovah's Wit-
       nesses, periods which are connected with the three presidents of
       the church, namely: 1) Russel (1881-1916); 2) Rutherford (1916-
       1942); and Knorr (1942-1970's). These periods are described and
       their differences noted.

1497. Strutt, Judith. "The Altar-Call Ritual in the Evangel Pentecostal
       Church, Montreal." RITUAL SYMBOLISM AND CEREMONIALISM IN THE
       AMERICAS: STUDIES IN SYMBOLIC ANTHROPOLOGY. Edited by N. Rose
       Crumrine. Greeley: Museum of Anthropology, University of North-
       ern Colorado, 1979, part 2, pp. 179-93.

       Describes a typical Sunday service at a Pentecostal church in
       Montreal, Canada. The author gives an account of her reception
       before the service actually began. She divides the service into
       three parts. The first part encourages personal, bodily expression
       in gestures and other bodily movements and, through the soloist,
       introduces the theme of individual apartness, loneliness, and per-
       sonal experience. The second part is dedicated to church business
       and announcements by the pastor. The final part consists of the
       sermon and the altar-call accompanied by singing and speaking in
       tongues. The ritual is interpreted as a rite of passage with the
       congregation sitting between the altar (symbolizing entrance to
       life in Jesus) and the lobby (symbolizing entrance from the life of
       sin). The entire service creates a society in microcosm. It is
       appealing because it stresses experience with its power and rewards.

1498. Swales, J. K., and Hugh V. McLachlan. "Witchcraft and the Status
       of Women: A Comment." BRITISH JOURNAL OF SOCIOLOGY 30 (1979):
       349-58.

       Criticizes Anderson and Gordon's views of European witchcraft
       (see items 1109-10). Their basic interpretations, that witches
       were used as scapegoats and that the difference between English and
       other European witch trials can traced to the relative social
       status of women, are challenged. Using extensive materials from
       Scottish witch trials, the authors attempt to show that Anderson
       and Gordon's conclusions are naive and hastily reached.

1499. Tapp, Robert B. "Dimensions of Religiosity in a Post-Traditional
       Group." JOURNAL FOR THE SCIENTIFIC STUDY OF RELIGION 10 (1971):
       41-47.

       Investigates the religiosity of Unitarian Universalists through a
       questionnaire sent to over 12,000 church members in the United
       States and Canada. The following factors are among the areas cov-
       ered: 1) personal beliefs and values; 2) social-ethical values;
       3) participation in church functions; 4) values regarding psycho-
       logical development; 5) esthetic values; 6) the educational func-
       tions of the church; 7) the church as a source of personal friend-
       ships; and 8) sectarian attitudes.

1500. Theobald, Robin. "From Rural Populism to Practical Christianity:
        The Modernization of the Seventh-Day Adventist Movement."
        ARCHIVES DE SCIENCES SOCIALES DES RELIGIONS 60.1 (1985): 109-30.

        Attempts to shed some light on a major paradox in the Seventh-Day
        Adventist Movement, namely its preoccupation with otherworldly
        goals coupled with its involvement in mundane affairs. The author
        describes the movement's origins and early development, outlines
        its eschatology, and then draws attention to the changes that have
        occurred in the movement over the years. It is held that when
        Seventh-Day Adventism moved from its rural setting to urban areas,
        it had to rethink its evangelistic programs to meet the needs of
        its more educated audience.

1501. Theobald, Robin. "The Politicization of a Religious Movement:
        British Adventism Under the Impact of West Indian Immigration."
        BRITISH JOURNAL OF SOCIOLOGY 32 (1981): 202-23.

        Assesses the impact of Seventh-Day Adventism on West Indian immi-
        grants in Great Britain. The similarities between Black Pentecos-
        talism and Seventh-Day Adventism are outlined. The author looks
        into the Adventist evangelistic center in London and the publica-
        tion of a brief history that includes a section on the effects of
        British Adventism on immigrants from the Caribbean. He observes
        that in Great Britain there is a polarization between Black Seventh-
        Day Adventists and the leaders of the movement. Adventism has
        acquired overt and organized political dimensions that were due
        partly to the movement's intensive "this-worldliness" and to its
        financial structure in Britain.

1502. Theobald, Robin. "The Role of Charisma in the Development of So-
        cial Movements: Ellen G. White and the Emergence of Seventh-Day
        Adventism." ARCHIVES DE SCIENCES SOCIALES DE RELIGIONS 49
        (1980): 83-100.

        Argues, in the context of Seventh-Day Adventism, that "the notion
        of charismatic authority can have explanatory value in relation to
        the origins and development of social movements" (p. 84). The
        essential features of charismatic authority as developed by Weber
        and other sociologists are reexamined. The author insists that the
        social dimension of charismatic domination, namely the charismatic
        community, should not be ignored. The emergence of Seventh-Day
        Adventism as a charismatic community is traced. The integrative
        role of Ellen White, the routinizatiion of charismatic power, and
        the subsequent decline of her authority are discussed. Her influ-
        ential position and function in the movement today are specified.

1503. Theobald, Robin. "Seventh-Day Adventists and the Millennium."
        SOCIOLOGICAL YEARBOOK OF RELIGION IN BRITAIN 7 (1974): 11-13.

        Studies Seventh-Day Adventism in the context of the wave of reli-
        gious revivalism in early nineteenth-century America. The author
        discusses the movement's development and its eschatology. The
        failure of the prophecy that the Second Coming was to be on October
        22, 1844, and the consequences of this failure, particularly its

reinterpretation by modern Adventists, are examined. Cultural,
rather than political or economic, deprivation brought about by
rapid social change, waves of immigrants, and large-scale movement
of the population to the frontier, is an important factor in understanding Adventism.

1504.   Thomas, Curlew O., and Barbara Boston. "Natural History of the
        Transformation of the Black Muslim Movement." FREE INQUIRY IN
        CREATIVE SOCIOLOGY 14 (1986): 73-76.

        Discusses the transformation of a revolutionary sect into a Black,
        conservative Islamic organization. The origins of the Black Mus-
        lims are described in terms of nativistic and revivalistic move-
        ments. Several stages in the movement's development are identified
        and the effects of socioeconomic conditions on the movement are
        examined. The author thinks that the "Muslim practices of thrift,
        sobriety, frugality, and self-denial have unwittingly upgraded
        their (that is, the movement's members) socioeconomic status" (p.
        76), thus facilitating its transition to an Islamic organization.

1505.   Thomas, Darwin L. "Family in Mormon Experience." FAMILIES AND
        RELIGIONS: CONFLICT AND CHANGE IN MODERN SOCIETY. Edited by
        William V. D'Antonio and Joan Aldous. Beverly Hills, CA: Sage,
        1983, pp. 267-88.

        Briefly presents the view of the family in Mormon teachings and
        then examines it in the largely social context, taking into account
        family size, sexual attitudes and behavior, age at marriage, di-
        vorce, sex roles, and socialization. Social-science research on
        various features of Mormon family are reviewed. Some speculations
        are made regarding the outcome of the encounter between the Mormon
        family and the larger American society.

1506.   Thomas, Keith. "The Relevance of Social Anthropology to the His-
        torical Study of English Witchcraft." WITCHCRAFT ACCUSATIONS AND
        CONFESSIONS (item 324), pp. 47-79.

        Examines "some of the basic functions of English witchcraft be-
        liefs and accusations in the light of anthropological studies of
        witchcraft elsewhere" (p. 47). After discussing the definitional
        problem, the author describes the reasons given for the accusations
        of witchcraft and the process of identifying witches. He thinks
        that witch beliefs throw light on the weak points in the social
        structure. During the sixteenth and seventeenth centuries, hostil-
        ity between the witches and the accusers could not be settled by
        legitimate means. The author combines a functional interpretation
        of the role of witch beliefs with a theory of social and intellec-
        tual change that was occurring during this period.

1507.   Thompson, William E. "Deviant Ideologies: The Case of the Old
        Order Amish." QUARTERLY JOURNAL OF IDEOLOGY 10.1 (1986): 29-33.

        Concedes that the Old Order Amish is a deviant subculture but
        argues that their deviancy is not caused by their religious ide-
        ology but by their cultural lifestyle, that is, by "the way they

translate their religious ideology into their everyday behavior"
(p. 29). The author describes the Amish as religious conformists
and points out their beliefs are very similar to those of many
mainstream Christian denominations. In putting their beliefs into
practice, however, they develop deviant social norms in language,
dress, rejection of modernity, strong sense of community, and the
practice of "shunning," that is, avoiding economic and social relationships with outsiders.

1508. Thompson, William E. "Old Order Amish in Oklahoma: Rural Transi-
        tion in Urban Society." FREE INQUIRY IN CREATIVE SOCIOLOGY 12
        (1984): 39-43.

        Examines how the Old Order Amish communities have struggled to
        resist the national movement of urbanization and industrialization
        and to maintain their face-to-face interactions and informal social-
        control mechanisms. The author explores two Amish communities, one
        in Oklahoma, the other in Kansas, and applies the symbolic-inter-
        actionist approach to understand how they actually "create their
        sense of social structure" (p. 39), perpetuating a social world
        that makes sense to them. It is theorized that the success of the
        Amish in maintaining their traditional agrarian culture is due to
        the pragmatism of their farmers who have accepted changes but rede-
        fined their meaning to fit the religious and cultural values of the
        community.

1509. Thompson, William E. "The Oklahoma Amish: Survival of an Ethnic
        Subculture." ETHNICITY 8 (1981): 476-87.

        Describes the lifestyle of the members of a small Old Order Amish
        community and the problems they face in preserving their religious
        and cultural identity under the impact of modern society. These
        Amish perceive the encroachment of modernity, the interventions by
        the government and by private enterprise, and the scarcity of farm
        land to be their major difficulties. The disenchantment with Amish
        lifestyle experienced by the young and the impact of tourism are,
        to a lesser degree, also problematic. The Amish endeavor to main-
        tain their lifestyle by minimizing the impact of all external fac-
        tors. Some modern adaptations, such as the use of tractors for
        farming, some division of labor, and more frequent use of hospital
        services, have become common among the Amish who reinterpret their
        use to reinforce traditional values.

1510. Titon, Jeff Todd. "Some Recent Pentecostal Revivals: A Report in
        Words and Photographs." GEORGIA REVIEW 32 (1977): 579-505.

        Gives an ethnographic account of two typical Pentecostal revivals
        in the Unites States. The author provides a brief historical in-
        troduction and several statistics that show the growth and decline
        of membership in some major Protestant denominations and in the
        Pentecostal movement between 1960 and 1975. A prophecy in tongues
        and its interpretation are transcribed.

1511. Trevett, Christine. "Woman, God, and Mary Baker Eddy." RELIGION
        14 (1988): 143-53.

Reflects on the writings of the founder of Christian Science, Mary Baker Eddy, in the context of the contemporary interest in the role of women in religion. Eddy's views on women and the family are sketched. Two current themes, namely the sole use of the term "Father" to address God and the concept of personhood in relation to sexuality and spirituality, were important issues to Mrs. Eddy. The fact that she refers to God by several names and the way she uses the person of Eve in her theology are a challenge to the traditional assumptions about the nature and role of women in society.

1512. Troyer, Henry. "Review of Cancer Among Four Religious Sects: Evidence That Lifestyles are Distinctive Sets of Risks Factors." SOCIAL SCIENCE AND MEDICINE 26.10 (1988): 1007-17.

Examines the relationship between cancer and lifestyles among four religious sects, namely the Amish, the Hutterites, the Mormons, and Seventh-Day Adventists. The dietary characteristics (meat consumption and use of coffee, tea, alcohol, and tobacco) of each group are considered. The author concludes that all these religious groups "experience an overall reduced rate of cancer when compared with the respective control groups" (p. 1009). The bibliography lists 93 items and contains materials for future study of the relationship between sect lifestyle and health.

1513. Turner, Christopher B. "Revivalism and Welsh Society in the Nineteenth Century." DISCIPLINES OF FAITH: STUDIES IN RELIGION, POLITICS, AND PATRIARCHY. Edited by Jim Obelkevitch, Lyndal Roper, and Raphael Samuel. London: Routledge and Kegan Paul, 1987, pp. 311-23.

Discusses the reasons why the industrial parts of Wales were so receptive to the evangelistic waves of the nineteenth century. Several features of Welsh revivalism are first described. The social tensions of the time had an effect on the preachers who warned their listeners that divine retribution was imminent. A number of cholera epidemics, together with the harsh conditions in which the coal miners worked, influenced to some degree the success of revivalism.

1514. Turner, Donald Lloyd. "Success Through Prayer Power: Theories of Self Help in American Religion." ANGLISTIK UND ENGLISCHUNTER-RICHT 25 (1985): 169-84.

Overviews the practice of healing in the Judeo-Christian tradition, focusing on the New Thought Movement during the Third Great Awakening in the nineteenth century. The views of Phineas Quimby, Warren Felt Evans, and Mary Baker Eddy are outlined. The author observes that New Thought always played an important role in American revivals, both in the nineteenth and twentieth centuries. Billy Graham, Norman Vincent Peale, and Robert Schuller are quoted as examples of the contemporary religious revival that represents the interests and message of the New Thought tradition.

1515. Wallis, Roy. "On Misunderstanding 'Status': A Reply to Zurcher and Kirkpatrick." SCOTTISH JOURNAL OF SOCIOLOGY 2 (1978): 247-51.

Continues the debate over the interpretation of moral crusades as a form of defense of the social status of those involved in them. The author points out that the disagreement between himself and Zurcher and Kirkpatrick (see items 525-26) stems largely from the meaning they ascribe to the word "status." Wallis thinks that these two authors use "status" to refer to social hierarchy, in which case he rejects their interpretation of moral crusades as a confirmation of the participants' social position.

1516. Wallis, Roy. "Moral Indignation and the Media: An Analysis of the NVALA." SOCIOLOGY 10 (1976): 271-95.

Studies the nature and activity of a moral crusade, namely the "National Viewers' and Listeners' Association" (NVALA) in Great Britain. The origin and development of this movement, and its ideology, structure, and tactics are described. With its members coming mainly from the bourgeois and respectable working class, the NVALA supports the norms and values that are embodied in the "Protestant Ethic," which, it is claimed, is being eroded by television. The NVALA is said to be a "moral reform movement" that stresses "cultural fundamentalism."

1517. Wallis, Roy. "Processes in the Development of Social Movements." SCOTTISH JOURNAL OF SOCIOLOGY 1.1 (1976): 81-93.

Interprets a British moral crusade, namely the National Festival of Light, as a social movement. Its emergence under the inspiration of a young Christian evangelist, Peter Hill, and its development till its 1971 London rally are recorded. The changing goals and leadership of the movement after that rally are discussed. The author contends that this movements "suggests that rational-legal administration may come to predominate as the charismatic leadership vacates the direction of the movement in the face of threatened routinization" (p. 93).

1518. Wallis, Roy, and Richard Bland. "Purity in Danger: A Survey of Participants in a Moral-Crusade Rally." BRITISH JOURNAL OF SOCIOLOGY 30 (1979): 188-208.

Reports on the National Festival of Light held in Trafalgar Square, London, on September 25, 1976. A short history of this Christian evangelical movement, founded by Peter Hill with the aim of combating pornography, is given. The authors examine and criticize three theories about moral crusades, namely: 1) that they are a form of expressive politics; 2) that they are a type of status defense; and 3) that they are aimed at some kind of assimilative and coercive reforms that impose legal and social standards of morality. Most of the participants viewed the crusade as a religious attempt to persuade people to reform, even though the rally appeared to stress a coercive approach to moral change. Morality, evangelism, and solidarity were the combined reasons for their presence at the rally.

1519. Ward, David A. "Towards a Normative Explanation of 'Old Fashioned Revivals.'" QUALITATIVE SOCIOLOGY 3 (1980): 3-22.

Decries the common tendency among scholars to explain revivals by
stressing their psychological and psychopathological aspects. A
normative framework is proposed as an alternative to explain revivals in the Holiness Church. The social significance and cultural
norms that play a role in the conversion process are stressed.
Four propositions are constructed: 1) the sinner and the revival
culture must interact; 2) structural facilities must be established
for the convert to learn the Christian way; 3) structures must be
present through which the individual might express himself or herself in the appropriate manner; and 4) the passage from salvation
to sanctification is an orderly one. The author insists that the
renewal behavior must be observed as a social process through the
method of participant observation.

1520. Washington, Joseph R. BLACK SECTS AND CULTS. Garden City, NJ:
        Doubleday and Company, 1972. xii, 176 pp.

        Examines Black sects and cults in their historical and social
        settings. In spite of the variety of expressions that are found in
        these religious groups, the author detects a fundamental and common
        ethic that unites Black people and gives continuity to their reli-
        gions. The distinctions between the Black church, sect, and cult
        are discussed. Black cults are not just religious movements but
        also political, social, and economic ones, since their prophets
        seek salvation and power for Blacks in all areas of life. Lack of
        structure, charismatic leadership, and mystical experience are
        among the main features of cults. The African roots of Black reli-
        gion, the established sects (Methodists and Baptists), the perma-
        nent sects (Holiness and Pentecostal churches), and Black cults
        (like Father Divine's Peace Mission Movement and Daddy Grace's
        United House of Prayer for All People) are among the areas covered.

1521. Wayland-Smith, Ellen. "The Status and Self-Perception of Women in
        Oneida Community." COMMUNAL STUDIES 8 (1988): 18-53.

        Reexamines the position of women in the nineteenth-century Oneida
        Community using several primary sources not previously considered
        by researchers. After evaluating previous studies on the topic of
        women in this controversial commune, the author discusses John
        Humphrey Noyes's position as patriarch of the commune. In Oneida,
        traditional and radically new sex roles were blended together and
        the masculine definition of morality and adulthood common at the
        time rejected. The communal dimension was stressed at the expense
        of the individualistic and egocentric trends in American culture.
        Because of Oneida's different system of identity formation, the
        author thinks that the community was a "comfortable environment for
        many women." However, women were not more liberated than men; they
        did not enjoy a privileged status, but neither did they play a
        noticeable subordinate role.

1522. Webb, Bernice Larson. "A Study of Voodoo Mail-Order Advertising in
        Louisiana." LOUISIANA REVIEW 2 (Summer 1973): 65-71.

        Surveys Voodoo products that are available in mail-order cata-
        logues. The author divides such products into ten categories:
        1) bones and blood; 2) books; 3) botanicals; 4) candles and

incense; 5) clothing and equipment; 6) household supplies; 7) the
human image (Voodoo dolls); 8) in the Boudoir; 9) lucky little
gadgets; and 10) magic stones. Items 3, 4, 6, 7, and 8, which are
the most commonly used, are described. Voodoo is an ancient cult
that has survived in modern times.

1523. Webster, A. J. "Scientific Controversy and Socio-Cognitive Meton-
ymy: The Case of Acupuncture." ON THE MARGINS OF SCIENCE
712), pp. 121-37.

Advances the view that the social and conceptual processes in the
practice of acupuncture must be taken together. The development of
the controversy over acupuncture and the latter's contemporary
status are described. The author dwells on the competition that
exists between orthodox medicine and acupuncture, which can both be
considered as specialized techniques of healing.

1524. Weigle, Martha. BROTHERS OF LIGHT, BROTHERS OF BLOOD: THE PENI-
TENTES OF THE SOUTHWEST. Albuquerque: University of New Mexico
Press, 1976. xix, 300 pp.

Presents a comprehensive study of a lay religious organization
within the Roman Catholic Church, an organization made up almost
exclusively of men of Hispanic descent who live primarily in
Northern New Mexico and Southern Colorado. The author first
sketches the physical setting of the Brotherhood and then outlines
their historical background and development and describes their
organization and ritual in some detail. She analyzes the folklore
about ghostly penitents and indicates the general significance of
penance and the experience of the sacred. Largely historical and
ethnographic in nature, this book applies the anthropological
theory of rites of passage to the Brothers of the Blood.

1525. Weisbrot, Robert. FATHER DIVINE AND THE STRUGGLE FOR RACIAL
EQUALITY. Urbana: University of Illinois Press, 1983. 241 pp.

Decries the attempts to depict Father Divine chiefly as a cult
leader, a depiction which has distorted the mission he founded.
The author prefers to stress the perspective that Father Divine
"was one of those rare cult figures who derived his greatest sense
of power and purpose from helping to shape society according to his
ideas of justice" (p. 8). The origin of Father Divine, his rise to
prominence in the 1930's, and the establishment of his Peace Mission
are described. Attention is drawn to his reform plans, his goal of
racial integration, his vision of a new economic order, and his
political involvement for racial justice. Father Divine's relationships with the Black community and other Black cult leaders and
with society at large are examined. During his own lifetime his
Peace Mission developed from a mass movement to a formal sect with
an elaborate bureaucracy.

1526. Weisman, Richard. WITCHCRAFT, MAGIC, AND RELIGION IN SEVENTEENTH-
CENTURY MASSACHUSETTS. Amherst: University of Massachusetts
Press, 1984. xiv, 267 pp.

Explores "the social processes underlying support and resistance
to collective action against witchcraft in seventeenth-century
Massachusetts" (xiii). After an overview of the historical data,
the author speculates on the social meanings of witchcraft. The
process of witch identification before and after the Salem trials
is outlined and the official response to these identifications
analyzed. New England witchcraft is said to present "the unusual
spectacle of a form of deviance in which collective mobilization
against a perceived problem proved to be more divisive than unifying" (p. 185). Several appendices list the legal actions, defama-
tion suits, and the allegations and confessions of witchcraft. A
bibliography of primary and secondary sources is added (pp. 251-62).

1527. White, O. Kendall. "Mormonism in America and Canada: Accommodation
      to the Nation-State." CANADIAN JOURNAL OF SOCIOLOGY 3 (1978):
      161-81.

      Contends that Mormonism established itself permanently in North
      America only after it abandoned its ideal of the Kingdom of God on
      earth and accepted the concept of the "nation-state." After re-
      viewing Mormon origins in the context of American culture, the
      author dwells on what he calls the "Mormon capitulation." The
      Mormon 1890 manifesto "legitimized the change from a posture of
      resistance to the nation-state to one of accommodation without the
      repudiation of the polygamy doctrine" (p. 173). Mormonism has
      become a denomination or church that supports the existing social
      order.

1528. White, O. Kendall, and Daryl White. "A Critique of Leone's and
      Dolgin's Application of Bellah's Evolutionary Model to Mormon-
      ism." REVIEW OF RELIGIOUS RESEARCH 23 (1981): 39-53.

      Criticizes Robert Bellah's model of religious evolution in five
      stages (primitive, archaic, historic, early modern, and modern) and
      its application by some contemporary scholars to Mormonism. The
      authors claim that Bellah's elaborate scheme has an implicit Pro-
      testant bias and that the opinion of Dolgin (item 1236) and Leone
      (item 1359) that Mormonism is an example of modern religion is
      untenable. Although nineteenth-century Mormonism may have exhib-
      ited a thisworldly theology, locating moral responsibility in the
      individual (which is a major feature of modern religion), later
      developments show a return to pessimism and dualism, which are
      characteristics that belong to Bellah's earlier religious stages.
      Moreover, the institutional organization of Mormonism never resem-
      bled modern religion as defined by Bellah.

1529. White, O. Kendall, and Daryl White. "Abandoning an Unpopular
      Policy: An Analysis of the Decision Granting the Mormon Priest-
      hood to Black." SOCIOLOGICAL ANALYSIS 41 (1980): 231-45.

      Discusses the factors that influenced the relatively recent change
      of Mormon policy regarding the ordination of Blacks to the priest-
      hood. The adaptation to environmental pressures, the logical out-
      come of established organizational practices, and the resolution of

internal contradictions are the major forces that led to the change
of policy. Among the references are citations to studies on Mormon
attitudes towards Blacks.

1530. Whitley, Oliver R. "Life With Alcoholics Anonymous: The Methodist
Class Meeting as a Paradigm." JOURNAL OF THE STUDIES OF ALCOHOL
38 (1977): 831-48.

Studies a metropolitan Denver Alcoholics Anonymous group and
reaches the conclusion that it can be called a "para-religious
group, utilizing identifiable religious resources in the efforts to
achieve its goals" (p. 831). The author describes the liturgy of
Alcoholics Anonymous, discusses the social import of its charter,
and investigates its nonprofessional group therapy. He observes
that the meetings of Alcoholics Anonymous are similar to the Methodist class meetings. Alcoholics Anonymous provides "a demytholo-
gized and secularized form of religious pietism" (p. 848).

1531. Whitworth, John M. GOD'S BLUEPRINTS: A SOCIOLOGICAL STUDY OF THREE
UTOPIAN SECTS. London: Routledge and Kegan Paul, 1975. xiii,
258 pp.

Presents a sociological study of the Shakers, the Oneida Community, and the Bruderhof. In each case the author 1) analyzes the
circumstances under which the group came into being and the nature
of its original teachings, 2) discusses the development of the
belief system and the group's self-conception, 3) considers the
formal organization of the sect, 4) describes the composition of
the members, and 5) examines the sect's relationship with the outside world. The social prerequisites for the growth of utopian
sectarianism, together with the social control and internal dynamics in sectarian groups, are among the topics discussed. A short
bibliography (pp. 249-55) includes works published by members of
the three sects and some basic studies.

1532. Whitworth, John M. "The Shakers--Ideological Change and Organizational Persistence." SOCIOLOGICAL YEARBOOK OF RELIGION IN BRIT-
AIN 8 (1975): 78-102.

Traces the development and structure of Shaker communitarianism,
to relate the Shaker organization to utopian concepts, to trace the
change this concept underwent, and to explain why the Shakers survived for over 150 years in spite of their many problems. An account of the English origins of the Shakers and their migration to
America is provided. Unsuccessful attempts to revitalize the sect
and the consequent stagnation are among the topics discussed.

1533. Whitworth, John M. "The Doukhobors, the Hutterites, and the Cana-
dian State." RELIGION AND POLITICS: ACTS OF THE 15TH INTERNA-
TIONAL CONFERENCE ON THE SOCIOLOGY OF RELIGION. Lille, France:
C.I.S.R., 1972, pp. 207-28.

Focuses on several issues between two religious sects and the
Canadian government, namely the refusal of sect members to perform
military service, their noncompliance with tax laws and with land,

marriage, and death registrations, and their attitudes toward education. The author maintains that these two sects, the Doukhobors and the Hutterites, embody two types of introversionism. He outlines some of the major similarities and differences between them and discusses their respective history and relationship with the Canadian government. He thinks that the persecutions by civil authorities has reconfirmed the Hutterite commitment to the sect's lifestyle but may have contributed to the decline of the Doukhobors.

1534. Whitworth, John M. "The Bruderhof in England: A Chapter in the History of a Utopian Sect." A SOCIOLOGICAL YEARBOOK OF RELIGION IN BRITAIN 4 (1971): 84-101.

Consists of an account of one stage in the development of a utopian sect whose response to the world has been withdrawal from society to establish a new, perfect world order. The sect examined is the Society of Brothers (the Bruderhof), a pacifist, communitarian, evangelistic group established by Eberhard Arnold in Germany in 1920. The history of the sect is sketched in four mian phases: 1) development since 1935; 2) establishment in England and migration to Paraguay in the years 1935-41; 3) reestablishment and expansion in England between 1942 and 1958; and 4) dissolution, brought about by internal quarrels, of the English colonies between 1958 and 1966. Three communities, comprising some 100 members, survive in the United States, where they maintain their separation from contemporary society that is condemned as a place of selfishness, greed, violence, and sexual corruption.

1535. Whitworth, John M., and Martin Sheils. "From Across the Black Water: Two Imported Varieties of Hinduism." NEW RELIGIOUS MOVEMENTS: A PERSPECTIVE FOR UNDERSTANDING SOCIETY (item 551), pp. 155-172.

Examines two Eastern religious movements in the United States, namely the Ramakrishna Vedanta Society (established in 1896) and the Hare Krishna Movement (founded in the early 1970's). The ways in which both groups satisfy the aspirations of their adherents are explored. The two movements are similar because both were founded by a charismatic leader, both are based on orthodox Hindu teachings, both regard the present age as corrupt, and both aim at enlightening the West with Eastern religious wisdom. They differ, however, in some of their specific teachings, in the paths to salvation they offer, in the structure of their communities and lifestyles, in the social makeup of their membership, and in their attitudes towards society. The authors maintain that those who seek refuge from the stress of life in these movements are not necessarily exhibiting signs of pathology.

1536. Wiesel, Barbara B. "From Separatism to Evangelism: A Case Study of Social and Cultural Change Among Franconia Conference Mennonites." REVIEW OF RELIGIOUS RESEARCH 18 (1977): 254-63.

Assesses and documents the causes and consequences of radical change among the Mennonites in Pennsylvania. Rather than belonging to a stable culture, the Mennonites have made a relatively successful effort to control the pace of change, thus maintaining their

original worldview. The historical background of this sect is
given, with special reference to the changing rules of the Franconia Conference and the changing environment of the Franconia
Township. Over the years these Mennonites abandoned their stress
on separation from, and nonconformity with, the larger culture and
began engaging themselves in missionary work. The author suggests
several strategies (like the new ethnography) for the study of
sects like the Amish and the Hasidic Jews.

1537. Williams, Cyril G. TONGUES OF THE SPIRIT: A STUDY OF PENTECOSTAL
GLOSSOLALIA AND RELATED PHENOMENA. Cardiff: University of Wales
Press, 1981. xiii, 276 pp.

Gives an account of the origins and development of glossolalia
from Biblical times up to the modern Pentecostal movement. One
chapter is dedicated to the resurgence of Pentecostalism in the
mainline churches since the mid-1960's. An outline of the most
prominent features in this revival is provided. Contemporary research, the results of which are summarized, has centered on four
major topics: 1) the personalty of those who speak in tongues;
2) their conditions; 3) the functions of glossolalia; and 4) the
form of glossolalic utterances. A substantial bibliography (pp.
241-68) is added.

1538. Williams, Melvin D. COMMUNITY IN A BLACK PENTECOSTAL CHURCH: AN
ANTHROPOLOGICAL STUDY. Pittsburgh: University of Pittsburgh
Press, 1974. xii, 202 pp.

Presents a study of the Zion Holiness Church, an affiliate of the
international group known as the Church of the Holy Christ. After
giving a short history of the church, the author examines its organization, activities, symbolic expressions, community relationships, and the behavioral dynamics of its members. He maintains
that the "critical task of Zion is to assimilate the social distance which usually accompanies social mobility" (p. 174). The
church has succeeded in maintaining an equilibrium between conflict
and solidarity and in providing a community and a network of social
interactions that respond to the social and economic upheavals that
poor, Black, and discriminated-against people face in the process
of migration and urbanization.

1539. Williams, Melvin D. "Food and Animals: Behavioral Metaphors in a
Black Pentecostal Church in Pittsburgh." URBAN ANTHROPOLOGY 2
(1973): 74-79.

Describes and analyzes the symbolic system of a Black Pentecostal
Church, called Zion, that was established by migrants from the
rural South. It it argued that its symbol system, which is replete
with references to farm life and food, "helps create, determine,
and delineate the interactional system among its members" (p. 74).
Animals and food are used in preaching and in the communication
between the members and some of the attributes ascribed to God are
expressed in similar symbolic language. Such linguistic peculiari-
ties give the members of the Church of Zion a distinct identity
and enable them to integrate rural symbols with their contemporary
urban life.

1540. Wilson, Bryan R. "A Sect at Law: The Case of the Exclusive Breth-
       ren." ENCOUNTER 60.1 (1983): 81-87.

       Argues that, in spite of religious freedom which modern states
       guarantee, religious minorities are not always treated equally.
       The author illustrates his point with reference to the way the
       Charities Commission in England dealt with the Exclusive Brethren,
       a branch of the Plymouth Brethren. A brief history of the Brethren
       and the various internal conflicts and schisms is given. The legal
       debate as to whether the Exclusive Brethren can be registered as a
       religious trust and the consequent quasi-judicial inquiry into the
       sect are discussed.

1541. Wilson, Bryan R. "Why Prophecy Failed." NEW SOCIETY 43 (January
       26, 1978): 183-84.

       Reflects on the failure of the Jehovah's Witnesses prophecy that
       the world would come to an end in 1975. The impact of this pro-
       phetic disappointment is seen in the decline of the sect's annual
       rate of growth in almost every country. Most Witnesses, however,
       have not abandoned their faith, but rather reinterpreted the pro-
       phetic declaration and increased their missionary efforts. The
       author speculates that with the passage of time there may be a
       return to the high rate of growth that prevailed before 1975.

1542. Wilson, Bryan R. "Sect or Denomination: Can Adventism Maintain Its
       Identity." SPECTRUM: A QUARTERLY JOURNAL OF THE ASSOCIATION OF
       ADVENTIST FORUMS 7.1 (1975): 33-43.

       Describes the various features of sectarianism and defines the
       sect's concern with salvation in sociological terms, that is, in
       the sense that sect members are saved from the world, from the
       destiny facing other people, and from society. Different responses
       to the world--conversionist, revolutionist, introversionist, manip-
       ulationist, thaumaturgical, reformist, and utopian--are outlined.
       The conversionist sect is the one "which most causes the individual
       to alter his whole orientation to the world" (p. 38). The differ-
       ences between Seventh-Day Adventism and other sectarian bodies with
       a strong adventist-revolutionist orientation are discussed. Those
       factors (such as the existence of a professional ministry) that
       suggest that Seventh-Day Adventism is changing into a denomination
       are listed. Other factors, like the group's teaching on the Sab-
       bath, its claim to special revelation, and its dietary rules,
       remain serious obstacles to its developing into a denomination.

1543. Wilson, John. "Voluntary Associations and Civil Religion: The Case
       of Freemasonry." REVIEW OF RELIGIOUS RESEARCH 22 (1980): 125-36.

       Considers Freemasonry in the United States as a model of most
       fraternal orders that function as a link between the private and
       public spheres. Freemasonry draws its membership from a higher
       socioeconomic strata. Even its inactive members stress its values
       as a means of moral education and good citizenship. The author
       describes the Blue Lodge, the basic unit of the Scottish Rite Free-
       masonry, noting the education, occupation, family income, and

patterns of its members' largely apathetic involvement in the association. He suggests that this low level of participation is due
to the fact that membership in the Blue Lodge is a requisite for
membership in the Scottish and York Rites and in the Shrine, to
which members direct most of their activities. The paradox between
commitment to an idea and lack of involvement is solved by the
postulate that Freemasonry functions as a Civil Religion. "Freemasonry has been a ritualized celebration of the American experience as filtered through the values and interests of the white
adult male" (p. 135).

1544. Wilson, John, and Harvey K. Clow. "Themes of Power and Control in
a Pentecostal Assembly." JOURNAL FOR THE SCIENTIFIC STUDY OF
RELIGION 20 (1981): 241-50.

Questions the contemporary functional interpretations of Pentecostal sects and attempts to understand them in terms of the symbolism of two of their prominent features, namely speaking in
tongues and spirit possession. A brief description of the beliefs
and rituals of a church belonging to the Holiness Movement is given.
The Pentecostal attitude towards work with its stress on the virtues of steady, hard work and sense of obligation to employers and
customers, is briefly outlined. The authors discuss the problem of
why rituals, in which people lose total control of self, are central
in Pentecostal gatherings. They argue that "the worship service in
part articulates the Pentecostal's concern with how much he is
really in control of his thoughts, desires, and feelings" (p. 249).
Ritual is not a compensation for lack of control; it rather symbolizes it and enables the participant to deal with it.

1545. Wilson, J. Hiram. "Visions of Heavens: Religious Community in a
Swedish Commune." ANTHROPOLOGICAL LINGUISTICS 23 (1981): 245-61.

Examines, from a structural point of view, a religious text from
the writings of the Janssonist Movement, a religious commune of
Swedish origin, that thrived in Henry County, Illinois between
1846 and 1861. The author shows how the belief system of this sect
is expressed in the religious text (a psalm) that contains several
implicit oppositions. He attempts to uncover the logic of the
meaning hidden in these oppositions and points out that the psalm
"is a statement of the role of the sect in history and religious
metahistory" (p. 250). A short bibliography and the text in question are included.

1546. Wilson, Michele. "Voodoo Believers: Some Sociological Insight."
JOURNAL OF SOCIOLOGY AND SOCIAL WELFARE 9 (1982): 278-83.

Discusses the beliefs and practices regarding Voodoo in a southern United States city. Various examples of how and where Voodoo
works are given. The author stresses the need to recognize the
fact that belief plays an important part in the cause, cure, and
perception of illness. From her perspective as a Christian, she
thinks that is it essential to look on Voodoo not as a superstitious belief system or a sign of mental illness, but rather as a
worldview that has repercussions on the believers' lives.

1547. Wimberley, Ronald C., Thomas C. Hood, et al. "Conversion in a
      Billy Graham Crusade: Spontaneous Event of Ritual Performance?"
      SOCIOLOGICAL QUARTERLY 16 (1975): 162-70.

      Examines contemporary religious revivals or crusades that have
      the total change (conversion) of direction in the individual's life
      as their primary purpose. Reflecting the view that crusade conver-
      sions are attempts to resolve status problems, the authors, in line
      with most contemporary sociological thought, argue that conversion
      is an institutionalized stand taken by those who respond to evange-
      lization. The crusade "becomes a ritualized opportunity for people
      to show what they claim to be, namely bona fide Christians" (p.
      163). Evidence from Billy Graham's crusades is adduced to show
      that most of those who convert at his meetings are ritually re-
      affirming existing values rather than spontaneously rejecting old
      ones and accepting new ones. Three areas are examined: 1) the
      religious background of those who attended crusades; 2) the selec-
      tivity of decision makers by age; and 3) the ritualized method of
      attracting and labeling converts at the meetings. Crusades are
      "ritualistic, integrative, value-affirming experiences" (p. 168).

1548. Wolfe, James. "Three Congregations." THE NEW RELIGIOUS CONSCIOUS-
      NESS (item 614), pp. 227-44.

      Studies three "deviant" Christian congregations that, like the
      Jesus People and the Catholic Church, are responding to the "ambi-
      guities in American culture." The consequences of these churches,
      namely Glide Memorial Methodist Church, St. John's Church, and
      Grace Church, on the counterculture are discussed. Glide Church
      was the only one where the new culture predominated in the style of
      worship. The author thinks that this "demonstrates that the possi-
      bility for creative renewal in the church remains alive" (p. 244).

1549. Wood, Michael, and Michael Hughes. "The Moral Basis of Moral Re-
      form: Status Inconsistency vs. Culture and Socialization as Ex-
      planations of Anti-Pornography Social Movement Adherence."
      AMERICAN SOCIOLOGICAL REVIEW 49 (1984): 86-99.

      Discusses two major sociological theories that have been advanced
      to explain the rise of moral reform movements: 1) the theory of
      status discontent or inconsistency, which interprets involvement in
      such movements as an expression of the incongruous social positions
      their members occupy; and 2) the theory of culture and socializa-
      tion that stresses that moral reform movements result from cogni-
      tion processes and judgments and must, therefore, be explained in
      the context of their members' sociocultural backgrounds. The
      authors' research suggests that neither status inconsistency nor
      deprivation are necessary to explain the rise of these movements,
      though they may account for the behavior of "moral entrepreneurs"
      or of their leaders. It is concluded that prior education in
      belief and ideology of the members is sufficient to explain the
      periodic waves of moral reform movements.

1550. Wright, Peter. "A Study of the Legitimization of Knowledge: The
      'Success' of Medicine and the 'Failure' of Astrology." ON THE
      MARGINS OF SCIENCE (item 712), pp. 85-101.

Reflects on the loss of astrology's influence to medical science
by the year 1700. The author suggests that this change is best
understood "as a reflection of the ideological and political power
of the professions practicing them and not as a result of the truth
or effectiveness of the knowledge they utilized" (p. 86). Medicine
and astrology are seen as two professional practices with different
social positions. Both are classified as cognitive systems that
should be evaluated not for their effectiveness, but for their contribution to the ideological structuring of a meaningful world.

1551. Wright, Peter. "Astrology and Science in Seventeenth-Century
       England." SOCIAL STUDIES OF SCIENCE 5 (1975): 399-422.

Looks at some of the difficulties in distinguishing scientific
from nonscientific explanations and the way in which such a distinction is made. Science and magic are said to be based on quite
different systems of cognition. Astrology and science in seventeenth-century England are used to illustrate these systems.
Astrology at the time not only provided an explanatory model for
the intelligentsia, but also influenced every level of society. The
author suggests that astrology was "not simply a cosmology, but
also a craft whose practices gave rise to particular professional
interests" (p. 413). Astrology's opponents (many of whom were
clergymen) did not attack its cosmological assumptions but its
practical applications. Astrology functions primarily as a system
of interpretation. The author also offers an explanation for the
decline of astrology by the late seventeenth century. His approach
takes people's interest in astrology seriously and does not dismiss
it as a superstition or pseudoscience.

1552. Zablocki, Benjamin D. THE JOYFUL COMMUNITY: AN ACCOUNT OF THE
       BRUDERHOF, A COMMUNAL MOVEMENT NOW IN ITS THIRD GENERATION.
       Baltimore: Penguin Books, 1971. 362 pp.

Presents a study of a communal society known as the Bruderhof,
consisting of a federation of three colonies in the states of.New
York, Pennsylvania, and Connecticut. The author gives an account
of the movement's beliefs and rituals and traces its history from
its origins in 1920 under its founder Eberhard Arnold till the
early 1960's in several stages. The practice of communism, the
power of the Bruderhof, and its leadership and social control are
among the main topics dealt with. The kind of people who join the
movement, their conversion experience, the effects of membership,
and the condition of those who leave are discussed. The author
maintains that the Bruderhof's model of utopia is unlikely to
become widespread, but its has important lessons for utopianism in
general and society at large. He includes a short appendix on
research methodology (pp. 331-33) and a basic bibliography (pp.
334-42).

1553. Zaretsky, Irving I. "In the Beginning Was the World: The Relation-
       ship of Language to Social Organization in Spiritualist Churches."
       RELIGIOUS MOVEMENTS IN CONTEMPORARY AMERICA (item 727), pp. 166-
       219.

Maintains that Spiritualists have a particular vocabulary, a kind
of ritual language, used when church-related topics are discussed.
Arguing that language is one main key for understanding culture and
social organization, the author attempts to decode the information
imparted by a Spiritualist movement in California. A description
of the church is provided and the role of language analyzed with
special attention being paid to the context in which the unique
vocabulary is used. It is maintained that, through the verbal exchanges in their religious language, Spiritualists create the
social organization of their church that, in turn, promotes the
language. The social structure of the church can only be understood in terms of the speech used to define roles and statuses,
spiritual development of members, and church activities.

1554. Zaretsky, Irving I. "The Language of Spiritualist Churches: A
        Study of Cognition and Social Organization." CULTURE AND COG-
        NITION: RULES, MAPS, AND PLANS. Edited by James A. Spradley.
        San Francisco: Chandler Publishing Company, 1972, pp. 355-96.

Presents the theory that "through their verbal exchanges in the
idiom of the argot (i.e., the special vocabulary), Spiritualists
create the social organization of the church--the roles, statuses,
and hierarchical relationships that articulate the church as a
social institution" (p. 357). The author describes the organization and belief system of Spiritualist churches, draws up a typology of them, and discusses the role of language. He gives, in
schematic form, examples of the kind of special terms used in
Spiritualist churches.

1555. Zygmunt, Joseph F. "Jehovah's Witnesses in the U.S.A.--1942-76."
        SOCIAL COMPASS 24 (1977): 45-57.

Examines the following four aspects of the recent developments
among the Jehovah's Witnesses: 1) the changing relationship to
secular authorities and other religious groups; 2) their accommodation to a rising membership (with, for instance, the introduction
of a new system of eldership); 3) their attempts to revitalize
their millenarian attitudes; and 4) their new strategies (such as a
more rigorous enforcement of moral standards) to maintain their
separation from the world.

1556. Zygmunt, Joseph F. "Prophetic Failure and Chiliastic Identity: The
        Case of Jehovah's Witnesses." AMERICAN JOURNAL OF SOCIOLOGY 75
        (1970): 926-48.

Presents an analysis of the impact of the millenarian hopes of
Jehovah's Witnesses throughout the movement's history. The early
belief system and collective identity are discussed. One feature
of the group's long-term adaptation can be seen in its abandonment
of a date-centered chiliasm that had prevailed for half a century
and had led to five prophetic failures. The author outlines the
patterns that response to such failures generally followed and the
identity changes that accompanied the patterns.

B.   STUDIES ON NEW CULTS AND RELIGIOUS MOVEMENTS

1557.   Aagaard, Johannes.   "Guru and God."   UPDATE: A QUARTERLY JOURNAL OF
NEW RELIGIOUS MOVEMENTS 1.2 (1977): 8-14.

Explores the Hindu meaning of the term "guru" with special reference to a movement called Yoga Trust led by Swami Narayanananda in
Gylling, Denmark.   This guru's books and the contents of his dar-
shans or satsangs are examined.   Gurus, according to the author,
establish   a total bond between themselves and their disciples, a
bond that involves absolute obedience on the part of the followers
who actually treat their gurus as gods or saviors.

1558.   Aagaard, Pernille.   "The Children of God's Attitudes Towards Politics."   UPDATE: A QUARTERLY JOURNAL OF NEW RELIGIOUS MOVEMENTS
2.1 (1978): 31-37.

Attempts to give an idea of the political system favored by the
Children of God with copious citations from the Mo Letters.   The
author states that this movement must be understood as part of the
counterculture of the 1960's.   He describes the members' negative
attitude to America and Europe (except England).   The Children of
God have an ambivalent attitude to Moamar Gaddafi, the ruler of
Libya.   They admire him for his plans to build a godly society, yet
they consider him to be a likely candidate for the person of the
anti-Christ.

1559.   Abilla, Walter D.   THE BLACK MUSLIMS IN AMERICA: AN INTRODUCTION TO
THE THEORY OF COMMITMENT.   Nairobi, Kenya: East Africa Literature
Bureau, 1977.   ix, 98 pp.

Gives an overview of the Black Muslim Movement in the United
States, focusing on members in the Cleveland, Ohio area.   The
author analyzes the character of those who remain in the movement,
the features of the authority system of Black Muslim leadership,
and the economic condition of those who join.   He finds that the
nature of the members' commitment is not determined by the position
one occupies in the movement's structure.   Commitment is measured
by using the following variables: 1) attendance at temple services;
2) financial contribution; 3) selling of literature; 4) bringing
new members to the temple; 5) ratio of friends in the Nation of
Islam as opposed to friends outside the movement; 6) length of
membership; and 7) attendance at Black Muslim activities.

1560.   Abraham, Gary.   "The Protestant Ethic and the Spirit of Utilitarianism: The Case of EST."   THEORY AND SOCIETY 12 (1983): 739-77.

Discusses the presence of small self-help groups in the United
States in the context of Weber's idea of "hygienic utilitarianism"
that provided the necessary foundation for his theory of the Protestant ethic and later became independent of its religious matrix.
The author considers one contemporary group, namely Erhard Seminars Training (EST), now known as The Forum, as an example of such

utilitarianism. The ideology of EST is described and it is suggested that its principles and practices are best understood as
"one modern response to problems of individual suffering" (p. 750).
EST's ideology has its origins in ascetic Protestantism, even
though its goals are secular and practical.

1561. Adams, Robert Lynn, and Robert Jon Fox. "Mainlining Jesus: The New
        Trip." SOCIETY 9.4 (1972): 50-56.

        Investigates the Jesus Movement, concentrating on one institution
        called Gethsemane Chapel in Orange County, Los Angeles. The reli-
        gious services held in this chapel and activities at several Jesus
        communes are described. The Jesus Trip, according to the authors,
        is tailored for adolescents and provides them with the necessary
        peers, rituals, creeds, and programs; it is an attempt to resolve
        the crisis of sexuality and replace the use of drugs. The authors
        see a continuity between the drug culture and the Jesus experience
        in that both are antiestablishment and stress subjective experi-
        ence. Unlike the drug experience, however, the Jesus Trip revolves
        around Jesus and is limited in scope with less variety; it also
        represents an ideological swing from the far left to the far right;
        and it adopts a different view of sexuality with a distinctly
        authoritarian viewpoint. While the drug experience is a quest, the
        Jesus Trip is a panacea for all human problems. The authors think
        that the Jesus Trip is rather faddish.

1562. Adams, Richard, and Janice Hacken. "Anticultural Culture: Life-
        spring Ideology and Its Roots in Humanistic Psychology." JOURNAL
        OF HUMANISTIC PSYCHOLOGY 27 (1989): 501-17.

        Examines "the social and ideological premises of Lifespring
        Training and their implications for bringing about social change"
        (p. 504). Lifespring, a Human Potential Movement, is based on the
        anticultural ideology that 1) believes that culture stifles indi-
        viduals and inhibits the realization of their potential, 2) rejects
        the view that legitimate values exist outside people, and 3) conse-
        quently trains its participants to avoid or transcend the power
        that culture has on them. Humanistic psychology is, according to
        the authors, the basis of this anticultural trend. It is shown how
        Lifespring illustrates the "anticultural culture" in practice with
        its stress on subjectivism, which focuses on the inner nature and
        insight of the individual. The authors think that Lifespring "is
        likely to lead people to be more unreflectively a part of their own
        culture" (p. 513).

1563. Adler, Margot. DRAWING DOWN THE MOON: WITCHES, DRUIDS, GODDESS-
        WORSHIPERS, AND OTHER PAGANS IN AMERICAN TODAY. Boston: Beacon
        Press, second revised and enlarged edition, 1986. lv, 595 pp.

        Presents an informative and detailed historical study on the
        origin of neo-Paganism and Witchcraft that are seen as attempts to
        create nonauthoritarian and nondogmatic religious systems. The
        author gives an account of the Pagan polytheistic worldview and
        ritual and of the way people become pagans. She outlines the cur-
        rent Wiccan revival in its many different forms and examines the

re-emergence of several pagan religious groups, including the Church
of All Worlds. She sees a relationship between the feminist movement and neo-Paganism. One chapter reviews the theories that explain the growth of new magical and religious groups. A number of
pagan rituals and a lengthy, comprehensive survey of resources (pp.
475-551) are included in the appendices.

1564.   Adler, Moshe. "Alienation and the Jesus Freaks." JUDAISM 23
        (1974): 287-97.

Maintains that one of the reasons why Jews defect from their
religious tradition and join Christian sects might be "alienation
from self," that is, a sense of having no personal worth and no
real home. Negative association with Judaism can reinforce self-
alienation and develop a failure-oriented picture of the universe,
leading the individual to defect to another reassuring worldview.
The author thinks that the Jewish Jesus trip is a painful symptom
of some of the contemporary problems of Jewish life and culture.

1565.   Adorno, Theodore W. "The Stars Down to Earth: The Los Angeles
        Times Astrology Column." TELOS 19 (1974): 13-90.

Presents a comprehensive sociological study of the daily astrology column in the LOS ANGELES TIMES, namely "The Astrological
Forecasts" by Carroll Righter. The basic situation in which the
column appears and the way it differs from astrological magazines
are outlined. The author unveils the underlying psychology of the
forecasts, observing that Righter caters to the narcissistic, anx-
ious, and dependent individual. Astrology, it is stated, encourages
an intellectual attitude that is expressive of "disoriented agnos-
ticism." Its basic structure can be reduced to the division of
labor.

1566.   Ahern, Jeffrey. "Five Karmas, or Anthroposophy, in Great Britain."
        UPDATE: A QUARTERLY JOURNAL OF NEW RELIGIOUS MOVEMENTS 6.4 (1982):
        68-77.

Describes the "esoteric identity" of Anthroposophy, focusing on
its membership in Great Britain. The application of its founder's
(Rudolph Steiner) system in the well-known Waldorf Schools, magical
agriculture and horticulture, spiritual dance, speech formation,
and spiritual science are sketched. Anthroposophy, which is the
organizational offspring of Theosophy, has a large membership in
India and a small following in Europe and in the United States.
The secretive School of Spiritual Science, located near Basel,
Switzerland, the Christian Community (the Anthroposophical Church)
with its extensive rituals, the village communities in Camphill,
Scotland, and the Anthropological Society in Britain are described.
These four branches of the society together with the school at
Goetheanum in Switzerland are the five karmas.

1567.   Ahlberg, Sture. MESSIANIC MOVEMENTS: A COMPARATIVE STUDY OF THE
        SABBATIANS, THE PEOPLE'S TEMPLE, AND THE UNIFICATION CHURCH.
        Stockholm: Almquist and Wiksell, 1986. 128 pp.

Explores the typical traits that separate messianic movements
from other prophetic ones. Three movements are compared, namely
those led by Sabbatai Sevi in the seventeenth century and by Jim
Jones and Reverend Moon in the twentieth. Each movement is briefly
described and their main features outlined. The main thrust is to
understand the self-proclaimed messiahs psychologically. The
author thinks that they are all antinomian in character, which
might make them criminals. He examines the techniques used in Jim
Jones' People's Temple and concludes that the term "brainwashing"
adequately describes the indoctrination process used to maintain
membership. The Unification Church uses similar techniques to
elicit commitment without the use of violence. A functional analysis of messianism is adopted, the most observable social function
being its replacement of the nuclear family by the extended family.

1568. Albrecht, Mark. "Gnosticism, Past and Present: An Examination of
        the Parallels Between Radha Soami Teachings and Hellenistic Gnos-
        ticism." UPDATE: A QUARTERLY JOURNAL OF NEW RELIGIOUS MOVEMENTS
        5.3-4 (1981): 19-34.

        Explores a fast-growing movement in the West, namely the Radha
        Soami, a syncretistic religion that was established in North India
        in 1861. An overview of ancient Gnosticism is given and then com-
        pared with the teachings of Radha Soami about God, the cosmos,
        human nature, eschatology, and salvation. The author holds that
        the conditions that gave rise to hellenistic Gnosticism are very
        similar to those of modern Western society. In both instances the
        traditional social, political, and religious frameworks were break-
        ing down due to the expansion of a uniform language and civiliza-
        tion. An interview between several Western writers on the new
        cults and Charan Singh, the guru of the largest of the Radha Soami
        sects in Beas, India, is transcribed (pp. 23-34).

1569. Alfred, Randall H. "The Church of Satan." THE NEW RELIGIOUS CON-
        SCIOUSNESS, pp. 180-202.

        Discusses the widespread interest in magical and satanic rituals.
        The author distinguishes between black and white witchcraft and
        then concentrates on the Church of Satan in San Francisco, a black
        magic group led by Anton Szandor LaVey. The main principles of
        Satanic philosophy, namely hedonism, magic, diabolism, iconoclasm,
        millenarianism, and the charismatic authority vested in the high
        priest, are described. The membership components and recruitment
        practices are analyzed. The author maintains that there is an
        element of conscious show business in Satanism. He thinks that the
        conflicts and contradictions within Satanism must be resolved in
        order to insure the survival of the Church of Satan.

1570. Ambrose, Kenneth P. "Function of the Family in the Process of Com-
        mitment Within the Unification Movement." THE FAMILY AND THE
        UNIFICATION CHURCH (item 1785), pp. 23-33.

        Describes the concept of commitment as related to the family in
        the Unification Church, using Kanter's model in her book COMMITMENT
        AND COMMUNITY (item 383). The various types of commitment--instru-

mental, affective, and moral--are visible in the theory and practice of the Unification Church. The author develops a model that
shows how the person who joins the movement progresses from close
personal ties with church members to commitment to the group and
finally to the acceptance of the ideology embodied in the DIVINE
PRINCIPLE. At this stage of involvement the member feels the need
to enter into a married relationship with a partner selected by the
Reverend Moon. A filter theory of mate selection is used to show
how the matched marriage overrides other factors (like attractiveness) in the choice of a partner. Marriage in the church stresses
the overriding goals of the institution to which all individual
aspirations are secondary. The family system strengthens a
person's commitment to the church's goals and values.

1571. Anderson, John. "The Hare Krishna Movement in the USSR." RELIGION
        IN COMMUNIST LANDS 14 (1986): 316-17.

        Traces the origin of the Hare Krishna Movement in the U.S.S.R. to
        an early convert, namely Anatoli Pinyayev. The relationship be-
        tween the state and the new religion is briefly outlined. The Hare
        Krishna Movement has spread throughout many different parts of the
        Soviet Union, in spite of the state's repressive measures that have
        led to the arrest and imprisonment of many of its members. The
        Soviet press has taken a negative view of the movement, linking it
        to espionage and to mental illness.

1572. Androes, Louis C. "The Rajneesh Experience: A Report." COMMUNAL
        SOCIETIES 6 (1986): 101-17.

        Provides a brief biographical sketch of Bhagwan Shree Rajneesh,
        the founder of the Rajneesh Movement, and then selects one signifi-
        cant and typical aspect of his teachings, namely "work as worship,"
        to understand the movement. The author links Rajneesh's thought to
        Indian mystical ontology as depicted in the Advaita (nondual or
        monistic mysticism). The definition of work, play, worship, medi-
        tation, celebration, and enlightenment as expressed by Rajneesh are
        then explored and interpreted in the context of a religious, agri-
        cultural, environmental, and communal society. A typical day in
        the life of a sannaysin at Rajneeshpuram is described.

1573. Anthony, Dick, and Thomas Robbins. "The Effect of Detente on the
        Growth of New Religions: Reverend Moon and the Unification
        Church." UNDERSTANDING THE NEW RELIGIONS (item 667), pp. 80-100.

        Views the Unification Church as a sectarian version of Civil
        Religion that is disintegrating in Western culture. The main
        theories of this church regarding the place of America in God's
        plan and the role of the Church and Reverend Moon in the struggle
        between democracy and communism are outlined. The goal of the
        Unification Church to establish a worldwide benevolent theocracy is
        underscored. The author interprets the church's position in the
        context of dualistic themes found in several world religions.

1574. Anthony, Dick, and Thomas Robbins. "The Meher Baba Movement: Its
        Effect on Post-Adolescent Social Alienation." RELIGIOUS MOVE-
        MENTS IN CONTEMPORARY AMERICA (item 727), pp. 479-501.

Presents a brief outline of a movement founded by Meher Baba, an
Indian spiritual master who claimed to be an avatar. The authors
pursued the anthropological method of participant observation in
their investigation of this group, a method which they think is
well suited to the study of systems of meaning. The main hypothesis advanced is that the Baba Movement "performs basic expressive
and communal functions which are increasingly marginal in bureaucratized 'adult' instrumental milieux" (p. 479). Such functions
were previously performed by the drug culture of the 1960's. Most
Meher Baba lovers are said to have been involved in the counterculture movement with which they had become disillusioned. The
universalism of this movement has been used as an effective device
to legitimize the structural social changes that are taking place
in Western culture.

1575. Anthony, Dick, Thomas Robbins, Madeline Doucas, and Thomas E. Curtis.
      "Patients and Pilgrims: Changing Attitudes Towards Psychotherapy
      of Converts to Eastern Mysticism." AMERICAN BEHAVIORAL SCIENTIST
      20 (1977): 861-86.

Describes the experiences with psychotherapy of converts to the
Meher Baba Movement and to Guru Maharaj Ji's the Divine Life Mission. These converts have, as a rule, found traditional psychotherapy unable to help them in their difficulties and turned to
Eastern mysticism. Three stages in the individual history of these
converts are noted: 1) preconversion experience with psychotherapy;
2) spiritual awakening leading to involvement in one of the two
groups; and 3) reentry into psychotherapy. The authors hold that
"the monistic symbolic universe of Eastern mysticism converges with
some of the assumptions of modern psychotherapy" (p. 880). Some of
the psychological benefits of involvement in Eastern religious
movements are mentioned.

1576. Aphek, Edna, and Yishai Tobin. "On Image Building and Establishing
      Credibility in the Language of Fortune-Telling". EASTERN ANTHRO-
      POLOGIST 36 (1983): 287-308.

Discusses various aspects of the sociolinguistics and rituals
used by male palm readers in Israel in the context of the increase
of interest in different methods of fortune-telling, faith healing,
and the occult in different parts of the world. Three major categories of fortune-tellers are described, namely: 1) the classic
type, whose language is substandard and informal; 2) the type who
manifests all the effects of the Western specialist or expert and
whose language is educated and scientific; and 3) an intermediary
type who combines an educated language with informality. Brief
transcripts from sessions with four different fortune-tellers are
given. It is argued that "the use of language in its social contexts, as well as the linguistic and non-linguistic devices used
to establish credibility, play an important role in the fortune-
teller's influencing of his client" (p. 301).

1577. Aphek, Edna, and Yishai Tobin. "Cartomancy." ENCYCLOPEDIC DICTIO-
      NARY OF SEMIOTICS. Edited by Thomas T. Seboek et al. New York:
      Mouton de Gruyter, 1986, pp. 99-100.

Lists briefly the various interpretations given to cartomancy, a form of divination based on the reading of Tarot cards or modern decks. Among the meanings given to such fortune-telling is a social semiotic one in which the linguistic, social, and cultural aspects are taken into account. The author thinks that applying the "semiotic system," which views the relationship between the cartomanist and his or her client, is necessary for understanding cartomancy.

1578. Aphek, Edna, and Yishai Tobin. "The Language of Cartomancy: A Sociolinguistic Perspective." PROCEEDINGS 1: AILA 81 (Sixth International Congress of Applied Linguistics). Edited by Bengt Sigurd and Jan Svartvik. Lund, Sweden: Wallin and Dalholm, 1981, pp. 436-37.

Presents some of the results of a research project investigating the function of language in the encounter between fortune-tellers and cartomanists and their clients. The language used by fortune-tellers is categorized into three major divisions. Cartomancy must be interpreted in the context of the linguist, extralinguistic, social, and cultural settings in which it takes place. The dyadic encounter between the cartomanist and his or her client are part of the fortune-telling process. The language of fortune-telling is a form of persuasive language, which influences both one's reason and emotions.

1579. Aphek, Edna, and Yishai Tobin. "A Linguistic Analysis of the Language of Palm Reading: A Preliminary Analysis." ANGEWANDTE SOZIOLINGUISTIK. Edited by Matthias Hartig. Tubigen: Gunter Narr Verlag, 1981, pp. 165-88.

Gives an account of the authors' research on the language used by fortune-tellers and presents a thorough analysis of three male palm readers. The terminology employed during the readings is recorded and excerpts from the palm-reading sessions are given. Three linguistic elements of the ritual are noted: 1) extralinguistic elements; 2) elements from persuasive communication; and 3) elements from the discourse itself. It is concluded that the language of fortune-telling is a subcategory of persuasive language.

1580. Ashworth, C. E. "Flying Saucers, Spoon-Bending, and Atlantis: A Structural Analysis of New Mythologies." SOCIOLOGICAL REVIEW 28 (1980): 353-76.

Discusses the nature and appeal of "popular science," a form of knowledge that has its roots in the general public rather than in the institutions of higher learning. The claims, concerns, and cosmologies of popular science are described and a structural theory is presented to account for their increasing influence. The author explores the common links between popular topics like alchemy, the Bermuda Triangle, the Druids, astral projection, Transcendental Meditation, UFOs, and water divining. Stonehenge and the Shroud of Turin are taken as examples of popular science and dealt with in some detail. In like manner, two cosmological myths, von Daniken's view of UFOs and the theory of Atlantis, are said to be,

respectively, examples of Judeo-Christian millenarianism and Greek
materialism on the one hand, and platonic eclecticism on the other.
Popular science takes anomalies and offers absolute answers. It
resolves contradictions in terms of human experiences when conventional religion and science are unable to offer any solutions.

1581. Atkinson, Paul. "The Symbolic Significance of Health Foods."
       NUTRITION AND LIFESTYLES. Edited by Michael Turner. London:
       Applied Sciences Publishers, 1979, pp. 79-89.

       Discusses, from an anthropological point of view, the social
       values, beliefs, and meanings that are generally associated with
       health foods. The symbolism of food operates on two levels: 1) it
       marks fine distinctions between social occasions, groups, and indi-
       viduals and 2) it provides a way of expressing the relationship of
       human society with the natural world. The trend to adopt natural
       "health" foods, as opposed to artificial foodstuffs made by human
       hands, is related to alternative movements and ideologies or cultic
       milieus. It relies heavily on the distinction between nature and
       culture, particularly the modern, industrial, scientific culture
       that has developed in the West.

1582. Babb, Lawrence A. "Sathya Sai Baba's Magic." ANTHROPOLOGICAL
       QUARTERLY 56 (1983): 116-24.

       Explores the role of the miraculous in the international cult of
       Sathya Sai Baba, one of the most important religious figures in
       modern India. The author gives a brief biography of this guru and
       examines the credibility of his miracles and the attractive quali-
       ties of his teachings. Arguing that his miracles are not essen-
       tially a recruiting device, the author points out that the miracles
       are mainly a vehicle for his relationships with his devotees and
       follow a pattern very familiar in Hindu devotional worship. The
       miracles are also performed with an apparent capriciousness that is
       reminiscent of the Hindu view that the gods are playful. The inde-
       terminancy of Baba's miracles does not disconfirm his claims, but
       rather exemplifies his divine attributes.

1583. Baer, Hans A. "Black Spiritual Israelites in a Small Southern
       City." SOUTHERN QUARTERLY 23.3 (1985): 103-24.

       Presents a study of a relatively new branch of the Spiritual
       Israel Church and its Army. An overview of the history, beliefs,
       and rituals of the church is provided. Its roots are said to lie
       in two large Afro-American religious traditions, namely Black
       Judaism and Black Spiritualism. The first leader of the church
       served as pastor, prophetess, healer, social worker, employment
       counselor, and friend of her congregation. The political-religious
       hierarchy of the Black Israelites is outlined and the functions of
       the various members noted. The author thinks that the dimensions
       of protest and accommodation that this sect symbolizes and expres-
       ses are closely related.

1584. Bainbridge, William Sims. "Science and Religion: The Case of Sci-
       entology." THE FUTURE OF NEW RELIGIOUS MOVEMENTS (item 579), pp.
       59-79.

Argues that while Scientology has no discernible cultural continuity with the Judeo-Christian tradition, it claims a close relationship with science (particularly with its use of the E-meter in
auditing). Scientology has two great strengths, namely 1) in the
popular science fiction subculture, and 2) in its harmony with
contemporary scientific cosmology. The role of Ron Hubbard as a
science fiction writer is outlined and his achievement in the field
compared with other popular science fiction writers is evaluated.
One of the major attractions of Scientology is that it makes the
human being, rather than God, the center of existence. The author
thinks that some religions like Scientology will be a major force
in the future of Western civilization.

1585. Bainbridge, William Sims. SATAN'S POWER: A DEVIANT PSYCHOTHERAPY
      CULT. Berkeley: University of California Press, 1978. vii,
      312 pp.

      Presents a sociological monograph on a Satanic cult that the
      author calls pseudonymously "The Power," (which is usually taken
      to refer to The Process Church of the Final Judgment). The author
      provides a history of the cult from its birth in England in 1963
      under Edward de Forest to its peak in 1974 when it had spread to
      other parts of Europe and to North America. Its emergence is de-
      scribed as that of "a deviant subculture born from conventional
      middle-class English society through the mechanisms of a pseudo-
      psychotherapy group" (p. 14). The communal lifestyle of the Power's
      members, the initiation process, the symbols and rituals of the
      cult, and the various therapeutic practices are described. The
      author gives an account of the great schism of 1974, in which the
      leader was ejected from the group and formed his own new cult,
      while the majority of the members formed a new organization called
      The Establishment Church of the Apocalypse. The decline and fur-
      ther splintering of de Forest's group is traced in detail.

1586. Bainbridge, William Sims. "Chariots of the Gullible." SKEPTICAL
      INQUIRER 3 (Winter 1978): 33-48.

      Examines the reason why so many people react favorably to the
      myth of ancient astronauts, particularly the one proposed by Erich
      von Daniken. Questionnaires given to over 200 university students
      were intended to test the following four theories that have been
      proposed to explain why Daniken's theory is acceptable: 1) the
      strain theory that maintains that these beliefs legitimize desires
      that conformity cannot satisfy; 2) the control theory that renders
      a person free to commit delinquent acts because his or her ties to
      convention have been broken; 3) the cultural deviance theory that
      explains deviant behavior as a conformity to a set of standards not
      accepted by the society at large; and 4) the trait theory that sees
      the deviation as an expression of individual characteristics. The
      author finds the last two mentioned theories more promising than
      the first two. People who accept von Daniken's theory are inter-
      ested both in the occult and in the scientific exploration of space.

1587. Bainbridge, William Sims, and Daniel H. Jackson. "The Rise and
      Decline of Transcendental Meditation." THE SOCIAL IMPACT OF THE
      NEW RELIGIOUS MOVEMENTS (item 725), pp. 135-57.

Provides a basic ethnographic description of the Transcendental Meditation Movement in the U.S.A. in two major phases, from the mid-1960's to the peak year of 1975 and from 1975 to the present day. During its first phase, the movement was a socially accepted client cult for meditators but a deviant cult for its teachers. During the second phase there was "an intensification of the supernatural element as a response to the decline in initiations" (p. 151). The substantial drop in recruitment is believed to have led to an intensification of its religious element in the form of the Siddhi Program. Transcendental Meditation changed from a client cult to a cult movement, which contributed to its further decline.

1588.   Bainbridge, William Sims, and Rodney Stark.   "Friendship, Religion, and the Occult."   REVIEW OF RELIGIOUS RESEARCH 22 (1981): 313-27.

Examines "how religious beliefs and practices become salient for dyadic personal friendships" (p. 313). After studying members of various churches and sects, the authors conclude that occult beliefs and attitudes (which include various forms of meditation, interest in astrology and the consultation of one's horoscope, and belief in extrasensory perception and psychic healing) are crucial for personal relationships only if they are linked with social movements or strong, formal organizations.

1589.   Bainbridge, William Sims, and Rodney Stark.   "Scientology: To Be Perfectly Clear."   SOCIOLOGICAL ANALYSIS 41 (1980): 128-36.

Advances a theory to explain the apparent success of Scientology in raising 16000 of its members to a superhuman level of functioning known as "clear." It is argued that empirical evidence does not support this claim and that the state of "clear" "is not a state of personal development at all, but a social status conferring honor within the cult's status system and demanding certain kinds of behavior from the person labeled clear" (p. 128). Ron Hubbard's social mechanisms used to establish and defend the status of "clear" are discussed. Scientology caters to those people who suffer from chronic unhappiness or inability to perform at the level set for themselves. It does not solve the underlying problems; it merely "cures the complaints by ending the person's freedom to complain" (p. 134).

1590.   Baird, Robert D.   "ISKCON and the Struggle for Legitimation." BULLETIN OF THE JOHN RYLANDS UNIVERSITY LIBRARY OF MANCHESTER 70.3 (1988): 157-69.

Describes three approaches that the Hare Krishna Movement has used to achieve social and legal recognition: 1) the U.S. Courts, where the movement has struggled for acceptance as a bona fide religion; 2) the courtship of scholars' approval, which includes scholarly publications and sponsoring of conferences; and 3) the adoption of a positive approach to other religious traditions, which stresses dialogue and interfaith contacts.

1591.   Baird, Robert D.   "The Response of Swami Bhaktivedanta."   MODERN INDIAN RESPONSES TO RELIGIOUS PLURALISM. Edited by Harold Coward. New York: State University of New York Press, 1987, pp. 105-27.

Examines the attitudes and reactions to religious pluralism of
the founder of the Hare Krishna Movement. After outlining some
principles that guide the treatment of Swami Prabhupada's treatment
of other religions, the author assesses his views on religion in
general. Prabhupada maintains that all religions, though containing some truth, are incomplete. He is somewhat harsh in his evaluation of all religions outside devotion to Krishna. The author
thinks, however, that as the Hare Krishna Movement is transformed
from a sect to a denomination, Prabhupada's milder statements will
become more prominent in the movement's relationship with other
religions.

1592. Baird, Robert D. "Religious or Non-Religious: TM in American
       Courts." JOURNAL OF DHARMA 7 (1982): 391-407.

Discusses the contention of proponents of Transcendental Meditation that TM is not a religion but an educational method that offers many benefits that are scientifically verifiable. The theoretical basis of this form of meditation, called the Science of
Creative Intelligence, is explained. The arguments presented in a
New Jersey law suit that challenged the teaching of a TM course in
some public schools are described. Two main reasons were adduced
that led the court to decide that Transcendental Meditation was a
religion: the content of the course it taught was equivalent to
religious teachings, and the "puja" (a service in which the mantra
is assigned to a new meditator) was clearly an example of religious
ritual.

1593. Bak, Felix. "The Church of Satan in the United States." ANTO-
       NIANUM 50.1-2 (1975): 152-93.

Describes in some detail the Church of Satan founded by Anton
Szandor LaVey and considered by the author as "the most rampant of
all forms of Satanism in the U.S.A." (p. 153). After a brief biographical sketch of LaVey, the author summarizes the main beliefs
and rituals of the church. He considers the Satanic Movement as a
"social danger."

1594. Balch, Robert W. "When the Light Goes Out, Darkness Comes: A Study
       of Defection From a Totalistic Cult." RELIGIOUS MOVEMENTS: GENE-
       SIS, EXODUS, AND NUMBERS (item 692), pp. 11-55.

Continues the author's study of the members of a totalistic UFO
cult who had given up their allegiance (see items 1595-98). By
incorporating participant-observation data with the disillusioned
believers' accounts of their own defection, the researcher drew up
a complete description of the group's history, organization, beliefs, and membership careers from recruitment to defection. The
following factors leading to defection are explored: 1) the crack
in consensual validation; 2) demoralizing experiences; 3) vacilla-
tion; 4) behavioral disengagement; 5) departure; 6) floating; 7)
reentry; and 8) cognitive reorganization. Since defectors engage
in a process of "symbolic bridge-building," it is suggested that
the rate of defection and the character of the retrospective accounts "are closely related to the opportunities for bridge-building talk during everyday conversations between members" (p. 55).

1595.   Balch, Robert W.   "Bo and Peep: A Case Study of the Origins of
        Messianic Leadership." MILLENNIALISM AND CHARISMA (item 711),
        pp. 13-72.

        Considers, with reference to a UFO cult, how a would-be prophet
        progresses from an apparently normal individual to a full-fledged
        religious visionary. The author questions how the two leaders of
        this religious movement, Marshall Herff Applewhite and Bonnie Lu
        Nettles, were transformed into Bo and Peep, who called themselves
        the Two Witnesses, and how this change led to the formation of the
        UFO cult. Descriptions of the research method followed by the
        author, of the main features of the cult, and of the background of
        its founders are given. The author suggests the following ana-
        lytical categories for comparing gurus, prophets, and messiahs: the
        background characteristics; the precipitating crises; the weakening
        of social bonds; the onset of paranormal experiences; the turning
        point; the self-initiated withdrawal; the awakening to higher
        reality; the revelation; the reentering of the world; the dis-
        appearance of symptomatic behavior; and the creation of social
        reality. The author finds this analysis consistent with Bainbridge
        and Stark's model (item 740). He concludes that "a new religion,
        at least in its early stages, may be largely a projection of its
        leader's personality" (p. 68).

1596.   Balch, Robert W.   "Looking Behind the Scenes in a Religious Cult:
        Implications for the Study of Conversion." SOCIOLOGICAL ANALYSIS
        41 (1980): 137-43.

        Studies a UFO cult lead by two people, named Bo and Peep, who
        claimed to be the two witnesses mentioned in the New Testament Book
        of Revelation (chapter 11). The author gives a brief description
        of the group and of the participant-observation method used to
        collect data. The focus was on observing the daily lives of the
        adherents and on the roles they adopted when they became members.
        It is argued that the first step to join a cult is to learn how "to
        act as a convert by outwardly conforming to a narrowly proscribed
        set of role expectations" (p. 142). Genuine convictions develop
        later, even though members may never overcome their doubts about
        the cults' beliefs and goals. The common, public impression of
        cult members as glassy-eyed zombies was actually adopted by the UFO
        people when they addressed nonmembers. It is postulated that
        dramatic behavioral changes in converts could result from the rapid
        learning of new roles rather than through sudden changes in person-
        ality (brainwashing).

1597.   Balch, Robert W.   "Salvation in a UFO." PSYCHOLOGY TODAY 10.5
        (October 1976): 58-66, 106.

        Presents a brief description of a small UFO cult, led by two
        individuals who adopted the names Bo and Peep, and who were
        attracting people by their promise of salvation in flying saucers.
        The authors joined the group for a while and followed them in their
        travels to various mountains in expectation of the coming salvation
        in UFOs. The adherents of this cult were encouraged to adopt a
        "bland look" so that they "wouldn't be seen as just another bunch

of kooks" (p. 58). Cult members had been religious seekers for a
long time before they joined. Their rather spartan lifestyle is
described. There was little, if any, indoctrination or coercion,
and the members' doubts were openly discussed. Those who dropped
out of the group were not shattered by their experience; they
thought that their temporary membership had been beneficial.

1598. Balch, Robert W., and David Taylor. "Seekers and Saucers: The Role
       of the Cultic Milieu in Joining a UFO Cult." AMERICAN BEHAVIORAL
       SCIENTIST 20 (1977): 839-60.

       Examines a small UFO cult, led by two prophetic figures (Bo and
       Peep) who claimed to be members of the kingdom of heaven sent to
       save people through the advent of UFOs. The authors, who joined
       the cult as hidden observers for seven weeks, examine the social
       organization of this religious movement and describe its recruit-
       ment methods. They suggest that those who became members saw their
       actions as a continuation of their spiritual quest, without the
       need of first establishing social ties with any of its adherents.
       The lifestyles of premembers was such that it led them to join a
       new religious group. They had been "religious seekers" and as such
       were not disoriented, but rather "socially oriented to the quest for
       personal growth," a growth which the UFO cult would accelerate.
       While joiners suffered from "psychic deprivation," the authors
       maintain that this deprivation was to some degree generated by the
       very role of being a seeker.

1599. Balswick, Jack. "The Jesus People: A Sociological Analysis."
       RELIGION AMERICAN STYLE. Edited by Patrick McNamara. New York:
       Harper and Row, 1974, pp. 359-66.

       Points out that the Jesus Movement unites two opposite life-
       styles, those of the Hippie subculture and of Christian Fundamen-
       talism. Several counterculture symbols have been incorporated into
       the movement, which stresses subjective religious experience, re-
       jects rationalism, encourages pragmatism, relies heavily on the
       authority of the Bible, and reacts against the organized church.
       The author, writing in the early 1970's, sees the future of the
       Jesus Movement as rather bleak. He thinks that it could either be
       taken over by the organized churches or else become another insti-
       tutionalized born-again Christian movement.

1600. Balswick, Jack. "The Jesus Movement: A Generational Interpreta-
       tion." JOURNAL OF SOCIAL ISSUES 30 (1974): 23-42.

       Proposes a "generational" interpretation of the Jesus People that
       sees them as differing both from the older generation and from their
       age-peers in the counterculture. As ex-members of the countercul-
       ture, Jesus People still exhibit many of its features, like subjec-
       tivity, informality, and spontaneity. As religious converts, they
       share some characteristics with fundamentalist Christians, like
       their belief in the inerrancy of the Bible, the stress on commit-
       ment to Jesus, and their insistence that there is only "one way" to
       God. The similarities and differences between the Jesus People and
       1) the older Christian fundamentalists, 2) the organized church,

and 3) the youth culture are discussed in some detail. The author
consists the Jesus People as a religious sect-movement, yet still
remaining within the tolerant limits of the normative structure of
American society. Some speculations on the future of the movement
are made.

1601.   Barker, Eileen. "Quo Vadis?: The Unification Church." THE FUTURE
        OF NEW RELIGIOUS MOVEMENTS (item 579), pp. 141-52.

        Lists several problems that the Unification Church and other new
        religions are likely to face in the next two decades. Three major
        areas of change which have had an impact on the Unification Church's
        direction are discussed: 1) the demographic shift in the movement's
        composition of membership; 2) the change in its leadership and
        structure; and 3) the theological reinterpretation of its messi-
        anic and millennial hopes.

1602.   Barker, Eileen. "Being a Moonie: Identity With an Unorthodox
        Orthodoxy." DISCIPLINES OF FAITH: RELIGION, POLITICS, AND PATRI-
        ARCHY. Edited by Jim Obelkevitch, Lyndal Roper, and Raphael
        Samuel. London: Routledge and Kegan Paul, 1987, pp. 211-25.

        Refutes the common view that by joining the Unification Church
        a person loses his or her identity. It is argued that while the
        church's belief system does not fit into traditional orthodox
        Christianity, its religious values can be regarded as orthodox. It
        is the author's opinion that the potential Moonie comes from a
        background "liable to foster preference for an identity compatible
        with the values of religious orthodoxy" (p. 216). The author also
        discusses the following four aspects of identity that are impeded
        by modern society and nurtured by the Unification Church: 1) spiri-
        tual self-development; 2) self-realization through others; 3) self-
        control; and 4) continuity or self-perpetuation. Some members of
        the Unification Church have found an orthodox identity in an unor-
        thodox movement.

1603.   Barker, Eileen. "Defection From the Unification Church: Some
        Statistics and Distinctions." FALLING FROM THE FAITH (item 578),
        pp. 166-84.

        Points out the difficulty in accurately accounting for the number
        of defections from the Unification Church and gives a few statistics
        that show that there is a high rate of defection and that the turn-
        over rate in membership has remained constant over the last ten
        years. Focusing largely on the church in Great Britain, the author
        classifies those who leave into the tasters, apostates, rejects,
        and deprogrammees, and the kind of defection into clean-breaks,
        sharp breaks with active antagonism, breaks with the maintenance of
        some contact, and returns to the church. She concludes that the
        apostates may have joined the Unification Church for different
        reasons than those who stayed and may have been more independent
        and critical. Some of the findings of Wright and Piper (item 1034)
        are contradicted.

1604.   Barker, Eileen. "Why Witness?" Evangelism From a Unificationist
        Perspective." THE NEW EVANGELISTS (item 587), pp. 148-60.

Makes some generalizations about the Unification Church's official doctrinal position, the policy and practice of evangelization,
the way its members perceive their views, and the functions it has
for its membership. Though the Unification Church's position is
that evangelization is good for God, for the world, for those being
evangelized, and for the evangelizers themselves, not all Moonies
accept their task with fervor and some do their best to avoid it
for a variety of reasons. The author distinguishes between evangelizing, when Moonies talk to other people about their church, and
witnessing, a broader method for making the church known through
conferences and contacts with the clergy of other denominations,
for example. She stresses the effects that witnessing has on the
Unification Church. By propagating their faith, Moonies strengthen
their own belief system, but also create tension with outsiders.

1605. Barker, Eileen. "A Short History, But Many Changes: A New Reli-
gious Movement." GILGUL: ESSAYS ON TRANSFORMATION, REVOLUTION,
AND PERMANENCE IN THE HISTORY OF RELIGIONS. Edited by R. Shaked,
D. Shulman, and G. G. Stroumsa. Leiden, The Netherlands: E. J.
Brill, 1987, pp. 36-44.

Outlines some of the changes that have taken place in the Unification Church from 1975 to 1985. Reinterpretation of beliefs (such
as those relating to the millennium), reformulation of the boundaries between church members and outsiders, demographic and economic changes, the rise of bureaucratization, and the growth of factions within the movement are among the areas covered.

1606. Barker, Eileen. "Unification Church." THE ENCYCLOPEDIA OF RELI-
GIONS (item 18), vol. 15, pp. 141-43.

Provides a rather brief history of the Unification Church and an
overview of the lifestyle of those who become full-time members.
Its theology is said to be "one of the most comprehensive to be
produced by a contemporary new religion" (p. 141). Some of the
main themes of the DIVINE PRINCIPLE, the Unification Church's text
that offers a reinterpretation of the Bible, are described.

1607. Barker, Eileen. "The Unification Church ('The Moonies')." THE
ENCYCLOPEDIA OF WORLD FAITH. Edited by Peter Bishop and Michael
Darton. London: Macdonald Orbis, 1987, pp. 151-53.

Gives an brief overview of the Unification Church and outlines
its beliefs, worship, and organization.

1608. Barker, Eileen. "People Who Attend Unification Church Workshops
and Do Not Become Moonies." RELIGIOUS MOVEMENTS: GENESIS, EXO-
DUS, AND NUMBERS (item 692), pp. 65-93.

Argues that factors brought by prospective members to the Unification Church workshops often determine whether they end up joining
the church or not. The author uses the methods of participant
observation and questionnaire analysis to study those people who
decide not to commit themselves to the church. The following areas
are examined: the first contact with the Moonies; the sex, age, and

social class of the participants; their protection from, and pro-
pensity to, conversion; the workshop experience; and the nonconver-
sion experience. Bearing in mind that over 90 percent do not join,
the view that participants in Unification Church workshops are
converted by irresistible techniques of manipulation is challenged.

1609. Barker, Eileen. THE MAKING OF A MOONIE: BRAINWASHING OR CHOICE?
       Oxford: Blackwell, 1984. ix, 305 pp.

       Presents a major monograph on the Unification Church that seeks
       to explain the process of becoming a Moonie. After describing her
       methods of collecting data, the author gives a historical sketch of
       the church, outlines its theological beliefs that are generally
       available to outsiders, and relates the process of meeting church
       members and attending workshops. Among the main topics dealt with
       are the brainwashing issue, the use of deception, control environ-
       ment, and "love-bombing" (that is, the showering of attention on
       guests) to gain members, and the kind of people who actually join
       the movement. The author suggests that there are some predisposi-
       tions and social experiences that might lead certain individuals to
       be persuaded that the Unification Church has answers to many pres-
       sing problems. To the question as to whether Moonies join freely
       or not she maintains that the evidence "would lead to suggest that
       the answer lies considerably nearer the rational-choice pole on
       the continuum than it does to irresistible-brainwashing pole" (pp.
       250-51).

1610. Barker, Eileen. "Doing Love: Tensions in the Ideal Family." THE
       FAMILY AND THE UNIFICATION CHURCH (item 1785), pp. 35-52.

       Raises the question of how the Unification Church, which aims at
       creating a unified world where the ideal family could flourish, has
       been accused of bringing division and tension within many families
       of its own members. The ideal family in Unification theology and
       the conflict which this theology creates are discussed. The Rever-
       end Moon's own family relationships are described. The author
       remarks that the tension between Unification Church members and
       their families should not cause surprise among historians and soci-
       ologists of religion. Adherence to a belief system that changes
       one's status and demands duty and service to others leads to isola-
       tion and familial estrangement. The leaders of two major religions,
       Jesus and the Buddha, are quoted as examples. It is pointed out
       that the ideal family, as proposed by the Unification Church, does
       not exist, since its members have to live in isolation from the rest
       of society and the environment. Tensions and conflicts between
       Unification Church members and their parents are thus unavoidable.

1611. Barker, Eileen. "Who'd Be a Moonie?: A Comparative Study of Those
       Who Join the Unification Church in Britain." THE SOCIAL IMPACT
       OF THE NEW RELIGIOUS MOVEMENTS (item 725), pp. 59-96.

       Gives a brief history of the Unification Church and an account of
       the methods used to answer the question of why people join it.
       Healthy family backgrounds, educational training, and religious
       upbringing are examined. The period prior to becoming a member is

assessed. The author's research led her to think that members
believed that before joining the church, they had been of no value
to themselves and had no close friends, but that after becoming
members, life improved enormously. The cultural role of "seekers"
that the members had previously adopted is considered to be have
been an important factor in leading them to the Unification Church.
Home Church membership, which is intended for those who have converted to the church but have not been willing to become fully
committed, is also considered. It is concluded that members to
this church come from "basically secure and comfortable, possibly
over-protective, backgrounds" (p. 93) and from among those young
adults who have been disillusioned with the religion of their upbringing.

1612. Barker, Eileen. "Free to Choose: Some Thoughts on the Unification
      Church and Other Religious Movements, II." CLERGY REVIEW 65
      (1980): 392-98.

      Provides a general description of the Unification Church in Great
      Britain. The process of being a "Moonie" is briefly outlined. The
      author thinks that the work asked of this church's members is hard,
      but it can be also perceived as a challenge. The conflict between
      parents and their children who have joined the movement and the
      freedom of choice the latter have are discussed. This article is
      the second of a series (see item 549) that maintains that those
      who join new religious movements are still exercising some measure
      of freedom.

1613. Barker, Eileen. "Whose Service is Freedom: The Concept of Spiritual
      Well-Being in Relation to the Reverend Moon's Unification Church."
      SPIRITUAL WELL-BEING (item 660), pp. 153-71.

      Depicts the ideal concept of spiritual well-being as expressed in
      the Unification Church, whose members are encouraged to strive for
      self-realization through self-transcendence. The church's reasons
      for rejecting modern Western society are outlined. Two pictures of
      members of the Unification Church are sketched, namely one in which
      members are brainwashed robots who have become so depersonalized
      that they cannot achieve transcendence, the other where members
      live happily and securely in a spiritual family where there is
      opportunity for self-fulfillment and transcendence. The Church
      strives to create a world that is a sharing religious community and
      a structured hierarchical organization, is led by a charismatic
      messiah, proposes an articular theology, and strives for a mundane
      challenge, the realization of the kingdom of God on earth.

1614. Barker, Eileen. "Living the Divine Principle: Inside the Reverend
      Sun Myung Moon's Unification Church in Britain." ARCHIVES DE
      SCIENCES SOCIALES DES RELIGIONS 45 (1978): 75-93.

      Questions how and why people remain affiliated to the Unification
      Church. More specifically, the author explores 1) how a person
      accepts the theology of, and maintains his or her commitment to, the
      Unification Church and 2) why the group as a whole persists. She
      rejects the view that psychological inadequacy and/or brainwashing

explain why people remain attached to the movement and insists that
some kind of conversion takes place whenever a young adult joins
the church. The group survives because it has some positive functions. After giving a brief outline of the major theological principles of the Unification Church, the author discusses the control
and development of the individual and group solidarity.

1615. Bastien, Joseph W., and David G. Bromley. "Metaphors in the
       Rituals of Restorative and Transformative Groups." PROCEEDINGS
       OF THE ANNUAL MEETING OF THE ASSOCIATION FOR THE SCIENTIFIC STUDY
       OF RELIGION, SOUTHWEST, 1980. 9 pp.

       Argues that rituals serve important functions for the social
       organization in which they occur, because they structure both indi-
       vidual and collective experiences. This is illustrated with refer-
       ence to the rituals of two groups, namely the Society for Creative
       Anachronism and the Unification Church. The origins, goals, and
       central metaphors of these two organizations are compared. The
       implications of the use of metaphors for redefining time and space,
       creating social organization, and transforming individual identities
       are examined. The Society for Creative Anachronism is essentially
       a restorative group, since its members seek to create what they
       perceive to be valued elements of their cultural tradition. The
       Unification Church, on the other hand, is a transformative organi-
       zation that is future-oriented with the goal of bringing in a new
       utopian order.

1616. Bauman, Richard, and Neil McCabe. "Proverbs in an LSD Cult."
       JOURNAL OF AMERICAN FOLKLORE 83 (1970): 218-24.

       Discusses the esoteric kind of proverb parody used in the initia-
       tion rites of a small LSD cult in Dallas, Texas in the late 1960's.
       Various stages of the ritual of initiation into the mysteries of
       the cult are described and the proverbs repeated during the cere-
       monies are listed. This ritual is interpreted as a rite of passage.
       The proverbs are paradoxical and refer to situations that are the
       opposite of the familiar. The function of the proverbs is compared
       to that of the Zen Koan.

1617. Beckford, James A. "Talking of Apostasy, or Telling Tales and
       'Telling' Tales." ACCOUNTS OF ACTION: SURREY CONFERENCES ON
       SOCIOLOGICAL THEORY AND METHOD. Edited by G. Nigel Gilbert and
       Peter Abell. Aldershot, Hampshire, England: Gower Publishing
       Co., 1983, pp. 77-97.

       Attempts to understand how the Unification Church's ideology and
       social structure lead members to withdraw from it and to return to
       their previous lifestyle. The author explores the special problems
       that come into play when the apostates' point of view is examined
       and summarizes his interpretation of the accounts given by apos-
       tates and their relatives. He finally reflects on his own strate-
       gies for understanding the stories that apostates recount. It is
       maintained that the apostates' accounts must be interpreted with
       constant reference to what is said by those who are still active
       participants in the movement.

1618. Beckford, James A. "Through the Looking-Glass and Out the Other
       Side: Withdrawal from Reverend Moon's Unification Church."
       ARCHIVES DE SCIENCES SOCIALES DES RELIGIONS 45 (1978): 95-116.

       Outlines briefly the status of the Unification Church in Great
       Britain and then critically surveys the main sociological theories
       that have been advanced to understand its presence. Several lines
       of investigation are discussed: 1) the reasons that lead people to
       join its ranks; 2) the movement's affinity with some features of
       the social structure; and 3) the attitudinal changes that its mem-
       bers undergo. The author suggests that research should focus on
       the stages of affiliation, practice, and withdrawal. A large part
       of this paper is dedicated to the author's strategy for studying
       the process of withdrawal from the Unification Church.

*   Beckford, James A. "Two Contrasting Types of Sectarian Organiza-
       tion." Cited above as item 1144.

1619. Beckford, James A. "A Korean Evangelistic Movement in the West."
       THE CONTEMPORARY METAMORPHOSIS OF RELIGION. Acts of the 12th
       International Congress of the Sociology of Religion, The Hague,
       The Netherlands, 1973. Lille, France: C.I.S.R., 1973, pp. 319-35.

       Attempts to present a sociological understanding of the Unifi-
       cation Church (the United Family) and to see it in the context of
       wider theoretical issues. The history of the movement and its New
       Age teachings as put forth in Reverend Moon's THE DIVINE PRINCIPLE
       are sketched. The author holds that the "importance of United
       Family beliefs lies in their potential for transforming an osten-
       sibly inward-looking, transcendentalist outlook in a disciplined
       commitment to practical goals" (p. 328). The distinctive traits of
       the United Family raise questions about its classification and
       comparability with other new religious movements, particularly
       because it combines Christian with Buddhist views as well as mil-
       lennialism with a communal lifestyle and organization.

1620. Ben-Yehuda, Nachman. "The Revival of the Occult and of Science
       Fiction." JOURNAL OF POPULAR CULTURE 20.2 (1986): 1-16.

       Suggests that the rise in interest in the occult and science
       fiction are indicative of a "new quest for elective centers" that
       provide the dynamics for reinstalling meaning in a changing world
       in which human beings are depersonalized. Several factors that
       make modern occultism and science fiction suitable for this task
       are examined. Both can meet some of the functions that have been
       traditionally assigned to religion, that is, they help people cope
       with existential problems and provide a basis for community. Both
       occultism and science fiction are seen as "anti-demystification"
       trends.

*   Berger, Alan A. "Hasidism and Moonism: Charisma in the Counter
       Culture." Cited above as item 1154.

1621. Berger, Bennett M. THE SURVIVAL OF THE COUNTER CULTURE: IDEOLOG-
       ICAL WORK AND EVERYDAY LIFE AMONG RURAL COMMUNARDS. Berkeley:
       University of California Press, 1981. xiv, 264 pp.

Aims at giving a partial ethnography of a commune in rural California, a commune which the author refers to as The Ranch, concentrating on some of its more revealing beliefs and practices. Three major areas are the focus of attention: 1) the relationship between adults and youngsters, especially their equal footing; 2) pastoralism, where living in harmony with nature is encouraged and the impending doom of the cities is expected, and 3) intimacy, which covers the relationships between the sexes, including group marriage, bisexuality, feminism, and serial monogamy. The commune embodies the core beliefs of the counterculture, namely pastoralism, anarchism, romantic bohemianism, an apocalypse in the near future, the practice of Asian religious mysticism, and interest in American Indian lore. An appendix on the ethnographic method (pp. 223-41) and a short bibliography (pp. 243-49) are included.

1622.   Bergquist, Susan L. "The Revival of Glossolalic Practices in the Catholic Church: Its Sociological Implications." PERKINS JOURNAL 27.1 (1973): 32-37.

Discusses the Catholic Charismatic Renewal where the practice of speaking in tongues occupies a significant role. The author draws a profile of the person who joins the movement, stressing the religious background of those who responded to her questionnaires and interviews. Certain linguistic patterns of glossolalia are outlined. It is speculated that the movement is, in part, a reaction against the "God is Dead" Movement of the 1960's and that those who become members are trying to reconstruct the spiritual aspect of the church that they feel has been neglected. Concerns about "spiritual elitism" within the movement are voiced.

1623.   Berliner, Howard S., and J. Warren Salmon. "The Holistic Alternative to Scientific Medicine: History and Analysis." INTERNATIONAL JOURNAL OF HEALTH SERVICES 10 (1980): 133-47.

Traces the emergence of the Holistic Health Movement, which is an outgrowth of the counterculture and of the Human Potential Movement and which has been influenced by Chinese medical practices, nineteenth-century Western health practices, and Eastern philosophies. The author points out that the rise of scientific medicine had led to the demise of a prior holistic view of health. The revival of holistic medicine expresses a popular dissatisfaction with scientific medicine, whose organizational forms and practical contents are being challenged. The Holistic Health Movement is a reaction to the "degenerative social and psychological conditions of the day" (p. 145).

1624.   Berliner, Howard S., and J. Warren Salmon. "The Holistic Health Movement and Scientific Medicine: The Naked and the Dead." SOCIALIST REVIEW 43 (January/February 1979): 31-51.

Attempts to understand the political and theoretical meaning of the Holistic Health Movement. After exploring the historical background and current state of traditional scientific medicine, the authors discuss the rise of the Holistic Health Movement, the success of which they attribute to the crisis in scientific medicine.

Two major features of Holistic Health are discussed, namely: 1) the assumed unity of body, mind, and spirit and 2) the belief that disease is not purely biological. Most Holistic Health practices "contain heavy doses of mysticism and charismatic elitism" (p. 45). They further ignore politics and fail to see a connection between disease and social relationships. Some valuable features of the Holistic Health Movement are discussed and possible improvements in scientific medicine suggested.

1625. Berliner, Howard S., and J. Warren Salmon. "The New Realities of Health Policy and Influences of Holistic Medicine." JOURNAL OF ALTERNATIVE HUMAN SERVICES 5 (June 1979): 13-16.

Discusses the reasons behind the shift in federal policy regarding health care and funding. The authors' view is that this shift has created a health crisis that has led to changes in the way people view health services. The stress of changing lifestyles that are injurious to health has led to the emergence of Holistic Health, which includes Eastern meditation, parapsychology, and folk medicines. The many features of the Holistic Health Movement are outlined and the impact on current medical practices assessed.

1626. Blake, Joseph A. "Ufology: The Intellectual Development and Context of the Study of Unidentified Flying Objects." ON THE MARGINS OF SCIENCE (item 712), pp. 315-37.

Discusses the emergence of the study of UFOs as a science and compares it with conventional or normal sciences. UFOs have been accounted for in two general ways, namely either as natural phenomena or as occurrences that lie beyond the confines of science. Though experiences of UFOs can be traced to the distant past, UFO as a category "derives from, and specifically refers to, a series of waves (of sightings) following one another more or less continuously since 1947" (p. 316). Ufology is analyzed in its theoretical formulations, its methods, and scope. In assessing the social context of ufology three areas are explored, namely the journalistic press, the scientific community, and those who experience UFOs. It is maintained that ufology is "an intellectual product of social groupings not of an intellectual elite" (p. 333).

1627. Blood, Linda. "Shepherding/Discipleship: Theology and Practice of Absolute Obedience." CULTIC STUDIES JOURNAL 2 (1986): 235-45.

Discusses a Christian movement known as "S/D" (Shepherding/Discipleship), or "New Covenant," or "Total Commitment," which exacts the submission of members to the church and its elders. The ideology of the movement and some of the practices that control the lives of its members are described. Obedience, tithing, and recruitment are among the topics covered. The author holds that the cultic beliefs and practices of this church are countercultural; they specifically reject the "respect for personal independence and for each person's right to conduct his life according to his own reasoned judgment" (p. 245).

1628. Bocking, Brian. "Reflections on Soka Gakkai." SCOTTISH JOURNAL OF RELIGIOUS STUDIES 2.1 (1981): 38-54.

Presents an outline of the relationship between Nichren Shoshu, a
700-year-old Japanese Buddhist sect, and Soka Gakkai, a well-known
organization of lay Buddhists affiliated with it. The expansion
program of Soka Gakkai, which started in 1966, is described and an
account of the controversy between Nichren Shoshu priests and Soka
Gakkai members given. Three major doctrinal differences between
the two groups are explored.

1629. Bord, Richard J., and Joseph E. Faulkner. THE CATHOLIC CHARIS-
MATICS: THE ANATOMY OF A MODERN RELIGIOUS MOVEMENT. University
Park: Pennsylvania State University Press, 1983. x, 162 pp.

Analyzes the Catholic Charismatic Renewal from sociological and
sociopsychological perspectives, focusing on those social structures that shape human motivations and behavior. The study is
divided into three major parts. Part I provides an outline of the
movement's origin, a description of its main features, and a summary of the methods used to study it. Part II examines the movement from two perspectives: the collective behavior, which stresses
the social-psychological states of individuals, and the resource-
mobilization approach, which centers on the social structural conditions that favor the development of the movement. Part III looks
toward future trends. The authors argue that, while the Catholic
Charismatic Renewal will continue for at least this generation, its
influence has already waned because there are more avenues for
expressing traditional values than there were when it first came
into being. The authors think that, though the movement has maintained its connection with the institutional church, the questions
which it posed to this church are still relevant.

1630. Bord, Richard J., and Joseph E. Faulkner. "Religiosity and Secular
Attitudes: The Case of Catholic Pentecostals." JOURNAL FOR THE
SCIENTIFIC STUDY OF RELIGION 14 (1975): 257-70.

Explores the relationship between abstract belief systems and
specific social attitudes with the goal of determining the socio-
political views of the believers. The research is limited to the
Charismatic Renewal in the Catholic Church. Three factors, namely
the degree of orthodoxy, the level of commitment in the institutionalized Church, and the depth of involvement in the Pentecostal
Movement, are treated as independent variables, while social attitudes regarding abortion, birth control, Women's Liberation Movement, and U. S. involvement in Vietnam, are among the dependent
variables considered. The conclusion reached is that "religiosity
indices are associated only with those social attitudes having
direct implications for ongoing doctrinal or church-related considerations" (p. 257).

1631. Borowski, Karol H. "The Modern Renaissance Commune." SOCIETY 25.2
(1988): 42-46.

Describes the Renaissance Movement, a contemporary communal-
revival organization centered in Massachusetts, and analyzes its
functions and relationship to society at large. The ideology of
the movement, founded by Michael J. Metelica, and its goals to

establish an environment complementary to life are specified. The
movement's growth and consequent tensions and conflicts with society are among the main topics dealt with. The gradual change of
society's hostile attitude to the movement is attributed to the
movement's acceptance of some rules and restrictions imposed by
civil authorities, to its community projects that benefited all,
and to the transfer of its center to the town.

1632. Borowski, Karol H. "The Renaissance Movement in the U.S.A. Today:
An Account of Alternative Religion in Popular Media." SOCIAL
COMPASS 34 (1987): 33-40.

Gives a brief history of the Renaissance Movement found in 1967
by Michael J. Metelica and discusses its relationship with the
popular media. The movement developed a religious system of
beliefs and practices and became an alternative religion aiming for
a New Age consciousness. Religious music, the publication of a
magazine, and other artistic and commercial enterprises were used
to promote the movement's goals, aspirations, and values. The use
of the media performed the function of "celebrating and reinforcing
group integrity."

1633. Borowski, Karol H. ATTEMPTING AN ALTERNATIVE SOCIETY: A SOCIOLOG-
ICAL STUDY OF A SELECTED COMMUNAL REVITALIZATION MOVEMENT IN THE
UNITED STATES. Norwood, PA: Norwood Editions, 1984. xii, 281 pp.

Explores the origin and development of a modern commune that
came into being as the "Brotherhood of the Spirit Commune" and
eventually evolved into the "Renaissance-Church Community" in Massachusetts. The author relates the story of its founder, Michael
J. Metelica, and of the initial gathering of high school and college dropouts who followed him with the intention of supporting one
another in the atmosphere of a communal lifestyle. It is argued
that participation in communes results from sociocultural conditions that do not satisfy the needs of individuals; that ideology
and leadership are fundamental factors for the movement to develop
and thrive; and that all the phases of this particular movement had
some features common among alternative societies. The author maintains that this commune could not develop into such an ideal society
because of the restrictions imposed by the larger society, the
limitations of its own leader, and the internal crises that beset
it. A substantial bibliography is attached.

1634. Borowski, Karol H. "From the Tree House to the 2001 Center: The
Renaissance Movement in the United States." COMMUNAL SOCIETIES 4
(1984): 121-30.

Describes a contemporary commune in the U.S.A. (known initially
as the "Brotherhood of the Spirit" and later as the "Renaissance
Church or Community") as "a spontaneous, conscious, and collective
attempt to create an alternative society by revitalizing values and
institutions of a Gemeinschaft-like society" (pp. 122-23). The
origin of the movement in the late 1960's under Michael J. Metelica,
its growth and development, its recruitment tactics, and its adap-
tations for survival are described. Its ideology, based largely on

THE AQUARIAN GOSPEL, and its leadership that was largely charismatic) were crucial to the movement's continuity and change. The
author concludes that this movement illustrates that social movements are brought about largely by conflict.

1635. Bradfield, Cecil David. NEO-PENTECOSTALISM: A SOCIOLOGICAL ASSESS-
       MENT. Washington, DC: University Press of America, 1979. vii,
       75 pp.

       Reflects on the emergence of the neo-Pentecostal (Charismatic)
       Movement within the mainline Christian churches in the 1960's and
       shows how it is linked with the Holiness Movement and with classi-
       cal Pentecostalism. The author examines these movements in the
       context of Glock's theory of deprivation (item 94) and the tradi-
       tional church-sect theory. He concludes that the Charismatic
       Renewal has not developed into the pattern predicted by this theory
       and cannot be explained in terms of social and/or economic depriva-
       tion. Other forms of deprivation may, however, be useful in under-
       standing its rise and appeal. Neo-Pentecostals are concerned about
       social and religious change and sense that they "have lost control
       of their way of life and of their own fate" (p. 60); they are per-
       vaded by a spirit of "escapism" and worried about depersonalization
       trends in contemporary society.

1636. Braum, Kirk. RAJNEESHPURAM: THE UNWELCOME SOCIETY. CULTURES COL-
       LIDE IN A QUEST FOR UTOPIA. West Linn, OR: Scott Creek Press,
       1984. 238 pp.

       Presents an essentially journalistic account of how the founda-
       tion of Rajneeshpuram in Oregon in 1981 brought about a confronta-
       tion between two cultures, namely conservative Christianity and an
       alien Eastern religious group. The efforts of the followers of
       Rajneesh to create a utopia are compared to similar religious and
       communal experiments in American history. The sense of panic,
       intolerance, prejudice, and emotional attacks against Rajneeshpuram
       are vividly described. A picture of the lifestyle of the guru and
       his disciples and of their major beliefs and practices is provided.
       Among the topics discussed are whether and in what sense the Raj-
       neesh Foundation can be called a cult.

1637. Breckwoldt, R. "The Hare Krishna Movement in Australia." AUSTRA-
       LIAN AND NEW ZEALAND JOURNAL OF SOCIOLOGY 9.2 (1973): 70-71.

       Provides a brief overview of the Hare Krishna Movement in Austra-
       lia, giving a general picture of its ideology and ritual, the roles
       and identity of its members, and its interactions with society at
       large. This sect, according to the author, offers a lifestyle for
       those who feel alienated from modern Western culture. It offers a
       setting in which a new and more satisfying identity is created and
       strengthened.

1638. Brewer, Mark. "Erhard Seminars Training: 'We're Gonna Tear You
       Down and Put You Back Together.'" PSYCHOLOGY TODAY 9.8 (August,
       1975): 35-40, 80, 88.

Maintains that EST is "no ordinary California Cult" but a "multi-million dollar corporation." A typical EST training session is described. The author sees EST as a popular psychology trip that is similar to a classical conversion experience or brainwashing which creates a feeling of a "mysterious or deeply cleansing ordeal."

1639. Brissett, Dennis, and Lionel S. Lewis. "The Natural Health Food Movement: A Study of Revitalization and Conversion." JOURNAL OF AMERICAN CULTURE 1.1 (1976): 61-76.

Attempts to understand the meaning system of health food users by studying the movement's literature. The Natural Health Movement depicts America in a state of nutritional deficiency and promotes natural food not just for nutritional value, but also as a means of improving one's material and spiritual life. The following are among the many beneficial results that flow from a natural food diet: improvement of body function; prevention and better treatment of illness; enhancement of one's appearance; and betterment of both mind and psyche. Promoters of a natural food diet argue that it contributes to long life, proper sexual functions, and psychological balance.

1640. Bromley, David G. "Financing the Millennium: The Economic Structure of the Unificationist Movement." JOURNAL FOR THE SCIENTIFIC STUDY OF RELIGION 24 (1985): 253-74.

Makes a survey of the way in which economic resources are generated in the Unification Church and the process by which, and purpose for which, these resources are expended. The meaning of the Church's economic structure is then assessed. The ideology of the Unification Church and its economic policies are outlined and its various profit-making organizations in the United States, South America, and Asia are listed, showing the organization of its business enterprises and leadership patterns. A significant amount of revenue generated is channeled to further the Church's religious, social, and political agenda. The author compares the Unification Church to other religious organizations, interprets its economic structure in terms of the features of world-transforming movements, and identifies the unique features of Unification economics. He states that it "has created an economic conglomerate to underwrite its theological agenda" (p. 272). Much of the success depends on its solid economic base, a strategy which has brought about serious legal problems for the movement.

1641. Bromley, David G., Bruce Bushing, and Anson D. Shupe. "The Unification Church and the American Family: Strain, Conflict, and Control." NEW RELIGIOUS MOVEMENTS: A PERSPECTIVE FOR UNDERSTANDING SOCIETY (item 551), pp. 302-11.

Examines, in the context of the Unification Church, two major questions: 1) what social conditions have been responsible for the conflict between the new religious movements and the larger society? and 2) how did this conflict lead to the persecution of some of the new religious groups? After discussing the allegations against the Church, the authors explore the sources and dynamics of strain and

sketch the anticult ideology of those parents who banded together
for solidarity, mutual support, and resolution of their common
problems. Two strategies used to suppress the Unification Church
are identified: support for those who attempt deprogramming and
alliance with other institutions that have greater sanctioning
(legal and social) powers. The anticult activity has brought
about a "siege mentality" within the Unification Church, a mentality which made the goals of the anticult movement more difficult
to achieve.

*   Bromley, David G., and Anson D. Shupe, editors. KRISHNA CONSCIOUS-
         NESS IN THE WEST. Cited above as item 580.

1642.   Bromley, David G., and Anson D. Shupe. "MOONIES" IN AMERICA: CULT,
         CHURCH, AND CRUSADE. Beverly Hills, CA: Sage Publications, 1979.
         268 pp.

         Deals with one of the most publicized and controversial of the
         new religious movements, the Unification Church, and attempts to
         view it from the perspective of the resource mobilization theory
         that stresses the organization aspects of social movements. The
         book is divided into three parts dealing with 1) the birth of the
         movement and its arrival in the United States, 2) the movement's
         growth and development from 1970 onwards, and 3) its conflict with
         society, particularly with the Anti-Cult Movement, and its efforts
         to defend itself, respectively . The church's leadership, orga-
         nization, and techniques for recruiting new members and for solic-
         iting public acceptance are among the topics covered. The authors
         judge the church to be a "world-transforming movement." Some spec-
         ulation about its future is offered.

1643.   Bromley, David G., and Anson D. Shupe. "'Just a Few Years Seems
         Like a Lifetime:' A Role Theory Approach to Participant Observa-
         tion in Religious Movements." RESEARCH ON SOCIAL MOVEMENTS,
         CONFLICTS, AND CHANGE 2 (1979): 159-85.

         Contends that the common motivational theory that is used to
         explain the rapid affiliative change of those who join new reli-
         gious movements has several limitations. The authors propose the
         application of the concepts of role theory and complex organization
         as an alternative approach. The Unification Church is taken as a
         test case for this theory. After briefly summarizing the main
         points in both the motivational and role models and describing the
         method used, the authors discuss the organizational goals and the-
         ology of the Unification Church. The affiliative process is exam-
         ined and divided into five components: 1) predisposing factors; 2)
         attraction; 3) incipient involvement; 4) active involvement; and 5)
         commitment. The authors argue that the predisposing factors are too
         varied and complex to be explained by alienation, that the motiva-
         tional model has little to offer after the initial contact between
         the individual and the group, and that behavioral change occurs
         before change of belief and commitment.

1644.   Bromley, David G., Anson D. Shupe, and Donna L. Oliver. "Perfect
         Families: Visions of the Future of a New Religious Movement."
         CULTS AND THE FAMILY (item 644), pp. 119-29.

Points out that the family is central in the conflict between
parents of cult members and the new religious movements because
1) the new movements serve many of the functions of the family, and
2) the anticult movement is composed mainly of parents of individuals who have joined one of the new groups. The family structure
advocated by the Unification Church is outlined, stressing the
Church's view of marriage with its implications on the way in which
partners are chosen. The integration of family and religious life
is the expectation of most members of the Unification Church. The
authors observe that tension between collective and individual
needs that characterized many communal groups throughout history is
also manifested in the Unification Church.

1645. Brooks, Charles R. " A Unique Conjuncture: The Incorporation of
        ISKCON in Vrindaban." KRISHNA CONSCIOUSNESS IN THE WEST (item
        580), pp. 165-87.

Examines the Hare Krishna settlement in New Vrindaban, near
Moundsville, West Virginia and its meaning both in the Hindu tradition and in the Hare Krishna Movement in the West. The author
first considers Vrindaban as a "celestial place in the phenomenal
world." Secondly, he delineates the relationship between Vrindaban
and Gaudiya Vaishnavism. Thirdly, he describes the meaningful role
of pilgrimage that Vrindaban has in the mind of the devotees. And,
lastly, he gives an account of the caste system that operates in
the settlement. Vrindaban, where Western converts and Hindu immigrants interact, is a social and religious institution. Though
ISKCON enjoys high status in Vrindaban, "its members have not been
fully accepted as Brahmins due to the refusal of the Brahmin community to accept them as social equals" (p. 184).

1646. Brown, Colin. "How Significant is the Charismatic Movement?"
        RELIGION IN NEW ZEALAND SOCIETY. Edited by Brian Colless and
        Peter Donovan. Edinburgh, Scotland: T. and T. Clark, 1980, pp.
        99-114.

Sketches the growth of classical Pentecostalism and the recent
Charismatic Renewal Movement in New Zealand and offers speculations
regarding the causes for their emergence and their long-term implications for religion in general. Classical Pentecostalism is growing in respectability and acceptability because converts are not
required to make a complete break with normal social life and to
adopt a hard puritanical ethic. The following reasons for the
popularity of the Charismatic Movement are adduced: 1) the tendency
among young adults to express emotions more freely and to stress
religious experience; 2) the clear-cut conservative stance that the
movement has taken in an age of religious and cultural changes; and
3) a desire for a more intimate form of community. The Charismatic
Movement may aid the cause of Christian renewal, encourage concern
for social issues, introduce informality and warmth in worship, and
strengthen the general drift to conservative politics and religion.

1647. Brown, Karen McCarthy. "Voodoo." THE ENCYCLOPEDIA OF RELIGION
        (item 18), vol. 5, pp. 296-301.

Explains Voodoo as an African-based, Catholic-influenced religion that is practiced mainly in Haiti and that immigrants have brought with them to the United States. The diversity within Voodoo, including some differences between urban and rural beliefs and practices, are delineated and the African and Catholic elements sorted out. Major Voodoo beliefs about the spirits, the human person, and the dead are outlined and its ceremonies and magical practices explained.

1648. Bruce, Steve. "Ideology and Isolation: A Failed Scots Protestant Movement." ARCHIVES DE SCIENCES SOCIALES DES RELIGIONS 28 (1983): 147-57.

Gives a detailed account of a militant Protestant movement in Scotland founded by Jack Glass in 1965. A short biographical sketch of Glass is provided and his efforts to start a Protestant crusade described. His attempts to join forces with Brian Green (a Baptist pastor in London) and Ian Paisley in Northern Ireland are examined. Different structural conditions in the three countries are, in the author's view, responsible for Glass's failure. The ideologies of Glass and Paisley are contrasted. Glass accepted the sectarian position that other Protestant organizations are not legitimate. When his movement, failed he stuck to his exclusivist stand, for it provided the most satisfying explanation and justification for the failure.

1649. Bruce, Steve. "A Witness to the Faith: Dilemmas of 'Evangelism' as Rhetoric and Reality." SCOTTISH JOURNAL OF SOCIOLOGY 2 (1978): 163-73.

Discusses the evangelizing goals and methods of a university Christian union and suggests that in its failure to attract many converts, the very lifestyle of its few members may be interpreted as a form of evangelization. The author's research was conducted on a Scottish university campus where the Christian union was part of a larger nationwide organization of campus ministry. The organized ministry of the union is described and its failure assessed. The members of the union, aware of their lack of success to attract converts, developed a social life that had little contact with outsiders and a view of evangelism as a form of "witnessing" that stresses social control over existing members.

1650. Bruch, Hilde. "The Allure of Food Cults and Nutrition Quackery." JOURNAL OF THE AMERICAN DIETIC ASSOCIATION (October 1970): 316-20.

Argues that the recourse to medical quackery and cultic practices must be understood as an attempt to fulfill the needs of suffering people. The author thinks that the field of nutrition "appears to be particularly vulnerable to distortions into fads and cults" (p. 318). Scientifically minded nutritionists have paved the way for faddism since they have sometimes preyed on people's fear and anxiety in order to promote good eating habits. It is contended that quackery expresses the relative failure of the scientific approach and that, in some cases at least, even the application of orthodox medicine may have a magical effect.

1651.   Bryant, M. Darrol. "Unification Eschatology and American Millen-
        nial Tradition: Continuities and Discontinuities." A TIME FOR
        CONSIDERATION (item 1652), pp. 262-74.

        Compares and contrasts the eschatology of the Unification Church
        with the traditional millenarian views of the Great Awakening.
        After outlining the Unification Church's views as contained in the
        DIVINE PRINCIPLES, the author draws attention to the similarities
        and differences.

1652.   Bryant, M. Darrol, and Herbert W. Richardson, editors. A TIME FOR
        CONSIDERATION: SCHOLARLY APPRAISAL OF THE UNIFICATION CHURCH.
        New York: Edwin Mellen Press, 1978. xi, 317 pp.

        Presents 11 essays on various aspects of the Unification Church.
        Three types of analysis, namely cultural, theological, and heuris-
        tic are pursued. Though largely favorably inclined towards the
        movement, these essays represent the views of scholars from differ-
        ent denominational backgrounds.

        Contains items 1651, 1686, 2138, 2209.

1653.   Burfoot, Jean. "The Fun-Seeking Movement in California." OF GODS
        AND MEN (item 550), pp. 147-64.

        Examines the modern fun-seeking movement and its relationship to
        the new religious movements. Fun-seeking, in the author's view,
        has much in common with "ecstatic religion," an outbreak that is
        directly related to social structural processes in modern Western
        society. A triple process of differentiation, disenchantment, and
        alienation is discussed. Fun has the power of healing the self by
        removing differentiation, reintroducing irrational elements and
        play thus creating enchantment, and combating alienation by remov-
        ing the divisions of labor. The author believes that "the emer-
        gence of fun-seeking marks the separation of individuals from old
        systems of social meaning" (p. 60). Fun (or ecstatic energy) may
        find expression in ideological communities. The author illustrates
        her major points with reference to several examples from California.

1654.   Burr, Angela. I AM NOT MY BODY: A STUDY OF THE INTERNATIONAL HARE
        KRISHNA SECT. New Delhi, India: Vikas Publishing House, 1984.
        vi, 301 pp.

        Presents an anthropological study of the Hare Krishna Movement
        "as an outstanding example of a social protest group which uses
        religion as its medium" (p. 2). The belief system and social
        structure of this Hindu group are examined and the background of
        those who join it explored. Special attention is given to the
        claim of the devotees that they are essentially spirit-souls and
        not materialistic bodies, a statement that the author thinks
        reveals a lot about the social problems of Western society. By
        analyzing the role of the body in Western culture and the view that
        the Hare Krishna Movement has developed about it, the author draws
        attention to an important symbol in the West. She shows how the
        Hare Krishna express their ideology in ritual, dress, sexual rite,

treatment of hair, bodily movement, and dance. There is also a
discussion of whether those who join the movement are converted or
brainwashed. In general, this book does give not a very positive
assessment of the movement.

1655. Campbell, Horace. "Rastafari: Culture of Resistance." RACE AND
       CLASS 22 (1980): 1-22.

       Contends that it is naive to look on the Rastafari Movement as a
       religious worldview that deifies Haile Selassie and looks for a new
       apocalypse. The movement is rather an international culture with
       Ethiopia as a symbol of African resistance and Black nationalism.
       The contribution of Marcus Garvey and the rise of the first Rasta-
       farians are outlined. The resurgence of the Rastafarian Movement
       in Jamaica since the 1960's and its struggle with the civil authori-
       ties are described. Rasta became the culture of the masses by the
       mid-1970's. The author refutes the view that the Rastafari Movement
       is apocalyptic with violent tendencies, a view that is often de-
       picted in the media. He insists that the social context of the
       movement is more important than its metaphysical aspects.

1656. Carey, Sean. "The Indianization of the Hare Krishna Movement in
       Britain." HINDUISM IN GREAT BRITAIN: THE PERPETUATION OF RELI-
       GION IN AN ALIEN CULTURAL MILIEU. Edited by Richard Burghart.
       London: Tavistock Publications, 1987, pp. 81-99.

       Traces the emergence and development of the Hare Krishna Move-
       ment, stressing its traditional and orthodox components. The
       author seeks to determine why the movement is attracting young
       Indians in Great Britain by examining the success and failure of
       its proselytizing patterns. He attributes the attraction that the
       movement has for some Indians to its function as a mechanism for
       the preservation of social identity in a foreign land.

1657. Carey, Sean. "The Hare Krishna Movement and Hinduism in Britain."
       NEW COMMUNITY 10 (1983): 477-86.

       Examines the relationship between the Hare Krishna Movement and
       its Hindu clientele in Great Britain. The author first traces the
       history of this movement in the West and then examines the various
       services it provides for Hindus and the reasons why some young
       Indians have joined it. Several case studies of Indian recruits
       are presented. The author points out that the movement no longer
       has the Hippie culture as its recruitment base and has become more
       institutionalized, thus attracting some members with Hindu back-
       grounds especially through contact with the friendly communities of
       Krishna devotees.

1658. Carter, Lewis F. "The 'New Renunciates' of the Bhagwan Shree Raj-
       neesh: Observations and Identification of Problems of Interpret-
       ing New Religious Movements." JOURNAL FOR THE SCIENTIFIC STUDY
       OF RELIGION 26 (1987): 148-72.

       Presents a narrative description of the Rajneesh Movement by a
       "non-hostile outsider." The author aims at giving a balanced docu-
       mentation of the movement and at identifying the problems involved

in studying new religious groups. The Rajneesh Movement presents
special problems because "it is difficult to locate the movement
1) in physical space and time; 2) in terms of formal and legal
structures; and 3) in terms of ideology and historical-cultural
perspective" (p. 150). The major sources of information are identified: firsthand observation, secondhand accounts, books by and
about Rajneesh, and newspaper and magazine articles. A short history of the movement and a description of its recruitment practices,
initiation, beliefs, and practices are provided. The research team
that contributed to this essay found the followers of Rajneesh to
be intelligent, articulate, and manipulative. The movement thrived
on its notoriety; its unconventionality and instability combined to
expedite its demise.

1659. Cashmore, Ernest Ellis. "'Get Up, Stand Up': The Rastafarian Move-
        ment." DISCIPLINES OF FAITH: STUDIES OF RELIGION, POLITICS, AND
        PATRIARCHY. Edited by Jim Obelkevitch, Lyndal Roper, and Raphael
        Samuel. London: Routledge and Kegan Paul, 1987, pp. 412-31.

        Gives a description of the Rastafarian Movement that, since the
mid-1970's, "has grown staggeringly amongst the Black ghetto youths
of England's inner cities" (p. 412). After placing the ideological
origin of the movement in the philosophy of Marcus Garvey, the
author dwells on the popularity of Robert Nesta Marley, a musician
who played an important role in the spread of Rasta beliefs and
values. The Rastafarian Movement is a total way of life that reacts sharply against the colonialist domination of Black peoples.

1660. Cashmore, Ernest Ellis. RASTAMAN: THE RASTAFARIAN MOVEMENT IN
        ENGLAND. London: Allen and Unwin, 1979. xi, 263 pp.

        Investigates the social basis of the Rastafarian Movement in
England and traces its development in Jamaica. Special attention
is given to Marcus Garvey, its most important predecessor, and to
the Rastafarian interpretation of Garvey's ideas that changes his
millenarianism into a form of social protest. Postwar Jamaican
immigrants to England and the patterns of their adaptation are
described. The actual mechanisms that made the movement flourish
into an exclusive and elite group that clashed with civil authorities are discussed. The author finally relates the rise of Rastafarianism to the development of African consciousness. A short
basic bibliography is provided (pp. 249-56).

1661. Cashmore, Ernest Ellis. "The Rastaman Cometh." NEW SOCIETY 41
        (August 25, 1977): 382-84.

        Describes briefly the origin and ideology of the Rastafarian
Movement and its presence in London, England. The enthusiasm of
the members is one of the cult's main features. The author maintains that Rastafarians should not be dismissed as racist thugs.
They represent a reaction to racial discrimination and an attempt
to preserve their self-respect and sense of identity.

1662. Chidester, David. SALVATION AND SUICIDE: AN INTERPRETATION OF JIM
        JONES, THE PEOPLES TEMPLE, AND JONESTOWN. Bloomington: Indiana
        University Press, 1988. xv, 190 pp.

Attempts to reconstruct the worldview that animated the People's
Temple as a utopian community that finally self-destructed. The
author believes that by creating a religiohistorical interpretation of the Temple's worldview, light might be shed on Jonestown in
the context of the history of religion. After a short history of
the People's Temple, the author points out that most explanations
of its demise have relied on "the preoccupation with cognitive
distancing." He finds such an approach wanting and prefers, instead, "to identify systems for the classification of persons,
patterns of special and temporary orientation, and strategies of
symbolic appropriation, enjoyment, and inversion by which the religious worldview assumes its unique shape in the history of the
Peoples Temple" (p. 50). The Temple embodied a worldview with
which a human identity could be forged and a type of salvation
worked out. Suicide, in the author's view, became the final strategy when it became clear to the members that salvation in this
world was no longer possible.

1663. Chidester, David. "Stealing the Sacred Symbols: Biblical Interpre-
      tation in the Peoples Temple and the Unification Church." RELI-
      GION 18 (1988): 137-62.

      Compares the way two new religious movements, the Unification
      Church and the now-defunct People's Temple, have appropriated and
      interpreted one basic religious symbol, the Bible. The major dif-
      ferences in 1) the nature of the text, 2) the text's beginning
      story, 3) the eschatological battle between good and evil, and
      4) the nature of community are delineated.

1664. Chidester, David. "Rituals of Exclusion in the Jonestown Dead."
      JOURNAL OF THE AMERICAN ACADEMY OF RELIGION 56 (1988): 681-702.

      Argues that the funeral rituals of those who died in Jonestown
      are symbolical of "the possibility of dissolution of American soci-
      ety" (p. 683). The author examines the way the Jonestown tragedy
      was received, particularly in the rituals that accompanied the final
      burial of those who died at the People's Temple compound in Guyana.
      He describes the different rituals of exclusion at Dover, Delaware
      and San Francisco, California, the two main places where the bodies
      of the dead were returned to the United States. He concludes that
      these rituals of exclusion indicate how Americans came to terms
      with Jonestown by denying that its victims were sane, Christian, or
      American, thereby reinforcing the various boundaries that makes the
      United States a "legitimate human identity."

1665. Chryssides, George. "Divisive Unity: Marketing Unificationist
      Paradoxes." THE NEW EVANGELISTS (item 587), pp. 43-55.

      Attempts to demonstrate how the Unification Church came into
      being as a result of Christian proselytization and what kind of
      problems arose when its theology was preached outside Korea. The
      author explains that the Unification Church originated as a result
      of contact between a primal society (Korea) with a universal world
      religion, and then it turned into a new religious movement set
      against all religious or social backgrounds. The effects on its

proselytization methods as it changed are examined. It is pointed
out that the church's messianism fits into the traditional syncretistic messianic movements of Korea and must consequently be understood in the context of the political situation in Korea over the
last 200 years. To market the Unification Church overseas, two
techniques were introduced: 1) a quasi-rational element in the
persuasive methods employed by its missionaries; and 2) some theological adaptation to make its appeal more universal. Some of the
difficulties involved in the Church's goal to unify all religions
are discussed.

1666.   Clarke, Peter B. BLACK PARADISE: THE RASTAFARIAN MOVEMENT. Wel-
        lingborough, England: Aquarian Press, 1986. 112 pp.

        Presents a study of one of the estimated 500 new religions that
        have emerged in Great Britain since World War II. After an intro-
        duction that outlines some of the similarities that all new reli-
        gions share (like millenarianism, self-divinization, and the stress
        for the need for knowledge leading to certitude), the author de-
        scribes the background of the Rastafarian Movement, the place and
        influence of Marcus Garvey in the movement, and its rise and devel-
        opment in Jamaica and Great Britain. He holds that the Rastafarian
        Movement has changed dramatically since its inception from an
        exclusivist, introversionist position with regard to White society
        to one that increasingly emphasizes "the brotherhood of man under
        the Fatherhood of God."

1667.   Clarke, Peter. "The Sufi Path in Britain--The Revivalist Tenden-
        cy." UPDATE: A QUARTERLY JOURNAL OF NEW RELIGIOUS MOVEMENTS 7.3
        (1983): 12-16.

        Examines one aspect of Islamic mysticism in Britain, namely the
        revivalist trend. The presence of Sufism in Britain is briefly
        outlined and its origin traced to the late nineteenth century.
        Some Sufi movements in Britain are syncretistic and preoccupy them-
        selves with alternative healing methods, while others are exclusiv-
        ist and revivalist in orientation.

1668.   Collins, H. M., and T. J. Pinch. FRAMES OF MEANING: THE SOCIAL
        CONSTRUCTION OF EXTRAORDINARY SCIENCE. London: Routledge and
        Kegan Paul, 1982. x, 210 pp.

        Reflects on the author's extended experiments at the University of
        Bath, England on children who claimed they could bend metal by
        paranormal means. A history of research in the field in Great
        Britain and the United States is given and the opposition to it
        outlined. The compatibility of parapsychology with science is
        discussed at length and it is concluded that scientists can legiti-
        mately investigate paranormal phenomena. The authors contend that
        the Geller-associated scientific activity was revolutionary since
        it raised issues from within the scientific community itself. The
        aim is "to present the social study of science as a peculiarly
        straightforward and empirical way of studying the construction of
        knowledge" (p. 184). A bibliography is provided (pp. 195-204).

1669. Cooper, J. R. (Dharmachari Ratnaprabba). "A Re-Emergence of Bud-
       dhism: The Case of the Friends of the Western Buddhist Order."
       THE NEW EVANGELISTS (item 587), pp. 57-75.

       Gives an account of a new Buddhist movement that started in Brit-
       ain in the late 1960's and has since grown into a worldwide organi-
       zation. The author, a member of the movement, provides 1) a brief
       introduction to the principles of Buddhism; 2) the background to
       the organization; 3) an analysis of the relationship between the
       Western Buddhist Order and the Friends of this order; 4) a descrip-
       tion of the evangelization efforts of the Western Buddhist Order;
       and 5) an explanation of how an individual gets involved in the
       Friends of the Buddhist Order that, with the Buddhist Order itself
       as its nucleus, offers itself as a prototype for a new society.

1670. Coser, Rose Laub, and Lewis Coser. "Jonestown as a Perverse Utopia:
       A 'Greedy' Institution in the Jungle." DISSENT 26 (1979): 158-62.

       Describes the People's Temple in Jonestown as a utopian commune
       that was isolated from the outside world by design. It attracted
       people who saw society as a "desert devoid of love." The internal
       structure of the commune that made people dependent on their
       leader, Jim Jones, is described. Jonestown easily became a total
       institution that controlled the whole life of those who entered it.
       The author thinks that the remaking of personal values and the lack
       of solidarity within the group led to its final self-destruction.
       People's past values were destroyed by systematic humiliating ser-
       mons that included beatings, torture, mutual accusations, and pub-
       lic confessions. Jim Jones used sex to pull people apart and to
       rechannel emotional energies. Members of Jonestown were already
       "dead inside" before the tragedy. Their commune was a greedy in-
       stitution "which successfully 'devoured' its members by making
       total claims on them and by encompassing their whole personality"
       (pp. 61-62).

1671. Coulehan, John L. "Chiropractic and the Clinical Art." SOCIAL
       SCIENCE AND MEDICINE 21 (1985): 383-90.

       Points out that, although chiropractic is licensed all over the
       United States, it still remains in the eyes of medical commentators
       an unscientific healing cult. The author describes the main prac-
       tices of this alternative healing technique and suggests that the
       chiropractic-patient interaction contributes greatly to its healing
       effects. Chiropractic is an art that begins with the "faith that
       heals," that is, it relieves pain, diminishes anxiety, leads to the
       acceptance of one's role in life, and helps towards the acquisition
       of a positive mental attitude. Physicians, in the author's opin-
       ion, can learn from its success.

1672. Cozin, Mark. "A Millenarian Movement in Korea and Great Britain."
       SOCIOLOGICAL YEARBOOK OF RELIGION IN BRITAIN 6 (1973): 100-21.

       Gives brief descriptions of traditional Korean religion and of
       the new religions that have emerged after the Second World War and
       the Korean War. The origins and main characteristics of the Tong-Il

Movement of the Reverend Moon are outlined and its adjustment to
Western culture under the name of the Unified Family explored.
Those who are attracted to this new religion are said to have
knowledge of, or membership in, "spiritualistic circles." Members
establish a charismatic relationship with the movement's founder,
whose charisma is validated by the creation and repetition of a
series of myths that compare him to heroic Biblical figures and
tell of his suffering for his uncompromising faith.

1673. Culpepper, Emily. "The Spiritual Movement of Radical Feminist
      Consciousness." UNDERSTANDING THE NEW RELIGIONS (item 667), pp.
      221-34.

      Argues in favor of a radical feminist consciousness which has
      spiritual dimensions. Three main streams in the development of
      this awareness are explored: 1) feminist Witchcraft and the worship
      of the goddess; 2) woman-identified culture; and 3) woman-identi-
      fied chronicles, philosophy, and theory. Though this essay does
      not advance a sociological understanding of the women's movement,
      it makes a clear connection between the revival of Witchcraft and
      the rise in feminism in Western culture. Most of the new reli-
      gions, the author states, "offer only a pseudo-newness for women"
      (p. 220); they still advance the traditional patriarchal view of
      male-female relationship.

1674. Damrell, Joseph. SEARCH FOR IDENTITY: YOUTH, RELIGION, AND CULTURE.
      Beverly Hills, CA: Sage Publications, 1978. 231 pp.

      Presents an in-depth study of the Church of the Cosmic Liberty,
      a pseudonym for a Hindu-oriented new religious movement that is
      described as an Adventist, gnostic, and introversionist organiza-
      tion. After discussing the method of participant observation used
      to study this church, the author provides biographical descriptions
      of some of the main actors in the church and an outline of its
      history, ideology, daily life, social structure, and the roles and
      social contexts of its members. The author then describes two
      other kinds of youth religions and reflects on youth culture as a
      whole. He suggests that contemporary society is characterized by
      a prolongation of adolescence and a lack of social networks and
      structures and that the new religious movements are "improvisa-
      tions" that come into being to provide people with meaning for
      their actions, feelings, and ideas.

1675. Daner, Francine J. "Conversion to Krishna Consciousness: The
      Transformation from Hippie to Religious Ascetic." SECTARIANISM:
      ANALYSES OF RELIGIOUS AND NON-RELIGIOUS SECTS (item 713), pp.
      53-69.

      Describes the conversion to the Hare Krishna Movement in four
      major stages: 1) the predevotee stage, characterized by the rejec-
      tion of middle-class values and experimentation with different
      lifestyles; 2) the neophyte stage, in which the individual begins
      living in the temple and starts the socialization process into the
      movement's lifestyle; 3) the membership phase, during which the
      initiation ceremonies take place and the individual acquires a new

name, a new status, and a new, initial identity; and 4) the integrative stage, that of an advanced devotee who has successfully
integrated one's role and identity in the movement.

1676.   Daner, Francine J. THE AMERICAN CHILDREN OF KRSNA: A STUDY OF THE
        HARE KRISHNA MOVEMENT. New York: Holt, Rinehart, and Winston,
        1974. ix, 118 pp.

        Presents an anthropological study of the International Society
        for Krishna Consciousness as a revitalization movement. It is
        argued that the apparently disorganized lives of its members before
        their conversion supports the view that joining the group helped
        solved their identity and alienation problems. Besides giving an
        account of the advent in the U.S.A. of the founder of the movement,
        the author gives a concrete picture of the temple life with its
        daily routine and worship services. The political and economic
        structures, the socialization process, and the family arrangements
        are described. Several biographies and autobiographies are used to
        draw a profile of the kind of individual who would join the move-
        ment. Disenchantment with society, loss of individuality, lack of
        value orientation, and a feeling of isolation are among the fea-
        tures of those who find a meaningful existence in the temple.

1677.   Darrand, Tom Craig, and Anson D. Shupe. METAPHORS OF SOCIAL CONTROL
        IN A PENTECOSTAL SECT. Lewiston, NY: Edwin Mellen Press, 1983.
        vii, 223 pp.

        Studies, from multidisciplinary perspectives, a neo-Pentecostal
        congregation, referred to as the "Restoration" or "Latter Rain"
        (that is, of divine blessings), which split from the Pentecostal
        Assembly of Canada in the mid-1940's. The authors focus on the
        conscious and unconscious "conceptual systems of images through
        which social life is interpreted and around which social life is
        organized" (p. 2). Three areas of investigation are pursued: 1) a
        study of the key metaphors of the movement (that is, the "Taberna-
        cle," or sacred community of believers; 2) an exploration of disaf-
        filiation or apostasy from the movement; and 3) a historical and
        ethnographic outline of the sect. The authors also discuss one
        major methodological issue, namely the ethics of a "returning
        Latter Rain member-become researcher."

1678.   Davis, Devra Lee. "The History and Sociology of the Scientific
        Study of Acupuncture." AMERICAN JOURNAL OF CHINESE MEDICINE 3
        (1975): 5-26.

        Reflects on the increased interest in, and scientific research on,
        the practice of acupuncture, especially since the early 1960's and
        explores reasons why the present times are conducive to such a
        development. Several reasons to explain why acupuncture is now a
        respectable area for scientific research are advanced. Acupuncture
        is said to be a goldmine for those sociologists of science who
        investigate 1) the simultaneity of scientific discoveries and the
        conflicts over such discoveries and 2) the social structure of the
        scientific enterprise, especially the circumstances under which
        scientific research of acupuncture begins. Social scientists also

examine the social relationships involved in scientific research
and the part played by the state, the profession, and public in the
rise of acupuncture interest and research.

1679. Davis, Douglas. "Social Groups, Liturgy, and Glossolalia." CHURCH-
       MAN 90 (1976): 193-205.

       Takes an anthropological approach to the study of the relation-
       ships between glossolalia (that is a specific form of communicat-
       ion) and the social contexts and relations in which it occurs. Two
       types of religious institutions and liturgies are distinguished,
       namely the traditional churches (like Anglicanism) and the newly
       emerging sects (such as the current Pentecostal revival). The
       present charismatic experience has brought into being new patterns
       of social interaction with the consequent particular forms of lin-
       guistic usages. Glossolalia is a polar type of restrictive code,
       since it requires interpretation by someone other than the one who
       is actually speaking in tongues. It further "indicates the break-
       through of the conservative middle-class individual into the affec-
       tivity of religious community" (p. 202). The differences between
       glossolalia in classical Pentecostalism and in the contemporary
       Charismatic Renewal Movement are detailed.

1680. Davis, Rex, and James T. Richardson. "The Organization and Func-
       tioning of the Children of God." SOCIOLOGICAL ANALYSIS 37 (1976):
       321-39.

       Gives a brief description of the Children of God and a historical
       outline of their origin and development till the mid-1970's. Among
       the issues raised are the recent leadership problems the movement
       has had in Scandinavia, the practical difficulties in their commu-
       nal lifestyle, and their decision-making processes. The types of
       colonies, their internal structure, and their finances are also
       dealt with. Recent restructuring, with a deemphasis of "litness-
       ing," and a stress on personal witnessing, are assessed in the
       light of social factors. A period of consolidation with a more
       decentralized structure and a maturing of members are seen as indi-
       cators that conflict with the traditional churches and with the
       community at large will decrease. The authors see signs that the
       movement is becoming an international bureaucracy with Moses David,
       their founder, as its charismatic, rather than autocratic, ruler.

1681. Deadwyler, William H. (Ravindra-svarupa das). "Patterns in ISKCON's
       Historical Self-Perception." KRISHNA CONSCIOUSNESS IN THE WEST
       (item 580), pp. 55-75.

       Outlines the historical perception of the devotees of the Hare
       Krishna Movement from three different points of view: 1) the linear
       view of secular history; 2) the linear view of religious history;
       and 3) the cyclical view of history. The idea of tradition and its
       relationship to each of the above views of time is described.
       ISKCON's view of salvation history is experienced in a linear,
       sacred time. The devotees (which include the author) believe that
       the movement will become a dominant force in the modern world.

1682. Deadwyler, William H. (Ravindra-svarupa das). "The Devotee and the
       Deity: Living a Personalistic Theology." GODS OF FLESH, GODS OF
       STONE: THE EMBODIMENT OF DIVINITY IN INDIA. Edited by Joanne
       Punzo Waghorne and Norman Cutler. Chambersburg, PA: Anima Publi-
       cations, 1985, pp. 69-87.

       Explains the attitude of worship and service of the Hare Krishna
       devotees towards the images of God in their temples. The author, a
       member of this new movement, attempts to answer the question of why
       people brought up in Western culture would adopt the forms of an
       alien one. The philosophical and theological foundations for the
       belief that the deities are present in the temple are presented,
       showing how they are part of the religious world of the members of
       the movement.

1683. Dean, Geoffrey A., I. W. Kelly, James Rotton, and D. H. Saklofse.
       "A Guardian Astrology Study: A Critique and Reanalysis." SKEPTI-
       CAL INQUIRER 9 (1985): 327-338.

       Examines Professor A. Smithers' study on astrology that was pub-
       lished in the British daily newspaper, THE GUARDIAN, in March and
       April, 1984. The relationship between sun sign and occupation is
       confirmed by the authors who, however, disagree with the conclusion
       that it indicates genuine astrological effects. "Statistical fluc-
       tuation and self-attribution effects" are said to be better expla-
       nations of Smithers' results.

1684. Decter, Midge. "The Politics of Jonestown." COMMENTARY 67.5 (May
       1979): 29-34.

       Reflects on the tragic case of the People's Temple and suggests
       that its history reflects something common to Western culture.
       "Jim Jones is a figure with many counterparts who have in recent
       years been given places of honor among us" (p. 31). Whether seen
       as an aspect of religious insanity or as an outgrowth of the radi-
       calism of the 1960's, Jonestown is a reminder of the dark side of
       human nature and of how close we can get to revolutionary suicide.

1685. Dégh, Linda. "UFOs and How Folklorists Should Look at Them."
       FABULA 18 (1977): 242-48.

       Argues that looking at UFO phenomena from a folklorist's point of
       view might add a "sobering and stimulating" aspect to a rather
       frustrating debate. UFO cases, according to the author, fit into
       well-known, traditional folklore categories and UFO testimonies and
       pertain to standard folklore genre. She sees a connection between
       accounts of UFOs and common monster stories and considers the be-
       lief in superhuman saviors watching us from the sky as typical of
       the messiah pattern common in many religions.

1686. DeMaria, Richard. "A Psycho-Social Analysis of Religious Conver-
       sion." TIME FOR CONSIDERATION (item 1652), pp. 82-130.

       Examines in some detail the methods of conversion employed and
       the commitment evoked by the Unification Church and concludes that,
       while there are some dangers attached to these methods, their use

has been common in the history of religions. The author discusses
sudden religious experiences in the context of the accusation of
brainwashing and compares them to similar experiences in other
American revival movements, in EST, and in monastic institutions.

1687. Derks, Frans, and Jan Van der Lans. "The Abortive Death of A De-
       structive Cult." UPDATE: A QUARTERLY JOURNAL OF NEW RELIGIOUS
       MOVEMENTS 9.1 (1985): 13-21.

       Chronicles the birth of a cult lead by a tai-chi teacher (Jo
       Onvlee) in 1983 and its conflicts with the Dutch civil authorities.
       The main accusation against the cult was its mistreatment of chil-
       dren. Though opposition to the cult may have strengthened, there
       are no indications that it has grown in size. The legal battles
       were still in progress when this essay was published in early 1985.

1688. Derks, Frans, and Jan Van der Lans. "Sub-Groups in Divine Light
       Mission Membership: A Comment on Downton." OF GODS AND MEN (item
       550), pp. 303-308.

       Comments on Downton's theory on conversion to the Divine Light
       Mission (items 1690-91) and questions whether one can possibly
       identify all the stages in the conversion process that he lists.
       The authors maintain that there is a clear difference between those
       Divine Light Mission members who joined before 1975 and those who
       entered after that date and that Downton's theory is applicable
       to the former and not to the latter, who were not dropouts from
       society. The change in members coincided with organization and
       ideological changes within the mission, particularly the move to
       make Guru Maharaj Ji a personal savior.

1689. Dinges, William D. "Catholic Traditionalist Movement." ALTERNA-
       TIVES TO AMERICAN MAINLINE CHURCHES (item 603), pp. 137-58.

       Describes the Catholic Traditionalist Movement "as a reaction to
       the humanistic, horizontally-oriented, worldview construction that
       has gained ascendancy in the Roman Church" (p. 137). The author
       compares the Underground Church of the late 1960's, a church that
       was made up of liberal Catholics, with the Underground Church of
       the 1970's, a church that attracted conservative Catholics who re-
       fused to accept the reforms of the Second Vatican Council. Four
       major traditionalist organizations are described: 1) the Catholic
       Traditional Movement; 2) the Orthodox Roman Catholic Movement; 3)
       the Traditional Catholics of America (a splinter group from the
       first mentioned movement); and 4) the Society of St. Pius X. Sev-
       eral conservative, ideological themes are shared by all these move-
       ments. These movements are linked with periods of social-struc-
       tural strain that threatens sacred values and religious symbolism.

1690. Downton, James V. "An Evolutionary Theory of Spiritual Conversion
       and Commitment: The Case of the Divine Light Mission." JOURNAL
       FOR THE SCIENTIFIC STUDY OF RELIGION 19 (1980): 381-96.

       Develops a theory of conversion in 10 distinct types and 27 steps,
       based on an intensive study of the members of the Divine Light
       Mission, an Eastern religious group under the leadership of Guru

Maharaj Ji. After a brief description of the movement's origins,
beliefs, and practices, the author traces in some detail the stages
of those members who reported a dramatic personal change as they
were led to the "experience of knowledge" in their initiation ritual. These changes, which the author thinks are applicable to
other movements, are in many respects in harmony with Lofland and
Stark's theory of conversion (1965).

1691.   Downton, James V.   SACRED JOURNEYS: THE CONVERSION OF YOUNG AMERI-
         CANS TO THE DIVINE LIGHT MISSION.   New York: Columbia University
         Press, 1979. ix, 241 pp.

         Presents a study of the social and psychological dynamics of
         conversion to the Divine Light Mission, an Eastern religious move-
         ment led by Guru Maharaj Ji. The author first gives four case
         histories of conversions and then traces the stages in the conver-
         sion and commitment process of "premies" (i.e., converts). He main-
         tains that conversion is an evolutionary change, starting with
         disillusionment with established religion, involvement in the
         counterculture, and experimentation with drugs. He thinks that
         those who joined this movement have changed in several positive
         ways and have become less alienated, worried, and afraid, and more
         confident and peaceful. There is a chapter on defection from the
         movement and a section on the method used. The author's opinion is
         that the movement has waned, but that it will probably continue to
         offer an alternative to conventional religion.

1692.   Drakeford, John W.   CHILDREN OF DOOM: A SOBERING LOOK AT THE COM-
         MUNE MOVEMENT.   Nashville: Broadman Press, 1972. 143 pp.

         Constructs a typology of communes and then explores the Children
         of God as an example of a religious commune. One chapter is dedi-
         cated to nineteenth-century communes where subordination of the
         individual will to that of the group and the loss of privacy are
         among the main features. The Children of God are described as a
         radical religion. Their daily lifestyle and their views on life,
         marriage, and the family are described and compared to those of
         other communes. In the author's view, the Children of God "may
         offer one of the most potent alternatives to the drug culture" (p.
         80). Some of the religious and social problems raised by this
         group are considered.

1693.   Drummond, Lee.   "Jonestown: A Study in Ethnographic Discourse."
         SEMIOTICA 46 (1983): 167-209.

         Proposes to make anthropological sense of Jonestown by dwelling
         on the ethnographic events experienced by the author, who was in
         Guyana when the tragedy occurred. The author explains that, while
         Americans experienced Jonestown as a media event, the Guyanese felt
         like they were participating in a movie. Jonestown is described
         from three perspectives, namely those of history, of national
         policy, and of the popular culture of the country in which the main
         events took place. The author shows how rumors and stories about
         Jonestown reached Georgetown, the capital city of Guyana, and
         created a picture of the events that differed significantly from

the official American and Guyanese commentaries. He states that "the reality of Jonestown is the heterogeneous assemblage of impressions, reactions, and interpretations it has provoked; its madness opens a window on a multifaceted world of the cultural continuum" (p. 199).

1694. D'Souza, Dinesh. "Moon's Planet: The Politics and Theology of the Unification Church." POLICY REVIEW 32 (Spring 1985): 28-34.

Discusses the relationship between the political and theological views of the Unification Church and points to some areas where, in spite of its anticommunist rhetoric, the church might be in conflict with conservative trends. Four main tenets of Unificationism are outlined: 1) its apparent lack of concern with religious freedom; 2) its socialist trends; 3) its dislike of national boundaries; and 4) its one-world idealism. Moon's earthly empire and missionary outreach are briefly outlined.

1695. Dubisch, Jill. "You Are What You Eat: Religious Aspects of the Health Food Movement." THE AMERICAN DIMENSION: CULTURE MYTHS AND SOCIAL REALITY. Edited by Susan P. Montagu and W. Arens. Palo Alto, CA: Mayfield Publishing Company, second edition, 1981, pp. 115-27.

Considers health foods as a system of symbols and the health food way of life as an expression of a religious worldview. After a short account of the history of the Health Food Movement, the author describes its ideological content, drawing schematic comparisons and contrasts between the qualities of health and junk foods. She reflects on the social significance of the movement and suggests that a person who gets involved in it may experience "mazeway resynthesis" (see Wallace, item 137), that is, the creation of maps, values, and techniques that restore harmony and that usually accompany conversion to a revitalization movement. The Health Food Movement, like any new faith, criticizes the current social values and institutions and provides alternatives. It has sacred symbols, a convincing worldview, a system of purity and impurity, and the concepts of mana and taboo to guide its members to their choice of food. It has its temples (namely health food stores), its specialists, and its "sacred" writings. Like many religious movements, it calls people back to a "Golden Age."

1696. Duddy, Neil T. "The Community of Jesus." UPDATE: A QUARTERLY JOURNAL OF NEW RELIGIOUS MOVEMENTS 6.2 (1982): 64-94.

Describes the beliefs and activities of a Christian community on Cape Cod, Massachusetts. Its origin is traced to the foundation of Bethany House by Cay Anderson and Judy Sorenson, a house that became a center for Bible studies and fellowship. The author reflects on the physical and verbal isolation that new members experience at their introductory retreat and outlines the principles that guide the relationship between the leaders and their followers. Though largely theological in scope, this essay points out several social mechanisms of conversion that operate within the group.

1697. Dupertius, Lucy. "How People Recognize Charisma: The Case of Dar-
       shan in Radhasoami and Divine Light Mission." SOCIOLOGICAL ANAL-
       YSIS 47 (1986): 111-24.

       Criticizes the deterministic model of charismatic recognition
       that assumes that individuals are passive to charisma. Three
       levels of analysis of how charisma works are mentioned: 1) the
       cultural approach that investigates ways of learning and teaching
       charismatic recognition; 2) the interactional analysis method that
       looks at how both leader and followers contribute to the creation
       of a charismatic relationship; and 3) the phenomenological position,
       which the author adopts, that focuses on the "techniques people
       deliberately cultivate in learning how to recognize charisma" (p.
       113). The Indian roots of both Radhasoami and the Divine Light
       Mission are briefly traced. It is maintained that charisma can
       best be understood in terms of "darshan" (i.e., presence of the
       guru). Various aspects of "darshan" are examined. Charisma is
       seen as an active, conscious, and changing process that involves
       noncognitive modes of perception. The author suggests that many
       members of the Divine Light Mission might have learned how "to
       experience God" on their own, thus explaining why this religious
       group declined in the early 1980's.

1698. Easton, Barbara, Michael Kazin, and David Plotka. "Desperate
       Times: The Peoples Temple and the Left." SOCIALIST REVIEW 9
       (1979): 63-73.

       Maintains that the interpretation of the tragic events at Jones-
       town as the result of a paranoic madman is an inadequate solution
       that avoids answering the question of why people joined the Temple
       at all. In California, the People's Temple operated within the
       tradition of the evangelical church. It recruited members largely
       from areas of high unemployment, where drug and alcohol addiction
       were common problems. It provided security, meaning, and direction
       to its members who gave up their independence. The Temple gradu-
       ally developed strong leftist views. It became an organization
       that strove to be a model for a better society and used communitar-
       ian ideals, denunciations of racism, and attacks on capitalist
       tyranny to attract members. The relationship between the political
       left and the People's Temple are outlined. The authors hold that
       radical politics provided the impulse that made the Jonestown trag-
       edy possible.

*   Ebaugh, Helen Rose Fuchs, Kathe Richman, and Janet Saltzman Chafetz.
       "Life Crises Among the Religiously Committed: Do Sectarian Differ-
       ences Matter?" Cited above as item 1244.

1699. Ejerfeldt, Lennart. "Sociology of Religion and the Occult Revival."
       NEW RELIGIONS (item 555), pp. 202-14.

       Discusses four main themes in the current occult revival: 1) the
       social diffusions of occult beliefs and practices (superstitions
       like astrology, belief in premonitions and ghosts, and visits to
       palmists); 2) the occult revival as a "cult;" 3) the connection
       between the occult revival and the counterculture; and 4) the

occult revival and the new spiritual trends in the mainline churches.
The author maintains that the occult revival has led to new cults
are no longer a marginal phenomenon. Some of the major works on
the occult (that are included in the bibliography) are surveyed.
The author states that the new trends in Christian spirituality
(including the Charismatic renewal) "must certainly be considered
in connection with the occult revival, to some extent as due to the
same influences, but partially as a reaction to it" (p. 213).

1700.   Ellwood, Robert S. "ISKCON and the Spirituality of the 1960s."
        KRISHNA CONSCIOUSNESS IN THE WEST (item 580), pp. 102-13.

        Points to various interpretations of the key themes of the
        counterculture of the 1960's and relates them to the new religious
        movements. These themes are rock music, psychedelic experiences,
        an antitechnology perspective, self-discovery and human potential,
        and exploration of the psychic world. Though at first the Hare
        Krishna Movement stressed the alternative to the experience of
        drugs it offered its devotees, by the early 1980's its literature
        spoke more of love and community than of the experience of being
        "high." Various reasons that might lead an individual to join this
        movement are discussed. "Exploration was the deepest dynamic of
        the spirituality of the 1960's and is supremely epitomized in
        Krishna Consciousness" (pp. 112-13.)

1701.   Ellwood, Robert S. "Religious Movements and UFOs." THE ENCYCLO-
        PEDIA OF UFOS (item 67), pp. 306-308.

        Examines the religious responses to UFOs. People who have had
        UFO experiences often unite to form an organization that has simi-
        larities to a religious movement. The connection between UFOs and
        the holy is traced to the 1947 sightings. The 1950's was the
        Golden Age of UFO religion. A large percentage of those involved
        in UFO movements had a background in Spiritualism and Occultism.
        Three UFO religious movements, namely Understanding Incorporated,
        the Aetherius Society, and the UFO People, are briefly described.

1702.   Ellwood, Robert S. ONE WAY: THE JESUS MOVEMENT AND ITS MEANING.
        Englewood Cliffs, NJ: Prentice-Hall, 1973. vii, 150 pp.

        Studies the Jesus Movement within the context of American culture
        and in comparison with other frontier revivals both in the Eastern
        and Western traditions. The author first examines the American
        popular culture of the 1960's and the evangelical tradition in Amer-
        ica. He next describes the Jesus experience, giving a brief out-
        line of the movement's history and symbols. The Jesus Movement,
        he suggests, attempts to relate to history, which it aims at tran-
        scending, in three ways, namely by "living in apocalyptic expecta-
        tion, reintegrating the alienated into the values demanded by liv-
        ing in a deferred reward historical stream, demanding conversion of
        the places and persons who shape history" (p. 96). One chapter is
        dedicated to a study of the Children of God and another to several
        campus-related groups like the Inter-Varsity Christian Fellowship,
        the Campus Crusade for Christ, and the now-defunct Christian World
        Liberation Front. Several alternatives to the Jesus Movement, like

the Metropolitan Community Church in Los Angeles, Catholic Pentecostalism, the Mythopoeic Society, and the Process Church of the
Final Judgment, are also considered.

1703. Emmons, Charles F., and Jeff Sobal. "Paranormal Beliefs: Functional Alternatives to Mainstream Religion?" REVIEW OF RELIGIOUS
RESEARCH 22 (1981): 301-12.

Attempts to find out whether there is a correlation between the
decline of liberal Protestantism in the U.S.A. and the increasing
interest in paranormal phenomena. Occult beliefs are divided into
two categories, religious and nonreligious. The former act as
alternatives to religion; the latter are merely part of popular
culture. Using the Gallup poll as a source data, the authors explore popular paranormal beliefs on the afterlife, angels, devil,
the Loch Ness Monster, the Sasquatch, witches, ghosts, astrology,
ESP, precognition, déjà vu, and clairvoyance. Various Protestant
churches (Baptist, Lutheran, Methodist, Presbyterian, and Episco-
pal) as well as Catholics and Jews are included in the survey. The
authors find definite support for their position that, with some
qualifications, belief in paranormal phenomena does act as a substitute for religion.

1704. Emmons, Charles F., and Jeff Sobal. "Paranormal Beliefs: Testing
the Marginality Hypothesis." SOCIOLOGICAL FOCUS 14 (1981): 49-56.

Tests the hypothesis that marginality is positively associated
with paranormal beliefs among which is included the occult, psychic
phenomena, and some fundamentalist religious tenets. The authors
review some of the main social literature on the subject and conclude that it supports the position that religious involvement in
occult matters is deviant behavior and can be explained by the
theory of social deprivation. The following paranormal beliefs
were the primary focus of the authors' research: life after death;
angels and devils; the Loch Ness Monster; the Sasquatch (Bigfoot);
witches; ghosts; astrology; and extrasensory perception (including
precognition, déjà vu, and clairvoyance). Only two of these beliefs, namely angels and astrology, were found to be positively
linked with marginality.

1705. Endore, Guy. "Synanon: The Learning Experience." DEVIANCE:
STUDIES IN DEFINITION, MANAGEMENT, AND TREATMENT. Edited by
Simon Dinitz, Russel R. Dynes, and Alfred C. Clarke. New York:
Oxford University Press, second edition, 1975, pp. 528-32.

Discusses the drug rehabilitation organization known as "Synanon"
as "a school for a totally new way of living" (p. 528). The author
points out that Synanon has consistently stressed self-education
and reeducation. It further proposes an educational system that
inspires and makes sense. Some elements of this educational system
are briefly outlined.

1706. Erickson, Keith V. "Black Messiah: The Father Divine Peace Mission
Movement." QUARTERLY JOURNAL OF SPEECH 63 (1977): 428-36.

Explores the effects of rhetoric used by the founder of the Peace
Mission Movement, Father Divine (alias George Baker), in an attempt
to discover how so many people were convinced that he was God. A
brief history of the movement is given and the social, economic,
and religious conditions of his followers investigated. Father
Divine's unprepared speeches, judged by conventional standards of
rhetoric, border on the "crude and incomprehensible." His rhetorical strategies, like the use of fear, were rather refined, showing
an understanding of human emotions, attitudes, and behavior. He
faced two rhetorical tasks: one was to establish his credibility as
a divine person, the other to restructure the attitudes of his
followers. The themes of his discourses coincided with the major
problems of Harlem, thus giving his movement an appeal suited to
his audience.

1707. Erikson, William. "The Social Organization of a Commune." URBAN
       LIFE AND CULTURE 2 (1973): 231-56.

       Describes a modern religious commune (called "Shalom") in a Mid-
       western city in the United States, stressing the basic features of
       its organizational structure and activities. The commune is de-
       scribed as a sect made up of people who were disenchanted with
       their experience of organized Christianity. The author gives an
       account of its historical and demographic background, of its formal
       structure, including its finances, and its religious and cultural
       activities, including its proselytization techniques. He concludes
       that groups like Shalom survive only when the needs of their mem-
       bers are met.

1708. Evans, Hilary. "Ufos as Social and Cultural Phenomena." UFOS,
       1947-1987 (item 19), pp. 359-63.

       Points out that the UFO phenomenon has generated its own mythol-
       ogy, stereotypes, and cultural patterns and that it has raised
       questions similar to those about European witchcraft between the
       fourteenth and seventeenth centuries. The social responses to UFOs
       are examined under the following categories: 1) UFOs and the funda-
       mentalist Christian; 2) UFOs and private projection; 3) UFOs as
       folklore; 4) UFOs as supertechnology; and 5) UFOs and the skeptics.
       The author thinks that UFOs also constitute a cultic system of
       beliefs and practices that attracts certain types of people and
       that "to study UFOs is like studying pathological patients to dis-
       cover how the human mind works" (pp. 362-63).

1709. Fichter, Joseph H. THE HOLY FAMILY OF FATHER MOON. Kansas City,
       MO: Leaven Press, 1985. 155 pp.

       Presents a sociological analysis of the main structural features
       of the Unification Church, stressing particularly its ecclesiology.
       Among the topics covered are the reasons why people join the
       church, its ideal marriage system, its structure, and the view of
       the church as the Family of God. The main charges against the
       church are refuted. Entrance into the church is compared to join-
       ing a Catholic religious order. The author holds that, whatever
       the church's faults are, one has to recognize its systematic

program for the restoration of "old-fashioned morality," its stress
on chastity before marriage, and and its recognition of the manifold spiritual dimensions in the marriage relationship and in the
family.

1710. Fichter, Joseph H. "Families and Religion Among the Moonies: A
       Descriptive Analysis." FAMILIES AND RELIGION: CONFLICT AND
       CHANGE IN MODERN SOCIETY. Edited by William V. D'Antonio and
       Joan Aldous. Beverly Hills, CA: Sage Publications, 1983, pp.
       290-304.

       Discusses the Unification Church position that religion is the
       most important element in marital and family love and the practical
       consequences that flow from this belief. The ideals of marriage
       and the family are reflected in the church's theological creed,
       code of moral behavior, system of worship services, and the struc-
       ture of social relations. The Unification Church's ideal that its
       church can function as a large and happy family is similar, accord-
       ing to the author, to ideas cherished by the monks of a Benedictine
       abbey and the members of a charismatic community. The Reverend
       Moon has blended Confucian philosophy of the family and society
       with a theology of family life and relationships. Some specula-
       tions on possible future developments within the Unification Church
       are made.

1711. Fichter, Joseph H. THE CATHOLIC CULT OF THE PARACLETE. New York:
       Sheed and Ward, 1975. 183 pp.

       Examines the Catholic charismatic renewal as a social phenomenon,
       i.e., as a movement "to which human energy and ingenuity must be
       brought, goals established, plans made, communication developed,
       and structure built" (p. 18). Among the topics explored are het-
       erodoxy, changing membership, personal relationships among charis-
       matics, and beliefs in prophecy, miracles, and demons. The author
       thinks that the Catholic Charismatic Movement, in spite of its
       newness, retains much that is traditionally Catholic. The rise
       of the movement has come as a surprise to sociologists because 1)
       it has been inaugurated by lay Catholics, rather than the clergy;
       2) it attracts people from the middle-class; 3) it stresses emo-
       tional, rather than intellectual, aspects of faith; and 4) it has
       emerged in a scientific, rational culture.

1712. Fichter, Joseph H. "Liberal and Conservation Catholic Pentecostals."
       SOCIAL COMPASS 31 (1974): 303-10.

       Questions the social generalization that "people who are doctrin-
       ally orthodox belong to lower-class pentecostal sects, while people
       of higher socioeconomic status belong to mainline liberal churches"
       (p. 303). The author contests that data from Catholic Pentecostals
       indicates that members are orthodox and devout, have favorable
       social attitudes, and do not belong to the underprivileged social
       classes. People with contrasting social and religious attitudes
       participate in the Charismatic Movement, whose spiritual and devo-
       tional practices make little demand on their attitudes except in
       general terms of universal love and fellowship.

1713. Fine, Gary Alan. "Psychics, Clairvoyance, and the Real World: A Social-Psychological Analysis." ZETETIC 1.1 (1976): 25-33.

Tests ten professional psychics and compares them with ten Harvard and Radcliffe upperclassmen to determine whether the former made "qualitatively different predictions." It is concluded that not all who claim psychic powers actually have them and that some psychics could be better described as "entertainers." Claims of psychic ability are, in the author's view, a social phenomenon. "Being a psychic involves learning how to make 'psychic' predictions" (p. 31). Self-confidence in making predictions may also enhance credibility. Psychics serve the function of reducing uncertainty and anxiety in people's lives.

1714. Fischler, Claude. "Astrology and French Society: The Dialectic of Archaism and Modernity." ON THE MARGINS OF THE VISIBLE (item 700), pp. 281-93.

Traces the rise of interest in Astrology in France to Madame Soleil and investigates various kinds of criticism leveled against it. The author thinks that astrology rests on the ancient mode of thought called the "magico-analogical." He traces the development of mass astrology from a primitive magical science to the use of modern horoscopes. Contemporary astrology has been influenced by psychology and by the stress on the individual and has assumed the form of a relationship between a private astrologer and his or her client. Astrology ignores the idea of social class and pervades all strata of society, even though there are differences between the astrologies of the upper and lower classes. Astrology flourishes when ideological and cultural norms are weakened and magical thought prevails.

1715. Flinn, Frank W. "Scientology as Technological Buddhism." ALTERNATIVES TO AMERICAN MAINLINE CHURCHES (item 603), pp. 89-110.

Describes the main features of Scientology, which, according to the author, bears a close resemblance to Buddhism. The Scientology concept of "clear" is compared to the Buddhist "Bodhi" (i.e., the enlightened one). The transition from Dianetics to Scientology is discussed both in terms of the therapeutic sequence they follow and of the dynamics they utilize. Several characteristics that are central to Scientology's self-understanding are also outlined: 1) research vs. revelation; 2) standardness vs. infallibility and inerrancy; 3) knowledge vs. faith/reason; 4) "engram" vs. sin; 5) organization vs. charisma; 6) technique vs. ceremony; and 7) survival vs. salvation. Scientology represents one aspect of the West turning to the East.

1716. Flother, Eckart. "Bhagwan Shree Rajneesh." UPDATE: A QUARTERLY JOURNAL OF NEW RELIGIOUS MOVEMENTS 9.2 (1985): 12-20.

Gives an account of the rise of the Rajneesh Movement with special reference to the events at Rajneeshpuram, Oregon. The luxurious lifestyle of the guru and some of the contradictory views he espoused are described. The author believes that there are clear parallels between Rajneeshpuram and Jonestown.

1717. Fontaine, Carole. "Brightening Up the Mindworks: Concepts of
       Instruction in Biblical Wisdom and Rinzai Zen." RELIGIOUS EDUCA-
       TION 79 (1984): 590-600.

       Examines what Biblical literature says about the tasks and ef-
       fects of instruction and compares it with the teaching of Rinzai
       Zen. Both Zen and the Bible are intensely concerned with the
       transmission of certain perspectives on experience. The use of the
       Koan as a teaching technique in Zen is described. Though the Bible
       and Zen use different metaphors to express different cultural world-
       views and goals, they both pursue a similar aim, namely to bring
       together traditional orientations towards the experiences of being,
       feeling, and knowing.

1718. Foss, Daniel A., and Ralph W. Larkin. "Worshipping the Absurd: The
       Negation of Social Causality Among the Followers of Guru Maharaj
       Ji." SOCIOLOGICAL ANALYSIS 39 (1978): 157-64.

       Analyzes the basis of Guru Maharaj Ji's appeal to ex-participants
       of the youth movement of the early 1970's. The Divine Light Mis-
       sion, which he founded, is seen as a "highly incongruent, even self-
       contradictory organization" whose leader is "worshipped for his
       seemingly nonsensical and unpredictable behavior" (p. 158). This
       Hindu mission appeals to those who were in a state of confusion and
       despair before joining it, because it deified the incomprehensible
       nature of the world while providing an ideology which gave ultimate
       meaning to life. The "premies" (devotees of the guru) were led to
       a noncausal belief system that was mirrored in their guru, himself
       a figure of ambiguity, contradiction, and irrationality.

1719. Fox, Phillis. "Social and Cultural Factors in Beliefs About UFOs."
       UFO PHENOMENA AND THE BEHAVIORAL SCIENTIST (item 622), pp. 20-42.

       Explores the reasons why people believe in flying saucers, focus-
       ing on the social and cultural factors that influence people who
       claim contact with extraterrestial vehicles and astronauts. The
       author discusses the cultural beliefs that are compatible with
       beliefs in UFOs and the social interaction that supports them. Some
       aspects of American culture, like the interest in space travel over
       long distances, make the presence of UFO visitors very plausible.
       The author thinks that the very lack of satisfactory explanations
       by experts of UFO sightings supports UFO beliefs.

1720. Friedrich, Otto. "New Age Harmonies." MAGIC, WITCHCRAFT, AND
       RELIGION (item 652), pp. 412-19.

       Points out that some elements of the New Age Movement, which
       combines spirituality and superstition, have been in existence for
       centuries. The various features of the New Age Movement, such as
       astrology, channeling, and healing, are reviewed with reference to
       specific people who are immersed in the movement's thinking and
       practices. Various reactions to, and interpretations of, the move-
       ment are given. The New Age is seen by many as a barometer of the
       disintegration of American culture. Originally published in TIME
       magazine (December 17, 1987), this article provides a popular
       account of the New Age.

1721. Fritscher, John. POPULAR WITCHCRAFT. Secaucus, NJ: Citadel Press,
       1973. 192 pp.

       Presents a descriptive study of witchcraft as part of popular
       culture, which is seen as essentially "neophiliac," that is, in love
       with the new. Witchcraft has the qualities to appear new and the
       attractiveness to be commercialized. Legends of sorcery and witch-
       craft, the casting of spells, records of interviews with practicing
       witches, and LaVey's Church of Satan are among the topics covered.

1722. Galbreath, Robert. "Explaining Modern Occultism." THE OCCULT IN
       AMERICA: NEW HISTORICAL PERSPECTIVES (item 849), pp. 11-37.

       Selects four basic problems that illustrate the difficulties
       involved in explaining modern occultism, namely: 1) the definition
       of the occult; 2) occult revival throughout history; 3) the occult
       as a manifestation of historical crises; and 4) the occult as a
       form of irrationalism. The author argues that the most familiar
       causal explanation of modern occultism, namely that it is a mani-
       festation of economic, social, and religious crises, is not self-
       evident. He points out that the occult is not irrational or un-
       scientific. It is rather an attempt to answer metaphysically
       questions that are beyond scientific investigation. The question
       whether the occult can be called "marginal" is also raised.

1723. Gambill, Karen Cruse. "Biographical Variables in the Hare Krishna
       Movement." PROCEEDINGS OF THE SOUTHWEST CONFERENCE FOR ASIAN
       STUDIES. Edited by Edward J. Lazzerini. University of New
       Orleans Press, 1980, pp. 155-57.

       Studies the members of the Hare Krishna Movement who live in a
       city temple in New Orleans and in a farming commune in Carriere,
       Missouri. After examining the age, sex, education, marital status
       and number of children in both locations, the author concludes that
       the devotee "is frequently a recent convert who is young, male,
       single, above average in education, and comes from a large family.
       He is typically independent, self-sufficient with little or no
       commitment to an established religious belief system and has exper-
       imented with drugs" (p. 157). These findings are in general agree-
       ment with the earlier results of Judah.

1724. Garrigues, E. L. "The Sokagakkai Enshrining Ceremony: Ritual Change
       in a Japanese Buddhist Sect in America." EASTERN ANTHROPOLOGIST
       28 (1975): 133-45.

       Studies the relationship between ritual form and social context
       with reference to a Buddhist sect that has established itself in
       the United States of America. The historical roots of the movement
       in thirteenth-century Japan and its presence in the West since the
       early 1960's are briefly sketched. The recruitment techniques and
       the ritual process of integration are discussed, bringing out some
       of the main differences between the Japanese and American branches
       of this movement. Because of the lack of priests in the U.S.A.,
       the usual priest-administered and temple-centered conversion rites
       are not possible. Instead, the dramatic conversion to Soka Gakkai

is highlighted by the individual's act of receiving and enshrining
the Gohonzon in a personal ceremony at home. The author thinks
that this shows how Soka Gakkai has adapted to its new environment
in the West.

1725. Gelberg, Steven J. (Subhananda dasa). "Exploring an Alternative
        Reality: Spiritual Life in ISKCON." KRISHNA CONSCIOUSNESS IN THE
        WEST (item 580), pp. 135-62.

        Presents an insider's perspective of life in the Hare Krishna
        Movement. After giving the historical and theological background
        of the movement, the author examines its spiritual life and experi-
        ence by analyzing its main characteristics, including its ascetic,
        personalistic, and meditational dimensions. A typical day in the
        spiritual life of a Hare Krishna devotee is outlined, stressing the
        theological rather than the social nature of the activities per-
        formed. The author suggests that the social scientist "should take
        more seriously the experiential ambience of the religious groups
        they wish to study" (p. 157).

1726. Gelberg, Steven J. (Subhananda dasa). "The Fading of Utopia:
        ISKCON in Transition." BULLETIN OF THE JOHN RYLANDS UNIVERSITY
        LIBRARY OF MANCHESTER 70.3 (1988): 171-83.

        Observes that since the death of the founder of ISKCON in 1977,
        the Hare Krishna Movement has been in decline due to the following
        factors: 1) the political and spiritual effects of its founder's
        death; 2) the activities of the Anti-Cult Movement; 3) decreased
        financial stability; 4) aging membership; 5) insecurity among mem-
        bers; 6) a stress on the need to build up the institution; 7) the
        rise of internal bureaucracy; and 8) a crisis of authority and
        disenchantment with the leadership and the consequent internal
        turmoil. Most of the essay is dedicated to explaining the last-
        mentioned factor. The 1980's reform movement within ISKCON is
        described. The author states that, in spite of all its problems,
        the movement has shown a "surprising resilience," though its future
        remains uncertain.

1727. Gelberg, Steven J. (Subhananda dasa). "The Future of Krishna Con-
        sciousness in the West: An Insider's Perspective." THE FUTURE
        OF NEW RELIGIOUS MOVEMENTS (item 579), pp. 187-209.

        Assesses the future prospects for the Hare Krishna Movement in
        the light of Stark's model (see item 956) of success or failure
        for new movements, a model that applies four major criteria to
        determine whether a new religious movement will succeed. The
        author thinks that these criteria, namely cultural continuity,
        effective mobilization, internal perception of success, and network
        ties, betray a quantitative bias and omit some important internal
        elements. The spiritual goals of a movement, its spiritual depth,
        its political cohesion, and effective leadership are essential
        criteria discussed by the author.

1728. Gelberg, Steven J. (Subhananda dasa).   "ISKCON After Prabhupada:
        An Update on the Hare Krishna Movement." ISKCON REVIEW 1 (1985):
        7-14.

Assesses the impact of Prabhupada's death (in 1977) on the movement he founded. The author provides "a brief overview, a summary,
a broad outline of ISKCON's evolution in the years between its
founder's death and the present" (p. 7). The reasons why the movement's solidarity and vitality haven't faded are outlined. Some
potentially disruptive changes in administrative and spiritual
leadership are discussed. The growth of the movement in size and
influence, both in India and in the Western world, are sketched.
Some reflections on future prospects are made.

1729. Gelberg, Steven J. (Subhananda dasa), editor. HARE KRISHNA, HARE
      KRISHNA: FIVE DISTINGUISHED SCHOLARS ON THE KRISHNA MOVEMENT IN
      THE WEST. New York: Grove Press, 1983. 276 pp.

      Transcribes the editor's interviews with the following five
      scholars who have contributed to the study of the Hare Krishna
      Movement in the West: Harvey Cox; Larry D. Shinn; Thomas J.
      Hopkins; A. L. Basham; and Shrivatsa Goswami. Among the topics
      discussed are the issues of brainwashing and deprogramming, the
      reasons why people join the movement, its historical background,
      its social and psychological contexts, and its theological signifi-
      cance. A short bibliography (pp. 267-72) includes the works of the
      movement's founder.

1730. Gillen, Paul. "The Pleasures of Spiritualism." AUSTRALIAN AND NEW
      ZEALAND JOURNAL OF SOCIOLOGY 23 (1987): 217-232.

      Questions the deprivation theory of cult formation because it
      does not explain why people join such groups at all. The author
      proposes the view that individuals join cults or sects because they
      take pleasure in their activities; in other words, becoming a mem-
      ber of a marginal religious group is one way of spending one's
      leisure time. A group of Spiritualists from Sydney, Australia
      is studied precisely to illustrate this theory. Spiritualism is
      judged to be not an unrealistic escape from the dreariness of the
      material world, but rather a form of enjoyment. Spiritualists
      participate in the thrill of the gnostic quest, entertain them-
      selves in several cognitive and textual games (such as mediumship),
      and simply enjoy the pleasure of companionship, competition, and
      caring found in Spiritualist groups.

1731. Goldstein, David N. "The Cult of Acupuncture." WISCONSIN MEDICAL
      JOURNAL 71 (October 1972): 14-16.

      Describes briefly the new interest in acupuncture in the Western
      world and adopts a view that acupuncture depends on a faith system.
      If the practice of acupuncture relies on the susceptibility of the
      patient, or on the power of suggestion, or on reliance on the prac-
      titioner's wisdom, then it should be listed with other faddish
      treatments like zone therapy and the use of copper bracelets.
      According to the author acupuncture is a "cult technique." It is a
      mysterious procedure that should not be confused with medicine.

1732. Goldstein, Michael S., Carol Sutherland, Dennis T. Jaffe, and Josie
      Wilson. "Holistic Physicians and Family Practitioners: Similar-
      ities, Differences, and Implications for Health Policy." SOCIAL
      SCIENCE AND MEDICINE 26 (1988): 853-61.

Lists the main features of holistic medicine, which is usually
judged to be at odds with orthodox medical practices. The authors
explore the possibility of integrating the two systems of healing
through a survey of physicians from the American Holistic Medical
Association and of a group of family physicians. They conclude
that there is little difference between them in their "sociodemographic characteristics." The evaluation by these healers and
doctors of 25 healing techniques (including meditation, spiritual
healing, and acupuncture) is recorded. It is concluded that
holistic and mainstream medicine are compatible, since their
differences are only a matter of degree.

1733. Goodman, Felicitas D. "Prognosis: A New Religion?" RELIGIOUS
       MOVEMENTS IN CONTEMPORARY AMERICA (item 727), pp. 244-54.

Examines, in the context of a Pentecostal church where trance was
a central feature, the manner in which the supernatural dimension
is incorporated within it. It is further speculated whether cultural change can result from the birth of a new religious movement.
Four phases of the cult, from the beginning to its dissolution, are
specified: 1) the onset, 2) the gathering of momentum, 3) the peak,
and 4) the platform stage. The author concludes that cultural
change is unaffected by the upheaval.

1734. Gordon, David F. "The Role of the Local Social Context in Social
       Movement Accommodation." JOURNAL FOR THE SCIENTIFIC STUDY OF
       RELIGION 23 (1984): 381-95.

Examines two Jesus People groups in the local community setting
in which they flourished. The context is held to be important,
because it helps explain the group differences in the internal
organizational features and because it directs our attention to the
interactive and symbolic aspects of the movements' development. A
brief history and description of each group--one urban, the other
suburban--is provided. Several internal group characteristics,
such as beliefs and values, goals and incentives, and leadership,
are examined. The various aspects of the local social context,
with its setting, local resources, symbolic environment, and the
relationship of the group with its neighbors, are explored. The
author concludes that the local social contexts influenced the
development of the groups by providing different kinds of membership, leadership, and resources.

1735. Gordon, David F. "Dying to Self: Self-Control Through Self-Aban-
       donment." SOCIOLOGICAL ANALYSIS 45 (1984): 41-55.

Examines the process of self-abandonment in two Jesus People
groups, focusing on the consequences on the self. The role of the
self in the salvation experience of these born-again Christians is
explored and analyzed. The author explains how this process enhances the individual's self-control by applying an interactionist
view that sees the convert as belonging to a social milieu, which
stimulates growth in self-esteem, self-consistency, self-efficacy,
and self-authenticity. Various interrelated stages of self-transformation are outlined. The Jesus person is dissatisfied with life

before his conversion. Through self-abandonment, he or she is lead
to a self-reconstruction and self-authentication that actually
makes him or her a better person.

1736. Gordon, David F. "Identity and Social Commitment." IDENTITY AND
RELIGIONS. Edited by Hans Mol. Beverly Hills, CA: Sage Publications, 1978, pp. 229-41.

Explores the relationship between identity and commitment in the
context of two Jesus People groups in a major United States city.
Jesus People, in the author's opinion, find identity in a hierarchical structure that provides "identity foci at several levels
going from the cosmological through social and group to the individual" (p. 231). The religious community has a central place in the
person's self identity and relationship to others. The author
observes that the two groups studied share a religious ideology,
historical origins, and some social characteristics. They differ,
however, in several areas. One is a communal organization that
encourages relationships within the group; the other stresses the
need to wear distinctive clothing, to witness to others, and to
retain one's contacts outside the group. An explanation of these
differences is proposed.

1737. Gordon, David F. "The Jesus People: An Identity Synthesis." URBAN
LIFE AND CULTURE 3 (1974): 159-78.

Attempts to solve the paradox of the Jesus People, namely that
many young adults return to those values which they had earlier
rebelled against. The view advanced in this essay is that the
activities, beliefs, and lifestyle of the Jesus People "synthesize
and reconcile otherwise contradictory aspects of a young person's
life" (p. 159). After a short description of the Jesus People
Movement, the author identifies various types of identity changes
that a convert might experience. This Movement is considered to be
a suitable way of solving the problems of young adults. Through
participation in this movement, the individual arrives at an "identity synthesis" by combining a conventional view of morality with
the subjective, expressive, and ecstatic qualities of youth culture.

1738. Gordon, James S. THE GOLDEN GURU: THE STRANGE JOURNEY OF BHAGWAN
SHREE RAJNEESH. Lexington, MA: Stephen Greene Press, 1987.
viii, 248 pp.

Offers a biographical account of the author's experience with,
and study of, a new religious movement that has created controversy
in, and been suppressed by, many countries. The author first describes his meeting with Rajneesh in Poona, India, then relates his
move with his disciples to Oregon in the summer of 1981, when Rajneeshpuram was founded, and finally tells the story of the breakup
of the community in September 1985. Though the author's account
tends to be sympathetic, he admits that as Rajneesh's personal
power and charisma increased, the imbalances and distortions of his
movement multiplied. In Gordon's opinion, this guru became a sa-
distic person who was also contemptuous, cruel, and wasteful.
Though not much social analysis is attempted, this book provides
some valuable inside information on Rajneesh and his followers.

1739. Grace, James H. SEX AND MARRIAGE IN THE UNIFICATION CHURCH: A
       SOCIOLOGICAL STUDY. New York: Edwin Mellen Press, 1985. 284 pp.

       Examines Unification Church beliefs and practices pertaining to
       sex and marriage, practices that are unique in American religious
       history and that contribute to the building and maintaining of the
       commitment of members in a hostile environment. The author focuses
       on the sex values and roles, the preparation for, and participation
       in, the sacramental mating ceremony, and the life of partners after
       the communal wedding rite. Three levels of analysis are pursued:
       1) an examination of the organizational structure which reflects
       the Unification Church's approach to sex and marriage as a commit-
       ment mechanism; 2) an exploration of the process of personal inter-
       action within the group from a phenomenological perspective; and
       3) a study of the church in terms of the roles of its members. The
       author rejects the use of a reductionistic psychological theory to
       explain sex and marriage in the Unification Church and prefers
       to use Kanter's approach (see item 383) that sees the church's
       approach to sex and marriage as a mechanism that enhances involve-
       ment in the group's goals.

1740. Grattan-Guinness, I. "Ufology and Its Social Predicaments."
       ANNALS OF SCIENCE 33 (1976): 205-210.

       Comments on Mimi Hynek's work on the flying-saucer debate (see
       THE SPECTRUM OF UFO RESEARCH, Chicago: J. Allen Hynek Center for
       UFO Studies, 1988) and argues that it "exemplifies very well many
       of the social issues of science which now attract so much interest"
       (p. 208). Among these issues are listed the relationship between
       fringe sciences and the scientific establishment, the emergence of
       popular organizations (flying-saucer clubs), and the role of entre-
       preneurs.

1741. Gutwirth, Jacques. "Jews Among Evangelists in Los Angeles." JEW-
       ISH JOURNAL OF SOCIOLOGY 24 91982): 39-55.

       Studies Messianic Judaism in Los Angeles and focuses on the Open
       Door Messianic Jewish Congregation, a branch of the Open Door Com-
       munity Church under the leadership of Robert Leslie Hymes. The
       author describes both the congregation and its parent church. He
       thinks that the Jewishness of the Jewish House Church, unlike that
       of the majority of Jewish Christians, is "skin-deep rather than
       fundamental." The well-defined lines of discipline and commitment
       that distinguish the Open Door Community Church from the rest of
       society have undeservedly earned the church the designation of a
       "cult." Most of this church's members are ethnic and marginal.
       The recruitment of Jews acts "as a link with the world of the
       established middle classes whose values the church has taught
       them to appreciate, and whose ranks they wish to join" (p. 53).

1742. Hall, John R. "Jonestown and Bishop Hill: Continuities and Disjunc-
       tions in Religious Conflict." COMMUNAL STUDIES 8 (1988): 77-89.

       Compares and contrasts the religious conflicts that occurred in
       Jonestown with those at Bishop Hill, the latter being a small vil-
       lage in Northern Illinois where a Swedish Lutheran immigrant sect

under Eric Jansson experienced violence and religious turmoil. The
similarities between Eric Jansson and Jim Jones are outlined and
the events that led to the former's assassination and the latter's
suicide are considered. In spite of the many differences, the
author observes that they both shared a history of struggle with
society at large. The conflicts that ensued over relatives who
joined the movements led to frustration and antagonism. The theme
of apocalyptic struggle was present in the rhetoric of both leaders.

1743. Hall, John R. "Collective Welfare as Resource Mobilization in
        Peoples Temple: A Case Study of a Poor People's Religious Social
        Movement." SOCIOLOGICAL ANALYSIS 49 (Supplement 1988): 44-77.

        Suggests that the mobilization of resources in new religious
        movements has to be understood in combination with the way in which
        these resources are allocated, monitored, and administered. The
        People's Temple at Jonestown is taken as an example of how finances
        are managed in a religious corporation. The People's Temple,
        through its control of all the money used by the group, became a
        "greedy institution" that made total demands on the individuals who
        joined it. In so doing, the Temple created great conflicts with
        the outside world, especially with defectors. It did not, however,
        demand the complete control of its members' financial resources
        simply as an effort to increase its margin of profit. It rather
        formed a sociological community, a bureaucracy with a more personal
        touch, and offered one possible solution to alienation.

1744. Hall, John R. "The Impact of Apostates on the Trajectory of Reli-
        gious Movements: The Case of Peoples Temple." FALLING FROM THE
        FAITH (item 578), pp. 229-50.

        Points out that despite the different interpretations of Jones-
        town offered by scholarly and popular literature, both indicate
        that the intense conflict that existed between the People's Temple
        and its opponents is a necessary component of any historical expla-
        nation of Jonestown. The author outlines the boundaries between
        the members of the People's Temple and apostates, proposes a socio-
        historical model of apostasy, and summarizes the situational his-
        tory of the Temple and of Concerned Relatives (an organization of
        apostates who left the movement before it moved to Guyana). The
        author's main argument is that the "conflictual interaction" be-
        tween the People's Temple and its opponents pushed the Temple
        leaders towards the ritual of mass suicide. The conflict created
        conditions similar to those that led to the collective martyrdom of
        politicoreligious sects.

1745. Hall, John R. GONE FROM THE PROMISED LAND: JONESTOWN IN AMERICAN
        CULTURAL HISTORY. New Brunswick, NJ: Transaction Books, 1987.
        xx, 381 pp.

        Attempts to present a picture of Jonestown as an intelligible
        cultural event and not as a morality play acted out in a series of
        atrocity tales about a deranged leader. The book is divided into
        three parts. The first examines the leader of the Temple and shows
        how the origins of his church were embedded in three streams of

American culture. The second part looks at the organization of the
People's Temple, focusing on its economics, social control, and
public relations. The last part traces the final period of Jonestown's history from its conflict with its detractors, its subsequent migration to Guyana, and its last days. The migration itself
is explained by general social dynamics rather than by some unique
paranoic feature of the movement or its leaders.

1746. Hall, John R. "Apocalypse at Jonestown." SOCIETY 16 (September/
        October 1979): 52-61.

        Maintains that historical parallels to Jonestown, and explana-
        tions that portray Jim Jones as an irrational charismatic and his
        followers as a group of brainwashed individuals, do not help us
        understand the tragedy, either sociologically or religiously. The
        author proposes the view that the People's Temple at Jonestown was
        an apocalyptic sect that leaned heavily on "the post-apocalyptic
        tableau of other-worldly graces" (p. 173). The goal of establish-
        ing a heaven on earth was frustrated and voluntary suicide was
        conceived as a way of overcoming that frustration. The origins of
        Jonestown are considered and its religious development examined.
        The members of Jones's group suffered from a persecution complex
        common among worldly sects. Jonestown, however, differed from any
        other religious group because it was racially more thoroughly inte-
        grated and pursued a distinctly communist ideology. These two
        factors made the individuals feel unique and at the same time nur-
        tured a deep sense of persecution. The mass suicide enabled the
        members of Jonestown to abandon the "apocalyptic hell" they had
        created and seek immortality.

1747. Hall, Robert L. "Sociological Perspectives on UFO Reports." UFOS--
        A SCIENTIFIC DEBATE. Edited by Carl Sagan and Thornton Page.
        Ithaca, NY: Cornell University Press, 1972, pp. 213-23.

        Focuses on reports of UFO sightings and elaborate beliefs linked
        with them and outlines the controversies about, and analyses of,
        such beliefs. The author first applies to the UFO phenomenon
        social scientific knowledge on the process of rumor, mass hysteria,
        and hysterical contagion. Then, he discusses "the plausibility of
        systematic misconception" in UFO reports. Finally, he makes some
        observations on the responses of scientists to the UFO phenomenon.
        Various forms of scientific resistance to UFOs are identified and
        discussed.

*   Hampshire, Annette, and James A. Beckford. "Religious Sects and
        the Concept of Deviance: The Mormons and the Moonies." Cited
        above as item 1293.

1748. Hann, Robert R. "Werner Erhard's 'Est'--A Religious Movement?"
        QUARTERLY REVIEW: A SCHOLARLY JOURNAL OF REFLECTIONS ON MINISTRY
        2 (Fall 1982): 78-95.

        Discusses whether EST (now called "The Forum") is a religion in
        spite of the insistence of its directors that it is primarily an
        educational institution. The author examines 1) Werner Erhard both

as the founder of EST and its ongoing source, 2) the movement's
function as a transformatory experience, and 3) its beliefs and
practices that involve the deep commitment of some of its graduates.
He concludes that EST has many features of a religious movement and
that its values and sense of community are similar to those of a
traditional church. EST does function as a source of ultimate
meaning for a majority of its graduates. The author, himself an
EST graduate, thinks that "involvement in EST has been both temporary and reportedly beneficial" (p. 93).

1749. Harder, Mary W. "Sex Roles in the Jesus Movement." SOCIAL COMPASS
        26 (1974): 345-53.

        Investigates the roles of men and women in an isolated Jesus
        commune which the author calls the Christ Commune, pseudonymously.
        The author observes that there is a relative absence of role con-
        flict and that the submissive position of women is in sharp con-
        trast with the aspirations encouraged by the Women's Liberation
        Movement in Western culture. The commune is characterized by sim-
        plicity of organization and role structure as well as by a rather
        uncomplicated worldview. In opposition to the values stressed in
        the West, competition, material gain, and educational achievement
        are rejected. Sex roles are defined precisely and easily differen-
        tiated. The role distinctions are justified on a scriptural basis.
        Women are expected to be submissive to men, to engage in traditional
        women's work, and to be nonaggressive, nurturing, self-effacing,
        and sensuous. The manner in which members are socialized into the
        commune is briefly described.

1750. Harder, Mary W., James T. Richardson, and Robert Simmonds. "Life
        Style: Courtship, Marriage, and Family in a Changing Jesus Move-
        ment Organization." INTERNATIONAL REVIEW OF MODERN SOCIOLOGY 6
        (1976): 155-72.

        Investigates one of the oldest and most well-organized groups in
        the Jesus Movement, a group that had grown to 1000 members, most of
        whom lived in communal houses in different parts of the U.S.A. The
        researchers discovered that this group is marked by the clarity,
        consensus, and consistency of the social roles of its members.
        They report on the changes in courtship habits, marriage patterns,
        and family roles that have occurred over a five-year period. The
        following changes are recorded: 1) a loosening of heterosexual
        contact norms; 2) an implementation of birth control practices;
        3) a redefinition of the role of women; 4) the replacement of mar-
        ried couples' houses by the traditional nuclear family living
        arrangement; and 5) an expansion to include noncommunal family
        units. The effects these changes might have on the organization
        are discussed.

1751. Harder, Mary W., James T. Richardson, and Robert Simmonds. "Jesus
        People." PSYCHOLOGY TODAY 6.7 (December 1972): 45-50, 110-13.

        Describes the attitudes and practices of a Jesus People group,
        namely the Christ Commune, with regard to sex, drugs, and liquor.
        A profile of a member of this Christian fundamentalist movement is

drawn. The Jesus People, when compared to college students, are
alienated from, and disinterested in, society. They are further
non-competitive, anti-intellectual, and otherworldly. Moreover,
they are significantly less defensive and self-confident and scored
lower on achievement, dominance, and endurance. The mechanisms
that are responsible for the personality change of the Christ Commune are discussed.

1752. Hardin, Bert, and Gunter Kehrer. "Some Social Factors Affecting
the Rejection of New Belief Systems." NEW RELIGIOUS MOVEMENTS:
A PERSPECTIVE FOR UNDERSTANDING SOCIETY (item 551), pp. 267-83.

Offers a model, based on a study of the Unification Church in
Germany, of how society goes about rejecting new belief systems,
which demand some commitment. Four characteristics of a belief
system are identified: 1) content (ideology); 2) degree of commitment in time, money, and emotion; 3) related social action; and 4)
the "carrier" (i.e., the amount and form of organization and the
training of individuals). The cooperation of the individual citi-
zen, the established churches, the mass media, and government institutions is deemed necessary to constitute social rejection. In
Germany, all these forces came together to contribute to a common
strategy understandable by all. The Unification Church was accused
of being a threat to economic stability and to the social welfare
system.

1753. Hardin, Bert, and Gunter Kehrer. "Identity and Commitment." IDEN-
TITY AND RELIGION: INTERNATIONAL, CROSS-CULTURAL APPROACHES.
Edited by Hans Mol. Beverly Hills, CA: Sage Publications, 1978,
pp. 83-96.

Studies the belief system of, and commitment to, the Unification
Church in Germany in terms of the identity they give to the members. After an analysis of the concepts of belief and commitment
and of the relationship between commitment and personal identity,
the authors explore the world of the Unification Church. The
author suggests that this church crystallizes the identity of its
members around three foci that require active commitment, namely:
1) the true parents, Reverend and Mrs. Moon; 2) the community; and
3) Korea, from which country the church originated. Various stages
of identity building are discussed. The requirement of total commitment and the success in building strong groups on a local level
are related to the high level of dedication elicited from members.

1754. Hargrove, Barbara W. "On Studying the 'Moonies' as a Political
Act." RELIGIOUS STUDIES REVIEW 8 (1982): 209-13.

Reviews several major works on the Unification Church and observes that the political climate in which the studies were done
must be taken into consideration. Earlier works on this movement
were less polemic. The anticult movement had a noticeable impact
on studies intended to be objective reports on the Unification
Church. Scholarly, social-scientific works on this church seem to
discredit the rather naive descriptions and interpretations that
are often made of the movement and its members.

1755. Harper, Charles L. "Spirit-Filled Catholics: Some Biographical
       Comparisons." SOCIAL COMPASS 21 (1974): 311-24.

       Attempts to determine the causal factors leading to the rise of
       Catholic Pentecostalism by presenting several in-depth interviews
       with its members. Four life histories are outlined. Some common
       hypotheses used to explain participation in the movement are re-
       jected as inadequate. A detailed analysis of several features,
       namely early socialization, growing ambivalence towards the tradi-
       tional church, search for options, the turning point, and continued
       commitment, is presented. Various stages of development are out-
       lined. The author thinks that the movement, in spite of some ten-
       sions with the institutional church, actually supports it.

1756. Harrison, Michael I. "Commitment and Routinization in a Social
       Movement." JOURNAL FOR THE SCIENTIFIC STUDY OF RELIGION 17
       (1978): 456-60.

       Comments on McGuire's paper (item 1851), which is judged to be
       faulty on three counts: 1) it overstresses the role of glossolalia;
       2) it fails to provide illustrative and interpretative materials;
       and 3) it does not consider the possibility that her conclusions on
       commitment differ from those of other researchers. While agreeing
       with McGuire's view that speaking in tongues is but part of an
       extended process of commitment, the author questions her stress on
       formal testimonies given in Pentecostal meetings. It is suggested
       that the importance of the individual act of speaking in tongues
       may have declined as the movement became more structured and as the
       interaction between members, including giving testimony, acquired a
       greater significance.

1757. Harrison, Michael I. "The Maintenance of Enthusiasm: Involvement
       in a New Religious Movement." SOCIOLOGICAL ANALYSIS 36 (1975):
       150-60.

       Studies the Catholic Charismatic Renewal in order to find how its
       participants sustain their focus on their initial experiences. The
       behavioral involvement, the regular pentecostal activities, the
       spiritual gifts (speaking in tongues, prophecy, and healing), the
       Christian community, personal religious life, and elite activities
       are described. The Catholic Charismatic Movement has successfully
       confronted the tension between the experience of religious conver-
       sion and the "routinized patterns of worship and organization" (p.
       158) through charismatic friendship networks and an intense devo-
       tional life. The movement has become increasingly organized in its
       religious expressions and its leadership has adopted a hierarchical
       structure. These developments, the author thinks, might lead mem-
       bers to seek religious experience elsewhere.

1758. Harrison, Michael I. "Sources of Recruitment to Catholic Pentecos-
       talism," JOURNAL FOR THE SCIENTIFIC STUDY OF RELIGION 13 (1974):
       49-64.

       Describes the impact of situational factors on recruitment to the
       Catholic Charismatic Movement. After a brief discussion on the
       emergence of the movement, the author examines the religious and

socioeconomic predispositions of those who join, the personal relationships between members, and the outside obligations that members
maintain. Basing his reflections on a study of Catholic Charismatic groups in three cities (Ann Arbor, Flint, and East Lansing)
in Michigan, he concludes that three factors contribute to the
successful recruitment of new members to the movement: 1) the sharing of the movement's problem-solving perspective; 2) the absence
of conflicting social obligations; and 3) the presence of social
relationships between members.

1759. Harrison, Michael I. "Preparation for Life in the Spirit: The
        Process of Initial Commitment to a Religious Movement." URBAN
        LIFE AND CULTURE 2 (1974): 387-414.

        Analyzes the way Catholic Charismatic groups, particularly those
        in Ann Arbor, Michigan, are organized in such a way as to attract
        individuals to become members. The procedure used to encourage
        newcomers to seek baptism in the Holy Spirit and to develop ties
        with the movement is first examined, showing how the leaders play a
        key role in engendering commitment. Various processes underlying
        the development of initial commitment are summarized and compared
        with those found in other movements. Two main settings that pro-
        mote initial commitment are described: informal contacts and
        friendships with members and prayer meetings. The baptism of the
        Holy Spirit is the public expression of commitment. The Catholic
        Charismatic Movement, unlike some other new groups, does not elicit
        complete conversion or total commitment of its members. Those who
        develop an intense allegiance to the movement usually take up a
        leadership role.

1760. Harrison, Michael I., and John K. Maniha. "Dynamics of Dissenting
        Movements Within Established Organizations: Two Cases and a Theo-
        retical Interpretation." JOURNAL FOR THE SCIENTIFIC STUDY OF
        RELIGION 17 (1978): 207-24.

        Examines why the American Neo-Pentecostal Revival of the 1960's,
        with its obvious Protestant stress on individual inspiration and
        its roots in Evangelical theology, flourished in the Roman Catholic
        Church and barely survived in the Episcopal Church. Three condi-
        tions that determine whether a reforming movement will remain in-
        corporated in the parent body or separate from it are suggested:
        1) the extent of integration of the reform group into its parent
        body; 2) the power of the parent body to control the dissenting
        group; and 3) the ability of the parent body to absorb the dissent-
        ing movement. Two Neo-Pentecostal congregations--one Catholic, the
        other Episcopal--are studied and the integration of the Pentecos-
        tals into their parent church, the power of this church over the
        new Pentecostals, and the way dissent is handled are observed.

1761. Harvey, David A. "TV Preacher Jimmy Swaggart: Why Does He Say
        Those Awful Things About Catholics?" THE GOD PUMPERS (item 604),
        pp. 87-100.

        Explores the sectarian behavior of TV evangelist Jimmy Swaggart
        and suggests that his belligerent style actually helps him "mobi-
        lize resources from people who watch his program and attend his

crusades" (p. 89). This he successfully achieves by raising the
level of consciousness of shared interest, by creating opportunities for collective action, including the donation of funds, and by
arousing feelings of solidarity. The attacks against Catholics and
other religious groups are seen as a rhetorical strategy to mobi-
lize resources.

1762. Hashimoto, Hideo, and William McPherson. "Rise and Decline of Soka
      Gakkai: Japan and the United States." REVIEW OF RELIGIOUS RE-
      SEARCH 17 (1976): 82-92.

      Discusses one of the new Japanese religions in the framework of
      the view that unconventional religions are on the edges of culture
      and can be explained by the common sociological and anthropological
      theory of deprivation. A brief history of Soka Gakkai is given and
      its growth in membership, both in Japan and in the United States
      between 1951 and 1970, is described in some detail. After outlin-
      ing some of the movement's main doctrines, the authors conclude
      that Soka Gakkai "illustrates the tendency of social movements to
      move from prophecy to agitation to consolidation" (p. 91). While
      Soka Gakkai may become another Buddhist sect in mainstream Japanese
      culture, its fate in the United States may be more precarious.

1763. Hayashida, Cullen T. "Isolation of Leadership: A Case Study of a
      Precarious Religious Organization." REVIEW OF RELIGIOUS RESEARCH
      17 (1976): 141-52.

      Studies an evangelical Christian youth organization at the Uni-
      versity of Hawaii. The members of this group acknowledge the fact
      that they are separated from the outside world, which considers
      them deviant and which reacts towards their behavior with some
      hostility. The author found the organization precarious both be-
      cause of its divergent belief system and its structural instability.
      He suggests that those members of the group that rank higher in the
      organization are more isolated from the sociocultural environment.
      Members tend to avoid conflict with nonmembers by minimizing con-
      tacts with them.

1764. Heelas, Paul. "Exegesis: Methods and Aims." THE NEW EVANGELISTS
      (item 787), pp. 17-44.

      Describes a new religious movement called "Exegesis" that oper-
      ated a standard seminar or program under the name of "Infinite
      Trainings" between 1976 and 1984 The author examines the group's
      rather secret, low-keyed recruitment methods and argues against
      both the conspiracy approach and the marketplace theory. Instead,
      he maintains that the evangelization techniques of Exegesis were
      influenced by the fact that the movement tried to attract people to
      distinctive and unusual experiences. The author thinks that re-
      cruitment to Exegesis relied heavily on the positive psychological
      effects of the seminars, which were aimed not at imparting doctrine,
      but at creating an experience. This approach, according to the
      author, made Exegesis appear secretive and devious.

1765. Heenan, Edward. "Which Witch: Some Personal and Sociological Im-
      pressions." MYSTERY, MAGIC, AND MIRACLE (item 631), pp. 105-18.

Describes the author's encounter with two people involved in witchcraft and/or Satanism. The first, a Dr. Herbert Sloane, is a witch in Toledo, Ohio, who found the Our Lady of Endor Coven--The Ophtic Gnostic Cultus of Baal Sathanus. This group is classified as a white Satanic cult that is rather small in size. The second is a nouveau witch, Robert Kennedy, of Dayton, Ohio, who led the Rainbow Coven that followed the rituals of THE BOOK OF SHADOWS. The two groups are contrasted, the first being an example of Satanism, puritanism, and authoritarianism, the second of occultism, libertarianism, and egalitarianism. Several factors useful in examining the differences within Witchcraft are listed.

1766.   Heeren, John W., and Marylee Mason. "Seeing and Believing: A Study of Contemporary Spiritual Readers." SEMIOTICA 50 (1984): 191-211.

Examines spiritual reading as one level of common religiosity, that is, a layer of religious beliefs and practices underlying the established churches. Rather than looking at fortune-telling as a form of divination, the authors focus on spiritual readings as interactional situations. Three fields of discourse in these readings are distinguished: 1) interview; 2) visionary style; and 3) everyday talk. This essay focuses on the second type of discourse and describes the various forms (such as interrogative and declarative) and content of visionary utterances.

1767.   Heeren, John W., and Marylee Mason. "Talk About Visions: Spiritual Readings as Deviant Work." DEVIANT BEHAVIOR: AN INTERDISCIPLINARY JOURNAL 2 (1981): 167-86.

Considers spiritual reading or fortune-telling as deviant behavior, bearing in mind that its practice does not fully deviate from legal or community norms. Though some fortune-tellers may use fraud and exploitation, they might still be providing an important service to their clients. The authors center on "the interactive processes involved in spiritual readings as they actually appear in the context of communication" (p. 169). They explore the setting and props mobilized by readers and the typical linguistic forms they use. The principal elements of a spiritual reading are outlined and it is concluded that a tacitly shared set of beliefs, a common religion, is the context in which the interview with a reader takes place. It is pointed out that the reader's performance depends on the proper responses of the client. A brief comparison between spiritual readers and psychotherapists is made.

1768.   Hegy, Pierre. "The Invisible Religion of Catholic Charismatics." RELIGIOUS SOCIOLOGY: INTERFACES AND BOUNDARIES. Edited by William H. Swatos. New York: Greenwood Press, 1987, pp. 115-23.

Examines Catholic Charismatic groups in Long Island, New York with the aim of finding out those aspects of religious experience that have been neglected by sociologists and those sociological concepts that are not understood by those involved in the Charismatic movement. By employing the method of participant observation, the author concludes that sociologists have often failed to realize that religion and the church have an invisible aspect and that

their typologies make little sense to members of religious groups.
Similarly, the much used dichotomy between the sacred and the profane is a sociological construct with little relevance when applied
to the daily life of Charismatics. The author stresses the need to
study religious experience and faith development.

1769. Hegy, Pierre. "Images of God and Man in a Catholic Charismatic
      Community." SOCIAL COMPASS 25 (1978): 7-21.

      Stresses the importance of analyzing the images of God and of the
      human being in different societies and then explores these images
      in a white, Catholic Charismatic community in the metropolitan New
      York area. An outline, based on interviews, of the images of God
      in this community is divided into two main sections, namely: 1) the
      God of wrath and 2) the God of love, or of the heart. The author
      discusses the image of the human person that is implicitly con-
      tained in the stress on submission to charismatic leaders (mind
      manipulation) and on the passivity to God's gifts (that limits
      intellectual growth and inhibits emotional development). He holds
      that the Charismatic Movement needs a new imagery of the human per-
      son as a free creature; otherwise it will be nothing but a new form
      of deviancy.

1770. Heinz, Donald. "The Family: The New Christian Right's Symbolism
      for a Lost Past, the Unification Movement's Hope for a Second
      Advent." THE FAMILY AND THE UNIFICATION CHURCH (item 1785), pp.
      67-85.

      Focuses primarily on the role and function of the family in the
      political and social program of the New Christian Right and to a
      lesser degree on the family's place in the theology and practice of
      the Unification Church. The Christian Right sees the family as "an
      image of a lost or neglected universal order" (p. 74) and the chaos
      of sexuality and of a Godless world as part of the current social
      problems. By stressing the family, the situation is rectified and
      order restored. The Unification Church's view of the family bears
      some resemblance to this Christian position. Both movements see
      the family as one basic paradigm of the cosmic order, the divine
      presence, and the way God relates to people. Both consider the
      family to be a fundamental social and religious unit. And both
      unite the family, society, the nation, and God in one unified sys-
      tem of orderliness.

1771. Heinz, Donald. "The Christian World Liberation Front." THE NEW
      RELIGIOUS CONSCIOUSNESS (item 614), pp. 143-61.

      Attempts to understand the now-defunct Christian World Liberation
      Front as a Jesus Movement of the late 1960's and early 1970's. The
      image of Jesus as an alternative to the counterculture who is ex-
      perienced in life and who is expected to return soon is described.
      The author points out that there are several views of Jesus within
      the group and that the meanings assigned to Jesus often tend to be
      rather individualistic. Some critique of this movement is offered.

1772. Hewes, Hayden, and Brad Steiger, compilers and editors. UFO MIS-
      SIONARY EXTRAORDINARY. New York: Pocket Books, 1976. 173 pp.

Presents a journalistic account of a UFO cult led by "The Two,"
namely Bo and Peep (see items 1594-98). A transcribed interview
with the two leaders and a prepared, official statement on their
teachings are included. Steiger presents his view of flying saucer
prophets who seem to reveal essentially the same revelatory message
throughout the history of the human race. Though not a social-
scientific study in the strict sense, both writers, who seem to be
believers in UFOs, have collected invaluable ethnographic data on a
religious movement which has all but vanished.

1773. Hexham, Irving. "Yoga, UFOs, and Cult Membership." UPDATE: A
       QUARTERLY JOURNAL OF NEW RELIGIOUS MOVEMENTS 10.3 (1986): 3-17.

Attempts to relate cultic beliefs in the West to popular cultural
ideas. After a short discussion on the effects that secularization
has had on Western society, the author states that young adults
tend to look for religious alternatives in a culture where the role
of Yoga and other Hindu beliefs have become common. Three basic
beliefs accompanying Yoga are examined: Karma, reincarnation, and
astrology. New Age beliefs and beliefs in flying saucers are seen
as a new mythology that makes cults attractive to unsuspecting
young people. Several explanations of the rise of this "new irra-
tionalism," which is a return to a prescientific worldview, are
examined. The development of one's critical faculty and a serious
religious education program are necessary for combating the cults.

1774. Hexham, Irving. "The 'Freaks' of Glastonbury: Conversion and Con-
       solidation in an English Country Town." UPDATE: A QUARTERLY
       JOURNAL OF NEW RELIGIOUS MOVEMENTS 7.1 (1983): 3-12.

Researches a group of young people who call themselves "freaks"
and who visited or settled in the small Somerset town of Glastonbury in England from 1967 to 1972. These freaks, who claimed to be
on a spiritual quest in a town traditionally known as a center of
pilgrimage, formed a common bond through the use of the drug called
LSD. The gradual process of becoming a "freak" is examined. Those
freaks who settled in Glastonbury went through a process of change
that the author thinks "can be better understood as part of a
consolidation process which enabled the freaks to live in society
and yet remain, in their own eyes, different" (p. 8). The partial
acceptance of the freaks, especially by the business community,
influenced them to direct their behavior into more acceptable channels and to associate themselves with more established spiritual
traditions.

1775. Hiernaux, Jean-Pierre, and Jean Remy. "'Socio-Political' and
       'Charismatic' Symbolics: Cultural Change and Transmission of
       Meaning." SOCIAL COMPASS 25 (1978): 145-63.

Discusses involvement in sociopolitical problems and commitment
to charismatic movements as extensions of the traditional ascetic
symbolism. The contemporary Charismatic Renewal has been promoting
elaborations of classic religious forms.

1776. Hoffman, Eva. "Est--The Magic of Brutality." DISSENT 24 (1977):
       209-12.

Suggests that EST (Erhard Seminary Training) is not a mystery or a naive pseudoreligion, but "a sophisticated scenario for enacting and assuaging disaffections" (p. 209). The rather spartan training that EST uses is a combination of "every mind-bending technique" (such as Zen, Gestalt, and Transcendental Meditation) that enjoyed popularity in the 1970's. A magical meaning ascribed to this synthesis is one of EST's attractive features. EST seems to train people to be nothing but machines--competitive, hostile, and barren of affective and moral vocabulary. In a recessionist economy, people "respond to therapies that endorse materialistic incentives, arouse the will to act, and urge the virtues of unprotesting discipline" (p. 212).

1777. Hollenweger, Walter J. "Pentecostalism and Black Power." THEOLOGY TODAY 30 (1973): 228-38.

Stresses the relationship between Black Power and Black Pentecostalism and points out that the latter is more involved in social and political action that its White counterpart. Maintaining that the study of Pentecostalism must include all of its forms, including the current Charismatic Renewal, the author argues that it can no longer be held that it attracts the spiritually and materially poor. Pentecostalism is "revolutionary" because it includes all people and not just the intellectual elite or the theologically educated.

1778. Hollowman, Regina E. "Ritual Opening and Individual Transformation: Rites of Passage at Esalen." AMERICAN ANTHROPOLOGIST 76 (1974): 265-80.

Discusses an Encounter/Gestalt workshop at the Esalen Institute in Big Sur, California and interprets it as a rite of passage. The author briefly explains her role as participant-observer of a movement with which she felt some affinities and in which she became personally involved. The background to Esalen, namely the Human Potential Movement, and the various activities performed during the five-day workshop--baths, massage, Rolfing, and Arica exercises-- are described. Leadership and group norms, liminality as a group state, and individual transformation are among the main topics discussed. The workshop is seen as a rite of passage ritual "whose goal is psychological transformation and whose means are the mobilization of automatic as well as cognitive processes by cultural techniques which manipulate context and interpersonal interaction" (p. 276). The worldview of the dominant culture is contrasted with that of Esalen.

1779. Holmes, Barbara. "Status Hierarchy and Religious Sanctions: A Report on the Krishna Cult." HUMAN MOSAIC 7 (1973/1974): 31-45.

Describes a local house temple of ISKCON, stressing the religious authority that dominates the lives of the devotees. The daily schedule is examined and interpreted as an example of how spiritual status is differentiated by an informal hierarchy of spiritual qualities that are measured by the member's length of time in the movement. The author used interviews, direct observation, and

participant observation in her study and found the latter somewhat
taxing, since the devotees were interested in converting her to
their ideology and lifestyle.

1780. Hopkins, Joseph M. "Children of God—Update." UPDATE: A QUARTERLY
       JOURNAL OF NEW RELIGIOUS MOVEMENTS 4.4 (1980): 42-45.

       Tries to assess the state of the Children of God in the late
       1970's. The author thinks that membership in this movement has
       declined. Various changes introduced by the leader, Moses David,
       are described. Many parallels between the Children of God and the
       People's Temple are noted, especially the spiritual, mental, and
       bodily manipulation and the paranoid hatred of the outside world.
       The Children of God, however, may not end up in the same tragic way
       as Jonestown because their members are dispersed in various
       countries.

1781. Hopkins, Thomas J. "The Social and Religious Background for Trans-
       mission of Gaudiya Vaisnavism to the West." KRISHNA CONSCIOUS-
       NESS IN THE WEST (item 580), pp. 35-54.

       Provides the historical background for understanding the advent
       of the Hare Krishna Movement in the West. The social and religious
       conditions of nineteenth-century Bengal are traced and the contri-
       butions of the religious leaders of the period outlined. The reli-
       gious thought and devotion of Bhaktivedanta Swami Prabhupada, the
       founder of ISKCON, is said to conform to the traditional openness
       of Bengali Vaisnavism, even though at times he seemed somewhat
       unorthodox.

1782. Horowitz, Irving Louis. "The Politics of the New Cults: Non-Pro-
       phetic Observations on Science, Sin, and Scholarship." SOUNDINGS
       62.2 (1979): 209-19.

       Attempts "to deepen the discussion of what the Moon phenomenon
       represents in the post-Jonestown era." The main feature of the
       Unification Church and other movements is their quest to be civil
       religions that deny the principle of separation of church and state.
       The Unification Church's goal of creating a new theocratic world
       order is discussed. Several responses to this new movement are
       assessed. The Unification Church is, in the author's view, an
       authoritarian organization that is incompatible with the democratic
       principles of the West.

1783. Horowitz, Irving Louis, editor. SCIENCE, SIN, AND SCHOLARSHIP: THE
       POLITICS OF REVEREND MOON AND THE UNIFICATION CHURCH. Cambridge:
       MIT Press, 1978. xviii, 290 pp.

       Presents a collection of documents and articles on the political
       activities and goals of the Unification Church. The materials are
       divided into four areas: 1) the theoretical and theological under-
       pinnings of the movement (in which section two speeches of the
       Reverend Moon are included); 2) the metaphysics of Reverend Moon
       (in which section the World Council of Churches' document that
       evaluates the movement from a Christian theological viewpoint is

reproduced); 3) the politics of Moon, where the activities of his
church in Korea and in the U.S.A. are discussed; and 4) the psychology and sociology of Moon. Different perspectives of the movement are well represented by both its critics and admirers.

Contains items 1073, 1944, 1961, 2008.

1784. Hummel, Reinhart. "Guru, Miracle Worker, Religious Founder: Sathya
        Sai Baba." UPDATE: A QUARTERLY JOURNAL OF NEW RELIGIOUS MOVE-
        MENTS 9.3 (1985): 8-19.

        Gives a description of the Sathya Sai Baba Movement. A short
        biography of its founder, from his birth in 1926 till he became an
        avatar at the age of 13 and his arrival in the West in the mid-
        1970's is provided. The activities of the movement and the forms
        of meditation recommended by the guru, who is the center of worship,
        are described. The author speculates on the functions of the guru-
        avatar, which he sees as a means "of recharging and revitalizing the
        religious traditions that have become powerless, or are perceived
        as powerless, with his energy" (p. 15). He also observes that
        there is an anti-Christian dimension in all guru movements, a di-
        mension that can be attractive to some Christians.

1785. James, Gene G., editor. THE FAMILY AND THE UNIFICATION CHURCH.
        New York: Rose of Sharon Press, 1983. xviii, 269 pp.

        Presents 15 essays on the novel structure of the family in the
        Unification Church. Four major topics are addressed: 1) conflict
        and commitment, where the factors and problems leading to involve-
        ment in the church as well as the difficulties between members and
        their families are considered; 2) comparisons between the theory
        and practice of marriage and the family in the Unification and
        other groups, including the Hutterites, the New Christian Right,
        and the American Muslim Mission; 3) the responses to the Unifica-
        tion Church as seen by its members; and 4) theological and philoso-
        phical assessments and consequences of Unification Church teachings.

Contains items 1386, 1570, 1610, 1770, 1872, 2130.

1786. Johnson, C. Lincoln, and Andrew J. Weigert. "An Emerging Faith
        Style: A Research Note on the Catholic Charismatic Renewal."
        SOCIOLOGICAL ANALYSIS 39 (1978): 165-72.

        Applies the Glock's theory of deprivation (item 94) to the Cath-
        olic Charismatic Renewal. The following areas pertinent to this
        movement are explored: 1) the background variables of its members;
        2) the movement's view that American society is in a state of moral
        decay; 3) its reaction to renewal within the Catholic Church after
        Vatican II; and 4) the theological orientation and commitment of
        the members. The researchers conclude that the Catholic Charis-
        matic Renewal satisfies the individual's ethical and psychic depri-
        vations. The movement is not seen as potentially schismatic but
        rather as an emerging lifestyle. Fichter's findings on Catholic
        Charismatics (see item 1711) are partly confirmed (even though the
        authors use a different definition of orthodoxy).

1787.   Johnson, Doyle Paul. "Dilemmas of Charismatic Leadership: The Case
        of the People's Temple." SOCIOLOGICAL ANALYSIS 40 (1979): 315-23.

        Constructs a theory of charismatic leadership that centers on the
        strategies adopted by the leaders to strengthen their positions and
        to resolve the difficulties brought about by their rules. The
        theory is then applied to Jim Jones who led his followers of the
        People's Temple to the tragic mass suicide and murder in Guyana.
        Several of the strategies, such as the leader's efforts to make the
        members dependent for their social, emotional, and material needs,
        are described. The author maintains that the leader must create
        "rituals so dramatic and overpowering in their emotional effects
        that it would be difficult to stage them without sincerity" (p.
        319). It is argued that this approach provides an interpretation
        of the social dynamics of Jim Jones' People's Temple and enables us
        to reach a better understanding of this movement and its tragic end
        than do theories of Jones' psychopathology and social deficiencies
        of the environment in which the members lived.

1788.   Johnson, Gregory. "The Hare Krishna in San Francisco." THE NEW
        RELIGIOUS CONSCIOUSNESS (item 614), pp. 31-51.

        Provides an overview of the Hare Krishna Movement with a brief
        account of its origins in the U.S.A. and a description of its world-
        view, based on the author's research in the Haight-Ashbury district
        of San Francisco, California. Three sources of commitment to the
        Hare Krishna Movement are the physical inducements of the Temple
        living, the interpersonal strategies of recruitment, and the expo-
        sure to many rituals. Joining the movement implies that a person
        surrenders all aspects of his or her previous identity, especially
        the use of all illegal drugs, in exchange for spiritual transcen-
        dence. Membership provides collective validation and fellowship as
        well as regulated emotional attachments. The success of the move-
        ment is attributed to its apocalyptic ideology and its participa-
        tory rituals. Those who join fulfill, to some degree, their
        aspirations for an alternative community and sustain their quest
        for a limited "psychedelic-utopianism." The question raised is
        whether the movement reaffirms one's preexisting deviant lifestyle
        or reconciles one with society.

1789.   Johnston, Hank. "The Marketed Social Movement: A Case Study of the
        Rapid Growth of Transcendental Meditation." PACIFIC SOCIOLOGICAL
        REVIEW 23 (1980): 333-54.

        Examines the rapid growth of Transcendental Meditation and sug-
        gests that the size and international character of the movement is
        an important measure of its success. Rejecting as inadequate the
        grievance and social mobilization models, the author advances the
        view that Transcendental Meditation is a marketed social movement
        which uses 1) sophisticated promotional and recruiting techniques,
        2) a radical change in the status of membership, 3) participation
        as a product package, and 4) the extension of membership as the
        dominant goal of the movement. Transcendental Meditation moved
        from being a cultic organization to a business enterprise that
        offers a packaged deal--where the initiation process is rather

costly, but easy to go through (a fee, a short course, and a brief
ceremony), and where increasing efforts (like the Siddhi program)
are made to maintain interest and commitment. Member grievances
are dealt with within the organization itself. The author thinks
that this approach can be applied to other movements like EST and
Silva Mind Control and to groups like the Cousteau Society and
Common Cause.

1790. Jorgensen, Danny L. "Divinatory Discourse." SYMBOLIC INTERACTION 7
       (1984): 135-53.

       Examines occult practices as dramatic performances between an
expert and a client. Relying on data from a study of Tarot divination and focusing on the interaction between the participants and
on the method used to advance and confirm occult knowledge, the
author lays the ground for a study of the differences and similarities between occult claims and other forms of knowledge. The
structure and significance of the Tarot cards is explained and
the type of exchanges between the reader and his or her client
outlined. The author holds that theories based on psychosocial
deprivation, marginality, and alienation "fail to provide an
adequate explanation of occult claims and practices" (p. 146).

1791. Jorgensen, Danny L. "Psychic Fairs: A Basis for Solidarity and
       Networks Among Occultists." CALIFORNIA SOCIOLOGIST 6 (Winter
       1983): 57-75.

       Presents a study of psychic fairs that not only generate economic
support for occult groups, but also "serve as a fundamental basis
for social solidarity" (p. 58) among those who are part of the
occult community. The author focuses on the networks and groups of
occultists that tend to form "local cults." An account is given of
the types of psychic fairs and of those who take part in them. The
various rules that define and organize membership in fairs and the
activities of those who participate are analyzed. The importance
of psychic fairs for the esoteric community is stressed.

1792. Jorgensen, Danny L. "The Esoteric Community: An Ethnographic In-
       vestigation of the Cultic Milieu." URBAN LIFE 10 (1982): 383-407.

       Describes and analyzes the organization of an "esoteric commu-
nity" and then discusses its nature. The author gives an account
of the community that consisted of about 35 groups linked by a
complex of social networks sharing one common feature, namely
marginality with respect to the larger society. The composition of
the group is defined and the roles played by psychic fairs and by
the readers who figure prominently in them are underscored. Three
segments of this community are distinguished: the esoteric (stress
on knowledge claims), the psychic (emphasis on those who earn part
or all of their income from the sale of esoteric goods and/or services), and the spiritual (focus on religious or quasi-religious
groups where morality or the supernatural are prominent). The
author sees the interest in esoteric thought as a general movement
in the U.S.A. today. He points out that the emergent beliefs and

practices of the esoteric community deal with recurrent human problems, such as self-understanding, human relationships, and well-
being.

1793. Jorgensen, Danny L. "Networks of Occultists: Comment on Stark and
        Bainbridge." AMERICAN JOURNAL OF SOCIOLOGY 87 (1981): 427-30.

        Refutes Stark and Bainbridge's view (item 969) that the occult
        is not a real subcultural phenomenon. These authors, it is argued,
        fail to see the different dimensions of the occult, misinterpret
        some of the studies they quote, and make generalizations too
        quickly from limited data. Jorgensen maintains that the network
        model can be applied to occult groups. A short response by Stark
        and Bainbridge is included (pp. 430-33).

1794. Jorgensen, Danny L. "The Social Construction and Integration of
        Deviance: Jonestown and the Mass Media." DEVIANT BEHAVIOR: AN
        INTERDISCIPLINARY JOURNAL 1 (1980): 309-32.

        Explains the role of the media in defining and interpreting devi-
        ance with special reference to the tragic events that led to the
        suicide and massacre at Jonestown, Guyana in 1978. The image of
        the People's Temple presented by the media, the factors that led
        to a partial interpretation of Jonestown, the manner in which the
        events were seen as deviant, and the role of experts and public
        officials in explaining the bizarre happenings are the areas
        explored. It is maintained that Jonestown became a media event.
        Reports of the sequence of events involved an "inordinate amount of
        attention, a selective emphasis on some aspects of the happenings,
        the contexualization of events, the reduction of complex issues to
        simple ones, and the selective use of expert opinion to support and
        advance an emergent interpretation of deviance" (p. 313).

1795. Jorgensen, Danny L., and Lin Jorgensen. "Social Meanings of the
        Occult." SOCIOLOGICAL QUARTERLY 32 (1982): 373-89.

        Criticizes sociological theories of the occult, focusing atten-
        tion on the use of Tarot cards that are believed to represent a
        sacred text and to hold the symbolic key to arcane wisdom. Using
        the method of participant observation, the authors delve into the
        Tarot's divinatory purpose, the people who have recourse to it, and
        the relationships that exist between these devotees and practitio-
        ners of other occult activities. The involved in the occult often
        form cult-like groups in which practitioner-client relationships
        flourish. The authors do not think that the occult poses any ser-
        ious threat or challenge to science or religion.

1796. Judah, J. Stillson. HARE KRISHNA AND THE COUNTERCULTURE. New
        York: John Wiley and Son, 1974. xii, 301 pp.

        Presents one of the earliest studies of the Hare Krishna Movement
        in the West that links the success of the movement to the counter-
        culture of the 1960's. After exploring the history and literary
        antecedents of the movement, the author describes the beliefs and
        lifestyle of those who join it. Several chapters are dedicated to

showing how Hare Krishna devotees were part of the counterculture
before their conversion and how they abandoned their traditional
faith to dedicate themselves to an Eastern religious group. The
crises of personal distress and loss of meaning are among the factors contributing to the conversion process. Some speculations on
the future of the movement are made.

1797. Judah, J. Stillson. "The Hare Krishna Movement." RELIGIOUS MOVE-
       MENTS IN CONTEMPORARY AMERICA (item 727), pp. 463-78.

       Outlines briefly the principal beliefs, devotional practices, and
       lifestyle of the members of the Hare Krishna Movement. The author
       holds that the movement satisfies many of the needs of its members.
       Its rapid geographical expansion and its attraction to young adults
       suggest that it offers them something lacking in the established
       churches, "a vertical dimension and an experiential element."
       Several values found in ISKCON are particularly relevant to those
       Western youths who enlist in the movement. Among these values are
       included a philosophy of nonviolence, a happiness achieved without
       addiction to drugs, and an absolute spiritual authority.

1798. Juergensmeyer, Mark. "Radhasoami as a Trans-National Movement."
       UNDERSTANDING THE NEW RELIGIONS (item 667), pp. 190-200.

       Examines the Berkeley, California chapter of Radhasoami, a mod-
       ern manifestation of the Sant Mat tradition of Northern India,
       which has influenced new religious groups like Eckankar, the Divine
       Light Mission, and Ruhani Satsang. The international diffusion of
       Radhasoami is outlined and its arrival and development in the U.S.A.
       in the early nineteenth century is traced. All branches of Radha-
       soami, in spite of its obvious Indian roots, contain international
       elements, which make it transcultural in its expressions. Several
       elements, such as its stress on social service and on the spiritual
       aspects of the family, that appeal to its Indian and American mem-
       bers alike are mentioned. Radhasoami provides a means of shedding
       the limitations of national identity and of transcending the paro-
       chial claims of traditional cultures.

1799. Junnonaho, Martti. "The Divine Light Mission as a Religious Counter-
          Culture." TEMENOS 18 (1982): 54-68.

       Explores the features of counterculture movements of which the
       Divine Light Mission is taken as a typical example. After a brief
       outline of the origin and development of this new religious move-
       ment, the author gives an account of its presence and activities in
       Finland. Like other new movements in Finland, the Divine Light
       Mission has gone through several stages: "at the beginning great
       enthusiasm and many supporters, followed by a leveling out of ac-
       tivities and transition from public presence to peace and tranquil-
       lity" (p. 63). In its early days, the Mission attracted frustrated
       young adults looking for a religious alternative to the hippie
       movement and provided its adherents with spiritual meaning and an
       otherworldly view of reality that is not found in contemporary
       Western culture.

1800. Kandel, Randy F., and Gretel H. Pelto. "The Health Food Movement:
       Social Revitalization or Alternative Health Maintenance System?"
       NUTRITIONAL ANTHROPOLOGY: CONTEMPORARY APPROACHES TO DIET AND
       CULTURE. Edited by Norge W. Jerome, Randy F. Kandel, and Gretel
       H. Pelto. Pleasantville, NY: Redgrave Publishing Company, 1980,
       pp. 327-63.

       Discusses the current interest in health foods and vegetarian
       diets and attempts to understand the biobehavioral change linked
       with diet and nutrition. The author states that use of health
       foods is "a significant social phenomenon." Basing their reflec-
       tions on research carried out in the greater Boston area in the
       early 1970's, the authors apply the major features of social move-
       ments to the Health Food Movement and explore the spiritual and
       mystical themes connected with special diets and foods. Two formal
       types of Health Food Movement, namely revitalization cults and
       other communication-distribution centers, and various kinds of
       participants, such as independent dieters, peripheral social mem-
       bers, and full participants, are described. The channels of commu-
       nication within the movements are outlined and several case studies
       are provided. The Health Food Movement functions both as a revita-
       lization movement and as an alternative health maintenance system.

1801. Kenney, J. Frank. "ISKCON Ethics as a Significant Factor in Con-
       version to Krishna Consciousness." PROCEEDINGS OF THE SOUTHWEST
       CONFERENCE FOR ASIAN STUDIES. Edited by Edward J. Lazzerini.
       New Orleans: University of New Orleans Press, 1980, pp. 161-63.

       Adduces data from a study of converts to the Hare Krishna Move-
       ment to support Heirich's contention (item 366) that "the content
       of the new vision is a significant factor in religious conversion
       in terms of validating previous experiences" (p. 161). The three
       devotees examined by the author were already living an ascetic
       lifestyle prior to their conversion. Though careful not to make
       generalizations from just a handful of case studies, the author
       thinks that the data point to the relevance of ideological content
       in conversion experiences.

1802. Khalsa, Kirpal Singh. "New Religious Movements Turn to Worldly
       Success." JOURNAL FOR THE SCIENTIFIC STUDY OF RELIGION 25
       (1986): 233-45.

       Studies three religious movements, namely the Healthy, Happy, and
       Holy Organization (3HO), the Divine Life Mission, and Vajradhatu,
       and discovers that the last two mentioned have developed an ideol-
       ogy which looks on success in moneymaking ventures as religiously
       significant. Material prosperity is considered by members of these
       movements to be a reflection of a positive, healthy state of mind
       which is cultivated by the practice of meditation. The author
       thinks that the socioeconomic background of the membership of both
       groups (who tend to recruit people who are well-educated and cul-
       turally sophisticated) has contributed to this development. The
       resource mobilization theory is used to explain why both the Divine
       Life Mission and Vajradhatu turned their attention to material
       wealth while the 3HO Foundation with the same kind of membership

has rejected worldly success and achievement. The turn to material
satisfaction might indicate a return to the values of Western culture, namely utilitarian individualism, capitalistic enterprise,
and financial advancement.

1803. Kilbourne, Brock K. "Equity or Exploitation: The Case of the Uni-
        fication Church." REVIEW OF RELIGIOUS RESEARCH 28 (1986): 143-50.

        Investigates the allegedly exploitative practices of many of the
        new religious movements, particularly the Unification Church. The
        author attempts to find out whether members of this group felt ex-
        ploited by comparing them with members of two established tradi-
        tions, namely the Catholic and Presbyterian Churches. Two basic
        questions were asked in a survey of the members of the three groups:
        1) whether and to what degree was there fair exchange between them-
        selves and their respective churches?; and 2) what kind of career
        goals did they have? The results did not support the exploitation
        hypothesis. Several new religions, however, may provide different
        ways in which career goals can be incorporated with their commit-
        ment. The stress placed by some of the new religions on faith and
        on a philosophy of self-growth might facilitate positive interde-
        pendence in the work place.

1804. Kilbourne, Brock K., and James T. Richardson. "The Communalization
        of Religious Experience in Contemporary Religious Groups." JOUR-
        NAL OF COMMUNITY PSYCHOLOGY 14 (1986): 206-12.

        Compares members of the Unification Church with those from Cath-
        olic and Presbyterian Churches with regard to the religious impor-
        tance each group attaches to communal experiences. The members of
        the Unification Church valued such experiences more than the mem-
        bers of the mainline churches. For the Moonies, there is a close
        connection between their religious faith and their experience of
        community.

1805. Kirkpatrick, R. George, Rich Rainey, and Kathryn Rubi. "An Empiri-
        cal Study of Wiccan Religion in Postindustrial Society." FREE
        INQUIRY IN CREATIVE SOCIOLOGY 14.1 (1986): 33-38.

        Examines the demographic elements of contemporary Witchcraft and
        its social and philosophical attitudes and ideologies. The authors
        find that those who become involved in Witchcraft register high on
        the scale of normlessness and powerlessness and rather low with re-
        gard to traditional family values and conservative issues. "Pagan
        Witches are under-rewarded status discontents who care little for
        money and much for knowledge and balance of nature" (p. 37).

1806. Knott, Kim. MY SWEET LORD: THE HARE KRISHNA MOVEMENT. Welling-
        borough, England: Aquarian Press, 1986. 112 pp.

        Presents an account of the Hare Krishna Movement from the view-
        point of those involved in it. Besides giving a brief history
        of the movement and an outline of its beliefs and practices, the
        author describes the devotee's worldview. One chapter analyzes
        the social background of those who join the movement and the type

of commitment demanded of the members. Social reactions to the movement, particularly in Great Britain, are explored. The author maintains that the Hare Krishna Movement is not a new religious group nor just another contemporary cult. Further, it has changed substantially since it was founded in the late 1960's. It is rather a traditional, dynamic, and adaptable religion offering those who join it a complete religious life.

1807. Kohn, Rachael L. E. "Ethnic Judaism and the Messianic Movement." JEWISH JOURNAL OF SOCIOLOGY 29 (1987): 85-96.

Discusses the emergence of Messianic Judaism that was formally established in 1975 when the Hebrew Christian Alliance of America adopted a new name, the Messianic Jewish Alliance of America. The developments that led to this change are outlined. Those who join this movement are characterized by a high degree of quest after the spiritual life they found wanting in their experience of Judaism. Secularization tendencies within Judaism are held to be partly responsible for the movement's attractiveness.

1808. Kopelman, Loretta, and John Moskop. "The Holistic Health Movement: A Survey and Critique." JOURNAL OF MEDICINE AND PHILOSOPHY 6 (1981): 209-35.

Discusses the nature and significance of the Holistic Health Movement in the West. The common themes that underlie this popular movement are first outlined. The authors, using such examples as reflexology and iridiology, suggest that the Holistic Health Movement differs from orthodox medicine in that the former does not rely on the scientific method. They contrast Holistic Health Medicine to holism in biology and social science and criticize its main tenets, some of which carry implicit moral and religious assumptions.

1809. Kranenburg, Reender. "Benjamin Creme and Maitreya the Christ." UPDATE: A QUARTERLY JOURNAL OF NEW RELIGIOUS MOVEMENTS 9.1 (1985): 50-55.

Describes briefly the activities of a Scottish painter, Benjamin Creme, who from 1980-1982 preached the message that the coming of Maitreya the Christ was imminent. Though his prophecy did not materialize, the small movement he started is still active, at least in the Netherlands. The author places Creme's views within the Theosophical tradition, his main teachings being similar to those of Alice Bailey. Creme's main appeal has been to those interested in the occult esoteric tradition.

1810. Kreuziger, Frederick A. THE RELIGION OF SCIENCE FICTION. Bowling Green, OH: Bowling Green University Popular Press, 1986. 160 pp.

Claims that science fiction functions as a religion and that it is dominated by apocalyptic thought. The author first draws some parallels between biblical and secular apocalyptic thought, stressing its imagery and symbolism and its function of providing hope in a crisis situation. A model to take into account the wide range of

apocalyptic beliefs in science fiction is developed. The author
thinks that science fiction may be viewed as the secular apocalyptic of modern times that has come into being as a response to contemporary rapid social change.

1811. Kronenfield, Jennie J., and Cody Wasner. "The Use of Unorthodox
      Therapies and Marginal Practitioners." SOCIAL SCIENCE AND MEDI-
      CINE 16 (1982): 1119-25.

Studies the extent of the use of unorthodox therapies by patients
suffering from rheumatic disorders and concludes that some elements
of folk medicine are still popular in most segments of the American
population. The authors suggest further research to assess the
situation more thoroughly.

1812. Kvideland, Karin. "Symbols and Their Functions in the Children of
      God." TEMENOS 15 (1979): 41-49.

Examines the various kinds of symbols used by the Children of God
(Family of Love) and concludes that their functions are not religious. Since the Children of God have chosen certain words, ges-
tures, and actions and assigned to them unique meanings that are
not found in traditional Christianity, the author suggests that the
function of the symbols is to maintain the group's identity and to
foster communication between members.

1813. Kvideland, Karin. "Children of God in Bergen." NEW RELIGIONS
      (item 565), pp. 154-74.

Traces the origin and development of the Children of God (Family
of Love) in Bergen, Norway in the early 1970's when they had little
success. The author describes the daily activities of the small
community and explains their growth by applying the deprivation
theory. The Children of God appeal to young people who are un-
happy with, and frustrated by, the lives they lead. The ways they
use the letters of their founder (usually referred to as "Mo's
Letters") and the Bible are examined and it is concluded that their
scriptures help establish an indisputable authority both within and
outside the movement.

1814. Lane, Ralph. "The Catholic Charismatic Movement in the United
      States: A Reconsideration." SOCIAL COMPASS 25.1 (1978): 23-35.

Accounts for the origin and nature of the Catholic Charismatic
Movement in its American background, Post Vatican II Catholicism.
Though most sociologists think that this movement will eventually
become routinized, the author sees certain indications that might
require a reevaluation of the direction the routinization might
take. Two types of influential adherents to the movement are distinguished: 1) laymen, who have leadership roles from the start and
who stress the need of a more identifiable community with its own
rules; and 2) mainly clerical members who saw the movement as a
prayer group within the structure and theology of the Catholic
Church. The author observes that a structural shift seems to be
occurring in the movement. Pressures within it exist for a more

accommodative position as opposed to the intense, exclusive, or closed character of several communities. An emphasis on the group at a new organizational level is also observable.

1815. Lane, Ralph. "Catholic Charismatic Renewal." THE NEW RELIGIOUS CONSCIOUSNESS (item 614), pp. 162-79.

Describes the beginnings and activities of the Catholic Charismatic Movement, stressing its prayer meetings, other related activities, and organization. The social context in which the movement emerged is then explored. The Christian Family Movement, the Young Christian Students, Young Christian Workers, and the Cursillo are seen as the forerunners of the Catholic Charismatic Movement. In the United States, the Catholic Charismatics have many parallels with neo-Pentecostal groups, both of which are indistinguishable from traditional Pentecostal revivals that led to the formation of new sects. Some reflections on the future direction the movement might take are offered.

1816. Lang, Anthony. SYNANON FOUNDATION: THE PEOPLE BUSINESS. Cotton-wood, AZ: Wayside Press, 1978. 269 pp.

Introduces the reader to the "most successful institution for the rehabilitation of narcotics addicts and a futuristic society whose members live fulfillingly and exuberantly without dope, crime, or violence" (p. 1). After a short outline of Synanon philosophy, the author describes the reeducation center in its early stages and its development into the full-fledged movement called the Synanon Foundation. The last phase of the movement, which saw the establishment of a corporation with the founder Charles Dederich as president, is depicted as a social movement. Synanon has became an experimental community concerned with societal problems rather than those of the individual. People involved in the movement now pursue its goals with quasi-religious intensity.

1817. Lasaga, Jose I. "Death In Jonestown: Techniques of Political Control by a Paranoid Leader." SUICIDE AND LIFE-THREATENING BEHAVIOR 10 (1980): 210-13.

Understands the Jonestown tragedy as "a collective delusional process." Several basic techniques of political control used by Jim Jones are briefly described: 1) management of property and income; 2) weakening of family ties; 3) the establishment of a sociopolitical caste system; 4) control of exit from Jonestown; 5) restriction of verbal expression; 6) cognitive control; 7) and emotional control. The People's Temple, in the author's view, was conceived as a cult but eventually developed into a "messianic sociopolitical movement."

1818. Latkin, Carl A., Richard Hagan, Richard A. Littman, and Norman D. Sundberg. "Who Lives in Utopia?: A Brief Report on the Rajneeshpuram Research Project." SOCIOLOGICAL ANALYSIS 48 (1987): 73-81.

Summarizes the results of a research project aimed at investigating Rajneeshpuram, the Oregon community founded by the followers of the Indian guru Bhagwan Shree Rajneesh. Demographic data (age,

sex, family structure, religious orientation, education, and place
of residence) relating to the composition of the members are recorded. Those who live in the communal setting have a healthy
self-perception, since they report low levels of depression, high
social support, and general satisfaction with their lifestyle.
Some similarities and differences between residents at Rajneeshpuram and members of other new religious movements are noted.

1819. Lebra, Takie Sugiyama. "Reciprocity-Based Moral Sanctions and
       Messianic Salvation." AMERICAN ANTHROPOLOGIST 74 (1972): 391-
       407.

       Suggests a way of understanding salvation as experienced through
       conversion to a messianic sect, namely Tensho-kotai-jingu-kya (the
       Dancing Religion), a relatively new Japanese religion imported to
       Hawaii in the early 1950's. It is argued that reciprocity generates
       moral sanctions that become open to charismatic influence, which
       brings with it several types of manipulation and social interven-
       tion. The author maintains that in this religious sect, which was
       founded by Mrs. Sayo Kitamura, guilt and indignation, aroused after
       conversion, made converts susceptible to manipulation, thus making
       all kinds of charismatic persuasions, from psychiatric inducement
       to ideological brainwashing, effective.

1820. Lebra, Takie Sugiyama. "Religious Conversion as a Breakthrough for
       Transculturation: A Japanese Sect in Hawaii." JOURNAL FOR THE
       SCIENTIFIC STUDY OF RELIGION 9 (1970): 181-94.

       Discusses the conversion of a group of Japanese Americans in
       Hawaii to a deviant sect introduced from Japan, namely Tensho-
       kotai-jingu-kya (the Dancing Religion). The author's main argument
       is that "faith triggers acquisition of freedom from secular con-
       straint and, at the same time or after a time lag, enables the
       individual to become better adjusted to the secular environment"
       (p. 183). The Americans who joined this new religion went through
       the process of deculturation and resocialization. Three charac-
       teristics of the converts, namely 1) responsiveness to social
       action, 2) striving for success, and 3) lack of spontaneity and
       flexibility, are changed and rechanneled to serve the goals of the
       sect.

1821. Levi, Ken. "Jonestown and Religious Commitment in the 1970s."
       VIOLENCE AND RELIGIOUS COMMITMENT (item 653), pp. 3-20.

       Maintains that there is a connection between religious violence
       and social cohesion. Several sectarian features that might lead to
       violence, such as total control, loyalty to the leader, and isola-
       tion, are examined and examples given from various new religious
       movements. The situation at Jonestown is described. Like all
       those who engage in religious violence, the members of the People's
       Temple relied heavily on their belief in an afterlife and on out-
       side hostility. Many people at Jonestown believed that they were
       performing an act of revolutionary suicide when they followed the
       orders of their leaders and drank poison. The author thinks that a
       paranoid milieu, like that at Jonestown, leads many sects to engage
       in acts of violence.

1822. Levin, Jeffrey S. "Commitment in a Successful Yoga Community."
       PROCEEDINGS OF THE THIRD ANNUAL CAROLINA UNDERGRADUATE SOCIOLOGY
       SYMPOSIUM. Edited by Martha Carter. Florence, SC: Francis
       Marion College, 1980, pp. 175-84.

       Examines the Himalayan International Institute for Yoga Science
       and Philosophy (with its headquarters in Homesdale, Pennsylvania),
       using Kanter's model of mechanisms of commitment (item 383). The
       community's dual existence as 1) an institute to promote unity
       between Eastern and Western mysticism and 2) an Eastern-oriented
       religious commune is examined. The Institute is said to be a suc-
       cessful community, scoring high on sacrifice, mortification, and
       transcendence.

1823. Levin, Jeffrey S., and Jeannine Coreil. "'New Age' Healing in the
       U.S." SOCIAL SCIENCE AND MEDICINE 23 (1986): 889-97.

       Examines one form of alternative healing known as "New Age Heal-
       ing." The authors first dwell on the meaning of the New Age and
       link it to the emergence of several medical, spiritual, and socio-
       cultural developments. They attempt to distinguish New Age healing
       from other nonallopathic modes of curing. Three types of New Age
       healing methods are mentioned: 1) one stresses the means of attain-
       ing somatic or psychosomatic health or well-being and is largely
       concerned with bodily health; 2) another emphasizes the need to
       study esoteric techniques as a way to health and concentrates on
       mental well-being; 3) the last type is based on Eastern imports and
       is directed towards healing the human soul. There are 85 refer-
       ences to works about, or related to, New Age Healing (pp. 896-97).

1824. Lewis, Jeanette. "Death Concerns and Other Belief Systems Vari-
       ables Among the Hare Krishna." PROCEEDINGS OF THE SOUTHWEST
       CONFERENCE FOR ASIAN STUDIES. Edited by Edward J. Lazzerini.
       New Orleans: University of New Orleans Press, 1980, pp. 151-54.

       Surveys the attitudes towards death of Hare Krishna members in
       two locations, namely a New Orleans temple and a Mississippi farm
       commune. The author found that the devotees registered generally
       low or moderate on concerns with death. Those who were highly
       involved in Krishna Consciousness and who conceived of themselves
       as being close to Krishna had low or moderate death anxiety.

1825. Lewis, William F. "The Rastafari: Millennial Cultists or Unregen-
       erate Peasants." PEASANT STUDIES 14.1 (1986): 1-26.

       Provides a brief description of the Rastafari Movement and re-
       evaluates the millennial paradigm that social science has adopted
       to understand its ideology and activities. The essay's main thrust
       is to show the link between Jamaican peasantry and the emergence of
       the movement. The author holds that that the Rastafari Movement
       deviates from the modern state and persists in its original peasant
       identity.

1826. Lieberman, Paul. THE FIG BLOSSOMS: MESSIANIC JUDAISM EMERGES.
       Indianola, IA: Fountain Press, 1977. 122 pp.

Presents a short account of modern Messianic Judaism that began in 1967 and began to flourish in 1975. One chapter is dedicated to a sketch of the history of early Messianic Judaism. Some of the basic themes of the contemporary revival are described without much theological sophistication.

1827. Lindt, Gillian. "Journeys to Jonestown: Accounts and Interpretations of the Rise and Demise of the People's Temple." UNION THEOLOGICAL SEMINARY QUARTERLY 37 (1981-1982): 159-76.

Examines the literature on the People's Temple and divides it into three major categories: 1) media coverage and books that draw heavily on press reports; 2) published autobiographies and confessions of apostates; and 3) works analyzing and interpreting the movement. Those writings that attempt to make some sense out of the Jonestown tragedy are further subdivided into 1) government reports, 2) political themes, 3) psychological interpretations; and 4) sociological analysis. The author observes that an investigation of the movement's religious character has not been comprehensively treated. This essay contains a useful bibliography covering materials until around 1980.

1828. Lipson, Julienne G. "Jews for Jesus: An Illustration of Syncretism." ANTHROPOLOGICAL QUARTERLY 53 (1980): 101-110.

Argues that the Jews for Jesus, a Hebrew-Christian missionary organization, provides an excellent example of classical syncretism, that is, "the process of reinterpreting and recombining cultural elements that occurs whether change is introduced from inside or outside a cultural system" (p. 101). The Jews for Jesus grew out of both the Jesus Movement and the Hebrew-Christian Missionary Movement. As an organization, the Jews for Jesus is a hybrid entity with multiple functions. A brief outline of the movement's ideology and rituals is given. The author thinks that the Jews for Jesus Movement is also syncretistic in the newer sense, that is, in that it is similar to other youth-culture movements that integrate elements from diverse value systems and unite opposing social roles.

1829. Locke, Ralph G. "Who Am I in the City of Mammon?: The Self, Doubt, and Uncertainty in a Spiritualist Cult." PRACTICE AND BELIEF: STUDIES IN THE SOCIOLOGY OF AUSTRALIAN RELIGION. Edited by Alan W. Black and Peter E. Glasner. Boston: Allyn and Unwin, 1983, pp. 108-33.

Explores "some of the dimensions of indeterminacy in mediumship," focusing on an urban Spiritualist cult, namely The Sanctuary, founded by Mrs. Trudy Lucas who, in 1954, migrated from England to Freemantle, Australia. After a brief historical overview of Spiritualism and of some of the main social studies of the phenomenon, the author describes the Sanctuary's origin, development, and organization and analyzes the conflicts within it. The author maintains that "liminality" is a relevant concept for understanding Spiritualism.

1830. Lofland, John. "Social Movement Culture and the Unification Church." THE FUTURE OF NEW RELIGIOUS MOVEMENTS (item 579), pp. 91-108.

Explores social movement organizations comparatively, focusing on
their effects on culture. These movements can generate rich or
poor cultures that vary along three lines, namely in their elaboration, expressiveness, and compassion (i.e., civility and humane-
ness towards outsiders). Using the Unification Church as a key
example, the author traces these variations. He concludes, among
other things, that 1) some religious movements are actually richer
than others; 2) religious movement organizations may promote more
robust cultures than political ones; 3) those movements that offer
members satisfaction and other adaptive resources are likely to be
the successful ones; and 4) cultural richness fosters continuity,
mobilization, and secularization. The cultural patterns of the
Unification Church have been "relatively elaborate, quite richly
expressive, and only moderately compassionate" (p. 106). Greater
secularization within the ranks of this church might hinder its
success.

1831. Lofland, John. "White-Hot Mobilization: Strategies of a Millenar-
        ian Movement." DYNAMICS OF SOCIAL MOVEMENTS (item 522), pp. 157-
        66.

Describes and contrasts two periods of a millenarian sect, i.e.,
an initial dormant state followed by one of extensive mobilization.
The sect, named by the author "Divine Precepts" and now generally
accepted to be the Unification Church, is said to be in a state of
"white-hot mobilization" because of its extensive program of evangelization, its deployment of full-time, totally dedicated members
to promote its ideology and lifestyle, its investment of a significant proportion of its resources to achieve its goals, and its
expenditure of large sums of money. Several generalizations on
this intense mobilization are made: 1) it is rather rare and
results from a combination of different factors; 2) it is "self-
terminating," in that its members grow weary and the host society
reacts negatively; 3) it stresses the recruitment and training of a
model elite group of people; and 4) it depends on the context for
its success.

1832. Lofland, John. DOOMSDAY CULT: A STUDY OF CONVERSION, PROSELYTIZA-
        TION, AND MAINTENANCE OF FAITH. New York: Irvington Publishers,
        enlarged edition, 1977. xii, 362 pp.

Analyzes the first five years in America (1959-1964) of a new
religious movement that the author calls "Divine Precepts" (that
is, the Unification Church). The author examines conversion to the
movement, the recruitment and socialization processes employed, and
the way faith and hope are maintained. Five historical periods are
distinguished: 1) slow growth and obscurity (1957-1971); 2) aggressive growth and social acceptance (1971-1974); 3) faltering and
social attack (1975-1976); 4) retreat and prosecution (c. 1977-
1979); and 5) enclaves and quasi-obscurity. In each period the
author outlines the membership, beliefs, organization, evangelization methods, morals, foreign connections, and relationship of the
movement with American culture.

1833. Lofland, John. "Becoming a 'World-Saver' Revisited." AMERICAN
        BEHAVIORAL SCIENTIST 20 (1977): 805-18.

Updates the author's research on the conversion efforts of a
millenarian movement that the author labels "Divine Precepts" (the
title used to refer to the Unification Church in its early stages).
The process of recruiting new members is described in five "quasi-
temporary phases," namely: 1) picking-up; 2) hooking; 3) encapsulating; 4) loving; and 5) committing. The encapsulating stage is
further analyzed in another five stages or elements: 1) absorption
of attention; 2) collective focus; 3) exclusive input; 4) fatigue;
and 5) logical, comprehensive cognitions. The earlier model (item
215) is applicable to the newer efforts by the church to recruit
members. Yet it is rather passive and antiinteractionist. The
author favors a more active, interactionist model to study conversions to the new religious movements.

1834. Long, Martha. "Is Satan Alive and Well in Northeast Arkansas?"
      MID-AMERICAN FOLKLORE 13.2 (1985): 18-26.

      Investigates a legend which was circulating in Northeast Arkansas
      during the Halloween season of 1984, namely that young children
      were being abducted by a group of devil worshipers. Several stories
      told about these worshipers are reproduced. The author summarizes
      the persisting interest in Satan in contemporary society. She
      thinks that devil worshipers can be used as scapegoats for societal
      problems and criminal acts.

1835. Luhrmann, T. M. "Witchcraft, Morality, and Magic in Contemporary
      London." INTERNATIONAL JOURNAL OF MORAL AND SOCIAL STUDIES 1.1
      (1986): 77-94.

      Discusses contemporary ritual magic in Great Britain and distin-
      guishes between four types of magical practices, namely: 1) Western
      mysteries ritual magic; 2) ad hoc ritual magic; 3) witchcraft; and
      4) paganism. Most people who practice magic come from educated,
      middle-class backgrounds and are concentrated in London. Most of
      those involved in these activities insist that they are practicing
      white magic and that their intentions are morally upright. "The
      ethical intention lessens the dissonance between the practice of
      magic and the practitioners' intellectual and social environment"
      (p. 86).

1836. Luhrmann, T. M. "Persuasive Ritual: The Role of the Imagination in
      Occult Witchcraft." ARCHIVES SOCIALES DES SCIENCES RELIGIONS 60
      (1985): 151-70.

      Studies the contemporary occult sciences in England and examines
      manuals that are used to train people in the magical arts. The
      author describes the magical subculture which is a small part of
      the New Age Movement and explores the occult by being initiated
      into several groups that practice witchcraft. Ritual actions per-
      formed in witchcraft rites are distinguished into words, gestures,
      and imagination. Some major anthropological studies on witchcraft
      are reviewed and it is concluded that the contexts in which the
      magic rites are performed both give meaning and provide force to
      the ritual utterance. Several examples from a standard manual
      of witchcraft are adduced to illustrate the place of controlled

imagination in creative persuasive rituals that are found not only
in Western magical rites, but also in some traditional religious
practices (like the Spiritual exercises of St. Ignatius Loyola).

1837. Lynch, Frederick R. "'Occult Establishment' or 'Deviant Religion'?: The Rise and Fall of a Modern Church of Magic." JOURNAL
FOR THE SCIENTIFIC STUDY OF RELIGION 18 (1979): 281-89.

Reports on research on an occult organization, pseudonymously
called the Church of the Sun, which practiced magic in the "Egyp-
tian Kabbalistic tradition" (a fusion of the pagan religion of
ancient Egypt and Jewish mystical and esoteric beliefs). The evolution of the church is traced from its early phase of pan-Chris-
tian mysticism (and latent occultism) to a middle period, namely
occultism, and finally to paganism and magic. The social and
psychological characteristics of its members and ex-members are
described, focusing on their social and religious predispositions,
the tensions and turning points at the time of their initial contact with the church, and the reasons for their continued involvement. It is concluded that those who joined represented the middle
class and occult establishment whose members are seeking a deeper,
more mystical, and more complex understanding of their lives.

1838. MacDonald, Jerry Paul. "'Reject the Wicked Man:' Coercive Persuasion and Deviance Production. A Study of Conflict Management."
CULTIC STUDIES JOURNAL 5 (1988): 59-121.

Describes how a fringe Christian sect, which the author calls
"Oasis," "manages the conflict associated with grievances and nonconformity" (p. 59). The author provides a brief history of the
group between 1970 and 1987, gives a view of its utopian goals, and
shows how some sect members achieve elite status within the sect.
The process whereby a member comes to be considered deviant by the
group and the manner in which such departure from the norm is
handled are analyzed in detail. By emphasizing the concepts of
"coercive persuasion" and "deviance production," the author shows
how this sect "reinforces commitment to the group by manufacturing
loyalty 'crises' designed to stigmatize and ultimately expel non-
conformists while reinforcing conformity within the membership,
which is the primary purpose of the manufactured crises" (p. 59).

1839. Maesen, William A. "Watchtower Influences on Black Muslim Eschatology: An Exploratory Study." JOURNAL FOR THE SCIENTIFIC STUDY
OF RELIGION 9 (1970): 321-25.

Suggests that in the early 1930's the Black Muslims were influenced by the eschatological teachings of the Watchtower Bible and
Tract Society. Several doctrinal similarities are listed: 1) the
belief that the end of time has been deferred; 2) the conviction
that the millennium is now beginning; 3) the idea that the Battle
of Armageddon is soon to come and that 144,000 people will survive;
4) the hope of a new world on earth; and 5) the rejection of the
immortality of the soul. Some reasons for this early influence are
advanced.

1840. Martin, David. "The Political Economy of the Holy Ghost." STRANGE
       GIFTS: A GUIDE TO CHARISMATIC RENEWAL. Edited by David Martin
       and Peter Mullen. Oxford: Blackwell, 1984, pp. 54-71.

       Examines how charismatic beliefs in the action of the Holy
       Spirit are related to the exercise of social power and describes
       the ways charismatics think the Holy Spirit operates in today's
       world. Mainline churches and sects understand designated function-
       aries and corporate authorities differently. Sects invoke the
       spirit to modify or reject tradition and to place new revelation in
       scriptural context. Pure spontaneity, like speaking in tongues, is
       conceived as an intrusion of the Spirit. Contrary to the practice
       in mainline churches, sects maintain that authority is more arbi-
       trary and that it is invested in charismatic individuals rather
       than in hierarchies. Sectarian phenomena, in the author's view,
       are clearly related to the exercise of power in the church.

1841. Martin, Ilse. "Inequality, Chastity, and Sign Endogamy." SEX
       ROLES IN CONTEMPORARY AMERICAN COMMUNES (item 705), pp. 82-110.

       Examines the rules that structure the relationship between men
       and women in a commune founded in 1970 by a disciple of Paramahansa
       Yogananda of the Self-Realization Fellowship and called, pseudony-
       mously, the "New Age Brotherhood." A brief description of the
       commune that consists of about 200 members divided into four sepa-
       rate communities is given. The following three concepts as they
       are perceived and put into practice by the members are analyzed:
       1) inequality, where male dominance and female submission is the
       norm; 2) chastity, which limits sexual relationships between cou-
       ples until God calls them to conceive; and 3) sign endogamy, which
       implies that ideal couples should be soul mates, that is, born
       under the same astrological sign. The author points out that the
       charismatic leader of the Brotherhood believes that the system of
       inequality is "an attempt to re-establish a balance of masculine
       and feminine forces in the universe" (p. 109).

1842. Marty, Martin E. "The Occult Establishment." SOCIAL RESEARCH 37
       (1970): 212-30.

       Examines the new wave of interest in the occult or metaphysical
       beliefs and practices in the U.S.A. The author traces the origin
       of such concerns to the Spiritualist Churches of the middle of the
       nineteenth century. Astrology, telepathy, clairvoyance, dream
       interpretation, and UFO sightings are among the topics included in
       the occult establishment, which attempts to adduce scientific evi-
       dence in support of the existence of these phenomena. One common
       element in conventional religion, namely the stress on community,
       is missing in the occult, which concentrates on the individual life
       and "other-worldly" concerns. The occult, according to the author,
       satisfies the religious needs of many people.

1843. McBride, James. "The Far East, The Far West, and the Second Coming:
       The Unification Church in America." RELIGION AND SOCIETY IN THE
       AMERICAN WEST: HISTORICAL ESSAYS. Edited by Carl Guarneri and
       David Alvarez. Lanham, MD: University Press of America, 1987,
       pp. 449-76.

Presents an overview of the Unification Church, focusing on its beliefs and ultimate purpose, its attractive powers, its perceived mission in America, and its future prospects. The author, who considers this church as part of America's Fourth Awakening, thinks that its recent consolidation and its efforts to gain legitimacy will shift the public focus away from the issues of brainwashing and deprogramming to its economic and political activities.

1844. McClure, Kevin. "UFO Cults." UFOS: 1947-1987 (item 19), pp. 346-51.

Examines several UFO cults including the one led by Mrs. Keech (see item 91) and the following organized groups: 1) the One World Family (located in California under Allen-Michael Noonan); 2) the Institute for Cosmic Research, founded by "Gordon" in the State of Michigan; 3) Light Affiliates, led by Robin McPherson in British Columbia; 4) the Human Individual Metamorphosis, under Bo and Peep (M. H. Appleworth and Bonnie Nettles) that was based in California (see items 1594-98); and 5) the Aetherius Society that was founded and is still directed, from its headquarters in Los Angeles, by George King. The author thinks that these religious cults "warrant our interest, and maybe our sympathy." They do not deserve, however, "a great deal of our time."

1845. McFerran, Douglass. "Witchcraft: The Truth About the Old Religion." LISTENING: JOURNAL OF RELIGION AND CULTURE 9.3 (1974): 105-111.

Attempts to show that contemporary witches are merely trying to revive an ancient religion and should not be confused with Satanists. The author reflects on the recent interest in Witchcraft and observes that the number of covens is quite limited. He distinguishes between occultism as an urban phenomenon that functions as an antidote to bureaucracy, and Witchcraft that is more comparable to shamanism.

1846. McGaw, Douglas B. "Meaning and Belonging in a Charismatic Congregation: An Investigation into Sources of Neo-Pentecostal Success." REVIEW OF RELIGIOUS RESEARCH 21 (1980): 284-301.

Analyzes the group behavior and beliefs of a (Presbyterian) neo-Pentecostal congregation in Hartford, Connecticut, in order to determine its appeal and the commitment of its members. Neo-Pentecostalism differs from its traditional (classical) counterpart in that the former's membership is largely made up from the upper-middle class. It further maintains communication with the mainline denominations and cuts across Protestant-Catholic denominational lines. Several measures of meaning (belief) and belonging (group behavior and practices) are outlined and the structure, ideology, and community life of this congregation described. The author thinks that the members' commitment to the group is enhanced by the fact that the congregation provides meaning and belonging, the former giving the rationale and justification for the Charismatic Movement's existence, the latter supplying an effective mechanism for building community. The degree of meaning and belonging is compared with those found in mainline Protestantism.

1847. McGaw, Douglas B. "Commitment and Religious Community: A Compari-
       son of a Charismatic and a Mainline Congregation." JOURNAL FOR
       THE SCIENTIFIC STUDY OF RELIGION 18 (1979): 146-63.

       Compares a Presbyterian Charismatic community with a mainline
       congregation of the same denomination in order to analyze the reli-
       gious commitment of the respective members. The author argues that
       community and meaning are co-equal elements of commitment and that
       the latter is the central concept in understanding church growth
       and vitality. The idea of commitment is explained and the methods
       used in the research project are outlined. Meaning and belonging
       are found to be stronger in the Charismatic congregation. This
       article is basically a different and slightly shorter version of a
       more recent publication by the author.

1848. McGaw, Douglas B., with Elliot Wright. A TALE OF TWO CONGREGATIONS:
       COMMITMENT AND SOCIAL STRUCTURE IN A CHARISMATIC AND MAINLINE
       CHURCH. Hartford, CT: Hartford Seminary Foundation, 1980. viii,
       110 pp.

       Describes and analyzes the role of congregational social struc-
       tures and organizations in determining strong or weak commitment
       ties among church members. Two New England congregations, a United
       Presbyterian church and a Charismatic community within the same
       Protestant denomination were chosen for comparison. After giving
       the historical background and the relevant demographic features,
       the following social mechanisms that lead to commitment are exam-
       ined: 1) closure (recruitment and socialization of new members);
       2) strictness (ongoing socialization, work arrangements, beliefs,
       and practices); 3) authority; and 4) social cohesion (including the
       lifestyle of members, group contacts, and interpersonal relation-
       ships). It is concluded that the social mechanisms were much
       stronger and more rigidly enforced in the Charismatic community.

1849. McGee, Michael. "Meher Baba--The Sociology of Religious Conver-
       sion." GRADUATE JOURNAL 9.1-2 (1974): 43-71.

       Examines the origins and dynamics of the Meher Baba Movement
       based on the author's research in Chapel Hill, North Carolina from
       1967-1974. The counterculture drug-oriented movement is seen as
       the background to the emergence of this movement. The philosophy
       of the founder is discussed and a picture of a typical follower is
       sketched. The author observes that it would be unwise to attempt
       to understand Baba Lovers solely in terms of the drug culture. The
       conversions of ten of these followers are then examined in some
       detail and the place Baba has in their lives is stressed. John
       Lofland's conversion model (see, for example, item 215) is used to
       analyze these conversions. Converts to this new religious movement
       are described as mostly "unbalanced" people who had become alien-
       ated from society and who are now reaccepting its norms while
       rejecting its philosophy. Their conversion has enabled them to
       accept an integrated system of values and actions.

1850. McGuire, Meredith B. PENTECOSTAL CATHOLICS: POWER, CHARISMA, AND
       ORDER IN A RELIGIOUS MOVEMENT. Philadelphia: Temple University
       Press, 1982. ix, 270 pp.

Presents a monograph on the Catholic Charismatic Renewal with the intention of finding out how new religious movements are related to the secularization of society, of understanding the place of religion in contemporary culture, and of illuminating "the relationship of the individual to the larger society and sources of meaning and identity" (p. 4). After outlining her methodological procedures, the author describes the movement's central beliefs and practices and analyzes the process of conversion, commitment, and socialization in a Catholic Charismatic prayer group. A detailed examination is made of the rituals and the use of language. Two chapters are dedicated to the beliefs about illness, health, and healing. The cultic and sectarian aspects of the movement are analyzed with reference to the "covenant communities." The author also attempts to determine what this movement reveals about the significance of religion in contemporary society.

1851. McGuire, Meredith B. "Testimony as a Commitment Mechanism in Catholic Pentecostal Prayer Groups." JOURNAL FOR THE SCIENTIFIC STUDY OF RELIGION 16 (1977): 165-68.

Reports on Catholic Pentecostal prayer groups that were studied by participant observation and by the use of interviews with key members. It is observed that the conversion process was a gradual development rather than a sudden dramatic event. Testimony and tongue-speaking as commitment mechanisms are compared. The latter is judged to be an important symbol of commitment, but the former tends to be a major dramatic commitment instrument. Testimony, in which ordinary language is used, is, thus, more important than the anomalous speech of glossolalia.

1852. McGuire, Meredith B. "The Social Context of Religiosity: 'Word-Gifts' of the Spirit Among Catholic Pentecostals." REVIEW OF RELIGIOUS RESEARCH 18 (1977): 134-47.

Studies seven Catholic Pentecostal groups in northern New Jersey, using the methods of participant observation and unstructured interviews with key members. A brief description of the Catholic Pentecostal understanding of prophecy is given and the social context of prophecy is analyzed. The general structure of the prayer groups with the roles of those who speak and confirm prophecy and those who speak in, and interpret, tongues, are discussed. Speakers of prophecy validate their authority in the prayer group, while those who speak in tongues promote a sense of awe and mystery. The interpreters of glossolalia and the confirmers of prophecy offer an authoritative and supportive role, respectively. Prophecy is seen as performing many functions, including the reinforcement of the stratification and authority structures within the group. The author relates these Pentecostal themes to the liberalizing trends after Vatican Council II and to the rapid social change and unrest in our times.

1853. McGuire, Meredith B. "Toward a Sociological Interpretation of the 'Catholic Pentecostal' Movement." REVIEW OF RELIGIOUS RESEARCH 16 (1975): 94-104.

Investigates seven nonuniversity Catholic Pentecostal prayer groups in northern New Jersey and suggests a number of factors that account for their attractiveness to "middle-class, educated, active Catholics." These factors, which express a need for security, are identified as follows: 1) perceived crisis in church and society; 2) need for strong authority; 3) anomie; 4) dualism; 5) doubt about one's salvation; 6) inability to cope with change; and 7) escapism. The author points out that the movement has certain sociopsychological functions, especially the affirmation of two values, namely the meaningfulness of a small, personal community of believers and the relevance of Christianity in the modern world. Catholic Pentecostals are a cognitive minority that affirms mystery and miracles that Vatican Council II seems to have downplayed. Many of the characteristics of cognitive dissonance are manifested in Catholic Pentecostalism, the emergence of which is interpreted as one response to the problem of belief in modern society.

1854. McGuire, Meredith B. "An Interpretative Comparison of Elements of Pentecostal and Underground Church Movements in American Catholicism." SOCIOLOGICAL ANALYSIS 35 (1974): 57-65.

Explains how, in spite of their differences, these two movements attract middle-class Catholics and thus do not fit into the common sociological theory that such movements are based on socioeconomic deprivation. The features of Catholic Pentecostalism and of the Underground Church are briefly described. The author maintains that both were triggered by Vatican Council II and by general social unrest and have the "function of making possible religious belief and commitment in a society in which such belief and commitment are increasingly difficult and uncommon" (p. 62). The groups' responses to ambiguity and change appear to account for the differences between them.

1855. McGuire, Meredith B. "Toward a Sociological Interpretation of the 'Underground Church' Movement." REVIEW OF RELIGIOUS RESEARCH 14 (1972): 41-47.

Examines numerous Christian communities (mainly composed of dissenting Catholics) that are known by such names as "The Underground Church," the "Free Church," and the "Group Church." The author's aim is to determine whether the emergence of these groups is related to the contemporary problem of religious belief. She speculates that these new church communities, together with religious communes and the neo-Pentecostal movement, question the process of secularization, which does not take religious beliefs for granted. Two specific features of the Underground Church, namely the sense of a sacred cosmos (miracle) and the stress on liturgy (mystery), seem to go counter to the secularization trend. These dissenting religious movements fulfill important sociopsychological functions: they maintain "a dissonant definition of reality" and counteract the "privitization of religious meaning" (p. 46).

1856. McGuire, Meredith B., with Debra Kantor. RITUAL HEALING IN SUBURBAN AMERICA. New Brunswick, NJ: Rutgers University Press, 1988. xii, 324 pp.

Presents a sociological study of alternative healing systems in middle-class suburban America. The many groups included are divided into the following five types: 1) Christian; 2) Metaphysical; 3) Eastern Meditation and Human Potential; 4) psychic and occult; and 5) technique practitioners (used mainly for comparisons). The author outlines the belief systems of each of the first four groups. The following areas are described: 1) ideas about health and well-being; 2) notions of illness and healing; 3) causes of illness; 4) diagnostic approaches; 5) sources of healing power; 6) healing and health practices; and 7) therapeutic success, therapeutic failure, and death. The roles of alternative healers and the attitudes towards orthodox medicine are also accounted for. The author provides a description and interpretation of the use of metaphor, symbolic language, and specific alternative healings. She thinks that "these movements may be related to a new mode of individualism, a new form of connection between the individual and society" (p. 16). There are appendices on the methods used in this study (pp. 259-82) and on the interview schedules (pp. 283-91). The footnotes contain copious references to books and articles on the subject, but there is no separate bibliography.

1857. McIver, Shirley. "UFO (Flying Saucer) Groups: A Look at British Membership." ZETETIC SCHOLAR Nos. 12/13 (1987): 39-57.

Discusses whether UFO groups are largely a religious phenomenon and explores the differences between UFO research organizations and UFO contactee cults. The author first looks into the membership of UFO research groups in Great Britain, particularly the British UFO Research Association, and outlines the social background of their members, the experiences and opinions that are linked with belief in UFOs, and the religious beliefs of UFO groups. The members of research groups differ from the social dropouts associated with some of the UFO contactee groups. The author argues that involvement in a research organization should not be identified with involvement in a religious cult, in spite of the similarities in interests, beliefs, and experiences that members of both groups share.

1858. McKee, Janet. "Holistic Health and the Critique of Western Medicine." SOCIAL SCIENCE AND MEDICINE 26 (1988): 775-84.

Examines the prevailing sociological critique of both the holistic view of health, which is often said to be unscientific and mystical, and Western medicine, which is frequently accused of neglecting the social influences of disease and health. The author endeavors to show how Western medicine reflects the capitalistic system of the West and suggests that holistic health practices may not be acceptable to traditional doctors because they pose a challenge to the Western model of health. Fifty-two references are included (pp. 782-84).

1859. McLeod, John. "The Social Context of TM." JOURNAL OF HUMANISTIC PSYCHOLOGY 21.3 (1981): 17-33.

Examines the social context in which Transcendental Meditation is learned and the social process by which people actually become meditators. The author maintains that most people who join this

movement already know something about it even before they attend
the introductory lectures. The career of the meditator, the teaching of the meditation technique, the negotiating of the meaning of
enigmatic experiences, and the significance of the mantra are all
discussed with reference to the social contexts. The mantra, for
instance, is seen not only as a means of expanding one's consciousness, but as a powerful symbol of one's inner life and allegiance to
a social group, a leader, and a system of thought" (p. 27). Some
implications of the sociological analysis of Transcendental Meditation are outlined.

1860. Mead, Margaret. "The Occult: On the Edge of the Unknown." MAGIC,
       WITCHCRAFT, AND RELIGION (item 752), pp. 379-82.

       Explores various reasons why many young people are interested in
       occult knowledge and practices that belonged to long-dead civiliza-
       tions. Besides the fascination with past knowledge and extraordi-
       nary powers, the impersonality and detachment of modern science
       plays a crucial role in the occult revival which provides, among
       other things, a sense of participation in a larger spiritual whole.
       Both scientists and occultists, according to the author, can con-
       tribute to the expansion of our knowledge of human capabilities.

1861. Méheust, Bertrand. "UFO Abdunctionists as Religious Folklore."
       UFOS: 1947-1987 (item 19), pp. 352-58.

       Provides several examples of UFO abductions to illustrate the
       patterns that are part of the stories about people being abducted
       by alien beings. The author seeks to identify the underlying
       structure behind these accounts and finds similarities to other
       stories from folklore and ethnology. The theme of death and re-
       birth with its recurrent motifs and reinterpreted symbols is found
       in all these stories. Abductions are one form of religious expe-
       rience disguised in a technological imagery acceptable to contem-
       porary Western culture.

1862. Melton, J. Gordon. "The Contactees: A Survey." THE SPECTRUM OF
       UFO RESEARCH. Edited by Mimi Hynek. Chicago: J. Allen Hynek
       Center for UFO Studies, 1988, pp. 99-108.

       Examines the accounts of over 100 individuals who claim to have
       had a close encounter of the third kind with people from outer
       space. These contactees are divided into three periods: 1) from
       1750 till the early twentieth century; 2) during the 1950's; and
       3) from 1960 to the present. The author lists and compares the
       features of these narratives. He concludes that flying saucer
       stories fit into the pattern of occult religion and that, conse-
       quently, the contactees should be considered as participants in an
       occult religious movement.

1863. Melton, J. Gordon.   "The New Age Movement." ENCYCLOPEDIA HANDBOOK
       OF CULTS IN AMERICA (item 44), pp. 107-21.

       Gives an overview of the New Age Movement, tracing its origin and
       historical development. Its varied expressions since it began to
       be announced in the early 1970's are briefly sketched. The author

thinks that the New Age Movement "is among the most difficult of
the recently prominent religious groups to grasp, particularly
because it is a movement built more around a vision and an experience rather than doctrine or a belief system" (p. 112-13). After
assessing its current status, he gives a basic bibliography and a
list of some New Age groups and teachers.

1864. Melton, J. Gordon. "The Revival of Astrology in the United States."
      RELIGIOUS MOVEMENTS: GENESIS, EXODUS, AND NUMBERS (item 692), pp.
      279-99.

      Explores the rise of the occult in the United States since the
      eighteenth century, with special reference to astrology. The de-
      velopment of astrology in the nineteenth and early twentieth cen-
      turies is briefly traced. The author thinks that "the rise of
      astrology, and of the occult community in general, calls into ques-
      tion the idea of a new religious consciousness" (p. 293). Astrology
      is placed within the context of occult sciences and both are traced
      to Eastern religions. Astrology provides a scientific outlook on
      life and gives the individual a purposeful, optimistic, and spiri-
      tual worldview.

1865. Melton, J. Gordon. "Thelemic Magick in America." ALTERNATIVES TO
      AMERICAN MAINLINE CHURCHES (item 603), pp. 45-68.

      Gives a brief historical account of the "Ordo Templi Orientis," a
      psychic group that practices sex magic and other occult rituals as
      developed by Aleister Crowley, and that was founded by Charles
      Stansfeld Jones, a Canadian occultist. The origins of this occult
      group is traced to the revival of magic and particularly to the
      Brotherhood of Eulis, the Rosicrucian Inner Court. The "Magick of
      Thelema" is seen as a substitute for religion. The author thinks
      that magic "is essentially superstitious because it attributes
      'powers' to an object or person which cannot be so attributed" (p.
      83).

1866. Melton, J. Gordon. "Toward a History of Magical Religion in the
      United States." LISTENING: JOURNAL OF RELIGION AND CULTURE 9.3
      (1974): 112-23.

      Traces the historical background of the magical religious commu-
      nity that represents "a significant minority tradition in America."
      The following six different groups have their origins in the nine-
      teenth century: 1) the folk magic ritual tradition; 2) neo-Paganism
      and Witchcraft; 3) ritual magic; 4) Satanism; 5) Voodoo (and its
      cousins, Santeria and Macamba); and 6) Hoodoo (the root-doctor
      tradition). Various sources of magical religion are discussed and
      contemporary trends in the various groups that comprise the magical
      community are outlined. The magical community is a "national phe-
      nomenon" that is located primarily in urban areas and structurally
      held together by several periodicals and national organizations.

1867. Menzel, Donald H. "UFO's—The Modern Myth." UFO'S: A SCIENTIFIC
      DEBATE. Edited by Carl Sagan and Thornton Page. Ithaca, NY:
      Cornell University Press, 1972, pp. 123-82.

Proposes the view that accounts of UFOs are myths, that is,
stories constructed to explain what cannot be understood. Though
reports of modern flying saucers actually began in 1947, there was
a ready-made tradition behind them. Several examples are given to
illustrate the author's main thesis. In a lengthy appendix (pp.
146-82), the author gives samples of UFO stories and discusses UFOs
in art and in the Bible.

1868. Messer, Jeanne. "Guru Maharaj Ji and the Divine Light Mission."
        THE NEW RELIGIOUS CONSCIOUSNESS (item 614), pp. 52-72.

Describes an new Eastern religious group in America led by a
young guru. The ideology of the movement with its stress on the
experience of knowledge and meditation is briefly outlined. It is
pointed out that the change of consciousness that the devotees go
through in the initiation process expresses itself in increasing
happiness, greater amiability, improved flexibility and interaction, and other beneficial personality changes. A description of
the international, national, and local activities of the mission,
with its superficial bureaucracy and organization, is provided.
The author also reports on the way its finances are managed. He
also shows how personnel are used in such a free-flowing manner that
the movement "has little chance to predict or control income or
staffing" (p. 68).

1869. Michael, R. Blake. "Heaven, West Virginia: Legitimation Techniques
        of the New Vrindaban Community." KRISHNA CONSCIOUSNESS IN THE
        WEST (item 580), pp. 188-216.

Examines three major activities that have been used by the Hare
Krishna Movement's New Vrindaban Community in West Virginia to gain
acceptance and legitimation by society at large: 1) the pursuance
of theological and scholarly dialogue through publications, conferences, and research projects; 2) conformity to secular values (such
as pragmatism, hard work, and success); and 3) service to the Hindu
immigrant community (who have supported New Vrindaban with funds
and pilgrimages). The relationship between these activities and
ancient Hindu tradition is discussed. The author stresses the role
of Indo-Americans in making New Vrindaban's efforts work.

1870. Mickler, Michael L. "Future Prospects of the Unification Church."
        THE FUTURE OF NEW RELIGIOUS MOVEMENTS (item 579), pp. 175-86.

Discusses, from an insider's point of view, the future of the
Unification Church and criticizes the following three assumptions
that underlie the theory that sects develop into churches: 1) new
religious movements are passive with regard to their future; 2)
their development implies deviation from their original faith; and
3) the first-generation movements become churches. The author
proposes a development process in four stages, namely: 1) a preliminary stage of social unrest; 2) a popular stage; 3) a formal stage
or "crucial point;" and 4) an institutional stage. He thinks that
the Unification Church has entered the third stage in which its
members are divided into four major ideological subgroups, namely
liberal, prophetic, theocratic, and cultic. He believes that the

church will survive "by accommodating more moderate demands of
intra-organizational subgroupings and subchanneling more radical
impulses into controlled settings" (p. 184)

1871. Mickler, Michael L. "Charismatic Leadership Trajectories: A Com-
        parative Study of Marcus Garvey and Sun Myung Moon." PROPHETIC
        RELIGION AND POLITICS (item 358), pp. 35-51.

        Suggests that charismatic leadership should be seen as a set of
        processes. After a short critical review of Max Weber's theory
        of charisma, the author compares two charismatic leaders, namely
        Marcus Garvey and the Reverend Sun Myung Moon, and the charismatic
        process of both through three stages: 1) self-stigmatization;
        2) dramatization; and 3) criminalization. The author thinks that
        organizational consolidation and routinization within the Unifica-
        tion Church may diminish its social impact.

1872. Mickler, Michael L. "Crisis in Single Adults: An Alternative
        Approach." THE FAMILY AND THE UNIFICATION CHURCH (item 1785),
        pp. 161-73.

        Reflects on the contemporary situation of single adults in Amer-
        ica and points out that there is "an ambiguity between increased
        social acceptance of singleness as a lifestyle and systematic psy-
        chological maladjustment among single adults" (p. 165). The crisis
        in American singles is located in the inadequacy of the two modes
        of being single, namely nonvocational (the model of self-fulfill-
        ment) and vocational (the model of self-sacrifice). The Unifica-
        tion Church offers an alternative approach integrating both models
        within a normative pattern of God-centered family values.

1873. Middleton, Roger. "Demons and Devotees: Hare Krishna and the
        Transformation of Consciousness." MARGINS OF THE MIND (item
        664), pp. 196-213.

        Reports on a study of a Hare Krishna Temple in a London suburb.
        After describing the religious heritage of the movement, the author
        dwells on the transformation of consciousness for which members
        strive and on the methods used to maintain their new identity. One
        way of protecting the boundaries of the Hare Krishna world is the
        insistence that the local inhabitants are "demons." A new spiri-
        tual consciousness is "created, sustained, and protected through
        rituals, regulations, and rules which give everyday routines of
        social relationships, working, and eating a spiritual significance"
        (p. 204). The Hare Krishna Movement rejects both Western society
        and the counterculture. The author suggests that participation in
        the Hippie culture is a state of liminality, while membership in
        the movement is a form of "communitas." He observes that there is
        a clear correspondence between the firmness of social boundaries in
        the Hare Krishna Temple and the sense of pollution.

1874. Miller, David L., Kenneth J. Mietue, and Richard A. Mathers. "A
        Critical Examination of the Social Contagion Image of Cultural
        Behavior: The Case of the Enfield Monster." SOCIOLOGICAL QUAR-
        TERLY 19 (1978): 129-40.

Examines, with special reference to a monster sighting in a rural
community in Illinois, the theory of "social contagion" that holds
that "under certain conditions, widespread masses of people rapidly
and unanimously adopt patterns of behavior that are intense, unwit-
ting, and non-rational" (p. 129). A chronology of the events of
the sightings at Enfield, Illinois is given. Rather than relying
on the theory of social contagion, the author suggests that a better understanding can be achieved by considering the different
kinds of involvement in the event, the availability of the population for participation, the manner in which the event grows or
recedes in scope, and the kind of effects it has on institutionalized social behavior. People's behavior with respect to millennial
movements, reports of monsters, and flying saucer sightings and
encounters comes into being by a process common to more familiar
social phenomena.

*   Miller, Timothy. "Families Within a Family: Spiritual Values of
       Hutterites and Unificationists." Cited above as item 1386.

1875. Mills, Edgar W. "Cult Extremism: The Reduction of Normative Disso-
       nance." VIOLENCE AND RELIGIOUS COMMITMENT (item 653), pp. 75-87.

       Summarizes the events of Jonestown under six headings: 1) recruit-
       ment of vulnerable people; 2) isolation; 3) undermining trust rela-
       tionships; 4) heightening of frustration; 5) suppression of alter-
       natives; and 6) legitimation of violence. The author discusses "a
       major source of normative order in groups and illustrates how its
       breakdown can create conditions in which the probability of violent
       action is very high" (p. 20). The roles of "legitimated inconsis-
       tency" and "normative dissonance" within the group are analyzed.
       The violence at Jonestown originated from its leaders who used the
       mounting frustration they generated in their followers to propel
       the members of the cult to suicide and murder.

1876. Mitchell, Dave, Cathy Mitchell, and Richard Ofshe. THE LIGHT ON
       SYNANON: HOW A COUNTRY WEEKLY EXPOSED A CORPORATE CULT--AND WON
       THE PULITZER PRIZE. New York: Seaview Books, 1980. xi, 307 pp.

       Gives a personal account of how the owners of a local newspaper,
       THE LIGHT, in Marin County, California investigated the activities
       of Synanon, a drug-treatment and rehabilitation program that devel-
       oped into a cultic organization. Synanon's relationship with the
       press and legal battles are described. The authors' view is that
       as Synanon developed from a community offering an alternative life-
       style to a cult, a marked distinction between the leaders and mem-
       bers emerged, the former enjoying better living conditions while
       increasing demands on the ordinary membership.

1877. Mo, Huang Sung. "The Unification Church From a Sociological Per-
       spective." RESEARCH ON THE UNIFICATION CHURCH. Edited by Lee
       Hang Nyong. Seoul, Korea: Song Hua Press, 1981, pp. 217-56.

       Views the Unification Church as a social entity subject to socio-
       logical analysis. Four major questions are the subject of this
       essay: 1) what makes the church a unique organization different

from other religious groups?; 2) what characterizes and motivates
the group activities of the members?; 3) what kind of relationship
can the church develop with the mainline culture?; and 4) what
conflicts are generated by the church's ideology and lifestyle? A
lengthy discussion (pp. 233-56) among various scholars is included.

1878. Moment, Gairdner B. "From Utopia to Dystopia: The Jonestown Trag-
        edy." UTOPIAS: THE AMERICAN EXPERIENCE (item 425), pp. 215-28.

        Explores the significance of the Jonestown tragedy, focusing on
        such questions as whether the People's Temple is just another exam-
        ple of a bizarre pathology common to all utopias or whether it
        reveals something about contemporary religion and society. The
        author outlines the similarities and differences between Jonestown
        and other utopias. The members of the People's Temple, once they
        moved to Guyana, became "truly captives" under the powerful domin-
        ion of their leader Jim Jones. It is argued that the People's
        Temple appealed to those people who felt a vacuum in their lives.
        The experiment of Jones was transformed from a successful enter-
        prise in San Francisco to the tragedy of self-destruction in Guyana.

1879. Moody, Edward J. "Magical Therapy: An Anthropological Investiga-
        tion of Contemporary Satanism." RELIGIOUS MOVEMENTS IN CONTEMPO-
        RARY AMERICA (item 727), pp. 355-82.

        Studies the First Church of the Trapezoid (Church of Satan) in
        San Francisco, California. The kind of people who join this church
        and the reasons why they become members of a group that automati-
        cally exposes them to social sanctions are among the areas investi-
        gated. The author defends the view that the magic practiced by
        Satanists helps them achieve their desires, namely money, fame,
        recognition, and power. He describes two magic rituals, the "Invo-
        cation of Lust" and the "Shibboleth Ritual," to show how Satanists
        go about fulfilling their desires and he explains their emergence
        in our times as the result of attempts by some people "to regain a
        sense of control over their environment and their lives" (p. 381).

1880. Moody, Edward J. "Urban Witches." CONFORMITY AND CONFLICT: READ-
        INGS IN CULTURAL ANTHROPOLOGY. Edited by James P. Spradley and
        David W. McCready. Boston: Little, Brown, and Co., 1971, pp.
        280-90.

        Discusses contemporary Satanism in the United States and explores
        both the reasons people take part in Satanic rituals and the bene-
        fits that might accompany membership in a Satanic Church. The
        rituals and beliefs of Satanism (or black magic) are described.
        People who get involved in the black arts may be motivated by a
        sense of alienation and social inadequacy, attracted because of
        personal psychological problems, or drawn by a desire to seek
        thrills. Satanic churches are secret societies in which people can
        perform socially disapproved of behavior in a natural and normal
        fashion.

1881. Moore, John. "The Catholic Pentecostal Movement." SOCIOLOGICAL
        YEARBOOK OF RELIGION IN BRITAIN 6 (1971): 73-90.

Attempts to analyze the origin, development, and social character
of the Catholic Charismatic Renewal. Its historical roots in classical Pentecostalism are traced and its cultural and ecclesiastical
milieu sketched. A sociological analysis of the movement is presented in four main areas: 1) an explanation in terms of collective
behavior; 2) a typology of the movement in terms of cults; 3) an
outline of factors that are crucial for its diffusion; and 4) the
reaction of the establishment. The author thinks that the Catholic
Charismatic Renewal is a cult movement in that it represents a
break with religious tradition, has its basis in mystical experience, and is concerned with the problems of the individual rather
than those of the group. It began as a local cult and became a
permanent cult with a missionary center and headquarters. It exists in an ambivalent relationship with the Catholic Church from
which it sprung.

1882. Morgan, Peggy. "Methods and Aims of Evangelization and Conversion
to Buddhism, With Particular Reference to Nichiren Shoshu Soka
Gakkai." THE NEW EVANGELISTS (item 587), pp. 113-30.

Examines, from a broadly phenomenological perspective, not only
how Buddhist groups like Nichiren Shoshu fit into the general Buddhist tradition, but also how Buddhism is being transplanted in
Great Britain. Hospitality, generosity, and openness are the key
methods that Nichiren Shoshu uses for its well-planned evangelization. The missionary activities of, and the conversion process to,
this relatively new religious movement are seen in the context of
the missionary goals of Buddhism. Nichiren Shoshu tends to stress
the personal experience of those who have joined its ranks. The
unique chanting of the Nichiren Shoshu liturgy is discussed.

1883. Mörth, Ingo. "Elements of Religious Meaning in Science Fiction
Literature." SOCIAL COMPASS 34 (1987): 87-108.

Points out that transcendent, fantastic, and utopian elements are
shared by science fiction and religion. The author outlines the
meaningful concepts in the world of science fiction and the disenchantment with religion that involvement in science fiction con-
notes. Science fiction writers often create a world where the
normal empirical boundaries of time, space, society, and knowledge
no longer exist. Based on the plausibility of UFOs landing on
earth, several science fiction religions (such as Scientology) and
UFO cults (such as the Aetherius Society) have come into being, the
former offering "a cosmically unrestricted life by means of God-
like Thetans inside each of us" (p. 105), the latter promising the
salvation of the human race through a charismatic figure who is the
contact person with extraterrestrial beings.

1884. Mullan, Bob. LIFE AS LAUGHTER: FOLLOWING BHAGWAN SHREE RAJNEESH.
London: Routledge and Kegan Paul, 1983. 204 pp.

Presents a descriptive study of one of the most controversial
cults, that founded by Bhagwan Shree Rajneesh in Poona, India, and
transplanted to the West in 1980. A brief biographical sketch of
the founder is provided. His teachings regarding the religion of

the "sannyasin," the meaning of enlightenment, the importance of
sex, and the role of the master are described. A profile of those
who join the movement and a description of its main and communal
lifestyles are given. One chapter is dedicated to the now-defunct
Oregon settlement, Rajneeshpuram. The conflicts between the movement and the State of Oregon are also dealt with. The author sees
this movement as a world-affirming religion. It is part of the
Human Potential Movement and fits into the so-called "new narcissism." Those who join it are children of the 1960's who are trying
to make moral sense of their lives.

1885. Musgrove, Frank. "Dervishes in Dorsetshire: Re-Alignment With
       Reality." MARGINS OF THE MIND (item 664), pp. 168-95.

       Studies an English commune of Islamic mystics in the Cotswolds,
       England, as an example of the reversal of the secularization pro-
       cess or a stage in the transformation of the counterculture of the
       1960's. The religious heritage of the dervishes is described. The
       author thinks that their presence in England is not surprising,
       since there is a striking parallelism between ecstatic social move-
       ments in thirteenth-century Europe, seventeenth-century England,
       and the Anglo-American counterculture of the 1970's. The author
       describes his visits to a Sufi commune, the lifestyle of the mys-
       tics he met, and the conversations he had with them. The commune
       they voluntarily joined is an example of marginality. Membership
       in a Hippie commune may have been a liminal phase prior to commit-
       ment to a commune of Sufi mystics.

1886. Myers, James E. "Rajneeshpuram: The Boom and Bust of a Buddha-
       field." MAGIC, WITCHCRAFT, AND RELIGION (items 652), pp. 366-75.

       Provides an account of a controversial religious movement that
       established a large settlement in the State of Oregon. After a
       brief biography of its founder, Chandra Mohan Jain (Bhagwan Shree
       Rajneesh), the author describes the guru's experiments in Poona,
       India and his establishment of his movement in the West. The
       collapse of the organization at Rajneeshpuram is also covered.
       Several explanations, mostly psychological, of this somewhat exotic
       movement are summarized. The author thinks that though Rajneesh
       has not yet found a permanent home, his movement will persist.

1887. Nederman, Cary J., and James Wray Goulding. "Popular Occultism and
       Critical Social Theory: Exploring Some Themes in Adorno's Cri-
       tique of Astrology and the Occult." SOCIOLOGICAL ANALYSIS 42
       (1981): 325-32.

       Discusses the relationship between popular occultism and contem-
       porary society in the context of Adorno's theory of the occult as a
       projection onto the stars of the structural contradictions of in-
       dustrial society, contradictions which are reflected in the practi-
       cal advice given in astrology columns (see item 1565). Apparent
       irrational phenomena (like the reading of Tarot cards and tea
       leaves) serve the social functions of justifying and legitimizing
       the status quo. Astrology columns and occult manifestations stress

the importance both of fate and individual accountability. "Popular occultism thus serves as an irrational rationalization of what advanced industrial society cannot itself rationalize" (p. 329).

1888. Neitz, Mary Jo. CHARISMA AND COMMUNITY: A STUDY OF RELIGIOUS COMMITMENT WITHIN THE CHARISMATIC RENEWAL. New Brunswick, NJ: Transaction Books, 1987. xxi, 294 pp.

Presents a study of the Catholic Charismatic Renewal in two major parts. Part One describes the movement and attempts to understand its belief system in its social context. The conversion process, the experience of God, and family symbolism are among the topics pursued. Part Two studies the movement in American culture, comparing it with some of its antecedents and with current social movements. The Catholic Charismatic Renewal is one way in which the Catholic Church is adapting to American culture, since it shares many elements with contemporary self-awareness movements and can be considered to be part of the culture of narcissism. The focus on healing, however, enables the Charismatic Renewal to transcend both the individualism and narcissism of modern culture. Among the appendices are included several guidelines for interviewing members of the movement.

1889. Nelson, Geoffrey K. "A Comment on Pilarzyk's Article 'The Origin, Development, and Decline of a Youth Culture Religion.'" REVIEW OF RELIGIOUS RESEARCH 21 (1979): 108–109.

Replies briefly to Pilarzyk's view (item 1924) of how the Divine Light Mission changed from a local to a centralized cult and why the attempts of its leader to transform the movement into a sect failed. It is argued that the rise of this movement must be understood in the light of the youth culture religion of the 1960's and that it developed into a cult as it adapted to Western culture. The decline of the movement is attributed to Guru Maharaj Ji's loss of charisma following the break with his family in India.

1890. Nelson, Geoffrey K. "Toward a Sociology of the Psychic." REVIEW OF RELIGIOUS RESEARCH 16 (1975): 166–73.

Reports on a survey conducted in an English town where ten percent of the population claimed to have had some psychic experience. These kinds of experiences, which are found in all human societies, are attributed to paranormal or supernatural causes. The author examines the occupation, class, sex, and social mobility of psychics. He suggests that an explanation of such events is best sought in the "effect of differential socialization in social classes and, in particular, in the socialization into occupational roles" (p. 171). Thus, in British society, the male role tends to repress psychic abilities, while the female role encourages them. Mobility and marginality were also found to be linked positively with psychic experiences.

1891. Nielson, Donald A. "Charles Manson's Family of Love: A Case Study of Anomism, Puerilism, and Transmoral Consciousness in Civilizational Perspective." SOCIOLOGICAL ANALYSIS 45 (1984): 315–37.

Attempts to understand the Manson Family in terms of "civilizational processes and structures of consciousness." Three types of
consciousness are distinguished and described, namely the sacromagical, the faith structure, and the rationalized structure. The
Manson Family represented a regressional shift from a rationalized
structure to an alternating stress on the sacromagical orientation
(characterized by play, puerilism, and millennialism) and on the
faith orientation (characterized by radical anomism, antinomianism,
spiritual perfection, and transmoral consciousness). Rather than
view Manson as unique, the author thinks that from a civilizational
perspective he is one example of a "recurrent type." Groups like
the one he founded come into being whenever there is sociocultural
dislocation that challenges the meaning normally ascribed to the
world.

1892. Nordquist, Ted A. ANANDA COOPERATIVE VILLAGE: A STUDY OF THE BE-
       LIEF, VALUES, AND ATTITUDES OF A NEW AGE COMMUNITY. Uppsala,
       Sweden: Borgstroms Tryekeri, 1978. 177 pp.

       Presents a study of Ananda Cooperative Village, a California-
       based commune founded and directed by Swami Kriyananda, a disciple
       of Swami Paramahansa Yogananda who in 1920 established the Self-
       Realization Fellowship. The history and development of the vil-
       lage, its initial internal struggles, the beliefs, values, and
       attitudes of its members who originally belonged to the counter-
       culture movement, and their commitment to a specific ideology are
       among the topics described. The author concludes that the people
       he studied are "involved in a redefinition of reality according to
       their beliefs, values, and attitudes" (p. 155).

1893. Norman, William H. "Asceticism or Mysticism: Transcendental Medi-
       tation." SOCIOLOGICAL SPECTRUM 1 (1982): 315-31.

       Argues that, although Transcendental Meditation is based on East-
       ern otherworldly mysticism, it still serves to reinforce an inner-
       worldly ascetic orientation. Using Weber's distinction between
       asceticism and mysticism (the former being a means to resolve ten-
       sion through mastery, the latter through resignation or adjustment),
       the author describes the elements of otherworldly mysticism and
       its affinity to inner worldliness. This new movement, according to
       the author, attracts people who are looking for some instrument to
       master their environment, particularly their stress-anxiety levels
       generated by contemporary Western culture.

1894. Novak, Michael. "Jonestown." AMERICAN ENTERPRISE INSTITUTE, Re-
       print No. 94 (March 1979): 1-10.

       Contains five short commentaries on Jonestown, which is described
       as a cult of socialism that was dominated by an antiindividualism
       orientation and excessive egalitarianism. Jonestown was a messi-
       anic cult that indoctrinated its members and destroyed the family,
       thus leading to its tragic end.

1895. Novak, Philip. "The Buddha and the Computer: Meditation in an Age
       of Information." JOURNAL OF RELIGION AND HEALTH 25 (1986): 188-92.

Argues in favor of the use of meditation, especially Zen Buddhist, in an age of information. It is the author's view that meditation trains one's capacity for attention, increases recognition of patterns, and enhances coordination between modes of human intelligence, such as intuition and reason. Meditation can be "a tool for balance and sanity in an electronically overstimulated civilization" (p. 192).

1896. Nugent, Donald. "The Renaissance and/of Witchcraft." CHURCH HISTORY 40 (1971): 69-78.

Compares the rise of the occult in the Renaissance period to its reemergence in modern times. The modern occult revival is related to the counterculture. The author maintains that the Renaissance was "the golden age of witchcraft" that has two universal features, namely sexuality and power. The new age of witchcraft is broadly associated with the end of the nineteenth century. Modern witchcraft cuts across social class. Witchcraft in both periods came into being in times of social despair.

1897. O'Brien, Leslie N. "A Case Study of the 'Hare Krishna' Movement." PRACTICE AND BELIEF: STUDIES IN THE SOCIOLOGY OF AUSTRALIAN RELIGION. Boston: Allyn and Unwin, 1983, pp. 134-53.

Examines the Hare Krishna Movement in Melbourne, Australia to find out why people join the group and what kind of problems they encountered in becoming members. The author concludes that his investigations confirm the research of other scholars in America who discovered that Hare Krishna members are largely ex-hippies who now claim that participation in the movement gives them a better "high" than drugs ever did. He discusses the six mechanisms used for maintaining a Krishna identity: 1) total control of the individual; 2) suppression of past statuses; 3) denial of the moral worth of the old self; 4) active participation in one's own resocialization; 5) various sanctions; and 6) intensification of one's peer support group. The conflicts that the movement had with the Melbourne Central Business District and with the legal authorities are described. The author thinks that the perceived harassment that the Hare Krishna members felt heightened the group's solidarity.

1898. O'Brien, Leslie N. "Some Defining Characteristics of the Hare Krishna Movement." AUSTRALIAN AND NEW ZEALAND JOURNAL OF SOCIOLOGY 9.2 (1973): 72-73.

Gives a brief sketch of the Hare Krishna Movement in Melbourne, Australia. The author suggests that "devotees of Krishna have encountered a 'reality flaw,' perceived it as problematic, and have actively sought a 'solution' in a viable alternative" (p. 72). Hare Krishna members seem to have reacted not to material deprivation, but to discrepancies between the humanistic ideals of Western society and the actual realities of inequality and impersonality. The Hare Krishna Movement provides a workable alternative to Western culture.

1899. O'Brien, Marc S., and William B. Barkston. "The Moral Career of a
       Reformed Compulsive Eater: A Study of Conversion to Charismatic
       Authority." DEVIANT AUTHORITY: AN INTERDISCIPLINARY JOURNAL 5
       (1984): 141-50.

       Examines how participation in a weight control group can be a
       means for coming to grips with the Western social stigma of obe-
       sity. The authors see this kind of group as a "converting agent."
       They describe its philosophy that considers overeating as a sin
       and constructs a typology of participants. Lofland's distinction
       (see item 1832) between predisposing and situational conditions for
       conversion are applied to the weight control group.

1900. O'Donnell, Christopher O. "Neo-Pentecostalism in North America and
       Europe." NEW RELIGIOUS MOVEMENTS (item 589), pp. 35-41.

       Reflects on the impact of the Charismatic Renewal, particularly
       within the Catholic Church. The main characteristics of those who
       join this movement are sketched, drawing attention to their middle-
       class backgrounds and to the predominance of women in all charis-
       matic functions. Several major theological and social issues are
       discussed. The author thinks that the movement has now become
       marginalized.

1901. Ofshe, Richard. "The Rabbi and the Sex Cult: Power Expansion in
       the Formation of a Cult." CULTIC STUDIES JOURNAL 3 (1986): 173-
       89.

       Analyzes one aspect of the social organization of a small, name-
       less cult, showing how its leader, a rabbi, developed techniques
       for recruiting and controlling his followers. The author outlined
       the cult's development and focuses on how its leader used hypnosis
       to persuade a woman to join the cult.

1902. Ofshe, Richard. "The Social Development of the Synanon Cult: The
       Managerial Strategy of Organizational Transformation." JOURNAL
       FOR THE SCIENTIFIC STUDY OF RELIGION 41 (1980): 109-27.

       Reviews the history of Synanon in four stages, namely those of:
       1) a voluntary association that functioned as an alternative to
       Alcoholics Anonymous (January to September 1958); 2) a therapeutic
       community for treating drug addicts (1958-1968); 3) a social move-
       ment and alternative society which demanded a lifetime commitment
       (1969-1975); and 4) a religion which assumed the features of a
       regular church (from 1975 to the present). The author contends
       that the transformations of Synanon were not phases of a natural
       evolutionary process, but were rather "used strategically to control
       the organization and to achieve managerial goals" (p. 115). Some
       of the problems that Synanon encountered with government agencies,
       particularly the Internal Revenue Service, are described. A short
       but useful bibliography with references to a number of legal cases
       is included.

1903. Ofshe, Richard. "Synanon: The People Business." THE NEW RELIGIOUS
       CONSCIOUSNESS (item 614), pp. 116-37.

Describes Synanon in its two analytically distinct social entities, namely a corporate entity with no owners or stockholders and
a community of people who formed an unusual pattern of social organization. The history of Synanon is sketched and its function as a
therapeutic community analyzed. Three groups of people are said to
make up the community: 1) adults with a long history of drug addiction and criminal behavior; 2) young adults who are drug users; and
3) "squares," referring to those who do not have a drug problem.
The relationship between the corporate entity and the community is
described. Most of the members of Synanon are transients. Those
who stay permanently join the administrative staff. The author
thinks that Synanon "probably does some good for the people who
have a transient contact with it" (pp. 137-37).

1904. Ofshe, Richard, et al. "Social Structure and Social Control in
      Synanon." JOURNAL OF VOLUNTARY SOCIAL ACTION 3 (1974): 67-76.

Discusses the function of the "Synanon Game" as it developed from
a drug rehabilitation program to a total society. The authors
argue that Synanon functions as a game in the sense that it undergoes minor changes and periodic major reorganizations and aims at
changing people's values and behaviors. The individual commitment
process and the consequences of commitment on the organization are
explored. Synanon controls individual behavior by the abolition of
privacy through monitoring one's behavior, by the "no-contract"
rule (that is, the prohibition against agreements not to manifest
each other's faults in public), and by magnifying deviance by insisting that not following minor regulations is a serious breach.

1905. Oh, John Kie-Chang. "The Nichiren Shoshu of America." REVIEW OF
      RELIGIOUS RESEARCH 14 (1972): 169-77.

Reflects on the presence of a new Japanese religious movement in
the United States. The movement's genesis and evolution as well as
its major religious tenets are briefly accounted for. A profile of
an American member is sketched. Over 50 percent of those who join
Nichiren Shoshu are between the ages of 21 and 40. The majority
learned about the movement through a friend. Among the most frequent reasons given for joining are the earnestness and sincerity
of missionaries and the superior doctrine of the church. Some
claim that joining the movement led to the solution of their personal problems. Others mentioned their dissatisfaction with their
religion and disagreements with their parents as causes for their
decisions to change their religious affiliation. The author records the length of time people have been involved in Nichiren
Shoshu, their prayer life in the movement, and the methods for
gaining new converts.

1906. Olsen, Flemming Falkenberg. "AAO--An Anachronistic Organization."
      UPDATE: A QUARTERLY JOURNAL OF NEW RELIGIOUS MOVEMENTS 2.1
      (1978): 43-50.

Examines a new quasi-religious movement called the Action Analytic Organization (AAO). Though there is no organizational system
that monitors the various groups that adhere to the philosophical

and political ideals of this movement, the AAO forms a unified
community that advocates, among other things, a unique lifestyle
that includes a common free sexuality. The AAO has an inner structure that includes strong leadership and a spiritual life.

1907. Omohundro, John T. "Von Daniken's Chariots: A Primer in the Art of
      Cooked Science." ZETETIC 1.1 (1976): 58-68.

      Describes the interest in UFOs as a kind of new religious move-
      ment in that it manifests a "humorless fanaticism, prophets, a new
      world view, and a stiff distaste for the Establishment" (p. 59).
      The author criticizes von Daniken's theory about the history of the
      human race and the visits of space people to earth for misrepre-
      senting scholarly fields like anthropology and archaeology. Von
      Daniken's views are both anthropocentric and ethnocentric.

1908. Oosterwal, Gottfried. "The Children of God." UPDATE: A QUARTERLY
      JOURNAL OF NEW RELIGIOUS MOVEMENTS 3.1-2 (1979): 35-44.

      Gives a descriptive historical account of the Children of God/
      Family of Love with a short biography of its founder, David Berg.
      The reaction to the movement, polarized into two groups--one sup-
      porting it, the other denouncing it--is outlined. The main fea-
      tures of the movement are the warm fellowship and the new meaning
      of life it offers to those who join. The author states that most
      of its members come from those young adults who are lonely, con-
      fused, and alienated.

1909. Pace, Enzo. "Charismatics and the Political Presence of Catholics
      (The Italian Case)." SOCIAL COMPASS 25 (1978): 85-99.

      Examines the Charismatic Movement in Veneto, a traditional Cath-
      olic region in Italy, and its relationship to the politicoreligious
      situation in the country. The geographical features of the area
      are summarized and the structural backgrounds of two charismatic
      groups are analyzed. The social dynamics of the movement are seen
      in terms of the tension and conflict between church groups, ideo-
      logical stands, and contrasting leadership (one exercising charis-
      matic, the other institutionalized, authority). The Charismatic
      Movement represents "a functional separation in the system of
      alliances between the Catholic Church and the Catholic Political
      Party in power, between the private and the public, and between the
      personal and the political" (p. 95). The political relevance of
      the Charismatic Movement is discussed.

1910. Palmer, Susan J. "Charisma and Abdication: A Study of the Leader-
      ship of Bhagwan Shree Rajneesh." SOCIOLOGICAL ANALYSIS 49
      (1988): 119-35.

      Applies Wallis's model of charismatic leadership (item 2055) to
      the founder of the Rajneesh Foundation, Bhagwan Shree Rajneesh,
      whose career is outlined in several stages. Two aspects of charis-
      ma, performance and responsibility, are distinguished, the former
      referring to the charismatic leader's ability to demonstrate extra-
      ordinary powers, the latter his willingness to provide direction

for the movement. The author thinks that Rajneesh excelled in
charismatic performance, but was rather weak in charismatic responsibility. His abdication of responsibility is partly understood as
the behavior of a prophet of the exemplary type (like Krishnamurti
and Gurdjieff).

1911. Palmer, Susan J. "The Cult of Birth: Natural Childbirth and Femi-
       nine Charisma." WOMEN AND MEN. Edited by Greta Hofmann Nemiroff.
       Toronto: Fitzhenry and Whiteside, 1987, pp. 224-44.

       Argues that the Natural Childbirth Movement "can be termed a cult
       in that it has its own sets of myths and rituals" (p. 225). Two
       alternative religious communities, the Farm, founded by Steven
       Gaskin in Tennessee, and the Institute for the Development of the
       Harmonious Human Being, founded by E. J. Gold in California, are
       described and the ways their members ritualize birth outlined. The
       concerns that the rituals surrounding birth reveal and the prevail-
       ing magical themes that prenatal preparations and birth experiences
       express are explored. The author suggests that the cult of birth
       in the feminist movement points to a "turning to the self as a
       source of sacred power."

1912. Palmer, Susan J. "Purity and Danger in the Rajneesh Foundation."
       UPDATE: A QUARTERLY JOURNAL OF NEW RELIGIOUS MOVEMENTS 10.3
       (1986): 18-29.

       Explores the meaning of body rituals in the Rajneesh Foundation.
       After a brief history of Rajneeshism, the author identifies two
       kinds of rites used simultaneously in Rajneeshpuram, namely puri-
       fication and healing rituals. Diet is the central symbol of
       pollution. Bhagwan's dynamic meditation contains a ritual which
       purifies people from anger, pain, and frustration. Sex functions
       both as a purification rite and as a meditation ritual. The
       segregation of the devotees in a remote commune is also aimed to
       protect them from pollution from the outside world. Purification
       and healing rituals express a response to external and internal
       sources of threat. The Foundation is another attempt "to achieve a
       kind of immortality and create an elite race through the ritual
       control of sexuality" (p. 29).

1913. Palmer, Susan J. "Community and Commitment in the Rajneesh Founda-
       tion." UPDATE: A QUARTERLY JOURNAL OF NEW RELIGIOUS MOVEMENTS
       10.4 (1986): 3-15.

       Examines and interprets the stages of development in the Rajneesh
       utopian commune in Oregon, particularly the dramatic shift between
       1981 and 1985. After a brief survey of Rajneesh's early biography,
       the author, following Kanter's procedure (item 383), describes the
       community mechanisms used by all communes. She reflects on the
       guru's silence, the pattern of worship, the "AIDS apocalypse," the
       establishment of communes in various parts of the world, the Bud-
       dhafield (the belief in a hidden spiritual community), and those
       therapists who have shaped the sexual and social mores of the com-
       mune. Three main weaknesses are said to have contributed to the
       downfall of Rajneeshpuram: 1) the leader's own weakness; 2) the

2) internal conflict between the elite members of the commune and
the rest of the members; and 3) the response to persecution.
Kanter's theory, in spite of its usefulness, does not explain why
Rajneeshpuram failed.

1914. Parsons, Arthur S. "Messianic Personification in the Unification
       Church." JOURNAL FOR THE SCIENTIFIC STUDY OF RELIGION 25 (1986):
       141-61.

       Applies the method of participant observation to study the role
       system within the Unification Church. The therapeutic ideology of
       the "heart," elaborated by the Moonies, the communal ideal of a
       personalized family, the two fundamental role-sets the Church uses
       (i.e., Father/Child and Abel/Cain), and the organization of these
       role-sets in a therapeutic but hierarchical apparatus of charis-
       matic relationships are described. The author believes that the
       Unification Church has succeeded in integrating authority (reli-
       gious fundamentalism) and personalism (narcissism) into a thera-
       peutic religion.

1915. Parsons, Arthur S. "Redemptory Intimacy: The Family Culture of the
       Unification Church." COMMUNAL SOCIETIES 5 (1985): 137-75.

       Presents a study of the "overall normal patterns and structure of
       the Church" and "the everyday role expectations and performances of
       the Moonies" (pp. 137-38). The author first describes the role
       system in the Unification Church, focusing on its ideology and main
       themes and their consequent practical applications. He concludes
       by reflecting on the relationship between the Church and contempo-
       rary society. Rather than seeing the Unification Church as diamet-
       rically opposed to Western culture, the author suggests that the
       "Moonies give redemptory value and communal form to some of the
       highly secular and antinomian tendencies of 'modernism'" (p. 174).

1916. Parsons, Arthur S. "Yoga in a Western Setting: Youth in Search of
       Religious Prophecy." SOUNDINGS: AN INTERDISCIPLINARY JOURNAL 57
       (1974): 222-35.

       Studies a Kundalini Yoga group in Boston with the aim of under-
       standing the meaning and consequences of the group's efforts and of
       clarifying the relationships between Kundalini Yoga and classical
       Yoga, modern Christianity, and secular society. The author shows
       how the members of this group translated the classical Eastern
       practice of Yoga into a Western setting. He maintains that the
       meaning of Yoga in the West can only be understood in the context
       of the secular and Christian background of those who join the group.

1917. Patel, Mahesh S. "Evaluation of Holistic Medicine." SOCIAL SCIENCE
       AND MEDICINE 24 (1987): 169-75.

       Discusses the contemporary interest in holistic and alternative
       medical practices such as acupuncture, homeopathy, and ayurvedic
       medicine. The traditional structure of the Western, scientific
       health care system is reviewed and the problems of applying these
       techniques to holistic medicine specified. Various ways of compar-
       ing the results of different medical systems are suggested.

1918.   Pentikainen, Julia.   "Revivalist Movements and Religious Contra-
        cultures in Finland."   NEW RELIGIONS (item 565), pp. 92-100.

        Examines the first revivalist movements in Finland that took
        place before industrialization. Four major movements are distin-
        guished: 1) evangelism (middle of the nineteenth century); 2) re-
        vivalism (eighteenth and nineteenth centuries); 3) Knee-Praying
        (eighteenth century); and 4) Laestadianism (middle nineteenth cen-
        tury). The religious leaders and their followers of all these
        movements are explored. In a final, section the author deals with
        the rise of "new religious splinter groups or contracultures" (p.
        114), which include Transcendental Meditation and the Divine Light
        Mission.

1919.   Petersen, Donald W., and Armand L. Mauss. "The Cross and the Com-
        mune: An Interpretation of the Jesus People." RELIGION IN SOCIO-
        LOGICAL PERSPECTIVE (item 352), pp. 261-79.

        Discusses the conditions that activated the Jesus Movement and
        the processes whereby people were recruited to join it. A brief
        description of the Jesus People is given and the data analyzed in
        order to determine the kind of people attracted to the movement.
        The authors apply Glock's theory of deprivations (item 94) to the
        Jesus Movement and conclude that ethical, psychic, and social de-
        privations have contributed to its growth. They find that the
        following forms of social deprivation are particularly operative:
        nonacceptance or nonaffiliation with traditional religion, a sense
        of loss, and a need for an alternative status system.

1920.   Petranek, Charles F. "Recruitment and Commitment." SOCIETY 25.2
        (1988): 48-51.

        Reviews the problems of recruitment and commitment to a religious
        organization in the context of the Unification Church. The type of
        person who joins this church is defined in terms of Lofland and
        Stark's analysis (item 215). Members of this new church are re-
        socialized and reeducated in a manner analogous to seminary stu-
        dents preparing for the priesthood. Deep commitment to their
        faith, the tendency to see the world in religious terms, a naive
        and innocent quality, similarity in dress, and the severance of
        ties with former friends are among the shared characteristics.

1921.   Phelan, Michael. "Transcendental Meditation: A Revitalization of
        the American Civil Religion." ARCHIVES DE SCIENCES SOCIALES DES
        RELIGIONS 48.1 (1978): 5-20.

        Describes Transcendental Meditation as a revitalization movement
        in American culture that came into being following a period of
        increased individual stress and cultural distortion. The author,
        using Wilson's typology of sects (see item 1023), classifies this
        movement as a "manipulationist sect" that has created social prob-
        lems because it strives to become legitimate by having recourse to
        tradition and science. "TM disciples are ethically oriented, cul-
        turally conservative individuals who have selected Transcendental
        Meditation as a means of dealing with stress because alternative
        counter-culture groups are opposed to traditional values" (p. 19).

1922. Picardie, Justine, and Dorothy Wade, "New-Born Christianity." NEW
        SOCIETY 78 (December 5, 1986): 14-16.

        Gives an account of a prayer meeting at which a charismatic (or
        born again) preacher, Steve Ryder, addressed an audience in London.
        The authors observe that the Charismatic Renewal is well-estab-
        lished in many parts of Great Britain. They contend, however, that
        the revival has not addressed itself to serious social issues and
        has become an end in itself.

1923. Pilarzyk, Thomas. "The Cultic Resilience of the Divine Light Mis-
        sion: A Reply to Nelson." REVIEW OF RELIGIOUS RESEARCH 21 (1979):
        109-112.

        Responds to Nelson's critical comment (item 1889) on the author's
        original essay on the Divine Light Mission (item 1924). It is
        maintained that the shift in the Mission's recruitment and member-
        ship patterns indicates a slow but increasing differentiation of
        the movement from its youth culture origins. The Divine Light
        Mission continues to serve as a cultic "mediating structure" in
        postindustrialized societies. The organizational shifts that have
        taken place since 1975 imply that the Mission will continue to be a
        somewhat tenuous, world-affirming, centralized cult.

1924. Pilarzyk, Thomas. "Conversion and Alteration Processes in the
        Youth Culture: A Comparative Study of Religious Transformations."
        PACIFIC SOCIOLOGICAL REVIEW 20 (1978): 379-406.

        Explores the different ways in which young adults changed their
        worldviews through participation in a new religious movement.
        Concentrating on converts to the Hare Krishna Movement and the
        Divine Light Mission, the author examines the converts' apprehen-
        sion of social reality. Three transformations are analyzed: 1) the
        reinterpretation of one's preconvert state as one of discontent,
        crisis, alienation, or suffering; 2) the process of resocializa-
        tion processes; and 3) the expression of one's commitment after
        one's conversion. Two types of radical religious change are dis-
        tinguished, namely sectarian conversion (of which conversion to
        the Hare Krishna Movement is an example), and cultic alternation
        (of which conversion to the Divine Light Mission is an example).
        The difference between conversions to the two groups lies, in part,
        in the degree of subjective change in worldview, lifestyle, and
        biography of converts.

1925. Pilarzyk, Thomas. "The Origin, Development, and Decline of a Youth
        Culture Religion: An Application of Sectarianization Theory."
        REVIEW OF RELIGIOUS RESEARCH 20 (1978): 23-43.

        Integrates various theories of sectarianism to study the growth
        and decline of new religious movements and to clarify those factors
        central to the process of sectarianization. The cultural, environ-
        mental, and intraorganizational factors of one particular group,
        namely the Divine Light Mission, are examined to trace the cult's
        initial success and subsequent decline. The movement's organiza-
        tion, decisions, goals, and collective actions are the most crucial

factors necessary to explain how the movement evolves. The guru's
actions, such as lessening the restrictions of ashram life, his
insistence on his role as the only true spiritual master, and the
internalization of the movement, insured a greater sectarianism.
But the precariousness of the Divine Light Mission's beliefs was
among the internal factors that led to its failure to become a
sect.

1926. Pilarzyk, Thomas, and Cardell K. Jacobson. "Christians in the
      Youth Culture: The Life History of an Urban Commune." WISCONSIN
      SOCIOLOGIST 14 (1977): 136-51.

      Gives an account of the origin and development of a Jesus People
      commune in Milwaukee, explores some of the functions it fulfilled,
      and examines the factors that led to its growth and eventual demise.
      The authors think that these Jesus People, in rejecting both tradi-
      tional religion and society and the counterculture, had to develop
      other forms of religious expression. Changes in leadership, re-
      cruitment patterns, and socialization techniques, together with
      organizational conflicts, led to insoluble problems. The commune
      never became a stable organization. Reasons for the commune's fail-
      ure can be traced both to the inadequacy of charismatic authority
      and administrative leadership as well as to the group's millennial
      eschatology and belief system.

1927. Poher, Claude, and Jacques Vallee. "Basic Patterns in UFO Observa-
      tions." FLYING SAUCERS REVIEW 21.3-4 (1975): 8-13.

      Examines a wave of UFO phenomena that was reported in 1973 and
      early 1974 and looks for patterns among those people who claimed to
      have sighted these flying saucers. The authors are convinced that
      the witnesses actually saw objects in the sky or on the ground, but
      think that these objects have features that are quite different
      from commonly observed natural phenomena. Most UFO observations
      occurred between five and nine in the evening and at sites not
      marked by high population density. Further, there is "nothing
      abnormal about the age distribution and group membership of the
      witnesses of such events, which follow patterns that can be
      explained from sociological factors alone" (p. 12).

1928. Poling, Tommy H., and J. Frank Kenny. THE HARE KRISHNA CHARACTER
      TYPE: A STUDY OF THE SENSATE PERSONALITY. Lewiston, NY: Edwin
      Mellen Press, 1986. 184 pp.

      Presents a psychological study of Hare Krishna devotees, taking
      into account some sociological factors. After a brief historical
      introduction, the authors summarize earlier research on the subject
      and outline their own method. They give a description of the move-
      ment's lifestyle and a personality profile of its members. While
      describing the devotees as having a "sensate personality," the
      authors observe that two situational factors relevant to conver-
      sion, namely the contact aspect and the sensate structure of the
      movement, must be taken into consideration. They conclude that the
      persons attracted to the movement are predisposed to accept its
      extensive and lengthy indoctrination program, but they find no
      evidence that the members are being coerced or brainwashed.

1929. Poloma, Margaret. "Pentecostals and Politics in North and Central
       America." PROPHETIC RELIGIONS AND POLITICS: RELIGION AND THE
       POLITICAL ORDER (item 358), pp. 329-52.

       Maintains that the "Charismatic Movement worldwide is character-
       ized by political passivity" (p. 346) and that this inactivity,
       particularly in the area of public issues, is actually fostered by
       Charismatic ideology. Pentecostalism tends toward a democratic-
       capitalist system, providing a private system of meaning, though it
       also has the potential of becoming a revolutionary political force.

1930. Poloma, Margaret. THE CHARISMATIC MOVEMENT: IS THERE A NEW PENTE-
       COST? Boston: Twayne Publishers, 1982. 284 pp.

       Describes the ideology and emerging institutions of the Charis-
       matic Movement and attempts to assess its potential impact on reli-
       gion and society. The theories that have been advanced to explain
       the rise of the movement are examined. The author holds that the
       movement is "a significant part of the Fourth Great Awakening,
       which could be an important agent of social change" (p. 35). It
       marks a sacralization process that coexists with current secular-
       ization trends. The author deals with the strategies of recruit-
       ment and initiation, with the relationship between the movement and
       the healing profession, the media, and the mainline churches, and
       with its views of social issues and political action. Some of the
       problems the movement faces, such as the routinization of charisma
       and internal divisions and conflicts, are discussed. A lengthy
       bibliography (pp. 249-80) is appended.

1931. Poloma, Margaret. "Christian Covenant Communities: An Adaptation
       of the Intentional Community for Urban Life." A READER IN SOCI-
       OLOGY: CHRISTIAN PERSPECTIVES. Edited by Charles P. De Santo.
       Scottsdale, PA: Herald Press, 1980, pp. 609-30.

       Examines a contemporary intentional community, a covenant commu-
       nity within the Catholic Charismatic Renewal, focusing on the
       nuclear family as the foundation for its development. The author
       describes the origin, sense of purpose, commitment to community
       goals, and socialization mechanisms of this charismatic group she
       calls "Mana Community," which was founded in the late 1960's. She
       discusses its structural features and main problems.

1932. Porterfield, Amanda. "Feminist Theology as a Revitalization Move-
       ment." SOCIOLOGICAL ANALYSIS 48 (1987): 334-44.

       Applies the anthropological theory of revitalization movements to
       explain feminist theology as a new and influential religious move-
       ment in contemporary America. The functions of this movement, its
       contexts, and the stages of development are explained. The femi-
       nist movement is a reform movement within American society and is a
       means of coping with personal and social stress. The author applies
       the stages of a revitalization movement to the feminist movement.

1933. Posner, Tina. "Transcendental Meditation, Perfect Health, and the
       Millennium." SICKNESS AND SECTARIANISM (item 643), pp. 94-112.

Describes how Transcendental Meditation is presented as a solution to all human problems leading to a perfect society. This new
movement has utopian and communitarian aspects, though it fits
better in Wilson's category of a "manipulationist" sect (see item
1023) that provides a method of salvation seen as the ability to
realize the good things of life. Transcendental Meditation has
evolved from a program to alleviate stress to a philosophical and
theological system of knowledge. It is an excellent example of a
cult that has been transformed into a sect. The Age of Enlighten-
ment--a major goal of the movement--is described. Members of this
movement believe they have discovered a method that will lead to a
breakthrough to the millennium.

1934. Poytress, Vern S. "Linguistic and Sociological Analyses of Modern
       Tongue-Speaking: Their Contributions and Limitations." WEST-
       MINSTER THEOLOGICAL JOURNAL 42 (1980): 367-88.

Distinguishes various kinds of free vocalization, including
speaking in tongues, and summarizes social-scientific research on
the subject. Whether free vocalization can be learned, whether it
can lead to a state of trance, and whether it can be considered a
language are among the issues discussed. The miraculous or divine
nature of speaking in tongues is dealt with in the context of contemporary Christian glossolalia.

1935. Preston, David L. "Meditative Ritual Practice and Spiritual Con-
       version-Commitment: Theoretical Implications Based on the Case of
       Zen." SOCIOLOGICAL ANALYSIS 43 (1982): 257-70.

Suggests that the nature of spiritual conversion and commitment
could be determined by an analysis of ritual which has "important
non-cognitive consequences." The author holds that conversion
should not be treated just as a process of learning a new role, set
of rules, or worldview. Zen, a form of Buddhist meditation that
the author himself practiced, is chosen as an example to test his
hypothesis. Scientific studies on meditation are briefly outlined
and the setting and ritual practice of meditation described from an
insider's point of view. The author concludes that: 1) meditation
has noncognitive results that affect the individual's behavior and
2) the organization of the ritual leads the practitioner to self-
actualization.

1936. Preston, David L. "Becoming a Zen Practitioner." SOCIOLOGICAL
       ANALYSIS 42 (1981): 47-55.

Studies the process of conversion and commitment to a new religious movement. The Zen setting is described and the consequences
of the meditative practices discussed. The author contends that
the practice of Zen has certain physiological results that take
place over the entire period of participation and that, therefore,
there is a learning process in which the practitioner comes into
contact with the effects of meditation. The Zen meditator learns
how to sit properly to produce the symptoms, to recognize them as
a result of sitting, and to assign meaning to them. Learning to
become a Zen meditator is compared to becoming a marijuana user.

Though it often occurs in a communal setting, Zen meditation is a
form of individual reflection, thus reducing the stress on social
relationships that are so important in many other new religious
movements.

1937.   Price, Maeve.   "The Divine Light Mission as a Social Organization."
        SOCIOLOGICAL REVIEW 27 (1979): 279-96.

        Proposes the view that the Divine Light Mission, in order to
        maintain its purity of belief, has acquired some rudimentary orga-
        nization and is moving towards the status of a sect. A brief
        account of the movement's history is presented with a special focus
        on the membership in Great Britain. Three phases in this history
        are noted: 1) rapid expansion through evangelization (conversionist
        phase); 2) conflict and recession; and 3) concentration on the
        morale and salvation of the members (the current introversionist
        phase). The mission has survived because it has continued to meet
        the fundamental psychological and social needs of its adherents.
        The author foresees a further decline in the movement unless its
        organizational problems are solved.

1938.   Price, Maeve.   "Divine Light Mission in a Festive Mood."   NEW
        SOCIETY 9 (June 1977): 500-501.

        Gives a description of the festival organized by the Divine Light
        Mission in 1977 in Great Britain. The author focuses on the type
        of people who attended and of the activities of "satsang" and "dar-
        shan." He interprets the Mission as a religious organization that
        provides "a simple creed and absolute answers, peace of mind, a
        sense of belonging, and the chance of experiencing ecstasy" (p. 501).

1939.   Quarantelli, E. L., and Dennis Wenger.   "A Voice From the Thir-
        teenth Century: The Characteristics and Conditions for the Emer-
        gence of a Ouija Board Cult."   URBAN LIFE AND CULTURE 1 (1973):
        379-400.

        Studies a Ouija Board cult as it developed, became semiinstitu-
        tionalized, and eventually dissolved. Dating the emergence of the
        Ouija Board from the middle of the nineteenth century, the authors
        suggest that the use of the board contains playful and serious
        elements. The Ouija Board cult's existence is traced to two facil-
        itating conditions common to all cults, namely structural condu-
        civeness and stress.

1940.   Ralston, Helen.   "The Typologies of Weber and Troeltsch: A Case
        Study of a Catholic Religious Group in Atlantic Canada."
        ARCHIVES DE SCIENCE SOCIALES DES RELIGIONS 50.1 (1980): 111-27.

        Argues that the contributions of Weber and Troeltsch to the
        nature and basis of religious organizations are still relevant and
        useful for understanding contemporary religious developments. The
        author illustrates this by an analysis of an experimental Catholic
        organization (which the author calls "Atlantis") that has emerged
        as a practical expression of post-Vatican II developments. She
        outlines the history and social context of the movement, which has

certain sect-like features while remaining integrated in the structure of the Catholic Church. The movement's membership, organization, authority system, and decision-making process are among the
topics covered.

1941. Rehorick, David Allen. "Subjective Origins, Objective Reality:
       Knowledge, Legitimation, and the TM Movement." HUMAN STUDIES 4
       (1981): 339-57.

       Examines the social process through which members of Transcen-
       dental Meditation construct an objective reality. The author dis-
       cusses this movement's position that knowledge is experientially
       based and points to the TM Siddhi techniques to show how meditators
       use concrete referents to describe their experiences. Transcen-
       dental Meditation has adopted socially sanctioned, scientific lan-
       guage and methods to demystify its practices and to downplay the
       spiritual aspects of the movement. He sees a gap between the inner
       core of meditators and both the average meditator and the general
       public, the former being open to those advanced techniques that
       promise a more rapid evolution of consciousness.

1942. Reidy, M. T., and James T. Richardson. "Roman Catholic Neo-Pente-
       costalism: The New Zealand Experience." AUSTRALIAN AND NEW ZEA-
       LAND JOURNAL OF SOCIOLOGY 14 (1978): 222-30.

       Summarizes the major areas of study of American neo-Pentecostal-
       ism and then compares them with data taken from the New Zealand
       scene. The author sees Catholic Pentecostalism in terms of "order
       deprivation," by which he means the the participants in the move-
       ment perceive the structure of their society as disorganized.
       Pentecostalism is "a conservative reaction to rapid social and
       cultural change" (p. 228).

1943. Remy, Jean, and Emile Servais. "The Functions of the Occult and
       Mysterious in Contemporary Society." THE PERSISTENCE OF RELI-
       GIONS (item 806), pp. 69-81.

       Places the occult "in the sociological category of illegitimate
       practices, and in the particular sector of that category where the
       illegitimate combines with the sacred" (p. 69). The authors con-
       sider the socioeconomic conditions that favor the interest in
       occult matters and argue that the occult thrives among the middle
       class in times of cultural insecurity.

1944. Rice, Berkeley. "The Pull of the Moon." SCIENCE, SIN, AND SCHOL-
       ARSHIP (item 1083), pp. 227-41.

       Reflects on the rise of the Unification Church in the United
       States and its effects on Western society. Besides a brief histor-
       ical overview, the author outlines the movement's recruiting pro-
       gram, the steps a person takes before becoming a member, and the
       familial conflicts that have ensued. Religious cults, in the
       author's view, seem to be the opiate of the people in the 1970's.

1945. Rice, Berkeley. "Messiah From Korea: Honor Thy Father Moon."
       PSYCHOLOGY TODAY 9.8 (1976): 36-47.

Describes the Unification Church, which has blossomed in a time
of recession and turmoil, as the hottest and most controversial new
religion in terms of growth, wealth, organization, and membership.
The origin of the church, its appeal, and its training program are
explored and the societal reaction to it discussed. The author
thinks that conversion, rather than brainwashing, might explain
more accurately what happens when a young recruit joins this new
religious movement.

1946. Richard, Michael P., and Albert Adato. "The Medium and the Mes-
      sage: A Study of Spiritualism at Lily Dale, New York." REVIEW OF
      RELIGIOUS RESEARCH 22 (1980): 186-97.

Presents a field study of Spiritualism in New York State. The
various classifications of Spiritualism as a cult, sect, or denomination are discussed and it is concluded that the label of religious sect is the more appropriate one. Though Spiritualism is not
strictly Christian, it does reflect some pietistic values of nineteenth-century America. The role of the medium, the character of
those who visit the church, the social stigma that spiritualists
are still subjected to, and the implication of spiritualism for
mental health are the main topics taken into consideration. The
authors' view is that spiritualism is "a syncretistic sect which is
formally and traditionally based on a belief in the possibility of
communicating with the dead, but which is substantively committed
to the development of all psychic abilities that might help oneself
and others" (p. 197).

1947. Richardson, James T. "People's Temple and Jonestown." JOURNAL FOR
      THE SCIENTIFIC STUDY OF RELIGION 19 (1980): 239-55.

Compares the People's Temple to other new religious movements.
The following eight areas in which the Temple differed from other
new religious movements are discussed: 1) its social location and
time of the beginning of the church; 2) the features of its members
and of possible recruits; 3) its organization and operation; 4) its
techniques of social control and contact with nonmembers; 5) its
methods of resocialization; 6) its ideology; 7) its general orientation; and 8) its ritual. The author finds some major differences
between Jonestown and other new religious groups and questions the
tendency in some quarters to see it as a paradigm of the new cults.
He further rejects the simplistic psychological interpretation that
Jim Jones was a crazy person and all his followers were brainwashed.

1948. Richardson, James T. "From Cult to Sect: Creative Eclecticism in
      New Religious Movements." PACIFIC SOCIOLOGICAL REVIEW 22 (1979):
      139-66.

Attempts to apply Wallis's theory (item 998) of development from
cult to sect to the Jesus Movement. After a brief description and
evaluation of Wallis's theory, the author outlines a general evolutionary model, taking into account additional factors, such as the
various ties that individual members of a cult have with outside
groups. Several bridges--ideological, experiential, behavioral,
and affective--between the cultic and sectarian experience are

also noted. The Jesus Movement made a transition from a cult-like organization to a more recognizable and acceptable form. By attempting to bring order out of chaos, a self-appointed leader often starts the movement's direction toward becoming a sect.

1949.   Richardson, James T. "The Jesus Movement: An Assessment." LISTEN-
        ING: JOURNAL OF RELIGION AND CULTURE 9.3 (1974): 20-42.

Argues that the Jesus Movement "has made some permanent and important contribution to the religious landscape and to American Culture" (p. 21). The author advances a historical and sociologi-cal explanation of the movement, drawing attention to its struc-tural cohesiveness and strain, its patterns of belief, its style of leadership and activities, and its methods of social control. He finds that American society has extended a largely favorable re-sponse to the movement, probably because the movement shares basic values and goals with society at large. He deduces from an exami-nation of the characteristics of those who join the movement that they have a "dependency-prone personality." The effects and future of the Jesus Movement are briefly discussed.

1950.   Richardson, James T. "Causes and Consequences of the Jesus Move-
        ment in the United States." THE CONTEMPORARY TRANSFORMATION OF
        RELIGION: ACTS OF THE 12th INTERNATIONAL CONGRESS ON THE SOCIOL-
        OGY OF RELIGION, The Hague, The Netherlands, 1973. Lille, France:
        C.I.S.R., 1973, pp. 257-69.

Endeavors to construct a theoretical model to explain why and how the Jesus People Movement came into being in the late 1960's in the United States. The author applies the model of "value-added per-spective," which holds that collective behavior takes place only because of the configuration of six major determinants, namely structural cohesiveness, structural strain, growth and spread of a generalized belief, precipitating factors, mobilization of partici-pants for action, and social conditions. The Jesus Movement may have lessened the social unrest so common in the 1960's and could also contribute to the status quo of society. It is postulated that the movement, which might affect both the church at large as well as the family structures, will not last long but will in the long run merge with the institutional church.

1951.   Richardson, James T., and Rex Davis. "Experiential Fundamentalism:
        Revising Orthodoxy in the Jesus Movement." JOURNAL OF THE AMERI-
        CAN ACADEMY OF RELIGION 51 (1983): 397-425.

Attempts to assess the belief structure and ideology of the Jesus Movement in terms familiar to both theology and sociology. A de-scription of the general beliefs of the movement is given and the primacy of experience is discussed. Because of the stress on the experiential dimension, the focus on fundamentalism was rather diluted in most Jesus People groups. The author describes in some detail the beliefs and practices of the Children of God (Family of Love) and analyzes their nontheological reasons for the custom of "flirty fishing."

1952. Richardson, James T., and M. T. V. Reidy. "Form and Fluidity in
      Two Contemporary Glossolalic Movements." ANNUAL REVIEW OF THE
      SOCIAL SCIENCES OF RELIGION 4 (1980): 183-220.

      Compares the Neo-Pentecostal (Charismatic) Movement with the
      Jesus Movement and concludes that the latter should be considered a
      part of the former. After drawing up the similarities and differ-
      ences between the two religious groups and discussing the mutual
      influences, the author examines their organizational forms. A
      distinction between cult, sect, and religious order in both move-
      ments is explored to specify the "locus of legitimated authority."
      Schisms, mergers, and coalitions are said to be ways in which new
      religious movements grow and change.

1953. Richardson, James T., and M. T. V. Reidy. "Neo-Pentecostalism in
      Ireland: A Comparison with the American Experience." SOCIAL
      STUDIES: IRISH JOURNAL OF SOCIOLOGY 5 (1976-77): 243-61.

      Summarizes the research conclusions on American neo-Pentecostal-
      ism under the headings: 1) social characteristics of participants;
      2) types of recruitment mechanisms; 3) sociopsychological and
      psychological correlates of members; 4) organization and function
      of movement; 6) consequences of participation; and 7) belief system.
      The Irish neo-Pentecostal movement as it developed both in the
      Republic of Ireland and in Northern Ireland is then described and
      compared with its counterpart in the United States. The authors
      find that the social-psychological and psychological correlates
      with affiliates, the movements' organization, and the consequences
      on those joining it are very similar. The religious differences
      between the two Irelands, however, have left an impact on their
      belief systems, an impact not felt in the United States.

1954. Richardson, James T., Robert B. Simmonds, and Mary W. Stewart.
      "The Evolution of a Jesus Movement Organization." JOURNAL OF
      VOLUNTARY ACTION RESEARCH 8.3-4 (1979): 93-111.

      Examines the changes that took place in one Jesus Movement group,
      exploring its goals, leadership structure, support methods, living
      arrangements, membership training and resocialization, and evangel-
      ical techniques. (This paper is derived from the authors' book on
      the Jesus People, ORGANIZED MIRACLES, item 1956.)

1955. Richardson, James T., and Mary Stewart. "Conversion Process Models
      and the Jesus Movement." AMERICAN BEHAVIORAL SCIENTIST 20 (1977):
      819-38.

      Explores various models of conversion from the data gathered in
      the authors' prolonged investigation of the Jesus Movement. The
      pioneering work of Lofland and Stark on conversion (item 215) is
      evaluated. Two other perspectives are added: 1) a "physiological"
      one that includes "the use of elements and activities to affect the
      body and mind in ways that furnish some meaning for the person"
      (pp. 823-24), and 2) a "conventional" one that is used to solve
      personal problems like getting a divorce. One situational factor,
      namely the formation of affectional ties between potential converts
      and group members, is briefly examined.

1956. Richardson, James T., Mary White Stewart, and Richard B. Simmonds.
       ORGANIZED MIRACLES: A STUDY OF A CONTEMPORARY, YOUTH, COMMUNAL,
       FUNDAMENTALIST ORGANIZATION. New Brunswick, NJ: Transaction
       Books, 1979. xxviii, 368 pp.

       Presents an in-depth study, carried out over a period of six
       years, of a major Jesus Movement group called Christ Communal
       Organization. The material is divided into five parts: 1) an out-
       line of the history and ideology of the organization and an analy-
       sis of the changes that have occurred since its foundation; 2) a
       description of the culture and daily life of its members; 3) a
       general overview of the participants, with special reference to
       their social backgrounds prior to joining the movement; 4) a criti-
       cal examination of conversion models in the social sciences; and
       5) an application of Kanter's model of commitment to this Jesus
       Movement group. One of the appendices deals at length with the
       methods employed in this research project (pp. 295-327). A bibli-
       ography is included (pp. 349-61).

1957. Richardson, James T., Mary White Stewart, and Richard B. Simmonds.
       "Conversion to Fundamentalism." SOCIETY 15.4 (1978): 46-52.

       Looks at the process whereby people join new religious movements
       and focuses specifically on one group, the Christ Communal Organi-
       zation. Several elements necessary for the formulation of a model
       of conversion are identified and discussed: prior socialization;
       perceived personal difficulties; the belief that a certain group
       may be able to help solve personal problems; the lack or loss of
       meaningful ties to society; and the development of affective ties
       between potential converts and members of a new religion. The
       authors claim that people who had no religious socialization would
       be prone to affiliate with a new religious movement "at a time when
       alternatives to problematic situations seemed unavailable" (p. 52).

1958. Rigby, Andrew, and Bryan S. Turner. "Findhorn Community, Centre of
       Light: A Sociological Study of New Forms of Religion." SOCIOLOG-
       ICAL YEARBOOK OF RELIGION IN BRITAIN 5 (1972): 72-86.

       Presents a study of a non-Christian, deinstitutionalized commune
       that is "pioneering a way of life into the New Age" (p. 76). The
       religious views of Findhorn, with its stress on mysticism, are
       described. The authors think that to categorize Findhorn as a cult
       that borrows ideas from Christian mysticism would be misleading.
       Findhorn has introversionist themes and adventist notions, the
       latter expressed in almost Zoroastrian terminology. The growth of
       a vegetable garden, the increasing number of its visitors, and the
       impressive community center all testify to the movement's success.
       The development of the belief system of, and lifestyle at, Findhorn
       are not, however, paralleled by an equal elaboration of their
       ritual system. Though the commune is a millennial sect, it does
       not have a concept of an elite and makes no attempt to convert new
       members. The authors find no sociological models that fit the new
       religion at Findhorn.

1959. Robbins, Thomas. "Reconsidering Jonestown." RELIGIOUS STUDIES
       REVIEW 15.1 (1989): 32-37.

Reviews the scholarly appraisals of Jonestown with special reference to two recent publications (see items 1662 and 1745). The
author observes that the first wave of sociological reactions to
Jonestown produced only a handful of publications. Recent studies
are attempting to analyze the events at Jonestown, stressing how
absolutely different, psychologically, politically, and religiously,
it was from Western society. The author maintains that for an
understanding of Jonestown, comparison with other movements in history is necessary. A useful, up-to-date bibliography is included.

*   Robbins, Thomas. "Religious Mass Suicides Before Jonestown: The
       Russian Old Believers." Cited above as item 1439.

1960. Robbins, Thomas, and Dick Anthony. "Getting Straight With Meher
       Baba: A Study of Mysticism, Drug Rehabilitation, and Post-Adoles-
       cent Role Conflict." JOURNAL FOR THE SCIENTIFIC STUDY OF RELI-
       GION 11 (1972): 122-40.

       Examines, in the context of a study of a Meher Baba center in
       Myrtle Beach, South Carolina, the commonly held view that certain
       new religious movements recruit people who had been drug users and
       facilitate their resocialization or termination of drug abuse. The
       authors give a brief description of the movement, whose members had
       been part of the counterculture of the 1960's and had become dis-
       satisfied with its lifestyle. Drugs, according to the authors, are
       not compatible with utopian mystics and are unable to express com-
       munal and utopian ideals in depth. The Meher Baba movement is an
       effective strategy for coping with alienation. Through its belief
       in a sacred cosmos defined in terms of an immanent divinity, the
       movement helps its members make the transition from social aliena-
       tion to social integration.

1961. Robbins, Thomas, Dick Anthony, Madeline Doucas, and Thomas Curtis.
       "The Last Civil Religion: Reverend Moon and the Unification
       Church." SOCIOLOGICAL ANALYSIS 37 (1976): 111-25.

       Argues that "a decline in the plausibility of civil religion will
       produce divisive and disciplined civil religious 'sects'" (p. 111).
       It is maintained that the Unification Church has arisen as a re-
       sponse to the cultural fragmentation of mass society. A brief
       description of the Unification Church is provided, with particular
       focus on its proselytizing techniques, communal lifestyle, sources
       of appeal, and civil religion themes. The authors consider the
       Unification Church to be a revitalization movement that stresses
       theistic beliefs and anticommunist patriotic values in an increas-
       ingly secularized cultural environment. The success of the church
       is attributed to the need for a viable Civil Religion.

1962. Rochford, E. Burke. "Factionalism, Group Defection, and Schism in
       the Hare Krishna Movement." JOURNAL FOR THE SCIENTIFIC STUDY OF
       RELIGION 28 (1989): 162-79.

       Analyzes the collective forms of disengagement from the Hare
       Krishna Movement, focusing on their temple in Los Angeles. The
       internal conflicts that followed the death of their charismatic

leader in 1977 are described. Three main areas are discussed:
1) the crisis in the Los Angeles community following his death;
2) the developments that led to factionalism and schism; and 3) the
rise and failure of "Kirtan Hall," a sectarian group founded in
1979 by ex-Hare Krishna members.

1963. Rochford, E. Burke. "Dialectical Processes in the Development of
       Hare Krishna: Tensions, Public Definition, and Strategy." THE
       FUTURE OF NEW RELIGIOUS MOVEMENTS (item 579), pp. 109-122.

       Examines the possibility that the Hare Krishna Movement might
       achieve success in the West if it develops a working relationship
       with society at large. This Hindu Movement is taken as an example
       of a deviant religion that rejects societal values and consequently
       lives in a high degree of tension with society. Three strategies
       that are now being used by the members of the Hare Krishna Movement
       to elicit a more positive public response are discussed: 1) align-
       ing the movement's goals and values with Hinduism; 2) engaging in a
       public welfare program; and 3) making attempts to inform the public
       of the movement's activities. The author believes that, since these
       efforts have not really been successful, the Hare Krishna Movement
       will have to increase its accommodation to society, thereby running
       the risk of succumbing to secularization. He thinks, however, that
       ISKCON's strategies reflect a commitment to sectarian values that
       will resist accommodation.

1964. Rochford, E. Burke. HARE KRISHNA IN AMERICA. New Brunswick, NJ:
       Rutgers University Press, 1985. xiv, 324 pp.

       Examines the growth and development of the Hare Krishna Movement
       in America. The author divides his treatment into three parts.
       The first is introductory and deals 1) with the author's research
       methods (particularly those of participant observation, surveys,
       and systematic observation) over a six-year period and 2) with a
       brief survey of the movement's history, religious beliefs, and
       organization. The second considers membership and participation.
       The final part traces the movement's development, its use of public
       places to generate resources, and the various adaptive strategies
       that its leaders and members have used to survive in the face of
       internal and external conflicts. The author's account is aimed at
       refuting the brainwashing theory of cult membership. Some specula-
       tions on the future of the movement are finally made.

1965. Rochford, E. Burke. "Recruitment Strategies, Ideology, and Organ-
       ization in the Hare Krishna Movement." SOCIAL PROBLEMS 29 (1982):
       399-410.

       Criticizes the social-psychological reasons--alienation, the
       search for meaning, deprivation, tensions, personal problems, and
       societal troubles--that have been frequently adduced to explain why
       people join new religious movements. The author prefers another
       approach that focuses on how people make contact with members of
       new movements and vice versa. Recruitment is thus seen in terms of
       interaction and relationship, rather than cognition and individual
       psychology. The ideology and organization of a movement are often

shaped by its recruitment strategies and opportunities. This line of inquiry is applied in a study of the Hare Krishna Movement. The types of contacts people have with the movement, the sociospatial dimensions of its recruitment practices, the expansion and modification of the movement, and the critical role of its sympathizers are among the areas investigated through a survey of over 200 Hare Krishna devotees. It is concluded that opportunistic exploitation of local conditions, rather than ideology or structure, is responsible for the growth of the Hare Krishna Movements in the U.S.A.

1966. Romarheim, Arild. "The Aquarian Christ." BULLETIN OF THE JOHN RYLANDS UNIVERSITY LIBRARY OF MANCHESTER 70.3 (1988): 197-207.

Examines the way the new religions (particularly Theosophy and Spiritualism) view Christ. A general picture of Christ is drawn under the following four headings: 1) the holistic framework; 2) the Easter mystery; 3) Jesus in the East; and 4) Spiritualist channels. New Age Religion offers an integration of the individual human soul and the fundamental oneness of the cosmos. It presents quite a different Jesus from that accepted and preached by traditional Christianity and thus attracts those who are opposed or hostile to the established churches.

1967. Rosch, Paul J., and Helen M. Kearney. "Holistic Medicine and Technology: a Modern Dialectic." SOCIAL SCIENCE AND MEDICINE 21 (1985): 1405-409.

Gives a comprehensive overview of two trends in American medical practice, namely the increase in medical technology and the growth of the Holistic Health Movement. The latter, in the author's estimation, is having an impact on the traditional doctor-patient relationship. The authors think that a functional synthesis of the two trends should be encouraged.

1968. Rose, Steve. JESUS AND JIM JONES. New York: Pilgrim Press, 1979. 232 pp.

Classifies religious institutions into three types of faith, namely institutional, intentional, and insular. In the latter instance, in which the People's Temple can be classified, "members are not merely giving free assent but are committing large areas of self to an authority system that is dominant and that radically confines autonomy" (p. 110). This author's tendency is to view Jim Jones as a deranged, paranoid personality. One chapter compares him to Father Divine. Documentation of Jim Jones' life and activities and references to many primary sources are included in a long series of appendices (pp. 119-227).

1969. Rose, Susan D. "Women Warriors: The Negotiation of Gender in a Charismatic Community." SOCIOLOGICAL ANALYSIS 48 (1987): 245-58.

Examines the theological view of the family of the New Christian Right, drawing data from a study of an independent charismatic group (the Covenant Community) in upstate New York. The author investigates why women and men join a religious group that stresses

traditional family and sex roles and how these norms are actually
put into practice. Women who become members of the Covenant Community hope "to surrender themselves to their men as a resolution of
conflict rather than choose to protest against the demands for
sacrifice on the part of women" (p. 251). They have chosen a religious answer to sex roles as a compromise, while insisting that men
should be actively involved in family life and child care.

1970. Rowe, Michael. "Soviet Pentecostalism: Movement for Emigration."
       RELIGION IN COMMUNIST LANDS 5.3 (1977): 170-79.

       Reflects on documents distributed by Soviet Pentecostals that
       assess the situation of Pentecostalism in the U.S.S.R. The picture
       presented is one of continuous persecution of the Pentecostal mi-
       nority since the 1930's. The conflicts between the demands of the
       communist regime and Pentecostal beliefs are also revealed.

1971. Ruhela, S. P., and Duane Robinson, editors. SAI BABA AND HIS MES-
       SAGE: A CHALLENGE TO BEHAVIORAL SCIENCES. Delhi, India: Vikas
       Publishing House, 1976. xx, 329 pp.

       Presents a collection of essays that endeavor to understand the
       phenomenon of Sai Baba from sociological, historical, and psycho-
       logical points of view. It is the editors' main contention that
       new tools to grasp the religious nature of Sai Baba's behavior and
       message are needed. Besides a biographical sketch of this contem-
       porary, popular Hindu holy man, this volume includes selections
       from Sai Baba's writings and several essays by devotees who experi-
       enced his miraculous powers. A short bibliography is added.

1972. Russell, Jeffrey Burton. "Witchcraft." THE ENCYCLOPEDIA OF RELI-
       GION (item 18), vol. 15, pp. 415-23.

       Presents a historical view of the concept of witchcraft and shows
       how simple sorcery, diabolical witchcraft, and the pagan revival of
       the twentieth century are distinct phenomena. Four schools of
       interpretation of witchcraft are distinguished, the last mentioned
       being the more commonly held view: 1) witchcraft as a superstitious
       invention of ecclesiastics who used it to augment their wealth and
       power; 2) Witchcraft as a survival of the old pagan religion of
       pre-Christian Europe; 3) witchcraft as part of the social history
       of Europe; and 4) witchcraft as an idea that has evolved through
       the centuries. The most recent revival of witchcraft, which has a
       few connections with sorcery and practically none with satanism, is
       sketched and its main features outlined. The author estimates that
       "the overall world number of witches must be fewer than a hundred
       thousand" (p. 22). Modern neopagan Witchcraft is, in the author's
       view, a naive, genial, nature religion.

1973. Saliba, John A. "The Guru: Perceptions of American Devotees of the
       Divine Light Mission." HORIZONS 7 (1980): 69-81.

       Examines the attitudes of the members of the Divine Light Mission
       towards their guru, Maharaj Ji. Three important areas are explored:
       1) the identity of the guru in the eyes of his followers; 2) the

mission that the guru claims for himself and his devotees assigned
to him; and 3) the devotional attitudes that the devotees manifest
towards him. The author attempts to present the attitudes of the
devotees (or "Premies") as a feature of the worldview they adopt
when they join the Mission. The devotion to the guru stresses the
personal dimension of religion and can be contrasted to the institutional religious forms that his followers had abandoned.

1974. Salmon, J. Warren, and Howard S. Berliner. "The Holistic Health
        Movement: Challenges to Health Care and Health Planning." AMERI-
        CAN JOURNAL OF ACUPUNCTURE 8 (1980): 197-203.

        Outlines the alternative modes of healing that are challenging
        orthodox medicine and reflects on some of the implications that
        they may have on contemporary culture. They authors sketch the
        rise of the Holistic Health Movement which includes such practices
        as acupuncture, biofeedback, bioenergetics, massage, meditation,
        rolfing, spiritual healing, and yoga. These methods differ from
        medicine in that they stress subjective experience, use a "non-
        invasive approach to therapy," and prefer a nontechnological
        perspective. People, according to the authors, have recourse to
        alternative medicines in times of crises and when they are dissat-
        isfied with modern present health care institutions. Health policy
        issues are discussed. The authors favor an integration of alterna-
        tive and holistic techniques with the mainstream medical system.
        This essay contains many references to studies on alterative heal-
        ing and holistic medicine.

1975. Samarin, William J. "Making Sense of Glossolalic Nonsense." SOCIAL
        RESEARCH 46 (1979): 88-105.

        Argues that the metalinguistics of glossolalia must be explored
        to give a complete picture of Pentecostal beliefs and behavior.
        Basing his reflections on studies on neo-Pentecostalism in the
        United States, the author thinks that glossolalia is a vocal phe-
        nomenon that can be produced by all. He further holds that it is
        a normal occurrence and does not have to be linked with altered
        states of consciousness. Various explanations of glossolalia are
        discussed and it is concluded that, since the phenomenon usually
        occurs in a social context, its social meaning determines to some
        extent both its form and usage. The need to understand how glosso-
        lalists themselves make sense of their own speech is stressed.

1976. Sawatsky, Rodney. "The Unification Church: Some Preliminary Sug-
        gestions for Historical and Social Scientific Analysis." EXPLOR-
        ING UNIFICATION THEOLOGY. Edited by Susan Hodges and M. Darroll
        Bryant. New York: Edwin Mellen Press, 1978, pp. 179-200.

        Suggests that the Unification Church can, from a social-scientif-
        ic perspective, be categorized as a sect that might become another
        denomination. The author reflects on the social implications of
        the church's doctrine that the Kingdom of God "comes through per-
        fected parents producing perfected offspring" (p. 185). Questions
        about the sociology of marriage and the possible routinization of
        charisma when the Reverend Moon dies are raised. A discussion
        between several scholars and church members is included.

1977. Schultz, Michael K. "Sociological Aspects of UFOs." ENCYCLOPEDIA
       OF UFOS (item 67), pp. 339-41.

       Points out that the UFO phenomenon has given rise to social move-
       ments and charismatic leaders and has generally elicited social and
       political debates. Various issues raised by UFOs are identified
       and the reasons why the UFO phenomenon is difficult to analyze
       explained. Three types of UFO groups have emerged: 1) religious
       cults (like the Aetherius Society and the Cosmic Circle of Fellow-
       ship); 2) platform societies that are more general groups that
       provide an opportunity for discussing UFOS (such as the Space Age
       Center and the Great Lakes Identified Flying Saucers Objects Asso-
       ciation); and 3) investigatory groups (such as the J. Allen Hynek's
       Center for UFO Studies in Chicago) that conduct serious research
       and examine claims of UFO sightings.

1978. Schwartz, Paul Anthony, and James McBride. "The Moral Majority in
       the U.S.A. as a New Religious Movement." OF GODS AND MEN (item
       550), pp. 127-46.

       Describes the worldview of a contemporary fundamentalist movement
       that focuses on the struggle with modernism and with the secular-
       ization tendencies of modern culture. The Christian New Right has,
       contrary to older forms of fundamentalism, found a compromise be-
       tween "the technical aspect of modern rationality and the eternal
       truth of biblical morality" (p. 30). Both the counterculture and
       neofundamentalism are rooted in the dissatisfaction with the
       effects of the modern secular culture and life. An appendix (pp.
       139-45) contains a "resource packet on the Christian New Right"
       that includes the names of organizations (with the locations of
       their respective headquarters, their officers, membership statis-
       tics, publications, and affiliate organizations).

1979. Scott, Gini Graham. THE MAGICIANS: A STUDY OF THE USE OF POWER IN
       A BLACK MAGIC GROUP. New York: Irvington Publishers, 1983. iii,
       219 pp.

       Explores various issues that have come to the fore with the in-
       crease in magical beliefs and practices since the early 1970's by
       examining a magical-religious group called, pseudonymously, the
       Church of Hu. The belief system, the ritual practices, and struc-
       ture and hierarchical system of this church are described. The
       social background of the members and the effect that magic has on
       their lives are discussed. The author compares the Church of Hu to
       a suburban White Witchcraft group called the Church of Empowerment.
       She maintains that magic, that is, the use of supernatural forces
       to manipulate events, increases the members' power in its various
       forms (like aggression and domination). Magic fulfills psychologi-
       cal needs, but it also endangers the interests of the group, creates
       problems with outsiders, and leads to selfishness, isolation, and
       alienation.

1980. Scott, Gini Graham. CULT AND COUNTERCULT: A STUDY OF A SPIRITUAL
       GROWTH GROUP AND A WITCHCRAFT ORDER. Westport, CT: Greenwood
       Press, 1980. xi, 213 pp.

Presents a comparative ethnography of the Inner Peace Movement
and the Aquarian Age Order, two occult groups that performed different internal and external functions while sharing some common
beliefs in paranormal forces. The author tries to show how "their
different values, norms, and behavior patterns have reflected their
respective mainstream and counterculture perspectives" (pp. 91-10).
The common monistic belief system of both groups, their daily life,
the experiences they encourage, the process of becoming a member,
and the way people leave each group are described. The differences
between them are schematically outlined. One of the appendices is
dedicated to the author's research methods. The author states that
cult involvement can be another expression of religious freedom
only if the cult does not control the individual or seems susceptible to violent excesses.

1981. Shepherd, Gordon. "The Social Construction of a Religious Proph-
       ecy." SOCIOLOGICAL INQUIRY 57 (1987): 394-414.

Discusses the prophetic claims of an individual, Charles Edward
Harris, who in August 1981 moved to Bradford (a small town in Arkansas) and proclaimed that God had given him the mission of preaching to the people when the water beneath the bridge he was painting
turned into ice on December 13. The author's interviews with
Harris are summarized and the community's interest in, and judgment
of, his self-proclaimed divine task to convert souls are recorded.
Various interpretations of Harris' behavior are examined. The
author thinks that the clergy "contributed significantly to the
community process of negotiating and constructing a plausible
conception of Harris and his activities" (p. 409). When his prophecy did not materialize, Harris interpreted his failure as a sign
that it was not God's will for the lake to freeze and that his
message had to be seen symbolically. The prophetic utterance became "objectified and internalized in the ongoing social construction of reality" (p. 413).

1982. Shinn, Larry D. "The Search for Meaning in Conversion to ISKCON."
       KRISHNA CONSCIOUSNESS IN THE WEST (item 580), pp. 118-34.

Stresses the need to take into account the basic conscious elements in all conversions and examines several instances of conversion to the Hare Krishna Movement to show how the individual's
search for meaning plays a key role in the conversion process.
Sudden conversions to the Hare Krishna Movement are rather rare.
The author attempts to understand conversion to ISKCON by using the
model of six stages of faith elaborated by James W. Fowler in his
book STAGES OF FAITH: THE PSYCHOLOGY OF HUMAN DEVELOPMENT AND THE
QUEST FOR MEANING (San Francisco: Harper and Row, 1981). Sections
of this paper are taken from Chapter Seven of the author's book on
the Hare Krishna (item 1983).

1983. Shinn, Larry D. THE DARK LORD: CULT IMAGES AND THE HARE KRISHNAS
       IN AMERICA. Philadelphia: Westminster Press, 1987. 204 pp.

Presents a study of the Hare Krishna Movement that directly re-
futes the popular cult images in America. Relying on many interviews with members of the movement, the author gives a description

and interpretation of the lifestyle of an Eastern religion that is
both ideologically and emotionally attractive. The outline of the
book is constructed in such a way as to counteract the anticult
thesis that a greedy guru and his successors seduce new converts
into complete submission by brainwashing techniques. The place of
the guru in the Hare Krishna Movement, the recruitment and socialization procedures, the daily schedule of the devotees, and the
theology of the movement are among the areas covered. Some speculations on the future of the movement are finally made.

1984. Shinn, Larry D. "The Future of an Old Man's Visions: ISKCON in the
       Twenty-First Century." THE FUTURE OF NEW RELIGIOUS MOVEMENTS
       (item 579), pp. 123-40.

       Discusses the possibilities of the success or failure of the Hare
       Krishna Movement in the context of its complex nature and the in-
       ternal and external factors that come to bear on it. The author
       holds that the various expressions of the movement in different
       countries and the independent nature of individual temples can have
       an impact on the movement's cohesion. Further, the problem of the
       transference of charismatic authority from the guru to the Govern-
       ing Body Commission has already resulted in some disputes within
       ISKCON, leading to several schisms, and raised the issue of whether
       the movement can continue to recruit sufficient members. The anti-
       cult activities as well as the support from Indian immigrants will
       also help determine the movement's future. The author maintains
       that the founder's charisma has already been effectively trans-
       ferred and institutionalized, thus assuring the movement's future.

1985. Shinn, Larry D. "Changing Patterns in ISKCON's Membership." ISKCON
       REVIEW 1.1 (1985): 24-25.

       Summarizes the results of a study on Hare Krishna Members in Amer-
       ican and in India and observes that modern devotees claim a more
       positive family experience than had been recorded by earlier re-
       searchers (Judah, item 1796, and Daner, item 1676). The author
       explains this discrepancy in terms of a "maturation of faith."

1986. Shinn, Larry D. "Conflicting Networks: Guru and Friend in ISKCON."
       RELIGIOUS MOVEMENTS: GENESIS, EXODUS, AND NUMBERS (item 692), pp.
       95-114.

       Discusses the guru-client and friendship relationships in ISKCON
       in terms of the social network elaborated by Stark and Bainbridge
       (item 969). Their theory, the author claims, supplements the
       deprivation theories of cult formation. ISKCON has endeavored to
       build communities marked by a sense of "communitas," which involves
       more than fellowship. The ideology behind the guru-disciple rela-
       tionship as well as the ritual and practice connected with it are
       described. It is argued that in spite of its flaws, this model of
       community building elicits a very high degree of commitment. The
       author concludes that "the social network theory needs to be modi-
       fied to allow for the vertical as well as the horizontal types
       of community building the guru/disciple relationship represents"
       (p. 112).

1987.   Shinn, Larry D. "Auroville: Visionary Images and Social Conse-
          quences in a South Indian Utopian Community." RELIGIOUS STUDIES
          20 (1984): 239-53.

          Attempts to answer the question of how "the 'unitary vision,'
          which the founder and charter of Auroville expounded, is related to
          the social and physical disorder that had characterized Auroville
          from its beginning" (p. 239). The underlying concepts or images
          that produced this situation in Auroville (the utopian village in
          South India that has several branches in the West) are explored.
          The very concept of such a city and the spatial and social reali-
          ties that exist are discussed. The failure of Auroville is studied
          in the context of Kanter's study of commitment and community (item
          383).

1988.   Shinn, Larry D. "The Many Faces of Krishna." ALTERNATIVES TO
          AMERICAN MAINLINE CHURCHES (item 603), pp. 113-35.

          Observes that the processes of affiliation to the Hare Krishna
          Movement are varied and that the religious and spiritual dimensions
          involved in joining and participating in the movement are often
          ignored by social scientists. The author compares his observations
          on Hare Krishna devotees with those of Judah (item 1796) and with
          converts to the Unification Church (see Baker, item 1609). The
          story of one Hare Krishna convert is related in detail to show that
          current theoretical formulations to explain why people join the
          movement are not easily applicable to individual cases. Central to
          the conversion to the Hare Krishna Movement is "the experience of a
          'relationship' with a sacred power" (p. 133).

1989.   Shupe, Anson D. "'Disembodied Access' and Technological Constraints
          on Organizational Development: A Study of Mail-Order Religion."
          JOURNAL FOR THE SCIENTIFIC STUDY OF RELIGION 15 (1976): 177-85.

          Shows how unconventional religious groups can rely on the regular
          postal service to communicate with their members and enhance their
          organizational growth. The outcome of depending on "disembodied
          access" strategies that do not use face-to-face encounters are
          explored. Information was gathered from 27 religious groups whose
          leadership communicated with the membership solely or almost exclu-
          sively through the mail. Many of these groups advertise in occult
          and astrological magazines and periodicals and tend to be syncre-
          tistic in their religious belief and practices. Such groups, in
          the author's view, resemble the cults of gnosticism or mystery
          religions of the ancient Mediterranean world. Proselytization,
          commitment maintenance, and distribution of charisma are discussed.
          It is concluded that the opportunities for organizational growth
          within these fringe religions are limited.

1990.   Simmonds, Robert B. "Conversion or Addiction: Consequences of
          Joining a Jesus Movement Group." AMERICAN BEHAVIORAL SCIENTIST
          20 (1977): 909-24.

          Explores reasons why people, many pursuing drug-oriented life-
          styles, would be converted to a fundamentalist Christian belief
          system. Previous research on the subject is outlined and the

research method used described. Basing his reflection of standard
psychological tests given to converts at different periods in their
lives, the author concludes that the personality profile of the
Jesus People is consistent with research on religious people in
general and that there is little evidence that a personal change
occurred in those who remained in the group for a while.

1991. Simmonds, Robert B., James T. Richardson, and Mary W. Harder. "The
        Jesus People: An Adjective Check List." JOURNAL FOR THE SCIEN-
        TIFIC STUDY OF RELIGION 15 (1976): 323-37.

        Presents the results of a personality assessment of a fundamen-
        talist Jesus Movement commune. The authors suggest that their
        results generally point to a "maladjustment pattern of self-
        conception." The implications of the data for the origin of the
        Jesus Movement are discussed in the context of four of Glock's
        general types of deprivations (see item 94) and the traditional
        economic deprivation theory common to sect analysis.

1992. Simmonds, Robert B., James T. Richardson, and Mary W. Harder.
        "Organizational Aspects of a Jesus Movement Community." SOCIAL
        COMPASS 21 (1974): 269-81.

        Examines the structural elements of a group within the Jesus
        Movement, identified pseudonymously as "Christ Commune." This
        study tries to understand the relationship between the movement and
        the dominant society, the attractive features of the group, and the
        prospects for its survival. A brief history of the group and a
        description of its various centers and residences and belief system
        are provided. The corporate structure of the group with its
        authoritarian system, the sex roles that the members adopt, the
        training of new recruits, and the functioning and maintenance of
        the group are among the areas covered.

1993. Simón, Armando. "The Zeitgeist of the UFO Phenomenon." UFO PHE-
        NOMENON AND THE BEHAVIORAL SCIENTIST (item 622), pp. 43-59.

        Looks at the UFO phenomenon as a cultural expression of the
        "spirit of the times" and examines how science fiction films and
        this spirit influence each other. The growth of English-language
        films on science fiction topics is traced to various social factors.

1994. Simon, Steven. "Synanon: Towards Building a Humanistic Organiza-
        tion." JOURNAL OF HUMANISTIC PSYCHOLOGY 18.3 (1978): 3-20.

        Attempts to analyze, from an insiders perspective, "the organiza-
        tional status of Synanon from the point of view of the central role
        of the Synanon game" (p. 4), that is a multidimensional approach
        designed to break down communication barriers. A historical per-
        spective, which compares the two phases of Synanon from 1958 to
        1968 and from 1968 to 1978, respectively, is given. The complex
        nature of the interaction roles in the context of organizational
        life is examined. It is argued that the lifestyle at Synanon "may
        constitute one of the few extant and viable models of the good,
        healthy, and humanistic organization" (p. 14).

1995. Singer, Barry, and Victor A. Benassi. "Occult Beliefs." AMERICAN
        SCIENTIST 69.1 (1981): 49-53.

        Maintains that the increase in the belief in occult phenomenon in
        the West is not a fad but an indication that the occult has become
        a pervasive part of Western culture. The authors do not totally
        reject the validity of such beliefs, but they think that psychologi-
        cal and sociological reasons are sufficient to explain why so many
        people are having recourse to the occult. Distortion by the media,
        deficiencies in human reasoning, social uncertainty, and recent
        developments in American religious practices are at the basis of
        occult beliefs. Shortcomings in scientific education are also
        partly responsible for the persistence of occultism, which is often
        a form of pseudoscience.

1996. Singer, Merrill. "The Social Context of Conversion to a Black
        Religious Sect." REVIEW OF RELIGIOUS RESEARCH 30 (1988): 177-92.

        Contends that the "preoccupation with the inner content of con-
        version experiences to the neglect of the context of that trans-
        formation represents a flawed turn in our efforts to understand
        conversion" (p. 177). To illustrate the importance of broader
        psychosocial, political, and economic influences on conversion the
        author studies recruitment to the Black Hebrew Israelite Nation.
        Richardson's proposal (see item 911) of "paradigm shift," a con-
        cept that downplays deprivation, is first examined and the socio-
        economic conditions of the sect members of this sect discussed. It
        it argued that the demands that conversion to this group entail
        have to be understood in the framework of racial discrimination and
        economic exploitation of Black Americans. Deprivation predisposes
        the individual to conversion, but does not determine it.

1997. Singer, Merrill. "Life in a Defensive Society: The Black Hebrew
        Israelites." SEX ROLES IN CONTEMPORARY AMERICAN COMMUNES (item
        705), pp. 45-81.

        Examines the relationship between the sexes in a Black Hebrew
        Israelite Community (which now calls itself the "Original Hebrew
        Israelite Nation") and theorizes that complete male supremacy in
        this group may actually contribute to communal cohesion. The
        author attempts to show this by an analysis of the sect's origin,
        development, and current system of organization. The following
        main features are described: 1) centralized authority; 2) communal
        living; 3) community boundaries; and 4) family organization and sex
        roles. It is argued that sex roles developed in response to sever-
        al historical factors, including the sect's migration, first to
        Liberia and then to Israel. The rigid subordination of women "was
        part of the overall defensive adaptation which emerged in the Black
        Hebrew Community in response to post-migration disunity and to the
        perception of outside opposition" (p. 77). The result was a unique
        arrangement in which polygynous marriage was combined with attempts
        to block exclusive attachments.

1998. Singer, Merrill. "The Social Meaning of Medicine in a Sectarian
        Community." MEDICAL ANTHROPOLOGY 5 (1981): 207-32.

Studies the role of medicine in the social system of the Black
Hebrews in Israel. A brief description of this sectarian community
and an analysis of its medical system, with their beliefs about the
etiology of illnesses and divine healing, are provided. The author
holds that, besides contributing to social control, the Black Hebrews' medical system has the function of maintaining and stabiliz-
ing the community "by (a) serving as an arena for the ventilation
of stress, (b) acting as a defense mechanism against the experience
of powerlessness, and (c) providing support for core values, beliefs, and statuses" (p. 208).

1999. Singer, Merrill. "The Function of Sobriety Among Black Hebrews."
JOURNAL OF OPERATIONAL PSYCHIATRY 11 (1980): 162-68.

Discusses the relationship between anxiety and abstention from
alcohol among the Black Hebrew Community in Israel. The author
briefly sketches the origins of this religious group and its migration, first to Liberia and then to Israel. Because of their strained
relationship with the Israeli government, the Black Hebrews have
become rather defensive and have developed "rigid boundaries, high
centralized authority, and a strict code of morality" (p. 164).
The high level of tension in the Black Hebrew Community has led to
its condemnation of the use of excessive alcohol rather than to an
indulgence in heavy drinking to relieve anxiety. The author argues
that the Black Hebrews prohibit drunkenness "as a means of maintaining an optimum level of community tension" (p. 167).

2000. Smith, Jonathan Z. "The Devil in Mr. Jones." IMAGINING RELIGION:
FROM BABYLON TO JONESTOWN. Chicago: University of Chicago Press,
1982, pp. 102-20.

Outlines the main facts about Jonestown from the birth of its
founder, Jim Jones, in 1931 till the tragedy in Guyana in 1978.
The author uses two models to illuminate the events that shocked
the public, namely the ancient Dionysian cult of Greece and the
Cargo cults of Melanesia.

2001. Snow, David A. "Organization, Ideology, and Mobilization: The Case
of Nichiren Shoshu of America." THE FUTURE OF NEW RELIGIOUS
MOVEMENTS (item 579), pp. 153-72.

Examines how the organizational structure and ideology of Nichiren Shoshu of America play a decisive role in recruiting members
and maintaining their high level of commitment. An overview of
this movement's historical development, goals, and values is first
provided. The means employed to generate solidarity, maintain
enthusiasm, and encourage dedication are then explored. It is
shown how Nichiren Shoshu has combined the benefits it promises
individuals with collective action for the common good. Some distinctive "ideological inducements" for joining and working for the
common cause are outlined.

2002. Snow, David A. "A Dramaturgical Analysis of Movement Accommodation:
Building Idiosyncrasy Credit as a Movement Mobilization Strategy."
SYMBOLIC INTERACTION 2 (1979): 23-44.

Discusses two problems in relation to social movements, namely
their outward-reaching strategies and tactics and their adaptation
and accommodation to the environment. The author focuses on one
contemporary religious movement, the Nichiren Shoshu of America,
and describes how it sought to establish a viable relationship with
the larger society. Nichiren Shoshu is similar to many religious
movements that stress salvation, since it teaches that personal
transformation is the key to social transformation. It differs for
other movements in that it believes that salvation can be achieved
by ritual acts and witnessing without a personal savior or messiah.
Its attempts to become a respected and legitimate organization
consisted in showing outsiders that its values and conduct were in
conformity with those of the larger society (a strategy the author
calls "dramatic ingratiation").

2003. Solomon, Trudy. "Integrating the 'Moonie' Experience: A Survey of
        Ex-Members of the Unification Church." IN GODS WE TRUST (item
        683), pp. 275-95.

        Discusses, in the context of the Unification Church, the brain-
        washing issue and looks at the processes of conversion and depro-
        gramming as the extreme points on a social-influence continuum.
        The author reports on a survey of 100 former Unification Church
        members. She explores their conversion and subsequent disaffilia-
        tion by force and their application of the brainwashing model to
        explain their original recruitment. The following types of inter-
        ventions that led to disaffiliation are examined: deprogramming;
        rehabilitation therapy; and various combinations of these methods.
        The way the ex-Moonie conceptualizes his or her experience in the
        Church depends on the method of exit and the degree of contact with
        the Anti-Cult Movement. The attitudes of ex-members who have been
        deprogrammed varies from enthusiasm to disgust.

2004. Spencer, John. "UFOs and the Public." UFOS: 1947-1987 (item 19),
        pp. 328-37.

        Points out that knowledge of UFOs has developed with the advance-
        ment in technology and can be analyzed in five areas: 1) factual
        (the evidence that UFOs provide an instance of advanced technology);
        2) factual (the suggestions that scientific research has made pro-
        gress by copying UFO techniques); 3) subterfuge (referring to
        secret UFO invasions); 4) credibility (mainly of the eyewitnesses);
        and 5) the "Hollywood" effect (implying that films about UFOs might
        actually stimulate UFO sightings).

2005. Stein, Susan. "Parapsychologists' Belief in and Explanation for
        the Unidentified Flying Object Phenomenon." JOURNAL OF OCCULT
        STUDIES 1 (1977): 158-70.

        Reports on a questionnaire sent to 20 parapsychologists aimed at
        measuring their interest in UFOs. The results were compared to
        those of a similar inquiry mailed to 140 psychologists (of which
        only 14 responded). "The results of this study do not seem to
        indicate that parapsychologists have any more or less unusual
        attitudes or experiences with UFOs than any other disinterested
        member of society" (p. 167).

2006. Stevens, Phillips. "Some Implications of Urban Witchcraft Beliefs."
       NEW YORK FOLKLORE 8.3-4 (1982): 29-42.

       Reflects on some of the social, legal, and ethical implications
       of Witchcraft beliefs and practices in contemporary urban areas in
       Western society. The author holds that both sorcery (evil magic)
       and witchcraft (sympathetic magic) are basically sociological prob-
       lems and, though widespread, tend to remain secretly practiced. He
       expounds the common anthropological view that social stress tends
       to contribute to the increase of witchcraft beliefs and practices
       among culturally marginal people. Specific cases are mentioned to
       illustrate the legal and clinical implications of witchcraft.

2007. Steward, James R. "Cattle Mutilations: An Episode of Collective
       Delusion." ZETETIC 1.2 (1977): 55-66.

       Provides a detailed account of a rash of cattle mutilations in
       Northeast Nebraska and Eastern South Dakota in the fall of 1974.
       These mutilation stories were recorded at a period when UFO and
       monster sightings were also being reported. Several explanations
       of the mutilations are briefly considered: 1) they were the work
       of a Satanic cult; 2) they were experiments being carried out by
       extraterrestrial visitors; and 3) they were perpetrated by small
       animal predators. The author explains the episodes as "a classic
       case of mild mass hysteria" (p. 59). Several factors, like the
       plight of the cattle market at the time and the lack of informa-
       tion, aggravated the problem and encouraged belief that Satanic
       cults or UFO people were responsible for the slain cattle.

2008. Stiebing, William H. ANCIENT ASTRONAUTS, COSMIC COLLISIONS, AND
       OTHER POPULAR THEORIES ABOUT MAN'S PAST. Buffalo, NY: Prometheus
       Books, 1984. viii, 207 pp.

       Describes popular theories about the Deluge, the existence of
       Atlantis, cosmic catastrophes, ancient astronauts, the mysteries of
       the Egyptian pyramids, and early voyages to the Americas. These
       accounts about human history are widely held by those who are in-
       volved in the occult or in the New Age Movement. They contain
       common features like an antiestablishment rhetoric that attacks
       particularly professional scholars. These "popular theories func-
       tion the way myths do in primitive cultures" (p. 171). They pro-
       vide simple answers to unresolved issues to those people who have
       "a low tolerance of psychological discomfort." They are popular
       because of their antiestablishment and antiintellectual rhetoric.
       And they also bind those who adhere to them into a special commu-
       nity that feels persecuted by those scholars who discard their
       views as unrealistic.

2009. Stone, Donald. "The Charismatic Authority of Werner Erhard."
       MILLENNIALISM AND CHARISMA (item 711), pp. 141-75.

       Provides a brief account of the format and content of the EST
       training program and then examines the source of the charisma of
       the founder of EST. The following charismatic qualities of Erhard
       are mentioned: 1) magical power; 2) revelations; 3) exemplary

prophet; 4) heroism; 5) iconoclasm; 6) acknowledging his followers
by pointing out their individual successes in, and contributions
to, the movement; 7) teaching them how to validate their miracles.
Some of the structures of EST are examined. EST is depicted as a
bureaucratic game, espousing both social accommodation and individual challenge. Followers of Erhard interpret their involvement as
important for both their immediate and ultimate welfare--a goal
constantly encouraged both in the course of the EST program and in
Erhard's talks.

2010. Stone, Donald. "Social Consciousness in the Human Potential Move-
       ment." IN GODS WE TRUST (783), pp. 215-27.

       Inquires whether the Human Potential Movement, which stresses
       that people are responsible for their lives, "contributes to social
       isolation by converting public issues into private failings" (p.
       216). The results of a survey of attitudes about poverty and fail-
       ure are recorded with special reference to EST graduates. The
       author finds that involvement in political and community affairs
       among those who participate in the Human Potential Movement tends
       to be rather low. His findings, however, do not indicate that
       these individuals are less sensitive to social issues. He thinks
       that the Human Potential notion of change is somewhat mystical,
       thus deemphasizing resistance and striving and stressing personal
       experience. To what extent this could lessen social awareness is
       not clear.

2011. Stone, Donald. "The Human Potential Movement." SOCIETY 15.4
       (1978): 66-68.

       Points out that the quest for self-awareness has become the new
       panacea for the problems of our age. Those new movements that
       stress experiences, like EST, Transactional Analysis, Transcenden-
       tal Meditation, and Zen, have been accused of contributing "to
       social isolation by converting public issues into private feelings"
       (p. 66). The attitudes of EST graduates, particularly their view
       of moral responsibility, are explored. The author concludes that
       there is no evidence that these movements lead to social irrespon-
       sibility. He has reservations, however, about the ability of some
       human potential groups like EST to provide a workable ethic for the
       present cultural conditions in the West.

2012. Stone, Donald. "The Human Potential Movement." THE NEW RELIGIOUS
       CONSCIOUSNESS (item 614), pp. 52-77.

       Overviews the many growth movements, body-awareness techniques,
       Eastern spiritual disciplines, and Western-style mind training that
       many middle-class Americans are turning to for a more direct expe-
       rience of living. The growing emphasis on transpersonal and spiri-
       tual experiences has been partly due to Eastern-oriented techniques
       like Psychosynthesis, EST, and Arica. The participation rates in
       these movements in the San Francisco Bay Area are surveyed and the
       varieties of attraction to these groups are discussed. The author
       thinks that there are also some structural features of the Human
       Potential groups that are appealing, such as the relatively low

level of commitment, the stress on personal authority, and the more
respectable position that these groups have in society. Those who
join the Human Potential Movement are seeking a way out of a highly
rationalized and technological society.

2013. Stones, Christopher R. "The Jesus People: Fundamentalism and
        Changes in Factors Associated With Conservatism." JOURNAL FOR
        THE SCIENTIFIC STUDY OF RELIGION 17 (1978): 155-58.

Administers psychological tests of religious beliefs to differen-
tiate Biblical fundamentalists and to measure conservative factors
like attitudes towards church authority. The author concludes that
Jesus People tend to become more fundamentalist in their interpretation of the Bible, but less conservative in general. They prefer
to submit to the Bible rather than to church authority. Compared
to members of mainline churches, the Jesus People are less militaristic, less ethnocentric, and less racially prejudiced.

2014. Story, Ronald D. "Von Daniken's Golden Gods." ZETETIC (Fall/
        Winter 1977): 22-35.

Challenges von Daniken's theory that superbeings from outer space
bestowed the rudiments of human culture and civilization. The
author offers some explanation of why von Daniken's theory is so
popular. It is suggested that his views are attractive because
they do away with the concept of human evolution, they support the
common belief that God is a superbeing faraway among the stars,
they reconcile modern science with a literal interpretation of the
Bible, and they reinforce the theme of salvation.

2015. Story, Ronald D. THE SPACE-GODS REVEALED: A CLOSE LOOK AT THE
        THEORIES OF ERICH VON DANIKEN. New York: Harper and Row, 1976.
        xviii, 139 pp.

Presents a critical scientific response to von Daniken's theory
that intelligent beings from outer space came to earth many millen-
nia ago and created human beings in their likeness. The interpretation of the archaeological data brought forth to buttress this
view is examined and refuted. The author interprets von Daniken
reconstructions as a new mythology couched in the symbols of space
technology. This new mythology has the function of helping people
"adapt to a sometimes confusing and mystifying world" (p. 119). An
appendix by Robert S. Ellwood reviews the literature on UFOs and
the Bible (pp. 121-25).

2016. Strauss, Roger. "Scientology 'Ethics': Deviance, Identity, and
        Social Control in a Cult-Like Social World." SYMBOLIC INTER-
        ACTION 9 (186): 67-82.

Presents the view that Scientology "not only shares but glorifies
the essential values, motives, and rationality of American capitalist society" (p. 68). Its system of ethics (social control) insti-
tutionalizes a contextual model linking deviance, identity, and a
reference group. Relying on both his two-year experience as a

Scientologist and his training as a sociologist, the author aims at understanding rather than debunking Scientology. The following areas are briefly outlined: the culture of Scientology; its organization and internal social structure; and its method of social control, which includes a criminal justice system. The similarities and differences between Scientology ethics and the interactionist theory are discussed.

2017. Stupple, David. "The 'I AM' Sect Today: An Unobituary." JOURNAL OF POPULAR CULTURE 8 (1975): 897-905.

Gives a brief historical outline of the I Am Movement and argues that it is currently showing strong signs of vitality and experiencing a revitalization in the form of a splinter group known as the Summit Lighthouse currently under the leadership of Elizabeth Claire Prophet. The structure and dynamics of the I Am Movement are examined. A short description of the Summit Lighthouse is provided and the two groups are compared. The author remarks that the success the Summit Lighthouse is having shows how "the extravagant claims of the I Am are still marketable today when delivered in effective contemporary media" (p. 903).

2018. Stupple, David, and Abdollah Dashti. "Flying Saucers and Multiple Realities: A Case Study in Phenomenological Theory." JOURNAL OF POPULAR CULTURE 11 (1977): 479-93.

Studies a mail order firm, the Saucerian Press, which disseminates literature on flying saucers. This press has helped in the proliferation and elaboration of folklore on UFOs and functions as an information center for flying saucer hobbyists. A short history of the press since its foundation in 1959 by Gray Baker is given. The author explores the demographic features of the Press's customers, their beliefs, and the extent of their integration into a community of believers in UFOs. Various beliefs about flying saucers are examined. Those who buy the literature of the Saucerian Press are not members of a cult since they are bound together only by this one common source of information. Flying saucer folklore, according to the authors, is a "subuniverse of experience" and not a religion.

2019. Sugarman, Barry. "Reluctant Converts: Social Control, Socialization, and Adaptation in Therapeutic Communities." SECTARIANISM: ANALYSES OF RELIGIOUS AND NON-RELIGIOUS SECTS (item 713), pp. 141-61.

Examines the "Concept Houses," that is, those therapeutic, community-oriented drug dependency treatment programs in the United States. Several similarities between these groups and sects are noted, namely: 1) a total dedication to the moral and spiritual improvement of the members; 2) the use of public confession and mutual criticism; 3) a hierarchy of authority based on moral or spiritual superiority; and 4) methods for punishing deviants and for generating ecstatic states. Social control and social life inside one Concept House are described with specific reference to the boundaries separating the house from the outside world, to its

ideology in which its members are indoctrinated, and to the treatment of confrontation and conversion. Concept Houses, like many
sects, perform the function of a temporary haven for those who will
eventually join the mainstream society.

2020. Swallow, D. A. "Ashes and Powers: Myth, Rite, and Miracle in an
       Indian God-Man's Cult." MODERN ASIAN STUDIES 16 (1982): 123-58.

Presents a study of the Sathya Sai Baba Movement that has made
its way from India to the West. A lengthy biography of the guru is
drawn, tracing the origins of the movement and the magical powers
he claims to possess. Sathya Sai Baba's belief that he is the
reincarnation of Sai Baba (an Indian holy man who died in 1918) and
the incarnation of several Hindu gods, particularly Siva, are discussed in the context of Hindu mythology and ritual. The author
explains the rise of this new religious movement in India as a
consequence of the concerns with purity and pollution in a culture
where modern changes are challenging the traditional views of the
caste system. To his Eastern devotees, Sathya Sai Baba stresses the
need to return to the service of "dharma," while to his Western
followers he represents a critique of the rational and empirical
tradition of Western culture.

2021. Taylor, David. "Becoming a New People: Recruitment of Young Ameri-
       cans into the Unification Church." MILLENNIALISM AND CHARISMA
       (item 711), pp. 177-230.

Presents a study of the recruitment practices of the Unification
Church in the San Francisco Bay Area in California. The author
employed the participant-observation method in his study of the
creative community project which, though an integral part of the
church, is not advertised as such. After a brief description of
the church, the initial recruitment procedures--contacting prospective candidates in public, inviting them to dinner, and encouraging
them to a weekend of retreat and activities--are outlined. Group
activities, expressions of love toward prospects, control of communication, propaganda lectures, and testimonies are all employed
in the process leading to final commitment. The author summarizes
the efforts of the Unification Church members as follows: they must
"1) present a sincere dramatic performance; 2) establish a trust of
potential members; 3) legitimize social control; 4) provide an
exhilarating atmosphere; and 5) allow participants to act out the
role of membership" (p. 224).

2022. Taylor, Donald. "Charismatic Authority in the Sathya Sai Baba
       Movement." HINDUISM IN GREAT BRITAIN: THE PERPETUATION OF RELI-
       GION IN AN ALIEN CULTURAL MILIEU. Edited by Richard Burghart.
       London: Tavistock Publications, 1987, pp. 119-33.

Examines the "relationship between institutional authority in the
Sai Movement and the gratuitous power of its founder and leader
Sathya Sai Baba" (p. 119). The author discusses the interrelationship between two kinds of authority, namely that of Sai Baba's
charismatic leadership and of the organizational structure of the
movement itself. He maintains that, while Sai Baba's charisma is

taken for granted, his authority is open to routinization leading
to the eventual ascendancy of legal rational authority. The two
main activities of the movement, namely devotion (directed towards
the guru) and service (an extension of his ministry of healing),
are described. It is shown that Sai Baba's authority, although it
enjoys primacy among his devotees, is not immune from both internal
and external challenges.

2023. Taylor, Donald. "Sathya Sai Baba Movement in Britain." THE NEW
       EVANGELISTS (item 587), pp. 77-93.

       Traces the origin of the Sathya Sai Baba Movement in India and
       its arrival in Great Britain in 1966 through the activity of a Mr.
       and Mrs. Sitaram who became the prototype devotees of the Indian
       guru. The process by which one becomes a devotee is described. In
       Britain, the movement is well organized and has over 50 centers.
       Two types of devotees are distinguished, namely Hindus and non-
       Hindus. The former, coming from South India and Sri Lanka, found
       the movement a haven against the threat of the Western seculariza-
       tion and a means of giving them identity and solidarity in a for-
       eign land. The latter form part of the cultic movement that has
       spread to the West. The introduction of organization controls,
       however, led to a shift in the recruitment of non-Hindu devotees by
       1975. This shift led to changes in the aims and methods of the
       Sathya Sai Baba Movement in Britain, changes which transformed the
       movement from being Hindu-oriented to adopting a more inclusive
       orientation with less explicitly Hindu activities.

2024. Taylor, Rosemary C. R. "Alternative Medicine and the Medical En-
       counter in Britain." ALTERNATIVE MEDICINES (item 687), pp. 191-
       228.

       Examines popular alternative medical treatments, such as acupunc-
       ture, chiropractic, homeopathy, naturopathy, and psychic healing,
       with the aim of discovering why they have aroused so much interest
       in Western culture in the last decade. The author thinks that the
       growth of these medicines in Great Britain and in the United States
       is an ambiguous phenomenon. Though the number of people having
       recourse to them has increased and some legal obstacles to their
       growth have been removed, it is still hard to determine whether
       they form a unified medical system. Their popularity is related
       to the changing nature of the medical encounter, which is weak in
       patient participation and which has shown signs of deterioration.

2025. Techter, David. "PSI: Past, Present, Future." JOURNAL OF POPULAR
       CULTURE 5 (1971): 647-54.

       Distinguishes four distinct traditions or orientations among
       those who experience paranormal phenomena (PSI): 1) the path of
       spiritual unfoldment (including such groups as Yoga societies, Zen
       Buddhism, the Spiritual Frontiers fellowship, and the Association
       for Research and Enlightenment); 2) Spiritualism; 3) Occultism; and
       4) psychic research. The explorations in the last three mentioned
       areas are surveyed. In spite of the failure of parapsychology to
       win scientific endorsement, the author thinks that the interest in
       PSI and in its practical applications will continue to grow.

2026. Thompson, Judith, and Paul Heelas. THE WAY OF THE HEART: THE RAJ-
       NEESH MOVEMENT. Wellingborough, England: Aquarian Press, 1986,
       139 pp.

       Presents an ethnographic account of a controversial religious
       movement, namely that founded by Bhagwan Shree Rajneesh. After a
       historical overview of the movement from the birth of its leader in
       1931 up to early 1986, the author describes its radical teaching,
       its therapeutic techniques, and its forms of meditation, especially
       the Dynamic Meditation, all of which are intended to transform a
       person into a mature and balanced individual. The experience of
       becoming a follower of Rajneesh is recorded through interviews with
       several devotees. An account of the daily life in the various
       communities is given and the differences between the British and
       Rajneeshpuram settlements noted. In discussing Rajneesh's ideas on
       freedom, the author expresses the view that members of Rajneesh-
       puram had become "too conditioned." The conflicts brought about by
       this guru and the lifestyle he promoted are examined.

2027. Tipton, Steven M. "Making the World Work: Ideas of Social Respon-
       sibility in the Human Potential Movement." OF GODS AND MEN (item
       550), pp. 165-85.

       Suggests that EST is important to some of those who participate
       in its activities because it transmits to them a system of moral
       norms, values, and attitudes. The author describes the EST ideol-
       ogy of transforming the institutions of socialization and its
       modest millenarian goals. EST places responsibility squarely on
       the individual. Since (like Buddhism) it teaches a monist, univer-
       sal philosophy, its stress on individual identity and moral respon-
       sibility is expressed in terms of "service" to all humanity.

2028. Tiryakian, Edward A. "Toward a Sociology of Esoteric Culture."
       AMERICAN JOURNAL OF SOCIOLOGY 78 (1972): 491-512.

       Starts by examining the sociological literature on the occult
       revival in modern society, particularly among the youth of the
       counterculture, and points out that the interest in the occult goes
       against the secularization process. The revival of the occult can
       be interpreted as a spiritual reaction against contemporary ration-
       alistic society and as a new religious and cultural revitalization.
       Esoteric culture may function as a vehicle of social change and as
       a major inspirational source of cultural innovation.

2029. Tobey, Alan. "The Summer Solstice of the Health-Happy-Holy Organi-
       zation." THE NEW RELIGIOUS CONSCIOUSNESS (item 614), pp. 5-30.

       Describes an Eastern religious movement in the United States,
       namely the Healthy, Happy, Holy Organization (known as 3HO) of Yogi
       Bhajan, the roots of which lie in Kundalini and Tantric Yoga and in
       the Sikh religion. A historical background to the movement is
       provided and a day in the life of a member described. The essay
       focuses on the organization's most important national gathering,
       the Summer Solstice Sadhana held in the San Francisco Bay Area in
       1973. This meeting is aimed at strengthening the members' personal

commitment to the work of the movement. The people who join 3HO
are surveyed in order to determine their reasons for joining, the
state of their present commitment, and their change of lifestyle.
The idealistic ethic of the movement is explained and its prospects
briefly discussed.

2030. Truzzi, Marcello. "Astrology as Popular Culture." JOURNAL OF
      POPULAR CULTURE 8 (1975): 906-11.

      Comments on the rise of interest in astrology in the United States
      since the late 1960's. The author thinks that the popularity of
      astrology is due to the fact that it is a belief system that meets
      the needs of many people. Two factors in particular account for
      its present popularity: 1) "its ancient and public-domain character
      which allows for the free and widespread dissemination of its ideas
      and symbols;" and 2) "its current separation from religion" (p.
      908). Various levels of astrological beliefs are distinguished.
      For those deeply involved, astrology requires less scientific veri-
      fication and provides a general metaphysical worldview.

2031. Truzzi, Marcello. "Towards a Sociology of the Occult: Notes on
      Modern Witchcraft." RELIGIOUS MOVEMENTS IN CONTEMPORARY AMERICA
      (item 727), pp. 628-45.

      Discusses the occult as a subdivision of the sociology of knowl-
      edge. Three broad types of occultists or levels of involvement are
      distinguished: 1) concern with the study of anomalies or mysterious
      occurrences with minimal involvement; 2) concern with "some inex-
      plicable relationships between events" (p. 632), relationships that
      are present but unknown to normal science; and 3) concern with the
      belief in, and study of, scientifically anomalous events and rela-
      tionships. The last mentioned is accompanied with a belief system
      such as Witchcraft or Satanism. Some analytical dimensions of
      modern Witchcraft are then discussed. The definition of Witch-
      craft, its moral, ontological aspects, and its legitimate standing
      are among the areas covered.

2032. Truzzi, Marcello. "Nouveau Witches." HUMANIST 34.5 (1974): 13-15.

      Examines the modern interest in Witchcraft and distinguishes
      between magical technology (or esoteric magical practices) from
      Witchcraft as a religion. Solitary and group-affiliated Witches
      differ in that the former practice magic on their own, the latter
      do so with others in a coven to which they belong. There are White
      and Black Witches, the latter being often identified as Satanists.
      The author thinks that White Witchcraft has had its peak while
      prospects for the growth of the Anton LaVey's Church of Satan look
      promising.

2033. Truzzi, Marcello. "The Occult Revival as Popular Culture: Some
      Random Observations on the Old and Nouveau Witch." SOCIOLOGICAL
      QUARTERLY 13 (1972): 16-36.

      Reflects on the rising interest in occult matters and on several
      interpretations that see this rise as one "of great cultural signi-
      ficance and as reflecting serious social conflicts and strains of

macroscopic import" (p. 16). Five major foci of occult interest
are mentioned, namely: 1) astrology; 2) Witchcraft and Satanism; 3)
parapsychology and extrasensory perception; 4) Eastern religious
thought; and 5) esoteric beliefs (such as in monsters and UFOs).
The first two areas mentioned above are explored in some detail.
The various levels of involvement in astrology and types of Witches
and Satanists are explained. The author thinks that the interest
in astrology and Satanism represents not a "search for a new spiritual meaning, but only a disenchantment with religious orthodoxy"
(p. 28).

2034. Truzzi, Marcello. "Definitions and Dimensions of the Occult: To-
       wards a Sociological Perspective." JOURNAL OF POPULAR CULTURE 5
       (1971): 635-46.

       Discusses various definitions of the occult, which is usually
       equated by scientists with mystical and antinaturalistic world-
       views. The occult deals with anomalous phenomena that contradict
       common sense or institutionalized knowledge. Five major dimensions
       of the occult are discussed: 1) the substance of occult beliefs; 2)
       the source of the occult label; 3) the authority of occult claims;
       4) the source of occult knowledge; and 5) the functions of occult-
       ism. No clear, simple analysis of the social and psychological
       functions of the occult emerges, though its role as mediator be-
       tween science and religion is fairly obvious.

2035. Tysol, Maryon. "The Great British Witch Boom." NEW SOCIETY 70
       (October 18, 1984): 92-94.

       Describes briefly contemporary Witchcraft, a pagan religion that
       involves the use of ritual magic. The author believes that Witch-
       craft in England is not restricted to a few villages and to the
       lunatic fringe. She adopts the psychological perspective that
       contemporary Witchcraft appeals to people who have lost control of
       their own lives. Witchcraft is a social phenomenon that points to
       psychological needs that British society is failing to meet.

2036. Van der Lans, Jan, and Frans Derks. "Premies versus Sannyasins."
       UPDATE: A QUARTERLY JOURNAL OF NEW RELIGIOUS MOVEMENTS 10.2
       (1986): 19-27.

       Compares two Eastern religious movements, namely the Divine
       Light Mission and Rajneeshism, and sees them as excellent examples
       of successive phases of the youth culture. Both movements have an
       Indian guru as their object of devotion and both require the rejec-
       tion of one's previous lifestyle. In spite of similar doctrines,
       the religion of Rajneesh is more radical in the separation of its
       members from the dominant worldview, incorporates various forms of
       meditation, and is more interested in sexuality, bodily experiences,
       and social interaction. These differences have led to the recruit-
       ment of members from different populations. The educational level,
       religious background, and preconversion experiences of converts to
       both groups are compared. The "premies" (devotees) of Guru Maharaj
       Ji of the Divine Light Mission tend to pursue the path of individ-
       ual experience, while the "sannyasins" of Bhagwan Shree Rajneesh
       prefer the path of interpersonal relationship.

2037. Van Fossen, Anthony B. "How Do Movements Survive Failures of
       Prophecy?" RESEARCH IN SOCIAL MOVEMENTS, CONFLICTS, AND CHANGE
       10 (1988): 193-212.

       Examines a contemporary French Messianic Movement called "The
       Universal Christian Church," founded by Georges Roux in the early
       1950s. The author's intention is to explain how such religious
       movements survive prophetic failure and deny, forget, or reinter-
       pret contradictory events. He finds the theory elaborated by Fes-
       tinger and his fellow researchers (item 91) inadequate and reduc-
       tionistic and turns to anthropological sources for insight into new
       theories. He suggests that, in order to survive failure, a move-
       ment must become more hierarchical, demote unreliable believers, and
       elevate the prophet's original disciples to higher roles and
       statuses within the movement. Contradictions are met by changing
       ethical, epistemological, historical, and spatial awareness.

2038. Van Fossen, Anthony B. "Prophetic Failure and Moral Hierarchy: The
       Origin of a Contemporary French Messianic Movement." UNDER THE
       SHADE OF A COOLIBAH TREE: AUSTRALIAN STUDIES IN CONSCIOUSNESS.
       Edited by Richard A. Hutch and Peter G. Fenner. Lanham, NY:
       University of America Press, 1984, pp. 239-78.

       Offers some theoretical speculations on the relationship between
       the failure of prophecy and a movement's change and adaptation in
       the context of a French Messianic Movement, which stresses nonmedi-
       cal healing. Four phases of the movement are outlined: 1) healing
       (Christmas 1953 to September 1953); 2) spirit communication (Octo-
       ber 1953 to July 1961); 3) quest for immortality (July 1961 to
       Christmas 1979); and 4) pursuit of universal artistic creativity
       (Christmas 1979 to the present time). The author points out that
       the movement created "an evergoing moral hierarchy which served to
       excuse crucial failures of its healing prophecy" (p. 245). Moral
       deficiency and culpability were used to explain both disease and
       the failure to cure it. Five phases in the movement's moral hier-
       archy, each with its own religious symbolism, actions, and social
       organization, are outlined. The bibliography contains many primary
       sources in French.

2039. Van Fossen, Anthony B. "Oral Tradition, Myth, and Social Struc-
       ture: Historical Perception in a French Messianic Movement."
       SOCIAL ANALYSIS No. 4 (September 1980): 38-50.

       Examines the French Messianic Movement founded by Georges Roux
       and focuses on the process of creating oral and mythical tradi-
       tion. A summary of the movement's origin and development is given
       and an attempt to understand it in terms of anthropological theory
       made. The author provides an account of the movement's view of its
       own history. Relying particularly on the work of Mary Douglas, he
       discusses the conditions under which oral tradition emerges. The
       bibliography includes references published in French newspapers and
       magazines.

2040. Volinn, Ernest. "Eastern Meditation Groups: Why Join?" SOCIOLOGI-
       CAL ANALYSIS 46 (1985): 147-56.

Studies a Yoga ashram in New England and concentrates on how
people are attracted to join it. The author observes that members
are discouraged from developing interpersonal relationships with
outsiders. New members are drawn into the ashram not because of
some organizational effort, but rather because individuals decide
to do so on their own. Several reasons that led individuals to
commit themselves without inducement from ashram members are explored: 1) the predispositions, namely a mental and psychotherapeutic orientation and structural availability; 2) the need to
break with their present condition, especially that of drug dependency; and 3) the search for an alternative "high" experience.

2041. Wagner, Jon. "Male-Supremacy: Its Role in a Contemporary Commune
        and Its Structural Alternatives." INTERNATIONAL REVIEW OF MODERN
        SOCIOLOGY 6.1 (1976): 173-80.

        Investigates a utopian commune (called pseudonymously "Haran")
        in Ohio that was founded by a religious visionary and charismatic
        leader. The patriarchal system of the commune is described. The
        author points out that the misogynist, male-supremacist ideology
        of this group "actually helps keep the community together" and is
        also one possible way "of discouraging two-person intimacy and thus
        contribute to group cohesiveness" (p. 180).

2041. Wagner, Melinda Bollar. METAPHYSICS IN MIDWESTERN AMERICA. Colum-
        bus: Ohio State University Press, 1983. xi, 229 pp.

        Presents an anthropological study of the Spiritual Frontiers
        Fellowship in the mid-1970's. After a brief overview of the new
        metaphysics, the author describes this fellowship, which flourishes
        mainly in the Midwest and attracts largely middle-class and
        middle-aged people. The ideology and goals of the group and its
        recruitment practices are among the topics dealt with. The primary
        function of the Spiritual Frontiers Fellowship is "the alleviation
        of individual meaninglessness." The Fellowship is a mirror of
        American culture, reflecting both individualism and pragmatism.

2043. Wagner, Melinda Bollar. "Spiritual Frontiers Fellowship." ALTER-
        NATIVES TO AMERICAN MAINLINE CHURCHES (item 603), pp. 45-68.

        Explores the Spiritual Frontiers Fellowship, a metaphysical orga-
        nization that, unlike most cults, does not offer its members a
        sense of community, but provides a flexible "meaning" in a changing
        world. This movement encourages not only spiritual growth, but also
        psychic phenomena and spiritual healing. A brief history of the
        movement and its main tenets are provided. The movement's stress
        on individual autonomy and self-realization is underscored. Its
        functions are to alleviate individually felt meaninglessness by the
        pursuit of self-realization, to dispel one's sense of guilt, and
        to deal with hypertension and drinking. The movement mirrors two
        common attractive features of contemporary American cults, namely
        individualism and pragmatism.

2044. Walker, Andrew. "Fundamentalism and Modernity: The Restoration
        Movement in Britain." STUDIES IN FUNDAMENTALISM. Edited by
        Lionel Caplan. London: Macmillan, 1987, pp. 195-210.

Examines the emergence of a new fundamentalism or "Restoration-
ism" in Great Britain, which unlike its earlier manifestations, is
linked to the middle class. The author sees the Restoration Movement as part of a broader revival, the "House Church Movement."
The belief and ritual of the Restoration Movement, which can be
classified as a sect, are described. In spite of accusations that
the movement is a brainwashing cult, the author thinks that it is a
form of benevolent paternalism rather than a totalitarian system.
He attempts to understand the movement in relation to evangelical
revivalism and the Catholic Charismatic Renewal.

2045. Walker, Andrew. RESTORING THE KINGDOM: THE RADICAL CHRISTIANITY OF
      THE HOUSE CHURCH MOVEMENT. London: Hodder and Stoughton, 1985.
      303 pp.

      Studies the House Church Movement or the Kingdom People or the
      Restoration. Adopting a sociological perspective, the author dis-
      cusses the origin of the movement, its links with the Charismatic
      Renewal and with some Baptist and Pentecostal denominations, and
      its split into two groups in 1976. He describes the movement's
      radical principles, its social structure, and the religious life of
      its members. The sectarian features of the House Church Movement
      are then examined in the light of Wilson's study of sects (item
      1023). Both the Catholic Apostolic Church and the Christian Breth-
      ren can be viewed as forerunners of the Restoration. Several per-
      sistent attacks against the movement are outlined. The author
      thinks that it will eventually merge with classical Pentecostalism.

2046. Walker, Andrew. "From Revival to Restoration: The Emergence of
      Britain's New Classical Pentecostalism." SOCIAL COMPASS 32
      (1985): 261-71.

      Examines the emergence of a new sect, namely the House Church
      Movement, that is sometimes wrongly identified with the Charismatic
      Renewal. The author maintains that the former belongs both theo-
      logically and sociologically to classical Pentecostalism. The two
      restoration groups that have emerged in Great Britain since the
      early 1970's are described as indigenous sectarian movements. Their
      distinctive doctrine of restorationism and their sectarian signifi-
      cance are examined. Restorationism, it is held, is "a sensible
      sociological method" of resisting the perceived watering-down of
      faith in modern times.

2047. Walker, Andrew. "Pentecostal Power: The 'Charismatic Renewal Move-
      ment' and the Politics of Pentecostal Experience." OF GODS AND
      MEN (item 550), pp. 89-108.

      Charts the emergence of the neo-Pentecostal Movement in the West,
      particularly in Great Britain, and points out its main features and
      its similarities to classical Pentecostalism. Three stages in the
      Charismatic Renewal are identified: 1) Anarchic Pentecostalism
      (1965-1975); 2) Consolidation, Broadening Horizons, and Official
      Recognition (1975-1980); and 3) Factions and Fractions (1980-1985).
      The author thinks that the neo-Pentecostal Movement in Great Brit-
      ain will continue to decline, both in the number of participants

and in their fervor. It will split into many factional groups and
many of its members will follow the path of itinerant evangelists
or become involved in the House Church Movement. An outline of the
main charismatic views on Christian life, secular society, and the
future of Christianity as they changed over the three stages of
development is provided.

2048. Walker, Andrew. "Sociological and Lay Accounts as Versions of
    Reality: Choosing Between Reports of the 'Charismatic Renewal
    Movement' Amongst Roman Catholics." THEORY AND SOCIETY 2 (1975):
    211-33.

    Describes four kinds of reports that one finds about Catholic
    Charismatics, namely those by: 1) Roman Catholic antagonists; 2)
    Charismatic apologists; 3) Protestant Pentecostal adversaries; and
    4) sociological researchers. The first three descriptions are of
    practical concern to Christians of different religious persuasions
    who need to make sense of the emergence of a Pentecostal Movement
    within the Roman Catholic tradition. One sociological study of
    Catholic Pentecostalism (Moore, item 1881) is analyzed. The prob-
    lem of adequacy in describing the Pentecostal phenomenon and the
    difficulties involved in choosing one descriptive version rather
    than another are discussed.

2049. Walker, Andrew, and James S. Atherton. "An Easter Pentecostal
    Convention: The Successful Management of a 'Time of Blessing.'"
    SOCIOLOGICAL REVIEW 9 (1971): 367-87.

    Presents a study of a Pentecostal gathering at Easter in England.
    The authors think that such meetings are "Dionysian highlights in
    the Pentecostal calendar" (p. 367). The major terms "fundamental-
    ism," "revival," and "blessing" are explained, the last mentioned
    referring to the experience of attending the meeting. The various
    services held during the convention are described. They are said
    to have the function of providing opportunities for members to
    achieve spiritual and social status within their own assemblies.

2050. Wallis, Roy. "Hostages to Fortune: Thoughts on the Future of
    Scientology and the Children of God." THE FUTURE OF NEW RELI-
    GIOUS MOVEMENTS (item 579), pp. 80-90.

    Suggests that speculation on the future of new religions should
    be based on an understanding of their appeal. Two new religious
    movements, namely Scientology and the Children of God, are examined.
    The former is a world-affirming movement that can be considered a
    response to the enduring condition of capitalist society, while the
    latter is a world-rejecting response to social marginality. Their
    sources of success and discernible trends that might indicate where
    their respective futures lie are discussed. Scientology has been
    successful, because it addresses the issue of unfulfilled human
    potential; it will continue to develop as an institutionalized and
    socially accommodated organization, but with declining membership.
    The Children of God, on the other hand, cater to those suffering
    from anxiety, depression, and deprivation; its survival might be
    seriously threatened when their founder and leader dies.

2051.   Wallis, Roy. "Religion as Fun?: The Rajneesh Movement." SOCIO-
        LOGICAL THEORY, RELIGION, AND COLLECTIVE ACTION. Edited by Roy
        Wallis and Steve Bruce. Belfast: Queen's University, 1986,
        pp. 191-224.

        Gives an account of the basic teachings of Rajneesh and points
        out that his stress on enjoyment and comfort led to his success in
        the West. The devotees of this unorthodox guru are "a group who
        had largely pursued particular careers because of expressive and
        creative interests and a desire for autonomy and freedom from the
        restrictions of commercial and bureaucratic employment" (p. 204).
        The development of Rajneeshism, which was formally declared a reli-
        gion with a priestly hierarchy, is described. The author maintains
        that this movement has succeeded in embodying elements of three
        types of religious movements, namely the world-affirming, world-
        rejecting, and world-accommodating, though by the middle of the
        1980's it seemed to be stressing the world-rejecting stance.

2052.   Wallis, Roy. "The Dynamics of Change in the Human Potential Move-
        ment." RELIGIOUS MOVEMENTS: GENESIS, EXODUS, AND NUMBERS (item
        692), pp. 129-56.

        Describes some of the main features of the Human Potential Move-
        ment and analyzes the changes that have occurred over the last two
        or three decades. The milieu within which the movement is located
        is depicted. It is argued that its main characteristics, namely
        proliferation, eclecticism, commercialism, professionalism, and
        spiritualization, "form a syndrome arising out of the fundamental
        difficulties and dilemmas posed by the precariousness of the move-
        ment" (p. 145). The author, disagreeing to some degree with Stark
        and Bainbridge's theory (item 478), maintains that increased spiri-
        tuality is caused by the movement's diffuse belief system and by
        its fundamental individualism.

2053.   Wallis, Roy. "Betwixt Therapy and Salvation: The Changing Form of
        the Human Potential Movement." SICKNESS AND SECTARIANISM (item
        643), pp. 23-51.

        Describes the main features of the Human Potential Movement,
        locating the milieu in which it flourished and the connection be-
        tween its various component groups. Five major characteristics are
        identified: "1) eclecticism; 2) inflationary proliferation of ideas
        and practices; 3) commercialization; 4) professionalization; and
        5) a drift towards spirituality" (p. 24). The theory of Stark and
        Bainbridge (item 478) that explains the transition from secular to
        religious forms is disputed. The author thinks that spirituality,
        rather than being a substitute for secular values, provides an
        explanation of past achievements and a chance to gain additional
        values. The movement, which is fundamentally precarious, overlaps
        with many other disciplines in its use of physical and meditative
        practices, its interest in occultism, its concern with social
        change, and its involvement with additional counseling and therapy.

2054.   Wallis, Roy. "Researching the Children of God: A Reflection and
        Review." UPDATE: A QUARTERLY JOURNAL OF NEW RELIGIOUS MOVEMENTS
        9.2 (1985): 32-37.

Reviews W. Douglas Pritchett's book, THE CHILDREN OF GOD/FAMILY
OF LOVE: AN ANNOTATED BIBLIOGRAPHY (New York: Garland, 1985) and, in
the process, reveals the author's (Wallis's) relationship with the
movement's leader during his participant-observation research. The
difficulties in studying this movement, which went underground in
1983 and which has gone through many changes since its founding,
are underscored. Besides criticizing the bibliography for several
flaws, Wallis rejects Pritchett's view that the founder's charisma
was effected by "societal control" or was "an inducement to further
deviance."

2055. Wallis, Roy. "Charisma, Commitment, and Control in a New Religious
      Movement." MILLENNIALISM AND CHARISMA (item 2055), pp. 73-140.

Examines the Children of God, a religious movement whose character and development have been entirely controlled by its charismatic founder, David Berg. The author 1) outlines the background
to the movement's development; 2) presents the major attributes of
the charismatic authority of its founder; and 3) discusses the
process of institutionalization. He demonstrates at some length
the substantial modifications that have occurred in the movement's
beliefs, practices, organization, and lifestyle. Charisma is inherently unstable and tends to become institutionalized with time.
Charismatic leaders can respond to the demand for this development
in four ways: acquiescence, encouragement, displacement, and resistance. Berg's behavior represents the reaction of resistance that
is expressed, especially in the frequent changes that have taken
place in the Children of God.

2056. Wallis, Roy. "The Social Construction of Charisma." SOCIAL COM-
      PASS 29 (1982): 25-39.

Attempts to show, through a study of the Children of God, " the
social nature of the emergence, recognition, and maintenance of a
charismatic identity" (p. 26). Charisma is a form of interaction
in which each party secures its own status. It is argued that the
rise of charismatic leaders, their success, and the relationships
they establish with their followers are better explained in sociological terms. A biography of David Berg, the founder of the Children of God, is given and his transformation from an evangelist
into a prophet is described. Two elements are said to be crucial
to this transformation: 1) his withdrawal from the main body of
believers with whom he continues to communicate only by letters;
and 2) the success of the movement and its lifestyle, a success
which validated his charisma. Berg has maintained his charismatic
status by a system of exchanges with followers who were singled out
for special attention.

2057. Wallis, Roy. "Yesterday's Children: Culture and Structural Change
      in a New Religious Movement." THE SOCIAL IMPACT OF NEW RELIGIOUS
      MOVEMENTS (item 725), pp. 97-133.

Traces the cultural and structural changes that have taken place
in the Children of God/Family of Love. The essay is divided into
two parts: 1) developments in the movement, where the history of

the group is outlined from its beginnings in the late 1960's till
the late 1970's; and 2) comparative analysis, where the group is
seen as a political-social organization and compared to other religious groups. The author holds that the Children of God Movement
has "undergone a rapprochement with the churches and society of a
kind normally subsumed under the notion of denominationalization"
(p. 117). The following factors are also observed: the movement's
original recruitment base: 1) the rising age of its current members; 2) the difficulties it encountered from the anticult sentiment and activities; and 3) and its internal dynamics. Movements
like the Children of God have remained essentially sectarian
because of their authoritarian conception of truth.

2058.   Wallis, Roy. "Coping With Institutional Fragility: An Analysis of
        Christian Science and Scientology." SALVATION AND PROTEST (item
        709), pp. 25-43.

        Discusses the transition of loosely organized cults to cohesive,
        authoritarian sects, using Christian Science and Scientology as
        examples. The two movements are briefly introduced and then ana-
        lyzed in terms of three distinct problems acutely felt by "manip-
        ulationist" movements, namely those of ideological precariousness,
        authority, and commitment. The two movements in question developed
        a strategy for sectarianization through the elaboration of a trans-
        cendental ideology and the focusing of commitment upon the leader
        and the central organization.

2059.   Wallis, Roy. "Sex, Marriage, and the Children of God." SALVATION
        AND PROTEST (item 709), pp. 74-90.

        Aims at clarifying the structural and motivational elements in
        the sexual and marital lives of the Children of God. The develop-
        ment in this movement from a puritanical form of marriage and the
        family to a system that permits a wider range of sexual activities
        is briefly described. The way the movement uses "flirthy fishing"
        as a mode of witnessing and the consequences of their activities
        are explained. Two main issues are explored: 1) why are members of
        the Children of God prepared to sacrifice their wives to other
        men?, and 2) why are female members willing to enter pluralistic,
        short-term, sexual relationships? The ideology and lifestyle of
        this group tends to minimize the economic, social, and psychic re-
        percussions that normally accompany extramarital sexual relations
        in Western culture.

2060.   Wallis, Roy. "Fishing For Men." HUMANIST 38.1 (1978): 14-16.

        Gives a description of the practice of "flirty fishing," a kind
        of "sophisticated prostitution business," which was adopted by the
        Children of God/Family of Love as an evangelizing technique. The
        women who are involved in this method do not ask for payment and
        make it a point to convey their message to the men to whom they
        render service. The author explores the rationale behind this
        custom and the various motives of the women that lead them to
        justify it. The fact that flirty fishing is considered a sacrifice
        leads to the conclusion that the women members of the Children of
        God are not really having a life of "unbridled promiscuity."

2061. Wallis, Roy. "Recruiting Christian Manpower." SOCIETY 15.4
       (1978): 72-74.

       Discusses the view of sexuality in the Children of God/Family of
       Love. The practice of "flirty fishing," a new form of proselytiz-
       ing developed between 1973 and 1975, is described. The author
       attempts to understand how this unusual practice came into being
       and how the members of the movement justify it. The theological,
       historical, and prophetic arguments adduced in its favor and the
       incentives that led to its development are outlined.

2062. Wallis, Roy. THE TOTAL ROAD TO FREEDOM: A SOCIOLOGICAL ANALYSIS
       OF SCIENTOLOGY. New York: Columbia University Press, 1977. xiv,
       282 pp.

       Presents an in-depth study of Scientology, one of the most con-
       troversial new religious movements. The author first offers a
       typology of religious groups and a theory of how cults develop into
       sects. The emergence of Dianetics (the forerunner of Scientology),
       the nature and development of its beliefs and practices, and the
       character of its followers are explored. The tension and strain
       inherent in the movement and the way its leaders try to deal with
       them are considered. Dianetics, a lay therapeutic system, devel-
       oped into Scientology, a new religious system complete with its own
       beliefs and practices and organizational structure. Its relation-
       ship with society at large and its impact on religion are assessed.
       "Scientology emerged as a religious commodity eminently suited to
       the contemporary market" (p. 247).

2063. Wallis, Roy. "Dianetics: A Marginal Psychotherapy." MARGINAL
       MEDICINE (item 715), pp. 77-109.

       Maintains that those healing practices in Western society that
       fall outside traditional medical and psychiatric practices provide
       "an insight into the strains and tensions generated by industrial
       societies" (p. 77). An account of Dianetics, the precursor of
       Scientology, is given, focusing on its theory and practice, the
       members who join it and their motivations, and its social organiza-
       tion and development. The major causes of the decline of Dianetics
       and its eventual demise and transformation into Scientology were
       1) the financial crisis brought about by the loss of many recruits
       and 2) the tensions within the organization itself. The author
       suggests that social mobility as well as an emphasis on individual
       achievement contributed to Scientology's success in the United
       States.

2064. Wallis, Roy. "Observations on the Children of God." SOCIOLOGICAL
       REVIEW 24 (1976): 807-29.

       Disagrees with Kanter's functional view (item 384) that millen-
       nial ideas merely provide a justification for support and mainte-
       nance of a community. It is argued that, at times, the movement's
       development into a social organization is dependent on its leader's
       millennial, revelatory vision. The Children of God are taken as an
       illustration of the author's position. Four phases in this group's

development are distinguished, namely: 1) the Children of God as "a prophetic, gathered remnant" (1968-1969); 2) "the New Nation and Subsistence Communitarianism" (1970-1971); 3) "evangelical millennialism" (1971-1972); and 4) "colportage (i.e., the solicitation of funds) and routine proselytization," which marks the introduction of functional rationality. These changes, accompanied by internal opposition and defections, were carried out according to the dictates of Moses Berg, the movement's founder and leader, who believed that his actions were revealed to him by God.

2065. Wallis, Roy. "'Poor Man's Psychoanalysis?': Observations on Dianetics." ZETETIC 1.1 (1976): 9-24.

Gives an account of the emergence of Dianetics, its theory, and its therapeutic methods that were believed to resolve psychosomatic illnesses. This paper is essentially a shorter version of the author's essay on Dianetics (item 2063).

2066. Wallis, Roy. "Scientology: Therapeutic Cult to Religious Sect." SOCIOLOGY: THE JOURNAL OF THE BRITISH SOCIOLOGY ASSOCIATION 9 (1975): 89-100.

Criticizes various concepts of cult, particularly that of Glock and Stark (item 97), as inadequate and proposes a new typology based on respectability or deviance and unique or pluralistic legitimacy. The central feature of a cult is "epistemological individualism," while that of sect "epistemological authoritarianism." Their respective appeal is illustrated with reference to Scientology which, according to the author, developed from a cult (Dianetics) to a sect (Scientology). Cults are considered to be precarious and transitory institutions that become sects when, and if, authority becomes centralized.

2067. Wallis, Roy. "The Aetherius Society: A Case Study of the Formation of a Mystagogic Congregation." SOCIOLOGICAL REVIEW 22 (1974): 27-44.

Suggests that the Aetherius Society, a new magicoreligious group, provides material for the study of Weber's neglected concept of the "mystagogue" and explores the career of its founder, George King, as an example of a mystagogic individual. The Society's beliefs and practices, which are related to those of Theosophy, are described. Though Dr. King defines his sources of legitimation in magical terms, his message does have an ethical content. The motivations for joining the Aetherius Society are ascribed, in part, to cognitive insecurity in the face of forces beyond human control and to the desire to alleviate the deteriorating world condition. The author maintains that the Aetherius Society has been institutionalized through monopolizing access to charismatic legitimation, elaborating a theodicy, and subordinating spiritual healing to evangelistic and ritual goals" (p. 42).

2068. Wallis, Roy. "The Sectarianism of Scientology." SOCIOLOGICAL YEARBOOK OF RELIGION IN BRITAIN 6 (1973): 136-65.

Considers Scientology in the light of various, commonly ascribed
sectarian features, namely: 1) voluntary and achieved nature of
membership; 2) exclusiveness; 3) self-conception as elect; 4) hostility towards the social environment and the state; 5) the priesthood of all believers; 6) ethical and ascetical character; and
7) totalitarianism. The author thinks that the second, third, and
seventh items mentioned above are those sectarian criteria best
applicable to Scientology.

2069. Wallis, Roy. "A Comparative Analysis of Problems and Processes of
Change in Two Manipulationist Movements: Christian Science and
Scientology." THE CONTEMPORARY METAMORPHOSIS OF RELIGION: ACTS
OF THE TWELFTH INTERNATIONAL CONGRESS ON SOCIOLOGY OF RELIGION.
Lille, France: C.I.S.R., 1973, pp. 407-22.

Discusses the process of development of religious movements from
loosely structured, ephemeral groups to organized sects in the
context of Christian Science and Scientology, two groups that have
successfully made the transition. A brief description of both
groups is given. Three major areas are discussed: the doctrinal
precariousness, the problem of authority, and the issue of commitment. Both Christian Science and Scientology are precarious groups
because their doctrine is syncretistic. Moreover, both have had to
face challenges to the authority of their respective leaders--to
which they have responded by using "effective mechanisms for isola-
ting teachers and practitioners" (p. 417) and by restructuring the
process of decision making. Finally, both have encountered difficulties in maintaining the commitment of their members--to which
they have responded by offering specific services, by fostering
wider theoretical and doctrinal concern (gnosis), and by stressing
the practitioner-client relationship.

2070. Wangerin, Ruth Elizabeth. "Women in the Children of God: 'Revolutionary Women' or 'Mountain Maid.'" WOMEN IN SEARCH OF UTOPIAS
(item 459), pp. 130-39.

Describes the position of women in the Children of God. Under
their prophetic leader's "Patriarchal tribalism," women tend to be
assigned household and secretarial jobs, even though they are
rarely bossed around by men. Mothers appeared to be better off
primarily because of group support. "All women in the Berg family
were important leaders and administrators in COG" (p. 135). In
this movement, the dichotomy between virgin and whore is eliminated
and many converts from Christian fundamentalism and Roman Catholicism experience a radical change in the sexual liberties women
enjoyed, since sex is given a theological significance. The introduction of "flirty fishing" and the effect it had on the role of
women is discussed. Both men and women participate in this evangelizing method, which is not often done for sacrifice and which com-
plicates sexual and marital arrangements within the movement itself.

2071. Ward, Hilary. THE FAR-OUT SAINTS OF THE JESUS COMMUNES: A FIRST-
HAND REPORT AND INTERPRETATION OF THE JESUS PEOPLE MOVEMENT. New
York: Association Press, 1972. 192 pp.

Examines the Jesus Movement in relation to early gnosticism and
to the emerging new consciousness. Writing about his personal
encounters with members of the movement from various communes, the
author discusses integration within communes, the Jesus People's
view of sex, their doctrines and links with the occult, and their
finances. Several organizations, like the Children of God, the
Local Church, and the Way International, are labeled "occult Jesus
People groups." One chapter is dedicated to the Children of God,
a movement that has a "cultic, almost rigid, denominational structure." The short bibliography (pp. 187-90) lists some of the early
works on the Jesus Movement.

2072. Warren, Donald I. "Status Inconsistency Theory and Flying Saucer
      Sightings." SCIENCE 170, No. 3958 (November 5, 1970): 599-603.

Maintains that UFO sightings "can be described within the context
of the societal position of particular individuals" (p. 599).
After explaining the concept of status inconsistency and outlining
some of its features, the author attempts to show how UFO sightings
are linked to status frustration. In other words, those who see
UFOs feel deprived of the social status they should possess and
their visions of flying saucers "are a form of escape into unreal-
ized and perhaps unrealizable consistent situations" (p. 601).

2073. Watson, G. Llewellyn. "Social Structure and Social Movement: The
      Black Muslims in the U.S.A. and the Rastafarians of Jamaica."
      BRITISH JOURNAL OF SOCIOLOGY 24 (1973): 188-204.

Compares two contemporary social movements that have different
social structures, with the aim of finding out how protest and discontent are related to those structures. The author examines, in
turn, the Black Muslims and the Rastafarians, both groups having
strong elements of millenarianism and otherworldly orientation.
He draws several parallels between them, particularly the fact that
both emerged out of a situation of racial oppression and class and
status deprivation. He suggests that the Marxist approach to social
relationships, an approach that stresses both the structural and
ideational elements of the social system, can be profitably used to
understand these two movements.

2074. Wedow, Susanne M. "The Strangeness of Astrology: An Ethnography of
      Credibility Processes." THE AMERICAN DIMENSION: CULTURAL MYTHS
      AND SOCIAL REALITIES. Edited by W. Arens and Susan P. Montague.
      Sherman Oaks, CA: Alfred Publishing Co., 1976, pp. 181-93.

Examines the theories that explain the persistence and survival
of the occult in Western culture and concentrates on a neglected
aspect, namely "the analysis of actual interactional scenes in
which the use of a system of knowledge occurs" (p. 183). The
author maintains that, by exploring how astrology maintains its
authority even though science and common sense reject its conclusions, the researcher can study the belief and practice surrounding
astrology as a system of knowledge. She maintains that belief in
astrology is sustained through the interaction between the client
and the astrologer.

2075. Weightman, Judith M. "A Sociological Perspective on Indemnity."
       RESTORING THE KINGDOM. Edited by Deane William Ferm. New York:
       Paragon House, 1984, pp. 113-22.

       Examines the Unification Church's teaching that it is necessary
       to restore human beings to their proper relationship with God
       through a payment or indemnity, which is concretized in their fund-
       raising activities that have become the basis for the church's
       plans for world transformation. The author examines the implica-
       tions of this connection between money-raising (works) and theology
       (faith, conversion). The self-sacrificial attitude of Unification
       Church members can, in the author's view, limit their relationship
       with the larger society. It could also have serious effects within
       the movement; that is, could impede institutional development by
       driving talented people whose ideals of self sacrifice lead them to
       avoid doing precisely those things that they are most suited to do.

2076. Weightman, Judith M. MAKING SENSE OF THE JONESTOWN SUICIDES: A
       SOCIOLOGICAL HISTORY OF THE PEOPLES TEMPLE. New York: Edwin
       Mellen Press, 1983. 213 pp.

       Argues that the suicides in Jonestown constituted a meaningful
       event to its members and investigates how the practices at the
       People's Temple inculcated such a belief. After giving a history
       of the Temple, which was both a political and a religious entity,
       the author analyzes the appeals of this new sect and its mechanisms
       for eliciting commitment that made the Temple a world apart. The
       charismatic nature of its leadership is examined and its implica-
       tions on the Temple's fate assessed. The socialization of members
       is discussed in the context of two explanatory models, namely the
       brainwashing theory and the sociology of knowledge. The responses
       to the suicides are finally examined as atrocity stories. It is
       maintained that a sociology of knowledge approach provides a better
       understanding of Jonestown and takes "seriously the potential with-
       in us all for just such an act" (p. 1). A bibliography of books on
       Jonestown and newspaper reports and magazine articles covering the
       main events of the tragedy is included (pp. 213-17).

2077. Weiman, Gabriel. "The Prophecy That Never Fails: On the Uses and
       Gratifications of Horoscope Reading." SOCIOLOGICAL INQUIRY 52
       (1982): 274-90.

       Explores the growing popularity of astrology columns as means of
       satisfying human needs, more specifically as a way a catering to
       modern existential anxiety and thus to the desire to reduce ambigu-
       ity and to exercise control over one's destiny. Anxiety indices
       among horoscope readers and nonreaders are measured and compared
       and it is concluded that a high anxiety trait is directly associ-
       ated with horoscope reading. Two stages in the use of horoscopes
       are identified, namely existential anxiety, followed by "locus of
       control." The following elements expose the horoscope's advantage
       in decreasing anxiety: authority; pseudorationality; pseudo-
       individualization; anxiety arousal and cure; conformity; and a
       quasi-scientific approach.

2078. Weinberger, Morris, William M. Tierney, James Y. Greene, and P.
       Albert Studdard. "The Development of Physician Norms in the
       United States: The Treatment of Jehovah's Witnesses Patients."
       SOCIAL SCIENCE AND MEDICINE 16 (1982): 1719-23.

       Discusses the medical issues raised by Jehovah's Witnesses, who
       refuse blood transfusions and examines the socialization process
       regarding the doctor's norms in dealing with specific cases. The
       authors investigate whether these norms, if they exist, vary with
       the physician's training and individual experiences and how the
       doctors become aware of this particular medical issue. The legal
       problems that might arise when treating Jehovah's Witnesses are
       dealt with and the need to make doctors aware of alternative thera-
       pies is underscored.

2079. Weldon, John. "The Strange World of Est." UPDATE: A QUARTERLY
       JOURNAL OF NEW RELIGIOUS MOVEMENTS 5.3-4 (1981): 53-65.

       Contains a description of Erhard Seminar Training, which is said
       to be "an intensive sixty-hour seminar of psychological indoctrina-
       tion designed to restructure a person's world view" (p. 53). After
       a brief biographical outline of Werner Erhard, the founder of EST,
       the author discusses the EST experience and its effects, its phi-
       losophy, and its potential for misuse. The author maintains that
       EST has serious social implications because it justifies immoral
       behavior. In spite of the heavy indoctrination techniques employed
       by EST, it should not be identified with the same kind of brain-
       washing used by North Koreans on their prisoners during the Korean
       War, since the element of involuntary confinement is not present in
       EST. Though EST claims to be nonreligious, it teaches a worldview
       that is incompatible with Christianity.

2080. Welles, Chris. "The Eclipse of Sun Myung Moon." SCIENCE, SIN, AND
       SCHOLARSHIP (item 1783), pp. 243-58.

       Maintains that, in spite of its claims to the contrary, the move-
       ment founded by the Reverend Moon is waning and wonders "whether he
       ever had the power and influence even remotely resembling that
       which has been widely attributed to him" (p. 244). The author
       discusses at some length the financial state of the Unification
       Church, questioning where the money comes from, where it is allo-
       cated, and whether the church can continue its successful fundrais-
       ing forever. He states that the church has difficulties maintain-
       ing its membership. Many of its members simply walk away because
       they get tired of the strict spiritual regime and become dispirited
       by the church's concern with private gain rather than with the
       improvement of social conditions.

2081. Westley, Frances R. "Interpersonal Contamination: Pollution Fears
       in the Human Potential Movement." STUDIES IN RELIGION 11 (1982):
       149-62.

       Applies anthropological theory to understand the contradiction
       which participants in the Human Potential Movement experience with
       regard to social contact. Many groups, like Arica, Silva Mind

Control Psychosynthesis, Shakti, EST, and Scientology, offer their
adherents new and unencumbered relationships with other people,
while at the same time employing methods that seem to focus on the
self. The social origins of pollution beliefs are outlined and
then examined within the Human Potential Movement. It is also
suggested that the work of Irving Goffman (INTERACTIONAL RITUAL,
New York: Doubleday, 1967) can be used to describe the symbolic
relationship between the individual and social order, purity, and
danger. Members of the Human Potential Movement are ambivalent
in that they both want community and fear it. Their ambivalence
derives from a fear of pollution, a fear that symbolizes personal
and social confusion that follow the breakdown in "international
codes and identity maintenance institutions in society" (p. 162).

2082. Westley, Frances R. "Search for Surrender: A Catholic Pentecostal
      Renewal Group." AMERICAN BEHAVIORAL SCIENTIST 20 (1977): 925-40.

Studies the ritual of sharing and the process of commitment in a
small Catholic Charismatic group in the Montreal area. After a
brief description of the movement and the method employed, the
author explores three elements in the experience of a charismatic
person, namely: 1) the shifting of responsibility; 2) the taking on
of responsibility for others: and 3) the relinquishing of self-
responsibility. The sharing of individual experiences increases
one's commitment to the group. This particular charismatic group
failed to reach the "ecstatic trance stage," the stage of "surren-
dering," in which people speak in tongues and witness miracles in
their midst. Hostility of church authorities and lack of strong
leadership are the main factors that led to this failure.

2083. Westrum, Ron. "Knowledge About Sea Serpents." ON THE MARGINS OF
      SCIENCE (item 712), pp. 293-314.

Discusses the origin of the much-debated data on sea serpents
(like the Loch Ness Monster) that is just one of the many anomalies
in which Western Society has recently shown a lot of interest. The
ways in which reports on sea monsters become public are studied.
The author records the number of sea monsters sighted between 1880
and 1966. He thinks that many factors, including the social class
of those who experience such phenomena and the social demands for
monster sightings, may affect the reporting. Knowledge on sea
serpents depends on a rather diffuse system of social intelligence.

2084. Westrum, Ron. "Social Intelligence About Anomalies: The Case of
      UFOs." SOCIAL STUDIES OF SCIENCE 7 (1977): 271-302.

Examines the debunking of UFOs by scientists, concentrating on
"the social system which intervenes between those who have anomaly
experiences and scientists who make decisions as to whether anomalies exist or not" (p. 272). The experiences of UFOs are first
considered. Then the manner in which these experiences become
reports are traced. And, finally, what happens to these reports as
they pass through the normal social channels is investigated.
Various explanations of UFOs are discussed. The author points out
that UFO experiences are contagious. He examines the roles played

by the news media, the Air Force, and amateur investigators in dis-
seminating information. The nonscientific process involved in
social intelligence about UFOs is typical of information about
other anomalous events, like the sightings of the Loch Ness Monster.

2085. Westrum, Ron. "A Note on Monsters." JOURNAL OF POPULAR CULTURE 8
(1975): 862-70.

Gives a brief survey of the nature and scope of "monster literature" and of the speculations regarding its social meaning. One
common approach to the belief in monsters (such as sea serpents,
the abominable snowman, and the Loch Ness Monster) is to include it
with occult phenomena, particularly UFO manifestations. "Occult
devotees often look upon accounts of monsters as supporting their
view that science cannot entirely explain the world" (p. 868).

2086. Westrum, Ron, David Swift, and David Stupple. "Extraterrestrial
Intelligence: The Social Impact of an Idea." PEOPLE IN SPACE:
POLICY PERSPECTIVES FOR A "STAR WARS" CENTURY. Edited by James
Everett Katz. New Brunswick, NJ: Transaction Books, 1985, pp.
178-93.

Studies the response of American society to the possibility of
the existence of, and contact with, extraterrestrial intelligence.
The following three subcultures based on such an idea are explored:
1) religious groups whose members believe that their leaders have
made contact with, or receive messages from, space beings, like the
Aetherius Society and the Unarius Foundation; 2) UFOlogists, who
investigate alleged sightings of flying saucers, such as the Aerial
Phenomena Research Organization (APRO) and the Mutual UFO Network
(MUFON); and 3) scientific organizations that conduct research on
UFOs by trying to interpret radio signals from outer space, such as
the Search for Extraterrestrial Intelligence (SETI). The author
describes the membership, social structure, norms, and ideology of
these groups and explores the relationships between the them.

2087. White, Charles J. "The Sai Baba Movement: Approaches to the Study
of Indian Saints." JOURNAL OF ASIAN STUDIES 31 (1971-1972):
863-78.

Stresses the need for firsthand observation and data collection
when one is studying the lives of Indian saints. Four general
traditional roles, those of guru, ascetic, avatar, and saint, are
first described. The historical antecedents to the Sathya Sai Baba
Movement are considered and a short biography of this miracle-work-
ing saint is given. Several methodological issues are discussed
and a three-level approach (namely collection of data, organization, and intention) proposed.

2088. White, James W. THE SOKAGAKKAI AND MASS SOCIETY. Stanford, CA:
Stanford University Press, 1970. xiii, 376 pp.

Discusses the political significance of the Soka Gakkai Movement
in Japan. The first part outlines the origins, structure, and
politics of the movement and describes its beliefs, political
goals, internal government, and recruitment and indoctrination

practices. The second part explores the concept of "mass movement" with reference to the rise of Soka Gakkai. Though this Japanese movement has rejected political activity outside Japan, this study throws some light not only on the movement's origin, but also on the manner in which it has spread and accommodated itself to others outside Japan.

2089. Whitehead, Harriet. RENUNCIATION AND REFORMULATION: A STUDY OF CONVERSION IN AN AMERICAN SECT. Ithaca, NY: Cornell University Press, 1987. 297 pp.

Unites insights from symbolic studies, structural psychology, and descriptions of religious experiences in an effort to draw an ethnographic portrait of the beliefs and controversial techniques of Scientology. The author gives an overview of the Church of Scientology in the early 1970's and traces its evolution from the earlier days of Dianetics in the 1950's. The role of "auditing" as a visionary technique that propelled this movement into prominence is discussed. The religious and psychotherapeutic practices of Scientology are understood in terms of renunciation. Scientology methods and beliefs are analyzed and the process of fitting the concepts to experiences explained. Comparisons are made between the Scientologist, the mystic, and the individual who undergoes psychotherapy and it is concluded that the basic ingredients of conversion or transformation are similar in all three cases.

2090. Whitehead, Harriet. "Reasonably Fantastic: Some Perspectives on Scientology, Science Fiction, and Occultism." RELIGIOUS MOVEMENTS IN CONTEMPORARY SOCIETY (item 727), pp. 547-87.

Argues that Occultism is not an irrational mode of thought, but rather an attempt to synthesize intellectual, emotional, and apprehensional orientations that human beings use to relate themselves to the ultimate conditions of existence. The author thinks that the early beliefs of Scientology had an occult orientation and that science fiction, from which Scientology is derived, is closely connected with the occult. Ron Hubbard, the founder of Scientology, used this occult orientation and gave it an intellectual and emotional experience it had not enjoyed for centuries, and by so doing he made Scientology an appealing religious option.

*   Whitworth, John, and Martin Sheils. "From Across the Black Water: Two Imported Varieties of Hinduism." Cited above as item 1535.

2091. Wikstrom, Lester. "Happy Hookers for Jesus: Children of God's Sex Revolution." UPDATE: A QUARTERLY JOURNAL OF NEW RELIGIOUS MOVEMENTS 1.3-4 (1977): 59-63.

Gives a brief summary of the Children of God's custom of "flirty fishing," which was introduced in 1977. Several quotes from Moses Berg's letters (the so-called MO Letters) are cited to illustrate this novel custom and its justification.

2092. Wilson, Bryan R., and Karel Dobbelaere. "Unificationism: A Study of Moonies in Britain." BRITISH JOURNAL OF SOCIOLOGY 37 (1987): 184-98.

Seeks to determine whether the negative reaction generated by the
activities of a relatively small group of Unification Church members in Great Britain is justified. Those who join this Church,
the methods used to recruit them, and the effects on family relationships are examined. The authors conclude that the common view
that Moonies are brainwashed is not substantiated by their findings
and that the fear portrayed in press reports is unwarranted.

2093. Wilson, Stephen R. "Becoming a Yogi: Resocialization and Decondi-
tioning as Conversion Processes." SOCIOLOGICAL ANALYSIS 45
(1984): 301-14.

Examines the conversion process in the context of new religious
movements and describes two types of such processes among members
of the Kripalu Yoga Ashram founded by Yogi Amrit Desai. The author
shows how individuals become affiliated with the movement and then
deepen their commitment. The practice of yoga as a means of freeing the human personality from social conditioning and of "letting
go" (that is, the "shakti experience") and of learning to deal with
growth situations is explained. The author links his findings to
Lofland and Sknovod's typology of conversion motifs (items 865-66).

2094. Woodrum, Eric. "Religious Belief Transformation: A Study of This
Worldly Religion." SOCIOLOGICAL INQUIRY 55 (1985): 16-37.

Examines the distinctive content and form of religious belief
systems in new movements, focusing on Transcendental Meditation
whose central themes, their relationship to otherworldly counterparts, and their process of change, are analyzed. Many of these
themes, like practical utilitarianism and worldliness, are not new.
Transcendental Meditation is a thisworldly oriented religion that
reflects the decline of traditional otherworldly religions. Those
who attack the new religions are merely using them as "convenient
scapegoats for disagreeable social changes" (p. 34). The author
thinks that the new religious movements often help their members in
their task of adaptation and integration.

2095. Woodrum, Eric. "Religious Organizational Change: An Analysis Based
in the TM Movement." REVIEW OF RELIGIOUS RESEARCH 24 (1982):
89-103.

Contributes to the understanding of religious organizational
change by studying the history of Transcendental Meditation over a
ten-year period. The author identifies three periods in the history of this movement: 1) the spiritual-mystical period (1961-1965);
2) the counterculture period (1965-1970); and 3) the secularized,
popular religion period (1970-1980). He relates certain belief
systems, including the reinterpretation of spiritual practices, to
organizational changes. Since 1970, the TM movement has relied on
secular, utilitarian motivations in their recruitment campaigns.
Its current claims of reducing stress and anxiety, with the accompanying physical benefits, give the impression that the movement
is not a mystical religion that stresses spiritual evolution, but
rather a scientific organization dedicated to physical and psychological well-being.

2096. Woodrum, Eric. "The Development of the Transcendental Meditation
       Movement." ZETETIC 1.2 (1977): 38-48.

       Traces three phases in the development of Transcendental Medita-
       tion (see item 2095). The concern with practical matters has
       enabled the movement to acquire an entrenched and accepted status
       in the West. Two types of participants are distinguished: the
       average meditator, who seeks the material benefits of the practice
       of meditation without accepting the whole belief system, and the
       fully committed person, who still believes in the mystical and sal-
       vational aspects of Transcendental Meditation. Some projections on
       the future of the movement are made. The author thinks that it
       will "stabilize as a denominational popular religion" (p. 48).

2097. Woods, Richard. "Satanism Today." SOUNDINGS IN SATANISM. Com-
       piled by F. J. Sheed. New York: Sheed and Ward, 1972, pp.
       92-104.

       Presents a descriptive account of the rise of interest in the
       occult, focusing on Satanic beliefs and rituals. Various groups,
       like LaVey's Church of Satan and the Process Church of the Final
       Judgment, are chosen as representative of Satanism, which the
       author considers to be "an important facet of contemporary reli-
       gious consciousness" (p. 104). Satanism, in the author's view,
       attracts young people who feel oppressed and who are weary of the
       current political scene, of the problems of technology, and of the
       weakness of organized religion.

2098. Woods, Richard. "The Occult: Counter Culture Religion." LISTEN-
       ING: JOURNAL OF RELIGION AND CULTURE 6.2 (1971): 117-26.

       Reflects on the significance of the occult revolution in Western
       culture. The main features of this revolution are described and
       the difference between occultism and ordinary experience specified.
       The author maintains that the occult is a manifestation of the rise
       of the counterculture movement.

2099. Wuthnow, Robert. "Astrology and Marginality." JOURNAL FOR THE
       SCIENTIFIC STUDY OF RELIGION 15 (1976): 157-68.

       Tests two major explanations of astrology, namely: 1) it is a
       part of the counterculture that appeals to educated young adults as
       an alternative worldview; and 2) it is mainly a phenomenon found
       among socially marginal individuals, like the uneducated and unem-
       ployed, who use it as a copying mechanism. The author's research
       in the San Francisco Bay Area confirms that casual interest in
       astrology is widespread and is found mainly among the socially-
       marginal--unemployed, unmarried, overweight, ill, and lonely peo-
       ple. Some connection between attraction to astrology and involve-
       ment in the counterculture was also observed. The author thinks
       that astrology functions as a substitute for more conventional
       religious commitments.

2100. Young, Wendy Warren. "The Aims and Methods of 'Est" and 'The Cen-
       ters Network.'" THE NEW EVANGELISTS (item 587), pp. 131-47.

Presents a study of EST in Britain, an organization now known as "The Centers Network" or "The Society for Contextual Studies and Educational Seminars." After an overview of Erhard's business, the author outlines the technology of personal transformation and the historical development of the organization he founded. EST grew out of the Human Potential Movement of the 1960's and belongs to the same family as Arica, Gestalt Therapy, Assertive Training, and Actualization. It is a "world-affirming, quasi-spiritual movement" that aims at personal enlightenment and social transformation. An account of EST training and its recent (1985) change into an new organization called "The Forum" is provided. Personal contact is the method of recruitment used by this new movement.

2101.   Zimmer, Troy A. "Belief in UFOs as Alternative Reality, Cultural Rejection, or Disturbed Psyche." DEVIANT BEHAVIOR: AN INTERDIS-CIPLINARY JOURNAL 6 (1985): 405-19.

Examines three interpretations of UFO beliefs that are widespread in Western culture: 1) they are held by science fiction advocates who are interested in occult phenomena and/or mysticism; 2) they express the feeling of rejection of, or alienation from, one's culture; and 3) they are ascribed to by mentally or psychologically disturbed, troubled, or maladjusted individuals. The author con-cludes that his research supports the first explanation.

C.   THE RESPONSE TO THE CULTS: STUDIES ON ANTI-CULT MOVEMENTS

2102.   Acock, Alan C., Charles Wright, and Kay McKensie. "Predicting Intolerance: The Impact of Parent's Own Tolerance vs. Social Class and Religious Fundamentalism." DEVIANT BEHAVIOR: AN IN-TERDISCIPLINARY JOURNAL 3 (1981): 65-84.

Examines, in the context of racial, ethic, religious, and polit-ical factors, the intolerance parents have of cultural and reli-gious deviance, with the aim of developing some means of predict-ing their behavior. Three areas are considered: 1) the parents' level of tolerance; 2) the socioeconomic status of the families involved; and 3) the religious beliefs of the parents and their offspring. The authors conclude that "religious beliefs provide the pivotal role in explaining intolerance" and that "such beliefs act as a mechanism by which the relevant orientation is engendered and sustained" (p. 79).

2103.   Alexander, Francesca, and Michele Rollins. "Alcoholics Anonymous: The Unseen Cult." CALIFORNIA SOCIOLOGIST 7 (1974): 33-48.

States that Alcoholics Anonymous has many attributes of a cult and explores how it works. Nine brainwashing methods, common to both Alcoholics Anonymous and other cults, are examined: 1) milieu control; 2) mystical manipulation; 3) purity; 4) confession; 5) sacred science; 6) loading of language; 7) stressing stress of doctrine over person; 8) dispensing of existence; and 9) love

bombing. Alcoholics Anonymous offers some alcoholics what they
need, namely understanding, absolute rules to live by, and escape
from loneliness and social isolation. It could help alcoholics of
certain psychological types, such as those who accept the intimacy
demanded by the group and are willing to sacrifice their individual identities.

2104. Anderson, Alan. "A Study in the Sociology of Religious Persecu-
       tion." JOURNAL OF RELIGIOUS HISTORY 9 (1977): 247-62.

Explores the patterns and forms of persecutions leveled against
the early Quakers by examining the suffering records they compiled
in Lancashire. There are records of a high degree of physical
violence and the frequency of assaults on Quakers who tried to
preach or spread their message. The roles played by the justices
and the informers are analyzed and illustrated by court cases.
The author discovers that the type and intensity of the attacks
changed over the years. He suggests that one effect of the persecutions "was undoubtedly to drive Quaker meetings into a tighter,
more self-contained and inward-looking organization, into a
closely-knit community enforcing rigid endogamy" (p. 262).

2105. Androes, Louis C. "Cultures in Collisions: The Rajneesh Search
       For Community." COMMUNITIES 71-72 (1986): 49-54.

Gives a brief historical account of the Rajneesh Movement in the
United States, particularly its presence in Oregon. The interrelationships between its members and the other social groups (the
media, the 1000 Friends of Oregon, the elected public officials,
the appointed public officials, and the local citizenry) are outlined. The behavior of Rajneesh's followers was impatient, abra-
sive, separatist, and confrontational and naturally led to resent-
ment and conflict. Their tendency to seek conflict with the local
inhabitants and with public officials was one major reason for the
commune's demise. The upheaval surrounding the final weeks of the
Rajneesh community is common to many communal efforts. Some speculations on the future of the Rajneesh Movement are made.

2106. Anthony, Dick, Thomas Robbins, and Jim McCarthy. "Legitimizing
       Repression." SOCIETY 17.3 (1980): 39-42.

Considers the various reasons that have been adduced to justify
the deprogramming of cult members who are believed to have been
brainwashed by the cult that recruited them. It is contended that
the "metaphor of brainwashing is best understood as a social weapon which provides a 'libertarian' rationale for the suppressing of
unpopular social movements and belief systems" (p. 40). Brainwashing is the medical model of psychopathology or deviant behavior and appeals to a scientifically oriented society in the state
of moral crisis.

2107. Barker, Eileen. "A Moral Responsibility of the Media in the Con-
       struction and Maintenance of Conceptual Boundaries." GLOBAL
       OUTREACH: GLOBAL CONGRESS ON THE WORLD RELIGION. Edited by
       Henry O. Thompson. Barrytown, NY: Unification Theological Semi-
       nary, 1987, pp. 237-53.

Maintains that the media not only provide information, but also
contribute "to the construction of the actual lens through which
we see the world and which we rarely think of testing for prese-
lected filters or distortions" (p. 238). The author discusses the
concept of social reality and the classification system necessary
to order that reality. Because mass communication plays a leading
role in the development of our concepts and attitudes, it carries
the burden of moral responsibility. Media coverage of the new
religious cults, such as the Unification Church, is taken as an
example to illustrate how it influences and formulates our opinions.

2108.   Barker, Eileen. "The Conversion of Conversion: A Sociological
        Anti-Reductionistic Perspective." REDUCTIONISM IN ACADEMIC
        DISCIPLINES. Edited by Arthur Peacocke. Guilford, Surrey,
        England: SHRE and NFER-Nelson, 1985, pp. 58-75.

        Argues against the brainwashing view of cult conversion that has
        been adopted by some psychologists and psychiatrists. Basing her
        reflections on her study of the Unification Church, the author
        discusses the various levels of explaining conversion and insists
        that individuals must be considered conscious actors. The follow-
        ing four variables that are operative in the conversion process are
        discussed: 1) the individual; 2) the alternative an individual has
        of remaining a member of the wider society; 3) the choice of join-
        ing an alternative religious group; and 4) the social context. She
        concludes that conversion to the Unification Church cannot be re-
        duced to psychology, biology, or medicine.

2109.   Barker, Eileen. "The British Right to Discriminate." SOCIETY
        21.4 (1984): 35-41.

        Compares the place religion has in two societies, namely Great
        Britain and the United Sates of America, and the different inter-
        pretations each country gives to the principle of religious free-
        dom. Specific cases involving the Unification Church and Scien-
        tology are given to illustrate the divergent societal responses
        and the legal problems involved.

2110.   Barker, Eileen. "With Enemies Like That: Some Functions of Depro-
        gramming as an Aid to Sectarian Membership." THE BRAINWASHING/
        DEPROGRAMMING CONTROVERSY (item 2127), pp. 329-44.

        Shows how deprogramming, while returning some cult members to
        their original lifestyle and belief system, also reinforces the
        hold of the cult over its remaining members and strengthens their
        commitment and fervency. Two testimonies of cult members are
        distinguished: 1) the public witness that stresses the good fea-
        tures of the cult; and 2) the testimony of those who return after
        a failed deprogramming experience and confirm the image of the
        outside world as a corrupt and hopelessly evil place. The author
        describes in some detail the second type of testimony showing how
        it contributes to the image of a persecuted community of true
        believers. Moreover, deprogramming contributes to the mistrust
        between parents and their offspring. A 1976 deprogramming manual
        called POWER (People's Organized Workshop on Erstaz Religion) is
        examined.

2111. Beckford, James A. CULT CONTROVERSIES: THE SOCIETAL RESPONSE TO
       NEW RELIGIOUS MOVEMENTS. New York: Tavistock Publications, 1985.
       viii, 327 pp.

       Provides an account of the current cult controversy and traces
       its development. Relying on interviews with many cult and ex-cult
       members and on scientific publications, the author provides brief
       descriptions of four of the more controversial cults, namely the
       Unification Church, Scientology, the Children of God, and the Hare
       Krishna Movement. Sociological approaches to these new movements
       are outlined. The author explains how this method tries to explain
       not why people believe, but rather how their beliefs are cultivated
       and managed in the new movements and also how the cults become
       entangled in controversy. Recruitment and disengagement processes
       are examined mostly in the context of members of the Unification
       Church. The public responses to the new religions in Great Brit-
       ain, France, and West Germany are sketched.

2112. Beckford, James A. "The 'Cult Problem' in Five Countries: The
       Social Construction of Religious Controversy." OF GODS AND MEN
       (item 550), pp. 195-214.

       Questions the opinion that new religious movements operate like
       multinational businesses, since it does not take into account the
       fact that cults are perceived as posing different kinds of problems
       in diverse countries. The author considers the ways in which cult
       behavior has been affected by the cultural and legal framework of
       five countries, namely the United States of America, Great Brit-
       ain, France, the Federal Republic of Germany, and Japan. He finds
       that whether the cults are considered a form of religious deviance,
       an expression of totalitarianism, or a threat to the social order,
       moral norms, and values depends on the sociocultural context.

2113. Beckford, James A. "'Brainwashing' and 'Deprogramming' in Britain:
       The Social Sources of Anti-Cult Sentiment." THE BRAINWASHING/
       DEPROGRAMMING CONTROVERSY (item 2127), pp. 122-38.

       Describes the Anti-Cult Movement in Britain "as a necessary pre-
       liminary to a sociological understanding of the vehemence of the
       anti-cult feeling" (p. 122). Restricting his comments largely to
       the Unification Church, the author examines the activities of two
       anticult organizations, namely "The People's Organized Workshop on
       Ersatz Religion" (POWER) and "Family Action, Information, and Res-
       cue" (FAIR), the second being the one still very active in the
       1980's. Several differences between anticultism in Great Britain
       and the United States are mentioned and illustrated by case studies.
       The author maintains that there are social conditions that lead
       relatives of cult members to formulate a brainwashing image and to
       use it to justify deprogramming.

2114. Beckford, James A. "The State and Control of New Religious Move-
       ments." RELIGION AND THE PUBLIC DOMAIN: ACTS OF THE 17TH INTER-
       NATIONAL CONFERENCE FOR THE SOCIOLOGY OF RELIGION, London, 1983.
       Paris, France: C.I.S.R., 1983, pp. 115-30.

Discusses the relationship between, and possible control of, the
state and the new religious movements, such as the Unification
Church, Scientology, the Hare Krishna Movement, the Divine Light
Mission, and the Children of God. The author thinks that state
control of these movements has been indirect, bureaucratic, and
rather similar to control over other comparable institutions.
Lack of official policy and laws aimed at the new religions tend
to create public distrust and paranoia. He suggests that the
treatment of the new cults has been benign when compared to that
afforded such groups as the Hutterites, the Mormons, and the
Shakers. The new movements, in their effort to establish themselves, have complained against government interference, but they
have not been singled out for special repressive treatment.

2115.   Beckford, James A. "The Public Response to New Religious Movements
        in Britain." SOCIAL COMPASS 30.1 (1983): 49-62.

        Examines, under five headings, how the general public in Great
        Britain has reacted to the presence of new religious movements or
        cults: 1) the establishment of religion; 2) the anticult campaign;
        3) the procult campaign; 4) the mass media and the cults; and
        5) policy implications. The distinctive strategies that the cults
        have adopted in response to the public outcry are also outlined.

2116.   Beckford, James A. "A Typology of Family Responses to a New Reli-
        gious Movement." CULTS AND THE FAMILY (item 644), pp. 41-55.

        Presents a study on the ways close relatives of members and ex-
        members of the Unification Church have responded to their involve-
        ment in this controversial movement. Three types of responses are
        recorded: incomprehension, anger, and ambivalence.   Parents are
        stunned by, and are unable to react to, their offspring's decision,
        or else they counteract angrily, or, finally, they sadly accept
        their children's new way of life. It is contended that each type
        of reaction corresponds to the family relationship at the time
        affiliation to the Unification Church took place.

2117.   Beckford, James A. "Beyond the Pale: Cults, Culture, and Conflict."
        NEW RELIGIOUS MOVEMENTS: A PERSPECTIVE FOR UNDERSTANDING SOCIETY
        (item 551), pp. 284-301.

        Examines popular sentiment towards unpopular cults and attempts
        to unearth the kinds of deep-rooted concerns that give rise to
        hostility towards them. In so doing, the author hopes to understand
        the British response to the change of ideology, religion, and life
        style that the cults openly espouse. People who join cults are
        judged to be abnormal in the sense that they are: 1) brainwashed;
        2) harmful to self; 3) controlled; 4) infantile; 5) drifting; 6)
        fanatical; 7) artificially committed; and 8) family-indifferent.
        On the other hand, normal people who do not join a cult are said
        to be 1) freethinking; 2) self-concerned; 3) autonomous; 4) adult;
        5) purposeful; 6) balanced; 7) genuinely committed; and 8) family-
        oriented. Three major conclusions are drawn: 1) there is an under-
        lying logic in anticult feeling; 2) cult critics are not necessar-
        ily irrationally fearful or prejudiced; and 3) anticultism should
        not be dismissed as a witch hunt.

2118.   Beckford, James A.   "Cults, Controversy, and Control: A Comparative
        Analysis of the Problems Posed by New Religious Movements in the
        Federal Republic of Germany and France."   SOCIOLOGICAL ANALYSIS
        42 (1981): 249-64.

        Focuses on the practical response to the major cults (namely the
        Unification Church, Scientology, the Divine Light Mission, the
        Children of God, the Hare Krishna Movement, and Transcendental
        Meditation) in West Germany and France. The author considers the
        religious history, local problems, and the modes of social control
        in each country. He concludes that 1) the way the "cult problem"
        is conceived depends on the particular country's social, political,
        and cultural conditions; 2) the social networks that have influ-
        enced anticult feeling must be taken into consideration; and 3) the
        issue of the civil rights of cults has not figured prominently in
        either France or West Germany. In comparison, the more rigid sepa-
        ration of church and state in the United States of America has
        militated against state intervention and control of the cults, but
        the level of overt conflict with them has been higher in the United
        States than in the other two countries.

2119.   Beckford, James A.   "Politics and the Anti-Cult Movement." ANNUAL
        REVIEW OF THE SOCIAL SCIENCES OF RELIGION 3 (1978): 169-89.

        Points out that a fairly uniform understanding of religious cults
        in the West can be found among social scientists, lawyers, and the
        general public. The reactions to the cults are related to far-
        reaching changes taking place in industrialized societies. Since
        the responses to the cults are political, one can make the follow-
        ing conclusions: 1) the controversy is not a frivolous one, but
        rather based on fundamental issues; 2) anticultism is not an irra-
        tional and highly subjective impulse, but a legitimate position
        regarding collective behavior; and 3) the cults themselves should
        be taken more seriously.

2120.   Beckford, James A., and Melanie A. Cole.   "British and American
        Responses to New Religious Movements." BULLETIN OF THE JOHN
        RYLANDS UNIVERSITY LIBRARY OF MANCHESTER 70.3 (1988): 209-24.

        Outlines and compares the images of new religious movements found
        in print media accounts in Britain and the United States. The
        effects of these accounts on the public response is then discussed.
        Journalists, according to the authors, tend to present a highly
        unfavorable image of the cults. Wallis's view (item 2214) that the
        public images of the cults in the two countries are related to
        constitutional, legal, political, and administrative differences,
        is refuted. The authors maintain that outbursts of violence
        against the cults in the United States cannot be explained solely
        by procedural matters and suggest various other factors that must
        be considered in order to understand this element of violence.

2121.   Bellah, Robert N., and Frederick E. Greenspahn, editors.   CIVIL
        RELIGION: INTERRELIGIOUS HOSTILITY IN AMERICA.   New York: Cross-
        road, 1987.   x, 235 pp.

Presents a collection of essays that discuss conflict and tensions between religious groups in America. Four major areas are
covered: 1) Jewish-Christian; 2) Protestant-Catholic; 3) liberal-
conservative; 4) emergent religious groups (cults). The societal
conflict between the new cults and the traditional religious and
social groups is put in a broader historical perspective. The view
that modern cults are dangerous and threatening novelties has parallels in the religious conflicts that have taken place throughout
the history of America. "Hostility," the editors claim, "is a sign
of underlying insecurity, a sense not only of personal danger, but
of religious uncertainty, with deep-seated social and psychological
concerns masked by theological language" (ix).

Contains items 2141, 2195.

2122. Biermans, John T. THE ODYSSEY OF NEW RELIGIOUS MOVEMENTS: A CASE
       STUDY OF THE UNIFICATION CHURCH. Lewistown, NY: Edwin Mellen
       Press, revised and expanded edition, 1988. xix, 357 pp.

       Assesses the current debate surrounding the Unification Church,
       particularly the allegation that its members are brainwashed and
       that the Reverend Moon controls every aspect of their lives. The
       author, himself a lawyer and member of the Unification Church,
       considers in turn the question of religious bigotry in historical
       perspective, the brainwashing myth, and the issue of deprogramming.
       He compares the attack on Unification Church members and their
       conversion experience to similar phenomena in other religious tra-
       ditions and finds similarities between anti-Catholicism, anti-
       Semitism, and anticultism. The role of the media, which have been
       rather sensational in their reports on the new movements, and the
       legal problems that the Unification Church has faced are discussed.
       A brief criticism of the anticult approach and a summary of the
       major court decisions involving the Unification Church are provided.

2123. Bromley, David G. "Hare Krishna and the Anti-Cult Movement."
       KRISHNA CONSCIOUSNESS IN THE WEST (item 580), pp. 255-92.

       Examines the impact of the Anti-Cult Movement on the Hare Krishna
       Movement by tracing the development of the fear of the cults, the
       emergence of organized opposition against them, and the use of
       mental health images to arouse a negative reaction against them.
       Two prominent legal cases, those involving Edward Shapiro and Robin
       George, are reviewed. The ideological orientation of the Anti-Cult
       Movement that evolved out of such cases rejects religious commit-
       ment that threatens family solidarity, removes individuals from
       their normal networks, and renounces secular rationalism. The
       strategic development of the Anti-Cult Movement into the formative,
       expansionist, and professional stages is traced. The author sees
       the conflict between this movement and ISKCON as a reflection of
       "more profound cultural tensions between secular/individualistic
       and sacred/communal lifestyles" (p. 287).

2124. Bromley, David G. "Deprogramming as a Mode of Exit From New Reli-
       gious Movements: The Case of the Unificationist Movement." FALL-
       ING FROM THE FAITH (item 578), pp. 185-204.

Examines the method of deprogramming as one way in which a person disengages from a new religious movement. After a description of the Anti-Cult Movement, the role of Ted Patrick in utilizing and diffusing the practice of deprogramming is outlined. Nearly 600 cases of attempted deprogramming of Unification Church members (of which 400 were successful) that occurred between 1973 and 1986 are analyzed. The author observes that there has been a steady drop in the rate of successful deprogrammings as the average age of church members increases. Since the news media have tended to report successful deprogramming attempts, the brainwashing mythology has been reinforced.

2125.   Bromley, David G. "Cults, Crusaders, and the Constitution." LAWS OF OUR FATHER: POPULAR CULTURE AND THE U.S. CONSTITUTION. Edited by Ray B. Browne and Glenn K. Brown. Bowling Green, OH: Bowling Green State University Press, 1986, pp. 167-86.

Argues that the cult scare "has created conditions necessary to morally override normally unassailable proscriptions" (p. 168) and that the rise of the Anti-Cult Movement can be considered a "violation of a constitutional taboo." The author sees some parallels between the Catholic scare of the nineteenth century and the contemporary reaction against the new cults. He describes the emergence of the Anti-Cult Movement and its legal campaigns against the new movements, campaigns which challenge the religious nature of the cults, impede their public fundraising efforts, attempt to define them as charitable organizations, and accuse them of violating the individual's autonomy.

2126.   Bromley, David G., and Bruce C. Bushing. "Understanding the Structure of Contractual and Covenantal Social Relations: Implications for the Sociology of Religion." SOCIOLOGICAL ANALYSIS 49 (Supplement 1988): 15-32.

Distinguishes between contractual and covenantal social relations, a distinction that parallels the traditional sociological contrast of tribal versus industrial types of social relationships. It is the authors' view that Western society has adopted a state-authorized contractual form of social relationship, while the new religious movements have opted for the covenantal type. The differences and conflicts between the two types of relationship are discussed in the context of the contemporary cult controversy.

2127.   Bromley, David G., and James T. Richardson, editors. THE BRAINWASHING/DEPROGRAMMING CONTROVERSY: SOCIOLOGICAL, PSYCHOLOGICAL, LEGAL, AND HISTORICAL PERSPECTIVES. New York: Edwin Mellen Press, 1983. 367 pp.

Edits a collection of essays that examine from different academic perspectives the current debate about the recruitment and socialization of new cult members and the attempts to return them forcibly to their previous lifestyle and belief system. An introduction by James Richardson explores traditional and contemporary views of conversion and maintains that the brainwashing hypothesis has not been proved. It is concluded that no absolute generalizations can

yet be made on the effects that the new religious movements might
have on their members. A bibliography is appended (pp. 345-67).

Contains items 944, 1033, 2110, 2113, 2133, 2174, 2209.

2128. Bromley, David G., and Anson D. Shupe. "Public Reaction Against
       New Religious Movements." CULTS AND NEW RELIGIOUS MOVEMENTS
       (item 611), pp. 305-34.

       Examines "the sources, dynamics, and consequences of the public
       reaction" to the cults in the United States. After a review of the
       response to other religious groups (such as Roman Catholics, the
       Mormons, the Jehovah's Witnesses, the Quakers, the Mennonites, and
       Christian Science) in other periods of history, particularly the
       nineteenth century, the authors summarize responses that families,
       the churches and other religious organizations, the government, and
       the media have made to the new cults. Various factors that have
       escalated the problem to a global issue and changed it from a con-
       flict of interest to a social scare are examined. The authors hold
       that the subversion mythology of cult activity has failed to under-
       stand that the presence of the new religions is the result of "com-
       plex macrostructural factors" that leave individuals with little
       influence.

2129. Bromley, David G., and Anson D. Shupe. "The Future of the Anticult
       Movement." THE FUTURE OF NEW RELIGIOUS MOVEMENTS (item 579), pp.
       221-34.

       Studies the contemporary anticult movement to identifying those
       factors that influence its internal growth and external impact on
       society. Three stages of this movement--the formative, expansion-
       ist, and institutional--are identified. Various components of the
       movement, such as its membership base, ideology, and strategy, are
       considered. The authors think that the movement will most likely
       "decline into relative obscurity and impotence," though it "could
       develop into a regulatory organization with a public mandate to
       monitor deviant practices by a wider range of religious groups"
       (p. 233).

2130. Bromley, David G., and Anson D. Shupe. "The Archetypical Cult:
       Conflict and the Social Construction of Deviance." THE FAMILY
       AND THE UNIFICATION CHURCH (item 1785), pp. 1-22.

       Argues that the Unification Church has become a symbol of the
       ideal cult because of its conflicts with other powerful groups and
       the activities of the Anti-Cult Movement. The background to the
       conflict is briefly sketched. Several sources of friction, like
       the family, the mainline churches, and the government, are singled
       out. The problems generated by the conversion of young adults to
       the Unification Church reached public attention because of the
       leaders' own activities, the group's work, and its location and
       mobility. For a variety of reasons, the Unification Church became
       the symbol of evil and the target of the Anti-Cult Movement, which
       originally came into being as a limited response to converts to the
       Children of God. It is the authors' view that the stereotypical
       image of the cult "bore little resemblance to reality" (p. 20).

2131. Bromley, David G., and Anson D. Shupe. "Repression and the Decline
       of Social Movements: The Case of the New Religious Movements."
       SOCIAL MOVEMENTS OF THE SIXTIES AND SEVENTIES (item 343), pp.
       335-47.

       Points out that social repression has been one of the many
       factors that have contributed to the decline of new movements like
       the Unification Church. After a brief description of this Church's
       theology and structure and of the Anti-Cult Movement, the authors
       dwell on the sources of conflict that are inherent in the Unifica-
       tionist Movement, namely its demand for total commitment and its
       goal of an imminent transformation of the social order. Much of
       the resistance to the Unification Church can be traced to the Anti-
       Cult Movement that received support from both fundamentalist and
       mainline Christian churches. The Anti-Cult Movement acquired some
       government support for its legal campaigns against this movement.
       Though little government action against the cults has been taken,
       the activities of the Anti-Cult Movement created a lot of public
       attention and made its brainwashing theory popular. The media also
       aided the Anti-Cult Movement's goals by the sympathetic coverage of
       its conferences and news reports and its negative portrayal of the
       Unification Church.

*   Bromley, David G., and Anson D. Shupe. "The Tnevnoc Cult." Cited
       above as item 1172.

2132. Bromley, David G., Anson D. Shupe, and Bruce C. Bushing. "Repres-
       sion of Religious 'Cults.'" RESEARCH IN SOCIAL MOVEMENTS, CON-
       FLICTS, AND CHANGE 4 (1981): 25-45.

       Examines the sources of strain between the Unification Church and
       other major institutions in the United States and the repressive
       social measures that are consequently taken. Religion and the
       family are identified as the two main sources of conflict. Those
       who participate in the Anti-Cult Movement are usually the relatives
       of cult members and members of fundamentalist Christian groups, the
       former attempting to exert social pressure against the cults, the
       latter stressing the need to warn Christians of the dangers of
       cultic involvement. The support given to the Anti-Cult Movement
       by the churches, the government, and the media is discussed. The
       success of the movement against the new religions has been largely
       due to its alliance with other institutions. The Unification
       Church has little power to resist either the sanctions imposed on
       it or the label of deviancy. The authors argue that once the
       study of a social movement moves from a sociopsychological per-
       spective to an organizational one, repression becomes an important
       concern.

2133. Bromley, David G., Anson D. Shupe, and J. C. Ventimiglia. "The Role
       of Anecdotal Atrocities in the Social Construction of Evil." THE
       BRAINWASHING/DEPROGRAMMING CONTROVERSY (item 2127), pp. 139-59.

       Discusses the use of atrocity stories about cults that are meant
       to evoke outrage, authorize punitive sanctions, and mobilize social
       action against those who appear to violate human rights and basic

social values. The authors examine a whole range of atrocity
tales told by opponents of the Unification Church and show how
these stories are employed to discredit the movement and to arouse
hostile sentiments against the cults in general. Several values
that the cults are accused of violating are mentioned. Atrocity
tales, according to the authors, "help construct a moral basis for
otherwise immoral actions" (p. 160).

2134. Bromley, David G., Anson D. Shupe, and J. C. Ventimiglia. "Atrocity
        Tales, the Unification Church, and the Social Construction of
        Evil." JOURNAL OF COMMUNICATION 29.3 (1979): 42-53.

        Discusses the conflict between marginal religious groups (the
        Unification Church in particular) and society. It is argued that
        one effective strategy in the "war of accusations" is the atrocity
        tale, a story that evokes moral outrage, justifies punitive sanc-
        tions, and encourages control efforts. The logic used to justify
        and rationalize the negative labeling of cult members is described.
        Six types of atrocities—physical, psychological, economic, asso-
        ciative, political/legal, and general cultural—are surveyed. The
        most frequent accusation has been the imputation of psychological
        harm to one's freedom and autonomy. Statements by ex-cult members,
        who had been deprogrammed, provide the ultimate authorization for
        the negative reaction to the cults.

2135. Cannon, Charles A. "The Awesome Power of Sex: The Polemic Campaign
        Against Mormon Polygamy." PACIFIC HISTORICAL REVIEW 34 (1974):
        61-82.

        Examines the polemic literature directed against Mormon polygamy
        with the aim of finding out the popular attitudes towards sex in
        America. The "Mormon Problem," as polygamy was referred to, was
        debated on several levels, including the economic, political, theo-
        logical, and moral. The article focuses on the moral critique of
        Mormon polygamy, since this clearly reveals the public attitudes
        towards sex and the family. The author questions the charge of
        unbridled sexuality that was often leveled at the Mormons. He
        points out that the campaign against Mormon polygamy "allowed Amer-
        icans to express vicariously their repressed desires at the same
        time that they reinforced the rigid sexual values of the existing
        order" (p. 82).

2136. Cherry, Charles L. "Enthusiasm and Madness: Anti-Quakerism in the
        Seventeenth Century." QUAKER HISTORY 74 (1984): 1-24.

        Shows how Quakers were persecuted and how they responded to the
        many attacks against them. The author's main point is that Quakers'
        concern for mental illness was a result of the persecutions they
        suffered. George Fox's attitude towards mental illness is outlined
        at some length. Because of their doctrine of the Inner Light and
        their innate tolerance of eccentricity, Quakers were bound to
        attract people with unstable minds, people who were treated com-
        passionately by Fox who attempted to cure them. The many attacks
        against the Quakers are described in two periods, those between
        1655-1670 and 1670-1700, respectively. The author thinks that the

Quakers were not irrational. However, their "implied deviation from social norms left them open to attack and identified them in many minds with the kind of religious enthusiasm leading to social disorder" (p. 23).

*   Cohen, David Steven. "The 'Angel Dancers': The Folklore of Religious Communitarianism." Cited above as item 1213.

2137. Collins, Harry M., and T. J. Pinch. "The Construction of the Paranormal: Nothing Unscientific Is Happening." ON THE MARGINS OF SCIENCE (item 712), pp. 237-69.

Examines the processes employed to establish the existence of paranormal phenomena. The focus is on the tactics used by parapsychologists to gain scientific recognition and by scientists to discredit them. Parapsychologists employ the symbolic and technical hardware of science, a tactic described as one of "metamorphosis" of "being scientists." Critics, on the other hand, refuse to accept the claims of parapsychology, which they associate with spiritualism and the occult. They consequently marshal philosophical arguments against it, accuse it of triviality and fraud, and question its methods. The result is that parapsychologists find it difficult to publish their research results in orthodox scientific journals. The refusal by scientists to consider paranormal phenomena buttresses their view that nothing is really taking place, that is, that paranormal occurrences are nothing else but psychological ones.

2138. Cox, Harvey. "Deep Structure in the Study of New Religions." UNDERSTANDING THE NEW RELIGIONS (item 567), pp. 122-37.

Reflects on the attacks on new religious movements and discovers recurrent "deep structures" that underlie the criticism and condemnation leveled at them. The author identifies four central themes or myths that express primal religious and spiritual fears, namely: 1) the subversion myth; 2) the myth of sexual and behavioral deviancy; 3) the myth of "dissimilation," which implies that the members of the new religions are not truthful; and 4) the myth of the evil eye, which implies people cannot possibly join cults freely.

2139. Cox, Harvey. "Myth Sanctioning Religious Persecution." A TIME FOR CONSIDERATION: A SCHOLARLY APPRAISAL OF THE UNIFICATION CHURCH (item 1652), pp. 3-19.

Gives a slightly different version of another essay in which the author explores mythological themes behind the persecution of new religions. In this version, he mentions five myths that have been used to justify persecution: 1) the subversion myth; 2) the orgy myth; 3) the "dissimilation" myth; 4) the evil eye myth; and 5) the benevolent inquisitor myth. The positive and negative functions of each myth are briefly alluded to and some psychological interpretations are advanced.

2140. Eck, Diana L. "Response of the Church to New Religious Movements: A Report From North America." NEW RELIGIOUS MOVEMENTS AND THE CHURCHES (item 577), pp. 138-56.

Discusses the suspicious and hostile response of the Christian
Church to the new cults and identifies four issues that must be
taken into consideration in order to understand this reaction.
These issues are 1) otherness (or religious pluralism), 2) heresy,
3) illegal and deceptive activities of the cults, and 4) cult ideology. Some specific responses are examined. The author describes
some of the resource centers in the United States for the study of
new movements. She observes that a shift in focus is already taking place with the New Age Movement being perceived as a cultural
movement towards Eastern ideology and values and as a greater danger than the cults.

*   Enroth, Ronald, and Neil T. Duddy. "Legitimation Processes in Some
         New Religions." Cited above as item 599.

2141.   Foster, Lawrence. "Cults in Conflict: New Religious Movements and
         the Mainstream Religious Traditions in America." UNCIVIL RELI-
         GION: INTERRELIGIOUS HOSTILITY IN AMERICA (item 2121), pp. 185-204.

         Explores some of the reasons why cults or new religious movements
         in the U.S.A., have created tensions with the mainstream religions
         and often encountered less hostility in America than in other parts
         of the world. The nineteenth-century Mormons are taken as an exam-
         ple of the complex reactions to new religious movements. In the
         U.S.A. cults have generally acquired a measured of acceptability as
         long as they lived within the limits of American pluralism. The
         reasons for hostility have been the cults' criticism of the domi-
         nant religious beliefs, their challenge to the established order,
         and their unusual social practices. The author thinks that the
         diversity of religious groups has inhibited conflict.

2142.   Hargrove, Barbara. "Evil Eyes and Religious Choices." SOCIETY
         17.3 (1980): 20-24.

         Considers two types of origin of the charge of brainwashing,
         namely: 1) the kind of activity of cult members that leads to such
         charges, and 2) the accusers' cultural and experiential basis for
         interpreting this activity as a result of brainwashing. The main
         issue as to whether those who join a new religious movement are
         manipulated to give their commitment or genuinely converted is
         discussed. The author compares the accusation of brainwashing to
         that of bewitchment. Brainwashing is the evil eye theory appropri-
         ate to modern scientific culture.

2143.   Harper, Charles L. "The Social Construction of Malevolence: Re-
         thinking Theories of the New Religions." FREE INQUIRY IN CRE-
         ATIVE SOCIOLOGY 6.1 (1988): 3-13.

         Critically reviews recent theories of the new religious movements
         and argues that they "do not adequately recognize the historic
         nature of cults in America" (p. 5) and fail to ignore the fact that
         they have become a widely recognized social problem. The shift
         from a largely marginal to a less marginal recruitment base is one
         of the main reasons for the unpopularity of the cults. Cults no
         longer attract people from society's fringes; rather, they draw them

from the mainstream and make them marginal. The author thinks that
both the Unification Church and the Anti-Cult Movement have undergone modifications over the last decade and that the cult controversy will soon be resolved.

2144. Harper, Charles L. "Cults and Communities." JOURNAL FOR THE
       SCIENTIFIC STUDY OF RELIGION 21 (1982): 26-38.

       Stresses the need to conduct research on the dynamic relation-
       ship between cults and their community environments. Three new
       religious movements--the Unification Church, Scientology, and the
       Assembly (of Born-Again Christians) in Omaha, Nebraska--are
       discussed in terms of their goal orientations and the ways they
       relate to the community at large. All three groups face the same
       problem, namely how to survive and maintain a distinctive and
       deviant mission in the context of a hostile or indifferent social
       world. The author applies movement-organization theory to analyze
       the way in which the relationship between cults and society affects
       the development and transformation of religious groups. He consid-
       ers several factors that influence this relationship and concludes
       that those religious groups that exist in a hostile environment
       are likely to undergo some change, depending on they way the handle
       hostility.

2145. Harper, Charles L. "The Cult Controversy: Values in Conflict."
       PROCEEDINGS: ASSOCIATION FOR THE SCIENTIFIC STUDY OF RELIGION,
       SOUTHWEST, 1981. 8 pp.

       Discusses the current controversy over the cults in terms of
       conflicting value systems. It is maintained that the debate has
       brought to the fore diverse and irreconcilable conceptions of
       social reality, ideology, and morality. The critical view of the
       new religious movements is briefly presented. Both cult members
       and those involved in the Anti-Cult Movement define each other in
       terms of a manifestation of evil in the world. The advantages of
       dialogue between both groups is stressed. The author suggests that
       the cult controversy is indicative of the contradictory values that
       exist in American culture.

2146. Harper, Charles. "Love Our Children: An Ethnography of Anti-Cult
       Organizations." PROCEEDINGS: ASSOCIATION FOR THE SCIENTIFIC
       STUDY OF RELIGION, SOUTHWEST, 1981. 6 pp.

       Describes the origin and growth of an Omaha-based, anticult orga-
       nization called "Love Our Children," in terms of its goals, social
       functions, and activities. Founded in 1976, this organization
       stresses education, advice, action, and encouragement among its
       goals. Several changes within the group are outlined. Its members
       have served the function of providing advice and emotional support
       to families of cult members.

2147. Heyd, Michael. "The Reaction to Enthusiasm in the Seventeenth Cen-
       tury: Towards an Integral Approach." JOURNAL OF MODERN HISTORY
       53 (1981): 258-80.

Discusses the negative reactions to various religious sects such as the Quakers and millenarian groups, a reaction that fits into Weber's concept of "disenchantment of the world." By studying these reactions in the seventeenth and eighteenth centuries, the author hopes to find "a clue for an understanding of some of the social and political motives behind the European elite's increasing reluctance to resort to supernatural explanations of daily occurrences and historical events" (p. 259). The author suggests that the reaction to religious enthusiasm was related to changing literary forms, evolving medical theories, and modern scientific discoveries. The term "enthusiasm" became a derogatory label and was employed to refer to movements that attacked both church authority and traditional professions and learning and to imply a psychological type of person who was marked by unreasonableness and lack of self-control. Its use points to significant aspects and changes in the mentality of the established elite.

2148. James, Gene G. "Brainwashing: The Myth and the Reality." THOUGHT: A REVIEW OF CULTURE AND IDEA 61 (1986): 241-57.

Discusses, with reference to major writers on the subject, the theory and practice of brainwashing, particularly as it was practiced by the Chinese and North Korean Communists to elicit forced confessions and ideological conversions. The author then shows how brainwashing has been extended to include religious conversion, group therapy, and psychoanalysis. The following elements of brainwashing are described: imprisonment; fear of death; induction of stress and fatigue; humiliation; interrogation; self-analysis; confession; reward and punishment; and indoctrination. It is argued that, after studies like those of John Lifton (THOUGHT REFORM AND THE PSYCHOLOGY OF TOTALISM, New York: Norton, 1961), the concept of brainwashing should never have been applied to the unpopular new religious movements. Brainwashing seems based on the evil eye theory of religious conversion. The so-called brainwashing practices of the Chinese and North Koreans have little in common with the recruiting techniques of the new movements. The author states that brainwashing has been employed as a tool to legitimize oppression.

2149. Kelley, Dean M. "Religious Liberty and Socio-Political Values: Legal Threats to Conversion in the United States." NEW RELIGIOUS MOVEMENTS AND THE CHURCHES (item 577), pp. 89-116.

Argues in favor of protecting "freedom of thought, conscience, and religion." Pointing out that religion provides an explanation of the ultimate meaning of life, the author suggests that the new religious movements may be reaching those people who are outside the influence of conventional religion. The opposition to the new movements, particularly the Anti-Cult Movement's attack on conversion, is discussed. The method of deprogramming is described and attempts to legalize it are documented.

2150. Kilbourne, Brock K. "A Reply to Maher and Langone's Statistical Critique of Kilbourne." JOURNAL FOR THE SCIENTIFIC STUDY OF RELIGION 25 (1986): 116-23.

Presents a lengthy defense of the author's use of statistical
analysis in examining the effects cults have on their members.
Maher and Langone's critique (item 2160) is refuted in detail.
Several statistical tables are produced to buttress the author's
position that cults do not have dire psychological effects on those
who join them.

2151.   Kilbourne, Brock K.   "The Conway and Siegelman Claims Against Reli-
        gious Cults: An Assessment of Their Data." JOURNAL FOR THE
        SCIENTIFIC STUDY OF RELIGION 22 (1983): 380-85.

Challenges the theory of Flo Conway and Jim Siegelman, popularized
in their book SNAPPING: AMERICA'S EPIDEMIC OF SUDDEN PERSONALITY
CHANGE (New York: J. B. Lippincott, 1978), that maintains that
cults have a psychopathological effect on their members. The
author concludes that the data produced to support their theory
rather favors the opposing view, namely that cults might have a
therapeutic effect on those who join them.

2152.   Kilbourne, Brock K., and James T. Richardson.   "Cultphobia."
        THOUGHT: A REVIEW OF CULTURE AND IDEA 61 (1986): 258-76.

Comments on the impact that the Anti-Cult Movement has had on
research on the cults and demonstrates that the psychopathological
argument, which holds that cult members are psychologically disturbed before, during, and after being involved in a cult, can be
applied to the members and sympathizers of the Anti-Cult Movement.
The rise of "cultphobia," an extreme, fearful reaction to cults,
is then described as another psychological disease. Cultphobia
"may be the stress reaction of individuals who feel their way of
life is under attack by the very presence of another social category of people, the cults" (p. 263).

2153.   Kilbourne, Brock K., and James T. Richardson.   "Cults Versus the
        Families: A Case of Misattribution of Cause?" MARRIAGE AND
        FAMILY REVIEW 4.3-4 (1982): 81-101.

Discusses the view that holds that new religious groups are a
threat to the institution of the family, a view that may be an
overreaction to the contemporary cultic phenomenon. The following
areas are covered: 1) the social literature on conversion; 2) the
effects of historical forces and stresses on the family; 3) the
diversity of family forms in American culture; and 4) the research
on the impact the new religious movements are having on the family.
The authors argue that the strains on the family are more correctly
attributed to social conditions than to the rise of the cults.

2154.   Kirkpatrick, Lee A.   "The Conway-Siegelman Data on Religious Cults:
        Kilbourne's Analysis Reassessed (Again)." JOURNAL FOR THE SCIEN-
        TIFIC STUDY OF RELIGION 27 (1988): 117-21.

Continues the debate on the data amassed by Conway and Siegelman
to confirm their view that cults have deleterious effects on their
members. Kilbourne's rebuttal of their argument (item 2151) is
criticized. The author raises issues about the interpretation of

the data by Conway and Siegelman and by Kilbourne. The random
sample of all possible cults as well as the small sample size lead
to the conclusion that "only the most tentative conclusions are
warranted at present" (p. 121).

2155. Kranenborg, Reender. "Churches' Response to Innovative Religious
       Movements of the Past." NEW RELIGIOUS MOVEMENTS AND THE CHURCHES
       (item 577), pp. 119-32.

       Dwells on the way in which the Protestant churches of the Nether-
       lands have responded to sects and cults between 1860 and 1960. The
       following movements and the societal reactions to them are briefly
       described: Jehovah's Witnesses; Christian Science; the Sufi Order;
       Theosophy; and the Lou Movement. The author states that: 1) real
       interest in new religious movements has been minimal; 2) very few
       efforts have been made to engage members of these movements in
       conversation; 3) the refutation of the movements has been exclu-
       sively theological; 4) the sociology of religion has been largely
       neglected; and 5) the innovative aspects of the movements have
       been almost totally ignored. Several practical recommendations
       are made to remedy what the author believes to be an inadequate
       and mistaken approach to the new religious movements.

2156. Langone, Michael D. "Cults, Evangelicals, and the Ethics of Social
       Influence." CULTIC STUDIES JOURNAL 2 (1985): 371-88.

       Discusses two main issues that the activities of the cults have
       raised, namely: 1) the proper place for proselytizing; and 2) the
       ethical boundaries of proselytization. Four kinds of influences,
       that is, educative, advisory, persuasive, and coercive, are distin-
       guished. The author insists that every profession that seeks to
       change people's behavior must be guided by an ethical code and must
       be held accountable for its practices.

2157. Levine, Edward M. "Deprogramming Without Tears." SOCIETY 17.3
       (1980): 34-38.

       Describes the process by which young adults are recruited and
       indoctrinated into cults as one characterized by deceit, threat,
       and manipulation. Cults provide "a clear sense of purpose, dispel
       confusion and uncertainty, and provide them [i.e., the recruits]
       with direction, stability, and an intensely sought-after inner
       peace" (p. 35). Cults, however, take over full control of the
       minds and lives of their members, whose use of reason is replaced
       with irrational considerations. Judicious deprogramming undoes
       these harmful effects of cult indoctrination by making cult members
       confront false claims and rationalizations. Cults may be symptoms
       of a social condition that leads people to "escape from freedom."

2158. Lewis, James R. "Apostates and the Legitimation of Repression:
       Some Historical and Empirical Perspectives on the Cult Contro-
       versy." SOCIOLOGICAL ANALYSIS 49 (1989): 386-96.

       Examines the attitudes of former members of various new religious
       movements and discovers a correlation between anticult views and
       exposure to anticult socialization, which includes the recitation

of atrocity tales about the cults. Such stories, it is pointed
out, can be found in anti-Catholic, anti-Mormon, and anticult
rhetoric. The author records some typical responses on recruitment, brainwashing, the leader's lifestyle, the cult's worldview,
and the Anti-Cult Movement. He maintains that deprogramming and
exit counseling provide ex-members with a stereotyped, negative
view of cults.

2159. Lewis, James R., and David G. Bromley. "The Cult Withdrawal Syn-
        drome: A Case of Misattribution of Cause?" JOURNAL FOR THE
        SCIENTIFIC STUDY OF RELIGION 26 (1987): 508-22.

        Examines the evidence brought forth to support allegations of
        cultic brainwashing, namely the negative testimony of former mem-
        bers, most of whom had been deprogrammed. The data adduced in sup-
        port of the view that cult membership is psychologically harmful is
        also questioned. The authors outline a role-theory approach that
        shows Conway and Siegelman's information disease theory to be both
        inadequate and misleading. They maintain that the source of emo-
        tional disturbance in former cult members lies in the dynamics of
        the exit process rather than in cult practices.

2160. Maher, Brendon A., and Michael D. Langone. "Kilbourne on Conway
        and Siegelman: A Statistical Critique." JOURNAL FOR THE SCIEN-
        TIFIC STUDY OF RELIGION 24 (1985) 325-26.

        Agrees with Kilbourne's critique (item 2151) of Conway and
        Siegelman's statistical data on the effect of cult membership, but
        complains about Kilbourne's use of the same data to reach the oppo-
        site conclusions. Maher and Langone insist that the available data
        cannot possibly be used to show that the effects of cult membership
        are beneficial. The need to apply adequate measures, samples, and
        statistics is underscored.

2161. Marciano, Teresa Donati. "Families and Cults." CULTS AND THE
        FAMILY (item 644), pp. 101-17.

        Discusses, in the context of contemporary sociological theory,
        the various family issues that arise when a young adult joins a new
        religious movement. The claims that parents have on their child-
        ren, family boundaries and the cults, the opposition of the family
        to their offspring's decisions, and the deprivation theory of cult
        formation are among the topics covered. The author maintains that
        the weight of scholarly opinion does not support the alarmist view
        that cults are a danger to the individual and to society.

2162. McDowell, Josh, and Don Stewart. UNDERSTANDING THE CULTS. San
        Bernardino, CA: Here's Life Publishers, 1982. 199 pp.

        Presents basically an apologetic work that is typical of the
        evangelical and fundamentalist Christian response to the cults.
        Though restricting its characterization of a cult to a form of
        "theological aberrancy," the authors assume some of the anticult
        rhetoric in their insistence that cults have strong leaders who
        control the lives of their followers with sometimes disastrous

consequences. A simple typology, distinguishing orthodox from nonorthodox Christianity, is adopted. Among the groups described and
exposed for their unorthodox and irreligious beliefs and practices
are the following: the Hare Krishna Movement, the Mormons, EST,
Theosophy, Transcendental Meditation, the Children of God, the
Unification Church, the Way International, the Worldwide Church
of God, Christian Science, and Unity. An annotated bibliography,
mainly of anticult literature, is added (pp. 189-99).

2163.   Melton, J. Gordon. "The Attitude of Americans Toward Hinduism From
        1883 to 1983, With Special Reference to the International Society
        for Krishna Consciousness." KRISHNA CONSCIOUSNESS IN THE WEST
        (item 580), pp. 79-101.

        Traces the history of Hinduism in America and the societal re-
        sponse to it in four phases: 1) the late nineteenth century, which
        signaled the entry of Hinduism in America after the World Parlia-
        ment of Religions in Chicago in 1893; 2) the period between 1920
        and the late 1930's, during which two anti-Hindu crusades erupted;
        3) the period from the late 1930's up to 1965, during which time
        attacks against Hindu religious groups diminished and when those
        who joined them "were pictured as socially marginally-psychopathic,
        sexually maladjusted, deviant, or social failures" (p. 88); and 4)
        from 1965, when the law restricting immigration for those of Asian
        descent was repealed. The last period is marked by the rise of the
        Hare Krishna Movement and the responses to it, which changed from
        one of cordiality and curiosity to one of hostility. The move-
        ment's response to this hostility is briefly sketched.

2164.   Melton, J. Gordon. "Violence and the Cults." NEBRASKA HUMANIST
        8.2 (1985): 51-60.

        Summarizes the results of a survey on violence associated with
        new religious movements that was conducted by the Institute for the
        Study of American Religion. Several guidelines were established to
        help evaluate reports on violence. Three types of violence are
        distinguished, namely that: 1) against cults; 2) between related
        cults; and 3) initiated by cults. The causes of cult violence are
        explored and some suggestions for its reduction proposed.

2165.   Oliver, Donna L. "Apostates in the Anti-Catholic Movement." PRO-
        CEEDINGS OF THE ASSOCIATION FOR THE SCIENTIFIC STUDY OF RELIGION,
        SOUTHWEST, 1981. 8 pp.

        Discusses the role of Catholic apostates who joined the anti-
        Catholic movement in the early nineteenth century. Apostates have
        often been used as resource persons in attempts by counter move-
        ments to mobilize resources. The cases of Maria Monk and Rebecca
        Reed, two of the best-known apostates in the 1930's, are brought
        forth as examples. The diverse manners in which these young women
        became sisters in a Catholic convent are examined. The novitiate
        was an intensive socialization process and the communal life of the
        convent resembled the lifestyle of the new religions. The ficti-
        tious accounts of Monk and Reed were attempts to portray their
        recruitment as the result of deception and exploitation. The

disaffiliation from the convent, the consequent recruitment of the
two ex-nuns by anticult organizations, and the reconstruction of
their defection are analyzed. The author thinks that the accounts
of modern apostates from new religious movements deserve a more
critical examination than they have received so far.

2166. Palefreman, Jon. "Between Skepticism and Credulity: A Study of
      Victorian Scientific Attitudes to Modern Spiritualism." ON THE
      MARGINS OF SCIENCE (item 712), pp. 201-36.

      Outlines the history of the interaction between science and spir-
      itualism in Victorian times. Modern spiritualism in England is
      traced to the middle of the nineteenth century, and the debates
      that took place then are overviewed with reference to the main
      protagonists. It is argued that the special interests of magicians
      influenced the fortunes of Spiritualism in the 1860's and 1870's.
      Scientists who taught at colleges and universities developed a
      hostile reaction to Spiritualism, which they called a "pseudo-
      science." Some scientists, however, conducted experiments on
      Spiritualism with the hope of providing evidence of life after
      death. The interaction between science and Spiritualism was highly
      complex and no uniform scientific response was possible.

2167. Pankratz, Loren. "Magician Accuses Faith Healers of Hoax." JOUR-
      NAL OF RELIGION AND HEALTH 26 (1987): 115-24.

      Discusses the findings of James Randi, who concluded that popular
      American faith healers (mediums and psychics) are fraudulent. The
      author reviews the history of the conflict between charlatans and
      their exposers, particularly the debate regarding Spiritualism in
      the nineteenth century and psychics and faith healers in the twen-
      tieth. The guidelines of the National Council Against Health Fraud
      are recommended.

2168. Petranek, Charles F. "The Social Psychology of the Unification
      Church's Recruitment and Commitment: Socialization or Brainwash-
      ing." COMMUNAL STUDIES (item 354), pp. 332-41.

      Attempts to answer the question of why people are so quickly
      converted to the Unification Church. The issue of whether these
      converts are socialized or brainwashed is examined. The author
      considers the predispositions of those who join the movement, the
      interpersonal communication between members, and the selective
      process that takes place before an individual is accepted into the
      church. It is concluded that the conversion pattern of a "Moonie"
      is one that has choice, even though the church used sociopsycho-
      logical techniques to hasten the process of conversion.

2169. Reay, Barry. "Popular Hostility Towards Quakers in Mid-Seven-
      teenth-Century England." SOCIAL HISTORY 5 (1980): 387-407.

      Explores the hostility towards Quakers, particularly the motives,
      attitudes, and behavior of the popular antagonism of the seven-
      teenth century. The causes of the hostility, according to the
      author, may have been partly political and partly the result of

ignorance. Xenophobia, the fear and distrust of strangers, may
have also been responsible for the animosity shown to the Quakers
who, compared to their contemporaries, were more mobile and often
found themselves traveling in remote provincial areas. Quakers,
who were frequently accused of sorcery and witchcraft, were considered to be intruders and might have become at times "scapegoats for
the tension generated by a society in flux" (p. 394). Commercial
rivalry might also have played a part in the general anti-Quakerism
mood of seventeenth-century England.

2170. Richardson, James T. "Consumer Protection and Deviant Religion: A
        Case Study." REVIEW OF RELIGIOUS RESEARCH 28 (1986): 168-79.

        Describes the various ways in which government authorities have
        attempted, under pressure from the Anti-Cult Movement, to curtail
        the activities of the new religions. The author concentrates on
        one tactic, namely that of "consumer protection," an approach that
        argues that, while people are free to believe whatever they like,
        their religious practices are subject to regulation. Religion is
        treated as a consumer good from which the public has sometimes to
        be protected. The attempts made in the early 1980's by the Nevada
        State Legislature to pass an Anti-Cult Bill are discussed.

*   Richardson, James T. "New Religious Movements in the United States:
        A Review." Cited above as item 676.

2171. Richardson, James T. "Conversion, Brainwashing, and Deprogram-
        ming." CENTER MAGAZINE 15 (1982): 18-24.

        Reflects on two legal, controversial issues that have surrounded
        the new religions, namely their financial and tax status and their
        recruitment practices, which have resulted in accusations of brain-
        washing. Recent studies on the sociology of conversion are summa-
        rized. The difference between the current sociological view of
        conversion and some contemporary psychological interpretations are
        discussed. The author thinks that the brainwashing theory gives a
        rather naive answer to a very complex problem and that deprogrammers
        have adopted the same tactics they have accused their opponents of
        using.

2172. Richardson, James T., editor. "Brainwashing." SOCIETY 17.3 (1980):
        19-50.

        Edits a series of essays that discusses the brainwashing issue,
        which has been in the forefront of public debate on the cults. The
        articles examine the various problems raised by deprogramming prac-
        tices. Divergent points of view on whether members of cults are
        brainwashed are expressed.

        Contains items 2106, 2142, 2157, 2206.

2173. Richardson, James T., Mary W. Harder, and Robert B. Simmonds.
        "Thought Reform and the Jesus Movement." YOUTH AND SOCIETY 4
        (1972): 185-202.

Examines thought control or brainwashing in relation to the Jesus Movement, focusing on one particular group that had been in existence for four years. Some similarities between brainwashing and the techniques of socialization used by several religious groups are briefly described. The resocialization of prisoners of war is compared to that of converts to the Jesus Movement and some major differences are noted. The main elements of religious totalism are contrasted with thought control and the similarities and differences recorded. The fundamentalism of the Jesus Movement is said to be a good example of religious totalism.

2174. Richardson, James T., and Brock Kilbourne. "Classical and Contemporary Applications of Brainwashing Models: A Comparison and Critique." THE BRAINWASHING/DEPROGRAMMING CONTROVERSY (item 2127), pp. 29-45.

Contends that the brainwashing rhetoric of the 1950's and 1970's share the following features: 1) an ideal perspective; 2) a meta-theoretical structure; 3) a stage-theory explanation of attitudinal and behavioral change; and 4) methodological approaches. Four classic models of brainwashing are distinguished. In spite of their differences, they all share the assumption that change in belief precedes behavioral change. Some apparently new models applied by some scholars to the new religions are actually modifications of earlier ones. In the authors' view, the negative concept of "cult syndrome" is employed to discredit new ideas, social reform, and alternative lifestyles that threaten the members of mainline culture.

2175. Richardson, James T., and Barend van Driel. "Public Support for Anti-Cult Legislation." JOURNAL FOR THE SCIENTIFIC STUDY OF RELIGION 23 (1984): 412-18.

Conducts an exploratory study in Washoe County, Nevada, to find out the support of the general public for legislation exercising some control over new religious movements. The attitudes towards such legislation by party affiliation, age, and religious preference are recorded. It is concluded that the regulation of the new religions is a controversial issue and more research is needed.

2176. Robbins, Thomas. "Church-State Tensions and Marginal Movements in the United States." CHURCH-STATE RELATIONS: TENSIONS AND TRANSITIONS. Edited by Thomas Robbins and Roland Robertson. New Brunswick, NJ: Transaction Books, 1987, pp. 135-49.

Identifies certain tendencies in American culture that contribute to the intensification of the main issues involving cults. State regulation of church matters is discussed in the context of the following cases: 1) the legal suit for tax fraud against the Reverend Moon; 2) the state interference in the financial affairs of the Church of God; and 3) the case brought against Southwestern Baptist Theological Seminary for allegedly not following equal employment regulations. The author explores the legal implications of the accusation of mind control by new cults.

2177. Robbins, Thomas. "Objectionable Aspects of 'Cults': Rhetoric and
       Reality." CULTIC STUDIES JOURNAL 2 (1986): 358-70.

       Reflects on the accusation of "interpersonal foul play" of which
       the cults have been accused. The author considers deception, emo-
       tional manipulation, autonomy and coercion, the breaking up of
       families, and the charge of heresy. He suggests that, although
       cults and sects often appear to be countercultural, they often
       change over time and accommodate themselves to mainstream culture.
       He advises that issues like dangerous healing methods and child
       abuse should not be dealt with as cult issues, but as broader
       social problems.

2178. Robbins, Thomas. "'Uncivil Religions' and Religious Deprogramming."
       THOUGHT: A REVIEW OF CULTURE AND IDEA 61 (1986): 277-89.

       Discusses the emerging patterns, legal status, and underlying
       sociological elements of the American phenomenon of religious de-
       programming. The major trends in this relatively new practice of
       forcefully rescuing devotees from cults are outlined with reference
       to several fundamentalist and charismatic churches or groups. The
       author questions the efficacy of the "brainwashing" allegations in
       "revolving-door cults." He examines the legal aspects of such
       deprogramming and finds the situation rather confused. In American
       society, Civil Religion praises the virtues of tolerance and plu-
       ralism, virtues which those people who favor deprogramming have
       apparently abandoned.

2179. Robbins, Thomas. "Goodbye to Little Red Ridinghood." UPDATE: A
       QUARTERLY JOURNAL OF NEW RELIGIOUS MOVEMENTS 10.2 (1986): 5-18.

       Deals with those theories of cult movements that exaggerate the
       role of mind control or brainwashing in eliciting the conversion
       of unsuspecting people. The author thinks that the brainwashing
       theory negates responsibility and opts for sociological and psycho-
       logical explanations which account better for the available data on
       ex-cult members.

2180. Robbins, Thomas. "Are Conflicting Images of 'Cults' Susceptible to
       Empirical Resolution?" SCIENTIFIC RESEARCH AND NEW RELIGIONS
       (item 645), pp. 138-48.

       Reviews some of the author's previous arguments (see item 2183)
       that brainwashing allegations are used to generate forced conver-
       sions are interpretations rather than factual accounts of what
       happens. Robbins suggests that empirical research might resolve
       the question about the new cults. Longitudinal studies of volun-
       tary defections, the establishment of a recorded ethnological bank
       (on the model of the Human Relations Area Files), and the avoidance
       of specialized or select examples are some of the ways that can
       help illumine many aspects of cults and lessen the academic con-
       flicts about their activities and meaning. It is pointed out,
       however, that since the debates are essentially interpretative,
       they are not subject to a decisive empirical judgment.

2181. Robbins, Thomas. "Government Regulatory Powers and Church Autonomy: Dissident Groups as Test Cases." JOURNAL FOR THE SCIENTIFIC STUDY OF RELIGION 24 (1985): 237-52.

Presents "an analysis of the increasing proliferation of church autonomy conflicts in the United States" (p. 239). The author thinks that such conflicts have become more common because of the expansion of state control and regulation and because of an increase in religious pluralism. He explores the legal issues with reference to the commercial and financial practices of the Unification Church and the Church of God.

2182. Robbins, Thomas. "Religious Movements and Church Autonomy Conflicts." NEBRASKA HUMANIST 8.2 (1985): 40-60.

Examines the recent increase in the number and intensity of church-state conflicts in the United States, conflicts which have been aggravated by the evangelical revival. The expansion of the State's regulatory apparatus and the diversification of religious activities and functions are two contemporary trends that account for the increase in legal cases over church and state autonomy. Conflicts between the church and the state are most intense when the issues are the therapeutic practices and the financial and commercial enterprises of the new religions. Accusations of mind control are becoming more frequent in civil law suits and raise the issue of the free exercise of religion.

2183. Robbins, Thomas. "Constructing Cultist 'Mind Control.'" SOCIOLOGICAL ANALYSIS 45 (1984): 241-56.

Examines the "rhetorical conventions, underlying assumptions, interpretative frameworks, and epistemological rules" (p. 241) behind the accusation that cults use brainwashing techniques. The author's opinion is that allegations that cults are coercive, that they exploit the vulnerable, and that they use deceptive methods to recruit members are not open to empirical verification. While not denying that the cults have created social conflicts that rightly create concerns and have used heavy-handed recruitment and indoctrination practices, the author holds that the view that cult members are brainwashed and their members psychologically imprisoned is an arbitrary assumption that cannot be proved.

2184. Robbins, Thomas. "Marginal Movements." SOCIETY 21.4 (1984): 47-52.

Explains how the tradition of religious liberty and the separation of church and state affect the conflicts between religion and public authority in the United States, particularly when these conflicts involve marginal movements. Various examples, such as the conviction of the Reverend Moon on charges of fraud, are discussed. The author observes that the accusation of "mind control" has been directed towards less esoteric religious groups. He thinks that the current hostility to the new religious movements is based on their "extreme diversification and aspiring omnicompetence."

2185. Robbins, Thomas. "Church, State, and Cult." SOCIOLOGICAL ANALYSIS 42 (1981): 209-226.

Maintains that the presence of highly cohesive and authoritarian cults raises serious social and legal issues. The ambiguities of the "mind control" theory, which has been at the basis of many law suits, are discussed. The author insists that the problems brought about by cults cannot be properly understood if they are treated as medical or mental health issues. He views the cults as "basically legitimate organizations which meet genuine needs of individuals and perform vital functions for participants" (p. 214). Cults are seen as structures that mediate between the individual and the larger institutions of modern society and that provide face-to-face contact among people who share similar values. They make possible communal fellowship and restore a person's identity that has been fractured by modern culture. Three policy considerations are advanced in favor of 1) the regulation of the gap between the churches and the new movements, 2) the dependency and exploitation of cult members, and 3) the conflict resolution by the state. The current controversies over cults are, in the author's view, closely related to current church-state issues.

2186. Robbins, Thomas. "Cults and the Therapeutic State." SOCIAL POLICY 10.1 (1979): 42-46.

Examines the attacks against religious cults, such as the Unification Church, Scientology, and Synanon, and the demands for legal action based on psychiatric arguments. The author discusses the state's interest in, and rights over, an individual and suggests that any conversion might involve a personality change. The stereotyping of cults as organizations that destroy one's freedom of choice, control one's mind, and pursue sinister goals "is clearly derivative from the demonological conceptions of the Unification Church" (p. 45). The author considers the potential of violence that exists with respect to 1) voluntary and involuntary exodus from the cults, 2) relationships with hostile neighbors, 3) child custody, and 4) kidnaping and deprogramming.

2187. Robbins, Thomas, and Dick Anthony. "Deprogramming, Brainwashing, and the Medicalization of Deviant Religious Groups." SOCIAL PROBLEMS 29 (1982): 283-97.

Discusses the brainwashing theory of cult recruitment and shows how the opponents of cults use the medical model of pathology and involuntary behavior to justify therapeutic intervention and to neutralize civil liberties arguments. The authors outline the process of deprogramming and summarize its legal status. They suggest that the medical profession (particularly psychologists and psychiatrists) indirectly view the new cults as "competitors." The social-scientific arguments against the medicalization of cults are presented. A useful bibliography is included (pp. 293-97).

2188. Robbins, Thomas, and Dick Anthony. "Religious Movements and the Brainwashing Issue." VIOLENCE AND THE CULTS (item 653), pp. 133-38.

Points out that the Jonestown tragedy has shifted public attitude against the cults in general and has been interpreted as a vindication of the theory of brainwashing. The authors discuss this theory and point out some of its weaknesses when it is applied to the new religious movements. They reject an underlying premise of the theory, namely that no person in his or her right mind could voluntarily commit oneself to a deviant ideology and lifestyle. In a culture pervaded by anomie, they argue, "one cannot really infer manipulation or brainwashing from seemingly irrational patterns of self-renunciation and asceticism" (p. 138).

2189. Robbins, Thomas, and Dick Anthony. "Cults, Brainwashing, and Counter-Subversion." ANNALS OF THE AMERICAN ACADEMY OF POLITICAL AND SOCIAL SCIENCE 446 (November 1979): 79-80.

Compares current anticult sentiment and activity and finds that it has parallels in the nineteenth-century reactions to Masons, Mormons, and Catholics. The fear that new religions are subversive and conducive to violence is demonstrated with reference to contemporary anticult literature. The new cults are believed to be dangerous because they control the minds of their adherents. Both past and present critics of religious revivals draw their conclusions from accounts of ex-converts. The Anti-Cult Movement is criticized for propagating overgeneralized stereotypes of cults and for adopting the same authoritarianism and intolerance of which they accuse the cults. The authors interpret the rise of the new movements as the result of the decline of American Civil Religion, a decline that has created cultural confusion and moral ambiguity.

2190. Robbins, Thomas, and Dick Anthony. "New Religions, Families, and Brainwashing." SOCIETY 15.4 (1978): 77-83.

Discusses the reactions to the new religious movements, focusing on the theory that cult members are brainwashed. The authors think that brainwashing is a metaphor for "a social weapon which provides a libertarian rationale for persecuting unpopular social movements and ideologies" (p. 78). Three aspects of brainwashing are dealt with: 1) the subjectivity of the brainwashing (or mind control) notion; 2) the concealed concern for certain belief systems; and 3) the involuntary nature of unpopular belief. The authors refute the view that the decline of family is due, in part, to the presence of the new movements. They suggest instead that this decline predates the rise of the cults and that attacks on these might contribute to increased hostilities between parents and their offspring. They point out, however, that a few of the new religious movements exercise tight information control over their members, a control that can easily be interpreted as totalistic.

*   Robbins, Thomas, William C. Shepherd, and James McBride, editors. CULTS, CULTURE, AND THE LAW. Cited above as item 684.

2191. Saliba, John A. "Christian and Jewish Religious Responses to the Hare Krishna Movement in the West." KRISHNA CONSCIOUSNESS IN THE WEST (item 580), pp. 119-37.

Describes three possible types of religious responses to new movements, namely: 1) relative neglect, which ignores or dismisses the problem raised by the so-called cults; 2) apologetic activity,

which takes a confrontational approach; and 3) attempts at dialogue, which is aimed at mutual understanding and cooperation. The
religious evaluation of the Hare Krishna Movement and the reasons
usually adduced to explain its success are outlined. In spite of
the fact that the religious response to the cults and to the Hare
Krishna in particular has been dominated by negative apologetic
arguments and influenced by legal and social campaigns of the Anti-
Cult Movement, the author observes that there have been some balanced nonbelligerent evaluations of the Hare Krishna Movement.

2192. Sandon, Leo. "Responding to the New Cult Politics." SOUNDINGS 62
       (1979): 323-28.

       Reflects on Horowitz's concern with the Unification Church and
       its involvement in political matters (item 1782). While agreeing
       that this church's political theory and practice have some unsa-
       vory implications, the author thinks that Horowitz is overreacting
       to the perceived danger of cults.

2193. Schwartz, Lita Linzer. "Parental Responses to Their Children's
       Cult Membership." CULTIC STUDIES JOURNAL 3 (1986): 190-203.

       Surveys the emotional reaction of the parents of cult members and
       some of the measures they took to return their offspring to a more
       traditional lifestyle. Among the measures described are deprogram-
       ming, court-ordered guardianship, exit counseling, law suits, and
       family therapy.

2194. Shepherd, William C. TO SECURE THE BLESSINGS OF FREEDOM: AMERICAN
       CONSTITUTIONAL LAW AND THE NEW RELIGIOUS MOVEMENTS. New York:
       Crossroad, 1985. 155 pp.

       Discusses some of the legal problems raised by the presence of
       the new religious movements and by the public's response to them.
       The main constitutional issues, the legal foundations of individual
       rights, and the laws governing forcible deprogramming are among the
       topics covered. A basic bibliography (pp. 136-44) and a table of
       legal cases (pp. 145-47) are added.

2195. Shupe, Anson D. "Constructing Evil as a Social Process: The Unifi-
       cation Church and the Media." UNCIVIL RELIGION: INTERRELIGIOUS
       HOSTILITY IN AMERICA (item 2121), pp. 105-18.

       Explains that in the sociological study of conflicts between
       religious groups antisocial or deviant behavior is seen as a con-
       struct by people who are in power. The Unification Church is taken
       as a classic example of how evil can become a social construct and
       how heresy can be used as means of imputing evil. Public awareness
       of the Unification Church has gone through the following five dif-
       ferent stages, each corresponding to a different perception of evil:
       1) latent (preconstruction); 2) benign; 3) skeptical; 4) accepted
       malicious; and 5) postmalicious. The author thinks that "the
       mythology of Moonism says more about the society that reacted to
       the Unification Church than about the objective features of the
       group" (p. 216).

2196. Shupe, Anson D. "The Routinization of Conflict in the Modern Cult/
       Anticult Controversy." NEBRASKA HUMANIST 8.2. (1985): 26-39.

       Examines the trend to institutionalize the cult controversy,
       which the author sees as part of a larger religious conflict and
       division. It is pointed out that, while the early stage of the
       cult controversy was marked by "deviance amplification," recent
       events have been characterized by a deamplification process that
       has been hastened by three factors, namely: 1) the use of the media
       by both groups; 2) the need of both sides to appear legitimate in
       the eyes of the public; and 3) the state's sovereignty that imposes
       limits on the conflict. Due to the pressures of the courts, the
       conflict has been restricted mostly to a symbolic level. The reli-
       ance on the media for disseminating one's point of view has led to
       internal developments that include the abandonment of extreme
       strategies, thus institutionalizing the conflict.

2197. Shupe, Anson D., and David G. Bromley. "Social Responses to Cults."
       THE SACRED IN A SECULAR AGE (item 623), pp. 58-72.

       Discusses the counter response to the new religious movements in
       order to broaden "our understanding of both the role of the sacred
       in a secular society and the developmental process which new reli-
       gious groups typically follow" (p. 59). The conflict between the
       new movements and the Anti-Cult Movement is interpreted as a strug-
       gle between the sacred and the secular. The organizational struc-
       tures of the countermovements are determined by their specific
       objections to the new groups, by the very nature of these groups,
       and by the legal limitations. Brainwashing is seen as the secular
       equivalent of spirit possession—in both cases the individual lacks
       the free will to make a decision and is held captive by force. The
       authors believe that the study of the Anti-Cult Movement, a study
       that exists in a symbiotic relationship with the new religions, is
       essential for an understanding of how and why new groups come into
       being and develop.

2198. Shupe, Anson D., and David G. Bromley. "Apostates and Atrocity
       Stories: Some Parameters in the Dynamics of Deprogramming." THE
       SOCIAL IMPACT OF THE NEW RELIGIOUS MOVEMENTS (item 725), pp. 179-
       215.

       Examines the influence that apostates have had on the general
       public attitudes towards the new religions. Basing their reflec-
       tions on data from the Unification Church, the authors consider in
       sequence the sources of strain between families and the cults, the
       dynamics of deprogramming, and the social context of apostasy and
       atrocity tales. The justification for deprogramming and the fac-
       tors that influence the dynamics and results of deprogramming are
       discussed. It is argued that there has never been "a reliable,
       standard 'therapeutic' deprogramming procedure which invariably
       'restored free thought' and which restored offspring to their fami-
       lies" (p. 188). Those apostates who joined anticult groups took
       part in two kinds of activities directed towards cult members.
       They either became involved in counseling procedures that helped
       members reevaluate their commitment or they participated in coer-
       cive deprogramming. Apostates provided the inside stories to

support the brainwashing theory and to discredit the movements'
claim to legitimacy. The recounting of these tales has in fact
had a great impact on the development of the cults themselves.

2199. Shupe, Anson D., and David G. Bromley. "Shaping the Public Response
      to Jonestown: People's Temple and the Anti-Cult Movement." VIO-
      LENCE AND THE CULTS (item 653), pp. 105-32.

      Provides a short history of the Anti-Cult Movement and describes
      its ideology and organization. The events of Jonestown are traced
      and their effects on the Anti-Cult Movement assessed. The authors
      hold that the Jonestown tragedy reinvigorated the declining cam-
      paign against the cults; it revitalized its members and boosted its
      credibility. The Anti-Cult Movement used Jonestown to buttress the
      view that the cults are dangerous institutions and to support the
      claim that brainwashing led to violence. Though Jonestown made the
      connection between the cults and violence more plausible, no legal
      action against the cults in general has been taken.

2200. Shupe, Anson D., and David G. Bromley. THE NEW VIGILANTES: DEPROGRAM-
      MERS, ANTI-CULTISTS, AND THE NEW RELIGIONS. Beverly Hills, CA:
      Sage Publications, 1980. 267 pp.

      Examines in some detail the loose coalition of groups known col-
      lectively as the Anti-Cult Movement (ACM). The authors have two
      objectives in mind, namely "to analyze the ACM from an organiza-
      tional perspective and to delineate the process whereby the ACM
      sought to initiate the construction and imposition of deviant
      labels upon the new religions" (p. 13). The sociocultural back-
      ground of the movement is given and the sources of strain between
      it and the new religions located. The ideology of the ACM, center-
      ing around the two metaphors of possession and deception, is de-
      scribed and its two components, the anticult association and the
      deprogrammers, are considered and their impact assessed. One chap-
      ter is dedicated to the Jonestown tragedy and to its revitalization
      of the ACM. The authors maintain that a study of the Anti-Cult
      Movement, which is a relatively small movement, will contribute to
      our understanding of social movements in general.

2201. Shupe, Anson D., and David G. Bromley. A DOCUMENTARY HISTORY OF THE
      ANTI-CULT MOVEMENT. Arlington: Center for Social Research, Uni-
      versity of Texas, 1980. (374) pp.

      Presents a collection of 102 documents relating to the activities
      of the Anti-Cult Movement. These documents are divided into four
      main sets: 1) those issued by family-based, anticult associations;
      2) those that pertain to the religious response; 3) those that
      record government actions; and 4) those drafted by educational
      institutions. In an introductory chapter the origin, ideology,
      organizational development, and limited success of the Anti-Cult
      Movement are reviewed. In a postscript, the authors, who describe
      themselves as "personae non gratae" to the members of this move-
      ment, reflect briefly on the problem of collecting the documents
      and on the limitations of this volume.

2202. Shupe, Anson D., and David G. Bromley. "Reverse Missionizing: Sun
       Myung Moon's Unificationist Movement in the United States." FREE
       INQUIRY IN CREATIVE SOCIOLOGY 8 (1980): 197-203.

       Considers the Unification Church's presence in the United States
       as an example of an Eastern religious movement that has expanded
       its mission to include the Western world. Three areas of conflict
       are identified and discussed: 1) the divergence of theological
       traditions; 2) the clash of organizational structures; and 3) the
       new movement's insensitivity to Western society's broader cultural
       heritage. A short summary statement of the Unification Church's
       stance is given and the challenge that its theology presents to
       established religion considered. Moon's doctrine and goals are not
       merely ecumenical; they are rather monolithic, in the sense that
       they aim to do away with religious pluralism and the consequent
       religious toleration in the West. His attempts to unify church and
       state as well as science and religion are an added cause for con-
       cern. The church's proselytizing tactics have amplified resistance
       to its presence and influence and alienated both conservative and
       liberal Christians.

2203. Shupe, Anson D., and David G. Bromley. "The Moonies and the Anti-
       Cultists: Movement and Countermovement in Conflict." SOCIOLOGI-
       CAL ANALYSIS 40 (1979): 325-34.

       Considers the structural conditions under which a countermove-
       ment emerges and the tactics it adopts to combat the movement it
       opposes. The following features of world-transforming movements
       like the Unification Church are described: 1) the provocation of
       ideological conflict; 2) a pan-institutional organizational style;
       3) the use of economic resources drawn from the larger society; and
       4) the recruitment of new members and socialization practices based
       on the belief in an imminent social change. The institutional
       sources of the Anti-Cult Movement, namely the family and religion,
       are described. Finally, the Anti-Cult Movement is examined as a
       countermovement with its own organization, ideology, strategy, and
       tactics. The authors state that this movement's activities against
       the Unification Church have been generally successful.

2204. Shupe, Anson D., and David G. Bromley. "Witches, Moonies, and
       Evil." SOCIETY 15.4 (1978): 75-76.

       Describes those common features of the accusations made against
       both the contemporary cults in the United States and witchcraft in
       the seventeenth century. Five dimensions are briefly listed: 1)
       the location of the source of evil (brainwashing or the devil); 2)
       the vulnerability of those who succumb to the evil sources (young
       adults or women); 3) the antisocial intentions of those who pro-
       mote evil (greed for money or interpersonal resentment); 4) the
       methods of identifying the presence of evil (psychological or phys-
       ical marks); and 5) the ways by which this evil can be combated and
       neutralized (deprogramming or exorcism). The authors maintain that
       "accusations of possession by evil tend to occur when there is a
       weakening in traditional norms of reciprocity" (p. 76).

2205. Shupe, Anson D., Bert Hardin, and David G. Bromley. "A Comparison
       of Anti-Cult Movements in the United States and West Germany."
       OF GODS AND MEN (item 550), pp. 177-93.

       Attempts to explain the main differences between anticult activ-
       ities in two different countries, more specifically, to understand
       why West Germany has witnessed a larger formal institutional re-
       sponse than the United States of America, even though the latter
       country has a more organized Anti-Cult Movement and more people
       actually involved in the new religious movements. The Anti-Cult
       Movements of each of the two countries are described and their
       differences are understood in terms of their respective religious
       traditions, tolerance of alternative lifestyles, and church-state
       relations. The authors conclude that in West Germany, one can more
       accurately talk of an anticult sentiment. They think that the
       United States government might follow West Germany in responding
       formally to the presence of the new movements.

2206. Shupe, Anson D., Roger Spielmann, and Sam Stigall. "Cults of Anti-
       Cultism." SOCIETY 17.3 (1980): 43-46.

       Examines the origin, structure, and ideology of the Anti-Cult
       Movement that by the early 1980's had grown into a full-scale cen-
       tralized movement. Its inception is traced to FREECOG (Free the
       Children of God Movement) and to several other independent groups
       (such as the Spiritual Counterfeits Project, Love Our Children,
       Inc., Citizens Engaged in Freeing Minds, and Return to Personal
       Choice Inc.), all of which came into being in the early 1970's.
       Several participants in Anti-Cult Movement are distinguished: the
       immediate relatives and friends of former and present cult members;
       ex-cultists; and various professionals, including clergymen, psy-
       chiatrists, psychologists, and social workers. The activities of
       the Anti-Cult Movement are described and its deprogramming rationale
       explained. The authors think that the Anti-Cult Movement will, in
       the long run, be affected by the amount of accommodation that mar-
       ginal religions reach with American society.

2207. Shupe, Anson D., Roger Spielmann, and Sam Stigall. "Deprogramming:
       The New Exorcism." AMERICAN BEHAVIORAL SCIENTIST 20 (1977):
       941-56.

       Maintains that the application of conservatory laws in cases
       involving cult members has social implications for the freedom of
       religion. The authors report on those organizations supporting
       deprogramming and compare their interpretation of the phenomena of
       commitment to marginal religions and the programming of their mem-
       bers to demonic possession and exorcism respectively. Basing their
       reflections on research carried out among anticult organizations
       that include relatives and friends of cult and ex-cult members, the
       authors depict the rationale adopted to justify forced deconver-
       sion. They suggest that the qualifications of exorcists in early
       Christianity were similar to those of contemporary deprogrammers.
       The process of deprogramming itself bears a close resemblance to
       the accounts of brainwashing or radical resocialization and in-
       cludes the element of physical coercion that is found in the
       recruitment and conversion of new cult members.

2208. Swan, Rita. "Faith Healing, Christian Science, and the Medical
        Care of Children." NEW ENGLAND JOURNAL OF MEDICINE 309.29
        (December 23, 1983): 1639-41.

        Outlines the Christian Science view of medicine and holds that
        the church aims at maintaining its independence from the medical
        establishment and at acquiring recognition for its own method of
        handling illnesses. The author argues that the United States De-
        partment of Health and Social Services and various state legisla-
        tures are actually promoting faith healing. She strongly insists
        that this procedure should be reversed and that legislation be
        enacted to force parents to provide medical care for their children
        and to prosecute faith healers. In so doing, she brings to the
        fore one of the most important issues pertaining to the societal
        response to some alternate religious movements. (This essay was
        later reprinted in UPDATE: A QUARTERLY JOURNAL OF NEW RELIGIOUS
        MOVEMENTS 8.3-4, 1984, pp. 3-9.)

2209. Taylor, David. "Thought Reform and the Unification Church." THE
        BRAINWASHING/DEPROGRAMMING CONTROVERSY (item 2127), pp. 173-90.

        Studies the conversion methods used by the Unification Church and
        discovers some similarities between them and brainwashing tech-
        niques employed on prisoners-of-war in China and North Korea. The
        way church members attract new recruits through direct contact, the
        establishment of personal relationships, and weekend training ses-
        sions are described as a socially structured process leading the
        prospective novice through successive stages of commitment. The
        main themes used in classical brainwashing are examined in relation
        to their applicability to the Unification Church. Noticing that
        there are some major similarities and differences between the
        methods used by the Unification Church and communist countries, the
        author concludes that the Unification Church uses psychological
        rather than physical coercion. The susceptibility of the church's
        recruits is a crucial factor in the conversion process. It is
        insisted that converts to the Unification Church are active parti-
        cipants in the process.

2210. Testa, Bart. "Making Crime Seem Natural: The Press and Deprogram-
        ming." A TIME FOR CONSIDERATION: A SCHOLARLY APPRAISAL OF THE
        UNIFICATION CHURCH (item 1652), pp. 41-79.

        Examines a series of six newspaper articles that were written by
        Josh Freed and published under the title "The Moon Stalkers" in the
        MONTREAL STAR. The author's aim is to determine how various models
        for representing a public controversy were used. He concludes that
        the author combined investigative reporting, advocacy journalism,
        and the new journalism (where the writer makes reflective responses
        and judgments on what is being reported). It is concluded that
        these articles did not provide a news report, but rather created or
        perpetuated a myth.

2211. Thorp, Malcolm R. "Sectarian Violence in Early Victorian Britain:
        The Mormon Experience, 1837-1860." BULLETIN OF THE JOHN RYLANDS
        UNIVERSITY LIBRARY OF MANCHESTER 70.3 (1988): 135-47.

Examines "the documented instances of popular disturbances
against the Mormons, with the specific intention of determining
the frequency and the intensity of such activities" (p. 135). The
author finds parallels between the treatment of Mormons in nineteenth-century Britain and that of Primitive Methodists and Millerites. Violence against the Mormons, he explains, was senseless,
triggered only by sectarian antipathy. The many sectarian conflicts between 1830 and 1840 and their decline by the 1850's are
recorded. The persecutions seemed to have consolidated the Mormon
self-image of an elite religious group, but did not increase their
level of internal cohesion.

2212.   Van Driel, Barend, and James T. Richardson. "Print Media Coverage
        of New Religious Movements: A Longitudinal Study." JOURNAL OF
        COMMUNICATION 38.3 (1988): 37-61.

        Examines the media's strong influence in the debate on the cults
        from 1972 up to 1984. The following publications were selected for
        content analysis: the NEW YORK TIMES, the LOS ANGELES TIMES, the
        SAN FRANCISCO CHRONICLE, NEWSWEEK, TIME, and the U.S. NEWS AND
        WORLD REPORT. The amount of attention given to the new religious
        movements and comparable groups (like Christian Science, the
        Jehovah's Witnesses, the Salvation Army, and the Amish and Hutter-
        ites) is schematically outlined and the contexts in five selected
        time periods examined in detail. Forty-two percent of the cover-
        age on new movements involved the Unification Church. The tenor of
        the print coverage is determined, in part, by the discussions on
        the atrocities committed by the new cults, which are portrayed as
        being "a less than integral part of U.S. society" (p. 55).

2213.   Van Driel, Barend, and James T. Richardson. "Categorization and
        New Religious Movements in American Print Media." SOCIOLOGICAL
        ANALYSIS 49 (1988): 171-83.

        Investigates the media's representation of the new religions or
        cults. The dimensions of sect and cult as used in social-scien-
        tific literature are schematically laid out. It is pointed out
        that in social scientific literature as well as in dictionaries and
        encyclopedias, the terms are given value-free definitions, though
        British sources give a more negative connotation to the term "sect"
        than American sources do. The following newspapers and weekly news
        magazines between November 1973 and April 1984 were examined: NEW
        YORK TIMES, WASHINGTON POST, SAN FRANCISCO CHRONICLE, NEWSWEEK,
        TIME, AND U.S. NEWS AND WORLD REPORT. The authors outline the main
        characteristics of cults as portrayed in these publications, which
        rarely make an attempt to carefully define cult and sect and which
        seem to ignore the scholarly efforts to study marginal religious
        organizations.

2214.   Wallis, Roy. "Paradoxes of Freedom and Regulation: The Case of New
        Religious Movements in Britain and America." SOCIOLOGICAL ANALY-
        SIS 48 (1988): 355-71.

        Explores the different reactions to the new religious movements
        in Britain and the United States, particularly from the point of
        view of the legal issue of freedom of religion. In the United

States, the relationship between society and the new movements has
been more confrontational, leading to the rise of a strong Anti-
Cult Movement with deprogramming as a professional enterprise.
Besides, in the United States, the new religions themselves have
exhibited some violent behavior (Jonestown and the abuse of children in several groups being excellent examples) not recorded elsewhere. The author explains these features with reference to the
relative size of the two countries and to their diverse political
institutions. The cohesive and centralized system of Great Britain
has extensive power to monitor and intervene in the affairs of the
new religions. The institutionalized religious freedom that prevails in the United States, on the other hand, allows new religious
movements the freedom to behave in ways that give rise to public
outcries. The Anti-Cult Movement in the United States, with its
forceful deprogramming strategy and legal suits, serves as an
alternative means of social control of fringe movements.

2215. Wallis, Roy. "How and Why Does the Treatment of New Religions
      Differ in Britain and America." UPDATE: A QUARTERLY JOURNAL OF
      NEW RELIGIOUS MOVEMENTS 10.1 (1986): 3-9.

      Points out that the relationship between the new religions and
      the wider society seems more confrontational in the U.S.A. than in
      Great Britain. Government intervention, court cases, and counter-
      attacks by the new movements have been more frequent and prominent
      in America where religious freedom is embedded in the Constitution.
      It is argued that the major differences between the political and
      institutional machinery of the two mentioned countries help explain
      the diverse encounters between the cults and the British and Ameri-
      can societies, respectively. In Britain greater control is exer-
      cised at an earlier stage, thus discouraging reactions by the new
      movements, reactions that can lead to stronger societal disapproval.

2216. Wallis, Roy. "Societal Reaction to Scientology: A Study in the
      Sociology of a Deviant Religion." SECTARIANISM: ANALYSIS OF
      RELIGIOUS AND NON-RELIGIOUS SECTS (item 713), pp. 86-116.

      Examines the relationship between Scientology and the mass media
      and state agencies that have tended to view its activities in a
      manner approaching "moral panic." A brief history of the social
      reaction to Scientology since its birth as Dianetics in the 1950's
      is given. The author points out that, because Scientology has an
      ambiguous status in the sense that the boundaries between church,
      business, science, and psychotherapy are not clearly drawn, it has
      become a source of cognitive anomaly and psychological anxiety. He
      favors the deviance-amplification model to explain the development
      of Scientology and the societal reaction to it.

2217. Weimann, Gabriel. "Mass-Media Occultism: The Role of the Media in
      the Occult Revival." JOURNAL OF POPULAR CULTURE 18.4 (1985):
      81-88.

      Proposes the view that modern news media has helped spread inter-
      est in occult topics, ranging from astrology to parapsychology.
      The causes for the media's generous coverage of the occult and the

effect this coverage might have on its audience are examined.
Occult events are compatible to "journalistic considerations,"
because they are soft news containing human interest stories, "not
necessarily timely." They provide an unusual, mysterious angle to
the news. The mass media also caters to the demands for "secondary
superstition." It has a reinforcement effect on occult beliefs and
attitudes. It further bestows prestige and legitimizes status,
plays a part in reconstructing reality, and acts as a catalyst to
the climate of opinion, thus playing "a crucial role in the revival
and perpetuation of the occult" (p. 86).

2218.   Westrum, Ron. "UFOs and Scientists." UFOS: 1947-1987 (item 19),
        pp. 324-27.

        Examines the response of the scientific community to the UFO
        phenomenon. The author outlines briefly the scientific investiga-
        tions of UFO reports since the late 1940's and the various groups
        that are currently studying UFO sightings. He favors some scien-
        tific involvement in UFO investigations.

2219.   Whitlock, F. A. "Witch Crazes and Drug Crazes: A Contribution to
        the Social Pathology of Credulity and Scapegoating." AUSTRALIAN
        JOURNAL OF SOCIAL ISSUES 14 (1979): 43-54.

        Observes some similarities between the current concern for drugs
        and the hunt for drug users and the witch craze and hunts of the
        sixteenth and seventeenth centuries. The author sees some similar-
        ities between the practice of witchcraft and the use of drugs in
        that both are employed to alter consciousness and both are linked
        with evil. After a brief description of the European witchcraft
        beliefs and practices, the author turns to contemporary efforts to
        fight drugs, particularly in Australia. It is pointed out that the
        nineteenth-century tolerance of drugs has changed. The author
        thinks that both witches and drug users are scapegoats for the
        collective fantasies of society.

AUTHOR INDEX

(Numbers refer to bibliographical entries.)

Kenney, J. Frank, 1801, 1928.
Kent, Stephen A., 847-48, 1336-37.
Kephart, William M., 391-92.
Kern, Louis, 1338-39.
Kerr, Howard, 849.
Khalsa, Kirpal Singh, 1802.
Khoshkish, A., 1340.
Kies, Cosette N., 37.
Kilbourne, Brock K., 393, 645,
    850-51, 1803-4, 2150-53, 2174.
Killian, Lewis M., 394.
King, Christine E., 1341.
King, Kay Atkinson, 1342.
King, Morton, 108.
King, Robert R., 1342.
King, Winston L., 852.
Kirkpatrick, Lee A., 2154.
Kirkpatrick, R. George, 525-28,
    1805.
Kistler, Robert C., 1220.
Kitzinger, Sheila, 210.
Klandermans, Bert, 395-96.
Klapp, O. E., 109.
Klein, Gary, 1251.
Kloss, Peter, 110.
Knott, Kim, 1806.
Knudsen, Dean D., 320, 853.
Kohn, Rachael L. E., 1343-44, 1807.
Kolmerten, Carol A., 1345.
Kopelman, Loretta, 1808.
Kowalewski, David, 646.
Kranenborg, Reender, 1809, 2155.
Karushaar, Otto F., 425.
Kreuziger, Frederick, 1810.
Kring, Hilda Adam, 1346.
Krippner, Stanley, 397.
Kroll-Smith, J. Stephen, 1347.
Kronenfeld, Jennie J., 1811.
Kunz, Phillip, 937, 1812-13.
Kurtz, Ernest, 1348.
Kvideland, Karin, 854, 1812-13.

La Barre, Weston, 38.
Lane, Christel O., 647, 1349.
Lane, Ralph, 1814-15.
Lang, Anthony, 1816.
Lang, Gladys Engle, 211.
Lang, Kurt, 211.
Langone, Michael D., 855, 2156,
    2160.
Lanternari, Vittorio, 856.
Larkin, Ralph W., 398, 796-97,
    1718.

Larner, Christina, 1350.
LaRuffa, Anthony L., 1351.
Lasaga, Jose, I., 1817.
Lasch, Christopher, 399.
Latkin, Carl A., 1818.
Laue, James H., 212.
Lauer, Jeanette C., 402.
Lauer, Robert H., 400-2.
Lauer, Roger M., 648.
Law, Henry, G., 769.
Lawless, Elaine J., 1352-54.
Lawren, Bill, 649.
Lawton, George, 213.
Lebra, Takie Sugiyama, 403,
    1819-20.
Lee, Carleton L., 1355.
Lee, John A., 650-51.
Lee, Shu-Ching, 1356.
Leger, Daniele, 404.
Lehmann, Arthur C., 652.
Leininger, C. Earl, 857.
Leonard, Bill J., 1357.
Leone, Mark P., 1358-60.
Levack, Brian P., 1361.
Levasseur, Martine, 559.
Levi, Ken, 653, 1821.
Levin, Jeffrey S., 1822-23.
Levine, Edward M., 858-59, 2157.
Levine, Saul V., 654.
Lewis, I. M., 405-6.
Lewis, James R., 860, 1074,
    2158-59.
Lewis, Jeanette, 1824.
Lewis, Lionel S., 1639.
Lewis, Russel E., 1362.
Lewis, Warren, 861.
Lewis, William F., 1825.
Lieberman, Paul, 1826.
Liebman, Charles, S., 862.
Lincoln, C. Eric, 214, 1363.
Linden, Ingemar, 1364.
Lindt, Gillian, 1827.
Lindsey, Donald B., 1296.
Lipp, Wolfgang, 407.
Lippy, Charles H., 39-40.
Lipset, S. M., 111.
Lipson, Julienne G., 1828.
Littman, Richard A., 1881.
Liu, William T., 217.
Ljungdahl, Axel, 655.
Lo, Clarence Y. H., 41.
Locke, Ralph G., 1829.
Lofland, John, 215, 408, 656,
    863-66, 1365, 1830-33.
Long, Martha, 867, 1834.

INDEX OF SECTS, CULTS, AND NEW RELIGIOUS MOVEMENTS

(Numbers refer to bibliographical entries to major works
on individual sects, cults, and new religious movements.)

Communes (cont.),
   in France, 404.
   and monasteries, 1305.
   secular, 392.
   and sensitivity training, 414.
   and sexual practices, 415, 1969,
     2041.
Concept Houses, 2019.
Concept therapy, 651.
Concord group, 190.
Conference on New Religions
   (University of Nebraska), 720.
Confession (religious), 367.
Confucius, 288.
Congo, Charismatic leaders in, 1021.
Contraculture movements, 152, 339.
Conservative churches,
   growth of, 294, 298, 389-90.
Conservatory laws and the cults,
   2207.
Conversion, 58-59, 155, 160, 215,
   296, 337, 480, 484, 607, 634,
   642, 645, 665, 689, 738, 746,
   749, 786, 802, 807-9, 844, 846-
   47, 850-51, 857, 865-66, 868,
   870-71, 897, 911, 913, 915,
   936-37, 949, 952, 955, 975,
   1019, 1030, 1138, 1274, 1284,
   1324, 1327, 1394, 1448, 1647,
   1755, 1786, 1788, 1796, 1832-
   33, 1849, 1924, 1935-36, 1955,
   1988, 2019, 2108, 2168, 2171,
   2189.
   bibliographies, 55, 850.
   and psychotherapy, 392.
   and socialization, 451.
   sociology of, 366.
     bibliography, 65.
   types of, 857
   typology of, 122.
Conway, Flo, 2151, 2154, 2160.
Copeland, Kenneth, 359.
Cosmic Circle of Fellowship, 1977.
Cosmology of cults, 531, 534.
Counterculture Movements, 41, 44,
   309, 316, 422, 433, 470, 502-
   3, 505, 513, 523, 614, 762,
   772, 778, 796, 821, 863, 930,
   995, 1037, 1045, 1047.
   and the Jews, 542.
   and religion, 390
Cox, Harvey, 1729.
Creationism, 571.
Creme, Benjamin, 1809.
Cretans, 459.

Crime and cultism, 279.
Cross, Whitney, 1442.
Crouch, Paul, 359.
Crowley, Aleister, 1865.
Crusades, 109.
Culture crisis, 398, 788, 790.
Cult leaders, 842, 859.
   bibliography, 45.
Cults (see New Religious Movements),
   and America Culture, 852, 855,
     858.
   and attitudes towards AIDS, 672.
   bibliographies, 38, 54, 60, 63,
     66, 70, 551, 581, 598, 604,
     727, 893, 918.
   of celebrities, 109.
   and social networks, 695.
   theories of, 829 ff.
   typologies of, 59, 103, 335,
     432, 546, 595, 600, 626, 638,
     641, 674, 731, 740, 744, 761,
     770, 783, 984, 914, 990-93,
     995, 1027.
   and psychotheraphy (see
     Psychotherapy).
   and violence (see Violence).
Culture crises and new religions,
   735, 756.
Cumbres (NH), 383,
Cursillo Movement,
   bibliography, 1373.

Da Free John (see Laughing Man
   Institute).
Daner, Francine J., 1985.
Danish commune, 371.
Decline of the new religions, 2131.
Dederich, Charles, 1816.
Defection,
   from mainline churches, 373-75,
     462, 578, 749, 832, 2165.
   bibliographies, 362, 558, 578,
     649, 835.
   from convents, 1142-43.
   from Mormonism, 115, 1001-2,
     1031, 1361.
   from new religious movements,
     203, 205, 478, 649, 666, 837-
     38, 844, 860, 865, 917, 929-30,
     932, 1296, 1503, 1517, 2003,
     2111.
   from social movements, 142.
De Harr, Richard, 359.

ESP phenomena, 417, 436, 691,
    1061, 1588.
EST, 532, 587, 627, 630, 663, 675,
    680, 710, 735, 828, 991, 1064,
    1686, 2037, 2081, 2162.
Essenes, 291, 371.
    and women, 445.
Ethics in research, 121.
Ethnoscience, 1087-88.
Evangelical Christianity, 44, 1332.
Evangelical Movement, 1851.
Evangelical Sects, 147.
Evans, Warren Felt, 1514.
Evil eye theory and brainwashing,
    2142.
Exegesis, 630.
THE EXORCIST (movie), 277.

Fabian Society, 1186.
Failure of communes, 392, 493.
Failure of new religious movements,
    1013, 1648.
Failure of prophecy, 91, 154, 530,
    884, 994, 1003, 1197, 1291,
    1478, 1541, 1556, 1981, 2077.
Fairfield, Richard, 471.
Faith healing, 537, 651, 716, 933,
    1025, 1576, 2208.
Falwell, Jerry, 357, 359, 552, 604,
    649.
Family Action, Information, and
    Rescue (FAIR), 2113.
Family conflicts and the cults,
    644, 872, 929, 943, 1034,
    1048, 1206, 1440, 1457, 1505,
    1570, 1610, 1641, 1785, 2153,
    2160, 2177, 2190, 2194.
Family in communes (see Communal
    Societies).
Family of Love (see Children of
    God).
Family response to the cults,
    typology of, 2216.
Family violence among Quakers,
    1177-78.
Fanaticism, 862.
Farrad, Wali, 159.
The Farm, 828.
Farrakhan, Louis, 1371.
FATE magazine, 734.
Father Divine and Jim Jones, 1968.
Father Divine Movement, 44, 109,
    114, 1117, 1128, 1196.

Fear of cults, 2152.
Female deity in Mormonism, 1296.
Feminism in sects, 728.
Festinger, Leon, 884, 994, 1003,
    1134, 1478.
Fichter, Joseph, 1786.
Fieldwork (see also Participant
    Observation), 110, 1068, 1070.
Films and filmstrips on new
    religious movements, 63.
Finances and the cults (see also
    Tax Issues), 767, 942, 2171,
    2176, 2176.
Findhorn, 455, 669.
    women in, 459.
Finney, Charles Grandison, 1199.
Flagellants, 168.
"Flirty Fishing" (see also Chil-
    dren of God), 1905, 2060-61,
    2091.
Flying saucers (see UFOs).
Folklore and UFOs (see Mythology).
Folk medicine and healing, 192,
    238, 278, 376, 716, 1234,
    1310-11, 1314, 1625.
Folk religion, 378.
Forest, Edward de, 1585.
Fortune-telling, 439, 1576-77,
    1608-9, 1766-67.
The FORUM (see EST).
Fourierites, 447.
Fowler, James W., 1982.
Fox, George, 205, 288, 2136.
France, communes in, 504.
Free the Children of God (FREECOG),
    676, 2206.
Freed, Josh, 2210.
Freemasonry, 675.
Freudian psychotherapy as a cult,
    964.
Frideres, James S., 1422.
Frustration and the cults, 41.
Functionalism and the cults (see
    also Deprivation), 151, 1011,
    1014.
Fundamentalism, 274, 358, 412, 426,
    927, 944, 1599-600.
    Islamic, 358, 779.
Fundamentalist sects, 146, 222-23,
    1438.
Fundraising, 581, 678.
Future of new religious movements,
    594, 727, 839, 1629, 1727,
    1870, 1984, 2050, 2080.
Future of religion, 346, 352.

Humanistic psychology, 540.
Humbard, Rex, 359.
Hurley, George E., 1117.
Hutter, Jacob, 1356.
Hutterites, 23, 291, 338, 368-69,
    392, 661, 1785.
    old people in Hutterite
        societies, 310.
    bibliography, 1313.
    and women's roles, 1425.
Hynek, J. Allen (see Center for UFO
    Studies).
Hypnosis, 481, 704.

I Am Movement (Society), 44, 112,
    114, 696.
I Ching, 618, 971.
Icarians,
    and sex and marriage, 428.
Identity crisis, 765, 796.
Ikeda, Daisaku, 1024.
Impact of cults on mainline
    churches, 825.
Inquisition and witch scare, 1152.
Institute for Harmonious
    Development, 629.
Institute for Psychic Integrity,
    663.
Institute for the Study of American
    Religion, 676.
Integral Yoga Institute, 60, 572,
    606.
Interactionist analysis of
    movements, 400, 1328, 1411.
International Conferences on the
    Unity of Sciences, 1063, 1073,
    1076.
Internationalists (Toronto), 897.
Irving, Edward, 1329.
Islam, 138, 956.
    fundamentalism in, 358, 779.
Ivory Coast, charismatic
    leadership in, 1021.

Jain, Chandra Mohan (Bhagwan
    Rajneesh), 1886.
Jansenists, 317.
Jansson, Eric, 1249, 1742.
Janssonists,
    bibliography, 1249.
Japanese religion, 942.

Jasper Community, 107.
Jehovah's Witnesses, 75, 109, 114,
    144, 146-47, 162, 295, 389,
    632, 646, 661, 672, 723-24, 884,
    933-34, 938, 1138, 1839, 2155.
Jesuits, 317, 1303.
Jesus, 288, 675.
Jesus Movement, 60, 452, 567, 724,
    726, 789, 879, 984, 1085,
    1548, 2071.
    bibliographies, 34, 51, 1956.
    interpretation of, 34.
    research on, 452.
Jesus People (see Jesus Movement).
Jewish Messianic movements, 153,
    523, 1246.
Jews,
    in American culture, 888.
    and the counterculture, 442.
    and the cults, 943, 2191.
John Birch Society, 441.
Johnson, Benton, 957, 966.
Johnson, President, 883.
Joho Shinshu Buddhist sect, 446.
Jones, Charles Stansfeld, 1865.
Jones, Jim, 842, 1363, 1396, 1567,
    1670, 1684, 1787, 1899, 1917,
    2000.
    and Father Divine, 1968.
Jonestown (see People's Temple).
Judah, J. Stillson, 1723, 1988.
Judaism, 131, 138.

Kabbala, 633, 945.
Kanter, Elizabeth Moss, 347, 359,
    477, 1570, 1739, 1913, 1956,
    1987, 2064.
Karma, 1773.
Kaufman, Herman, 188.
Keech, Mrs., 91, 994.
Kelley, Dean, 295.
Kennedy, Robert, 1765.
Kenney, Elizabeth, 201.
Kibbutzim, 291, 338, 369.
Kilbourne, Brock K., 2154, 2160.
King, George, 994, 1844, 2067.
King, Martin Luther, 288.
Kingsway Community, 455.
Kirkpatrick, R. George, 496.
Kitamura, Sayo, 1819.
Koinonia Community, 342.
Krishnamurti, 21, 597, 667, 1910.
Kundalini Yoga, 2019.